INTERNATIONAL ENCYCLOPEDIA OF ECONOMICS OF EDUCATION

SECOND EDITION

Resources in Education

This is a new series of Pergamon one-volume Encyclopedias drawing upon articles in the acclaimed *International Encyclopedia of Education, Second Edition*, with revisions as well as new articles. Each volume in the series is thematically organized and aims to provide complete and up-to-date coverage on its subject. These Encyclopedias will serve as an invaluable reference source for researchers, faculty members, teacher educators, government officials, educational administrators, and policymakers.

The *International Encyclopedia of Economics of Education, Second Edition* contains 87 articles on the economics of education. It provides an understanding of where the economics of education has been, where it is heading, and where it needs to go in the future to provide further insights into the human role in production and the production of human skills valued in the labor market.

The economics of education has been expanded into new areas of research and has deepened and changed its analysis of traditional areas, such as educational finance, the production of knowledge, and the relation between education and economic growth. In the past decade theories have been modified and new concepts have appeared. These developments are covered by the scope of this Encyclopedia. A complete bibliography and further reading at the end of each article provide references for further research. Extensive name and subject indexes are also included.

Other titles in the series include:

POSTLETHWAITE (ed.)
International Encyclopedia of National Systems of Education, Second Edition

ANDERSON (ed.)
International Encyclopedia of Teaching and Teacher Education, Second Edition

TUIJNMAN (ed.)
International Encyclopedia of Adult and Continuing Education, Second Edition

PLOMP & ELY (eds)
International Encyclopedia of Educational Technology, Second Edition

DeCORTE & WEINERT (eds)
International Encyclopedia of Developmental and Instructional Psychology

KEEVES (ed.)
International Encyclopedia of Educational Research, Methodololgy, and Measurement, Second Edition

INTERNATIONAL ENCYCLOPEDIA OF ECONOMICS OF EDUCATION

SECOND EDITION

Edited by

MARTIN CARNOY
Stanford University, CA, USA

PERGAMON

UK   Elsevier Science Ltd, The Boulevard, Langford Lane, Kidlington, Oxford OX5 1GB, UK

USA   Elsevier Science Inc, 660 White Plains Road, Tarrytown, New York 10591-5153, USA

JAPAN   Elsevier Science Japan, Tsunashima Building Annex, 3-20-12 Yushima, Bunkyo-ku, Tokyo 113, Japan

---

Second edition 1995

Library of Congress Cataloging in Publication Data
International encyclopedia of economics of education / edited by Martin Carnoy. — 2nd ed.
    p.   cm. — (Resources in education)
  Rev. ed. of: International Encyclopedia of economics of education, 1st ed. 1987.
  Draws upon articles in International encyclopedia of education, 2nd ed., with revisions as well as new articles.
  Includes bibliographic references and index.
  1. Education—Economic aspects. 2. Industry and education. 3. Human capital. 4. Educational planning. 5. Income. I. Carnoy, Martin. II. International encyclopedia of economics of education (Oxford, England) III. International encyclopedia of education, 2nd ed. IV. Series: Resources in education (Oxford, England)
LC65.I58   1995
338.4'737—dc20   95-45387

British Library Cataloguing in Publication Data
A catalogue record for this book is available from the British Library.

ISBN 0–08–042303–5 (alk. paper)

Printed and bound in Great Britain by Cambridge University Press, Cambridge, UK.

Contents

Contents

Contents

Contents

Acknowledgements

I would like to thank, first and foremost, all those colleagues who contributed to this volume, and Pia Lindquist Wong who helped me edit many of the manuscripts as they came in. I am also indebted to Barbara Barrett, Michèle Wheaton, Glenda Pringle, and Peter Frank, the editors at Elsevier Science Ltd., who made the volume possible. Intellectual inspiration for continually deepening my understanding of education comes from my wife, Jean MacDonell, a teacher and administrator in Santa Clara County's primary schools, and my children, David, Jon, and Juliet.

The Economics of Education, Then and Now

Economics of Education, Then and Now

M. Carnoy

In the early 1960s, at the dawn of the economics of education, Theodore Schultz wrote:

> The economic value of education rests on the proposition that people enhance their capabilities as producers and as consumers by investing in themselves and that schooling is the largest investment in human capital. This proposition implies that most of the economic capabilities of people are not given at birth or at the time when children enter upon their schooling. These acquired capabilities are anything but trivial. They are of a magnitude to alter radically the usual measures of the amount of savings and of capital formation that is taking place. They also alter the structure of wages and salaries and the amount of earnings from work relative to the amount of income from property. There are long standing puzzles about economic growth, changes in the structure of wages and salaries, and changes in the personal distribution of income that can be substantially resolved by taking account of investment in human capital. (Schultz 1963 pp.10–11)

This proposition has taken us a long way. Economists have filled the framework of the human capital paradigm with analyses of the returns to education and training, with explanations of individuals' behavior in the labor market and firms' labor investment behavior, with studies of human capital's contribution to economic growth, and research on the impact of the quality of schooling on returns to education. They have also gone beyond Schultz's labor market focus in the early 1960s to analyze schools as firms—to study the "efficacy" of the educational enterprise. Because of all this research, today we know much more about the relation of education to productivity, which tended to be an assumed relationship in the early 1960s; about the behavior of individuals and firms regarding investment in education and training; and about the very tenuous relationship between school inputs and the acquisition of knowledge by children.

The new knowledge has not come too soon. Since the 1960s enormous changes have taken place in the world economy that shape the institutions that economists of education study, and the changes have put human capital even more at the center of the development process. Revolutionary transformations in the demand for goods and the way they are produced have affected long-term national growth possibilities, how governments relate to their national economies, and how national economies relate to each other. The world economy is becoming more competitive, more global, and increasingly dominated by information and communications technology. This has made human capital—as technical knowledge and the capacity to respond rapidly to change—an even more crucial input into the production process.

Yet these changes also suggested that economists of education needed to look in new ways at the *meaning* of human capital and its role in economic growth and labor markets. They required economists of education to reexamine the formation of human capital in schools and in job training. This reanalysis had to take place for both those who accepted the strictest neo-classical version of the human capital concept and those who had challenged it over three decades.

The concept of human capital and its role in development that Schultz described and that paradigm box that economists of education have filled with their research regarded development as a continual process. Countries, firms, and schools were classified as successful or unsuccessful economic units according to their capacity to move rapidly along a predetermined trajectory and to adapt rapidly to social and economic models imported from outside the unit. Growth was perceived as depending on the acquisition from external sources of capital, technology, and organizational efficiency and superimposing them on a predetermined structure of production. In these views of exogenously stimulated growth or efficiency, human resources were usually only considered in quantitative terms—as available labour of varying quality to be combined with existing capital and technology in relatively low added-value activities.

Technology, in turn, was seen by theorists as rigidly tied to a trajectory in which it could enter at various stages. Technology already utilized in industrialized countries or more technically advanced firms entered economic units to recreate the conditions which were already a part of existing practice in those more developed units.

This model of the growth process was part of a generalized "assembly-line" view of the organization of production. As a view of production, it was incorporated into both orthodox human capital models and heterodox labor market theory that characterized firms as "contested terrains" and labor markets as segmented. Today, it seems highly reductionist. In it human capital plays no role in *creating* new technology and new practices *endogenous* to economic units.

The closest that traditional human capital models came to viewing educated labor as playing such a role was in Welch's and Schultz's work in the early 1970s on "adjustment" to innovation and price changes—what Schultz called "adjusting to economic disequilibrium" (Schultz 1975). These studies are very revealing. Welch's work on resource use in US agriculture showed farmers with more education getting greater gains in income from the more efficient allocation of resources (Welch 1970). Schultz went on to argue that farmers with more education not only adjust more rapidly to price changes but also to technological changes—that they tend to adopt the new technology sooner and are more likely to make the economic changes dictated by the new technology so as to increase their income. This ability to adjust to change and to adopt new ways of doing things, according to Schultz, is the result of skills acquired in school.

But although these studies implied that such skills made workers more productive across industries and jobs, Schultz's and Welch's empirical tests were only applied to the role of education in adjusting to disequilibrium by *individual agricultural entrepreneurs*, not to the role of education in raising productivity by workers in assembly-line factories. Even for these individual farmers, it was those with university education who did significantly better during the process of change. Indeed, so far there is no hard evidence that more schooling does raise industrial worker productivity—only that higher levels of schooling are associated with higher wages. Why and how workers produce more because they acquire knowledge in schools is still subject to considerable controversy. The best case is that schooling increases students' cognitive knowledge and that such knowledge is relevant to the skills needed to be productive in work. Yet, empirical verification for even the relationship between more school knowledge and increased productivity is almost non-existent. It is generally believed that investment in schooling leads to higher productivity, but researchers have not, as scientists, made a persuasive empirical case for such causality.

From the standpoint of human capital theory, it made perfect sense that the skills which made self-employed farmers more productive would also make employed workers more productive. The neoclassical conception of labor markets characterizes employed workers as having similar kinds of individual choices as the self-employed, both as consumers and producers. But the segmentation theory of labor markets—contemporary with Welch's and Schultz's work—characterized employed and self-employed individuals as quite different (Gordon et al. 1982). It assumed that employers and employees have different interests, that employer decisions on the use of human capital are conditioned by power/control considerations as well as profit maximization, and that employed workers' decision-making in the workplace is severely restricted by employer-employee power relations. Unlike human capital theory, segmentation theory at least allowed for the possibility that a firm's decision-making configuration is alterable—not necessarily technologically "fixed." Modelling the firm as a hierarchical social organization also helped explain why no empirical study succeeded in showing that increased individual productivity in manufacturing or service firms was linked to individual employees' schooling. The capacity to "adjust to disequilibrium" available to individual farmers and entrepreneurs making their own decisions is normally not available to employed workers with assembly line jobs.

Applying this insight from segmentation theory to Schultz's and Welch's work, it might be expected that productivity increases due to education would be greater when those who obtain education enter occupations where they can make decisions; for example, small farmers rather than farm laborers or small-scale entrepreneurs rather than employed semi-skilled workers. This interpretation of schooling's contribution to increased productivity assumes that a person with the additional education is in a position to make better decisions. In most work situations, the decision-making function is usually restricted to those who are self-employed or in a high-enough employed position to have decision-making responsibility.

With the advent of new technologies and new, flexible organizations of production, these arguments about human capital in the production process have to be taken much farther. The adjustment to equilibrium argument does suggest that the economic returns to education should be higher to employed workers in job situations where they are counted on to make judgments rather than simply follow orders. This may have always been true, even in the hierarchical, specialized organization of production in the assembly-line factory; yet, in the new organizations of production associated with the new international economy and the information age, it has become somewhat more obvious that this is the case. In so many words, relations in the workplace are not only crucial to productivity, but the human capital-productivity relation is wrapped up in the social relations between management and labor.

Assume that the highest payoff to human capital comes when labor is able to participate in making decisions, and that the advent of flexible production rewards endogenous innovation and learning-by-doing. Assume also that innovation and learning on the job are improved by a better educated and trained labor force and by organizations of production that promote participation. In that case, the contribution of human capital to higher productivity and economic growth depends largely on two factors: (a) management-labor relations that allow for greater participation by workers in decision-making, particularly in developing new ways to produce products and services; and (b) innovation networks among firms and between firms and other innovation institutions, including human capital-intensive educational and public administration institutions that help produce innovation. Thus, not only does the quality of human capital condition innovation and the utilization of technical and productive knowledge, but the organization of production and innovation is fundamental to the effectiveness of human capital in contributing to these processes.

Moving away from assembly-line, input-output models of production to models of endogenous innovation and learning-by-doing, which assume that productivity increase is a self-generating process endogenous to firms and economies, has major implications for the economics of education in all the areas that we study. Five areas will be considered.

First, the change shifts the focus on the relation between education and productivity—what Schultz called the economic value of education—to a much more complex set of relationships between the *potential* human capacity to produce more economic output and its *realization* through organizations of work that are both geared to realize that capacity and to innovate using their human capacity. Thus the payoff to education is conditioned not only by technology, but by information, ideology, political power, property rights, citizenship rights in the workplace, and the willingness of organizations to innovate constantly. When a main source of productivity increases may be endogenous to the production process, residing in the organizational arrangements between employers, managers, and employees and the focus that those arrangements place on autonomy and innovation, the actual role of education in raising productivity may depend more on these arrangements than on the higher cognitive skills associated with more schooling. In that sense, the "residual" that so fascinated development economists in the 1950s and 1960s becomes the black box that needs to be unraveled even when years of schooling, formal training, and job experience of the labor force are taken out of it.

Second, there are major implications of the changing production systems for the relationship between education and *income*. Most of the emphasis in this discussion in the 1990s has been on "skill mismatch." Since the new information economy requires a more highly skilled labor force, it is argued, the incomes of the lower skilled, lower educated are under downward pressure, thus producing an increasing payoff to skills. But there are alternative views. One is that technology has played a major role in affecting wage growth, but not through increasing demand for more skilled labor. Rather, the new information technology has helped increase the effective supply of low-skilled and mid-skilled labor by giving firms much greater capacity to locate production in lower-wage countries and to contract out to small, low-wage suppliers. Improved telecommunications have increased capital mobility and decentralization of production. Indeed, the number of low-skilled jobs in the developed countries remained remarkably stable between the mid-1980s and the mid-1990s. While it is true that the relative wages of the low-skilled in countries such as the United States have fallen, the absolute real wages of the college-educated (the high-skilled) are about the same as they were 20 years ago, and manufacturing wages did not rise to reflect increased manufacturing productivity in the 1980s and early 1990s.

Furthermore, other countries, such as Korea, went through the same type of industrial restructuring and technological change in the 1980s as the United States, with a completely different change in wage structure. In Korea, wages of the low-skilled rose sharply relative to wages of the high-skilled in the period 1986–91, partly as a result of a slowdown in the supply of low-skilled workers coming from rural areas and rapid increases in education, especially at the university level. An equally important factor, however, was the increased strength of the union movement which arose as part of increasing pressures for democratizing the political system. This also pushed government to implement higher minimum wages, and firms to equalize wage structures (Nam 1994). This suggests that the new information technology does not inherently create an increased wage spread between higher and lower skilled labor. Demand for higher skilled labor may be increasing relative to demand for lower skills, but wage changes also depend on effective labor supply and the bargaining power of labor in wage setting.

This discussion of "skill mismatch" has important implications for analyses of education and labor markets. Rates of return to higher levels of education appear to be increasing relative to rates to investment in lower levels. But in the United States, for example, where rates have been measured since 1939, the rise in rates to higher education brought them back to levels that had already been achieved in the late 1960s after they had declined in the 1970s. The difference is that in the 1960s, rates of return to university education rose even as real incomes to high school graduates were rising; in the 1980s, college premiums rose mainly because the real incomes of high school graduates fell. Furthermore, there is now considerable evidence that the share of lower skilled jobs decreased in various United States industries but the share of low-wage jobs increased (Howell and Wolff 1991). The case that wages of the lower educated are falling relative to the higher educated just because of the differential demand for different levels of skills is hardly a strong one.

In Korea, the return rate to higher education rose rapidly relative to the rate to investment in secondary and middle-level schooling until the mid-1980s, and then declined, as in the United States in the 1960s, during a period when real incomes to all levels of education were rising. The results of studies in various countries of changes in rates over time also suggest that the "universal rule" of higher rates to lower levels of schooling and lower rates to higher levels of schooling due to declining marginal return to capital is not valid. As lower levels of schooling expand rapidly, the payoff declines relative to the payoff to higher levels. Further, the ranking of rates seems to depend on the overall wage structure, which in turn may depend mainly on the political bargaining power of labor. There may just not be a "universal rule" in the payoff structure for education. Moreover, changes in the world economy are such that in each country, depending on its place in the international division of labor, the structure of rates of return to education may be different. This implies that new educational strategies may have to be increasingly based on local possibilities for tying into a rapidly changing but all-pervasive world economy rather than any hard-and-fast investment rules.

A configuration of rates of return in which rates are lower to investment in lower levels of schooling and higher for university education raises questions about an old issue for economists of education. In the late 1960s and in the 1970s, a debate raged about what it was about schooling that contributed to higher incomes. Was schooling primarily a "legitimation" of knowledge acquired outside of schooling (in the family and in relationships with peers) and situated in pupils' socioeconomic environment? Or was there a real and separate contribution of schooling to pupil's knowledge that was independent of such "outside" forces? Further, did socioeconomic environments condition schooling choices, so that schooling acted as a screening mechanism, and its income value was to its selection capability, or were schooling choices primarily the result of pupil "preferences" independent of socioeconomic background, for additional investment in schooling? That debate was never resolved, but it was thought that declining rates of return were an indication that screening was less likely. Now the issue raises its head again, and the question is the same: does the income payoff to schooling result mainly from barriers to entry, or is it mainly a payoff to the greater cognitive knowledge acquired by individuals freely choosing to invest in more schooling?

In the globally competitive economic environment of the 1990s, most economists would expect a shift away from schooling as a screen to schooling as "pure" human capital. A highly competitive economy could hardly afford to "waste" resources on screening. Yet the results of the rate-of-return studies suggest that in rapidly industrializing societies access to higher levels of schooling is increasingly restricted (in relative terms) as lower levels of schooling expand and the payoff to higher education rises relative to lower levels. Does this indicate a disjuncture between the market and public policy? Or is the private sector labor market primarily interested in having schools act as a screening mechanism even under conditions of increased competition? Indeed, it may very well be that increased global competition could put more value on schooling as a screen. Employers might value formal schooling especially for its risk-reducing screening capacity, and risk-reduction may be even more valuable under highly competitive conditions.

The other approach to this issue is through analyses of the relationship between pupil achievement in school and productivity and income. Economists of education have long debated this point as well. Again, changes in the world economy should result in greater rewards to cognitive knowledge than in the past. If business rhetoric is any indicator, managers are increasingly interested in rewarding the best and the brightest. This means that pupils who achieve better than others at any level of schooling should have higher productivity and higher income in work than pupils who achieve less well. But showing that such a relationship exists has proven elusive, and when shown, the size of the effect is relatively small—a large increase in pupil achievement (for example, one standard deviation of an achievement test) may result in a few percentage points on higher observed income. There is mixed evidence about whether this relationship has become stronger in the more competitive global economic environment.

So even if it can be shown that those who take more schooling are scoring higher on school achievement tests (therefore, allegedly bringing more cognitive knowledge to their work and earning higher incomes than those with less schooling), those who take the same amount of schooling yet score much higher on tests, earn little more, if any income, than those who score much lower. Do employers have faith in more cognitive knowledge only when it is sanctioned by additional years of schooling and a diploma, or is something else at work here? Moving into new organizations of production processes should have changed these relationships, but economists have not been able to discern much about how these changes are taking place, if they are at all.

Third, there is a more macroeconomic aspect to the implications of moving away from an assembly-line, simple input-output model of the economy. In the past, economists argued that seeking a more equal income distribution conflicted with maximizing economic growth through a long stage of development associated with the take-off and the climb to sustained growth. The "inverted-U" of increasing income inequality during industrialization was posed as a natural outcome of the shift from agricultural subsistence production to the increasingly specialized, increasingly diversified labor force implicit in Tayloristic industrial production and high level services. It was also assumed specifically that a high fraction of the labor force in such production could remain unskilled for two or more generations as nations gradually built up their industrial capacity and passed into higher levels of manufacturing sophistication—this again being based on a model of industrial development as it occurred in the nineteenth and early twentieth century.

The first clue that this conception of the relationship between income distribution and economic development might be wrong came when income distribution was studied in individual countries over time rather than across countries. Such research showed that large changes in income distribution came quickly, generally in periods of major economic shocks (such as the Great Depression or a war) and when a government made radical changes in distributive policies. The connection between rising levels of education and more equal income distribution was positive, but not large. Further, there was no evidence that in capitalist economies government equalization policies per se had a negative effect on economic growth. This, it should be remembered, was research that pertained to an era when traditional assembly-line industrialization was still dominant.

In the 1980s, some analysts challenged the economic growth-distribution trade-off in terms of the new global information economy. Research on Japan (Johnson 1982) and comparisons between Latin America and the "Four Tigers" in Asia (Castells 1989) suggested two things: a well-organized, activist state involved in promoting by means of incentives the new kinds of organizations and innovativeness needed to compete in the world economy almost certainly had a positive effect on economic development, and a more equal income distribution probably also had a positive effect on growth, other things equal. Later the idea that more equal income distribution is associated with state policies that rapidly expand high-quality education from the bottom up linked human capital formation to the "virtuous circle" of economic growth with *increasing* income equality (Birdsall and Sabot 1993). If new types of organization at the level of the firm are needed to be constantly innovative and to increase productivity, perhaps the most successful economies are also characterized by state policies that emphasize greater participation and equality in the context of promoting more education and provide incentives to firms to innovate under conditions of more equal wages. Countries such as Korea, Taiwan, and Singapore supply good examples of such policies. Their success not only affirms the important role of high quality public education in preparing labor for modern competitive, flexible production systems, but also the crucial role of the "developmentalist state" in guiding the process of development.

Fourth, moving away from the assembly-line model of educational production adds a completely new dimension to the production-function models of schools and educational systems and even those micro models of education that attempt to analyze the achievement productivity of classrooms in terms of time use. If any process depends on relations between the people doing the producing, it is the teaching-learning process inherent in school production. Learning is a product of interactions, and the quality of interactions is crucial to learning. There is no explicit wage contract between students and teachers that defines what school is bound to produce. Furthermore, teachers are virtually unsupervised in their production activities, and a major part of the production of education takes place jointly outside the school in other institutions—the family and the community—that are even less structured like an assembly plant than schools. Yet the public sector and many private schools attempt to make teaching and learning an assembly line, factory process, and economists analyze them as if teaching and learning were guided by the rules of a hierarchical factory production system.

That does not mean that there are no elements of assembly-line production in schooling and learning. Repetition does work to produce learning. But the point is that if economists are to try to understand what goes on in the process of formal education, they should come to terms with the reality and complexity of that process and model its complexity, not assume that it works like a production process that can already be modeled.

To capture the relationship between schooling and families' behavior toward children and toward children's school learning requires understanding what may be called "joint production." Researchers have shown, for example, that when families can and do provide good nutrition and health care to their children and spend more time talking with them, and paying attention to them in positive ways at an early age, this makes them inherently much better learners. Later, when children go to school, their family's participation also affects learning in school.

Capturing the complexity of this process also means doing a better job of understanding the organizational relationships in the family and in school as they pertain to pupils' learning. Just as in the case of flexible production in private, for-profit firms, participation in decision-making and innovation by teachers and parents (and students) is almost certainly a crucial factor in the productivity of the teaching-learning process.

The policy implications of economists' research in

explaining how to improve school achievement are only as good as their understanding of what goes on in schools. This leads to the fifth implication for the content of the economics of education. Many economists are wedded to ideological notions of "public" and "private." Many jump to the conclusion that public education is inherently inefficient, or at least inherently more inefficient than private education. This comparison between private and public is, it may be argued, not very useful and largely misleading in most parts of the world. The vast majority of schools are publicly run and publicly financed. Yet they also have a large *private* financing component in the form of parental contributions of fees, school supplies, uniforms, transportation, and books. Private schools in all countries but the United States are largely publicly financed or aided, but also have a large private contribution component. Indeed, it is only in certain developed countries such as the United States where publicly financed and managed public education is at all clearly separated from privately run and privately financed, private education.

The emphasis in the 1980s on private education as an alternative to public also proved counterproductive in a wider sense. Economists of different political persuasions now generally agree that markets and competition are important for economic growth. But economists also need to be reminded that the public sector, when even moderately well run, is just as indispensable as the private sector to growth. In part, its indispensable role centers on the human capital-based innovation and learning system that is now required for progress in the new world economy. All of the high-growth Asian "NICs" (newly industrializing countries) including China, have in common with Japan, Germany, France, and Scandinavian countries a highly interventionist state that "manages" their economic growth process in a variety of ways, from a system of subsidies to direct and indirect rewards and sanctions over production units.

A second point is worth making: although markets and competition are important in allocating resources efficiently, there is no evidence that competition between public and private schools itself improves the performance of public or private schools. The case of Chile is informative. There, fully subsidized private schools have existed for more than 10 years and have flourished, even in low-income areas. The results for public education have not been at all positive, and lower economic class pupils do no better in private than in public schools (Tedesco 1992). It may be that the production of schooling is such that competition itself has no impact on children's learning because teaching and learning are an inherently cooperative endeavor, not necessarily responsive to the pressures of competition.

From this it should be deduced that in the present world economy, a public-private *partnership*, guided by a human capital-intensive, politically stable, decentralized, honest, and accountable public bureaucracy

is crucially important in guiding and assuring capital formation and equitable investment in public services in a politically democratic market economy. Indeed, it is difficult to imagine the sustainability of growth in a market economy without a reasonably efficient public sector that regulates and controls the market, assures some measure of the equitable distribution of the fruits of growth, and coordinates the investment process.

Public education plays a triple role in this coordination. First, it forms the backbone of the innovation and learning-by-doing systems that are required for competing in the new world information-based economy—publicly financed education is crucial to producing the human capital needed for those systems. Secondly, publicly managed education is fundamental to producing a notion of the collective goals that the public sector intends to achieve. The importance of collective goals has always been stressed, but in the new world economic situation its economic meaning has become much more apparent. Thirdly, in public goal-oriented societies, public education is also largely responsible for producing the efficient, collectively oriented public bureaucrats who will guide these human capital-based economies.

Economists of education are strategically placed to understand this changing nature of the public–private partnership, precisely because education is so central to it. Yet this means that they must regard the *public* in public education as part of the process of mobilizing families, students, and firms to act for larger social goals, and doing so in a way that draws the private voluntarily into these goals. To develop this understanding, they must have a firm grasp of theories of public-private relations, how these influence human capital formation, and how and why practice in such relations has changed over time.

Economists of education have done a great deal since the 1960s to show that Schultz and others were correct in their intuition that education is an important input into the production process. However, economists will have to go far beyond those early models to understand the role of education in the present-day development process.

This volume attempts to provide an understanding of where the economics of education has been, where it is heading, and where it needs to go in the future to provide further insights into the human role in production and the production of human skills valued in the labor market.

To achieve these goals, the volume is divided into seven further sections: Education and Labor Markets; The Benefits of Education; Education, Economic Growth, and Technological Change; Education, Income Distribution, and Discrimination; The Production of Education; Evaluating Educational and Training Investment; and Financing Education. Although there is some overlap between the sections, this division provides a general typology of the main themes in the economics of education, and gives the reader a map for understanding its main debates.

Each section features articles that summarize the past generation of work in that subset of the field, going back in time to review the work that has traditionally defined it. The section also includes articles that cover critiques of the traditional approaches to the subject. For example, in education and labor markets, the human capital approach is carefully analyzed (in a number of articles), but so is the screening hypothesis and the literature on dual and segmented labor markets. Finally, each section includes reviews of more recent theoretical perspectives that should influence economics of education in the future.

The underlying idea, of course, is to *build* on the past rather than to consider it obsolete. Many of the original ideas in the economics of education, such as the option value of education and downward substitution of higher levels of education for lower, tend to be forgotten, and then miraculously resurrected as archaeological finds. Students of economics of education should understand the debates in this field as they unfolded in their original incarnation, how they have changed over time, and why they have changed. In most cases these debates reflect larger theoretical disagreements in the economics profession as a whole, but the economics of education can continue to make a singular contribution to them. For example, the possibly changing role of skills in labor markets has important implications for growth theory and for the relationship between economic growth, technological change, and income distribution. Increasingly sophisticated models of education production would be important for understanding the production process in both private firms and in the public sector. And the role of competition in the market for quasi-public goods such as education could be greatly illuminated by more in-depth study of the provision of private education.

The articles in this volume should be viewed as the foundation for such future contributions. By summarizing what economists have already learned about education and training and presenting their most recent thinking on these subjects, these works serve to define paradigms and issues for both those who have long been involved in the field and those who are entering it now.

References

Birdsall N, Sabot R 1993 *Virtuous Circles: Human Capital Growth and Equity in East Asia*. Policy Research Department, World Bank, Washington, DC

Castells M 1989 High technology and the new international division of labour. *Labour Soc.* 14

Gordon D, Edwards R, Reich M 1982 *Segmented Work, Divided Workers*. Cambridge University Press, Cambridge

Howell D, Wolff E 1991 Trends in the growth and distribution of skills in the US workplace, 1960–1985. *Industrial and Labor Relations Review* 44(3): 486–502

Johnson C 1982 *MITI and the Japanese Miracle*. Stanford University Press, Stanford, California

Nam Y S 1994 Women, schooling, and the labor market: Changes in the structure of earnings inequality by gender in Korea, 1976–1991 (Doctoral dissertation, Stanford University)

Schultz T W 1963 *The Economic Value of Education* Columbia University Press, New York

Schultz T W 1975 The value of the ability to deal with disequilibria. *J. Econ. Lit.* 13: 872–6

Tedesco J C 1992 Nuevas estrategias de cambio educativo en America Latina. *Boletin Proyecto Principal de Educacion en America Latina y el Caribe* 28: 7–24

Welch F 1970 Education and production. *J. Pol. Econ.* 78: 35–59

Education and Labor Markets

Introduction

M. Carnoy

The core of the economics of education is found in the relationship between education and labor markets. Human capital itself is defined in terms of the value that markets place on the work done by individuals who have invested in varying amounts of formal schooling, formal on-the-job training, and informal training. So economists have focused on understanding the underlying reasons for the higher value the market apparently places on higher levels of schooling and training, on whether that higher value is attributable directly to what is learned in schooling and training, and on how this higher value affects individual investment behavior.

Major early contributions by Theodore Schultz, Gary Becker, and Jacob Mincer argued that there was a direct link between the marginal productivity of labor and investment in education and training (including acquired work experience) during an individual's lifetime. Such human capital models assumed that individuals as producers were differentiated primarily by that investment, and that human capital investment decisions were made freely by individuals responding to labor market incentives and individual time preferences. A number of entries in this section develop this conception of the functioning of the labor markets; Keith Hinchliffe, Maureen Woodhall, Richard Freeman, Sherwin Rosen, and Mary Jean Bowman all review the arguments underlying human capital concepts and their relation to neoclassical notions of the labor market for skills.

By the 1970s the earlier conception was challenged by several alternative views of how labor markets worked. Some of these challenges came from within the framework of the neoclassical paradigm, arguing that there existed imperfections in labor markets that significantly affect the relationship between education and marginal productivity. In brief, labor's marginal productivity in such alternative models is set by the institutional conditions of work. The "pay-off" to individual workers' education and training in the form of higher productivity depends on the institutional conditions under which these skills are employed.

Because of market imperfections, different conditions can exist side-by-side in the marketplace. The internal labor market model discussed by Peter Doeringer, the technological segmentation model suggested by Maria Tueros' entry on informal labor markets, and the screening models reviewed by Wim Groot and Joop Hartog, all argue that the relationship between education and productivity/wages differ significantly in parts of the labor market characterized by different technological and organizational conditions of work. Implicitly, such models also suggest that where (e.g., in which type of firm) individuals with the same education get jobs has a major effect on the amount of further training they receive, and hence, on the value placed on their work.

Other challenges went further, arguing that the nature of labor markets as described by neoclassical economists operated quite differently "in the large" from what the human capital model claimed. The labor market could be characterized less as a level bargaining table between individual owners of physical capital and those delivering labor skills than a sociopolitical arena heavily influenced by social power relations where employers treated various social class/gender/race/ethnic groups differently from White males, even when individuals from these various groups had invested equally in human capital. Segmentation theories based on this social concept of labor markets viewed the value of education as much by these "power" characteristics of labor as by marginal productivity. Thus, Gregory de Freitas' entry and those by Ignacio Llamas and Glaura Vasquez de Miranda, the underlying critique of human capital is much more profound than those challenging it from within the neoclassical paradigm.

The division of labor markets into different strata, or segments, implies that the constraints on choice are rooted in the nature of social and political power relations, not just the technical or bureaucratic structure of firms and schools. According to this critique, these social relations of production dominate the value that the market places on education, and, in turn,

9

the amount invested in education by individuals from various social class, gender, race, and ethnic groups is conditioned by their position in the social structure.

In his entry Mark Blaug makes a somewhat different critique of the human capital model. He argues that the wage contract cannot specify precisely what the employer expects the employee to do for the wages received. Therefore, to a significant degree the work the employee carries out is a matter of negotiation and motivation, both in terms of extracting labor (by the employer) and delivering labor (by the employee). Employers and employees demand and take education on the basis of better defining this grey area of expectations, but education's role in wage determination seen this way may have little to do with the cognitive skills assumed by the human capital model. The incomplete contract, according to Blaug, also has important implications for the relationship between human capital and economic growth: for a similar investment in education, some economies may increase productivity more rapidly than others because of more positive management-labor relations; in other words, how workers and managers, regardless of skills, complete the employment contract.

Samuel Bowles and Herbert Gintis explore this notion of "agency" in the labor market relation further. If the firm is an arena of "contested exchange," as they claim, the education-wage relationship may differ considerably from the neoclassical assumption of greater cognitive skills producing higher marginal productivity, hence higher wages. Bowles and Gintis spell out the alternative in which employees and employers contest wages. They argue that there is little evidence that cognitive skills as such are related to either productivity or wages, but considerable evidence of wide variation in wages awarded to employees with similar skills in varied bargaining situations.

The entries in this section suggest the major contributions made by human capital theory to understanding the role of education and training in labor markets, and the major challenges to that theory made over the years, including the most recent challenges from Blaug and Bowles and Gintis. When the concepts of incomplete contracts and contested exchange are added to the phenomena of internal labor markets and labor market segmentation, a picture emerges of the economic value of schooling that is far removed from the simplistic belief that education makes workers more productive and that employers pay them more because they are more productive. Why educated workers are more likely to get good jobs and how much they produce when they get those jobs appears to depend on a host of factors that are deeply imbedded in much more subtle labor market relations. It may be that these subtleties make a greater contribution to individual worker, firm, and economy-wide productivity than higher levels of education in the labor force.

Work and Education

H. M. Levin

In most societies, education and work are intimately connected. Schooling is the main institutional experience shared by the young, while work is the principal institutional experience of adults. Most jobs and occupations have educational requirements for entry and advancement, and the organizational forms of schooling correspond closely with the organizational forms of work. Further, schooling attainments represent an important mechanism for determining social and occupational mobility from generation to generation. Although the term education is sometimes used interchangeably with schooling, it is important to note that schooling is not the only form of education. However, schooling represents such a dominant aspect of education in modern societies that the convention of equating education and schooling in the advanced industrialized societies will also be adopted here.

1. Connecting Education and Work

Every society has specific forms of work which derive from the particular ways in which the society is organized. In traditional societies, adults must be able to produce directly the food, clothing, and shelter they require for subsistence. In non-traditional societies, adults must be able to function as workers in large and bureaucratic enterprises in which most jobs are unconnected with the production of daily needs and where work is often broken down into highly routinized and repetitive tasks under a vast division of labor. Today, a small proportion of employers has moved to team production where workers receive substantial training and participate in decisions. In each situation, societies can only reproduce their forms of work from generation to generation if the young are educated to perform in appropriate work roles by the time that they attain adult status. Exposure to work tasks from an early age and placement in local work apprenticeships have been the dominant forms of preparation for work under preindustrial circumstances. Although schools existed prior to the Industrial Revolution, few children attended them and they were not crucial experiences for the world of work except for those who would enter the so-called learned professions of law, medicine, teaching, and the ministry.

1.1 Contemporary Work Organization

The traditional sources of preparation for adult responsibilities, such as family, church, apprenticeships, and community, are no longer adequate for preparing the modern worker. It is generally accepted that an important reason for the rise of universal and compulsory schooling was the need to inculcate the young with the attributes necessary to work in modern work enterprises.

To a very large degree in all societies, the basic forms of formal education or schooling correspond to the basic forms of work organization. This can be seen more clearly if modern work organizations are described in terms of their general features (Perrow 1970 Chap. 3). First, they tend to be large, hierarchical, and impersonal. Modern small firms tend to be considerably larger than the small workshops, farms, and commercial establishments of early capitalism. Much, if not most, of the labor force in capitalist societies is found in enterprises with several hundred or even several thousand employees.

Hierarchy in the modern workplace is exemplified by the fact that most firms are organized along the principle of military organization with responsibilities set out according to the level of the organization at which the individual is employed as well as the nature of the position at that level. Each employee is placed in a command structure in which he or she must be responsive to persons higher up and must often supervise those below. In addition, such firms are pyramidal, in that there is a large number of workers at the bottom of the firm working under close supervision and pervasive rules and regulations. At the top of the enterprise, a few executives are charged with overall decision making for the enterprise, and at the intermediate levels there are other groups of workers with both work duties and supervisory responsibilities. The position of the worker in the hierarchy determines his or her authority, status, pay, and the opportunities for promotion to other levels. The impersonality of the modern work organization is reflected in the fact that relations among workers are expected to be "matter-of-fact" and businesslike rather than highly personalized. Workers are expected to work together efficiently not because they like each other or have other attachments, but because they are paid to interact with each other in established ways that enhance the overall control of the organization and its output.

Second, rather than workers participating fully in the creation of a complete product or service, modern workplaces are usually characterized by a minute division of labor in which the vast majority of workers execute only a few routinized tasks. Although there have been some deviations from this pattern in the

"new productive work organization" (Osterman 1992, Womack et al. 1990), the typical production of goods and services is still divided and subdivided into a large number of simple operations which enable careful and close supervision to ensure that each worker is performing adequately the few tasks to which he or she has been assigned. This fragmentation of work originated in the late nineteenth century under the inspiration of "scientific management" and its progenitor Frederick Taylor (Nelson 1975, Haber 1964), and it has been an inexorable characteristic of the workplace as newer technologies have often been designed around further simplification of work tasks and their skill requirements (Flynn 1988, Spenner 1985). In postindustrial societies this trend has spread from manufacturing and industrial production to wholesale and retail trade, health services, office work, and the service industries generally (Braverman 1974). The advent of the microcomputer has further enhanced the ability to replace relatively skilled work roles with unskilled ones, although the technology can also be used to support more democratic workplaces (Levin 1987).

A third feature of the workplace is the emphasis on motivating workers through extrinsic rewards rather than through the intrinsic quality of the work experience. Since most workers are given little control over the process and product of their own work activity, there is little that is intrinsically attractive about most jobs. Therefore, work organizations must use other devices to get the work performed, such as constant supervision under which workers must obtain favorable ratings to achieve continuing employment, wage increases, and promotion. Further, workers must compete with other workers for these benefits, a competition that can be particularly fierce under conditions of high unemployment.

A final feature of modern work organization is the degree to which work and occupations are segregated by sex and other personal characteristics. In most societies, females are found overwhelmingly in those occupations that appear to be extensions of the household (e.g., waitresses, maids, seamstresses, elementary-school teacher, nurses) and in office work. They are less likely to be found in high-level professional and supervisory positions than men. In addition, many societies are characterized by similar forms of segregation as various racial groups, "guest workers," immigrants, and persons from rural origins are found in the least attractive and lowest paying jobs.

In summary, the modern work organization is highly complex, places a great deal of control over the activities of workers, and determines the nature of work tasks according to the requirements of the enterprise and its owners rather than according to the human needs of its workers. Workers are often placed in antagonistic relations to one another, and they have little or no control over the nature of their own work activity. In addition, certain social groups are typically found at the bottom of the work hierarchy while other groups are found in the middle and at the top.

Although it is often assumed that such forms of work are necessary for achieving high levels of productivity and consumption, there is some evidence that they evolved primarily because they enabled control of the work enterprise to be centralized under capitalist owners and managers (Marglin 1974). As the government sector expanded, or as the ownership of capital was transferred to the state as in the socialist countries, the government also adopted similar forms of organization for similar reasons. Supervision and control of the work process are enhanced by the monitoring of simple and repetitive tasks arrayed among different levels, with each successive level in the hierarchy responsible for the one below it (Alchian and Demsetz 1972). Recent evidence suggests that moving towards greater worker involvement in decisions can result in greater productivity than in more conventional forms of work organization (Bonin and Putterman 1987, Bonin et al. 1993, Levine and D'Andrea Tyson 1990, Jones and Svejnar 1982).

1.2 Contemporary School Organization

Given this general description of the workplace, it is possible to outline some features of schooling and their correspondence with work enterprises. Organizationally, schools are hierarchical and bureaucratic with highly centralized control of the overall institution through central school boards, administrators, and school-level directors, head teachers, or principals. Teachers supervise a work process that is relatively uniform and usually organized according to grade levels. The work process for teacher and student has been set out well in advance of the implementation of the schooling activity and without the involvement of the major participants. The design and planning of the curriculum, pedagogy, sequence of courses, selection of textbooks, and methods of evaluation are usually set out by a political and administrative process with the assistance of technical specialists. The implementation and evaluation of the process are generally carried out by classroom teachers and other professionals who have authority over students by virtue of their superior positions in the hierarchy. Each course is generally divided into units and subunits which are followed sequentially and often learned by rote to enable success on standardized tests of the units. Students have little control over the use of their time and little input into the learning process, but are mainly expected to respond correctly to the demands placed upon them.

Control of student activities and the basis for student motivation is provided through an elaborate system of extrinsic rewards and other sanctions such as grades, promotions, and access to later educational opportunities in a world where such educational accomplishments translate directly into opportunities for economic and occupational status. For the vast majority of the population, schooling is pursued for rewards that are external to the educational activity rather than because of the direct satisfaction received from the activity itself. Like most workers, students, too, are alienated from the process and product of their own efforts and are placed in direct competition with their fellow students for schooling rewards and for favor in the eyes of their supervisors. Only rarely do schooling activities yield satisfaction of an intrinsic nature, since they are planned, controlled, supervised, and evaluated by an organizational approach and process over which the student as little or no control.

Finally, schooling corresponds to the workplace in its treatment of persons from different social-class backgrounds, race, and sex. In the workplace the most remunerative, powerful, and highest status positions are generally occupied by persons who themselves have considerable educational advantages and come from higher social class origins. In the schools, persons from less advantaged backgrounds generally receive less education and schooling of a poorer quality than those from more advantaged backgrounds. For many countries this is also true for the children of immigrants and rural inhabitants, racial and ethnic minorities, and females.

Children from higher socioeconomic origins are more likely to be found in elite, private schools or higher quality public schools with better trained teachers, smaller classes, superior facilities, and better instructional materials than their less advantaged peers. In addition, tracking or streaming within schools on the basis of "aptitudes" generally functions to assign children from more advantaged families to academic and honors programs, and those from less advantaged families to basic and vocational preparation. The former programs tend to lead to university and the most prestigious jobs and professions, while the latter is designed to prepare students for relatively unskilled work or limited vocational training in technical institutes or community colleges.

In many obvious ways, the structure of the schooling experience and that of the workplace correspond, although it must be noted that correspondence is never complete, as other dynamics also influence the nature of schooling. However, it is useful to distinguish several functions of the schooling process that contribute to the formation of workers, and in doing so, to the reproduction and expansion of the production process.

First, schools produce both general cognitive skills and specific vocational ones that correspond to the skill requirements for entry at different job levels. Second, they produce those behaviors, habits, values, and awareness of social processes among children that will predispose them to accept the conditions and social relations which predominate among work organizations. Third, the schools legitimate the differential preparation and certification of the young for work roles according to class, race, and sex as these are reflected in the inequalities of the work hierarchy.

Finally, schooling plays a major role in reproducing the ideology of the forms of work that characterize a society as well as workplace justice. In this respect students learn that in the capitalist workplace, rewards are allocated according to individual effort and productivity and that social mobility is limited only by educational attainments and efforts in both school and in the workplace.

2. Theories of Education and Work

Theories of the relation between education and work can be either positive or normative. Positive approaches represent attempts to explain the observed connections between education and work and how they developed. In contrast, normative approaches tend to focus on what should be the relation between education and work. That is, normative theories emphasize an ethical or moral approach to the issue rather than attempting to explain what exists or has existed. Educators are particularly concerned with the normative view, since it has important implications for designing the structure and content of schooling, that is, what should be taught and how. Social scientist and educational planners are especially concerned with positive theories for explaining the relation between education and work. For social scientists, this relationship is an important puzzle that needs to be understood; for planners, it is necessary to grasp the behavioral connections that link education and work in order to plan and implement educational reforms that are designed to prepare the young better for the workplace.

2.1 Normative Theories

The two principle normative theories regarding the relation between education and work differ primarily according to the role accorded to each in shaping the other. One theory is predicated on the view that a major function of schools should be the preparation of workers in the appropriate numbers, and with suitable skills and behaviors, to serve the system of production. The implication of this theory is that the schools should be designed for "social efficiency" by preparing workers for the existing economic order. The criterion of success is the degree to which the schools provide trained personnel to fill the needs of firms. To a large degree the field of educational planning is based upon this assumption about the relation between education and work, and most planning tools assume that patterns of curriculum and enrolment, as well as the quality of instruction, should be measured against the needs for trained workers (Blaug 1970 Chap. 5). That is, the system of education is considered to be subservient to the system of production and its needs for workers, and the criterion for educational planning and implementation is its fidelity to the requirements of the workplace. This view also underlied the human capital theory of investment in schooling and the development of vocational schooling.

However, a starkly contrasting view is that the schools should serve the ideals of providing a moral education dedicated to human development and democratic ideals without reference to the needs of the workplace. This view is largely embodied in the thought of John Dewey and "progressive education." Dewey (1916) argued that by creating ideal social communities in the school, the eventual growth of youth into adulthood would transform adult society along similar principles. Dewey rejected instrumental views of schooling in which an educational activity was predicated upon producing a specific educational "output." Rather, his concern was that the educational process itself should be the central focus such that schooling activities would be undertaken only because of their intrinsic goodness. Progressive education was to be child-centered rather than based upon preparing youth for the stark realities of adult life. Each child was to be given a maximum opportunity to develop its talents through exposure to a wide range of experiences in which democratic participation and intrinsic satisfaction were the principal guidelines for the choice of educational activities. Dewey opposed the use of schools to prepare workers for an existing work order that he considered to be unequal, unjust, and alienating even though acknowledging that good work skills could be an important "by-product" of the educational process.

2.2 Positive Theories

The theory of human capital represents the simplest explanation of the relation between education and work (Becker 1964). Schooling, formal on-the-job training, and work experience represent investments in skill development and enhancement that lead to higher workplace productivity that is rewarded in labor markets with higher earnings. Welch (1970) has claimed that there are two effects from education which increase productivity. First, education creates a worker effect which enables a worker to increase his or her productivity in terms of the speed and quality of work outcomes by virtue of greater literacy, knowledge, and proficiencies in undertaking specific tasks within the context of work organizations. Second, an allocation effect results from gains in productivity of better educated workers making decisions that will improve the allocation of and utilization of resources in the firm, including the allocation of the worker's own time. It is derived from processing information on costs and productivities of different allocation strategies and using these to make decisions. Schultz (1975) has referred to this effect within the context of worker adjustment to disequilibrium situations in which education enhances the capabilities of individuals to obtain access to, understanding of, and productive use of information. In addition to these two direct effects, more education enables an individual to benefit from more advanced training and occupational placement which will enhance productivity in its own right.

Accordingly, individuals and societies invest in education to raise productivity and earnings, and both entities will invest in schooling to the point where the present value of any additional investment is exactly equal to the present value of the investment returns. Evidence of this relation is the positive relation between education and earnings throughout the world. Sometimes economists use a measure of the internal rate of return to compare investments in education with those of other alternatives (Psacharopoulos 1973). Economists are also concerned about whether on-the-job training is specific to a firm or can be generalized to an industry or a large number of employments. Although the theory of human capital does not address the issue of correspondence directly, it does imply that since investment returns are the ultimate guide for educational decisions, families and societies will attempt to make certain that education is vocationally relevant.

In contrast, sociologists have devoted considerable attention to the close correspondence between the organization of schools and that of the workplace. However, in many ways they differ in their explanation of how this relation developed historically and why it exists today. Important distinctions include whether the explanation is based upon the general reproduction of workers through the schools, or whether it emphasizes a social class-based approach to reproduction; whether the theory is based on a Marxian framework of class conflict; whether the emphasis is on the reproduction of skills and qualifications or other aspects of worker reproduction; and whether the state is considered explicitly in the formulation of the theory. A general theory of reproduction of workers that ignores social-class distinctions is that of the United States functionalists in sociology as reflected in the work of Inkeles (1966), and Dreeben (1968). The functionalist perspective is one that has been adopted by many anthropologists and sociologists to organize cultural and social phenomena in order to understand how they are functional to a society (Malinowski 1945). According to this view, all societies must develop means of preparing the young to be competent adults (Inkeles 1966). In modern societies, competency for the workplace requires that youth receive experiences which prepare them for the systems of work organization, control, and hierarchy characteristic of the workplace and replicated in the schools (Dreeben 1968). Essentially, the schools are viewed as the single most important agency of socialization for creating competent adult workers for modern work institutions. In support of this view, Inkeles and Smith (1974) found that for a sample of six countries the amount of schooling experience was the best predictor of those attitudes "which may be required of workers and the staff

if the factory is to operate efficiently and effectively" (p.19).

The functionalist approach has a normative counterpart in the use of schooling for social efficiency. The former theory explains the functioning of schools in these terms, while the latter advocates that schooling be used in this way. However, the functionalist framework has two major shortcomings as an explanatory theory of correspondence between education and work. First, it neither identifies a mechanism by which correspondence is supposed to take place, nor does it offer historical validation of its approach. Rather, it is a static analysis of the logical connections between two institutions rather than an analytical and dynamic explanation. Although both schools and workplaces have changed over time, the dynamics of change are not evident in the functionalist explanation. Second, the functionalist approach ignores the systematic differences in adult competencies and the treatment by the schools and workplace of races, sexes, and persons from different social-class backgrounds: why is it that socialization for adult competencies differs according to these factors?

For these and other reasons, a number of alternative explanations or modifications of the functionalist approach have been proposed. Most of these have been Marxist in orientation. The most important non-Marxian contribution that attempts to incorporate the reproduction of social classes into the education and work relation is that of Bourdieu and Passeron (1977). They view the main function of schooling as the reproduction of the hierarchical and power relations between different groups or classes. The reproduction is carried out through the system of values, norms, and language of the schools as well as a system of selection which is based upon class criteria. The major criticisms of functionalism also apply to Bourdieu and Passeron in that the origins of inequality, and the dynamics by which the schools function to reproduce it, are not explicit in their theory. Instead, the schools are viewed as operating in a mechanistic way with no mention of the origin or forces that create their motion. Marxian approaches provide a dynamic framework which has been used by a large number of authors to explain the connections between education and work. The Marxian view places the productive system at the center of the explanation as well as the class conflict between capitalists who own the means of production and workers who must sell their labor to capitalists to obtain income. In order for capital to expand, capitalists must extract surplus value beyond the wages paid to workers. In order to do this, the capitalist owners and their managers have adopted production techniques designed around a minute division of labor, hierarchy, and both bureaucratic and technical control of the production process (Edwards 1978, Braverman 1974). This approach divides workers against each other in competition for jobs and promotions, while routinizing the extraction of a surplus from the labor input. The cost to workers is high in the form of "deskilling" of the work process and in the loss of control by the worker of both the process and product of his own work activity–the Marxian concept of alienation (Marx 1964, Ollman 1971, Braverman 1974). While the structural contradiction of "struggle of opposites" between capital and labor is mediated by the form of production adopted by the capitalist, the capitalist still must face the challenge of obtaining workers who will be acclimated to the system of work relations that awaits them.

In general, the Marxist explanation sees the schools as instrumental in preparing wage labor that will be properly inculcated with the skills, values, and attitudes to accept the capitalist order and to contribute to capital accumulation. The precise explanations of what schools do differ among the theorists, with some emphasizing the formation of ideology (Apple 1979, Althusser 1971, Baudelot and Establet 1971), others the creation of skills or qualifications pertinent to capitalist production, such as the German participants in the *Prokla* debate (Broady 1981), and yet others focusing on the social relations of production (Bowles and Gintis 1976). What the theories have in common is their emphasis on a dominant capitalist class molding the structure and agenda of the schools either directly or indirectly to reproduce exploitable labor power for the needs of capital expansion and to mediate the contradictions of capitalist production.

Bowles and Gintis (1976) have analyzed the educational system in the United States within the type of framework set out by Poulantzas (1973, 1975) in his early writings. According to their analysis, the educational system serves to perpetuate the existing relations of economic life and cannot be used as an independent agent to transform economic relations, since schools developed historically to meet the needs of capital for an exploitable and dominated labor force. Rather than focusing on ideology or skill formation, Bowles and Gintis focus on the preparation of the young for the social relations of production. They attempt to show historically that the social relations of capitalist production were replicated in the structure and social relations of schooling in America, and that major changes in production were always followed by corresponding changes in schools. What is particularly important about the Bowles and Gintis work is their attempt to explore in both concrete and historical terms the correspondence between the structures of the workplace and of schools as well as its implications.

Their explanation does not, however, account for the fact that schools tend not just to mirror the workplace, but also to have characteristics that are rather different. Most notably, even within their overall pattern of correspondence, schools tend to be more equitable and democratic than work organizations. There are more constitutional protections in the schools than in the workplace, in such societies as the United States, and in virtually all societies there are greater opportunities for upward educational mobility than for upward occupational mobility. How can these differences be explained, and what are their implications for the work-education relationship?

2.3 Education, Work, and the State

To answer these questions, it is necessary to return to the role of the state in capitalist societies. Unlike some of the more mechanistic instrumentalist or structuralist interpretations of the capitalist state (Althusser 1971, Miliband 1969), in which it is assumed that the state is strictly an instrument of the capitalist class, more sophisticated analyses view the state as an arena for continuing struggle between capital and labor and among segments of each (Carnoy 1982, Carnoy and Levin 1985, Dale 1982, Poulantzas 1978). The legitimacy of the state depends upon its ability to provide popular reforms while at the same time meeting the needs for private capital accumulation. But, reconciling both sets of needs is often impossible. Accordingly, a contest must ensue between capital and labor and among segments of both capital and labor to mold the structure and actions of the state on behalf of class and subclass interests.

Schools are situated within the state and are characterized by the same internal contradictions between the demands for popular and egalitarian reforms and the pressures of capital accumulation. That is, schools are in opposition to themselves in being organized to satisfy the needs of two masters with conflicting goals. This internal contradiction is mediated by school policies which represent an attempt to meet the needs of both the democratic and egalitarian aspects of schooling, and the authoritarian and hierarchical ones that are needed for reproducing labor for capitalist firms (Carnoy and Levin 1985). However, the mediation of the underlying contradiction and struggle creates an autonomous dynamic for the schools that is neither under the control of capital nor of labor. Thus, although the influence of capitalist ideology and practice on the operations of schools can explain their correspondence with the workplace, such factors are unable to explain the fact that schools are far more equal and provide more opportunities for upward mobility than the workplace. Indeed, longitudinal comparisons within many societies show that education has become more equally distributed over time, while during the same period income distribution has been unchanged or has become more unequal (e.g., see recent results for Latin America in Lustig 1995). Further, educational opportunities for females and economically disadvantaged groups are generally far superior to those in the workplace.

2.4 Overproduction of Educated Workers

The outcome of the struggle between the forces shaping education for mobility, equality, and democracy and those pushing the schools to reproduce wage labor

15

with the appropriate characteristics and in the appropriate proportions for the economy, can deviate substantially from a loyal path of correspondence. Perhaps the most important manifestation of this departure is the tendency for the educational system to produce a larger number of educated workers than can be absorbed by the economic system at appropriate occupational levels. The widely held ideology of education under capitalism is that equality of democratization of opportunity is reflected in educational opportunity and the possibility of upward mobility through a school system that provides equal opportunities to all. Since access to jobs depends crucially on the amount of schooling that is attained, it is necessary only to achieve a high enough level of educational attainment to obtain high income and employment status. The result is that the perceived status of more schooling in conjunction with political pressures on the educational system to expand in order to accommodate all aspirants will tend to expand the number of educated persons beyond the availability of appropriate jobs in the economic system. This outcome may be accelerated by the fact that even though the earnings and employment opportunities for highly educated persons such as university graduates may decline over time, the earnings and employment opportunities for less educated persons may deteriorate even more. Thus, the profitability of obtaining a university degree may rise, even if real incomes for all young persons entering the labor market are declining relative to the experiences of their older cohorts (Levin and Kelley 1994).

This phenomenon may have severe consequences for the workplace as relatively young and underutilized workers respond to a frustrating situation in ways that are injurious to productivity. Since the early 1970s there has been a productivity crisis in post-traditional societies like the United States that cannot be explained wholly by conventional factors (Denison 1979). Increasingly it is hypothesized that there may be ties between the rise of an overeducated workforce and declines in productivity (Tsang 1986, Tsang and Levin 1985). The most notable concerns seem to be that the frustrations and work dissatisfaction of the overeducated may contribute to such costly phenomena as worker absenteeism, turnover, alcoholism, drug usage, wildcat strikes, and deterioration of product quality (Tsang et al. 1991). In summary, although there is a general pattern of correspondence between the schools and the workplace, the struggle over school policy will tend to create an historical dynamic for schooling that may deviate substantially from strict correspondence (Irizarry 1980). That divergence may create obstacles to further capital accumulation unless the schools and the workplace are pulled back into correspondence. At such points of major disjuncture, both school and workplace reforms will be proposed once again in order to create a smooth pattern of reproduction of workers for capitalist production (Carnoy and Levin 1985).

3. Education and Workplace Reforms

Within this framework, it is possible to understand what types of educational and workplace reforms might develop and which ones might be adopted. Several educational reforms have been proposed in recent years in several countries to mold the schools to meet the needs of the workplace. Workplace reforms have also been proposed and initiated to integrate the "new worker."

3.1 Educational Reforms

Two prominent educational reforms that seem to address the growing disjuncture are career education and recurrent education. Career education represents a broad attempt to integrate more fully the worlds of education and work (Hoyt 1972). Particular strategies include attempts to increase career guidance and student knowledge on the nature and availability of existing jobs; to improve the career content of curricula; to provide periods of work and schooling interspersed through the secondary schooling cycle; and to inculcate students with a more realistic understanding of what to expect in the workplace. At the university level, the movement toward career education takes the form of reducing the availability of nonvocational courses and fields of study as well as changing university governance to increase the voice of the business community. Obviously, an important element of this strategy is to reduce "unrealistically high" expectations for high level careers and to guide students into more attainable ones.

Recurrent education and lifelong learning refer to establishing patterns of postsecondary training that recur over a lifetime rather than completing advanced education and training prior to entering the labor force (Levin and Schutze 1983). Presumably, a typical pattern would entail entry to the labor force after the completion of secondary school with further education and training provided, as needed, for career mobility through education leave as well as on-the-job training. This approach would replace the more traditional one in which many persons take advanced training or university education immediately after secondary completion, entering the labor market only at the end of formal studies. A large range of training and educational options would be developed with greater flexibility in terms of schedule and entry requirements than traditional postsecondary alternatives. This proposal would also match more closely the needs of employers with the educational system, and it would tend to reduce the number of persons with educational levels in excess of those required for available jobs by lessening the initial demand for university degrees prior to labor market entry.

If these reforms were implemented, they might have a major effect on reducing overeducation and "unrealistic" career expectations. However, there are reasons why they have not met with substantial success. First, no matter how realistic the schools are about the available jobs, most families have no alternative other than education for providing opportunities for their children. Without an alternative route for social mobility, it is unlikely that parents and students will become more "realistic." Further, recurrent education can only work successfully if there are a large number of entry-level jobs available to secondary school graduates and if career mobility can proceed on the basis of part-time and intermittent study. However, the relative lack of positions for persons with only secondary school credentials is one of the important inducements to moving directly to postsecondary schooling to obtain better job options. The opportunity cost of undertaking more advanced education and training is very low when few jobs are available at lower levels of training. Moreover, it is very unlikely that persons who take entry-level positions will ever have the same access to professional and managerial positions through recurrent education that persons with traditional educational credentials have. Stock clerks, office workers, and unskilled workers do not become executives, lawyers, and engineers through part-time and recurrent education, because most employers do not accept part-time study while holding low-level jobs as equivalent to full-time study for those careers. That is, a major change would have to take place in labor markets in terms of availability of entry-level positions and employer attitudes for recurrent education to be more widely adopted.

Attempts in the 1980s and 1990s to provide better workplace training for those who will not get university degrees has also been focused on apprenticeships and on imparting more academic content to vocational education. Inspired by the German apprenticeship system, attempts have been made to adapt the system to other countries (Hamilton 1990). However, a shortage of jobs requiring apprenticeships and providing training ladders as well as a reluctance by enterprises to establish apprenticeship training have limited their expansion. That is, major changes in job structures and training responsibilities by employers in conjunction with schools must be undertaken rather than just changes in Schools. Vocational education has increasingly shifted in the United States and Western Europe to postsecondary courses through community colleges and technical institutes that build specialized and job-oriented training on an academically oriented secondary education. At the same time it is being recognized that secondary vocational training often needs more academic content to provide the general skills which will benefit workers in adapting to new technologies. But, all educational strategies to improve the fit between education and work suffer from the fact that responsibility for change must be situated in the workplace as well as the school, if new educational approaches are to be effective. For example, Bishop (1989) has found that United States employers do not seem to obtain information on grades or examination results from job applicants, even though he argues that such information predicts worker productivity. Thus, many students–and particularly those going directly from secondary schools to the job market–may not have direct incentives to put in the effort to learn in secondary school in the absence of greater employer focus on such accomplishments.

3.2 Workplace Reforms

As the educational path diverges from that of the workplace, it is more likely that changes in the workplace will be the major mechanism for reestablishing correspondence. The disruptive potential of overeducation for productivity and capital accumulation has created the need for addressing worker challenges in the workplace itself. One of the most prominent movements in this direction is that of increasing worker participation by establishing various forms of workplace democracy to increase the intrinsic involvement and satisfaction of workers and their commitment to work. In individual enterprises and plants of many countries, attempts have been made to reduce costly worker absenteeism and turnover, and increase productivity by expanding worker participation in the decision process (Levin 1987). Around the world, automakers, for example, have emphasized a team assembly approach in which small teams of workers, in consultation with management, are responsible for scheduling production of subassemblies, training, quality control, maintenance of machinery, and hiring (Logue 1981). Job rotation is also typical under this arrangement. These changes are based upon the sociotechnical approach to reorganization of the workplace in which teams become the basic unit of production (Susman 1976), and dramatic improvements have been reported in worker turnover and quality control (Logue 1981).

In Germany and in Sweden there are national laws that require the participation of workers in the major decisions affecting their working lives. Such laws have been a major priority of the labor-oriented social-democratic parties of those nations, but they are also being recognized increasingly by employers as a basis for keeping workers loyal to firms and involved in their operations. Germany not only requires that workers be represented on the boards of directors of the larger firms, but all firms with five or more employees must establish work councils (Svejnar 1982, Furstenberg 1977). Work councils have the right to handle grievances, administer social-welfare provisions for the company, supervise the enforcement of applicable labor laws, and to negotiate with management on wages and working conditions, hiring and firing, work rules, and such changes in the plant as those emanating from shifts in technology, mergers, and introduction of new work methods.

If these changes are widely adopted and implemented as a way of countering the problems created by relatively overeducated workers and increasing competition created by the worldwide spread of new technologies, they can have profound effects for education. The emphasis on collective decision-making and greater worker participation would suggest educational changes in the direction of greater group decision-making in the schools, emphases on the attainment of, at least, minimal skills and competencies for all students, collegial training where students tutor other students, and a much greater emphasis on cooperative skills and problem-solving (Carnoy and Levin 1985, Levin and Rumberger 1989). That is, the changes that take place in work organization will be replicated in the educational system so that the basic reproduction of labor proceeds more smoothly and in correspondence with the system of work. Of course, this newly established correspondence may be undermined in the future as the separate dynamics created by conflict and struggle within education and work continue.

This does not mean that educational changes will be found only in the schools. These methods require considerable training in the workplace to take advantage of new methods of production. Clearly, a new combination of education and training will be needed to meet the needs of this transformed workplace (Secretary's Commission on Achieving Necessary Skills 1991). If the schools resist the necessary changes, other institutions will arise to accommodate the changes or existing institutions will modify their functions to embrace new roles.

4. Conclusion

In summary, historical changes in the organization of work have led to major changes in the organization of education generally and schooling specifically. As struggles in production between capital and labor over the labor process and the product of labor have ensued, new techniques of production have arisen to mediate the underlying contradictions between capital and labor and to sustain capital accumulation. Historically such changes in the work process have been followed by supportive changes in the schools and in the overall system for reproducing labor as capital has gained a temporary primacy in its influence over educational policies. However, what has often been ignored in analyses of education and work is the fact that schools also represent an arena of struggle creating their own autonomous dynamic that will tend to diverge from a pattern of correspondence and undermine the accumulation process itself. At such historical junctures there will be a flurry of reforms of both work and education that will push to reestablish correspondence once again (Carnoy and Levin 1985).

In such a system, the relation between education and work will be forever changing, although following predictable laws of motion. It is the dynamics of this underlying dialectic which confound the assumptions of educational planners and reformers who are charged with planning the educational system to meet the needs of the workplace. History has shown that despite the best intentions of the planners, the system "plans" itself, and the consequences are often the opposite of what was expected.

Developments in understanding the relation between education and work suggest a rich research agenda. It is important to explore the specific historical dynamics of class struggle within the state and schools, and how they have influenced patterns of worker reproduction. Within the schools it is crucial to establish the dynamics by which educational change occurs in terms of both internal struggle within education and the return to correspondence with changes in the workplace. Educational and workplace reforms must be evaluated according to how they fit the overall patterns of correspondence and how they respond to divergences in that pattern. The respective roles of schools, families, on-the-job experiences, and other influences on the molding of worker traits are not well understood and need further examination and elaboration. Finally, the implications of these dynamics must be better understood, if the role of educational planning is to be become more effective than it has been in the past.

References

Alchian A A, Demsetz H 1972 Production, information costs, and economic organization. *Am. Econ. Rev.* 62: 777–95

Althusser L 1971 *Lenin and Philosophy and Other Essays.* Monthly Review Press, New York

Apple M W 1979 *Ideology and Curriculum.* Routledge and Kegan Paul, London

Baudelot C, Establet R 1971 *L'Ecole capitaliste en France.* Maspero, Paris

Becker G S 1964 *Human Capital: A Theoretical and Empirical Analysis, with Special Reference to Education.* Columbia University Press, New York

Bishop, J 1989 Incentives for learning: Why American high school students compare so poorly to their counterparts overseas. In: Commission on Workforce Quality and Labor Market Efficiency, *Investing in People,* Background Papers, Vol. 1. Department of Labor, Washington, DC

Blaug M 1970 *An Introduction to the Economics of Education.* Allen Lane, Baltimore, Maryland

Bonin J, Putterman L 1987 *Economics of Cooperation and the Labor-Managed Firm.* Harwood Academic Publishers, New York

Bonin J, Jones D, Putterman L 1993 Theoretical and empirical studies of producer cooperatives: Will ever the twain meet? *J. Econ. Lit.* 31: 1290–1320

Bourieu P, Passeron J-C 1977 *Reproduction in Education, Society and Culture.* Sage, Beverly Hills, California

Bowles S, Gintis H 1976 *Schooling in Capitalist America: Educational Reform and the Contradictions of Economic Life.* Basic Books, New York

Braverman H 1974 *Labor and Monopoly Capital: The Degradation of Work in the Twentieth Century*. Monthly Review Press, New York

Broady D 1981 Critique of the political economy of education: The Prokla approach. *Econ. Ind. Democracy* (2): 141–89

Carnoy M 1982 Education, economy and the state. In: Apple M W (ed.) 1982 *Cultural and Economic Reproduction in Education*. Routledge and Kegan Paul, Boston, Massachusetts

Carnoy M, Levin H M 1984 *Schooling and Work in the Democratic State*. Stanford University Press, Stanford California

Dale R 1982 Education and the capitalist state: Contributions and contradictions. In: Apple M W (ed.) 1982 *Cultural and Economic Reproduction in Education*. Routledge and Kegan paul, Boston, Massachusetts

Denison E F 1979 *Accounting for Slower Economic Growth: The United States in the 1970's*. Brookings Institution, Washington, DC

Dewey J 1916 *Democracy and Education: An Introduction to the Philosophy of Education*. Macmillan, New York

Dreeben R 1968 *On What is Learned in School*. Addison Wesley, Reading, Massachusetts

Edwards R C 1978 *Contested Terrain: The Transformation of the Workplace in the 20th Century*. Basic Books, New York

Flynn P M 1988 *Facilitating Technological Change*. Ballinger, Cambridge, Massachusetts

Furstenberg F 1977 West German experience with industrial democracy. *The Annals* 431: 44–53

Haber S 1964 *Efficiency and Uplift: Scientific Management in the Progressive Era, 1880–1920*. University of Chicago Press, Chicago, Illinois

Hamilton S 1990 *Apprenticeship for Adulthood*. Free Press, New York

Hoyt K B 1972 *Career Education: What Is It and How To Do It*. Olympus, Salt Lake City, Utah

Inkeles A 1966 Social structure and the socialization of competence. *Harv. Educ. Rev.* 36: 265–83

Inkeles A, Smith D H 1974 *Becoming Modern: Individual Change in Six Developing Countries*. Harvard University Press, Cambridge, Massachusetts

Irizarry R L 1980 Overeducation and unemployment in the Third World: The paradoxes of independent industrialization. *Comp. Educ. Rev.* 24: 338–52

Jones D C, Svejnar J (eds.) 1982 *Participatory and Self-Managed Firms*. Lexington Books, Lexington, Massachusetts

Levin H M 1987 Improving productivity through education and technology. In: Burke G, Rumberger R (eds.) *The Future Impact of Technology on Work and Education*. Falmer Press, London and New York

Levin H M, Kelley C 1994 Can education do it alone? *Econ. Educ. Rev.* 13: 97–108

Levin H M, Rumberger R 1989 Education, work and employment in developed countries: Situation and future challenges. *Prospects* 19: 205–24

Levin H M, Schutze H (eds.) 1983 *Financing Recurrent Education: Strategies for Improving Employment, Job Opportunities, and Productivity*. Sage, Beverly Hills, California

Levine D I, D'Andea Tyson L 1990 Participation, productivity, and the firm's environment. In: Blinder, A S (ed.) *Paying for Productivity*. Brookings Institution, Washington, DC

Logue J 1981 Saab/Trollhattan: Reforming work life on the shop floor. In: Swedish Information Service, *Working Life in Sweden*. Swedish Information Service, New York

Lustig N 1995 *Coping with Austerity, Poverty, and Inequality in Latin America*. Brookings Institution, Washington, DC

Malinowski B 1945 *The Dynamics of Cultural Change: An Inquiry into Race Relations in Africa*. Yale University Press, New Haven, Connecticut

Marglin S A 1974 What do bosses do? *Review of Radical Political Economy* 6: 60–112

Marx K 1964 *The Economic and Philosophic Manuscripts of 1844*. New World Paperbacks, New York

Miliband R 1969 *The State in Capitalist Society*. Weidenfeld and Nicolson, London

Nelson D 1975 *Managers and Workers: Origins of the New Factory System in the United States, 1880–1920*. University of Wisconsin Press, Madison, Wisconsin

Ollman B 1971 *Alienation: Marx's Conception of Man in Capitalist Society*. Cambridge University Press, Cambridge

Osterman P 1992 *How Common is Workplace Transformation and How Can We Explain Who Adopts It?* Sloan School of Management, Massachusetts Institute of Technology, Cambridge, Massachusetts

Perrow C 1970 *Organizational Analysis: A Sociological View*. Wadsworth, Belmont, California

Poulantzas N A 1973 *Political Power and Social Classes*. New Left Books London

Poulantzas N A 1975 *Classes in Contemporary Capitalism*. New Left Books, London

Poulantzas N A 1978 *L'Etat, le pouvoir, le socialisme*. Presses Universitaires de France, Paris

Psacharopoulos G 1973 *Returns to Education: An International Comparison*. Jossey-Bass, San Francisco, California

Schultz T W 1975 The value of the ability to deal with disequilibria. *J. Econ. Lit.* 12 (3): 827–46

Secretary's Commission on Achieving necessary Skills 1991 *What Work Requires of Schools*. US Department of Labor, Washington, DC

Spenner K I 1985 The upgrading and downgrading of occupations: Issues, evidence, and implications for education. *Rev. Educ. Res.* 57: 125–54

Susman G I 1976 *Autonomy at Work: A Sociotechnical Analysis of Participative management*. Praeger, New York

Svejnar J 1982 Codetermination and productivity: Empirical evidence from the Federal Republic of Germany. In: Jones D, Svejnar J (eds.) 1982 *Participatory and Self-Managed Firms*. Lexington Books, Lexington, Massachusetts

Tsang M 1987 The impact of underutilization of education on productivity: a case study of the U.S. Bell Companies. *Econ. Educ. Rev.* 6: 239–54

Tsang M, Levin H M 1985 The economics of overeducation. *Econ Educ. Rev.* 4: 93–104

Tsang M, Levin H M, Rumberger R W 1991 The impact of surplus schooling on worker productivity. *Industrial Relations* 30: 209–28

Welch F 1970 Education in production. *J. Pol. Econ.* 78(1): 35–59

Womack J P, Jones D T, Ross D 1990 *The Machine that Changed the World* Rawson Associates, New York

Education and the Labor Market

K. Hinchliffe

This entry focuses on relationships between the educational characteristics of individuals and the characteristics of the jobs they enter (or fail to enter). First, some evidence is briefly given, from both developed and less developed countries, of the close associations between age, educational background, occupational status, and earnings from employment. How this evidence is then interpreted, and in particular how alternative theories describe the process of the absorption of school leavers into the occupational labor force, is the subject of the second section. Finally, some aspects of youth and school-leaver unemployment are discussed.

1. Age, Education, Occupation, and Earnings

Education, occupational status, and earnings from employment have been shown in a wide range of studies to be positively interrelated, in countries adopting many different types of socioeconomic system and at different levels of economic development. Earnings functions and path analyses of the effects of individuals' background characteristics on occupational attainment and earnings have invariably indicated that, while much of the variance remains unexplained, the largest single indicator is education. Jencks et al. (1985), utilizing perhaps the largest amount of data for such a study, concluded that for men aged between 25 and 64 years in the United States, the number of years of education was the best single predictor of the eventual occupational status of a labor force entrant. The results of similar (but less sophisticated) studies in a large number of less developed countries made since the early 1970s show the same general findings, often even more strongly. Turning to earnings, Psacharopoulos (1975) demonstrated that for the OECD industrial countries, average earnings of secondary- and primary-school leavers show a differential of 40 percent, while higher education graduates receive on average 77 percent more than secondary-school leavers. In the less developed countries, the differentials through the 1960s and 1970s were much wider (Hinchliffe 1975), though they did narrow significantly in several countries over the 1980s (Lindauer et al. 1988).

Empirical studies of the interrelationships between education and earnings have usually included a third variable—age. Age–earnings profiles demonstrate that, for all educational levels, earnings rise with age up to a maximum and then level off. Further, the higher the educational level, the steeper the rise in earnings. The result, for both developed and less

developed countries, is that while average earnings in wage employment vary significantly by educational level for all age-groups, they do so most prominently in the older age-group. Another general finding is that the distribution of earnings at each educational level is wider for older workers, particularly for those with higher education. Finally, increments of age and education also appear to have different effects depending on type of occupation, with the effects being larger for professionals than for manual workers.

The earnings differentials by educational level, and the earnings functions, which have been calculated for less developed countries, have largely been restricted to observations of individuals in the formal wage sector. While this sector is the one entered by the majority of those with higher education qualifications, in many countries the rural and urban informal sectors still contain most of the labor force, and even most school leavers (Hinchliffe 1986). Detailed studies of the relationship between education and earnings in the rural sector are few. A review of 18 surveys in 13 countries relating the educational level of farmers to their productivity, however, suggests that 4 years of schooling may be capable of raising productivity by around 10 percent a year (Lockheed et al. 1980, Cotlear 1989). Surveys of urban informal sector workers have been more numerous in recent years and have strongly demonstrated a positive association between education and earnings. Several of these studies, however, have omitted consideration of other possible earnings-related factors. Recent World Bank studies for Peru are an exception (Suarez-Berenguela 1987).

In summary, the large number of empirical investigations into the relationships between education, occupation, and earnings from employment which have been conducted since the 1960s in both high- and low-income countries have resulted in two major findings. The first of these is that the main criteria used by employers to recruit new entrants into the occupational structure are level and type of education. To formalize this, minimum educational requirements are generally set for each occupation. Second, there is a very close correlation between an individual's educational attainment and his or her level of lifetime earnings. Explanations of these observations, however, vary widely. Each is based on a different theory of the operation of labor markets.

2. Alternative Theories of the Labor Market

Explanations of the interface between individuals with specific educational characteristics and the nature and remuneration of the jobs they enter are each one part of more general theories of labor markets. In this section, the different interpretations of the empirical conclusions presented above are discussed.

Three major approaches may be identified. The first is grounded on the argument that the educational system operates in such a way that it directly adds to an individual's cognitive abilities. These abilities range from basic numeracy and literacy at one end of the scale to a greater capacity for logical and analytical reasoning at the other. These increased abilities lead to higher earnings. A second approach also maintains that schools are effective in changing a person but that the important changes are not those of cognitive abilities. Class background is here seen as the major determinant of occupation and income, and the educational system is said to operate in such a way that it develops different sets of productivity-related personality traits among children from different social classes. This both legitimizes the distribution of jobs, which simply perpetuates the existing structure of social class, and also increases the productivity of all classes in their ascribed occupations. Traits produced by schools in those individuals who will fill low-paid jobs include punctuality, obedience, and respect for authority, while traits induced in those destined for high-status occupations include self-reliance and the ability to make decisions. Finally, there is a set of approaches which directly questions the view that through the development of either cognitive abilities or personality traits, schools increase the potential productivity of individuals. Rather, the educational system is said to act simply as a selection mechanism to sort out those who possess non-school-related characteristics such as intelligence and motivation, which are in some way connected to productivity. Schooling itself does not affect productivity.

These views of the educational process can in turn be placed in the wider context of the labor market theories to which they are related. In orthodox neoclassical economics, following on from the composition of demand for goods, individual firms derive a demand schedule for labor (relating amounts of labor demanded to different wages) and labor is employed up to the point where marginal productivity is equal to the industry wage. In models up to the late 1950s, labor was regarded as homogeneous. With the development of human capital theory this was no longer assumed, and labor demand has come to be interpreted in a set of markets in each of which there is a demand for specific productivity-determining worker characteristics, among which education and training are the most important. In response to these demands, individuals are assumed to compare the costs of acquiring the relevant characteristics with the expected increase in earnings. As a result of these comparisons, individuals invest in themselves and the aggregation of these decisions determines the supply of human capital. If the demand for productivity-determining characteristics exceeds the supply at a given wage rate, the rate will then rise and, in turn, supply will increase and demand fall. Conversely, if supply exceeds demand the wage will fall and employment increase. Thus, according to human capital theory, the labor market is capable of continually absorbing workers with ever-higher levels of education and training, provided that education-specific earnings are flexible downwards and the labor market is a single continuous one. This approach to the operation of labor markets may be termed "the wage competition model."

Since the early 1970s, a wide range of labor market theories has been developed at variance with the orthodox neoclassical/human capital school. The theories have emerged largely in response to a number of empirical observations in the United States labor market, which were deemed to be at odds with the implications of orthodox theory. These include the persistence of poverty and income inequality, the failure of education and training programs to raise the incomes of the poorest groups, continual upgrading of the qualifications required for jobs, and continuing discrimination against sections of the labor force (Cain 1976). The interpretations of labor market functioning which have come to compete with orthodox theory may be divided into labor market segmentation and job competition models.

Segmentation models are discussed in detail elsewhere (see *Segmented Labor Markets and Education*). The basic contention behind these models is that the labor market is characterized by a number of segments, each of which has different conditions of employment and which recruits from among separate sections of the labor force. To some theorists, the types and numbers of jobs in each segment are determined by technological requirements; to others, segmentation occurs as the result of conscious actions by employers to divide the working class and reduce class consciousness. The latter view has two implications for education. First, educational expansion among those groups consigned to the secondary labor markets characterized by low pay, insecurity, and poor working conditions will not lead to increased earnings. Second, this view links up with the approach to education described above, which argues that the role of the education system in capitalist society is to reproduce existing class relations by legitimizing the stability of intergenerational occupational status and developing different sets of personality traits among the different groups in society necessary for a hierarchical occupational structure. The technological interpretation of segmented labor markets also has some features which tend toward this approach, but at the same time it shares some of the arguments associated with the job competition model described below.

In the third view of education described above it is argued that schooling merely acts as a screening device which helps employers to choose between people who have very different capabilities and who are competing for a small number of jobs. According to this view, educational credentials are essentially signals which indicate the varying levels of "raw" intelligence, motivation, and so on—factors which affect future productivity or "trainability." These credentials may accurately predict future work performance but they do not directly add to it. Several attempts have been made to describe in detail the interrelations between schooling and the labor market based on this simple concept of screening. One of the most widely discussed is the job competition model associated with Thurow and Lucas (1972), which was developed to counter the wage competition view of the United States labor market. This model is based on the uncertainty which surrounds the hiring of labor. Given the problems of accurately predicting the future performance of job applicants and the fact that most job-specific skills are learned on the job, employers use educational qualifications as proxies for those characteristics which facilitate training. In the model, two sets of characteristics determine an individual's income. One set determines the job structure in the economy and the other an individual's relative position in the queue for jobs. Job structure is regarded as technologically determined, and a central feature of the model is that productivity is seen as an attribute of jobs rather than of people. Consequently, wages are based on the characteristics of jobs rather than the characteristics of people in them. Workers are distributed across job opportunities according to their position in the queue.

Potential workers arrive on the labor market with several background characteristics, the most important of which is amount of education. While these are insufficient to allow the worker to take an immediate part in the production process, they do affect the cost of training. Potential workers are then ranked in a queue according to their expected training costs. Based on such a queue, jobs are distributed with employers offering high-productivity jobs to those at the head and working down. In contrast to the wage competition model, which regards the labor market as a market for matching demands and supplies of job skills, the job competition model sees it as a market for matching trainable individuals with training ladders.

The theories of job competition and screening, in their various forms, have important implications for educational policy. As high-productivity jobs become scarce, competition to get to the head of the queue intensifies and the amount of education required increases. A leapfrogging process develops whereby the demand for education by individuals increases the more difficult it becomes for each education group to secure jobs. The effect of education expansion is neither a fall in occupational wages nor an increase in jobs. What does result is that educational qualifications for jobs lower in the hierarchy rise and the more highly educated are then recruited to jobs that would have been filled in the past by the less educated.

While the surplus of a particular educated group does not affect occupational wage levels, it does result in a lower average wage for the group. However, since the "bumping" process, once triggered, extends right down the occupational ladder, wage differentials—and hence the incentive to acquire further amounts of education—may not decrease. However, if jobs are performed no differently by those with different levels of education, the social returns to this educational expansion are negative. If, on the other hand, all job entrants are not perfect substitutes in this sense, and either levels of productivity within particular jobs can be affected by the individual or training costs do differ between individuals in line with their educational qualifications, the social returns to investment in education may be positive. In this case the returns result more from an occupation selection mechanism than from an increase in the quality of labor.

The labor market theories into which the various views of education have been placed were formulated primarily for analyzing the labor markets of developed market economies. In the labor markets of many less developed countries there are two major differences. Employment in the formal wage sector is proportionately very much smaller and, within this, the public sector tends to have a more important place. This dominant role of the public sector has often been used to argue that the job competition model is an even more appropriate model to apply to these countries than the wage competition one. In virtually all less developed countries, the public sector is the largest single employer and, for secondary-school leavers and above, the majority employer. Public sector employment has been strongly sought not only for the level of wages—which, while offering large but declining differentials at the highest levels, may be below those in the private and parastatal sectors—but also for the long-term security. Wage levels in the public sector are set administratively every few years and the criteria adopted rarely allow supply factors much influence. The results tend to be inflexibility with respect to nominal wage levels and differentials. In addition, in order to appear impartial and as a way of coping with the selection of recruits from a large number of potential applicants, emphasis tends to be placed predominantly on formal educational qualifications for recruitment. As a result of both these factors, the problem of surpluses of educated labor is not resolved by wage changes (as implied in the wage competition model) but is rather thrown back onto the educational system to solve by continuously expanding qualifications (as implied in the job competition model).

3. School-leaver Unemployment

An issue which has been given considerable attention, particularly in less developed countries, since the 1960s is school-leaver unemployment. On the labor supply side two features dominate: the historically high growth rate of new entrants to the labor market and their increasing level of qualifications. The average annual rate of growth of the population across all less developed countries between 1960 and 1980 was 2.2 percent, three times the nineteenth-century growth rate of modern developed countries. One result is that around 40 percent of the population in many countries is below the age of 15 years. Not only are new entrants more numerous than those retiring, they are also on average much better educated as a result of the rapid expansion of primary and secondary schooling since the 1960s. Looked at in terms of employment opportunities, not only is the required number increasing, but their quality is also expected to increase. These combined pressures place great stress on labor markets, particularly in urban areas.

The most conspicuous feature of urban unemployment in less developed countries is the concentration on the young (and even more so on young females), with the rate for the 15–24 years age-group often being more than three times greater than for the total labor force. Given the age profile of the unemployed and the expansion of secondary and higher education since the early 1970s, it is not surprising that the unemployed tend to be relatively well-educated. While there are countries which do not fit the overall pattern, the available evidence appears to show a positive relationship between levels of urban open unemployment and education up to the end of secondary schooling followed by a reduced rate among tertiary graduates (Squire 1981). This pattern also appears to correspond with variations in the period of job search, a measure which is arguably more useful than open unemployment rates for identifying employment "problems". Since the 1980s unemployment rates in most developed countries have reached levels higher than at any time since the peaks of the 1930s. Once again rates of unemployment have been higher for females and for the 16–24 years age-group as a whole. During the periods when overall unemployment has increased, its concentration among the young has intensified relative to other age-groups. In contrast to the experiences in less developed countries, the relationship between unemployment and education appears to be a more straightforward negative one.

Disagreements over the appropriate analytical (and hence policy) treatment of school-leaver unemployment, and in particular the willingness of young people to offer themselves for employment, have tended to be sharp. This is particularly so in debates concerning less developed countries. Over time there has been a shift away from placing the whole responsibility on the schools themselves and on the antimanual work aspirations which they were alleged to produce through inappropriate curricula and teaching methods, toward a greater emphasis on the effect of wage differentials. Wide differentials are said to provide a rationale for extensive periods of job search. In this interpretation of school-leaver unemployment, changes in school practices may be desirable but will not in themselves result in altering school-leaver aspirations and eliminating unemployment. Particularly in countries where labor market information is scarce, unemployment has widely come to be regarded, at least in part, as a rational period of job search with its duration depending on the relative strength of three factors: (a) the higher the level of education an individual receives, the wider the variance of possible wage offers and therefore the longer the likely period of job search; (b) the higher the level of education an individual receives, the higher the opportunity costs through income forgone while unemployed and therefore the shorter the likely period of job search; and (c) the greater the amount of financial support from the individual's family, the longer the period of job search. While periods of job search are undertaken by the individual to increase the likelihood of finding a higher paid job, in practice the increased amount of labor market information is expected to reduce "inappropriate" aspirations to a more "realistic" level.

See also: Education and Labor Markets in Developing Nations; Education, Occupation, and Earnings; Education and Earnings

References

Cain G G 1976 The challenge of segmented labor market theories to orthodox theory: A survey. *J. Econ. Lit* 14: 1215–57

Cotlear D 1989 The effects of education on farm productivity. *J. Dev. Planning* 19: 73–99

Hinchliffe K 1975 Education, individual earnings and earnings distribution. *Journal of Development Studies* 11: 149–61

Hinchliffe K 1986 *Monetary and Non-monetary Returns to Schooling in Africa*. Education and Training Department Discussion Paper No. 46. World Bank, Washington, DC

Jencks C et al. 1985 *Who Gets Ahead? The Determinants of Economic Success in America*. Basic Books, New York

Lindauer D L, Meesook O A, Suebsaeng P 1988 Government wage policy in Africa: Some findings and policy issues. *World Bank Res. Obs.* 3: 1–25

Lockheed M E, Jamison D T, Lau L J 1980 Farmer education and farm efficiency: A survey. *Economic Development and Cultural Change* 29: 37–76

Psacharopoulos G 1975 *Earnings and Education in OECD Countries*. OECD, Paris

Squire L 1981 *Employment Policy in Developing Countries: A Survey of Issues and Evidence*. Oxford University Press, New York

Suarez-Berenguela R 1987 *Peru: Informal Sector, Labor Markets and Returns to Education*. LSMS Working Paper No. 32. World Bank, Washington, DC

Thurow L C, Lucas R E B 1972 *The American Distribution of Income: A Structural Problem.* Joint Economic Committee of the United States Congress, Washington, DC

Further Reading

Blaug M 1973 *Education and the Employment Problem in Developing Countries.* ILO, Geneva

Knight J B, Sabot R 1990 *Education, Productivity and Inequality: The East African Natural Experiment.* Oxford University Press, Oxford

Schultz T P 1988 Education investments and returns. In: Chenery H, Srinivasan T N (eds.) 1988 *Handbook of Development Economics.* North-Holland, Amsterdam

Human Capital Concepts

M. Woodhall

The concept of human capital refers to the fact that human beings invest in themselves, by means of education, training, or other activities, which raises their future income by increasing their lifetime earnings. Economists use the term "investment" to refer to expenditure on assets which will produce income in the future, and contrast investment expenditure with consumption, which produces immediate satisfaction or benefits, but does not create future income. Assets which will generate income in the future are called capital. Traditionally, economic analysis of investment and capital tended to concentrate on physical capital, namely machinery, equipment, or buildings, which would generate income in the future by creating productive capacity. However, a number of classical economists, notably Adam Smith pointed out that education helped to increase the productive capacity of workers, in the same way as the purchase of new machinery, or other forms of physical capital, increased the productive capacity of a factory or other enterprise. Thus, an analogy was drawn between investment in physical capital and investment in human capital.

The concept was not fully developed, however, until the early 1960s when the American economist Theodore Schultz analyzed educational expenditure as a form of investment (Schultz 1961), the *Journal of Political Economy* in the United States published a supplement on "Investment in Human Beings" in 1962, and Gary Becker published a book with the title *Human Capital* (Becker 1964, 2nd edn. 1975) which developed a theory of human capital formation and analyzed the rate of return to investment in education and training.

Since that time the concept of human capital has dominated the economics of education and has had a powerful influence on the analysis of labor markets, wage determination, and other branches of economics, such as the analysis of economic growth, as well as expenditure on health care and the study of migration. For it is recognized that these also represent investment in human capital, since they can help to determine the earning capacity of individuals, and therefore increase their lifetime incomes.

However, investment in human capital remains a controversial issue. Attempts to measure the rate of return to investment in education have been attacked by critics who argue that education does not increase the productive capacity of workers but simply acts as a "screening device" which enables employers to identify individuals with higher innate ability or personal characteristics which make them more productive. A summary of this controversy is given below, together with a brief review of research on investment in education and some other applications of the concept of human capital. However, more detailed treatment of all these issues is provided in separate entries (see *Rates of Return to Education; Screening Models and Education*).

1. Measuring the Rate of Return to Investment in Human Capital

When economists refer to expenditure on education and training as investment in human capital, they are doing more than pointing to analogies between education and investment in physical capital. They are asserting that it is possible to measure the profitability of investment in human capital using the same techniques of cost-benefit analysis and investment appraisal that have been traditionally applied to physical capital.

The profitability, or rate of return on investment, is a measure of the expected yield of the investment, in terms of the future benefits, or income stream generated by the capital, compared with the cost of acquiring the capital asset. Cost-benefit analysis is designed to express all the costs and benefits associated with an investment project in terms of a single figure, the rate of return, which shows the rate of interest at which the present discounted value of future income is exactly equal to the present discounted value of costs. This enables different projects to be compared and an optimum investment strategy consists of identifying and investing in projects offering the highest rate of return, or profitability.

If money devoted to education, training, or health care is regarded as investment in human capital, since it raises the lifetime earnings of workers who are better educated and trained or more healthy than other workers, then techniques of cost-benefit analysis can be used to compare the economic profitability of different types or levels of education, of on-the-job compared with off-the-job training, or of different types of medical treatment. It should also be possible to compare rates of return to investment in human capital and physical capital, in order to discover whether it is more profitable to invest in men and women or machines.

Investment in human capital produces benefits both to the individual and to society as a whole. The individual who takes part in education or vocational training benefits by increasing his or her chances of employment and by increased lifetime earnings. These additional earnings, after allowance for payment of taxes, can be compared with the direct and indirect costs of education that must be borne by the individual, including fees, expenditure on books or equipment, and earnings forgone while in school, college, or university. This provides a measure of the private rate of return to investment in education or other form of human capital.

Both the costs and benefits of education also affect society as a whole, since society benefits from the increased productivity of educated workers. Throughout the world this is recognized by governments who pay some or all of the costs of education, and provide free or subsidized tuition in schools or higher education institutions. The costs and benefits to society can be compared by means of the social rate of return.

The question of the profitability of different types and levels of education and training, and the question of the relative yield of investment in human capital and physical capital, have attracted a considerable amount of research activity since the 1960s, as well as provoking fierce disagreements among economists and educational planners. Psacharopoulos reviewed attempts to measure the social and private rate of return to investment in education in 32 countries (Psacharopoulos 1973) and more recently has twice updated this survey of research on the returns to education by analyzing the results of cost-benefit analysis of education in 44 and 61 countries respectively (Psacharopoulos 1981, 1985).

Estimates of social and private rates of return to educational investment, based on surveys of the earnings of workers of different educational levels in 44 countries in the period from 1958 to 1978 reveal, according to Psacharopoulos (1981 p. 326), four underlying patterns:

(a) The returns to primary education (whether social or private) are the highest among all educational levels.

(b) Private returns are in excess of social returns, especially at the university level.

(c) All rates of return to investment in education are well above the 10 percent common yardstick of the opportunity cost of capital.

(d) The returns to education in less developed countries are higher relative to the corresponding returns in more advanced countries.

2. The Profitability of Human Capital versus Physical Capital

The rates of return that are reviewed by Psacharopoulos are summarized in Table 1, which shows the average private and social rate of return for primary, secondary, and higher education in less developed, intermediate, and economically advanced countries. These rate of return estimates refer to single years, and therefore do not show how rates of return change over time, although the average rate of return is calculated from estimates for years which range over a 20-year period. However, there are very few countries

Table 1
Average returns to education by country type and level (percent)

Region/Country type	Social			Private		
	Primary	Secondary	Higher	Primary	Secondary	Higher
Africa	26	17	13	45	26	32
Asia	27	15	13	31	15	18
Latin America	26	18	16	32	23	23
Intermediate	13	10	8	17	13	13
Advanced	—	11	9	—a	12	12

Source: Psacharopoulos 1985
a Not available because of lack of a control group of illiterates

25

Table 2
Returns to human and physical capital by type of country
(percent)

Type of country[a]	1960s		1970s	
	Human	Physical	Human	Physical
Developing	20	15	15	13
Advanced	8	10	9	11

Source: Psacharopoulos 1985
a Developing countries included in the table are Mexico, Colombia, Venezuela, Chile, Brazil, India, the Philippines, Ghana, Kenya, Uganda, and Nigeria. Advanced countries are United States, United Kingdom, Canada, the Netherlands, and Belgium

for which it is possible to calculate rates of return on an historical time-series basis. Data exist on earnings of workers in the United States classified by educational level since 1939. Estimates of rates of return to secondary and higher education between 1939 and 1976 suggest that the returns to education are falling, although not by a large amount. Data from Colombia also suggest that between 1963 and 1974 the returns to education declined, but still remained profitable.

The results of all these studies confirm that expenditure on education does represent investment in human capital, and that it is a profitable investment, both for the individual and for society, although some critics deny that the earnings of educated workers provide an adequate measure of the economic benefits of education. It is difficult, however, to answer the question of whether human or physical capital represents the more profitable form of investment.

An early attempt to answer this question was called "Investment in men versus investment in machines" (Harberger 1965), and this is still a matter that is of vital concern to economists and planners. Psacharopoulos examined estimates of the returns to physical capital in both developed and developing countries and concluded: (a) the returns to both forms of capital are higher in developing countries, which reflects the differences in relative scarcities of capital in either form in developed and developing countries; and (b) human capital is a superior investment in developing countries but not in developed countries, as indicated by the reversal of the inequality signs in Table 2 (Psacharopoulos 1985 p. 591).

3. How Does Human Capital Increase Workers' Productivity?

The earliest explanations of the concept of human capital suggested that education or training raised the productivity of workers, and hence increased their lifetime earnings, by imparting useful knowledge and skills. However, this assumption was soon attacked by critics who argued that the higher earnings of educated workers simply reflected their superior ability, rather than the specific knowledge and skills acquired during the educational process. In addition, it was argued that highly educated workers are more likely to come from higher social class groups in society, and to work in urban rather than rural areas. Many estimates of rates of return to education therefore adjust the observed earnings differentials of educated people to allow for the influence of other factors on earnings.

Since ability is one of the main factors that may determine earnings, this is often called the "ability adjustment" or alternatively the "alpha coefficient," where "alpha" (α) represents the proportion of the extra earnings of the educated, which is assumed to be due to education. Regression analysis and earnings functions suggest that an appropriate value for the α coefficient is between 0.66 and 0.8 (Psacharopoulos 1975). Further details of research on this problem, together with an explanation of earnings functions, will be found elsewhere (see *Education and Earnings*).

More recently, however, critics have gone further, and have argued that education does not improve productivity by imparting necessary knowledge and skills, but simply acts as a screening device, which enables employers to identify individuals who possess either superior innate ability or certain personal characteristics, such as attitudes towards authority, punctuality, or motivation, which employers value and which are therefore rewarded by means of higher earnings.

This argument is called by various names in the literature, including the "screening" or "filtering" hypothesis, or alternatively the "certification" or "sheepskin" argument, since it is suggested that education simply confers a certificate, diploma, or "sheepskin," which enables the holder to obtain a well-paid job without directly affecting his or her productivity. This argument has attracted considerable controversy, but has been refuted by a number of economists who argue that while a "weak" version of the screening hypothesis is undoubtedly true, since employers do use educational qualifications in selecting employees, as a proxy for other characteristics, there is no evidence to support the "strong" versions of the hypothesis, that education has no direct effect on productivity. The fact that employers continue to pay educated workers more than uneducated throughout their working lives refutes this (Psacharopoulos 1979).

Even if the "strong" version of the screening hypothesis is rejected, and it is difficult to see why a cheaper means of identifying workers with desired characteristics has not been developed if education really had no effect on productivity, it is nevertheless true that the idea of education as a screen or filter has been important in influencing recent directions in research in the economics of education. Blaug (1976) in a review of research on investment in human capital, which he describes as a "slightly jaundiced survey" of the empirical status of human capital theory, predicts that

> in time, the screening hypothesis will be seen to have marked a turning point in the "human investment revolution in economic thought," a turning point to a richer, still more comprehensive view of the sequential life cycle choices of individuals. (Blaug 1976 p. 850)

The reason why the screening hypothesis is important is that it has focused attention on the precise way in which education or other forms of investment in human capital influence productivity, and has served as a reminder that education does far more than impart knowledge and skills. The reason why employers continue to prefer educated workers is that not only does the possession of an educational qualification indicate that an individual has certain abilities, aptitudes, and attitudes, but the educational process helps to shape and develop those attributes. In other words, it is now increasingly recognized that education affects attitudes, motivation, and other personal characteristics, as well as providing knowledge and skills.

This means that the concept of investment in human capital is still valid, but it must be extended to include activities which affect personal attributes as well as skills, and it must recognize that such activities increase workers' productivity in complex ways.

4. Accounting for Economic Growth

One of the first applications of human capital theory was the attempt to explain the sources of economic growth and identify the factors that constituted the "residual" after increases in physical capital and labor had been measured. Two different approaches in the early 1960s by Denison (1962) and Schultz (1961) had both demonstrated that investment in human capital, particularly education, could explain a substantial proportion of the growth rate in the United States and other advanced economies, including Canada and the United Kingdom. This type of analysis was extended to include cross-national comparisons of more than 30 countries, and also to include other indicators of human capital (see *Education and Economic Growth*).

Summarizing this research, Psacharopoulos (1984) concluded that when the indirect effect of education on other social welfare indicators was taken into account, the contribution of education to economic growth was even larger than Schultz and Denison had suggested. The interrelations between education and fertility, life expectancy, and child mortality, for example, lead Psacharopoulos to conclude that traditional growth accounting estimates "are likely to underestimate the true contribution of education to economic growth and social welfare in general" (Psacharopoulos 1984 p. 346).

More recently Schultz (1989) has reviewed research on the contribution of human capital to economic growth and summarized the results in terms of seven propositions including:

(a) The human capital that people in developed modern economies have accumulated consists predominantly of specialized human capital.

(b) During the process of economic modernization the rate of increase in human capital is higher than that of reproducible physical capital.

(c) Human capital enhances the productivity of both labor and physical capital.

He finally concludes that "investigations show that specialization, specialized human capital, increasing returns, and economic growth go hand in hand" (Schultz 1989 p. 222).

Psacharopoulos (1989) analyzed time series data for nine countries and concluded that, in general, rates of return to education decline over time, following educational expansion, but that this decline is not sufficient to suggest that further educational expansion would be unprofitable, particularly in developing countries.

5. Other Forms of Investment in Human Capital

Other forms of investment in human capital also develop the personal attributes that help to determine a worker's productivity. On-the-job training and work experience and the process of job search, including migration, as well as health care, can all increase earning capacity, and can therefore be regarded as investment in human capital. Blaug's survey of research on human capital links all these activities together.

> The concept of human capital, or "hard core" of the human-capital research program is the idea that people spend on themselves in diverse ways, not for the sake of present enjoyments, but for the sake of future pecuniary and nonpecuniary returns... All these phenomena—health, education, job search, information retrieval, migration and in-service training—may be viewed as investment rather than consumption, whether undertaken by individuals on their own behalf or undertaken by society on behalf of its members. What knits these phenomena together is not the question of who undertakes what, but rather the fact that the decision-maker, whoever he is, looks forward to the future for the justification of his present actions... The human-capital research program has moved steadily away from some of its early naive formulations ... it has never entirely lost sight of its original goal of demonstrating that a whole range of apparently disconnected phenomena in the world are the outcome of a definite pattern of individual decisions having in common the features of forgoing present gains for the prospect of future ones. (Blaug 1976 pp. 829, 850)

Recent resources suggest that all these different forms of human capital formation are interrelated. For example, education, health, and improved nutrition interact in their effects on income. Moreover, education and training can increase the profitability of other forms of investment, for example, agricultural extension programs (Psacharopoulos and Woodhall 1985).

See also: Rates of Return to Education; Education and Economic Growth

References

Becker G S 1975 *Human Capital: A Theoretical and Empirical Analysis, with Special Reference to Education*, 2nd edn. National Bureau of Economic Research, New York

Blaug M 1976 The empirical status of human capital theory: A slightly jaundiced survey. *J. Econ. Lit.* 14: 827–55

Denison E F 1962 *The Sources of Economic Growth in the United States and the Alternatives Before Us.* Committee for Economic Development, New York

Harberger A C 1965 Investment in men versus investment in machines: The case of India. In: Anderson C A, Bowman M J (eds.) 1965 *Education and Economic Development.* Aldine, Chicago, Illinois

Psacharopoulos G 1973 *Returns to Education: An International Comparison.* Elsevier, Amsterdam

Psacharopoulos G 1975 *Earnings and Education in OECD Countries. Organisation for Economic Co-operation and Development, Paris*

Psacharopoulos G 1979 On the weak versus the strong version of the screening hypothesis. *Economic Letters* 4: 181–85

Psacharopoulos G 1981 Returns to education: An updated international comparison. *Comp. Educ* 17: 321–41

Psacharopoulos G 1984 The contribution of education to economic growth: International comparison. In: Kendrick J W (ed.) 1984 *International Comparison of Productivity and Causes of the Slowdown.* Ballinger, Cambridge, Massachusetts

Psacharopoulos G 1985 Returns to education: A further international update and implications. *J. Hum. Resources* 20 (4): 583–604

Psacharopoulos G 1989 Time trends of the returns to education: Cross-national evidence. *Econ. Educ. Rev.* 8 (3): 225–31

Psacharopoulos G, Woodhall M 1985 *Education for Development: An Analysis of Investment Choices.* Oxford University Press, New York

Schultz T W 1961 Investment in human capital. *Am. Econ. Rev.* 51: 1–17

Schultz T W 1989 Investing in people: Schooling in low income countries. *Econ. Educ. Rev.* 8 (3): 219–23

Internal Labor Markets and Education

P. B. Doeringer

Internal labor markets are a prominent organizational feature of the labor market landscape in industrialized countries and are characteristic of the large-enterprise sector in developing countries. Internal labor markets serve an important function in developing skills and enhancing labor productivity, and they have implications for educational policy, labor mobility, and income distribution. The most widely studied internal labor markets are those for blue-collar jobs in large manufacturing plants, but internal labor markets are found in most other sectors and occupations.

1. The Origins of Internal Labor Markets

The typical example of an internal labor market in the United States is that described in Doeringer and Piore (1971). Work tasks are organized into well-defined jobs and jobs are arranged into the hierarchical promotion and training ladders that define the structure of the internal labor market. Internal labor markets are linked to external labor markets through a limited number of entry jobs that require relatively little enterprise-specific skill. Once hired into an internal labor market, workers receive special employment privileges, including employment rights over "outsiders" and rights

to training, promotion, and career advancement. Access to the training and career employment benefits of internal labor markets commonly has a demographic dimension as well. The educationally disadvantaged, racial minorities, and females generally participate less than educated White males in the earnings advantages provided by employment in internal labor markets.

A major cause of the distinction between internal and external labor markets is investment by workers and firms in on-the-job training. Such investments are inevitable where job skills are specific or idiosyncratic. But even where skills are not specific, internal labor markets may provide important efficiencies in training and labor market information. In addition, internal labor markets can improve upon external labor market efficiency where there are imperfections in information and where contracts between workers and their employers cannot fully account for uncertainty. (See Williamson 1975. For other interpretations of internal labor markets see Willis 1986.)

Workers and employers are presumed to make their human capital investments through schools or workplaces depending upon the relative costs and benefits of alternative training mechanisms (Mincer 1974). In the case of on-the-job training, however, these costs and benefits may reflect institutional influences, as well as the traditional human capital considerations that apply in competitive labor markets. These institutional factors include the manner in which work is organized within internal labor markets, the extent to which firms that provide training also earn excess profits or other quasi-rents, and the power of workers to raise wages and otherwise increase their share of profits and quasi-rents.

In addition to providing training, raising labor productivity, and increasing the earnings of trained workers, internal labor markets affect a large set of other labor market outcomes. For example, schooling and on-the-job training interact to improve the rate at which career earnings rise with work experience. Conversely, workers who receive little schooling also tend to receive little on-the-job training and exhibit little career earnings growth. Different patterns of job changing are associated with the distinction between general and enterprise-specific skills—promotion within internal labor markets is more common than mobility among firms where skills are specific, while labor mobility can involve moving among firms where skills are general. Finally, on-the-job training and the efficient organization of internal labor markets can contribute to the growth of national output and income (Denison 1985).

1.1 The United States

Internal labor markets are not solely the product of efficient choices of technology and training methods by employers and workers. They must also be understood in the historical context of the political economy of industrialization (Edwards 1979).

In the economy of the United States, for example, on-the-job training preceded schooling as a source of skill. Prior to the Industrial Revolution, the economy relied on family-based training (for household production), on craft union apprenticeships for the skilled trades, and on on-the-job training for skilled workers and their helpers in small enterprises.

With industrialization, production shifted from homes and small shops to factories. Early factories, however, were organized more as a collection of small contracting shops, each under the direction of skilled foremen, than as integrated production systems, so that the skill development process continued to resemble that of the apprenticeship and small shop systems more than the hierarchical internal labor market of the modern factory (Jacoby 1985).

Mass production technologies transformed these loose coalitions of craft-based contractors into modern factories. Initially, management concerns with human resources concentrated more on the job simplification techniques of scientific management than on creating efficient training mechanisms (Jacoby 1985). The low skill content of work, combined with high rates of labor turnover, deterred the formation of workplace training systems and internal labor markets.

Progressive managers came to realize during the early 1900s, however, that there were limits to job simplification and that the costs of training were often significant, particularly where high rates of labor turnover and labor unrest often meant extra training investments in replacement workers. As a result, employers began to pay greater attention to skill development and turnover reduction (Jacoby 1985).

The vocational education movement of the early 1900s, as well as craft apprenticeship programs, offered ready models for systematic training at the industrial workplace. Larger companies began to develop a variety of formal schooling opportunities for their employees, ranging from English language education for recent immigrants to formal vocational schools for training skilled workers, and employer-sponsored apprenticeship programs were a common way of blending classroom training with on-the-job training for skilled crafts in the factory (Jacoby 1985).

The new managerial prescription for controlling labor turnover and reducing strikes during this period involved changing the values and work attitudes of working-class (and often immigrant) employees, as opposed to improving the incentive structures of the employment relationship. Managers saw employer-sponsored social service programs for workers and their families, as well as factory schools, as the appropriate instruments for improving the work ethic (Jacoby 1985).

The growing ability of factories to standardize products and mechanize production further shifted the occupational structure of the factory from skilled to semiskilled jobs during the early twentieth century. At the same time, however, skills became more specific to the technology and work organization of each firm so that training costs and labor turnover continued to be the principal human resource problem in industry (Slichter 1919).

During the 1920s, leading-edge companies decided to remedy these problems by replacing vocational schooling with on-the-job training that was limited to the relatively narrow skills needed for specific job classifications (Jacoby 1985). In place of social programs for educating workers in proper work habits, these companies adopted the economic incentives of career employment and pensions to control turnover and reduce labor strife.

The commitment to on-the-job training and career employment opportunities focused management attention on the introduction of systematic skill-building techniques and on the efficient structuring of internal labor markets. Hierarchical internal labor markets in which workers moved from low-skilled entry jobs to progressively more skilled jobs during their lifetimes resulted from the marriage of on-the-job training efficiencies with career employment incentives (Jacoby 1985).

With the advent of widespread industrial unionism in the 1930s, organized labor also began to favor internal labor markets, rather than apprenticeship craft training, as a source of job skills. Over the next three decades, systematic internal labor market hierarchies were diffused throughout manufacturing by a number of forces—the tendency of managers to emulate "best practice" personnel arrangements in other companies, the bargaining objectives of industrial unions, and the exigencies of wage and labor market controls administered during the Second World War.

The historical positioning of internal labor markets as a central instrument for providing job skills for career employees therefore reflects the character of American schooling, the evolving technology and organization of work in manufacturing, and the policy choices made by government, business, and organized labor. Despite growth in the level of schooling and an increase in formal skill training programs in the postwar United States economy, internal labor markets remain synonymous with skill accumulation, career employment, and earnings profiles graded according to age or seniority (Doeringer and Piore 1971).

2. Internal Labor Markets and the Transition from School to Career Jobs

The presence of internal labor markets has sharply circumscribed the role of the schooling system in human capital formation and has also shaped the character of labor mobility in the American economy. As in the nineteenth-century economy, education and training in internal labor markets is a ready substitute for that in schools, but schools are limited in their ability to substitute for internal labor markets. As recently as the mid-1980s, workforce surveys confirm that internal labor market training is of equal or greater importance than schooling for occupations ranging from production work to sales and administration (US Department of Labor 1985).

Further evidence of the limits of schools as skill training institutions comes at the point of transition from school to work. Instead of preparing workers to acquire career jobs immediately upon graduation, schooling in the United States is followed by transitional employment in "bridge jobs," that is, jobs in firms without internal labor markets that require few skills (Osterman 1980).

During the period of bridge job employment, young workers may change jobs through the external labor market. Once career employment is attained, however, workers will only infrequently change firms and will instead attain earnings growth through job changes within their internal labor markets. Young workers who are unsuitable for bridge jobs, or who lack the employment networks that provide access to such jobs, find work in secondary labor market jobs where there is little or no on-the-job training (Osterman 1980, 1991).

2.1 Career Employment Transitions in Other Industrialized Countries

While the provision of on-the-job training is common to internal labor markets in other national settings, the content of jobs, the hierarchical configuration of internal labor markets, the relationship between schools and internal labor markets, and the patterns of internal and external job changing, are often very different. Some countries (such as the United Kingdom and France) closely approximate the experience in the United States while others (such as Germany and Japan) illustrate rather different combinations of schooling and internal labor market arrangements (Germe 1986, Osterman 1991).

2.1.1 Germany. Secondary schooling in Germany primarily involves vocational schools and graduates routinely move into an apprenticeship program with a single company prior to obtaining their first career job (Maurice et al. 1984, Osterman 1988). Apprenticeships provide a systematic means of combining schooling with on-the-job training and are a well-defined bridge between schooling and career employment. They also involve the certification of occupational competency that can be used in the labor market at large so that German workers often establish career employment in a company that is different from the one in which they received their apprenticeship training.

This "dual system" of occupational training through both schools and workplace apprenticeships leads to the structuring of external and internal labor markets along an occupational dimension. In this blended model of occupational and internal labor market training, job content tends to be broadly defined and skills tend to be general. Moreover, schools play a continuing role in the upgrading and mobility of labor because promotions within internal labor markets, as well as external job changing, are often accompanied by further schooling and skill certification. This lifetime pattern of workers moving back and forth between schooling and work to achieve upward mobility between broad occupational strata within (and across) internal labor markets means that the insider–outsider distinction is less sharp in Germany than in other industrialized countries (Maurice et al. 1984).

2.1.2 Japan. The internal labor markets of large Japanese firms represents yet another distinctive case. As in the United States and France, Japanese schools emphasize general education. But in Japan, there is a more direct link between educational attainment in a general school system and entry level jobs in the internal labor market (Koike 1984, Rosenbaum and Kariya 1989, Aoki 1990).

Graduates selected for employment in large firms move directly into an internal labor market with little or no transitional employment period in bridge jobs. Once inside an internal labor market, workers have a virtual guarantee of lifetime employment and traditionally there has been little interfirm mobility among the tenured workforce (Koike 1984).

Between guaranteed career employment in an internal labor market and a structure of pay that is steeply graded by age and seniority, Japanese internal labor markets give the outward appearance of being an extreme version of the internalization of labor market functions (Hashimoto and Raisian 1985). However, unlike the internal labor markets found in the United States and other Western countries, Japanese internal labor markets have broad job definitions and little explicit job hierarchy (Aoki 1990). Instead, workers are part of production teams that share tasks in a flexible way and there is frequent rotation of workers among work teams and departments. These flexible work assignments provide workers with extremely broad internal labor market training, familiarity with the overall production process, and the ability to respond rapidly to the skill demands of new technologies and changing product markets.

The Japanese model of the internal labor markets has been credited with creating Japan's industrial workforce and helping to speed the industrialization of Japan. The Japanese model, with its flexible work organization and seniority-based pay system, is also thought to contribute to high levels of labor productivity and to the high responsiveness of Japanese firms to changing economic conditions (Aoki 1990). The contemporary Japanese internal labor market model, however, has tighter links with schools and depends more on the presence of a tier of smaller vendors with weaker internal labor markets, than did the internal labor markets that helped industrialize Japan.

2.2 Developing Countries

The ability of internal labor markets to substitute for vocational schooling, and even to be able to provide basic education and general skills, has particular importance for human resources development in developing countries where education and training infrastructures are frequently inadequate. The Japanese model of lifetime employment and flexible training is often seen as the prototype to be adopted in the developing country context because of its successful role in helping Japan to become a world economic power (Dore 1974). In practice, however, the Japanese model often requires adaptations that reflect national differences in school systems, labor market regulations, employment networks, the structure and capacity of small-scale enterprise, and the cultural attitudes of workers (Doeringer and Terkla 1992, Doeringer 1988).

3. International Evidence on Internal Labor Markets and Earnings

Much of what is known about on-the-job training in internal labor markets comes from detailed case studies of firms and local labor markets (Osterman 1984). However, the consequences of internal labor markets, and their relationship to schooling can also be seen in the patterns of life-cycle earnings that emerge in different countries (Psacharopoulos 1985).

In a wide range of both industrialized and developing countries for which human capital analyses of earnings are available, two regularities in lifetime earnings patterns can be observed. Earnings rise systematically with education, lending support to the human capital interpretation of schooling, and postschooling earnings rise over time in a manner that is consistent with the contribution of internal labor markets to enhancing labor productivity and pay.

National differences in internal labor markets are also reflected in earnings patterns. Good examples of such differences are the United States and Japan. The internal labor market employment guarantees and age/seniority pay practices in Japan clearly impart a steeper profile to career earnings than is found in the United States (Hashimoto and Raisian 1985).

4. Alternative Explanations: Power, Control, and Class

While internal labor markets make important contributions to training, efficiency, productivity, and earnings, they can also be interpreted as control mechanisms for weakening labor power and for extracting gains in labor productivity from the workforce (Edwards 1979, Goldberg 1980). Conversely, workers and unions try to amend internal labor market structure to favor their interests.

According to this radical interpretation, schools play a role in the development of work attitudes and serve as channeling mechanisms for feeding new labor market entrants into segmented labor markets (Bowles and Gintis 1976, Rubinson 1986). Working-class schools and vocational or "general" school tracks condition students to acquire qualities of punctuality, attendance, and the acceptance of authority (Bowles and Gintis 1976). College-track educational programs also promote the acceptance of authority, but they teach problem-solving and encourage a somewhat greater independence of thought as well.

Students who are educated to be reliable employees and to accept authority have qualities that reduce the costs and add to the efficiency of on-the-job training for production jobs in internal labor markets. Similarly, those who are educated in problem-solving can be most efficiently incorporated into managerial internal labor markets. However, those for whom such conditioning is unsuccessful are seen as having "underclass" attitudes that makes them less suited for employment in internal labor markets where training investments are made (Doeringer and Piore 1971).

31

Schools and internal labor markets therefore mirror societal relationships among economic and social classes and are an indicator of working-class power (Maurice et al. 1984). Internal labor markets can be seen as an extension of class relationships because employers design them both to conform to the skills and attitudes produced by schools and to control workers by providing them with incentives for identifying with the interests of the firm.

5. Implications for Policy

Because training within internal labor markets can profoundly influence labor earnings, productivity, and economic growth, the analysis of internal labor markets is central to education policy. The policy significance of internal labor markets ranges from technical issues of labor market forecasting to broad concerns with income distribution and national competitiveness.

For economic forecasting and planning, for example, it is important to know which occupations are associated with craft-like employment systems (where skills are general and highly transferable among employers) and which are part of hierarchical internal labor markets. The former is an appropriate potential target for vocational schooling and apprenticeship training, whereas the latter can only be reached through comparatively unskilled entry jobs for which educational qualifications are relatively less important (Dunlop 1966).

For curriculum planning, internal labor markets often mean that worker qualities which are difficult to quantify are more important than cognitive knowledge for obtaining career employment. Reliability, a strong work ethic, tolerance for repetitive work, the ability to work in teams, and problem-solving capacity are examples of such qualities. However, the specific mix of these qualities demanded will depend upon the technology, work organization, and the management cultures of specific firms, as well as societal attitudes (Doeringer and Terkla 1992).

Internal labor markets are also important when education policy is concerned with earnings and the distribution of earnings. While the content and structure of the education system may have little short-term effect upon established internal labor markets, both history and international comparisons suggest that the schools and educational policy can shape internal labor market structure and the level of on-the-job training investments in new firms and new industries. The success of such policies in fostering internal labor markets can, in turn, affect the aggregate mix between career and dead-end employment in the economy.

Finally, internal labor markets can be a critical instrument for national competitiveness. The training and productivity-enhancing structure of internal labor markets, even those that are well-established, is not fixed. Employers continually seek to redesign internal labor markets and human resources development systems to lower unit labor costs. One way of lowering costs is to simplify jobs, reduce skills, and reduce training costs; a second way is to enhance skills and raise labor productivity.

The historical record suggests that job simplification has come to receive less emphasis than human resources development as a strategy for maintaining competitive labor costs as countries industrialize. The experience in the United States in the 1980s of adjusting internal labor markets to a more competitive global economic environment, however, illustrates how these productivity-enhancing internal labor market practices are now in jeopardy (Doeringer et al. 1991).

Internal labor markets in the United States are being threatened by head-to-head competition from "employment-at-will" firms that have rejected internal labor markets and career employment in favor of a transient employment relationship in which little or no training investments are made at the workplace. At present, these employment-at-will relationships are gaining ascendancy because of their flexibility and lower costs of human resources development.

While employment-at-will firms are competitive, they do nothing to enhance the labor productivity or growth. Instead, they rely upon a pool of previously trained workers made available by the downsizing and closing of internal labor markets. If internal labor markets should eventually be replaced by employment-at-will firms, the skill gap traditionally filled by on-the-job training and other forms of workplace human resources development will have to be met by an already overburdened public education system.

The economy of the United States is at a crossroads between a system of skill development and productivity enhancement that is based on internal labor markets and an employment-at-will system that makes little contribution to skill and productivity. In the short term, this choice appears to be dictated by considerations of employment flexibility and business competitiveness. In the long term, however, the choice is between two different, but equally competitive, growth paths—one offering high wages and high productivity and the other offering low wages, slow productivity growth, and a labor market with high turnover and little postschooling investment in on-the-job training.

These choices are not unique to either the United States economy or to the period of economic change taking place in the early 1990s. They have been present in the United States since the Industrial Revolution and are readily apparent in the widespread policy debates over the superiority of regulated or free market approaches to human resources development in both industrialized and developing countries.

See also: Education and Earnings; Screening Models and Education; Education and the Labor Market; Education and Labor Markets in Developing Nations; Segmented Labor Markets and Education; The Wage Contract and Education; On-the-job Training

References

Aoki M 1990 Toward an economic model of the Japanese firm. *J. Econ. Lit.* 28: 1–27
Bowles S, Gintis H 1976 *Schooling In Capitalist America.* Basic Books, New York
Denison E F 1985 *Trends In American Economic Growth.* Brookings Institution, Washington, DC
Doeringer P B 1988 Market structure, jobs, and productivity: Some observations from Jamaica. *World Dev.* 16(4): 465–82
Doeringer P B et al. 1991 *Turbulence in the American Workplace.* Oxford University Press, New York
Doeringer P B, Piore M J 1971 *Internal Labor Markets and Manpower Analysis*, D C Heath, Lexington, Massachusetts
Doeringer P B, Terkla D G 1992 Japanese direct investment and economic development policy. *Econ. Development Q.* 6(3): 266–72
Dore R P 1974 The labour market and patterns of employment in the wage sector of LDCs: Implications for the volume of employment generated. *World Dev.* 2(4/5): 1–7.
Dunlop J T 1966 Job vacancy measures and economic analysis. In: National Bureau of Economic Research 1966 *The Measurement and Interpretation of Job Vacancies: A Conference Report.* Columbia University Press, New York
Edwards R C 1979 *Contested Terrain: The Transformation of the Workplace in the Twentieth Century.* Basic Books, New York
Germe J F 1986 Employment policies and the entry of young people into the labor market in France. *British Journal of Industrial Relations* 24(1): 29–42
Goldberg V 1980 Bridges over contested terrain. *J. Economic Behaviour and Organization* 1: 249–74
Hashimoto M, Raisian J 1985 Employment Tenure and Earnings Profiles in the United States and Japan. *Am. Econ. Rev.* 75(4): 721–35
Jacoby S M 1985 *Employing Bureaucracy: Managers, Unions, and the Transformation of Work In American Industry 1900–1945.* Columbia University Press, New York
Koike K 1984 Skill formation systems in the U S and Japan: A comparative study. In: Aoki M (ed.) 1984 *The Economic Analysis of the Japanese Firm.* North Holland, Amsterdam
Maurice M, Sellier F, Silvestre J J 1984 The search for a societal effect in the production of company hierarchy: A comparison of France and Germany. In: Osterman P (ed.) 1984
Mincer J 1974 *Schooling, Experience, and Earnings.* National Bureau of Economic Research, New York
Osterman P 1980 *Getting Started: The Youth Labor Market.* MIT Press, Cambridge, Massachusetts
Osterman P (ed.) 1984 *Internal Labor Markets.* MIT Press, Cambridge, Massachusetts
Osterman P 1988 *Employment Futures: Reorganization, Dislocation, and Public Policy.* Oxford University Press, New York
Osterman P 1991 Is there a problem with the youth labor market and if so how should we fix it? Sloan School, MIT, Cambridge, Massachusetts (mimeo)
Psacharopoulos G 1985 Returns to education: A further international update and implications. *J. Hum. Resources* 20(4): 583–604
Rosenbaum J E, Kariya T 1989 From high school to work. Market and institutional mechanics in Japan. *Am. J. Sociol.* 94(6): 1334–64
Rubinson R 1986 Class formation, politics, and institutions: Schooling in the United States. *Am. J. Sociol.* 92(3): 519–48
Slichter S H 1919 *The Turnover of Factory Labor.* D Appleton, New York
US Department of Labor 1985 *How Workers Get Their Training.* Government Printing Office, Washington, DC
Williamson O E 1975 *Markets and Hierarchies: Analysis and Antitrust Implications.* The Free Press, New York
Willis R J 1986 Wage determinants: A survey and reinterpretation of human capital earnings functions. In: Ashenfelter O, Layard R (eds.) 1986 *Handbook of Labor Economics.* North Holland, Amsterdam

Further Reading

Carnoy M, Levin H M 1985 *Schooling and Work in the Democratic State.* Stanford University Press, Stanford, California
Kohn M 1969 *Class and Conformity.* Dorsey Press, Georgetown, Washington, DC
Koike K 1988 *Understanding Industrial Relations In Modern Japan* (tr. Mary Suso) St Martin's Press, New York
Lindbeck A, Snower D 1986 Wage setting, unemployment, and insider–outsider relations. *Am. Econ. Rev.* Papers and Proceedings: 235–39
Marsden D, Ryan P 1986 Where do young workers work? *British Journal of Industrial Relations* 24(1): 83–102.
Montgomery D 1987 *The Fall of the House of Labour.* Cambridge University Press, Cambridge
Simon H A 1991 Organizations and markets. *J. Economic Perspectives* 5(2): 25–44
Wachter M L, Wright R D 1990 The economics of internal labor markets. *Industrial Relations* 29(2): 240–62
Wilson W J 1987 *The Truly Disadvantaged: The Inner City, The Underclass and Public Policy.* University of Chicago Press, Chicago, Illinois

Screening Models and Education

W. Groot and J. Hartog

1. Introduction

Screening theory refers to a range of theories that have in common the fact that they challenge the human capital assumption of the productivity-augmenting role of education. The general term "screening" is often used in two connotations: to indicate that education acts as a signal for pre-existing abilities and as a means for the already better off to get the best jobs. In the first form—where education acts as a signal—wages still equal marginal productivity in equilibrium. In the second form—a view which can be ascribed to Berg (1970) and Thurow (1970) and which we may term the "credentialist" view of education—education only serves as an admission ticket for certain professions. The existence of a relation between productivity and wages is questioned. Since productivity is not altered by schooling, neither is total output raised. In this view education is wasteful as it has an effect on the distribution of income only. The credentialist view is not strongly formalized.

According to the "signaling" view, education yields useful information to identify individuals with a higher expected productivity. This set of theories includes the filtering theory (Arrow 1973), the screening theory (Stiglitz 1975), and the signaling theory in the strict sense (Spence 1973, 1974a, 1974b; Riley 1976, 1979b). Henceforth screening will be identified with signaling. The theories are molded in formalized models. According to this view the (empirical) relation between education and wages is a result of the productivity-identifying role (instead of the productivity-augmenting role in the human capital theory) of education (see Davies and MacDonald for a comparison of the implications of the human capital and signaling models). In this theory, the extent to which education also has a productivity-augmenting effect is left as an open question. In either case, educational achievements serve as signals for employers and result in an efficient allocation of employees to a diversity of jobs.

2. Theory

The signaling theory as developed by Spence (1973) starts from the following assumptions: (a) Individuals differ in productivity, productivity is fully person-specific and not affected by schooling; (b) more schooling entails more costs, schooling costs are lower for the more productive; (c) individuals know their productivity, firms do not (asymmetrical information); and (d) educational qualifications can be observed

without cost. Firms cannot observe individuals' productivity, and instead use schooling qualifications for hiring decisions and for setting individual wages. Firms assume that the individuals with more schooling are the more productive. Since they can observe total output for the entire workforce, they can use this as probabilistic information to check whether this assumption is correct in the aggregate. Hence, an equilibrium can only exist if more productive individuals indeed choose more schooling. Individuals will invest in schooling as long as the benefits outweigh the cost. With a proper wage structure, schooling will be worthwhile for high-productivity individuals, but not for low-productivity individuals: offered wages are identical, but schooling cost is higher for the low-productivity individuals. The wage gain from schooling should be sufficient for high-productivity/low-cost individuals and insufficient for low-productivity/high-cost individuals. Thus, schooling may effectively separate high-productivity and low-productivity individuals, and the firms' belief regarding the relation between schooling and productivity may be upheld by individuals' decisions. Finally, individuals take rational decisions on schooling, just as in the human capital theory.

The model assumes that the more able have an absolute advantage in all jobs over the less able. Stiglitz (1975) terms this "hierarchical screening": there is an unequivocal order of productive capacities which is revealed by education. In Stiglitz's own screening model, education identifies productive traits of individuals. The costs of schooling do not vary with capabilities but are equal for all individuals. The returns to schooling do, however, vary with (innate) capabilities. If the screening costs are not prohibitive, more productive workers attain higher expected lifetime earnings by investing in schooling.

Although the assumptions of the screening model are somewhat different from those of the signaling/filtering model, the predictions about the optimal investment in education and the relation between education and productivity are similar.

Wages are solely determined by observable characteristics such as educational qualifications. However, in the signaling theory, wages will also be equal to the expected value of the marginal productivity of employees. The proof of this assertion runs as follows. As employers eventually get to know the productivity of those they have appointed, they will be able to observe the relation between education and productivity of workers. Employers have rational expectations about workers' productivity. This implies that the wage offers to workers equal their expected marginal productivity. Competition will ensure that the wages of employees, which are determined by educational qualification, equal marginal productivity. In this way, the educational signaling mechanism generates a wage which equals the expected value of the marginal product.

Despite this, educational signals do not necessarily have a productivity-augmenting effect. If productive traits are not altered by schooling, education does not lead to higher productivity. In this view investments in education do not determine the size of the total output, but merely the distribution of it: individuals invest in education to obtain a greater share in total output. If education only serves as a screen, the gross social returns to education are zero because of its distributional effects. The net social returns are negative, as investments in education imply social costs which are not matched by higher total output (Stiglitz 1975 p. 285).

The private returns to investment in education are positive for those with more capabilities. In an economy without screening, all employees would receive the same wage equal to the average marginal product. As a result of screening, workers with more capabilities receive more than average, while those with less capabilities receive less than average. Stiglitz speaks of the private returns of screening as "the individual's capturing of his 'ability rents' which in the absence of screening he shares with others" (Stiglitz 1975 p. 186). Spence (1974b) shows that it may be in the individual's interest to form coalitions for promoting screening.

There are three mechanisms by which the productive traits of employees become public knowledge (Stiglitz terms them "screening mechanisms"): selection by educational institutions, educational achievement, and self-selection.

The educational system sorts individuals in two ways: by admission requirements and by grading. The group into which the individual is sorted by the educational system provides information for the employer about the individual.

A second screening mechanism is educational achievement: within a homogeneous educational program a standard test yields information by which individuals can be compared.

An important source of information is self-selection of individuals. If individuals have more information about their capabilities than employers and some have a (comparative) advantage in one task over another, there are gains to be obtained in selecting oneself for a job in which this trait is rewarded. As noted by Spence (1973), the self-selection mechanism yields signals to the market. This mechanism is emphasized in Akerlof's "theory of lemons" (Akerlof 1970). So, even if education in itself has no productivity-augmenting effect, it can be productivity-augmenting by sorting workers into various jobs. This may be termed the "allocation-effect" of screening.

Schooling can both be productivity-augmenting and act as a signal of (innate) capabilities. The human capital theory and the screening theory are therefore not mutually exclusive. Mincer states that: "The productivity and screening functions of schooling are not mutually exclusive in a world of imperfect information, given that ability is an input in the educational process. The controversy, if any, concerns the relative importance of the productivity and screening functions of schooling in affecting earnings" (Mincer 1980 p. 125). Moreover, as emphasized by Davies and MacDonald (1984), the information generated by schooling may be socially valuable. If the schooling system did not sort individuals by ability, the labor market would have to solve the problem of optimal allocation by reassigning individuals as information gradually emerges with experience. Hence, the prevention of such ignorant, suboptimal initial job assignments has benefits which may be compared with the cost of schooling.

3. The Empirical Results

The empirical research on the validity of the screening hypothesis has focused on testing (some of the extreme) empirical implications of this hypothesis and on assessing the productivity and informational components of education. The hypothesis that the individual financial returns to schooling exceed the social returns based on productivity effects is hard to test, because the true productivity effects of schooling are hard to measure.

In empirical work two implications of the screening hypothesis have been distinguished: the Wiles hypothesis and the sheepskin argument. Both implications are derived from the credentialist variant of the screening hypothesis. These two implications will be discussed in turn.

The Wiles hypothesis (Wiles 1974) states that if the screening hypothesis is correct, there should be no wage difference between workers with qualifications which exactly match the requirements of the profession they work in and workers with equal qualifications working in other professions. If the screening hypothesis is correct, (specific) human capital does not affect performance in a job: according to this view productivity is fully job-specific. The Wiles hypothesis is a logical corollary to the credentialist variant of the screening theory.

The Wiles hypothesis has been tested by Miller and Volker (1984) and by Arabsheibani (1989). Miller and Volker used data for Australia on starting salaries for academics with a technical education and an economics education. They found that economists working in an economic profession were not paid significantly more than those with a technical education working in an economic profession. This corroborates the screening hypothesis. However, the starting salary of males with a technical education working in a technical profession was more than 5 percent higher than the starting salary of economists in a technical profession. This, conversely, is a corroboration of the human capital theory. For women in a technical profession, Miller and Volker found no differences between educations.

Arabsheibani used a sample of Egyptian graduates. It was found that a premium was paid in starting salaries when education was useful in the job. This finding supports the human capital view. Moreover, it was discovered that when education was specifically job-related the premium was high, whereas the premium was low when there was a less specific education–occupation relationship.

The sheepskin argument holds that, if education serves as an admission ticket or credential for a better job with higher earnings, there is a premium for completion of a course with a certificate. Preliminary school leavers or dropouts would, averaged over their years of schooling, have a lower return to education than those who completed their course with a certificate: "… graduation from a course should provide more evidence of ability and staying power than mere attendence for a number of years" (Layard and Psacharopoulos 1974). The sheepskin argument has been tested by Layard and Psacharopoulos (1974), Hungerford and Solon (1987), Hartog (1983), and Groot and Oosterbeek (1990).

Layard and Psacharopoulos compared the returns on education of dropouts with the returns for employees who have completed their education. They concluded that there are no significant differences in the returns to education between these two groups. However, Hungerford and Solon pointed out that Layard and Psacharopoulos do not take account of the timing of the decision to drop out. Hungerford and Solon looked for discontinuities in the relation between years of education and earnings. Comparing year-to-year returns they found that the rate of return in the first year and in the final year is higher than in the intervening years. The first finding confirms the prediction by Arrow (1973) that admittance to higher education (college) itself yields an income benefit. The discontinuities in the rates of return are taken as a corroboration of the sheepskin hypothesis.

Hartog (1983) estimated an earnings equation and a job-level equation, by taking as explanatory variables the highest educational level and a dummy which indicated whether this level was completed with a certificate. At the lower general level and the higher general level (high school) nongraduation does not influence earnings or job level. At the lower vocational level, the extended vocational level, and extended general level, a certificate has an effect on job level but not on earnings. At the higher vocational and university levels, a certificate influences both earnings and job level. However, at these levels there is no premium on a certificate as such: earnings lost per year not attended (years still to go to the diploma when dropout occurs) are roughly equal to what graduates earn per year of attendance.

Groot and Oosterbeek (1990) divided actual years of education into effective years (i.e., the shortest, most efficient path to attaining a certain level of education), inefficient routing years (i.e., skipping and repeating classes, and years spent inefficiently), and dropout years (i.e., years spent in education without receiving a diploma). This division is such that the actual number of years of education is equal to the sum of effective years, repeated years, (minus) skipped years, inefficient years, and dropout years. This decomposition allows a test of the screening theory against the human capital theory. The test relies on two predictions of the screening theory: (a) the sheepskin hypothesis that years spent in education without obtaining a degree should not increase earnings, and (b) a more rapid completion of a degree signals greater ability and should therefore lead to higher earnings.

For males, the results strongly support the human capital theory and refute the predictions of the screening hypothesis. Skipped years have a significantly negative influence on future earnings. According to the screening hypothesis this effect should be positive, since skipping a class gives a positive signal to potential employers, whereas within a human capital framework the finding can be explained as the manifestation of a less than thorough understanding of the curriculum. Repeated years have no effect on future earnings. This is in accordance with the human capital theory, whereas the screening hypothesis predicts a negative effect because of the negative signal which repeated years give to employers. The absence of influence on earnings from inefficient years of education agrees with both the human capital and screening predictions. Finally, a positive return on dropout years emerges. This is in line with the human capital theory and refutes the sheepskin version of the screening theory.

When data relating only to women are also examined, all results are in line with the human capital predictions and refute the screening theory.

Both the Wiles hypothesis and the sheepskin argument implictly test whether the credentialist version of the screening theory is tenable. However, education can both be productivity-augmenting and can provide information about ability. As stated by Machlup (1984) the controversy is not whether education acts as a sorting mechanism, but whether this is the sole function of education. In this respect Psacharopoulos (1979) made a distinction between the weak and the strong version of the screening hypothesis. According to the weak version, employers offer higher starting wages to the more highly educated because of imperfect information on expected productivity. According to the strong version of the screening hypothesis, this wage differential between the higher and lower educated does not vanish with tenure. As noted by Psacharopoulos (1979), few doubt the validity of the weak version, rather it is the validity of the strong version which is debatable.

Direct testing of the strong version of the screening hypothesis has been performed by Taubman and Wales (1973), Layard and Psacharopoulos (1974), Wolpin (1977), Psacharopoulos (1979), Cohn et al. (1987), Dolton (1986), Mendes de Oliveira et al. (1989), and Rao and Datta (1989). The direct test entails whether the partial effect of education on wages decreases with years of work experience, controling for other productive traits.

Psacharopoulos and Layard (1979) compared earnings by educational level for a 33-year old and a 47-year old in the United States. They found that the relative earnings differential between these two ages increases with the level of education. Similar findings were reported by Cohn et al. (1987) and Psacharopoulos (1979). These findings confirm the strong version of the screening hypothesis.

Indirect tests of the strong version are performed by earnings comparisons between industries or professions where screening is supposed to be important and industries and professions where screening does not play a role. More specifically, these tests involve comparing wages in the market sector with wages in the private sector, and wages of employees with wages of the self-employed. It is assumed that screening is relatively more important in the public sector and wage sector than in the private sector and the self-employment sector. As the self-employed do not have to invest in educational signals for potential employers, it is expected that employees invest more in education to attain a higher job level than the self-employed. This hypothesis has been tested by Riley (1979a), Katz and Ziderman (1980), Cohn et al. (1987), Wolpin (1977), and De Wit and Van Winden (1989). Riley and Katz and Ziderman found evidence in favor of the screening hypothesis. Riley (1979a) found that the self-employed have less education than the employed, other things being equal. Cohn et al. found only small differences in years of education between employees and the self-employed by job level. Wolpin also found that (nonprofessional) employees and the (nonprofessional) self-employed acquire similar amounts of schooling. On the other hand, Wolpin found that the self-employed have considerably higher productivity than employees as measured by earnings. However, this might be due to earnings of the self-employed that include a return to capital as well. From these findings Wolpin concluded that the strong version of the screening theory has to be rejected. Riley found that in the screened occupations (mainly teaching occupations) education gives a better explanation of earnings than in the unscreened occupations (mainly managerial occupations). De Wit and Van Winden estimated a switching regression model on earnings for employees and the self-employed, controling for ability. For employees they found positive returns to schooling and a premium on obtaining a certificate. For the self-employed they found no significant returns on schooling and no evidence of a

premium on a certificate. These findings confirm the screening theory.

Taubman and Wales (1973) tested the screening hypothesis by comparing the expected and actual distribution of education over occupations. The expected distribution is determined by the income distribution by occupation and is defined as the probability that an individual with a given educational level can earn a higher wage in a certain occupation than in any other occupation. Taubman and Wales found that the actual probability that an individual with an intermediate level education ends up in a low-paid occupation is higher than the expected probability, while for the higher educated the actual probabilities almost equal the expected ones. From this finding Taubman and Wales concluded that education is used as a screening device to prevent lower educated workers from entering well-paid occupations.

Perlman (1988) tested the screening hypothesis by comparing the actual and expected unemployment rates by level of education. The expected (or standardized) unemployment rate by level of education is defined by the unemployment rate in an occupation multiplied by the share of a certain educational level in this occupation. This generates the unemployment rate that would prevail for an educational group if its members had the average unemployment rate for each occupational group to which it belonged. The results show that for higher educated people the actual unemployment rate is lower than expected, while for the lower educated the unemployment rate exceeds the expected rate. This suggests negative screening or selection of lower educated workers.

Albrecht (1981) tested the screening hypothesis by using data on job applicants at the Volvo company in Sweden. Applicants were distinguished by their educational background and their informational level (i.e., the amount of information the employer has on the job seeker). The information level was determined by the ways job seekers came into contact with the firm. In decreasing order of informational content, these were (a) through a recommendation by a Volvo employee to the employer and an invitation to apply, (b) through the job agency, or (c) through an advertisement or an open application. If the signaling hypothesis is correct, employers will, in their hiring decision, make more use of the educational background of an applicant if the informational content of the applicant is less. The results showed that Volvo preferred applicants with more schooling, and slightly preferred applicants with a higher informational content. However, education does not serve as a substitute for lack of information on the applicant. This implies that education is not considered to be a perfect screening mechanism by employers in their hiring decision.

Finally, some studies have yielded results that confirm both the screening theory and the human capital theory of education. Rao and Datta (1989) concluded that both the strong and the weak version of the screening hypothesis hold good for India, as well as the human capital prediction of decreasing marginal returns to schooling. Dolton concluded from data on the United Kingdom that the human capital theory and the screening theory should not be seen as mutually exclusive but rather as complementary: "In conclusion there are reasonable grounds to support a compromise interpretation of the education–income association which gives credence to both human capital theory and screening theory but supports an extreme version of neither" (Dolton 1986 p. 30).

4. Conclusion

In 1976 Blaug concluded his survey of human capital theory with the prediction that: "... in all likelihood, the human capital research program ... will gradually fade away to be swallowed up by the new theory of signaling" (Blaug 1976 p. 850). So far this prediction has not been corroborated. Although the human capital theory is perhaps not as dominant as it was in the 1960s and 1970s, it still stands firm, while the signaling theory has lived a much more marginal existence. During the 1980s, interest in the screening theory appeared to be on the wane. Research has taken other directions: the investment in information has been analyzed by the so-called "information theory" (see Hartog 1981, MacDonald 1980, 1982, Davies and MacDonald 1984, Weiss 1983) and the formation of information on productive qualities has been emphasized in matching theory (Jovanovic 1979a, 1979b, 1984). The lack of developments in the area of the theory of the transfer of information or signaling theory, led Freeman (1986) to remark that "following Spence's analysis a theoretical literature on screening/sorting models flourished briefly" (Freeman 1986 p. 360).

The results of empirical research do not conclusively discount the screening theory. Education seems to have signaling aspects. However, the strong version of the screening theory, which states that the signaling aspect of education prevails over the entire career, must be rejected. Evidence suggests support for the weak version of the screening hypothesis, namely that employers pay highers starting wages to the higher educated because of incomplete information on productivity.

See also: Internal Labor Markets and Education; Education and Earnings; Education and the Labor Market; Segmented Labor Markets and Education; Education and Labor Markets in Developing Nations; The Wage Contract and Education

References

Akerlof G 1970 The market for "lemons": Quality uncertainty and the market mechanism. *Q. J. Econ.* 84: 488–500

Albrecht J W 1981 A procedure for testing the signalling hypothesis. *J. Publ. Econ.* 15: 123–32

Arabsheibani G 1989 The Wiles test revisited. *Economics Letters* 29(4): 361–216

Arrow K J 1973 Higher education as a filter. *J. Pub. Econ.* 2: 193–216

Berg I 1970 *Education and Jobs: The Great Training Robbery.* Praeger, New York

Blaug M 1976 The empirical status of human capital theory: A slightly jaundiced survey. *J. Econ. Lit.* 14: 827–55

Cohn E, Kiker B F, Mendes de Oliveira M 1987 Further evidence on the screening hypothesis. *Economics Letters* 25(3): 289–94

Davies J, MacDonald G 1984 *Information in the Labour Market: Job-Worker Matching and Its Implications for Education in Ontario.* Ontario Economic Council Research Studies, Ontario

Dolton P 1986 Signalling and screening in the graduate labour market. Economics research paper 134. Department of Economics and Commerce, University of Hull, Hull

Freeman R 1986 Demand for education. In: Ashenfelter O, Layard R (eds.) 1986 *Handbook of Labor Economics I.* North Holland, Amsterdam

Groot W, Oosterbeek H 1990 Does it pay to take the shortest way? *Research Memorandum 9013.* Faculty of Economics and Econometrics, University of Amsterdam, Amsterdam

Hartog J 1981 Wages and allocation under imperfect information. *De Economist* 129: 311–23

Hartog J 1983 To graduate or not: Does it matter? *Economics Letters* 12: 193–99

Hungerford T, Solon G 1987 Sheepskin effects in the returns to education. *Rev. Econ. Stat.* 69: 175–77

Jovanovic B 1979a Job matching and the theory of turnover. *J. Pol. Econ.* 87(5): 972–90

Jovanovic B 1979b Firm-specific capital and turnover. *J. Pol. Econ.* 87(6): 1246–60

Jovanovic B 1984 Matching, turnover, and unemployment. *J. Pol. Econ.* 92(1): 108–22

Katz E, Ziderman A 1980 On education, screening and human capital. *Economics Letters* 6: 81–88

Layard R, Psacharopoulos G 1974 The screening hypothesis and the returns to education. *J. Pol. Econ.* 82(5): 985–98

MacDonald G 1980 Person-specific information in the labor market. *J. Pol. Econ.* 88(3): 578–97

MacDonald G 1982 A market equilibrium theory of job assignment and sequential accumulation of information. *Am. Econ. Rev.* 72(5): 1038–55

Machlup F 1984 *Knowledge: Its Creation, Distribution, and Economic Significance: The Economics of Information and Human Capital.* Princeton University Press, Princeton, New Jersey

Mendes de Oliviera M, Cohn E, Kiker K 1989 Tenure, earnings and productivity. *Oxford B. of Econ. Stat.* 51: 1–14

Miller P W, Volker P A 1984 The screening hypothesis: An application of the Wiles test. *Economic Inquiry* 22 (1): 121–27

Mincer J 1980 Human capital and earnings. In: Atkinson A B (ed.) 1980 *Wealth, Income and Inequality,* 2nd edn. Oxford University Press, Oxford

Perlman R 1988 Education and training: An American perspective. *Oxford Review of Economic Policy* 4(3): 82–93

Psacharopoulos G 1979 On the weak versus the strong version of the screening hypothesis. *Economics Letters* 4: 181–85

Psacharopoulos G, Layard R 1979 Human capital and earnings: British evidence and a critique. *Rev. Econ. Stud.* 46: 485–503

Rao M J M, Datta R C 1989 The screening hypothesis and the marginal productivity theory. *Economics Letters* 30(4): 379–84

Riley J 1976 Information, screening and human capital. *Am. Econ. Rev.* 66 254–60

Riley J 1979a Testing the educational screening hypothesis. *J. Pol. Econ.* 87(5): 227–52

Riley J 1979b Informational equilibrium. *Econometrica* 47(2): 331–59

Spence M 1973 Job market signaling. *Q. J. Econ.* 87: 355–74

Spence M 1974a Competitive and optimal responses to signals: An analysis of efficiency and distribution. *J. Econ. Theo.* 7: 296–332

Spence M 1974b *Market Signaling: Information Transfer in Hiring and Related Screening Process.* Harvard University Press, Cambridge, Massachusetts

Stiglitz J E 1975 The theory of "screening," education, and the distribution of income. *Am. Econ. Rev.* 65: 283–300

Taubman P, Wales T J 1973 Higher education, mental ability, and screening. *J. Pol. Econ.* 8(1): 28–55

Thurow L 1970 *Investment in Human Capital.* Wadsworth, Belmont, California

Weiss A 1983 A sorting-cum-learning model of education. *J. Pol. Econ.* 91(3): 420–42

Wiles K 1974 The correlation between education and earnings: The External-Test-Not-Content hypothesis (ETNC). *High. Educ.* 3: 43–57

Wit G de, Winden F van 1989 An empirical analysis of self-employment in the Netherlands. Research paper 89.02. Research Institute for Small and Medium-Sized Business, Zoetermeer

Wolpin K I 1977 Education and screening. *Am. Econ. Rev.* 67: 949–58

Segmented Labor Markets and Education

G. DeFreitas

Labor market segmentation exists when workers of comparable productivity receive significantly different opportunities and job rewards. The concept has been widely used in attempts by economists and sociologists to explain the persistence of poverty, involuntary unemployment, interindustry wage differentials, and race and sex discrimination. The impact of education on wages and job mobility has been a central issue in the ongoing debates between neoclassical and segmentation theorists since the 1960s.

1. The Theory of Dual Labor Markets

The original model of labor market segmentation emerged from economic research on low-income urban populations in the 1960s. Doeringer and Piore (1971) argued that the labor market is divided into two separate submarkets: the "primary" and the "secondary" segments. The former is characterized by jobs offering relatively high wages and fringe benefits, good working conditions and training, promotional paths governed by seniority, and protection from arbitrary dismissal. Jobs in the secondary sector are, in contrast, low-paying with few benefits, training, or promotional chances, poor working conditions, and frequent quits and discharges.

To account for the origins of this bifurcation, Doeringer and Piore drew upon the concept of "internal labor markets" introduced in the 1950s by John Dunlop, Clark Kerr, and others of the institutional school of industrial relations. Jobs in the primary market are characterized by largely firm-specific skills, acquired by means of on-the-job training. The major share of the costs of such training are typically borne by the employer and the payoff period on his or her investment is a positive function of the length of tenure of each worker. In consequence, primary sector firms pay wages systematically higher than the marginal productivity of the individual worker in order to minimize costly quits by trained employees.

In addition to skill specificity and on-the-job training, workplace customs are assigned a key causal role in the formation of internal labor markets. Long-term employment relationships generate unwritten rules about such matters as what constitutes "just cause" for disciplinary actions and "fairness" in job assignments and relative wage levels.

Wage determination is based on each job's value within the the firm's internal wage hierarchy, on job evaluations, and on customary wage relativities. The influence of competitive forces emanating from the "external market" (e.g., through community wage surveys) is of distinctly secondary importance. Since wages are attached to specific jobs rather than to individual workers, the economic value of education is not primarily a result of its impact on labor productivity. Instead, educational credentials are used by employers to screen out less trainable, less reliable job applicants. Better educated workers generally stand to benefit from greater access to primary sector jobs and promotional ladders, but the returns to education for those left behind in the secondary sector are lower or even nil.

Most unemployment is concentrated in the secondary sector and reflects not a shortage of vacancies but the often short-term nature of the available work, the low costs to employers of firing workers, and the high quit rates of some low-wage workers. In the primary sector it is in the interests of both employers and employees to maintain a stable employment relationship, so unemployment in this sector is of the involuntary sort generated by cyclical contractions. The high turnover of the secondary work force is attributed to a complex interaction between jobs and workers. On the one hand, the nature of an employer's product market or of the product's technology may discourage the formation of internal labor markets offering continuous employment. For example, firms subject to high variability of product demand and/or product design, such as in the clothing industry, are unlikely to provide specific training when production periods tend to be so brief and unpredictable that returns cannot be captured sufficient to outweigh training costs.

However, even if it is assumed initially that all workers have similar levels of work commitment and that the instability of secondary jobs reflects employer preferences, eventually workers in unstable, undesirable jobs without rewards for punctuality or regular attendance will themselves develop work traits unacceptable to primary sector employers. According to this "feedback hypothesis," as these behavioral traits become reinforced through working in secondary jobs, subsequent employers are more likely to adapt the structure of work and production to an unskilled, unreliable work force than to risk training workers who might quit well before investment costs have been recouped.

2. Radical Segmentation Theories

Whereas Doeringer and Piore (1971) presented a time-specific analysis stressing the technological causes of segmentation, radicals incorporated segmentation into a broader historical and political framework in which divisions within the labor force play a functional role in perpetuating capitalist control of the labor process (Gordon et al. 1973, 1982). The destruction of many skilled crafts and the expansion of factory production in the nineteenth century were associated with the progressive homogenization of the labor force. To combat the resulting increase in class consciousness and worker militancy, employers consciously created segmented internal labor markets as part of a "divide and conquer" strategy. This process began in the 1920s but was not fully consolidated until after the Second World War. The proliferation of separate job ladders, though accelerated by the growing importance of firm-specific training, was primarily a means to draw artificial distinctions between workers to prevent those in more desirable jobs from making common

cause with those at the bottom. As oligopolistic corporations with stable product markets and internal labor markets consolidated their power over small business the gap between their primary sector workforce and secondary sector laborers widened.

Soon after the appearance of Doeringer and Piore's work (1971), Gordon et al. (1973) argued that the strict dualist image required modification to take account of the complex variety of employment in the primary sector. They distinguished between skilled crafts jobs, as "subordinate primary" and "independent primary" jobs. The latter are higher-level jobs involving considerable individual initiative and often professional standards of work. The "subordinate primary" tier consists of routinized factory and office jobs with little individual responsibility entrusted in the worker.

An alternative theory of the role of education was also proposed. Bowles and Gintis (1976) presented an historical analysis to demonstrate the emergence of a "correspondence principle" between the types of education offered to students from different class backgrounds and the labor sector in which they are expected to be ultimately employed. Youths from low-income homes are more likely to be channeled into schools (and tracks within each school) that stress attitudes and behavioral traits appropriate to the secondary sector, and quite dissimilar from those emphasized to upper-income students in their schools. "Premarket segmentation" in education thereby circumscribes their postschool opportunities and reproduces and justifies the prevailing economic hierarchy.

On the issue of racial discrimination, radical economists have disputed both human capital and statistical discrimination models. The former is faulted for assuming that the "tastes" of discriminators are formed independently of economic interests and for its fundamentally incorrect view of the roles played by competition and profit maximization. The latter is said to exaggerate the typical firm's costs in screening job candidates. A great deal of information is usually readily available through schooling and previous job references, job-related tests, and observation of new employees during an initial probationary period with the firm. Less prejudiced personnel officers would be expected to use these inexpensive informational sources to correct any systematic misperceptions about individual job applicants based on racist stereotypes.

Contrary to the view of employer discrimination as imposing costs on the firm, Reich (1981 Chap 4) concluded from empirical tests of both 1960 and 1970 census data that high-income groups tended to benefit from employment discrimination against Blacks, while most White workers lost out. He explained this as reflective of employers' greater ability to hold down wages and forestall unionization efforts when the labor force is weakened by racial divisiveness.

3. Neoclassical Theory and Segmentation

From the start, segmentation theory was considered by its proponents to be an alternative to the conventional neoclassical model of the labor market. This long-dominant view was founded on the idea that competitive pressures make labor markets generally function like continuous auctions between atomistic buyers and sellers of labor. Business firms' demand for labor is based on each worker's marginal productivity, and is inversely related to the real wage rate. Labor supply reflects workers' utility-maximizing behavior in the face of work yielding disutility, and is a positive function of the real wage. Competition is said to insure that employers pay each worker a real wage equal to his marginal product, and at the same level offered by any other employer. Aside from short-run bouts of "frictional" unemployment, competitive forces move the wage rate up or down to equate labor demand and supply at the full employment level.

In the 1960s the neoclassical model of labor supply was expanded from a simple theory of hours worked to one of labor quality as well. According to "human capital" theorists, differences in worker productivity are shaped by each individual's decisions on how much schooling, training, healthcare, and other "self-investments" to undertake. The human capital investment decision is based on comparisons of, for example, the expected costs of additional schooling and the expected resultant stream of future earnings (appropriately discounted). Better educated individuals will tend to be more skilled and more productive as workers, and competitive pressures will assure them compensatory wage premiums. In the debates of the 1960s over the causes of poverty and racial income differentials, human capital explanations emphasized the below-average education levels of low-income groups and gave top priority to corrective schooling and training policies.

Most segmentation theorists explicitly dispute key elements of neoclassical theory. Internal labor markets are said to insulate much of the primary work-force from competitive forces and give both employers and employees incentives to minimize turnover. With wage levels attached to jobs rather than to workers, human capital choices by individuals have limited influence on earnings. The presence of fixed employment costs of recruiting and training and of greater worker bargaining leverage generally result in violation of the neoclassical assumption of equality between each worker's marginal productivity and the wage.

3.1 Critiques of the Original Dualist Model

In the two most influential attacks on the dualist theory of the early 1970s, Cain (1976) and Wachter (1974) challenged its views on neoclassical theories and its claim to represent a competing paradigm. They characterized it as being little more than a modern continuation of the postwar institutional economists'

efforts to focus attention on sociological and policy aspects of the employment relationship and to contest the importance of marginal productivity in wage determination.

Both Cain and Wachter contended that dualists have misrepresented neoclassical theory as too narrow and supply-driven to accommodate institutional realities and demand effects. Thus Wachter argued that, while price theory and maximizing behavior are central to the conventional model, neoclassical economists with his "broader view" recognize the role of internal labor markets and unions, and see the economy as "built of industrial and demographic segments" (Wachter 1974 p. 641). However, contrary to Doeringer, Piore, and others, he argued that the internal labor market is primarily an efficient organizational response to firm-specific jobs and training, and is thus not inconsistent with neoclassical theory. Internal labor markets serve to expedite recruiting, minimize costly turnover, minimize bargaining, and maximize on-the-job training opportunities among workers in long-term contact. Even if education is mainly a screen, it must be a valuable index of actual or potential productivity or employers would have abandoned it. Beyond the entry level, promotional ladders act as continous screening mechanisms for efficiently selecting only the most productive for advancement.

Cain and Wachter charged that dualist authors failed to support empirically their most ambitious claim: that a strict primary–secondary division of jobs exists, with little upward mobility possible for secondary workers (see below). They do, however, credit them with one original insight: the feedback hypothesis of interdependence between job characteristics and workers' behavioral traits.

3.2 A Neoclassical Model of Stratification

In the early 1980s a number of young neoclassical economists took a fresh look at these earlier debates and sparked a strong revival of theoretical and empirical research on segmented markets. Looking back over a decade of economic turmoil, they shared a common dissatisfaction with conventional assumptions of automatic market clearing and sought microeconomic foundations for these macroeconomic problems. For example, Bulow and Summers (1986) attempted to integrate Keynes's argument about wage relativities with key aspects of segmentation, and "efficiency wage" models. They began with the assumption that the involuntarily unemployed are those who cannot find a job at a wage equal to that currently paid to other workers with the same qualifications. The persistence of such wage differentials is attributed primarily to labor market segmentation. The more that workers are concerned with fair pay relativities, the more likely they are to queue for higher paying primary sector jobs. But the question then arises about why high-wage employers do not lower their pay level to clear the labor market. Unions are one obvious reason, but sizable interfirm wage differences are known to persist even in nonunion areas. "Efficiency wage" considerations are the suggested explanation.

The basic idea underlying the efficiency wage is that employers have an incentive to pay above-market wages because of the positive productivity effects they yield. Higher wages help to raise morale, reduce shirking on the job, and make workers less likely to be absent or quit. If employers have the goal of minimizing labor cost per unit of output (i.e., per "efficiency unit") then they will adopt a long-term strategy of maintaining the firm's wages above the market-clearing level. This explanation implies that some workers forgo low-wage work while waiting for a job paying wages commensurate with their skill level.

Lang and Dickens (1988) suggested that, while the dual labor market concept has been "largely atheoretical," efficiency-wage models now make feasible a neoclassical rendering of dualism. They base this on the "dual economy" approach, developed largely by sociologists from an idea introduced by Averitt (1988). This distinguishes between jobs by their location in "core" and "periphery" industries. Core sector firms can be identified by their market power, high capital–labor ratios, stable product demand, and monopoly rents. Their tendency to pay efficiency wages leads to worker queues for core but not periphery employment, and thus a persistent failure of labor markets to clear.

Efficiency-wage research thus far differs in many ways from much of the segmentation literature. The neoclassical assumption of perfectly competitive product markets is generally accepted, and little is said about the role of unions or the importance to employers of union-avoidance as a motive for above-equilibrium wages. Nor is there any historical or institutional analysis of the origins of this pay system. At the same time, the claimed compatibility between neoclassical and segmentation models is open to debate. For example, even Lang and Dickens (1988) conceded that Piore's feedback hypothesis is fundamentally at odds with the core neoclassical assumption that individual preferences are exogenous. The contrasts with radical segmentation theory (generally ignored by all these authors) are far more numerous.

4. Empirical Findings

4.1 First-generation Research

The earliest studies of labor market segmentation focused on the late 1960s, a period of unusually low unemployment and high wage growth and labor mobility. The data samples examined were typically limited to cross sections and excluded women. It is evident, with hindsight, that these factors contributed to the ambiguity and weak generalizability of some initial results.

The empirical basis of Doeringer and Piore's (1971) concept of the dual labor market was a series of open-ended interviews with management and union officials, and with urban poverty and manpower agencies. Though their subjects commonly perceived a split labor market for the poor and nonpoor, the unconventional data source was the target of much criticism by economists. A number of studies (surveyed by Rosenberg 1979) soon followed which used standard data and statistical methods to test whether the wage-setting mechanism in the primary sector differed as predicted from that in the secondary sector. For example, Osterman (1975), after subdividing urban male workers according to the stability and autonomy of their occupations, estimated separate wage regressions for each sector. He concluded that wage determination differed significantly between sectors and that additional education was rewarded in primary but not in secondary jobs.

Cain (1976) criticized this approach for truncating the sample of workers on the dependent wage variable. Restricting some to low-wage jobs prevents observation of those who obtain higher wages only by upward mobility to the primary sector. This would, he argued, cause a systematic downard bias in the estimated wage effects of human capital variables in the secondary subsample.

A second empirical approach used factor analysis of job and industry characteristics to determine if they could be grouped by a single bimodally distributed variable. Studies such as that of Buchele (1976) tried to avoid sample selection bias by classifying jobs according to exogenous variables rather than earnings. Though his methodology and sample (middle-aged White males) differed from Osterman's, he too found that the earnings payoff to age and education were significantly positive in the primary sector alone. Yet he also found that secondary workers average 11.3 years of tenure with their employer. Although this was 3–4 years less than primary workers, it is far more than would be expected from the image of unstable, high-turnover workers given in early dualist literature.

In addition to testing within-segment wage-setting, Carnoy and Rumberger (1980) investigated worker mobility from 1965 to 1970. To define segments, they used United States Labor Department information on the specific training and autonomy characteristics of detailed census occupations. Substantial upward mobility from the secondary sector was found for this period, both for Whites and Blacks. Blacks, however, were significantly less likely than Whites to escape that sector and Blacks in primary jobs were nearly twice as likely to experience downward mobility. College education contributed to upward mobility for Whites only, though Blacks with vocational education had some advantage over other Black secondary workers.

Carnoy and Rumberger's earnings analysis showed that secondary workers averaged 30 percent lower annual wages than primary subordinate workers.

Within-segment wage equations revealed no significant returns to college education or to most work experience for either Whites or Blacks in the secondary sector. The authors disputed any influence of truncation bias, noting that even if it did depress estimated coefficient magnitudes it would not affect statistical significance. This can now be seen as a transitional study: though still based on 1970 data, it expanded beyond earlier work to pursue a longitudinal focus and to include results for women and Hispanics.

Several studies in developing countries, such as Singapore, Brazil, Mexico, Peru (Carnoy 1980), and Cameroon (Clignet 1976) suggested the existence of more clearly segmented labor markets and a more dominant role than in highly industrialized economies for labor market formality–informality and education in delineating segments (for a review of these studies, see *Education and Labor Markets in Developing Nations; Income Distribution and Education*).

4.2 Second-generation Studies

As new data sources and statistical techniques became available in the late 1970s and early 1980s, segmentation theory began to be re-evaluated for a wider variety of time periods, demographic groups, and countries. Two of the most surprising new confirmations of the theory came from neoclassical economists. Dickens and Lang (1985) tested an "endogenous switching model with unknown regimes," which avoided the need for *a priori* segment assignments as well as sample truncation bias. From their analysis of 1980 adult males they concluded: "Our results provide considerable support for the view that there are two distinct labor markets—a primary labor market with a wage profile similar to that predicted by human capital theory, and a secondary market with a completely flat (low) wage profile." They also found that the crowding of non-Whites into secondary jobs accounted for over 40 percent of the wage gap between Whites and non-Whites.

Heckman and Hotz (1986) used Heckman's own sample-selection corrections to study the 1983 earnings of adult males in Panama. While being critical of much dualist theory and research, they nonetheless reported significant differences in the wage-setting mechanisms of high-wage and low-wage groups and of different regions.

Intersectoral mobility was re-examined by Rosenberg (1981) with observations on a large sample of adult American men in the period from 1966 to 1975. He found that much of the occupational advancement seen in the late 1960s boom was short-lived. One-fifth to one-fourth of Whites and Blacks fell from the primary jobs gained at that time back to the secondary level. Rosenberg interpreted this as being consistent with a view of secondary workers as a labor reserve drawn periodically into the high-wage sector to absorb excess demand.

Though women, youth, and immigrants were long presumed to be disproportionately represented in secondary jobs, remarkably little was done to test this until the mid-1980s. A growing body of evidence is now available on the occupational segregation of working women (Hartmann 1987, Buchele 1981), immigrant clustering in "ethnic enclaves" and "immigrant-intensive industries" (Portes and Bach 1985, DeFreitas 1991), and youth concentrations in low-wage industries in the United States and Europe (DeFreitas et al. 1991).

These new studies, the expanding segmentation research in Europe (Berger and Piore 1980, Wilkinson 1981), and new historical analysis of postwar occupational trends (Reich 1984) have led many to replace the early "strict dualism" with a more eclectic and dynamic approach. In Piore's words: "As the range of research problems has expanded it became clear that a broader typology was needed, one that expressed discontinuity rather than dualism" (Berger and Piore 1980 p. 16). Segmentation has increasingly been viewed not as a stable, clear-cut division between good and bad jobs, but as a labor market *process* (Ryan 1981). Different labor force groups become compartmentalized in different ways in different countries. Moreover, it is a dynamic process which manifests itself in diverse forms over time. It is still, however, identifiable from evidence of similarly skilled workers receiving significantly different employment opportunities and rewards.

5. Conclusion

Although it is more than two decades since dual labor market theory was first proposed in the late 1960s, it remains a subject of great controversy. The widening of the scope of the research agenda promises to produce a more diverse array of historical, sociological, and economic studies in a growing number of national settings. If these further intensify the continuing debates between the conventional and segmentation perspectives, it will only provide more evidence of the importance of the issues in contention, both to an understanding of labor markets and to economic and educational policy.

See also: Education, Occupation, and Earnings; Race Earnings Differentials; Education and the Labor Market; Internal Labor Markets and Education; Education and Labor Markets in Developing Nations; Human Capital Concepts; Screening Models and Education; The Wage Contract and Education; Education and Productivity; Income Distribution and Education

References

Averitt R 1988 The prospects for economic dualism: A historical perspective. In: Farkas G, England P (eds.) 1988
Berger S, Piore M 1980 *Dualism and Discontinuity in Industrial Societies.* Cambridge University Press, Cambridge

Bowles S, Gintis H 1976 *Schooling in Capitalist America: Educational Reform and the Contradictions of Economic Life*. Basic Books, New York

Brown C, Pechman J (eds.) 1987 *Gender in the Workplace*. Brookings Institution, Washington, DC

Buchele R 1976 Jobs and workers: A labor market segmentation perspective on the work experience of young men. (Doctoral dissertation, Harvard University)

Buchele R 1981 Sex discrimination and labor market segmentation. In: Wilkinson F (ed.) 1981

Bulow J, Summers L 1986 A theory of dual labor markets with application to industrial policy, discrimination, and Keynesian unemployment. *J. Labor Econ.* 4(3): 376–414

Cain G 1976 The challenge of segmented labor market theories to orthodox theory: A survey. *J. Econ. Lit.* 14(4): 1215–57

Carnoy M 1980 Segmented labor markets: A review of the theoretical and empirical literature and its implications for educational planning. In: Carnoy M, Levin H, King K 1980 *Education, Work, and Employment*, Vol. 2. UNESCO/IIEP, Paris

Carnoy M, Rumberger R 1980 Segmentation in the US labour market: Its effects on the mobility and earnings of whites and blacks. *Cambridge Journal of Economics* 4(2): 117–32

Clignet R 1976 *The Africanization of the Labor Market: Education and Occupational Segregation in the Cameroun*. University of California Press, Berkeley, California

DeFreitas G 1991 *Inequality At Work: Hispanics in the US Labor Force*. Oxford University Press, New York

DeFreitas G, Marsden D, Ryan P 1991 Youth employment patterns in segmented labor markets in the US and Europe. *Eastern Economic Journal* 17(2): 223–36

Dickens W, Lang K 1985 A test of dual labor market theory. *Am. Econ. Rev.* 75(4): 792–805

Doeringer P, Piore M 1971 *Internal Labor Markets and Manpower Analysis*. Heath, Lexington, Massachusetts

Farkas G, England P (eds.) 1988 *Industries, Firms, and Jobs: Sociological and Economic Approaches*. Plenum Press, New York

Gordon D, Edwards R, Reich M 1973 A theory of labor market segmentation. *Am. Econ. Rev. Papers and Proceedings* 63(2): 359–65

Gordon D, Edwards R, Reich M 1982 *Segmented Work, Divided Workers: The Historical Transformation of Labor in the United States*. Cambridge University Press, Cambridge

Hartmann H 1987 Internal labor markets and gender: A case study of promotion. In: Brown C, Pechman J (eds.) 1987.

Heckman J, Hotz V J 1986 An investigation of the labor market earnings of Panamanian males: Evaluating the sources of inequality. *J. Hum. Resources* 21(4): 507–42

Lang K, Dickens W 1988 Neoclassical and sociological perspectives on segmented labor markets. In: Farkas G, England P (eds.) 1988

Osterman P 1975 An empirical study of labor market segmentation. *Industrial and Labor Relations Review* 28(4): 508–23

Portes A, Bach R 1985 *Latin Journey: Cuban and Mexican Immigrants in the United States*. University of California Press, Berkeley, California

Reich M 1981 *Racial Inequality: A Political–Economic Analysis* Princeton University Press, Princeton, New Jersey

Reich M 1984 Segmented labour: Time–series hypotheses and evidence. *Cambridge Journal of Economics* 8(1): 63–81

Rosenberg S (ed.) 1979 A Survey of Empirical Work on Labor Market Segmentation. Working Paper Series 138, University of California, Davis, California

Rosenberg S 1981 Occupational mobility and short cycles. In: Wilkinson F (ed.) 1981

Ryan P 1981 Segmentation, duality and the internal labour market. In: Wilkinson F (ed.) 1981

Wachter M 1974 Primary and secondary labor markets: A critique of the dual approach. *Brookings Papers on Economic Activity* 3: 637–80

Wilkinson F (ed.) 1981 *The Dynamics of Labour Market Segmentation*. Cambridge University Press, Cambridge

The Wage Contract and Education

M. Blaug

All wage labor under capitalism is hired in accordance with an explicit or implicit employment contract. This contract is typically "incomplete" in as much as it specifies the duration of work and the rate of pay but not the intensity and quality of effort. The incompleteness of the hiring contract is not an accidental feature of the relationship between employer and employee; it is a necessary feature which can be mitigated but which can never be wholly eliminated.

It is impossible to complete the employment contract for the simple reason that workers, unlike machines, must be given an incentive to work effectively. Labor is the only human input in the productive process and the hire of labor at a time rate implies a conscious willingness to work at a minimum level of intensity, a willingness which cannot be adequately written down in a contractual agreement. If that were not bad enough, there is the further difficulty that much of output in modern production systems is carried out by teams, in which case output cannot be unambiguously traced to individual workers. The United States labor movement used to fight for higher wages and better working conditions under the slogan "a fair day's work for a fair day's pay." Even leaving aside the question of what constitutes "a fair day's pay," the incompleteness of the employment contract in an industrial society can be neatly expressed by saying that there is no natural way of determining the meaning of "a fair day's work." In short, labor power under capitalism is not, as Marx claimed, a commodity like any other; if it were it would be bought and sold subject to a contract that would fully specify all the characteristics of the commodity being traded. Unfortunately, this is not the case where labor is concerned.

1. Some Implications

The standard manner in which employers attempt to complete the employement contract is by the combination of carrot and stick: the carrot is the promise of continuing employment and eventual promotion to higher rates of pay; the stick is the threat of instant dismissal. Both the carrot and the stick imply full knowledge of the worker's effort throughout the working day. Clearly, such knowledge is out of the question but intermittent first-hand monitoring by supervisors, accompanied by quality checks at nodal points in the production process, serves to evaluate individual workers where possible, or the average performance of a team of workers in the case of batch production. Since most plants even in the same industry are to some extent unique, these performance ratings of workers rarely involve cardinal comparisons; at best, they rank workers ordinally as in a tournament. It follows that if workers act in concert, say, by slowing down in unison, even constant monitoring may not be effective in preventing shirking and malingering.

The management of a labor force, therefore, necessarily involves a strategy of "divide and rule," particularly if the presence of trade unions impels collective rather than individual wage bargaining. The most effective way of preventing workers from synchronizing their work efforts is to promote sexual, racial, and ethnic stratification of the labor force, which in any case merely reproduces the sexual, racial, and ethnic discrimination existing in the outside world. This is not to say that sexism and racism are inherent in capitalist society but simply that where there is sexism and racism, it proves to be most convenient for the requirements of efficient personal management.

2. Marxist Treatment

It is a curious fact that the incompleteness of the employment contract under capitalism as well as its significance for industrial relations is part and parcel of Marxian economics, radical economics and, in recent years, mainstream economics. The origin of the idea is undoubtedly Marx's analysis of "the valorization of the labor process" in Volume 1, Chapter 7 of *Das Kapital*. The employment contract, Marx argued, is an entirely voluntary exchange of labor power for

wages and, being voluntary, should benefit both parties to the transaction. However, in the course of the process by which labor is combined with raw materials and capital goods to produce a salable product, profit emerges as the difference between the value of labor power and the net value of the final product; this difference is surplus-value, said by Marx to be due entirely to the "exploitation" of labor. This surplus-value does not emerge naturally but only if workers are coerced to produce enough to exceed their own subsistence requirements as expressed in the wage payment. It is this extraction of surplus-value from workers that Marx labels the "valorization" of the labor process. The apparently free employment contract under capitalism in effect masks "the despotism of the work place," an authoritarian control of production by capitalists, which for Marx is both the key to the nature of profits and the key to the technical dynamism of capitalism.

In essence, although expressed in rhetorical language, this is the heart of the thesis of the incomplete employment contract. Marx's discussion of the labor process was long neglected by his followers but in recent years, particularly since the publication of Braverman's *Labor and Monopoly Capital* (1974), the variety of ways by which management controls the labor force has been a subject of vigorous study by Marxists (Littler 1990).

3. Radical Treatment

Radical economists in the United States have built an entire paradigm on the need of capitalists to secure labor discipline on the factory floor. "What do bosses do?" asked Marglin (1974) in a famous paper; his answer was that they exercise coercive social power over the production process, and that is just about all they do. Indeed, he traced the origin of the division of labor in the eighteenth-century factory, not to the superior efficiency of occupational specialization or the technical advantages of a hierarchical organisation of production, but simply to the desire of capitalists to "divide and rule" the work force. From the point of view of economic growth, he implied, labor-managed enterprises would have proved just as effective as the typical factory of the Industrial Revolution.

Similarly, because there is a fundamental conflict of interest between workers and capitalists in maintaining the employment relationship, capitalists actively promote sexual and racial discrimination in the labor market. For radical economists, therefore, the problem is not to explain why there is discrimination against women and Blacks under capitalism but how anyone could imagine that sexism and racism could ever be eliminated in a capitalist society (Reich 1981).

Analysis of sexism and racism as inherent features of capitalism is intimately associated with the concept of segmented labor markets (SLM), which is perhaps the most important contribution that radical economists have made to economics. The theory of SLM is not itself radical in origin and was first broached by United States labor economists of the Institutionalist School in the 1920s, culminating in the famous distinction by Doeringer and Piore (1971) between "internal" and "external" labor markets. Normally, one thinks of hiring labor as a process of recruiting workers on a labor market that is external to the firm. But a great many jobs in firms are filled internally by promotion. If the occupational structure of a typical business enterprise is thought of as a pyramid with a lower stratum of shop-floor workers, surmounted by a thinner stratum of supervisors, and then by an even thinner stratum of managers, new workers are recruited at only two or three "ports of entry," namely, at the base and at the apex of the pyramid; all other vacancies are filled from within the company by drawing on the "internal labor market." Apart from misleading language—an administrative process of filling vacancies by internal promotion has none of the characteristics of a market process—this notion of an "internal labor market" captures an important, perhaps increasingly important, feature of job placements in a modern industrial society.

The idea of SLM builds on, but is distinct from, the concept of internal labor markets. The institutionalists' version of SLM refers to a contrast between two sectors of the economy, the so-called "primary" labor markets of large corporations (with trade unions, job security, and steady career prospects) and the "secondary" labor markets of small business (with no unions, dead-end casual jobs, and high turnover rates); such a dichotimization of labor markets is said to be due to certain structural changes in the twentieth-century economy of the United States. In radical theories of SLM, however, segmentation, apart from involving three rather than two strata, is not so much a matter of contrasting sectors of economic activities but rather of contrasting categories of workers within each and every firm in every sector. In other words, segmentation runs to some degree through all capitalist enterprises (Edwards 1979) and this is precisely why sexism and racism are judged to be endemic to capitalism.

4. Orthodox Treatment

All this might be dismissed as merely so much radical chic were it not for the fact that all such Marxist and radical ideas are echoed in the "new" orthodox labor economics of the 1970s. In standard neoclassical economics, labor and capital are treated as perfectly symmetrical inputs purchased on spot markets, which are somehow combined in a "black box" called the firm. Ronald Coase argued that firms are nonmarket institutions in which authoritarian allocation replaces the price system; firms are "command economies" in miniature. More recently, the rise of human capital theory fundamentally altered the way in which

economists view the recruitment of labor. The simple investment concept—that individuals, like firms, spend now through schooling and on-the-job training to reap rewards later, thereby producing an upward tilt to age-earnings profiles—directed attention to lifetime considerations in methods of payment to labor. The fact that the process of recruiting labor and assigning them to different tasks in the enterprise involved considerable transaction costs which accounted for many well-attested characteristics of labor markets, generated a wholly new style of labor economics in the 1970s (e.g., Alchian and Demsetz 1972). Nevertheless, it was developments in macroeconomics rather than microeconomics that really gave the theme of the incomplete employment contract a central place in the agenda of neoclassical economics.

Keynes had demonstrated that macroeconomic equilibrium might well be an unemployment equilibrium, in which case the economic system lacked a stabilizing mechanism that would automatically generate full employment. But why did the labor market fail to clear in the presence of involuntary unemployment? To say that both money and real wages were rigid downwards for institutional reasons and hence that Keynesian equilibria are quantity-constrained rather than price-constrained equilibria, seemed arbitrary and ad hoc. In short, Keynesian macroeconomics lacked a microeconomic foundation in standard rational choice theory. Thus arose the idea of formulating a Keynesian unemployment equilibrium that would meet all the analytical requirements of Pareto-optimal Walrasian general equilibrium theory.

5. Invisible Handshake

The formal development of the notion of an "implicit contract" mutually agreed upon by workers and employers, and capable of demonstrating that all unemployment is fundamentally voluntary, appeared independently but more or less simultaneously in the mid-1970s in three papers by Bailey, Gordon, and Azariadis (also see Azariadis 1987). The first problem was to show that layoffs are preferred to work-sharing in times of depression even by workers, not to mention managers. Why else is a fall of aggregate demand always associated with layoffs and never with work-sharing? The answer is that workers are risk-averse and are unwilling to contemplate a future income profile that fluctuates with aggregate demand. Hence risk-neutral firms relieve their employees of the market risk of unemployment when aggregate demand declines in return for the right of management to make allocative decisions about the use of labor, including discretion about the volume of employment. Another way of expressing the same idea is to note that the employment contract is in part an insurance contract that protects workers from fluctuations in their marginal product, and hence their wages, as a consequence of output fluctuations. As a result the employment contract takes on the character of a personal agreement over a long period of time between a worker and a firm rather than the impersonal instantaneous spot exchange characteristic of old-style labor economics.

This game-theoretic formulation of the conundrum of involuntary unemployment is not entirely convincing because some workers will be laid off when demand slackens and they will presumably be worse off even if there is a dole. However, just as deferred compensation or "less pay now for more pay later," and fringe benefits that improve with length of service, are management tools for discouraging shirking on the part of workers, so the promise of continuing employment or security of job tenure becomes yet another incentive to individual workers (Lazear 1987). In other words, every worker expects to be one of the "insiders" who will be kept on when demand slackens and in that sense it is perfectly rational for utility-maximizing workers to accept unemployment for some as a preferable alternative to sharing whatever work is available, which implies a drop in earnings in a recession or depression.

There is a multiplicity of views on the employment contract, and the 1970s and 1980s saw a number of other ways of explaining the persistence of involuntary cyclical unemployment within the constraints of the Walrasian paradigm. One of these was the so-called efficiency wage hypothesis, which appeared in a great number of papers written around 1980. The efficiency wage hypothesis is a corollary of the "principal–agent problem" applied to the labor-hiring process. A principal–agent problem arises whenever someone, the principal, wants a task carried out and hires someone else, the agent, to do it but cannot continuously observe or perfectly infer the agent's action and cannot assume that the self-interest of the agent is identical to his or her own (Stiglitz 1987). In the case to be considered, the principals are the firm's managers or owners and the agents are the workers. Since their interests are not necessarily the same, the problem is to provide workers with an incentive to work efficiently in accordance with managerial instructions. The stick for achieving that result is, as mentioned earlier, the threat of being dismissed. However, dismissing a worker imposes the cost of recruiting, placing, and evaluating a new worker and hence it may be profitable for firms to pay existing workers a wage which on average exceeds the wage that could be earned elsewhere. The penalty for workers who are caught shirking is now not just unemployment but also the loss of the wage premium paid by the firm. Thus, the total wage payment is an "efficiency wage" in the sense that firms are better off paying it and workers are better off receiving it, and yet it is a nonmarket clearing wage in excess of the competitive wage that on average would be necessary to get them to supply their labor.

There is a striking overlap between these orthodox explanations of unemployment equilibrium and typical radical explanations of chronic unemployment under capitalism (Stiglitz and Shapiro 1986, Reich and Devine 1981). However, orthodox economists pay little attention to, and sometimes even deny, the likelihood of a conflict of interest between workers and capitalists in maintaining the employment relationship, whereas radical economists understandably emphasize the "contested terrain" of industrial relations (Edwards 1979). There is little doubt that if workers controlled production, they would choose more job enrichment and more frequent job rotation, that is, a lower division of labor than capitalists now do. In general, there is no reason to believe that the worker's goal of maximizing the pecuniary and nonpecuniary rewards of labor always gives the same results as the capitalist's goal of maximizing profit. Moreover, workers prefer collective rather than individual labor contracts and in this sense too the interests of workers and capitalists are bound to clash.

Personnel managers have long devised a variety of "incentive contracts" to induce workers to cooperate in the maximization of the joint welfare of all members of the firm. Nevertheless, in the words of Okun (1981 p. 86), "the basic problem of the need for trust (in the employment relation) and the inherent reasons for distrust is not soluble. Distrust is a pervasive fact of ... the career labor market." In the end, the employment relation boils down entirely to a sense of attachment between employer and employees. In Okun's memorable phrase (1981 p. 89), employers must rely on "an invisible handshake" to take the place of "the invisible hand" that fails to operate in labor markets.

6. Interim Summary

When a firm hires a worker it hopes to obtain a reliable, achievement-motivated and committed employee; the worker on the other hand hopes that the firm seriously intends to provide not just a casual job, but a long-term career. Both sides to the bargain will try to create reliable expectations about their own intentions, which simply cannot be spelled out explicitly in a written contract. It is in this sense that the term "incomplete employment contract" is used.

The incompleteness of employment contracts has enormous significance for the idiosyncratic character of labor markets, a fact which has struck numerous observers as far back as Adam Smith. The necessity of relying on an implicit rather than on an explicit contract is certainly not confined to labor markets: it arises, for example, in insurance markets, in capital markets, in tenant—landlord relationships, and indeed in every transaction in which the quality of an input is a major element of output. Nevertheless, no implicit contract is as pervasive or as central to the fortunes of an economy as the implicit employment contract.

Economists have been discussing the sources of economic growth and the reasons for the unequal rates of growth of different countries for over 200 years. Natural resources, capital investment, the growth of the labor force, technical progress, management styles, all have been canvassed as keys to economic growth. However, the *quality* of the labor force, its attitudes to work and leisure, its willingness to submit to discipline, are rarely mentioned as factors in a country's economic performance. Such factor do figure in radical writings on the causes of the so-called "productivity slowdown" in the United States economy (e.g., Sherman 1976, Gordon 1981) but a more far-reaching analysis of differential rates of growth of, say, the United Kingdom and Germany or Italy and Japan has yet to be undertaken. Why does Germany grow faster than the United Kingdom economy? Possibly for no other reason than that German workers have a sense of loyalty to German firms that British workers do not have to British firms. Why are the economies of Eastern Europe at a stand still? A major reason is that workers in these economies, long accustomed to perfect job security, have virtually stopped working. Marx was quite correct to argue that unemployment is vital to the survival of capitalism; what he did not realize is that it is equally vital to the survival of socialism! The secret of economic growth lies not in the questions traditionally studied in economics. It lies in industrial relations.

7. Screening and Signaling

What has all this to do with education? Simply this: the process of hiring workers poses a problem of "asymmetric information," that is, information not equally available on both sides of a market. For example, employers possess superior information about their demand for labor, but workers possess superior information about their willingness to supply labor. Employers face the problem of predicting the future performance of job applicants in the absence of any accurate measure of the worker's past performance. Of course, the employer can require a certain number of years of work experience, but it will be experience in a different firm under different circumstances and in the case of young recruits, there may well be no prior experience. In the event, the employers will find it advantageous to use certain "filters" in selecting workers. The first is age as a proxy for work experience. The second is sex as a proxy for labor force commitment. The third is marital status, again as a proxy for commitment and perhaps eagerness for continued employment. The fourth and final filter is provided by educational qualifications—and various hypotheses have been advanced to explain what they act as a proxy for.

It could be argued, somewhat crudely, that so long as production is hierarchically organized in large enterprises, what is required at the bottom of the job pyramid is the ability to take orders, while at the top of the pyramid what is required is the ability to give orders. Employers have learned from past experience that there is a general concordance between the attributes required at various levels of the occupational pyramid and educational attainments. In that sense, educational credentials act as surrogates for qualities which employers regard as important, predicting a certain level of job performance without, however, making any direct contribution to it. This is the so-called "screening hypothesis" according to which education acts merely as a filter to identify workers with desirable work habits. Screening by employers in terms of educational qualifications then creates an incentive on the part of employees to produce the "signal" that maximizes the probability of being selected, namely, the possession of an educational qualification. In short, "signaling" is the other side of the coin of "screening."

This screening–signaling hypothesis gains cogency once it is recognized that employers value education not so much for what educated workers know than for how educated workers behave. The economic value of education is not what it is usually supposed to be. The point can test be made by summarizing Benjamin Bloom's *Taxonomy of Educational Objectives* (1956), a book that is still the veritable bible of curriculum reformers the world over. Bloom made the extraordinary claim that the objectives of all curricula in any subject at any stage of education can be exhaustively classified into three categories, namely: (a) "cognitive knowledge," (b) "psycho-motor skills," and (c) "affective behavioral traits." By cognitive knowledge, Bloom meant the sum of memorized facts and concepts that are supposed to be crammed into the student's head; by psycho-motor skills, he meant the manual dexterity and muscular coordination that a student is supposed to acquire; and by affective behavioral traits, he meant the values and attitudes shaping behavior, which a student is supposed to take away with him or her at the completion of a course. The same idea had been expressed much earlier in much simpler language by a famous philosopher of education, Johann Heinrich Pestalozzi. Pestalozzi said that all education touches either the "head," the "hand," or the "heart" of the pupil and these three "Hs" correspond exactly to Bloom's more forbidding terminology.

When it is said that education is economically valuable, that it makes people more productive, most people think immediately of the first "H," cognitive knowledge. The assumption, in other words, is that it is the educated worker's knowledge of certain facts and concepts that makes him or her valuable to employers. This might be called "the pilot fallacy": in order to fly a plane you need a pilot, and flying a plane requires cognitive knowledge (and some psycho-motor skills) which can only be learned by formal training. But what employers really value in most workers is "affective behavioral traits," such as punctuality, persistence, attentiveness, responsibility, achievement-drive, cooperativeness, compliance, and so on. The cognitive skills required to carry out most jobs in industry and agriculture are learned on the job. What formal education does, therefore, is not so much to train workers as to make them trainable.

It is a curious fact that these crucial behavioral traits which largely account for the economic value of education cannot be efficiently conveyed directly but only as a by-product, as a "hidden agenda," of an educational process directed at cognitive knowledge. Imagine a class in punctuality; it would be possible but it would also be immensely tedious and probably ineffective. But punctuality is powerfully fostered by an educational process rigidly tied to a timetable throughout every moment of the school day. One of the greatest problems in running a factory in a newly industrialized country is that of getting workers to arrive on time and to notify the plant manager when they are going to be absent; the lack of punctuality in the work force can raise labor costs in a developing country by as much as 50 percent over a developed country. This is a simple but telling example of the phenomenon in question: The economic value of education resides much more in the realm of behavior than in the realm of cognitive knowledge.

The notion that most jobs in a modern economy require high levels of literacy and numeracy, and increasingly so as industry becomes more computerized, is simply erroneous. It lies behind the frequent tendency to "vocationalize" secondary education in the fond belief that this will increase the employability of school leavers; this despite the fact that vocational school graduates almost always experience higher unemployment rates than academic school graduates. The very distinction between "academic" and "vocational" education, in which only the latter is supposed to be geared to the needs of the labor market, plants the suggestion that much, if not most, education is economically irrelevant. But the "hidden curriculum" of teacher–pupil relations in academic-style education has as much to do with the world of work as the explicit curriculum of mental and manipulative skills in vocational education. The frequently repeated research finding that few workers ever make specific use of the cognitive knowledge acquired in schools thus indicates, not some sort of monstrous mismatch between education and work, but the pivotal role of effective behavioral traits in job performance. The truth of the matter is that most jobs in a modern economy require about as much cognitive knowledge and psycho-motor skills as are necessary to drive an automobile!

8. Some Implications of Screening and Signaling

The screening hypothesis neatly accounts for the fact that earnings rise with additional education; it even explains why so many educational qualifications appear to be unrelated to the type of work that students eventually take up; and it certainly helps to explain why the educational explosion that began in the 1950s has had so little effect on equalizing the distribution of income.

If education acts merely as a filter to separate the wheat from the chaff, the steady expansion of, say, higher education dilutes the significance of a degree and induces employers to upgrade the hiring standards of jobs previously filled by university and college graduates; graduates will then be worse off in absolute terms. But if secondary schooling is expanding at the same time, so that secondary school leavers are likewise being squeezed into lower-level jobs, earnings differentials between the two cohorts may nevertheless remain more or less the same. What is true of these two categories of labor is true of every category: the expansion of postcompulsory education is simply passed down the line and results in a chronic core of unemployed school leavers without, however, much visible effect on the distribution of earned income from employment.

The screening hypothesis clearly has dramatic implications for educational policy. The difficulty with the hypothesis is that it comes in two versions, a strong version and a weak one. In its strong version, it is virtually untenable, whereas in its weak version, it is difficult to pin down with any precision. The strong version of the screening hypothesis asserts that education merely identifies students with particular attributes, acquired either at birth or by virtue of family background, but does not itself produce produce or improve those attributes. It is difficult to conceive how this strong version of the hypothesis could possibly be true. After all, colleges screen twice, once when they select students for admission and a second time when they pass or fail students at the end of an educational cycle. If there is screening in the strong sense, only the first screen serves any useful economic function, whereas the second is just a piece of window dressing designed purely to create employment for teachers. But as every teacher knows, the correlation for any individual student between predicted and actual success in education is by no means perfect: selection for admission to courses is wrong almost as often as it is right. In other words, "good" students have to be discovered, and it takes a protracted sequence of hurdles, such as any educational cycle provides, to identify the traits and attributes that lead to success. The notion that they are present, only waiting to be sifted out by some ingenious filter, and that any filter will do, schooling being simply one, is a naive psychological fallacy.

In addition, the strong version of the screening hypothesis implies that there is little reward to an uncompleted degree or certificate, or at any rate that the extra rewards of, for example, two years of university education are much less than two-thirds of the rewards of a completed university degree. In other words, educational credentials act like a "sheepskin" that disguises the true difference between dropouts and graduates. Similarly, strong screening implies that, whatever differences in starting salaries between university graduates and secondary school leavers, the gap in the two salary streams gradually disappears with additional years of work experience. Employers may use educational qualifications as a screen at the time of hiring when they are ignorant of the true abilities of potential workers but, as time passes, they can actually observe workers' job performance and reward them in accordance with their personal abilities. Finally, strong screening makes it difficult to understand why employers have not sought to replace the educational system by a cheaper screening mechanism. Surely it is cheaper to incur the costs of testing the abilities of individual workers by a battery of psychological aptitude tests, say, than to pay all university graduates more simply because they are university graduates.

Thus, the strong version of the screening hypothesis carries with it at least three definite empirical implications (Blaug 1987 pp. 118–22). All of these three implications, however, are firmly refuted by the evidence. First, the private rate of return to education for university dropouts sometimes actually exceeds the yield of a completed university degree. Second, the effect of years of education on personal earnings generally rises rather than falls with additional years of work experience. Business firms and government departments do sometimes test individual workers at the point of recruitment; nevertheless, in no country in the world have such independent testing services effectively replaced the role of educational credentials in screening out job applicants. Third, education ought to have no effect on personal earnings when it comes to the self-employed since there is little point in self-screening. As a matter of fact, however, the impact of years of education on earnings is as great for self-employed accountants, doctors, and lawyers as it is for wage and salary earners. Of course, that may be due to screening by the customers of self-employed professionals, which in turn leads professional associations of accountants, doctors, and lawyers to press for increased educational qualifications under state occupational licensing laws. Nevertheless, the evidence on the association between education and earnings for the self-employed does cast some doubt on screening in its stronger versions.

All these refutations, however, are invalidated if the screening hypothesis is given a weaker interpretation. Employers face information costs in recruiting suitable workers and assigning them appropriately to different tasks. Every new worker takes days or weeks to reach an adequate level of performance and thus mistakes in hiring are costly in terms of output forgone, not to mention the administrative costs of posting vacancies, sorting applicants, and inducting successful recruits. It is therefore hardly surprising that employers resort to stereotypes like age, sex,

color, ethnic background, marital status, work experience, and educational credentials to predict job performance. For crucial jobs like those of supervisors, junior managers, and executives, it may pay to engage in expensive search procedures, including the use of aptitude tests, to select a particular candidate from among a group of job applicants with similar characteristics. But for most jobs, it is cheaper to rely on group characteristics. But for most jobs, it is cheaper to rely on group characteristics and to run the risk of occasional error. Thus, the use of educational qualifications as a hiring screen is a species of a larger genus of "statistical discrimination" in the hiring of labor: the costs of truly identifying the talents of potential workers forces employers to discriminate against atypical members of social groups. The fact that educational qualifications stand out among all the other stereotypes as being legally permitted and generally approved—most people regard educational meritocracy as being perfectly fair and legitimate—only encourages screening by education on the part of the employers.

So interpreted, the "screening hypothesis" is a label for a classic information problem in a labor market. So far, however, the discussion has only dealt with hiring at the point of recruitment and nothing has been said to explain the association between education and earnings during the entire working life of individuals. Granted that employers will pay more to better educated workers when they know nothing about their individual aptitudes, why should they almost invariably continue to do so when they have had ample opportunity to monitor their performance over long periods of time?

One explanation may be the existence of "internal labor markets" in many business firms and government departments. In such enterprises, workers tend to be recruited not to a job but to a career path and this means that any advantages at the point of recruitment tend to be converted into persistent advantages throughout a working life with the company. In this way, the use of educational qualifications as a screen at the point of hiring becomes an effective screen throughout the period of association with a particular enterprise. Even if the worker leaves the company to work elsewhere, the next employer is likely to give credit both for previous experience and for previous earnings, which perpetuates the earlier link between schooling and earnings. In summary, the notion of "statistical discrimination" in hiring and the presence of "internal labor markets" taken together are perfectly capable of explaining why highly educated people earn more on average than less educated people even though they may not be inherently more productive.

The term "on average" is used advisedly. Clearly, employers do make mistakes in hiring and discover in due course that some university graduates are worse than others. Consequently they do not promote such graduates or only promote them more slowly; alternatively, they may transfer them to a different job from the one for which they were recruited. Contrariwise, the jobs of "high flyers" may be enriched over time or combined with other jobs into a new job title. Therefore, a study of the structure of personal earnings by education and occupation in any modern economy reveals: (a) a strong positive association between earnings and education when expressed in terms of averages; (b) considerable variance in the association between education and earnings, such that the worst paid university graduates actually earn less than the best paid secondary school leavers, and so on for all other educational cohorts; and (c) a considerable variance for every occupational category, however finely defined, in the years of schooling of incumbents of that occupation. Such evidence is accountable by an element of "statistical discrimination" at the hiring stage and the presence of "internal labor markets" of various degrees of strength in many private companies and government departments.

9. Conclusion

Add together the concept of the incomplete employment contract, the phenomenon of internal labor markets, the notion of labor market segmentation, and the fundamental socialization function of schools in inculcating definite values and attitudes, and a picture emerges of the economic value of schooling that is far removed from the simplistic belief that education makes workers more productive and that employers pay them more because they are more productive. It may well be that schooling increases the productivity of individuals by making them more effective members of a production team or better able to handle machines and materials. On the other hand, it would matter little if this were not so, provided that everyone believed it to be true (as is indeed the case). What is important is that every worker accepts the principles on which some are paid more and some less. Even if these payments are in reverse order of the true spot marginal products of individual workers (assuming that these could ever be identified), the maximization of the output and minimization of the costs of the firm depend critically not on the scale of individual rewards but on the mutual consent of all workers in the enterprise. In short, screening by educational qualifications is economically efficient not because "good" students are always "good" workers but because educational credentialism avoids the inherent conflict of interests between workers and employers.

It is no wonder, then, that labor markets tend to react to changes in effective demand by adjusting quantities rather than prices, and numbers employed rather than wages. Layoffs in a slump threaten the morale of the work force less than an across-the-board cut in wages,

particularly if the layoffs are concentrated among certain "inferior" groups, like young trainees, women, or Blacks. Likewise, fresh hiring in a boom generates the expectation of promotion among older workers, which is even more effective in raising morale than an actual promotion. Thus, labor markets are inherently capable of continually absorbing workers with ever higher levels of education simply by adjusting the customary educational hiring standards for jobs. However, such adjustments, precisely because they must be seen to win general approval, take time. A rapid flooding of a labor market with, say, university graduates may well produce graduate unemployment, whereas the same numbers could have been absorbed if they had been forthcoming at a slower rate. Similarly, a sudden glut of university graduates produces graduate unemployment because employers have misgivings about hiring overqualified applicants who tend to feel underutilized, making them ineffective workers. But declining job opportunities force university graduates to adjust their job aspirations downwards. In time, therefore, holders of bachelors' degrees will cease to feel themselves to be overqualified for, say, secretarial posts and in that sense the original objection to hiring them for such jobs will lose its force. Once again, it is not an absolute oversupply of university graduates but a rapid increase in that supply that causes graduate unemployment.

On the other hand, there is no real sense in which a given level of education in the economically active population of a country can be said to be technically "required" to permit the achieved level of economic growth of that country. Such an argument grossly exaggerates the contribution of manipulative and cognitive skills in the performance of economic functions, ignores the fact that such skills are largely acquired by on-the-job training, and utterly neglects the vital role of suitable personality traits in securing the "invisible handshake" on which production critically depends. In short, educational policies may be fitted to literally any level or rate of economic growth and cannot be justified in terms of those patterns of growth. Education does make a contribution to economic growth, not as an indispensable input into the growth process, but simply as a framework which necessarily accommodates the growth process.

See also: Internal Labor Markets and Education; Segmented Labor Markets and Education

References

Alchian A A, Demsetz H 1972 Production, information costs, and economic organization. *Am. Econ. Rev.* 62 (2): 777–95

Azariadis C 1975 Implicit contracts and underemployment equilibria. *J. Pol. Econ.* 83: 1183–1202

Azariadis C 1987 Implicit contracts. In: Eatwell J et al (eds.) 1987 *The New Palgrave. A Dictionary of Economics*, Vol.2. Macmillan, London

Bailey M N 1974 Wages and employment under uncertain demand. *Rev. Econ. Stud.* 41: 37–50.

Blaug M 1987 *The Economics of Education and the Education of an Economist.* Edward Elgar, Aldershot

Bloom B S et al. 1956 *Taxomony of Educational Objectives.* David McKay, New York

Braverman H 1974 *Labor and Monopoly Capital: The Degradation of Work in the Twentieth Century.* Monthly Review Press, New York

Coase R H 1988 *The Firm, the Market, and the Law.* University of Chicago Press. Chicago Illinois

Doeringer P, Piore M 1971 *Internal Labor Markets and Manpower Analysis.* Heath, Lexington, Massachusetts

Edwards R C 1979 *Contested Terrain. The Transformation of the Workplace in the Twentieth Century.* Basic Books, New York

Gordon D F 1974 A neoclassical theory of Keynesion unemployment. *Econ. Inquiry* 12:431–5g

Gordon D M 1981 Capital-labor-conflict and the productivity slowdown. *Am. Econ. Rev.* 71 (2): 30–35

Lazear E P 1987 Incentive contracts. In: Eatwell J et al (eds.) 1987, Vol. 2 London

Littler C R 1990 The labor process debate: A theoretical review. In: Knights D, Willmot H (eds.) 1990 *Labor Process Theory.* Macmillan, Basingstoke

Marglin S 1974–75 What do bosses do? The origins and functions of hierarchy in capitalist production. *Rev. Rad. Pol. Econ.* 6(2): 60–112; 7(1) 20–37

Okun A M 1981 *Prices and Quantities.* Blackwell, Oxford

Reich M 1981 *Racial Inequality: A Political-Economic Analysis.* Princeton University Press, Princeton, New Jersey

Reich M, Devine J 1981 The microeconomics of conflict and hierarchy in capitalist production. *Rev. Rad. Pol. Econ.* 12(4): 27–45

Sherman H J 1976 *Stagflation: A Radical Theory of Unemployment and Inflation.* Harper and Row, New York

Stiglitz J E 1987 Principal and agent. In: Eatwell J et al. (eds.) 1987, Vol. 3

Stiglitz J E, Shapiro C 1986 Equilibrium unemployment as a worker discipline device. In: Akerlof G A, Yellen J L (eds.) 1986 *Efficiency Wage Models of the Labor Market.* Cambridge University Press, Cambridge

Agency and Efficiency Wage Theory

S. Bowles and H. Gintis

Until the late 1980s the economics of education labored under the burden of a microeconomic framework that, far from illuminating the economic consequences of and influences on education, systematically obscured fundamental aspects of the economy-education nexus. Most important, the concept of production in conventional neoclassical economic theory is technocratic, representing the transformation of inputs into outputs as a process governed not by social relationships but by the laws of physics and chemistry. However, since the late 1980s a new theory of production and labor markets has emerged, one evocative of the substance if not the mode of expression of Marx's reasoning concerning the social relations of production and the conflict between worker and employer over the pace of work, or as he put it, the "extraction of labor from labor power." This new body of microeconomic theory, as this article will show, provides a more adequate basis for the economics of education than the conventional neoclassical model underlying the human capital approach. Conventional neoclassical economics will be called the "Walrasian paradigm" (after one of its great founders, Leon Waldras), to distinguish it from later developments. For summaries of what can be termed "post-Walrasian" economics, see Stiglitz (1987) and Bowles and Gintis (1990, 1993). An early critique of human capital theory based on an early version of post-Walrasian microeconomic theory was presented in Bowles and Gintis (1975).

1. The Missing Dimension

Missing in the Walrasian view of production is any notion of the social setting in which production takes place or of the class and other social dimensions of the production process. The concept of "power", for example, is absent from Walrasian economic theory: one can peruse the indexes of dozens of economics texts without encountering the term. More surprising, there is no entry for "power" in the massive (and heterodox) *New Palgrave* encyclopedia of economics. Similarly, because Walrasian economics represents the exchange of one's labor for a wage as no different from buying a shirt, the theory has no place for concepts such as "work norms", "alienation of labor", and other dimensions of the employment experience. Missing from this "thin" view of the production process is both the cultural and political dimension: the theory simply assumes away the manner in which the workplace is both a learning environment and an arena for the exercise of power. As a consequence, schooling has been represented simply as a means of transmitting production-related cognitive skills to the next generation and as an influence of the degree of equality through its de facto redistribution of the claims on income that these skills are said to represent. Those who recognized that schools exert broader cultural or political effects (often critics of the schools) rarely considered the importance of these effects for the functioning of the production process itself.

A compelling economic theory of the social relations of production is implicit, however, in recent developments in microeconomic theory. The purpose in this entry is to make this new theory explicit, primarily by investigating the microeconomic theory of power and the implications this bears for the way the exercise of power in the production process may be shaped by schooling. In doing this the approach of the authors to what they term "contested exchange" will primarily be drawn upon. Related contributions (cited above) support a similar analysis. The authors will also draw upon the recently flourishing econometric literature in labor economics.

Power is treated as the capacity of some agents to influence the behavior of others in their favor through the threat of imposing sanctions. In this usage, power may be exercised over the formation of the preferences of others as well as over more traditional objects of economic conflict such as the distribution of income (on the concept of power over the preferences or interests of others, see Lukes 1974). While liberal social theory in general, and Walrasian economics in particular, have confined the exercise of power to the activities of governments and other actors capable of resorting to physical coercion, power, in the sense of command over others implied by the above definition, is transparently present in the economy wherein the hands of bankers allocating credit or employers directing the activities of employees. The hiatus between rudimentary observation and liberal economic theory in this case may be traced to a peculiarity of the Walrasian model: the assumption that the terms of exchanges can be written into contracts enforceable at no cost to the exchanging parties, thereby obviating any role for the exercise of power by economic actors in the enforcement of the contracts into which they have entered.

2. Contested Exchange

Perhaps the most notable, if strikingly counter-intuitive, political implication of the Walrasian model is that the location of decision-making authority within the enterprise (its political structure) has neither allocative nor distributive effects in competitive equilibrium, and hence may be considered irrelevant to economic theory. Paul Samuelson (1957 p.894) has expressed the matter more succinctly: "in a perfectly competitive model," he wrote, "it really doesn't matter who hires whom; so let labor hire 'capital.'"

The absence of power in the Walrasian model is based in the presumption that supply equals demand in competitive equilibrium, for when markets clear, agents' transactions are equivalent to their next best alternatives. From this it follows that agents lose nothing by abandoning their current transaction in favor of the next best alternative. In this situation, no agent can impose sanctions on another. For instance, if the

labor market clears, the manager of a firm cannot use the threat of dismissal to control the behavior of an employee, since by assumption, a discharged worker can find equally desirable employment elsewhere.

Yet as shall be demonstrated, post-Walrasian developments in the microeconimics of information, transactions costs, and principal agent relationships allow the demonstration of the fact that even in competitive equilibrium a market economy sustains a system of power relations, and that such power relations explain otherwise inexplicable aspects of the capitalist economy.

Consider agent A who purchases a good or service from agent B. The exchange is called "contested" when B's good or service possesses an attribute that is valuable to A, is costly for B to provide, yet is not fully specified in an enforceable contract. Exogenous enforcement is absent when there is no relevant third-party enforcer (as when A and B are sovereign states), when the contested attribute can be measured only imperfectly or at considerable cost (work effort, e.g., or the degree of risk assumed by a firm's management), when the relevant evidence is not admissible in a court of law (such as an agent's eye witness but unsubstantiated experience), when there is no possible means of redress (e.g., when the liable party is bankrupt), or when the number of contingencies concerning future states of the world relevant to the exchange preclude writing a fully specified contract. In such cases the ex post terms of exchange are determined by the monitoring and sanctioning mechanisms instituted by A to induce B to provide the desired level of the contested attribute.

3. The Labor Market as Contested Exchange

An employment relationship established when, in return for a wage, the worker B agrees to submit to the authority of the employer A for a specified period of time in return for wage w. While the employer's promise to pay the wage is legally enforceable, the worker's promise to bestow an adequate level of effort and care upon the tasks assigned, even if offered, is not. Work is subjectively costly for the worker to provide, valuable to the employer, and costly to measure. The manager-worker relationship thus is a contested exchange. The endogenous enforcement mechanisms of the enterprise, not the state, are responsible for ensuring the delivery of any particular level of labor services per hour of labor time supplied (for a complete mathematical exposition, see Bowles and Gintis 1994).

Faced with the problem of labor discipline the employer may adopt the strategy of "contingent renewal," promising to renew the contract of the employee if satisfied with his or her performance, and to dismiss the worker otherwise. To be effective such a strategy requires two conditions: the employer first must adopt a system of monitoring to determine with some degree of accuracy the work effort levels of the employees, and second must be able to impose a costly sanction against those whose effort levels are found wanting.

The imposition of a costly sanction requires that the worker be paid a wage sufficiently high that he or she would prefer to retain the job, given the alternatives available (e.g., unemployment insurance and job search followed by a new job). For any given wage, the worker will determine how hard to work by trading off the marginal disutility of additional effort against the effect that additional effort has on the probability of retaining the job and thus continuing to receive the employment rent. As a result of this employer wage-setting strategy, in competitive equilibrium the expected well-being of the employed worker must exceed that of the worker without the job. The difference between the two is termed an "employment rent". The employment rent must be positive for a contingent renewal strategy to be effective, otherwise the sanctions are without force. The employer will determine the optimal wage by trading off the cost of increasing the wage against the additional work effort that the employment rent elicits from workers, or perhaps the reduced monitoring costs that a higher wage allows.

Where employers adopt contingent renewal strategies two results will follow. First, the workers will work harder than they would have in the absence of the threat of the sanction. Second, workers without jobs would prefer to have them, but cannot obtain them by promising to work as hard as the currently employed for lower wages (the promise is not believable). The first result indicates that A's enforcement strategy is effective. The second indicates that the labor market does not clear in competitive equilibrium: workers holding jobs are not indifferent to losing them, since there are identical workers either involuntarily unemployed, or employed in less desirable positions.

Does employer A have power over worker B in this situation? As has been seen, in equilibrium there will exist unemployed workers identical to B who would prefer to be employed. Thus A's threat to dismiss B is credible and dimissal is costly to B. Hence A can apply sanctions to B. In addition, A can use these sanctions to elicit a preferred level of effort from B, and thus to further A's interests. Finally, while B may be capable of applying sanctions to A (e.g., B may be capable of burning down A's factory), B cannot use this capacity to induce A to choose a different wage, or to refrain from dismissing B should A desire to do so. Should B make A a take-it-or-leave-it offer to work at a higher than equilibrium wage, or should B threaten to apply sanctions unless A offers a higher wage, A would simply reject the offer and hire another worker. Thus A has power over B.

The presentation of the theory of contested exchange thus far has focused on the question of power in production, but its implications for the cultural aspect of the production process are evident. Because the exercise of power by employers is based on the threat of termination, for example, any collusion among workers that raises the costs of the employer's attempt to discipline a worker through termination will reduce profits. Thus employers benefit if workers are divided by race, sex, credentials, and other differences, and are oriented towards competition rather than collaboration. Similarly, because the new microeconomics of production dramatizes the enduring conflict between worker and employer, it also makes clear that the interest of profits will be served if workers' objectives and norms can be brought into line with the objectives of their employer, for example, by affirming rather than avoiding hard work.

To clarify the implications of the contested labor exchange approach for the economics of education one needs to model the production process more explicitly. The strategic interaction of the employer and the worker makes clear that the production process is a social, as well as, technical relationship that cannot adequately be described as a transformation of inputs into outputs: the production process also concerns the manner in which labor inputs are elicited from their owners. The standard technical representation of the production process is the "production function," which in a simple application might describe the input-output relationships among capital goods inputs, K, labor inputs, L, and output, Y, or,

$$Y = f(K,L), \tag{1}$$

where labor inputs are measured as hours of labor hired, n, times a measure of the average skill of labor, q, or $L = qn$. Schooling affects production, according to this view by raising q, or possibly by improving technology and altering the function f in a favorable manner.

However, because the employment relationship is a contested exchange, a second functional relationship is needed; this is called the "labor extraction function" for it describes the manner in which the employer disciplines labor so as to elicit the labor input from the worker. By the reasoning of the previous paragraphs, the amount of labor input depends not only on the skill of labor and the hours of labor hired, but also on the level of work effort performed per hour of work, e: or $L = qen$. The level of effort per hour, in turn, depends on the amount of monitoring of the work process done by the employer (or the employer's representatives), m, and the employer's wage offer (relative to the workers other income earning alternatives), w, as well as numerous other influences on the worker's degree of commitment or alienation from the job, the worker's degree of solidarity with other workers, and the like. Because these latter influences represent the social construction of the worker, they will be referred to collectively by the variable s. So the labor extraction function is:

$$e = e(m,w,s). \tag{2}$$

Thus, while the Walrasian economic model underlying the human capital school confines the influence of schooling on production to its effects on the production function, the contested exchange approach adds a second influence: the impact of schooling on the labor extraction function; that is, on *s* and on the function *e* itself. It will be seen that this dual representation of production as both social and technical yields important insights.

4. New Microeconomic Foundations for the Analysis of Education

Contested exchange, along with related contributions to the new microeconomics, makes at least six contributions to the economics and politics of education.

The first is its capacity to illuminate the surprisingly weak role of cognitive characteristics of workers in accounting for the positive relationship between schooling and economic success. Conventional thinking on this question holds that schooling enhances cognitive abilities and that those with more schooling are therefore more cognitively capable, and further that it is these capabilities that explain the superior economic success enjoyed in labor markets by the more highly schooled. However, this interpretation finds little factual support. Setting aside the complex issue of causality, no measure of cognitive capacity (nor any in combination) statistically explains more than a small fraction of individual differences in incomes of occupational status. It is not meant to suggest, of course, that cognitive and other skills are unnecessary for high levels of productivity. What is germane to the explanation of income differences is whether the relevant skills are economically scarce, and whether they are the effect of schooling. Further, it is possible that unmeasured cognitive capacities might account for a larger share of economic success, but are not persuaded by those who merely assume that unexplained differences can be attributed to "skills" or "abilities."

If it were the case that schooling contributes to individual economic success primarily through its contribution to (measured) cognitive capacities, then one would expect that differences in income among individuals with similar cognitive scores would be substantially unrelated to differences in their level of schooling. However, this also is not the case: the statistical relationship between level of schooling and economic success is highly significant even when cognitive test scores are "held constant." The authors' econometric research on these questions (using data from the 1960s) demonstrated that most of the statistical association between schooling and income cannot be accounted for by the common correlation of these variables with cognitive ability: it was found that for various samples of workers the economic returns to schooling are substantial even for workers with similar levels of cognitive achievement. The authors' own study of the relatively greater importance of

noncognitive aspects of schooling is presented in Bowles and Gintis (1976 pp. 125–51), and in Gintis (1971). An appendix in Bowles and Gintis (1976) summarizes the results of every study available at that time allowing a similar calculation. Each of the 11 cases confirms the authors' findings. A recent study of United States labor markets provides further support for this position. Camerone and Heckman (1993) found that while high school graduates receive substantially more income than high school dropouts, those who receive high school equivalency certificates through a process of examination in the cognitive content of the high school curriculum rather than through school attendance receive barely more than the dropouts. The probable implication is that the economic return to schooling is at best weakly related to mastery of the curriculum material that makes up the equivalency test. More recent studies have confirmed this.

Using data primarily from the 1980s, Maxwell (1994) found that for both Black and White male workers, more than half of the statistical relationship between schooling and wages is independent of measured cognitive ability. In a study using older data, Bishop (1989 p. 181) found that "the higher levels of GIA (general intellectual achievement) that are associated with schooling account for 29 percent of the total effect of schooling on weekly earnings." These results are inconsistent with the conventional view, but as will be seen, are readily explained within the contested exchange framework.

Second, by clarifying the social as well as technical nature of the production process, contested exchange provides some clues concerning what it is about schooling that explains its correlation with economic success. Bishop's conjecture is suggestive: "The large direct effect of schooling (on weekly earnings, independently of the GIA score). . . suggests that schooling develops or signals other economically productive traits such as discipline, reliability, perseverance, and occupationally specific skills." Bishop's conjecture can be confirmed, at least in part, if one penetrates the black box of schooling to observe the personality traits that appear to be rewarded in both workplaces and schools.

In Bowles et al. (1975), for example, it was found that students' grades were strongly correlated with measures of personality, with the strongest positive correlations being those that are easily motivated by the contested exchange view of the endogenous enforcement problem at work. Controlling for three cognitive test scores, the best predictors of grades were the traits described by the adjectives: persevering, dependable, consistent, identifies with school, emphasizes orders, punctual, defers gratification, externally motivated, and predictable. Other traits were penalized in grading: creative, aggressive, and independent. In a remarkable study of workers' supervisor ratings and employee personality traits, Edwards (1976a, 1976b) found virtually identical correlations (these results are reported in Bowles and Gintis (1976). These findings support the cultural and political conception of the workplace suggested by the theory of contested exchange, and are inexplicable by the human capital approach based on the older neoclassical framework.

Third, partly for reasons just elucidated, an economics of education based on contested exchange rectifies an earlier excessive preoccupation of both liberal and Marxist analysis with the overt content of schooling: the curriculum. By motivating a focus upon the experience of schooling and its relationship to the social structure of the production process, the contested exchange model provides a consistent analytical framework for understanding the school as an arena of structured social interaction. It also dramatizes the need for measurements of school effectiveness going beyond achievement scores and other cognitive performance indices.

Fourth, in contrast to the traditional neoclassical model in which profit maximization induces employers to pay workers with given characteristics a given wage, employers in the contested exchange model may act strategically in both setting wages and selecting workers on the basis of characteristics having little or nothing to do with productivity. Discriminatory hiring practices based on race, sex, or educational credentials may therefore impose little or even no cost on the employer. Indeed, if discrimination contributes to labor discipline, by fostering divisions and reducing the bargaining power of workers, for example, discriminatory employers may be rewarded by higher profits in the process of competition rather than penalized (as in the neoclassical model).

The empirical importance of divide and rule strategies cannot be assessed. Labor historians have identified cases in which racial tensions have weakened labor's bargaining position, and there is some evidence that employers appear to have fostered these tensions in their hiring practices (see Edwards et al. 1982), but this evidence does not allow an overall assessment of the importance of divisions among workers as a contribution to profitability.

In providing both a motive for discriminatory practices and in demonstrating that competitive pressures do not preclude discrimination, contested exchange thus suggests a much broader scope for educational credentials unrelated to productivity in the labor market. However, good evidence on the role of credentials per se, is difficult to come by, and the authors remain agnostic as to their importance in the allocation and remuneration of jobs. For example, Kane and Rouse (1993) found that possession of a BA degree contributes significantly to both the hourly earnings and the occupational prestige level achieved by male workers independently of the number of college credits earned. But is this a credential effect? Among workers with sufficient credits for graduation, are those with and without degrees likely to be identical in other relevant respects?

Fifth, the contested exchange model illuminates the relationship between employment rents, schooling, and rent-seeking activities. As has been seen, the term "rent" is the appropriate description of the difference between the living standards enjoyed and anticipated by those holding jobs and those workers whose job has been terminated: it represents an income above the employed workers' next best alternative. These rents may be seen as the prizes to be had in the labor market, and one would anticipate that workers seek to enhance their probability of winning a prize, even adopting costly strategies to do so.

If educational credentials, years of schooling, cognitive achievement, or other aspects of schooling are used by employers as job screening methods, workers will engage in schooling as a rent-seeking activity. The theory of rent seeking, pioneered by critics of governmental activities that limit competition in the economy, can thus be used to illuminate the role of schooling in strategies of job-seekers even in perfectly competitive labor markets. Of course, schooling and other rent-seeking activities need not be unproductive or wasteful. However, identifying rent seeking as an aspect of the motivation for schooling does emphasize the fact that where labor market rents exist, powerful incentives promote additional schooling, credentials and the like quite independently of any productivity effects.

Sixth, by demonstrating that racial and other divisions among workers may support higher levels of profits, the new microeconomics may help identify some of the difficulties and obstacles likely to be encountered by attempts to eliminate racial and other forms of discrimination, not only in labor markets, but in schooling as well. By providing a theoretical foundation for the theory of segmented labor markets, the theory contributes also to the understanding of the closely associated pattern of racial and other divisions in schooling opportunities and experiences.

5. Conclusion: School Reform and Educational Policy

As the twentieth century closes, the economics of education has come full circle, returning to many of the themes that gave impetus to the discipline during its early years in the 1950s and 1960s. Chief among these are twin convictions that improvements in schooling can be a powerful force both for improved productivity and other measures of macroeconomic performance and, as well, for a greater measure of equality of economic opportunity.

Two bodies of research have contributed to these convictions. The first is the compelling new evidence that the statistical association between schooling and economic success is not (as many once thought) simply the result of the differential ability of other characteristics of those who attain higher levels of education

(Ashenfelter and Krueger 1992, Angrist and Krueger 1991, Kane and Rouse 1993). Card 1993, survey six recent studies in this area, all pointing strongly to a substantial association between schooling and earnings independently of covarying measures of ability). On the basis of this research, one can confidently label schooling an asset, one whose (often costly) acquisition yields an economic return. However, economists have made little progress in establishing that this asset yields returns to its owner because it is productive in the standard sense of yielding greater outputs for a given level of inputs, thereby affecting the production function defined above. The fact that employers pay more for more schooled workers strongly suggests that schooling contributes to profits; but whether it does this by altering the production function or the labor extraction function cannot be determined on the basis of available evidence.

The second body of research has shown that the 1980s witnessed a major increase in economic returns to schooling (particularly college), and a substantial increase in the level of inequality in (before tax) earnings. Because educational assets are unequally held, an increase in the returns to the asset *ceteris paribus* clearly increases inequality. Thus, the coincidence of these two trends is commonly taken to imply that increased inequality is primarily the result of an increased scarcity of skills, and that enhancing the skills of low-wage workers and thereby equalizing the holdings of the educational assets is an effective means of redressing the trend towards inequality.

However, no such inference is warranted, for two reasons. First, it is not known what explains the returns to schooling, as has been seen, and therefore it is not known why the returns increased: given that the college educated tend to earn more, *anything* that enhanced the earnings of the top income groups would almost certainly yield evidence of an increased return to college education. A possible explanation is that something learned in college became more valuable in the production process, but one is hard pressed to find reasons why this explanation should be privileged in the absence of empirical support.

Second, most of the increase in inequality took place among workers with similar levels of schooling, not between workers with different levels of schooling (see Juhn et al. 1993; Katz and Murphy 1992 document the rise in what is termed "residual inequality," namely that which obtains within rather than between groups of workers classified by education, experience, and sex; see also Levy and Murnane 1992). Thus even *if* the higher earnings of the better educated were attributed to increased scarcity of skills, this would not account for most of the increase in inequality. It is a common leap of faith among economists to attribute these within-group differences to "unmeasured skills." Thus Juhn et al. (1993 p.423) say "we view this increase in within-group wage inequality as a trend toward higher

skill prices." Katz and Murphy (1992 p.43) write: "we use the dispersion of relative wages within our gender-education-experience cells as a measure of the spread in relative wages across different skill levels within the cells." However, lacking any evidence that incomes within these groups are the result of productive skills, these within-group differences are better understood simply as unexplained differences. Katz and Murphy do concede that the low earners in a given cell might not be the "least skilled" but rather the "least lucky," but proceed to interpret within-cell inequalities as the result of skill differences. Thus the case for both the increased returns to skill interpretation of growing inequality and the improved skill training prescription for productivity enhancement remain unconvincing.

The importance of skills in the production process is not at question here. Moreover, more than sufficient reason can be found for improving skill training in schools and providing all children with equal opportunities for effective learning. However, it is doubtful that skill training comes close to exhausting the connection between schooling and production. As has been seen, contested exchange and related approaches provide a microeconomic foundation for the proposition that the relationship between schooling and the economy is ensured at least as much through its *form* as its *content*, the social relations of the educational process. To the extent that education prepares students to be "good workers," it does so through a *correspondence* between the social relations of production and the social relations of education. Like the division of labor in the enterprise, the educational system is a graded hierarchy of authority governed by a system of external rewards (wages in the case of the economy and grades in the case of schools). While these attributes make sense from the standpoint of contested exchange, they are inexplicable if the sole function of schools is cognitive development, as is implied by the conventional Walrasian economic model.

Contested exchange thus explains why the egalitarian and humanistic expectations of liberal educators are often disappointed, for it shows why it is so difficult for schools simultaneously to promote full personal development and social equality, while integrating students into the economy. The hierarchical order of the school system, often admirably geared towards preparing students for their future positions in the economic hierarchy, limits the development of those personal capacities involving the exercise of reciprocal and mutual democratic participation and reinforces social inequality by legitimating the assignment of students to inherently unequal "slots" in the social hierarchy.

Contested exchange helps identify what it is that limits the effectiveness of egalitarian and humanistic school reforms. By explaining that the hierarchical nature of the production process is a result of profit maximizing strategies of employers engaged in a conflict of interest with workers rather than an inexorable result of either technological imperatives or differences in human capabilities, the theory provides a social rather than biological or technological interpretation of the limits of progressive education. The contested exchange model of production dramatizes the possibility that egalitarian and humanistic education are impeded not by some defect in human nature or infirmity of advanced industrial society, but by the structure of economic life.

Education may nonetheless play a critical part in advancing equality. First, for most parents and children quality schooling is a highly valued end in its own right; a redistribution of opportunity for quality schooling would be egalitarian even if it did not effect later earnings. Second, policies which improve the quality of education and broaden access by children of low-income families to higher levels of education will have two effects: higher incomes will be conferred on those who receive the additional quality or quantity of schooling, and the additional supply of educated labor will tend to depress the returns to schooling. The first effect will support higher levels of intergenerational mobility, while the second will generate a more equal distribution of income. A more circumspect view of role of schools in generating job relevant skills thus is consistent with a strong endorsement of egalitarian educational policy.

References

Angrist J D, Krueger A B 1991 Does compulsory school attendance affect schooling and earnings? *Quarterly Journal of Economy* 106(4): 979–1014

Ashenfelter O, Krueger A 1992 Estimate of the economic return to schooling from a new sample of twins. National Bureau of Economic Research Working Paper No. 4143. NBER, Cambridge, Massachusetts

Bishop J 1989 Is the test score decline responsible for the productivity growth decline? *Am. Econ. Rev.* 79(1): 178–97

Bowles S, Gintis H 1975 The problem with human capital theory. *Am. Econ. Rev.* 65(2): 74–82

Bowles S, Gintis H 1976 *Schooling in Capitalist America.* Basic Books, New York

Bowles S, Gintis H 1990 Contested exchange: New microfoundations for a political economy of capitalism. *Politics and Society* 18(2): 165–222

Bowles S, Gintis H 1993 the revenge of HOMO ECONOMICUS: Contested exchange and the revival of political economy. *Journal of Economic Perspectives* 7(1): 83–102

Bowles S, Gintis H 1994 Escaping the efficiency equity tradeoff: Productivity enhancing redistributions. In: Epstien G, Gintis H (eds.) 1994 *Macroeconomic Policy After the Conservative Era.* Cambridge University Press, Cambridge

Bowles S, Gintis H, Meyer P 1975 The long shadow of work: Education, the family, and the reproduction of the social division of labor. *The Insurgent Sociologist* (Summer)

Camerone S, Heckman J 1993 The nonequivalency of high school equivalency. National Bureau of Economic Research Working Paper No. 3804. NBER, Cambridge, Massachusetts

Card D 1993 Earnings, schooling and ability revisited. (mimeo) Princeton University, Princeton, New Jersey

Edwards R 1976a Personal traits and "success" at school and work. *Educ. Psychol. Meas.*

Edwards R 1976b Individual traits and organizational incentives: what makes a good worker? *J. Hum. Resources*

Edwards R, Gordon D, Reich M 1982 *Segmented Work, Divided Workers.* Cambridge University Press, Cambridge

Gintis H 1971 Education, technology, and the characteristics of worker productivity. *Am. Econ. Rev,* 61(2): 266–79

Juhn C, Murphy K, Pierce B 1993 Wage inequality and the rise in returns to skill. *J. Pol. Econ.* 101(3): 410–42

Kane T, Rouse C 1993 Labor market returns to two- and four-year college. National Bureau of Economic Research Working Paper No. 4268. NBER, Cambridge, Massachusetts

Katz L, Murphy K 1992 Changes in relative wages, 1963–1987. *Quarterly Journal of Economy.* 107:35–78

Levy F, Murnane R 1992 US earnings levels and earnings inequality: A review of the recent trends and proposed explanations. *J. Econ. Lit.* 30: 1333–81

Lukes S 1974 *Power: A Radical View.* MacMillan, London

Maxwell N L 1994 the effect on Black-White wage differences of differences in the quality and quantity of education. *Industrial and Labor Relations Review* 47(2): 257

Samuelson P 1957 Wages and interest: A modern dissection of Marxian Economics. *Am. Econ. Rev.* 47: 885–912

Stiglitz J 1987 The causes and consequences of the dependence of quality on price. *J. Econ. Lit.* 25: 1–48

Job Information and Education

S. Rosen

Information about the labor market and about the availability or likely availability of jobs is required by, respectively, public decision makers and individuals. This entry approaches the provision of information from the perspective of the economics of information. The subject is concerned with how information affects resource allocation; how economic agents and institutions cope with imperfect information; and how social organizations arise which improve information networks and economize on the acquisition of information. The state of information confronting a decision maker is an important constraint in all economic problems, because knowledge of the factors that influence costs and returns are key ingredients in assessing the best course of action in any given situation. Since the economics of education is largely concerned with the future income consequences of educational choices among individuals, the important role of job market information in educational decision-making is apparent.

1. Information and Resource Allocation

From the perspective of economics, decisions about the provision of education can be thought of as producing human capital; that is, as generating skills and knowledge broadly conceived in terms of students who have market value when they enter the workforce. These decisions turn on a comparison of the cost of education with its expected return. Neither component can be known with certainty, though the assessment of returns may be more uncertain than the assessment of costs, because the former extend further into the future. The financial return to schooling is the flow of additional income it helps to produce. This flow consists of two components: first, the amount and types of additional skills produced by schooling; second, the valuation of those skills in the future, usually measured by the wage prospects for the period during which the skills will be employed. Both the amount of skill creation and its unit value (wage rate) in each year of labor market activity during which those skills are put to work determine the flow of expected income attributable to schooling decisions. This defines the return side of educational decision-making. The probability of error in assessing alternatives is obviously related to the quality of information about both components. Improved specific and general information about the job market reduces probable divergence between anticipated and actual returns. It also increases the efficiency of educational investments by reducing the probability of unfavorable outcomes.

The British economist Alfred Marshall (1842–1924) pointed out many years ago that the payback period of educational investment can be very long. For those contemplating professional or vocational education for a particular skilled trade or profession, the skills acquired might be employed for as long as 40 or 50 years. For this reason, assessments of expected returns require projections and predictions of specific skill valuations, possible future obsolescence, and depreciation well beyond the period for which current information can be tolerably extrapolated. Consequently, the certainty with which future income prospects can be inferred falls as those prospects are pushed further into the future.

This situation, however, is initigated by another factor. A crucial component in any personal decision about skill education is the expected present value of future income, discounted at the marginal rate of return to investment. The force of discounting greatly reduces the weight of income prospects that occur many years from the present. Thus, the anticipated additional income in the first decade or two of work experience is the most important factor to be considered.

Lengthy payback periods are certainly not unique to educational investments. They also characterize most nonhuman fixed capital investments. Examples are public works, buildings, and additional production capacity. Issues concerning increasing uncertainty as the time span lengthens are also relevant for such investments. However, there is an important difference between the two. Business investment activities in the private sector are placed in the hands of a relatively small cadre of highly trained and highly skilled professionals. These people continually obtain market feedback on the wisdom of their judgments. They repeatedly revise and revalue their decisions as new information becomes available. Educational decisions, on the other hand, are squarely in the hands of young people and their parents. They are usually made in the early stages of life, before the acquisition of significant practical experience, and do not continually recur. There is much less room for obtaining decision skills through repetition and experience because the major decisions typically are made only once or twice in a person's life. The costs of rectifying errors are sufficiently large that third and fourth chances do not occur for most people. It is also often difficult to renounce an erroneous decision. For all these reasons, a considerable volume of uncertainty is likely to cloud personal educational investments.

2. Information about Jobs

In developed economies a variety of formal and informal social institutions have arisen to deal with these problems, providing the information network necessary for efficiency. Guidance counseling, testing, and job placement services are widely available. The school system itself communicates some knowledge of work environments and the nature of different types of occupations. Many governments actively forecast and publish current and expected employment trends, national needs, and probable shortfalls or surpluses across job categories. Many trade and professional associations collect data on members' incomes, the volume of new entrants, and on retirements, and disseminate them through the press and by other means. Finally, family and friends communicate knowledge of the world of work to young people. This is a particularly important source of information. Studies of the schooling choices that people make show significant effects derived from family background. Children of parents who are highly educated are themselves likely to be more highly educated. Similarly, studies of intergenerational job mobility find that a person is more likely to enter and remain in the occupation of a parent than any other occupation.

While the financial aspects of educational choices are of principal concern to economists, equally important elements of returns take nonpecuniary forms. It is at this point that the analogy between human and nonhuman capital fails to work. Since human capital is embodied in people and cannot be dissociated from the content and environment of the workplace, alternative "consumption elements" of various jobs and skills are a very important aspect of choice. Yet many of these consumption elements cannot be perfectly identified in advance. In the language of the economics of information, this aspect of work is more akin to an "experience good" than to a pure "search good." It is virtually impossible for a person to know all relevant nonpecuniary considerations involved in a specific job, general occupation, or skill before gaining direct personal experience. This point is fully borne out by all available data on job and occupational mobility. These data invariably show that the greatest amount of job change and flux is among people in the early stages of the work life cycle. For the most part these people are sampling alternative possibilities, to seek out their most appropriate job and occupational match in the economy; that is, to obtain their proper niche in society. Because of the personal elements involved, it is virtually impossible for this kind of knowledge to be perfectly communicated in advance of actual experience.

Broadly considered, education is the social process by which knowledge is conveyed to students by the intermediate agency of teachers. It is in the nature of things that the knowledge transferred becomes increasingly specialized and advanced as formal education proceeds. In fact, learning becomes most specialized after people actually cease formal instruction and enter the labor market, where very specific job skills are acquired. In the early stages of formal schooling only very general skills are communicated and developed, and these are not strongly differentiated among students. As the educational process continues and general skills are developed, a great deal of sorting gradually takes place. The educational system offers ever greater variety and options for more specialization. The menu of choices available to students continually expands. These choices also involve quality dimensions. However, it is not only the pure transfer and development of skills that are involved here.

An equally important role of education is to identify the special talents and proclivities of students. By being exposed to varieties of knowledge, students receive valuable information about themselves, about their tastes, their talents and natural abilities, and about their capacities. It is perhaps insufficiently recognized that the use of grades by educational institutions operates in two ways. Grades not only provide external certification of achievement levels,

they also serve as an important feedback mechanism for students' self-assessment of their goals. They therefore guide individual sequential decisions about which paths to follow toward conformable work activities in later life. Viewed in this way, an important function of education is to assist people in finding their proper place in the economic system and to help them to locate those areas in which they will be most successful and productive. Nevertheless, there is no perfect substitute for personal experience, so this kind of information cannot be other than imperfect and incomplete.

As a general rule, imperfections in information become more important as the degree of specialization increases. There are two main reasons why this is so. First, general knowledge about a broadly defined occupation is more easily communicated without extensive personal experience than information about the subspecialties within it. For example, most people have a good idea of what medical practitioners do, but it is much more difficult to obtain accurate information about various medical specialties until one has actually entered medical training. Second, every economic society is in a constant state of flux and change. There are continual changes in the allocation of resources through changes in the relative demands of consumers, the introduction of new production techniques and new goods, the geographic shifts of population, and so forth. These signal corresponding changes in relative demands for various skills, which alter the expected returns of different types of education. Two components of these changes must be distinguished: those that are more or less predictable and anticipated, and those that are unanticipated and which contain greater elements of surprise. A good example of changes that can be anticipated are the results of fluctuations in birthrates and family structure. These will affect the age structure of a population for many years and have obvious implications for the demand for teachers, geriatric social workers, and other professions that have a direct bearing on the age composition of the populance. As an example of the second component, unanticipated changes in raw materials prices in the early 1970s greatly altered the relative demands for people with complementary skills, such as automobile mechanics and geologists.

The economic organization of educational resources and the manner in which education is structured are affected by all of these forces. The general principle rests on the tendency for resource allocations to be organized as efficiently as possible, in this case to maximize the social and private returns to education. The long-run anticipated types of change have obvious consequences for the magnitude of resources that are devoted to alternative types of schooling. For example, the reduction in the relative numbers of students between the early 1970s and the early 1980s in the United States resulted in a weak market for teachers and a substantial reduction in resources spent on teacher training. These types of ebbs and flows are practically inevitable in all societies.

3. Factors in Decision-making about Jobs

In the light of likely shortcomings of information used in educational choices, a natural first question to ask is to what extent do choices reflect current and anticipated market conditions? This does not directly address the magnitude of information constraints, but it does provide some indirect evidence. For if large variations in market conditions do not affect choices then informational inefficiencies may be large. However, if entry is fairly sensitive to conditions, then it may be presumed that information flows are relatively efficient and do not seriously constrain investment efficiency.

Rational choice of education maximizes its expected utility in life. In addition to expected future wage and employment prospects in various occupations and their consumption and nonpecuniary characteristics, prospective entrants' self-assessments of their talent and prospects for success in various fields are very important factors affecting choice. This is especially the case in those occupations in which there is substantial variation in personal success. Some practitioners are more successful than others in the same trade throughout their working lives. Where a person fits into the distribution of outcomes can affect lifetime wealth to an enormous extent.

In many occupations there are great variations in success, but extreme manifestations arise in those fields such as music, acting, and writing, where the incomes of successful practitioners are large but are concentrated among relatively few people. Here the chances of success are small and most entrants must ultimately quit the field to ensure financial stability. An entrant must continually update and revise assessments of the likelihood of success, based on the accumulated personal record up to that point. Obviously, people choosing these professions expose themselves to great risks of failure. They do so because the rewards of success are so great, even though few achieve them. However, the possibilities of leaving these professions for safer alternatives place limits on potential losses and reduce the risk. This *option value* of leaving actually encourages the entry of young people to try their hand, because they have enough time ahead of them to make the prospects of starting another career tolerable, should the first choice terminate in failure.

There remain unresolved questions about whether young people make accurate self-assessments of their talents and abilities in the fields they choose. It is always difficult to be objective about oneself and occupational choices are made necessarily at a stage in life when extensive experience is lacking. In commenting about the highly arbitrary nature of

success in many fields, the Scottish economist Adam Smith (1723–90) observed a tendency in young people to overestimate their chances. The economic principle of revealed preference, whereby a person's preferences are, in part, "revealed" by observed choices, supports the point: timid and self-doubting individuals tend to be repelled from occupations where the variance of outcomes is great and substantial personal investments are at stake. Persons with more optimistic self-assessments are more likely to enter such fields. As Smith put it, "conceit" is a more prevalent sentiment than pessimism among new entrants in such fields as law and medicine. Little systematic empirical evidence is available on the personal outlooks of new entrants. However, there is an increasing tendency for college graduates to gain work or life experience before entering professional and graduate schools, partly in an effort to reduce errors in career choices.

4. Earnings Prospects and Enrollment

There is more substantial evidence about the influence of general earnings prospects and related matters, especially on choices for higher education and also for entry into the skilled professions.

Between the mid-1940s and mid-1960s there was a great rise in the number of college-trained workers in the United States. The rise, however, had little effect on the rate of return to college education, which was maintained in the 10–12 percent range. Productivity advances of this period increased the demand for college-trained personnel; the supply responded appropriately and the rate of return remained relatively constant. However, from the late 1960s and continuing into the 1970s the slowdown in productivity and other deteriorating market conditions reduced the demand for highly educated labor, thereby reducing the rate of return. The demand for college attendance also dropped, mostly because the size of college-eligible cohorts became smaller. Yet the fraction of these cohorts going to college also dropped significantly in response to the lower rate of return—a clear indication of sensitivity to conditions. The rate of return to college increased greatly in the 1980s and reached some of the highest levels ever recorded. Relative enrollments rose along with returns.

School enrollment rates of White and non-White youths exhibit remarkably different patterns over this period. The general pattern for Whites followed the course described above. However, college and high-school completion among non-Whites increased from the early 1970s. At the same time, civil rights legislation, court decisions, and changing attitudes increased the demand for skilled Black males, so increasing their rate of return to schooling. In direct response there were increased completion levels among members of this group and an improvement in the quality of public education provided for them.

A third example of educational choice responding to employment prospects concerns women. The growth of women's participation in the labor market and a marked increase in professional job prospects for women have raised their enrollment in professional schools and institutions of higher learning.

Empirical research on individuals' choice of college generally finds that earning expectations are an important determinant of behavior. Such research also reports a substantial positive elasticity of response. This has even been discovered in the choice of college major (main subject of study), where changing income prospects among the specific fields with which subjects are associated have effects in the expected direction. These and many other studies also find that family background has a great influence on career choices, though often because family financial constraints affect the ability to finance a college education.

Research of a more aggregative nature on the numbers of entrants into specific fields such as law, engineering, medicine, and teaching have produced a variety of results that are less easily summarized. However, virtually all of them find that earnings expectations influence the number of people choosing to enter them. Early studies found that current starting salaries were major determinants of entry and that entrants seemed to behave myopically, causing irrational cycles of entry and wages. For, if young people overreact to prevailing market conditions, then too great an influx into fashionable fields tends to occur, driving down the wages of entrants, making their previous decisions appear erroneous, and unduly deterring subsequent entrants. Later studies have tried to test more sophisticated models of expectations, treating current entrants as if they expected many future entrants to follow them if demand conditions warranted. These second generation models have found some success for law, and for primary and secondary teaching.

5. Education and Adaptability at Work

Analysis of unanticipated changes interacts with the degree of educational specialization. It is therefore necessary to broaden the concept of human capital to include both general and vocational dimensions. The latter is associated with specific job skills, whereas the former is identified with flexible skill capacity that can be put to use in a variety of ways. General education develops the capacity to learn new things and to adapt to changing circumstances and environments. The division of educational production between these two components itself responds to uncertainty in the economic environment. In a static world the capacity to adopt new ways of doing things has no value and the content of education is more skill-specific. The value of general education is much higher in a world that is forever changing but in which the precise nature of the changes cannot be anticipated in advance.

The empirical issues raised in this connection are subtle and difficult. However, a growing body of evidence suggests the importance of this decomposition. The most direct evidence relates to the profitability achieved and choices of production methods made by farmers and farm-managers. Throughout the world, more highly educated farmers control more resources and earn more than the less educated. By itself this merely says that the rate of return to education justifies its cost for people engaged in agriculture. However, numerous case studies have examined the actual mechanisms by which these greater gains come about. Since the 1950s, there has been a rapid pace of technical change in agricultural technology. The more educated are found to adopt the most productive innovations and to eliminate the least productive techniques more quickly than the less educated, who tend to stick with more traditional and obsolete methods. The more educated also have greater access to new research results and are able to process that information better than the less educated.

Studies of age–earnings profiles among high-school and college graduates tend to confirm this result in a more general setting. The available evidence suggests that the job market skills possessed by the more educated are subject to greater depreciation and obsolescence rates than the skills possessed by the less educated. However, the implied production functions for learning suggest that more educated people are more efficient learners, in the sense that they acquire new job-related skills more quickly and at less cost. It is therefore socially desirable that the more educated tend to sort themselves into jobs where their comparative advantage in learning has the largest effect, namely those activities where technical and other changes occur at greater rates.

Finally, a host of studies investigating nonmarket implications of education are consistent with its effects on adaptability and superior information processing. For example, the highly educated are more efficient at maintaining their health: surveys show that voluntary exposure to health risks, such as cigarette smoking, is lower for the more educated. Similarly, it is well documented throughout the world that the education of women leads to reduced infant mortality.

In conclusion, the economic approach to education suggests that there are important feedbacks between information about job markets and efficient human capital investments. Not all of the detailed interactions have been addressed in the empirical literature. However, indirect evidence from a variety of sources suggests that major informational imperfections do not seriously impede the tendency toward efficient resource allocation in this area of economic life. This conclusion is supported by three main findings: that variations in school enrollments correlate with current and expected market conditions; that highly educated people hold jobs requiring greater flexibility and adaptability to changing economic circumstances; and that education appears to improve consumption and nonmarket productivities in a variety of ways consistent with better information-processing capacities.

Bibliography

Berger M 1988 Predicted future earnings and choice of college major. *Indust. and Labor Rel. Rev.* 41(3): 418–29

Freeman R B 1971 *The Market for College Trained Manpower: A Study in the Economics of Career Choice.* Harvard University Press, Cambridge, Massachusetts

Freeman R B 1975 Legal cobwebs: a recursive model of the market for new lawyers, *Rev. Econ. and Stat.* 57(2): 171–79

Freeman R B, Brenaman D W 1974 *Forecasting the PhD Labor Market: Pitfalls for Policy.* National Board of Graduate Education, Washington, DC

Johnson W 1978 A theory of job shopping. *Q. J. Econ.* 92(2): 261–78

Laband D N, Lentz B F 1985 *The Roots of Success: Why Children Follow in Their Parents' Occupational Footsteps.* Praeger, New York

Murphy K M 1986 Equilibrium specialization in the labor market. Unpublished doctoral dissertation. University of Chicago, Chicago, Illinois

Pashigian P 1977 The market for lawyers: The determinants of the demand for and supply of lawyers. *J. Law and Econ.* 20(1): 53–85

Siow A 1984 Occupational choice under uncertainty. *Econometrica* 52(3): 631–45

Rosen S 1976 A theory of life earnings. *J. Pol. Econ.* 84(4): S45–S67

Rosen S 1977 Human capital: A survey of empirical research. In: Ehrenberg R G (ed.) 1977 *Research in Labor Economics,* Vol 1. JAI Press, Greenwich, Connecticut

Rosen S 1992 The market for lawyers. *J. Law and Econ.* 35

Schultz T W 1975 The value of the ability to deal with disequilibria. *J. Econ. Lit.* 13(3): 827–46

Welch F 1970 Education in production. *J. Pol. Econ.* 78: 35–59

Willis R, Rosen S 1979 Education and self-selection. *J. Pol. Econ.* 87(5): S7–S36

Zarkin G A 1985 Occupational choice: An application to the market for public school teachers. *Q. J. Econ.* 100(2): 409–46

Demand and Supply Elasticities for Educated Labor

R. B. Freeman

The elasticity of demand for educated labor measures the percentage change in the number of workers with specified levels of education demanded by employers per percentage change in the wage of these workers (with other wages and input prices assumed to be fixed). It is a central concept in the analysis of the market for labor skills, as it represents the responsiveness of employers to price incentives to employ workers of varying levels of education.

The elasticity of supply of educated labor measures the percentage change in the number of workers with specified levels of education who enter the labor market per percentage change in wages. It can also reflect the response of students and their families to changes in the price of schooling. The results of a number of studies suggest that employers are responsive to changes in the relative prices of graduates with different amounts of schooling and that students and their families are responsive to changes in the cost of going to school and the returns to investing in schooling.

1. The Elasticity of Demand

When the elasticity of demand is relatively small, as in case (a) of Fig. 1, enormous changes in wages are needed to induce employers to alter the number of workers hired. In this case, responses to wage changes can be practically ignored and demand for labor analyzed as if it did not depend on wages. By contrast, when the elasticity of demand is moderate, the concept is a critical element in understanding the effect of economic changes on demand for labor and wages, as in case (b) in Fig. 1. When the elasticity of demand is near infinite, it is probably not useful to think of educated labor as a distinct input in production at all, since it is likely that other inputs are perfectly substitutable for it, as in case (c) in Fig. 1.

The magnitude of the elasticity of demand for educated labor depends critically on the extent to which educated labor is substitutable for other inputs in production. The ease of substitutability is generally measured by the elasticity of substitution, defined as the percentage change in the number of educated workers relative to the amount of other inputs (say, less educated workers) per percentage change in the wages of educated workers relative to the price of other inputs (say, the wages of less educated labor). Formally, if E_1 measures the number of educated workers and E_0 the number of other inputs and if W_1

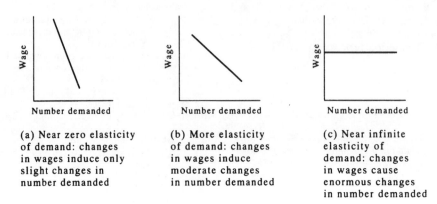

(a) Near zero elasticity of demand: changes in wages induce only slight changes in number demanded

(b) More elasticity of demand: changes in wages induce moderate changes in number demanded

(c) Near infinite elasticity of demand: changes in wages cause enormous changes in number demanded

Figure 1
Elasticity of demand for educated labor

and W_0 are the respective factor prices, the elasticity of substitutions σ is

$$\sigma = - (\%\Delta E_1/E_0)/(\%\Delta W_1 /W_0)$$

where $\%\Delta$ measures percentage changes. In analyses that treat employer demand responses at a given level of output, the elasticity of demand is just a function of elasticities of substitution. When the level of output varies in response to changes in prices, the elasticity of demand for educated labor, like other inputs, depends on the elasticity of demand for the final product as well.

The elasticity of substitution between more and less educated workers (or other inputs) has been at the center of analyses of demand for educated labor for two reasons. First, because the validity of widely used "fixed coefficient" methods for forecasting educational demands or "needs" and the potential economic worth of educational planning to meet such demands or needs hinges critically on the size of the elasticity. Standard "fixed coefficient" forecast methods assume zero elasticities of substitution in order to focus on the impact of changes in the composition of industries on the demand for educated labor. The greater are actual elasticities, the less valuable are such forecasts. Similarly, planning education to meet future labor market demands is useful only if elasticities of substitution are small; if the elasticities are large, employers can readily substitute less educated for more educated labor, so that even accurate planning will be of little economic value. Second, the elasticity of substitution between more and less educated labor is important in analyzing the impact of changes in relative supplies of workers on the distribution of earnings. When the elasticity is high, large increases in the supply of graduates relative to nongraduates will have little effect on their relative wages. When the elasticity of substitution is small,

large increases in the relative supply of graduates will cause sizable changes in relative wages and thus will alter the distribution of earnings.

Given these issues, it is not surprising that economists have undertaken empirical studies designed to measure the elasticity of substitution between more and less educated or skilled workers. Because the number of workers with varying levels of education is predetermined in any given year by supply decisions made years earlier (due to the length of training), most analyses actually examine the inverse of the elasticity of substitution, the elasticity of complementarity which measures the percentage change in relative wages due to percentage changes in relative supplies. While it is reasonable to assume that supplies are fixed in analyses that treat time-series data, this assumption is less defensible in comparisons across geographic regions at a point in time: within a country, educated workers who migrate to a particular area can migrate elsewhere in response to wage incentives and thus cannot be regarded as exogenous to wage determination across countries, differences in supply may reflect responses to differences in the rewards to education that persist over time, weakening the assumption that supplies can be taken as independent of the wages. Accordingly, some studies have also used "simultaneous equations" techniques to estimate the relevant elasticities of substitution. In these studies, demand and supply of educated labor are estimated conjointly in a system.

Table 1 summarizes the findings of the most important empirical studies on the elasticities of substitution between more and less educated labor. Initial work on elasticities of substitution focused on cross-sectional data, with most attention given to transnational comparisons. While the early evidence on states of the United States supported relatively moderate elasticities (Johnson 1970, Welch 1970),

Table 1

Estimates of the elasticity of substitution between highly educated and less educated workers[a]

Study	Sample	Elasticity of substitution
Bowles (1969)	countries	202
Johnson (1970)	states, USA	1.3
Welch (1970) (agriculture sector)	states, USA	1.4
Dougherty (1972)	states, USA	8.2
Psacharopoulos and Hinchcliffe (1972)	developed countries	1000
	less developed countries	2.1–2.5
Tinbergen (1974)	countries	0.6–1.2
	states	0.4–2.1
Freeman (1975a)	years, USA	1.0–2.6
Fallon and Layard (1975)	countries	0.6–3.5
Grant (1979)	Standard Metropolitan Areas (SMAS)	1.2

a Definitions of highly educated to less educated vary somewhat between samples. All except Fallon and Layard treat college relative to some other group. Fallon and Layard relate groups with 8 or more years of education to less than 8

the work of several analysts led many to believe that the elasticity was rather high, sufficient to yield practically horizontal demand curves. Bowles (1969) produced, in particular, an elasticity between workers with some college education and those with 8 to 11 years of school of 202, and smaller but still sizable elasticities (6 to 12) between other educational groups. With a sample of 28 states from the United States, Dougherty (1972) obtained a more moderate but still high estimate of over 8. Psacharopoulos and Hinchcliffe (1972) divided the international sample by degree of development, obtaining an essentially infinite elasticity (implying perfect substitutability at the relevant wage ratios) in the developed countries but a more modest value in the less developed countries.

As the relative earnings of graduates remained constant or increased in the 1950s and 1960s, despite increased supplies of graduates from colleges and universities, these estimates were generally accepted as being in accord with reality. Some viewed them as casting serious doubt on the concept of educational bottlenecks as a barrier to economic growth and on the value of the fixed coefficient model of labor demand, then being used by the Organisation for Economic Co-operation and Development, among others, to analyze the graduate and skilled worker labor markets for the purpose of educational planning.

In the 1970s, concurrent with the observed decline in the relative earnings of college graduates through-

out the developed world, analysts began to reexamine these results. New estimates based on better data and models provided a very different picture of the elasticity of substitution between educated and less educated labor. Nobel Laureate Jan Tinbergen (1974) amplified the country and state analyses to take account of the likely simultaneous determination of relative wages and relative supplies in cross sections and obtained quite different results from Bowles and Dougherty using their data sets. His elasticities ranged from 0.50 to 2.00, which were consistent with the earlier cross-state work of Welch and Johnson in the United States. Freeman (1975b) used time-series data for the United States to estimate the effect of the growth in the number of college graduates relative to high school graduates on their relative earnings and obtained estimated elasticities of a similar magnitude, ranging from 1.0 to 2.6. Fallon and Layard (1975) examined a large cross section of countries with the comparable results shown in Table 1. Grant (1979) developed estimates in a complete translogarithmic systems equation which included capital in the analysis and obtained a value of 1.2. All told, the current evidence suggests a value of the elasticity of substitution between more and less educated labor in the range of 1.0 to 2.0. This magnitude is consistent with changes in the supply of graduates altering their relative earnings and does not invalidate the potential economic worth of educational planning based on fixed coefficient models.

A large number of additional studies on substitution among groups of workers have used occupational disaggregation. While these results show a wider range than those given for educational groups in Table 1, the estimates are consistent with elasticities of substitution between highly educated and less educated workers of 1–2. In the Hamermesh and Grant (1979) review of 20 estimates of elasticities of substitution between production (blue-collar) and nonproduction (white-collar) workers, the mean estimate was 2.3, with half the studies yielding estimates below 1.0 and half above that value.

The relationship between capital and more educated or skilled labor and the relationship between capital and less educated or skilled labor have also been studied as important elements in the demand for labor of varying educational qualities. The key hypotheses in this work had been that capital is less substitutable (more complementary) for educated than for less educated labor (Griliches 1969). If this is the case, increases in capital raise the demand for educated labor relative to less educated labor and changes in the price of capital cause employers to alter employment of the less educated more than employment of the more educated. The extant evidence appears to support this hypothesis. Of the 12 studies in Hamermesh and Grant's review article (1979), eight showed capital to be more easily substituted for blue-collar labor than for white-collar labor, and half indicate that white-collar labor is actually complementary with capital, so that changes in the price of capital raise demand for white-collar labor rather than reduce it. The only study to examine labor by education also shows lower substitutability between the more educated and capital than between the less educated and capital (Grant 1981).

With moderate elasticities of substitution between educated and less educated labor, and with relatively small (or even oppositely signed) elasticities of substitution between more educated labor and capital, current evidence suggests that the elasticity of demand for educated labor is of a moderate magnitude. In terms of Fig. 1, the evidence suggests that case (b) represents actual labor markets. Hence, analyses of the impact of economic changes or policies on employment or wages of educated labor cannot ignore the employment response to changes in wages.

2. Elasticity of Labor Supply

The human capital "revolution" in economic thinking about labor supply directed attention to the magnitude of supply elasticities. One key assumption of the human capital model is that individuals make investments in education in response to market incentives, which should be revealed in significant elasticities of the supply of educated labor.

Efforts to estimate elasticities of supply of educated labor have taken several forms. Some studies in the United States have analyzed the impact of the salaries of college workers relative to high school workers on the proportion of the young enrolled in college; some have focused on the effect of college tuition and scholarship charges on enrollments, while others have studied the relation between salaries in specific occupations and the relative number of young persons choosing to study the disciplines leading to those occupations. Several of the studies have used time-series data to estimate supply elasticities, identifying supply behavior from demand behavior by the fact that, because education takes a number of years, the decision to study in a field depends on salaries and related market conditions prior to the individual's graduation into the job market. Other studies have compared the relative number of persons obtaining different levels or types of education across geographic areas to salaries in these areas. Another body of literature has concentrated on the decision of individuals to enroll in higher education and/or the type of education or institution they choose.

The various studies have yielded generally consistent results regarding the magnitude of the elasticities of supply of educated labor, in the range of around 1 to 2. The studies for the United Kingdom are comparable to those for the United States. The study by Mattila (1982), which is the only one to estimate responses to calculated rates of return rather than starting or average salaries, yields figures analogous to studies using these measures of incentives. All told, the various studies reveal considerable responsiveness, which goes a long way to accounting for observed swings in the proportion of young persons enrolled in college in postwar years. The studies indicate, further, that elasticities of supply to specific fields tend to be higher, in general, than elasticities of supply to higher education as a whole. Surveys of students regarding the importance of salary and career considerations in their educational decisions buttress these conclusions: a large number take explicit consideration of monetary factors in decision-making (see Table 2).

Studies of responses to changes in tuition rates, summarized by McPherson (1978), tell a similar story. All of the reviewed studies found that tuition charges affected enrollment, with a magnitude that roughly indicates that a change in tuition charges of US$100 would alter the proportion enrolled by perhaps 0.8 or so percent. Translated into an elasticity of response, the tuition-elasticity of enrollment is about 0.3 (McPherson 1978 p.181). Since tuition takes up only a fraction of the salaries received by students, this low number makes intuitive sense and is, indeed, consistent with a supply elasticity in the range of 1 to 2.

As for elasticities for supply to specific fields of study, a substantial literature has examined time-series fluctuations in enrollment and degrees. Supply elasticities have been estimated for a wide variety of professional specialties: physics (Freeman 1976b), economics (Hansen et al. 1980), engineering (Freeman 1976a, Sirbu et al. 1978), law (Freeman 1975a, Freebairn and Withers 1979, Pashigan 1977) and teachers (Zarkin 1982) in the United States; teachers in the United Kingdom (Zabalza 1979), engineers, scientists, commerce graduates in Australia (Fisher 1983, Miller and Volker 1983) among other areas. The principal result of this work is that supply elasticities to various professions are quite sizable and, in conjunction with observed wage changes, explain a large proportion of the changes in degrees and enrollments.

Many studies distinguish between short-run and long-run elasticities of response. The short-run response is defined as the percentage change in one year's supply due to a change in economic incentives; the long-run response represents the percentage change in supply a number of years in the future—assuming the new wage pattern persists. As a rough generalization, short-run supply elasticities are typically below 1, while long-run elasticities are in the range of 3 to 4. The long-run responses tend to exceed those estimated for college enrollments overall, presumably because any given field can attract persons from other college fields as well as from persons on the margin between attending college and working.

There is some evidence that the supply of educated labor to specialties such as engineering fluctuates according to "cobweb types" dynamics in which a large supply in one period depresses wages and market opportunities, which in turn reduces enrollment and

Table 2
Estimates of the supply of persons to higher education

Studies of responses to salaries

Study	Sample	Elasticity response to salaries
Tinbergen (1974)	countries	0.54–2.64
Freeman (1975c)	time series, USA	1.3–1.7
Freeman and Hansen (1983)	time series, USA	1.82
Willis and Rosen (1979)	Individuals in NBER-Thorndike sample, USA	about 2.00
Pissarides (1979)	time series, UK	1.12–1.31
Dolphin (1981)	time series, USA	0.7
Mattila (1982)	time series, USA	0.86–1.39

Studies of responses to tuition

Study	Sample	Response of enrollment rate per US$100 change in tuition
Corazzini et al. (1972)	National cross section	0.62
Hopkins (1974)	State cross section	0.75
Barnes (1978)	Individual students	1.53
Radner and Miller (1975)	Individual students	0.05
Kohn et al. (1974)	Individual students	0.92
Hoenack (1967)	High school districts	0.71
Hoenack and Weiler (1975)	Individual students	1.46
Spies (1973)	Individual students	0.05
Campbell and Siegel (1967)	Time series	0.20
Bishop and van Dyck (1977)	Individual students	0.90

Source: All studies listed in bibliography. Lower panel from McPherson M 1978 p. 181, Tables 3–9

future supply, thereby raising wages and improving conditions, and so on. The impact of this market dynamics on supply in engineering can be seen in the swings in enrollment in Fig. 2. Estimates of the supply and demand elasticities in the market do, however, indicate that these fluctuations are stable and dampened (Freeman 1976a, Freeman and Hansen 1983), which means that it takes considerable shocks to set off supply responses that greatly overshoot the appropriate levels in the market.

Similar studies in developing countries have used household consumption data to estimate the effect of changing tuition charges on children's school enrollment among families of different income levels. This elasticity of the "demand for education" is some fraction of the price elasticity of the supply of educated labor, depending on the size of tuition payments relative to the income earned by graduates of primary and secondary schools.

Jimenez (1987, 1989) reviewed a number of studies that estimate price elasticities of demand for education. Various measures are used as a proxy

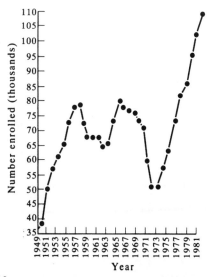

Figure 2
First-year enrollments in engineering in the United States

67

Table 3
Estimates of the supply of persons to education: studies of responses to tuition in developing countries

Study	Dependent variable	Price measure	Price elasticity
Malawi (1983)	Household enrollment ratio	Total household cost	−0.52
Malaysia (1976)	Population of schoolchildren	Distance to secondary school	
	age 6–11		−0.039
	age 12–18		−0.012
Mali (1982)	Enrollment ratio	Fees to parents	−0.98
		Distance to school	−0.26
Peru (1989)	Enrollment ratio	School fees	
		poorest 75%	−0.13/−0.45
		wealthiest 25%	−0.05/−0.18
Philippines (1968)	Years of completed schooling	Mean wage for children	
		age 7–14	−0.05
		age 15–19	−0.008

Sources: Jimenez 1987 (Malawi, Malaysia, Mali, Philippines); Gertler and Glewwe 1989, Jimenez 1990 (Peru)

for the price of education to families, such as the distance to school (Malaysia, Mali), fees to the parent association (Mali), the mean wage for children (Philippines), the total household cost (Malawi), and school fees (Peru). The dependent variable also varies, from the population of schoolchildren (Malaysia) to the household enrollment ratio (Malawi) to the enrollment ratio (Mali) to the years of schooling completed (Philippines). The results are summarized in Table 3.

The price elasticities of demand vary enormously in part because the measures of schooling demand and costs also vary so greatly. When the enrollment decision is used to measure demand, as in Mali, Malawi, and Peru, the price elasticity is in the 0.2–1.0 range. Since costs are only a small fraction of salaries received by school completers, the implicit elasticity of supply is quite high. When price elasticity of demand is measured for different income groups and at different levels of price, it produces the expected result of much more inelastic demand for the highest income quartile of families than for the lowest 75 percent of families. The higher the price of schooling, the more elastic the demand (Gertler and Glewwe 1989).

See also: Education and Productivity; Education, Occupation, and Earnings; Vocational Education and Productivity; Education and Earnings; Income Distribution and Education

References

Bowles S 1969 *Planning Educational Systems for Economic Growth.* Harvard University Press, Cambridge, Massachusetts

Dougherty C R S 1972 Estimates of labour aggregation functions. *J. Pol. Econ.* 80 (6):1101–19

Fallon P R, Layard P R G 1975 Capital–skill complementarity, income distribution, and output accounting. *J. Pol. Econ.* 83 (2): 279–301

Fisher W L 1983 *Occupational Choice in a Constrained Labour Market: The Australian Case of Highly Skilled Labour.* Conference Paper No. 27, Bureau of Labour Market Research, Canberra

Freebairn J W, Withers G A 1979 Welfare effects of salary forecast error in professional labour markets. *Rev. Econ. Stat.* 61: 234–41

Freeman R B 1975a Legal cobwebs: A recursive model of the labor market for new lawyers. *Rev. Econ. Stat.* 57 (2): 171–79

Freeman R B 1975b Overinvestment in college training? *J. Hum. Resources* 10 (3): 287–311

Freeman R B 1976a A cobweb model of the supply and starting salary of new engineers. *Independent Labor Relations Review* 29 (2): 236–48

Freeman R B 1976b *The Overeducated American.* Academic Press, New York

Freeman R B, Hansen J 1983 Forecasting the changing market for college-trained workers. In: Taylor R, Rosen R, Pratzner F (eds.) 1983 *Responsiveness of Training Institutions to Changing Labor Market Demands.* National Center for Research in Vocational Education, Ohio State University, Columbus, Ohio

Gertler P, Glewwe P 1989 *The Willingness to Pay for Education in Developing Countries: Evidence from Rural Peru.* World Bank, Washington DC (Living Standards Measurement Study, Working Paper No. 54)

Grant J H 1979 Substitution among labor, labor and capital in United States manufacturing. Doctoral dissertation, Michigan State University

Grant S 1981 *Separability and Substitution among Labor Aggregates and Capital*, Wellesley College Working Paper No. 40, Wellesley College, Massachusetts

Griliches Z 1969 Capital–skill complementarity. *Rev. Econ. Stat.* 51 (4): 465–68

Hamermesh S, Grant J 1979 Econometric studies of labor–labor substitution and their implications for policy. *J. Hum. Resources* 14 (4): 518–42

Hansen W L, Newburger H B, Schroeder F J, Stapleton D C, Youngday D J 1980 Forecasting the market for new PhD economists. *Am. Econ. Rev.* 70 (1): 49–63

Jimenez E 1987 *Pricing Policy in the Social Sectors: Cost Recovery for Education and Health in Developing Countries.* Johns Hopkins University Press, Baltimore, Maryland

Johnson G 1970 The demand for labor by educational category. *South Econ. J.* 37 (2): 190–204

Mattila J P 1982 Determinants of male school enrollments: A time–series analysis. *Rev. Econ. Stat.* 64 (2): 242–51

McPherson M 1978 The demand for higher education. In: Breneman D W, Finn C E (eds.) 1978 *Public Policy and Private Higher Education.* Brookings Institution, Washington, DC

Miller P W, Volker P A 1983 *Starting Salaries and Designations of Graduates of Australia.* Department of Economics, Australian National University, Canberra

Pashigan B P 1977 The market for lawyers: The determinants of the demand for and supply of lawyers. *J. Law Econ.* 20 (1): 53–85

Psacharopoulos G, Hinchliffe K 1972 Further evidence on the elasticity of substitution among different types of educated labor. *J. Pol. Econ.* 80 (4): 786–92

Sirbu M et al. 1978 *Improved Methodologies for Forecasting New Entrants in Science and Engineering.* Center for Policy Analysis Report No. CPA–78–15, Center for Policy Alternatives, Cambridge, Massachusetts

Tinbergen J 1974 Substitution of graduates by other labour. *Kylos* 27 (2): 217–26

Welch F 1970 Education in production. *J. Pol. Econ.* 78 (1): 35–59

Zabalza A 1979 The determinants of teacher supply. *Rev. Econ. Stud.* 46 (1): 131–47

Zarkin G 1982 Occupational choice: An application to the market for public school teachers. Doctoral dissertation, University of Chicago, Chicago, Illinois

Further Reading

Barnes G T 1978 Determinants of the college going and college choice decision. University of North Carolina, Greensboro, North Carolina

Bishop J, van Dyck J 1977 Can adults be hooked on college? Some determinants of adult college attendance. *J. Higher Educ.* 48 (1): 39–62

Campbell R, Siegel B N 1967 The demand for higher education in the United States, 1919–1964. *Am. Econ. Rev.* 57: 482–94

Corazzini A J, Dugan D J, Grabowski G 1972 Determinants and distributional aspects of enrollment in US higher education. *J. Hum. Resources* 7 (1): 39–59

Dolphin A M 1981 The demand for higher education. *Employment Gazette* July: 302–05

Freeman R B 1975c Supply and salary adjustments to the changing science manpower market: Physics, 1948–73. *Am. Econ. Rev.* 65 (1): 27–39

Hoenack S A 1967 Private demand for higher education in California. Doctoral dissertation, University of California, Berkeley, California

Hoenack S A, Weiler W C 1975 Cost-related tuition policies and university enrollments. *J. Hum. Resources* 10 (3): 332–60

Hopkins T 1974 Higher education enrollment demand. *Econ. Inq.* 12 (1): 53–65

Jimenez E 1989 Social sector pricing policy revisited: A survey of some recent controversies. In: Fischer S, de Tray D (eds.) 1989 *Proceedings of the World Bank Annual Conference on Development Economics, 1989.* World Bank, Washington, DC

Kohn M G, Manski C F, Mundel D S 1974 *An Empirical Investigation of Factors which Influence College-going Behaviors.* Rand, Santa Monica, California

Pissarides C A 1979 *Staying on at School in England and Wales — and Why 9% of the 1976 Age Group Did Not.* London School of Economics and Political Science Discussion Paper No. 63, London School of Economics, London

Radner R, Miller L S 1975 *Demand and Supply in US Higher Education.* McGraw-Hill, New York

Sato R, Koizumi T 1973 On the elasticities of substitution and complementarity. *Oxf. Econ. Pap.* 25 (1): 44–56

Spies R 1973 *The Future of Private Colleges: The Effect of Rising Costs on College Choice.* Industrial Relations Section, Princeton University, Princeton, New Jersey

Willis R J, Rosen S 1979 Education and self-selection. *J. Pol. Econ.* 87 (5 Pt. 2): S7–S36

On-the-job Training

M. J. Bowman

The term "on-the-job training" is used in several overlapping ways, all of which are usually focused on postschool learning. The first section of this entry discusses briefly the scope of and variations in on-the-job training as discussed in the descriptive and nontechnical literature. The second and third sections deal with the meanings and treatments of on-the-job training in human capital investment theory and its applications. Attention is then turned in the fourth section to a well-known view of institutional adaptations associated with on-the-job training in a dynamic context, characterizing some of the work on what have come to be labeled "internal labor markets" (internal, that is, to particular firms or agencies). Finally, the largely unseen informal economy is noted along with the training and learning activities that go on in its many crannies.

1. On-the-job Training in Nontechnical Usage

At one extreme the term on-the-job training is used quite literally to refer to organized instruction in the workplace. Somewhat less narrowly (and more often) it covers job-related training sponsored by an employer or required as a condition of promotion even when conducted on other premises and irrespective of whether direct outlays are covered by the individual or by the employer.

Remarkably little attention is given in most discussions that use the term in this way, to the many variants of apprenticeship and modifications over time with changes in economic structures. Nevertheless, apprenticeship training in great variety and with all degrees of formalization has remained of critical importance in both the less and the more developed countries. It is important not only for the more traditional manual skills but for other skills as well; indeed, recipients of doctorates have absorbed large amounts of apprentice training in the process of acquiring competence in research. Apprenticeship clearly constitutes a form (or set of forms) of on-the-job training even in a relatively narrow definition of that term. This is normally recognized where apprenticeship programs are developed as part of an organized government policy, but it is often ignored when apprenticeship arrangements evolve spontaneously and their structure remains relatively informal. These biases in what comes to be included have had counterparts in analyses of labor market and of human resource development. Fortunately, this fact is coming to be more adequately recognized in some of the less developed countries (LDCs).

Meanwhile, increasing alertness has emerged among both planners and researchers to the fact that time in school and time in the labor force need not be, and often are not, separated by a sharp divide. The long-established German system of extended part-time vocational education for young people in their first jobs is a striking example. If the vocational training is related to the jobs held and promotions in them, this is unambiguously a variant of on-the-job training. A quite different but equally interesting type of arrangement is exemplified by the *Servicio Nacional de Aprendizaje* (SENA) in Colombia and the complex of related programs in Brazil, in which some students are individually sponsored by firms that will employ them later or may be employing them at intervals during the training program. In the United Kingdom the university-level polytechnics provided "sandwich courses" which interspersed academic training with periods at work, an approach since adopted by some other countries. The list is easily extended.

Yet another step toward generalization about what is counted as on-the-job training is the inclusion of much of the wide range of activities encompassed in what has sometimes been called "nonformal education" (public or private) and in the vogue for "recurrent education," which was pioneered in Sweden and evoked varying responses elsewhere from about 1970 onward. Much of this type of training is indistinguishable in practice from activities commonly labeled as on-the-job training though often it might be more accurately termed "out-of-a-job training in hope of a job."

The common element that brings together a diverse array of activities under the broadly defined umbrella term on-the-job training is not, in fact, whether the training is received by an individual virtually as part of the job (whether in the workplace or elsewhere). Rather, what seems to be common to all cases is the training of active members of the labor force with the purpose of improving career prospects. There are costs involved in such training, however those costs may be shared. On-the-job training entails investment in the human capital of men and women who have already joined the labor force. These investments are oriented toward their futures in paid or (less often) in independent employment.

2. Opportunity Costs and On-the-job Training

Studies of schooling as an investment constitute only one element in human capital theory. A seminal contribution to that theory came with Becker's incorporation of investments in human beings on through the postschool years into a theory about investments in schooling (Becker 1962, 1983). There were two essential elements in Becker's formulation. The first was the application of an old and powerful concept that lies at the heart of economic theory, the concept of opportunity cost, to the costs of spending time in school or training—commonly referred to in the literature on human capital as forgone earnings. The second element was the analytical distinction made between general and specific training of human capital. While opportunity costs are entailed in both sorts of human capital formation, the most direct applications in empirical work on earning streams deal only with the general (portable) components of learning and earning in the school years and in later years. Though presented initially in terms of time diverted from earning to learning, analysis was subsequently expressed in "time-equivalent units" and emphasis shifted to the importance of experience as an indicator of potentials for on-the-job training. Earnings are forgone when a person takes a job on which he or she will receive lower immediate pay but a compensating increase in the value of his (or less often her) portable investment in acquisition of that human capital. It does not matter, at this level of analysis, whether the accumulation of human capital occurs through formal instructional programs or in the most informal ways through cumulative experience on a job in which a person learns by doing. There may very well be a mixture of both elements of learning, as there has always been in apprenticeship for the skilled crafts and as there is, in fact, in much white-collar employment. In any case, estimates of the extent of investment through forgone earnings were designated on-the-job training in the first empirical forays by Mincer (1962), a designation that has been carried over into much subsequent work.

The initial formulations, along with most of the theoretical and empirical models that followed in the later 1960s and the 1970s, viewed the investments individuals make in themselves as outcomes of a sequence of decisions made implicitly at frequent intervals. Along with the further simplifying assumption that marginal rates of return to schooling and to postschool investments were equal, this way of formulating the process allowed researchers to estimate the time path of investments and returns over a man's life. (Analysis for women, incorporating periods out of the labor force, came later.) Experiments have been conducted that dispense with the assumptions of the equality of marginal rates of return to schooling and to postschool investments, and skill obsolescence has been brought into the picture. This initial and simplest model remains at the core of these refinements, however, and it must suffice here.

Using the Mincerian approach in its initial form, it is possible to separate out the schooling and on-the-job training components of earning streams (Mincer 1962, 1974, Bowman 1968, 1974). Suppose that two male populations have been matched as far as socioeconomic background, health, innate ability, and so forth are concerned, but that one of these populations has completed the ith level of schooling whereas the other has completed schooling $i + m$. The focus of comparison is formed by the schooling and on-the-job training components that account for the differences in the average earning streams of these two populations. In analyzing this problem, two highly simplified models may be devised.

2.1 Model 1

Earnings differentials match differences in productivity; they are determined solely by differences in schooling; those earning differentials are realized immediately; and productive capacity is maintained intact until its complete demise. Designating the cost of schooling increment m as Cm and the rate of return on that investment as Rm, the incremental earning path will be unchanging at the value $RmCm$. Starting from an earning path for no schooling and adding to

those earnings incrementally for each increment of schooling would give the earning path for a person with schooling $i + m$. Taking $(i + m) = j$ gives the line labeled Yj^* in Fig. 1 for earnings over the period from $t=0$ to $t=T$, when earnings cease.

2.2 Model 2

The potential productivity differentials determined by schooling are the same as in Model 1, taking effect immediately and being sustained intact throughout working life. In addition, however, there are opportunity-cost investments in on-the-job learning, which account for the concavity of observed earning streams. The internal rate of return to an increment of schooling m and rates of return to associated postschool investments are equal. The curve Yj which includes effects of investments in the postschool accumulation of human capital, intersects Yj^* from below because of the forgone earnings in the early years. The point of intersection is known in economics following Mincer (1974) as the "overtake point," at which observed earnings (which are net of opportunity-cost investments in oneself) come to match and then to surpass the return to investments of the individual in on-the-job training. If the assumptions of model 2 are retained, which are Mincer's assumptions (Mincer 1962, 1974), the area $(J - A)$ is the undiscounted aggregate net return to investments of the individual in on-the-job learning or training. The area $(A + B)$ is the undiscounted gross return to the investment in schooling, and the net contribution of schooling is $(A + B - C)$. The undiscounted total net contribution of investments in schooling and on-the-job training is thus $(B + J - C)$ and the postschool proportion of this total is $(J - A) (B + J - C)$ (see Fig. 1).

Model 2 is a powerful simplification and the ratio

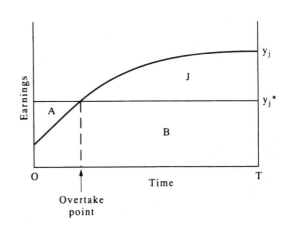

Figure 1
Earnings paths

71

$(J - A)$ $(B + J)$ with or without a correction for C can be a useful descriptive statistic even when the assumptions of the model are challenged. In any case, challenges must arise in any careful consideration of empirical findings using age cross-section data. Other problems of specification aside, each observation of people of a given age at a given calendar date is an observation referring to members of a particular and hence necessarily unique cohort.

3. "General" Training and the Individual as Investor

The models laid out thus far refer only to that part of on-the-job training that is implicitly financed and returns on which are received by the individual. The share of investment costs borne and the returns received by a firm or employing agency will not show up in the individual's earning stream. In the terminology of human-capital theory, only "general" human capital is picked up in the above formulation. "Firm-specific" human capital is not.

There are two main overlapping concepts of general training or learning. The first of these, which may be designated here for convenience as general I training, refers to the acquisition of capabilities or traits that have value over a wide range of uses and activities. The most general of all training is in literacy and numeracy, usually acquired in elementary schools. Most fundamental in general training is learning to learn. Persons with a foundation in the most general capabilities will be more readily trainable in many more specialized skills. By the same token, such training is the foundation of capabilities to communicate effectively, to seek out and interpret information, and to adjust to changing situations and opportunities. What is often regarded as specialized training may be classified as general I, however, in that it may be useful in a wide range of uses and diverse settings; carpentry and clerical skills are examples. Indeed, such skills may be far more general in their applications than the supposedly "general" education popularly associated with graduates of Oxford or Cambridge universities who were recruited by the British Foreign Office.

What might be designated here as general II training is the concept associated with human capital theory. General human capital (in contrast to specific human capital) is portable. In other words, the general human capital embodied in a person can be applied in agencies other than the one in which the capabilities were acquired. General I training is necessarily also portable, but portability does not necessarily imply general I training or capabilities. A doctor may have been trained in a highly specialized skill, such as open heart surgery; this is hardly a general I type of skill, but the heart surgeon is not limited to practice in the hospital in which he or she received his or her training. The skills embodied in the heart surgeon are portable,

and hence in this sense general. So are the skills of a cook or a barber (as are, in most industrialized economies, those of semiskilled operatives in textile factories), however specialized these skills may be.

General skills defined in terms of portability have a central place in the treatment of learning in school and at work as parts of an integrated theory of human capital. This was first refined by Becker (1962) and has been applied empirically by Mincer (1958, 1962, 1974), in the interpretation of the concave shapes of earning paths over a man's (and to a lesser degree a woman's) life. Taking as a first example the employer providing the training, the following situation may be hypothesized. If this employer paid the trainee full-time wages without regard to the time spent on learning and the direct costs of the instruction, but the trainee then went to another employer, carrying the full value of the newly acquired human capital, the first employer would get no return on his or her investment in training. Indeed, the employer would not make that investment unless he or she could shift the costs onto the trainee. What happens in the extreme case of completely general formation of human capital is then a shift of the investment cost to the trainee in the form of partially forgone earnings. In effect, the employer sells and the employee buys the increments to the individual's portable human capital.

An essential element in this theoretical construct is the concept of opportunity costs, or "forgone earnings," whether in attending school or later on. Thus the individual may take a job that yields only small earnings at first if by doing so he or she can build up general human capital from which greater returns can be expected later on. The difference between current earnings in this job and what could be earned initially in a dead-end job is the opportunity cost incurred as an investment by the individual in the acquisition of human capital. (Forgone earnings when attending school is simply a special case of opportunity-cost investments in oneself.) Readiness to bear the full opportunity costs of earnings forgone in school or at work depends on the extent to which the individual can carry the compensating accumulation of human capital elsewhere—that is, on the portability of the skills acquired. It follows from this view of labor markets that the steeper the gradient of earnings and the lower the associated initial earnings, the greater must be the postschool investments that people are making in themselves. At least, this is the case so long as the human capital is fully portable.

To the extent to which the accumulation of human capital in an employee is specific to the firm (nonportable) the situation is changed. While earning paths may still provide rough clues to the costs borne by individuals and the returns on those investments, they cannot capture that part of the costs of on-the-job training that is ultimately borne by the employer, or the employer's share in the rewards.

4. Firm-specific Training and the Sharing of Costs and Returns

The term "specific training," as it has been used in human capital theory since Becker's seminal work (1962, 1983), carries the precise meaning of nonportability. This is not the same thing as specialized training, which may or may not be portable. Rarely does anyone acquire specific human capital without at the same time acquiring at least some additions to his or her general human capital. A secretary, for example, may be of greater value as he or she comes to know the informal communication networks in which the boss participates. More generally, productivity in an enterprise depends not only on the aggregate of capabilities of individuals taken separately, but also on the development of effective interaction patterns and team work; an individual who has become integrated into joint activities and ways of doing things has acquired specific human capital that makes him or her more valuable than a new recruit to the enterprise, but that human capital cannot be carried elsewhere.

Both the firm and the individual have a stake in the accumulation of specific human capital, and the result spelled out in human capital theory is a sharing of the costs of and returns to the formation of such capabilities. Other things being equal, a large admixture of firm-specific relative to general (portable) human capital would be reflected in flatter life-earnings paths than where the proportion of portable human capital is higher. Other things are rarely equal, however.

5. Firm-specific Human Capital and Labor Market Structures

It is not enough to look at on-the-job training from the perspective of either individuals or firms as investors in some given institutional context, for institutions themselves both affect and are affected by the processes of human resource development. Multiple endogenous variables are at issue here. For one thing, there is usually a much greater investment in the firm-specific skills of men than of women; flatter age–earning curves will be observed in enterprises that hire a relatively large number of women, even though these enterprises are likely also to be characterized by little firm-specific human capital. Even considering men only, arrangements that foster the development of firm-specific human capital are often in turn fostered by the enlargement of such capital as a substantial component in the assets of both the firm and its individual personnel. Such arrangements include management practices and personnel policies that discourage turnover of a firm's labor force through resignations and layoffs alike. Both the costs of and the returns to investments in human resource formation at work are shared by employers and employees, since both have an interest in stabilizing the association. As

Oi showed many years ago (1962), labor then becomes a "quasi-fixed factor of production."

The relative importance of firm-specific human capital (and hence of the formal or informal training through which such capital is acquired) depends in part on the size of an economy. In a small country in which there is only one textile mill, for example, skills learned by operators in that mill may be specific to it so long as there are substantial barriers (formal, cultural, or linguistic) to international migration. However, this also illustrates the fact that what makes a skill specific may often depend as much on institutional constraints on mobility as on the nature of a skill (Bowman 1965). The development of customs that have constrained mobility between firms in Japan are frequently cited in discussions of specific human capital. The degree of uniqueness of the Japanese situation and of its limitations on interfirm mobility are often exaggerated, however, even as analogous situations elsewhere are ignored. Moreover, substantial investments in firm-specific human capital do not mean a lack of flexibility in the development and allocation of human resources where internal labor markets are large and well-developed.

Stability in attachments between firms and their employees and the formation of firm-specific human capital are mutually supportive features of labor markets, both "external" and "internal," but most obviously and directly of internal labor markets. This means, among other things, an extension of time horizons in the formal or implicit terms of contracts between employer and employee. The longer those horizons, the greater the scope for variations in trade-offs over time. Investments in and returns to on-the-job training can come to be confounded in earnings data by arrangements that constitute in part an internal capital as well as an internal labor market, the internal capital market performing a hidden function of lending and borrowing between firm and employee that is adapted in part to the economic life cycles of consumption and earnings. This phenomenon is especially important for interpretations of the workings of Japanese internal labor markets as agencies of human resource development. Those markets often differ substantially from internal provisions but with quite different management–labor relations and sources of seniority arrangements. Nobody who is at all familiar with management and personnel policies in Japan would question the importance of on-the-job training in its firms.

In sum, when human capital theory is applied to analysis of the rational behavior of firms as well as of individuals in a world in which training and human capital are a mixture of the general and the specific, the importance of association between on-the-job training and long-term commitments is underlined. Rough measurement by methods applicable to general training may still have its uses, but some of the elegant optimal control models run into severe problems. One direction that further work has taken has been a shift toward greater emphasis on the new economics of information and the "matching" of firms and employers in search processes. This has reduced somewhat the attention given to investments by either individuals or firms in on-the-job training, but without challenging the earlier work. Meanwhile research on life-cycle earnings and learning at work has been enriched by studies of the participation in the labor force by women and of the effects of interruptions in the continuity of their employment on subsequent life-earning prospects.

6. On-the-job Training and Institutional Adaptation to Change

The term "internal labor market" is entirely appropriate to analysis of adjustments by firm and individual in human capital theory. That term is more often used in other contexts, however, and it has spread rapidly since about 1970. In so doing, it has taken on at least as many variants as on-the-job training, especially in the sociological literature, as is amply demonstrated in Berg (1981). Of greatest interest here, however, must be the line of thought stimulated by Doeringer and Piore (1966). The focus in this and in related subsequent work is on how economic institutions adapt to provide education and training for adults in skills that come into being and are increasingly demanded by innovative change in a dynamic economy. In some respects the work by Doeringer and Piore stands at the opposite extreme from the optimal control models stimulated by human capital theory. It gives far more explicit attention to economic change and far less to life-cycle experiences. It provides good descriptive analyses of some of the institutional options in adjustment to and furtherance of innovative change.

It is often supposed that this line of work runs counter to human capital theories. Perhaps, however, this is instead a case of potential complementarity of endeavor, but with insufficient communication among economists who have started from different initial perspectives. After the investigation of internal labor markets that he and Doeringer had conducted for the United States Department of Labor, Piore wrote:

> the training process yields one explanation for the rigidity of internal wage structure and the use of seniority to govern promotion and lay off. Without the protection which these provide, experienced workers would be reluctant to cooperate in training, for fear that the competition of newly trained workers would undermine income and job security. (Piore 1968 p.439)

This conclusion points to relationships ignored in most of the human capital literature. At the same time, it bypasses completely the whole question of the part managements and personnel policies may play in the creation and modification of incentive structures in the work force, along with related questions about the nature of labor unions and contrasts in their histories and modes of operation in different countries (and even within a single country). It also bypasses, perhaps for the same reasons, the question of what may be the incentives to workers and to employers to invest in the formation of human capital. One result has been a failure in most of the literature on internal labor markets to probe more deeply into the ways in which costs of labor turnover (resignations as well as layoffs) and investments in on-the-job training may be affected by, and may themselves affect, other aspects of institutional structures and behavior. To the extent that economists have approached these questions, they have worked primarily from a combination of human capital theory and search theory.

7. On-the-job Training in the Invisible Economy

It is undoubtedly the case that on-the-job training, however defined, is of crucial importance not only for economic growth but for the sustained viability of an economy in the modern world. What, if anything, governments could or should do about it is a matter of hot debate in both industrially advanced countries and LDCs. Meanwhile, consideration of the training and learning that takes place in the less visible sectors of the economy is what has most often been neglected. This neglect characterizes even the research on Japan, despite the proliferation of painstaking studies of labor efficiency in larger firms in that country. Most serious, however, has been a propensity to ignore the importance of learning systems that have evolved informally in many of the LDCs when public policy has given scope for the exercise of ingenuity in the unseen eddies of economic life. Such training and learning tends to elude conventional quantitative counts. It is an integral factor in determining age–earning streams, but no analysis at the level of aggregation that has characterized empirical estimates in the human capital tradition will illuminate these facets of the life of a people. A few sallies into this large but largely unexplored territory have shown that it may be much richer than commonly has been supposed. Work by King (1977) on Kenya is an illuminating example, but the Kenyan government has not penalized initiative in the informal sectors of the economy as some of the LDCs have. It is not known how much on-the-job training goes on in the less developed countries, or to what extent such activities are inadvertently discouraged (or encouraged) by public policies.

References

Becker G S 1962 Investment in human capital: A theoretical analysis. *J. Pol. Econ.* 70(5, Part 2): 9–49
Becker G S 1983 *Human Capital: A Theoretical and Empirical Analysis with Special Reference to Education*, 2nd edn. University of Chicago Press, Chicago, Illinois

Berg I E (ed.) 1981 *Sociological Perspectives on Labor Markets*. Academic Press, New York

Bowman M J 1965 From guilds to infant training industries. In: Anderson C A, Bowman M J (eds.) 1965 *Education and Economic Development*. Aldine, Chicago, Illinois

Bowman M J 1968 The assessment of human investments as growth strategy. In: Joint Economic Committee, 90th Session of the US Congress 1968 *Federal Programs for the Development of Human Resources*. US Government Printing Office, Washington, DC

Bowman M J 1974 Learning and earning in the postschool years. In: Kerlinger F N, Carroll J B (eds.) 1974 *Review of Research in Education*, Vol. 2. Peacock, Itasca, Illinois

Doeringer P B, Piore M J 1966 *Internal Labor Markets, Technological Change, and Labor Force Adjustment*. Report submitted to the Office of Manpower Policy, Evaluation, and Research, US Department of Labor, Cambridge, Massachusetts

King K 1977 *The African Artisan: Education and the Informal Sector in Kenya*. Heineman, London

Mincer J 1958 Investment in human capital and personal income distribution. *J. Pol. Econ.* 66(4): 281–302

Mincer J 1962 On-the-job training: Costs, returns and some implications. *J. Pol. Econ.* 70(5 Pt. 2): 50–79

Mincer J 1974 *Schooling, Experience, and Earnings*. Columbia University Press, New York

Oi W Y 1962 Labor as a quasi-fixed factor. *J. Pol. Econ.* 70(6): 538–55

Piore M J 1968 On-the-job training and adjustment to technological change. *J. Hum. Resources* 3(4): 435–49

Vintage Effects and Education

S. Rosen

The term "vintage" is borrowed from capital theory in economics and applied to the economics of education: education is viewed as human capital which enhances innate skill and productivity. In the production of new capital there is a chronological element, because each new generation of machinery embodies improved design. For example, rapid advances in technology in the digital computer industry have continually raised computational speed, and power while at the same time reducing computational costs. Specific productivity improvements are built into each new generation or vintage. Vintage effects are associated with productivity differentials across successive generations of graduates or cohorts with a given level or type of schooling. For these reasons they are sometimes called "cohort effects," a term which is used interchangeably with "vintage effects" in the economics literature. The capital value of schooling is reflected in the sequence and pattern of income associated with it over the work life cycle.

1. Measurement of Vintage Effects

To keep the issues clear conceptually, one might consider the generation of graduates of one level of school in the United States in any one year who choose to enter the labor market upon graduation; for example the class of high-school graduates in 1951 who do not continue on to college. This group would be labeled the 1951 vintage of high-school graduates. If the average annual real earnings (i.e., deflated by a price index to remove the general effects of inflation) of members of this group are observed for each year subsequent to graduation and plotted on a graph with average earnings on the ordinate and years of labor market experience on the abscissa, the resulting curve will show a characteristic pattern of increasing earnings with experience. When the same procedure is undertaken for high-school completers in a different year, say the class of 1961 (i.e., the 1961 vintage), and plotted on the same graph as for the 1951 vintage, this curve will also show the characteristic shape. However, it will not be identical in location to the earlier vintage. Generally speaking, it will begin at a higher level and may also have a slightly different slope. The average difference in earnings for each year of experience between these cohorts is the first-order estimate of the vintage effect. Second-order effects are captured by interactions of vintage with the experience gradient of the earnings profile. The same procedure may be repeated for other levels or types of school completion. The generalization to n vintages ($n > 2$) is straightforward.

2. Interpretation of Vintage Effects

While measurement of vintage effects is clear enough from this kind of exercise, the meaning of the estimates admits a variety of interpretations, which are not mutually exclusive. In part—perhaps in major part—the estimates reflect secular change in the real wage of all workers, independent of the quantity and quality of schooling. That is, the return to all skills generally increases over time because of general economic growth and productivity advances in the economy. Each successive generation tends to be wealthier than past generations for this reason alone. Since the average United States real wage rose around 1.5–2 percent annually from the Second World War to the early 1970s, an annual average vintage effect of that magnitude serves as a benchmark for the expected magnitude of these effects in that country.

Second, intercohort differences may be partially attributable to improvements in educational technology. These are true vintage effects and can be broadly classified into two groups. First, there may be shifts in the educational production function through technological innovations in teaching methods and in resources that improve methods of communicating existing knowledge. Examples are improvements in information transfer through such devices as computer-assisted teaching, better teacher quality, and better teaching environments. Second, the content of materials taught changes periodically through advances in knowledge. This is perhaps of greater importance for advances in technical and vocational subject matter than for general education and humanities. For example, the contents of engineering and medical education have changed markedly over the years as the state of knowledge in those fields has developed. Since each new generation of graduates tends to obtain access to the latest methods and theories, a corresponding rate of obsolescence of older vintages is implied. Few satisfactory estimates of these important effects exist in the literature, though the 2 percent increase mentioned above suggests that they must be substantially smaller than that on average. However, this does not rule out considerable variation across disciplines.

Third, there may be systematic changes in student quality among completion levels over time. There are forces working in two directions. Insofar as improvements in teaching technology and knowledge permeate all levels, successive generations at each level embody more knowledge and human capital. On the other side of the coin, the underlying abilities of students by grade completion may change. For example, at the beginning of the twentieth century only a very small proportion of cohorts attended college, whereas a much larger percentage attended in the 1990s. The college populations of the 1990s must exhibit a substantially different distribution of underlying abilities than did the elite group almost a century earlier. The same is true of high school graduates.

Fourth, there are difficult statistical problems isolating vintage or cohort effects from earnings data because age or working experience has important independent effects on earnings. Multicollinearity problems are caused by linear dependencies between calendar time and age, which have an independent effect on earnings through work experience. The term "multicollinearity" denotes a situation where two variables are themselves so closely correlated that it is impossible to isolate the independent effects of each. While these dependencies may not be exact, they are often too close to yield reliable estimates. Nonlinear effects may be better identified under these circumstances, but caution and care are necessary here as well. For example, erroneous specification of the curvature of earnings–experience profiles can cause misleading inferences on vintage effects because specification bias in experience effects tends to spill over to estimated vintage effects and bias them as well. These inference problems have been compounded by the lack of growth in real wages in the United States during the 1970s and 1980s. This altered the shape and the level of experience–earnings profiles over time in much different ways than had occurred in the past.

Finally, the lifetime returns on a given type of education may depend on the number in any given generation who choose it. In this case vintage effects are inversely related to the size of cohorts. If members of different cohorts with the same level of schooling are imperfect substitutes in production, the real wage prospects at each point in the life cycle may be affected by considerations of supply. Recent estimates suggest the members of the United States baby boom birth cohorts of the 1950s have suffered from the volume of their numbers, due to increased intracohort competition for career advancement at each step in the work life cycle. The estimates show a reduction in the rate of return to higher education among these vintages compared with earlier vintages because of their large numbers. There may be, in addition, important interactions with changing labor force participation rates among men and women and affirmative action programs addressed to improve the economic status of minorities. However, observations on later cohorts of graduates are limited by their relatively sort earnings histories, because many of these people had not been in the labor force for very long. With incomplete record length it is difficult to distinguish between perturbations in the curvature of the experience-earnings profiles and shifts in the profile itself. The passage of time and lengthier earnings histories will enable investigators to obtain a firmer resolution of this important issue.

Bibliography

Berger M C 1984 Cohort size and earnings growth of young workers. *Ind. Lab. Relations Rev.* 37(4): 582–591

Berger M C 1985 The effect of cohort size on earnings growth: A reexamination of the evidence *J. Pol. Econ.* 93(3): 561–573

Freeman R B 1977 The decline in economic rewards to college education. *Rev. Econ. Stat.* 59(1): 18–29

Freeman R B 1979 The effect of demographic factors on the age-earnings profile. *J. Hum. Resources* 14(3): 289–318

Kosters M H (ed.) 1991 *Workers and Their Wages: Changing Patterns in the United States.* AEI Press, Washington, DC

Murphy K M, Plant M 1988 cohort size and earnings in the United States. In: Lee R D, Arthur W B, Rodgers G (eds.) 1988 *Economics of Changing Age Distributions in Developed Countries* Clarendon Press, Oxford

Murphy K M, Welch F 1992 The structure of wages. *Q. J. Econ.* 107(1): 285–326

Rosen S 1975 Measuring the obsolescence of knowledge. In: Juster F T (ed.) 1975 *Education, Income and Human Behavior.* Report of the Carnegie Commission on Higher Education and the National Bureau of Economic

Research. McGraw-Hill, New York

Rosen S 1976 A theory of life earnings. *J. Pol. Econ.* 84(4): S45–S67

Taubman P, Wales T 1974 *Higher Education and Earnings: College as an Investment and a screening Device.*

Carnegie Commission on Higher Education. McGraw-Hill, New York

Welch F 1979 Effects of cohort size on earnings: The baby boom babies' financial bust. *J. Pol. Econ.* 87: S65–S97

Internal Migration and Education

R. H. Sabot and P. L. Wong

1. Introduction

The spatial redistribution of labor that accompanies economic growth and structural change is observable both in individual countries over time and in different countries at varying levels of development. A decreasing share of total output from agriculture and an increasing share from manufacturing and services are associated with a decrease in the proportion of the labor force employed in agriculture and rural areas, implying a net migration to urban centers (Berry and Sabot 1978).

Educational factors have been shown to be significant in the complex decision-making process that precedes migration to urban areas. There is educational selectivity in internal migration due to the greater concentration in urban areas of the demand for skills acquired in school. Todaro (1976) observed a strong positive relationship between the propensity of rural residents to migrate and their level of education in many countries at different levels of development. Arthur (1991) found that rural households in Ghana considered level of education to be one of the more important criteria used to determine which family member(s) will migrate to urban areas. Because it is believed by the family that those members with higher skills levels are more likely to find work in the urban labor market, those possessing higher education levels are typically the first to migrate from the rural areas. Sahn and Alderman (1988) also indicated that in Sri Lanka those rural residents with higher education levels were the most likely to migrate to urban areas.

However, the relationship between education and internal migration extends beyond this trend of educational selectivity. Several studies have shown that individuals and families migrate to urban areas in pursuit of the more abundant and higher quality educational opportunities available there. Lemel's (1989) research in Turkey indicates that rural residents believe that higher levels of education generally result in greater lifetime earnings and higher status jobs. Because opportunities to obtain higher levels of education often exist only in urban areas, individuals and/or families migrate to urban areas to pursue education, with the ultimate goal of improving earning potential,

which may or may not be realized in the urban area. A review by du Toit (1990) of the theoretical models for internal migration and the examples that he provides from Mexico and Cuba also suggest that migration from rural areas to urban areas is the result of a calculated decision-making process in which educational *and* economic opportunities in urban areas are seen as interrelated and significant "pull" factors. Finally, Gugler (1986) suggested that families migrate to urban areas (or more urbanized) areas to provide members with greater educational opportunities, in the hope that these opportunities will be translated into increased access to higher status and higher salaried jobs.

Educational selectivity may be constant, but the educational level of migrants has tended to increase over time, particularly in the 1970s and the early 1980s. There are two reasons for this. On the one hand, the concentration of labor demand increases in skilled manual and white-collar occupations—a corollary of urbanization and the change in the sectoral composition of output that characterizes development. On the other hand, as investment in rural areas has increased, so school enrollment rates, and consequently the relative supply of educated labor, have risen—another regular feature of development (Chenery and Syrquin 1975).

There is some evidence, however, that this pattern is being transformed by the increasingly more significant role played by the informal/subsistence sector in urban areas in developing countries. This urban informal sector also attracts rural residents and does *not* require high levels of education for job placement (Cole and Sanders 1985). Research on this subject is in its early stages and therefore it is unclear whether the informal sector serves as a transition to modern sector employment, a means of sustenance while education is pursued, or a final employment destination in and of itself (Cole and Sanders 1985, 1986, Todaro 1986).

2. Microdeterminants of Educational Selectivity

From the perspective of the individual rural resident, education and migration both represent investments in human capital in the sense that both entail costs

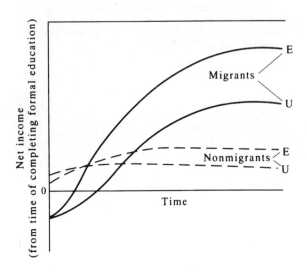

Figure 1
Earnings over time of educated (E) and uneducated (U) migrant and nonmigrant workers

borne in anticipation of enjoying returns in the future. For investment in migration or education to occur, rural residents must expect monetary benefits (higher earnings) and nonmonetary benefits, appropriately discounted, to exceed the costs. Moreover, migration and education are complementary: investing in one enhances the returns to investment in the other, as is illustrated in Fig. 1.

The income of rural workers who have just completed their formal education and begun to work is lower than that of uneducated workers, who entered the labor market earlier as agricultural producers. Their greater training and natural ability, however, combined with better contacts with those in control of the supply of credit, enables the educated to use their resources more efficiently, to be more innovative, and thus to raise their income above that of the uneducated. Production functions relating the amount of farm output to the level of each input, including farmer's education, have been estimated in more than 10 countries at different levels of development. Though the results vary, the overall conclusion is that the productivity of small farmers with elementary education is substantially higher than the productivity of uneducated farmers (Jamison and Lau 1982). There are no studies of the effects of postprimary education on agricultural productivity in the developing countries, but the expectation, particularly in low- and middle-income countries, is that diminishing returns set in at above low levels of education.

The net income of migrants is negative at first, because direct costs of migration must be borne during the period of moving and searching for a job.

Subsistence during the period of job seeking is likely to be the most important of these costs and to be positively related to the rate of urban unemployment. The income of the educated becomes positive before that of the uneducated. It also rises more steeply and to a higher level, reflecting the greater access of the educated to urban wage employment and the higher starting wages and returns to employment experience in the preferred occupations open to them. Earnings functions that relate wages of urban employees to various individual characteristics, including educational attainment, have been estimated in more than 40 countries (Psacharopoulos 1973). These functions indicate that a strong positive relationship between years of education and earnings is a universal characteristic of earnings structures.

Both rural and urban incomes rise with educational attainment. The evidence indicates, however, that the lifetime earnings of the educated are, as depicted in Fig. 1, higher in urban than in rural areas. For the educated rural resident the economic advantage of migration is thus more obvious; the present value of urban benefits dominates the rural stream. If the educated and the uneducated apply a similar discount to future income, expected net returns to migration will be higher for the educated. Because the educated are from higher income households for whom the costs of credit and the aversion to risk may be lower, the discount rate may be lower for the educated than for the uneducated, reinforcing the conclusion that the educated reap higher returns from migration.

Analysis of the relationship between migration rates and education is further complicated by the difficulty of separating economic from noneconomic costs and returns. The educational system may select individuals who are relatively open to change or who come from families that have urban-oriented values on occupation and consumption. Alternatively, education may alter the preferences of rural residents, increasing their preference for urban jobs and an urban mode of living. Differences in the psychic costs and returns of migration to groups with different amounts of education may make educated rural residents more willing to move in response to a given economic return to migration. Of course, a higher rate of migration among the educated may be due both to movement along a migration function and to a shift in the function.

Though the behavioral analysis of migration is in its infancy and there are significant unresolved problems of data, measurement, and specification (Schultz 1982), migration functions estimated in more than 10 countries empirically confirmed the foregoing propositions. Rates of migration for various geographic and demographic subgroups of the rural population are related to rural–urban income differentials, to probabilities of urban employment, to educational opportunities in urban areas, and to distance. The sign on the destination wage elasticity is generally positive, that on the origin wage elasticity negative, confirming that rural residents respond to economic opportunities in their migration decisions (Yap 1977, Berry and Sabot 1978). Some studies have shown that extreme poverty may preclude investing in migration irrespective of expected returns, suggesting that the shape of the relationship between migration and source area incomes is an inverted "U". In the few studies where such a determination has been possible, it has been shown that higher rates of migration among the educated are due to higher economic returns and lower costs (Levy and Wadycki 1974, Barnum and Sabot 1977). It has also been demonstrated, controlling for economic costs and returns, that migration rates are still higher among the educated, lending support to the hypothesis that the educated have different preferences (Barnum and Sabot 1977). However, as mentioned above, this trend may be changing because of the increasing importance of the informal sector in the urban labor market.

3. *Suboptimality of the Rate and Composition of Migration Flows*

There is little doubt that internal migration and, in particular, the educational selectivity of migration are beneficial for economic growth. They contribute to the process whereby labor moves from activities in which productivity is low to activities where productivity is high. This move does not imply, however, that the rate or composition of migration flows is optimal. The premium earned by more educated urban employees may exceed the difference between more and less educated workers in productivity—as a consequence, for example, of government or union influence on wage structures and hiring rules. This implies that the gap between more and less educated rural residents in the private returns to migration exceeds the gap in social returns and that the educational selectivity of migration may be greater than is optimal for economic growth.

Growing urban unemployment among school-leavers in developing countries may be a manifestation of above-optimal migration of the educated. The urban structure of wages may be slow to adjust to the increased supply of (migrant) school-leavers that results from educational expansion. Rural school-leavers may then be encouraged to migrate and wait for jobs in well-paid urban occupations rather than immediately accept a rural job that pays significantly less; if the income difference is high enough and the probability of obtaining a higher paid job sufficiently large, a period of job seeking or unemployment will yield a higher expected lifetime income. This pattern is a variant of what has come to be known as the Todaro model (Todaro 1969).

In the 1970s and early 1980s it was thought that neither the social nor the private costs associated with excess migration were as serious as might appear,

since the unemployed were young, had few dependents, and were often supported by their families, and since most of them eventually found sources of employment (Berry and Sabot 1978). Various studies from that era demonstrated that the social rate of return to investment in education might have been high despite large numbers of educated unemployed (Psacharopoulos 1973).

Since the early 1980s, as urban areas in developing countries have exploded with rural migrants, it has become increasingly clear that the migration trends are problematic. Although some social benefits of rural–urban migration are clear (e.g., migrants provide cheap labor, they contribute to the economy through their consumption of goods and services, and they pay taxes), significant social costs are also incurred (Arthur 1991). Arthur's evidence from Ghana indicated that increased rural–urban migration has practically overwhelmed the cities' ability to provide essential services such as housing, transportation, water, and sewage. Gugler (1986) also stated that high rates of rural–urban migration have resulted in the overburdening of urban labor markets already characterized by unemployment and underemployment and have increased demand for urban housing and services in areas where they were already considered inadequate.

See also: Economics of the Brain Drain; Education and Labor Markets in Developing Nations

References

Arthur J A 1991 Interregional migration of labor in Ghana, West Africa: Determinants, consequences and policy intervention. *Review of Black Political Economy* Fall 1991: 89–103
Barnum H N, Sabot R H 1977 Education, employment probabilities and rural–urban migration in Tanzania. *Oxf. Bull. Econ. Stat.* 39: 109–26
Berry A, Sabot R H 1978 Labor market performance in developing countries. *World Dev.* 6: 1199–242
Chenery H B, Syrquin M 1975 *Patterns of Development, 1950–1970.* Oxford University Press, London
Cole W E, Sanders R D 1985 Internal migration and employment. *Am. Econ. Rev.* 75(3): 481–94
Cole W E, Sanders R D 1986 Internal migration and employment: Reply *Am. Econ. Rev.* 76(3): 570–72
du Toit B M 1990 People on the move, rural–urban migration with special reference to the Third World: Theoretical and empirical perspectives. *Human Organization* 49(4): 305–19
Gugler J 1986 Internal migration in the Third World. In: Pacione M (ed.) 1986 *Population Geography: Progress and Prospect.* Croom Helm, London
Jamison D T, Lau L L 1982 *Farmer Education and Farm Efficiency.* Johns Hopkins University Press, Baltimore, Maryland
Lemel H 1989 Urban skill acquisition strategies: The case of two Turkish villages. *Human Organization* 48(3): 252–61

Levy M E, Wadycki W J 1974 Education and the decision to migrate: An econometric analysis of migration in Venezuela. *Econometrica* 42: 377–89

Psacharopoulos G 1973 *Returns to Education: An International Comparison.* Elsevier, Amsterdam

Sahn D E, Alderman H 1988 *The Effects of Human Capital on Wages, and the Determinants of Labor Supply in a Developing Country.* North-Holland, Amsterdam

Schultz T P 1982 Notes on the estimation of migration decision functions. In: Sabot R H (ed.) 1982 *Migration and the Labor Market in Developing Countries.* Westview Press, Boulder, Colorado

Todaro M 1969 A model of labor migration and urban unemployment in less developed countries. *Am. Econ. Rev.*: 138–48

Todaro M 1976 *Internal Migration in Developing Countries: A Review of Theory, Evidence, Methodology, and Research Priorities.* International Labour Organisation, Geneva

Todaro M 1986 Internal Migration and Urban Employment: Comment. *Am. Econ. Rev.* 76(3): 566–69

Yap L 1977 The attraction of the cities: A review of the migration literature. *J. Dev. Econ.* 4: 239–64

Economics of the Brain Drain

H. G. Grubel

This entry treats the economics of the brain drain. First, it gives a definition of the concept and explains why it is of such great political and emotional importance. It then discusses the motives of brain drain migrants and the problems of measuring the size of brain drain flows. The final parts consist of a study of the welfare effects of the brain drain and some policy proposals for dealing with it.

The material presented here draws heavily on scholarly works dealing with the economics of the brain drain by Adams (1968) and Grubel and Scott (1977) and on works with a more general emphasis on the economics of human capital and migration such as those by Schultz (1963), Becker (1964), and Psacharopoulos (1973). Blume (1968) and Dedijer and Svenningson (1967) are bibliographies of early writings on the brain drain. Recent publications concerning the brain drain are indexed under the heading "International Migration" (code F22) for journals and "International Factor Movements" (code F2) for books in the *Journal of Economic Literature*.

Public concern over the brain drain arose during the 1980s and into the 1990s as a result of the special circumstances of some countries. For example, China was faced with large numbers of nonreturning students as a result of the political upheavals of the late 1980s. Emigration of scientists and engineers from the former Soviet Union can be expected. The brain drain is a concern for territories within countries, such as Catalonia which seek greater independence from central government. However, these problems have not given rise to a literature containing new theoretical insights or empirical results of broad general interest.

1. Definition and Historical Background

The concept of the brain drain is popularly used to refer to the migration of highly skilled individuals who are trained in one country and take up residence and work in another. Such migration has taken place throughout history, but it became the focus of public attention during the early 1960s when the United States embarked on a major increase of expenditure on science and engineering in order to meet the Soviet challenge symbolized by the launching of Sputnik. This increased expenditure created an excess demand for highly skilled personnel that was met by immigration at a time when, generally speaking, United States laws severely limited the inflow of foreigners.

At the same time, developing countries launched major efforts to industrialize and other industrial nations attempted to catch up with the technological and scientific standards of the United States. The loss of highly skilled workers was believed to frustrate these countries' efforts at economic development and the brain drain became a widely discussed political issue. During the late 1960s and 1970s the brain drain from developing countries to Western Europe and multinational organizations also became sizable and the phenomenon was recognized as a more general problem.

For economic science the brain drain is a component of two separate traditional fields of study: migration and human capital. In the terminology of these fields it involves the crossing of international borders by human capital in the form of migrants. The value of this human capital is not recorded in conventional statistics on the international balance of payments.

It is worth noting that there are other forms of human capital flows across borders which are not considered to be part of the brain drain. Examples of this phenomenon are a professor who delivers a lecture abroad or an engineer who works on a foreign construction site. Payment for these services enters balance of payments statistics. On the other hand, individuals who study abroad and return to their home countries also transfer human capital across borders which is not reflected in international balance of payments statistics. Foreign study is often discussed in the context of the brain drain but stricltly speaking it is not part of the basic phenomenon, either conceptually or in terms of public policy concerns.

The preceding considerations suggest that the economics of the brain drain might be called less emotively the economics of unrecorded international human capital flows associated with permanent migration. However, the use of the term "brain drain" is so well-established that it is advantageous to continue its use even in analytical and quantitative studies of the phenomenon.

2. Motives for Migration of Highly Skilled Workers

Motives for migration generally—and of students and highly skilled workers in particular—are complex. However, the following considerations dominate the decision to migrate by persons with high levels of training: prospects for real income, professional opportunities, working conditions, and sociological–cultural aspects of life. The migrant considers each of these four elements by comparing conditions between the native land and foreign countries. Personal tastes and circumstances as well as costs of transaction and travel enter individuals' decisions to migrate.

The basic calculus is known to many people from personal experience or can readily be envisaged. In practice it is made very difficult by uncertainties surrounding all decision variables and the need to discount future prospects in both the countries of emigration and immigration. It is facilitated by the fact that migration can usually be reversed if uncertain events turn out unfavorably. Formal models of the decision-making calculus are found in the literature noted below.

2.1 Survey Studies

One type of empirical research on the motives of brain drain migrants tends to be based on questionnaires designed and administered by sociologists. For a massive study using this approach see Glaser (1973). Such studies have tended to find that respondents give professional opportunities as their primary motive, while earnings and living conditions are relatively unimportant. Skepticism has been expressed about the meaning of these findings, since respondents may well have been rationalizing their motives and have been conditioned to do so by social pressures in their home countries. It is simply not socially acceptable to leave one's home country and the source of finance for one's education in order to enjoy a higher living standard abroad. On the other hand, going abroad for better research opportunities, is a more socially acceptable motive.

2.2 Economists' Studies

Economists who have studied migratory patterns have found support for the basic economic models applicable to all migration: people move in order to maximize the present value of their expected earnings net of costs of moving and adjustment. In particular, the propensity to become a brain drain migrant is an increasing function of differences in income at home and the countries of destination.

These economists' findings on the motives for the brain drain point to the difficulties of solving it in the short run through government policies. Restrictions on international travel can stop the emigration of highly skilled persons but only at high cost in terms of equity and efficiency. Raising incomes of highly skilled persons in the country of emigration creates inefficient and inequitable income gaps between trained and untrained people.

3. Magnitude of Brain Drain Flows

Initially, during the 1960s, evidence on the magnitude of the brain drain was primarily anecdotal. Newspapers provided a fund of supposedly representative stories. Efforts by scholars to quantify the phenomenon were frustrated by the lack of easily accessible and suitable data. The most readily available data for any kind of quantification were those of the United States Immigration and Naturalization Service. They showed that there were indeed large numbers of highly skilled migrants who acquired United States immigration visas. In some fields such as nursing and medicine the numbers represented sizable proportions of total United States graduates with such skills. For skills other than medical, however, the flows by and large represented relatively small proportions of the stocks of professionals and of the number of newly trained personnel in the United States and most other countries receiving the emigrants.

Using the United States statistics on flows and multiplying the number of migrants by the estimated present value of their earnings due to higher education, that is, their human capital value, produced figures that were large relative to United States foreign aid, especially in the case of India. This fact was used by some politicians to dramatize the problem of the brain drain and to demand action by the United States or by the world at large to remedy the resultant injustices. As will be seen below, it is highly misleading to compare flows of foreign aid and migrating human capital in order to make inferences about welfare effects and moral debt relationships.

3.1 Problems with United States Immigration Statistics

Later research, as summarized by Friborg (1975), revealed that the United States immigration statistics and the early uses they were put to failed to reflect three important aspects of the brain drain. First, a substantial proportion of immigrants to the United States were individuals who had obtained part or all of their higher education in the United States and were financed by United States funds or their own work. Therefore, their migration was the result of the general willingness of the United States to permit immigration to take place and to open its educational institutions to foreigners. Both of these policies were welcomed by most people during the period when living and educational standards in the United States exceeded those of the rest of the world, typically by a large margin.

Information on the educational background of brain drain migrants was obtained through analysis of the biographies of United States scientific and technical personnel kept by the National Science Foundation. This analysis showed that a foreign Ph D was held by only one-third of foreign-born United States scientists.

Second, the United States statistics failed to record return flows of highly skilled people to their native or to third countries. At the same time, no countries keep records of returning natives classed by education levels. Therefore, information on net flows could be obtained only from statistics on stocks specifically assembled for this purpose or obtained from other data sources in the countries losing brain drain migrants. Thus, military and church records in some European countries showed that for some professions during the 1960s emigration to the United States tended to be matched by large return flows. As a result, net migration averaged only about 30 percent of the gross. Analogous data for developing countries are not available.

Third, the United States immigration data contained no information on the number and human capital value of migrants returning to their home or native countries after study in the United States. Since the brain drain is just one aspect of the international circulation of human capital and can be seen as simply a cost of foreign student training, the value of student capital gains should be compared to the value of the genuine brain drain capital losses for individual countries. A special survey of Canadian economists in Canada and in the United States revealed that even though Canada suffered a deficit on its conventional brain drain account, its overall human capital account was positive by a large margin because many Canadians obtain graduate degrees in the United States (see Grubel and Scott 1977).

The continuous and accurate measurement of presently unrecorded international human capital flows is highly desirable, since the existence of such information would permit a more rational discussion of, and policies for control of, the brain drain. However, the required basic data are not collected routinely and the cost of new data collection procedures is very high. Therefore it is highly unlikely that official statistics will be generated soon, especially since the subject appears to have lost some of its public appeal in the major industrial countries. We may expect, instead, to receive sporadic information generated by special research efforts of scholars in the tradition of the study noted in the preceding paragraph.

4. Welfare Effects: Short-run Output Effects

When a country unexpectedly loses a highly skilled person through emigration there are likely to be short-run adjustment costs. These costs arise from the fact that efficiency requires an optimal mix of human capital with physical capital and unskilled labor. Thus when a supervising engineer suddenly leaves a plant, in the extreme case machines and labor have to remain idle until a replacement is found. Typically, however, engineers are not totally indispensable and output of firms deprived of some of their human capital drops only to a certain extent. In addition, temporary losses can be eliminated if the departure of the engineer is known in advance and a replacement has been trained.

The argument just presented in the context of an individual firm or plant also applies in its basic outline to society as a whole. The main difference is that replacements of skilled persons cannot simply be hired from other jobs but require time-consuming education. They may therefore involve longer periods of inefficient operating procedures. However, if emigration can be predicted it is possible to plan education levels to avoid such short-run shortages of skilled people.

In the real world, short-run adjustment costs are likely to be minor since there is a high elasticity of substitution between different types of human capital. In addition, in some countries like India, emigration losses have been quite predictable and often permitted the hiring of highly skilled workers who otherwise would have been unemployed. In the case of such countries short-run losses are small or zero.

5. Long-run Output Effects

Long-run output effects of the emigration of human capital can usefully be analyzed with the help of what is known as the generalized theory of capital. According to this model, society can invest its stock of capital in knowledge, and human and physical capital. Markets, competition, and laws protecting the rights to the ownership of knowledge capital result in a tendency for society's output to be maximized. In technical terms, in efficient equilibrium the marginal productivity of each capital form is the same and equal to the interest rate. One implication of this neoclassical model is that the three types of capital can be added up to find the overall endowment of labor with capital.

This model can be used to study the long-run output effects of the brain drain. A country may be hypothesized which is initially in efficient equilibrium in its use of the three types of capital. Assuming that this country loses a certain amount of human capital and labor through emigration, then a reallocation of society's remaining capital stock is likely to be necessary and to involve the short-run adjustment costs noted above. The *total* output of that country will be lowered. However, for rational assessment of the welfare effects of the brain drain it is essential to consider what effect this loss of labor and capital has on the per capita output of the remaining population.

It turns out that under relatively simple and standard assumptions about the nature of the production function, total output per capita in the country of emigration may be raised, lowered, or remain unchanged. It will be lowered if the amount of human capital lost when the average emigrant leaves is greater than the original overall capital per worker in the home country. This is the case simply because under these conditions the country's stock of capital per worker is lowered. Since productivity and output are an increasing function of the overall capital–labor ratio, the smaller ratio brought about by the emigration leads to lower labor productivity and reduced income per capita.

The same reasoning can be applied to the cases where emigrants take with them different amounts of capital. Average output remains unchanged if the emigrants' capital per person equals the country's initial overall stock of capital per worker. The output is raised if emigrants take away less than the average.

An interesting result of this model is that the emigration of unskilled workers, who do not divest the country of any capital, always raises output per capita of the remaining workers. This fact may well explain why there is so rarely any opposition to the emigration of unskilled workers. Another interesting result stems from the estimate that in the mid-1960s the human capital value of two years' university training in India was roughly equal to the average of human and physical capital of all Indian workers. This result implies that the loss of persons with that level of education left unchanged India's capital stock and therefore also output per worker.

The preceding model, if applied in a logically obvious fashion to assess the long-run output effect of brain drain immigration, leads to the same possible outcomes. The immigration of highly skilled persons can raise, lower, or leave unchanged the per capita income in the country of settlement. Because of the high opportunity cost of advanced education in industrial countries, it is likely that the immigration of professional and scientific personnel raises overall capital–labor ratios and incomes per capita.

The preceding model simplifies a complex process

in many ways but provides a useful focus and directs attention to the essential aspects of the migration of highly skilled persons.

6. Welfare Effects

6.1 The Nationalist Model

The brain drain became the source of much public concern in the 1960s and continues to form a major element of discussions at the United Nations Commission for Trade and Development (UNCTAD) and other UN agencies because of the following perception of the welfare effects and inequities (see UNCTAD 1979). The population of a country taxes itself to finance the operation of institutions of higher learning or the study of citizens abroad. This collective investment in education is made in expectation of general returns to society: the country's total output is raised, the productivity of cooperating factors of production is increased, a greater tax base permits raising more revenue to be spent on further development and on welfare projects, and the country as a whole moves into the modern age improved by science and technology and accompanying externalities. Moreover, competitive selection processes of education tend to provide education to the most gifted and dynamic young people who are sources of leadership generally and carriers of desirable genetic material.

Given these expectations of return from investment in the education of young people, their emigration or failure to return from study abroad represents a serious loss. Basically, the investment has been wasted and what makes this waste particularly pernicious is that it involves great inequities. For example, in developing countries people with low and average incomes have lowered their incomes to finance education, the benefits of which now accrue to the emigrants who live in relative opulence in industrial countries and add to the further development and tax base of peoples who already have incomes that are a multiple of those who financed the migrants' education. Projects for the provision of very basic technology and medical services in developing countries suffer or have to be abandoned because of the lack of skilled personnel, while those same brain drain migrants contribute to the unnecessary luxury of technical and medical projects in industrialized countries.

This nationalistic viewpoint often quantifies the effects of the brain drain by measuring the value of income earned by brain drain migrants in their countries of new residence. This sum is then considered to represent the inequitable transfer of resources from poor to rich nations. Under reasonable assumptions, the value of this transfer from some developing countries has been estimated to exceed the value of the foreign aid received from the industrial countries which received the brain drain migrants.

6.2 The Internationalist View

Economists have approached the analysis of the welfare effects of the brain drain by building logically rigorous models based on simple and widely accepted principles of economics. The resultant model and conclusions have become known as the internationalist approach for reasons that will become obvious. The basics of this model are as follows.

Consider a world of nation-states in which all people are paid an income equal to the value of their contribution to the nation's output. This assumption reflects one of the cornerstones of modern price theory and is known as the marginal productivity theory of factor incomes. It implies that there are no externalities from work so that a skilled person provides no benefits to society other than those for which payment is received. This assumption is unrealistic and will be relaxed below. As a second basic initial assumption consider that in this hypothetical world all education is financed privately by parents.

In the world described by such assumptions, the emigration of one or a small number of highly skilled persons leaves unchanged the welfare of those left behind. The migrants take with them both their contribution to and their claim upon the country's output, which are of equal value. In the country of immigration, the brain drain migrants earn an amount equal to their contribution to output. They use their earnings to buy what they have produced. As a result, the incomes of the people in the country of immigration are unchanged.

The migrants, however, raise their own incomes. From this analysis follows the important fundamental conclusion that migration generally, and the migration of highly skilled people in particular, raises world output and welfare: the income of the migrants is raised and that of the population in the receiving and sending countries is unchanged.

6.3 Role of Education Financing

The basic model above may be amended by introducing the fact that the education of children is typically undertaken by taxpayers. The analysis is facilitated by considering first the case where all education is financed by parents. Under this assumption, all obligations arising from education are between members of a family. Emigration of the educated leaves unchanged the welfare of those citizens who are not members of the emigrant's family. The basic results of the model are unchanged, except that there is some effect on the welfare of the emigrant's family.

The welfare effect on the emigrant's family can be viewed from two polar positions. Under the first, the education of children is considered to be an investment good which yields returns when the children look after the welfare of their parents in old age. Emigration of the educated person reduces, increases, or leaves unchanged the welfare of the family, depending on the transfers which the emigrants make from abroad. In the case of emigrants from developing countries resident in industrial countries, it is likely that their higher incomes permit them to send to their families more rather than less of the expected return on the investment in their education. Under these conditions, the welfare of the family will be raised. In principle, however, the outcome is indeterminate.

Under the second basic view children are a consumption good. Parents have a moral obligation to raise and educate their offspring, as their parents, and indeed every generation of parents, have done. The obligation of every productive generation is not to their parents but to their own children. Under this view, educated emigrants leave no obligations behind because they take along their offspring. There is no change in the welfare of the families who financed their education or in that of the rest of the population.

These two views of the nature of the obligation arising from education can readily be translated into the more realistic situation where it is financed by the government rather than the family. Under the investment view, emigrants owe repayment to the government. The obligation is payable through taxes which are used to provide public pensions, medical care, and similar welfare programs for the elderly. These payments are equivalent to those children providing for their aged parents in the absence of modern government programs. Under these assumptions, emigration involves a clear-cut reneging on a moral obligation. It lowers the welfare of those left behind who face an increased tax burden to take care of the elderly.

Under the consumption view of children, on the other hand, those left behind do not suffer a reduction in welfare since the emigrants take along with them both their contributions to taxes used for financing education and their children on whom this tax money would have to be spent.

This discussion shows that there exists no simple and unique assessment of the welfare effects of migration due to the public financing of education. However, the model increases an understanding of the public and largely political debate. The investment view of children and education probably dominates attitudes in developing countries while the consumption view appears to dominate attitudes in industrial countries. If this judgement is correct it may help to explain why concern over the inequities of the brain drain is so much more prevalent in developing than in industrialized countries.

6.4 General Government Taxes and Services

The basic approach to the analysis of government-financed education of emigrants can readily be applied to all government services. Emigrants reduce tax revenue and demand for all government services simultaneously. They thus leave unchanged tax burdens on those remaining behind. By analogy, there are no gains to taxpayers in countries of immigration.

There may be some secondary effects on welfare if the taxes paid exceed the value of benefits received. Typically, however, educated high-income taxpayers also demand high levels and quality of legal, police, pension, education, and similar services. The basic model also needs modification if government services are provided through large, fixed investment, and migration affects average costs. However, expenditures on such major government programs as defense and roads are fixed only in the short run and long-run average costs are likely to be constant.

6.5 Externalities from Work of Migrants

Highly educated people are believed to provide societies with many positive externalities through leadership and contributions to the arts, sciences, and culture generally. To the extent that this is true, the emigration of highly trained individuals lowers the welfare of those left behind. It also raises welfare in countries of immigration.

However, the importance of these externalities is debatable. Most artistic, scientific, and technical contributions are rewarded through salaries or the sale of copyrighted publications and patents. They typically leave uncompensated only those contributions to nationalistic feelings of pride held predominantly by an intellectual and artistic elite. The production of pure knowledge that cannot be patented is usually an international good, the benefits of which accrue to the world as a whole including the home country of the brain drain emigrant. The real benefits of a scientific breakthrough leading to a cancer cure, for example, accrue to Indians whether an Indian scientist does the research in the United States or in his or her native country.

It is also misleading to consider the scientific and other achievements of brain drain migrants in their new countries of residence and infer that the real benefits or glory of their achievement would have accrued to their home countries if they had not emigrated. In many instances, these achievements would not have been possible in the home countries because of the lack of support facilities, colleagues, and other factors contributing to scientific and artistic productivity.

Highly skilled persons may also occasionally be considered to create negative externalities. At certain periods of history, academics (particularly the academic proletariat of underemployed intellectuals) have provided the stimulus for civil unrest and revolutions that turned out not to have been in the long-term interest of countries. The emigration of such highly skilled potential revolutionaries may then have positive externalities for their home countries.

6.6 Nonmarginal Flows

The analysis of welfare effects tacitly assumed that migration involved small numbers and therefore could be treated as marginal. As noted above, brain drain flows have been and are marginal by almost all standards. However, cumulatively through time, such flows can reach a size where they should be considered to be nonmarginal. Under these conditions, the following modification of the basic model and conclusions are necessary.

First, nonmarginal migration changes the relative income of capital and labor. For example, the emigration of a large number of persons with human capital above the average capital per person lowers the capital–labor ratio in the losing country. As a result, labor income falls relative to the income of capital. This analysis might easily be applied to differnt assumptions about the amount of capital taken away by emigrants. It can also be applied to the study of the effects of migration on income distribution in the receiving country.

The assessment of the importance of these income redistribution effects on welfare depends not only on their magnitude but also on the analyst's views about the merit of given relative incomes of labor and capital. Nonmarginal brain drain migration probably lowers the relative wages of unskilled labor and raises returns to capital in developing countries, whereas it does the opposite in industrial countries. Widely held ethical norms about income distribution in the postwar years are likely to regard these changes as undesirable. Their presumed existence is probably responsible for much of the concern over the effects of the brain drain among leaders of developing countries and in the forums of international organizations.

Second, in the standard models of consumer and producer surplus, nonmarginal changes generate deadweight losses or gains in welfare measured by triangles often referred to as "Harberger triangles." In commonsense terms, these effects reflect the changed opportunities of economic agents to engage in welfare-enhancing market exchange. They have been estimated to have relatively minor effects on welfare by most students of the subject and are predominantly a concern of scholars.

6.7 Benefits from Mobility

In the technical and quantitative discussion of the economic effects of the brain drain, sight is often lost of the fact that it is part of the general phenomenon of the international circulation of human beings that includes travel for business, recreation, and study, all of which involve stays abroad of varying length. As noted above, some of the seemingly permanent brain drain migration involves stays of limited duration and there is some practical ambiguity between study, advanced training, and permanent migration.

The international circulation of people generally provides enormous benefits to humanity. The educational experiences of travel are widely recognized. Most contemporary leaders in all fields of human endeavor have studied or worked abroad temporarily during their careers. Contact among people of different nationalities raises tolerance and understanding and thus lowers the risk of international conflict. There is no doubt that without the international circulation of people the world would be a much less attractive place. The brain drain, which involves some people extending or making permanent their stay abroad, may usefully be considered as part of the cost, much like the cost of transportation, that has to be incurred in order to derive these benefits.

7. Policy Recommendations

Given the public concern over the brain drain and the political rhetoric it generates in international organizations, there have been surprisingly few solid policy proposals on either how to reduce it or how to deal with its consequences. Those policy recommendations that do exist fall into three categories.

First, there are those policies that would reduce the incentives without interfering with the flow of students and professionals in any way. The basic objective of these policies is to raise the incomes and working conditions of highly skilled people in countries that suffer from the brain drain. These policy recommendations are unrealistic in that, given the scarcity of resources and many different development objectives of most countries, raising highly skilled peoples' incomes and expanding research facilities are not the most important priorities. Moreover, it would lead to inequities and inefficiencies. The creation of international research institutes where scientists from developing countries might obtain temporary work and update their skills has been proposed but has failed to find sponsors.

Second, there have been proposals to make the immigration policies of countries that gain from the brain drain less discriminatory in favor of highly skilled people, and to make it more difficult for students and temporary visitors to obtain permanent resident status.

United States and Canadian policies have been made less discriminatory in favor of highly skilled migrants. This was done mainly as part of a more general attempt to reduce discrimination in economic and social policies. It probably had less influence on the level of the brain drain than did changes in science policies and overall economic prosperity. However, the governments of industrial countries have resisted all pressure from more radical elements in developing countries to initiate straight forward procedures whereby foreign students and other highly skilled persons can be extradited at the request of their native countries' governments. There has been concern about the abuse of such procedures for political purposes. Developing countries have generally attempted to use legal means to assure the return of students sponsored by official sources, but they have no effective leverage to secure the return of privately sponsored students. Except for

countries of the Soviet bloc prior to 1989–90, none have ever introduced prohibitions on travel to prevent the brain drain.

The third set of proposals is aimed at redressing the inequities which are alleged to arise, according to the nationalistic view, from the debt on educational outlay owed to the losing countries. One set of proposals suggests bilateral intergovernmental compensation agreements. Such an approach might encourage the development of international specialization in the production and export of human skills.

Another widely discussed set of proposals requires that brain drain migrants be assessed for a special tax surcharge which is transmitted to the countries in which they were educated, either directly or through some international organization. The main problem with these proposals is that they involve law enforcement and tax agents of one country, say the United States, in the enforcement of the laws and judgments of another country, say India, without allowing the individual any opportunity to appeal against judgments reached in the foreign country. These proposals have not been adopted, though they have been discussed intensively through the initiative of J Bhagwati (see Bhagwati and Martington 1976).

See also: Immigrants' Economic Performance and Education; Internal Migration and Education

References

Adams W (ed.) 1968 *The Brain Drain*. Macmillan New York

Becker G 1964 *Human Capital. A Theoretical and Empirical Analysis, with Special Reference to Education*. Columbia University Press for the National Bureau of Economic Research, New York

Bhagwati J, Martington M (eds.) 1976 *Taxing the Brain Drain: A Proposal*, Vols. 1, 2. North Holland, Amsterdam

Blume S 1968 "Brain drain"—a look at the literature. *Universities Quarterly* 22: 281–90

Dedijer S, Svenningson L 1967 *Brain Drain and Brain Gain: A Bibliography on Migration of Scientists, Engineers, Doctors and Students*. Research Policy Program, Lund

Friborg G 1975 *Brain Drain Statistics: Empirical Evidence and Guidelines*. NFR Report No. 6 Swedish Research Council Committee on Research Economics, Stockholm

Glaser W A 1973 *The Migration and Return of Professionals*. Bureau of Applied Social Research, Columbia University, New York

Grubel H, Scott A 1977 *The Brain Drain: Determinants, Measurement and Welfare Effects*. Wilfred Laurier University Press, Waterloo

Psacharopoulos G, Hinchliffe K 1973 *Returns to Education: An International Comparison*. Elsevier, Amsterdam

Schultz T 1963 *The Economic Value of Education*. Columbia University Press, New York

UNCTAD 1979 *The Reverse Transfer of Technology: A Survey of its Main Features, Causes and Policy Implications*. Publication sales No. E.79.II.D.10, United Nations, New York

Public Sector Employment and Education

K. Hinchliffe

The public sector as a source of employment for graduates of the education system is the focus of this article. In many countries, particularly low income ones, the public sector is the majority or main employer. The nature of public sector employment has been widely discussed in the literature on labor market segmentation and its role in determining several wider aspects of both employment and earnings structures, and the consequent effect on parts of the educational process, remains contentious.

Since the late 1960s, a great deal of attention in labor economics has concentrated on the supposed existence of segmented labor markets and the attempted refutation of this supposition by neoclassical/human capital economists. In segmentation theory, most public sector employment is viewed simply as one component of what is termed "primary segment employment" and shares the characteristics of that segment along with parts of the bureaucratized private sector. In the first section of this entry, therefore, broad elements of segmentation theory including hiring practices and internal labor markets are introduced and discussed as they relate to jobs in the primary segment. Despite this emphasis in the literature differentiating between job characteristics rather than between employment sectors (public/private), some economists continue to be concerned with wage and employment determination in the public sector under nonprofit-maximizing conditions and with comparing the outcomes to those in the private sector. This work is discussed in section 2. Finally, attention is concentrated on the public sector in less developed countries (LDCs). This separate treatment results from arguments that the public sector's dominance as an employer in these countries has particularly important repercussions on earnings levels and structures, the demand for schooling, and the structure and quality of education itself.

1. Segmentation Theory and the Public Sector

Until the late 1960s, the general issue of public versus private earnings and conditions of employment was not accorded a great deal of attention in the economics literature on developed market economies where the "prevailing wage rate" model had been used. In this model the public sector is simply regarded as just another price-taker accepting a market-determined rate. Regardless of differences in types of goods and services produced, the technology used, and profitability and ownership of establishments, the model supposes that competition in the labor market will ensure that all workers with the same economic characteristics will receive similar rates of pay. If differentials occur between the public and the private sectors, they are interpreted as the results of short-term adjustment lags. This is one of several positions associated with neoclassical economic theory which labor market segmentation theory has come to contest.

Segmentation theory, with its central feature of a dual labor market, attempts to refute neoclassical assumptions of the existence of a single continuum of both workers and firms operating under conditions of perfect competition. In contrast, it asserts that the labor force is fragmented into groups with specific and permanent characteristics (race, sex, class, etc.) and that members of these groups face different sets of working conditions, which in turn are determined by a differentiated structure of labor demand. At its simplest, a dual labor market has been defined as one in which:

(a) there is a pronounced division of jobs into higher and lower paying sectors, or primary and secondary segments;

(b) mobility across the boundary between these sectors is restricted;

(c) higher paid jobs are tied to promotional ladders while lower paid jobs have fewer opportunities for promotion; and

(d) higher paying jobs are relatively stable, while lower paid jobs are unstable (Loveridge and Mok 1979).

While there are variations among theorists as to the causes of segmentation ranging from technological determinism on the one hand to the conscious division of the working class on the other, all segmentation theories attempt to establish that there are at least two types of job, each with "distinct criteria for hiring and advancement, supervisory procedures, working conditions and wage levels, and each with generally different groups who fill the jobs" (Carnoy 1977 p. 32). While the public sector invariably includes jobs requiring a very wide variety of skills and offering wide variations in pay, as well as many jobs in which only some of the criteria listed above are appropriate (e.g., stable but low paid), there is general agreement that the majority fall into the primary segment.

A central feature of segmentation models, and one which is said to be particularly relevant to a description of the public sector, is the existence of internal labor markets in primary segment jobs. Hiring practices in the public sector and in the large private concerns center around sex, race, and particularly, educational qualifications. Whether these are used as proxies for cognitive or noncognitive productivity-enhancing characteristics, for measures of individuals' trainability, or simply as measures to divide the work force is still debated. However, once hired into the primary segment, workers become part of an internal labor market, that is, a fully developed labor market specific and internal to each employing institution and largely isolated from labor markets outside.

While being an important part of recently constructed segmentation models, the concept of the internal labor market and the structure of rules determining entry to and exit from this market, plus the "seniority ladders" and "job clusters" which allow for movement within it, were first developed by Kerr in the early 1950s (Kerr 1954). According to segmentation theorists, members of internal labor markets are relatively insulated from the competitive pressures of the external labor market and well-developed promotional ladders exist for them. An explanation of the development of internal labor markets based on the necessity for enterprise-specific skills to be developed, and the cheaper training costs of individuals already in an establishment, has been provided by Doeringer and Piore (1971). In addition, worker stability is encouraged by the seniority promotion system which regulates promotion along finely regulated job ladders. To the economic rationale behind the operation of internal labor markets, Doeringer and Piore also add "custom and practice," arguing that relative wages along job ladders are defined in this way rather than by reference to supply and demand. Finally, the development of internal labor markets that appear to favor the existing labor force is said to be encouraged by the trade unions and, indeed, a widely observed feature of primary segment employment is the very high level of unionization.

It is commonly argued that in several respects the public sector typically appears to contain many of the features associated with primary segment employment. Hiring practices are largely centered on the "objective" criterion of educational qualifications (which rise over time as education expands), security of employment is high, opportunities to enter this sector at the higher levels are few and internal promotion prevalent, and salaries are fixed administratively more by reference to custom and practice than to supply and demand. However, as the next section implies, not all economists completely share this view of the workings of the labor market.

2. Earnings Comparability in the Public and Private Sectors

Several empirical comparisons of public and private sector earnings have been made. These have generally utilized broad averages for the two sectors or have made comparisons of the pay associated with a given range of jobs. Fewer comparisons have been made of the earnings of public and private sector employees on the basis of their levels of education and experience. Reder's (1975) presentation of United States data for 1959 and 1969 is one exception. Among his conclusions is that, for virtually all age groups, public sector average hourly earnings are above those in the private sector. Introducing years of schooling into the comparison leads to the opposite result for all workers in each category, in as much as the private sector invariably pays the highest wages. However, disaggregating the work force by gender and racial groups results in this positive differential between private and public sector holding only for White males and not for females or for Blacks of either sex.

In the early 1980s, Psacharopoulos (1983) compared public and private sector earnings in six countries: the United Kingdom, Greece, Portugal, Brazil, Colombia, and Malaysia. Some of the results of this cross-national comparison are as follows:

(a)   Average earnings in the public sector are significantly higher than in the private sector.

(b)   Comparing earnings by educational level, differentials between public and private sectors are positive at the lower levels of education but are negative in three of the six countries at higher education levels.

(c)   Within both employment sectors (public and private) differentials increase by educational level but are widest for all educational level comparisons in the private sector.

(d)   When age, as a proxy for experience, is considered and earnings regressions fitted, the resulting private rates of return are higher for those people employed in the private sector in all countries.

(e)   The different prices received by the two sets of workers for their education and experience were found to be statistically significant, implying that the earnings-determining process is structurally different in the two sectors.

Some of these findings are used by Psacharopoulos in an attempt to discredit the screening, job competition, and dual labor market hypotheses and to refute the view that the public sector dominates the entire earnings structure. Each of the arguments and interpretations put forward, however, would be strongly contested by advocates of these positions. This entry confines itself to noting that, in the context of the previous section, it is not totally appropriate to argue that because education-related average earnings are higher in the private sector, this runs counter to a basic prediction of the dualist hypothesis. This would only follow if all public sector jobs were defined as being in the primary segment. Earnings in the primary segment of the private sector may be so much greater than those in the public sector that the lower earnings in the private secondary segment are not capable of dragging average private sector earnings down to the public sector average. Equally important, the fact that private sector earnings are higher than those in the public sector for qualified labor does not necessarily mean that the public sector is passive and follows the behavior of the private sector. It is equally feasible to suppose that the public sector does set earnings levels but because of the greater security of employment and automatic promotion in that sector, private employers have to offer a higher wage. Many segmentation theorists argue that while all workers probably receive less than their marginal product, the relative gap between marginal product and earnings is greatest for those with low levels of schooling (Carnoy 1977 p. 161).

3. The Public Sector in Less Developed Countries

Despite the continued strong advocacy of the neoclassical "prevailing wage rate" model in industrialized market economies and isolated attempts to argue that the public sector in the less developed countries (LDCs) simply responds to earnings structures in the private sector, a conventional wisdom has developed which maintains that the public sector in these countries totally dominates the entire labor market. This is then said to result in the public service significantly influencing earnings structures for the educated work force and, through the emphasis on qualifications in hiring practices and the response of raising qualification requirements in the face of a surplus of school leavers, having undesirable effects on the ways in which schools operate (Dore 1976).

A description of public sector employment in the early 1980s in LDCs is given by Squire (1981). Figures presented for the public sector's share in the total labor force range from 1 percent in Upper Volta (now Burkina Faso) to 25.7 percent in Trinidad and Tobago. Naturally, as shares of the wage labor force they are higher. The 11 countries described by Squire have an average of around 16 percent of their wage labor force in the public sector. None of these countries is in sub-Saharan Africa. According to Lindauer et al. (1988) public service employment as a percentage of total formal sector employment in 1983 was 16 percent in Liberia, 34 percent in Mali, 37 percent in Zambia, 43 percent in Nigeria, and 45 percent in Senegal. To these can be added a further figure of between 5 and 38 percent in parastatal employment. Workers with a secondary school education and above are even more concentrated in this sector. During the 1970s and early 1980s annual growth rates of public sector employment in African countries were often substantial, reaching 15–16 percent in Ghana and Nigeria.

Wages in the public sector are set according to administratively determined pay scales which tend to relate directly to educational certificates. Many studies written in the 1960s—particularly directed at countries in Africa and the Asian subcontinent—argued that not only did these pay scales fail to reflect existing labor market conditions and changes in them, but also that they dominated pay arrangements in the private sector. A further concern was that earnings structures appeared to reward general education, leading to clerical jobs more than technical education which, it was contended, was more relevant to the needs of the LDCs. The International Labour Organisation (1971) pointedly noted, for instance, that in Sri Lanka an assistant clerk received 40 percent more than an unskilled engineering worker in both 1948 and 1967, despite the substantial growth of secondary school-leaver unemployment over this period. It has been on the basis of observations such as this that early critics of the rate-of-return approach to educational planning in LDCs partly based their case. According to Balogh and Streeten (1963 p. 102), a high observed rate of return would simply show "that pay scales in the civil service, universities and professions are still governed by the traditional standards of a feudal or colonial aristocracy and by natural or artificial restrictions" since earnings differentials in no way reflect competitive labor market conditions.

From the premise that the public sector dominates the labor market and determines the levels of wages, it has frequently been argued that these levels remain impervious to changing conditions in the labor market and that, as a result, excess supply or unemployment does not lead to a fall in wages. Consequently, the blame for the continuation or growth of school-leaver unemployment is often attributed directly to the public sector where, it is claimed, the solution can also be found. Squire (1981) provides a good example:

> The rapid expansion in educational output has not elicited the appropriate response in public pay scales and, given the slow rate of adjustment in job expectations, the result has been unemployment. Given that the public sector both determines the supply of educated workers (through its educational policy) and the demand for such (through its role as employer) the solution to the problem of educated unemployment is within the immediate sphere of policy influence. (Squire 1981 p. 121).

The assumption that the central position of the public sector in the labor market in LDCs results in that sector both dominating earnings structures and paying excessive wages which are inflexible downwards is being increasingly questioned. As regards the latter contention, since the late 1970s there have been substantial falls in real wages across most African and Latin American countries following severe bouts of economic recession which have resulted in the increases of periodic awards being below the levels of inflation (Jamal and Weeks 1988). For example, in Sudan between 1975 and 1983 real salaries fell by 11–15 percent annually. In many cases, public service incomes have fallen by significantly more than the fall in real average per capita incomes and by more than those in the rest of the formal sector, or primary segment (Lindauer et al. 1988). Further, while incomes of government employees have fallen in general, those of the more educated have tended to fall furthest with a squeezing of differentials resulting from the granting of equal absolute wage increases across all categories of employee. The evidence across Africa points to considerably higher incomes (often double) in both the private and parastatal sectors than in the public sector for workers with comparable levels of education or skills. More recent work conducted within the World Bank utilizing data up to 1988 for 12 countries in Africa, Latin America and Asia again suggests the significant downward flexibility of real wages in the formal sector.

Another feature of the public sector labor market in the LDCs is the pronounced emphasis on schooling qualifications in both hiring and determining starting salaries. Both Dore (1976) and Foster (1977) have pointed out that as a result of the public sector's relatively large size in these countries, the effect that this has both throughout the labor market and on the degree of social mobility for those few who are able to acquire high-level qualifications is far greater than in the more industrialized market economies. Another important aspect of public sector employment practices concerns promotion. Blaug (1973) draws attention to a survey of university students in Sri Lanka showing that a majority of them preferred public sector employment because of the greater personal freedom and job security it afforded. This, he maintains, is a result of job performance rarely being assessed and internal promotion being virtually automatic. Recent evidence suggests that job security in the public service has been seriously eroded since the early 1980s.

The use of paper qualifications by the public service is perfectly understandable, given the high level of ignorance of the potential qualities of job applicants and the very high costs of assessing the performance of people in jobs. As Blaug (1973) argues, it is fruitless to suggest the abolition of pay scales tied to educational qualifications unless there is also a suggestion of what to put in their place. One suggestion has been a greater amount of job specification, which would define the components of jobs and the specific knowledge and skills required to perform them. Taking another path, it has been suggested that the answer lies in a mixture of earlier starts to careers with as much selection as possible within the employing organization and,

where preemployment selection has to occur, the use of tests which cannot be extensively prepared for (Dore 1976).

See also: Internal Labor Markets and Education; Segmented Labor Markets and Education

References

Balogh T, Streeten P 1963 The coefficient of ignorance. *Bull. Oxf. Univ. Stat.* 25 (2): 99–107
Blaug M 1973 *Education and the Employment Problem in Developing Countries.* International Labour Organisation, Geneva
Carnoy M 1977 *Segmented Labour Markets: A Review of the Theoretical and Empirical Literature and its Implications for Educational Planning.* International Institute for Educational Planning (IIEP), Paris
Doeringer P B, Piore M J 1971 *Internal Labor Markets and Manpower Analysis.* Heath, Lexington, Massachusetts
Dore R P 1976 *The Diploma Disease: Education Qualification and Development.* Allen and Unwin, London
Foster P J 1977 Education and social differentiation in less developed countries. *Comp. Educ. Rev.* 21 (2–3): 211–29
Jamal V, Weeks J 1988 The vanishing rural–urban gap in sub-Saharan Africa. *Int. Lab. Rev.* 127(3): 271–92
Kerr C 1954 The Balkanization of labor markets. In: Bakke E W (ed.) 1954 *Labor Mobility and Economic Opportunity.* MIT Press, Cambridge, Massachusetts
Lindover D L, Meesook O A, Suebsaeng P 1988 Government wage policy in Africa: Some findings and policy issues. *World Bank Res. Obs.* 3: 1–25
Loveridge R, Mok A L 1979 *Theories of Labor Market Segmentation: A Critique.* Nijhoff, The Hague
Psacharopoulos G 1983 Education and private versus public sector pay. *Lab Soc.* 8(2): 123–34
Reder M 1975 The theory of employment and wages in the public sector. In: Hamermesh D S (ed.) 1975 *Labor in the Public and Nonprofit Sectors.* Princeton University Press, Princeton, New Jersey
Squire L 1981 *Employment Policy in Developing Countries: A Survey of Issues and Evidence.* Oxford University Press, New York

Further Reading

Elliott R F 1991 *Labor Economics: A Comparative Text.* McGraw-Hill, London
Knight J B, Sabot R H 1987 Educational expansion, government policy and wage compression. *J. Dev. Econ.* 26: 201–21

Education and Labor Markets in Developing Nations

I. Llamas

Developing countries are characterized by dualism in their labor markets. Markets are divided between formal and informal sectors. These can be generally characterized as having high and low wages, respectively. They can also be identified as treating the education of those who work in them differently.

This entry analyzes labor market structures and how markets reward educational investment. Specifically, the analysis suggests that labor markets are segmented, that segmentation emerges from demand-side forces, and that the productive traits that define the quality of labor are rewarded differently in the two segments.

1. Formal and Informal Sectors

The concept of "developing countries" is applied to a wide diversity of nations with equally great diversity in the functioning of their wage determination institutions. In spite of such variation, labor markets in almost all developing countries are divided between formal and informal sectors. This dualism results from significant asymmetries and discontinuities within their economic systems. There are institutional asymmetries between formal and informal labor markets because they operate with two different labor settings, which generate significant differentials between their workers' productivity and wages. Moreover, the perceptible limitation of labor mobility between formal and informal sectors suggests the existence of labor market discontinuities (Kanbur and McIntosh 1987).

The International Labour Office (ILO) has been the principal supporter of the notion that developing societies' labor markets are divided between formal and informal sectors. The ILO defines the informal sector in negative terms as including "all economic activities which are not effectively subject to 'formal' rules of contracts, licenses, taxation, labor inspection, etc." (ILO 1987 Vol.1 p. 25). In contrast, the formal sector is defined as public and private sector employment that offers working conditions based on formal rules. There is not a perfect clear division between sectors, largely because of the multiple criteria used for their differentiation.

As in dualist models of economic development, the labor market sectors are interrelated. The informal sector may constitute a labor "reserve army," which sets the supply price of labor for the formal sector. The informal sector performs the role of an actual "reserve army" for the formal sector because workers acquire experience and training which become productive human capital when they move into formal activities (see *Education and Informal Labor Markets*). This reserve represents labor awaiting integration into the formal sector. Such labor may be working alternately in both formal and informal sectors (Hallak and Caillods 1981 p. 25). The informal sector can supply goods and services to households and firms in the formal sector, and may compete with the formal sector in retailing and in commodity production (ILO 1987 Vol.1 p. 26, Godfrey 1986 p. 141).

In both sectors there is a segmentation of workers and the payoff to human capital varies depending on the sector and the labor segment in which individuals are located. Labor segmentation is created by the demand for labor which is differentiated by wages and working conditions at the workplace. Segmentation is analyzed as defining differentiated labor markets with their own rules of wage determination.

The labor segmentation approach is compatible with the division of the economy between formal and informal sectors. The notion of dualism views a developing society as divided into two interrelated sectors. Labor segmentation refers to a differentiation of economic opportunities and rewards among objectively comparable groups of workers. It suggests a process of division and isolation of different social groups. This methodological approach is opposed to the neoclassical theory, which treats the labor market as a unified entity in which the allocation of labor is regulated by price mechanisms, and where employer and employee meet each other as equals. Neoclassicists assume that labor markets treat all workers with the same skills in exactly the same way. Contrarily, the labor segmentation approach shows that the rewards to workers depend not only on their productive traits (supply side of the market) but also on the structural working conditions or the sector in which they find an occupation; that is, the demand side of the market (Carnoy 1980, LLamas 1987 p. 15).

The dual model for the analysis of the economies of developing countries and the labor segmentation approach have the same theoretical foundations. Both are derived from historical observations of the existent asymmetries and discontinuities in society, and both have emphasized the demand side as the driving force that has shaped such features. Deficient capital accumulation (deficient demand for labor) determines the relative size of the formal sector of the economy. Labor segmentation is created by the functioning of labor demand, which lays the foundation for differentiation of economic opportunities and rewards among objectively comparable groups of workers.

2. Deficient Capital Accumulation, Expansion of Educational Systems, and Labor Markets

The lack of capital accumulation limits the size of the formal-modern sector. Besides, the dynamic of this sector depends upon capital-intensive, foreign-imported technology which has meant that its economic growth does not necessarily result in job expansion. In contrast, developing countries have experienced a rapid expansion of their educational systems in the 1970s and 1980s. This expansion has outrun the labor requirements of the formal sector. The interplay of these factors with a significant rural migration to the urban areas has produced: (a) underemployment of higher-educated workers; (b) employers' upgrading of the educational requirements for workers at all levels of job entry, reinforced by the decline in educational standards; (c) a dissatisfaction in a great majority of the population, who are unable to find the route to upward mobility; and (d) political institutions that are losing legitimacy as a consequence of the worsening of these unsolved economic and social problems (Fägerlind and Saha 1983, LLamas 1989).

The employment problem of developing countries is focused on urban underemployment. The high growth rates of population, the insufficient dynamism of the formal sector, the expansion of the educational system, and the use of education as one of the principal allocators of workers to jobs imply that the uneducated, the unskilled poor and poorest are pushed even further toward unemployment and underemployment. This mass of laborers finds its source of wages and income in the low-income and low-productivity jobs of the informal sector. Thus, the informal sector appears as a residual sector that is mainly constituted of the surplus labor that cannot find a job in the formal sector. Migrants from rural to urban areas, women, and young workers are overrepresented in urban surplus labor.

Migrants constitute a substantial part of the informal sector. They suffer mostly short periods of open unemployment because of their low aspirations and expectations, which move them to accept low-paid jobs and poor working conditions. They are concentrated in casual jobs. These facts in part explain how it happens that more educated people have longer periods and higher rates of unemployment than the less educated in many urban areas of the developing countries. It also seems that more educated workers are likely to face a wider dispersion of potential offers. Thus they behave rationally in investing more time in the search for work because the potential returns to further search are higher (Harris and Sabot 1982). In addition, the more educated have the possibility of relying for longer periods of time on support from their extended families (Blaug 1973).

The participation rates of women in the economically active population have grown during the 1970s and 1980s, in both developing and developed countries. The low income and standards of living of the greater part of the population in developing countries have limited the access of women to schooling. Women constitute a significant part of rural–urban migration and enter the urban market through low-level, low-paid, and casual jobs. Many women enter the labor market through domestic employment. They also constitute the main body of workers in labor-intensive, export-producing manufacturing firms that are becoming established rapidly and in increasing numbers in developing economies with a surplus of labor. Export-oriented firms in electronics and clothing mainly recruit female labor. On average, women earn less than men, whatever the economic activity. Young workers, 20–24 years of age or less, experience longer periods of unemployment in both developed and developing countries. In modern stratified societies, young women with little education are usually at the bottom of the employment ladder and older, more experienced, and highly educated men at the top.

3. Education and Labor Segmentation

The role of education in the market is difficult to perceive because it is an investment organically embedded in human beings. In the labor market, workers offer a package of several productive traits: education, training, experience, ability, and so on. These traits influence workers' productivity and wages.

The role of education in the allocation of workers to specific jobs with specific wage rates has to be explained by the functioning of specific markets. There exist different theories dealing with the role of education in the labor markets (see *Education and the Labor Market; Internal Labor Markets and Education; Segmented Labor Markets and Education*). The standard economic approaches that assume a universal application in both developed and developing countries have failed to grasp the complexities of lower income economies because they were primarily elaborated in developed countries to model and explain their own labor market structure and labor trends. Based on the heterogeneity and asymmetries of developing economies, some economists have conceived dualistic models (Lewis 1954, Fei and Ranis 1964, Harris and Todaro 1970).

Neoclassical economics assumes a continuous labor market with wage competition among workers. Labor segmentation approaches suggest the existence of two or more essentially distinct labor markets with little labor mobility between them. Workers of equal human capital do not receive equal wages because of the segmentation on the demand side of the labor market. The most familiar version of this approach divides the market into two segments: a primary and a secondary sector. As an outcome of the segmentation process, the primary sector has been divided between subordinate and independent primary segments. Primary jobs require and develop stable working habits, wages are high, and job ladders exist; these jobs encourage abilities such as creativity and problem-solving. Subordinate primary jobs are routinized and encourage workers' dependence on external rules and authority. Secondary jobs do not require, and often discourage, stable working habits; wages are low; turnover is high; job ladders are few. Secondary jobs are mainly filled by women and young workers.

3.1 Empirical Studies

There is empirical evidence that the human capital traits of individuals make a substantial monetary difference when they are productively employed in the formal sector of the economy. In the informal sector, schooling has a significant positive effect on workers' earnings but, on average, lower than the effect it has on the earnings of the workers in the formal sector see *Education and Informal Labor Markets*). These differences are generated by the process of labor segmentation.

There are several econometric studies on labor market segmentation in developing countries. In Latin America, Velloso (1975) in Brazil, Toledo (1977) in Peru and Lobo in Mexico (see Carnoy et al. 1969) estimated the rewards to human capital characteristics; that is, education and labor market experience (as measured by age). The results of these studies are analytically summarized in Carnoy (1980). The studies used data for urban males and their segment definitions represent the formal sector of those economies. The three studies found that education and work experience are significant variables in explaining earnings in all labor segments and that work experience (or age) has a lower reward in the secondary segment. Toledo and Lobo found that formal schooling is more highly rewarded in the primary independent and primary subordinate segments than in the secondary segment. These results support the hypothesis of the existence of labor segmentation.

In Singapore, Liu (1975) applied the same segmentation model to the data derived from a survey of industrial establishments. He found that schooling has more than five times higher payoff for primary workers than for secondary. Labor market experience is rewarded in both primary and secondary segments but the reward is lower in the secondary segment. The effect of training on earnings is not significant for primary workers but it is for secondary (Carnoy 1980).

Other researchers have modeled the segments of the labor market in a different manner. In Cameroon, Clignet (1976) studied the labor market in the modern or formal sector. He divided the workforce into two segments: manual and nonmanual workers. He found that formal schooling is more important in determining the income level in nonmanual jobs and that work experience produces a higher reward in the nonmanual segment than in the manual one (Carnoy 1980). In Mexico, LLamas (1987) studied segmentation of the Mexican industrial labor market. He divided industry into large and small size plants. In order to compare relatively homogeneous labor, segments were defined according to identical occupations. They were also defined with direct reference to the class structure. Thus, the working class included manual labor, office employees, and semispecialized sales agents and those at low levels of specialization. Semiautonomous workers were represented as different from the working class since it is assumed that they retain some control over their direct labor processes and some autonomy in their work pace and productivity. The intermediate position between the capitalists and the working class included managers, administrators, and professionals. The monetary returns to similar levels of education were estimated for each segment. The smallest monetary return

corresponded to the semiautonomous workers and the biggest to the intermediate positions. The returns to the segments of the working class were in between those two values.

The segmentation approach assumes that mobility of workers between segments is limited. Those workers in secondary jobs, characterized by low pay and poor working conditions, are trapped. Among the previously mentioned studies, only Liu and Clignet estimated workers' mobility. They found that mobility between primary and secondary jobs was restricted and that it depended more on education and work experience than on other variables. Additionally, a study in Coimbatore, India, found relatively little movement of workers from the small-scale business sector to large-scale firms. In Bombay, mobility from casual to regular employment was also found to be limited. These results show that many workers find themselves trapped in low-status and low-paying jobs (ILO 1987 Vol. 3 p. 124).

These results do not permit a clear affirmation of the superiority of the labor market segmentation approach over the human capital theory. The relationship between education and wages for different groups of workers could in fact be interpreted according to the dictates of the human capital paradigm. The labor market segmentation approach, however, does provide useful insights into how labor markets work in developing societies, characterized by structural heterogeneities and discontinuities.

3.2 Training for Workers in Formal and Informal Sectors

It is socially and individually profitable for workers to acquire training when they have a job either in the formal sector or in the informal sector. The improvement of workers' skills seems to make an important contribution to more productive employment. A study by the World Bank estimated the rate of return for graduates of Colombia's national training system, SENA (*Servicio Nacional de Aprendizaje*). This institution was set up by Colombia's ministry of labor with the purpose of training workers who have a job in the formal sector (ILO 1987 Vol. 3 p. 18). The study concluded that:

(a) The overall financial rate of return for SENA courses was clearly higher than the average rate obtained by investing in physical capital, and it also exceeds the rate of return to secondary education in Colombia.

(b) The rate varies according to the length of the courses: it is higher for long programs and for students who have greater experience and basic school training. Therefore, it appears to be a complement rather than substitute for other forms of investments in human capital. The training given to the worker participants in the program was useful not only for a better work performance but also for promotion.

The radical transformation of the world economy from the 1970s is changing the international division of labor and the national conditions of labor markets in both developed and developing countries (see *Education and the New International Division of Labor*). In developing countries there is a growing number of firms that are establishing their own training centers. These focus on specialized occupations as a way of keeping pace with the personnel needs of technological change.

Technological change alters the demand for specific occupations and skills and creates demand for new ones. The large firms or groups of firms in the formal-modern sector adjust to changing patterns of labor demand by generating the conditions for training, retraining, and conversion of workers' skills.

For workers in the informal sector, the most effective training programs seem to be those that are realized in the same informal sector, just as the best training for becoming a worker in the formal sector is within the formal sector itself (see *Education and Informal Labor Markets*); also Hallak and Caillods 1981 p. 125).

4. Educational Policy and Economic Development

The firms from advanced capitalist countries will probably be locating their labor-intensive processes of production in the labor-surplus economies to take advantage of their relative low wages and lax working conditions. However, these economies cannot rely on their labor surplus as if it were a permanent comparative advantage. It might become rapidly exhausted as a consequence of the increasing automation in production.

Multinational enterprises decide where to move, what and how to produce on the basis of their own estimated profits. An essential element that influences this estimate is the existence of "good" workers in quantity and quality. Education is the most important factor that affects the quality of labor supply. This is why educational policy plays a relevant role in any strategy for economic growth and development. What kind of education should governments promote? What kind of workers' skills and behavior must be stimulated in order to attract capital and create an increasing labor demand? The answers depend on the development strategy of developing countries.

Education seems to play an important role in selecting workers for the formal sector. One probable consequence of the arrival of young educated workers in the labor market will be to push the less educated out of the formal sector, and push them into the search for jobs in the informal sector or into open unemployment.

When secondary education becomes generalized, it is likely that the school-leavers will enter the informal sector in large numbers (Hallak and Caillods 1981 pp. 62, 108). Therefore, the educational policy of developing countries will affect the skill formation of potential workers in both sectors.

In the foreseeable future, developing countries will continue to be divided between formal and informal sectors; dualism will persist. The educational system has to instill attitudes and cognitive abilities that will enable individuals to face job uncertainty and to adjust to changes in labor markets. Individuals have to view education as a permanent process—as a means of adapting themselves to a rapidly changing world. Primary and secondary education must be devoted to the development of fundamental skills in the labor force—advanced literacy and numeracy—and the capacity for problem-solving and decision-making. General education seems to be more suitable than vocational education for working people of both sectors for inculcating the required attitudes and abilities (Psacharopoulos 1985).

See also: Segmented Labor Markets and Education; Education and the New International Division of Labor

References

Blaug M 1973 *Education and the Unemployment Problem in Developing Countries*. International Labour Office, Geneva

Carnoy M, Lobo J, Toledo A, Velloso J 1969 *Can Education Policy Equalise Income Distribution in Latin America?* International Labour Office, Geneva

Carnoy M 1980 Segmented labor markets. In: Carnoy M, Levin H, King K 1980 *Education, Work and Employment*, Vol. 2. UNESCO/IIEP Paris.

Clignet R 1976 *The Africanization of the Labor Market: Education and Occupational Segmentation in the Cameroons*. University of California Press, Berkeley, California

Fägerlind I, Saha L 1983 *Education and National Development: A Comparative Perspective*. Pergamon Press, Oxford

Fei J C H, Ranis G 1964 *Development of the Labor Surplus Economy: Theory and Policy*. Irwin, Homewood, Illinois

Godfrey M 1986 *Global Unemployment: The New Challenge to Economic Theory*. Wheatsheaf, Brighton

Hallak J, Caillods F 1981 *Education. Training and the Traditional Sector*. UNESCO/IIEP, Paris

Harris J, Sabot R 1982 Urban unemployment in LDCs: Towards a more general search model. In: Sabot R (ed.) 1982 *Migration and the Labour Market in Developing Countries*. Westview, Boulder, Colorado

Harris J R, Todaro M P 1970 Migration, unemployment and development: A two-sector analysis. *Am. Econ. Rev.* 60(1): 126–42

International Labour Office (ILO) 1987 *World Labour Report*, Vols. 1–4. International Labour Office, Geneva

Kanbur R, McIntosh J 1987 Dual economics. In: Eatwell J, Milgate M, Newman P (eds.) 1987 *The New Palgrave:*

A Dictionary of Economics. Macmillan, Houndmills, Basingstoke

Lewis W A 1954 Economic development with unlimited supplies of labour. *Manchester School of Economics and Social Studies* 22: 139–91

Liu Pak Wai 1975 Education and socioeconomic status in labor market segmentation: A case study in Singapore. Paper presented at the OECD Development Centre, Paris.

Llamas I 1987 Education and income determination in a segmented labor market: Analysis of the Mexican industrial sector. (Doctoral dissertation, Stanford University, Stanford, California)

Llamas I 1989 *Educación y mercado de trabajo en México.*

Universidad Autónoma Metropolitana (UAM), Mexico City

Psacharopoulos G 1985 Returns to education: A further international update and implications. *J. Hum. Resources* 20: 583–604

Toledo A 1977 Education, employment and the distribution of labor income in Peru between 1961 and 1972. (Doctoral dissertation, Stanford University, Stanford, California)

Velloso J 1975 Human capital and market segmentation: An analysis of the distribution of earnings in Brazil, 1970. (Doctoral dissertation, Stanford University, Stanford, California)

Education and Female Labor Force Participation in Industrializing Countries

G. V. De Miranda

In the industrializing countries, between 1950 and 1980, a significant proportion of the adult female population was incorporated into the labor force. This happened, for example, in most Latin American countries, although at different speeds. This increase was largely a consequence of changes in women's attitudes toward the labor market. Other explanatory factors have also been identified: social transformation in societies, economic development, specific characteristics of family structure, increases in the educational levels of populations, and changes in societies' cultural characteristics. Supply factors have also played a significant role in driving women toward the labor market. Many variables seem to have had contradictory effects in different socioeconomic contexts, because of cultural differences or different stages of development.

Although some trends toward gender equality have become evident, discrimination continues to exist. The labor market still belongs predominantly to men. Mainly because of cultural factors, women are still thought of as secondary and occasional workers. This entry analyzes the relationship between education and female labor force participation in industrializing countries, with a focus on Latin America. It is especially concerned with education as a determining factor of female wage labor.

1. Theoretical Background

Different approaches have been used to explain female labor force participation. Neoclassical economic theories assume that men and women have equal access to job opportunities and compete on an equal basis in the labor market (Anker and Hein 1986). They emphasize gender differences which affect productivity and labor supply. Such variables are connected with human capital (investment in schooling and work experience), personal characteristics, and family and socioeconomic status. Higher levels of participation are dependent on the levels of investment in human capital. However, this approach has provoked a great deal of criticism on account of the data used to prove the effect of each factor and therefore requires the use of artificial assumptions.

Theories dealing with labor market segmentation are based on different principles. They emphasize factors related to the structure of the labor market and the different ways in which men and women are distributed into separate segments within the market. In this approach the labor market is stratified and institutional barriers separate the layers. The primary market is composed of the best jobs, whereas co-workers from the lower social classes are concentrated in the much less attractive jobs of the secondary market. One criticism states that analyses of female occupations in such an approach underestimate market mechanisms and overestimate segmentation forms of the labor market (Lobo 1992).

Another approach can be found in the Marxist tradition, which analyzes capitalist development. The transference of the production of goods and services from homes to factories segregates women into the private domain, while men are privileged with mastery of the public domain, including labor market participation. Therefore, economic development affects women's labor. According to this interpretation, women have formed an industrial reserve army that comes into play during economic crises or in special situations. Some studies, however, have questioned this interpretation (Aguiar 1983).

A final approach is the "social relation of gender," which considers women's position as a consequence of submission and oppression to which they have been historically subjected. Cultural aspects rather than biological ones prevent women from working under conditions equal to those of men.

2. Methodological Aspects

Few studies consider the broader context of women's labor force participation. There is, for example, little multivariate analysis in the literature. The emphasis is on descriptive analysis and case studies (Barrig 1988), making generalizations difficult.

In addition, there has been a broad discussion in Latin America about the inadequacies of methodology and processes for collecting data on female participation (United Nations 1982). Some changes were introduced in the 1970 and 1980 demographic censuses in many Latin American countries in order to obtain more accurate and precise information and make more evident the contribution of women to the labor force.

3. Female Labor Force Participation

Between 1970 and 1990, a great expansion of the educational system in Latin America contributed to the reduction of differences in schooling experienced by men and women. In spite of the nonuniversality of primary and secondary schooling in many countries, gender differences in educational attainment almost disappeared.

In the case of higher education, women became more numerous than men in many important universities in Brazil, despite their concentration in those disciplines that usually lead to female occupations. The increase in the levels of female labor force participation in Latin America was evident in the period 1970–90. In Brazil, the total number more than doubled in absolute terms. In other Latin American countries similar trends were observed. However, it is possible that these higher levels of female participation were due to changes introduced in the methodologies used in census and household samples to measure participation.

3.1 Organization of Productive Activity

Changes in the organization of productive activity play a central role in changes in the gender division of labor. Different combinations of productive forces and social relations of production affect female labor force participation. In precapitalist production, the family was the basic unit of production and played a central role in the productive system. When production shifted from the family to the industrial enterprise, family members had to sell their labor power. This had a great impact on the gender division of labor. Men became the major source of commodity labor power, while women assumed full responsibility for domestic

reproduction and maintenance of that labor power.

In Brazil, analyses of the rural sector show that the country has moved from being an essentially agrarian productive structure to one in which manufacturing is not only sophisticated but has become the leading sector. In agriculture, interrelated changes in rural property, in technology, in the types of crops cultivated in each region, and in the relations of production have resulted in changes in female labor force participation (Miranda 1983). Similar phenomena are mentioned by Sautu (1983) for Peru and Lattes (1983) for Argentina.

In most rural areas, women's and children's work within the family unit has always been significant for the subsistence of the whole family group. Thus, when the major part of the labor force is occupied with subsistence or small-scale agriculture, female participation is usually high, since this kind of production more easily allows women to combine domestic responsibilities with agricultural work. At a later stage of development, as the transformation in the structure of production reaches the countryside, and agriculture in its turn becomes more commercialized and capitalized, a progressively increasing migration of peasants to urban areas takes place, thus decreasing rural population. There has then been a substitution of men for women in the larger properties while the employment of both male and female workers decreases with the introduction of new technologies.

Within the urban sector historical trends in female labor force participation seem to be linked to industrialization and urbanization. Both phenomena have caused deep changes in employment structure, but seem to have affected women more than men. Industrial expansion initially reduced female participation, first through the substitution of manufactures for handicraft, second, as a result of changes in the gender structure of employment. The latter happened because the number of factories increased, production diversified, and new advanced technologies were introduced.

Technological changes in the production process have shown that when machines are introduced in the traditional sectors, women are replaced by men, since men are usually placed in charge of machines. In an analysis of manufacturing industry in Brazil, Lobo (1992) observed that as a result of mechanization, women lost their jobs to men, even in those industries in which previously they had had absolute hegemony, such as the textile industry.

Following this same line of thought, Barrig (1988) observed for Peru that there was a higher demand for female laborers in the consumption goods industry than in the more advanced technological sectors because of women's low technical performance with machines. Among the explanations for lower demand for female labor in manufacturing industries in Peru, Scott (1986) and Barrig (1988) pointed to laws that protected female labor and provided women's labor with benefits. These sorts of laws can be found in other Latin American countries.

An historical study of female labor force participation also reveals a tendency to concentrate women in service industries; that is, in the tertiary sector. This sector has helped to open up new opportunities for women in areas such as education, clerical work in the modern sector and in state services. However, on the other hand, it has served to keep a large proportion of women in domestic service. Unlike the mechanized sectors of production, low-level services are less susceptible to technological changes and employ predominantly low-wage persons (especially women), who are intensely exploited and oppressed.

In the 1980s this tendency was maintained at an increasing rate. The concentration of workers in the service sector can be explained by the increase in available labor, the incapacity of the productive forces in the modern industrial sector to absorb excess labor, and a new tendency toward the tertiarization of the economy. In order to reduce costs of labor, enterprises began to hire labor power from other service firms. These human resources were usually not highly qualified and unrelated to production. For almost all types of services, women were generally hired.

Additionally, women were losing jobs in peasant farming areas in Latin America at a rate higher than women in Africa and Asia. They tended not to find jobs in the industrial sector. As a result, they "start working in the informal sector as domestic servants, petty vendors, market women, and even as prostitutes. These were survival strategies that women tried to work out in order to eke out a living" (Safa 1983 p. 4).

Madeira and Singer (1973), when analyzing female labor force participation in Brazil, detected that the transformation processes of women in the labor force occurred in accordance with historical stages. In the first stage, subsistence activities, manufacturing, and small-scale commerce were dominant and agriculture was the principal productive activity. In the second stage, when the agrarian economy became capitalist, manufacturing and small-scale commerce were supplanted by modern factories, large-scale stores, warehouses, and supermarkets. In this stage, men replaced women on the large farms and female participation tended to decline, since women were not hired in the new industries in the same proportion. In the third stage, development of the productive forces reached a level that allowed the liberation of women from the domestic setting. Their participation tended to increase again, principally in the service sector which developed as a consequence of industrial expansion.

In the underdeveloped regions of Brazil and other Latin American countries, a high percentage of women have worked in agriculture, which historically demonstrates the female contribution to the labor force. These stages also proved to be present in other regions. Using the "U" curve, Barrig (1988) in Peru and Wainerman and Lattes (1981) in Mexico, analyzed female participation in relation to industrial development. Under this formulation, participation levels were high in both the advanced and the primitive stages of industrialization but lower in the intermediate ones, thus confirming the historical stages mentioned above.

Although this phenomenon has been present in different countries it can also be observed that each one experienced these changes in different periods. In Argentina, for example, Lattes showed that "the upsurge in female labor in economic activities began timidly in the 1950s and is clearly seen during the 1960s, after a secular declining trend" (1983 p. 73). In Brazil the same phenomenon occurred at least a decade later.

It is possible to conclude that there is no consensus regarding the role of economic development in female labor force participation. While some authors see development contributing to the marginalization of women in the process of production, others argue that it promotes the transition of the active population from the traditional to modern economy.

3.2 Socioeconomic Conditions and other Factors

Entrance into the labor force is decided by the intersection of family variables. Women's wage work depends on the role they perform in the family, as well as on their family's position in the social structure. The unemployment of husbands, for example, is a factor that has led to two contradictory effects: it has encouraged women either to look for jobs in the labor market (the "added worker" hypothesis) or to proceed in the opposite direction, that is, to stay out of wage labor (the "discouraged worker" hypothesis). Which hypothesis is correct?

In Brazil unemployment rates are usually very high because of certain structural characteristics of the economy that have resulted in a low capacity to absorb the available labor force. The country experiences frequent periods of economic recession. In a situation with this combination of factors, married women might be discouraged from working. In practice, however, the large rise in participation by married women in the 1980s could indicate the strong effect of the added worker hypothesis. The same was observed in Peru. Jurado et al. (1985) have shown that industrial recession caused an increased presence of women in the labor market, mostly in services and in the informal sector.

Female labor force participation is also affected by social class conditions. According to Saffiotti (1978), women's position in the labor market and the discrimination to which they are subject vary with social stratification in each society. Whereas upper-class women work for reasons other than economic necessity, the lower classes work no matter what social expectations they have. Variables such as age, marital status, fertility rates, and the presence of children at home are also significant factors in studying female participation, since the labor force is drawn from populations with different demographic, cultural, and economic conditions.

An analysis of female participation in Brazil based on 1970s census data (Miranda 1983) confirmed both the hypothesis that participation is closely connected to marital status and that single women tend to exhibit higher participation rates. However, one of the greatest changes that has occurred involves the number of married women who enter the labor force. It doubled from 1970 to 1990 although it remained lower than the level of participation by single women. The same was observed by Lattes in Argentina, where "married women made the most significant contribution to labor force growth in young cohorts of all regions" (1983 p.74).

The explanation for this fact lies in the reduction of lower- and middle-class salaries which therefore demanded women's contribution to family income, in changes in employers' attitudes toward female work (Bruschini 1986), in the expansion of child-care centers, and in the decrease in fertility rates. There is, however, no consensus with regard to the effects of fertility rates on female participation. Silva (1979) showed its effect on female labor in Brazil, while Lattes argued that in Argentina "differences in the level of fertility trends do not seem to be related to participation trends" (1983 p.73).

Levels of participation in the labor market also reflect age effects. Time and cross-sectional effects were observable in the case of Brazil in 1970 (Miranda 1983). Time effects were manifested in a claim which postulates that younger generations tend to show higher levels of participation, since they are affected by different factors which prove to have a positive effect on female participation. The cross-sectional effect is the age effect per se, which means that women at a certain age exhibit a certain pattern of participation.

While the curve of participation rates by age for men are reduced only at the age of retirement, in the case of women the rates usually decline after the age of 25, most obviously reflecting marriage and maternity as determinant causes (Bruschini 1986, Sautu 1983). In an age cohort study in Argentina, Lattes (1983) showed that several generations of women have increased their participation after age 25.

3.3 Education

Many studies have suggested that the education of women has been by far the most important factor in bringing about changes in their status all over the world. Since the 1970s in Latin America the importance of education has been emphasized especially for its role in the preparation of individuals for citizenship or for life in modern society.

The human capital approach emphasizes the social investments made in formal schooling and job training. Thus, the level of capital accumulated by persons

would explain their position in the labor market. Since women have generally accumulated less human capital than men, for various reasons, it is possible to understand their lower levels of participation and occupational segregation. Since, however, the differences in the number of years of schooling by gender had almost disappeared by the 1980s and the number of years of work for women had also increased, the human capital approach proves to be inadequate for explaining gender differentiation in the labor market in the early 1990s.

Another explanation claims that education has historically been interpreted as having a close connection with the structure of production. When the family was the unit of production, the skills necessary for production were usually transmitted by adults to boys and girls through working together, although some differentiation existed in the types of tasks that were assigned to them. When the factory became the center of production it was necessary to socialize the workers to meet the needs of production (Levin 1978). Therefore, a highly differentiated education for social classes and genders was developed. Men have been socialized for certain professions or oriented toward production whereas women's socialization has been oriented to household activities and to the reproduction of labor power.

In the above context the roles played by schools in the early 1990s can be defined as being associated with the transformation of social relations, as well as with the maintenance of the contradictions in social stratification and the gender division of labor. According to Levin (1978) the first function performed by schools was related to production or the reproduction of skills required for production. Within the context of a set of social and organizational relationships, schools had to produce both general and vocational skills that corresponded to the requirements imposed by production. Nevertheless, when trying to transmit skills to male and female students, schools followed the preexisting gender lines of the social division of labor.

A second function is related to the reproduction of the social relations of production. The conditioning of youth to an organizational context dominated by hierarchy, specialization, competition for rewards, and alienation from the process and product of their schooling activity tended to reproduce the social relations of the capitalist workplace (Levin 1978).

As a third function, Levin relates the reproduction of an ideology of education in which education is an appropriate allocator of occupational position and a mechanism for social mobility and equality. Within this perspective, schools and the credentials they provide are seen as a legitimate device for allocating occupations within the structure of production. The early socialization of boys and girls in the family and later in schools has seemed to be geared to the traditional places of boys and girls in society.

For women, a fourth function can be added. When women's education was restricted to the upper social classes it had no exchange value, only use value, since women were not supposed to sell their labor power. Therefore, there was no reason to develop their skills. However, as the educational system later expanded and industrialization developed, requiring the incorporation of a simultaneously cheap and educated labor force, female education began to incorporate exchange value as well.

During the first half of the twentieth century, the content of female education in the Brazilian education system, which remained restricted to women of higher social classes, was limited to the arts and domestic activities. This improved their ability to perform familiar and other social roles, but did not increase their ability to work in the labor market.

The schooling system has been one of the most important mechanisms for the development of skills and the inculcation of norms and values to new generations. As such, it has been the most appropriate process for the reproduction of specific forms of capitalist accumulation in each society. That reproduction, however, does not follow a predetermined path nor is it an automatic consequence of the needs of capital accumulation. Rather, in each specific social system this reproduction is mediated by class conflicts and contradictions, in which various alternative systems of education, linked to the contending social forces, dispute with each other.

Finally, schools have had a significant role in the preparation of citizens for democratic societies. Irrespective of gender, each person has to be able to participate in the political, economic, and social spheres of modern societies. A more optimistic perspective sees schooling as an important mechanism for social transformation toward modernity.

In the literature dealing with the relationship between schooling and the labor force it is possible to observe some tendencies in the industrializing countries of Latin America in the late twentieth century. They include the following.

(a) Education has a positive effect on female labor force participation (Miranda 1983, Rosemberg 1982).

(b) Female labor force participation varies with the number of years of schooling. This tendency was observed in Argentina and Chile (Elizaga 1974), Brazil (Miranda 1983, Bruschini 1986, Lewin 1980) and Peru (Barrig 1988).

(c) Higher levels of schooling usually lead to higher levels of occupation. Education is an important determinant of the type of occupation (Del Valle 1976). However, frequently women are engaged in activities incompatible with the education level achieved (Miranda 1983, Rosemberg 1982). The more the level of schooling has increased, the

more the number of women adequately employed has also increased (Del Valle 1976).

(d) The impact of schooling on female labor force participation varies according to social class. This variation was detected in the Brazilian case (Miranda 1983) and was demonstrated by Fernandez (1983) in the case of Peru. He noticed that for the middle classes education can be viewed as a channel which provides social mobility, whereas for the lower classes it does not provide sufficient access to better and more stable jobs.

(e) Women have continued to be concentrated in traditionally female occupations. It is possible to infer from this segregation that cultural factors are still relevant determinants of gender discrimination in the labor market (Bruschini 1986). It is important to mention that this segregation has not disappeared with the introduction of increased years of schooling for women.

(f) Higher levels of education have been associated with higher levels of salary—however, with inequality between men's and women's wages. Many studies have revealed that although women had more schooling and training than men they continued working for lower salaries (Barrig 1988, Del Valle 1976). In Brazil (Miranda 1983) it was clear that access to higher education did not imply wage equality since women in the liberal professions earned, on the average, less than half of a man's salary for the same job. Salary differentials have been more evident among professionals than among clerical employees.

(g) Scott (1986), in a household sample in Lima, Peru, provided evidence that there was a higher percentage of women with secondary education among the unemployed than with no schooling or with lower levels of schooling. Del Valle (1976) also showed that there were more unemployed women than men and the reason for this was linked to education.

(h) Barrig (1988) showed that in Lima female participation in the modern and informal sectors of the economy was not characterized by great differences in level of education. In the latter sector, women with secondary schooling had higher levels of participation. This was due to the expansion of education. However, because of circumstances such as lower labor demand, higher levels of women's schooling did not guarantee access to better jobs.

(i) Education has also had a positive effect in reducing discrimination against married women in the labor force. An analysis of the levels of participation of married and single women in Brazil revealed that differences were more perceptible among those with lower levels of schooling (Miranda 1983).

4. Conclusion

In the 1970s and 1980s there was an accelerated rise in female labor force participation in Latin America. This rise was a consequence of changes in women's attitudes toward working and of other factors such as education. It was also evident that supply factors played a significant role in driving women toward the labor market. Industrialization and the increase of commerce and services in the tertiary sector opened new opportunities for women's employment, especially in the more developed regions of Latin America.

Nevertheless, it is possible to confirm that several patterns of female labor force participation have existed in the region. Many factors seem to have had contradictory effects in different socioeconomic contexts, either because of cultural differences or because of different stages of development. Although some trends toward equality have been evident, it can easily be observed that discrimination has persisted, that the labor market has continued to belong predominantly to men, and that women, especially because of cultural factors, have been considered secondary and occasional workers, with their "natural" working place being in the home.

Education has tended to exert a positive force over female labor force participation since it has greatly facilitated female involvement in the labor force. However, its role has been contradictory, not only in Brazil but also in other Latin American countries. First, there can be no guarantee that the universalization of schooling for all social classes will continue to have a strong effect on female labor force participation. Education will probably not continue to play as positive a role, and its effect is likely to be reduced. Second, since education has played an important role in the reproduction of social structures, it is probable that it will continue to reinforce the gender division of labor for many decades. It is only by changing the ideology of gender roles which has permeated social and educational systems that it will be possible to reach some sort of equality in labor force participation.

References

Aguiar N 1983 Women in the labor force in Latin America: A review of the literature. In: El-Sanabary N M (ed.) 1983 *Women and Work in the Third World: The Impact of Industrialization and Global Economic Interdependence.* Center for the Study, Education, and Advancement of Women, University of California, Berkeley, California

Anker R, Hein C (eds.) 1986 *Sex Inequalities in Urban Employment in the Third World.* St Martin's Press, New York

Barrig M 1988 *Investigación sobre Empleo y Trabajo Femenino: Una Revisión Crítica.* ADEC–ATC. Lima

Bruschini C 1986 *Mulher e Trabalho: Uma Avaliacao Da Decada Da Mulher.* Nobel Conselho Estadual de Condicão Feminina (CECF), São Paulo

Del Valle D 1976 *Factores Determinantes de la Participación de la Mujer en el Mercado de Trabajo.* Ministerio de Trabajo, Lima (mimeo)

Elizaga J C 1974 The Participation of Women in the Labor Force in Latin America: Fertility and other factors. *Int. Lab. Rev.* 109(5/6): 519–38

Fernandez H 1983 Notas sobre la problematica de la educacion y empleo en el Peru. In: Henriques N, Iguiniz J (eds.) 1983 *El Problema del Empleo en Peru.* Pontificia Universidad Catolica del Perú, Lima.

Jurado J, Vargas V, Suares F 1985 Crisis Económica, Ingressos Familiares y Dinámica Ocupacional de la Mujer. In: UNICEF 1985 *Estudios sobre la Participación de la Mujer en la Economia Peruana.* UNICEF and Ministerio de Trabajo de Perú, Lima

Lattes Z R D 1983 *Dynamics of the Female Labor Force in Argentina.* UNESCO, Paris

Levin H M 1978 The dilemma of comprehensive secondary school reform in Western Europe. *Comp. Educ. Rev.* 22(3): 434–51

Lewin H 1980 Educacão e Forca de Trabalho Feminino no Brasil. *Cadernos de Pesquisa* 32: 45–49

Lobo E S 1992. O Trabalho como Linguagem: O Genero do Trabalho. In: Costa A C, Bruschini C (eds.) 1992 *Uma Questao de Genero.* Editora Rosa dos Tempos, São Paulo

Madeira F, Singer P 1973 *Estrutura de Emprego e Trabalho Feminino no Brasil: 1920–1970.* Cadernos Centro Brasileiro de Analise e Planéjamento, São Paulo

Miranda G V 1983 Human resources development and FLFP in Brazil. In: Streeten P, Mayer H 1983 *Human Resources, Employment, and Development,* Vol. 2. Macmillan, London

Rosemberg F et al. 1982 *A Educacão da Mulher no Brasil.* Global, São Paulo

Safa H I 1983 Women and the international division of labor. In: El-Sanabary N M (ed.) 1983 *Women and Work in the Third World: The Impact of Industrialization and Global Economic Interdependence.* Center for the Study, Education, and Advancement of Women, University of California, Berkeley, California

Saffiotti H I B 1978. *Women in Classes Society.* Monthly Review Press, New York

Sautu R 1983 Economic development and patterns of female labor participation in Latin America. In: El-Sanabary N M 1983 *Women and Work in the Third World: The Impact of Industrialization and Global Economic Interdependence.* Center for the Study, Education, and Advancement of Women, University of California, Berkeley, California

Scott A M E 1986 Economic Development and Urban Women's Work: the case of Lima, Peru. In: Anker R, Hein C (eds.) 1986

Silva L M 1979 *A Participacao da Mulher Casada na Forca de Trabalho: Compatibilidade entre Suas Atividades Extra-domesticas e o Numero de Filhos.* CEDEPLAR, Belo Horizonte

United Nations Economic Commission for Latin America and the Caribbean (CEPAL) 1982 La Mujer en el Empleo y el Trabajo Domestico. In: *Cinco Estudios sobre la situación de la Mujer en América Latina.* CEPAL, Santiago

Wainerman C, Lattes Z R D 1981. *El Trabajo Feminino en el Banquillo de los Acusados.* Terranova, Mexico City

Further Reading

El-Sanabary N M 1983 *Women and Work in the Third World:*

The Impact of Industrialization and Global Economic Interdependence. Center for the Study, Education, and Advancement of Women, University of California, Berkeley

Jensen J, Hagen E, Reddy C 1988 *Feminization of the Labor Force: Paradoxes and Promises.* Polity Press, Cambridge

Educational Expansion and Labor Markets

G. S. Fields

Educational systems have been expanded throughout the world. The entry of additional educated persons into the labor market would be expected to affect labor market conditions, both for those with the education level in question and for others. Different models of the labor market consequences of educational expansion are presented in this entry. It does not, however, seek to model the *reasons* for educational expansion, be these political forces, a premeditated plan, or other factors. Nor is it proposed to set out the actual ways in which rational educational planning should be undertaken.

1. The Basic Framework

Although there is a continuum of educational levels, for the present analysis it is useful to think in terms of just two types of people: educated and uneducated. (In countries where everyone receives a basic level of education, it may be more helpful to think in terms of two groups: better educated and less educated.)

When the number educated is relatively limited, those few who have education are able to get very good jobs. However, when the educational system expands and the educated labor force increases, the additional educated people typically are not able to get jobs as good as their predecessors did when education was relatively scarce. This has been widely observed in countries as diverse as the United States (see the studies cited below), Turkey (Krueger 1971), India (Blaug et al. 1969), Kenya (Boissiere et al. 1985), and others (Skorov 1968). Sometimes the deterioration in labor market conditions is manifested in open unemployment of the educated, while at other times it is reflected in falling earnings within the occupations in which the educated are typically employed, and at yet other times in the systematic movement of the educated into steadily lower job categories.

Basic supply and demand analysis explains the fall in the earnings of the educated following educational expansion. The attractiveness of the job for educated people is summarized in a single variable, termed "wage," here abbreviated as W_{ed}. Other things being equal, the supply of educated labor S_{ed} is a positive function of the wage for educated people W_{ed}, and the demand for educated labor D_{ed} is a negative function of W_{ed}. In the standard textbook model of labor economics (e.g., Ehrenberg and Smith 1991), the wage W_{ed} equates the amount of educated labor supplied and demanded; it is thus termed the "market-clearing wage," denoted W^*_{ed} in Fig. 1.

Starting with an initial supply-of-educated-labor curve S_{ed}, an initial demand-for-educated-labor curve D_{ed}, and an initial wage W^*_{ed}, what is the effect of educational expansion? Take first the educated persons' labor market. The supply of educated labor curve shifts rightward from S_{ed} to S'_{ed}, since there are now more educated persons available to work at any given wage. According to the standard analysis, the labor market reaches a new equilibrium when the wage *falls* from W^*_{ed} to W'_{ed}, an amount just sufficient to employ all the extra educated people.

As for the uneducated persons' labor market, educational expansion means that there are now fewer uneducated people. Basic supply and demand analysis suggests that, now that uneducated persons are relatively more scarce in the labor market, their relative economic position should improve. As shown in Fig. 2, the supply of uneducated persons would shift leftward from S_{uned} to S'_{uned}. For a given demand for labor curve D_{uned}, and with market wage determination, this analysis predicts that the wage for uneducated workers would be expected to *rise*, from W^*_{uned} to W'_{uned}. This has happened in some places but not in others. Empirical evidence is presented below in Sect. 3. First, though, alternative models are presented.

2. The Market-clearing Labor Market Model: Theme and Variations

This section presents models in which the wage for each type of labor (better educated and less educated)

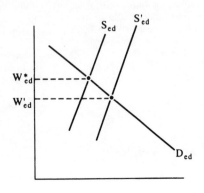

Figure 1
Educated labor market

adjusts upward or downward to clear each market. The labor supply and demand equations and the market-clearing wage equation are, for the educated persons' labor market,

$$S_{ed} = f(W_{ed}, X_1), \quad f_1 > 0, \tag{1}$$

$$D_{ed} = g(W_{ed}, X_2), \quad g_1 < 0, \tag{2}$$

$$f(W^*_{ed}, X_1) = g(W^*_{ed}, X_2) \tag{3}$$

and, for the uneducated persons' labor market,

$$S_{uned} = h(W_{uned}, X_3), \quad h_1 > 0, \tag{4}$$

$$D_{uned} = i(W_{uned}, X_4), \quad i_1 > 0, \tag{5}$$

$$h(W^*_{uned}, X_3) = i(W^*_{uned}, X_4). \tag{6}$$

Educational expansion entails a shift of the labor supply curves. The labor demand curves may also change as well.

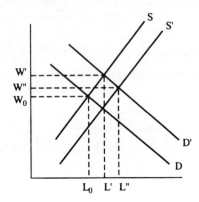

Figure 3
Educated labor market

The case where the supply curves shift but the demand curves do not is depicted graphically in Figs. 1 and 2. As already explained, that model predicts a fall in the wage of educated persons and an increase in the wage of uneducated persons.

Variants on the model would postulate that, at the same time that educational expansion shifts the labor supply curves, there is a shift in the demand curve for educated labor, in the demand curve for uneducated labor, or in both. Such shifts might be exogenous or endogenous.

An exogenous shift in the demand curve might arise, for example, because the country improves its capacity to export, thereby shifting the derived demand for labor rightward. Figure 3 shows the changes in labor market conditions for educated workers. Denoting a wage/employment pair by {W, L}, the educated workers' labor market would change from {W_0, L_0} to {W', L'} if there were no educational expansion and from {W_0, L_0} to {W'', L''} if there were an educational expansion. Comparing {W', L'}

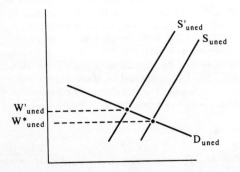

Figure 2
Uneducated labor market

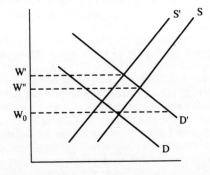

Figure 4
Uneducated labor market

with $\{W'', L''\}$, we see that the educational expansion results in a lower wage for the larger number of educated persons employed. Figure 4 shows, similarly, that for uneducated workers, educational expansion brings about a higher wage for the smaller number of uneducated persons employed.

The analysis is made more complicated if the shift in the labor demand curve arises endogenously for reasons which are associated with the educational expansion itself. This might happen, for example, if educated workers consume a relatively large percentage of goods produced by educated people. Provided that the marginal propensities to consume the two goods are both strictly between zero and one, the shift in the demand-for-educated-labor curve would be less than the shift in the supply-of-educated-labor curve, so it would still be the case that the wage of educated workers would *fall* due to educational expansion.

The models described in this section share the assumption that the wages of educated and uneducated labor rise or fall to clear their respective labor markets. If they do not, the labor market consequences of educational expansion are very different. Such models are taken up in the next two sections.

3. Nonmarket-clearing Wages: The Case of Labor Market Stratification

By definition, a wage is nonmarket-clearing if it is too high or too low relative to the market-clearing wage. It is often said that the wage levels in the jobs traditionally filled by educated workers lie above the market-clearing levels. As a result, there are not enough jobs available for all educated persons seeking to work.

The question then arises: What happens to the

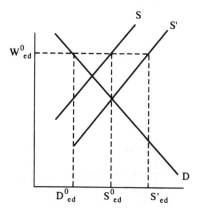

Figure 5
Educated labor market

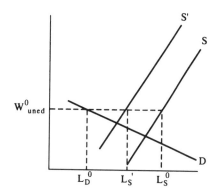

Figure 6
Uneducated labor market

educated persons who do not get hired for these jobs? Suppose that they continue to seek the better jobs, enduring a spell of unemployment until they get hired. This case is called the "labor market stratification model" (Fields 1974) because the educated persons occupy the higher stratum of jobs, the uneducated persons occupy the lower stratum, and neither group crosses over into the other stratum.

In the case of labor market stratification, the wage of educated persons is set at a level above the market-clearing one. Eqn. (3) is replaced by

$$W_{ed} = W_{ed}^0 > W_{ed}^*. \qquad (3')$$

The educated labor market in this case is depicted in Fig. 5. The unemployment brought about by the higher-than-market-clearing wage is the difference between the amount of labor supplied at wage W^0 (S_{ed}^0) and the amount demanded at that wage (D_{ed}^0).

The effects of educational expansion are very different in this case from the market-clearing case. When the labor supply curve shifts from S_{ed} to S'_{ed}, employment of educated workers does *not* increase. This is because the wage does not fall, and so employers will not want to employ the additional supply of labor. Instead, the effect of educational expansion is to increase educated unemployment.

This is the essence of the analysis offered by Blaug et al. (1969) and Blaug (1973) to explain unemployment of college graduates in India. As more people get educated and enter the labor market, competition for the limited number of jobs becomes even keener. New graduates might experience unemployment lasting months or even years until they are finally hired for such a job.

As for those without education, educational expansion means that there are fewer of them. If their wages are set by supply and demand, as in Fig. 2, the leftward shift of their labor supply curve would result in an increase in the wages of those who remain uneducated. But if their wages are also set at higher-than-market-clearing levels, so that initially some of them were unemployed, the amount of unemployment amongst the uneducated is reduced by educational expansion (from $L_s^0 - L_D^0$ to $L_s' - L_D^0$ in Fig. 6).

Another variant is possible. Rather than having completely rigid wages, a sticky wage adjustment process might be postulated. An example is a partial adjustment model of the form

$$\Delta W_{ed}^Q(t) = \eta[W_{ed}^Q(t-1) - W_{ed}^*(t-1)], \qquad (7)$$

$$0 < \eta < 1.$$

With this wage adjustment process, the economy always has educated unemployment, because the wage that actually prevails in the market, W_{ed}^Q, is always above the wage that would clear the market, W_{ed}^*. However, educational expansion under this variant lowers W_{ed}^* which, by Eqn. (7), lowers W_{ed}^Q in the next period. This means that, unlike the rigid wage case, educational expansion in the sticky wage case leads with a lag to an increase in educated employment.

4. Nonmarket-clearing Wages: The Case of Bumping

"Bumping" is a term first applied in education analysis by Fields (1972). The bumping model described below is developed formally in Fields (1974). The basic idea of bumping is similar to the notion of "job competition" put forth by Thurow (1975) and of "filtering down" used by Knight and Sabot (1990).

In the bumping model, as in the labor market stratification model described in the last section, education is a requirement for the better paying jobs, the wage of which is set above market-clearing levels. Workers without education can only be hired for lower paying jobs. There is, however, one very important difference between the bumping model and the labor market stratification model: in the bumping model, educated workers would be willing to accept lower-level jobs if it pays them to do so, whereas in the labor market stratification model, the educated and uneducated always remain in distinct labor market strata.

The bumping model consists of two labor markets, called "skilled" and "unskilled." In skilled jobs, education is required. The labor market for workers in the skilled jobs is depicted in Fig. 5. Educational expansion increases the supply of educated labor. This will shift the supply curve of labor to the skilled labor market rightward provided that at least some of the newly educated workers enter the queue for skilled jobs.

However, educated workers may have another possibility. Suppose they are at least somewhat more

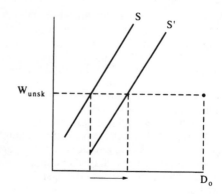

Figure 7
Labor market for educated persons in unskilled jobs

productive than the less educated workers in the unskilled jobs. Whether they are very much more productive or only marginally more productive does not really matter: at a given wage for unskilled jobs W_{unsk}^Q, employers would wish to hire the better educated workers preferentially for these lower level jobs if they are *any* more productive, be it for reasons of human capital formation in the schools, screening by the schools of persons with greater innate ability, or sociological factors.

Would the better educated workers want to be hired for such jobs? If the choice is between strategy (i), that of seeking a job at the skilled wage (W_{sk}) but with a low probability of success (p), versus strategy (ii), being hired preferentially for a job at the unskilled wage (W_{unsk}) with no unemployment, the better educated workers might choose option (ii) when the competition for skilled jobs becomes sufficiently fierce. The decision between these options depends upon a comparison of the expected wages associated with the respective labor market strategies. Under one formulation, the expected wage for an educated person who adopts strategy (i) is

$$V_{(i)} = W_{sk}\, p$$

while for someone adopting strategy (ii), it is

$$V_{(ii)} = W_{unsk}.$$

It would be in an educated person's interest to switch labor market strategies if these expected values were unequal; hence, $V_{(i)} = V_{(ii)}$ is an equilibrium condition. Under more complicated formulations, the logic is similar but the mathematical expressions are more complicated; see Fields (1974) for details.

Figures 7 and 8 depict the effects of educational expansion on the unskilled labor market. Employers

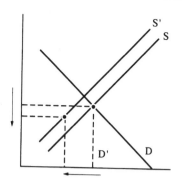

Figure 8
Labor market for uneducated persons in unskilled jobs

which have direct empirical applicability, as shown in the next section.

5. Educational Expansion and the Labor Market: The Case of the United States

The United States presents a study in contrasts. Educational expansion had different labor market effects in the 1980s from those it had previously shown. This suggests that different models pertain to the United States case at different times.

First, take the case of late 1960s and the 1970s. During this period, the percentage of the labor force who were college graduates increased. For instance, among white males, in 1973, the ratio of college graduates to high school dropouts was 0.82; in that same year, the ratio of college graduates to high school graduates was 0.56. As a result of educational expansion, the corresponding ratios had risen to 1.46 and 0.76 in 1979 (Blackburn et al. 1990 Table 6). At the same time, the ratio of college graduates' earnings to high school graduates' earnings fell (Freeman 1976, Blackburn et al. 1990 Table 1). The narrowing of the college graduate/high school graduate earnings differential as a result of an increased supply of college graduates is precisely what would be predicted from the basic human capital model presented in Figs. 1 and 2 above.

In the 1980s, however, a different pattern emerged. The labor force became better educated. Male and female college enrollment rates went up for 20- and 21-year olds (US Department of Education). Among workers aged 25–64, college graduates became more numerous (Blackburn et al. 1990 Table 6). Despite the increased relative abundance of college graduates, the ratio of college graduates' earnings to high school graduates' earnings rose for both males and females

are demanding a certain number of workers D^0 for unskilled jobs at wage W_{unsk}. If a larger number of educated workers offer their labor in the unskilled labor market (a shift of the labor supply curve from S to S' in Fig. 7), they get hired preferentially. As a result, *fewer* unskilled jobs are available for uneducated workers. The demand curve for their labor shifts to the left. Figure 8 illustrates the case where the leftward shift of the labor demand curve for the less educated workers is large enough to *reduce* the uneducated workers' wages. This outcome is only a possibility, not a necessity.

Depending on the various parameters of the model, an expansion of the educated labor force (L_{ed}) may affect the net present value of education (PV_{ed}) in any of the three ways shown in Fig. 9. Only the pattern shown in Fig. 9(c) is possible in the standard market-clearing model discussed in Sect. 2. In this way, the bumping model admits a wider set of possibilities,

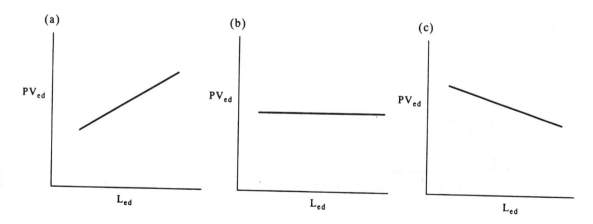

Figure 9
Alternative patterns of present value of being educated, as a function of the number educated

(Bound and Johnson 1992 Figs. 1 and 2). For the first time in the recent history of the United States, the earnings of the least educated workers (those with high school education or less) fell absolutely, with the decline being largest for the youngest (Blackburn et al. 1990 Table 1, Freeman 1989 p. 1).

The conjunction of these three phenomena—a fall in the earnings of the least educated, both absolutely and relatively, during a time when the least educated were becoming relatively scarcer due to educational expansion—is inconsistent with the market-clearing model presented in Sect. 2. A different explanation must be sought.

The answer is found by considering the demand side of the labor market along with the supply side. It appears that the greater availability of well-educated workers in the 1980s meant that employers could hire those with more education in preference to those with less. If preferential hiring took place in large numbers throughout the economy, the least educated would then have been pushed to the end of the queue for the available jobs. The demand curve for their labor would have shifted leftward as a result. If the leftward shift of the demand curve for their labor was greater than the leftward shift in the supply of their labor, their earnings would have fallen.

What has just been described mirrors the bumping model presented in Sect. 4. According to this model, educational expansion causes poorly educated workers to get bumped out of jobs for which they had previously been hired and into poorer ones. It may be predicted that if educational expansion continues into the future, those workers in the United States who have little education will continue to earn less, both in relative terms and, if the economy continues to stagnate, in absolute terms as well.

6. Educational Expansion and Labor Markets: Evidence from Kenya

Many of the changes in labor market conditions reported for the United States also hold for Kenya. Kenya underwent an exceptionally rapid educational expansion, which had the effect of creating greater competition for skilled jobs. The newly educated could not get the same kinds of jobs as those previously educated had managed to secure for themselves. The result was bumping: after a time, those educated workers unable to get high-level jobs sought lower level jobs, for which they have been hired preferentially (Carnoy and Thias 1971, Knight and Sabot 1990). Fields (1972) developed the bumping model based on patterns in Kenya in the late 1960s and early 1970s. Subsequent evidence shows that

substantial bumping continues. However, unlike the United States, educational expansion in Kenya has driven down the earnings of educated workers, reduced the private returns to schooling, and narrowed the educated–uneducated earnings differential.

See also: Education and the Labor Market; The Wage Contract and Education; Income Distribution and Education; Rates of Return to Education

References

Blackburn M L, Bloom D E, Freeman R 1990 The declining economic position of less skilled American men. In: Burtless G (ed.) 1990 *A Future of Lousy Jobs? The Changing Structure of US Wages*. Brookings Institution, Washington, DC

Blaug M 1973 *Education and the Employment Problem in Developing Countries*. International Labour Organisation, Geneva

Blaug M, Layard P R G, Woodhall M 1969 *The Causes of Graduate Unemployment in India*. Allen Lane/Penguin, London

Boissiere M, Knight J B, Sabot R H 1985 Earnings, schooling, ability, and cognitive skills. *Am. Econ. Rev.* 75(5): 1016–30

Bound J, Johnson G 1992 Changes in the structure of wages during the 1980s: An evaluation of alternative explanations. *Am. Econ. Rev.* 82(3): 371–91

Carnoy M, Thias H 1971 The rates of return to schooling in Kenya. *East. Africa Econ. Rev.* 3(2): 63–103

Ehrenberg R, Smith R 1991 *Modern Labor Economics. Theory and Public Policy*. Harper Collins, New York

Fields G S 1972 Private and social returns to education in labor surplus economies. *East. Africa Econ. Rev.* 4(1): 41–62

Fields G S 1974 The private demand for education in relation to labor market conditions in less-developed countries. *The Economic Journal* 84(336): 906–25

Freeman R 1976. Academic Press, New York

Freeman R 1989 Labor market tightness and the declining economic position of young less educated male workers in the United States. Unpublished paper, Harvard University, Cambridge, Massachusetts

Knight J, Sabot R 1990 *Education, Productivity and Inequality*. Oxford University Press, Oxford

Krueger A 1971 Turkish education and manpower development: Some impressions. In: Miller D R (ed.) 1971 *Essays in Labor Force and Employment in Turkey*. Ankara

Skorov G 1968 Highlights of the Symposium. In: UNESCO 1968 *Manpower Aspects of Educational Planning*. UNESCO/IIEP, Paris

Thurow L 1975 *Generating Inequality*. Basic Books, New York

US Department of Education (various years) *Digest of Education Statistics*. Office of Educational Research and Improvement, Washington, DC

Education and Informal Labor Markets

M. Tueros

This entry examines the functions that education plays in the performance of informal labor markets. It first reviews some characteristics of the concept of the informal sector and its uses in labor market analysis. It then proceeds to discuss evidence linking education with labor market outcomes seeking to derive consequences for the formulation of policies related to the improvement of working conditions in the informal sector. The relationship between the level and types of skills required by informal sector occupations and their sources is focused on. Finally it treats some general issues of educational policy for informal sector needs from the viewpoint of standard educational planning criteria.

1. The Informal Sector in Labor Market Analysis

Since its introduction in the early 1970s, the informal sector concept has received considerable attention in labor market analysis, especially from research on structural changes and adjustments to labor market in developing countries. The use of the informal sector as a conceptual tool basically assumes that it is a structural feature of the labor market that may be identified by *a priori* criteria and characterized by its linkages. The approach taken here views the informal sector as a set of activities aimed at income generation, performed in production, trade, or services sectors, and carried out by small-scale establishments with few wage-earning workers, with labor composed mostly of family or apprentice workers, who have little capital and no legal recognition. The diverse emphases of researchers on one or more aspects of this concept have elicited a multiplicity of empirical approaches that generate confusing data. Despite these drawbacks, the informal sector/modern sector dichotomy is accepted as explaining some of the complexity and trends in labor dynamics within the urban economy.

An increasing number of studies on the informal sector have stressed its linkages to problems of employment, income distribution, and satisfaction of needs. They have shown that:

(a) The informal sector plays a key role in urban and national employment, accounting for 30 to 60 percent of the urban labor force, depending upon the developing region considered (e.g., PREALC 1978). Its rate of growth is also considerably larger than that of modern employment.

(b) A major characteristic of informal activities is the heterogeneity of technical and human capital, which is still not adequately addressed in the research on forms of production and labor.

(c) Informal activities face a number of constraints that hinder the maximization of use of productive factors. These constraints are embedded in the regulatory framework and the business environment that circumscribe informal labor activities.

The analysis of the impact of education in the informal labor market entails a choice of methodological approaches that allow for its unique characteristics as a labor market. Standard neoclassical assumptions of most labor market analysis refer to the meeting of labor supply and demand in an unrestrained context, with wages fixed as a result of competitive pressures. This scarcely applies to informal sector labor conditions where most labor is comprised either of unwaged workers, or of self-employed people in one-person units. Consequently the usual methodology based on estimations of human capital earnings functions lacks fundamental precision when applied to informal labor markets analysis and should be modified accordingly. Among the alternative models of informal sector labor markets that have been proposed, there are those based on the assumption of labor participation as a self-selection process (e.g., Grotaeert 1990), of the job search as a probabilistic process, and of the structural segmentation of labor markets (Souza and Tokman 1978, Carnoy et al. 1980). Another methodological issue that arises when approaching the special characteristics of informal labor markets is the adequacy of individual earnings as the unit of analysis as opposed to informal establishments' revenues: individual entrepreneur's earnings dependent on personal factors including education do not explain all sources of informal income, which is also a function of production inputs in addition to those in the human capital equation.

2. Education, Earnings, and Mobility in the Informal Sector

Regardless of the way the informal sector is modeled, research has shown consistent results about the role performed by educational factors on informal labor markets. It seems that, compared to modern sector employees, human capital factors account for smaller amounts of earnings variation in informal sector workers. This has been shown in African countries such as Côte d'Ivoire (Vijverberg 1988) as well as in Latin America (for Chile, see Romaguera and Paredes

1987, and for Peru, see Moock et al. 1990). On average, human capital factors explain 15–40 percent of income variation in informal earnings, but as much as 60 percent in the case of modern labor market samples. There is also evidence of a "credential effect" of schooling on informal earnings, in which its impact increases when an educational level is completed as compared to equivalent school attainment but with no completion of educational level (Tueros 1992).

The impact of training on earnings follows a rather different pattern, showing high contributions in the modern sector but scanty or even negative ones on informal activities (for instance Arriagada 1990). In general, literacy and numeracy developed by schooling constitute basic skills for informal work, and the higher the school level attained, the greater the effect on informal income. On the other hand, the kind of specific occupational training geared to modern enterprise characteristics that most informal operators acquire is hardly relevant to their special training needs.

An issue that requires more attention is the impact of education on social mobility to and from the informal sector. By analyzing intragenerational mobility patterns between first and present occupation, Pastore (1981) in Brazil has shown that schooling and experience are strong determinants of mobility from the informal to the formal sector, and a main factor in the permanence of formal sector occupations.

3. Education as a Factor in the Performance of Informal Enterprises

The studies reviewed utilized household surveys and individual earnings as units of analysis. Another perspective can be taken from the analysis of economic efficiency in informal establishments. At the enterprise level, the relationship between education and economic efficiency has distinctive characteristics depending upon several factors. One such factor is scale of operations and the distinction between formal and informal sector activities. By definition, informal businesses work with technologies characterized by low capital intensity, flexibility of operations, and high specificity in terms of their markets. Consequently, educational requirements for informal sector occupations are necessarily different from those of the formal sector. In most countries, schooling, particularly its vocational variety, directly addresses only the demands of formal industrial activities, from curriculum to discipline and social organization (as the literature on "correspondence" has shown). Vocational education is scarcely relevant to the needs of the informal sector, where production conditions are labor-intensive, and more exhausting, risky, and exploitative than in the formal sector. Training would have to be highly functional to these characteristics if there is a chance that, given the low rate of profit

extraction, its benefits would exceed its relatively high costs.

3.1 Schooling Factors in Informal Production

While analysis of schooling factors in production enterprises has usually been undertaken in modern sector contexts, there are no clear-cut results concerning its relevance to nonmodern settings. When nonfarm informal production is analyzed in a profits or an earnings function, the usually clear positive contribution of schooling to explained variation in informal individual earnings samples decreases noticeably. On average, contribution of human capital variables varies from 5 to 15 percent of informal enterprises' revenues or profits. An increasing number of studies show that the less productive or poorer the enterprises' sample is, the smaller the impact of formal education factors (Maldonado 1987 on the informal sector of sub-Saharan African countries). They also show that in some cases (e.g., the World Bank "family enterprises" studies, see Vijverberg 1988, Moock et al. 1990), the impact of formal education or training is close to insignificant. It is difficult to explain the differences between informal sector individuals' and enterprises' equations unless some new interpretation is adopted. In other words, it could be argued from a modified human capital viewpoint that the voluntary choice of most qualified people for modern employment (or, in the case of many females with considerable investment in human capital, employment in unwaged household employment) diminishes overall productivity in the informal sector. Empirically, this decrease is accounted for as a consequence of truncated general population samples and is treated in self-selection bias models such as Grootaert (1990). Alternatively, it can be posited as a result of internal segmentation of informal sector production forms, in which the positive educational impact on semicapitalist informal enterprises' profits is offset by the negative or insignificant impact of educational factors on incomes in a larger number of noncapitalist informal units (Tueros 1992).

3.2 Training and Informal Enterprises

Standard human capital theory would predict that, given a direct positive effect of schooling on productivity, an additional direct and strong positive role of informal training on informal output would be expected. Moreover, from the human capital distinction between general and specific training, and given the poor supply of formal (general) educational opportunities for informal workers, a greater role for potential and real job experience than formal schooling would not be surprising. However, empirical results show that vocational training does not seem to have any impact whatsoever on the productivity of informal enterprises (Moock et al. 1990 on Peru, Vijverberg 1988 on Côte d'Ivoire). The implication is that either educational factors combine in other proportions than those in the modern sector, or that optimization in the production function is constrained by a different set of institutional settings than in formal production.

3.3 The Human Capital Model and Informal Production

If the analysis is kept within the limits of individual production units, it is increasingly clear that standard human capital or production function models will be insufficient to account for its variation. Research shows that other aspects of entrepreneurial behavior are as important, in addition to entrepreneur's individual characteristics, in explaining differences in economic performance. However, this evidence has been shown only in the anthropological literature. In order to improve the explanatory capacity of production function models of efficiency on a cross-section of informal production units, variables related to the role played by family, gender, neighborhood, professional, regional, and other social networks in which the informal entrepreneur finds most of his or her resources and markets need to be taken into account.

In general, education contributes positively to economic payoffs in informal firms. For reasons discussed above, this relationship would more likely hold in the "efficient" units than in others. There will be some structural factors interacting with this relationship, like technological complexity, market niche where the firm operates, and other background variables. It is also likely that the trade-off between education and economic efficiency would not follow a linear pattern. For example, the "minimum threshold" of formal schooling needed to produce an economic impact found in several vocational education studies might be useful in order to enlarge the understanding of the effects of education in the informal economy.

Nevertheless, some qualifications need to be made. Conventional schooling does not seem to have a relevant impact beyond a basic minimum requirement of literacy and numeracy when success in informal business depends on skills other than an academic education. For instance, it is insignificant in trade occupations, where what is needed is a good knowledge of the market segment in which the firm is operating (neighborhood, family clients, etc.), which does not require schooling, although it does require a highly specific learning process. On the other hand, if the firm uses machinery or has a complex, highly symbolic work process, schooling would be an advantage for its workers because they would possess relevant skills (literacy, numeracy, mechanics, etc.) that are expected to be provided by schools. As more than half of informal firms are in urban service activities and no more than 15 percent in manufacturing on the average in Latin America (PREALC 1978) and Africa, it might be said that school-acquired skills exert only a low influence in the determination of economic efficiency. However, it can also be argued

that, as is consistent with the internal heterogeneity characteristic of the sector, those firms with higher productivity will be more susceptible to the influence of their entrepreneurs' and workers' schooling than those less efficient, as some evidence shows (Fluitman and Oudin 1992). Efficient informal units would accept more readily the kind of skills that conventional vocational schooling develops because more complex technology could be incorporated to production processes if labor were more schooled.

4. Educational Systems and Informal Sector: Criteria of Policy Analysis

Some of the criteria of educational policy analysis can be helpful in assessing the value of educational systems for informal sector workers. Educational services for informal operators are appreciated in new ways if perspectives such as equity and efficiency are applied to them.

4.1 Equity

The issue of equity deals with some of the hardest problems in the human resources aspect of informal sector work. An initial problem is presented by the highly unequal opportunities of access to education, regardless of form, that prevail among the diverse groups that compose the informal sector. However, it could be argued that it is not always their socioeconomic background that makes the difference. One of the few homogeneities of the informal sector is the poverty of its workers. Inequity in access to education by informal workers is related mostly to gender, although migration condition and age can play some role. Similarly, gender is associated with discrimination in rewards to equivalent work. Some evidence is given by Merrick (1976), who shows that in Belo Horizonte, Brazil, an informal sector male worker, aged 35–49 years, with incomplete primary education, gets 55 percent of the income he could earn working in the formal sector. If the worker is female, she only gets 47 percent. Despite the high proportion of women in informal work and low levels of formal or nonformal educational achievement across the sector, women as a group have consistently less education (basic, vocational, or otherwise) and work experience. They also are limited to a few occupations and activities, mostly related to domestic skills, which are among those with the lowest productivity and income (Hallak and Caillods 1981).

4.2 Internal Efficiency

The internal efficiency perspective estimates whether a given educational delivery system is effective in providing the cognitive learning required for informal sector occupations. Most of formal education services, either vocational or academic, show low internal efficiency, as formal education seems to offer small cognitive relevance for informal work. Yet there is increasing research regarding areas such as literacy and numeracy skills in informal occupations whose applications in curricular change could enhance schooling's relevance for informal work. It also seems that a good knowledge of the environmental properties of the market in which the firm is operating (neighborhood, family clients, etc.) is critical for the success of the business. This requires a highly practical learning process (MacLaughlin 1979) which might also become a subject of curricular change in formal vocational schools.

4.3 External Efficiency

The issue of external efficiency is concerned with how education influences actual economic performance, both of individuals in the informal labor market and of informal establishments in goods and services markets. It seems that formal education has a range of influences in determining income levels in the informal sector, and that it is subject to contextual qualifications. Schooling would appear to be a good determinant of informal sector earnings, although gender, experience, and the productivity tier of the workplace seem to be even more important as predictors. However, as discussed above, education loses much of its impact on efficiency when nonlabor determinants of income are accounted for, as shown in studies on informal enterprises.

A view to economic efficiency would also deal with how cost-effectiveness analysis of educational programs can be useful in this regard. For informal sector work, the most cost-effective educational programs seem to be those in the category of on-the-job training, because, while providing most of the skills required for an informal sector job, their costs are minimal, both from social and private criteria. On the other hand, vocational education appears to be highly inefficient, with both high costs (especially social ones) and low benefits. In fact, the increasing numbers of technical education graduates who eventually opt for self-employment suggests that the rationale of vocational education investment should be revised, at least in countries with declining modern sectors.

In summary, depending on a number of factors, including the size of specific activities, the level of economic development, and the degree of access to the educational system, informal sector development in a given area will require unique links between human resources policy institutions and the informal labor force. It will draw more heavily on one or another educational subsystems for its skills development. For instance, in East African countries, the informal sector is concentrated in productive activities rather than in services; vocational training is often a high-status alternative to academic education, and few informal workers receive formal vocational training.

In addition, basic primary education is widespread and cheap, while vocational schools are scarce, expensive—from a social point of view—and highly selective, and functional to the needs of modern employment in the private or public sectors. Thus, it is no surprise that vocational education students use their skills to obtain administrative jobs instead of applying them to production occupations. In this context, indigenous apprenticeship systems answer more efficiently than other educational structures the training demands of informal production.

A different picture can be obtained in contemporary Latin America. In a country such as Argentina, with a long-established industrial base and a highly educated work force, vocational education is reasonably available and has low prestige in comparison to academic education. It was therefore understandable that the long economic recession that afflicted the country drove most vocational education graduates into self-employment, rather than cause them to look for jobs in large private or public enterprises with shrinking numbers of openings. Here, a reinforcement of traditional vocational systems seems to be the appropriate policy response to informal sector training problems.

These examples illustrate how difficult the prospects are for educational policy when informal sector demands are also taken into account. The act of coupling highly heterogeneous educational needs with a supply provided by a no less varied set of educational institutions has proven to be a highly difficult task. It is increasingly urgent, however, to develop systemic alternatives to satisfy the educational demands of a sector that might hold the key to equitable economic development in many areas of the developing world.

References

Arriagada A 1990 Labor markets outcomes of non-formal training for male and female workers in Peru. *Econ. Educ. Rev.* 9(4): 331–42

Carnoy M et al. 1980 Segmented labor markets: A review of the theoretical and empirical literature and its implications for educational planning. In: Hallak J, Caillods F (eds.) 1980 *Education, Work and Employment II.* UNESCO/IIEP, Paris

Fluitman F, Oudin X 1992 *Skill Acquisition and Work in Microenterprises: Evidence from Lomé, Togo.* Vocational Training Branch, International Labour Organisation, Geneva

Grootaert C 1990 Returns to formal and informal vocational education in Cote d'Ivoire: The role of the structure of the labor market. *Econ. Educ. Rev.* 9(4): 309–17

Hallak J, Caillods F 1981 *Education Training and the Traditional Sector* UNESCO, International Institute for International Planning, Paris

MacLaughlin S D 1979 *The Wayside Mechanic: An Analysis of Skill Acquisition in Ghana.* Center for International Education. University of Massachusetts, Amherst, Massachusetts

Maldonado C 1987 *Petits Producteurs Urbains d'Afrique Francophone: Programme Mondial de l'Emploi*. International Labour Organisation, Geneva

Merrick D 1976 Employment and earnings in the informal sector of Brazil: The case of Belo Horizonte *Journal of Developing Areas* 10(3): 337–53

Moock P, Musgrove P, Stelcner M 1990 *Education and Earnings in Peru's Informal Nonfarm Family Enterprises*. PPR Working Paper No. 236. The World Bank, Washington, DC

Pastore J 1981 Mobilidade social sob condicoes de segmentacao de mercado no Brasil. *Estudos Econ.* 6(3): 21–42

PREALC (Regional Employment Program for Latin America) 1978 *Sector Informal: Funcionamiento y Politicas* PREALC (ILO), Santiago

Romaguera P, Paredes R 1987 *Modelos de Capital Humano y Segmentación* Documentos de Trabajo No. 306. PREALC-ILO, Santiago

Souza P R, Tokman V 1976 The urban informal sector in Latin America *Int. Lab. Rev.* 114(3): 355–63

Tueros M 1992 *Education heterogeneity, and productive efficiency in Peru's informal sector* dissertation, Unpublished doctoral, Stanford University, Stanford, California

Vijverberg W 1988 *Profits from Self-Employment: A Case Study from Côte d'Ivoire*. LSMS Working Papers. The World Bank, Washington, DC

Further Reading

Fluitman F (ed.) 1989 *Training for Work in the Informal Sector*. International Labour Organisation, Geneva

Hultin M 1987 *Vocational Education in Developing Countries: A Review of Studies and Project Experience*. Education Division Documents No. 34. Swedish International Development Authority (SIDA). Education Division, Stockholm

King K J 1990 Training for the urban informal sector: Issues for practioners. In: Turnham D, Salame B, Schwartz A (eds.) 1990

Turnham D, Salome B, Schwartz A 1990 *The Informal Sector Revisited*. OECD publications, Paris

Tokman V 1990 The informal sector in Latin America: Fifteen years later. In: Turnham D, Salome B, Schwartz A (eds.) 1990

SECTION III

The Benefits of Education

Introduction

M. Carnoy

When economists first began taking education seriously as a source of economic growth, they focused much of their attention on the economic benefits of education. Their quest was for evidence that, with other things being equal, more educated workers had a higher rate of productivity than less educated workers. Beyond presenting that evidence, economists suggested that education might have nonpecuniary and external pecuniary effects—educated workers not only had higher productivity and incomes themselves, but also enjoyed other benefits and increased others' ability to produce and have more enjoyable lives. Thus, more education had external income and consumption effects—for example, increasing a population's wealth, reducing crime, and reducing fertility rates, would lead to population growth.

Lewis Solmon's opening entry in this section categorizes and summarizes the arguments that have been made regarding such benefits. He claims, persuasively, that the benefits to educational investment include a wide range of pecuniary and nonpecuniary gains, both to the individuals who invest in it (higher incomes, being able to think critically) and to the society as a whole (higher productivity, innovation, better health) that also accrue to others than those who invest in education. He warns the reader, however, that differences in individuals with different educational attainments cannot all be attributed to different educational experiences, and that this has clouded the broad issue of how large the benefits of education really are.

It has been a tall order finding hard evidence for some of these claims for the benefits of education, almost irrespective of whether differences in individuals should be attributed to education. Increased productivity associated with more educated labor has been measured mainly for independent farmers, as Martin Carnoy, Peter Moock, and Hodan Addou show in their entries. There is little or no evidence that employees who work in teams or on assembly lines and have invested more in education systematically outperform their colleagues. One reason for that may be, Carnoy

argues, because generally production line workers or group production workers produce in teams, making it difficult to identify individual contributions to higher productivity (see also Mark Blaug, in his analysis of the incomplete labor contract). Such workers also tend to have little decision-making power, lowering the potential impact of workers' investment in schooling. Unlike individual farmers, self-employed entrepreneurs, or employees with at least some autonomy (such as researchers and university professors, whose decision-making capacity can have considerable effect on their output), most production and service employees are required to perform tasks in which productivity depends on a whole set of external conditions, including the productivity of other workers in the firm or plant. Nevertheless, there may be some evidence that workers with specialized skills may produce more than those without such skills in production line jobs, as Weifang Min argues in his entry assessing differential productivity in a Chinese automobile plant.

Because of the difficulty of obtaining productivity data for the employed labor force in any economy, in the past, economists quickly fell back to using earnings data for individuals with varying amounts of schooling to measure the primary economic benefits of education. The use of earnings was based on the argument that with perfect competition and full information, wages equal marginal productivity. Piero Cipollone's and Toshiaki Tachibanaki's entries review both the argument for using earnings as a proxy for productivity in estimating the economic payoff to education and the major results that economists have found relating education to higher earnings. Beginning with those two entries, the rest of the contributions to this section review the case for economic benefits to education primarily in terms of earning differences between those with more or less schooling, lower and higher quality schooling, and those with different kinds of education.

The estimates of economic benefits measured in terms of differential earnings have been subject to enormous controversy in the economics of education. Besides the problem of whether earnings differences are isomorphic with productivity differences, the main issue confronting economists has been whether earnings differences associated with different amounts of education reflect the effect of that education on earnings, or rather reflect the impact of other, unmeasured variables correlated with additional schooling. Early on, economists identified some portion of these earnings benefits as returns to "ability" differences between individuals taking more and less schooling. The "ability" specter has continued to hang over such estimates. Part of ability differences may also be associated with differences in the quality of schooling, as Carnoy argues in his second entry in this section. The benefits usually associated with the amount of education taken may also include benefits to the quality of education taken. Thus, the difference in earnings between workers who have completed college versus those who have completed high school probably includes the benefits of the higher quality high school (and primary) education taken by those who complete college compared to those who do not. This implies that the return to college completion is less than a simple comparison of earnings differences between the two levels.

The payoff to different kinds of schooling (vocational versus academic versus nonformal education) may be quite different and also may benefit different social groups of individuals. In addition, there may be greater benefits to schooling when accompanied by complementary forms of education, such as apprenticeship. Yue-Ping Chung, Stephan Hamilton and Robert Glover, and Ana Maria Arriagada and Pia Wong address these issues in their entries. They highlight yet another thorn in the side of economists: trying to assign benefits to schooling as an investment as separate from other income-enhancing investments. Returns to schooling are inexorably bound to the way that schooling is allocated among different groups of students and to the training opportunities in work that schooling affords to these groups. Employers have often argued that much of schooling is worthless in the job market, yet they use it to select workers for training into different kinds of jobs.

Finally, there are nonpecuniary and "external" effects of a schooled labor force and population that may be quite large, although in some cases, second generational. Walter MacMahon analyzes the consumption benefits of education, which he regards as the nonmonetary returns accruing from education to the individual throughout his or her lifespan, including improved health and improved consumption behavior. Barbara Wolfe summarizes the argument and the model for analyzing external returns. She suggests that additional education increases productivity in the home as well as the marketplace, including a mother's education's effect on family health, which also improves the health of others. The fact that parents' education can increase their children's cognitive development means that they will do better in school, reducing the cost of schooling them to given level of achievement. Crime may also be reduced, reducing social costs considerably. Laura Gibney reviews the case for another important externality—lower fertility rates in societies with rapid population growth rates. Lower fertility provides a direct benefit to women as well as an external benefit to others competing for scarce resources. Its environmental effects are also an externality in the long run. The main issue is whether lower fertility is linked to more education—Gibney reviews the case that it is. David Stern argues that because of risk, firms may under-invest in the education and training of workers. The issue here is *who* captures benefits, as well as their size.

Since most of the nonmonetary and external payoffs to additional schooling have eluded the easily interpreted earnings measure, they have rarely been included in the overall returns to education. Even so, MacMahon argues that consumption benefits of education may be large, reaching 50–60 percent of the monetary returns expected by students in the United States from their higher education. Social benefits and externalities, such as those analyzed by Wolfe and Gibney, may also be large, especially over the long run.

Benefits of Education

L. C. Solmon and C. L. Fagnano

Any discussion of educational benefits must start with two basic observations. The first is that people with more education usually differ from those with less education, though it is a matter of debate as to how far this results simply from education. The second observation is that individuals change as they obtain more schooling. Yet to what extent are changes the result of schooling? To what extent are they the effects of maturing generally or of other experiences unrelated to education? Ideally, study of these issues should consider two groups of individuals similar in all respects except for the fact that one experienced a particular type of education and the other did not. If advantages were observed only for those with the educational experience, then it would be possible to attribute those advantages to the education, since no other factors could account for the differences.

In the real world, as opposed to the ideal world of educational and social science research, it is impossible to study two identical groups, one with and one without education. In the first place, in situations where certain individuals or groups of individuals reach a certain level of education and other individuals or groups do not, there are clearly significant differences other than educational attainment between the individuals or groups. This has resulted in many attempts to hold constant statistically factors which differ between attenders and nonattenders, but which cannot be held constant by selection of experimental and control groups directly. The problem with attempts at statistical control is that one can never be certain that all important differences have been taken into account, because many factors may be either unthought of or unmeasurable.

1. The Dimensions of Educational Benefits

For all levels of education, the discussion of educational benefits must begin by asking a number of questions. The first of these is: who will benefit? There are several potential beneficiaries of the educational process. The first and most obvious is the student. However, even here it is impossible to look at benefits to students as a homogeneous group. Individuals enter the educational process with a variety of complementary and/or hindering characteristics which will either help or impede them in achieving what they seek. Thus individual characteristics of students must be considered in conjunction with benefits. One of the fundamental policy questions in this area is: what happens if certain students are able to benefit more or less from a particular type of education? Should different resources be provided for those with different needs, or does equality of educational opportunity demand that equal resources be provided for unequal students?

In addition to the students themselves, other groups of beneficiaries must be considered, such as others in society (nonstudents) who may or may not invest in the education of a student either directly (as in the case of family and friends) or indirectly (as in the case of individuals who support education by paying taxes). Benefits to individual students are easy to conceptualize: the student who learns to read in school is better-off than were he or she unable to read. In economic jargon this is known as a "private benefit" of education. The economist distinguishes private benefits from social benefits. Social benefits are ones that accrue to people other than those being educated. If a student graduates from medical school he or she will obviously obtain the benefits of high income and the satisfaction of curing the sick. However, if that medical doctor were to pursue a research career and eventually develop a cure for a major disease, the beneficiaries of his or her education would be not only be the doctor who received income and acclaim, but also those who were saved from the disease by his or her discovery. Society is clearly better-off because of the education of that individual, and the individual has not appropriated all of the benefits of his or her education for him- or herself: others derive (social) benefits above and beyond those (private benefits) received by the individual doctor.

Basic economic analysis leads to the inference that if decisions are made by individuals who base their actions on the personal costs and benefits of education, and if net social benefits are produced by education, from society's perspective insufficient education will be purchased unless there is subsidy to potential purchasers. It is important to know what benefits accrue not only to students but to society at large in order to devise policies that achieve the socially optimal amount of education.

Most of the literature merely distinguishes between private and social benefits as discussed above. However, there is a third important group of beneficiaries from education at each of its levels: namely, those in the institutions who teach, administrate, and provide other services. This is important, because in many cases decisions are made within a school not for the benefit of students or society but for the benefit of those employed there.

At the elementary-school level, salaries are generally paid on the basis of degree attainments and seniority, not on the basis of an individual teacher's ability to impart knowledge or other educational benefits to students. At the level of higher education many compulsory courses in the humanities are maintained primarily to ensure that humanities faculties are able to maintain minimum class sizes in fields in which enrollments are declining. Additionally, administrators often decide to erect new buildings and expand the size of institutions, even if alternative uses of funds in developing a new curriculum or improving the quality of a smaller institution might have greater educational benefits to students. However, the former choices might lead to greater acclaim and individual power for particular administrators. It is therefore vital when evaluating educational decisions to ask in whose interest decisions have been made. By doing so, it will soon be discovered that, at all levels of education, decisions made can have a very different impact on individual students, on society at large, and on people employed in the institutions. This helps to explain why certain objectives (or what some people regard as objectives) are not achieved in various educational settings.

Once the potential recipients of educational benefits have been identified, the various types of benefits should be considered. Certain benefits are explicit goals of educational institutions, such as enabling a grammar-school student to have a certain facility in reading, or ensuring that the chemistry graduate understands the various ways in which elements can be combined to form chemical compounds. In addition to benefits that are explicit goals, there can be unsought results or side effects, which may also be beneficial. Few colleges would admit to the explicit function of being a dating service, but one side-effect benefit of going to college for many individuals is the opportunity of meeting a future spouse during the college years.

Certain general aptitudes and characteristics are thought to result from attending school. These include an understanding of the value of democracy as opposed to a dictatorial form of government and the ability to think critically and reason well. Although various educational institutions would admit to the hope that their students would acquire these characteristics, they do not usually offer courses entitled "Appreciating Democracy" or "Thinking Critically." These skills might be the indirect effects of courses in civics, social studies, history, philosophy, English literature, and other subjects. Depending upon the degree of explicitness with which a goal is held, it may be more difficult to determine whether the goal is achieved. For example, most students obtain reading scores, thanks to the explicit nature of the desire to teach students to read. On the other hand, the appreciation of democracy or the ability to think critically are less measurable.

Whether the result of explicit or indirect behavior of students and educational institutions, a variety of possible educational benefits have been considered in the literature. These have been categorized according to whether they are psychological or behavioral; cognitive or affective; vocational or nonvocational; monetary or nonmonetary. It must be kept in mind that benefits of any of these types might accrue to students, society at large, or to those employed within the educational institutions.

Consideration of these categories of benefits again makes it clear that some are easier to identify than others. In their constant desire to conduct cost–benefit analyses, economists tend to consider benefits that can be evaluated in monetary terms. One school of economics views education in part as an investment in human capital, whereby expenditures of money and time are made to acquire education which increases individual productivity, value in the labor market, and income (Schultz 1963). However, vocational or monetary outcomes are only one type of benefit, and perhaps not the most important type. Others must be considered. There are also numerous psychological, behavioral, cognitive, and affective impacts of schooling, but these are very difficult to identify and, once identified, even more difficult to evaluate.

The problem is how to identify, assess, measure, and evaluate the benefits of education. As has already been noted, differences in individuals with different educational attainments cannot all be attributed to different educational experiences. The observation that a college graduate earns more than one with only a high school education should not lead to the conclusion that going to college necessarily yields higher income. It is possible that the college graduate is more intelligent and motivated than the high school graduate and that

the college graduate would have earned more even had he or she not attended college. The problem is that basic intelligence, and more so motivation, are factors that affect income but are very difficult to isolate and measure.

The central issue of educational benefits is the question of what changes are effected by the educational experience. Methodologically, this implies that pre- and post-test measures on individuals are required that will identify changes caused by education. This has come to be known as the "value-added approach." In essence, knowing an individual's initial attributes and aptitudes would lead to a predicted achievement in some test or other. At the end of an educational experience one could determine actual achievement. By comparing the actual to the predicted achievement, one could observe the impact of the educational experience in this dimension. Even when that is done, if such a change is observed, it may not be attributable to the educational experience itself. Certain changes in individuals may be the result of normal maturation, which would have occurred with or without attendance at school. Other changes may be a function of such diverse factors as changes in national economic conditions or a divorce in the student's family. Thus, there is a need to net out or account for other noneducational factors which might confound the link between the educational experience and the changes observed in the students.

Assuming that this approach revealed that attendance at a particular institution led to a gain in a certain type of knowledge for a student, the question then becomes: how can the worth of such an achievement be evaluated? This issue is addressed by Bowen (1977) in his classic treatise *Investment in Learning*. There he asks: "What is the worth of the changes in individuals wrought by higher education?" Bowen suggests five different ways of making such a calculation, and applies each methodology specifically to higher education. His first way of evaluating changes in individuals is to argue that whatever is being spent on higher education is a measure of its worth; "the total expenditure on higher education would not have been made unless the students and their families, the citizenry, and philanthropic donors collectively thought the returns justified the outlays. ... Nevertheless, that American people do devote $85 billion of resources each year to higher education is some evidence that they value it highly" (p. 438). Bowen was writing in 1977. It is worth noting that, a decade and a half after his observation, Americans increased their expenditure on higher education in real terms by over 20 percent. Since education's share of gross national product remained constant or rose slightly, Americans apparently continued to value higher education long after Bowen conducted his analysis.

Bowen's second approach was to investigate the reactions of clients to their own college education.

He concluded that "this evidence is far from conclusive—especially because the clients did not pay the whole cost. Yet the overwhelming favorable reaction of clients can only mean that something of great value was received by a larger majority of students" p. 439). Bowen's third approach is to consider the possible increases in the capital value of human beings resulting from higher education. However repugnant, individuals are valued in connection with claims for damages in cases of death and disability; they are valued by implication when decisions are made about expenditures intended to save lives, as in air or highway travel or workplaces; and people value their own lives when they make decisions to accept premium pay for risky work assignments. Bowen describes the literature on valuing human lives and points out that if it were possible to determine the extent to which, say, college graduates' lives are valued more highly than those with less education, one could aggregate across all college graduates to determine the extra value of human lives resulting from college education.

A fourth approach for estimating the value of college education is to look at the sources of growth in the United States over a particular period and determine the extent to which higher education was responsible for that growth. The well-known Denison (1962, 1964, 1974, 1984) approach of accounting for growth in national income has led to the conclusion that instructional activities have paid their way handsomely in the history of the United States. The fifth approach to estimating the value of college education is to look at the rate of return on investments in college education. The problem with this approach is that it only takes into account the earnings or the increased earnings potential enjoyed by students as the result of college attendance. (It must be remembered that there are numerous other potential educational benefits beside an individual's higher earnings.)

Each of these approaches—namely, expenditure levels, reaction of clients, the incremental value of human lives, the contribution to economic growth, and the rate of return—is applicable to elementary, secondary, college, and postgraduate education. The point is that although evaluation of benefits might be difficult, that should not preclude them from being considered; nor should it lead to the conclusion that benefits that are difficult to evaluate are not valuable.

After considering identification and measurement problems, there are still more questions to ask. An important one is: when do educational benefits occur? Some benefits occur during the educational experience itself. For example, the opportunity to enjoy an entertaining and stimulating class is an educational benefit. Certain types of educational benefits could be assessed by querying students during the time they are engaged in education. Similarly, the social benefits of having a local high school football game to attend occur during the educational experience. Other educational benefits can be identified upon completion of an educational program. For example, reading scores at graduation can be compared with those at entry, and the increment in reading scores of elementary-school children over, say, a year of schooling determined. The pretest–posttest methodology can be used not only to identify changes in knowledge but also to consider changes in attitudes and values.

Looking for educational benefits only during the years of schooling or upon completion precludes a realistic assessment of a wide variety of additional possible educational benefits. Numerous benefits accrue at times well past the completion of education. There are also serious questions of whether or not the effects of education are long-lasting. The point here is that by looking only at benefits that accrue during the schooling experience or at its conclusion may give quite inaccurate results.

The most vivid example of this would be the results obtained by comparing the salaries of a high school graduate who has been at work for 4 years with that of a college graduate entering his first job. It would be naive to expect that the earnings of the college graduate would necessarily exceed those of the high school graduate who has had four years more experience. Also, it is often observed that graduates from "higher quality" college programs often earn less at the beginning than graduates from "lower quality" programs. These apparent paradoxes can be explained by several factors. In particular, the individual with more education, or with better education, has usually demonstrated a comparative advantage in learning and so will take a job that enables him or her to continue learning while earning a living and beginning a career. Most employers are unwilling to incur the cost of educating employees, particularly when the employee is able to change employers at any moment. The way for more highly educated, or better educated, individuals to learn on the job is to take lower initial salaries to compensate the employer for the cost of providing additional education or training. The expectation is that, after several years, the individuals who have been investing by taking lower salaries while learning on the job will receive a payoff not only from formal schooling but also from the additional human capital acquired on the job. Thus, more educated individuals are observed to begin with lower salaries than less educated individuals, but over the years their salaries surpass those of people with less education, with the gap between the two groups widening over time.

If the educational benefit of higher earnings were to be evaluated at the time an individual with more or better education entered the labor market, it might be suggested that no educational benefit of this type existed because those with less or inferior education were earning more. It is necessary to observe income differentials after a substantial number of years in the labor market before it can be determined that there is an educational benefit in terms of higher income for the more highly educated.

Other impacts of education also occur some time after leaving college. It has generally been observed that the college years lead individuals to become increasingly more liberal in their political philosophy. However, other studies have shown that some years after their college experience, college graduates again become more conservative—indeed, even more conservative than they were upon entering college (Solmon and Ochsner 1978). This raises the question of whether the effect of education on political attitudes endures. It might be argued that the change to liberalism is a college impact (irrespective of whether it is a benefit) that is not enduring. Alternatively, the benefit under consideration might be identified as adopting a political philosophy that is in the student's best interest. During the college years, when educational subsidies and other types of support are a necessity, it is in the student's interest to advocate liberal causes. Afterward, when those liberal causes have to be financed by the individual's own tax payments, the educated person may see his or her interest as being served by a conservative ideology. In this sense, the understanding of different political philosophies might be viewed as an enduring effect of college. Finally, a student who would never have identified a course in English grammar as an educational benefit while struggling with the course might many years later recognize the tremendous value of that course when using the knowledge obtained to write the memoranda or speeches required in his or her particular line of work. Clearly, an assessment of educational benefits which stops at the time of graduation is an incomplete one.

Another question that must be asked is: what is it about education that caused or impeded the benefits? Is it the time in school? Is it the quality of the faculty staff, their teaching abilities, the physical plant, or other facilities? Is it the support services such as counseling, guidance, and the like? Is it the aptitude of students who attend? Or is it all of these things as they interacted with each other? In essence, much of the discussion of the impact or benefits of education at various levels to date has viewed education as a black box. That is, education is viewed as something people enter and leave. While in the box they change; but why they change is unknown.

Most studies that have attempted to identify particular factors such as quality of teachers and facilities generally have been forced to use highly aggregated measures of these inputs, thereby clouding the understanding of the actual interrelationship of particular factors with particular students. The most recent literature, particularly that dealing with educational impacts at the elementary or secondary school level, tends to emphasize the importance of looking at situations within schools and even within classrooms in order to understand what factors affect different students in different ways. There is clearly no universal answer to the question of what benefits accrue to whom during the educational process, nor will there be until it is known how individuals are affected by the various components of an educational experience.

2. Uses of Knowledge of Educational Benefits

The questions asked so far are fundamental to an understanding of the possible benefits of education at various levels. They are important because unless the benefits yielded by education are understood, various assessments and policy decisions will be made in a vacuum. It is necessary to know what benefits accrue from education in order to allocate resources not only among schools of various types and levels, but also between educational and other social programs. Educational benefits must also be appreciated in order to decide how to finance education at different levels. If benefits accrue to society in large amounts, this provides a justification for public subsidy. Alternatively, if virtually all benefits accrue to those who are educated, there are reasons to advocate self-financing of the education process, even if in the form of loans.

Educational benefits must also be identified in order to interpret the motivation of educators. What may seem irrational on one level may be explainable if it is appreciated that benefits accrue to those making the decisions. If those decisions are unjustified in terms of private and social educational objectives, action can be taken with full understanding of the situation. Basically, knowledge is required about educational benefits so that educational processes can be evaluated in terms of cost–benefit analysis (and associated resource allocation decisions) and in terms of assessing management.

The most overriding need to understand educational benefits is the result of the commitment of most countries to the achievement of equality of educational opportunity. In the first place, equal educational opportunity must be defined. Is it necessary for every student to attend any institution he or she chooses, or is it enough if every student has access to some but not all schools or colleges? Does access to the same amount of resources ensure equal opportunity? If so, does that mean that less able students should be given the same as more able students, even though more able students could reach the same levels of achievement with fewer resources? That is, does equal opportunity mean equal treatment in a particular educational institution, or does it mean that each student should have the right to equal educational benefits? If the latter is the case, those with less aptitude or less ability to obtain educational benefits might require a different treatment, particularly a treatment that might be more costly than that needed by other students to achieve the same end. But unless it can be understood what educational benefits have been obtained, it is impossible to assess the extent to which a country has moved toward equality of educational opportunity.

. Research on Benefits of Education

A considerable amount of research has been conducted on the educational benefits, impacts, and effects of each level of education. Yet for all levels, the research has focused on a very limited range of educational outputs and has not considered, in an empirical sense, a large number of other possible benefits. This section will summarize the major findings of the empirical research on educational benefits at both the elementary and secondary levels and at the higher education levels in the United States, where the research has been discussed in great detail. Some of the other possible benefits that have been discussed informally will also be considered, though they have rarely been documented and even more infrequently measured.

.1 Elementary and Secondary Education

The literature on educational effects typically asks whether or not schools with different resource levels (and hence different inputs) have correspondingly differential impacts on students, where impacts are measured by some type of standardized achievement test. From the Coleman Report of the early 1960s (Coleman and Moynihan 1966), the results of the surveys, individually and in combination, have most frequently been interpreted to demonstrate that school differences account for little of the variations in students' outcome measures (McPartland and Karweit 1979). However, these and other authors have concluded that the pessimism inherent in the statement that "schools bring little influence to bear upon a child's achievement that is independent of his background and general social context" (Coleman and Moynihan 1966, p. 325) is basically unwarranted (Madaus 1980). Readers are encouraged to study these two papers for an excellent perspective on the research on early school effects. It is sufficient to note here that most scholars now reject the findings that effects of school variables on student achievement are minimal, because the evidence provided in the studies is inadequate to reach such conclusions. As McPartland and Karweit (1979) emphasized:

> Each study is based on naturally occurring variations of environments found in existing public schools and uses student samples that are non-randomly distributed across schools. Because these studies do not meet the scientific standards for controlled experiments, methodological questions on the proper analysis and interpretation of non-experimental data apply to each of them. (p. 372)

The variety of criticisms of the school effects research can only be briefly listed here. The studies usually do not ask about the schools' objectives and then proceed to investigate the extent to which schools achieve these objectives. Schools certainly have many objectives other than to improve verbal ability or to maximize scores on standardized achievement tests. The dependent variables used in the most frequently cited studies probably do not represent either school achievements, even in such basic areas as reading or mathematics, or the appropriate goals of the schools and the teachers. Also, standardized tests are not linked to any common prescribed curriculum in the United States and so they are clearly testing some set of achievements that no single school particularly seeks. The test scores, therefore, come to reflect not achievement but how closely a particular school's curriculum parallels the curriculum implied by the test design.

The studies have also overlooked important environmental variations within the same schools, or have failed to measure the duration of exposure of different students to particular school factors. The typical model has implied that all students enter a black box (the school) and come out being somewhat different. In fact, different resources are targeted to certain students within the school (Oakes 1985). The characteristics of individual students must be linked with the teachers who actually taught them, rather than looking only at the impact of the average teacher. Yet the studies imply that all students within a school or school district are treated the same. Moreover, the learning consequences of additional instructional time and other resources may not be the same for all students, for all curricular units, or for all modes of classroom instruction. In sum, the variation of resources within schools available to students must be considered. Such work is dependent upon advances in research methodology that occurred from the mid-1980s onward. These will be discussed below.

The factors identified with school environment in the educational production function studies undertaken in the United States in the 1960s, 1970s and early 1980s tended to be fairly uniform throughout the country. These studies provided no information on how achievement related to school factors other than those in the restricted natural range. All schools have teachers with about the same level of education, classrooms with from about 10 to 45 students, and so on. It is not known if class sizes of 2 have different impacts from class sizes of 100 because there are not many of either size and rarely are the situations compared where a factor does and does not exist (e.g., all classrooms have a teacher). The small range of variation in the school measures causes two problems: since there is little variance in the explanatory variable, little of the variance in the dependent variable is explained, and nothing is known about the effects of variables with magnitudes outside the natural range.

There have also been a number of more technical problems with the school effects studies. When the aggregation level of certain background traits is too high, these can become confounded with measures of school resources. For example, it is clear how socioeconomic status might affect the achievement of a youngster (e.g., low socioeconomic status (SES) may

119

lead to low appreciation of education and hence low motivation to achieve and low actual achievement). But an aggregate measure of SES for the student body is probably highly related to the community's and school's resources. The SES measure is correlated with a school's funds, and if entered into a regression model before the resource measure will prevent the latter from demonstrating much effect.

The problem concerning ordering of variables deserves emphasis. In the absence of longitudinal data, information on students' home background has usually been used as a proxy for students' initial status (to control for the aptitudes the student brings to school). Home or background variables were entered first, and it was thus erroneously assumed that these influenced achievement only prior to and independent of school influences. In estimating the relative importance of nonschool and school variables, all of their shared variation was assigned to the nonschool factors, resulting in an underestimate of the school effects.

From the mid-1980s onward there were considerable methodological advancements in school effects research. Statisticians developed regression models for handling hierarchical data that produced more accurate estimates of school effects. Techniques pioneered by Aitkin et al. (1986), Raudenbush and Bryk (1986, 1988), and Wilms and Raudenbush (1989) to analyze cross-sectional and longitudinal hierarchical data (i.e., data collected on individual pupils grouped into schools) became employed more widely. Barr and Dreeben (1983) observed that schooling is conducted in layers or levels and that what happens at one level will affect what happens at subsequent levels. Burstein (1980) demonstrated that the individual child should be the primary unit of analysis and then variables measured at other levels (classroom, school, district) should be incorporated into the analytical model.

Later school effects studies looked at the types of curriculum delivered to students and compared general or comprehensive public schools with other types of schools. Typically, these studies looked at schools serving inner-city minority students who tended to be most at risk for school failure. What has been reported from these projects is that schools which accelerated the learning of at-risk students tended to have greater success than schools that concentrated on remediation of these same types of students (Levin and Hopfenberg 1991). Additionally, several studies demonstrated that the previously reported relationship between social background and school achievement is weaker in Catholic schools than in public schools (Coleman et al. 1981, 1982). Also, it was found that students attending Catholic and special-purpose schools tended to have significantly different educational outcomes than their public school peers. That is, the percentage of at-risk students in the Catholic and special purpose schools who graduated from high school, who took the Scholastic Aptitude Test (SAT) and who scored above the mean for their group was greater than for the same

types of students in typical public schools (Hill e al. 1990).

Using hierarchical linear modeling (HLM) tech niques, Lee and Bryk (1989) identified characte istics of high schools that encouraged academi achievement and promoted an equitable distributio of achievement across diverse social classes. Their re sults indicated that organizational differences amon Catholic and public schools exerted substantial im pacts on students' achievements. For example, a equitable distribution of high achievement is enhance when all students are required to take more academi courses. Additionally, when schools are small an resources unavailable for differentiating the academ ic program, this tends to promote broader academi achievement across all student groups. These finding supported the contention of other researchers tha the normative environment and academic organizatio found in Catholic and special-interest schools appear to promote academic achievement independent o background variables.

Unfortunately, the use of these multilevel model did not solve all the problems associated with schoo effects research. Measurement and specification er rors and the problem of multicollinearity continue to persist. (Multicollinearity is a problem confronte by statisticians and researchers in which two or mor factors, any of which may account for a phenomenon systematically vary together. In these circumstances it is not possible to determine the unique contributio of any of these factors to the phenomenon bein studied.) However, these new techniques did produc more precise estimates of variance between schoo and students, as well as estimates of the effects o background variables in reducing or explaining thes variables.

If conviction about the effectiveness of schools i imparting basic skills and knowledge to students ha not been strongly supported by data, the other allege benefits are supported even less. Schools have bee credited with certifying people as being eligible fo the next level of education. This could be a valuabl sorting function, but as high school graduation in th United States has become more dependent on tim spent and less on demonstrated achievement, and a admission to college has become more open an less based upon prior achievement, this function ha declined in value.

One basic rationale for the education of youngster has always been the custodial function. Schools kee children off the streets, reduce crime, free parent for work or leisure, and teach children the norm of civil society. The reader may decide if school still perform these functions, and if so, how valu able they are. Schools have similarly been credite with serving a socialization function: teaching chil dren how to get along, to share, to take turns, t dress, and to fit in. Whether this occurs and, if i does, whether it is a benefit are unclear. If any o these services were provided, both the students and the broader society would be affected. This is also the case with another long-alleged benefit, namely the entertainment services that a school provides for the community around it. These include athletic events, cultural activities, and extended educational programs.

In considering the benefits of precollege education other than providing knowledge and academically related skills and attitudes, it has become clear that many of them have become irrelevant to the mobile, heterogenous, mass-media society of the United States. These benefits were probably much more important at earlier stages in the social and economic development of the country.

3.2 Higher Education

The study of the benefits of higher education provides the opportunity to compare individuals who have achieved different numbers of years of schooling. That is, in addition to comparing those who attended different colleges, one can compare those with high school only to those who attend college without graduating, and to those with Associate of Arts degrees, bachelors' degrees, and postbaccalaureate training.

Economists focus on the private monetary or job- and career-related benefits received from colleges by those who attend and graduate not because they are only concerned with money, but because they want to see whether changes effected by college attendance enhance productivity (i.e., produce human capital) and thereby increase earnings. The questions are whether or not college attendance is likely to result in better jobs and higher earnings, and if so why?

The problem is of interest because the education–work fit has been the main justification for public support of higher education. Yet for the most part, career outcomes represent a private gain which should be purchased with private funds. Social benefits are the economic argument for public support. When the education–work fit seems less favorable, fewer people should be enrolling if labor market returns are all that matter, but subsidy moderates this. Subsidy should not be based on job outcomes, but it has been. Therefore, when the labor market becomes relatively less favorable for college graduates, subsidy declines, even though social benefits may still result.

What are the job-related benefits of higher education? The human capital theory (Schultz 1961) hypothesizes that the duration (quantity) and quality of education an individual obtains contribute to his or her human capital, which leads to greater productive capacity. It is also assumed that production capacity is reflected in higher earnings over a career if not immediately after graduation. An individual's human capital necessarily depends upon factors in addition to education (such as health, motivation, innate ability, and socioeconomic status). Thus the value of education in terms of earnings has been tested empirically

by looking at the partial correlation between earnings and the quantity and quality of schooling while holding constant as many other factors that might affect earnings as possible. From the early work of Becker (1983), which looked at highly aggregated census data from 1950, to the later studies of Taubman and Wales (1974), Solmon (1981), Rumberger, (1987), and Murphy and Welch (1989), each of which analyzed a different longitudinal database, the human capital model seems to have been validated: everything else being equal, those with more and better education seem to earn more.

Obviously the earnings–education correlation is always substantially less than perfect. This led Jencks (Jencks et al. 1972) to minimize the value of education for earnings. Jencks argued that "Economic success seems to depend on varieties of luck and on-the-job competence that are only moderately related to family background, schooling or scores on standardized tests … . Competence … seems in most cases to depend more on personality than on technical skills" (p.8). Of course, this argument merely points out that other factors that produce human capital are also important.

Other reasons for the imperfect relationship between education and earnings can also be suggested. There may be differences among educational programs in the extent to which they build human capital for the labor force (e.g., engineering courses) and the extent to which they provide consumption benefits unrelated to earning power (perhaps courses in the humanities). Similarly, jobs themselves yield not only monetary benefits, but also nonmonetary advantages. It is possible that advanced education might lead some people to highly desirable jobs that are relatively low-paying, but which have the attraction of providing other benefits such as satisfaction, challenge, and status. As examples, prestigious jobs in government and academe could be cited, which are often held by people who could be earning much more in other settings. The correlation between education and earnings may also break down somewhat when graduates produce a product or service that is not highly valued in the market. When demand for a product or service falls the price it can command also falls. For example, during the 1970s fewer students wanted to study the humanities than in the past. The supply of humanities teachers at that time exceeded the demand for them; therefore the wage rate for people with doctorates in the humanities fell (at least in inflation-adjusted dollars). This occurred even though the physical productivity of doctors in the humanities was not lower than it had been in the past (i.e., they could still teach the same things to the same number of students).

Finally, it is generally agreed that discrimination plays a role in preventing productivity from being reflected in higher earnings. The preference of certain employers for one type of worker (perhaps White males) over other types (perhaps women or minorities) would imply that at equal salaries the White males would be hired rather than equally productive women or minorities. Thus, for the latter groups to be hired by employers who discriminate, they must produce more to earn the same salary or accept lower salaries for equal productivity (Becker 1971). However, readers are warned to be cautious when deciding whether earnings differences are better explained by discrimination or productivity differences.

Some critics of the human capital model argue that the correlation between earnings and education is due to the fact that education, rather than enhancing productivity, serves merely as a screening device (Collins 1979, Dore 1976). One version of this argument claims that the more educated earn more because they are more productive but their productivity is due to nonschool factors. They would have been more productive than those with less education even had they not had as much schooling as they did. All education does is indicate to employers who is more productive. Thus, education is seen as no more than an expensive device for sorting the more from the less productive.

Another version of the screening argument is that employers think that college graduates are more productive even when they are not. This might result in those with more or higher prestige education being given special advantages, such as being put on a "fast track." Then they become more productive and successful even though education did not make them so.

The data, as much as they can, seem to support the argument that education serves to enhance productivity and thereby increases earnings, even though screening is also taking place (Layard and Psacharopoulos 1974, Chiswick 1973). From the mid-1970s the value of educational attainment (years) as a screen declined in the United States. Such a large proportion of college-aged people began to attend college, a college graduate was no longer a special person. Screening possibly then developed on the basis of quality of institution attended, major field of study, and grades.

Following the decline in the income advantage college graduates had over high school graduates in the mid-1970s, Freeman (1976) argued that the United States became an overeducated nation; that is, that too many people were getting too much schooling given the needs of the labor market. Immediately, several criticisms arose of Freeman's approach and of the work of others such as Berg (1971). Witmer (1978), after redoing Freeman's calculations, claimed to have found major errors. There were also problems with the way Berg defined "college level" jobs. Additionally, much of the decline in the high school–college wage gap was due to increases in wages for noncollege attenders working in craft industries or at minimum wage, both of which were irrelevant for people thinking of attending college. The 1980s witnessed a rebound in the rates of return to a college education which seemed to indicate that the experience of the 1970s was a temporary aberration in a general pattern of increasing returns to college education (Murphy and Welch 1989).

The "overeducated American" argument ignored the fact that unemployment for college graduates was substantially lower than for those who had not gone to college. It considered earnings only in the first job after college graduation, thus failing to recognize that if postschool on-the-job training is being acquired by college graduates, initial salaries will be misleading. In this case, the gap between college and high school salaries will widen over the years. Finally, the overeducation argument ignored the substantial nonmonetary benefits of college, which will be discussed below.

The fact remains that the United States system of higher education has been distinguished by the high proportion of the population that has experienced it. By the early 1970s, over 50 percent of the traditional college-aged population (18–21-year olds) had attended college, with others attending vocational programs in proprietary schools. There was also the prospect that many of those unable to attend immediately after high school would study at some college during their adult lives. Thus the question of oversupply should not have been unexpected in the American case (Cartter 1976). However, the benefits from college relating to income advantage and social prestige are inherently related to the supply and demand of college-educated workers. Whenever there is greater supply than demand the price will go down and when there is greater demand and less supply the price will go up. There were over 80 percent more holders of a bachelor's degree per dollar of gross national product per capita (i.e., a proxy for demand) available for jobs in 1976 than in 1960.

However, in the 1980s there was a rapid growth in the rate of return to a college education. Murphy and Welch (1989) reported that "from 1979 to 1986, the earnings differential expanded from 32 percent to about 70 percent, so that by 1986 college/high school earnings differentials were larger than ever" (p. 17). Again this was the result of the interplay between supply and demand. Between 1979 and 1986 there was a slowdown in the growth of the college population and an increase in the demand for college-educated workers.

Solmon (1981) asserted that years of schooling still pay off even in times of increasing supply. In college the major subject is important, as are quality of institution attended and grades; that is, college has always mattered even in regard to income. In 1977, 56 percent of 1970 freshmen regarded their jobs as closely related to their major subject, 19 percent as somewhat related, and 25 percent as not at all related. Most who held nonrelated jobs did so voluntarily, but this was less the case in later years. Those voluntarily in unrelated jobs were as satisfied as those in related jobs. Over 55 percent of those who held jobs related to their majors felt that their skills were not fully utilized. This implies that problems of underemployment are independent of the failure of the colleges to provide training that is relevant to work. Very few respondents to the survey were dissatisfied with their jobs. In 1977, 14 percent of 1970 freshmen were dissatisfied— far less than the 80 percent some were predicting— but only those employed full-time were considered. However, there may be a problem of college graduates involuntarily holding part-time jobs. Whether a particular job is a good one depends not only upon its links with education but also upon whether it provides the opportunity to use all one's skills, challenge, status, income, and opportunities for advancement.

Conversely, Rumberger (1986) suggested that additional schooling was not always automatically rewarded with higher earnings. According to Rumberger, schooling that is rewarded tends to be job-specific. That is, when workers acquire training based on their own or an independent judgment of what is needed on the job, that training is rewarded with higher salaries, while other non-job-specific training may not be so rewarded. According to Rumberger, "This suggests that additional schooling is not completely unproductive, but simply that jobs constrain the ability of workers to fully utilize the skills and capabilities they acquire in school" (p. 46).

In other countries the proportion of the eligible population that has attended college is usually much lower than in the United States. Thus, if everything else were equal, the college graduate in other countries might be less likely to find himself or herself unappreciated in the job market, or forced to take a less prestigious job than those held by previous graduates. However, the problems of overeducation can surely occur despite lower postsecondary participation rates if the requirements of the economic system are for fewer college graduates than are available. This might be the case in many less developed countries (for example, where the agricultural sector dominates or where industry does not require high technology). Additionally, in some less developed countries, large numbers of college graduates study disciplines where demand is low (e.g., arts, letters, humanities) rather than those where demand is high (e.g., science, engineering, and business).

In the United States, it is difficult to argue that any level of saturation at the undergraduate level could result in overeducation in a general sense, because vocational outcomes are such a small part of the total benefits of education at that level. With regard to the job market, what is necessary for the individual might be wasteful for the overall economy (e.g., a bachelor's degree may be required in order to teach fourth-grade history, but there may not be a need for another history teacher). However, other benefits do not have this zero-sum game characteristic: additional enjoyment of classes, respect for democracy, better health habits, or appreciation of culture obtained by one student does not deprive others of receiving the same benefits.

In other countries a college first degree is more likely to serve as the final professional credential. For example, in Brazil even law and medicine are practiced by college graduates without any postbaccalaureate training. To the extent that vocational aims overpower other personal and societal goals for undergraduate education, then mismatches between demand and supply for graduates for various professional fields and disciplines become more of a reason to question the growth in undergraduate education.

Certainly the nonmonetary benefits of college (and education in general) are at least as important as the job-related monetary benefits of college. Perhaps the best summary of the research into educational benefits as changes in individuals and changes in society is provided by Bowen (1977). In his summary "Is Higher Education Worth the Cost?" Bowen begins by pointing out that, "The primary purpose of higher education is to change people in desirable ways. These changes may, in turn, have profound effects on the economy and the society and even on the course of history. But in the first instance the objective is to modify the traits and behavior patterns of individual human beings" (p. 432). These effects may occur in a variety of areas, including creativity, family planning, childcare, quality of schools, appreciation of arts, culture and learning, health service, political participation, understanding of social issues, acceptance of social change, and a sense of common culture and social solidarity.

A second type of social impact "is achieved through the manifold activities that we have called research and public service" (Bowen 1977 p. 445). Universities also serve to preserve the cultural heritage and advance the civilization. In addition, they provide direct community services such as health care, libraries, museums, dramatic and musical performances, recreational facilities, and a consulting service. Higher education may also contribute to the quest for human equality.

These last benefits are vague, difficult to document, and even more difficult to evaluate. Related impacts of universities on society may be considered negative (e.g., if they produce research which culminates in the development of destructive weapons, if intolerance is the result of certain studies and so on).

Despite some minor shortcomings, Bowen's work has remained an authoritative voice regarding college effects. Indeed, a comparison of Pascarella and Terenzine's (1991) excellent and comprehensive review of the research with Bowen's 1977 work showed remarkably consistent findings. For example, Pascarella and Terenzine reported on college students' development of verbal, quantitative, and subject-matter competence by stating "our own estimates of the average gains in verbal and mathematical skills during college generally concur with those of Bowen" (p. 64). Regarding the personal adjustment and psychological well-being of college graduates they report, "Taken together, these estimates of average change are strikingly similar to the estimated overall change in psychological well-being reported by Bowen" (1977 p. 226). The same consistency is found regarding the attitude and value changes in graduates: "seniors as compared with freshman, place greater emphasis on the intrinsic value of liberal education and less on the instrumental value of education" (Bowen 1977 p. 273); and "estimates of magnitude of decline in traditional religious values are generally consistent with those reported by Bowen" (1977 p. 370).

4. Conclusion

Individuals are different and so all cannot expect to obtain all of the benefits that have been suggested. Some of the benefits become less potent as a level of education becomes less exclusive. There must also be negative impacts of schooling. Cost–benefit analysis must be undertaken by individuals in deciding whether the potential benefits they could receive from attending a particular educational institution are worth the costs. Similarly, society must ask whether the benefits it will receive from allocating public funds for education are worth as much as benefits that would be derived from alternative uses of these funds. The conclusion here is that for most individuals and for society as a whole, schooling is a good investment. However, like most economic goods, the incremental benefits from education probably get increasingly smaller after some point. Because substantial benefits derive from education it must be taken seriously, yet no one would be so rash as to claim that education can solve all of a nation's problems. Education is worth supporting, but too much cannot be expected of it.

See also: Consumption Benefits of Education; External Benefits of Education; Cost-Benefit Analysis; Rates of Return to Education

References

Aitkin M A et al. 1986 Statistical modelling issues in school effectiveness studies. *Journal of the Royal Statistical Society*, A 149 CD 1–43

Barr R, Dreeben R 1983 *How Schools Work*. University of Chicago Press, Chicago, Illinois

Becker G S 1971 *Economics of Discrimination*, rev. edn. University of Chicago Press, Chicago, Illinois

Becker G S 1983 *Human Capital: A Theoretical and Empirical Analysis, with Special Reference to Education*, 2nd edn. University of Chicago Press, Chicago, Illinois

Berg I 1971 *Education and Jobs: The Great Training Robbery*. Beacon, Boston, Massachusetts

Bowen H R 1977 *Investment in Learning: The Individual and Social Value of American Higher Education*. Jossey-Bass, San Francisco, California

Burstein L 1980 The analysis of multilevel data in educational research and evaluation. In: Berliner D C (ed.) 1980 *Review of Research in Education*. American Educational Research Association, Washington, DC

Cartter A M 1976 *PhDs and the Academic Labor Market*. McGraw-Hill, New York

Chiswick B R 1973 Schooling, screening and income. In: Solmon L C, Taubman P J (eds.) 1973 *Does College Matter?* Academic Press, New York

Coleman J S, Hoffer T, Kilgore B S 1981 *Public and Private Schools. An Analysis of High School and Beyond: A National Longitudinal Study for the 1980s*. National Center for Educational Statistics, US Department of Education, Washington, DC

Coleman J S, Hoffer T, Kilgore B S 1982 *High School Achievement: Public, Catholic and Private Schools Compared*. Basic Books, New York

Coleman J S, Moynihan D P (eds.) 1966 *On Equality of Educational Opportunity*. National Center for Educational Statistics, Washington, DC

Collins R 1979 *The Credential Society: An Historical Sociology of Education and Stratification*. Academic Press, New York

Denison E F 1962 *The Source of Economic Growth in the United States and the Alternatives Before Us*. Committee for Economic Development, New York

Denison E F 1964 Measuring the contribution of education, and the residual, to economic growth. In: ECD Study Group in the Economics of Education 1964 *The Residual Factor and Economic Growth*. Organisation for Economic Co-operation and Development, Paris

Denison E F 1974 *Accounting for United States Economic Growth 1929–1969*. The Brookings Institute, Washington, DC

Denison E F 1984 Accounting for slower growth: An update. In: Kendrick J (ed.) 1984 *International Comparisons of Productivity and Courses of Slowdowns*. Ballinger, Cambridge, Massachusetts

Dore R 1976 *The Diploma Disease: Education, Qualification and Development*. University of California Press, Berkeley, California

Freeman R B (ed.) 1976 *The Overeducated American*. Academic Press, New York

Hill P T, Foster G E, Gendler T 1990 *High Schools with Character* (R-3944-RC). The Rand Corporation, Santa Monica, California

Jencks C S et al. 1972 *Inequality: A Reassessment of the Effect of Family and Schooling in America*. Basic Books, New York

Layard R, Psacharopoulos G 1974 The screening hypothesis and the returns to education. *J. Pol. Econ.* 82(5): 985–98

Lee V E, Bryk A S 1989 A multilevel model of the social distribution of high school achievement. *Sociol. of Educ.* 62(3): 172–92

Levin H M, Hopfenberg W S 1991 Don't remediate accelerate! *Principal* 70(3): 11–13

Madaus G F 1980 *Schooling Effectiveness: A Reassessment of the Evidence*. McGraw-Hill, New York

McPartland J M, Karweit N 1979 Research on educational effects. In: Walberg H J (ed.) 1979 *Educational Environments and Effects: Evaluation Policy, and Productivity*. McCutchan, Berkeley, California

Murphy K, Welch F 1989 Wage premiums for college graduates: Recent growth and possible explanations. *Educ. Researcher* 18(4): 17–26

Oakes J 1985 *Keeping Track: How Schools Structure Inequality*. Yale University Press, New Haven, Connecticut

Pascarella E T, Terenzine P T 1991 *How College Affects Students: Findings and Insights from Twenty Years of Research*. Jossey-Bass, San Francisco, California

Raudenbush S W, Bryk A S 1986 A hierarchical model for studying school effects. *Sociol. Educ.* 59(1): 1–17

Raudenbush S W, Bryk A S 1988 Methodological advances in analyzing the effects of schools and classrooms on student learning. In: American Educational Research Association 1988 *Review of Research in Education.* American Educational Research Association, Washington, DC

Rumberger R W 1987 The impact of surplus schooling on productivity and earnings. *J. Hum. Resources*, 22(1): 24–50

Schultz T W 1961 Investment in human capital. *Am. Ec. Rev.* 51: 1–17

Schultz T W 1963 *The Economic Value of Education.* Columbia University Press, New York

Solmon L C 1981 New findings on the links between college education and work. *High. Educ.* 10(6): 615–48

Solmon L C, Ochsner N L 1978 New findings on the effects of college. In: American Association for Higher Education 1978 *Current Issues in Higher Education.* American Association for Higher Education, Washington, DC

Taubman P, Wales T 1974 *Higher Education and Earnings: College as an Investment and a Screening Device.* Report prepared for the Carnegie Commission on Higher Education and the National Bureau of Economic Research, General Series 101. McGraw-Hill, New York

Wilms J D, Raudenbush S W 1989 A longitudinal hierarchical linear model for estimating school effects and their stability. *J. Educ. Meas.* 26(3): 209–32

Witmer D 1978 Shall we continue to pursue universal higher education? In: Solmon L C (ed.) 1978 *Reassessing the Link between Work and Education.* Jossey-Bass, San Francisco, California

Education and Productivity

M. Carnoy

The economic case for educational investment hinges on the assumption that education contributes to increased worker productivity (Schultz 1961). Since productivity differences among workers are difficult to measure, economists have argued that in competitive labor/product markets, marginal productivity equals wages. They have relied on earnings differences as a proxy for such productivity increases and have shown that more education does, indeed, appear to be directly related to such earnings differences (Blaug 1972). Earnings-based weights have then been used to measure education's contribution to output and economic growth (Denison 1967). However, using the earnings proxy assumes away the issue of whether earnings accurately measure productivity, or whether more education actually leads to higher productivity.

This entry focuses directly on the education–productivity relationship. It reviews the arguments that have been advanced for the existence of that relationship and empirical studies that purport to measure it.

1. Why Does Schooling Contribute to Economic Output?

There are five major explanations of why schooling contributes to higher productivity, and these are outlined below.

1.1 The Human Capital Explanation

The original human capital discussion of educational investment argued that something happens in school that results in improved economic performance for those who have schooling, and especially for those who complete levels of schooling. In other words, individuals acquire skills in school that enable them to produce more. These skills are directly related to the characteristics that labor needs so as to use other production inputs, namely capital and land, more efficiently.

1.2 The Disequilibrium Explanation

This reasoning had shifted by the mid-1970s to what Theodore Schultz called "adjusting to economic disequilibrium" (Schultz 1975). Schultz built on Welch's (1970) study of resource use in United States agriculture, which found that farmers with more education received higher gains in income from the use of other resources (more efficient allocation of resources), and then went on to argue that farmers with more education also adjust more rapidly to technological changes. They tend to adopt the new technology sooner and are more likely to make the economic changes dictated by the new technology so as to increase their income. According to Welch and Schultz, this ability to adjust to change and to adopt new ways of doing things, is the result of skills acquired in school, although it should be noted that, in these studies, it was farmers with university education who did significantly better during the process of technological change.

This interpretation of schooling's contribution to increased productivity assumes that the person with the additional education is in a position to make better decisions. The decision-making function is usually restricted to those who are self-employed or in a sufficiently high position of employment to have decision-making responsibility. If Schultz and Welch are right, one would expect that productivity increases due to education would be greater when those who get education enter occupations where they can make decisions, for example, small farmers rather than farm laborers, or small-scale entrepreneurs rather than employed semiskilled workers. Yet the economic returns to education should also be higher to employed workers in job situations where they are relied up on to make judgments rather than simply follow orders (Levin 1987).

The notion of adjusting to disequilibrium also has implications for women's education. As women get more education, the economic payoffs to their schooling should be higher in those activities where they get more say about resource allocation and responses to change. One possible reason for the fact that development projects aimed at women have met with only partial success is their failure to give women decision-making power over resource use. On the opposite side of the coin, countries that do not provide equal education to women often fail to increase productivity in rural areas or in the informal sector because women are often the ones who make the decisions in the use of family resources or market the products produced at the farm.

1.3 The Skills Explanation

A third explanation is that higher productivity skills acquired in school are fundamental for a person to function effectively in modern production organizations (Bowman and Anderson 1963, Peaslee 1967). In the main, these skills are the ability to perform basic mathematical operations (numeracy) and the ability to read and write (literacy). These are the communicative arts of modern society. For traditional societies, the initiation of youth into adult roles enabled those societies to reproduce their culture and their economic survival. For modern societies, numeracy and literacy serve much the same purpose. These skills help people to produce material goods more effectively, especially where following directions and making judgments in work are concerned. Such qualities in the work force improve productivity and therefore economic output.

1.4 The Organizational Explanation

A broader version of the explanation is that schools as organizations socialize young people into functioning effectively in modern society (Inkeles and Smith 1974). This explanation argues that, by virtue of their very structure and the kind of behavior they demand from children, schools and classrooms prepare them to function well in employment situations. As "modern" institutions, schools teach children to work in response to modern stimuli and inculcate in them values and norms that are consistent with productive behavior in factories, banks, and even agricultural cooperatives. Schooled youth become more competent to deal with the requirements of an urban, industrialized society and with its institutional organizations.

By teaching young people how to be effective in modern organizations, schools help them to respond more quickly, willingly, and predictably to demands from supervisors. In addition a schooled youth may learn how to work effectively with others in an organizational setting—to be what is known as a "team player"—since that type of behavior is also rewarded in school.

1.5 The Trainability Explanation

Some studies argue that what is learned in school—whether cognitive skills or certain types of behavior—is not nearly as important to future productivity as simply succeeding at what school demands (Arrow 1973, Carnoy and Levin 1985). Success may mean learning the skills that school requires the child to learn, or completing a particular level of schooling. The very fact of "success" in school symbolizes social approval. It suggests that the young person is more likely to do well in the society beyond the school (Carnoy 1990). This conforms to the argument that education is a "filter," but even if it is a filter, success in school may confer a sense of probable success on the job. As long as this message is confirmed by experiences after graduating from school, such as being able to earn a livelihood, it makes individuals easy to convince that they can learn new tasks, make appropriate decisions and choices, and assume responsibility. These are all characteristics of a highly productive person.

Some would define these characteristics as "trainability," or "learnability." People who are successful in school are those who have shown that they can learn new things and carry them through. In effect, basic education is a training ground for further training or learning. Morever, the jobs or self-employment that provide the most training and learning require the most schooling to prepare young people to get them. This is not so much because of the mathematics and language skills they pick up, but rather because of the skills they acquire in learning how to learn. According to this argument, more education is related to higher productivity to the degree that it makes a high fraction of children "successful" in school.

This notion of "trainability" is consistent with the neoclassical human capital model, which assumes that individuals have free choice in deciding on the amount and kind of schooling that they take. In that case, an individual always feels "successful" in having completed the amount of schooling that is consistent with maximizing return on investment. The different amounts of schooling that are invested in define the degree of success in completing schooling tasks, hence the kind of jobs people can be trained for, and, in turn, their productivity (Rosen 1976).

However, there is a contrary view. If the amount of education individuals take is not just a function of individual choice, but also of the educational system's constraints and controls, education may act as a filter for selecting those relatively few children who can succeed at the tasks basic education places before them from the large majority of children who will "fail" at these tasks and will not complete schooling. If the "learnability" explanation is correct, this majority of failers, even if they are literate and numerate as a result of several years' attendance at school, consider themselves "failures" and are regarded as untrainable by the labor market. Because of the symbolism of their failure, they are indeed slower learners and unlikely to get work that requires further learning. As schooling expands, and the definition of "socially adequate" education changes to include more years of schooling, the filter becomes longer and the definition of school success and failure also changes. Even young people who complete secondary education but do not continue to university could eventually be made to feel unsuccessful, untrainable, and unlearning, as is the case in the United States.

2. Empirical Evidence

Studies attempting to relate productivity to either quantity of education, school-related skills, or student performance in school fall into three different categories: (a) correlational studies, (b) studies that measure individual educational attainment and individual productivity, and (c) studies that measure individual school-related achievement and individual productivity.

2.1 Correlational Studies

Economists have long argued that literacy and primary education are positively related to economic growth. The United Kingdom, Sweden, and the United States had all achieved relatively high rates of literacy (40–50%) just before their industrial revolutions. According to one study, no country with less than 40 percent adult literacy in 1955 had a per capita income higher than US $300 (equivalent to US $1400 in 1990), but literacy rates above 30–40 percent in and of themselves were not associated with higher per capita incomes. This suggests that unless a country is rich in a highly valued natural resource, such as petroleum or potash, a minimum level of literacy is a necessary although not a sufficient condition for economic development (Bowman and Anderson 1963).

Particularly after the Second World War primary school enrollment rates were more highly correlated with later per capita income than was either literacy or, to an even greater degree, postprimary enrollment rates (Bowman and Anderson 1963, Peaslee 1967). Throughout the developing world, primary school expansion in the 1950s and 1960s was associated with rapid increases in economic development in the 1960s and 1970s. Such correlation data suggest, but do not prove, a causal link between primary schooling of the population and economic growth (higher productivity) in some later period.

Another approach attempts to relate growth rates of developed countries in the post-Second World War era to increases in young adult IQ over a similar period (Bishop 1992). Using a variety of aptitude tests applied to large groups of young adults in the United States, Japan, and Western Europe between 1930 and the 1970s, Bishop correlates average annual gains on these tests to growth rates for nine countries. The results are rough but suggest that there is a positive and statistically significant relation.

2.2 Productivity Studies

Productivity measures are difficult to obtain (Metcalf 1985) and any estimate of the relationship between education and productivity is beset by limitations. Individuals who have completed different levels or amounts of education are generally in different types of jobs, producing different outputs.

However, in agriculture, more years of schooling do seem to result in higher output. A survey conducted for the World Bank of 18 studies that measured the relationship in low-income countries between farmers' education and their agricultural efficiency (as measured by crop production) concluded that a farmer with 4 years of elementary education was, on average, 8.7 percent more productive than a farmer with no education (Lockheed et al. 1980). The survey also found the effect of education to be even greater (13% increase in productivity) where complementary inputs, such as fertilizer, new seed, or farm machinery were available.

Further evidence on the effect of education in raising farmers' productivity appears in studies carried out in South Korea, Malaysia, and Thailand (Jamison and Lau 1982), and more recently in Pakistan, Nepal, Thailand, India, Bangladesh, and a number of Latin American countries (Jamison and Moock 1984, Moock and Addou 1992) (see *Education and Agricultural Productivity*). Other studies (Sack et al. 1980), although reporting mixed results, support the general conclusion that education contributes positively to agricultural productivity, especially when other inputs are available to farmers and land reform has created favorable conditions for a range of production choices.

In the United States, Welch's study of farmer response to technological change (new seeds and other new inputs) suggests that those farmers with higher education have higher earnings from farming (when other inputs are controlled for), respond more rapidly to adopting new inputs once they are available, and obtain higher yields from the use of such inputs (Welch 1970).

Several attempts have also been made to analyze the effect of education on productivity in industry (Berry 1980, Fuller 1970, Min 1987). Berry's review suggests that there is little conclusive evidence that education has a positive effect on productivity in urban jobs. Fuller's research in two electrical machinery plants in Bangalore, India shows that there is a positive effect of education and training on output, especially when that training is in-firm. Min's study of academically and vocationally educated workers in a Chinese automobile factory also shows a small, but statistically significant, increase in productivity associated with more education, and a 6–11 percent higher productivity for those with vocational schooling than for those with academic schooling.

Significant results for productivity–education relations in urban jobs are not easy to obtain because such studies necessarily measure these relations within a single occupation. Yet the main source of higher productivity for those who take more schooling is a move into different categories of jobs (where productivity can be higher), rather than an increase in productivity within the same job (Thurow and Lucas 1972). The more productive jobs also generally provide training that contributes to higher productivity, yet entrants to such jobs generally need to have completed certain levels of education to get them (Knight and Sabot 1990).

The difficulty of making productivity comparisons between different jobs also makes it difficult to assess what the education–productivity relation is. Even assuming that education is somehow responsible for higher productivity in more productive jobs, no study has been able to ascertain whether it is the skills associated with more schooling or the socialization into competence that produces higher productivity in those jobs, although there are some data that suggest a much higher correlation in the United States between socioeconomic background and earnings than between IQ and earnings (not productivity) when years of schooling are controlled for (Bowles and Gintis 1976). Economists have also failed to identify the skills learned at school—beyond adult IQ—that contribute to higher productivity (Carnoy and Carter 1976). An analysis of the adult IQ (achievement)–productivity relationship is presented below.

The more years of schooling completed, the higher the probability that individuals will find work in the formal sector or will stay in that sector once they get a job in it (Tueros 1992). Even so, in many countries the formal sector is growing so slowly that the more important issue is whether schooling contributes to worker productivity in the informal sector. Almost every developing country has a large informal labor market, where production takes place in small-scale units, using labor-intensive technology, and where workers are employed, paid, and dismissed without any regulation or control by government. The informal market is the result of urban growth without corresponding industrialization or increased formal employment in commerce and services.

A detailed study of the informal labor market in Peru shows that in both informal and formal sectors, education contributed to higher earnings, and in some cities, such as Lima, completing primary education seemed to be more significantly related to earnings in the informal sector than in the formal (Tueros 1992) (see *Education and Informal Labor Markets*). Within Peru's informal sector, the entrepreneur's education—especially if he or she has completed secondary education or above—is associated with a positive effect on the firm's profits. These results contradict the widely accepted idea that formal schooling is only relevant to economic performance in the formal sector. They also suggest that the technological and business problems faced by an entrepreneur in such small, informal enterprises requires at least some years of secondary education to increase profitability. This "threshold" effect of secondary education on productivity corresponds to the threshold effect of primary education on productivity in agriculture (Jamison and Lau 1982). Moreover, as Jamison and Lau noted for Asian farms, it is the education of the entrepreneur that really counts for profitability in the informal sector, not the education of the workers.

2.3 Student School Achievement and Productivity

In the United States, no significant relation has been found between school achievement and earnings for a given amount of schooling completed (Bishop 1992), possibly as a result of the following factors: (a) employers do not collect information on school performance, (b) there is no national examination in the United States that would yield such information at relatively low cost, and (c) only a small proportion (about 3%) of United States workers are subject to employer-administered tests prior to employment.

Similar insignificant results of childhood and adult aptitude (a proxy for school achievement) on earnings obtain from Swedish longitudinal data (Tuijnman 1989). In the Swedish case, earnings at various ages are closely related to youth education and home background, but not to scores on tests administered at age 10 and 20.

Bishop argues, however, that in those United States firms or enterprises where tests are administered, a significant relation does exist between an individual's school-acquired skills and productivity. He argues further that if it can be shown that scores on tests measuring school-subject aptitude are associated with higher productivity, then "better" education would necessarily raise productivity. Bishop cites two kinds of studies conducted in the United States: (a) US Army trainability ratings, and (b) studies that measure the relation between supervisor ratings and individual employer-administered examination scores in mathematics, verbal ability, and vocational skills. He concludes that early aptitude and the skills learned in school (achievement), as measured by adult aptitude, do have an important effect on both job productivity and trainability, even though these same test scores have insignificant effects on earnings.

In the case of test score effect on final grades in United States armed forces' training programs, Bishop's estimates from others' studies shows that mathematical knowledge and arithmetical reasoning subtests had a highly significant impact on grades, with verbal and science subtests showing less impact.

Bishop's estimates using employer test data indicate that even when years of schooling, relevant job experience, and tenure in the present job are accounted for, mathematical achievement, perceptual ability, and psychomotor ability are significantly related to job performance, as measured by supervisors ratings, in a wide range of broadly defined occupations. Verbal ability is only significant in clerical occupations. Years of schooling do not have a significant effect because of the low variance in schooling of those in each occupational set, but age and relevant work experience do produce sufficiently higher supervisor ratings for older, more experienced workers with low test scores to do better than younger, brighter ones. This suggests that, even if supervisor job performance ratings were considered unbiased estimates of productivity, 4 years of tenure in the job, or age or relevant experience, would offset the "productivity" effect of one standard deviation difference on these test scores.

In addition, controlling for test scores, years of schooling, experience, and tenure does not annul the very large and significant negative effect on ratings in all jobs of being Black and, in some types of jobs, of being female or Hispanic. Black operatives and Black high-skill clerical workers suffer a negative job rating impact equal to two standard deviations on the mathematics component of the employer test. Female craft workers and operatives also suffer a "productivity" penalty of two standard deviations of mathematics score. Such results alone should raise serious doubts about the validity of supervisors' ratings as a proxy for productivity and about the meaning of the test score–productivity relation. Why should Black workers have much lower productivity when mathematical ability, for example, is accounted for?

3. Conclusion

For a variety of reasons, most economists agree that there is a positive relationship between the quantity and quality of individuals' education and job productivity, but proving it has been an elusive enterprise. Empirical studies of the self-employed in agriculture and informal labor markets show that there is a significant, albeit not especially large, effect on productivity from more schooling. However, similar effects in industrial jobs have not been measured. Attempts to link what is learned in school (achievement or adult aptitude) to productivity through supervisors' ratings have been fairly successful but are subject to severe problems which cast doubt on their validity. The principal role of school achievement on productivity is probably through its effect on how much schooling individuals take: this finding further highlights the immense complexity of trying to

compare the productivity of employed workers with different amounts of schooling working in different kinds of jobs.

See also: Education and Economic Growth

References

Arrow K 1973 Higher education as a filter. *J. Pub. Econ.* 2(3):193–216

Berry A 1980 Education, income, productivity and urban poverty. In King K (ed.) 1980 *Education and Income.* World Bank, Washington, DC

Bishop J 1992 *The Economic Consequences of Schooling and Learning.* Mimeo, Economic Policy Institute, Washington, DC

Blaug M 1972 The correlation between education and earnings. What does it signify? *Higher Educ.* 1 (1):53–76

Bowles S, Gintis H 1976 *Schooling in Capitalist America.* Basic Books, New York

Bowman M J, Anderson C A (1963) Concerning the role of education in development. In Geertz C (ed.) 1963 *Old Societies and New States: The Quest for Modernity in Asia and Africa.* The Free Press, New York

Carnoy M 1990 *Opening the Door: Education and Productivity.* Film sponsored by ILO, presented at the Education For All Conference, Jomtien, Thailand (distributed by ILO, Geneva), 17 mm, VHS/PAL

Carnoy M, Carter M 1976 *Theories of Worker Productivity and Income Distribution.* Center for Economic Studies, Palo Alto, California (mimeo)

Carnoy M, Levin H M 1985 *Schooling and Work in the Democratic State.* Stanford University Press, Stanford California

Denison E 1967 *Why Growth Rates Differ: Postwar Experience in Nine Western Countries.* The Brookings Institution, Washington, DC

Fuller W P 1970 Education, training and worker productivity: A study of skilled workers in two factories in South India. Unpublished doctoral dissertation, Stanford University, Stanford, California

Inkeles A, Smith D 1974 *Becoming Modern: Individual Change in 6 Developing Countries.* Harvard University Press, Cambridge, Massachusetts

Jamison D, Lau L 1982 *Farmer Education and Farm Efficiency.* Johns Hopkins University Press, Baltimore Maryland

Jamison D, Moock P 1984, Farmer education and farm efficiency in Nepal: The role of schooling, extension services and cognitive skills. *World Dev.* 12 (1): 67–86

Knight J B, Sabot R 1990 *Education, Productivity, and Inequality: The East African Natural Experiment.* World Bank/Oxford University Press, New York

Levin H M 1987 Improving productivity through education and technology. In: Burke G, Rumberger R (eds.) 1987 *The Future Impact of Technology on Work and Education.* Falmer Press, London

Lockheed M, Jamison D, Lau L 1980 Farmer education and farmer efficiency: A survey. *Econ. Dev. Cult. Change* 29 (1): 37–76

Metcalf D 1985 *The Economics of Vocational Training: Past Evidence and Future Considerations.* World Bank Staff Working Paper No. 713. World Bank, Washington DC

Min W 1987 The impact of vocational education on productivity in the specific institutional context of China: A case study. Unpublished doctoral dissertation, Stanford University, Stanford, California

Moock P, Addou H 1992 *Education and Productivity*. World Bank, Washington, DC (mimeo)

Peaslee A 1967 Primary school enrollments and economic growth. *Comp. Educ. Rev.* 11(1): 57–68

Rosen S 1976 A theory of life earnings. *J. Pol. Econ.* 84(4 Pt.2): S45-S67

Sack R, Carnoy M, Lecaros C 1980 Education y desarrollo rural en America Latina. In: Banco Interamericano de Desarrollo 1980 *Problemas del Financiamiento de la Educacion en America Latina*. Banco Interamericano de Desarrollo, Washington, DC

Schultz T W 1961 Investment in human capital. *Am. Econ.*

Rev. 51(1): 1–17

Schultz T W 1975 The value of the ability to deal with disequilibria. *J. Econ. Lit.* 13(3): 827–46

Thurow L, Lucas R 1972 *The American Distribution of Income: A Structural Problem*. Joint Economic Committee of the US Congress, Washington, DC

Tueros M 1992 Education and informal labor markets in Peru. Unpublished doctoral dissertation, Stanford University, Stanford, California

Tuijnman A 1989 *Recurrent Education, Earnings, and Well-being: A Fifty-Year Longitudinal Study of a Cohort of Swedish Men*. Almqvist and Wiksell International, Stockholm

Welch F 1970 Education in production. *J. Pol. Econ.* 78(1): 35–59

Education and Agricultural Productivity

P. R. Moock and H. Addou

Since the 1960s, a large number of studies have analyzed the effects of formal education on agricultural productivity. Most have estimated a "marginal product" of education by means of production function analysis. Some have looked also at education's "allocative effect" on agricultural productivity, in terms, for example, of a farmer's willingness to adopt profitable new technologies. This entry reviews the empirical literature in this area since 1978, picking up where an earlier survey (Lockheed et al. 1980) left off.

1. Education's Worker and Allocative Effects

It is argued that education should enhance both technical and allocative efficiency in production. Welch called these the "worker" and "allocative" effects of education. The worker effect is education's marginal product, "the increased output per change in education, holding other factor quantities constant" (Welch 1970 p. 42). It is education's contribution to the quality of the individual as a worker. The notion here is that increased education permits a worker to produce more output using any given quantity of physical inputs.

The allocative effect of education, on the other hand, refers to the more educated farmer's "ability to acquire and to decode information about costs and productive characteristics of other inputs" (Welch 1970 p. 42). A central aspect of the allocative effect is "the capacity to evaluate and adopt profitable new technologies" (Cotlear 1989 p. 75), for example the diversification of production to include different crops for sale, or the use of high-yielding hybrid seeds in lieu of traditional, home-grown seeds. Increased formal education enhances the worker's ability to make optimal decisions about the selection of outputs produced and also about the inputs used to produce particular outputs. Some

studies have argued that the allocative effect is probably more important than the worker effect in terms of overall value added. (Dhakal et al 1987, Jamison and Moock 1984, Pudasaini 1983.)

Studies on education and agricultural production commonly include years of formal schooling completed as one of several independent variables used to explain production levels or technological choice. The largest number of studies specify an engineering (single crop) or gross revenue production function to estimate education's contribution. Most make use of a Cobb–Douglas (C-D) function, in which dependent and independent variables are expressed as logarithmic transformations. Most use ordinary least squares (OLS) regression analysis to estimate the function. This approach has been used because the statistical results are efficient and easy to interpret. The regression coefficient on any input in a log-log production function can be taken to be the constant elasticity of this factor in the production process.

Several studies have compared education's effects on agricultural productivity under traditional and modernizing conditions. Education has been found to be more effective in a modernizing environment, as Schultz (1975) reasoned should be the case.

The remainder of this entry is organized as follows. Section 2 recounts the findings up to and including the late 1970s as summarized in the earlier survey by Lockheed et al. (1980). Section 3 reports criticism in subsequent literature of the early studies and the survey. Section 4 summarizes the results of 14 studies published since 1978 analyzing 29 data sets from 12 countries in Africa, Asia, and the Americas and looking at the effect of education on agricultural productivity. The studies to be discussed are described in Table 1.

Table 1

Studies published since 1980 and included in this survey

Author	Date	Country studied, year in which data collected, and sample characteristics
Azhar	1988	Pakistan, 1976–1977; entire irrigated region of Pakistan; data taken from survey conducted jointly by Pakistan WAPDA and World Bank; number of observations for high-yielding variety crops (1,370 wheat and 665 rice) and traditional crops (727 cotton and 720 sugarcane)
Butt	1984	Pakistan, 1977; 1,787 farms across the Indus Basin; survey jointly conducted by Pakistan WAPDA and World Bank; wheat, sugarcane, cotton, and sugar
Cotlear	1989	Peru, 1982–1983; 555 rural households in three regions of Peruvian highlands with varying degrees of technology: a modern region (the valley of Yanamarca), a traditional region (the pampa of Sangarara), and an intermediate region (the plateau of Chinchero)
Dhakal, Grabowski, and Belbase	1987	Nepal, 1973–1974; 600 farm families from six villages of the Nuwakot district in Nepal; maize, millet grown in the upland and in the lowland, paddy and wheat; data from Calkins (1976)
Duraisamy	1990	India, 1981–1982; 461 farm households in 12 villages in two development districts of Tamil Nadu; detailed information of 323 cultivated farms; analysis of paddy production
Grabowski and Pasurka	1988	Northern United States, 1860; sample of 109 farms; data: secondary source
Jameson	1988	Paraguay, 1976; 1,053 farms in eastern Paraguay; administered by Ministry of Agriculture and Livestock and USAID; focus on farm production, employment, and income
		Dominican Republic, 1976; 1,802 farms across the country; administered by Secretariat of State for Agriculture with USAID; focus on farm production, employment, and income
		Guatemala, 1974; 1,548 farms across the country; survey conducted by Ministry of Agriculture and USAID; analyze effects of credit on income, output, and employment
		Bolivia, 1977; 750 farms from Chiquisaca, Tarija, and Potosi; collected by USAID and Ministry of Rural Affairs and Agriculture; concentrated on farm income
Jamison and Moock	1984	Nepal, 1977–1978; 683 households in six panchayats of Bara district and six panchayats of Rautahat; early paddy, late paddy, and wheat; part of World Bank Research Project
Kalirajan and Shand	1985	India, 1977; random sample of 91 farmers in the Tamil Nadu State; growing high-yielding paddy varieties
Khandker	1986	Bangladesh, 1985; 364 farm households in Rangpur, Bogra, Sherpur, Tangail, Comilla, and Dhaka districts
Moock	1981	Kenya, 1971; 152 maize farmers in Vihiga division of Kakamega district in Kenya's Western Province
Phillips and Marble	1986	Guatemala, 1974; 1,348 small farmers across the country, excluding Peten region; survey administered by the Ministry of Agriculture with USAID support; analyze effect of credit on income, output, and employment
Pudasaini	1983	Nepal, 1981; random sample of 205 farmers of the Bara district (modernizing Terai) and 149 farmers of Gorkha district (traditional hill regions)
Ram and Singh	1988	Burkina Faso, 1980; 51 households from seven villages of the Mossi plateau area; part of a regional development project; data collected by personal interviews and questionnaires

2. Early Findings

In a review of the literature up to 1978, Lockheed et al. (1980) developed a useful meta-analytic framework for examining the role of education in farm production. The authors were able to conclude that education has a positive effect on farmers' efficiency. To reach this conclusion, they reanalyzed 37 data sets from 18 studies in 13 countries. The studies they surveyed all used production functions to test the hypothesis that farmers' education influences farm productivity; outputs were regressed against factor inputs and education indicators.

The survey found that education was positively associated with farm production at the 0.05 probability level in 15 of 37 tests of the worker effect hypothesis. The regression coefficient was positive but not statistically significant in 16 other cases; in 6 cases, the coefficient was small but negative. The overall conclusion derived from the studies surveyed by Lockheed et al. (1980) was that, holding physical inputs constant, output could be expected to be about 7 percent higher on farms where the farmer had completed 4 years of elementary schooling as compared with no education at all.

The survey also reported evidence to support Schultz's hypothesis that the returns to education in production are greater in a modernizing environment. When the partial relationship between education and farm production was measured against degrees of modernization, the authors were able to conclude that "the percentage gain as a result of 4 years of education is 10% higher in a modernizing environment than in a traditional environment" (Lockheed et al. 1980 p. 57).

Finally, the survey looked at the relationship between the farmer's exposure to agricultural extension services and farm output in 16 data sets. The survey reported that the regression coefficient on extension contact was significantly positive in eight cases, in one the coefficient was negative, and in the other seven there was no apparent effect of extension services on productivity.

3. Critique of Early Empirical Research

Work carried out in the 1980s has questioned the interpretations of Lockheed et al. as well as the empirical studies on which their survey was based. The survey has been criticized for its use of inadequate ad hoc classifications to define modernizing agriculture and for its inattention to the question of whether the observed relationship between education and agricultural productivity might not be the result of other factors related to both education and production, such as family background or land quality. Although some of the early studies used locational indicators as approximate control variables, most failed to include direct measures of such factors. Their absence from the analysis may have led to erroneous or exaggerated conclusions (Jamison and Moock 1984, Cotlear 1989).

The survey's "optimistic" conclusion regarding the impact of education on agricultural productivity has been further questioned in light of the fact that, although over 50 percent of the data sets surveyed by Lockheed et al. showed a positive association, this statistical effect was significant at the 0.05 level in only about half of these cases (Phillips and Marble 1986). Efforts to replicate findings on other sets of data have been only moderately successful in providing a consistent and strong relation, according to some critics (e.g., Jameson 1988).

Work in the 1980s has indicated the limitations of using either an engineering or gross revenue production function. Much of the effect of education on farm profits may be missed by taking this approach, since it measures only the worker effect and neglects

the allocative effects on: (a) outputs produced, and (b) inputs selected. Several 1980s studies have suggested that education's total effect can be measured by estimating a value-added function, and the three separate effects (worker and two allocative effects) then measured by also estimating gross sales and engineering functions (Dhakal et al. 1987, Phillips and Marble 1986, Pudasaini 1983). "By simple manipulation the three effects can be separated out" (Phillips and Marble 1986 p. 259). This requires more information, however, than most data sets actually contain, a problem encountered by most advocates of the complete approach (e.g., Pudasaini 1983, Phillips and Marble 1986).

The specification of the relationship between agricultural inputs and output as a C–D production function has also been subject to criticism. The restrictive assumptions implied by this specification have been questioned, including constant production elasticity of factor inputs and unitary elasticity of substitution between all pairs of inputs. Other authors have criticized the use of OLS regression analysis, as this approach results in estimation of an "average" function, with "efficient and inefficient farms ... mixed in together so that the concept of inefficiency has no meaning" (Grabowski and Pasurka 1988 p. 316). Such critics argue for the use of a nonparametric estimation technique such as linear programing.

4. Studies in the 1980s

Studies published since the late 1970s have attempted to address some or all of the criticisms directed at the earlier studies reviewed by Lockheed et al. The 12 studies reviewed in this entry confirm, for the most part, the story that education has a positive effect on farmer efficiency. Table 2 reports the coefficients of education on productivity, listing the non-education variables controlled for in the regression equation and indicating whether or not the estimate relating to education is statistically significant at the 0.05 probability level. The table includes 78 tests of hypotheses relating to education's effects, drawing upon 29 data sets in 14 countries.

4.1 Years of Formal Schooling

Many of the findings reported in Table 2 are for the variable years of school completed. All but one of the 26 regression coefficients on this variable are positive and 15 (58 percent) are statistically significant at the 0.05 level.

4.2 Levels of Formal Schooling

Fourteen regressions in Table 2 show the differential effects of "a few years" of school versus "more years," the cutoff between the two levels coming after three, four, five, or six years completed, depending on the study. All of the studies in Table 2 treat different schooling levels as categorical (dummy) variables

Table 2
Estimates of education's effect in studies of small-farm production

Country location study: author and date	Output variable (logarithmic transformation)	Sample size	Other variables controlled for in equation	Education variable (logarithmic transformation of nonbinary variables)	Coefficient on educ. variable (*t*-statistic in parentheses)
Africa					
Burkina Faso: Mossi Plateau (Ram and Singh 1988)	Farm income	51	None	Years of school completed: HH head	0.096 (2.7)[a]
				Yrs of school completed: all HH members	0.086 (2.14)[a]
			Land, labor, input, use, age, sex, value of livestock, credit, soil type, crop rotation, marketing, capital assets, no. of children, no. of wives, migration	Years of school completed: HH head	0.030 (1.27)
				Years of school completed: all HH members	0.070 (3.27)[a]
Kenya: Kakamega District (Moock 1981)	Maize output per acre	101	Plant population, rate of phosphate and nitrogen, labor, soil, interplanted crop, crop damage, insecticide, hybrid seed, area planted, migration, age, loan recipient	1–3 years of school completed: farm manager	−0.118 (−1.82)
				4 or more years of school completed: farm manager	0.182 (1.61)[a]
				Index of extension contact	0.030 (2.50)[a]
				(4 years schl) × (extension contact)	−0.037 (−1.76)
Asia					
Bangladesh: Ranpur, Bogra, Sherpur, Tangail, Comilla and Dhaka (Khandker 1986)	Gross value of farm outputs less expenditure on purchased inputs	364	Land; predicted wages of head, spouse, and family members	Years of schooling: male head of HH	0.143 (1.69)[a]
				Years of schooling: heads' wife	0.003 (0.09)[a]
				Years of schooling: other HH members	0.019 (0.50)
India: The Coimbatore District in Tamil Nadu (Kalirajan and Shand 1985)	Paddy production	91	Labor, fertilizer, capital, HYV seed, insecticide, farm size	Years of school completed: farm manager	0.102 (2.54)[a]
India: East Coimbatore and North Salem of Tamil Nadu (Duraisamy 1990)	Paddy production	323	Land, wage, labor, fertilizer, animal input, value of capital services	> 4 yrs of school completed: farm manager	0.198 (2.93)[a]
				Extension dummy	0.130 (1.83)[a]
Nepal: Bara District (Pidasaini 1983)	Value of rice production	205	Land, family and hired labor, capital, age, schooling, machinery, bullock, use. fertilizer. farm	Years of school completed: manager	0.011 (1.10)
				Extension dummy	0.004 (0.13)

133

Table 2 continued

Country location study: author and date	Output variable (logarithmic transformation)	Sample size	Other variables controlled for in equation	Education variable (logarithmic transformation of nonbinary variables)	Coefficient on educ. variable (*t*-statistic in parentheses)
Nepal: Bara District (Pudasaini 1983)	Gross sales	205	Land, family and hired labor, capital, age, schooling, machinery, bullock use, fertilizer, farm size	Years of school completed: manager	0.030 (2.73)[a]
				Extension dummy	−0.013 (−1.00)
				(School) × (extension)	−0.001 (−0.50)
	Value added			Years of school completed: manager	0.050 (3.13)[a]
				Extension dummy	−0.008 (−0.42)
				(School) × (extension)	−0.003 (−1.00)
Nepal: Gorkha District (Pudasaini 1983)	Value of maize production	149	Land, family and hired labor, capital, age, schooling, machinery, bullock use, fertilizer, farm size	Years of school completed: manager	0.022 (1.29)
				Extension dummy	0.212 (0.99)
				(School) × (extension)	−0.004 (−1.33)
Nepal: Gorkha District (Pudasaini 1983)	Value of maize production	149	Land, family and hired labor, capital, age, schooling, machinery, bullock use, fertilizer, farm size	Years of school completed: manager	0.051 (4.25)[a]
				Extension dummy	−0.009 (−0.18)
				(School) × (extension)	0.001 (0.17)
	Value added			Years of school completed: manager	0.057 (4.57)[a]
				Extension dummy	−0.007 (−0.13)
				(School) × (extension)	0.000 (0.00)
Nepal: Bara and Rautahat Districts (Jamison and Moock 1984)	Value of early paddy production	443	Area cultivated, labor, percent female labor, percent male labor, animal use, capital, fertilizers, age, experience, SES background, occupation, numeracy, district	1–6 years of school completed: farm head	0.050 (0.63)
				> 7 years of school completed: farm head	0.152 (1.25)
				Recent contact with extension agent	0.007 (0.11)
				Percent of HHs in area with extension contact	0.202 (0.12)
	Value of late paddy production	284		1–6 years of school completed: farm head	−0.048 (−0.52)
				> 7 years of school completed: farm head	0.131 (1.08)
				Recent contact with extension agent	0.084 (1.01)
				Percent of HHs in area with extension contact	0.122 (0.48)

ble 2 continued

Country location study: author and date	Output variable (logarithmic transformation)	Sample size	Other variables controlled for in equation	Education variable (logarithmic transformation of nonbinary variables)	Coefficient on educ. variable (*t*-statistic in parentheses)
epal: Bara and utahat Districts mison and oock 1984)	Value of wheat production	345	Area cultivated, labor, percent female labor, percent male labor, animal use, capital, fertilizers, age, experience, SES background, occupation, numeracy, district	1–6 years of school completed: farm head	−0.108 (−1.32)
				> 7 years of school completed: farm head	0.271 (2.30)[a]
				Recent contact with extension agent	0.083 (1.26)
				Percent of HHs in area with extension contact	0.472 (2.85)[a]
epal: Nuwakot strict (Dhakal al. 1987)	Maize output in kilograms	600	Land, labor, farming experience, bullocks, family size, fertilizer	Average years of schooling of family members	0.036 (0.67)
	Gross sales				0.094 (2.17)[a]
	Value added				0.096 (2.23)[a]
kistan (Butt 1984)	Gross value of production	1,787	Land, labor, fertilizers, machinery, animal use, irrigation, age, schooling, owner operated	1–4 yrs of school: farm manager	0.070 (1.07)
				5+ yrs of school: farm manager	0.107 (2.43)[a]
	Wheat output per acre	1,156	Acreage, owner operated	1–4 yrs of school: farm manager	0.037 (0.54)
				5+ yrs of school: farm manager	0.186 (4.13)[a]
	Sugarcane output per acre	394		1–4 yrs of school: farm manager	0.0001 (0.00)
				5+ yrs of school: farm manager	0.002 (0.26)
	Cotton output per acre	704		1–4 yrs of school: farm manager	0.012 (1.05)
				5+ yrs of school: farm manager	0.202 (2.59)[a]
	Rice output per acre	604		1–4 yrs of school: farm manager	0.132 (1.14)
				5+ yrs of school: farm manager	0.212 (2.92)[a]
kistan (Azhar 1988)	Output of wheat	1,370	Land, labor, fertilizers, irrigation	Years of school completed: farm manager	0.018 (4.06)[a]
	Output of rice	665			0.015 (2.69)[a]
	Output of cotton	727			0.014 (1.61)

Country location study: author and date	Output variable (logarithmic transformation)	Sample size	Other variables controlled for in equation	Education variable (logarithmic transformation of nonbinary variables)	Coefficient on educ. variable (*t*-statistic in parentheses)
Latin America					
Bolivia (Jameson 1988)	Value of farm production	750	Land, labor, seed, fertilizer, animal use, and machinery	Years of school completed: farm manager	0.138 (2.36)[a]
Dominican Republic (Jameson 1988)	Value of farm production	1,802	Land, labor, seed, fertilizer, animal use, and machinery	Years of school completed: farm manager	0.006 (1.90)[a]
Guatemala (Phillips and Marble 1986)	Value of corn production	1,384	land, labor, seed, fertilizer, machinery, animal use	Years of school completed: farm manager	0.028 (1.31)
				1–3 years of school completed: farm manager	0.006 (0.17)
				4+ years of school completed: farm manager	0.065 (1.42)
Guatemala (Jameson 1988)	Value of farm Production	1,548	Land, labor, seed, fertilizer, animal use, and machinery	Years of school completed: farm manager	0.001 (0.40)
Paraguay (Jameson 1988)	Value of farm production	1,053	Land, labor, seed, fertilizer, animal use, and machinery	Years of school completed: farm manager	−0.006 (−0.31)
Peru: Valley of Yanamarca (Cotlear 1989)	Production of potatoes	254	Land, labor, animal, tractor, extension service, migration, credit, use of HYV	4–5 years of school completed: HH head	0.14 (1.27)
				6+ years of school completed: HH head	0.37 (3.52)[a]
				Recent extension dummy	0.09 (0.84)
Peru: Plateau of Chinchero (Cotlear 1989)	Production of potatoes	151	Land, labor, animal, tractor, extension service, migration, credit, use of HYV	4–5 years of school completed: HH head	0.13 (1.35)
				6+ years of school completed: HH head	0.24 (2.48)[a]
				Recent extension dummy	0.29 (3.42)[a]
Peru: The Pampa Sangarara (Cotlear 1989)	Production of potatoes	150	Land, labor, animal, tractor, extension service, migration, credit, use of HYV	4–5 years of school completed: HH head	0.13 (1.15) 0.05 (0.56)
				6+ years of school completed: HH head	0.11 (0.66)
				Recent extension dummy	
North America					
United States: Northern Region (Grabowski and Pasurka 1988)	Farm revenue	109	Land, age of head, family size	Literate: household head	0.108 (1.82)[a]

ther than as continuous (spline) variables. In most of
e studies, the missing category is "no education," al-
ough for his three Peruvian samples, Cotlear (1989)
mpares four to five years and six or more years with
ree years or less, which is the omitted category in his
gression equations.

When the schooling variable is collapsed in some
ch fashion, the prevailing result is that "a few
ears" of education shows no significant relation to
ricultural productivity (true in 13 of 14 tests of the
pothesis), whereas "more years" of schooling does
ow a relation (in 9 of 14 cases, or 64%). The impli-
tion of these findings is that some minimum level
educational attainment, often argued to be the level
which the recipient achieves functional literacy
d numeracy sufficient to be sustained over time, is
quired before any payoff is seen in the individual's
rformance as a farmer later in life.

3 Whose Education Is Relevant?

able 2 suggests that the statistical effect of education
production probably differs depending on whose
ucation is considered—that of the farm head, the
rm manager, or all family members. In 4 of 13 cases
1%), the education level of the "farm head" has
significantly positive regression coefficient in the
uation to explain farm output. The "farm manager,"
hom studies define as the person responsible for
e day-to-day technical decisions on the farm, may
r may not be the same person as the farm head but
probably the more relevant agent to be considered
hen analyzing the effect of education on agricultural
utput. The educational attainment of the manager is
ositively related to production in 21 of 55 tests (38%)
f the hypothesis.

A few studies have measured education as the aver-
ge educational attainment of all family members on
e farm. This variable shows a significantly positive
elation to farm output in four out of six tests of the
ypothesis. The farm manager or farm head, which-
ver may be the more relevant decision-maker, does
ot need to rely solely on his or her own expertise but,
ather, can draw upon the collective expertise of all
embers of the family. By this logic, perhaps the best
easure of education in the context of farm decision-
aking is that of the most educated family member—
hoever that person may be, and however junior in the
amily hierarchy. No studies in the sample, however,
ave looked at this alternative measure.

.4 Separate Estimates of Worker and Allocative
ffects

Much of the empirical research, including most of
he studies surveyed here, focuses on the worker
ffect of education, estimating a single crop or gross
evenue production function, in which factor inputs
re "held constant." Little or no attention is given
o the farmer's choice either of outputs produced or
actor inputs utilized. Many education and agricultural

economists would argue that an informed selection
of outputs and inputs is the essence of efficient farm
production and, *ipso facto*, that the allocative effect of
education is likely to be even more important than the
worker effect.

Some of the studies surveyed here, such as the
one by Jamison and Moock, which looked at paddy
(rice) and wheat farmers in the Nepal Terai (1984),
have specified probability (binary choice) models
to explain a farmer's adoption or nonadoption of
modern practices such as application of chemical
fertilizers or use of a high-yielding seed variety, the
profitability of which is assumed in the analysis.
A significantly positive coefficient on an education
variable in the logit or probit regression equation
used to estimate the choice model indicates the existence of an allocative effect as posited by Welch
and others.

For farm samples in other parts of Nepal, Pudasaini
(1983) and Dhakal et al. (1987) have described and
demonstrated an approach for actual quantification
of the allocative effect of education. By estimating
several equations and manipulating the regression
results, both studies are able to conclude that the
input selection effect is paramount among education's
contributions to the profit-making of farmers.

4.5 Traditional and Modernizing Environments

The Nobel Prize-winning economist T W Schultz has
argued (Schultz 1975) that education is likely to be
much more effective under modernizing (i.e., rapidly changing) conditions than under very traditional
and stable conditions. The survey by Lockheed et
al. (1980) bears this hypothesis out. Of the studies
surveyed here and summarized in Table 2, only
two explicitly compared different groups of farmers
who were living in more and less modern settings (Cotlear 1989) or who were engaged in more
and less modern farming activities (Jamison and
Moock 1984).

In Cotlear's Peruvian study, the statistical effect
of formal schooling was greatest in Yanamarca, designated as "modernizing," and it was nonexistent in
Sangarara, designated as "traditional." In Chinchero,
designated as "intermediate" on the traditional-to-
modern spectrum, the magnitude of the effect was
intermediate, that is, between those found in the first
two areas. For farmers in Nepal, Jamison and Moock
observed a significantly positive worker effect of formal schooling in the production of wheat, a recently
introduced crop, but not in the production of paddy, a
traditional crop grown by all farm families in Nepal for
countless generations.

4.6 Exposure to Agricultural Extension Services:
Farm

Fourteen findings reported in Table 2 are concerned
with the farmer's contact with the (government-
provided) agricultural extension services. Only three

of these (21%) are significant at the 0.05 level. Extension contact is quite crudely measured in most studies—nearly always a binary variable (recent contact or not) and self-reported by the farmers in the sample. This measure reveals nothing about the nature or the quality of the extension contact—the extension agent may have met with the farmer about some other matter and given no agricultural advice, or may have given bad advice. Even if correctly measured, extension contact is quite probably endogenous—less efficient farmers are visited more often by conscientious extension agents trying to enhance agricultural performance in an area.

4.7 Exposure to Agricultural Extension Services: Community

If extension exposure is measured, not by whether the individual farmer has been in contact with the extension services, but by the percentage of all farms in the same geographical area who have been in contact, then there is little chance that the individual's own farm performance is influencing the extension services received, and the question of endogeneity becomes moot. Moreover, it is quite likely that the impact of extension services on productivity in an area is indirect, at least in part. Extension services may affect productivity by changing the behavior of the most innovative

farmers first, who then provide a demonstration good farming practices for other farmers in the are Finally, these practices are adopted by the less inn vative farmers, whether or not they themselves ha been in direct contact with an extension agent (se Rogers and Shoemaker 1971). The impact of comm nity extension (percentage of farms reporting rece contact) is considered in a farm sample from Nep by Jamison and Moock (1984). In three tests of tl hypothesis, Jamison and Moock find one result to l significantly positive (for the "modern" wheat cro; and two to be not significantly different from zero (f the more traditional paddy crop in both the early ar late growing seasons).

4.8 Interaction Between Formal Schooling and Extension Contact

A small number of studies have investigated th interaction between formal schooling and extensio contact. It is not clear *ex ante* what this interaction ter is expected to look like. A positive interaction mig be assumed, implying that schooling and extensio contact are complements—more schooling enables farmer to benefit additionally from any given amou of extension exposure. On the other hand, a negativ interaction is also plausible, suggesting that schoolir

Table 3
Summary of findings in studies of education's effects

	Number of tests of hypothesis	Number of results significant at 0.05 level
Education variable		
Formal education, measured as:	26	15 (58%)
Years of school		
Dummy variables		
Some education	14	1 (7%)
More education	14	9 (64%)
Extension services received by:		
Household itself	14	3 (21%)
Community (households in area)	3	1 (33%)
Education × extension interaction	7	
Regression coefficient negative	5 71%	1 (20%)
Regression coefficient positive	2 29%	0 (0%)
Recipient of education/training		
Farm head	13	4 (31%)
Wife of head	1	0 (0%)
Farm manager	55	21 (38%)
Family members	6	4 (67%)
Region		
Africa	8	6 (75%)
Asia	53	18 (34%)
Americas	17	6 (35%)

and extension contact are substitutes—all farmers may benefit from extension contact, but the farmer with more schooling already has access to the information on best farming practices and benefits less from extension exposure than a farmer with less schooling. A zero nonsignificant interaction is also possible indicating that educational attainment and extension contact are both useful separately, but having the two in combination is no more useful in enhancing agricultural output than having either one by itself. In the sample of studies surveyed here, seven two-tailed tests are conducted of the hypothesis that there is a nonzero interaction between formal schooling and extension contact. For five the sign is negative (of which only one is significantly different from zero at the 0.10 probability level), and for two the sign is positive (neither of which is statistically significant).

5. Conclusion

There has developed since the 1960s a rich body of research on the relationship between education and agricultural productivity. Most of the empirical research has focused on samples of farmers in developing areas, where agricultural production is certainly more constrained by low levels of education than in more developed areas. Asian samples dominate the literature, probably because the data from Asia are better than from Africa or Latin America.

Although the findings include inconsistencies—they are particularly inconclusive in regard to nonformal education (namely, agricultural extension contact) as distinct from formal schooling—nevertheless, a reasonably clear pattern does emerge from the empirical literature, one that was first sketched by Lockheed et al. in their survey of studies through 1978. Much the same pattern is demonstrated here, based on 14 studies published since then. Table 3 summarizes the more recent findings, abstracting from Table 2 above.

In general, there is a positive relation between formal schooling and agricultural productivity. This relation is strong for educational attainment beyond some culturally defined threshold level, whereas it is weak or nonexistent for attainment below this level. The clear suggestion is that an individual who completes only a few years of school does not retain enough learning to benefit from it later as a farmer. Finally, the Schultzian hypothesis (the more modern and less traditional the farm activity which the farmer performs or the farming area in which the farmer lives, the stronger will be the relation between education and agriculture productivity) is generally borne out by studies conducted in the 1980s.

References

Azhar R A 1988 Education and technical efficiency in Pakistan's agriculture. *The Pakistan Development Review* 27(4), Pt. 2: 687–95

Butt M S 1984 Education and farm productivity in Pakistan. *Pakistan Journal of Applied Economics* 3(1): 65–82

Cotlear D 1989 The effects of education on farm productivity. *J. Dev. Planning* (UN Department of International Economic and Social Affairs) 19: 73–99

Dhakal D, Grabowski R, Belbase K 1987 The effect of education in Nepal's traditional agriculture. *Econ. Educ. Rev.* 6(1): 27–34

Duraisamy P 1990 Technical and allocative efficiency of education in agricultural production: A profit function approach. *Indian Economic Review* 25(1): 17–32

Grabowski R, Pasurka C 1988 Farmer education and economic efficiency: Northern farms in 1860. *Economics Letters* 28(4): 315–20

Jameson K P 1988 Education's role in rural areas in Latin America. *Econ. Educ. Rev.* 7(3): 333–43

Jamison D T, Moock P R 1984 Farmer education and farm efficiency in Nepal: The role of schooling, extension services, and cognitive skills. *World Dev.* 12(1): 67–86

Kalirajan K P, Shand R T 1985 Types of education and agricultural productivity: A quantitative analysis of Tamil Nadu rice farming. *The Journal of Development Studies* 21(2): 232–43

Khandker S R 1986 *Farmer Education and Farm Efficiency: The Role of Education Revisited.* Discussion Paper No. 506, Economic Growth Center, Yale University, New Haven, Connecticut

Lockheed M E, Jamison D T, Lau L J 1980 Farmer education and farm efficiency: A survey. *Economic Development and Cultural Change* 29(1): 37–76

Moock P R 1981 Education and technical efficiency in small-farm production. *Economic Development and Cultural Change* 29(4): 723–38

Phillips J M, Marble R P 1986 Farmer education and efficiency: A frontier production function approach. *Econ. Educ. Rev.* 5(3): 257–64

Pudasaini S P 1983 The effects of education in agriculture: Evidence from Nepal. *American Journal of Agricultural Economics* 65(3): 509–15

Ram R, Singh R D 1988 Farm households in rural Burkina Faso: Some evidence on allocative and direct return to schooling, and male-female labor productivity differentials. *World Dev.* 16(3): 419–24

Rogers E M, Shoemaker F 1971 *Communication of Innovations*, 2nd edn. Free Press, New York

Schultz T W 1975 The value of the ability to deal with disequilibria. *J. Econ. Lit.* 13(3): 827–46

Welch F 1970 Education in production. *J. Pol. Econ.* 78(1): 35–59

Further Reading

Bowman M J 1991 The formation of human resources for farming and household work as vocations: Lessons for less developed countries. *Econ. Educ. Rev.* 10(1): 1–5

Eisemon T O, Nyamete A 1988 Schooling and agricultural productivity in western Kenya. *Journal of Eastern African Research and Development* 18: 44–66

Griliches Z 1964 Research expenditures, education, and the aggregate agricultural production function. *Am. Econ. Rev.* 54(6): 961–74

Hayami Y, Ruttan V W 1970 Agricultural productivity differences among countries. *Am. Econ. Rev.* 60(5): 895–911

Jamison D T, Lau L J 1982 *Farmer Education and Farm Efficiency.* Johns Hopkins University Press for The World Bank, Baltimore, Maryland

Khandker S R 1988 Input management ability, occupational patterns and farm productivity in Bangladesh agriculture. *Journal of Development Studies* 24(2): 214–31

Moock P R 1976 The efficiency of women as farm managers: Kenya. *American Journal of Agricultural Economics* 58(5): 831–35

Pudasaini S P 1982 Education and agricultural efficiency in Nepal, Discussion Paper No. 82–3. The World Bank, Washington, DC

Schultz T W 1964 *Transforming Traditional Agriculture.* Yale University Press, New Haven, Connecticut

Stefanou S E, Saxena S 1988 Education, experience, and allocative efficiency: A dual approach. *American Journal of Agricultural Economics* 70(2): 338–45

Welch F 1978 The role of investments in human capital in agriculture. In: Schultz T W (ed.) 1978 *Distortions of Agricultural Incentives.* Indiana University Press, Bloomington, Indiana

Wu C C 1977 Education in farm production: The case of Taiwan. *American Journal of Agricultural Economics* 59(4): 699–709

Vocational Education and Productivity

Weifang Min

The value of different kinds of education for production has been the subject of continuous controversy. In the past 30 years numerous studies have been conducted to examine the economic rationale for the investment in secondary vocational education by comparing the performance of secondary vocational school graduates and general senior high-school graduates. This entry reviews the arguments regarding the impact of vocational versus general education in increasing worker productivity and presents the theoretical discussions and available empirical data with a case study of workers in a Chinese automobile plant.

1. Economic Relevance of Vocational Education

The linkage between education and productivity has been the subject of numerous studies in the literatures both of economics and of sociology. Many studies have examined how different levels of education and different types of education influence worker productivity. In particular, a significant number of studies exist which compare the productivity of vocational education graduates with that of general education graduates in both developed and developing countries of the world.

Most of these studies use earnings as a measure for productivity. A few use alternative proxies such as a worker efficiency rate or job performance (Fuller 1970, Godfrey 1977, Min and Tsang 1990). Most of the studies are cross-sectional in design. Some have examined the longitudinal differences in relative effectiveness of vocational and general education (Bolino and Uri 1982, Gustman and Steinmeier 1982, Hu et al. 1971, Meyer and Wise 1982, Tannen 1983).

The findings from these studies are mixed, with some showing higher earnings or productivity for vocational education graduates (Bolino and Uri 1982, Castro 1979, Corazzini 1968, Fredland and Little 1980, Freeman 1973, Gustman and Steinmeier 1982, Hu et al. 1971, Min and Tsang 1990, Newman and Ziderman 1991), and others showing no significant difference or negative results in comparison with general education graduates (Clark 1983, Fuller 1970, Godfrey 1977, Grasso and Shea 1978, Meyer and Wise 1982, Moock and Bellew 1988, Psacharopoulos and Loxley 1985, Rumberger and Daymont 1984). Some investigators have found that the economic effects of vocational education vary with programs, and the gender and ethnicity of students (Gustman and Steinmeier 1982, Li et al. 1981, Meyer and Wise 1982); and the effectiveness of vocational training depends upon the nature of the training received and the type of institutions providing it (Tannen 1983). Moreover, the estimated results can change significantly with the model employed and the time period studied (Gustman and Steinmeier 1982). In general, there is no consistent and convincing evidence in support of the presumed productivity advantage of vocational education over general academic education.

In addition to the mixed evidence in existing literature, there are some issues to consider in generalizing the results of these studies to other situations. First, most of the studies do not measure productivity directly but assume that productivity is reflected in individual wages. While the use of wages as a proxy for productivity is questionable for capitalist economies characterized by imperfect competition, it is even more problematic for the nonmarket economies (e.g., a centrally planned economy where wages are set and tightly controlled by the government). In such cases, wages would not be a valid measure of productivity.

Second, most of the studies have not taken account of the impact of work effort on productivity. The degree to which workers exert effort on their jobs could make a significant difference in productivity. Without taking account of the work effort variable, the linkage between education and productivity would ot be properly revealed. Thus, work effort is an nportant intermediate variable linking education and roductivity (Tsang 1987).

Third, most of the studies have taken the individual orker as the unit of analysis and have ignored the otential interaction among workers that might affect roductivity. In modern production, however, a large roportion of work is group work which can influence ow an individual worker behaves, in part by provid- ng incentives at the group level. Thus the impact of roup dynamics on individual productivity should be iken into account.

. *Education, Work Effort, and Productivity*

lost of the empirical work on the relationship be- veen education and productivity is based on human apital theory, which argues that education can raise ie productivity of an individual, primarily by increas- ng the individual's cognitive skills. Thus, there is a irect and positive relationship between education and roductivity. This relationship is usually estimated by elating earnings to human capital variables such as ears of formal schooling, work experience, and other n-the-job training variables.

Research on the relationship between education nd productivity has focused on work effort as an nportant intermediate variable relating the education f workers and their productivity (Tsang 1987). Work ffort is seen as a function of worker characteristics, ɔb characteristics, and the degree of match/mismatch etween these two sets of characteristics. Worker haracteristics include worker skills and abilities, type nd level of education, worker needs and expecta- ions, experience, age, and gender. Job characteristics nclude both physical aspects such as the nature of ɔb and its skill requirements, the reward structure nd promotional opportunities, and the physical en- ironment; and social aspects such as peer-group nteraction, supervision and the worker–supervisor elationship, the atmosphere for cooperation, and so orth. Two types of match/mismatch can be identified: n skill and in occupational expectations. If workers ind their skills to be underutilized in their jobs or heir occupational expectations unfulfilled, they may ɔecome dissatisfied and exert a lower level of effort, vhich results in lower productivity.

Education can affect worker characteristics by its nfluence on an individual's skills, needs, and expec- ations; it can also affect the job characteristics of a vorker by influencing the kind of jobs available to im or her as a result of his or her education. Through ts influence on both worker characteristics and job haracteristics, education can affect the degree of natch/mismatch between these two sets of character- stics, and thus influence work effort and productivity. ːducation can have both a direct and indirect effect on ɔroductivity.

This model of work effort has been applied to

the study of the impact of the level of education on productivity (Tsang 1987). It was found that workers with more education than their jobs require (i.e., underutilization of education) tend to exert lower work effort (proxied by job satisfaction) and have lower productivity. It is conceivable that the type of education (vocational or general) that workers receive can be related to differences in productivity among workers. To the degree that vocational education and general education socialize individuals with different skills, needs, and occupational expectations, the type of education may be correlated with work effort and productivity.

3. *Individual Behavior and Group Dynamics*

It should be noted that the Tsang–Levin model of work effort is based on individuals, not groups. Because of the possible interactions among individuals in work groups, an individual may perform differently under different group settings. The impact of the interaction among workers in a group on the relationship be- tween education and productivity has to be taken into account.

On the one hand, because much of the work in modern production, involves group work and provides some incentives at the group level, cooperation among group members is likely. For example, in a coopera- tive work environment those with more knowledge and skills may share that information with those with less knowledge and skills. This may equalize skill proficiencies among workers and may obscure the dif- ferences in productivity which arise from differences in the skill background of workers.

On the other hand, since the promotion of workers to a higher wage level within groups has been partially based on the evaluation of individual performance both in the production process and in the test of technical knowledge and skills, only a certain pro- portion of workers are promoted each year. In most countries, there exist remarkable differences between the lowest wages and the highest wages. This pro- motion policy is supposed to encourage workers to improve themselves technically, but it may also lead to competition among individual workers, thus maintain- ing individual differences in skills and productivity. Since both group-based incentives and individual- based incentives exist in the workplace, both group interactions and individual behaviors should be taken into account when estimating the impact of general versus vocational education on productivity.

4. *Hypotheses to be Tested*

Based on the above discussions, two hypotheses might be generated and tested empirically with a case study of workers in a Chinese automobile plant.

Hypothesis 1: Secondary vocational school graduates as factory workers holding jobs more closely related to their training tend to exert higher work effort and be more productive than general senior high-school graduates who hold the same jobs. This result might arise because vocational education graduates occupying jobs closely related to their training might have better matched occupation expectations. Since secondary vocational schools prepare students for employment after graduation, students in these schools (such as skilled worker training schools) expect to be employees of a certain type (factory workers, for example). General senior high-school graduates, however, are prepared for college, yet in most countries there are not sufficient college places for all of them. Some have to enter the labor market, and they do not have the appropriate technological and psychological preparation for the jobs they are embarking on. Thus, with respect to occupational expectation, vocational education graduates are better matched and they thus have higher work effort. Vocational education graduates may be more productive than general education graduates because the skills they acquired from the vocational programs may better meet the skill requirements of their jobs.

Hypothesis 2: A worker's educational background has a less significant impact on productivity in a more cooperative work group than in a less cooperative one. This may arise from individuals with more skills in a group with a high level of cooperation sharing their knowledge with less skilled colleagues. This equalizes skill proficiencies among members of the group, and obscures differences in productivity which result from the diverse educational background of the group. The impact of vocational education on productivity in a workplace with a high level of cooperation may be less significant than that with a lower level of cooperation.

4.1 A Case Study

These hypotheses were tested empirically by means of a case study conducted at an automobile plant in Beijing (Min and Tsang 1990). The sample included 413 skilled workers, of whom 299 were general secondary education graduates and 114 vocational secondary education graduates from the company-affiliated skilled worker schools sponsored by the automobile plant and jointly supervised by the Beijing Municipal Education Bureau and Labor Bureau. A total of 93 percent of these vocational school graduates considered themselves to be holding jobs related to their training. Data on level and type of education of the workers, work experience, gender, socioeconomic status, salaries, job satisfaction as a proxy of work effort, work efficiency as an indicator of productivity, cooperation among workers, and some other controlled organizational variables were collected in 1986 in the plant by a clustered sampling strategy.

Work efficiency reflects the amount of goods an services produced by a worker during a period of tim and is defined as:

$$\text{Work efficiency} = \frac{\text{actual output of a worker per period}}{\text{production quota for a worker per period}}$$

The production quota in the above ratio is a func tion of labor, equipment, technology, materials, an time. It reflects the physical conditions and inputs t production. Thus, work efficiency measures the per formance of the worker based on a given set of inpu and physical conditions of production per period. Th advantages of using worker efficiency as a measure c productivity are twofold: (a) it is a direct measure c worker productivity, and (b) since quotas are designe to take account of factors that might affect worke output other than the worker's contribution, wor efficiency holds constant those factors which coul affect worker performance but which are extraneou to the worker, such as machine capacity, availabilit of tools, and quality of materials. It thus enables th researcher to concentrate on the performance of worker (Fuller 1970).

Job satisfaction of workers is a function of work er characteristics and job characteristics and th match/mismatch between these two. It is measured b a five-item scale, on which the figure one denote the lowest level of satisfication and five the highes level. The reliability and validity of measures of jo satisfaction, cooperation among workers and othe organizational variables were tested by a pilot stud conducted by the present author. Both Cronbach' alpha (a reliability coefficient developed in the earl 1950s) and the inter-item correlation coefficient ha values well above 0.7, which were acceptable for a exploratory study.

The data were analyzed by a two-equation recursiv system. The first equation is a job satisfaction equatio in which job satisfaction is a function of the type c education, and other worker and job characteristics The second equation relates work efficiency to jo satisfaction, type of education, and other worker an job characteristics. The type of education is expecte to have a direct effect and an indirect effect (throug job satisfaction) on work efficiency. To examin the impact of the level of cooperation among grou members on the relationship between education an productivity, two subsamples are considered: individ uals working in groups with a high level of cooperatio and individuals working in groups with a low level o cooperation.

4.2 Empirical Results

Table 1 presents the regression results for the 41 workers surveyed. The dependent variable in Equatio

Table 1
Results of regression analyses for workers under 40 years old[a]

	Equation 1.1		Equation 1.2		Equation 1.3		Equation 1.4	
				Dependent variable				
	Job Satisfaction		Work Efficiency		Work Efficiency		Work Efficiency	
Job satisfaction	—		0.033	$(5.2)^b$	0.038	$(3.2)^b$	0.034	$(4.6)^b$
Worker characteristics:								
Level of education	0.051	(1.5)	0.011	$(2.9)^b$	0.006	(0.8)	0.012	$(2.5)^b$
Type of education	0.28	$(2.6)^b$	0.069	$(5.4)^b$	0.053	$(2.0)^b$	0.080	$(5.3)^b$
On-the-job training	0.022	(1.6)	0.008	$(4.7)^b$	0.006	$(2.0)^b$	0.008	$(3.9)^b$
Experience	0.016	(0.9)	0.025	$(6.6)^b$	0.024	$(3.6)^b$	0.027	$(5.1)^b$
Experience squared	—		−0.001	$(−4.6)^b$	−0.001	$(−2.7)^b$	−0.001	$(−3.0)^b$
Father's education	− 0.004	(−0.1)	—		—		—	
Mother's education	− 0.035	(−0.6)	—		—		—	
Gender	− 0.049	(−0.5)	−0.015	(−1.4)	−0.003	(−0.1)	−0.022	(−1.6)
Job characteristics:								
Salary	0.13	$(2.5)^b$	—		—		—	
Peer relationship	0.088	(1.4)	0.016	$(2.2)^b$	0.019	(1.4)	0.018	(2.0)
Leader–member relationship	0.032	(0.5)	0.004	(0.6)	0.013	(0.9)	0.013	(0.5)
Promotional opportunity	0.16	$(2.5)^b$	—		—		—	
Work autonomy	0.061	(1.1)	0.017	$(2.5)^b$	0.017	$(2.0)^b$	0.016	$(2.0)^b$
Cooperation among workers	0.15	$(2.1)^b$	0.038	$(4.4)^b$	—		—	
Constant	0.58		0.45		0.59		0.53	
R-squared	0.31		0.58		0.42		0.56	
N	413		398		155		243	

Source: Min and Tsang 1990 p. 357
a Numbers in parentheses are t-values   b Significant at 0.05 level

1.1 is job satisfaction. The estimated coefficient for the variable type of education is both positive and significant, showing that vocational school graduates holding jobs closely related to their training tend to be more satisfied with their jobs as factory workers than general education graduates, thus supporting Hypothesis 1. The coefficients for all the other independent variables were statistically insignificant except for the job characteristic variables for salary, promotional opportunity, and cooperation among workers which were statistically significant and positive.

The dependent variable in Equation 1.2 is work efficiency. Equations 1.1 and 1.2 constitute the recursive model for the 413-worker sample. From Equation 1.2 it can be seen that the type of education is positively and significantly related to work efficiency, indicating that vocational–technical graduates as factory workers holding jobs closely related to their training are more productive than general education graduates. Job satisfaction (as a proxy for work effort) is also positively and significantly related to work efficiency. Thus the type of education has a direct and indirect effect on productivity, also supporting Hypothesis 1.

Equations 1.3 and 1.4 are the work–efficiency equa-

tions for workers in more cooperative groups and less cooperative groups respectively. From the R-square values of these two equations, it can be seen that the individual-based model explains productivity significantly better for less cooperative rather than more cooperative groups. By comparing the coefficients in these two equations, it becomes clear the human capital variables reflecting individual differences in skills, such as type of education, level of education, on-the-job-training, and experience, are less significant and less strong in more cooperative groups. In particular, the coefficient for level of education is 0.012 and is significant in Equation 1.4; but it is only 0.006 and is insignificant in Equation 1.3. In addition, the coefficient for type of education in Equation 1.4 is 50 percent larger than the one in Equation 1.3. This result is consistent with Hypothesis 2. Thus, the level of cooperation among group members appears to affect the relationship between productivity and the skills of workers.

4.3 Discussion

The case study found that secondary vocational education graduates holding jobs closely related to their training are more satisfied with their jobs as factory workers, and more productive, than secondary general education graduates. A plausible reason for this is that vocational school graduates have better preparation for their jobs. The expectations and skills they acquire in vocational schools better match the job characteristics of factory work in the People's Republic of China.

Moreover, there is significant interaction between education and the level of cooperation among group members. In a work environment which is more cooperative, the education or skill background of workers becomes less important. This may be due to the sharing of knowledge and mutual assistance among workers that reduce individual differences in skills.

Furthermore, the results show work effort (proxied by job satisfaction) to be a significant factor affecting productivity. It is an important intermediate variable relating education and productivity. Thus, education can affect productivity directly through its human capital capacity; it can also affect productivity indirectly through the work effort variable. This indirect effect depends on the degree of match/mismatch of worker characteristics and job characteristics. If education socializes students in the skills, expectations, and needs that are consistent with jobs they find in the workplace, then education has a positive and significant indirect effect on productivity. If there is a significant level of mismatch in skills and expectations, the indirect effect can be negative (Tsang 1987). Since the indirect effect of education depends on a complex set of factors, the relationship between education and productivity is necessarily intricate, and is likely to vary under different conditions. This may partly explain the mixed evidence in research literature on the relationship between vocational education and productivity.

However, these conclusions are premature for several reasons. First, this case study relates to only one plant of the automobile industry. Further research is needed to determine if the findings are generally applicable to other plants in the same industry, and to other industries in China. It would also be revealing to study the productivity of graduates of vocational schools not affiliated with a company. In fact, this case study considered "user" graduates (i.e., those holding jobs closely related to their training) of well-established, company-affiliated vocational schools only. "Non-user" graduates from non-affiliated vocational schools might not perform as well. The findings of this case study may represent the upper limit of the productivity advantage of vocational education relative to general education. Further research should be undertaken to examine the case of "non-users" and non-affiliated vocational schools.

Second, even if the findings are generalizable to other plants and other industries at a particular point in time, the education–productivity relationship over time should be examined. It is conceivable that, in the long run, general education graduates might catch up and even surpass vocational education graduates in productivity. As a result of their general training general education graduates may be more flexible in handling a range of tasks and more adaptive to technologically induced changes in the workplace than vocational education graduates trained in specific skills. Time and rates of renewal of technologies of production will play a critical role. General education graduates may be more productive than vocational graduates in a dynamic environment after they have made an initial adjustment to their job.

Third, this study compares the relative productivity advantages of two types of education, without considering their respective costs. To inform decisions on efficient allocation of scarce resources, a cost benefit approach should be adopted. Further research should therefore examine the costs of different types of education.

Finally, the case study has been narrowly confined to a comparison of economic returns to different types of education; however, economic rationality is not the sole basis for education policy making in general and the vocationalization of secondary education in particular. Political and social considerations are also relevant. The vocationalization of secondary education in the broader context of the current educational reform in the People's Republic of China can be seen as part of an effort to rally popular support for the modernization policy of the new leadership, thus carrying both economic and political legitimation implications. In China, as well as in other countries, vocational streaming is a form of social stratification. It is also a commonly used strategy for reducing the social demand for higher education. Thus the vocationalization of secondary education reflects a reassessment of the social function of education in China. These various considerations should be properly balanced in arriving at an educational policy to promote national development.

See also: Returns to Vocational Education in Developing Nations; Education Production Functions

References

Bolino A C, Uri N D 1982 Vocational education: A human capital/productivity nexus? *J. Behav. Econ.* 11(2): 1–32

Castro M C de 1979 Vocational education and the training of industrial labor in Brazil. *International Labor Review* 118(5): 617–29

Clark D H 1983 *How secondary school graduates perform in the Labor Market: A Study of Indonesia.* World Bank Staff Working Paper No. 615, World Bank Washington, DC

Corazzini A J 1968 The decision to invest in vocational education: An analysis of cost and benefit. *J. Hum Resources* 3 (Supplement): 88–120

Fredland J E, Little R D 1980 Long-term returns to vocational training: Evidence from military sources. *J. Hum Resources* 15: 49–66

Freeman R B 1973 Occupational training in proprietary

schools and technical institutes. *The Review of Economics and Statistics* 56(3): 310–18

Fuller W 1970 Education, training and productivity: A study of skilled workers in two factories in south India. A Dissertation submitted to School of Education, Stanford University, Stanford, California

Godfrey M 1977 Education, training, productivity and income: A Kenyan case study. Discussion paper No.93. Institute of Development Studies, University of Sussex, Brighton

Grasso J, Shea J 1978 Vocational education and training: Impact on youth. Carnegie Council on Policies in Higher Education, Carnegie Foundation for Advancement of Teaching, New York

Gustman A L, Steinmeier T L 1982 The relation between vocational training in high school and economic outcomes. *Industrial and Labor Review* 36(1): 73–87

Hu T W, Lee M L, Stromsdorfer E W 1971 Economic returns to vocational and comprehensive high school graduates. *J. Hum. Resources* 6: 25–50

Li W L, Seitz P, Lewis M, Mertens D 1981 *Vocational Education Graduates in the Labor Market: Experiences of Young Workers*. National Center for Research in Vocational Education, Ohio State University, Columbus, Ohio

Meyer R H, Wise D A 1982 High school preparation and early labor force experience. In: Freeman R, Ellwood D (eds.) 1982 *The Youth Labor Market Problem*. University of Chicago Press, Chicago, Illinois

Min W, Tsang M C 1990 Vocational education and productivity: A case study of the Beijing General Auto Industry Company. *Economics of Education Review* 9: 351–64

Moock P, Bellew R 1988 *Vocational and Technical Education in Peru*. Population and Human Resources Department Working Paper, World Bank, Washington, DC

Newman S, Ziderman A 1991 Vocational schooling, occupational matching, and labor market earnings in Israel. *J. Hum. Resources* 26(2): 256–58

Psacharopoulos G, Loxley W 1985 *Diversified Secondary Education and Development: Evidence from Columbia and Tanzania*. Johns Hopkins University Press, Baltimore, Maryland

Rumberger R W, Daymont T N 1984 The economic value of academic and vocational training acquired in high school. In: Borus M (ed.) 1984 *Youth and the Labor Market*. W E Upjohn Institute for Employment Research, Kalamazoo, Michigan

Tannen M B 1983 Vocational education and earnings for White males: New evidence from longitudinal data. *Southern Economic J.* 50: 369–84

Tsang M C 1987 The impact of underutilization of education on productivity: A case study of US Bell companies. *Economics of Education Review* 6(3): 239–54

Education and Earnings

P. Cipollone

The relationship between earnings and schooling has been widely studied at both the theoretical and empirical levels. The relationship is simple to state: more educated people enjoy a higher level of earnings than people with a lower level of education. However, people with the same level of education do have different earnings depending on their race, gender, ethnicity, ability, and social background. This characteristic of earning structure seems to hold good regardless of the level of development of the economy and the institutional setting (e.g., planned or free market economy). Thus it is hardly surprising that many scholars since the late 1950s have been studying education and earnings in an effort to understand fully the economic forces underlying the empirical observed facts. Theoretical discussion has mainly investigated the possible reasons for earnings differentials among differently educated people. Empirical studies have attempted to test the different theories and, at the same time, to measure the earnings differentials due to education. This entry is a review of the main contribution to the debate.

1. The Empirically Observed Relationship Between Earnings and Education: Age–Earnings Profiles

Traditional economists describe the relationship between earnings and schooling by the use of so-called "age–earnings profiles." Traditional age–earnings profiles are simple relations which demonstrate how the structure of earnings of individuals is distributed across age and level of education, and in some cases, over gender, race, and ethnicity. Figure 1 represents stylized age–earnings profiles (Pencavel 1990). Although the age–earnings in Fig. 1 have been constructed using the mean earnings of males in the United States in 1987, they present some characteristics which are common to age–earnings profiles computed for other economies with different levels of development and different institutional arrangements.

The main characteristics of a stylized age–earnings profile are:

(a) The absolute level of earnings at any point in time is higher for people with a higher level of schooling.

(b) Age–earnings profiles are concave in age. That is to say, earnings increase with age at a decreasing rate, up to a maximum (usually between the age of 45 and 55) and then flatten or even decline. This pattern is observed for all the levels of schooling.

(c) The slope of the profile is positively correlated with level of schooling. In other words, before the

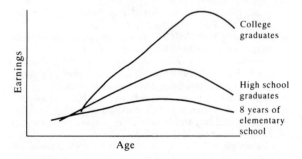

Figure 1
Stylized age–earnings profile by schooling[a]
Source: Pencave 1990

earnings peak is reached, the mean earnings of people with a higher level of schooling increases faster than those of people with a lower level of schooling. After the peak, the earnings of more educated people decline faster than those of less educated people.

(d) The maximum level of earning tends to be reached at a later age for people with a higher level of education.

(e) The earnings differentials for differently educated people tend to increase with the level of education. In other words, at any given age, the differential earnings associated with a given differential in years of education increases with the absolute level of schooling. For example, the difference in earnings between people with 12 and 8 years of schooling is lower than the difference in earnings between people with 16 and 12 years of schooling.

The evidence collected thus far (which is quite considerable since data are now available for more than 40 countries) has convinced economists that the characteristics outlined above are robust to changes in the level of economic development, the institutional setting, and the cyclical pattern of the economy. Therefore, economists have tended to regard the above characteristics as structural ones, and have devoted much effort to understanding the economic behavior behind them.

2. Caveats in the Interpretation of the Age–Earnings Profile

There are some significant caveats attached to the interpretation of the above characteristics. In fact, while cross-sectional surveys of individuals consistently reveal age–earnings profiles by level of schooling with

the features described above, this does not mean that these profiles are invariant over calendar time (Pencavel 1990). As stated above, the age–earnings profiles represent the structure of earnings for level of education and age of a given population at a given point in time rather than the evolution of the earnings of a given group of people over time. Indeed, age–earnings profiles are constructed from cross-sectional data rather than from longitudinal data. Therefore, there is no need for the true age–earnings profile of a given person (i.e., the evolution of the person's earning over his or her lifetime) to follow the pattern displayed in Fig. 1. Indeed, there exists a new stream of research, based on the so-called "synthetic cohort", which uses repeated cross-sections to construct the true age-earnings profile of a given cohort (Macurdy and Mroz 1991). The first results to emerge from this line of research show that while traditional age–earnings profiles, calculated from cross-sectional data, look very much like the stylized one given in Fig. 1, the real evolution of the income of different cohorts of workers over the eleven-year period 1978–87 has been completely different from the one predicted by traditional age–earnings profiles. Figure 2 presents the classical age–earnings profile based on cross-sectional data from the United States for the year 1987 (data obtained from the Current Population Survey). In addition, it presents three other curves which describe the earnings of college graduates who were 30, 40, and 50 years old in 1987 (i.e., cohorts of 1957, 1947, and 1937) over the 11-year period 1977–87.

Thus, the curve labeled "Age=40" represents the evolution of the median earnings of college graduates born in 1947, from the year when they were 29 years old (1977) to the year they were 40 (1987). The difference between the true evolution of earnings and the one predicted by the traditional age–earnings profile is striking. College graduates born in 1937 had de-

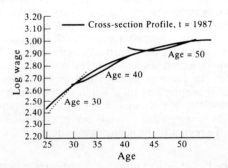

Figure 2
Cross-sectional profile and corresponding cohort profile for college graduates 1987
Source: Macurdy and Mroz 1991

clining earnings while still in their early forties. Their earnings went up again when this cohort was about 45 years old. This pattern is exactly opposite to the one predicted by the traditional age–earnings profiles. Even more interesting is the fact that for the younger workers (the 1957 cohort) earnings rose over the entire period 1977–87. The reason for these discrepancies is that the economic environment changes and affects people's wages in different ways, mostly depending on a person's age. For example, Pencavel (1990) noticed that in the United States labor market the college earnings premium of recent labor market entrants is much more volatile than the premium of people with a comparable level of skill but in the middle of their career. This means that downturn periods will have a greater effect on new entrants than on people already in the market. Thus, cohorts which enter in slow growth periods will be disadvantaged for their entire career since the next expansion period will alter their wages much less than those of new entrants. Despite these problems, many researchers still rely on the cross-sectionally based age–earnings profiles. There are several reasons for this practice:

(a) Synthetic cohort-based age–earnings profiles require a great deal of data (one cross-section every year) which are not available in many countries. This problem is particularly relevant in less developed countries.

(b) Inertia in the field. At the early stage of development of the economics of education literature, few data were available, even in the United States. Therefore, the pioneering researches of Mincer and Becker had to be based on single cross-sectional data.

(c) Finally, if the changes in the economic environment are not dramatic, or if their effects are the same across the market, then it is still possible to use single cross-sections to infer the evolution of the earnings of a single cohort.

3. The Leading Explanation for the Stylized Features of Cross-sectionally based Age–Earnings Profiles: The Human Capital Model

By far the most complete and developed theoretical model by which to understand the relationship between earnings and schooling is the human capital model (HCM) (Becker 1975, Ghez and Becker 1975, Mincer 1974). (For a full discussion of this model, see *Human Capital Concepts*.) In this entry, attention will be focused on how the HCM explains the stylized facts described in Sect. 1 above. These facts can be elucidated as follows:

(a) The level of earnings for differently educated people: According to the HCM, the school system is

an institution specialized in the production of training (Becker 1975). People attend school to acquire training which, in turn, is rewarded by the market with a higher level of wages. However, the relation between training and earnings is still not perfectly understood. Even among human capital theorists there is no generally accepted explanation for why training is rewarded by the market. Some authors stress the fact that training supposedly increases people's productivity. Thus people with a higher level of education produce more than those with a lower level of education regardless of the specific task they are performing. Other authors stress the fact that training is costly to acquire. Thus the supply of trained people is less than the supply of untrained people (simply because a trained worker can enter the market of untrained labor, while the inverse is not possible). Therefore, the payment of higher wages to more educated people is simply a premium to the scarcity of trained labor.

(b) Concavity in Age of the age–earnings profile: If school were the only channel through which people acquire training, and training did not depreciate, the age–earnings profiles would have a different shape from the one observed. Working from the premise that school is the only source of training, then, according to this hypothesis, the stylized age–earnings profile would be a step function with value zero from age 0 to graduation age and a constant value Y_s from graduation age to retirement age. People with higher education would have a higher Y_s. Indeed, in the absence of postschooling investment and depreciation, the human capital acquired during the schooling period would be constant with respect to age. Thus, earnings would be constant with respect to age since earnings are flows generated from the stock of human capital through an interest rate.

In reality, earnings grow with age because age is a proxy for the postschooling investment in human capital. Thus people continue to invest in training well beyond the formal schooling period and increase their stock of human capital while in the labor market through experience and on-the-job training. Earnings therefore keep growing with age because the human capital stock keeps growing with age. However, human capital depreciates over time, very much like physical capital, mainly because of the problem of obsolescence. Over time, new knowledge becomes available and often replaces or complements existing knowledge. Subsequently, a constant stock of human capital loses market value over time. As a result of this depreciation problem, the stock of human capital will increase as long as the gross investment in human capital is greater than the depreciation. Therefore, there are two variables which influence the evolution of the human capital stock over time: the depreciation of the stock which increases over time if the stock is increasing and decreases if the stock is decreasing, and the gross investment which depends on the decisions of individuals about time and resource allocation over time. This second variable declines over time for two reasons. The first is related to the fact that time is an input for the production of human capital and the price of time (wage rate) increases when human capital increases. Hence, as the consumers age and their stock of capital increases, they will invest less and less in acquiring additional human capital. The second reason for the decline of investment in human capital is that the later in life the investment occurs, the shorter the period in which the yield of the investment can be enjoyed by the investor. Thus the difference between gross investment and depreciation declines over time and even becomes negative. Therefore, the optimal path for the stock of human capital is one which first increases at a declining rate, and then declines.

(c) More highly educated people have a steeper age–earnings profile: This characteristic of the age–earnings profile is a consequence of the fact that time spent in acquiring postschool training declines with age. Indeed, the price effect discussed under (b) makes it relatively more convenient for the consumer to substitute time spent in training with time spent in market activities as the human capital stock and, hence, the wage increases. This price effect is stronger for people with higher levels of education. Thus the earnings profile will be steeper for the better educated as a result of the greater amount of time spent in the labor market. The slope would be even greater if the wages rate were a convex function of the human capital.

(d) The peak in earnings function occurs later in life for the profile of less educated people: This characteristic can be explained by stressing that experience, not age, is the variable which increases the human capital after the school period. Assuming that the maximum human capital stock is achieved after a period (years of experience) which is independent of the level of human capital acquired in school, then the age–earnings profile of more educated people peaks later in life simply because more educated people enter the labor market later. Hence, it is only later in life that more educated people attain the years of experience required for the human capital stock (and the earnings profile) to reach the maximum.

(e) Earning differentials are an increasing function of schooling: This characteristic has been noted by Mincer (1974 p. 10), who explained it with a model which assumes that consumers live a given

number of years. The explanation of the feature of the earnings profile relief heavily on this assumption of a fixed length of life. However, the same result obtained by Mincer can be obtained simply by observing that people who enter the labor market later in life have an expected working life which is shorter than that of people who enter the labor market earlier. In fact, because the probability of dying increases with age, the difference in the expected working life of two people who enter the labor market with one year of difference in age is smaller than one year. Moreover, in equilibrium, the present discounted value of two schooling investment plans must be the same. As a result, the differentials in earnings, at any given age, must be an increasing function of schooling because more educated people have a shorter expected working life.

4. Alternative Explanations

Thus far, the pure theory of human capital has been presented. However, empirical researches have shown that many other observed variables which strongly influence earnings also exist. These empirical findings cast doubt on the validity of HCM and have stimulated a stream of alternative theoretical works which explain the findings on political and sociological, as well as economic grounds (see *Internal Labor Markets and Education; Segmented Labor Markets and Education; Screening Models and Education*).

Among the observed variables which influence the relation between education and earnings, the most studied are gender (see *Gender and Occupational Segregation*), race and ethnicity (see *Race Earnings Differentials*), and ability. The following section will deal with the effect of ability on the relation between education and earnings.

5. Effect of Ability on Earnings

Even human capital theorists broadly agree that individuals differ in their ability to produce mainly because of innate ability or, as Mincer expresses it, preschool investment in human capital. This latter variable refers to the fact that even before school age children are exposed to different, more or less stimulating, environments (often referred to as "social background," or SES). Both innate ability and "cultural capital" foster people's ability to produce independently of formal schooling and the on-the-job training they will acquire later in life. Economists, therefore, while recognizing the existence of these independent sources of ability to produce, have tried to measure the component of earnings attributable to education and that which is attributable to ability. The body of literature which deals with this problem is often referred to as the "alpha coefficient literature". The alpha (α) coefficient is simply an adjustment factor which indicates the proportion of earnings which can be ascribed to education alone. Thus an α coefficient of 0.6 means that 60 percent of the earnings of a given person is attributed to her or his level of education. The standard way economists have estimated the α coefficient is by multivariate regression analysis of the log of earnings on schooling and some proxy indicating the ability of the individual. Thus the coefficient of the ability variable should indicate the contribution of ability to earnings. Using this technique, Becker found that the α coefficient is about 0.8 when only ability is used in the analysis. However when some indicator of social background is used, then the coefficient drops to 0.65 percent. Psacharopoulos, in reviewing several studies conducted in the United States, found an average α of about 0.77 (Psacharopoulos 1975).

The literature on the contribution of ability to earnings has begun to adopt a different approach from the one used by the α coefficient literature. On the basis of the observation that ability influences both earnings and years of schooling acquired by a person, this new body of literature attempts to construct and estimate a structural model which describes all the interactions among years of schooling, human capital acquired in school, ability, and earnings. In general, this approach specifies a set of simultaneous equations which describe the relations among these variables. An important example of such literature is the work of Knight and Sabot (1990) on Kenya and Tanzania. Knight and Sabot specify a three-equation model in which years of schooling is a function of the parents' level of schooling, the probability of being at school at age 14, and the reasoning ability of the individual. Cognitive achievement is described as a function of reasoning ability, year of schooling, and two dummies for urban birth and attendance of public school. Finally, earnings are described as a function of years of schooling, reasoning ability, cognitive achievement, and a linear and a quadratic term in years of experience.

The result of this study seems to confirm that the reduced form estimation of the model (i.e., the classical Mincerian earnings function, with ability among the explanatory variables) overestimates the contribution of education to earnings. In their view:

> in neither Kenya or Tanzania are the estimate return to experience affected by introduction of variables that measure (cognitive) achievement and reasoning ability. By contrast, the premium to secondary education declines by nearly two-thirds in both countries, and in Tanzania it is no longer significantly different than zero. In neither country is the influence of ability on earning large or significant. By contrast, in both countries the coefficient on achievement score is positive, significant, and large in relation to the coefficient on ability score. (Knight and Sabot 1990)

Thus, despite the complexity of the approach, the basic results do not vary greatly. The greater effect on earnings is given by some index of human capital investment. Ability, when defined independently from human capital, has a small part in explaining earnings differentials.

See also: Human Capital Concepts; Segmented Labor Markets and Education; Screening Models and Education; Race Earnings Differentials; Gender and Occupational Segregation; Internal Labor Markets and Education

References

Becker G S 1975 *Human Capital. A Theoretical and Empirical Analysis with Special Reference to Education*, 2nd edn. National Bureau of Economic Research, New York

Ghez R C, Becker G S 1975 *The Allocation of Time and Goods over the Life Cycle.* National Bureau of Economic Research, New York

Knight B J, Sabot H R 1990 *Education, Productivity and Inequality. The East African Natural Experiment.* Oxford University Press, Oxford

Macurdy T, Mroz T 1991 Measuring macroeconomic trends in wages from cohort specification. Stanford University, Stanford, California (mimeo)

Mincer J 1974 *Schooling Experience and Earnings.* National Bureau of Economic Research[2u]/[1u]Columbia University Press, New York

Pencavel J 1990 The contribution of higher education to economic growth and productivity: A review. Discussion Paper No. 191, Stanford Center for Economic Policy and Research, Stanford, California.

Psacharopoulos G 1975 *Earning and Education in OECD Countries.* Organisation for Economic Co-operation and Development, Paris

Education, Occupation, and Earnings

T. Tachibanaki

Education, occupation, and earnings are interrelated. Most analyses of these phenomena, however, have focused on either the relationships between education and earnings or that between education and occupation. The relationship between occupation and earnings has also been studied. There are several explanations for why these relationships have been studied separately. One important explanation is that the relationship between education and occupation has been researched mainly by sociologists, whereas the relationship between education and earnings has been researched largely by economists.

1. Factors Affecting the Determination of Earnings

The effect of education on the determination of wages and earnings has been analyzed by employing the concept of human capital. The concept emphasizes the importance of not only formal education but also job training. A basic premise behind the concept is that higher levels of educational attainment increase individuals' productivity and, consequently, their earnings capacity. Since formal education and job training are costly, it is impossible to invest in human capital endlessly. Many studies have been devoted to examining the effect of education on earnings within the framework of human capital theory.

The relationship between occupation and earnings has been analyzed extensively in many countries. It may be described as "pay difference by occupation" or "pay structure by occupation." It is important to stress that occupation is the variable that has received the most attention in studies investigating earnings difference. Researchers were interested in studying whether there were earnings differences between occupations by estimating the magnitudes of such differences, if any. They usually suggested social and economic reasons to explain occupational earnings differentials.

It is possible to conclude that difference of earnings by occupation can be observed in all societies in all periods of history. In modern times pattern of pay difference by occupation is common to many countries, particularly capitalist countries, suggesting that occupations which pay higher wages and those which pay lower wages do not differ significantly from country to country. For example, white–collar workers receive higher wages than manual workers in nearly all countries. This situation is found even when a wider range of occupations is considered. What kind of justifications can be offered to explain earnings difference by occupation?

Brown (1977) provides a useful survey of the causes for pay difference by occupation. The starting point for explaining pay difference by occupation can be found in the usual functions of supply and demand, consisting of both wage rates and the number of jobs available for any occupation. Economics asserts that the intersection of the supply and demand curves determines the equilibrium wage and the number of jobs for each occupation. When adjustments of both supply and demand for all occupations are made smoothly, nearly all occupations produce equilibrium wage rates. In some occupations, however, the effects of supply and demand are often limited for various reasons. This limitation is responsible for pay differences between

occupations. Several institutional and economic factors can be suggested that prevent free and perfect adjustments of supply and demand.

(a) Perfect monopoly in supply: the number of people available for a particular occupation is perfectly controlled by a group of people who engage in the same occupation. In other words, there is an entry barrier to working in a particular occupation to protect the benefits of workers already engaged in it. This is a variation of the guild system developed in medieval Europe. It continues to be commonly observed.

(b) License: a public authority grants special privileges to a particular occupation such that only people who have received licenses or other types of certification can engage in the occupation. Examples include medical doctors and airline pilots.

(c) Compensating wage differentials: some types of occupations involve dangerous tasks, require special physical abilities, or are located in unfavorable environments. It is expected that higher wages are paid in these occupations to compensate for unfavorable or excessively demanding working conditions. This concept is called "equalizing" or "compensating" wage differentials. The idea goes back to Adam Smith's *The Wealth of Nations* (published in 1776). The concept can be analyzed by supply–demand relations. It suggests that jobs or occupations that offer favorable working conditions attract many workers at lower wages than average wages, while jobs or occupations that offer unfavorable working conditions must pay premiums (i.e., higher wages) to compensate for such undesirable working conditions in order to attract workers. Examples of the working conditions concerned are: unsocial working hours, high risk levels, high skill levels, locations of factories and offices, and unemployment risk. This kind of theory can be explained by the demand–supply relationship between a firm and a worker who has certain preferences, and the number of firms and of workers. A simple economic equation can describe theoretically this idea of compensatory wage differentials, as Rosen (1986) has elegantly shown. The results of empirical observations are, however, considerably mixed, with only some supporting the theory.

(d) Risk: this refers to the personal traits of individuals that affect their choice of occupation. Individuals' attitudes toward risk have been included in studies by several economists, such as Friedman and Kuznets (1954) and Weiss (1972). Friedman, for example, suggested that skewness in earnings distribution arises from the fact that while most persons are risk averse, some persons are risk lovers. By employing Von Neumann and Morgenstern's notion of expected utility maximization, he was able to show that risk lovers choose an occupation in which there is a small chance of success at a higher income, while risk-averse people choose an occupation in which there is a large chance of receiving a lower income. Consequently, the degree of risk determines an individual's occupation, and thus produces the observed difference in earnings.

The effects of compensatory wage differentials caused by various occupations and the risk element are somewhat conflicting because the latter is a rationale for wage differentials, while the former is a rationale for equalizing wages by occupations. The actual earnings differentials by occupation may be a hybrid of the two. Discovering which of the two is dominant may be an interesting area for further empirical research.

(e) Imperfect or asymmetrical information: individuals in the labor market do not have perfect access to all available information. When they seek jobs they often lack sufficient information on both wage levels and the number of jobs available. Such imperfect information creates a distortion and causes pay difference by occupation.

(f) Formal education and training costs: several occupations require higher formal education or more training to obtain them and to perform the tasks involved successfully. Formal education and training incur cost; thus a proportion of workers cannot afford the education and training when they have to bear the cost. In such cases the situation may be observed where one group of people can engage in higher wage occupations because they were able to pay the cost, while another group of people is obliged to engage in lower wage occupations because they are unable to bear the cost.

(g) Ability: some jobs or occupations require special talent or ability, such as artistic activities and professional sport. Work in these fields cannot be gained through education and training alone. In other words, innate ability is essential. It is quite natural that extra money is paid to talented people in such fields because the supply is very limited.

(h) Regional immobility: even if information is perfect, there are significant transaction costs for both employers and employees, which restrict the movement of workers and/or offices or factories. This influences the determination of wages and produces pay differences: two identical people engaged in the same occupations but who live in different locations may receive different wages.

Other reasons may be advanced to explain pay differences by occupation. Among these is the "occupation matching" theory. This is influenced by the notion of "job matching," which emerged as an alternative explanation for several labor market phenomena explained by human capital theory. The job matching model arose from dissatisfaction with human capital theory in explaining the wage–tenure profiles and turnover–tenure relations. Human capital theory predicts the positive growth of wage by length of job tenure, but job matching theory proposes that this positive rate appears because only those workers who are well-matched to their jobs stay in their jobs. If workers who changed jobs because of mismatching were included, the positive wage growth would not appear. The occupation matching model is an extension of the job matching model. Therefore, it is likely that it can deny the human capital interpretation of the effect of education and job tenure on earnings, or it can give an alternative understanding of education in relation to earnings which has not been disclosed by the human capital model. Since these issues have not yet been exhaustively analyzed in the literature, fuller analyses and examinations of the relationship between the occupation matching model and earnings are tasks for the future (but see the pioneering work by Miller 1984).

2. Education and Occupation

The effect of education on determining a person's occupation can be analyzed from various perspectives. One approach is to examine the relationship between educational attainment and jobs obtained (or simply occupation). A second approach is to investigate the relationship between education and earnings without necessarily referring to occupation. The second approach was applied frequently when the concept of human capital was used to investigate the economics of education. Using this approach, the internal rates of returns to various education levels were estimated. It should be emphasized, however, that the first approach actually examined the effect of education on earnings because average earnings of each occupation are used to represent occupations quantitatively. In other words, jobs (or occupations) are ranked by their average earnings. Consequently, both the first and second approaches in fact applied the same approach, namely that of focusing on the relationship between education and earnings.

Apart from the relationship between education and earnings, it is important to explain the effect of "credentialism" and the "screening hypothesis" when the relationships between education, occupation, and earnings are investigated. They are particularly important for understanding the effect of education on the determination of occupation.

The screening hypothesis is sometimes referred to as "educational signaling," a concept proposed by Arrow (1973) and Spence (1973). It argues that education serves as an informational device for distinguishing between talented and untalented people. It does not indicate any direct effect of education on a person's skill. A person who has a higher educational attainment is judged to be an able person because he or she can purchase the educational signal on more favorable terms, whereas a less able person cannot. Credentialism is a more direct form of educational signaling, which guarantees certain benefits for a person who had a higher education or who graduated from a particular school or university. Some of the implications of these signaling and credential effects were described above in the discussion of the relationship between occupation and earnings. It should be remembered that education or education in a particular school is used as a prerequisite for certain occupations or for obtaining a higher status since it conveys a signal to employers of the job applicant's capability.

The relationship between the signaling hypothesis and occupation can be understood easily by considering occupations such as flying and law. There are often particular schools that produce pilots and lawyers. In Japan, pilots attend an airline pilots' school; in almost every country, lawyers must attend law school or university faculties. Those universities or schools select entrants (i.e., students) by means of tough physical and/or intellectual examinations. Students who are admitted and graduate from these schools convey, through their credentials, the information that they will conduct their professional lives successfully. Of course, several further examinations have to be passed even after eligibility to become a pilot or lawyer has been secured. The great majority pass such entry examinations after they graduate from these schools. Thus, the examinations are only formal matters. Graduation (i.e., education) is more important. The education of medical doctors also proceeds along similar lines.

It should be emphasized, however, that the meaning of educational screening, signaling, and credentialing is much more general than is suggested by the discussion in the previous paragraph. They signify a device for identifying more or less able persons. Three comments can be offered about the implications of the signaling aspect of education, following the arguments of Rosen (1987).

First, although the human capital interpretation of education and the signaling (or screening) interpretation of education are proposed on different theoretical grounds, they have very similar implications for the rational choice of schooling. In particular, empirical studies of income and schooling cannot distinguish between the human capital interpretation of education and the signaling interpretation of education. In other words, it is nearly impossible to identify which interpretation is more appropriate to explain empirical evidence of the relationship between education and earnings. This is due partly to the fact that a person's productivity or earnings capacity cannot be observed in the production process. Thus it is impossible to test directly the effect of education (i.e., schooling) on earnings capacity, as the theory of human capital proposes. Therefore, Rosen (1987) understands that schooling has little social value when it serves as a signal and much social value when it produces real human capital. Second, schooling contributes only a very marginal part of earnings differentials. Other important variables, such as ability, job tenure, and family background, contribute significantly to the variance of earnings. The limited explanatory power of schooling in the determination of earnings obscures the value of education as a signal. Third, if people are identified and classified properly by using schooling and education as a signaling device, it may be socially productive because such sortings of people are likely to allocate both talented and untalented people to the most relevant places in the market.

As was noted previously, the relationships between education, occupation, and earnings have traditionally been examined separately. When the comprehensive relationship between these variables is investigated by applying econometric techniques to individual survey data, a recursive-type simultaneous equation system is used. Typical examples of the endogenous variables are education, occupation, and earnings. The theory behind this system implies that education determines occupational attainment and occupation then determines earnings. If these observations together with other information on various exogenous variables are available, the ordinary least squares method or the two-stage least squares method can be applied, depending upon the correlation among the error terms. Representative examples are shown by Griliches and Mason (1972) for the United States, by Tachibanaki (1980) for France, by Hubler (1984) for Germany, and by Tachibanaki (1988) for Japan. Before discussing these issues, several observations should be made about this econometric approach.

First, many sociological studies strongly suggest that sociological background (such as father's or mother's educational attainment and occupational level and family income) are important determinants of an individual's educational level. Thus it is customary to consider social background variables prior to the determination of educational attainment (see Duncan et al. 1968).

Second, occupational level is a difficult variable for quantification. Several United States studies use the sociologist Duncan's socioeconomic index, which gives a weighted average of income and corresponding educational attainment for occupations in order to quantify occupations. Griliches (1976) posed a serious question concerning the introduction of occupation, claiming that it correlates with dependent variables, such as earnings or education. Thus, he urged ignoring occupation, if occupational attainment were quantified like Duncan's socioeconomic index.

This elimination causes an omitted-variable problem. Thus it would be preferable not to ignore occupation in a recursive type simultaneous equation system. A variable such as "prestige," which was used by Tachibanaki (1980, 1988), may be an alternative idea to quantify occupation. Needless to say, prestige is measured independently of education and/or income.

Third, when an estimate is made of the earning function which enters as part of a recursive simultaneous equation system, the ability (innate ability) of an individual cannot be ignored because it affects not only earnings but also occupation and other variables which may raise earnings capacity. This subject has received considerable attention, discussed in the following way.

Ignoring other variables, a simple earnings function can be written:

$$Y = \alpha + \beta S + \gamma A + u \qquad (1)$$

where Y is income, S is education and A is a measure of ability. When we ignore ability, we obtain a biased estimator of β as follows:

$$Eb_{YS} = \beta + \gamma b_{AS} = \beta + \gamma \, \text{cov}(AS)/\text{var}A, \qquad (2)$$

where the return to education is estimated with a bias. Thus, it is necessary to include A when ability has an independent positive effect on earnings, and the relationship between the excluded ability and included schooling variable is positive. However, Griliches (1977) proposed that the "ability bias" caused by the excluded ability was minor. Therefore, it is not so serious even if ability is excluded. Moreover, serious problems remain for the ability variable even if it is included. First, even if a popular variable such as IQ is included, there is a question about whether this indicates a proper measure of ability. A professional baseball player has a particular ability rather than IQ. Therefore the ability variable should be fairly multi dimensional. Second, even if we assume that IQ is a relevant measure, it includes considerable measurement errors. In other words, errors-in-variables may be more serious than the previous left-out-problem bias. "Ability" is a difficult subject and needs to be investigated seriously.

3. Conclusion

Although the above problems cannot be ignored, empirical estimates of earnings functions together with other variables which are included in recursive type simultaneous equation models suggest the following conclusions. First, the social background variable is a very important factor and affects a student's success. Second, education determines the level of occupational attainment fairly directly. In other words, the higher the educational attainment, the higher the occupational attainment. Third, both educational attainment and occupational achievement contribute to providing people with higher earnings. Fourth, many exogenous variables must be included to obtain a better estimate of earnings function, in addition to social background, education, and occupation. They include age, tenure, family status, region, religion, and working hours. Fifth, the recursive model is fairly successful in explaining the relationship between education, occupation, and earnings in Japan and European nations such as France and Germany judging from the estimated R^2 of earnings functions. However, the result for the United States is less impressive because the estimated R^2 of earnings functions are not so high but fairly low (0.1–0.3). In other words, there are "unexplained factors" or large residuals in the estimation of earnings functions in the United States (see, for example, Taubman 1975). Jencks (1972) once attributed this residual to "luck." The determination of which variables are left out in explaining earnings differentials in the United States requires investigation, even though more empirical studies have been made in the United States than in other countries.

Three important variables which need more attention in research are hierarchy (or position) in a firm, the size of firm, and industry. The first variable is strictly related to the relationship between supervisory job and incentive. The second is related to the ability of firms to pay higher wages, and the third is related to efficiency wage hypothesis. Representative works dealing with these variables include Lazear and Rosen (1981), Rosen (1982), Brown and Medoff (1989), Akerlof (1982), and Katz (1986).

See also: Human Capital Concepts; Education and Productivity; Education and Earnings

References

Akerlof G A 1982 Labor contracts as partial gift exchange. *Q. J. Econ.* 97(4): 543–69
Arrow K J 1973 Higher education as a filter. *J. Publ. Econ.* 2(3): 193–216
Brown C, Medoff J 1989 The employer size-wage effect *J. Pol. Econ.* 97(5): 1027–59
Brown H P 1977 *The Inequality of Pay*. Oxford University Press, Oxford
Duncan O D, Featherman D L, Duncan B 1968 *Socioeconomic Background and Occupational Achievement: Extensions of a Basic Model*. US Department of Health, Education and Welfare, Washington, DC
Friedman M, Kuznets S 1954 *Income from Independent Professional Practice*. National Bureau of Economic Research, New York
Griliches Z 1976 Wages and earnings of very young men. *J. Pol. Econ.* 84 (4 pt.2): 569–86
Griliches Z 1977 Estimating the returns to schooling: Some econometric problems. *Econometrica* 45: 1–22
Griliches Z, Mason W 1972 Education, income and ability. *J. Pol. Econ.* 80 (3 pt.2): S74–103

Hubler O 1984 Zur empirischen Uberüfung alternativer Theorien der Verteilung von Arbeitseinkommen. In: Bellman L, Gerlack K, Hubler O (eds.) 1984 *Lohnstruktur in der Bundesrepublik Deutschland*. Campus Verlag, Frankfurt

Jencks C 1972 *Inequality: A Reassessment of the Effect of Family and Schooling in Practice*. Basic Books, New York

Katz L 1986 Efficiency wage theories: A partial evaluation. In: Fischer S (ed.) 1986 NBER Macroeconomics Annual. MIT Press, Cambridge, Massachusetts

Lazear E P, Rosen S 1981 Rank–order tournaments as optimum labor contracts. *J. Pol. Econ.* 89(5): 841–64

Miller R A 1984 Job matching and occupational choice. *J. Pol. Econ.* 92(6): 1086–1120

Rosen S 1982 Authority, control and the distribution of earnings. *Bell Journal of Economics and Management Science* 13: 311–23

Rosen S 1986 The theory of equalizing differences. In: Ashenfelter O, Layard R (eds.) 1986 *Handbook of Labor Economics* Vol. 1. North-Holland, Amsterdam

Rosen S 1987 Human capital. In: Eatwell J, Milgate M, Newman P (eds.) 1987 *The New Palgrave: A Dictionary of Economics*, Vol. 2, Macmillán, London

Spence M 1973 Job market signalling. *Q. J. Econ.* 87(3): 355–74

Tachibanaki T 1980 Education, occupation and earnings: A recursive approach for France. *European Economic Review* 13: 103–27

Tachibanaki T 1988 Education, occupation, hierarchy and earnings. *Econ. Educ. Rev.* 7: 221–29

Taubman P 1975 *Sources of Inequality in earnings*. North-Holland, Amsterdam

Weiss Y 1972 The risk element in occupational and educational choice, *J. Pol. Econ.* 80(6): 1203–13

Benefits of Improving the Quality of Education

M. Carnoy

Economists generally assume that, along with investment in years of schooling, investment in higher quality education also produces higher productivity and wages in the workplace. The logic of this connection is derived from human capital theory, which argues that schooling increases productivity because it increased the productive attributes of labor; that is, the cognitive skills of potential workers. Any investment that increases cognitive skills therefore increases productivity and income, and the variance of cognitive skills in the labor force is a key explainer of the variance of productivity and wages. In other words, children of the same "native ability" with similar learning environments at home, and the same quantity of schooling, differences in the quality of schooling attended contribute to the variance in cognitive skills, hence to higher productivity in the workplace.

Are these assumed relations observed in the real world? Does higher quality of eduction, other things being equal, improve productivity and earnings? This entry develops a model to study the influence of educational quality on earnings and surveys the empirical evidence available in developing and developed economies.

The recent shift of interest among economists from the quantity to the quality of education as a source of higher productivity is linked historically to new "austerity" in government spending and to the concept that quality improvements in education could be less expensive than those of quantity, and also yield higher returns in the long term. This view is also linked to a recognition that, especially in low-income countries, merely increasing access to schools for increasing numbers of children does not guarantee any tangible effects of schooling, such as literacy or numeracy. High repetition rates and low completion rates of basic levels of schooling suggest low quality and high implicit costs per student to achieve target (cognitive) learning goals.

1. Measuring Educational Quality

One fundamental problem in assessing the role of educational quality on labor market outcomes is in measuring quality. Expenditures per pupil would ordinarily be a reasonable measure of quality. However it is difficult to estimate the proportion spent on individual pupils since such a high fraction of spending in schools goes to teachers' salaries which should in themselves reflect standards of quality and productivity. Nevertheless, spending per pupil in schools is often used as an indicator of educational quality (Fuller 1986). Other common measures are school repetition rates and completion rates. More repetition and less completion leads to lower standards of schooling. Often the cost per "completing pupil" is estimated, showing that in countries where repetition and dropout rates are high, the cost per pupil in terms of "learning outcomes" is also very high. Such an estimate also suggests that the costs of quality improvements may reduce cost per pupil substantially by reducing repetition and dropout rates. However, estimating quality of education through repetition and dropout rates is problematic because these rates may be set by the availability of places at the next level of schooling, not by the quality of education at the lower level. For example, if the first year of secondary school can accommodate only one-third of the total number of students entering the first year of primary schooling, some way has to be found to "cull" two-thirds of those entrants during their progress through primary education. Usually schools are given mandates to allow only a certain number of passes on the examinations at the end of each primary grade. Those who do not pass, repeat, and higher repetition does (intentionally) raise the dropout rate. But this would be the case even if the quality of education increased significantly, unless the number of places at secondary level expanded simultaneously.

Because of such problems, economists have increasingly relied on other indicators of educational quality (Fuller 1994). Generally, these are school inputs that have been shown to be correlated with pupil achievement when pupils' social class and ability are taken into account (see *Education Production Functions*; *Education and Productivity*). Such school inputs include teacher educational level (Behrman and Birdsall 1985, Fuller 1986) and cognitive skills, and the availability of textbooks, blackboards, computers, laboratory equipment, and other physical inputs. They also can include the amount of time (number of hours per day and number of days per year) the pupil goes to school, absenteeism, and the number of pupils per teacher in the classroom.

Assuming that pupils' native ability does not differ greatly among schools in different states or countries, educational quality for a given level of schooling is often measured by achievement test scores. Even though this combines the impact of the learning environment at home with the quality of schooling, it can be assumed that improving this in the larger sense also has an impact on labor market performance.

2. A Model for Measuring the Payoff to Higher Quality Education

Whatever measure of quality is used, the second fundamental problem in assessing the role of the quality of education in labor markets is to show that it has a measurable effect on productivity (wages). Improved school quality can impact labor market performance in two ways: (a) directly, through the effect on productivity of increasing cognitive skills for a given level of schooling; and (b) indirectly, through raising the probability that an individual will invest in additional years of schooling, thus increasing cognitive skills by spending more years in school. The two effects can be modeled as follows:

The economic benefit of schooling at age *i*, Y_i, can be expressed as a function of quality of schooling and the grade level attained. Other variables, such as the sex, race, or ethnic group could be included in the function, but for the sake of simplicity, these are omitted here. So,

$$Y_i = f(Q,G) \qquad (1)$$

In turn the grade level attained can be expressed as a function of quality of schooling and the initial endowment of the student *(C)*.

$$G = g(Q,C) \qquad (2)$$

The economic benefit due to an increase in schooling quality for a given student endowment is found by taking the derivative of Eqn. (1):

$$\frac{\delta Y_{ic}}{dY_i} = \delta Q + \left(\frac{\delta G}{\delta Q}\right)\left(\frac{\delta Y_{ic}}{\delta G}\right) \qquad (3)$$

The first part of the right side of the equation measures the direct effect of improving school quality and the second part, the indirect effect, can be viewed as an "option value" of better performance in school.

3. Estimating the Indirect Economic Effect of Improved School Quality

A great deal has been written about this second term of the option value, that is, doing better in school. This is the economic return from taking more schooling. It is generally positive and, in most countries, rather high, although it varies across levels of schooling (see *Education and Earnings*; *Rates of return to Education*).

Much less is known about the first term of the option value, that is, the change in the quantity of schooling taken for a given increase in quality of schooling. Many factors may enter simultaneously to affect retention, making it is difficult to isolate the effect on retention of improved school inputs or pupil performance per se. If the function of grading in a particular school system or in part of a school system is to select a fraction of students to go on, grading will be on the curve, and a certain percentage of students will fail, even if the quality of outcome increases. At levels of schooling that are "compulsory"—that is, everyone is expected to complete them—improving quality may, indeed, improve retention and completion rates. But an increase in student performance will have relatively little impact on additional schooling if, for example, the next level of schooling is expensive and intentionally limited to relatively few students. For example, the secondary school system in Brazil has traditionally been closed to large increases in enrollment because it was disproportionately private and the public system expanded slowly. Similarly, despite very large increases in Black Students' high school test scores relative to those of White Students in the United States during the 1980s, Black college enrollment hardly increased. High college costs and increasing poverty levels among Blacks might have effectively reduced the impact caused by increased achievement through attending higher levels of education (Carnoy 1994).

However estimates for young Black and White women in the United States using data from longitudinal surveys from a class of high school seniors in 1972 and, almost a decade later, seniors (in 1980) and second-year students (in 1982) suggest that the effect of more advanced high school reading test scores on students completing four years of college are significant and moderately large. For the 1972 class of students, one-half of a standard deviation higher test score from the mean raises the probability of enrolling in a four-year college by about 6 percentage points (mean enrollment 30%) for White women and about 5 percentage points for Black women (mean enrollment 25%). The results are somewhat lower for the second-year and senior students in 1980 and similar for the seniors for completing college in 1972 and 1980 (McElroy 1995). Thus, the option value of an increase in quality of education could be large, and more attention should be paid to measuring its magnitude.

There is also the question of how the product of the two terms of the option value of higher quality schooling might behave under different circumstances. If low academic performance has restricted the supply of graduates, both the increase in schooling taken with higher quality education and the economic payoff to taking increased schooling would probably be high, producing a very large indirect effect. This could be a case for improving high school performance for disadvantaged youth in the United States, or of improving primary schooling in most Latin American countries, where secondary schools are already prepared to accommodate increased enrollment. The payoff to college education in the United States and to secondary education in Latin America is also relatively high. However, if availability of places at the next highest level of schooling restricts completion of the previous level, or if low economic payoffs to additional schooling are an important factor in the dropout rate, the indirect effect of increasing educational quality would probably be small.

4. Estimating the Direct Economic Effect of Improved School Quality

Most attention has been paid to the first term of eqn. (3)—the direct economic effect of increased educational quality. Estimates have focused on the wage and income benefits of improved school inputs and on the wage benefits of improved pupil performance (school outcomes).

4.1. Estimates of the Contribution of Improved School Inputs to Economic Outcomes

Estimates of the relationship of school inputs to economic outcomes are relatively rare, but it is worth mentioning two. First, a study of Brazilian adults found that school quality measured by the level of

teachers' qualifications explained as much difference in adult earnings as did the actual amount of schooling they had taken over a certain number of years (Behrman and Birdsall 1985). Second, research in the early 1990s on the contribution of the relative "quality" of Black and White schools in the South to the relative income of Blacks shows a positive significant relationship between quality and income (Card and Krueger 1992a). Card and Krueger use three measures of school quality—the ratio of pupil to teachers, school term length, and teacher pay—to compare Black and White schooling quality, by state over a fifty-year period from 1915 to 1965. They find that men in particular who were educated in states with higher quality systems tended to earn a higher economic return for their years of schooling. The results also suggest that changes in school quality over time explain a high 45–80 percentage of the relative increase in the return to schooling for Black workers born in 1940–49 over those born in 1910–19, and this, in turn, explains about one-fourth of the convergence of Black and White payoffs to schooling between 1960 and 1980 (Card and Krueger 1992b).

4.2 Estimates of the Contribution of School Outcome (Higher Achievement Scores) to Economic Outcomes

Most studies estimating the impact of educational quality on economic performance use school output (pupil achievement) as a measure of quality. These studies show very mixed results. In some cases, when years of schooling, sex, social class, race, and other factors that are associated with outside-of-school effects on pupil performance in school are accounted for, higher achievement scores are related to higher earnings. In other cases, there is no relationship.

An early study of male earnings and secondary schooling in Tunisia (Carnoy et al. 1976) showed that when years of schooling are controlled for (socioeconomic background was not a significant explainer of salary differences), the effect of grade point average (GPA) in the last year of schooling reflected the earnings of a subsample of 17–25-year olds in the labor force with some years of secondary school, at least, as being positive and significant. A one standard deviation increase in GPA (about 2 points out of a possible 20 would result in a monthly higher income of 5.6 dinars (US$5.5)). This compared to a higher monthly earning of 6.3 dinars (US$6.2) for each year of schooling between 9 and 12 years. Thus, a one standard deviation increase in school performance is equivalent to one additional year of schooling. Although this represents a significant impact of better performance in school, the cost of increasing GPA by such a large amount could be much higher than keeping young people in school for an additional year, assuming that this is even a meaningful comparison.

In 1992, Knight and Sabot estimated the relationship between the cognitive ability of those completing secondary schooling and the cognitive ability of those completing primary schooling as well as the relationship between earnings, secondary school completion, and acquired cognitive ability in urban Kenya and Tanzania. They controlled for "early [preschool] ability." Their results show that in the sample from the two countries together for both men and women the combined effect on earnings of completing secondary school rather than finishing primary school and acquiring additional cognitive skills is to raise earnings by about 25 percent. This is equivalent to the total derivative dY in our Eqn. (1) above. The first term of Eqn. (1), however, is much smaller, raising earnings only by 2 percent. The total effect on earnings is higher in Kenya than in Tanzania, largely because in 1980, when the sample was taken, there was a much greater social class difference in Kenya than in Tanzania between those who completed secondary school and those who only completed primary school. In addition, earnings differences were smaller in Tanzania than Kenya. Knight and Sabot therefore conclude that their results suggest a major contribution of secondary education to cognitive knowledge formation, which ultimately reflects earnings.

The largest number of empirical studies on test score performance (cognitive ability) and labor market performance has been done in the United States. The commonly held notion that United States productivity is increasing more slowly than in Japan or West Germany because of United States students' lower test scores (Bishop 1989) is counteracted by a number of studies that show no relation between test score and productivity, nor between test scores and income in the United States economy. These fall into two categories: studies of workers by industrial psychologists that relate cognitive test scores to worker productivity (Schmitt et al. 1984; Bishop 1992), and studies by economists relating achievement test scores to earnings (Bishop 1992, Murnane et al. 1992). Both show only small earnings gains for very large gains in test scores.

A review of the relation between the General Ability Test Battery (GATB), used by the United States Employment Service to refer job candidates to prospective employers, suggests that only 6–7 percent of the variance in observed productivity by supervisors is associated with test scores (Levin 1993). Another study (Bishop 1992) argues that one standard deviation in a worker's GATB's mathematics achievement component is associated with 10–20 percent of a standard deviation from the mean performance (as measured by supervisors' ratings) in work establishment. But the regression equations from which this result is drawn explain a relatively low 11–17 percent of performance variance, even when work experience, tenure on the job, sex, and ethnicity are included as variables (Bishop 1992). Since one standard deviation in mathematics achievement represents a large difference in test score, the resulting increase in supervisors' rating is relatively small. Furthermore, Bishop's results suggest that

a few years' additional job tenure has an equivalent effect on job performance rating.

The relationship between test scores and earnings are just as tenuous. Based on his analysis of the 1972 National Longitudinal Survey (NLS) data, Bishop concludes: ". . . when years of schooling are held constant, achievement in science has no effect on wage rates, earnings or unemployment of young men and women. Achievement in mathematical reasoning has no effect on the wage rates and earnings of young men and only very modest effects on the wage rates of young women. Verbal competency has no effect on the wage rates of young men and women . . ." (Bishop 1992 p. 29). More recent empirical work by Murnane et al. (1992) comparing the 1978 wage rates of 1972 high school seniors sampled in the NLS, with the 1986 wage rates of 1980 high school seniors sampled in the High School and Beyond (HSB) survey, found that the wage difference associated with a one standard deviation difference in mathematics test scores among high school graduates who did not go on to college was 3 percent for males and 8.5 percent for females in 1978, and 7.4 percent for males and 15.5 percent for females in 1986. This suggests that the impact of mathematics achievement on earnings has risen, but remains relatively small, especially for males. Furthermore, Murnane et al. also show that a 1980 high school graduate who did not go on to college and whose test score was one standard deviation above the mean earned 75 cents per hour less, 6 years after graduation, than the wage rate in 1978 of a 1972 high school graduate whose test score was one standard deviation below the mean. Their results should be sobering for politicians who believe that higher academic standards are a panacea for low incomes. Declines in real wage rates for male high school graduates in the relatively short period of time between 1978 and 1986 (resulting from changes in the way labor markets valued high school education) were much greater than any increase in wage rates that might have been achieved even by huge (one standard deviation) improvements in average mathematics achievement.

A number of studies also suggest that rather than advanced high school level mathematics and science skills, adequate performance for workers in most jobs means acquiring basic skills at the eighth-grade level (Levin 1993). Much more important for high productivity may be high "team skills" (cooperativeness) and good "work habits"—worker competencies that employers claim are in much shorter supply than mathematics and reading skills (Capelli 1993), but are not tested on international achievement examinations.

Another method of assessing the contribution of school achievement to higher incomes is to look at changes over time in the relative test scores and incomes of young people from different groups. In the United States, Black pupils showed large gains in reading and mathematics scores in the late 1970s and early 1980s relative to White pupils (Carnoy 1994). Such gains should have had two effects: first, they should have made young Black high school graduates more valuable in the labor market relative to young Whites; second, they should have significantly increased Black college entrance and completion. The second effect was very small, as mentioned earlier. Young Blacks did not increase their enrollment in college until the very end of the decade.

There is a question as to whether or not 16–24-year old Black and Latino high school graduates would begin to see income gains in the mid- and late 1980s. If Murnane et al.'s (1992) research is correct, it would support the view that this vastly improved educational achievement by young Black people relative to Whites would have improved their relative wages. According to Murnane et al.'s results, if Black male youth were able to attain the same scores as Whites (they are now about one-half deviation apart), they could reduce about one-half the difference in income between Black and White male 24-year olds in 1986. But their research also suggests that higher mathematics skills do not in themselves yield higher wages, which could only be compared with those earned by graduates from the same year. The effect of improving mathematics skills therefore seemed to have a relatively small effect on earnings over time.

When this hypothesis was tested directly, average wages of young Black high school graduates (average age about 20–21 years old) did show gains compared to young Whites in the late 1980s and early 1990s (see Table 1). However, because the relative wages of Blacks first declined and then rose in the 1980s, they were more likely to be the result of business cycle demand for, rather than changing academic performance of, young Black workers. Relative wages could also have risen because of decreasing participation by young Blacks in the wage labor force— what economists call the "selection effect." Lower participation systematically eliminates an increasing proportion of the least employable young Blacks from earning any wages at all, hence raises the relative wages of those remaining, thus biasing upward estimates of gains. The pattern of relative wages over time shown in Table 1 does not fit a steady upward drift due to selection bias. Although the overall level of young Blacks' relative wages may be overestimated, the change in the level in the late 1980s is almost certainly due to real increases in the wages being offered to young Blacks compared to Whites. The conclusion is that large academic gains for Blacks relative to Whites in the 1980s may have had an effect on their relative incomes, but, if so, it is buried in the cyclical fall and rise of relative wages. This suggests that business cycles and relative unemployment rates have a greater impact on relative wages than secular increases in test scores.

The swing in relative wages of Blacks from the early 1970s to the early 1990s is not necessarily inconsistent with an argument for educational improvement lead-

Table 1
Ratio of minority to White mean hourly income, high school graduates at 20-years old, all workers with income, by ethnicity, gender and birth cohort, 1953–71

| Birth cohort | Gender/ethnic group | | | |
| | African-American | | Latino | |
	Males	Females	Males	Females
1953	0.87	0.98	0.89	0.98
1959	0.92	1.05	0.97	0.98
1962	0.75	0.97	0.87	1.04
1965	0.79	0.86	0.93	0.92
1967	0.90	0.86	0.96	0.98
1969	0.92	1.04	0.93	1.01
1971	0.90	0.92	1.01	0.98

Source: Carnoy 1994, Table 4.7

ing to higher wages. As Murnane et al. (1992) show, even as things get worse for male labor as a whole, if individual Blacks increase their test scores they will have an economic advantage over their lower-scoring colleagues. Irrespective of this fact, Table 1 suggests that young Blacks' wages are as much or more influenced by labor market forces out of their control than by the quality of their performance in high school.

This estimation of wages only accounts for the direct effect of better school performance. It does not include the indirect effect of better performance achieved by Blacks continuing on to college. Although in the short run, that effect appears to have been small, in the longer run, it could have a much more impressive impact on Blacks' wages through higher educational attainment.

5. Conclusion

Logically, improving the quality of schooling should have a positive impact on economic performance by improving the cognitive learning that goes on in a given amount of time in school. But as has been shown, the empirical results relating to showing any direct connection between school outcomes and economic performance, when years of schooling are taken into account, are not very convincing. More likely, if there is a significant relationship between standards of schooling and economic outcomes, it is indirect, coming as a result of students who stay in school longer, thus attaining more advanced levels of schooling and earning higher incomes. Such a result implies that improving the quality of schooling without simultaneously providing for the expansion of higher levels of schooling may have little effect on economic performance. It also raises issues about the "pure impact" of cognitive knowledge on economic performance. Such knowledge, if it is to be translated into higher wages the labor market for those acquiring it, may have carry some type of certification (such as school plomas) to convince employers of its existence.

ferences

hrman J, Birdsall N 1985 The quality of schooling: Quantity alone may be misleading. *Am. Econ. Rev.* 73 (5): 928–46

shop J 1989 Incentives for learning: Why American high school students compare so poorly to their counterparts overseas. In: Commission on Workforce Quality and Labor Market Efficiency 1989 *Investing in People*. Background Papers, Vol. 1. Department of Labor, Washington, DC

shop J 1992 *The Economic Consequences of Schooling and Learning*. Working Paper, No.91. Cornell University, New York

pelli P 1993 New work systems and skill requirements. Paper presented at Workshop on New Trends in Training Policy. ILO, Geneva

rd D, Krueger A 1992a School quality and Black/White relative earnings: A direct assessment. *Q. J. Econ.* 107 (1) 151–200

rd D, Krueger A 1992b Does school quality matter? Returns to education and the characteristics of public schools in the United States. *J. Pol. Econ.* 100, (1): 1–40

rnoy M 1994 *Faded Dreams: The Economics and Politics of Race in America*. Cambridge University Press, New York

Carnoy M, Sack R, and Thias H 1976 Middle-level manpower in Tunisia: Socioeconomic origin, schooling and economic success. In: Stone R, Simmons J 1976 *Change in Tunisia*. State University of New York Press, Albany, New York

Fuller B 1986 Is primary school quality eroding in the Third World? *Comp. Educ. Rev.* 30 (4): 491–507

Fuller B 1994 Quality of education in developing nations: Policies for improving. In: Postlethwaite T N, Husén T (eds.) 1994 *International Encyclopedia of Education*, 2nd edn. Pergamon Press, Oxford

Knight J B, Sabot R H 1990 *Education, Productivity, and Inequality: The East African Natural Experiment*. Oxford University Press for the World Bank, New York

Levin H M 1993 Education and jobs: a proactive view. Paper prepared for the 7th Annual Conf. on Education and Work. Ontario Institute for Studies of Education, Toronto (mimeo)

McElroy S 1995 The effect of teenage childbearing on women's educational attainment, labor force participation, and earnings. Unpublished PhD dissertation, Stanford University, Stanford, California

Murnane R J, Willett J B, Levy F 1992 *The Growing Importance of Cognitive Skills in Wage Determination*. Harvard Graduate School of Education, Cambridge, Massachussetts (mimeo)

Schmitt N, Gooding R Z, Noe R A, Kirsch M 1984 Meta-analyses of validity studies published between 1964 and 1982 and the investigation of study characteristics. *Personnel Psychology* 37: 407–22

External Benefits of Education

B. L. Wolfe

andard estimates of the returns to education include only a portion of the total effect of education. wo other types of economic benefits from education are usually omitted from such estimates: private nmarketed benefits and external nonmarketed (or blic) benefits. Nonmarketed private benefits are impcts of schooling valued by the individuals schooled, ut not included in their earnings differences associated with incremental years of schooling. External nefits are those benefits to members of society her than the persons schooled and their immediate mily. Nonmarketed private benefits are taken into count by individuals when making decisions on e amount of schooling to acquire; external benefits re not. Evaluation of the appropriate level of public vestment in schooling (really marginal increments r decrements, for example, whether there should be dditions to schooling such as more years of schooling, longer school year, or smaller class sizes) requires an nalysis of all returns to schooling, including external nefits.

Examples of nonmarketed private benefits are the entertainment or consumption value of education and the ability to achieve one's desired family size. Examples of external benefits are crime reduction and technological change. Examples of nonmarketed benefits with both private and external benefits are charitable donations, consumer choice efficiency, and individual and family health.

Traditionally, the amount of schooling provided has depended heavily on the public sector. In the United States, schooling is mandatory for children up to the age of 16 (older in some states), and is made available to all children by the public sector. At levels beyond the 12th grade, schooling is produced by the public and private sectors. All those attending public colleges and universities have their college education subsidized by the public sector; many students attending private institutions do so as well. In 1989 in the United States, 81.4 percent of the US $330.5 billion overall budget for schooling was public money, including 92.1 percent of the funds

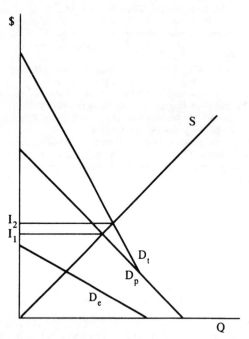

Figure 1
The demand and supply of education

mand and society's demand based on externalit[ie]
is D_t ($D_t = D_p + D_e$). The optimal level of resourc[e]
to be devoted to schooling is where total demar
(reflecting private demand and demand based [o]
externalities) equals costs, or I_2, where D_t equals
Since the optimal quantity to be provided differs wh[e]
externalities are included, it is important that they [b]
included in any evaluation of the amount of educatic
to be provided. (Since externalities can be positi[v]
or negative, in theory I_2 could be greater than, le[s]
than, or equal to I_1.)

The purpose of this entry is to provide a compr[e]
hensive catalog of the external effects of schoolin[g]
In evaluating these benefits care must be taken n[o]
to double-count benefits: benefits to the stude[n]
and immediate family are private benefits, where[a]
only those accruing to others in society are soci[al]
benefits or externalities.

This entry considers benefits that are extern[al]
and those that have both external and priva[te]
nonmarketed economic impacts. A third catego[ry]
of externalities that is quite different in nature-
spillover effects—is also discussed.

for elementary and secondary schooling. In many
other developed countries, the public sector supplies
an even greater share of elementary, secondary, and
postsecondary education. Wherever the public sector
is involved, the price charged for schooling tends to
be far below the marginal costs. Hence, evaluation of
the appropriate level of public investment in schooling requires an analysis of all returns to schooling,
including private marketed, private nonmarketed, and
external benefits. If external or social benefits are
not included, the estimated social payoff to additional
schooling will be biased, and decisions based on estimated private returns may lead to underinvestment (or
overinvestment) in education from the standpoint of
efficiency.

This problem is illustrated in Fig. 1. The vertical
axis measures benefit and cost in dollars and the horizontal axis measures units of schooling. The private
benefits (both marketed and nonmarketed) are reflected in the downward-sloping demand curve marked D_p
(private demand). The marginal cost of providing
education increases as more is provided and is reflected in the upward-sloping supply curve S. If the
amount provided depended only on private demand,
the optimal resources provided would be where D_p
equals S, or I_1. External benefits are reflected in
another demand curve D_e. The sum of private de-

1. Private Benefits with Externalities

Schooling increases productivity in the home as we[ll]
as in the marketplace. In the home, there are benefits [to]
oneself, one's spouse, and one's children which hav[e]
private and public aspects. Evidence exists that th[e]
health of family members is positively influenced b[y]
the education of the parents, particularly of the moth[er]
(The empirical evidence that the mother's schoolin[g]
has a greater influence than the father's on child healt[h]
provides evidence that the observed relationship do[es]
not have a straightforwardly genetic basis.) This rel[a]
tionship generally develops along two paths: the mo[re]
educated may get more health per unit of health inpu[t]
(productive efficiency), and they may have more info[r]
mation on the true effects of specific health inputs an[d]
hence select a better mix of inputs (allocative efficie[n]
cy) (Grossman and Joyce 1989, Pauly 1980). Thus, on[e]
of the mechanisms of the positive relationship betwee[n]
health and schooling appears to be through the positi[ve]
relationship between schooling and health knowledg[e]
(Kenkel 1991). While the individual and family un[it]
gain most from this effect, there are also public gain[s]
First, healthier people reduce the spread of disea[se]
(contagious illnesses in general), which improves th[e]
health of others. Second, healthier people miss wo[rk]
less often, which may improve the productivity of the[ir]
fellow employees. Finally, healthier people are likel[y]
to use less medical care, which reduces the overa[ll]
cost of such care. This influences the rest of socie[ty]
by reducing tax expenditures (or taxes) for priva[te]
employer-provided (or tax-financed) health insuran[ce]
and the expenditures of public insurance for medic[al]

are, such as Medicaid and Medicare in the United States. (For evidence of the effects of schooling on the individual's own health, see Grossman 1975, Leigh 1983, Berger and Leigh 1989, Kemna 1987, Grossman and Joyce 1989. For evidence of the positive influence of the individual's schooling on his or her spouse's health, see Auster et al. 1969, Grossman 1975, Grossman and Jacobowitz 1981. Finally, for evidence on the positive relationship between child health and parents' education, see Edwards and Grossman 1979, Behrman and Wolfe 1987, Shakotko et al. 1981, Grossman and Joyce 1989.)

For the individual, there also appears to be a lower prevalence of serious psychiatric disorders, such as schizophrenia, somatization disorder, and alcohol abuse and dependence (Robins 1984), among college graduates than among those with less education. The external benefits from reduced mental illness include lower Medicaid costs, reduced absenteeism, reduced demand for cash transfers, and probably fewer homeless persons.

Other dimensions of what economists term "child quality" also seem to be positively related to parents' schooling, and they also have external benefits. These other dimensions of child quality include improved cognitive development of one's children, including reduced probability of having a child who repeats a grade in school (Dawson 1991) and a reduced probability of having a child who exhibits antisocial behavior or hyperactivity. These decreased probabilities are likely to lead to a reduction in the public costs of providing education and an improvement in the learning or cognitive development of other children.

Another group of external benefits related to private nonmarketed effects of schooling are intergenerational in nature. The offspring of parents who have received more schooling (particularly mothers) are themselves less likely to give birth to an illegitimate child while in their teens, and are less likely to have children who receive welfare (An et al. 1991). More schooled parents are less likely to have children who do not graduate from high school, who postpone the use of prenatal care when pregnant, and who give birth to underweight infants. All of these factors tend to reduce public expenditures, particularly those for welfare and Medicaid.

Beyond the external effects derived from the influence of an individual's education on his or her family members are other nonmarketed private benefits with externalities. One of these, related to allocative efficiency as mentioned above, is the societal gain from an individual's improved consumer choice efficiency. Education augments knowledge and access to knowledge, namely to facts and ideas that are expected to increase the efficiency of the individual's choices regarding consumption activities and purchases. An example of such a choice that has an external benefit is the negative association between smoking and schooling. There is evidence that this link takes two forms:

a reduced probability of smoking and, among those who do smoke, less smoking per day among those with more schooling (Kenkel 1991). Reduced smoking decreases secondary exposure to smoke and hence may positively influence the health (including life expectancy) of others. Another example of efficiency associated with more schooling is better matching of marketable skills of individuals to jobs. There is some evidence that job search costs are reduced with more schooling and the associated increase in information of the more schooled individual (Metcalf 1973). While the more educated individual is the principal beneficiary of this improved matching, the reduction in transactions costs associated with a reduction in search time is also shared by the buyer (the employer and final buyer of the product or service).

There is also some evidence that schooling increases charitable giving, in terms of both volunteer time and financial donations (where income, the other prime determinant of donations, is a constant) (Hodgkinson and Weitzman 1988). For instance, in 1987 college graduates volunteered on average 3.3 hours per week and donated 1.9 percent of their income, as compared to 1.8 hours and 1.3 percent of income for high school graduates. There are some gains in psychological well-being to the donor from this benefit of schooling (donor utility), but more significant are the externalities—social gains—to the individuals who receive goods and services based on these donations. Moreover, such donations may add to the social cohesion of society. In evaluating this effect, the efficiency and distributional consequences of the special tax treatment of charitable donations must also be taken into account.

2. Aspects Contributing to the Public Good

A fundamental aspect of education contributing to the public good is its role in preserving and encouraging democratic freedoms. Individuals with education are expected to be more civilized and more tolerant of others. Persons with schooling are expected to vote, and to make an informed choice when doing so. This is the basis of the argument Thomas Jefferson used to obtain public responsibility for education. A more modern version of this can be found in the report *The State of America's Children, 1991* by the Children's Defense Fund:

> Substandard schools that serve poor and minority students reinforce the polarizing trends at work in our society. . . . This polarization heightens racial tensions and weakens Americans' sense of shared values and concerns. Citizens who feel isolated from the mainstream by a lack of education . . . are less likely to vote, participate in their communities and pass along to their children the values associated with informed citizenship. (Children's Defense Fund 1991 p. 85)

Comer (1988) shares this perspective in his work on inner-city schools in which he notes the importance of education in reducing future alienation and social inequities.

A related public benefit stems from the view that schooling improves the neighborhood: it provides children with socially acceptable norms and encourages them to display more socially acceptable behavior (Weisbrod 1962). This effect is also likely to entail more sustained societal benefits: recent studies of neighborhood effects (Wilson 1987) cite the negative influence on teenage behavior of growing up in areas with high unemployment or nonemployment and high rates of transfer recipiency (both positively associated with low levels of education of those in the community). Such negative influences include dropping out of school, drug and alcohol use, and idleness. All of these have negative consequences for the individual, the neighborhood, and society in general.

Other public benefits from education include the reduction of criminal activity, increases in social cohesion and technological change, and changes in income distribution. All these changes share the characteristic that they can simultaneously benefit numerous individuals, in other words they are nonexclusive benefits.

The public good aspect of education that has probably received the greatest attention from economists is the effect of schooling on economic growth, including increases in technological change, and in particular the diffusion of technology. The underlying principle of this is that more education leads to greater access to new information and greater ability to assimilate and access new ideas, concepts, and so on. In addition, education increases the ability to work productively in new situations. This is expected to lead to a greater willingness to experiment with new ideas, to understand the potential of new services or products, and hence to be leaders in the development and adoption of changing technology.

While some of the gain from new technology may be reflected in labor market earnings, there is evidence that willingness to take risks in research and development and to adopt new research brings benefits to society beyond the gains reflected in labor market earnings. For example, Wozniak (1987) argues that "early adopters of new technology must acquire and process a better quality and larger quantity of information than others" (p. 104). His empirical results, based on a group of farmers, is consistent with the view that "increases in education enhance innovative ability." He estimates that an additional year of schooling increases the probability of being an innovator by about 3 percent. The increase in technology should lead to increases in productivity, which provide gains to others in society. In fact, as long as there are, in general, complementarities between skills in production, society in general will gain from the increased schooling of some of its members. In addition to the contribution of education to technological change, the economic growth literature finds other contributions of education to economic growth. On the whole, these studies find that schooling makes a positive contribution and, at least in Western Europe, that its role has been increasing over time (Broer and Jansen 1989). A related body of literature finds that those with more schooling have lower levels and duration of unemployment and suggests that increased schooling is way to reduce unemployment, and hence the amount of income transfers to the unemployed (Ritzen 1987 Kiefer 1985).

The basic link between crime and schooling is that the more schooled person has better labor market earnings and so is less likely to choose to commit a crime (Yamada et al. 1991). (For white-collar crime, this analysis may not hold. For such crimes those with more education may be better able to see opportunities for individual gains. Note the recent financial market crimes in the United States and the BCCI banking scandal.) Factors working for the public good are the saved costs of protection and the overall increases in well-being which the public enjoys as a result of reduced actual crime or the threat of crime. For example, Ehrlich (1975) estimates that for each additional year of schooling in the community, there is a significant reduction in the probability of convicting and imprisoning offenders, which is taken to be a contribution to the reduction of crime. Consistent with this are Ehrlich's findings that adult prison inmates have limited education. Trumbull (1989) studied another population: released criminals. He found that among released criminals, those with more education were less likely to commit another crime than those with less education. A problem with all of these studies however, is that they may reflect the link between education and the probability of apprehension and/or conviction rather than a link between crime and education itself. A somewhat more direct link is found in the studies by both Ehrlich (1975) and Spiegelman (1968) as well as the link via unemployment and opportunity cost noted above. Spiegelman found that time spent in school appeared to be directly and negatively related to crime; that is, adolescents involved with schooling had a lower probability of committing a crime. Ehrlich refers to a study which shows that the delinquency rate among 14- to 17-year olds in school is far below that of those not enrolled.

3. Spillovers

Another quite different type of externality of education is the spillover effect it has on other communities, other localities, states, regions, countries, and so on. These types of spillover are different from the externalities discussed above, since the former are externalities in the sense that those who live in an area that did not contribute to the cost of the education provided receive the public benefits when a schooled person moves into the community. The community that funded the education loses these benefits. The result is an allocative inefficiency, insofar as the social benefits such as savings in welfare and medical costs, voter responsibility, and lower crime rates are lost to the community that financed the education if there is outmigration. If taxes increase with income, the greater (potential) tax payments of the more schooled person will also be lost to the community that funded the schooling. The result is likely to be a reduction in the public financing of education unless there is cost-sharing by larger units of government. Indeed, this forms the basis of the argument that state and federal governments or countries within a single geographical region, such as the European Community, should share the costs of education. Similarly, as long as immigration occurs, the same argument can also be advanced for investment by developed nations in the education system of developing nations.

See also: Benefits of Education; Consumption Benefits of Education; Cost–Benefit Analysis; Rates of Return to Education

References

An C B, Haveman R H, Wolfe B L 1991 Teen out-of-wedlock births and welfare receipt: The role of childhood events and economic circumstances. Institute for Research on Poverty, Discussion Paper 944–91

Antel J 1988 Mother's welfare dependency effects on daughter's early fertility and fertility out of wedlock. University of Houston, Houston, Texas (mimeo)

Auster R, Leveson I, Sarachek D 1969 The production of health: An exploratory study. *J. Hum. Resources* 4(4): 411–36

Behrman J, Wolfe B 1987 How does mother's schooling affect family health, nutrition, medical care, usage, and household sanitation? *J. Economet.* 36: 185–204

Berger M, Leigh J P 1989 Schooling, self-selection and health. *J. Hum. Resources* 24(3): 433–55

Broer D P, Jansen W J 1989 Employment, schooling and productivity growth. *De Economist.* 137(4): 425–53

Children's Defense Fund Staff 1991 *The State of America's Children, 1991* Children's Defense Fund, Washington, DC

Comer J P 1988 Educating poor minority children. *Sci. Am.* 259(5): 42–48

Dawson D 1991 Family structure and children's health and well-being: Data from the 1988 National Health Interview Survey on Child Health. *J. Marriage Fam.* 53: 573–84

Edwards L N, Grossman M 1979 The relationship between children's health and intellectual development. In: Mushkin S, Dunlop D (eds.) 1979 *Health: What Is It Worth? Measures of Health Benefits.* Pergamon Press, New York

Ehrlich I 1975 On the relation between education and crime. In: Juster F T (ed.) 1975 *Education, Income, and Human Behavior.* McGraw-Hill, New York

Grossman M 1975 The correlation between health and schooling. In: Terleckyj N E (ed.) 1975 *Household Production and Consumption.* National Bureau of Economic Research, New York

Grossman M, Jacobowitz S 1981 Variations in infant mortality rates among counties in the United States: The roles of public policies and programs. *Demography* 18(4): 695–713

Grossman M, Joyce T 1989 Socio-economic status and health: A personal research perspective. In: Bunker J, Genby D, Kehrer B (eds.) 1989 *Pathways to Health: The Role of Social Factors.* Kaiser Foundation, Menlo Park, California

Hodgkinson V, Weitzman M 1988 *Giving and Volunteering in the United States: Findings from a National Survey, 1988 Edition.* Independent Sector, Washington, DC

Kemna H J M I 1987 Working conditions and the relationship between schooling and health. *Journal of Health Economics* 6(3): 189–210

Kenkel D 1991 Health behavior, health knowledge, and schooling. *J. Pol. Econ.* 99(2): 287–305

Kiefer N 1985 Evidence on the role of education in labor turnover. *J. Hum. Resources* 20(3): 445–52

Leigh J P 1983 Direct and indirect effects of education on health. *Social Science and Medicine* 17(4): 227–34

Metcalf D 1973 Pay dispersion, information, and returns to search in a professional labour market. *Rev. Econ. Stud.* 40: 491–505

Pauly M 1980 *Doctors and Their Workshops: Economic Models of Physician Behavior.* University of Chicago Press for the National Bureau of Economic Research, Chicago, Illinois

Ritzen J 1987 Human capital and economic cycles. *Econ. Educ. Rev.* 6(2): 151–60

Robins L N 1984 Lifetime prevalence of specific psychiatric disorders in three sites. *Arch. Gen. Psychiatry* 41: 949–58

Shakotko R, Edwards L, Grossman M 1981 An exploration of the dynamic relationship between health and cognitive development in adolescence. In: Van der Gaag J, Perlman M (eds.) 1981 *Contributions to Economic Analysis: Health, Economics and Health Economics* North-Holland, Amsterdam

Spiegelman R G 1968 A benefit/cost model to evaluate educational programs. *Soc-Econ. Plan. Sci.* 1: 443–60

Trumbull W N 1989 Estimation of the economic model of crime using aggregate and individual level data. *Southern Economic Journal* 56(2): 423–39

Weisbrod B 1962 Education and investment in human capital. *J. Pol. Econ.* 70(5): 106–23

Wilson W J 1987 *The Truly Disadvantaged: The Inner City, the Underclass, and Public Policy.* University of Chicago Press, Chicago, Illinois

Wozniak G 1987 Human capital, information and the early adoption of new technology. *J. Hum. Resources* 22(1): 101–12

Yamada T, Yamada T, Kang J 1991 Crime rates versus labor market conditions: Theory and time-series evidence. National Bureau of Economic Research, Working Paper No. 3801

Further Reading

Haveman R, Wolfe B 1984 Schooling and economic well-being: The role of nonmarket effects. *J. Hum. Resources* 19(3): 377–407

Michael R 1982 Measuring non-monetary benefits of education: A survey. In: McMahon W, Geske T (eds.) 1982 *Financing Education: Overcoming Inefficiency and Inequity.* University of Illinois Press, Urbana, Illinois

Education and Fertility

L. Gibney

The expansion of schooling, particularly of females, is believed by many to be the most promising means of lowering high population growth rates. To understand the basis for this belief, this entry reviews some of the empirical evidence and theoretical explanations of the relationship between education and fertility (number of births). Explanations from different social science perspectives are presented, though primary emphasis is on those of economists.

1. Empirical Evidence

The relationship between education and fertility has been studied at both the macro and micro levels. At the macro level the focus has been on how changing levels of educational attainment in the population influence fertility levels, or on how the onset of universal education has influenced the demographic transition in societies from high to low fertility. At the micro level researchers have examined how individuals' level of educational attainment influences choices they make between having children and pursuing other options.

Evidence for the relationship between educational attainment and fertility has been mixed, though there is sufficient data to indicate that it is generally, but not universally, inverse: with increasing levels of education people have fewer children. The relationship varies depending on gender, residence in rural or urban areas, and countries' level of development.

1.1 The Influence of Gender

The inverse relationship is most pronounced for women. Numerous empirical studies during the 1970s and 1980s have demonstrated that female education has a stronger, and more consistently negative, relationship with fertility than any other single variable (Kasarda et al. 1986). The relationship holds for male education too, but less strongly (about one-third of that for women), and hardly at all when income is held constant. For women, on the other hand, the relationship between schooling and fertility increases when income is held constant, indicating that it is not simply a function of their economic position (Cochrane 1983). This pattern of having a smaller fertility differential according to husband's rather than wife's education is typical only in Africa and Asia; in Latin America the fertility differential is approximately the same size according to either husband's or wife's education (UN 1986).

1.2 Level of Development and Residence

Income levels and development stages of individual countries, as well as people's residence in urban or rural areas, affect the impact of education on fertility. With respect to residence, schooling has been shown to have a more negative effect on fertility in urban than in rural settings (Cochrane 1983). Plausible explanations for this include: greater employment opportunities, exposure to consumer goods and lifestyle alternatives to children, fewer traditional kinship norms, higher costs of raising children and lower economic returns from children, and greater access to contraception (Kasarda et al. 1986).

In terms of level of development, it is the middle-income developing countries (e.g., in the Middle East and South America) which seem to have the strongest monotonically inverse relationship between education and fertility. In the more developed Third World countries (some in Latin America and Asia) and in highly developed Western nations there is also generally a linear, inverse relationship, but with a smaller gradient because even women with little or no schooling have low fertility levels (Cochrane 1979, 1983, UN 1987). There are, however, studies indicating that several European nations have a curvilinear, U-shaped relationship between education and fertility. The average number of children born tends to be higher among the least and most educated women (Cochrane 1979).

In the poorest, most illiterate societies with overall high fertility (sub-Saharan Africa and certain Asian countries), women with a small amount of education often have higher fertility than those with no education. Fertility in those societies is only likely to fall at the completed primary or postprimary levels. Cochrane hypothesizes that this inverted U shape in less developed countries may be due to the fact that education "initially increases the ability to have live births, probably through improved health, better nutrition, and the abandoning of traditional patterns of lactation and postpartum abstinence" (Cochrane 1979 p. 9).

2. Theoretical Explanations

Education influences fertility in a complex fashion. While some researchers believe that education may have a "direct" effect on fertility via its impact on modern attitudes and behavior, generally the literature perceives its influence as "indirect." An argument for the links necessarily being "indirect" is the complicated and "often tenuous link between the teaching act and learning outcome and between these factors and smaller family size" (Kasarda et al. 1986 p. 95).

To understand the causal pathways via which education influences fertility, researchers have generally ocused on education's influence on the three determinants of fertility, originally incorporated in Easterlin t al.'s economic theory of fertility (1980). These re: (a) the demand for children or for an additional hild; (b) the potential supply of children; and (c) ontraceptive use.

.1 The Demand for Children

\ fundamental premise of microeconomic models of ertility, including the "new household economics" ipproach, is that couples make rational economic decisions pertaining to fertility, based on their desire to maximize utility (Leibenstein 1974, Easterlin 1985). The "implicit" weighing of the benefits/values and :osts/disvalues (both economic and noneconomic) of :hildren is of primary importance in determining the 'demand" for children or for an additional child, and ience for maximizing utility or satisfaction.

Studies have demonstrated that the economic utility »f children, and parents' perceptions of children as :conomically useful, is positively related to desired amily size and to contraceptive use. The economic itility of children usually comes from the work they >erform when they are young (assisting with house-iold chores, agricultural work, and the care of other :hildren), as well as the "bridewealth" they bring in ind the old-age security they provide for their parents. With increased education, the need and expectation »f economic benefits from children are typically re-luced (Mason 1984). Better educated women are able :o enter the formal labor market, gain more finan-:ial independence, and participate in old-age security »lans, all of which reduce the need for economic .upport from children. Further, Caldwell argues that nass schooling undermines traditional family norms »bliging children to help materially support their par-:nts, and once parents perceive their offspring as an :conomic burden rather than a source of economic »enefits they desire fewer children (Caldwell 1982).

The actual cost of childrearing increases for more :ducated parents because they tend to prefer few-:r, higher "quality," better educated children. These :hildren cost more to maintain and educate and iave higher consumption demands (Caldwell 1980). Moreover, better educated parents usually have higher >pportunity costs, in terms of the value of the activities ind expenditures they must forgo in order to spend :ime and funds in childrearing. Such opportunity costs ire thought to pertain mainly to women, for economic :heories of fertility have usually assumed that child-rearing time is largely provided by mothers, making :he cost of their time of primary importance. The nain choice is between occupational work and child-rearing; forgone earnings from occupational work are viewed as an important opportunity cost of employed women having many children. This assumed asso-:iation between female labor force participation and fertility has been widely examined and the results have been mixed. Studies have shown positive associations,

negative associations or no association at all between these two variables (Kasarda et al. 1986).

This idea of "role incompatibility," believed to exist among working women who are also raising young children, has been contested in the context of developing societies. Mueller argues that while children are time-consuming, childrearing need not necessarily interfere with occupational work. One reason for this is that it is more common in developing countries for relatives and older children to help the mother look after younger children, and many of the traditional jobs in which Third World women are engaged are compatible with child care (Mueller 1982). An additional reason why women's potential earnings ought not to be viewed necessarily as an opportunity cost of raising children is that there is a pervasive underemployment problem in many developing countries. Consequently, even with increasing levels of schooling, women may not perceive more work as a realistic alternative to more children.

It is important to note that in addition to economic opportunity costs there may also be "psychic" oppor-tunity costs involved in childrearing. Psychic oppor-tunity costs refer to the the value of the noneconomic, psychological rewards people derive from activities other than childrearing (e.g., leisure, employment), which they have to give up or reduce when raising children. These psychic costs are likely to be higher for more educated women because they tend to marry later, and hence have more time to experience alterna-tive sources of fulfilment to that of childrearing and to be exposed to nonfamilial values. Further, women with higher educational attainment have greater access to nonmenial employment which may offer psychologi-cal satisfaction, and a higher status within and outside the household. (This will, of course, only be the case in societies where such employment opportunities are available for women.) For less educated women with-out access to intrinsically satisfying employment, their source of status within the family and society, and of greatest fulfillment in life, will likely remain in child-rearing. As a result, they will experience lower psychic costs in raising children.

Finally, the tendency for women with higher levels of schooling to have more egalitarian conjugal rela-tions, characterized by the greater autonomy of women from their husbands and in-laws, may increase the psychic costs of childrearing. This is because couples in more egalitarian relationships reportedly look more to each other for emotional satisfaction than to their children (Caldwell 1982, Oppong 1983). Other means by which this marital egalitarianism may influence de-mand for children include: a lessening in the husband's machismo image, whereby frequent pregnancies are proof of his virility; the couple's increased concern about the health consequences to the wife of having an additional child; and an increase in the probability that a woman's fertility desires will be honored (Mason 1984). The latter will only influence fertility, however, when a woman's fertility desires are lower than her husband's.

2.2 The Supply of Children

The supply of children refers to the number of children a couple would have if family size were not deliberately limited by contraception or abortion; it depends on couples' "natural fertility" and the probability of their children surviving to adulthood. The supply of children is important vis-à-vis fertility, for couples will be strongly motivated to control their fertility through contraception when their supply of children equals or is greater than their demand.

Schooling has both a positive and negative effect on a woman's potential supply of children via its impact on several important variables. One of these variables is the age of marriage. In less developed countries female education has a fairly strong direct relation with age of marriage (for males the effect of education on age of marriage is less uniform and less strong), thereby reducing the number of years of exposure to pregnancy, and their potential supply of children (Cochrane 1979, Kasarda et al. 1986).

Another important variable is infant and child mortality. Mothers' and fathers' schooling reduces infant and child mortality, particularly in countries at moderate or low levels of mortality (Cochrane 1979, Caldwell 1982). This increases the potential number of surviving children, but may also reduce the demand for additional births as parents are less likely to feel the need to replace a lost child or to produce many children as a form of insurance in case some of them die. A variety of explanations has been offered for the negative relationship between education and infant mortality. These have ranged from very specific and practical explanations such as heightened awareness of personal hygiene and greater propensity to seek out modern healthcare for children, to less direct consequences of schooling pertaining to mothers' cognitive development and its effects on childcare.

In some environments schooling may increase the potential supply of children via its positive impact on maternal health, and its negative effect on both the observance of sexual postpartum taboos and the prevalence and duration of breastfeeding (Cochrane 1979). Schooling's negative impact on breastfeeding is considered primarily responsible for the slight rise in fertility which occurs along with a small amount of education for women in many developing countries (Kasarda et al. 1986). In most developing countries breastfeeding declines monotonically with education level. This has the effect of increasing fertility because the intensity and duration of breastfeeding have a strong positive influence on the length of postpartum amenorrhea (the inhibition of the return to ovulation after giving birth) (Bongaarts 1987). The reasons why education has this negative effect on breastfeeding are

unclear, though the modernizing influence of schooling has been suggested.

2.3 Contraceptive Use

The third primary issue which is addressed in studies examining schooling's influence on fertility is the relationship between education and contraceptive use. Cross-national data indicate that education differentials in contraceptive use are generally quite large, and that contraceptive use increases monotonically with increasing education (UN 1986). These differentials have been attributed to the cost—psychological, economic, and time—of gaining information on contraceptives, of obtaining the contraceptives themselves, and of using contraceptives. Women's schooling has a stronger positive relationship to contraceptive use than men's, probably due in part to the fact that the contraceptive methods in widest use are methods used by women (pills, IUDs, diaphragms, sterilization).

One means by which schooling may lower the cost of contraceptive use is by increasing access to family planning services. Indeed, schooling has been shown in a study by the *Centro Latinoamericano de Demografía* (CELADE/Community and Family Study Center 1972) to exert an indirect influence on access to family planning through higher income in Latin American cities. Another channel by which schooling is thought to have a negative effect on the cost of contraceptive use is by increasing knowledge about, and promoting favorable attitudes toward the use of contraception. Evidence of a strong direct relation between schooling and contraceptive knowledge cross-nationally (Cochrane 1979) indicates that schooling lowers the costs (financial and time) of obtaining knowledge about family planning methods. It also lower the psychic cost of using them by clarifying misinformation about potential side effects, and by promoting positive attitudes towards the regulation of fertility. Reviews of empirical studies indicate that there is almost uniformly a direct relationship between male and female schooling and favorable attitudes toward birth control (Cochrane 1979, UN 1986).

The contribution of education to marital egalitarianism and to the increased autonomy of women within the family are other suggested paths through which education promotes contraceptive use. This increased autonomy of women reportedly operates in favor of more contraceptive use as women feel less compelled to follow the dictates of their family or kinship group (Caldwell 1982). And marital egalitarianism is believed to weaken the sexual double standard which prevents women from using birth control because their husbands fear that they will engage in extramarital sex (Mason 1984). According to Kasarda et al. (1986), however, there is only "weak to moderate evidence" to support the claim that egalitarianism positively influences contraceptive use.

Finally, the demonstrated positive relationship between educational attainment and the extent of husband–wife communication about fertility and contraception has been cited as a partial explanation of schooling's impact on contraceptive use. Where such communication is present there is abundant evidence that it is positively related to contraceptive use and to duration and effectiveness of use. Communication is assumed to lead to greater empathy and to increase a couple's ability to act together to achieve fertility goals. However, studies have also shown that in the absence of congruence of attitudes between marital partners about desired family size and fertility control, discussions between spouses do not lead to the use of contraceptives (Kasarda et al. 1986).

3. Conclusion

Evidence of the relationship between education and fertility is clearly mixed, but a generally inverse relationship between female education and fertility appears prevalent. The relationship between maternal education and fertility may, of course, be due to other factors in women's lives. LeVine notes the possibility that:

> the more educated women had parents who were more educated, sophisticated, or otherwise privileged, from whom they acquired the attitudes attributed to schooling before going to school. That the more educated women married men of greater education, wealth, or distinctive values who made it possible in terms of material conditions and ideological influence for the women to acquire the maternal attitudes attributed to maternal schooling. (LeVine 1980 p. 101)

However, a number of large-scale studies demonstrate that the schooling of women has effects on fertility independent of maternal conditions, husbands' education, and other factors attributable to the external situation of the mother (LeVine 1987, UN 1986).

While maternal education on its own appears to have important effects on fertility, more research is needed, nonetheless, on how the relationship between maternal education and fertility is influenced by characteristics of the husband. More specifically, studies are required which examine how level of educational attainment along with other characteristics of both spouses influences the intervening variables leading to a couple's fertility, that is, variables such as conjugal roles, sexual behavior, household utility functions, and the couple's beliefs about family planning. To render such analysis feasible it is essential to gather data from men as well women, contrary to the trend of the 1970s and 1980s, which included only women in family planning surveys. Where possible, it would be useful for researchers to gather data from couples (through separate interviews of husbands and wives).

Models of the relationship between schooling and fertility also thoughtfully need to incorporate into the analysis contextual/community level factors, and the mechanisms via which these contextual factors influence fertility. There have been a few studies examining how rural–urban residence, and level of development of a subregion or country, influence the impact of schooling on fertility, and Caldwell and others have examined how level of schooling in a community as a whole influences individual fertility. However, no existing studies make systematic efforts to understand how the relationship between couples' schooling and their fertility is influenced by local socioeconomic, cultural, and institutional contexts. Such studies, along with the research suggested above—examining the influence of spouses' characteristics—may offer insights into why people with similar levels of schooling have very different fertility.

A final important limitation of the literature to date is its sole focus on the relationship between educational attainment—number of years, or degree obtained—and fertility. This focus is understandable, but it is essential to go beyond the examination of these demographic relationships to strive to gain insights into just how what goes on within schools influences fertility. Admittedly, understanding the relationship between what actually occurs in schools and adults' fertility-regulating behaviors is extremely difficult given the time lag between schooling and fertility-regulating behaviors, the lack of longitudinal data, and the seemingly intangible ways in which schooling influences later fertility. These difficulties no doubt explain the paucity of research on what LeVine (1987) terms "educational processes" influencing fertility. If further insights are to be gained into how schooling influences fertility, it is essential that ethnographic studies be conducted in schools and in familial situations (such as the one by LeVine in Mexico), which endeavor to identify the aspects of formal education influencing those "behavioral dispositions" and values which have a dampening effect on fertility.

See also: External Benefits of Education

References

Bongaarts J 1987 The proximate determinants of exceptionally high fertility. *Population and Development Review* 13(1): 133–39

Caldwell J 1980 Mass education as a determinant of the timing of the fertility decline. *Population and Development Review* 6(2): 225–55

Caldwell J 1982 *Theory of Fertility Decline*. Academic Press, New York

CELADE/Community and Family Study Center (eds.) 1972 *Fertility and Family Planning in Metropolitan Latin America*. University of Chicago, Chicago, Illinois

Cochrane S 1979 *Fertility and Education: What Do We Really Know?* Published for World Bank by Johns Hopkins University Press, Baltimore, Maryland

Cochrane S 1983 Effects of education and urbanization on fertility. In: Bulatao R, Lee R (eds.) 1983

Easterlin R, Pollak R, Wachter M 1980 Toward a more general economic model of fertility determination:

Endogenous preferences and natural fertility. In: Easterlin R (ed.) 1980 *Population and Economic Change in Developing Countries*. Chicago University Press, Chicago, Illinois

Easterlin R 1985 *The Fertility Revolution*. University of Chicago Press, Chicago, Illinois

Kasarda J, Billy J, West K 1986 *Status Enhancement and Fertility: Reproductive Responses to Social Mobility and Educational Opportunity*. Academic Press, London

Leibenstein H 1974 An interpretation of the economic theory of fertility: Promising path or blind alley? *J. Econ. Lit.* 12: 457–79

LeVine R 1980 Influences of women's schooling on maternal behavior in the Third World. *Comp. Educ. Rev.* 24(2): 78–105

LeVine R 1987 Women's schooling, patterns of fertility, and child survival. *Educ. Res.* 16(9): 21–27

Mason K O 1984 *The Status of Women: A Review of its Relationships to Fertility and Mortality*. Population Sciences Division, Rockefeller Foundation, New York

Mueller E 1982 The allocation of women's time and its relations to fertility. In: Anker R, Buvinic M, Youssef N (eds.) 1982 *Women's Roles and Population Trends in the Third World*. Croom Helm, London

Oppong C 1983 Women's roles, opportunity costs, and fertility. In: Bulatao R, Lee R (eds.) 1983

United Nations Department of International Economic and Social Affairs 1987 *Fertility Behavior in the Context of Development: Evidence from the World Fertility Survey* Population Studies No. 100, United Nations, New York

United Nations Population Division 1986 *Education and Fertility: Selected Findings from the World Fertility Survey Data*. United Nations, New York

Further Reading

Bulatao R, Lee R (eds.) 1983 *Determinants of Fertility in Developing Countries*, 2 vols. Academic Press, New York

Schultz T W (ed.) 1974 *Economics of the Family, Marriage Children and Human Capital*. University of Chicago Press, Chicago, Illinois

Consumption Benefits of Education

W. W. McMahon

The consumption benefits of education are treated in this entry as the nonmonetary returns accruing from education to the individual throughout his or her lifespan. As such, they include not only the nonmonetary satisfactions enjoyed by the student while in school, but also the contribution made by education to the efficiency of household production and final consumer satisfaction during leisure time before and after retirement, plus the contribution made by homemakers during the nonmarket time spent in household management and child rearing.

Many of these consumption benefits have been measured. This research has largely followed the lament by Schultz in surveying the earlier literature that "all these studies omit the consumption value of education ... It is a serious omission ... The available estimates of earnings from education in this respect all underestimate the real value of education" (1967 p. 300). The most fruitful empirical results have been achieved by use of the theory of household production as developed primarily by Becker (1975 pp. 67–68, 1976 Chap. 7) and as extended and surveyed by Michael (1972, 1982). The results of further empirical research, which are summarized below, find that education makes positive contributions to many types of nonmarket activities involving significant cognitive or education-related affective attributes—activities such as maintaining the health of family members, earning a higher rate of return on savings, improving the children's school achievement and preschool IQ, increasing the efficiency of household purchasing, and staying out of jail. Some studies find education counterproductive for the more mundane household (and workforce) tasks, since it causes time to be diverted from those tasks where education contributes less to productivity, such as dishwashing, mending, ironing, and the more time-intensive aspects of child rearing. For example, the findings of Lemennicier (1978) and Levy-Garboua and Jarousse (1978) are analogous to similar counterproductive effects found for comparable time-intensive tasks in the workplace by Rumberger (1981) and others.

The following material focuses on those studies that control in some way for the purely market benefits of education to avoid double-counting the satisfactions secured through the use of education in the workplace. This summary excludes nonmonetary satisfactions of the job (Duncan 1976), since these derive from the use of market time. The private consumption benefits from education considered below exclude externalities and spillover benefits which accrue to the society (or to other jurisdictions) above and beyond those that accrue to the individual. This entry also focuses on those microeconomic studies that test for measurable nonmarket effects—there is some work on the macro level, however, by Eisner and Nebhut (1981), McMahon (1981), and Kendrick (1979) that expands imputed values in the national income and product accounts to include an imputed value for the services of the education of homemakers in total consumption, and hence in total product and total productivity.

1. Consumption Benefits

Consumption benefits of education can be regarded as those that fall within the "new theory of consumer behaviour" (see, e.g., Becker 1976 pp. 87–150), even though most occur later in the life cycle and therefore can alternatively be viewed as a nonmonetary return on an investment. Higher earnings are a pure investment return, however, and hence are considered separately under investment returns (Psacharopoulos and Hinchliffe 1973, Psacharopoulos 1993) and under expected rates of return to education (McMahon and Wagner 1982). In considering consumption benefits, those studies will not be included that do not eliminate the benefits from education due to higher earnings.

1.1 Pure Current Consumption Effects

There are the current satisfactions enjoyed when schooling itself is enjoyable—particularly at high-school and college levels and in leisure-time courses—plus current services provided by local schools to the family such as hot lunches, community center services, and childcare. Although these can be observed, little has been done to measure them beyond one study by Lazear (1977) and aspects of some cost–benefit studies of daycare services by Gustafson (1978) and others.

1.2 Health

There is strong evidence that education contributes to better health. Numerous studies show that education is highly correlated with good health, and highly significant work by Grossman (1976) considerably refines this. He controls for the individual's income, IQ, health status as a teenager, and wife's schooling, to find an effect of education on health status by age 46 that is about 40 percent as strong as the effect of education on wages. He finds that the wife's schooling has an even bigger positive effect on the man's health than does his own schooling. Those with more education live longer; each additional year of schooling lowers the probability of death by 0.4 percent. Lando (1975) finds less work-disability, and in a later study, Grossman, again holding income and other factors constant, finds that the children of more educated women tend to have healthier teeth, are less likely to be anemic, and are less likely to be obese. Cochrane and her coresearchers estimate that one additional year of the mother's education is associated with a reduction of nine per thousand in infant mortality, and an additional year of the father's education with a reduction of one-half that amount (Cochrane et al. 1980). Although the positive effects of schooling on the individual's own health, and of the woman's education on the health of her

children are now well-documented, no study has yet examined the effect of the education of the husband on his wife's health.

1.3 Other Effects on Family Life

Leibowitz (1974), using Ben-Porath's well-known model of the household production of human capital over time, finds that a mother's education and preschool home investments in children significantly raise the child's IQ. Benson (1982) finds that families of high socioeconomic status tend to limit television viewing and pay more attention to whether or not the child does his or her homework, factors positively related to school achievement. The number of years of college planned by White male and by Black male college freshmen has been found by McMahon (after controlling for family income, ability, and all financial aids) to be positively influenced by the education of the parents (McMahon 1976 p. 322).

Ben-Porath neutrality implies that the young person's past education is productive in further education, as every school admissions officer knows, but also that this is only at the cost of its equal productivity in the market. This is not an issue when considering the productivity of education in the home during leisure time, however (since in this case there are no forgone earnings), or when considering how the education of the parents contributes to the further education of the child in exchanges within the family.

1.4 Returns on Savings

Solomon (1975) finds that the level of education among respondents in a survey of members of the Consumers Union, after controlling for income and occupation, has the strongest relation to choosing the best inflation hedge for their savings.

1.5 Consumption Behavior

Michael (1972, 1982) finds that those consumers with higher levels of education shift their spending patterns among consumption items, behaving as if they have more real income (over and above the higher money earnings that they also have). He estimates this real income effect of schooling on nonmarket production of consumption satisfaction to have an elasticity of 0.5, an effect about 60 percent as great as the comparable relation of schooling to money earnings.

1.6 Expected Consumption Benefits

From preliminary evidence, consumption benefits appear to average 50–60 percent of the monetary returns expected by students from their higher education. In a survey in which 5,000 students were each asked to appraise the value of the nonmonetary leisure-time returns to them relative to the expected monetary returns, McMahon (1974) finds that students in fields such as music placed the expected nonmonetary returns above the expected monetary returns, while those in medicine and business tended to place them far below. In a 1984 study, McMahon also finds that expected earnings tend to have a relatively stronger influence on most student and family educational investment decisions, an influence that is even more pronounced at the more advanced levels.

Within the sphere of nonmarket behaviour, however, education is more productive in some household activities than in others. Lemennicier (1978) challenges Michael's important simplifying assumption that education is technologically neutral among these activities—an assumption that eventually had to be challenged—which allows schooling to affect the relative price of time within the household. He finds that this causes time to be diverted from those types of activities which are time-intensive, so that in these activities education is counterproductive. He finds, for example, that a very large proportion of the time budgets of French housewives is occupied by dishwashing, and although he agrees with the positive effects of education on health, schooling, and saving behavior, which require cognitive and affective skills, the overall shifts away from dishwashing, mending, ironing, and analogous activities in the time budgets of the more educated French housewives leads him to conclude that education is counterproductive in these forms of household production. This is consistent with the now numerous research studies by Gustafson (1978), Levy-Garboua and Jarousse (1978), Ferber and McMahon (1979), and others documenting the time shifts of more educated women in Sweden, France, and the United States toward entry into the labor force.

1.7 Home Management

The simultaneous technological revolution within the home, however, may require even less time-intensive labor and increasing levels of education for effective home management which uses fewer hours. The advent of dishwashers, automatic washing machines, wash-and-wear clothing, and monthly payment of bills by check means that less time is required for such tasks than by earlier methods. However, they do require knowledge of home repairs and repair management, plus some accounting skills. Tele-shopping for groceries and sundries is now in use in 217 United States cities, tele-bill-paying and tele-banking are spreading, and home computers are now available at increasingly reasonable cost for managing household energy use, adjusting savings portfolios, teaching the children, preparing income tax returns, and even life-cycle planning—all requiring more (and changing) education for their effective use.

There are many studies, not all accompanied by adequate controls for differences in money income, which provide evidence that those with more education tend to adopt new products more quickly. Of those that do attempt to hold real income constant,

Mandell (1972) finds that those with more education adopted credit cards faster; Michael (1982) reports on several studies, including his own, that indicate that more educated women are more likely to use contraception and to have fewer unplanned babies; and Hettich (1972) finds that more educated women are more efficient in market search, with potential savings as the result of more efficient purchasing behaviour that raises the estimated rate of return to a college education by 1.5 percent. No study has yet examined whether or not persons with more education realize more of the deductions to which they are entitled on their income tax.

1.8 Affective Attributes Created by Education

As distinct from the more cognitive attributes, affective attributes affect productivity in consumption in addition to their effect on earnings.

The clearest measures are of the comparative advantage schooling confers in the selection of a desirable spouse. Michael (1982) develops the point that a person's own schooling and that of their mate are positively correlated by at least 0.4, making education a good investment in securing a spouse whose earning capacity and presumably other attributes also are more desirable. The amount of college education planned by students is also found to be positively and significantly related to "finding a spouse with college values" in a study by McMahon (1984), who controls for expected monetary returns, as well as for financial aids and other influences on student decisions. It is interesting that the coefficient for this expected nonmonetary return is four times as large, and the t-statistic twice as large, for men as it is for women students. Benham (1974) and Welch (1974) find that a wife's schooling raises her husband's annual earnings by about 3.5 percent.

Such affective returns from education as meeting, and conversing with more interesting people, capacities for entertaining guests, and community service (although the latter is an external benefit discussed elsewhere) are recognized by students and expected to be positive, although only meeting more interesting people was found by McMahon to have significant effects on student decisions. Becker (1981 Chap. 4) suggests that schooling can contribute to greater happiness in marriage, since it facilitates a more nearly optimal sorting among mates in the marriage market. However, women with more education are also more prone to divorce, generating disutility for the husband and children, a fact that Becker (1981 p.231) and others have usually associated with the growth in women's earnings that lessen the economic advantages of marriage, rather than with education per se.

Education facilitates readjustment for divorced persons with more education who are known to remarry more quickly. Furthermore, in the broader role stressed by Schultz (1975), it allows individuals to adapt more easily to changes at work, disequilibria in the job market, and new technology in the home. It also changes tastes—from drag racing or horse racing, for example, toward concerts and reading editorials. Yet the net effects of pure shifts in tastes on consumer satisfaction cancel out to some extent. Rather than concentrate on taste shifts, the research focusing on the effects on productivity in household production has been far more fruitful.

In summary, it has been seen that many good studies exist which provide evidence of positive consumption benefits of education—benefits (after holding earnings constant) to the family's health, schooling, return on savings, purchasing efficiency, home management skills, and affective sources of happiness. Against this, the counterproductive effects relating to divorce and to the time-intensive activities in the home requiring less skill must be netted out. Beyond testing for additional effects, further work is needed such as extending the work by Michael and others using shadow prices to impute values (both positive and negative) to each of these nonmonetary benefits for individual families, and also for total consumption and total product at the macro level in the national income and product accounts. These would have to include the value of education in facilitating adjustment to disequilibria, whether they be caused by market opportunties, divorce, or new technology within the family.

See also: Benefits of Education; External Benefits of Education

References

Becker G S 1975 *Human Capital: A Theoretical and Empirical Analysis, with Special Reference to Education*, 2nd edn. National Bureau of Economic Research, New York

Becker G S 1976 *The Economic Approach to Human Behavior*. University of Chicago Press, Chicago, Illinois

Becker G S 1981 *A Treatise on the Family*. Harvard University Press, Cambridge, Massachusetts

Benham L 1974 Benefits of women's education within marriage. In: Schultz T W (ed.) 1974

Benson C S 1982 Household production of human capital: Time uses parents and children as inputs. In: McMahon W W, Geske T G (eds.) 1982

Cochrane S, O'Hara D J, Leslie J 1980 *The Effects of Education on Health*. World Bank Staff Working Paper No. 105, The World Bank, Washington, DC

Duncan G J 1976 Earnings functions and non-pecuniary benefits. *J. Hum. Resources* 11: 462–83

Eisner R, Nebhut D H 1981 An extended measure of government product: Preliminary results for the United States, 1946–76. *Rev. Income Wealth* 27: 33–64

Ferber M A, McMahon W W 1979 Women's expected earnings and their investment in higher education. *J. Hum. Resources* 14: 405–20

Grossman M 1976 The correlation between health and schooling. In: Terleckyj N (ed.) 1976 *Household Production and Consumption*. Columbia University Press, New York

Gustafson S 1978 Cost benefit analysis of early childhood care and education. Working Paper, Industrial Institute for Economic and Social Research, Stockholm

Hettich W 1972 Consumption benefits from education. In: Ostry S (ed.) 1972 *Canadian Higher Education in the Seventies*. Information Canada, Ottawa

Kendrick J W 1979 Expanding imputed values in the national income and product accounts. *Rev. Income Wealth* 25: 349–63

Lando M 1975 The interaction between health and education. *Soc. Secur. Bull.* 38(12): 16–22

Lazear E P 1977 Education: Consumption or production? *J. Pol. Econ.* 85: 569–97

Leibowitz A 1974 Home investments in children. In: Schultz T W (ed.) 1974

Lemennicier B 1978 *Education et technologie de consommation. Incidences de l'éducation sur la consommation.* Centre de Recherche pour l'Etude et l'Observation des Conditions de Vie (CREDOC), Paris

Levy-Garboua L, Jarousse J 1978 *Education, aptitudes perceptives, et valeur extraite des choses familiales. Incidences de l'éducation sur la consommation.* Centre de Recherche pour l'Etude et l'Observation des Conditions de Vie (CREDOC), Paris

McMahon W W 1974 Policy issues in the economics of higher education and related research opportunities in Britain and the United States. *High. Educ.* 3: 165–86

McMahon W W 1976 Influences on investment by Blacks in higher education. *Am. Econ. Rev.* 66(2): 320–23

McMahon W W 1981 The slowdown in productivity growth: A macroeconomic model of investment in human and physical capital with energy shocks. Faculty Working Paper No. 752, Bureau of Economic and Business Research (BEBR), University of Illinois, Urbana, Illinois

McMahon W W 1984 Why families invest in education. In: Sudman S, Spaeth M (eds.) 1984 *The Collection and Analysis of Economic and Consumer Data; Essays in Honor of Robert Ferber*. University of Illinois Press, Urbana, Illinois

McMahon W W, Wagner A P 1982 The monetary returns to education as partial social efficiency criteria. In: McMahon W W, Geske T G (eds.) 1982

Mandell L 1972 *Credit Card Use in the United States*. Institute for Social Research, University of Michigan, Ann Arbor, Michigan

Michael R T 1972 *The Effect of Education on Efficiency in Consumption*. Columbia University Press/National Bureau of Economic Research, New York

Michael R T 1982 Measuring nonmonetary benefits of education. In: McMahon W W, Geske T G (eds.) 1982

Psacharopoulos G 1993 Returns to investment in education: A global update. Education and Employment Policy Research Working Paper No.1067, Latin American and Caribbean Region, The World Bank, Washington, DC

Psacharopoulos G, Hinchliffe K 1973 *Returns to Education: An International Comparison*. Elsevier, Amsterdam

Rumberger R W 1981 *Overeducation in the US Labor Market*. Praeger, New York

Schultz T W 1967 The rate of return in allocating investment resources to education. *J. Hum. Resources.* 2: 293–309

Schultz T W 1975 The value of the ability to deal with disequilibria. *J. Econ. Lit.* 13: 827–46

Solomon L C 1975 The relation between schooling and savings behavior. In: Juster F T (ed.) 1975 *Education, Income, and Human Behavior:* McGraw-Hill, New York

Welch F 1974 Comment. In: Schultz T W (ed.) 1974

Further Reading

Cohn E 1990 *The Economics of Education*, 3rd edn. Ballinger, Cambridge, Massachusetts
Haveman R, Wolfe B 1984 Schooling and economic well-being: The role of nonmarket effects. *J. Hum. Resources* 19(3): 377–407
Levhari D, Weiss Y 1974 The effect of risk on the investment in human capital. *Am. Econ. Rev.* 64(6): 950–63
McMahon W W, Geske T G (eds.) 1982 *Financing Education: Overcoming Inefficiency and Inequity*. University of Illinois Press, Urbana, Illinois

Mincer J 1963 *Social and Economic Factors in Spending for Public Education*. Syracuse University Press, Syracuse, New York
Mincer J 1974 *Schooling, Experience, and Earnings*. Columbia University Press for the National Bureau of Economic Research, New York
Schultz T W (ed.) 1974 *Economics of the Family: Marriage, Children and Human Capital*. University of Chicago Press, Chicago, Illinois
Weisbrod B A 1964 External benefits of education: An economic analysis. Research Report 105, Industrial Relations Section, Department of Economics, Princeton University, Princeton, New Jersey

Market Failure in Firm-based Education and Training

D. Stern

Most adult education and training occurs in schools or workplaces. The economic theory of markets holds that socially efficient amounts of education and training will be provided if students are free to buy as much as they are willing to pay for, and providers charge fees equal to marginal cost (the incremental cost of instructing the last student). An important exception to this principle is recognized if benefits accrue to people other than the students themselves, in which case some subsidy is warranted. Society may also subsidize some individuals' education for reasons of fairness. Payments by government for education provided by schools is based on these considerations of fairness or external benefits, considerations which may apply to both children and adults.

In workplace education or training, an additional reason for market failure is the fact that employers control how much will be provided. Most employers in nonsocialist economies are profit-seeking firms which can be expected to provide education or training only if they can profit from the investment. If a company pays for education or training, and if the employee subsequently leaves the firm, then the company will have lost its investment. Economists have given considerable thought to how employers and employees deal with this risk. This entry summarizes the economic theory and evidence on market failure in firm-based education or training (hereafter abbreviated FBET), and briefly discusses remedies.

1. How the Market is Supposed to Work: Becker's Hypotheses

Contemporary economic analysis of FBET begins with Gary S Becker's *Human Capital* (1964; 2nd edn.

1975). Becker originated the distinction between general training, which is "useful in many firms besides those providing it" (p. 19), and specific training, which "increases productivity more in firms providing it" (p. 26).

Becker hypothesized that "employees pay for general on-the-job training by receiving wages below what they could receive elsewhere" (p. 21). His argument was that "perfectly general training would be equally useful in many firms and marginal products would rise by the same extent in all of them. Consequently, wage rates would rise by exactly the same amount as the marginal product and the firms providing such training could not capture the return" (p. 20). If they tried to appropriate some of the return, the trained employee would quit and go to work for another firm.

"Why, then, would rational firms in competitive labor markets provide general training if it did not bring them any return? The answer is that firms would provide general training only if they did not have to pay any of the costs. Persons receiving general training would be willing to pay these costs since training raises their future wages. Hence it is the trainees, not the firms, who would bear the cost of general training and profit from the returns" (p. 20). In effect, employees buy general training from their employers. They prefer to buy it at work rather than going to school if complementarity between work and FBET makes learning at work more efficient than at a school.

A second hypothesis follows from the first. "Training has an important effect on the relation between earnings and age ... Trained persons would receive lower earnings during the training period because training is paid for at that time, and higher earnings at later ages because the return is collected then. The combined effect of paying for and collecting the return from training in this way would be to make the age-earnings curve of trained persons . . . steeper than that of untrained persons, the difference being greater the greater the . . . investment" (p. 23).

Mincer (1974) applied these ideas to estimating the rate of return to FBET.

1.1 Is there Really a Payoff from Firm-based Education and Training?

Economists have questioned whether FBET is responsible for the fact that earnings increase with age. Following critiques of the human capital theory of schooling (e.g., Arrow 1973, Spence 1973), which suggested that the economic payoff from schooling may be attributable to ability screening rather than to any effect of schooling on productivity, others began to apply similar thinking to FBET. In theory, even if individuals do not grow any more productive over time, earnings may still increase with seniority if such a wage structure discourages unproductive workers from joining the firm (Salop and Salop 1976, Nickell 1976) or deters them from "shirking" (Lazear 1981). Older workers may also earn more because they have had more time to find the jobs where they are most productive (Jovanovic 1979). Several studies (Topel 1986, Altonji and Shakotko 1987, Abraham and Farber 1987) found that seniority in a given firm appears to be less strongly associated with rising wages than is total experience in the labor market—which could be consistent with the idea that job matching rather than training is what causes earnings to increase with age.

However, these critiques are not based on direct evidence about FBET. They are either purely conceptual models or else based on indirect inferences from data on earnings, seniority, and job mobility. In contrast, a number of studies have found positive correlations between measures of FBET and subsequent wages. Using the Panel Study of Income Dynamics, Duncan and Hoffman (1979) and Brown (1989), among others, have found a positive association between FBET and subsequent earnings. Lillard and Tan (1986) found similar results using data from the 1983 Current Population Survey and the cohort of young men from the National Longitudinal Survey of Labor Market Experience (NLS). Lynch (1988) also corroborated the positive relationship between FBET and earnings in the NLS cohort of male and female youth. Tuijnman (1989) found adult education, including FBET, was positively associated with later earnings in the 50-year longitudinal study of men from Malmo, Sweden. And the Employment Opportunities Pilot Project (EOPP), which provided detailed measures of on-the-job training, also revealed a positive link between the amount of FBET and subsequent earnings among newly hired workers (Barron et al. 1989, Bishop 1991).

These latter studies leave little doubt that FBET leads to higher earnings, although they do not indicate exactly how much of the average rise in earnings with age results from FBET, as opposed to job matching or implicit long-term wage bargains.

1.2 Do Employees Really Pay for Their Own General Training?

Although direct evidence on FBET and earnings supports the hypothesis that training increases subsequent wages, the evidence does not seem to support Becker's other hypothesis, that employees pay for their own general training. Barron et al. (1989) found in the EOPP data that employees who received more training in their first three months on the job did not receive significantly lower wages. Yet most of the EOPP employers said they thought the training they gave would be useful in other firms. The absence of wage reduction during training therefore appears inconsistent with Becker's hypothesis. Likewise, Parsons (1985) found in the NLS data that young workers earned higher wages on jobs where they were acquiring skills which "would be useful in getting a better job."

The EOPP survey also estimated the increase in workers' productivity during their first two years. Barron et al. (1989) found that a given increase in the amount of training led to a productivity gain that was twice as big as the worker's wage increase. Bishop (1991), analyzing the same data, found an even bigger difference. Apparently employers are capturing a large share of the return from training. Since EOPP employers indicated that most of their training was general, these patterns are again inconsistent with Becker's hypothesis that employers cannot capture the return from general training.

Similarly, Feuer et al. (1987) discovered that scientists and engineers who had received formal education financed by their employers did not earn lower salaries than those who had paid for their own education. Since formal education is general training, this result also contradicts Becker. The authors consider it evidence in support of an alternative theory, that employers finance general training in order to encourage employees to invest in specific training (Glick and Feuer 1984).

Bishop (1991) suggests that employers may pay for training which is ostensibly useful in other firms because the other firms will fail to give an employee full credit for general skills acquired through FBET. One reason is that different firms require different kinds of general skills, and in different proportions. The particular package of general skills obtained in one firm therefore may be less useful in another firm.

Another reason why other firms may undervalue general skills and knowledge acquired through FBET is simply that it is difficult for other employers to find out about it. Katz and Ziderman (1990) point out that other firms would find it particularly difficult to discover the range of adaptive abilities a worker has acquired but which are not being displayed in the present job— what they call the "options value" of general training.

Bishop (1991) found that, even though formal and informal FBET have approximately equal effects on a new worker's subsequent productivity, formal training—which is more visible to other employers—leads to larger wage increases than informal training.

In sum, direct evidence on training and wages indicates that employees do not pay for most, if any, of their own general training, yet they do obtain higher earnings after they receive it. This implies a very high rate of return to general FBET for employees. In spite of that, employees are evidently reluctant to pay for general FBET because they fear that its value may not be fully recognized if they move to a different firm. This implies that markets will provide less than the optimal amount.

1.3 Other Possible Reasons for Market Failure

There would be other possible reasons for market failure in FBET even if employees did pay for their own general training as Becker hypothesized (Ritzen and Stern 1991). Uncertainty is one reason. An individual considering a possible course of training will often have only a vague idea of the benefits that are likely to ensue. Individuals who are averse to risk will invest less than if they were certain of the benefit. The risk is greater if general skills and knowledge acquired through FBET are more useful when combined with specific training—then separation from the current employer decreases some of the value of the general, in addition to the specific, FBET. Ritzen (1991) has demonstrated that, in theory, protecting individuals against risk would lead to more investment in FBET. In addition, liquidity constraints, and inability to borrow for the purpose of financing FBET, could prevent workers from paying for their own general training. Minimum wage laws may also prevent some workers from accepting wages low enough to finance their training.

Even if all bargains between individual employees and employers were efficient in the existing labor market, a different macroeconomic and institutional configuration might call for a different level of investment in FBET. Soskice (1989) and Streeck (1989) argue that cooperation among firms, possibly including the use of governmental power, can provide greater incentive for each firm to provide a socially efficient amount of FBET. One important piece of this cooperative bargain is a low aggregate rate of unemployment. When unemployment is low, firms have greater difficulty replacing workers they have laid off during temporary business downturns, so if business is slack they are more likely to retain workers and use the extra time for training. The expectation of stable employment also encourages both employees and firms to invest more in FBET. Full employment is conducive to more skill-intensive forms of production and management practices such as quality circles, systematic job rotation, and skill-based pay (National Center on Education and the Economy 1990, Stern and Benson 1991).

In contrast, when the overall rate of unemployment increases, workers become separated from firms where they have been trained, which immediately destroys the value of their firm-specific training. The loss of valuable firm-specific knowledge and skill due to recessions is a major market failure.

2. Remedies for Market Failure

When markets fail, collective action may provide a remedy. Among the possible public policies to remedy failure in the market for FBET are maintenance of full employment, imposition of a training obligation on firms, articulation of training standards to facilitate recognition of general training, and public subsidies.

A low aggregate rate of unemployment encourages investment in FBET. Governments in most industrialized countries list full employment as one of their goals. A few, including Sweden and Japan, have been notable in maintaining low unemployment in recent decades.

A more direct strategy for encouraging FBET is to require all employers to spend at least a certain minimum percentage of their payroll on providing it. France pioneered this policy in 1971 with a law initially requiring all firms employing 10 or more people to allocate at least 0.8 percent of their annual payroll to continued training; as of 1991 the required percentage had been raised to 1.2. In 1990 Australia enacted a similar law, requiring every enterprise with a payroll of A$200,000 or more to spend at least 1 percent on training, rising to 1.5 percent in 1992 (Australian Taxation Office 1990).

Defining standards for certifying worker competence can facilitate FBET by making it easier for firms to recognize the results of each other's training. This is a hallmark of apprenticeship systems as in Germany. Many countries are currently extending this idea to FBET (e.g., National Training Board 1991). Japan awards National Trade Certificates for skilled workers in 133 occupations (Koike and Inoki 1990).

Finally, governments may directly subsidize FBET. Such subsidies may be targeted to smaller firms, which tend to spend less on FBET, or to training certain types of employees who tend to receive less FBET, such as workers older than 50, and those with fewer years of initial schooling (OECD 1991).

See also: Education, Occupation, and Earnings; Cost-Benefit Analysis

References

Abraham K G, Farber H S 1987 Job duration, seniority, and earnings. *Am. Econ. Rev.* 77(3): 278–97
Altonji J G, Shakotko R A 1987 Do wages rise with job seniority? *Rev. Econ. Stud.* 54(3): 437–59
Arrow K J 1973 Higher education as a filter. *J. Pol. Econ.* 2: 193–216

Australian Taxation Office 1990 *The Training Guarantee— Your Questions Answered*. Australian Taxation Office, Canberra

Barron J M, Black D A, Loewenstein M A 1989 Job matching and on-the-job training. *J. Labor Econ.* 7(1): 1–19

Becker G S 1964 *Human Capital: A Theoretical and Empirical Analysis with Special Reference to Education*. Columbia University Press, New York

Bishop J H 1991 On-the-job training of new hires. In: Stern D, Ritzen J M M (eds.) 1991 *Market Failure in Training? New Economic Analysis and Evidence on Training of Adult Employees*. Springer-Verlag, Berlin

Brown J N 1989 Why do wages increase with tenure? On-the-job training and life-cycle wage growth observed within firms. *Am. Econ. Rev.* 79(5): 971–91

Duncan G J, Hoffman S 1979 On-the-job training and earnings differences by race and sex. *Rev. Econ. Stat.* 61(4): 593–603

Feuer M, Glick H, Desai A 1987 Is firm-sponsored education viable? *J Econ. Behav. Org.* 8(1): 121–44

Glick H A, Feuer M J 1984 Employer-sponsored training and the governance of specific human capital investments. *Quart. Rev. Econ. and Business* 24(2): 91–103

Jovanovic B 1979 Job matching and the theory of turnover. *J. Pol. Econ.* 87(5): 972–90

Katz E, Ziderman A 1990 Investment in general training. The role of information and labour mobility. *The Econ. J.* 100: 1147–58

Koike K, Inoki I (eds.) 1990 *Skill Formation in Japan and Southeast Asia*. University of Tokyo Press, Tokyo

Lazear E P 1981 Agency, earnings profiles, productivity, and hours restrictions. *Am. Econ. Rev.* 71(4): 606–20

Lillard L A, Tan H W 1986 *Private Sector Training. Who Gets it and What Are its Effects?* The Rand Corporation, Santa Monica, California

Lynch L M 1988 *Private Sector Training and its Impact on the Earnings of Young Workers*. (Working paper SSWP) Sloan School of Management, Massachusetts Institute of Technology, Cambridge, Massachusetts

Mincer J 1974 *Schooling, Experience, and Earnings*. National Bureau of Economic Research, New York

National Center on Education and the Economy 1990 *America's Choice: High Skills or Low Wages!* Report of the Commission on the Skills of the American Workforce. National Center on Education and the Economy,
Rochester, New York

National Training Board 1991 *National Competency Standards. Policy and Guidelines*. National Training Board Ltd., Canberra

Nickell S J 1976 Wage structures and quit rates. *Int. Econ. Rev.* 17(1): 191–203

Organisation for Economic Co-operation and Development 1991 *Employment Outlook 1991*, Chap. 5: *Enterprise Training*. OECD, Paris

Parsons D 1985 Wage determination in the post training period. In: Parsons D 1985 *Pathways to the Future*, Center for Human Resource Research, Ohio State University, Columbus, Ohio

Ritzen J M M 1991 Market failure for general training, and remedies. In: Stern D, Ritzen J M M (eds.) 1991 *Market Failure in Training? New Economic Analysis and Evidence on Training of Adult Employees*. Springer-Verlag, Berlin

Ritzen J M M, Stern D 1991 Introduction and overview. In: Stern D, Ritzen J M M (eds.) 1991 *Market Failure in Training? New Economic Analysis and Evidence on Training of Adult Employees*. Springer-Verlag, Berlin

Salop S C, Salop J 1976 Self-selection and turnover in the labor market. *Q. J. Econ.* 90(4): 619–28

Soskice D 1989 Reinterpreting corporatism and explaining unemployment: Coordinated and non-coordinated market economies. In: Brunetta R, dell'Aringa C (eds.) 1990 *Markets, Institutions and Cooperation. Labour Relations and Economic Performance*. Macmillan, London

Spence M 1973 Job market signaling. *Q. J. Econ.* 87(3): 355–74

Stern D, Benson C S 1991 Firms' propensity to train. In: Stern D, Ritzen J M M (eds.) 1991 *Market Failure in Training? New Economic Analysis and Evidence on Training of Adult Employees*. Springer-Verlag, Berlin

Streeck W 1989 Skills and the limits of neo-liberalism. The enterprise of the future as a place of learning. *Work, Employment & Society* 3: 89–104

Topel R 1986 Job mobility, search, and earnings growth. A reinterpretation of human capital earnings functions. *Res. Lab. Econ.* 8(A): 199–233

Tuijnman A 1989 *Recurrent Education, Earnings, and Well-Being: A Fifty-year Longitudinal Study of a Cohort of Swedish Men*. Almqvist and Wiksell International, Stockholm

Returns to Vocational Education in Developing Nations

Yue-Ping Chung

Vocational education has been the focus of educational development in many developing countries. However, there are controversies about its role in development planning, and research findings on its returns are not consistent. This entry reviews the results of some studies from the 1970s to the early 1990s on returns to vocational education in developing countries, and identifies some general patterns from these results. Aspects of both the supply side and the demand side are examined to explore why and when the return to vocational education is especially high or low. Particular attention is given to the effect and implications of employment in matched occupations.

1. Controversies in Vocational Education

Developing countries have a long history of devoting large resources to the development of vocational education. It has been estimated that about 60 percent of the US$1.6 billion of World Bank lending for education investment in the period 1963–76 and about 50 percent of the US$5.8 billion lending in 1977–86 were devoted to vocational education of some sort (Middleton 1988). Parallel to such enthusiasm for the development of vocational education is the long-standing controversy over the "fallacy" of vocational schools raised by Foster in 1965. He maintained that vocational education is considered by students and their parents as a second-rate education which leads to lower status employment; graduates from vocational schools do not work in the field they are prepared for; and the value of their specific skills cannot be realized in the workplace, and the investment in their training is thus wasted. After more than 20 years, Foster summarized this controversy as an "old soldier" that would never die (Foster 1987).

2. Economic Returns to Vocational Education

Though the costs of vocational education in developing countries are usually high (Tsang 1989), it is hoped that equipping young people with specific skills related to production would reduce unemployment and increase productivity in the workplace. That is, the economic returns to investment in vocational education would eventually exceed its costs. Hence, the explicit aim for the development of vocational education in development planning is mainly economic. Indeed, there is a large volume of literature on the economic aspect of vocational education. Both Metcalf (1985) and Haddad et al. (1990) have summarized studies in the area.

3. Criteria of Returns and Sources of Inconsistency

Different criteria have been used to measure the economic returns to vocational education in developing countries. They can be summarized in three major categories.

The first category uses direct measures of productivity. For instance, Fuller (1976) used a cardinal scale of worker efficiency to rate the productivity of workers in a factory in India. In a more recent study in the People's Republic of China, Min and Tsang (1990) designed a "work efficiency" ratio based on the actual output of a worker and his or her production quota to get a direct measure of his or her productivity in the workplace.

The second category focuses on employment status. The employment status most commonly examined is the employment or unemployment rate. Some studies use the probability of employment to adjust for the earnings of different groups (e.g., Arriagazzi 1972, Hinchliffe 1990). Other studies compare the occupation levels and the employment patterns of graduates from different streams of education (e.g., Pscharopoulos and Zabalza 1984). The third aspect of employment status is the rate of "matched employment." This is the percentage of graduates from a specific field of vocational education being employed in a related field of work. It has been used in a number of studies as an index of the success of the vocational programs concerned (e.g., Campbell et al. 1986, Chung 1992, Neuman and Ziderman 1991).

The third major category uses earnings as its criterion. Earnings are the most common measure of returns to investment in education and other aspects of human capital. In a labor market economy, earnings reflect productivity in the workplace, and are thus taken by many writers as the "ultimate" measure of economic returns to investment in human capital. Most of the studies reviewed here analyze the earnings function of a Mincerian type (e.g., Bellew and Moock 1990, Chung 1992, Tannen 1991). Some studies also combine the lifetime earnings stream projected from the earnings function, with costs data to estimate the social and private rates of return to vocational education (e.g., Grootaert 1990, Tannen 1991, Neuman and Ziderman 1991).

Other measures used in the evaluation of returns to vocational education include the reduction of dropout rate (e.g., Blaug 1976, Bishop 1989) and the likelihood of passing a government trade test (e.g., Godfrey 1977). All these measurement criteria are either directly or indirectly related to productivity, and have caused little disagreement. However, there is still confusion in the interpretation of the results of these returns analyses.

The first confusion arises from the different types of vocational education based on its modes of delivery (Middleton 1988, Dougherty 1989). There are: (a) formal vocational schools and diversified schools, (b) nonformal but structured firm-based apprenticeship and industrial training programs, and (c) informal short training courses run by various agents. Evaluation studies may consider any of these diverse programs, that is, the "target program" under consideration is different among different studies. The second confusion arises from the frame of reference for comparison. The most common reference used is the return to academic general education of equivalent level. However, there are also studies evaluating the returns to a certain type of vocational education with reference to another type, such as diversified schools versus conventional vocational schools (e.g., Pscharopoulos and Zabalza 1984). Confusions arise when the investigator cites the ineffectiveness of

Table 1
Distribution of major published studies on the returns to vocational education in developing countries

Results of the study	Number of studies
Returns higher than the reference	12 (44%)
Returns lower than or not different from the reference	10 (37%)
No basis to decide if returns are lower or higher	5 (19%)
Total	27

diversified schools to disprove the effectiveness of all forms of vocational education (e.g., Psacharopoulos 1991).

The third confusion arises from the perspective of the returns to be evaluated. There are different beneficiaries as the result of imparting specific skills to the worker. Usually, economic returns to investment in education can be considered from the private perspective and the social perspective. However, for the firm-based nonformal training programs and for most of the informal short training programs, the firm is directly involved. There are costs and benefits considerations for the firm in offering such training programs. Therefore, returns to firm-based vocational education can also be evaluated from the perspective of the firm (Cohen 1985).

4. Evaluation of Returns to Vocational Education

A general survey of major published studies on the returns to vocational education shows that there is a great diversity of "target programs" being evaluated and "reference programs" being used for the evaluation. However, the methods adopted for the evaluation are rather similar. The most frequently used methodology is the analysis of the earnings function, incorporating vocational education in the function as a dummy variable with reference to academic general education. Table 1 shows the distribution of some recent studies on developing countries.

It can be seen from the table that about the same number of studies show that vocational education generates higher economic returns as otherwise. It is suspected that this inconclusive picture represents the situation in the early 1990s fairly closely, and that the same result would be obtained even if more studies were identified and reviewed.

There may be different reasons for this inconsistency. The target programs under consideration are not the same; the times and countries, and hence the economic situations, of the program under study are not the same; finally, the

criteria of measurement and the methodology of analysis are not all the same.

5. Some Underlying Patterns

The results of the studies on returns to vocational education in developing countries are varied and would appear to disagree with each other. However, a closer examination of these studies reveals some general patterns.

5.1 Costs of Program

For those cases where rates of return to particular types of vocational education are low, the costs are usually high, compared with other educational programs. This is found both in the case of India (Fuller 1976) and Israel (Borus 1977).

5.2 Types of Program and Fields of Study

Most of the vocational programs that generate positive returns are the nonformal firm-based training programs, such as the apprenticeship program in Israel (Borus 1977, Ziderman 1989), the company apprenticeship training program in Malaysia (Cohen 1985), and the company-affiliated vocational school in the People's Republic of China (Min and Tsang 1990). No general pattern as to the cost-effectiveness of short courses compared with long courses emerged. For example, the earnings effect of the SENA (National Apprenticeship Service programs) in Colombia drops for the long courses and disappears for the short courses when selectivity bias is controlled for (Jimenez and Kugler 1988).

In the case of formal vocational schools, there are differences in the earnings effect among different fields of study. For example, in Colombia the average social rates of return for both diversified and conventional vocational schools were 9.9% percent for commercial programs, 12.3 percent for industrial programs, 7 percent for agricultural programs, versus

9.1 percent for the academic program (calculated from data in Psacharopoulos and Zabalza 1984). In Hong Kong, there was a higher earnings effect for vocational education for the commercial field (7.8%) and the electronic and electrical field (6.9%) of study over general education, but no effect for the textile and the mechanical fields (Chung 1992). In Brazil, Tannen (1991) found an earnings advantage of 4.7 percent for commercial education and 16.4 percent for industrial education, but no advantage for other vocational fields of study.

5.3 Level of Schooling

Workers with higher schooling level tend to benefit more from the informal and nonformal firm-based learning. In the case of India, Fuller (1976) found that workers with higher levels of schooling picked up the trade informally in the firm more readily. In the case of the People's Republic of China, Min and Tsang (1990) showed that the effect of company-affiliated vocational education on work efficiency was higher among the group with 12 years of schooling than the group with a lower level of schooling. However, conflicting results were found with SENA in Colombia (Puryear 1979). The positive earnings effect of SENA was associated with years of pretraining formal education in a nonlinear way. It dropped for those who possessed education beyond primary level and then increased for those who possessed more than nine years of formal education.

There are also conflicting results on the effect of formal vocational education on schooling levels. Tannen (1991) found a positive earnings effect in Brazil for vocational education at the primary level but no effect at the secondary level. On the other hand, Grootaert (1990) found that the earnings effect of vocational education in the Côte d'Ivoire was higher for higher schooling level than for primary level, though all levels of formal vocational education had low returns.

5.4 Effects of the Demand Side

The above three generalizations consider returns of vocational education from the supply side, that is, the type of specific skill and the level of schooling that vocational education produces. In the late 1970s Levin (1977) had already emphasized the importance of paying attention to the labor market conditions in research on vocational education. Inconsistencies across countries in the returns to vocational education with respect to different fields of study and different levels of schooling may be explained with effects from the demand side of the labor market.

There are three aspects of the demand side that have been considered by the various studies reviewed here: (a) the employment or unemployment rate which reflects the situation of the general economy; (b)

self-employment, employment in the private sector, and employment in the public sector which reflects influence of the state; and (c) employment in various industries which are undergoing different degrees of development and technological change.

Though some studies use the employment rate as a criterion for the measurement of returns to or success of vocational education, most studies include the employment rate in the analysis to control for its effect on earnings. For example, Hinchliffe (1990) found in Botswana that there was no earnings advantage for the Brigade and the City and Guilds training programs over general education, if the employment rates of the graduates from the two streams were not adjusted for. Borus (1977) qualified his findings on the earnings effect of vocational education in Israel by stating that the country was operating at full employment at the time when the data were collected. Arriagazzi (1972) included an adjustment for long-term employment and other factors in his recalculation of returns to vocational education in Chile based on the original International Bank for Reconstruction and Development (IBRD) data. As a result, he found a drastic drop in the rate of returns from about 50 percent to about 20 percent.

The sector of employment is also a crucial factor. The government may set a salary schedule for the civil workers according to educational qualifications. Tannen (1991) found that employment in the public sector in Brazil resulted in a wage some 7.5 to 19.5 percent lower. But this wage compression was not evident for employees with a college education. Many studies reviewed here have tried to analyze the earnings function separately for people employed in the private wage sector, the public wage sector, and for the self-employed (e.g., Kugler and Psacharopoulos 1989, Psacharopoulos and Steier 1988, Grootaert 1990). Grootaert found that formal and informal vocational education in Côte d'Ivoire prepared people for different careers in the formal and informal labor market respectively.

Different industries in a country may undergo different stages of development and have different degrees of technological change. The type of labor demanded and the labor productivity in high-tech industry may be very different (Carnoy 1985). Puryear (1979) found for Colombia that employment in larger firms, which were assumed to have a higher degree of technological change, resulted in higher earnings. Since there was a greater percentage of the SENA group employed in these larger firms, the regression coefficient of the SENA group rose from 0.48 to 0.56 if the size of employer variable was omitted from the earnings function. In exploring the earnings advantage of vocational education in Israel, Neuman and Ziderman (1991) included a series of dummy variables to control for the effect of employment in various economic sectors and industries. They found that employment in the industry, power generation, finance, and transport sectors had a significantly positive effect on earnings. Chung (1990) also found the mean log earnings for those who had 12 to 13 years of schooling in Hong Kong to be 2.62 in the commercial field of work, 2.41 in the electronic and electrical, 2.23 in the mechanical, and 2.06 in the textiles industries.

Conflicting results on the returns to different fields of studies and different schooling levels across several countries may also be explained with reference to the stage of development of the various industries and the structural change of the general economy in the various countries, which result in a demand for workers with different types and levels of training.

5. Effect of Employment Matching and Technological Changes

Perhaps the most prominent effect of the labor market conditions on returns to vocational education is employment in a matched field of work. It is apparent that in matched employment, skills acquired are utilized in the workplace to increase productivity. The studies on matched employment by Chung (1990), Min and Tsang (1990), and Neuman and Ziderman (1991) have demonstrated this point. They found that earnings of those vocational graduates working in fields related to their training, that is, the "users," were higher than for "nonusers," or the general education group.

These few studies on matched employment in developing countries bear out the results of some recent studies in the United States (Fredland and Little 1980, Rumberger and Daymont 1984, Campbell et al. 1986). In the study by Min and Tsang (1990), great care was exercised to identify the user group. Though graduates from company-affiliated vocational schools could be assumed to work in their related field, the investigators further screened the workers with interviews and questionnaires to identify the user group. They found that the user group had greater work effort and produced a 7 percent higher work efficiency.

In the study by Neuman and Ziderman (1991), schemes of direct and wider matchings were worked out based on the two-digit occupational codes reported in the population census of Israel. The user group and the nonuser group in each field of study were identified. Dummy variables representing the users and nonusers with reference to general education graduates were introduced into the earnings function to explore the effect of matched employment. The users had an 8 to 9.6 percent earnings advantage over the general education graduates, while the nonusers enjoyed no earnings advantage at all.

In the study by Chung for Hong Kong (1990), technical graduates from various fields of study were identified, namely, the mechanical, the electronic and electrical, the textile, and the commercial fields. The earnings function for each group of graduates was analyzed separately with a series of dummy variables representing their fields of employment. It was found that graduates from the commercial and from the electronic and electrical fields tended to have higher earnings if they entered employment in their matched field. It was also found that the field of work or the demand side was more important than the field of study or the supply side in wage determination.

In another study by Chung (1992), it was determined that earnings of vocational graduates in Hong Kong were higher than those of general education graduates by 6.6 percent in 1976 and 11 percent in 1981. However, when the dummy variable representing vocational education was broken down into a series of dummy variables representing the various fields of study, the earnings advantage remained significant only for the commercial and the electronic and electrical fields, and disappeared for the mechanical and the textiles fields. The study also demonstrated that the percentage of matched employment was 40 percent for the electronic and electrical field, 69 percent for the commercial field, 22 percent for the mechanical field, and 15 percent for the textiles field. The two fields of study that produced significant earnings advantage are related to the growing industries of Hong Kong at the time. That is, the earnings advantage of the vocational graduates is not only affected by employment in a matched field but also by whether the field of study is related to a growth industry or not. It would appear that vocational education in a field related to an industry which is expanding and thus undergoing rapid technological changes would increase the probability of its graduates being employed in a matched work field and increase their earnings.

The finding that matched employment yields higher returns is also consistent with the finding that firm-based training programs are particularly effective. Min and Tsang (1990) found that more than 90 percent of graduates of the company-affiliated vocational schools of the Beijing General Auto Industry Company were assigned jobs related to their training. Puryear (1979) also observed that sponsorship of the SENA apprenticeship by modern sector firms resulted in the allocation of the graduates to these firms. That is, there is a sort of "built-in" mechanism by which firm-based training programs place nearly all of their graduates in matched employment.

7. New Challenges for Vocational Education

It is clear to researchers in the field of the economics of education that there is no simple answer to the question of returns to vocational education. The question has to be expanded to ask which mode of delivery, at what level, for which fields of study, and, above all, under what labor market conditions; or, in the case of developing countries, at what stage of economic development? Most of these questions have to be approached from the demand side as well as the supply side of the labor market.

From the demand side, technological changes in the various industries would have great effects on the productivity of their workers, especially for those with training matched to the requirements of the work. Countries undergoing different stages of economic development would demand workers with different types and levels of education, and would most probably benefit from vocational education in different fields at different schooling levels. How can programs of vocational education be designed that would match the requirements of work, particularly in industries experiencing high technological change? How can one guarantee that vocational graduates will work in a field matched to their training? What entry schooling level to firm-based training programs is most beneficial, and for what industry? These questions will become new challenges in planning further development of vocational education. However, the supply of vocational education alone seems to be incapable of answering all these questions. Most answers have to be found in the operation both of the labor market and of society at large.

Finally, this entry has only addressed that part of the returns to vocational education which relates to efficiency. There is also the equity effect and the social integration effect of education to be explored. For example, Ziderman (1989) has pointed out that vocational education in Israel also serves the purpose of integrating new immigrants into the labor market. Many studies have demonstrated that vocational students usually come from lower socioeconomic status families (Puryear 1979, Borus 1977, Ziderman 1989). If vocational education is heavily subsidized and can finally generate higher earnings for its graduates, the equalizing effect of such education is obvious. However, this equalizing effect does not depend totally on the supply of vocational education. Again, the employment conditions and the wage structure in the labor market play a major role.

See also: Vocational Education and Productivity; Education and Earnings

References

Arriagazzi L 1972 Chile: evaluating the expansion of a vocational training programme. In: Coombs P H, Hallak J (eds.) 1972 *Educational Cost Analysis in Action: Case Studies for Planners*, Vol.1. UNESCO, IIEP, Paris
Bellew R, Moock P 1990 Vocational and technical education in Peru. *Econ. Educ. Rev.* 9(4): 365–75
Bishop J 1989 Occupational training in high school: When does it pay off? *Econ. Educ. Rev.* 8(1): 1–15
Blaug M 1976 The rate of return on investment in education

in Thailand. *Journal of Development Studies* 12(2): 270–84
Borus M E 1977 A cost-effectiveness comparison of vocational training for youth in developing countries: A case study of 4 training modes in Israel. *Comp. Educ. Rev.* 21(1): 1–13
Campbell P B, Basinger K S, Dauner M B 1986 Outcomes of vocational education for women, minorities, the handicapped, and the poor. The National Center for Research in Vocational Education, Ohio State University, Columbus, Ohio (mimeo)
Carnoy M 1985 High technology and international labour markets. *Int. Lab. Rev.* 124(6): 643–59
Chung Y P 1990 Educated mis-employment in Hong Kong: Earnings effects of employment in unmatched fields of work. *Econ. Educ. Rev.* 9(4): 343–50
Chung Y P 1992 Economic returns to vocational and technical education in Hong Kong. In: Chung Y P, Wong Y C (eds.) 1992 *The Economics and Finance of Education in Hong Kong*. The Chinese University Press, Hong Kong
Cohen S I 1985 A cost-benefit analysis of industrial training. *Econ. Educ. Rev.* 4(4): 327–39
Dougherty C 1989 *The Cost-Effectiveness of National Training Systems in Developing Countries*. World Bank PHREE Working Paper No. WPS171, World Bank, Washington, DC
Foster P 1965 The vocational school fallacy in development planning. In: Anderson C A, Bowman M J (eds.) 1965 *Education and Economic Development*. Aldine, Chicago, Illinois
Foster P 1987 Technical/ vocational education in the less developed countries. *Int. J. Educ. Dev.* 7(2): 137–39
Fredland J E, Little R D 1980 Long-term returns to vocational training: Evidence from military sources. *J. Hum. Resources* 15(1): 49–66
Fuller W P 1976 More evidence supporting the demise of pre-employment vocational trade training: A case study of a factory in India. *Comp. Educ. Rev.* 20(1): 30–39
Godfrey M 1977 Education, productivity and training: A Kenyan case-study. *Comp. Educ. Rev.* 21(1): 29–36
Grootaert C 1990 Returns to formal and informal vocational education in Côte d'Ivoire: the role of the structure of the labor market. *Econ. Educ. Rev.* 9(4): 309–19
Haddad W D, Carnoy M, Rinaldi R 1990 *Education and Development: Evidence for New Priorities*. World Bank Discussion Paper No. 95, World Bank, Washington, DC
Hinchliffe K 1990 The returns to vocational training in Botswana—research note. *Econ. Educ. Rev.* 9(4): 401–04
Jimenez E, Kugler B 1987 The earnings impact of training duration in a developing country. An Ordered Probit Selection Model of Colombia's *Servicio Nacional de Aprendizaje* (SENA). *J. Hum. Resources* 22: 228–47
Kugler B, Psacharopoulos G 1989 Earnings and education in Argentina: An analysis of the 1985 Buenos Aires household survey. *Econ. Educ. Rev.* 8(4): 353–65
Levin H M 1977 Vocational education and the labor market: Some research directions. In: The Planning Papers for the Vocational Study, Vol. 2. National Institute of Education, Washington (mimeo)
Metcalf D H 1985 *The Economics of Vocational Training: Past Evidence and Future Considerations*. World Bank Staff Working Paper No. 713. World Bank, Washington, DC

Middleton J 1988 Changing patterns in World Bank investments in vocational education and training: Implications for secondary vocational schools. *Int. J. Educ. Dev.* 8(3): 213–25

Min W, Tsang M C 1990 Vocational education and productivity: A case study of the Beijing General Auto Industry Company. *Econ. Educ. Rev.* 9(4): 351–64

Neuman S, Ziderman A 1991 Vocational schooling, occupational matching, and labor market earnings in Israel. *J. Hum. Resources* 26(2): 256–81

Psacharopoulos G 1991 Vocational education theory, VOCED 101: Including hints for 'vocational planners'. *Int. J. Educ. Dev.* 11(3): 193–99

Psacharopoulos G, Steier F 1988 Education and the labor market in Venezuela, 1975–1984. *Econ. Educ. Rev.* 7(3): 321–32

Psacharopoulos G, Zabalza A 1984 The effect of diversified schools on employment status and earnings in Colombia. *Econ. Educ. Rev.* 3(4): 315–31

Puryear J M 1979 Vocational training and earnings in Colombia: Does a SENA effect exist? *Comp. Educ. Rev.* 23(2): 283–92

Rumberger R W, Daymont T 1984 The economic value of academic and vocational training acquired in high school. In: Borus M E (ed.) 1984 *Youth and the Labor Market: Analysis of the National Longitudinal Survey.* W E Upjohn Institute of Employment Research, Kalamazoo, Michigan

Tannen M B 1991 New estimates of the returns to schooling in Brazil. *Econ. Educ. Rev.* 10(2): 123–35

Tsang M 1989 The costs of vocational training. The World Bank, Washington, DC (mimeo)

Ziderman A 1989 Training alternatives for youth: Results from longitudinal data. *Comp. Educ. Rev.* 33(2): 243–55

Further Reading

Arriagada A 1990 Labor market outcomes of non-formal training for male and female workers in Peru. *Econ. Educ. Rev.* 9(4): 331–42

Lauglo J, Närman A 1986 Diversified secondary education in Kenya: The status of practical subjects and their uses after school. Paper presented at the Vocationalising Education Conference, London 1986. University of London Institute of Education (mimeo)

Neuman S, Ziderman A 1989 Vocational secondary school can be more cost-effective than academic schools: The case of Israel. *Comp. Educ.* 25(2): 151–63

Economics of Apprenticeship

S. F. Hamilton and R. Glover

Apprenticeship is a means of teaching the knowledge and skills required in a recognized trade or occupation primarily by hands-on, work-based methods. Learning occurs as the apprentice observes, assists, and is taught by one or more skilled workers, assuming responsibility for progressively more challenging tasks until all the necessary skills are mastered. In many societies, apprenticeship is also a means of socializing young people to adulthood.

The *practice* of apprenticeship may be usefully distinguished from the *institution*. Learning by watching, helping, doing under supervision, and then doing independently is so natural and universal that the term "apprenticeship" may be properly used to describe a wide range of formal and informal learning arrangements, from the training of indigenous healers in simple societies (Jordan 1989) to training scientists.

In modern industrial societies, the institution of apprenticeship has some features that are not found in traditional societies. Although the workplace is the principal location for learning, related classroom instruction is part of the curriculum. Standards for the completion of apprenticeship are explicitly stated and apprentices who meet them are awarded certificates attesting to their achievements. A governance structure involving government, organized labor, and employers is rooted in law. The relationship between apprentices and their employer/trainers is formalized in a contract, which specifies apprentices' compensation and the duration or scope of training.

This entry addresses the institution of apprenticeship as a formal system that promotes and controls teaching and learning of occupational competence in workplaces. It discusses apprenticeship in two countries, the United States and Germany. In many respects, apprenticeship in the United States and Germany represent polar cases. Examining the extremes may help to clarify the possibilities and the issues that lie between. The United Kingdom and Canada have apprenticeship systems that are in many ways akin to that of the United States. Similarly, Austria, Switzerland, and Denmark have systems much like Germany's, as do several Eastern European countries (Adamski and Grootings 1989).

The apprenticeship system in the United States enrolls a small number of adults and very few youths. In Germany, the majority of older teenagers are apprentices. Apprentices in the United States gain applied academic knowledge and skills by means of "related instruction," usually in the form of evening classes. German apprenticeship is part of the educational system and is known as the "dual system" because instruction takes place both in the workplace and in the classroom. Apprenticeship programs in the United States are sponsored by labor unions or employers and approved by the federal or state department of labor. Germany has a complex collaborative system for involving employers, labor, and government in designing and overseeing apprenticeship.

The fundamental economic questions about the institution of apprenticeship can be stated in terms of its costs and benefits to employers, to apprentices, and to the society in which it is found, including government and the school system. After addressing these questions as they affect each country, the discussion turns to the same questions as they apply to current proposals that the United States adapt some elements of German apprenticeship.

1. Apprenticeship in the United States

American apprenticeship operates primarily as a training program for young adults. Unlike other nations, where apprenticeship is a program for teenage youths, in the United States and Canada the average starting apprentice is in his or her late 20s. In the United States, apprenticeship is best established in the unionized sector of commercial–industrial construction and in the maintenance departments of major manufacturers. Apprenticeship is not only an important source of training in these two industrial sectors, it is also highly concentrated there so that the two sectors account for nearly three-fourths of the roughly 250,000 registered civilian apprentices in the United States.

1.1 Costs and Benefits to Employers

Large firms that train apprentices primarily for skilled maintenance (e.g., plumbers, electricians, millwrights) expect to recoup their investment in training apprentices by employing those who successfully complete their training. The incentives for contractors who participate in union-sponsored apprenticeship programs are different. One is that their collective bargaining agreements with unions specify that they will train apprentices. A second is that they are allowed to pay apprentices lower wages than journeyworkers.

1.2 Costs and Benefits to Apprentices

There is good evidence that apprenticeship training pays off for workers who undertake it. Studies undertaken in the 1970s using employment and earnings data in health and welfare records of journeyworkers in union building trades have documented that individuals who completed apprenticeship worked more regularly and earned more than journeyworkers trained in other ways (Collins 1973, Marshall et al. 1975). Likewise, studies have demonstrated that individuals who have been trained in apprenticeships tend to advance to supervisory status and work more often in supervisory positions (Marshall et al. 1975). Subsequent research using longitudinal databases have confirmed

the association of apprenticeship with more stable employment and higher earnings (Cook et al. 1989, Hills 1982, Leigh 1989).

1.3 Costs and Benefits to Society

The presence of a body of skilled workers clearly benefits society, though that benefit is difficult to calculate. It is most obviously beneficial in productive work performed, but another even less tangible benefit derives from the sense of identity and social status that advanced work skills can give. Because little public money is invested in apprenticeships in the United States, the costs to society are low, especially as compared with school-based training in public community colleges or postsecondary vocational–technical institutes. The greatest public investment in apprenticeship is for veteran's benefits. Next in order of magnitude comes the cost of subsidizing related instruction. Administration of apprenticeship is the smallest public cost. Altogether, these costs totaled no more than a nationwide average of US $400 per apprentice during 1990. Hence, the cumulative total of public monies invested over a 4-year period amounts to no more than approximately US $1,600. At a marginal federal income tax rate of 28 percent, apprenticeship training need only boost earnings by US $1,429 per year to yield a return to the government equal to the public funds invested. Available studies show that effects of apprenticeship on earnings exceed this amount.

2. Apprenticeship in Germany

Apprenticeship is the predominant form of upper secondary education in Germany. Half to two-thirds of the youth population between the ages of 16 and 18 is enrolled. Apprentices constitute about 7 percent of the labor force, and some 370 occupations have apprenticeship programs. They cover a wide range of skill levels and occupations, for example, waiter, retail sales clerk, office helper, barber, dental office assistant, bricklayer, precision mechanic, and electronics technician. Apprentices also train for a multitude of middle-level office occupations such as secretary, bookkeeper, personnel officer, and inventory control specialist.

A typical apprenticeship lasts three years. On-the-job training is interpersed with school attendance, usually in a ratio of four days at work to one day at school every week. In addition to general academic subjects, apprentices study academic subjects in relation to their occupation and take practical shop or laboratory courses at school.

Both school instruction and on-the-job training follow regulations and curricula set out for the specific occupation by a national body, the *Bundesinstitut für Berufsbildung* (BIBB), which operates on the basis of consensus among employers, organized labor, federal and state (*Land*) governments. Apprentices demonstrate their mastery of the specified knowledge and skills by passing examinations halfway through and at the end of their training period. The examinations are devised and administered by the chamber responsible for the occupation. (All German employers are required by law to belong to a chamber.) Completing the requirements and passing the qualifying examination certifies that a person is prepared to enter the occupation at the level of a skilled worker.

Employment in many apprenticeable occupations is effectively limited to those holding apprenticeship completion certificates. A certified employee is legally entitled to all the rights and benefits granted to her or his occupation in collective bargaining agreements, establishing a floor beneath wages and benefits. Possession of the skilled worker's certificate confers social status as well. It is a formal recognition that its bearer has attained adulthood. To be a skilled worker is to hold a respectable station in society. Unskilled workers are socially marginal.

The German states pay for apprentices' schooling. Employers pay apprentices' wages and the costs of their on-the-job training. Apprentices' earnings are rather low, usually less than half of what skilled workers earn in the same occupation. The cost of training by employers cannot be calculated precisely, since it is too embedded in production and the costs vary too widely from one employer to another. Moreover, the question of employers' net costs, after apprentices' productive work has been subtracted, is a subject of controversy between organized labor and employers.

2.1 Costs and Benefits to Employers

German employers' costs can best be considered by distinguishing larger from smaller firms. In general, firms with 20 or more employees invest substantial sums in apprentice training. The largest and best spend as much as US $10–15,000 per year for each apprentice. These firms employ full-time trainers and provide on-site classrooms, shops, and laboratories. Apprentices are placed in a coherent sequence of worksites according to their learning needs and career interests. They have access to up-to-date equipment and well-qualified coaches. Large firms nearly always exceed official training requirements, providing their apprentices with far more than is needed to pass the qualifying examinations.

Firms employing fewer than 20 workers, which train one-third of apprentices, present a different picture. As they are unable to dedicate staff or space exclusively to instruction, and because they lack the diversity of worksites to provide a varied set of experiences, they tend to offer less thorough training. They also tend to rely on apprentices as inexpensive helpers, assigning them to tasks on the basis of production needs rather than instructional principles.

Contrasting larger with smaller firms highlights different sets of economic incentives for training apprentices. In the worst cases, which both unions and the employers' chambers try to eliminate, apprenticeship is exploitative. Young people work for low wages, perform routine tasks, and learn only what they can pick up on their own or during slack times. Employers benefit because they pay less for the performance of necessary tasks than they would in an open labor market and incur no training costs.

The economic issues surrounding the expensive and high quality training that the best firms provide are both more salutary and more interesting. Why would a business enterprise spend thousands of dollars to train young people who have no formal obligation to work for them? A British economist, Soskice (in press), has responded to this question by asking a series of related questions and answering them persuasively.

First, why do German firms seek highly skilled workers? The answer, Soskice proposes, is that leading German firms have positioned themselves in world markets as providers of high-quality goods and services that are customized, modified, and varied. Producing such goods and services requires a highly skilled workforce, which is assured by means of apprenticeship training. Corporations do not pay training costs by lowering profits. Rather, consumers ultimately absorb them. The choice of a profitable market niche makes this possible.

Second, why do German firms train their own workers rather than "poaching" them from other firms? One reason, according to Soskice, is that nationwide collective bargaining agreements covering occupational groups reduce employers' ability to buy off employees by offering higher wages. Another is that the workers who leave their training firm are likely to be the less skilled and less productive ones, leaving the poaching employer with less desirable workers. Another answer is that the net cost of training apprentices is susbtantially reduced by apprentices' willingness to work for low wages and by the firm's access to technical assistance from public bodies and associations.

2.2 Costs and Benefits to Apprentices

In return for their willingness to work at low wages, German apprentices gain access to jobs that pay well, are secure, and offer career ladders. A German sociologist, Lempert (1982), has concluded that apprenticeship provides a solid foundation for lifelong employment and career mobility. Examining the careers of 1,320 skilled workers in three occupations, Lempert reported that nearly all found their first full-time jobs in their training occupation and that two-thirds remained in jobs where they used the skills they had learned as apprentices. Whereas only about 5 percent lost status by shifting into unskilled jobs, about one-third gained status by becoming white-collar workers, often after further education.

2.3 Costs and Benefits to Society

An educational system both mirrors and shapes its society. The German educational system's strong emphasis on vocational training and its reliance upon work experience reflect German society's respect for skilled labor and for quality, which, in turn, support an export-driven economy.

The German state governments pay the costs of apprentices' schooling. Government subsidies are provided to some firms for training apprentices who would otherwise not be placed, such as those with physical and learning disabilities. The government also subsidizes the creation of multifirm training centers to improve the quality of instruction for apprentices in small firms. However, the greatest portion of the cost of apprenticeship is borne by employers (in the public and nonprofit sectors as well as the private sector). Enrolling a larger proportion of the youth population in full-time schools would clearly require much higher public expenditures. Hence, private employers are, in effect, directly subsidizing the society's cost for educating its youth.

German apprenticeship has another set of societal benefits. In addition to constituting a significant part of the educational system, apprenticeship prepares youth for adulthood. The presence of a recognized pathway from adolescence into adulthood via a strong social institution makes that transition less troubled in Germany than it is in the United States (Hamilton 1990).

A societal cost associated with apprenticeship is the rigidity it fosters in occupational roles and social status. This rigidity is currently under attack simultaneously from those who would democratize German society and those who would update vocational training to meet the demands of workplaces being transformed by new technology and heightened international competition. These forces have already succeeded in loosening the system, for example, by consolidating 42 metalworking occupations into six and by making more full-time school options available to apprentices.

Apprenticeship lays great stress on discipline, thereby potentially encouraging excessive deference to authority and unduly restricting the spontaneity and creativity of youth. Organized labor argues that corporations should not be granted as much power as they now have to shape the attitudes and behavior, particularly the political ideology of young people. However, a series of studies of apprentices' political beliefs failed to disclose a trend toward passivity attributable to employer influence (Hamilton 1987).

3. Proposals for Youth Apprenticeship in the United States

The idea that a form of "youth apprenticeship" should be created in the United States gained adherents at the beginning of the 1990s (Hamilton 1990, Lerman and Pouncy 1990, Nothdurft 1990). The long-term prospects of this idea are by no means clear, but it deserves attention here under the same headings that have been used in describing apprenticeship as it now exists in Germany and the United States.

3.1 Costs and Benefits to Employers

The question that is both most critical to the future of the nascent youth apprenticeship movement, and most difficult to answer, is whether and at what scale employers will support it. Without substantial and enduring support from many employers, the idea will simply disappear. One way in which the idea could become viable is as a solution to predicted shortages of highly skilled workers at the technician level in the 1990s. In this scenario, youth apprenticeship would become an important educational option for a significant proportion of high-school educated American youth, probably drawn from populations that would otherwise have attended 2-year technical and community colleges without also enrolling in apprenticeship.

A second scenario in which youth apprenticeship would thrive is the one outlined in the report *America's Choice: High Skills or Low Wages?* from the Commission on the Skills of the American Workforce. The report argued that in order to remain prosperous the United States must rapidly adopt the production and human resource strategy of Germany, Japan, and most other leading industrial powers, namely emphasizing the production of goods and services to which workers add high value. Such goods and services are more customized, produced in shorter runs, and require more judgment and skill from workers. If decision makers at many levels of business, government, and education in the United States choose to follow this strategy, then youth apprenticeship will be essential because it can educate those young people who do not learn well in conventional schools. However, United States employers lack the German tradition of training production-line workers, or cooperating among themselves and with organized labor for this purpose, and they lack the institutional support for apprenticeship that has evolved in Germany.

3.2 Costs and Benefits to Apprentices

For American youth who would be apprentices the costs are identical to those paid by German apprentices: chiefly forgone earnings. Until a system is established and functioning, the benefits are much less certain. However, those costs can be significantly reduced by linking apprenticeship to higher education rather than separating the two. So long as apprentices continue their education through two years of community college, as many proposals specify, then even if they are unable to recoup their investment immediately by taking well-paid and secure jobs in their area of training, they will have an educational credential with immediate value in the labor market and credit toward a bachelor's degree.

.3 Costs and Benefits to Society

There are two potential levels of societal cost in the creation of a youth apprenticeship system. If the United States follows the German model and expects employers to assume most direct training costs, then the greatest public costs will be in underwriting the research and development needed to design and implement a youth apprenticeship system and in creating and maintaining an institutional base for such a system. If, in contrast, government subsidies are used to encourage employers to train apprentices, the public costs would be enormous.

Without knowing more about the shape of a youth apprenticeship system in the United States, it is impossible to estimate those costs. Whatever the amount, a substantial portion must surely come from redirecting resources currently devoted to less effective approaches and consolidating the array of piecemeal programs currently dealing with related issues. Using rather than duplicating the institutions already devoted to vocational education and job training would contain society's costs.

The potential benefits include a well-educated workforce to increase the nation's prosperity and reduced alienation and disruptive behavior by youth, which would increase domestic peace and tranquility.

References

Adamski W, Grootings P (eds.) 1989 *Youth, Education and Work in Europe*. Routledge, London

Collins M F 1973 Assessing the benefit of apprenticeship training in construction: A case study of operating engineers apprentices and non-apprentices. International Union of Operating Engineers, Washington, DC (mimeo)

Commission on the Skills of the American Workforce 1990 *America's Choice: High Skills or Low Wages? The Report of the Commission on the Skills of the American Workforce*. National Center on Education and the Economy, Rochester, New York

Cook R F et al. 1989 *Analysis of Apprenticeship Training from the National Longitudinal Study of the High School Class of 1972*. Report prepared for the Bureau of Apprenticeship and Training, US Department of Labor and the National Training Program of the International Union of Operating Engineers, Westat Inc, Rockville, Maryland. Summarized in: Cook R F, Cairnes K L 1990 *The Impact of Participation in Apprenticeship: Proceedings of the Forty-Second Annual Meeting of the Industrial Relations Research Association*, December 1989, Atlanta, Georgia. Industrial Relations Research Association, Madison, Wisconsin

Hamilton S F 1987 Work and maturity: Occupational socialization of non-college youth in the United States and West Germany. In: Corwin R G (ed.) 1987 *Research in the Sociology of Education and Socialization 7*. JAI Press, Greenwich, Connecticut

Hamilton S F 1990 *Apprenticeship for Adulthood: Preparing Youth for the Future*. Free Press, New York

Hills S N 1982 How craftsmen learn their skills: A longitudinal analysis. In: Taylor R E, Rosen H, Pratzner F C 1982 (eds.) *Job Training for Youth*. National Center for Research in Vocational Education, The Ohio State University, Columbus, Ohio

Jordan B 1989 Cosmopolitical obstetrics: Some insights from the training of traditional midwives. *Social Science Medicine* 28 (9):925–44

Leigh D E 1989 *What Kinds of Training "Works" for Noncollege Bound Youth?* Report prepared for the US General Accounting Office, Washington, DC

Lempert W 1982 Ausbildung zum Facharbeiter: Startbahn oder Parkplatz, Aufzug oder Abweg? Max-Planck-Institut für Bildungsforschung, Berlin (mimeo)

Lerman R I, Pouncy H 1990 *Why America Should Develop a Youth Apprenticeship System. Progressive Policy Report*, No. 5 (March). The Progressive Policy Institute, Washington, DC

Marshall R, Franklin W S, Glover R W 1975 *Training and Entry into Union Construction*. Manpower R & D Monograph No. 39, US Department of Labor, Manpower Administration. US Government Printing Office, Washington, DC

Nothdurft W E (Jobs for the Future) 1990 *Youth Apprenticeship, American Style: A Strategy for Expanding School and Career Opportunities*, (Conference report December 7 1990, Washington DC). The Consortium on Youth Apprenticeship, Washington, DC

Soskice D in press The German training system: Reconciling markets and institutions. In: Lynch L (ed.) in press *Training and the Private Sector: International Comparisons*. University of Chicago Press, Chicago

Economics of Nonformal Training

A.-M. Arriagada and P. L. Wong

Occupational training outside of school has long been seen as an economically efficient alternative to more formal schooling, either academic or vocational (Coombs and Ahmed 1974, Papagiannis 1977). Transferring job-related skills to individuals, it has been argued, enhances both the probability of finding a job and of earning higher income once on the job. Logically, employers value such skills, are more likely to hire people who acquire them, and are willing to pay such employees more because occupational training increases productivity. Occupational training in a nonschool setting is also generally much less expensive than formal schooling and therefore may be characterized by higher cost-effectiveness or benefit-cost ratios (see *Cost-effectiveness Analysis; Cost–Benefit Analysis*).

1. Studies in Developing and Developed Countries

From an economic standpoint, then, the value of occupational training can be assessed in terms of its costs and the impact it has either on individuals' employment and income or in terms of other goals, such as skills or knowledge acquired. Early attempts at such assessments in developing countries were not particularly convincing in arguing for high benefits relative to costs (Coombs and Ahmed 1974).

For example, Coombs and Ahmed show that in Nigeria trainees took specialized courses 10 hours per week for a total of 3 years as an alternative to formal vocational education in order to pass a government trade certificate exam. About 30 percent were able to achieve the certificate through the short course, at a cost per successful student of about one-sixth the formal schooling cost. They conclude that the specialized courses are more cost-effective than traditional vocational education. Their evaluation of other training programs and of rural extension services yield more mixed results, primarily because the benefits of such programs are difficult to measure. Their evaluation suggests that costs of occupational training are generally much lower than those of formal education. But data on outcomes were difficult to obtain, making impossible any definitive comparison with traditional forms of acquiring job-related knowledge.

The impact on workers' incomes of occupational training programs relative to costs of training has been successfully evaluated with cost–benefit analysis. Puryear (1977) estimated rates of return to one of the best-known training programs in Latin America: Servicio Nacional de Aprendizaje (SENA) in Colombia. In SENA, already employed workers are sent by their firms for skills upgrading in industry-supported, government-run, short-term vocational training. Puryear found the payoff to be relatively high. However, he also found that such programs were successful because firms were committed to taking the workers back into their old jobs or better ones. Workers were sent to learn skills needed by the firms.

Later analysis of SENA's in-service training (Jimenez and Kugler 1987) indicates a positive effect of such training on the earnings of males already in wage employment and its complementarity with investments in other forms of human capital such as schooling and in-job experience.

Fuller (1970) found similar results in two electrical machinery firms in Bangalore, India. He used supervisors' ratings as a proxy for productivity and estimated the relation of workers' ratings to formal education, out-of-plant training courses, and in-plant training.

Out-of-plant short training courses had the largest payoff in terms of higher ratings. He concluded that such courses had a significantly higher benefit–cost ratio than formal education.

In the United States, early studies of occupational training for low-income, unemployed urban youth in the 1960s suggested very poor results (Vietorisz and Harrison 1970). These results were used to argue for the existence of segmented labor markets (see *Segmented Labor Markets and Education*). A number of studies have evaluated the impact on earnings of the Comprehensive Employment and Training Act (CETA) begun in 1973. Four program activities were offered by CETA: subsidized jobs in the public sector (PSE) on-the-job training (OJT), in which private employers were reimbursed for training costs in subsidized jobs, classroom training (CT), and work experience (WE). A review of results of the various studies matching follow-ups of CETA participants with control groups from census data suggests that PSE and OJT had the greatest impact on annual earnings, with estimates exceeding \$1,500 for some demographic groups (Barnow 1987). The estimates for CT were generally lower than for PSE or OJT, but there was a very broad range of estimated impacts. The most disadvantaged CETA participants were generally provided with WE, and most studies found a very small or negative impact from WE programs. In all these programs, there was substantial variation in benefits for different gender/ethnic groups, with Black women making significantly larger gains than white men.

Bloom (1987) confirmed the gender differences in gains from CETA programs. Unlike Barnow, he only looked at adult participants with a number of years of work experience. He measured annual earnings of the demographic comparison group and of the 1975 and 1976 CETA participant groups from 1964 to 1978 by gender. The results showed that for female participants, earnings dipped in 1975, then rose significantly to levels above the comparison nonparticipant group. For males, the dip in earnings also occurred, but their earnings only increased back to approximately their original trend line. Bloom concludes that CETA programs had a large impact on female earnings but not on male earnings. This seemed to be equally true for CT, OJT, and WE.

These studies in developing and developed countries suggest that occupational training programs have varied effects by gender, ethnic group, and type of program. Although they are relatively low cost, many of them also have minor impact on trainees' earnings capacity and employment possibilities. The studies also show that, apart from the CETA evaluations undertaken in the United States, definitive studies of occupational training are rare. Even the CETA evaluations focused primarily on earnings, not on increased employment probabilities—a variable that is important both in low-income countries and in low-income areas of developed countries.

2. An Assessment of Occupation Training in Peru

A study in Peru took account of both earnings and employment as dependent variables in assessing the impact of occupational training (Arriagada 1990). Since the 1960s successive Peruvian governments have supported three types of nonformal training programs: (a) job-based training programs—both on-the-job and off-the-job—provided by autonomous sectoral training institutions attached to public agencies; (b) postsecondary level programs made available through public and private technical institutes and universities, and through institutions managed by entrepreneurial or professional associations; and (c) proprietary institutions or private for-profit programs (*academes*). Government investment in these programs hinges on the presumption that occupational training will enhance both new and already employed workers' productivity and therefore increase their earnings. Using data from the Peruvian Living Standards Survey (PLSS), this study examined the effect of training on the employment and earnings of workers in urban areas in Peru, analyzing both by gender and by employment sector (i.e., public, private, self-employed).

Several patterns are indicated by the basic demographic data. Regardless of gender, individuals who pursued training were younger, possessed more education, and received higher wages than those who did not. Training was mostly sought by those with secondary schooling or more, which may suggest that skills imparted in secondary schooling did not adequately match those demanded by the labor market, where training was perceived as a complement to formal education. Conversely, those with less than secondary education (over 50 percent of the urban labor force in Peru) did not acquire job skills through the training system. The combination of these two patterns may indicate that exposure to secondary schooling predisposes individuals to future investment in education, which may take the form of job training (as in this case) or higher education. Finally, among urban males, job-based programs have the highest demand, and among urban females proprietary institutions (*academes*) have the highest demand.

In estimating the effect of training on employment choices, an employment choice model was used to give the probabilities of employment in the private and public wage sectors or in self-employment, relative to being elsewhere (i.e., not working, an unpaid family worker, or a farmer). In estimating the effect of training on earnings, the traditional human capital model was followed (Becker 1964, Mincer 1974). Special consideration was made in the calculations to account for selectivity bias that may have been caused by the fact that neither participation in the training programs nor women's participation in the labor force are random (Arriagada 1990).

In analyzing the data, a special specification that accounts for family characteristics was used for women, under the assumption that a woman works if offered a wage higher than her asking (reservation) wage. A woman's offered wage depends primarily on personal attributes such as age, formal schooling, job experience, and training, but her asking wage varies according to her marital status. Thus, a single woman's asking wage depends largely on personal characteristics whereas a married woman's asking wage is influenced by the needs of her family for additional income relative to the costs associated with her obtaining that additional income. Therefore, for married women, household consumption variables were included to proxy these costs (the number and ages of children, the composition of the household, husband's income, annual nonlabor income and remittances received by the family).

The results indicate that job training has no impact on a man's probability of employment in the private or self-employed sectors, but it does have a positive impact on his probability of working in the public sector. This can be explained by the lack of competitiveness and the role of credentials in the hiring processes of the public sector in Peru, in particular, and in developing countries, in general. For women, the data indicate that job training increases employment probabilities by 10 percent in the private sector, by 2 percent in the public sector, and by 5 percent in nonwage employment. This pattern suggests that for men, who have few barriers to labor market entry, one goal of pursuing job training may be career development rather than actually obtaining a job.

For women, on the other hand, it appears that the motivation to participate in training courses stems from the opportunities that such training might provide for actual entry into the labor market. The training provided may improve a woman's chances for employment by providing necessary skills, expanding her capacity to evaluate choices and increasing her self-confidence and willingness to engage in economic opportunities. Similarly, training may provide private sector employers with important indicators in the hiring process. These explanations would be consistent with prior research in developing countries showing that training most significantly affects women's employment status (Welch 1970, Barnow 1987, Bloom and McLaughlin 1982, Bassi et al. 1984, Ashenfelter 1978, Kiefer 1979).

To estimate the effect of training on earnings, the study employed the human capital model. For both men and women, the proxies used for formal education were three splines (i.e., those variables where the data are split into distinct subsets and separate estimates generated for each subset) for years of schooling at primary, secondary, and postsecondary levels, and type of school last attended (public or private). Labor market experience was measured by tenure in the current job (years), the usual measure of years of potential work for males, and age for females.

187

The standard model was also expanded to include several personal, family background factors, and place of residence. For self-employed individuals, the total capital of the business, the number of hired workers, and the number of family workers are also included. Finally, in designing the wage equation for women in private sector paid employment, consideration was paid to two workplace characteristics likely to affect women's wages: unionization and access to social security.

The results indicated that hourly wage rates of males in the private sector were positively and significantly affected by job-training programs. After controlling for the effects of schooling, work experience, background and the probability of entering training courses, wage increases due to training were found to be about 13 percent, on average. Training received through job-based programs raised wage rates more than 10 percent and training received in postsecondary training programs increased wage rates of salaried males by over 20 percent. In contrast, training sponsored by *academes* did not significantly affect wage rates for males.

The data also revealed that job training has no significant effect on the hourly wage rates of women in salaried employment. This difference can be interpreted in several ways. First, because of gender stratification in the labor market, men and women are employed in different sectors and therefore, are likely to train for different occupations and in different institutions. For example, most evaluation studies of institutional training programs show the greatest earnings gains for in-service industrial training in blue collar and supervisory level jobs, where few Peruvian women are employed (Employment and Immigration Canada 1982, Jimenez and Kugler 1987). Also, Peruvian women typically pursue training in proprietary institutions while Peruvian men attend occupation-based programs and technical institutes. Similarly, men tend to be employed in industries where hourly wage rates are higher and opportunities for career advancement are greater. It has proved difficult to reduce wage differentials and career profiles because of rising female labor force participation and institutional discrimination, respectively. Second, it is expected that increases in wage rates would to some extent be tied to increased labor productivity resulting from new skills learned in the training program.

It may be that the different effect of training on wage rates can be explained by the different types of training offered by each program. Women may be prevented by institutional factors from participating in the most successful training programs. Another explanation may be simply that some training programs are more convenient for women than for men, for reasons such as proximity to home, proximity to work and proximity to children's school (Coombs and Ahmed 1974). However, as the PLSS did not evaluate either the quality of the training programs or the equality of

access to them, it is not possible to make these distinctions. In addition, as mentioned above, the effects of training on women's wage rates may be indiscernible because of low rates of female participation in the labor force. In this situation, the effects of training would be more significant on labor market entry than on wage rates.

Finally, research in developed countries has shown that women who train for traditionally male occupations still do not earn more in those occupations than those women who train for traditionally female occupations (Strober 1982, Streeker-Seeborg et al. 1984). This suggests that there is discrimination in the labor market that negatively affects women's occupational attainment. Women's awareness of this discrimination may discourage their pursuit of training programs in these fields (Bergmann and Adelman 1973).

In discussing the results for the self-employed, several caveats are required. The self-employed only reported the nominal value of the "total earnings" obtained from the business. Thus, it is not clear whether "business income" reflects income earned by that individual or by all individuals in the firm. Also, reported income may be inaccurate because family businesses tend not to keep detailed accounting records; they often carry out a high proportion of nonmonetary transactions; and the household often consumes a significant amount of the goods and services produced by the enterprise. The specification of the wage equation for the self-employed requires additional caveats. First, returns to physical capital and assets should be separated from returns to labor inputs, and returns from other labor inputs should be separated from returns to the individual entrepreneur's human capital. Second, the wage equation for the self-employed should account for managerial ability and risk taking.

Despite the careful consideration of the factors noted above, the study reveals no effect of job training on self-employed earnings. A comparison across employment groups shows significant differences in the earnings structure of wage and self-employment activities, in the role of schooling in earnings determination, in the age–earnings profiles of the workers in each sector, and in the impact of job training on hourly earnings. There may be several explanations for this finding (Blau 1986, Psacharopoulos et al. 1987, Chiswick 1977, Soon 1987). First, because self-employed workers often perform a variety of tasks (allocative, supervisory, etc.) occupation-specific training programs may be too specialized (Fredland and Little 1981). Second, a positive effect of training may be hidden by a large group of retail vendors and hawkers in the sample, although estimates excluding this group of vendors revealed the same findings. Third, the relationship among wages, education and training for the self-employed may be highly nonlinear for the highest levels of education. However, when professionals were excluded from the sample, the results were not altered. Fourth, job training may have an indirect effect on wages rates, although specifications such as interaction terms of training with schooling, job tenure, and general experience did not support this argument.

None of the above arguments offers a convincing explanation for why, given the lack of effect, self-employed workers would pursue training. One could only surmise that the workers participated in training prior to entering the nonwage sector (i.e., while working in salaried employment), or that training for alternative jobs may be used as a hedge to cope with the unpredictability and instability of the Peruvian economy.

In summary, the research found that among males the effect of training on employment status is significant only in the public sector, and the effect of training on wages is significant only in the private sector. For males in private sector wage employment, training from job-based programs increases their wage rates by 10 per cent, training from postsecondary programs increases them by 20 percent, and *academes* training programs produces no increases.

Among women, nonformal training significantly enhances the employment probabilities in all sectors although its effect on wage rates is not significant. As explained, this is likely due to the low labor participation rates among women (relative to men), and may actually reflect the importance of these types of programs if they facilitate women's entry into the labor market. Also, the research reveals a differentiation among the three types of training programs, with men more likely to pursue training offered by job-based or postsecondary programs and women more likely to participate in programs offered through proprietary institutions. Exactly why this differentiation exists is not yet known but may be due to factors such as segmentation in labor market by industry sector, inequality of access to programs or institutional discrimination.

Training programs among the self-employed, regardless of gender, do not affect earnings or profits. This finding should not be interpreted as reason to dismiss training programs for the self-employed but merely to suggest a reconsideration of the types of services offered by training programs for this sector.

See also: Cost–Benefit Analysis.

References

Arriagada A M 1990 Labor market outcomes of non-formal training for male and female workers in Peru. *Econ. Educ. Rev.* 9(4): 331–42

Ashenfelter O 1978 Estimating the effect of training programs on earnings. *Rev. Econ. Stat.* 60(1): 47–57

Barnow B 1987 The impact of CETA programs on earnings: A review of the literature. *J. Hum Resources* 22: 157–93

Bassi L, Simms M, Burbridge L, Betsey C 1984 *Meas-uring the effect of CETA: Youth and the Economically Disadvantaged*. The Urban Institute Report, Washington, DC

Becker G 1964 *Human Capital: A Theoretical and Empirical Analysis, with Special Reference to Education*. Columbia University Press, New York

Bergmann B, Adelman I 1973 The 1973 report of the President's Council of economic advisors: The economic role of women. *Am. Econ. Rev.* 63(4): 509–14

Blau D 1986 Self-employment, earnings, and mobility in Peninsular Malaysia. *World Dev.* 14(2): 839–52

Bloom H 1987 What works for whom? CETA Impacts for Adult Participants. *Eval. Rev.* 11(4): 510–27

Bloom H, McLaughlin A 1982 *CETA training programs—Do They Work for Adults? US Congressional Budget Office and the National Commission for Employment Policy*, Washington, DC

Chiswick C U 1977 On estimating earnings functions for LDCs. *J. Dev. Econ.* 4: 67–78

Coombs P H, Ahmed M 1974 *Attacking Rural Poverty. How Nonformal Education Can Help*. Johns Hopkins University Press, Baltimore, Maryland

Employment and Immigration Canada (EIC) 1982 *Evaluation of Canada Manpower Training (Institutional)*. Program Evaluation Branch, Ottawa

Fredland J, Little R 1981 Self-employed workers: Returns to education and training. *Econ. Educ. Rev.* 1: 315–37

Fuller W P 1970 Education, training, and worker productivity: A study of skilled workers in two factories in South India. Unpublished doctoral dissertation, Stanford University, Stanford, California

Jimenez E, Kugler B 1987 The earnings impact of training duration in a developing country: An ordered probit selection model of Colombia's Servicio Nacional de Aprendizaje (SENA). *J. Hum. Resources* 22: 228–47

Kiefer N 1979 *The Economic Benefits from Four Employment and Training Programs*. Garland, New York

Mincer J 1974 *Schooling, Experience and Earnings*. National Bureau of Economic Research, New York

Papagiannis G 1977 Nonformal education and national development: A study of the Thai Mobile Trade Training School and its institutional effects on adult participants. Unpublished dissertation, Stanford University, Stanford, California

Psacharopoulos G, Arriagada A M, Velez E 1987 *Earnings and Education Among the Self-employed in Columbia*. EDT Discussion Paper No. 70, The World Bank, Washington, DC

Puryear J 1977 *Estudio Comparativo de la Formacion Profesional en Colombia: El Servicio Nacional de Aprendizaje*. CINTERFOR, Montevideo

Soon L Y 1987 Self-employment vs. wage employment: Estimation of earnings functions in LDCs. *Econ. Educ. Rev.* 6(2): 81–89

Streeker-Seeborg I, Seeborg M, Zegeye A 1984 The impact of nontraditional training on the occupational attainment of women. *J. Hum. Resources* 19(4): 452–71

Strober M 1982 The MBA: Same passport to success for women and men. In: Wallace R (ed.) 1982 *Women in the Workplace*. Auburn House, Boston, Massachusetts

Vietorisz T, Harrison B 1970 *The Economic Development of Harlem*. Praeger, New York

Welch F 1970 Education in production. *J. Pol. Econ.* 78(1): 350–59

Education, Economic Growth, and Technological Change

Introduction

M. Carnoy

The economics of education in its present form has its origins in economists' search for the sources of economic growth. In the 1950s, attempts to account for output growth through estimating increases in traditional inputs—specifically, person-hours of labor and physical capital stock—surprised economists by explaining only about one-half of total increases in output. Theodore Schultz, Edward Denison, Zvi Griliches, and others argued that important "unaccounted for" sources of output growth could be found in changes in the quality of these traditional inputs, sources that were usually grouped under a residual that Robert Solow identified as "technological change."

This section of the encyclopedia focuses on the continuing attempts by economists to explain economic growth and, more recently, changes in national productivity. With the shifts to a more competitive international environment and the development of information and communications technology, education has become an increasingly important variable in such explanations.

In the entry that begins the section, Norman Hicks summarizes the literature in original growth accounting approach and how economists measured education's contribution to increases in output using standard production function estimates. Until recently, such estimates were used to measure both the contribution of educational investment (human capital) and of "residual technological change"—increases in labor and capital productivity even when improvements in labor skills and physical capital improvement were accounted for. Economists making the estimates viewed technological change as *exogenous* to the production process. For example, Denison found that economies of scale resulting from the European Economic Union in the 1950s were an important explainer of increased productivity of labor and capital in Europe after the Second World War.

In the 1980s, however, with the new role played by science-based industries in worldwide economic growth, and the focus on process innovations in assembly line production, the idea took hold that technological change was *endogenous* to the labor force and management's organization of the production process. Increases in productivity were therefore largely external economies to improvements in the labor force, resulting from the increased capability of labor and management to innovate. In his entry on endogenous learning and productivity, Don Harris reviews this concept and proposes a model that would account for long-term changes in the "productivity gap" between national economies, purely in terms of differential changes in their capacity to innovate. Harris's model makes national investment in education even more important than in traditional production function analysis for reasons which are spelled out in the general introduction to this volume. Not only does more highly educated labor produce more output when combined with a given amount of physical capital, the larger the stock of human capital, the more likely labor will find ways to improve the production process and to develop new, highly profitable products.

The other four entries in this section look at the reverse side of the relationship between technological change and education. Whereas Hicks and Harris address the role of education in increasing productivity and as a source of technological change itself, Russell Rumberger and Kenneth Spenner discuss the controversial effect that technological change has on the demand for skills. Martin Carnoy in the first of his two entries, analyzes the symbiotic relationship between a nation's educational stock, its capacity to compete in the new global informational economy, and its position in the international division of labor. In the second of his entries, he reviews the kinds of changes that should take place in national systems of education in this new, changing division of labor.

The most recent view in economic circles is that the new information technology has increased the demand for highly skilled labor relative to low skilled labor because of the more complex requirements of information systems and flexible production. This view is challenged by those who argue that technological change progressively deskills tasks in order to lower wages and the bargaining power of labor in the wage contract. It is also challenged by the notion of "contested exchange," in which the bargaining power of various groups of labor plays as much if not more of a role than skills in determining the distribution of wages. Hence, wage distribution and skill mix can move independently of each other.

From a "micro" perspective, it is possible to observe deskilling at the process, plant, and even firm level, yet at the "macro" level, because of the growth of new product production, requiring, on average, higher skilled labor, the demand for these higher skills can increase sharply compared to the demand for lower skills. Indeed, this is the main argument for the changes in income and employment trends in Europe and the United States of the "skills mismatch" proponents. They claim that the expansion of more sophisticated products and production processes has increased the demand for highly educated labor much more rapidly than for less educated labor, especially in the advanced industrialized countries. Rumberger discusses these arguments from a "macro" perspective and Spenner, from a micro perspective. Neither finds convincing evidence that technological change produces a clear cut shift in skill demand up or down— towards more or less educated labor or towards deskilling or reskilling. Spenner concludes that technological change simultaneously produces deskilling and reskilling, often at different occupational levels in the same firm. Rumburger concludes that there is no evidence for new technology per se increasing the relative demand for educated labor. The growth of low skilled jobs in the United States economy has been just as impressive as jobs requiring university graduates.

Carnoy reviews these issues in an international context. Intensified global competition and the development of new information technology have altered the international division of labor, sharply increasing competition in the production of the most advanced technology among the highly industrialized economies, shifting manufacturing jobs from these economies to a group of newly developing countries in Asia. The changes have left Africa and parts of Latin America behind. Rapid educational investment during the past three decades as well as other forms of state macroeconomic "guidance" in these high flying Asian economies has apparently made a major contribution to their ability to compete with the more industrialized countries.

Carnoy also analyzes how changes in labor markets might (or should) influence educational reforms. The entry brings the argument full circle, from the discussion of education's contribution to economic growth to a discussion of how changes resulting from the dynamics of economic growth should impact educational reform.

Education and Economic Growth

N. L. Hicks

The attainment of high, steady rates of economic growth, measured by the growth rate of Gross National Product (GNP), has been an elusive goal for many countries. In attempting to understand the growth process, economists have examined the relative importance of various factors, including education, in the growth process. The contribution of education to growth is presumed to occur through its ability to increase the productivity of an existing labor force in various ways, including both technical training and general education. But exactly how education increases productivity, how important it is, and in what ways it is important, are difficult questions which remain unsettled. While a shortage of educated people might limit growth, it is not clear that promoting education will foster more rapid growth. Furthermore, it is not clear what kinds of education are best at assisting growth: general formal education, technical training, or informal education related to specific jobs.

In general, countries that have higher levels of income also have higher levels of educational attainment (see Table 1), but this cannot be interpreted to mean that education is a necessary cause of higher levels of output and income. Education is both an investment good and a consumption good. As income grows people demand more education, and can afford more education, both for themselves and more importantly for their children. Whether this education contributes to raising productivity is a debatable point. Education may become a kind of screening device used by employers to make hiring decisions. Faced with a large number of applicants for a given job, an employer tends to narrow his or her options by looking seriously only at those with the highest levels of education, even though high levels of education are not

Table 1
Education data: Selected countries

	Per capita income US$ 1980	Adult illiteracy rate % 1985	Enrollment rates % 1988		
			Primary	Secondary	Tertiary
Japan	23,810	a	102	95	30
Sweden	21,570	a	101	93	31
United States	20,910	a	100	98	60
France	17,820	a	114	94	35
United Kingdom	14,610	a	107	83	23
Korea, Republic of	4,400	—	104	87	37
Hungary	2,590	a	96	71	15
Brazil	2,540	22	104	38	11
Mexico	2,010	10	117	53	15
Tunisia	1,260	46	116	44	7
Philippines	710	14	110	71	28
China	350	31	134	44	2
India	340	57	99	41	—
Uganda	250	43	77	8	1
Bangladesh	180	67	59	18	5

Source: World Bank Staff 1991
a Less than 5 percent

necessary for the job. As a result the education level required to gain entry to certain jobs tends to move upward over time with little or no change in basic productivity (see *Screening Models and Education*).

1. Growth Accounting

In order to understand the contribution of education to growth, one first must understand the causes of growth and the growth process itself. Traditionally, economists have identified three factors of production: land, labor, and capital. In the growth process, land will presumably not change, so that the key factors are the growth of labor and capital. If the growth rates of labor and capital are weighted by their shares in total output, one can derive an index of the growth of factor inputs. If the growth of total output exceeds the growth rate of the index of factor inputs, then total factor productivity is rising. More formally, output (Q) is assumed to be a function of the stock of capital (K), the labor force (L), and the level of technical progress (A), which is also a measure of total factor productivity. Hence, $Q = f(K,L,A_t)$, where A is assumed to be a function of time, t. Recasting in terms of growth rates and transposing results in a production function of the type:

$$\frac{dA}{A} = \frac{1}{\varepsilon_{QA}} \frac{dQ}{Q} - \frac{\varepsilon_{QK}}{\varepsilon_{QA}} \frac{dK}{K} - \frac{\varepsilon_{QL}}{\varepsilon_{QA}} \frac{dL}{L} \qquad (1)$$

where ε = elasticity.

Thus the term dA/A is a residual between the growth of output and the growth of factor inputs, and measures total factor productivity. However, it can be affected fundamentally by errors in the measurement of output. For example, changes in the quality of the labor force can affect the results in a misleading direction.

The major work on growth accounting has been done by Denison (1967, 1979). In this work, labor inputs are adjusted to reflect changes in the age and sex composition of the labor force, changes in hours worked, and most importantly, for changes in education. The differentials in earnings at different education levels are assumed to reflect the added productivity of education. Denison acknowledges, however, that earnings differentials can also reflect unmeasurable factors such as ability and family background, and reduces these differentials by 60 percent to allow for these factors. This reduction factor, while somewhat arbitrary, is generally accepted by practitioners of growth accounting as a reasonable estimate, although it indicates that growth accounting itself is inclined to be a combination of an art and a science.

For the period 1948 to 1973, Denison estimates that total United States potential national income grew at an annual rate of 3.87 percent per year (Denison 1979 p. 105), while total factor input grew at a rate of 2.2 percent. The growth rate of labor inputs, making allowance for hours worked and so on, but excluding education, accounted for 28 percent of total growth. Education of the labor force accounted for 11 percent. Overall, however, both labor and capital inputs explain about 60 percent of total growth; the remaining 40 percent is accounted for by changes in factor productivity of output per unit of input. A certain part of this productivity growth Denison explains by improvements in resource allocation, changes in the legal and human environment, and economies of scale. There is a large residual, however, labeled "advances in knowledge and miscellaneous determinants," which accounts for about 29 percent of total growth. In Denison's words, "The advance in knowledge is the biggest and most basic reason for the persistent long-term growth of output per unit of input" (1979 p. 79). Broadly speaking, it can be said to constitute nonformal education, and technical and managerial knowledge, obtained in a variety of ways ranging from organized research to simple observation and experience. But the residual also includes other factors which are not advances in knowledge and which are not otherwise incorporated in the estimates, including statistical discrepancies and measurement errors.

If one combines the direct influence of education (11 percent) and the indirect influence of advances in knowledge (29 percent), a very large proportion of growth (about 40 percent) can be attributed to improvements in human capital or education broadly conceived. However, estimates made for the period after 1973 tell a different story. For the period 1973 to 1981, Denison's (1984 p. 5) estimates for the nonresidential business sector show total factor inputs growing at a rate of 2.1 percent per year, compared to only a 1.8 percent growth in total output; the result is a decline in productivity or a negative residual. Since it is unlikely that "advances in knowledge" were negative during the period, some other explanation is needed for the slowdown in productivity growth. While Denison examines 17 possibilities (1984 p. 24), including higher oil prices, higher inflation, and greater government regulation, he concludes that none of them offer a satisfactory explanation of the decline. While the decline in productivity thus remains a mystery, it raises questions about the previous estimates of the contribution of education and human capital improvements to the growth process.

Furthermore, a review of growth accounting exercises of various countries compiled by Bowman (1980) shows much lower contributions for education in other countries. In 22 countries having estimates for roughly the period 1950 to 1962, only in 4 did the direct contribution of education exceed 10 percent (Argentina, Belgium, United Kingdom, and the United States). In a survey of 29 countries, Psacharopoulos (1985) found that the direct effect of education explained an average of only 8.7 percent of total growth. For most countries, the direct effect of education seems to be a minor factor, and to be a smaller factor in countries having rapid growth rates. Moreover, the unexplained residual seems to be larger the higher the growth rate, that is, productivity itself grows faster when total output grows faster. For instance, Japan's growth averaged 10 percent per year during the period 1955 to 1968, of which only 39 percent could be attributed to the growth of factor inputs. Education

explained only 1.4 percent of total growth. However, these estimates may all understate the contribution of education since they do not distinguish between the need to maintain the existing stock of education in the labor force and its expansion. This downward bias could range, according to Selowsky (1969), between 40 and 90 percent, and will be higher in countries with rapid population growth rates.

2. Returns on Human Capital

Another approach which attempts to measure the impact of education on productivity consists of recasting education as an investment in human capital (see *Human Capital Concepts*). In theories developed by Becker (1964), Schultz (1961), and a host of others, it is assumed that rational people will attempt to invest in education up to the point where returns to them in terms of extra income are equal to the costs of undertaking education, including the income forgone while education is being undertaken (see *Education and Earnings*). Social returns to education will differ from private returns to the extent that recipients of education do not pay the full costs of this education. On the other hand, the social gains will be measured as pretax income, while the private gains will be net of taxes.

Decisions on investment in human capital generally relate to the amount of education to give children; income earners usually cannot afford to resume education on a full-time basis or may be barred from doing so. Parents must decide how much of present consumption to forgo in investing in the education or human capital of their children, which is counterbalanced by the real and expected income earned by more educated offspring. Expected returns from education, however, can vary in perception and in fact, and parents may be unwilling to take the risks associated with such long-term investments.

Returns to education have been calculated for many countries, and have been summarized by Psacharopoulos (1985) (see Table 2). His basic findings are that: (a) returns to primary school are higher than those to other levels of education; (b) private returns exceed social returns, particularly at the university level; (c) most rates of return are above 10 percent (a commonly accepted estimate of the opportunity cost of capital); and (d) returns to education were higher in the poorer countries, reflecting the greater scarcities of trained workers in these countries.

For developing countries, the high social returns found for primary education (27 percent) contrast sharply with the more modest returns for higher education (14 percent). This suggests that these countries may have overinvested in higher level education, and neglected primary education. Thus primary education in developing countries could make significant contributions to growth if new investments had returns close to the average rate

Table 2
Returns to investment in education (percent)

Country group	Primary	Secondary	Higher
Social returns			
Africa	26	17	13
Asia	27	15	13
Latin America	26	18	16
Intermediate	13	10	8
Advanced	—	11	9
Private returns			
Africa	45	26	32
Asia	31	15	18
Latin America	32	23	23
Intermediate	17	13	13
Advanced	—	12	12

Source: Psacharopoulos 1985

of return of 27 percent and if alternative investments earned only 10 percent. For the more advanced countries, the social rates of return for higher education averaged only 9 percent, suggesting that further rapid expansion of higher education would not be warranted. Further investments in higher education in developed countries could actually slow growth, if more productive investments elsewhere are forgone. Thus education's impact on growth depends on the level of development of both the economy and the labor force, and will be country- and time-specific. The whole process becomes self-equilibrating: an oversupply of a certain class of educated people will drive down salaries and lower prospective rates of return, which in turn will discourage entrants. Where systems of public education are well-developed, and financial markets permit borrowing against future earnings, rates of return on education will, in the long run, equal the rates of return on other productive assets. Thus, higher than normal rates of return reflect some sort of market imperfection, for example, in developing countries where education facilities may be unavailable, financial markets are relatively underdeveloped and people are unable, because of their low incomes, to sacrifice present consumption levels to finance education. In short, education is likely to be more important to economic growth in situations marked by underinvestment in human capital, limited supplies of skilled and educated workers, and relatively undeveloped education systems. Many would agree with Schultz (1975) that education is more likely to be important in modernizing environments than in traditional ones.

In all countries, the gap between private and social returns to education produces popular pressure on governments to expand public education beyond the optimal level. In the advanced countries, the private return to higher education averages 12 percent, compared to 9 percent for the social return. The gap between private and social returns is even greater in developing countries (see Table 2). Since this gap between social and private returns is greater at the university level, it is not surprising that there is an overinvestment in higher education, particularly in developing countries.

3. Cross-national Comparisons

Other cross-national evidence also supports the idea that human capital development in general, and education in particular, is an important element in explaining variations in growth rates and levels of per capita income. Krueger's study (1968) made a pioneering attempt to compare differences in per capita income between the United States and a wide range of other countries. The technique consisted of breaking down the labor force by age, education, and rural–urban areas for each country. If each of these categories had the same productivity as that of the United States, an estimate of "attainable income" can be derived. In most cases, even if countries had the same factor endowment as the United States, Krueger finds that they would attain a per capita income of only half of that of the United States level (see Table 3), with the balance being attributed to the different levels of development of human capital. Mexico, whose 1960 per capita income was 14 percent of that of the United States, serves as a useful illustration. If Mexico had the same endowment of land, capital and other resources as the United States, it would have had a per capita income level of 46 percent of the United States. Explained another way, 63 percent of the gap in per capita incomes must be explained by other differences, namely differences in human capital stocks.

It is worth noting, however, that Krueger does not equate human capital entirely with education. Other important differences include the age structure of the population, and the split between rural and urban areas. In most countries, attainable income is reduced by about 15 to 30 percent due to education deficiencies, or about half of the total gap explained by human capital differences. In the case of Mexico, education lowers attainable income by about 23 percent, compared to a total reduction attributable to human capital of 54 percent.

Increasingly, economists working in developing countries have been more concerned with policies that help reduce poverty and increase employment, in addition to promoting growth. Improving the basic health, education and nutrition of the poor is now seen as an important mechanism for increasing their welfare directly, and their productivity indirectly. This has led to a renewed interest in the "social sectors" consisting not only of education, but also of health services, water supply and sanitation, nutrition, and housing. Greater attention is now paid to protecting these sectors during periods of adjustment, although it is not clear whether these are investments in human capital or a form of consumption.

Table 3

Education and gaps in per capita incomes between the United States and other countries

Country	Per capita GDP as percentage of US value	Per capita attainable income with present human resources[a]	Percentage by which attainable income is reduced by gap in education[b]
United States	100.0	—	—
Canada	72.6	100.5	8.1
Israel	38.3	83.8	13.6
Japan	14.4	93.2	3.7
Puerto Rico	23.2	59.8	12.6
Jamaica	16.2	56.7	16.0
Panama	15.0	51.5	16.0
Mexico	14.2	45.6	22.9
Greece	12.5	71.2	28.6
Portugal	11.6	67.1	29.9
El Salvador	7.5	45.5	24.1
Honduras	7.5	36.6	23.9
Peru	7.3	51.1	18.3
Iran	7.2	39.8	33.2
Jordan	6.9	38.7	23.3
Malaysia	7.9	44.2	25.0
Indonesia	3.1	37.3	32.2
Korea, Republic of	4.7	44.3	24.8
China, Republic of (Taiwan)	3.9	48.5	21.6
Thailand	3.6	46.5	21.4
India	3.0	34.1	32.6
Ghana	7.7	38.0	30.3

Source: Krueger 1968
a Per capita income attainable with present human resources if the country has US per capita nonhuman resources b Controlling for age and sector

In a cross-national study, Hicks (1980) found that the rapidly growing developing countries were those that had above average performance in both literacy and life expectancy. Growth, of course, can add to the resources available for making improvements in health and education. In order to circumvent this cause and effect problem, he examined the growth of a sample of 75 developing countries for the period 1960 to 1977 and the respective levels of achievement in 1960 for life expectancy (an assumed health measure) and literacy. He found that literacy levels and growth are related. The top 12 countries (see Table 4) had an average per capita growth rate of 5.7 percent during the period, compared to 2.4 percent for all countries. These fast-growing countries started the period with above-average literacy levels. However, the fast-growing countries also have above-average income levels, and one would expect higher than average levels of literacy. But even if one adjusts for differences in income, these countries had literacy rates 12 percentage points higher than would

have been expected at their income levels.

Correlation analysis such as this suffers from many deficiencies, and the problem of identifying cause and effect remains. In addition, Hicks points out the strong correlation between literacy levels and life expectancy, suggesting that literacy may have an important influence on health and hygiene. In a more extensive study, Wheeler (1980) attempted to overcome the causality problems by using a system of simultaneous equations. While more rigorous, this approach reduces the number of countries that can be included in the analysis, since data must exist for all countries for all variables. His findings partially contradict those of Hicks, in that he does not find a strong association between the life expectancy or nutrition variables and growth. Rather, he regards changes in literacy as having a major impact on changes in output, and finds an important influence for literacy in reducing fertility. This finding supports the work of Cochrane (1980) and others who generally find that education and fertility reductions work

Table 4
Economic growth and life expectancy: Selected countries

	Growth rate 1960–77[a] %	Life expectancy 1960	Deviations from expected levels of life expectancy	Adult literacy 1960	Deviations from expected levels of literacy 1960[b]
Singapore	7.7	64.0	3.1	—	—
Korea, Republic of	7.6	54.0	11.1	71.0	43.6
Taiwan	6.5	64.0	15.5	54.0	14.2
Hong Kong	6.3	65.0	6.5	70.0	6.4
Greece	6.1	68.0	5.7	81.0	7.5
Portugal	5.7	62.0	4.7	62.0	1.7
Spain	5.3	68.0	1.8	87.0	1.2
Yugoslavia	5.2	62.0	4.7	77.0	16.7
Brazil	4.9	57.0	3.0	61.0	8.6
Israel	4.6	69.0	2.0	—	—
Thailand	4.5	51.0	9.5	68.0	43.5
Tunisia	4.3	48.0	−0.5	16.0	−23.8
Average: Top 12	5.7	61.0	5.6	64.7	12.0
Average: All countries	2.4	48.0	−0.0	37.6	−0.0

Source: Hicks 1980a

a Growth rate of real per capita GNP   b Deviations from estimated values and derived from an equation where life expectancy in 1960 (LIEX) and adult literacy in 1960 (LIT) are related to per capita income in 1960 (Y) in the following way: $LIEX = 34.29 + 0.07679Y − 0.0000430Y^2$ $R^2 = 0.66$; $LIT = 9.23 + 0.1595Y − 0.0000658Y^2$ $R^2 = 0.44$

together, but the evidence here is not always clear. Cochrane's work, for example, also suggests that in some instances, increased education at lower levels increases fertility, probably because of the effects of improved health and hygienic practices that come with increased education.

Wheeler's work has been extended by Marris (1982). Using data from 66 developing countries for the period 1965 to 1979, he estimates a model that confirms the previous findings on the importance of education for growth in developing countries. Furthermore, he finds a relatively weak role for investment, as normally measured in terms of the construction of fixed tangible assets. The estimated cost–benefit ratios for education (measured by primary enrollment rate) range in his model between 3.4 and 7.4, depending on one's assumptions on costs. By contrast, the cost–benefit ratios for investments in nonhuman capital ranged between 0.4 and 1.0. Romer (1990) identifies a significant relation between the change in literacy and the rate of investment in nonhuman capital, as well as the level of literacy and rates of investment in subsequent periods. More recent work by Lau et al. (1991) which integrates education variables into an aggregate production function framework for five developing country regions, notes a wide variability in the impact of education and growth. The effect of a one-year increase in the average educational attainment of the working age population ranges from a negative to more than 5 percent per year.

Finally, some mention needs to be made of some of the microlevel work on the influence of education.

These studies are important, because they can associate education differences at the worker level more directly with variations in worker productivity. A survey of studies on farmer productivity by Lockheed et al. (1980) covering various developing countries found that 4 years of education increased farmer productivity on average by 7.4 percent. This average centers around a fairly wide range, however, with several studies showing a negative correlation between education and productivity. The authors explain this by dividing the sample into modernizing/nonmodernizing subsamples. In nonmodernizing societies, marked by traditional and primitive farming methods, and little exposure to innovation and new methods, 4 years of education was found to increase production by only 1.3 percent, compared with 9.5 percent under modernizing conditions. Similar studies for more advanced countries also come to similar conclusions. In the United States, for instance, agriculture studies by Griliches (1964) and Welch (1970) suggest that a 10 percent increase in farmer education raises productivity by 3 to 5 percent, compared to only a 1 to 2 percent increase to be gained from a 10 percent increase in either land, fertilizer, or machinery. In a classic study of the Japanese textile industry, Saxonhouse (1977) found that in the period between 1891 and 1935 improvements in productivity occurred almost entirely because of modest changes in labor force characteristics and working conditions. He concluded that the standard production function which examines only the conventional inputs of capital and labor, and the rate of substitution between them, is deficient to the extent it ignores the nonconventional inputs of worker education, training, and experience.

4. Conclusion

The overall conclusion from the literature surveyed in this entry suggests a strong positive relation between human capital improvements and growth. Formal education is a major, but not the sole factor in improving human capital, which includes worker training and experience, as well as health and nutrition. Human capital variations appear to be a major element in explaining differences in productivity and productivity growth between countries. It is possible to have too much investment in education, just as it is possible to have too much investment in plant and machinery. The higher rates of return to education in developing countries suggests that investment in education makes most sense where the supply of educated labor is relatively scarce. However, developing countries appear to have made too much investment in higher education and too little in primary education. Overinvestment in education also appears a potential problem in some of the developed countries, such as the United States, whose current enrollment rates for higher education (60 percent) are double those of countries like Sweden and Japan. Overinvestment of this type is a particular problem in countries which subsidize higher education, and where, as a consequence, the private returns to education are substantially higher than the social returns.

See also: Education Production Functions; Education and Productivity; Returns to Vocational Education in Developing Nations

References

Becker G S 1964 *Human Capital: A Theoretical and Empirical Analysis with Special Reference to Education.* National Bureau of Economic Research, New York
Bowman M J 1980 Education and economic growth: An overview. In: King T (ed.) 1980 *Education and Income: A Background Study for World Development Report, 1980.* World Bank Staff Working Paper No. 402. World Bank, Washington, DC
Cochrane S H 1980 *Fertility and Education: What Do We Really Know?* Johns Hopkins University Press/World Bank, Baltimore, Maryland
Denison E F 1967 *Why Growth Rates Differ: Post-War Experience in Nine Western Countries.* Brookings Institute, Washington, DC
Denison E F 1979 *Accounting for Slower Economic Growth: The United States in the 1970s.* Brookings Institute, Washington, DC
Denison E F 1984 Accounting for slower growth: An update. In: Kendrick J W (ed.) 1984 *International Comparisons of Productivity and Causes of the Slowdown.* Ballinger, Cambridge, Massachusetts
Griliches Z 1964 Research expenditures, education, and the aggregate agricultural production function. *Am. Econ. Rev.* 54: 961–74
Hicks N 1980 Is there a trade-off between growth and basic needs? *Finance and Development* 17(2): 17–20
Krueger A O 1968 Factor endowments and per capita income differences among countries. *Economic Journal* 78: 641–59
Lau L J, Jamison D T, Louat F F 1991 *Education and Economic Growth: An Aggregate Production Function Approach.* World Bank PRE Working Paper No. 612. World Bank, Washington, DC
Lockheed M, Jamison D, Lau L 1980 Farmer calculation and farm efficiency: A survey. In: King T (ed.) 1980 *Education and Income: A Background Study for World Development Report 1980.* World Bank Staff Working Paper No. 402. World Bank, Washington, DC
Marris R 1982 Economic growth in cross-section. Department of Economics, Birkbeck College, London (mimeo)
Psacharopoulos G 1985 Returns to education: A further international update and implications. *J. Hum. Resources* 20(4): 583–604
Romer P M 1990 Human capital and growth: Theory and evidence. *Carnegie-Rochester Conference Series on Public Policy* 32: 251–86
Saxonhouse G R 1977 Productivity change and labor absorption in Japanese cotton spinning. *Q. J. Econ.* 91(2): 195–219
Schultz T W 1961 Investment in human capital. *Am. Econ. Rev.* 51: 1–17
Schultz T W 1975 The value of the ability to deal with disequilibria. *J. Econ. Lit.* 13(3): 827–46
Selowsky M 1969 On the measurement of education's contribution to growth. *Q. J. Econ.* 83: 449–63
Welch F 1970 Education in production. *J. Pol. Econ.* 78: 35–59
Wheeler D 1980 *Human Resource Development and Economic Growth in Developing Countries: A Simultaneous Model.* World Bank Staff Working Paper No. 407. World Bank, Washington, DC
World Bank Staff 1991 *World Development Report 1991.* World Bank, Washington, DC

Further Reading

Hicks N 1980 *Economic Growth and Human Resources.* World Bank Working Paper No. 408. World Bank, Washington DC
Jorgenson D W 1984 The contribution of education to US economic growth 1948–1973. In: Dean E (ed.) 1984 *Education and Economic Productivity.* Ballinger, Cambridge, Massachusetts
Nadiri M I 1972 International studies of factor inputs and total factor productivity: A brief survey. *Review of Income and Wealth* 18 (2): 129–54
Psacharopoulos G 1981 Returns to education: An updated international comparison. *Comp. Educ.* 17: 321–41
Tilak J B G 1989 *Education and Its Relation to Economic Growth, Poverty and Income Distribution: Past Evidence and Further Analysis.* World Bank Discussion Paper No. 46. World Bank, Washington, DC

Endogenous Learning and Economic Growth

D. J. Harris

The basic conception that motivates the analysis presented in this entry is that the development of knowledge and training of the labor force are crucial determinants of productivity growth. This idea is in keeping with the widely held view that education, broadly defined, is closely linked with an economy's productivity (see *Education and Economic Growth* and Easterlin 1981). But what precisely is the nature of that link and how does it generate changes in productivity in different economies over time? The specification of that link is a key element and distinctive feature of this analysis.

The traditional production function approach identifies the main sources of productivity increase as external to the production process: in increases in human capital, physical capital, and exogenous technological change (see *Education and Economic Growth*). However, this entry will take an alternative approach. The emphasis is placed on productivity increase as a self-generating process depending on specific activities geared to the production of new knowledge. Also emphasized is the embodied learning associated with production in the form of both learning-by-doing and learning-by-using. Productivity increase occurs when the production process itself generates new knowledge (education and training) and when education and training are incorporated as new knowledge in the production process. Thus, this approach keeps education and training as a central focus, but situated within the production process itself rather than as external inputs.

With this approach, a specific set of analytical questions is addressed. These questions arise from the empirical record of productivity growth among different world economies, both regional and national.

1. Convergence in Productivity Levels

Among a selected sample of advanced capitalist economies, a notable feature of the postwar experience of productivity growth is a tendency to convergence in productivity levels. This tendency has been identified and discussed by a number of observers (Abramovitz 1986, Baumol 1988, Maddison 1982, 1987, Matthews et al. 1982). However, the strength and generality of this tendency are a matter of dispute (Baumol et al. 1988, De long and Bradford 1988, Romer 1989, Dowrick and Nguyen 1989, Baumol et al. 1989). Even if it is accepted for a specific subsample of countries, it remains evident that there is great diversity in the actual pattern of experience of a wider class of countries, including developing countries, observed over the same period. Among this wider class, the coexistence

of both convergence and divergence can be found with no clear and unambiguous case for either tendency to prevail across the whole set of countries.

Owing to the absence of comprehensive productivity data for developing countries, per capita income figures which admittedly provide only a rough guide to productivity levels have to be relied on. The available data (World Bank 1992) show that, for much of the postwar period, the group of "middle income economies" have narrowed the gap relative to the top group of "industrial market economies." The most dramatic examples of this tendency are the countries constituting the so-called "Asian Miracle" (World Bank 1993). On the other hand, for the "low income economies" as a group, the gap has actually been increasing relative to the top. As to the actual magnitude of the gaps involved, in 1990 the ratio between the top and the bottom stood at 56:1 and between the top and the middle it was 6:1.

This record of experience in productivity growth poses deep problems for economic analysis. The overall picture is evidently much more diverse and complex than either a simple convergence thesis, or its opposite, a divergence and polarization thesis, would suggest. (For a penetrating discussion of some of the complex issues involved in analyzing the historical record of differential productivity growth among countries, see Abramovitz 1986 and Nelson 1981.)

As mentioned before, this entry addresses a specific set of analytical questions that this picture raises. The focus is on the nature of the so-called "convergence process" as such and, in particular, on the following questions. Under what circumstances does the process of productivity growth tend to converge or diverge? What are the factors that determine such convergence or divergence? If a productivity gap persists, what determines its ultimate size?

In order to provide an answer to this set of questions, "a model of a productivity race" will be developed in this entry, a model in which there are specified relationships governing the rate of productivity growth among different production units viewed as countries or regions. From these relationships it is possible to find certain characteristic conditions, related to the parameters of the productivity-increasing process. These conditions allow a direct inference concerning factors that determine the possibility of convergence/divergence among different units and the size of the gap, if any, that remains between them.

2. A Heuristic Model

This is a model of pure productivity growth. It abstracts essential features of productivity growth as an endogenous process, putting aside other factors that are usually considered to affect growth of output, such as saving/investment rates, aggregate demand, supply of labor, and natural resources.

The concept of productivity used here is the simple and well-defined concept of labor productivity; that is, average product per unit of labor. This bears comparison with the neoclassical concept of total factor productivity, measured as the ratio of output to a weighted index of (augmented) capital and labor inputs. All the well-known capital-theoretic problems implicit in the aggregate production function underlying that concept are avoided here by focusing on labor productivity. Actually, in this model it is assumed that labor is the only input in production, although there is an augmentation effect on the side of labor arising from experience. Correspondingly, factors related to "capital deepening" that have traditionally been used to account for productivity growth, whether one thinks of capital deepening either as increasing mechanization or as variation of the length of life of different vintages of capital, are left out of consideration. Other factors such as investment in human capital (formal education) are also ignored.

It is assumed that productivity increase is a "self-generating process." This self-generating feature derives from two conditions that are crucial to the model. First, it derives from the operation of what might be termed the "knowledge industry." This industry consists of the congeries of activities taking place within universities and research institutes, within the Research and Development (R&D) divisions of firms, in industrial laboratories, and in the activities of people tinkering in the basement. It therefore includes what is commonly referred to as "Research and Development" activity, but much else besides. Operationally, the output of this industry is embodied in technical blueprints, patents, professional and trade journals, books, videos, computer software, and the like. These outputs are linked to production, and hence to productivity, in many complex ways that defy detailed specification. Nevertheless, the link is clear and well-established. Conceptually, what this analysis seeks to capture is the crucial role of these activities as a determinant of overall productivity growth.

Freeman (1982) provides the most forceful statement of the argument supporting this view of the role of the knowledge industry as a key feature of the development of modern economies in the twentieth century. Freeman conceives what he calls "the Research and Development System" as "the heart of the whole complex." Even so, there are still considerable empirical difficulties in identifying exactly what constitutes this "system", as shown in National Science Foundation (1987). Machlup (1962) gives a much wider definition of the "knowledge industries" and estimates that 30 percent of the labor force in the United States economy is included in his definition.

Porat (1977) defines a similar category of "information occupations" to include about 50 percent of total occupations. (For relevant empirical evidence on the contribution of Research and Development to productivity growth, see Griliches 1986 and Mansfield 1980.) From the standpoint of ascribing causality, the relationships involved are considerably complex, as is argued forcefully by Nelson (1981).

Second, the self-generating feature of productivity growth derives from an intrinsic characteristic of the production process, namely that experience counts in some meaningful sense. In particular, it counts here towards further increase in productivity. In this respect, there exists a "learning effect", which is modeled here as both a learning-by-doing effect and a learning-by-using effect. This feature of the model also conforms well to ideas that have been demonstrated and documented in the literature (Arrow 1962b, Rosenberg 1982.)

This particular way of approaching the problem of productivity growth has the significant implication that every producing unit (country or region) has the capacity to generate its own productivity growth from its own activity of knowledge production and learning. This capacity is subject to a critical threshold effect that, as shown below, may operate to inhibit some units from starting up the process. Still, every producing unit has the capacity to pull itself up by its own bootstraps, so to speak, provided that the required minimum condition is met. Therefore, observed differentials in performance among units, instead of being reduced simply to arbitrary external factors, barriers, or limits, must be accounted for by factors that are internal to the productivity increasing process. Furthermore, once these factors are known, the conditions under which the process will tend to converge or to diverge can be identified, as well as what determines the asymptotic state of that process as regards the magnitude of the productivity gap. This is essentially the thrust of the analysis presented here.

For the purpose of this analysis, the following assumptions about knowledge as a commodity are made. First, it is permanent and indestructible and therefore does not depreciate over time. Second, it is a produced commodity, made by its own production process in the knowledge industry. Third, it is a high-powered commodity in that it has the capacity to increase the productivity of all industries including its own. Fourth, it generates significant externalities in the course of its production and use, in the strict sense that any producer can benefit from access to and use of a given total quantity of knowledge without diminishing the amount available to others. This externality feature of knowledge as a commodity implies that there are intrinsic problems of establishing property rights and hence of appropriation of income from its use. Thus, the idea of inferring a unique market-determined price of knowledge or an immediate connection with income of its owners is highly problematical. For this reason, it is worth emphasizing that no significance is assigned here to the pricing and income distribution side of the production of knowledge. (Some relevant issues concerning the conception of knowledge as a commodity with its own peculiar attributes are considered by Arrow 1962a and Nelson 1959.)

3. The Model

In constructing the relations of the model, a critical variable x, the stock of knowledge, which is the sum of all the flows of knowledge generated in the past is defined. Thus,

$$x = \int_0^\tau \dot{x}\, dt \qquad (1)$$

It would be straightforward to extend this formulation to allow for depreciation of the stock of knowledge, but this complication is not considered here. The essential point is that x is assumed to be a scalar. This notion of an aggregate of knowledge is used here for heuristic purposes only. A simple way of giving it a concrete representation is, for instance, as a number of blueprints or a number of patents. There are, of course, important theoretical and practical problems involved in constructing such an aggregate (as with many other aggregates commonly used in economic analysis) in a real-world context of heterogeneous knowledge commodities, but these problems are not considered here, and neither are they strictly relevant for present purposes.

The production characteristics of the knowledge industry are specified as follows:

$$\dot{x} = f(x,L) = \phi(x) \cdot L \qquad (2)$$

Here, the flow output of knowledge $\dot{x}$ is a function of the stock of knowledge x and the labor input L. The stock of knowledge represents an index of productive experience, which has a positive effect on production through a process of "learning by doing." The learning function is further specified to be a function $\phi(x)$ which is a multiplicative factor applied to the labor input. This formulation says simply that the track record of experience in producing knowledge, as measured by the cumulated stock of knowledge already produced, governs the productivity of labor in producing knowledge.

It is assumed that the average product of experience is greater than the marginal product and that the marginal product is positive:

$$\frac{\phi(x)}{x} > \phi' > 0 \qquad (3)$$

Thus, there is a kind of "diminishing returns" to experience. This assumption is intended to capture an idea that recurs in the literature, taking different forms. In its most common form it is the idea of running up against a frontier of technological knowledge, which essentially implies that beyond a certain point the yield of incremental efforts in Research and Development activity rapidly falls off (to zero in the extreme). It is sometimes tied to Wolff's Law referring to a general tendency to "retardation of progress" (Freeman 1982). It could also be derived from the idea of a "lock-in effect" arising from cumulative experience along a given trajectory of technological development (Dosi 1984, 1988). Or, it could be that there is a kind of "dead weight" of past experience connected with the social and institutional structures that it generates, such as "the accumulation of special interest groups" (Olson 1982). Whatever form it takes, this idea evidently entails the existence of some condition within the knowledge-producing industry that acts cumulatively to retard the process of increase in productivity. That condition may itself be considered to be of an essentially transitory nature if, over time, "major breakthroughs" in knowledge occur so as to expand the scope for productivity increases at any level of experience. Nevertheless, while recognizing its "short run" character in this sense, the analytical implications of this idea are worth exploring here.

The logic of this idea does not necessarily rule out the existence of an initial phase of increasing returns, but for simplicity this analysis focuses on the case of diminishing returns as an "ultimate" phase of the process. Also, it must be emphasized that, as presented here, there is nothing inherent in the idea of "diminishing returns to experience" that makes it a purely technological condition. Rather, it is considered to be an analytic expression for a wide range of social and institutional factors that are themselves the product of historical development.

It is further assumed that, in order to start up the knowledge industry, it is strictly necessary to have some positive amount of labour input to begin with:

$$L \geq L^* \qquad (4)$$

Thus there is a critical mass, or minimum threshold, of engineers, physicists, economists, and the like, that have to be assembled in order to run an effective knowledge-producing process. This assumption also captures an idea that is commonly found in the literature on research and development. It has the significant implication that any unit (country or region) which is unable, for whatever reason, to mount the required minimum scale of the activity is unable to gain the full advantages of the productivity-increasing process.

Assume that there is a second productive sector, the y-sector, that produces a consumption commodity. Output of this commodity, y, is produced by labor L_y. The labor employed in this sector is able to enhance its productivity by drawing on the total stock of knowledge accumulated from production in the x-

sector without diminishing the amount of it available to that sector. The same total stock of knowledge therefore enters into the production equation of both the x- and y-sector. In the x-sector, however, it represents a "learning-by-doing effect." whereas, in the y-sector, it incorporates a "learning-by-using effect." This learning-by-using effect is specified to be a multiplicative factor applied to the labor input, as follows:

$$y = h(x, L_y) = \psi(x) \cdot L_y \qquad (5)$$

Hence, there exists a two-sector economy, with a knowledge-producing and knowledge-using (consumption–good producing) sector. There is a degree of circularity in production insofar as the knowledge output reenters the productive process as the stock of experience, giving rise to learning effects in both sectors. There is an externality feature of knowledge associated with the fact that both sectors draw on the same total stock of knowledge to boost their productivity. Output of the consumption commodity, though forming part of the aggregate national income, drops out of the picture viewed from the standpoint of the total reproductive process. In the subsequent analysis, no attention is given either to consumption behavior or to movements of the aggregate national income: the focus is entirely on the production side, specifically on productivity growth which is uniquely connected with growth in the stock of knowledge.

Now, assume that there are two countries (or regions), A and B. Both have an established and viable knowledge-producing industry and a consumption-good industry. Issues involved in determining the pattern of trade and specialization in the countries are left out of this analysis, inasmuch as the pricing side of the picture (on which an account of comparative advantage must be based) is being ignored. Still, it is not unreasonable to suppose that both countries produce some of the same commodities, unless it should turn out that specialization according to comparative advantage yields a corner solution, which would be a very special case.

The assumption that production conditions are the same in both countries could be usefully dropped and the model extended to allow for differences in production conditions across countries. Country A is the leader in the strict sense that it has a greater stock of knowledge than country B, so that $x_A > x_B$. Correspondingly, A also has all-round higher levels of labor productivity. In addition, country A allocates relatively more labor to the knowledge industry than country B, so that $L_A > L_B$. Insofar as ther exists a gap in the stock of knowledge between country A and B, there is room for a one-way process of diffusion of knowledge from A to B. Assume that diffusion itself is costless in terms of labor and that the amount of knowledge transmitted to B at any moment is proportional to the size of the gap by a factor of proportionality equal to δ.

Accordingly, one has the following equations of production of knowledge in both countries:

$$\dot{x}_A = \phi(x_A) L_A , \; x_A > x_B \qquad (6)$$
$$L_A \geq L_B$$

$$\dot{x} = \phi(x_B) L_B + \delta(x_A - x_B) , \; 0 < \delta < 1 \qquad (7)$$

A convenient interpretation of the diffusion term in Eqn. (7) is that it represents a direct transfer from A to B that is costless to both A and B. It amounts, therefore, to a kind of "spillover effect" or pure externality. The parameter δ could then be taken as a measure of absorptive capacity in B, hence dependent on internal conditions within country B (such as range and depth of social infrastructure, size of the market, language skills, and policies of the national state). Or, δ could be a reflection of regulative measures and other institutional barriers in A to the export of knowledge. An alternative interpretation is that the diffusion term represents a flow of foreign investment from A to B; but this interpretation would raise further complications that cannot be pursued here. Whatever the case, it is supposed that this transfer has a direct impact on the current flow output of knowledge in B equivalent to the size of the transfer. The impact is assumed to be positive; but the possibility that it is negative could be introduced because of the existence of retarding effects from the transfer process. The latter case is an implication of the argument that relations between advanced and developing economies are characterized by a "structure of dependence" (Dos Santos 1970).

In practice, of course, there are likely to be significant resource costs of adoption of imported knowledge and of adaptation to local conditions. Insofar as these are accountable to labor costs, they can conveniently be absorbed into L^* for the importing country. A more complex treatment, consistent with the spirit of this model, and as a possible extension to it, would be to make diffusion itself a labor-using activity, subject to its own learning process.

The analytical problem that is posed now is the following: if both countries operate in accordance with the conditions specified in this model, what would be the associated pattern of productivity growth over time and what is the outcome of the process in the long run, as regards the size of the gap in productivity levels? Since productivity levels in both countries are uniquely related to the prevailing stock of knowledge, the analysis focuses on movements in this variable.

4. Dynamics of the Productivity Gap

Eqn. (6) and (7) constitute the key dynamic relationships indicating how the two countries evolve over time, starting from given initial conditions. To simpify the analysis and sharpen the results, let the learning function in both countries conform to the following linear relationship:

$$\phi(x_i) = a + bx_i, \ i = A, B; \ a > 0, b > 0 \qquad (8)$$

Then, by transforming Eqns. (6) and (7) to proportional rates of growth and subtracting one gets:

$$g_A - g_B = \frac{aL_B}{x_A}\left(\frac{L_A}{L_B} - \frac{x_A}{x_B}\right) + b\left(L_A - L_B\right) - \delta\left(\frac{x_A}{x_B} - 1\right) \qquad (9)$$

$$g_i = \dot{x}_i/x_i \ , \ i = A, B$$

For clarifying the properties of the underlying process, one can distinguish the following cases:

(a) $\qquad\qquad \delta = 0, L_A = L_B, x_A > x_B$

Here, A is the leader in the stock of knowledge, but the two countries are equal in every other respect, and there is no diffusion. In this case, Eqn. (9) simplifies to

$$g_A - g_B = \frac{aL_A}{x_A}\left(1 - \frac{x_A}{x_B}\right) < 0 \qquad (10)$$

Since $g_A < g_B$, the ratio x_A/x_B falls. There is a process of convergence to a steady state. However, the stocks of knowledge are never equalized; they diverge in absolute terms. The speed of convergence is determined by aL_A/x_A which reflects the role of diminishing returns to experience in A. In particular, a/x_A is the difference between the average and the marginal product of experience and it diminishes as experience grows. This result indicates that what dominates the process of convergence is diminishing returns to experience in the leading region. Thus, it appears that the leader leads not only in experience; it also leads the process of convergence by its slowing down from "aging" or "maturing" of experienc e.

(b) $\qquad\qquad 1 > \delta > 0, L_A = L_B, x_A > x_B$

This case allows for diffusion from A to B. Eqn. (9) now becomes:

$$g_A - g_B = \frac{aL_A}{x_A}\left(1 - \frac{x_A}{x_B}\right) - \delta\left(\frac{x_A}{x_B} - 1\right) < 0 \qquad (11)$$

Here again, $g_A < g_B$, the ratio x_A/x_B falls, and there is convergence in growth rates but not in absolute levels. The speed of convergence is augmented in this case by the existence of diffusion from A to B. Contrariwise, if $\delta < 0$, implying negative spillovers, it is easy to see that there is no convergence; x_A/x_B rises without limit.

(c) $\qquad\qquad 1 > \delta > 0, L_A > L_B, x_A > x_B$

This is the general case encompassing full differentiation among countries and diffusion of knowledge between them. The basic story which can be told in this case is as follows. For L_A/L_B sufficiently large in relation to x_A/x_B, country A has an advantage deriving from its larger allocation of labor to the knowledge industry. This advantage allows it to grow faster than B, so that x_A/x_B increases and, correspondingly, the productivity gap in-

creases. However, part of this advantage, as represented by the first term on the right-hand side of Eqn. (9), is diminished by growing experience (due to diminishing returns to experience) as x_A rises both absolutely and relatively to x_B. It is converted to a disadvantage as x_A/x_B comes to exceed L_A/L_B. This advantage is also diminished by the increasing contribution (represented by the third term on the right-hand side of Eqn. (9)) that the growing gap in the stock of knowledge makes to growth in B due to diffusion of knowledge from A to B. Both these factors contribute to reducing the difference in growth rates between A and B. Consequently, the magnitude of the gap in the stock of knowledge, while continuing to grow, approaches an upper boundary given by the critical ratio:

$$(x_A/x_B)^* = \frac{b}{\delta}(L_A - L_B) + 1 \qquad (12)$$

However, what if x_A/x_B is large enough to begin with, in particular, x_A/x_B exceeds this critical ratio? The logic of Eqn. (9) entails that, with such initial values of x_A/x_B, the growth advantage that A has from its larger allocation of labor to the knowledge industry is overpowered by the diffusion effect and the diminishing returns effect. The advantage in growth then shifts from A to B and this results in reducing the size of the gap between A and B in the stock of knowledge and, correspondingly, in productivity levels. In this case, the gap asymptotically converges from above to the critical ratio x_A/x_B^*.

Thus, no matter how small or large the initial gap in the stock of knowledge between leader and follower, this process operates to bring about convergence in terms of growth rates of the stock of knowledge. But, as to the size of the gap itself, there is a sharp asymmetry, as shown in Fig. 1. For small initial gaps, the size of the gap widens, up to some upper limit. For gaps that are large enough to begin with, that is, gaps larger than the critical ratio, there is a reduction in the size of the gap. However, whatever the initial size of the gap, there always remains a gap and it is positive. This result follows from the fact that the critical ratio is necessarily greater than 1, given that $L_A > L_B, b > 0, \delta > 0$. The magnitude of this permanent gap

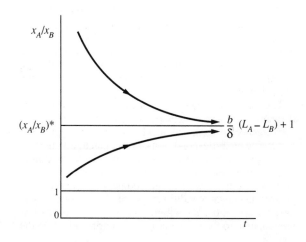

is uniquely determined by the difference in the allocation of labor to the knowledge industry, $L_A - L_B$, by the marginal product of experience, b, and by the diffusion parameter, δ.

(d) $\qquad\qquad 1 > \delta > 0, L_B < L^* < L_A$

If country B is unable to achieve the threshold size of allocation of labor to the knowledge industry, then it is unable to participate actively in the productivity race. It remains in a dependent status of receiving whatever spillovers it can get from those already in the race and its productivity level continues to fall further and further behind relative to the rest.

5. Conclusion

So far as the process of convergence/divergence in productivity growth is concerned, the analysis presented here identifies exactly what form that process takes and the conditions which affect the outcome.

The productivity gap is analyzed in terms of the relative size of the stocks of knowledge existing in the leader and follower countries. It is shown that, given some initial gap to begin with (no matter how big or small), the gap asymptotically approaches a definite size from above or below depending on initial conditions. Whether the gap increases or diminishes depends on how big the initial gap is. Thus, it is a matter of the exact degree of "relative backwardness" in a precise sense, specified in relation to the critical ratio $(x_A/x_B)^*$. In particular, only if the initial gap is "large enough" does convergence occur. In this respect, this result serves to give a certain precision to the well-known hypothesis of relative backwardness as a factor determining the tendency to convergence in productivity levels. Abramovitz (1986) provides a discussion of this hypothesis, along with several extensions and qualifications, and reviews some of the historical evidence pertaining to it. The general idea that the "degree of economic backwardness" is a significant factor governing the pace and direction of development was put forward by Gerschenkron (1952).

This result also replicates the diversity of the empirical record, insofar as that record exhibits the coexistence of dual tendencies of convergence and divergence. The coexistence of these two tendencies is shown here to be precisely connected with the cross-country distribution of initial conditions and paramater values around the critical ratio.

The analysis supports the need to maintain a sharp distinction between convergence in growth rates and convergence in terms of levels. In one class of cases depending on initial conditions, even though growth rates converge, levels diverge and the gap correspondingly widens, albeit to an upper limit.

It is evident also that the process of productivity growth, under the conditions specified here, operates to keep the size of the gap within bounds. This is for reasons related, first, to the existence of a "maturity" effect in the leading country associated with diminishing returns to experience. Second, it is related to the advantage that the follower country gains from the operation of a diffusion effect or of "spillovers" from the leader.

If the gap does not explode, it is never eliminated altogether. A certain positive size of the gap is permanently reproduced by this process. That size, given by the critical ratio $(x_A/x_B)^*$, is uniquely determined by specific conditions of the productivity-increasing process, namely; the marginal product of experience, b, the diffusion parameter, δ, and the difference in relative allocations of labor to the knowledge industry, $L_A - L_B$.

A special class of cases consists of those countries that are unable to mount the scale required to start up the productivity-increasing process. In such cases the gap increases without limit. The same result would occur if the diffusion parameter is negative, implying that there are retarding effects or negative spillovers from diffusion.

It is accepted that this analysis does not, nor does it attempt to, tell the whole story concerning the empirical record sketched in the first part of this entry. It does provide a heuristic framework with which to identify various essential elements of the story that need to be explored in greater depth, in seeking to explain the record of productivity growth.

As it stands, the model focuses on the character of the convergence/divergence process that occurs over a period of time appropriate to what one might call "a given technological paradigm," during which it might be said that the frontier of technological knowledge is relatively fixed. It is in that context that it would seem to make sense to talk about "diminishing returns to experience." However, in the long term, the paradigm does change and the frontier shifts out along with it. This introduces the possibility that, by leapfrogging, followers may overtake and surpass leaders, so that the pattern of leadership changes. It would remain to determine who leads and who follows under those conditions, and whether there is any tendency to convergence. This effect is not considered here and is intrinsically more difficult to model. (For an examination of the issues involved in the question of overtaking and of changing leadership, see Ames and Rosenberg 1963.)

Another effect not captured here, which may be considered a significant part of the empirical record of productivity growth, is the intersectoral effect associated, for instance, with a shift from agriculture to manufacturing industry, or from traditional manufacture to services. This aspect of the process is essentially eliminated at the highly aggregative level of this model. For the same reason, it is not possible to capture a significant dimension of the process that is related to the effect of commodity specialization among countries.

References

Abramovitz M 1986 Catching up, forging ahead, and falling behind. *Journal of Economic History* 46(2): 385–406

Ames E, Rosenberg N 1963 Changing technological leadership and industrial growth. *Economic Journal* 72: 13–31

Arrow K 1962a Economic welfare and the allocation of resources for invention. In *The Rate and Direction of Inventive Activity*. Princeton University Press, Princeton

Arrow K 1962b The implications of learning by doing. *Rev. Econ. Stud.* 29: 1955–73

Baumol W J 1988 Productivity growth, convergence, and welfare: What the long-run data show. *Am. Econ. Rev.* 76 (5): 1072–85

Baumol W J, Wolf E N 1988 Productivity growth, convergence, and welfare: Reply. *Am. Econ. Rev.* 78 (5): 1155–69

Baumol W J, Blackman S A B, Wolff E N 1989 *Productivity and American Leadership: The Long View*. MIT Press Cambridge, Massachusetts

De long B J 1988 Productivity growth, convergence and welfare: Comment. *Am. Econ. Rev.* 78 (5): 1138–54

Dos Santos T 1970 The structure of dependence. *Am. Econ. Rev.* 60 (2): 231–36

Dosi G 1984 *Technical change and Industrial Transformation*. St Martins Press, New York

Dosi G 1988 Sources, procedures, and microeconomic effects of innovating. *J. Econ. Lit.* 26: 1120–71

Dowrick S, Nguyen D-T 1989 OECD comparative economic growth 1950–85: Catch-up and convergence. *Am. Econ. Rev.* 79: 1010–31

Easterlin R 1981 Why isn't the whole world developed?. *Journal of Economic History* XLI (1): 1–17

Freeman C 1982 *The Economics of Industrial Innovation*. 2nd edn. MIT Press, Cambridge, Massachusetts

Gerschenkron A 1952 Economic backwardness in historical perspective. In: Hoselitz B F (ed.) 1952 *The Progress of Underdeveloped Areas* University of Chicago Press, Chicago, Illinois

Griliches Z 1986 Productivity, R&D and basic research at the firm level in the 1970s. *Am. Econ. Rev.* 70: 141–54

Machlup F 1962 *The Production and Distribution of Knowledge in the United States*. Princeton University Press, Princeton, New Jersey

Maddison A 1982 *Phases of Capitalist Development*. Oxford University Press, New York

Maddison A 1987 Growth and slowdown in advanced capitalist economies: techniques of quantitative assessment. *J. Econ. Lit.* 25 (2): 649–98

Mansfield E 1980 Basic research and productivity increase in manufacturing. *Am. Econ. Rev.* 70: 863–73

Matthews R C O, Feinstein C H, Odling-Smee J C 1982 *British Economic Growth 1856–1972*. Clarendon Press, Oxford

National Science Foundation 1987 *Science Indicators*. National Science Foundation, Washington, DC

Nelson R 1959 The simple economics of basic scientific research. *J. Pol. Econ.* 67: 297–306

Nelson R 1981 Research on productivity growth and productivity differences: Dead ends and new departures. *J. Econ. Lit.* 19: 1029–63

Olson M 1982 *The Rise and Decline of Nations: Economic Growth, Stagflation, and Social Rigidities*. Yale University Press, New Haven, Connecticut

Porat M U 1977 *The Information Economy: Definition and Measurement*. Vols. 1–9. USGPO, Washington, DC

Romer P M 1989 Capital accumulation in the theory of long-run growth. In Barro R (ed.) 1989 *Modern Macroeconomics*. Harvard University Press, Cambridge, Massachusetts

Rosenberg N 1982 *Inside the Black Box: Technology and Economics*. Cambridge University Press, Cambridge

World Bank 1992 *World Development Report 1992*. Oxford University Press, New York

World Bank 1993 *The East Asian Miracle*. Oxford University Press, New York

Education and Technological Change

M. Carnoy

Technological change has profound implications for production processes, the division of labor, and labor skills. This entry assesses the extent of available knowledge about the spread of technology, its impact on skills, its consequences for educational policy at different stages of technological diffusion, and conversely, the effect of education on both the use and development of new technology. For the sake of presentation, the discussion focuses on the new information technology, since it is this that represents the most modern wave of worldwide change in production processes.

1. Technological Diffusion

The new microelectronic technologies are diffused in three major forms: (a) through their consumption (electronic consumer goods, such as radios, calculators, television sets, videocassette recorders, and video games, and through telephone availability); (b) through the use of information and telecommunications technologies in the production of traditional goods and services; and (c) through the development and production of high technology products and processes themselves.

1.1 Consumer Electronics

Although the consumption of electronic goods is not usually regarded as technology diffusion, it does have an important impact on diffusion in three ways. First, there is a logical progression from the use of electronic and telecommunication products—even when imported—to their repair locally, and then to their local production. Second, there is a logical progression from the manufacture of simple electronic consumer goods to the manufacture of more complex computer and telecommunications systems, particularly when produced for export; both require similar quality control and production processes. Finally, and most important, certain electronic goods such as telephones also serve as the underlying infrastructure for a larger information–communication network.

The greater availability of telephones and improved worldwide communications have significant implications for the way developing economies can hook into the world economy. It is difficult to say precisely what "threshold" level of telecommunications access is needed for "high technification," but it appears to be approximately four to five telephone lines per 100 inhabitants.

1.2 Applications in Production of Traditional Goods and Services.

The diffusion of computers and telecommunications as investment goods employed in the production of goods and services represents a different level of technological use from consumer electronics and consumer telephone use. New technology brought into the production process enhances productivity and quality control and creates the possibility of producing new goods and services associated with the collection, treatment, and dissemination of information: new goods and services which in turn can increase productivity in existing industry.

The process of the technology diffusion through such applications is undoubtedly complex (Rosenberg 1976, Rogers 1983, Dosi 1988). Enterprises in different countries adopt new technologies at different rates depending on a number of factors, including the sector in which they are situated (Pavitt 1984). Economic and social variation at the national level (e.g., the position of labor unions, state macroeconomic policies, the role of exports in the economy) also play a significant role in technology diffusion, in addition to conditions in firms themselves (Edquist 1985, Edquist and Jacobsson 1988).

But for true technology transfer to occur, "learning by using" (Rosenberg 1982) has to result in the adaptation and production of applications domestically as a result of importing technology. This may begin with the development and production of software applications or adapting quality control processes, but may eventually spread to the import-substitution of hardware. It is the first of these activities (software applications using imported hardware) which turns out to be far more important in terms of productivity, and far more indicative of technology diffusion than hardware production (Bhalla and James 1984). Research in the People's Republic of China (Bianchi et al. 1988) and Mexico (Miller 1986) suggests that the importation of new technology, both in the form of hardware and software without accompanying training in the use of the technology and the management of associated production processes (including quality control), creates minimal technology transfer and minimal higher productivity linkages to other firms.

1.3 The Production of High-tech Products

The last link in the technological diffusion process is the domestic production of high-tech goods and services. Such production sometimes refers to both consumer microelectronics and microelectronics for business applications. However, the two types of production require very different levels of quality control and research and development spending (hence management and labor skills), and should therefore be separated.

The development of both consumer electronic production and, even more so, microelectronics production for business purposes, depends on the presence of one or more of several key factors: (a) the availability of the management and labor skills associated with the production of high-tech goods and services; (b) supply conditions which attract transnational corporations to locate part of their production in that country for export to the world market; (c) the existence of a domestic market for such goods and services, which may be in large part the result of previous technology use; alternatively, development may depend initially on consumption by the state as part of modernizing the state sector (where the state is itself a producer of goods and services), or on the need of traditional industries to compete internationally in the sale of their products by improving their production technology; and (d) a structure of economic incentives that make it worthwhile for producers of final products to source high-tech inputs domestically, and worthwhile for local suppliers to invest in the production of such inputs.

There are several different national models in the Third World which have attempted to capture the rents associated with domestic production of business microelectronics. The Brazilian and Indian models attempt to develop autarkic production in order to satisfy domestic demand and to export to other, less developed countries (Evans 1986, Agarwal 1985). Although their high-tech products are not competitive with the products of developed countries in terms of quality, they assure the development of a domestic industry and assure that these countries can move up the "learning curve" most rapidly by actually producing the new technology.

In the South Korean model, which applies to Hong Kong, Singapore, and Taiwan (and, to a lesser extent, Malaysia), the first phase of development was represented by foreign companies assembling goods in the country for export to their domestic markets (see Kim 1986, Amsden 1989, Henderson 1988, Henderson and Castells 1987, Salih and Young 1989). Then, due to considerable investment by the South Korean government in education and research and development, Korea first began to produce consumer electronics d other consumer goods of its own using high-technology production processes, and then moved into the production of computers, all for export. This was simultaneously accompanied by domestic consumption of these products.

A third model is found in Mexico (and, on the periphery of Europe, Spain). Mexico is in a special situation, since it borders on the world's largest economic market and also as it is historically a major recipient of United States foreign investment. In this model, foreign firms assemble high-tech products in Mexico for the Mexican market and for export to the United States and other Latin American countries. These firms are committed to hiring Mexican engineers and technicians ("learning by doing"), who, it is hoped, will eventually develop their own firms producing high-tech goods and services (Miller 1986, Montoya 1988, Warman and Miller 1988).

A fourth and final model is that of the People's Republic of China. Here, a huge potential domestic market for electronic and communications equipment is used to attract foreign firms into joint ventures to transfer technology, much as in the Mexican model. The difference between Mexico and China seems to be, however, that China is not attractive as an export platform for these foreign firms, although the Chinese would like it to be. And, unlike the Indians and Brazilians, China imports most of its new information technology for industrial applications in order to modernize manufacturing as rapidly as possible (Bianchi et al. 1988).

The data suggest that although diffusion has been limited, many developing countries in Asia and some in Latin America are already involved in the production and export of electronic goods and components. Many countries are importing new technologies. It is highly likely that production of new technologies in the developing world will increase, even though the research and development base for evolving and designing such products will remain concentrated in the Organisation for Economic Co-operation and Development (OECD) countries. This division of labor may change with the increasing importance of the software industry, which requires a much higher percentage of highly skilled labor.

Skill Effects

There is a long history of discussion among economists about the deskilling or reskilling effects of technology on labor. This discussion revolves around the issue of whether new technology decreases or increases the skills required in the workplace, hence lowering or raising the training and education needed by workers to do their jobs effectively. Without describing this literature in detail (see *Technological Change and Deskilling*) it is worthwhile summarizing its conclusions before going on to assess the wider relation between education and technology.

Spenner's review (1985) of results in the United States and Europe concludes that:

> There is no evidence that jobs, taken as a group, are experiencing dramatic upgrading and downgrading in terms of their skill requirements. This does not mean an absence of upgrading and downgrading changes but rather an approximate balancing in the direction and quantity of changes of an approximate conservation of total skill ... It is intriguing that there are more hints of downgrading in studies of skill as autonomy-control and more hints of upgrading in studies of skill as substantive complexity, suggesting the possibility of divergent aggregate trends in the two dimensions of skill. (Spenner 1985 p. 141)

Spenner argues that, "the impacts of technology on skill levels are not simple, not necessarily direct, not constant across settings, and cannot be considered in isolation" (p. 146). The same innovation in different firms can alter skill requirements in different ways.

No research on developing countries is as detailed as Spenner's. However, a recent set of case studies in Asian countries (International Labour Organisation 1988) of automation in the banking, engineering, electrical appliance, and printing industries confirm Spenner's conclusions that it is difficult to identify deskilling or reskilling with automation. It seems that the new jobs being created do not require higher skills, only different skills. It also appears that the most likely workers to be made redundant when automation is introduced are unskilled workers, although this varies according to country and labor legislation. In some cases, such as in South Korea, new unskilled jobs for women were created by automation.

Intuitively, it would seem likely that, as manufacturing and services adopt more complex forms of production, more complex skills would be required. Yet Spenner's review suggests that this may not be the case. Even as new jobs are created that do require higher level skills, just as many jobs (in absolute terms) may be created that require lower level or unchanged skills (Rumberger and Levin 1984).

The changes are made even more complicated by shifts in the gender of those employed in the new manufacturing industries and services. Labor in high-tech industries—where they have an important research and development or software component—tends to be more highly educated but also more gender-stratified than either that in traditional manufacturing or the labor force as a whole. This has important implications for technological job displacement in traditional industries combined with expansion of production of new technologies. Although the production jobs involved may require similar levels of skill, microelectronics production employs a female production labor force. Males are hired into technical jobs—relatively highly educated managers, engineers, sales personnel, and technicians—demanding a different set of skills to those displaced from traditional manufacturing. Therefore, in countries where new technologies applied in traditional industries and services "release" workers, and the production of new technologies employs workers, there is very little absorption of the first by the second.

3. Implications for Education and Training Policies

3.1 The Complementarity of Schooling, Training, and New Technology

Education and training policies are key elements in the process of change occurring in the world economy, but these policies should be different at different levels of development. What is the basis for formulating such policies?

The traditional tools for analyzing public educational investment have been labor force planning and rates of return. Labor force planning attempts to use input–output analysis to predict educational "needs," given projected industry growth, fixed education–skill ratios, skill–job ratios, and job–industry ratios. The method was flawed from the start because none of these ratios was in reality fixed. Spenner's (1985) discussion makes clear that education and skill demand are not necessarily the same. Rumberger's (1981) study argues that education in the United States is increasing much more rapidly than skill requirements. Yet there have been few if any measures of changing skill requirements in other economies; hence most analysts use average education as a proxy for the "capacity to produce," or skill "availability" in the labor force.

Rate-of-return analysis also has its problems, especially when social rates of return are used to predict which levels and what kind of education and training should be subsidized by the state in order to maximize economic growth. Rapid technological change may make social rates of return in the 1990s obsolete in terms of where countries want to be or will be one or two decades hence. The future direction of an economy may well depend on the kind of educational investments made before the payoffs to that education are realized. As economies shift from agricultural to manufacturing and services and the educational system expands, the social rate of return to higher levels of education is seen to rise relative to lower levels (Carnoy 1972, Carnoy and Marenbach 1975, Ryoo et al. 1991, Knight and Sabot 1990).

The association of education with "capacity to produce" is inherently correct, particularly in terms of five variables: literacy, numeracy, socialization to "competence," (Inkeles and Smith 1974), the self-confidence to learn new skills, and the ability to adjust to change (Schultz 1989). In addition, high-level science, medical, mathematical, and management skills needed for certain kinds of production of goods and services can be associated with university education. Societies whose population has these capabilities seem to be more able and willing to learn a wide range of skills related to working with "new" technologies (i.e. new to them). A better "educated" population is more trainable into new jobs. And it is more likely to adopt new technologies and increase their own productivity by using them (Welch 1970). Schultz calls this the "adjustment to disequilibrium" (Schultz 1989).

This complementarity between new methods of production and the capacity to produce that is implied in what schools are supposed to teach is the most powerful argument for more education. As Cohen and Tyson (1989) contend, a better educated labor force will create the conditions for investing in new kinds of production and new organizations of production. This argument probably holds even in relatively low income countries undergoing severe adjustments to the changing world economy.

Complementarity between education and new technology would contribute both to the diffusion of new growth-promoting technologies and to the employment-creation effect of technological change. A more literate, numerate, and socialized labor force would raise the rate of return to investing in new technology because it would be cheaper to train it to apply the new processes and to work in new kinds of work organizations. Moreover, in the case where labor is involved in making decisions on the use of new technology, it is more likely to use new technology and reap its benefits. An educated labor force would also represent one of the institutional conditions (in addition to a well-developed credit system, for example) required for the effects of technological change in particular firms and industries (lower prices or more employment and income) to spread to other firms and industries.

3.2 The Special Role of the University

Higher education plays a crucial role in technology transfer at two levels. First, it has the capability to develop the management skills required to utilize and organize the new technology; therefore, in terms of the analysis presented here, higher education is the key to the technology transfer process in those industries that use and produce information technology. Second, with the spread of science-based industries, the university is the site that can combine the basic research needed for the advance of such industries with the training of researchers and appliers of research for industry.

The rising rates of return in the larger, and higher educated, nonindustrialized countries (NICs) in part reflect this increasingly important economic role that the university plays in the labor force formation process. This role will increase in the future, especially in the NICs and the industrializing economies, and the more rapid the rate of growth and information-technology orientation of the economy, the more important the university's role.

However, most universities in developing countries are not organized to combine research and training of undergraduates and graduates in the way required by the new technology and new organization of production. In Brazil, for example, the federal universities are expensive and inefficient, and produce relatively few research–training connections. Much of the teaching is not oriented toward problem-solving. In addition, space is not sufficiently utilized, keeping many qualified students out of the university system. Universities in Argentina and Mexico are much cheaper and much more crowded, but are similar in their lack of research and research–training connections. China's universities are almost purely training institutions, with research delegated to research centers that offer little training. Most developing countries' universities will have to undergo serious reforms if they are to enter into the information age.

Most countries also need to expand greatly their research program in both the universities and industry. Brazil, Argentina, and to some extent Mexico, have engaged in basic scientific research in universities and particularly research institutes. However, this effort has been small compared to the industrialized countries (Castells 1991).

The most telling variable is the degree of cross-activity between training and research on the one hand, and practical industrial applications, on the other, in the three institutions that conduct research and training in most societies: (a) universities, (b) research institutes, and (c) private and public businesses. The greater the presence of both research and training, and application activities in each of these institutions, and the greater the interaction between institutions, the greater the return to research and higher education.

3.3 The New Technology and Training

Training is also a complementary investment to new technology. Yet it must be viewed as complementary both to capital (and the technology associated with capital) and education (and the "technology" associated with education). Training can be divided into: (a) in-school training, or vocational education; (b) on-the-job training, both general and specific, designed for a particular type of production process; and (c) learning by doing, a form of on-the-job training directly connected to the production process itself.

In-school training/vocational education is most distant from the production process. It is designed to provide general skills directly applicable to the production of goods and services, and therefore falls somewhere between schooling and training. From the educators' point of view it has the distinct advantage of "taking care of" students who need preparation for the world of work but who do not perform especially well in abstract academic education. The emphasis centers more on deciding which kind of schooling and training best produces complementarity with new kinds of technology and production processes. Is vocational education more complementary to new methods of production than academic? And is vocational education more complementary than on-the-job training or learning by doing?

Grubb (1987) argues that the new information technologies' impact on skill demand should push the educational system away from vocational concerns into more general preparation of the population to think critically. In theory, this would make workers able to deal with a variety of higher quality jobs that require thought and decision-making rather than the repetitive work that characterizes Fordist technology. This approach would argue for investing in higher quality academic education rather than specific vocational, even if the two could be produced at same cost. In general, long-course vocational education is as expensive (or more so) than even relatively high-cost academic schooling.

A recent World Bank monograph (Middleton et al. 1990) makes the case that in-school vocational education, both because of its cost and its use of obsolete equipment, is not as complementary to changing technologies as in-firm training. This suggests that a more effective way to provide training is through direct subsidies to firms rather than through indirect subsidies via vocational education.

Nevertheless, there is still a case for vocational education in certain situations: (a) in countries characterized by high economic growth, especially where private enterprises are willing to bear part of its cost, or in vocations for high-growth industries (Chung 1990); (b) in situations where enterprises send workers who are already employed to be trained partially at the company's expense (examples are SENA in Colombia and SENAI in Brazil, but it should be remembered that the analyses of these programs were done in relatively high economic growth periods); (c) in countries characterized by low growth and increasing or high unemployment, short-course, self-employment-oriented training designed for new occupations in agriculture or the informal labor market may yield high returns provided that they focus on broader, "business" skills such as marketing and sales in addition to traditional production or service skills.

What is the complementarity of in-plant training to new technologies? It is commonly agreed that training programs are an important feature of successful firms producing high-technology products and those that use high-technology intensive capital (see, e.g., Shaiken and Herzenberg 1987). Less clear is the relationship of training programs to employee education and to work organization. Recent research in Mexico found that plants providing in-plant training generally geared it to certain "target" levels of education, and those targets were used in labor force hiring (Carnoy 1989). This held for production workers, as well as for management trainees and industrial engineers. There appears to be a significant relationship between the technology embodied in capital and work organization, the "optimum" level of education required of different kinds of employees who work with that capital or in that organization, and the in-plant training programs provided, although that optimum level may vary historically as the formal educational system expands. This suggests that "trainability" is as much a function of what is actually learned in various levels of schooling (the mathematics, science, and language arts curricula) as of graduates' sense of self-worth and capability. The first is an absolute consideration; employers producing particular products and using particular technology have a clear image of the minimum literacy and numeracy skills required for in-plant training in certain jobs. The availability of those school skills might be a condition of initial investment in such production. The second is relative: that is, how graduates are measured and how they measure themselves compared to others who are the same age and who are also seeking work at that point in time. A graduate with nine years of schooling in Mexico may well have a greater sense of capability than a high-school graduate in the United States. This relative notion of education is generally called its "screening" feature. The simpler the technology and the more hierarchical the organization, the less the complementarity between in-school education, in-plant training, and physical capital.

Learning by doing, unlike in-plant training, can be complemented by capital and especially by work organization. Once again, many questions arise: what is the complementarity of in-school education to learning by doing? Do more highly schooled workers learn more by doing with given capital (and therefore become more productive) than less schooled workers? Is in-plant formal training complementary to learning by doing, or are they relatively independent learning processes? Are certain types of work organization more complementary to learning by doing, given the schooling of workers and managers, than others (see Levin 1987)? Are there minimum levels of previous learning by doing which are required with certain kinds of technology or in certain industries and not in others?

The last wave of new technologies, new organizations of production, changing employment conditions, and the development of new sectors of production suggest that the complementarity of general, formal schooling, in-plant training, and learning by doing to capital investment are increasing over time and that general schooling plus on-the-job training is more complementary to new technologies than vocational schooling. The former combination is more likely to equip workers with the flexibility they require in such changing conditions. The analysis across types of sectors outlined above also suggests that different levels and conditions of development necessitate different decisions regarding schooling and training, and that many countries face the threat of being excluded from the new information revolution unless they restructure their economies and expand education and training programs with a focus on general and high-quality skill formation. The larger NICs could also fall far behind unless they, too, focus on university reform and greatly increased research and research-oriented training in higher education.

See also: Technological Change and the Demand for Educated Labor

References

Agarwal S M 1985 Electronics in India: Past strategies and future possibilities. *World Dev.* 13 (3): 273–92

Amsden A 1989 *Asia's Next Giant: South Korea and Late Industrialization.* Oxford University Press, New York

Bhalla A S, James J 1984 New technology revolution: Myth or reality for developing countries? *Greek Econ. Rev.* 6 (3): 387–423

Bianchi P, Carnoy M, Castells M 1988 *Economic Modernization and Technology Transfer in the People's Republic of China.* Report No. 88–26. Center for Educational Research at Stanford, Stanford University, Stanford, California

Carnoy M 1972 The political economy of education. In: La Belle T (ed.) 1972 *Education and Development in Latin America and the Caribbean.* Latin American Center, UCLA, Los Angeles, California

Carnoy M 1989 *Opening the Door: Education and Productivity.* Film produced by the International Labour Organisation, Geneva (VHS videotape, distributed by ILO, Geneva), 17 min

Carnoy M, Marenbach D 1975 The return to schooling in the United States, 1939–1969. *J. Hum. Resources* 10 (3): 312–31

Castells M 1991 The university system: Engine of development in the new world economy. Paper prepared for the World Bank Seminar on Higher Education and Development, Kuala Lumpur (mimeo)

Chung Y-P 1990 The economic returns to vocational and technical education in a fast growing economy: A case study of Hong Kong. Unpublished doctoral dissertation, Stanford University, Stanford, California

Cohen S, Tyson L 1989 Technological change, competitiveness and the challenges confronting the American educational system. Berkeley Roundtable for International Economics, University of California, Berkeley, California (mimeo)

Dosi G 1988 Sources, procedures, and microeconomic effects of innovation. *J. Econ. Lit.* 26: (3) 1120–71

Edquist C 1985 *Capitalism, Socialism and Technology: A Comparative Study of Cuba and Jamaica.* Zed Books, London

Edquist C, Jacobsson S 1988 *Flexible Automation: The Global Diffusion of New Technology in the Engineering Industry.* Basil Blackwell, Oxford

Evans P 1986 State, capital, and the transformation of dependence: The Brazilian computer case. *World Dev.* 14 (7): 791–808

Grubb N 1987 Responding to the constancy of change: New technologies and future demands on US education. In Burke G, Rumberger R (eds.) 1987.

Henderson J 1988 High technology production in Hong Kong and the making of a regional 'core'. Paper presented at the International Symposium of Technology Policy in the Americas, Stanford University, California

Henderson J, Castells M 1987 *Global Restructuring and Territorial Development.* Sage, Beverly Hills, California

Inkeles A, Smith D 1974 *Becoming Modern: Individual Change in Six Developing Countries.* Harvard University Press, Cambridge Massachusetts

International Labour Organisation 1988 *Technological Change, Work Organization and Pay: Lessons from Asia.* Labor-Management Relations Series, No. 68. ILO, Geneva

Kim L 1986 New technologies and their economic effects: A feasibility study in Korea. Paper prepared for the United Nations University, New Technologies Centre Feasibility Study, Maastricht

Knight J B, Sabot R 1990 *Education, Productivity, and Inequality: The East African Natural Experiment.* World Bank/Oxford University Press, New York

Levin H 1987 Improving productivity through education and technology. In: Burke G, Rumberger R (eds.) 1987

Middleton J, Ziderman A, Van Adams A 1990 *Vocational Education and Training in Developing Countries.* World Bank, Washington, DC

Miller M 1986 High technology transfer: A case study of the Mexican computer electronics industry. Unpublished undergraduate honors thesis, Stanford University, California

Montoya A 1988 Telematics, knowledge and power in Mexican society: The policies of the Mexican State, 1970–1983. Unpublished PhD dissertation, Stanford University, California (mimeo)

Pavitt K 1984 Patterns of technical change: Towards a taxonomy and a theory. *Res. Policy* 13 (6): 343–73

Rogers E 1983 *Diffusion of Innovations,* 3rd edn. Free Press, New York

Rosenberg N 1976 *Perspectives on Technology.* Cambridge University Press, Cambridge

Rosenberg N 1982 *Inside the Black Box: Technology and Economics.* Cambridge University Press, Cambridge

Rumberger R 1981 *Overeducation in the US Labor Market.* Praeger, New York

Rumberger R, Levin H 1984 Forecasting the impact of new technologies on the future job market. *Technological Forecasting and Social Change* 27: 399–417

Ryoo J, Nam Y S, Carnoy M 1993 Rates of return to education in the Korea. *Econ. Educ. Rev.*

Salih K, Young M L 1989 Changing conditions of labour in the semiconductor industry in Malaysia. *Lab. Soc.* 14: 59–80 (special issue devoted to High Tech and Labor in Asia)

Schultz T 1989 Human capital in restoring equilibrium. Paper presented at the Conference on Human Capital and Economic Growth, Institute for the Study of Free Enterprise Systems, SUNY, Buffalo, New York

Shaiken H, Herzenberg S 1987 *Automation and Global Production. Automobile Engine Production in Mexico, the United States, and Canada.* University of California, Center for US–Mexican Studies, San Diego, California

Spenner K 1985 The upgrading and downgrading of occupations: Issues, evidence, and implications for education. *Rev. Educ. Res.* 55 (2): 125–54

Warman J, Miller M 1989 *Competividad de la Industria Electrónica Mexicana: Estudios de caso.* Friedrich Ebert Foundation, Mexico City

Welch F 1970 Education in production. *J. Pol. Econ.* 78(1): 35–59

Further Reading

Burke G, Rumberger R (eds.) 1987 *The Future Impact of Technology on Work and Education.* Falmer Press, London

Castells M 1985 New technologies, world development, and structural transformation: The trends and the debate. Department of City and Regional Planning, University of California, Berkeley, California (mimeo)

Rumberger R, Levin H M 1989 Schooling for the modern workplace. Background paper No.2 prepared for the Commission on Workforce Quality and Labor Market Efficiency, US Department of Labor, Washington, DC

Education and the New International Division of Labor

M. Carnoy

In the 1970s and 1980s the world economy underwent a radical transformation. It affected long-term national growth possibilities, the actual and potential roles that countries play in the world economy, and the strategies that governments must pursue to insure growth. Because the use and production of information are so important to these changes, education has been particularly impacted. The experience of both developed and newly industrializing countries suggests that education's importance as a source of growth has increased and that new educational policy approaches are required to realize this growth in an era of greater resource constraints and changing demands for labor skills.

No one is untouched by the change. Like every transformation, it creates new winners and losers. The winners understand the contours of the change earlier than others. They adapt to it and even exploit it when the particular nature and resources of their societies enable them to do so. Their educational strategies are generally harmonious with a coordinated national strategy for growth (Altbach et al. 1989, Amsden 1989). The losers become locked into widely varying patterns of economic, social, and political behavior that are incongruent when related to the kinds of action required in the new conditions. These patterns usually include anachronistic and incoherent educational strategies (Dahlman and Frischtak 1991).

211

This entry describes the main characteristics of the economic changes, assesses the corresponding changes in the international division of labor and its effects on the returns to schooling in various countries, and explores the potential for government intervention in shaping national development by responding to such changes through new educational investment strategies.

1. Changed World Economy

What are the main features of this changed world economy? First, higher productivity is increasingly generated from the application of knowledge and information applied to production, and such knowledge is increasingly science-based. This is not an entirely new phenomenon, since knowledge has always been critical in organizing and fostering economic growth. However, as economies become more complex, as consumption tastes worldwide become more varied, and as competition increases, new knowledge and information become more critical to the production and realization process.

Second, production in the advanced capitalist societies shifts from material goods to information-processing activities. This represents a fundamental change in the structure of advanced societies toward economic activities that focus on symbol manipulation in the organization of production and in the enhancement of productivity. The quality of information and the efficiency of acquiring it therefore become the strategic factors in both competitiveness and productivity for firms, regions, and countries.

Third, the organization of production and of economic activity in general change from mass standardized production to flexible customized production, and from vertically integrated large organizations to vertical disintegration and horizontal networks between economic units (Piore and Sabel 1986). Small and medium-size businesses have proven to be particularly good at adjusting to and developing new responses to the market's new demands for flexibility and customization. Yet large corporations have also been able to become more decentralized, both internally and in their relationship to networks of smaller, supplier firms. Thus large, multinational firms have been able to maintain themselves as the dominant actors in the new world economy, but only by becoming much more decentralized and flexible.

Fourth, the new economy is global (Porter 1990). Capital, production, management, markets, labor, information, and technology are organized across national boundaries. What is new is not so much that international trade is an important part of each nation's economy, but that a national economy works as a unit at the world level on real time. This gives a tremendous advantage to multinational firms, since they already have the knowledge required to produce and to market goods and services internationally. Nation-states remain important in organizing economic activities; yet their frame of reference for economic strategies can no longer be restricted to the national economy.

Fifth, these economic and organizational transformations have been taking place in the midst of one of the most significant technological revolutions in human history. Its core is information technologies—informatics, microelectronics, and telecommunications—surrounded by and aiding scientific discoveries in other fields, such as biotechnology, new materials, lasers, and renewable energy. All this has been stimulated by economic and organizational transformations on a global scale; simultaneously, the new information technology is indispensable for such transformations. It is the critical factor for developing flexibility and decentralization in production and management, since it assists production and trade units to function autonomously, yet also permits reintegration through information networks into a new economic "space of flows" (Castells 1993) (see *Education and Technological Change.*).

The revolution in information technology has combined with the organizational changes at the global level to produce a new worldwide Information Economy. Within the emerging global system, the structure and logic of the Information Economy defines a new international division of labor. The division is based less on the location of natural resources, cheap and abundant labor, or even capital stock and more on the capacity to create new knowledge and apply it rapidly through information processing and telecommunications to a wide range of human activities in ever-broadening space and time.

How does the new division of labor operate in the world arena? In the first instance, both the demand for new products and the capacity to create and produce them are still concentrated in the major industrial powers. Yet, there is a difference: United States hegemony, developed in a period when proximity to major markets and economies of scale in manufacturing dominated comparative advantage, has declined as other national economies, namely those of Japan and West Germany (at the core of the European Community), exploited their base of scientific knowledge and management skills in order to be able to compete successfully under the conditions of more flexible, export-oriented manufacturing production. As a result, United States hegemony has been transformed into a multipolarity of economic power among several dominant countries and regions.

Further, a second tier of efficient producers of electronic goods and high technology hardware has arisen in Asia, again built on a base of high-level technological and management skills and the commitment of national states to the promotion and application of those skills. The economies of countries such as South Korea, Taiwan, Hong Kong, and Singapore have made astonishing advances since the early 1960s. These countries (the newly industrializing countries or NICs), along with Japan, constitute the most dynamic pole of the new world economy.

At the other end of the spectrum, much of Latin America and Africa have suffered as a result of the changes in the world economy. The heavy borrowing that these national economies undertook to overcome their structural problems in the 1970s became a huge debt burden to them in the 1980s. This crippling debt rang the death knell of their traditional attempts to develop manufacturing to facilitate import substitution. Their financial crisis occurred just at the moment when large investments were needed for new imported technology, for new types of local production, for industrial reorganization, and for more schooling, training, and research. Effectively, debt burdens prevented such new investments, leaving many of the economies that might have participated in the type of transformation occurring in Asia—such as those of Brazil, Mexico, Argentina, Nigeria, and Venezuela—far behind in the change process. Other economies, such as those of the low-income, predominantly agricultural countries of Africa, Asia, and Latin America, were left further estranged from the world development process than they had been in the past.

As a result, the concept of the Third World as such has disappeared (Castells 1993). What used to be known as "Third World economies" have become different economic groups, redefined in terms of their relationship to the world economy by their ability to produce goods and services related to information. They can be divided into four groups: (a) the clear winners in the new international division of labor— the rapidly growing, newly industrializing countries of Asia; (b) the potential winners, such as Mexico (as part of the North American free trade area), Argentina, Brazil, Chile, Colombia, and Venezuela—the recovering, relatively highly educated Latin American societies; (c) the large continental economies of India and China, which are on their way to integration in the new world economy thanks primarily to their potentially massive markets and large stock of highly skilled human capital; (d) the clear losers—the Fourth World, comprised of marginal rural economies on all three continents and of Africa's and Latin America's sprawling urban peripheries.

What happens in the potential winner countries and in the large continental economies will depend largely on how they transform their economic and educational organizations and how they relate their existing but relatively underdeveloped research and development (R&D) to production. The potential situation of the Fourth World is more a function of creating totally new institutions and new bases of economic and social integration. There are serious questions as to whether the free-enterprise policies promulgated by the major international agencies will push the Fourth World in that direction or will leave it even worse off.

2. Changing Labor Market

These changes in the demand for and production of goods have changed overall conditions in the national labor markets of the developed countries and the Asian NICs. Similar changes should characterize national labor markets in other countries as they join the new world information economy. The main characteristics are as follows.

First, an increasing proportion of jobs are in what could be called high technology sectors or in "traditional" manufacturing and service sectors that use high technology and have been reorganized. In these sectors, innovation (R&D) is the key to the success of firms and economies in the new competitive environment. The most important jobs are those that require workers and managers to be innovative.

Second, an increasing proportion of jobs require "flexible response"; that is, they require workers and managers to be able to make decisions that are not the same every day or even every hour. The jobs also may require an update of knowledge even in the course of a single year on the job. For example, secretarial jobs increasingly require the use of new software and new tasks—thus, the "job" is constantly changing (Rumberger and Levin 1989, Levin 1987).

Third, because of increased competition and rapid reorganization, workers and managers may have to change jobs several times during their working lives. There is also increased subcontracting and hiring of part-time workers. Jobs are much less secure. Even in the European Community, with its elaborate labor laws, subcontracting and part-time employment are becoming increasingly popular ways of avoiding the payment of social benefits. An increasing part of the EC labor force is required to face frequent job changes.

Fourth, more women are coming into the labor market throughout the world. Many of the new jobs in service industries and in high tech production are being occupied by women—because of increased competition, employers are hiring women for jobs that were previously done by men. This process is set to continue, and it will continue to have profound social and educational effects.

Fifth, a large informal labor market has developed. Its existence is assured, and it may even grow, as competition and the restructuring of firms increase the subcontracting of production and services to firms with low labor costs and increase subcontracting for part-time labor services to employment agencies. Thus, dualities develop in the labor market. In Fourth World countries the majority of the urban labor force may be employed or self-employed in such informal markets.

3. Changing Payoff to Education

The increased importance of educated labor in production should, all other things being equal, raise the rate of return to investment in education. This implies that individuals and governments should, and will, invest more in education. However, since the social payoffs to education are relatively long-term and capital markets are highly imperfect for educational investment, both individuals and governments in many economies have either been unable, or have simply not been perceptive enough to make such investments in periods of low economic growth and decline in real income (Coombs 1985).

Given the nature of the new technology, the increase in payoff should be greater for the more educated than for the less educated. Especially in developed countries, the Asian NICs, and the "potential winners" described above, the value of investment in higher education should have risen relative to the labor-market value of investment in lower levels. At these lower levels, an increasing part of the return should reside in the "option value" of investing in the higher payoff, higher levels of education. In lower income countries, with correspondingly less-developed educational systems (i.e., the Fourth World), the returns to primary and secondary education may remain high, however, since many of the productivity-increasing job opportunities (as in agriculture, commerce, and simple manufactures) do not require university training and there is a relative dearth of labor educated at secondary or even primary level.

The evidence suggests that since around 1975 rates of return to investment in higher education in the NICs and the developed countries have risen relative to lower levels of schooling (Ryoo et al. 1993) (see *Rates of Return to Education*). In the United States real incomes of college graduates rose in the 1980s while those of high-school graduates fell. This resulted in rapidly rising relative rates of return to college education (Murphy and Welch 1989, Carnoy et al. 1990). Similar trends were observable in South Korea and Hong Kong. Yet other results show that in a country such as Kenya, which had not participated in the second tier of the information revolution, the payoff to primary schooling dropped sharply relative to secondary education in the 1970s (Knight and Sabot 1990), largely as a result of increasing demand for middle-level skills relative to the simpler skills associated with primary education (see *Educational Expansion and Labor Markets*).

Since workers are much more likely to change jobs during their working life in those societies that participate fully in the new world economy, to perform multiple tasks in whatever jobs they hold, and, in many countries, to end up in the informal labor market, greater flexibility in learning and a wider range of learning capabilities are needed for those newly entering the labor force. Logically, the payoff to investment in general education should rise relative to the payoff to vocational education, although vocational training in the skills required in rapidly growing sectors should continue to yield a high rate of return (Chung 1990) (see *Education and Technological Change; Technological Change and the Demand for Educated Labor; Returns to Vocational Education in Developing Nations*). The evidence suggests, however, that many of these same skills can be developed more cost-effectively through a combination of general education plus on-the-job training (Middleton et al. 1991).

One of the manifestations of the greater value to the individual and society of general education in the longer term is the customarily much flatter age–earnings profile of vocationally educated workers compared to the generally educated. The vocationally educated tend to start out with higher earnings, but fall behind as their work career progresses. The specificity of their training tends to make them less adaptable to economic changes. With the increase in the velocity of these changes, the vocationally educated will probably become increasingly penalized—governments that invest heavily in vocational education could be burdening their labor forces with relatively greater inflexibility.

With increased demand for labor flexibility and for the ability to learn different jobs over a lifetime, the quality of education should be a much more important factor in affecting labor productivity and economies' growth rates. Although evidence on this point is scarce, and these data should be interpreted with care, there appears to be some correlation between increases in the adult aptitude scores of national labor forces since around 1960 and national growth rates (Bishop 1992). These aptitude scores are more related to the *quality* of education rather than to years of schooling (Bishop 1992).

4. Role of National Governments

Although multinational corporations have become increasingly important in the Information Economy as innovators and bearers of advanced technology, national governments have remained crucial to each national economy's position in the new international division of labor. However, the roles of both of these actors have changed.

The shift to the application of information to material production in a global context as the principal source of the wealth of nations has made the skills embedded in multinational firms even more fundamental to a national economy's success. Their ability to process and use information on an international scale, and their very size (which suggest a capacity for mobilizing investment capital and, more importantly, for conducting research and development on new products and applications) make them powerful players in a world that places ever greater value on these capacities. Small and medium-size firms are often more flexible, more efficient producers or quicker to develop new products. Yet very little of the world's total

R&D is undertaken in such firms; ultimately the most successful ones necessarily become multinationals.

However, the nation-state's policies have a significant influence on multinationals' capacity to expand, for two reasons: (a) for most multinationals the home market has remained crucial to the capital accumulation process—national macroeconomic policies remain important for home market development; (b) the research and development capability of most multinationals has remained linked to home-based nation-state R&D policies, high-skill human capital development policies, and telecommunications policies (Carnoy 1993).

National governments therefore have remained crucial actors in the new world economy, but the conditions in which each of them acts have been altered. First, each has less leeway in focusing its policies purely on developing national markets. It is not enough to attract capital into most countries just to give investors access to the consumers and producers in that country. Second, a national government has to be much more concerned than in the past about acquiring or developing information technology that transforms its productive capacity—this technology resides in management skills, telecommunications, computer hardware and software, and the more general higher level engineering skills required to adapt and supervise the use of these new technologies. Even if the hardware element of such technologies is imported, it is crucial that the software (including management) is localized. This means that government policies concerning education, R&D, and incentives for adopting and developing new technologies must be much more aggressive than in an assembly-line type of industrialization.

Good management and organizing for technology adoption and development require more coherent public policies than simple resource exploitation or even assembly-line production. National government themselves therefore need to be better managed, clearer in their objectives, and more attuned to world information systems than was previously the case.

How have relationships between national governments and multinational enterprises changed? Because so many of the skills and so much of the hardware fundamental to participation in the Information Economy belong to multinationals, one of the most important new roles of national governments is bargaining with these technology carriers in order to transfer knowledge into the local economy. This is not an easy task. Multinationals are not anxious to transfer skills that generate the highest returns to others; most national governments have little bargaining power. This is a two-way street, however. Governments that are able to develop coherent *general* knowledge-acquisition strategies are more likely to be ready to learn "on-the-job" from multinationals, should they locate locally. Most multinationals also find it more economically advantageous to disperse skills across those countries where a high premium is placed on learning. Governments that have coherent national policies on information-technology acquisition are also more likely to know what to bargain for, and what their bargaining chips are (Newfarmer 1985, United Nations Centre on Transnational Corporations 1988, Carnoy 1993).

5. Educational Policies

The key elements for a successful educational policy under these new conditions are relevance, coherence, and participation. In the new international division of labor based on information, national economic possibilities depend increasingly on the population's capacity to adapt to rapidly changing conditions (flexibility, the capacity to learn new jobs, and the ability to use information), the innovative nature of the information, and its incorporation into the national economic project. In the countries that have responded most effectively to the new international division of labor, educational systems have been coherently utilized to move toward these goals.

5.1 Changing Academic Product

The academic product of schools has to change from managing facts and reproducing those facts to problem-solving and critical thinking. Studies have shown that even those in the informal labor market do significantly better when they receive more education (Tueros 1992). Since many workers in the informal labor market are self-employed, problem-solving skills and critical thinking are even more important to their success than for employed labor (see *Education and Informal Labor Markets*). Even though young people will stay in school longer on average, they need to develop critical thinking and problem-solving early, as part of their fundamental skills development.

There also has to be more focus on *general* academic rather than vocational skills for all students. The question of how to provide this—whether through practical problems or through a very theoretical, traditional curriculum—should be left to schools and teachers and customized for each child or groups of children. General skills are needed because of the need for a flexible labor force that can change tasks and even the type of work they do (Middleton et al. 1991).

In addition, socialization in schools has to change from strict obedience to *participation*. One important impact of the spread of information is increased pressure for democratization, even within the economy. Successful firms are increasingly relying on worker participation in decisions (Brown et al. 1993). The educational system must prepare them for this new role by socializing them in a more participative education.

Part of participation is the notion of creativity and innovation, rather than just following rules (Rumberger and Levin 1989).

5.2 Education and Increased Social Participation

Development has meaning in the contemporary world only if it extends through all strata of society. Such general, deep-seated development is required to mobilize savings and investment over the long term. "Deep development" is also needed to build up human resources for the new organizations and technologies associated with the information-based world economy. Deep development strategies hinge on the concept of social participation. Development with social participation means that development strategies derive from the population's needs and respond to them. It also means that development relies on widespread commitment by a nation's people to the national development project and, in turn, it can only occur if the population at large believes in it.

All-inclusive, high-quality schooling plays a crucial role in development with social participation. Schooling is almost universally valued. It represents people's connection to and involvement with potential economic improvement and social change. Market economies with more equal income distribution have an easier path to mobilizing savings for development and political support for long-term development programs. The Asian economies that did particularly well in the 1970s and 1980s had relatively equal income distributions. A large part of their success has been their extremely high savings rate and general support from all income segments of the society for postponing consumption and building productive capacity. This situation may be contrasted with that of Latin American countries, beset by highly unequal income distribution and resulting social conflict. The blame for Latin American societies' inability to mobilize high savings rates in the 1970s can be apportioned to the unequal distribution of income increases in the 1950s and 1960s. These unequal income increases, favoring a small percentage of the population, politically delegitimized the governments that attempted to produce development in this fashion. It reduced such governments' capability to mobilize savings and investment, and created instead a situation where groups increasingly conflicted with each other over the "spoils" of development. Simultaneously, the capacity to develop declined.

This scenario directly contradicts the widely held beliefs that economic growth is incompatible with more equal income distribution, that high growth rates "naturally" lead to more unequal income distribution, and that economic growth eventually produces more equal income distribution. A major reason for income equalization policies has been to establish political legitimacy for governments—especially democratically elected ones, but even for authoritarian ones, such as those of South Korea, Singapore, and Taiwan in the 1960s and 1970s—and to develop the political

support for long-term economic development policies especially ones that require society-wide, long-term economic saving and investment (Castells 1991a). When income and wealth are more equal, and the fruits of development are distributed more equally, the mass of the population is more committed to development policy.

Because more and more young people need some type of postsecondary education, schools must organize themselves to create high-quality primary and secondary education, both for those who arrive with skills already developed in the family *and* for those who do not. Expectations for disadvantaged children need to increase. There also needs to be a greater focus on girls' education—female workers have become crucial to export industries and financial services in the newly industrializing countries (NICs).

5.3 Tying Education into a Coherent National Innovation System

Those countries that have developed most rapidly in the global, information context of the new world economy have been able to tie their educational policies into an overall, coherent national innovation policy (Carnoy 1992, Castells 1991a, 1991b). For developed countries, this appears to mean making the higher educational system a functioning part of an R&D policy that both produces basic research and research-trained labor for R&D in industry. For developing countries, this also appears to mean the coordination of technological "catch-up," both through transferring technology by attracting multinationals' investment and through adapting foreign technology to local manufacturing, services, and agriculture (Okimoto 1984). This will entail an increase in the quality of primary and secondary educated labor as well as a change in the role of universities in most developing countries (Castells 1991b, Schwartzman 1984, Dahlman and Frischtak 1991).

See also: Education and Technological Change; Rates of Return to Education; Educational Expansion and Labor Markets; Economics of Nonformal Training; Education and Informal Labor Markets

References

Altbach P et al. 1989 *Scientific Development and Higher Education: The Case of the Newly Industrializing Nations.* Praeger, New York

Amsden A 1989 *Asia's Next Giant: South Korea and Late Industrialization.* Oxford University Press, New York

Bishop J 1992 The economic consequences of schooling and learning. Economic Policy Institute Washington, DC (mimeo)

Brown C, Reich M, Stern D 1993 Becoming a high-performance work organization: The role of security, employee involvement, and training. *International Journal of Human Resource Management* May

Carnoy M 1992 *Universities, Technological Change, and*

Training in the Information Age, mimeo. World Bank, Washington, DC

Carnoy M 1993 The changing role of multinationals: Whither the nation-state? In: Carnoy M, Castells M, Cohen S, Cardoso F H 1993 *The New Global Economy in the Information Age*. Pennsylvania State University Press, University Park, Pennsylvania

Carnoy M, Daley H, Hinojosa R 1990 *Latinos in a Changing US Economy*. Interuniversity Program for Latino Research, City University of New York, New York

Castells M 1991a *Four Asian Tigers with a Dragon Head: A Comparative Analysis of the State, Economy, and Society in the Asian Pacific Rim*. Instituto Universitario de Sociologia de Nuevas Tecnologias, Universidad Autonoma de Madrid, Madrid

Castells M 1991b The university system: Engine of development in the new world economy. Paper prepared for the World Bank Seminar on Higher Education and Development, Kuala Lumpur, June 30–July 4

Castells M 1993 The informational economy and the new international division of labor. In: Carnoy M et al. (eds.) 1993 *Reflections on the New World Economy in the Information Age*. Pennsylvania State University Press, University Park, Pennsylvania

Chung Y-P 1990 The economic returns to vocational and technical education in a fast growing economy: A case study of Hong Kong. Unpublished doctoral dissertation Stanford University, Stanford, California

Coombs P 1985 *The World Crisis in Education*. Oxford University Press, New York

Dahlman C, Frischtak C 1990 *National Systems Supporting Technical Advance in Industry: The Brazilian Experience*. World Bank, Washington, DC

Knight J B, Sabot R 1990 *Education, Productivity, and Inequality: The East African Natural Experiment*. Oxford University Press, New York

Levin H M 1987 Improving productivity through education and technology. In: Burke G, Rumberger R (eds.) 1987 *The Future Impact of Technology on Work and Education*. Falmer, London

Middleton J, Ziderman A, van Adams A 1991 *Vocational and Technical Education and Training*. World Bank, Washington, DC

Murphy K, Welch F 1989 Wage premiums for college graduates: Recent growth and possible explanations. *Educ. Researcher* 18(4): 17–26

Newfarmer R (ed.) 1985 *Profits, Progress and Poverty: Case Studies of International Industries in Latin America*. Notre Dame University Press, South Bend, Indiana

Okimoto D 1984 The political context. In: Okimoto D, Sugano T, Weinstein F (eds.) 1984 *Competitive Edge: The Semi-conductor Industry in the US and Japan*. Stanford University Press, Stanford, California

Piore M, Sabel C 1986 *The Second Industrial Divide: Possibilities for Prosperity*. Basic Books, New York

Porter M 1990 *The Competitive Advantage of Nations*. Free Press, New York

Rumberger R, Levin H M 1989 Schooling for the modern workplace. Paper prepared for the Commission on Workforce Quality and Labor Market Efficiency, United States Department of Labor, Washington, DC

Ryoo J, Nam Y S, Carnoy M 1993 Changing rates of return to education over time: The case of Korea, 1974–1988. *Econ. Educ. Rev.*

Schwartzman S 1984 The focus on scientific activity. In: Clark B (ed.) 1984 *Perspectives on Higher Education: Eight Disciplinary and Comparative Views*. University of California Press, Berkeley, California

Tueros M 1992 Education and informal labor markets in Peru. Unpublished doctoral dissertation, Stanford University, Stanford, California

United Nations Centre on Transnational Corporations 1988 *Transnational Corporations in World Development: Trends and Prospects*, Ref. ST/CTC/89. United Nations, New York

Technological Change and the Demand for Educated Labor

R. W. Rumberger

Countries throughout the world are experiencing rapid technological change. Computers and a host of other new technologies are not only providing a myriad of new products for consumers, they are also transforming the way work is performed. In both advanced industrial countries and developing countries, firms are using new technologies to improve worker productivity and increase their competitiveness in the global marketplace.

It is widely perceived that rapid technological change has a profound impact on the demand for educated labor. New technologies create new occupations and transform old ones. But how do these changes affect the skill and educational requirements of work?

The answer to this question has sparked widespread discussion and debate in both the policy communities and the research communities. The following discussion will outline this debate and then review the current research literature on two components of the demand for educated labor: the composition of jobs in the labor market and the skill requirements of existing jobs.

1. Framing the Debate

Technological change is only one of several factors that influence the demand for educated labor. Other factors are: (a) changes in the demand for goods and services, since the production of some goods and services requires more educated labor than the production of others; (b) changes in the costs of different categories of skilled labor relative to other factors of production such as capital, since employers can substitute among different factor inputs as their relative costs change; (c) changes in international competition, which can influence the level and composition of both exports and imports of goods and services which, in turn, influence domestic production and hence educational requirements of jobs; and (d) changes in work organization, since work can be organized in different ways that can either increase or decrease the levels and types of skills that workers need to perform their jobs and work within an organizational setting.

Technological change influences the demand for educated labor through its impact on each of the preceding factors. New technologies alter the demand for goods and services by introducing new products and changing the prices of existing products through productivity changes. They also alter the costs of both capital (products) and wages through their impact on worker productivity. Improved communication, transportation, and techniques of production have increased international competition by fostering a global marketplace where goods and services can be produced in both advanced industrial nations and newly developed nations. Technological change has facilitated new forms of work organization in which workers at a lower level have access to information that can give them more discretion and decision-making ability.

While there is little debate on the scope and rapidity of these changes, there is considerable debate on their impact. The predominant view in the policy community and among some in the research community is that the advanced economies of the world—the United States, Japan, and Western Europe—are entering a "post-industrial" period where traditional, low-skilled industrial jobs are increasingly being replaced by newer, high-skilled service jobs. In addition, the increased use of new technologies, such as computers, are raising the skill requirements of the many existing jobs where they are used (Johnston and Packer 1987, US Department of Labor 1989).

A contrary and less popular view, primarily advanced by radical economists, is that there is a secular trend in capitalist economies for employers to "deskill" jobs in order to lower labor costs and maintain control over the workforce (Braverman 1975, Zimbalist 1979).

A more agnostic view that partially supports both of the other two viewpoints is the one that is the most widely held in the research community. This view maintains that technology exerts a powerful influence on the skill and education requirements of jobs, but that the impact is not uniform (e.g., Wood 1982, Spenner 1988). Rather, in some cases skill requirements have increased, while in other cases the skill requirements have declined. This view supports a contingency perspective in which changes in skills have no predetermined direction, but rather depend on a host of specific and perhaps conflicting influences that may result in either the upgrading or downgrading of work skills.

Supporters of each perspective have presented a variety of evidence to support their claims. Yet the existing evidence is not sufficient or suitable to resolve the different perspectives.

2. The Problem with Existing Evidence

One difficulty in determining the adequacy of these competing perspectives is the lack of suitable data. In most countries there is a paucity of empirical data that directly assess the skill demands of work. Instead, many government agencies and researchers are forced to rely on two other, more widely available measures—educational attainment (qualifications) of workers or workers' earnings—as proxies for skill levels. The problem with both of these measures is that, while they are related to the educational demands of jobs, the relationships are neither simple nor straightforward.

Educational attainments represent the supply characteristics of workers. Since the amount of education that workers acquire may be influenced by social and political considerations as well as economic ones, the educational attainments of workers may not be perfectly matched to the educational demands of their jobs (Thurow 1975, Carnoy and Levin 1984). As a result, there can be a "mismatch" between the skill level of workers and the skill requirements of their jobs. When workers have more education and skills than their jobs require, the condition is referred to as "overeducation" or "underemployment" (Rumberger 1981, Tsang and Levin 1985). A growing body of research in the United States and other advanced countries suggests that overeducation does exist and that it can have adverse effects on job satisfaction and worker productivity (e.g., Tsang 1987, Hartog and Oosterbeek 1988). Other workers may have less skills than jobs require, a condition referred to as "undereducation," which may prevent them from securing employment in even low-skilled jobs (Rumberger and Levin 1989).

For similar reasons, earnings are not a suitable measure of skill demand. Earnings can be influenced by sociological factors (e.g., union bargaining power) as well as economic factors (Berg 1981). As a result, they are not directly related to worker productivity and skill demands, as human capital theory posits (Tsang and Levin 1985).

Even available data that directly assess the skill demands of work are deficient because they often rely on a single, aggregate measure of skills. In a major review of empirical research in the United States on skill changes prepared for the National Academy of Sciences, Spenner remarks that existing studies are limited in their coverage of the technologies and the time span covered. He also notes that the concepts and measures of skills in existing studies are poor (Spenner 1988 p. 159). Thus, existing research is limited as to how well it can measure changes in both the levels and types of skills that are needed to perform work.

Of course, some analysts argue that knowledge of distinct skill requirements for different jobs is unnecessary because it is claimed that worker productivity can be improved significantly in all jobs by simply increasing the general aptitude of workers. These claims have been challenged, however, in part because the ability tests used in the sampled occupations have largely been validated on correlates of work performance, such as job knowledge and supervisory ratings, rather than on actual measures of work performance (Gifford 1989). Moreover, to the extent that jobs differ in the abilities that they require, then the predictive validity of ability tests in one set of jobs would not readily apply to another set of jobs.

Even with limited data, a substantial body of research exists that attempts to assess the effects of technological change and its effects on the educational demands of work. Although much of the research discussed below comes from the United States, major studies have been carried out in other countries (e.g., Freeman and Soete 1987, Burke and Rumberger 1987, Matzner and Wagner 1990).

3. Reviewing Existing Evidence

In order to review the empirical evidence, it is important to distinguish between two types of changes that contribute to changes in the demand for educated labor: (a) changes in the composition of jobs in the economy, and (b) changes in the skill requirements of individual occupations. Changes in the composition of jobs in the economy—such as employment growth that favors high-skilled jobs over low-skilled jobs—can increase aggregate skill requirements in the economy even if the skill requirements of individual occupations do not change. Similarly, changes in the skill requirements of invidual occupations—such as increased skill requirements stemming from the increased use of new technologies—can raise aggregate skill levels even if there are no changes in the composition of jobs in the economy.

3.1 Changes in the Composition of Employment

The composition of jobs varies between countries and over time. Most advanced industrial countries have moved from economies largely based on agriculture in the last century to economies largely based on

manufacturing in the first half of the twentieth century and then to economies largely based on services in the latter part of the century. Technological change has hastened this transformation through the development of new machines and processes that have increased the physical capital used in agricultural and goods production and decreased the human capital. In the United States, for example, output in the manufacturing sector between 1960 and 1980 (in constant dollars) increased 104 percent, capital stock increased 109 percent, while employment increased only 21 percent (Rumberger 1984 Table 5).

This transformation has affected the skill and educational demands of work. Since the skill requirements for work are generally higher in the service sector than in the manufacturing or agricultural sectors, the growth of service employment has tended to increase the average skill demands of work in advanced industrial economies (Freeman and Soete 1987, Burke and Rumberger 1987, Matzner and Wagner 1990).

The growth of service employment is likely to continue. Employment projections in the United States indicate that virtually all future employment growth over the next decade will be in the service-producing sector (Rumberger and Levin 1989). Although the United States is one of the few countries to make econometric estimates of future job growth, employment growth in other industrialized countries is also likely to favor service employment.

In the United States, employment projections have been used to estimate the educational requirements of future jobs based on the schooling level of current job holders (e.g., Johnston and Packer 1987, Levin and Rumberger 1986). This is done by first computing the distribution of schooling of the existing labor force for individual occupations and then using occupational forecasts to estimate required schooling levels for the future economy. This procedure can only estimate the effects of compositional shifts on the demand for education since it assumes that the educational requirements of individual occupations will not change in the future. Moreover, it assumes that current job holders have the appropriate level of education that these jobs require which, according to the "mismatch" thesis discussed above, may not be the case.

Despite these limitations, the projections do provide some concrete estimates of the future demand for educated labor. Two sources of confusion surround their use, however. One comes from the practice of using figures on the fastest growing jobs in the economy as indicative of overall trends in educational requirements (e.g., Johnston and Packer 1987 p. 97). The problem with such a practice is that it tends to overstate changes in educational requirements because the fastest growing jobs generally require above-average education levels, but will generate few new jobs.

For example, the fastest growing jobs in the United

States economy over the next decade are concentrated in health and technical fields and require above-average education levels, yet these jobs are mostly in new fields that employ relatively few people so that these fast growth rates will actually produce few new jobs—less than 5 percent of all the new jobs projected between 1986 and 2000. In contrast, more traditional occupations that generally require lower education levels are expected to grow more modestly over this period on a percentage basis, but because they employ so many people, these modest growth rates will produce a substantial number of new jobs (Rumberger and Levin 1989).

A second source of confusion about the use of occupational projections concerns the practice of focusing only on new job growth as indicative of overall educational demand for future jobs. Although the focus on new jobs can reveal trends in the educational requirements, it is important to examine the educational requirements of both new jobs and existing jobs since the latter will provide more employment opportunities for future job seekers than the former. In the United States, for example, new jobs expected over the next decade have higher educational requirements than existing jobs, but because only one out of every six jobs by the year 2000 will be a new job, the overall educational requirements of all jobs in the year 2000 are likely to be quite similar to those at present (Rumberger and Levin 1989).

3.2 Changes in the Skill Requirements of Jobs

Perhaps the most controversial issue about skills concerns the question of whether technology tends to increase or decrease the skill requirements of jobs. This issue has been debated in earlier periods of technological change and is again being debated in both the research and policy arenas.

The common perception is that the rising use of computers and other new technologies in many occupations must be raising skill requirements of those occupations. But this assertion does not take account of the fact that most persons who use computers require no special skills. For example, warehouse clerks and supermarket checkout clerks typically use a computer readout device to read barcodes on products as they are purchased, sold, shipped, and received. But the use of this device requires no knowledge of computers. Word processing operators and office workers need only learn how to operate a new piece of office equipment, as they have done in the past, not how to program or understand computers. This training can be measured in hours or days, not weeks, months, or years.

A recent study of a national sample of almost 3,000 small businesses in the United States found that the average duration of training for a wide range of computer applications in offices by those without computer skills was only about 30 hours (Levin and Rumberger 1986). The same study found that interest

and enthusiasm, followed by reading and comprehension skills were far more important for learning to use the computer than extensive technical training. In general, the many workers in the United States who use computers in their jobs utilize standard computer packages that require very little previous education or training (Goldstein and Fraser 1985).

Reviews of past studies on the impact of technologies on skill requirements in the United States as well as Europe reach a similar conclusion: past technologies have tended to raise the skill requirements of some jobs while lowering the requirements of others, with a net result that aggregate skill requirements have not changed much (Rothwell and Zegveld 1979, Spenner 1988, Flynn 1988).

One reason the existing research literature presents such a mixed view is that technology and other workplace changes may affect work skills in different ways depending on the conditions and characteristics of the firms where the changes are introduced. For example, a study, by Jaikumar (1986) found major differences in the amount and type of labor employed between Japanese and United States firms that use the same automated manufacturing technology. Such evidence supports a contingency perspective that changes in skills have no predetermined direction, but rather depend on a host of specific and perhaps conflicting influences that may result in either the upgrading or downgrading of work skills.

Of course, the future may not look like the past. One major difference concerns the type of technologies and their capabilities. Whereas many past technologies enabled machines to reduce the physical requirements of work, present and future machines are more capable of displacing the mental requirements of work (Rumberger 1984). Nobel Laureate Wassily Leontief has pointed out that because computers and robots can now replace humans in the exercise of mental functions in the same way as mechanical power replaced them in the performance of physical tasks, "the role of humans as the most important factor of production is bound to diminish—in the same way that the role of horses in agricultural production was first diminished and then eliminated by the introduction of tractors" (Leontief 1983 pp. 3–4).

3.3 Net Impact

What has been the net impact of these two types of changes on the demand for educated labor? What are the prospects for the future?

In reviewing both kinds of historical evidence for the American National Academy, Spenner (1988) concluded that compositional shifts in the economy in the United States have tended to raise aggregate skill requirements, while technological effects on individual jobs have tended to lower skill requirements. The net result is that the educational demands have increased modestly over the last two decades. As for the future, the American National Academy of Sciences concluded that the empirical evidence was too fragmentary and mixed to support confident predictions about the impact of technological change on aggregate skill levels, but that existing "evidence suggests that the skill requirements for entry into future jobs will not be radically upgraded from those of current jobs" (Cyert and Mowery 1987 p. 103)

Although the available evidence suggests that the aggregate demand for educated labor has not changed appreciably since the early 1960s, there is some evidence that the *distribution* of skill demand has become more unequal over time, producing a more unequal distribution of earnings. A 1991 study found that the skill requirements of jobs in the United States increased much faster than the hourly or annual earnings of jobs over the period from 1960 to 1985. Furthermore, in the services sector, where most employment growth took place, both high-skill/high-wage jobs and low-skill/low-wage jobs grew faster than mid-level jobs, increasing the inequality of skills and earnings in the economy (Howell and Wolff 1991). However, a major review of other studies in the United States found that *income inequality* has increased more than *earnings inequality* and that demographic and structural factors were more responsible than technological change (Cyert and Mowery 1987).

4. Conclusion

Technological change is having a widespread impact on goods and services and how they are produced throughout the world. What is less clear is the impact of these changes on the demand for educated labor.

Despite the widespread perception that technological change is increasing the demand for educated labor, there is insufficient empirical data in most countries to support that view. Although the educational attainments of workers in most countries are rising (Psacharopoulos and Arriagada 1986), such a condition is not sufficient evidence that those increases are simply in response to increasing educational requirements of work.

The limited empirical evidence available, which is mostly based on studies undertaken in the United States, suggests that changes in the occupational structure of jobs towards service employment do tend to raise the demand for educated labor. However, changes in the skill demands of individual jobs have not systematically risen due to technological change or other factors. Rather, available evidence suggests that in some cases technological change has tended to raise skill requirements, while in other cases it has lowered them. The effect of both compositional changes and job changes has been to raise aggregate skill requirements of jobs, but not as much or as fast as commonly perceived.

See also: Technological Change and Deskilling; Education and Technological Change; Education, Occupation, and Earnings

References

Berg I (ed.) 1981 *Sociological Perspectives on Labor Markets.* Academic Press, New York

Burke G, Rumberger R W (eds.) 1987 *The Future Impact of Technology on Work and Education.* Falmer Press, London

Braverman H 1975 *Labor and Monopoly Capital: The Degradation of Work in the 20th Century.* Monthly Review Press, New York

Carnoy M, Levin H M 1984 *Schooling and Work in the Democratic State.* Stanford University Press, Stanford, California

Cyert R M, Mowery D C (ed.) 1987 *Technology and Employment.* Report of the Panel on Technology and Employment. National Academy Press, Washington, DC

Flynn P M 1988 *Facilitating Technological Change: The Human Resource Challenge.* Ballinger, Cambridge, Massachusetts

Freeman C, Soete L (eds.) 1987 *Technical Change and Full Employment.* Basil Blackwell, Oxford

Gifford B R (ed.) 1989 *Test Policy and the Politics of Opportunity Allocation: The Workplace and the Law.* Kluwer, Boston, Massachusetts

Goldstein H, Fraser B S 1985 *Training for Work in the Computer Age: How Workers Who Use Computers Get Their Training.* National Commission for Employment Policy, Washington, DC

Hartog J, Oosterbeek H 1988 Education, allocation and earnings in the Netherlands: Overschooling? *Economics of Education Review* 7: 185–94

Howell D R, Wolff E N 1991 Trends in the growth and distribution of skills in the US workplace, 1960–1985. *Industrial and Labor Relations Review* 44: 486–502

Jaikumar R 1986 Postindustrial manufacturing. *Harvard Business Review* 64(6): 69–76

Johnston W B, Packer A E 1987 *Workforce 2000: Work and Workers for the 21st Century.* Hudson Institute, Indianapolis, Indiana

Leontief W 1983 National perspective: The definition of problems and opportunities. In: National Academy of Engineering Symposium 1983 *The Long-Term Impact of Technology on Employment and Unemployment.* National Academy Press, Washington, DC

Levin H M, Rumberger R W 1986 Education and training needs for using computer in small businesses. *Educational Evaluation and Policy Analysis* 8: 423–34

Matzner E, Wagner M (eds.) 1990 *The Employment Impact of New Technology: The Case of West Germany.* Avebury, Aldershot

Psacharopoulos G, Arriagada A M 1986 The educational composition of the labour force. *International Labour Review* 125(5): 560–73

Rothwell R, Zegveld W 1979 *Technological Change and Employment.* St Martin's Press, New York

Rumberger R W 1981 *Overeducation in the US Labor Market.* Praeger, New York

Rumberger R W 1984 High technology and job loss. *Technology in Society* 6: 263–84

Rumberger R W, Levin H M 1989 Schooling for the modern workplace. In: Commission on Workplace Quality and Labor Market Efficiency 1989 *Investing in People: A Strategy for Addressing America's Workforce Crisis*, Background papers, Vol. 1. US Department of Labor, Washington, DC

Spenner K 1988 Technological change, skill requirements and education: The case for uncertainty. In: Cyert R M, Mowery D C (eds.) 1988 *The Impact of Technological Change on Employment and Economic Growth*. Ballinger, Cambridge, Massachusetts

Thurow L C 1975 *Generating Inequality*. Basic Books, New York

Tsang M C 1987 The impact of underutilization of education on productivity: A case study of the US Bell companies. *Economics of Education Review* 6: 239–54

Tsang M C, Levin H M 1985 The economics of overeducation. *Economics of Education Review* 4: 93–104

US Department of Labor, Commission on Workforce Quality and Labor Market Efficiency 1989 *Investing in People: A Strategy for Addressing America's Workforce Crisis*. US Government Printing Office, Washington, DC

Wood S (ed.) 1982 *The Degradation of Work*. Hutchinson, London

Zimbalist A (ed.) 1979 *Case Studies in the Labor Process*. Monthly Review Press, New York

Technological Change and Deskilling

K. I. Spenner

How does technological change alter the quantity and quality of jobs in parts or the whole of national economies? The answer to the question is of central importance to research and policy on education. Technological change directly and indirectly defines the demand for given mixtures of skills. A rapidly changing world of work implies different educational policies from one of little or slow change. In principle, technology and technological change shape the quality of the match between the skills and capabilities that workers bring to the labor force, and what jobs permit, demand, and allow. Technological change may constrain or enable new, more productive uses of human talent. Moreover, from the 1980s onward, technology and technological change have been directly implicated in the day-to-day conduct of education, for example, in issues surrounding computer literacy and the electronic classroom.

This entry defines technology broadly to include product and process distinctions, the "hard" materials, things, and machines of producing goods and services, as well as the "soft" but changing ways of organizing production, people, and ideas (Cyert and Mowery 1987). The first section reviews the major theoretical positions, the second section considers methodological issues in research on technological change and deskilling, the third section summarizes the aggregate and case study evidence and suggests a synthesis, and the final section discusses several research frontiers.

1. Theoretical Positions

1.1 Upgrading Arguments

The upgrading position stems from the industrialization thesis and neoclassical economics (Kerr et al.

1964, Standing 1984). According to this argument, the division of labor evolves along the lines of greater differentiation and efficiency in industrial societies. Technological changes increase productivity, requiring a broader variety of skills and higher average skills from the workforce. Automation and other forms of mechanization eliminate routine work. Jobs increasingly involve higher levels of complexity and discretion, both key dimensions of the skill demands of jobs, particularly white-collar, technical, and professional jobs, and in high-technology fields. Proponents of the industrialization thesis would cite the aggregate increase in levels of education and composition shifts in the occupational structure as evidence (Jaffe and Froomkin 1968, Bell 1973).

A related type of upgrading argument and line of evidence points to growing demand for managerial and professional workers in the 1980s and the rising wage-premium associated with a college degree. In the eyes of the human capital theorist, the rising wage-premiums are *prima facie* evidence of skill upgrading of the labor force, with technological change one of the generative factors.

Other versions of the upgrading thesis suggest that new technologies demand new forms of skill compared with the past, for example, with respect to computerization and flexible manufacturing systems, increased responsibilities for the whole of the production process, for teamwork and job interchangability, or higher abstraction skills and computer literacy (Adler 1992).

1.2 Downgrading Arguments

Downgrading arguments posit a decline in the quality and quantity of work because of changes in the nature of the labor process during the twentieth century (the web of social and technical aspects surrounding the activity of work). Technological change and automation are strategic instruments of managers, who use devices such as scientific management, numerical control, programmable automation, and the redesign of jobs to separate the execution of work from the conception of work (Braverman 1974, Wood 1982, Noble 1984). According to this argument, the job changes of the twentieth century include the dilution of traditional craft skills, and a growing mass of unskilled and semiskilled labor, particularly in clerical and selected white-collar fields. Other versions of the downgrading thesis point to a polarization in the changing labor force: differential growth of high-skill versus low-skill occupations and industries (Levin and Rumberger 1987), or deindustrialization, in which job loss and/or deskilling are secondary consequences of plant shutdowns, and national or international industry relocations.

Upgrading and downgrading studies consider a range of industrial market economies but concentrate on Canada, the United Kingdom, France, Germany, Japan, Sweden, and the United States (for reviews, see Cyert and Mowery 1987; Flynn 1988; Heidenreich 1993; Littler 1982; Spenner 1985, 1988; Wood 1989).

1.3 Mixed Change, Conditional, and Contingency Arguments

Mixed change arguments are more of a characterization of the empirical literature than a theoretical position: some sectors and jobs in the economy experience upgrading as a function of technological change, others experience downgrading, and the net result is little change in the skill requirements of work or offsetting trends in the composition of the occupational structure and the content of work (Horowitz and Herrnstadt 1966, Spenner 1979).

Conditional and contingency theories go beyond empirical description and specify a logic of one or more factors that condition the effects of technological change on jobs. For example, Flynn's (1988) model of the skill-training life cycle posits upgrading effects on jobs early in the life cycle of a technology. With the passage of time, the effects shift to mixed–neutral and then downgrading, as the technology is learned and segmented, as production processes are routinized, and as training shifts outside of firms to vocational and educational instutions. Form et al. (1988) postulate a multicomponent web of contingency factors that condition the effect of technological change on the quantity and quality of jobs. Depending upon measurement, the theory might generate 10s of conditioning factors, which comprise more a list of possibilities than a tight theory that answers the question "why?" Finally, the present author's synthesis of the empirical evidence postulates the uncertainty–contingency hypothesis discussed below (Spenner 1988). In brief, it states that technological change has no simple, single, or unitary effects on the quantity or quality of jobs. Rather, the effects of technological change on jobs are conditioned by market forces, by managerial strategies and actions, and by selected organizational factors.

2. Methodological Issues

Studies of technological change and upgrading–deskilling fall into two general types. Aggregate studies investigate the changes in skill levels of the economy over time, capturing a broad range of jobs. The upgrading tradition draws more upon aggregate studies. Case studies intensively investigate shifts in skill as a function of technological change in a narrower sampling of space, for example, for an occupation or in a single firm. Case studies have been more the domain of the downgrading tradition. The different designs have characteristic strengths and weakness, trading off population coverage for the ability to see the dynamics and detail of change.

A further distinction is helpful: the overall skill level of the economy or a subset thereof (i.e., jobs, firms) can change along two tracks, content and composition. Content changes refer to actual changes in the nature of jobs, apart from the numbers of workers in different types of jobs. Compositional changes refer to changes in the overall skill level that emanate from shifting distributions of workers to jobs, conceptually distinct from changes in the actual content of jobs. There is no logical reason why technological change need operate on skill levels in the same way or on the same schedule as for compositional and content changes. For example, the long-term effects of a technological change may be indirect and involve upgrading through job creation in certain industries (compositional shift). On the other hand, the short-term effects may involve content shifts in deskilling the jobs directly involved in the technological change.

Further, studies of technological change vary in their sampling of time and space. The case-study literature has concentrated heavily on manufacturing jobs, but has given relatively less attention to service industry jobs. Aggregate studies cover more jobs but only a few aggregate studies consider the era before the Second World War. The collected social science literature on technological change offers nothing approaching a full sampling of time and space for the twentieth century, particularly if one requires direct measures of skill at multiple points in time.

Finally, as economists have long known, "technology" is extraordinarily difficult to isolate and measure (Cyert and Mowery 1988). Technological change tends to occur in conjunction with a number of other changes, including changing factor conditions, supply–demand shifts, and larger demographic and social changes. Research designs often capture the gross effects of all changes but have difficulty isolating the net effects of technological change.

2.1 Meanings and Measures of Skill

The various meanings and measures of skill have been reviewed elsewhere (Spenner 1990). In general, substantial variability, but nonetheless progress, can be identified in the empirical research of the 1970s and

1980s. It is important to distinguish skill as a human attribute (internalized capabilities, forms of knowledge and so on) from the skill demands of jobs. A long tradition of research in education shows the match between the two is quite problematic, and is associated with issues of underemployment and overeducation (Berg and Gorelick 1970, Clogg and Shockey 1984, Smith 1986).

The research literature on technological change and skill changes offers a variety of conceptualizations of skill that vary on several issues (Spenner 1990 p. 400):

(a) social valuation; or what specific skills will be rewarded?

(b) social definition and construction; or what will custom, language, the construction of tasks, and the power of interested parties define as a skilled performance or job?

(c) supply, demand, and governance structures that determine transactions involving skills in people and jobs; or what logic—for example, efficiency or control—and what system (market, internal hierarchy) matches people to jobs, and translates technologies into mixtures of jobs with given skill demands and various forms of work organization?

The theoretical stance on these questions defines the conceptions of skill in the literature. For example, case studies in the downgrading tradition often assume strong forms of social construction of skill, key roles for managers in deciding valuation (versus the "market" or production functions), and control logics in addition to a logic of efficiency. Some of the variability in the findings of such studies may issue as much from variations in concepts and measures as it does from variation in the underlying phenomenon.

Measurement of job skills in the literature shows similar variability. Some studies continue to assume that the meaning of skill is so obvious that it need not be specified or measured but can be equated with education levels or labels for groups of occupations such as "white-collar," or "blue-collar." Other studies indirectly infer skill levels of jobs through wage levels. Studies of skill shifts and technological change in neoclassical economics provide illustration.

Since the early 1970s, research has relied increasingly on direct measures of skill, as provided by expert raters or systems (e.g., US Department of Labor 1977, Cain and Treiman 1981), or as provided through the self-reports of people about their jobs. Validity studies show a fairly reasonable degree of correlation between the two types of measure (for review see Spenner 1990). Nonetheless, each type of measure has strengths and weaknesses; progress in cumulative empirical research will require both.

A final measurement issue involves the specific dimensions of skill. Spenner (1990) shows studies that range from a single, often unspecified global dimension of skill, to one line of research that measures about 200 specific job features as dimensions of skill. Here too, the research of the 1980s shows some convergence on multidimensional concepts and measures (versus unidimensional), and on two to five or so different dimensions.

Theoretical and empirical research suggest at least two broader organizing dimensions of skill: substantive complexity and autonomy control. Substantive complexity refers to the level, scope, and integration of mental (cognitive), manipulative, and interpersonal tasks in a job, following the classic distinction by job analysts of functional foci of data, people, and things in human–task interfaces. Aggregate studies and studies in the upgrading tradition frequently investigate skill conceived and measured as substantive complexity. Autonomy control refers to the discretion or leeway in a job to control the content, manner, and speed with which a task is done. Downgrading and case studies often consider this dimension of skill. The two dimensions are correlated for jobs in the United States economy, and recent studies have suggested a figure in the range of r = 0.5 to 0.7 (Spenner 1990).

3. Summary of Aggregate and Case-study Evidence

In brief, the empirical literature fails to provide a single or simple answer to the question of how technolgical change alters the quantity and quality of jobs. For example, Flynn (1988) reviews nearly 200 case studies in economics and finds substantial variability in outcomes, which she organizes with the skill-training life cycle model suggested earlier. The aggregate studies that cover all or a large portion of the United States economy and that use direct measures of skill at multiple time-points now number about 15. The case-study literature includes literally hundreds of studies. The summary here reflects this set of major aggregate studies, and a nonrandom sample of an equal number of major (frequently cited) case studies (see Spenner 1988).

The aggregate study evidence suggests several conclusions. First, the rate of change of the skill levels of jobs in the United States economy is evolutionary rather than revolutionary. The Canadian evidence is similar (Myles 1988). Second, there is no clear evidence of widespread or massive downgrading, particularly in studies of skill as substantive complexity. To the contrary, there is more consistent evidence of slow aggregate upgrading, particularly since the Second World War, and perhaps since the beginning of the twentieth century. No aggregate study evidence precedes this time frame. Third, studies of compositional shifts show slower net aggregate change; studies of content shifts show more dramatic change, but again in both upgrading and downgrading directions, with the net change fairly small. Fourth, aggregate studies of autonomy control are in short supply and are mixed, providing some hint or suggestion of an aggregate compositional downgrading in the autonomy control of jobs, but more a function of the massive movement out of self-employed farming (higher autonomy control) and into bureaucratized work settings (less autonomy control) over the course of the twentieth century. The larger changes involve a complicated web of specific technological changes. Fifth, both studies based on self-report measures of skill and studies based on expert-system measures of skill support these general conclusions.

The case-study evidence affords a related set of conclusions (Spenner 1988). First, case studies show more volatility in skill transformations and find more instances of downgrading, perhaps because of the concentration on autonomy control, or additionally, because of sample selection in overstudying changing occupations, industries, and firms, and understudying stable ones. Second, case studies concentrate on content shifts in work, again reporting more change of both upgrading and downgrading varities, but devoting less coverage to skill change through compositional shifts. Third, case studies suggest regional, industrial, and other variations in skill transformations. Fourth, and perhaps most importantly, case studies suggest that the effects of technological change on the skill levels of work are not necessarily simple, direct, or constant across settings and firms, and cannot be considered in isolation, that is, in the absence of contingency factors.

In summary, the aggregate and case-study evidence fails to provide consistent corroboration of simple versions of upgrading or deskilling arguments. If anything, there is slightly more support for upgrading arguments in the area of compositional shifts and skill as substantive complexity, but this support deteriorates if consideration is expanded to content shifts and skill as autonomy control. Interestingly, when the conclusions about skill dimensions are juxtaposed, it is possible that the world of work at the end of the twentieth century compared with a century before is more complicated in terms of its substantive complexity, but with less autonomy control to meet more complicated task demands. This hypothesis awaits comprehensive test.

One way to summarize the collected empirical literature is the uncertainty–contingency hypothesis (Spenner 1988). This hypothesis disavows simple, single, or unitary effects of technological change on skills. Rather, it posits intrinsic uncertainty and contingency in the relationship between technology and jobs. The uncertainty and contingency are not only in the state of knowledge about the relationship, but are built into the very character of how technology creates, destroys, and alters jobs. Technological change defines a new range of options and possibilities; other social and economic forces determine the specific direction. The contingency factors fall into three general categories:

market forces, managerial prerogatives, and organizational cultures. Selected evidence, as outlined below, suggests that any one of the contingency factors or a combination of them are sufficiently powerful to alter or reverse (from net upgrading to downgrading, or vice versa) the effects of a technological change on the quality and quantity of jobs.

Market forces refer to classic economic dynamics of supply and demand, and the associated factor conditions in firms, industries, and sectors of the economy. For example, a resource-rich environment as defined in factor conditions and supply and demand levels may afford a more forgiving and expansive environment for content and compositional upgrading, whereas resource-lean environments might favor downgrading of job numbers and quality. Along these lines, Osterman (1986) found computerization in various industries led first to a stronger contraction in managerial and clerical labor, but after a number of years to lesser contraction, perhaps associated with bureaucratic reorganization and firms re-expanding into new products and markets over the longer term as a function of technological change.

Managerial prerogatives refer to the discretion of management to control the timing and nature of technological change. This includes decisions on whether to implement a technological change, what to implement, how to implement it, and who participates in the implementation (e.g., engineers, workers). A number of studies clearly suggest the central role played by managers. Kelley (1986, 1990) found differing managerial strategies produced all three outcomes—upgrading, downgrading, and mixed change—for the same technology change (computerized numerical control machinery) in a similar range of industrial settings in the United States, the United Kingdom, Germany, and Japan. Jaikumar (1986) found similar variability in outcomes as a function of managerial strategy and practice in the implementation of flexible manufacturing systems in Japanese and United States firms.

Organizational culture refers to the social and cultural system of the work environment in which technological change occurs. It includes classic demographic factors such as size, differentiation, hierarchy, and spans of control, but also belief systems and the norms and sources of power of different groups. Here too, there is suggestive evidence implicating a number of these factors.

Support for the uncertainty–contingency hypothesis comes more from a comparative overview of studies in the various disciplines than from a clear or comprehensive test in any single study. Further, the specific recipe of market forces, managerial strategies, and organizational cultures that produce upgrading or downgrading or more mixed results is not yet known. One of the main frontiers of research in this area will be to decipher this recipe for change, particularly if a parsimonious version exists. The major competing explanation to the uncertainty–contingency hypothesis for patterns in the empirical literature is Flynn's (1988) skill-training life cycle model. It explains the mixtures of upgrading and downgrading by stage in the life cycle of the technology: earlier stages produce upgrading and later stages produce downgrading. Studies that fail to control for life-cycle stage of technology produce a jumbled mixture of effects. The challenge to this explanation occurs in studies such as Kelley's (1986) and Jaikumar's (1986), in which the same technology at about the same life-cycle stage and in similar industrial settings still produces a range of effects, thus implicating other contingency factors such as managerial strategies.

4. Research Frontiers

The research literature on technological change and deskilling continues as an active, exciting, and fertile arena of ideas, with contributors from a number of disciplines including anthropology, economics, education, human systems engineering, managerial sciences, industrial psychology, and sociology. A number of frontiers shape future research.

First, while the 1980s research made considerable progress in moving toward replicable multidimensional concepts and measures of skill, considerable progress remains to be made. This includes national level-measurement and validation studies that regularly measure technological and job changes for sample universes, similar to other social indicator and assessment projects.

Second, better forums are needed to bring together ideas and contributors for publication and presentation. Research on technological change and skill change is truly interdisciplinary, yet often progress is slowed by lack of communication among contributors in different fields.

A third research frontier comprises arguments about a different future and new skills. The different future argument regards microelectronics and computerization as qualitatively different (Hirschhorn 1984). Earlier technological changes altered the physical dimensions of work; computerization has the potential to alter the intellectual requirements as well. The new skills argument is related, suggesting that new forms of work organization and high technology demand new forms of skill which are not adequately captured by earlier concepts and measures. Examples include teamwork or the requirements of a job to conceptualize an interrelated but remote system. Neither argument is resolved and both are in early stages of empirical investigation. The new skills argument depends centrally on the definition of skill. If a multidimensional conceptualization is at a sufficiently basic level (i.e., level, scope, and integration of mental, manipulative, and interpersonal tasks for substantive complexity), then it is not clear whether so-called "new" skills are

qualitatively new, or whether they are quantitatively different levels of basic dimensions.

Finally, as technology has integrated the global economy and shortened horizons of time and space, the investigation of skill and technological change increasingly involves a comparative dimension, with cross-national and transnational dynamics and mechanisms. These range from differences between countries at the simplest level, to technology transfer, labor mobility, and skill shifts across national boundaries as a function of technological change. Beyond these, future research will also likely yield insight into whether the recipe that governs how technology changes job skills, researched in industrial market economies, has some broader applicability—namely, to Third World settings, to centralized state socialist economies, or to societies undergoing transformation.

See also: Vocational Education and Productivity

References

Adler P S (ed.) 1992 *Technology and the Future of Work.* Oxford University Press, Oxford
Bell D 1973 *The Coming of Post-industrial Society: A Venture in Social Forecasting.* Basic Books, New York
Berg I, Gorelick S 1970 *Education and Jobs: The Great Training Robbery.* Praeger, New York
Braverman H 1974 *Labor and Monopoly Capital: The Degradation of Work in the Twentieth Century.* Monthly Review Press, New York
Cain P, Treiman D J 1981 The Dictionary of Occupational Titles as a source of occupational data. *Am. Sociol. Rev.* 46(3): 253–78
Clogg C C, Shockey J W 1984 Mismatch between occupation and schooling: A prevalence measure, recent trends and demographic analysis. *Demography* 21(2): 235–57
Cyert R M, Mowery D C 1987 *Technology and Employment: Innovation and Growth in the U. S. Economy.* National Academy Press, Washington, DC
Cyert R M, Mowery D C (eds.) 1988 *The Impact of Technological Change on Employment and Economic Growth.* Harper Business, New York
Flynn P M 1988 *Facilitating Technological Change: The Human Resource Challenge.* Ballinger, Cambridge, Massachusetts
Form W, Kaufman R, Parcel T, Wallace M 1988 The impact of technology on work organization and work outcomes: A conceptual framework and research agenda. In: Farkas G, England P (eds.) 1988 *Industries, Firms, and Jobs: Sociological and Economic Approaches.* Plenum, New York
Heidenreich M (ed.) 1993 *Computers and Culture in Organisations: The Introduction and use of Production Control Systems in French, Italian, and German Enterprises.* Edition Sigma-Rainer Bohn Verlag, Berlin
Hirschhorn L 1984 *Beyond Mechanization: Work and Technology in a Postindustrial Age.* MIT Press, Cambridge, Massachusetts
Horowitz M, Herrnstadt I 1966 Changes in skill requirements of occupations in selected industries. In: National Commission on Technology, Automation, and Eco-

nomic Progress 1966 *Technology and the American Economy, Vol. 2 Appendix: The Employment Impact of Technological Change*. US Government Printing Office, Washington, DC

Jaffe A J, Froomkin J 1968 *Technology and Jobs, Automation in Perspective*. Praeger, New York

Jaikumar R 1986 Postindustrial manufacturing. *Harv. Bus. Rev.* 64(6): 69–76

Kelley M R 1986 Programmable automation and the skill question: A reinterpretation of the cross-national evidence. *Hum. Syst. Man.* 6: 223–41

Kelley M R 1990 New process technology, job design and work organization: A contingency model. *Am. Sociol. Rev.* 55(2): 191–208

Kerr C, Dunlop J T, Harbison C, Myers C A 1964 *Industrialism and Industrial Man: The Problems of Labor and Management in Economic Growth*. Oxford University Press, New York

Levin H, Rumberger R 1987 Educational requirements for new technologies: Visions, possibilities and current realities. *Educ. Policy* 1(3): 333–54

Littler C R 1982 *The Development of the Labour Process in Capitalist Societies: A Comparative Study of the Transformation of Work Organization in Britain, Japan and the USA*. Heinemann, London

Myles J 1988 The expanding middle: Some Canadian evidence on the deskilling debate. *Can. Rev. Sociol.*

Anthropol. 25(3): 335–64

Noble D 1984 *Forces of Production: A Social History of Industrial Automation*. Knopf, New York

Osterman P 1986 The impact of computers on the employment of clerks and managers. *Ind. Lab. Rel. Rev.* 39(2): 175–86

Smith H L 1986 Overeducation and underemployment: An agnostic review. *Sociol. Educ.* 59(2): 85–99

Spenner K I 1979 Temporal changes in work content. *Am. Sociol. Rev.* 44(6): 968–75

Spenner K I 1985 The upgrading and downgrading of occupations: Issues, evidence, and implications for education. *Rev. Educ. Res.* 55(2): 125–54

Spenner K I 1988 Technological change, skill requirements and education: the case for uncertainty. In: Cyert R, Mowery D (eds.) 1988

Spenner K I 1990 Skill: Meanings, methods and measures. *Work Occup.* 17: 399–421

Standing G 1984 The notion of technological unemployment. *Int. Lab. Rev.* 123(2): 127–47

United States Department of Labor 1977 *Dictionary of Occupational Titles*, 4th edn. US Government Printing Office, Washington, DC

Wood S 1982 *The Degradation of Work? Skill, Deskilling and the Labour Process*. Hutchinson, London

Wood S 1989 *The Transformation of Work? Skill, Flexibility and the Labor Process*. Unwin Hyman, London

SECTION V

Education, Income Distribution, and Discrimination

Introduction

M. Carnoy

Education is directly related to the distribution of monetary rewards in two ways: first, the distribution of income in the labor force is at least partly a function of the distribution of formal schooling; second, those individuals with more schooling earn, on average, higher income than those with less schooling. From a human capital perspective, individual "early" ability and investment in education and training should explain a high proportion of both aspects of income distribution. In a perfectly competitive market with full information situated in a political system that faithfully represented the "common good", it might do just that. But in the absence of these conditions, the distribution of monetary rewards in the two senses mentioned above is significantly affected by the way the market treats individuals from different social class, ethnic, gender, and race groups. It is also affected by government macroeconomic policies concerning the overall distribution of income and this market treatment of various groups.

Jacques Velloso's entry begins this section by reviewing the literature on the tenuous relation between the distribution of education in the labor force, the average level of education in the labor force, and the distribution of earnings for labor. That literature suggests that in countries where the distribution of income is highly unequal, such as Brazil, the distribution of education, also highly unequal, is an important explainer of income distribution. But in countries, such as the United States, where income distribution and educational distribution are much more equal, the relation between the two is considerably weaker. Other factors—for example, the unemployment rate—are more important in explaining changes in income inequality.

What about causality? Do changes in the distribution of education in the labor force *lead* to changes in income inequality? Velloso argues that there is probably some causal relationship, but it is less clear than human capital theory predicts. Government macroeconomic policy and historical sociopolitical conditions explain educational and income distribution simultaneously in ways unaccounted for by human capital theory.

Much of the recent work on the relationship between education and income distribution, however, has appeared in analyses of the role of class, race, and gender in explaining income differences, and in explaining differential investment in education by these various groups. The underlying issue in these analyses (and also in the entries in this section) of group differences is whether class, race, and gender are proxies for ability and quality of schooling—"unmeasured skills"—differences, or whether they reflect labor market/social discrimination rooted in the structure of society. This discussion has gone on in the United States since before the Second World War, picked up momentum in the 1960s, and generated a whole new set of writings in the 1980s and early 1990s. With the recognition of the changing role of women in the global economy, the controversy has been extended to earnings differences and differential access to investment in schooling by men and women.

A number of important points regarding education, income differences among individuals, and overall degree of income distribution emerge from the discussion. First, family status, race, and gender continue to explain a significant amount of income variance, but such sources of inequality can and do change over time. Second, quality of formal education, especially in the case of race, probably explains part of the earnings differences between race groups. Third, unmeasured investment in education in the family before children enter school and while they attend school is still surely a factor in explaining income variation for individuals with the same amount of schooling and the amount of investment that individuals make in formal education. And as Barry Chiswick suggests in his entry, the cultural capital that certain (immigrant) groups bring to the labor market may also have a major influence on incomes.

But the entries by Velloso, Martin Carnoy, Myra Strober, Mariam Ferber, and Elizabeth King suggest that two other factors are also important in explaining race and gender differences in educational investment and earnings. These factors are as follows.

(a) Government-promoted changes in income in income distribution towards greater equality (for example, in the United States in the early 1940s and Korea in the late 1980s), or inequality (for example, Brazil in the 1960s and the United States in the 1980s) can favor or hurt low-income groups over and above any changes in the supply and demand for skills. In the United States in the 1940s, a significant "wage compression" that lifted low wages relative to high wages, along with a war-promoted shift from rural to urban jobs, were the major explanations for a large increase in Black earnings relative to White. The equalization of educational attainment and of educational quality for Blacks and Whites explained a small fraction of the gains Blacks made in the 1940s. In Korea in the late 1980s, government policy promoted raising low salaries relative to high salaries, and this had the largest impact of any factor on raising women's wages relative to men's during the period 1976–91, larger, for example, than the major increases in women's education compared to men's during the same period.

(b) "Market failure," as reflected in (i) differential access to schooling for different race and gender groups that allows dominant race group males to attain higher levels of schooling than the others,

hence access to higher paying jobs; and (ii) racial and gender wage discrimination, also contributes to earnings differences between groups, and government willingness or unwillingness to reduce both pay discrimination directly or barriers to investment in education by discriminated-against groups can have a significant effect on race and gender differences in earnings.

However, racial and gender wage discrimination may differ in important ways. Racial discrimination generally is observed both in some occupational segregation—where the dominant group has greater access to higher-paying occupations than the discriminated-against group even for those with the same level of education—and *within* occupations. But as Strober and Ferber argue, gender discrimination appears to manifest itself much more in occupational segregation, with women crowded into relatively few occupations, defined as female and relatively low-paid.

The entries in this section, then, suggest that a "market-determined" distribution of education may have some effect on wage distribution, but other factors may have as much or more. These other factors include the degree of race and gender discrimination in "access" (including financial) to schooling, the degree of gender and race discrimination in the labor market, and the degree of wage and income distribution acceptable politically in different periods of a nation's history.

Income Distribution and Education

J. Velloso

Approaches to the relationship between education and income distribution cover a wide range of perspectives. Conceptual frameworks in which choice and optimizing behavior play a key role contrast with approaches in which economic variables are closely intertwined with sociopolitical phenomena. This entry discusses major competing views and empirical results on the topic.

1. Approaches to the Distribution of Income

Analyses of income distribution are of two types. Research on the range of personal income inequality is concerned with relative differences in earnings accruing to individuals and households. Research on the functional distribution of income deals with the aggregate shares accruing to the factors of production, labor,

and capital. These two types of income inequality are indirectly connected: increases in the share of labor relative to that of capital tend to generate an equalization of personal income, since capital and property incomes tend to be concentrated in the highest income classes.

Current research on income inequality typically concentrates on the personal distribution of earnings from work, as opposed to earlier studies of classical political economy, which dealt with the functional distribution of total income in the process of capitalist development. The exclusion of income from sources other than work is a rather serious shortcoming since a significant fraction of the national product remains unaccounted for. In highly industrialized countries the share of earnings from labor ranges from 60 to 70 percent of the national product and in developing countries it is about 50 percent (Carnoy et al. 1979).

Approaches to the relationships between education and the personal distribution of earnings vary widely in their interpretations. Major sources of these differences are related to: (a) assumptions about the behavior of the labor market, including presumptions about the associations between schooling, productivity, and earnings, (b) perceptions (or lack thereof) on the inner workings of the capitalist firm, and (c) views on the nature of the state and of its interventions in the economy.

2. The Human Capital Approach

2.1 Conceptual Framework

The rationale of the human capital approach to the distribution of earnings applies to all sorts of training investments, but the discussion in this entry will deal with schooling investments only, which have been viewed as a major source of human capital. The approach assumes a rather homogeneous market for workers' education and the services derived therefrom. Individual choice, optimizing behavior, and such economic mechanisms as the price and quantity of the services supplied and demanded govern the market's operation. Skills imparted by schooling are held to increase worker productivity. Under competitive assumptions, in market equilibrium, wages equal marginal products. This implies a schooling–productivity–earnings causal chain. Additional schooling therefore entails higher earnings.

Emphasizing the supply side of the market, this approach postulates that the distribution of earnings depends on the distribution of schooling investments and on their returns. Shifts in the distribution of schooling, that is, changes in the personal characteristics of workers, entail changes in earnings inequality.

The formal model of schooling has been cast in a supply and demand framework in which the behavior of the relevant variables leads to different degrees of earnings inequality (Becker 1983). The supply of (funds to finance) schooling investments is seen as a function of the marginal interest cost of funds to finance them. Demand is viewed as a function of the marginal rate of return on these investments. Persons with more favorable social opportunities (supply conditions) tend to invest more in schooling, thanks to a larger availability of funds. Individuals with higher "ability" (demand conditions) also tend to invest more, as they have a greater capacity to benefit from these investments. This means that the distribution of earnings is more concentrated the more unequal the distribution of the supply and demand curves, that is to say the larger the negative correlation between them. This negative correlation may stem from a positive association between "opportunities and abilities."

It has been convincingly argued, however, that the formal model suffers from serious internal inconsistencies: the behavior of endogenous variables has been taken to be exogenously determined. The distribution of "abilities and opportunities"

> is merely a shorthand for the effects of early cognitive ability and parental background on the demand for formal schooling, both of which are endogenously determined variables in any intergenerational view of the process of human capital formation ... Thus, at best, the schooling model is incomplete and, at worst, it is misleading. (Blaug 1976 p.845)

2.2 Empirical Specifications and Studies

The intergenerational perspective mentioned above has not been taken into account by human capital analysts, either in earlier or in more recent studies. Earlier cross-sectional and time-series empirical studies were often based on an "earnings inequality function". Given some assumptions and simplifications regarding the relationships between investments in training and earnings, which include measuring investments in schooling in "time-equivalents" (empirically corresponding to years of schooling [S_j] of the jth individual) and impounding postschooling investments in the residual, the earnings inequality function is written:

$$\text{Var } \ln[Y_j] = f(r^*, \text{Var}[S_j]) \qquad (1)$$

where the distribution of earnings, measured by the variance of log earnings (Var $\ln[Y_j]$), is a positive and linear function of the average rate of return to schooling (r^*) and the inequality (variance) in years of schooling (Var$[S_j]$).

An alternative specification assumes that the rate of return to schooling is a random variable independent of years of schooling (Chiswick 1974, Mincer 1974):

$$\text{Var } \ln[Y_j] = f(r^*, \text{Var}[r_j], S^*, \text{Var}[S_j]) \qquad (2)$$

where the distribution of earnings is a positive function of the average size (r^*) and variance (Var$[r_j]$) of the returns to schooling, of the average level (S^*) and variance (Var$[S_j]$) of years of schooling.

Predictions of the human capital approach depend upon the specification that is adopted. According to Eqn.1, a reduction in the variance of years of schooling, presumably associated with the expansion of education, would lead to a decrease in the concentration of earnings. According to the specification of Eqn. 2 the same effect applies, but higher average levels of schooling are positively associated with an increase in income concentration. The net effect would depend upon the relative empirical magnitude of changes in the variance and in the average level of schooling.

Expanded versions of the human capital earnings inequality function typically decompose training investments into years of schooling and post schooling experience in the labor force (a proxy for on-the-job-training). Both the simplified and expanded versions, often standardized by an employment variable, have been used in empirical studies for a number of countries. In the United States, income inequality across the states has been found to be statistically associated with state differences in the distribution of schooling and in the average rates of return. Similar results were obtained for Canada (provinces), the Netherlands, and a few other countries (Chiswick 1974). With aggregate data at the state (province) level the model yielded a good statistical fit. In the United States positive associations were also found with cross-sectional individual observations. An expanded version of Eqn.1 standardized for employment was used (Chiswick and Mincer 1972). However, with individual observation, the statistical contribution of the schooling and rate of return variables (computed from the published results) was very small, about 15 percentage points of the statistically explained variance of log income. Predictions of changes in income inequality over time were made by switching to another specification, an expanded version of Eqn. 2 standardized for employment. The contribution of the schooling component was again quite small.

The specifications and empirical results of the earnings inequality function have generated considerable debate among human capital analysts. The core of this controversy lies in the effects of the distribution and of the average level of schooling on earnings inequality.

A cross-sectional study for 32 developed and developing economies found that the dispersion of schooling was positively associated with income inequality, as predicted by the human capital approach. Yet higher average levels of schooling exhibited a negative rather than a positive association, as predicted by Eqn. 2 (Winegarden 1979). More recent evidence contradicts earlier predictions and results. A linear relationship between earnings inequality and the schooling variables has not been sustained. In a cross-sectional study of 94 developing and developed countries, the average level of schooling was found to have a curvilinear (inverted U-shaped) relationship with the dispersion of years of schooling (Ram 1990). In developed economies the expansion of schooling, with a likely decrease in its inequality, appears to be statistically associated with a more equal distribution of income, but the same would not hold for less developed economies.

More recent work in the United States has focused on the concept of "unmeasured skills," as explaining income distribution changes in the 1980s (Juhn et al. 1991). Unmeasured skills refers to the quality of education. The analysis attempts to show that the bulk of increasing wage inequality has occurred in cohorts of workers with the same levels of education and that this is due to increased differentiation by educational quality. However, others have made estimates that appear to refute this argument (Card and Krueger 1993).

3. Education, Productivity, and Job Competition Approach

The controversy above takes for granted the existence of an education–productivity–earnings relationship. Although crucial for the economic meaning of the human capital approach, this remains largely an unverified assumption. Partial exceptions are given by some evidence related to the (allocative efficiency) effects of schooling of farm households in dealing with new and changing opportunities. However, these seem to apply only in the rare circumstances where competitive conditions are likely to hold.

In a different vein, a job competition approach argues that occupations directly connected with modern capital equipment are high productivity jobs. Productivity is an attribute of jobs and is technologically determined. Employers look for trainability, which is statistically associated with an individual's education and helps to determine his or her relative position in the queue for jobs and wages in the labor market. This means that if exogenous variables like the determinants of productivity are (at least) a partial determinant of the distribution of wages with respect to the supply characteristics of workers, then changes toward a more equal distribution of schooling do not imply changes in earnings inequality.

It has been argued that evidence on the behavior of the distribution of earnings sustains the job competition approach (Bluestone 1990). Substantial reductions in schooling inequality were not followed by a fall in the variance of log earnings in the United States between 1963 and 1987. Inequality in wages exhibited a U-shaped profile, declining substantially until 1978 but then reversing its path. Changes in the demand side of the market, and in the structural characteristics of the economy, as opposed to changes in the supply of personal characteristics of workers, are claimed to account for most of the observed trend. The increase in wage inequality would be mainly due to a shift in employment from goods production to services, a reduction in unionization, and the impact of international trade on the economy. These factors entailed changes in the share of employment in sectors with differentiated wage inequalities and different rates of pay with respect to schooling, which are presumed to be technologically determined.

This evidence appears to be inconsistent with the human capital approach. It underlines the relevance of macroeconomic variables and of structural shifts in changing earnings inequality as compared to changes in the personal characteristics of workers. It does not lend support to a widely applicable schooling–productivity–earnings relationship, but it does not necessarily corroborate the job competition model either, since no direct evidence is provided in regard to its tenets. Research efforts pursued along these lines seem to provide only a partial account of changes in earnings distribution.

4. Education and the Political Economy of Income Distribution

Studies concerned with the inner workings of capitalist firms have contributed to enlarging the understanding of what makes workers more productive, and of income determinants. These studies, when cast in a conceptual framework that deals with contradictory relationships between schooling, the needs of capitalist firms, and the roles of the state patterned after a political economy approach, appear to be a powerful tool for explaining changes in income distribution.

4.1 Education, Conflict, the Firm, and Labor Control

When labor is hired by firms the hiring contract is "incomplete" to the extent that it does not spell out the intensity and quality of the effort to be expended. Attempts to secure the cooperation of workers include monitoring and policing, promises of promotion and threats of dismissal. Employers may resort to an "invisible handshake" of trust and loyalty or to other available alternatives within the authoritarian allocation (rather than price) system of the firm. Collective contracts signed by workers through trade unions in order to compensate for the attempts to control the production process on the part of employers may in turn prompt them to exercise "divide and rule" strategies, for instance promising promotions (higher wages) to winners among competitors. Alternatively, employers may adopt such socially legitimate (or illegitimate) indicators as schooling diplomas (or gender/ethnicity) to allocate workers to different career paths (differentiated wage schedules) in the firm (Blaug 1985).

A combination of both strategies is likely to be preferred by employers to the extent that winners may be legitimated by their diplomas. This suggests that the pay-off to schooling does not necessarily depend on productivity nor on supply and demand relationships in a presumed competitive setting but rather on the firms' politics of labor control. Thus, income determination and, *ipso facto*, income distribution are mediated by the internal non-price allocation strategies within firms, by the role of unions, and by other variables. Schooling is just one of these many noneconomic variables.

A parallel but diverse view of labor control departs from the differences between wage-efficiency and wage-discipline approaches. Wage-efficiency approaches typically hold that wage incentives are sufficient to induce workers to increase their labor effort without complementary supervision. Alternatively, labor-discipline models contend that supervisory inputs are additionally necessary to monitor the intensity of labor services provided by production (Bowles 1985). Given the conflicts of interest between employers and production employees, pecuniary incentives can only extract labor effort if complemented by supervision. A key variable to appraise these competitive approaches is the intensity of supervision.

Available data across industries in the United States, using proxies for the intensity of supervision, tend to provide a strong, albeit provisional, support for the labor-discipline model (Gordon 1990).

Earlier studies based on a market segmentation approach to income determination highlighted the relevance of labor-discipline models. The more recent studies discussed here tend to uphold these models. They suggest the relevance of different capitalists' practices of labor control in wage determination and, therefore, in income distribution, although in this regard they have not scrutinized the role of schooling. This has been the task of wider concerns, which will be discussed below only briefly because of space limitations; the reader is referred to the sources quoted in the following section.

4.2 Education, Conflict, and the State

It has been pointed out that the roles performed by schooling with regard to the needs of capitalist firms are pervaded by contradictions, conflicts, and internal incompatibilities. While schools tend to reproduce the hierarchical and unequal relations prevailing in capitalist firms they also contribute to the expansion of economic opportunities for lower classes and groups (Carnoy and Levin 1985). This perspective has shed light on the processes of labor discipline in production and on other facets of the capitalist firms' setting. It has also revealed the historical nature of the relationships between schooling and work, which change as power conflicts among social classes and groups undergo changes in society at large.

When dealing with the nature of the state and the role of its intervention in the economy this perspective provides relevant clues to understanding changes in income distribution. The state is seen as an arena of struggle among social classes and groups. State policies respond to these conflicts. Education, an important allocator of social and economic roles, is a relevant tool for the reproduction of domination relationships as well as for democratic forces acting in the opposite direction. Thus, access to schooling is part and parcel of those power conflicts and so are changes in the distribution and in the average level of schooling attainment over time. Schooling and earnings relationships are mediated by these conflicts, in which state policies and the internal non-price allocation practices of firms (for example, politics of labor control) play a major role. Changes in the supply of workers' characteristics, such as schooling, may lead to minor but not to substantial shifts in the distribution of earnings over time, since these depend upon similar shifts in the balance of power among social classes and groups.

There is evidence to substantiate this conceptual framework, at least as far as developing countries are concerned. Research findings indicate that schooling has a positive and significant statistical association with earnings in countries such as Brazil, Peru,

Mexico, and Korea. Yet changes in the distribution and in the level of schooling have a relatively small statistical effect on the observed increases in earnings inequality over time in these three countries. Most of the shifts in earnings inequality over a ten-year period have not been accounted for by changes in variables related to the personal characteristics of workers. In Brazil, changes in the relative pay-offs to schooling stemmed mostly from the state's income policies, which benefited higher income groups. In Peru, gains obtained by the well-paid occupational groups at the expense of the lower-paid could not be attributed to changes in the personal characteristics of workers. The same applies to Mexico, where income differences between well-paid/poor economic sectors and rich/poor economic regions have increased.

In Korea, although an equalizing distribution of education played some role in equalizing income between 1976 and 1991, the major factor in income equalization was apparently the political changes in the 1980s, leading to government efforts to hold down wage increases for managers and professionals while promoting low-end wage increases through minimum wage policies and a general ideology of wage equalization (Nam 1994).

In fact, major shifts in earnings inequality appear to have been the outcome of government incomes policies affecting the reward to different levels of schooling, types of occupation, work sectors, and regions of a country. In the countries concerned, which represent a wide range of the political spectrum among economies in the process of capitalist development, Carnoy et al. (1979 p. 97) reported that "income distribution has been changing largely because higher income groups have been gaining income at the expense of lower income groups, not because more people in the labor force are acquiring characteristics which enjoy greater pay relative to which enjoy less."

Theory and research on the origins of shifts of income distribution and on the roles played by schooling in these changes have been making meaningful progress. As they have revealed, the scenario was more complex than that envisaged by straightforward relationships between schooling, productivity and earnings under competitive assumptions or, for that matter, between schooling, jobs, productivity, and earnings. The states' policies and the underlying conflicts among social classes and groups, in which schooling is a key variable, associated with the firms' politics of labor control, are increasingly being understood as major factors in explaining changes in income distribution over time. Research based on a political economy approach, as discussed, seems to be a most promising avenue for understanding these changes in each historical context in the process of capitalist development.

See also: Benefits of Education; Education, Occupation, and Earnings; Education and Earnings

References

Becker G S 1983 *Human Capital: A Theoretical and Empirical Analysis with Special Reference to Education*, 2nd edn. University of Chicago Press, Chicago, Illinois

Blaug M 1976 The empirical status of human capital theory: A slightly jaundiced survey. *J. Econ. Lit.* 14(3): 827–55

Blaug M 1985 Where are we now in the economics of education? *Econ. Educ. Rev.* 4(1): 17–28

Bluestone B 1990 The impact of schooling and industrial restructuring on recent trends in wage inequality in the United States. *Amer. Econ. Rev.* (80)2: 303–07

Bowles S 1985 The production process in a competitive economy: Walrasian, Neo-Hobbesian, and Marxian models. *Am. Econ. Rev.* 75(1): 16–36

Card D, Krueger A 1993 Trends in relative Black–White earnings revisited. *Am. Econ. Rev.* 83(2): 85–91

Carnoy M, Lobo J, Toledo A, Velloso J 1979 *Can Educational Policy Equalise Income Distribution in Latin America?* Saxon House, Farnborough

Carnoy M, Levin H M 1985 *Schooling and Work in the Democratic State*. Stanford University Press, Stanford, California

Chiswick B R 1974 *Income Inequality: Regional Analyses Within a Human Capital Framework*. National Bureau of Economic Research, New York

Chiswick B R, Mincer J 1972 Time series changes in personal income inequality in the United States since 1939, with projections to 1985. *J. Pol. Econ.* 80(3, 2): S34–66

Gordon D 1990 Who bosses whom? The intensity of supervision and the discipline of labor. *Am. Econ. Rev.* (80)2: 28–32

Juhn C, Murphy K, Pierce B 1991 Accounting for the slow-down in Black–White wage convergence. In: Kosters M (ed.) 1991 *Workers and Their Wages: Changing Patterns in the United States*. American Enterprise Institute Press, Washington, DC

Mincer J 1974 *Schooling, Experience, and Earnings*. National Bureau of Economic Research, New York

Nam Y S 1994 Women, schooling, and the labor market: Changes in the structure of earnings inequality by gender in Korea, 1976–91. Unpublished PhD dissertation, Stanford University, Stanford, California

Ram R 1990 Educational expansion and schooling inequality: International evidence and some implications. *Rev. Econ. Stat.* 72(2): 266–74

Winegarden C R 1979 Schooling and income distribution: evidence from international data. *Economica* 46: 83–7

Further Reading

Blaug M, Dougherty C, Psacharopoulos G 1982 The distribution of schooling and the distribution of earnings: Raising the school leaving age in 1972. *The Manchester School* 1(1): 24–40

Bowles S, Gintis H 1975 The problem with human capital theory: A Marxian critique. *Am. Econ. Rev.* 65(2): 74–82

Carnoy M 1980 Segemented labor markets. In: UNESCO (ed.) 1980 *Education, Work and Employment*, II. International Institute of Educational Planning – UNESCO, Paris

Green F, Weisskopf T E 1990 The worker discipline effect: A disaggregative analysis. *Rev. Econ. Stat.* 72(2): 241–49

Harrison B, Bluestone B 1988 *The Great U-Turn: Corporate Restructuring and the Polarizing of America.* Basic Books, New York

Jamison D T, Van der Gaag J 1987 Education and earnings in the People's Republic of China. *Econ. Educ. Rev.* 6(2): 161–66

Kakwani N C 1980 *Income Inequality and Poverty: Methods of Estimation and Policy Applications.* Oxford University Press, New York

Klees S 1989 The economics of education: A more than slightly jaundiced view of where we are now. In: Caillods F (ed.) 1989 *The Prospects for Educational Planning.* UNESCO IIEP Paris

Mincer J 1970 The distribution of labor incomes: A survey with special reference to the human capital approach. *J. Econ. Lit.* 8(1): 1–26

Psacharopoulos G, Woodhall M 1985 *Education for Development: An Analysis of Investment Choices.* Oxford University Press, New York

Sahota G S 1978 Theories of personal income distribution: A survey. *J. Econ. Lit.* 16(1): 1–55

Race Earnings Differentials

M. Carnoy

Earnings differentials between racial or ethnic groups exist in most societies. To the extent that they persist over time in democratic political conditions, they are of considerable concern, since they suggest that different groups are not getting either equal access to human capital investment opportunities or equal treatment in labor markets, or both.

The literature on such earnings differences has grown rapidly, especially in the United States, where the civil rights movement in the 1950s and 1960s drew attention to the unequal education and income of African-Americans and Latinos. Because of the social pressure exerted by the movement, detailed census statistics were collected that enabled researchers to estimate the existence of wage and schooling differences and to posit explanations for them. In other countries where such data are collected, the results also show distinct differences in economic performance between ethnic and race groups, suggesting that discovering differences is largely a function of data collection politics. Although the discussion in this entry focuses on the United States case, this is primarily because of the richness of the data available and the highly developed debate about explanations of differences. The methodology is applicable to other economies with minor changes for local conditions. Such a comparison is made with Israel, where European immigrants and those of Afro-Asian origin differ considerably in education and cultural background.

1. Race and Ethnic Earnings Differences in the United States

Data on race, ethnicity, and earnings in the United States are available for the period 1939–89, and can be analyzed by native- and foreign-born parentage (see Chiswick 1984 for the 1970 census breakdown). It is important in studying earnings differences to divide the data by gender: earnings differ by gender across groups and female labor force participation rates also differ among groups and over time.

The data suggest that certain ethnic groups, regardless of race, earn more than average, and more than the dominant White Anglo (non-Latino) majority. So, for example, Japanese-Americans, Chinese-Americans, and Jewish-Americans all earn more than Anglo-Whites, and this has been the case since at least the 1960s. African-Americans, Latinos, Filipinos, and Native-Americans are all examples of groups that earn considerably less, on average, than Anglo-Whites and have done so for as long as data have been available on such differences. Among Latinos there is also variation, with Mexican and Puerto Rican Latinos earning much less than those of Cuban origin.

Table 1 presents earnings data for the period 1939–89 according to ethnic group, race group, and gender group. The Asian-American and Latino groupings are broad and contain distinct subgroups that earn significantly more or significantly less than the group average. Estimates of earnings of Latinos of Mexican origin, Puerto Rican origin, and Cuban origin show that Cuban-origin Latinos earn more, on average, than those of Mexican or Puerto Rican origin. Part of the subgroup variation is due to large differences in the socioeconomic origins of different national groups that immigrated to the United States: for example, the first wave of Cuban-Americans who came to Florida in the late 1950s and early 1960s were professionals leaving Castro's Cuba. That group of immigrants was markedly different from the unskilled laborers from Mexico who immigrated throughout the same period, and especially after immigration laws changed in 1965.

Yet, despite this variation within broad groups, Table 1 suggests that: (a) there are important and persistent ethnic/race differences in earnings in the United States labor market, (b) these differences cut

Table 1
United States: Annual median earnings by education, race/ethnic group, and gender 1939–89[a] (full-time workers, current dollars, and percent)

Category	Year							
	1939	1949	1959	1969	1973	1979	1982	1989
All schools (male)								
White	1,356	3,001	5,438	8,633	11,038	17,389	21,343	28,578
Black	42	55	58	63	67	70	69	71
Latino	62	71	72	76	70	70	72	67
Asian-American	65	76	86	101	—	96	—	98
High-school graduates (male) (25–34 years)								
White	1,353	3,026	5,241	8,052	10,534	14,830	17,712	22,288
Black	58	73	69	73	81	80	83	80
Latino	88	83	82	85	85	89	88	85
Asian-American	75	85	99	100	—	86	—	89
College graduate (male) (25–34 years)								
White	2,719	3,760	6,788	10,549	12,076	18,394	22,301	31,279
Black	59	72	67	68	90	82	81	70
Latino	99	66	78	76	97	88	90	83
Asian-American	73	85	85	110	—	91	—	100
All schools (female)								
White	816	2,038	3,302	4,956	6,285	10,226	13,207	18,613
Black	39	57	63	77	87	91	91	90
Latino	61	87	75	90	85	87	85	82
Asian-American	83	89	99	113	—	109	—	109
High-school graduate (female) (25–34 years)								
White	935	2,212	3,470	5,121	6,118	9,523	12,114	15,421
Black	51	75	73	84	94	95	93	90
Latino	94	103	95	103	98	93	98	95
Asian-American	85	69	100	94	—	92	—	119
College graduate (female) 25–34 years								
White	1,128	2,491	4,378	6,336	8,059	12,448	16,026	23,732
Black	67	89	71	101	97	95	92	94
Latino	—	—	—	99	102	94	97	98
Asian-American	—	—	—	104	—	110	—	106

Source: US Department of Commerce, Bureau of the Census, Public Use Census Sample, 1940, 1950, 1960, 1970, 1980; Current Population Survey, March Sample, 1974, 1983, 1990
a Median estimated as mean of log income

across gender, and (c) they are subject to historical change. In the period before 1973, non-Anglo men and women made large gains relative to Anglos, and after 1973 these gains slowed down and reversed for some groups. Even with the changes, African-Americans and Latinos have remained at a much lower level of average income than either Anglos or Asian-Americans. It is also fairly evident from the table that, once education and age are accounted for, Latinos do relatively better than African-Americans.

The two important questions that the literature has addressed about these earnings differences, logically, are: (a) why do some groups do better or worse than others? and (b) what causes them to change over time?

2. A Model for Explaining Earnings Differences

The human capital model has typically been used to understand race and ethnic differences in earnings (Becker 1957, Freeman 1973, 1976, Hanushek 1981, Welch 1973, Chiswick 1984). This model

able 2

ercentage points of income gain that would result from qualizing minority education to White male education, by thnicity and gender, full time employed, 1939–89[a]

'ear	Latino males	Latina females	Black males	Black females	White females
939	29	18	27	22	–9
949	17	12	18	11	–8
959	15	10	15	9	–2
969	12	9	14	7	0
973	16	9	12	5	0
979	16	8	11	6	2
982	15	10	11	6	2
985	15	10	11	6	2
987	15	8	10	6	1
989	20	14	10	7	0

The education variable is measured in 1940, 1950, 1960, 1970, 1974, 980, 1983, 1986, 1988, and 1990; incomes refer to the previous ear—hence the years in the table refer to the income year. The education ap is estimated from a simulation using a regression equation with human apital variables (years of schooling, labor force experience, and, in census ears, native or foreign born). The percentages in the table should be read s the number of percentage points that a given group would have gained ist from getting the same distribution of education in its labor force as /hite males. A negative sign means that White females would receive ower incomes, all other variables equal, were education equalized with aat of White males (White females in the labor market in those years had igher average education than White males).
ource: Department of Commerce, United States Census, Public Use ample, 1940, 1950, 1960, 1970, 1980, and Current Population Survey, 974, 1983, 1986, 1988, 1990

haracterizes individual earnings as a function of ducation and experience in the labor force. Its remise is that earnings of various groups would be xplained largely, if not entirely, by their average ducation and experience. This still leaves the issue of /hy average education differs among different groups. s the difference voluntary, or the result of discrimina-ion in the supply of educational services? However, eaving this issue aside, if the human capital model is correct representation of the market for labor, then ace or ethnicity should play no significant role once he human capital of individuals is controlled for; that s, the coefficients of education and experience in the arnings function should be equal for all ethnic groups. he model is as follows:

$$\ln Y_i = a + b_j \sum_{j=1}^{m} S_{ij} + C_k \sum_{k=m+1}^{n} E_{ik} + e_i \qquad (1)$$

Vhere Y_i = income of individual i; S_{ij} = *dummy for chooling level j*; E_{ik} = dummy for experience level k; e_i = unexplained variance.

Other models are more elaborate, including the pos-ibility that earnings for different groups vary because f employment in different industries (with significantly ower or higher pay), in public versus private employ-ment, in different parts of the country, and because of differences in civil status, or in native versus foreign parentage (Carnoy et al. 1976, Farley 1986, Bean and Tienda 1988, Carnoy et al. 1990). Time worked per week or per year is also an important potential factor affecting earnings differences, since some groups may have higher average levels of involuntary unemployment and part-time employment than others.

Empirical results of cross-sectional studies in a single year show that schooling level attained is a signifi-cant explainer of earnings differences among groups. African-Americans, Latinos, and Native-Americans take significantly less schooling than Anglo Whites and particularly than Asian-Americans. The importance of education in explaining differences in income between various ethnic/gender groups can be simulated with log income equations, estimating how much equalizing education differences would equalize income between groups. For each year and each ethnic/gender group shown in Table 2, the figure in the table represents the percentage point increase in average income the group would have had if its education would have been equal to that of White males in the same year. For example, in 1939, Black males would have had 27 percentage points higher income if their education were equal to White males', taking account of age differences. White females, to the contrary, would have had 9 percentage points *lower* income if they had the same education as White males, implying that working White females were much more educated than males in the 1930s. Adding experience differences changes these percentages marginally, except for Latinos in the 1970s, when the Latino labor force became significantly younger than other groups. The additional effect of Latino experience decreased sharply in the 1980s.

Since the quantity of schooling and experience differ-ences explain only a portion of the "gap" in the earnings of Black and Latino workers compared to Whites, other factors must also be important. Among these may be in-dustry and region worked in (some industries and regions are significantly lower-paying than others), the quality of education taken by different groups (which could include differential investment in education at home), English language limitations (foreign birth), and labor market discrimination.

3. Earnings Differentials and Discrimination

Although education provides a powerful explanation for income differences among race or ethnic groups, empiri-cal estimates of the human capital equation suggest that the returns to both education and experience have been lower, historically, for non-White minorities (including Asian-Americans) than for Whites (see Hanushek 1981, Chiswick 1987, Carnoy et al. 1990). These lower returns can be interpreted as reflecting lower quality education received by minorities (Welch 1973, Card and Krueger 1992a, 1992b) and, in the case of the return to experience, choice of or access to jobs that have a smaller training

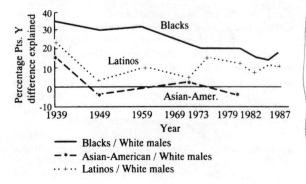

Figure 1
Minority–White full-time income gap explained by wage discrimination 1939–87

component, hence flatter experience–earnings profiles. There could also be a strong interaction between quality of schooling and access to training in jobs.

The difference in quality of education received may not only reflect differences in the quality of schools attended by different groups, but also the amount invested in them by their families and the interaction between family background and school performance. Because of the cumulative nature of learning before and during school and because of interaction effects, eliminating discriminatory practices in school access does not necessarily equalize outcomes (the quality of an individual's education). Differences in returns to education and in access to jobs with more training for different groups may also simply be the result of discriminatory practices in the labor market.

If it is assumed that all differences in returns to individual characteristics, such as education and experience, as well as differences in return to place of work (region, industry) for various race and ethnic groups are caused by discrimination, this discrimination can be estimated as the "residual" unexplained portion of income differences when characteristics are "equalized," through simulation, between whites and each minority group (see Carnoy et al. 1990, for the standard model of such a simulation).

The "discrimination rate" as measured by the residual when the schooling, experience, region of work, marital status, foreign/native birth, and industry of work are equalized to that of White full-time employed adult males fell significantly for full-time employed Black males between 1939 and 1982 and for Latino and Asian-American males between 1939 and 1969. The rate shown in Fig. 1 is measured as percentage points of the earnings gap for each group that is not "explained" when minorities are "made to look" like White males educationally, in terms of both experience and of place of work. In the 1980s, discrimination rates rose for all three groups. The rate is insignificant for Asian-Americans, and lower for Latinos than for African-Americans. In the 1980s, it represented about 16 percentage points of White male income for Blacks and 13 percentage points for Latinos. Part of this discrimination for Latinos is associated with foreign

birth, and this, in turn, may be a function of English language capability. When Latinos of Mexican origin are separated into native- and foreign-born, the corresponding discrimination rates for the native-born are 3 percentage points in 1960, 3 in 1970, and 6 in 1980, and for foreign born, 27 percentage points in 1960, 14 in 1970, and 14 in 1980 (Carnoy et al. 1990). The low discrimination rate for native-born Latinos of Mexican origin suggests that the main explanation of lower incomes for this group of Latinos is differences in education and that labor market barriers are less important among second-generation income earners.

Why labor market discrimination occurs has been the subject of considerable controversy. In his pioneering work on racial discrimination, Myrdal (1944) argued that it was historically institutionalized in the fabric of society and required public intervention to change. Becker's model of discrimination (1957) focused on the "taste for discrimination" on the part of White workers and owners of capital, which drives the earnings of Black workers down relative to White workers. Reich (1982) refutes the claim by Becker that White workers profit when there is discrimination, showing that the lowest White earnings are in those states where the greatest discrimination exists. He argues that labor market discrimination serves owners of capital, since it keeps all workers' wages lower.

4. Earnings Differences for Minority Women

Racial and ethnic earnings differentials vary by sex. Table 1 suggests that full-time employed minority women in the United States have come to earn approximately the same income as full-time employed White women when the level of schooling is the same, and, on an hourly basis, may actually earn more than White women (Chiswick 1987). Black male high-school graduates earned only 79 percent of the annual income of Whites in 1989, but Black women graduates earned more than 90 percent of full-time White female incomes. The figures are similar for Latino males and females.

If Black women and Latinos are subject to the same race/ethnic discrimination as men, why should they earn higher relative incomes when compared to their White gender counterparts? The answer lies partly in the gender segregation of the labor market and the willingness of White male employers to group minority and White women in the same category of labor. This was not always the case: Black female incomes were much lower than those of Whites in the 1940s and 1950s, when Black women were highly concentrated in domestic service. As Black women moved into manufacturing and clerical jobs and received much more schooling, the differences between White and Black female earnings tended to disappear.

Part of the answer also lies in the tendency for minority women to stay in the labor market permanently and therefore to accumulate seniority due to: (a) economic necessity (their husbands generally have lower education and lower income than White males), and (b) the greater likelihood of the women in some group—Blacks and Puerto Ricans—being single heads of household supporting children. In addition, Black women are much more likely than Whites or Latinas to work in the public sector, where female salaries are much higher than in the private sector. Public sector employment was especially important in the late 1960s and in the 1970s, when such employment was at its peak.

5. Explaining Changes in Earnings Differences Over Time

Why has the gap in earnings between minority groups changed over time? Table 1 shows that full-time employed Black males and females made large gains in relative earnings in the period 1939–79, especially in the 1940s and 1960s. The gains in the 1980s were negligible. Latino males and females also made big gains in the period 1939–69, but then lost ground. Asian-Americans made large gains in the 1940s, 1950s, and 1960s, but stopped gaining in the 1970s and 1980s.

The principal debate that has developed over these changes is whether they are the result of supply-side forces, specifically changes in the relative investment in human capital made by the different groups; or demand-side forces, specifically legal and direct employment intervention by government. Freeman (1976) maintained that the large gains in relative earnings of Blacks in the 1960s came as a result of the passage of the 1964 Civil Rights Act and subsequent federal employment legislation in 1965. Others (Heckman and Payner 1989, Donohue and Heckman 1991, Card and Krueger 1993) have supported this explanation. Smith and Welch (1989), on the contrary, have argued that the single best explanation for the gains in the period 1939–79 was the relative increase in Black education, and that federal intervention had only a minor effect, primarily in raising the earnings of young Black college graduates in the early 1970s. Card and Krueger (1992b) claim that about one-fourth of the gain in Black earnings attributed to government intervention in labor markets in the 1960s and 1970s is the result of improvements in Black education in the South in the 1930s and 1940s. Juhn et al (1991) argue that the slowdown in Black–White wage convergence in the 1980s was due to "unmeasured skill" effects, namely that the payoff to educational quality increased in the 1980s, and Blacks still received lower quality education than Whites.

If the analysis is done decade-by-decade in the 50-year period, the supply-side argument is weakened. Table 2 suggests that education gains by Blacks between 1939 and 1979 was correlated with a reduction in the Black–White earnings gap in those four decades. But other factors appear to have been much more important than education in that reduction. For example, Table 3 corrects that contribution of education differences to the income gap estimated in Table 2 for changes in the income distribution (specifically, the income weights attached to different levels of schooling) in each decade.

Table 3

Change in education gap adjusted for changing income weights, by decade, full-time workers, 1939–89 (percentage points of income)

Year	Latino males	Latino females	Black males	Black females
1939	29	18	27	22
1949	23	16	24	15
1949	17	12	18	11
1959	16	10	16	9
1959	15	10	15	9
1969	12	9	14	7
1969	12	9	14	7
1979	16	8	11	6
1979	16	8	11	6
1989	19	13	9	7

Source: see Table 2 for figures based on the education gap estimated using same year White male income weights. Figures in this table compare the education gap in 1939 with the gap in 1949 figures based on average education differences between ethnic groups in 1949 weighted by White male coefficients estimated using 1939 census data; compare the 1949 figures from Table 2 with 1959 figures based on average education differences in 1959 weighted by White male coefficients using 1949 census data, and so forth, for various census years. This permits comparison for each decade of the effect on income of the education gain net of changes in the distribution of income among education groups in that particular decade.

"Wage compression" in the 1940s was much more important than Black male educational gains in reducing the Black–White male income gap, and was as important as education for Latinos. Although Black males' education did not increase much relative to Whites in the 1940s and racial discrimination declined only slightly, the enormous increases in incomes for all low-income earners relative to high-income earners—irrespective of race—during that decade lifted Black male relative incomes more than in any decade since. In the 1940s, there was also a job shift from agriculture to manufacturing that had a powerful effect on Black male incomes. As a point of comparison, in the 1950s—a period of significant educational gains for minorities but no reduction in overall income inequality, much reduced sectoral job shift and no reductions in job discrimination—gains in relative income for Blacks were minimal. In the 1960s and particularly, the 1970s, Blacks made large education gains, but the major gains in income for Blacks came from the reduction in wage discrimination. In the 1980s, when the political climate on affirmative action changed, Black male and female incomes stopped rising relative to Whites'.

A similar analysis for Latino and Asian-American males and females suggest that education is a more important explainer of their relative income gains than

Table 4
Private rates of return to education, by level and ethnic group, full-time workers 1939–87 (annual rates, in percent)[a]

Category	Year							
	1939	1949	1959	1969	1973	1979	1982	1987
White Male								
HSC/ElemC	9.1	7.5	6.4	6.4	5.7	6.2	—	—
HSC/HSdrop	9.6	6.7	4.6	6.2	7.4	7.9	9.1	7.8
CollC/HSC	10.9	9.1	10.4	10.8	8.6	9.5	9.8	11.0
Black male								
HSC/ElemC	5.5	6.0	5.4	6.7	8.4	8.9	—	—
HSC/HSdrop	9.4	7.0	8.2	6.5	10.8	7.8	8.0	5.6
CollC/HSC	5.7	5.8	6.1	10.2	9.8	8.6	8.5	12.7
Latino								
HSC/ElemC	8.2	5.7	3.7	5.7	6.0	2.7	—	—
HSC/HSdrop	12.1	5.9	4.4	8.4	8.2	8.0	8.8	9.6
CollC/HSC	7.2	7.1	8.6	7.9	10.2	8.7	11.7	12.2

Source: Regression estimates using US Census Bureau, Public Use Samples, 1940, 1950, 1960, 1970, 1980, and Current Population Survey, 1974, 1983, and 1988
a These percentages are based on the coefficients of dummy variables of elementary complete (8 years of schooling), high school dropout (1–3 years of high school), and college complete (4 years of college), where the dependent variable is log income (wage earnings and self-employment income), and experience dummies and native/foreign birth are held constant. The left-out dummy is high school complete. The coefficients are divided by the appropriate number of years of schooling to obtain the figure shown here. The 1982 and 1987 high school dropout dummy includes all those who recorded less than high school complete. For Whites and Blacks, this averaged to approximately 9 years of schooling, and for Latinos, approximately 8 years

for Black males and females, although change in sector or work (shifts from agriculture to manufacturing) is also crucial in understanding their gains in the 1940s (Latinos and Asian-Americans) and 1950s (Latinos). Both groups also profited from reduced labor market discrimination in the 1940s and 1960s.

6. The Impact of Changing Returns to Different Levels of Schooling

As schooling in a society expands as a whole, rates of return to lower levels of schooling tend to decline relative to higher levels. In the United States, rates of return to schooling for minorities equalized with those for Whites in the 1970s (see Table 4), mainly, according to a number of analyses, because of government legislation to reduce discrimination in labor markets. Latinos and Blacks still earned less than Whites with the same amount of schooling since, even with equal (or higher) rates for minorities, they invested less (lower income forgone) in each level of schooling.

Moreover, the payoffs to college education in the United States fell sharply to all groups in the 1970s and then rose sharply in the 1980s (Murphy and Welch 1989), especially for younger age groups. This created a situation in the 1980s where those ethnic groups whose members tended to invest in college education saw their earnings

rise relative to those groups that had a lower percentage of college graduates. The opposite situation arose in the mid-1970s, when college rates fell, negatively affecting the earnings of young Whites and Asian-Americans relative to Blacks and Latinos.

One of the educational anomalies in the 1980s was the increased graduation rate from high school for Black males and females, but a declining percentage of these graduates going on to college and finishing college. This occurred even when the rate of return to college graduation increased sharply for Blacks (as it did for other groups). Whatever the reasons for the lower rate of Black (and Latino) college attendance, the impact on their relative earnings was negative. In effect, these two groups increased the number of years of schooling they were engaged in, but they were investing in levels of schooling where the rate of return was stagnant or falling. Whites and Asian-Americans, on the other hand, invested in college education, where the rate rose and remains high.

The phenomenon of changing rates of return to different levels of education over time—especially the "usual" case of declining marginal rates to investment in lower schooling levels relative to higher levels as the educational system expands—has important implications for the relative earnings of different ethnic groups in most countries, not just the United States. Those groups who are ahead of the average investment in education will tend to see their earnings rise over time relative to those groups which are behind the average, unless some other social change takes place that equalizes incomes in favor of the less educated. Thus, the less schooled groups not only have lower incomes because of their lower schooling, but their incomes relative to more schooled groups will also tend to decline as the payoff to lower levels of schooling falls relative to higher levels.

7. Comparing Results for Israel and Korea

Similar estimates have been made for Israel, where ethnic origin (European-origin versus North African–Asian-origin immigrants) is potentially a source of wage discrimination (Amirs 1983, 1988). The results of such estimates show that in the 1970s, the wage differential between the foreign born males of the two ethnic groups fell substantially from 25 to 16 percent mainly because of demographic factors, such as a change in the relative age structures and period of immigration of the two groups. Unexplained differentials (wage discrimination plus quality of schooling differences) also fell from 15 to 12 percent. When the same estimates are made for first-generation Israeli-born of North African–Asian and European extraction, the wage differential is shown to have become larger than for the foreign-born in the 1970s, rising from 26 percent in 1970–72 to 30 percent in 1980–82. This is explained mainly by an increasing age difference over the decade, with European-origin Israelis becoming increasingly older in relative terms. Nevertheless, the results also show that educational differences (larger than between the foreign-born of the two ethnic groups) continued to persist even though average levels in both groups rose significantly relative to their parents. The results also suggest that wage discrimination fell during the decade and was relatively low (about 6 percent in 1980–82).

Israel's systematic policy of social equalization has apparently succeeded in keeping wage discrimination against lower status ethnic groups low and even falling, but it has not succeeded in overcoming the impact of original intergroup economic and educational inequalities. Children of European origin continue to earn more than other ethnic groups largely because they are much more likely to attend and complete university.

Although recent results for Korea (Nam 1994) explain gender differences in income over time for a homogeneous ethnic group, the analysis supports the relative importance of income distribution changes in equalizing the incomes of low-paid groups (women, in this case) and high-paid groups (men). Nam shows that by far the single most explainer of more equal incomes for women in Korea in the period 1976–91 was the "wage compression" that occurred in 1986–91. Similar to the impact on Black–White incomes in the United States in the 1940s, equalizing income distribution lifted all low-income earners in Korea relative to high-income earners. Women, occupying a much higher proportion of low-income jobs, were disproportionately favorably affected

by the equalizing income distribution. Again, as in the United States, government policies and increasing union power, in addition to a dwindling supply of rural labor for low-skilled industrial jobs, were major factors in compressing wages.

References

Amirs 1983 Educational structure and wage differentials of the Israeli labor force in the 1970s. Discussion paper No. 83.07. Bank of Israel, Jerusalem

Amirs 1988 Trends in wage differentials between Jewish males of different ethnic origin during the 1970s. *Bank of Israel Economic Review* 63 (December): 52–75

Bean F, Tienda M 1988 *The Hispanic Population of the United States.* Sage, New York

Becker G S 1957 *The Economics of Discrimination.* University of Chicago Press, Chicago, Illinois

Card D, Krueger A 1992a Does school quality matter? Returns to education and the characteristics of public schools in the United States. *J. Pol. Econ.* 100(1): 1–40

Card D, Krueger A 1992b School quality and Black/White relative earnings: A direct assessment. *Q. J. Econ.* 107(1): 151–200

Card D, Krueger A 1993 Trends in relative Black–White earnings revisited. *Am. Econ. Rev.* 83(2): 85–91

Carnoy M, Girling R, Rumberger R 1976 *Education and Public Sector Employment.* Center for Economic Studies, Stanford, California

Carnoy M, Daley H, Hinojosa R 1990 *Latinos in a Changing US Economy.* Interuniversity Program for Latino Research, City University of New York, New York

Chiswick B R 1984 Differences in education attainment among racial and ethnic groups: Patterns and preliminary hypotheses. Paper presented at the National Academy of Education Conference on the State of Education, Washington, DC (mimeo)

Chiswick B R 1987 Race earnings differentials. In: Psacharopoulos G (ed.) 1987 *Economics of Education: Research and Studies.* Pergamon Press, Oxford

Donohue J III, Heckman J 1991 Continuous versus episodic change: The impact of civil rights policy on the economic status of Blacks. *J. Econ. Lit.* 29 (December): 1603–43

Farley R 1986 Assessing Black progress: Employment, occupations, earnings, income, poverty. *Economic Outlook USA* 13(3): 14–23

Freeman R 1973 Decline of labor market discrimination and economic analysis. *Am. Econ. Rev.* 63(2): 280–86

Freeman R 1976 *Black Elite: The New Market for Highly Educated Black Americans.* McGraw-Hill, New York

Hanushek E A 1981 *Sources of Black–White Earnings Differentials.* Stanford University, Institute for Educational Finance and Governance, Stanford, California

Heckman J, Payner B 1989 Determining the impact of federal antidiscrimination policy on the economic status of Blacks: A study of South Carolina. *Am. Econ. Rev.* 79(1): 138–77

Juhn C, Murphy K, Pierce B 1991 Accounting for the slowdown in Black–White wage convergence. In: Kosters M (ed.) 1991 *Workers and Their Wages: Changing Patterns in the United States.* American Enterprise Institute Press, Washington, DC

Murphy K, Welch F 1989 Wage premiums for college graduates: Recent growth and possible explanations. *Educ. Researcher* 16(4): 17–26

Myrdal G 1944 *American Dilemma: The Negro Problem and Modern Democracy*. Harper & Row, New York

Nam Y S 1994 Women, schooling, and the labor market: Changes in the structure of earnings inequality by gender in Korea, 1976–91. Unpublished Phd dissertation, Stanford University, Stanford, California

Reich M 1982 *Racial Discrimination*. Princeton University Press, Princeton, New Jersey

Smith J, Welch F 1989 Black economic progress after Myrdal. *J. Econ. Lit.* 27(2): 519–64

Welch F 1973 Black–White differences in returns to schooling. *Am. Econ. Rev.* 63(5): 893–907

Gender Differences in Earnings

M. A. Ferber

The male–female earnings gap has undoubtedly received more attention than any other indicator of women's position in the labor market and in the economy. In the advanced industrialized countries, where reliable data on earnings are available, this gap has been declining during the second half of the twentieth century, but at different times, at varying rates, and interspersed with brief reversals in some instances. The United States is one of a very few nations where it remained stubbornly at about the same level until the late 1970s. Since then it has narrowed at a sustained, albeit slow, pace. This entry examines these changes and their causes, then briefly discusses policies that might be used to hasten its further reduction.

1. Evidence

Table 1 provides information on the level of women's compared to men's hourly earnings in manufacturing for 13 countries from 1955–88. These data are widely thought to be representative of earnings in general. In all instances the proportion is higher at the end of the period than at the beginning. However, at one extreme it rose only from 44.7 percent to 48.5 percent in Japan, while at the other extreme it rose from 69.2 percent to 90.0 percent in Sweden. Data on hourly earnings are not available for the United States. The weekly earnings used are expected to show a somewhat larger male–female differential because on average, even among workers employed full-time, women work fewer hours than men. Nonetheless, the earnings gap in the United States appears to be greater than in the majority of European countries.

As can be seen from Table 2, in the United States the level of women's earnings compared to those of men working full-time, year-round, fluctuated narrowly around 60 percent for about three decades before 1980. Since then it has increased, reaching 71.1 percent in 1990. Similarly, the percentage, when expressed in terms of usual weekly earnings of full-time workers, which tends to be somewhat higher, rose from 61.3 percent in 1978 to 74.0 percent in 1991. The reasons for this difference in the ratios of annual and weekly earnings are discussed in considerable detail in Rytina (1983). The gap would, no doubt, be smaller for hourly wages, but such data are not available in the United States. Thus it is clear that the male–female wage gap has been narrowing over time.

Data for 1960–90 in Table 3 show that women's income (largely comprised of earnings) is lower than men's in all age groups, but that, with the exception of the oldest age groups, who were most likely to be disproportionately successful women with high earnings, the gap tends to increase with age. This reflects the fact that even in the 1990s women on average accumulate less experience than men. The figures also show that for those under age 45 the earnings gap began to close as early as the 1970s, and that it was the youngest women who experienced the greatest decline. In view of the rapid rise in the labor force participation rates of these cohorts, it is very likely that they will retain at least a substantial part of these gains over the life cycle. Therefore this evidence suggests that the decline in male–female earnings differentials is likely to continue.

There is a growing consensus that the relative improvement in women's earnings has been the result of a combination of supply and demand factors. As Smith and Ward (1989) point out, employment has been declining in the relatively male-intensive manufacturing sector, while the more female-intensive service sector expanded, at least prior to the recession of 1990, and again since then. At the same time, women's market skills and labor force experience have increased substantially. Between 1966 and 1991 the share of degrees awarded to women increased from 39.9 percent to 53.9 percent for bachelor's, from 40.4 percent to 53.5 percent for master's, from 15.4 percent to 37.0 percent for doctoral degrees, and from 3.8 percent to 39.0 percent for first professional degrees (US Department of Education 1993). Estimated years of labor market experience also increased, from 7.97 to 10.45 years for employed women aged 30, and from 10.57 to 13.51 years for employed women aged 40.

Nevertheless, differences remain in attitudes toward these developments. Neoclassical economists generally emphasize how much the situation has improved,

Table 1
Female-to-male hourly earnings in manufacturing, selected years 1955–88 (in percent)

	1955	1973	1982	1988
Australia[a]	69.0	69.4	78.2	79.6
Belgium	56.8	68.7	73.5	74.5
Denmark[b]	65.3	82.3	85.1	84.4
Finland[c]	67.6	71.7	77.1	77.2
France	–	76.8	77.7	79.2[k]
Germany, Fed. Rep.[d]	62.8	70.9	73.0	73.0
Greece	64.7[h]	65.5	73.1	78.0
Ireland	56.3	59.9	68.5	68.9
Japan	44.7	53.9	48.8	48.5[j]
Luxembourg	–	55.3	60.1	58.4
Netherlands	58.8	75.5	74.1	74.8
New Zealand	62.8	65.8[i]	70.8	74.6
Norway[a]	67.4	76.2	83.2	84.3
Sweden[e]	69.2	84.1	90.3	90.0
Switzerland[d]	63.7	65.4	67.0	67.5
United Kingdom	58.6	60.7	68.8	68.0
United States[f]	63.9[g]	61.7	65.4	70.2

Sources: Calculated from data in International Labour Organization *Yearbook of Labour Statistics* (various years). United States data are from Department of Labor *Employment and Earnings* (various issues); and Japanese data are from Organisation for Economic Co-operation and Development *Employment Outlook* (September 1988) p. 212
a Earnings of employees only   b excludes vacation pay   c includes mining and quarrying, electricity   d includes family allowances paid by employers   e includes holiday and sick pay, and value of payments in kind   f usual weekly earnings of full-time workers   g earnings of year-round, full-time workers   h 1961   i 1974   j 1986   k 1987

and the extent to which changes in women's own behavior have brought this about. Feminists, on the other hand, are more inclined to point to the substantial earnings gap that still exists, and to what extent external factors are responsible.

The scale of the remaining disparities may be observed in Table 4. It will be noted that in 1990 men who were high-school drop-outs earned more than women high-school graduates, and men with a bachelor's degree earned more than women with a master's degree.

2. Causes of the Earnings Gap

As suggested, there is much disagreement about the causes of the continuing earnings differentials. The dispute is mainly between those who emphasize only the importance of differences in work-related characteristics, such as education, training, work experience, and job tenure, and those who ascribe a significant role to discrimination as an additional factor.

The importance of differences in human capital is beyond dispute. Indeed, there is broad agreement that such differences account for a substantial portion of the earnings gap. In fact, there is growing recognition

Table 2
Median annual earnings and usual weekly earnings of full-time women workers as percent of men's earnings, selected years 1955–92

Year	Annual	Weekly
1955	63.4	—
1960	60.8	—
1965	60.0	—
1970	59.4	62.3
1975	58.8	62.0
1980	60.2	63.4
1985	64.6	68.2
1990	71.1	71.8
1991	—	74.0
1992	71.5[a]	

a Income rather than earnings
Sources: 1955–91, Blau and Ferber, 1992; 1992, US Bureau of the Census, *Money Income of Households, Families, and Persons in the Households, Families, and Persons in the United States*, 1992, Table 26

that the premium for more human capital has substantially risen in recent years (Blau and Kahn 1994). While there is no difference by gender in the number of years of schooling, even in the 1990s women tend to take different courses in secondary school, and to choose different majors in college. It is a well-documented fact that men have more experience and longer job tenure than women, and there is little doubt that they receive more on-the-job training. However, many important questions remain unresolved.

First, none of the numerous existing studies, even those that include information on a large number of variables, have succeeded in accounting for all of the disparities in earnings; often they explain little more than half of the differential, although evidence from the 1980s has improved on this figure (Blau and Beller 1988, Blau and Ferber 1987, Treiman and Hartmann 1981). The unexplained portion may be

Table 3
United States: Female-to-male incomes of full-time, year-round workers by age (in percent)

Age	1960	1970	1980	1990
25–34	65.1	64.9	68.6	79.1
35–44	57.6	53.9	56.2	68.9
45–54	58.0	56.3	54.3	61.4
55–64	64.5	60.3	56.7	62.6

Sources: O'Neill J[a32] 1980 Women and Wages. The American Enterprise 1 (November/December) p. 29, for data 1960–1980. US Bureau of the Census *Money, Income, and Poverty Status in the United States*, Consumer Income Series P-60, for 1989 data

Table 4
Median income of men and women working year-round, full-time by years of schooling, 1992[a]

Schooling	Men (US$)	Women (US$)
Less than 9 years	16,980	12,176
9 to 12 years	21,179	13,760
High-school grad.	26,766	18,648
Some college	31,413	21,967
B.A. degree	40,381	29,264
Master's degree	47,260	35,018
Profess. degree	73,942	44,405
Doctoral degree	56,590	43,699

a For population 25 years of age or older
Source: US Bureau of the Census, *Money Income of Households, Families and Persons in the United States*, 1992, Table 26

ascribed to real differences between men and women, say in talents, motivation, or energy expended, which are thought to influence productivity, even though they cannot be measured. For instance, Becker (1985) claims that because women do the bulk of housework they expend less energy per unit of time on their paid work. He does not, however, even attempt to provide any evidence to support this hypothesis, while Bielby and Bielby (1988) show that women actually report expending more effort on their jobs.

Alternatively, the cause may be discrimination resulting in reduced access to better paid jobs and promotions, and lower pay for work in women's occupations or for doing essentially the same work. The law requires equal pay for the same work. Nonetheless, wages for the same work frequently vary by industry and even by firm (Blau 1977). Also, there is a very high degree of gender segregation within individual establishments, as confirmed by Baron and Bielby (1984), who found that in 51 percent of 400 organizations, no men and women shared the same job title, while an additional 8 percent employed workers of only one sex. Such differences in job titles can obscure the fact that women and men may be performing substantially the same tasks.

One problem is that there is disagreement whether, and to what extent, differences in earnings by occupation are tainted by the tendency to devalue women's work. In general, wages are lower in female occupations, as illustrated in Table 5, and this is true even when such variables as years of education, training, and experience, as well as hours and weeks worked, are held constant. On the other hand, there may be differences in work environment, risks, stress, and so on, which are virtually impossible to measure.

A second difficulty is that when women and men make different career choices with respect to their education, the amount of time they plan to spend in the labor market, and the occupation they select, it is not clear to what extent these decisions are themselves influenced by existing discrimination, whether in society, because tradition dictates traditional choices, or in the labor market, where lesser opportunities offer lesser incentives.

3. Can Discrimination Persist?

Becker (1957) was the first to develop a formal theory which ascribed discrimination to tastes of employers, employees, and customers. This theory was first developed in reference to race alone, but it became clear that it could be readily applied to gender as well. In the version that involves employers, they are expected to indulge such tastes at the expense of sacrificing profits. Not surprisingly, this conjecture was challenged on the grounds that, in a competitive market, discriminating employers would not be able to hold their own against more efficient producers who hired workers on merit alone (see Arrow 1973, Cain 1986 among others). This difficulty is, however, circumvented by other versions of the theory. Some feminist theorists also argue that social pressures from other discriminating employers make it difficult for those who would themselves prefer not to discriminate (Nelson, forthcoming).

One such explanation is that, rather than disliking members of what may be termed the "out group," employers derive positive satisfaction from discriminating in favor of the "in group." In this case, they may be willing to settle for lower profits in the long run, and may refuse offers to buy them out at a favorable price (Goldberg 1982). Alternatively, it has been suggested that smooth social relations are very important for the efficient functioning of an enterprise, and are often difficult to achieve among a diverse labor force (Bergmann and Darity 1981).

Another related hypothesis is based on the propensity to discriminate among workers themselves. In this case, the employer either has no choice but to refuse to hire members of the out group, or to compensate workers in the majority group for having to associate with them. To the extent that all employers face the same situation and are unable to run their business solely with members of the out group, no single employer will be at a competitive disadvantage. This is generally likely to be the case because experienced workers would be needed, if only to train the newcomers. Alternatively, loss of efficiency may offset what is gained by paying lower wages. This could be one explanation for the somewhat puzzling phenomenon of gender- or race-segregated enterprises. As for the workers who practice discrimination, far from incurring costs, they will either gain directly in the form of higher wages, or indirectly, by facing less competition for their jobs. Thus, earnings differentials and/or employment segregation must be expected to result, and can be expected to continue in the long run.

A third possibility is that customers may tend to

Table 5
United States: Median weekly earnings of women full-time wage and salary workers in selected detailed occupations

	Total number (thousands)	Percent women	Earnings ($)
Professions			
Engineers	1,719	7.0	723
Natural scientists	356	22.8	635
Physicians	254	25.2	714
Lawyers	366	25.7	914
Operations and systems researchers and analysts	208	37.5	675
Teachers (elementary)	1,264	84.4	481
Teachers (special ed.)	222	84.7	489
Librarians	146	84.9	476
Registered nurses	1,075	92.7	516
Technical occupations			
Engineers and related technologists and technicians	854	18.6	479
Health technologists and technicians	909	79.0	367
Sales occupations			
Sales representatives (commodities except retail)	1,302	18.0	539
Sales workers, retail and personal services	2,683	58.8	229
Sales workers (apparel)	166	78.9	207
Administrative support (including clerical)			
Mail and message distribution	776	33.6	463
Secretaries, stenographers, and typists	3,842	98.4	310
Service workers			
Protective services	1,747	11.7	417
Health service occupations	1,438	87.6	236
Operators and fabricators			
Metal work and plastic work machine operators	438	17.8	382
Typesetters and compositors	50	66.0	328
Textile, apparel, and furniture machine operators	1,160	79.4	206
Laborers			
Handlers, equipment cleaners, helpers, and laborers	3,505	16.8	277
Hand packers and packagers	249	60.6	256

Source: US Department of Labor 1989 *Handbook of Labor Statistics*

discriminate. If they are willing to pay a higher price to indulge this taste, once again employers can afford to hire only members of the preferred group at higher wages, even in the long run, while other employers may hire members of the out group, as long as enough customers are willing to take advantage of the lower prices they can offer.

When "taste discrimination" in any of these forms results in exclusion of members of the out group from some occupations, industries, or enterprises, the result will be a greater supply of workers available to the remainder of the economy, causing "overcrowding" and lower wages (Bergmann 1974). This does not constitute an independent explanation of discrimination, but does shed additional light on how occupational segregation and wage differentials interact.

A different explanation for persistent discrimination does not rely on capricious preferences, but assumes knowledge on the part of employers that members of the preferred group of workers are, on average, more productive, although they are unable to predict accurately the productivity of individual workers. This is termed "statistical discrimination" (Phelps 1972, Arrow 1973, Aigner and Cain 1977, Borjas and Goldberg 1978).

When such behavior is based on sound information, it enables firms to maximize profits rather than interfering with this goal, and perhaps should not be considered discriminatory, even though the outcome may be unfair to individuals. Problems arise, however, when employers' decisions are based on popular beliefs rather than accurate knowledge or, more frequently, when they rely on information about past behavior that in times of rapid change is no longer relevant. In such instances, the consequences are particularly serious because of potential feedback effects (Arrow 1973). A good example of this is when women are not hired for jobs that have the potential for upward mobility because in earlier times they were unlikely to remain in the labor force, and then drop out because they do not have jobs making it worth their while to continue working.

Finally, there is "monopsony discrimination." This theory is based on the assumption that employers, in an effort to maximize profits, take advantage of any existing differences in the elasticity of supply of labor. Wages will be lower for the workers less likely to be influenced by changes in pay. More precisely, when marginal outlay and marginal revenue product are equated for each group, wages will be lower for the one with the less elastic supply of labor. Not only can such discrimination persist, but those who practice it would have a competitive advantage and could gain at the expense of other firms. The limitation on this explanation is that the labor supply of women is not necessarily less elastic than that of men, although this may be the case in local labor markets, because women are less likely to move to further their own careers. Moreover, there is legislation that may inhibit such practices.

4. Policy Issues

Econometric studies have been unable to resolve the question of the existence of discrimination. Therefore, other relevant information is worth considering. A good deal of direct proof of discriminatory attitudes has been accumulated, mainly by social scientists other than economists.

Evidence has come to light that identical résumés are viewed differently when male and female names are used (Fidell 1970, Riach and Rich 1987). Kanter (1977) discovered that "identifiable outsiders," especially when their numbers are small, are treated very differently in the workplace from members of the majority. Ferber (1986, 1988) showed that researchers are more likely to cite authors of the same sex. One study even disclosed that retail dealers charge far lower prices for cars to Whites than Blacks, and to men than women (Ayres 1991). In addition, employers have

been found guilty of discrimination in a great many court cases, even though they had the opportunity to provide testimony about unmeasurable characteristics of workers of the sort not generally accessible to researchers. Thus it is apparent that discrimination poses a real problem.

If remedies are to be found for the pay gap, it is not sufficient to establish that there is some discrimination. It is important to discover the main factors that are responsible for the large earnings differentials.

Considerable light is shed on this subject by Blau and Kahn (1992), who used micro data on nine industrialized countries (Australia, Austria, the Federal Republic of Germany, Hungary, Norway, Sweden, Switzerland and the United Kingdom, in addition to the United States) to analyze differences in the earnings gap which, as has been demonstrated above, is relatively large in the United States. They identified the following four elements within this gap, and determined the effect of each in the various countries:

(a) differences in observed characteristics,

(b) differences in the prices associated with these characteristics,

(c) unobserved characteristics and/or discrimination, and

(d) the overall level of wage equality.

The results of this study indicate that women in the United States had a relatively high level of measured characteristics related to productivity, as well as a high level of unmeasured characteristics and/or were subject to relatively little discrimination. The cause of the comparatively large earnings gap in the United States appears to be a very high degree of wage inequality, and one particularly unfavorable to workers with less than average levels of market skills. The inequality in earnings is further aggravated by the even greater disparity in benefits provided by employers, mainly contributions to social insurance and private pension, health and welfare funds. Such benefits constitute a substantial part of the package of rewards that employees receive, amounting to 28 percent of total compensation, including pay for time not worked (Ferber et al. 1991 p. 89).

The findings above suggest that a large part of the problem in the United States lies in the unusually decentralized wage-setting institutions, together with the particular nature and weakness of labor unions. Assuming these conditions are unlikely to change, the chief hope for further progress in reducing the earnings gap is likely to be continued growth in women's productivity-related skills and labor-force commitment. Although Blau and Kahn (1992) do not address the earnings gap by race and ethnicity, there is even more reason to assume that their conclusion applies to these groups, because they tend to have less education, and education of poorer quality. It must be recognized, however, that as long as women have primary responsibility for children, other family members in need of care, and the household, such progress will not be easy. Hence policies to help people to combine jobs and homemaking successfully would be particularly advantageous. For instance, employers could be urged or required to offer family leave, more nearly equal terms for part-time workers, flextime, flexible benefits, and assistance with child and elder care (Ferber et al. 1991). Such policies might even encourage men to take on a larger share of homemaking chores.

As long as there is widespread occupational segregation, equal opportunity legislation and affirmative action are also likely to be helpful in further opening up traditionally male fields to women, and equal pay for comparable work would raise the earnings of the large numbers of women who continue to be concentrated in predominantly female occupations (England 1992).

All of these approaches have been used to a greater or lesser extent, with some degree of success. Even without further progress in introducing and enforcing such policies, it is likely that the earnings gap will continue to decline slowly as women prepare themselves for spending more years in the labor market, get more training, and acquire more work experience. At the present pace, it will, however, be a very long time before the gender differential in earnings becomes so small that women who support families will no longer constitute the bulk of the population living below the poverty line in the United States.

See also: Education and Earnings

References

Aigner D J, Cain G G 1977 Statistical theories of discrimination in labor markets. *Industrial and Labor Relations Review* 30(2): 175–87

Arrow K J 1973 The theory of discrimination. In: Ashenfelter O A, Rees A (eds.) 1973 *Discrimination in Labor Markets*. Princeton University Press, Princeton, New Jersey

Ayres I 1991 Fair driving: Gender and race discrimination in retail car negotiations. *Harvard Law Review* 104: 817–72

Baron J N, Bielby W T 1984 A woman's place is with other women: Sex segregation in the work place. In: Reskin B F (ed.) 1984 *Sex Segregation in the Workplace: Trends, Explanations and Remedies*. National Academy Press, Washington, DC

Becker G S 1957 *The Economics of Discrimination*. University of Chicago Press, Chicago, Illinois

Becker G S 1985 Human capital, effort, and the sexual division of labor. *J. Labor Econ.* 3 (Supplement): S33–S58

Bergmann B R 1974 Occupational segregation, wages and profits when employers discriminate by race or sex. *Eastern Economic Journal* 1(2): 103–10

Bergmann B R, Darity W Jr. 1981 Social relations, productivity, and employer discrimination. *Month. Lab. Rev.* 104(4): 47–49

Bielby D D, Bielby W T 1988 She works hard for her money: Household responsibilities and the allocation of effort. *Am. J. Sociol.* 93(5): 1031–59

Blau F D 1977 *Equal Pay in the Office*. Heath, Lexington, Massachusetts

Blau F D, Beller A H 1988 Trends in earnings differentials by gender, 1971–1981. *Industrial and Labor Relations Review* 41: 513–29

Blau F D, Ferber M A 1987 Discrimination: Empirical evidence from the United States. *Am. Econ. Rev.* 77(2): 316–20

Blau F D, Kahn L M 1992 The gender earnings gap: Learning from international comparisons. *Am. Econ. Rev.* 82(2): 533–38

Blau F D, Kahn L M 1994 Rising wage inequality and the US gender gap. *Am. Econ. Rev.* 84(5): 23–33

Borjas G J, Goldberg M S 1978 Biased screening and discrimination in the labor market. *Am. Econ. Rev.* 65(5): 918–22

Cain G G 1986 The economic analysis of labor market discrimination: A survey. In: Ashenfelter O A, Layard R (eds.) 1986 *Handbook of Labor Economics*. North Holland, Amsterdam

England P 1992 *Comparable Worth: Theories and Evidence*. Aldine de Guiter, New York

Ferber M A 1986 Citations: Are they an objective measure of scholarly merit? *Signs. Journal of Women in Culture and Society* 11(2): 381–89

Ferber M A 1988 Citations and networking. *Gender and Society* 2: 82–89

Ferber M A, O'Farrell B, Allen L (eds.) 1991 *Work and Family. Policies for a Changing Work Force*. National Academy Press, Washington, DC

Fidell L S 1970 Empirical verification of sex discrimination in hiring practices in psychology. *Am. Psychol.* 25: 1094–98

Goldberg M S 1982 Discrimination, nepotism, and long-run wage differentials. *Q. J. Econ.* 97: 307–19

Kanter R 1977 *Men and Women of the Corporation*. Basic Books, New York

Nelson J A (in press) Feminism and economics. *Journal of Feminist Economics*

Phelps E S 1972 The statistical theory of racism and sexism, *Am. Econ. Rev.* 62: 659–61

Riach P A, Rich J 1987 Testing for sexual discrimination in the labour market. *Australian Economic Papers* 26(4): 165–78

Rytina N 1983 Comparing annual and weekly earnings from the current population survey. *Month. Lab. Rev.* 106(4): 32–38

Smith J P, Ward M 1989 Women in the labor market and in the family. *Journal of Economic Perspectives* 3(1): 9–24

Treiman D J, Hartmann H I 1981 *Women, Work, and Wages: Equal Pay for Jobs of Equal Value*. National Academy Press, Washington, DC

US Department of Education, National Center for Education Statistics, *Digest of Education Statistics*. US Government Printing Office, Washington, DC

Further Reading

Blau F D, Ferber M A 1986 *The Economics of Women, Men, and Work*. Prentice-Hall, Englewood Cliffs, New Jersey

Blau F D, Ferber M A 1992 Women's work, women's lives: A comparative economic perspective. In: Kahne H, Giele J Z (eds.) 1992 *Women's Lives and Women's Work*.

Parallels and Contrasts in Modernizing and Industrial Countries. Westview Press, Boulder, Colorado

Gunderson M 1989 Male–female wage differentials and policy responses. *J. Econ. Lit.* 27(1): 46–72

Symposium on Women in the Labor Market 1989 *Journal of Economic Perspectives* 3: 3–76

Gender and Occupational Segregation

M. H. Strober

Men and women in the labor force are not distributed equally across occupations. This inequality in distribution is termed occupational segregation: the labor market segregates women disproportionately into certain occupations, men into others. In general, the occupations that are disproportionately female tend to have lower earnings and lower rates of return on education, less security of employment and fewer opportunities for promotion than do the occupations that are disproportionately male. As a result, occupational segregation by gender is a major contributor to the female–male earnings differential. Occupational segregation also inhibits men and women from choosing occupations in accordance with their talents and tastes and may thereby decrease the overall efficiency and productivity of the economy and the well-being of those whose aspirations are restricted.

1. Explanations

Theories that explain how occupational segregation develops and persists are divergent. And few theories have examined when and why segregation changes. For a review of theories see Reskin (1984) and Reskin and Hartmann (1986).

Most explanations of occupational segregation are supply-side; that is, they point to women themselves as the cause of occupational segregation. Sociological and psychological theories suggest that women's own values, aspirations, attitudes, expectations and behaviors are the cause of occupational segregation. Similarly, human capital theory in economics views women's own choices about their educational attainment and work experience as responsible for their occupations and earnings.

Other sociological theories, as well as economic theories of discrimination, locate the cause of segregation with the employer, sometimes aided by customers or other employees or unions. Although dual-labor market theories place much less emphasis on individual choice and the operation of labor markets than does neoclassical economic theory, these theories, too, locate the cause of occupational segregation with the employer.

Theories put forth by Hartmann (1976) and Strober (Strober 1984, Strober and Arnold 1987) stress that both supply and demand factors are responsible for occupational segregation. In a context of society-wide gender power relationships, employers, male employees, and female employees all play a role in initiating and maintaining occupational segregation.

Based on her studies of elementary school teaching and banktelling, Strober (Strober 1984, Strober and Arnold 1987) has put forth the relative attractiveness theory of occupational segregation to explain how and why occupations change their gender designation. In brief, the argument is as follows. The factors that affect demand and supply in the labor market are embedded in societal power relations that include male dominance. Because of these power relationships, women and men have unequal access to occupations. In particular, unequal power relations in the society at large are reflected in the labor market by employers' preference for White male workers in "relatively attractive" occupations (to be defined below). This is not to say that any White man can find employment in any occupation he fancies; job offers depend not only on race and gender, but also on having the requisite skill to perform the job (or at least the requisite educational credential to be trained to perform the job) and may also depend upon age and other factors such as social class.

Given employer preferences, White men choose to inhabit those occupations that are most attractive to them, leaving the occupations that they find less attractive available for the other race–gender groups. Minorities and White women, like White men, attempt to maximize their "utility," but their occupational choices are constrained by employers' preferences for White men in the most attractive occupations.

The relative attractiveness of an occupation depends on four occupational attributes: (a) the monetary return on workers' investments in their education and labor market experience; (b) the working conditions of the occupation; (c) the degree of power, prestige, and status the occupation holds in the society at large; and (d) the potential for future rewards in the occupation.

When White men find an occupation becoming relatively less attractive as compared to other occupations requiring similar education and training, they begin to leave, or reduce their rate of entry. Women then begin to enter the occupation, thereby increasing their representation in it. Such an occupation may eventually become resegregated as a female occupation.

2. Measurement of Occupational Segregation

The most common measure of occupational segregation is the Index of Segregation, also called the Index of Dissimilarity, and the Duncan Index (Duncan and Duncan 1955), defined as:

$$\text{Index of Segregation} = 1/2 \sum_{i=1}^{n} |x_i - y_i|$$

where x = the percentage of women in the ith category of a particular occupation and y = the percentage of men in that same occupational category. The index ranges from 0, indicating complete integration, to 100, indicating complete segregation. The value of the index may be interpreted as the percentage of women (or men) that would have to be redistributed among occupations in order for there to be complete equality of the occupational distribution by gender.

The magnitude of the index is affected by the level of aggregation of the occupations. The greater the degree of disaggregation, the higher the index is likely to be; aggregation of occupations into fewer categories tends to mask segregation. For example, although the occupational category "professional, technical and related workers" was approximately gender neutral in the United States in 1990 (women accounted for 45 percent of the work force and 51 percent of professional, technical and related workers, see International Labour Organisation 1991), women and men were not distributed equally across the various professional and technical occupations aggregated to form this broad category. For example, in 1989, women accounted for 97.8 percent of prekindergarten and kindergarten teachers, and 94.2 percent of registered nurses, but only 7.6 percent of engineers and only 7.8 percent of clergy (United States Department of Labor 1990).

For 1981 in the United States, Jacobs (1989) reported the segregation index by gender at 40.0 when calculated across 10 major categories, 62.7 across 426 categories and 69.6 across more than 10,000 categories. Bielby and Baron (1984), in their study of approximately 400 establishments in California, found that in more than 50 percent of the establishments, occupations were completely segregated by gender and that only 20 percent of the establishments had segregation indexes lower than 90.

Because the index is sensitive to the degree of aggregation of occupations, and because the number of occupations often increases as an economy grows, analyzing changes in the degree of occupational segregation over time is complex. For instance, in the United States, the 1940 Census used 226 occupational categories while the 1980 Census used 503 (King 1992). Indexes based on the total number of categories used for each year

will understate the degree of segregation in the earlier year and therefore understate the decrease in segregation over time.

One way to deal with this problem is to aggregate jobs into broad categories and compare changes in these broad categories over time (Albelda 1986). But, as already noted, calculating the index based on broad categories of occupations masks segregation in component occupations. A second method of dealing with the problem is to include in the indexes only those occupations that are common to each year being studied (Blau and Hendricks 1979). However, to the extent that integration is higher (or lower) in new occupations than in existing occupations, indices calculated in this way will overstate (or understate) the degree of segregation in the later years and thus understate (or overstate) the reduction in segregation over time.

An additional measurement problem arises in making longitudinal comparisons of gender segregation broken down by race. Occupational categories in which women predominate are generally more aggregated than occupational categories in which men predominate. Men's occupations in the crafts are, for example, particularly disaggregated. As a result, segregation indexes show less racial segregation among women's occupations than among men's. To the extent that over time women's occupations become more finely defined, while men's occupations remain the same with respect to detailed definition, longitudinal comparisons of the segregation index may understate the decline in racial segregation among women relative to that among men (King 1992).

Comparing segregation across economies also presents difficulties. The only data that can be compared across countries are collected by the International Labour Organisation (ILO) for only the seven broadest categories of occupations: professional, technical and related workers; administrative and managerial workers; clerical and related workers; sales workers; service workers; workers in agriculture, forestry and fishing; and production and related workers, transport equipment operators and laborers. The measures of segregation for each country are therefore lower than those obtained from calculations with more refined data.

In countries where both women and men are heavily involved in agriculture, the index of segregation is likely to be low, even if, in fact, there is a great deal of gender segregation within agricultural employment. It is misleading to compare indexes for these countries with those for countries having a much smaller proportion of the labor force in agriculture. Moreover, when women do a great deal of agricultural work but are not included in the labor force, as is sometimes the case in the early stages of economic development, when the labor force participation rate of women may actually fall (Boserup 1974), indexes of occupational segregation, which are calculated on labor force data only, are not comparable across countries. A final component contributing to lack of comparability is that the work performed in occupations with a particular title (secretary, farmer, transport worker) varies greatly by level of economic development (Blau and Ferber 1992).

The index of segregation is calculated across occupational categories and hence provides a measure of horizontal gender or race–gender segregation. But occupations are also segregated vertically: women's representation in occupations is negatively related to occupational level, that is, women's representation is higher in the lower levels of an occupation than at the middle or upper levels. Vertical segregation is generally measured by comparing the percentages of women and men at various levels for particular occupations. However, there are no systematic data collected by occupational levels that permit the calculation of a single measure of vertical segregation for a country as a whole.

3. The Extent of Occupational Segregation by Gender and Changes Over Time

For the United States in 1988, using the most detailed occupational categories available in the Current Population Survey (CPS), King (1992) calculated that the index of segregation by gender was 56.7. Interestingly, the index was virtually the same for Black women and men (56.8) as for White women and men (56.7). When the index was calculated using only those 159 occupations that were found in the occupational coding system of the censuses for 1940 through 1980 as well as in the 1988 CPS, it was slightly higher: 60.9 for Black women and men and 60.4 for White women and men.

Comparable indexes of segregation by race are much lower (about 30 percentage points lower) than those for gender. Using the most detailed occupational categories, in 1988, among women, comparing Blacks and Whites, the index was 29.2. That is, 29.2 percent of Black women or White women would have had to change their occupation in order for Black and White women to be distributed equally across occupations. Among men, the comparable index was 31.8 (King 1992).

Over time, the index of segregation by gender has declined in the United States, but there is some disagreement about the pattern of the decline. In general there is agreement that between 1900 and 1960, the index was high—between 66 and 68—and relatively stable (Gross 1968). Between 1960 and 1970, the index fell about 3 percentage points (Blau and Hendricks 1979). In the next decade, 1970–80, the decline accelerated and the index fell about 8.5 percentage points (Beller 1984, Bianchi and Rytina 1986). In the 1980s, the decline continued, but at a slower pace than during the 1970s. Comparing the index computed on CPS data for 1983 with that computed on CPS data for 1987, the index fell about 2.4 percentage points (Blau 1989). (See King 1992 for a slightly different set of numbers.)

A breakdown of the index change into two effects—changes in gender composition within occupations and changes in the occupational mix of the economy—showed that between 1970 and 1980 about three-fourths

of the decline in the index was due to integration within occupations (particularly in professional and managerial occupations). Between 1983 and 1987, however, slightly less than two-thirds of the change was due to integration within occupations. Part of the reason for the slowdown in the decline of the index in the 1980s was that several occupations that had become more integrated in the earlier period began, in the 1980s, to be resegregated as women's occupations, creating a "drag" on occupational integration (Blau 1989).

In Italy the index of segregation has also declined over time. In 1901, it was 78.0. It declined slightly, to 74.0, by 1936. But the major decline (18.5 percentage points, to 56.0) came between 1936 and 1971. Between 1971 and 1981, the index declined slightly, 4 percentage points, to 52.0. A breakdown of the change in the index into two effects, changes in gender composition within occupations and changes in the occupational mix of the economy, showed that between 1936 and 1971, the two effects were about equal. However, between 1971 and 1981, almost two-thirds of the decline in segregation within occupations was offset by the increased share of total employment of occupations in which women were preponderant: teachers, clerical employees, and shop assistants (Bettio 1988).

Using the ILO data for various years during the 1980s, over the seven broad occupational categories, the index of segregation for the United States was 36.6. The index ranged from a low of 9.7 in China and 9.9 in Thailand to a high of 62.3 in Qatar and 60.2 in the United Arab Emirates (Blau and Ferber 1992). For all advanced industrialized countries, the segregation index was 39.5; its range was wide, from the low and mid-20s for Greece, Japan, and Portugal to the high 40s for Denmark, Ireland, and Luxembourg.

Moreover, the underlying patterns of segregation varied widely across countries. Some examples of this are as follows: women were a high of 64.0 percent of all professional and technical workers in the Philippines, but a low of 15.2 percent of workers in this category in Pakistan; women were a high of 39.2 percent of managers and administrators in the US Virgin Islands, but had no representation in this occupation in Comoros; women were a high of 84.5 percent of clerical workers in Bulgaria and a low of 3.1 percent in Pakistan; and, finally, were a high of 89.7 percent of sales workers in Haiti and a low of 1.1 percent in Qatar (Blau and Ferber 1992).

In Anker and Hein's (1986) study of ILO data, they found that in developing countries women's share of professional occupations is relatively high, and unlike in industrialized countries is often greater than their share of clerical employment. This is partly because in developing countries teaching and nursing, highly feminized occupations, represent a higher percentage of all employment in professional occupations. At the same time, women are underrepresented in developing countries in administrative/managerial occupations and in production occupations.

In a more detailed breakdown of occupations for Peru,

Cyprus, Ghana, India, and Mauritius, Anker and Hein (1986) found a large number of occupations that were almost exclusively male. This was true not only for countries where women constitute a small proportion of the nonagricultural labor force, but also where their share was relatively high.

In a case study of an urban labor market in Lima, Peru, Scott (1986) found a high degree of occupational segregation: out of 107 occupations, 44 were exclusively male, while only 13 were female-dominated.

A study of occupational segregation over time in Puerto Rico found that between 1950 and 1980, the segregation index fell considerably. For a set of detailed occupations present in all census years from 1950–80, the segregation index fell 23 percentage points over the period, from 80.06 in 1950 to 57.28 in 1980; for all detailed occupational categories for each census year, the index fell 19 percentage points, to 60.12 in 1980 (Presser and Kishor 1991).

3.1 Changes in the Gender Designation of Occupations

Elementary school teaching (Tyack and Strober 1981), and banktelling (Strober and Arnold 1987) in the United States and secretarial work in the United States (Davies 1984) and the United Kingdom (Cohn 1985) are examples of formerly male occupations that have been resegregated as women's occupations with concomitant losses in relative earnings and opportunities for upward mobility.

Reskin and Roos (1990) provide detailed case studies of 11 occupations in which women greatly increased their representation in the United States during the 1970s. Whether these occupations will resegregate as women's occupations remains to be seen.

In Ciudad Juarez, Mexico, when the first *maquiladoras* (foreign-owned border factories) opened in the late 1960s, the vast majority of factory operatives were women. Even in 1980–82, men held only 20 percent of such jobs. But, by 1986–87, after a downturn in the Mexican economy, employment provided by the *maquiladoras* became attractive to men and their percentage increased markedly. Estimates of the percentage of male production workers in the Ciudad Juarez *maquiladoras* in 1986–87 vary between 34 and 42 percent (Catanzarite and Strober 1993).

The phenomenon of gender resegregation in particular professions should also be studied at the disaggregate level in order to develop a better understanding of its effects. For example, in the United States, women have greatly increased their representation in the occupation of physician, from 7.5 percent in 1970 to 16.4 percent in 1989. But medicine provides a good example of the need to look at segregation at a detailed occupational level: women are not increasing their representation evenly across medical specialties, and the most lucrative specialties remain closed to women (Strober 1992).

Women are more concentrated than are men in the seven largest medical specialties. Of the 36 medical and surgical specialties listed by the American Medical Association, the top 7 account for 63 percent of male physicians, but 75 percent of women physicians. Moreover, women are particularly highly concentrated in two low-paid specialties: pediatrics and child psychiatry. At the other end of the spectrum, with the exception of obstetrics/gynecology, women are virtually absent from the highly paid surgical specialties (Strober 1992).

3.2 Vertical Segregation

Case studies of manufacturing plants in developing countries reveal the extent to which women workers are concentrated, not only into specific occupations, but also into particular sections and tasks within the hierarchically organized workplace. Horton and Lee (1988) examined the employment situation of women workers in Asian subsidiaries of the United States owned sector of the semiconductor industry. They found that women workers were at the lowest job levels. Similarly, Humphrey's (1985) study of blue-collar workers in manufacturing plants in Brazil showed that men and women were rarely found in the same department with the same job titles; women were excluded from almost all skilled occupations and even within semiskilled and unskilled occupations, women were concentrated on the lowest rungs of the occupational hierarchy.

In the United States, academia provides one example of vertical segregation. In 1989–90, women accounted for 27.4 percent of all faculty. However, they were concentrated in the lowest levels: 56.5 percent of instructors, 52.4 percent of lecturers, 39.5 percent of assistant professors, 26.4 percent of associate professors, and only 12.8 percent of professors were women (*Academe* 1990, as cited in Blau and Ferber 1992).

Another United States example concerns management. In 1990, although women accounted for 40.1 percent of all managers and administrators (ILO 1991), only half of one percent of the highest paid officers and directors in the 799 public companies on *Fortune* magazine's list of the 1,000 largest industrial and service companies were women. Out of 4,012 such people, only 19 were women (Fierman 1990). There is said to be a "glass ceiling" for women in management in the United States. Women are in jobs where they can "see" top management positions (that is, they are qualified to move into them and can picture themselves doing such jobs), but when they attempt to move into top management, they are prevented from doing so by strong structural forces and gender prejudices.

4. Conclusion

Several countries have made the elimination of occupational gender segregation a priority for public policy and have successfully used affirmative action policies to reduce such segregation. However, segregation is a dynamic process and occupations can resegregate. It is likely that in the near term, occupational segregation in the workplace will continue to mirror the gender power relationships in the society as a whole and that permanent reduction in occupational segregation will move hand in hand with fundamental shifts in societal power relationships between women and men.

References

Albelda R P 1986 Occupational segregation by race and gender 1958–81. *Industrial and Labor Relations Review* 39(3): 404–11

Anker R, Hein C 1986 Sex inequalities in Third World employment: Statistical evidence. In: Anker R, Hein C (eds.) 1986 *Sex Inequalities in Urban Employment in the Third World*. Macmillan, New York

Beller 1984 Trends in occupational segregation by sex and race, 1960–81. In: Reskin B F (ed.) 1984

Bettio F 1988 *The Sexual Division of Labor: The Italian Case*. Oxford University Press, New York

Bianchi S M, Rytina N 1986 The decline in occupational segregation during the 1970s: Census and CPS comparisons. *Demography* 23(1): 79–86

Bielby W T, Barron J N 1984 A woman's place is with other women: Sex segregation in organizations. In: Reskin B F (ed.) 1984

Blau F D 1989 Occupational segregation by gender: A look at the 1980s. Unpublished paper.

Blau F D, Ferber M A 1992 *The Economics of Women, Men and Work*. Prentice-Hall, Englewood Cliffs, New Jersey

Blau F D, Hendricks W E 1979 Occupational segregation by sex: Trends and prospects. *J. Hum. Resources* 14(2): 197–210

Boserup E 1974 *Women's Role in Economic Development*. St. Martin's Press, New York

Catanzarite L, Strober M 1993 Gender recomposition of the maquiladora workforce in Ciudad Juarez. *Industrial Relations* 32(1): 133–47

Cohn S 1985 *The Process of Occupational Sex-Typing: The Feminization of Clerical Labor in Great Britain*. Temple University Press, Philadelphia, Pennsylvania

Davies M W 1984 *Woman's Place is at the Typewriter: Office Work and Office Workers, 1870–1930*. Temple University Press, Philadelphia, Pennsylvania

Duncan O D, Duncan B 1955 A methodological analysis of segregation indexes. *Am. Sociol. Rev.* 20(2): 210–17

Fierman J 1990 Why women still don't hit the top. *Fortune* July 30: 40–64

Gross E 1968 Plus ça change ...? The sexual structure of occupations over time. *Soc. Problems* 16(2): 198–208

Hartmann H I 1976 Historical roots of occupational segregation: Capitalism, patriarchy and job segregation by sex. *Signs: Journal of Women in Culture and Society* 1(3 Pt. II): 137–69

Horton J, Lee Eun-Jin 1988 Degraded work and devaluated labor: The proletarianization of women in the semiconductor industry. In: Smith J, Collins J, Hopkins T K, Muhammad A (eds.) 1988 *Racism, Sexism, and the World System*. Greenwood Press, New York

Humphrey J 1985 Gender, pay and skill: Manual workers in Brazilian industry. In: Ashfar H (ed.) 1985 *Women, Work and Ideology in the Third World*. Tavistock Publications, London

International Labour Organisation (ILO) 1991 *Yearbook of Labour Statistics*. ILO, Geneva

Jacobs J A 1989 *Revolving Doors: Sex Segregation and Women's Careers*. Stanford University Press, Stanford, California

King M C 1992 Occupational segregation by race and sex, 1940–88. *Mon. Lab. Rev.* 115(4): 30–36

Presser H B, Kishor S 1991 Economic development and occupational sex segregation in Puerto Rico: 1950–80. *Pop. Dev. Rev.* 17(1): 53–85

Reskin B F (ed.) 1984 *Sex Segregation in the Workplace. Trends, Explanations and Remedies*. National Academy Press, Washington, DC

Reskin B F, Hartmann H I (eds.) 1986 *Women's Work, Men's Work: Sex Segregation on the Job*. National Academy Press, Washington, DC

Reskin B F, Roos P A 1990 *Job Queues, Gender Queues. Explaining Women's Inroads into Male Occupations*. Temple University Press, Philadelphia, Pennsylvania

Scott A M 1986 Economic development and urban women's work: The case of Lima, Peru. In: Anker R, Hein C (eds.) 1986

Strober M H 1984 Toward a theory of occupational segregation. In: Reskin B F (ed.) 1984

Strober M H 1992 The relative attractiveness theory of gender segregation: The case of physicians. *Proceedings of the Annual Meetings of the Industrial and Labor Relations Research Association*, pp. 42–50

Strober M H, Arnold C 1987 The dynamics of occupational segregation among banktellers. In: Brown C, Pechman J A (eds.) 1987 *Gender in the Workplace*. The Brookings Institution, Washington, DC

Tyack D, Strober M H 1981 Jobs and gender: A history of the structuring of educational employment by sex. In: Schmuck P, Charters W W (eds.) 1981 *Educational Policy and Management: Sex Differentials*. Academic Press, New York

United States Department of Labor 1990, *Employment and Earnings*, Vol. 37. Washington, DC

Further Reading

Walby S 1986 *Patriarchy at Work: Patriarchal and Capitalist Relations in Employment*. Polity Press, Cambridge

Economics of Gender and Occupational Choices

E. M. King

1. Introduction

Evidence across countries and across regions reveals regular patterns in school enrollment ratios and literacy rates that are divided along gender lines. In the developing world, excepting Latin America and the Caribbean as a region, the enrollment ratios of females lag behind those of males. In the poorest of these countries, educational progress since the 1960s, though enjoyed by both sexes, has not eradicated this gender gap. Consequently, in 1990, the enrollment ratio of girls aged 6–11 years is estimated to be 12 percentage points lower than (or three-fourths) the enrollment ratio of boys of the same age; the enrollment ratio of girls aged 12–17 years was only two–thirds; and of those aged 18–23 years, less than one-half. The cumulative effect of these gender disparities in enrollment rates is that the literacy rate of adult women (aged 25–44 years) in developing regions is lower than that of adult men (see Fig. 1). The gender gap in education is also evident from the clustering of female students in certain fields of study, fields which are different from those seemingly favored by male students.

These disparities between the sexes are a product of different factors. A major factor is the labor market in which educated women are likely to earn less than comparably educated men. But even when the labor market returns for women are at least as high as those for men, the opportunity cost of schooling for older girls may be great enough to cause them to drop out of school since older girls are responsible for cooking, housework, and the care of younger children. Studies have shown that traditions and values which define sex roles or discriminate between the sexes influence the behavior of parents and of providers of education, resulting in an underinvestment in the education of females.

The discussion below begins with theoretical models in the economic literature that offer some explanations for the gender gap in education. It then proceeds to survey the findings of empirical studies for developing countries.

2. Theories and Models

Why does the gender bias in education arise? The meager economic literature on this topic has focused primarily on why parents might treat sons and daughters differently when allocating the family's resources. The reasons for teachers or school principals being less or more supportive of female pupils in classwork (a contributing factor recognized by educators) have not been included in economic models.

Several studies have found that parents tend to favor sons in certain societies. For example, in South Asia, boys receive preferential treatment even with respect to food and healthcare, resulting in lower mortality and better anthropometric indicators for them (Behrman and Deolalikar 1990, Rosenzweig and Schultz 1982, Sen 1984).

Without appealing to assumptions regarding preferences of parents, the standard household choice model in economics explains why daughters might systematically obtain less schooling than sons. In

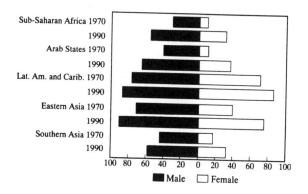

Figure 1

Sex differences in adult literacy rates

Source: UNESCO Compendium of Statistics on Illiteracy 1990

a Population age group 25–44

brief, it states that parents will choose the level of their sons' and daughters' education such that the benefits of educating sons relative to daughters must equal the relative cost of educating them. The benefits are usually equated to income transferred to parents (here termed the "parent-centered" model). Costs include out-of-pocket expenses such as school fees, textbooks, and uniforms, as well as the opportunity cost of children's time spent at school.

If costs associated with schooling were reduced sufficiently for girls relative to boys, girls' schooling levels would rise even without a corresponding increase in relative returns to educating daughters (as might happen if women's wages rose). Building a school in a rural community may reduce the opportunity cost of school time differently for boys and girls depending on differences in the value of their time. Moreover, even if out-of-pocket expenses and value of time were identical, the relative cost of educating girls may still fall if parents are more averse to long travel by their daughters.

The returns to parents from their children's education depend on both the effect of education on the child's income and the rate at which the child's income is transferred to the parents. Although the returns to schooling go first to the student, the decision and the resources usually belong to parents, certainly in the early school years. Because of the sequential and cumulative nature of investments in education, schooling decisions in the early ages are critical. Thus, the perception of parents is a crucial factor. They may anticipate that the earnings prospects for their daughters are poorer than for their sons. Alternatively, custom and social norms may dictate that sons, rather than daughters, take responsibility for their parents. When girls "marry out" of their own family into their husband's family, parents can recoup little, if any, of the returns from their daughters' education.

Less education for girls than boys does not

necessarily imply underinvestment. The issue of underinvestment arises only because there is a judgment that the optimal level of education for girls is higher than that dictated by individual decisions. In the parent-centered model above, this would be true from the individual child's point of view because parents base their decision on the remittances they would obtain from their children, not on the benefits that children would reap. In an alternative specification of the model (the "altruistic parents" model), parents might care not only about their own level of consumption but also about the potential standard of living that their children can achieve (Becker 1974, 1976). Assuming that education improves one's standard of living, parents would thus invest in their children's education at levels beyond those suggested merely by considerations about income remittances.

Variants of the standard household choice model have not included the nonincome intergenerational benefits from education as they differ for sons and daughters. Evidence summarized in the next section suggests that these benefits may be much larger for daughters than for sons. Yet if parents ignore these nonincome benefits when they make their decisions, or are ignorant about the differences in these returns by gender, then daughters will continue to be given less education than their brothers.

In addition, it is possible that family decision-making is quite different from the picture conveyed by these models. A basic assumption of the standard economic model is either that family members have the same preferences or that the preferences of parents are similar. However, experience indicates that these assumptions do not represent typical household behavior. Mothers and fathers frequently have different preferences with respect to consumption and human capital investments within the family, and outcomes depend on the degree of participation in these decisions by mothers. Bargaining models of choice explicitly consider the possibility and the results of cooperation and conflict within the family (Manser and Brown 1980, McElroy 1990, Folbre 1986).

Furthermore, the issue of social underinvestment suggests the presence of externalities. By "externalities" are meant the benefits (or costs) from education above and beyond those enjoyed by the individual or the family. Are the externalities from educating girls larger than those from educating boys? In the parent-centered model, benefits reaped by children but not transferred to parents are "external" to the decision-making. In the altruistic parents model, there may still be externalities if there are benefits that accrue to society at large without being reflected in the incomes or welfare of those who have been educated. For example, does increasing the school enrollment of girls in rural areas raise economic production or lengthen life in those regions in greater proportion than the increases in girls' income or life expectancy,

Table 1
Private rates of return to education in Latin America: Estimates from earnings functions

Country	Men	Women
Argentina	0.091	0.109
Bolivia	0.071	0.065
Brazil	0.147	0.156
Chile	0.126[a]	0.108
Colombia	0.120	0.099
Costa Rica	0.101	0.129
Ecuador	0.097	0.091
Guatemala	0.129	0.101
Honduras	0.153	0.140
Jamaica	0.123	0.202
Mexico	0.132	0.109
Panama	0.072[a]	0.098
Peru	0.094[a]	0.071
Uruguay	0.099	0.079
Venezuela	0.091	0.111

a These estimates are drawn from various chapters of Psacharopoulos and Tzannatos 1991. They are the coefficient estimates on the variable 25 years of completed schooling in a regression with logarithmic hourly or weekly wage rates in the main job as the dependent variable. Other included variables are postschool experience, experience squared, and logarithmic hours of work. All estimates are statistically different than zero at better than the 1 percent confidence level. The estimates for women have been corrected for sample selection bias (i.e., the probability of nonemployment) while those for men have not (except where indicated)

and are such improvements greater than those which increases in boys' enrollment produce?

3. Benefits from Women's Education

Gender disparities are costly both for national development and for the welfare of the family. What does female education contribute to development? How does the gender gap in education affect this relationship? There is a growing body of literature which examines the benefits of educating women within and outside the home.

3.1 Production and Social Welfare

Education enhances women's economic productivity in farm and nonfarm work. In a study of farmers' efficiency, the gain in productivity from education was found to be higher for women than men (Jamison and Lau 1982). Studies on the determinants of wage earnings have found the rates of return to education for women not to be systematically lower than for men once labor force participation and work experience have been taken into account. For example, Table 1 illustrates the findings for Latin American countries. Given that some discriminatory employment practices against women have limited their work opportunities, such as entry barriers for married women—explicit or

Table 2

Differential effects of father's and mother's education on child schooling (elasticities at means from regression estimates)

Variables	Males		Females	
	Father	Mother	Father	Mother
Pakistan	.30[a]	.05[a]	.29[a]	.14[a]
Indonesia	.13[a]	.07[a]	.10[a]	.12[a]
Philippines	.07[a]	.11[a]	.07[a]	.15[a]
Peru	.100[a]	.078[a]	.079[a]	.111[a]
Ghana	.034[a]	.007[a]	.034[a]	.007[a]

Sources: King et al. 1986; King and Bellew 1989; Glewwe 1991

a Significantly different from zero at the 5 percent level. Other variables in the regressions include parents' occupation and land wealth, and child's age and birth order. In the Ghana study, the coefficients were constrained to be equal for males and females

implicit—in certain occupations, these rates of return serve to emphasize further education's positive effect on women's market work.

In the home, women's education exerts a large influence on various aspects of family welfare. A more educated mother raises a healthier family; she can better apply improved hygiene and nutrition practices. Education can substitute for community health programs among women who are informed about healthcare and personal hygiene, and also complement such programs via an increase in their income and in the recognition of the value of these services. A study of the determinants of children's chronic malnutrition in the Philippines found that mother's schooling appeared to attenuate the negative effects of poor community sanitation and water supply (Barrera 1990).

Another important benefit is that a mother's education improves the educational attainment of her children, particularly that of daughters. Table 2 summarizes the results of studies in several countries. After controlling for various other factors such as parents' occupation and wealth and school characteristics, the mother's and father's education levels were found to have different effects on children's schooling. In Pakistan, where women's education levels are very low, the mother's education has no discernible effect on the son's education, but a small positive effect on the daughter's. In Indonesia, the mother's education has half the effect of the father's on sons but a slightly larger effect on daughters. In the Philippines, the effect of the mother's education is about twice that of the father's, and larger for daughters. Likewise, in Peru, the effect of the mother's schooling is larger than that of the father's for daughters, but smaller for sons.

Table 3 demonstrates the effect of mother's schooling on measures of students' achievement. These data show that the mother's schooling can have a large positive effect on mathematics achievement scores, student motivation, and study habits. Unfortunately, the few studies available in this area do not compare the relative effects of the mother's and father's education.

There are other benefits from women's education. For example, among the better educated women in Latin America and Asia, fertility rates have declined and are approaching desired levels as a result of the higher prevalence of contraception (Cochrane and Sai 1991). Moreover, the education of the wife has a stronger negative effect on fertility (by a factor of almost 3) than does the education of the husband.

3.2 The Effect of the Education Gender Gap

The benefits discussed above are clearly evident even at the country level. A handful of studies have examined cross-national data and have found significant gains from educating women for economic growth and for social development. For example, the *World Development Report 1991* (World Bank 1991) documents the educational achievement of women as the most important variable in explaining changes in infant mortality in the developing world. An extra year of schooling for women is associated with a 2-percentage point reduction in the rate of infant mortality.

Hill and King (1993) examine the effect not only of women's schooling levels but also of the gender gap

Table 3

Effects of mother's education on school achievement

Country/sample size	Coefficient
Thailand	
Post-test math achievement	.97[a]
Parental support (1 = high)	−.07[b]
Motivation to succeed (1 = low)	.06[a]
Hours on homework	.23[e]
Thailand[e]	
Single-sex schools	1.91[b]
Coeducational schools	1.41[c]
Malawi	
Math test score	−.23[d]
Language test score	.41[d]
Philippines	
Math achievement score	
= 1 if mother's education <10; 0, otherwise	3.29[d]
= 1 if mother's education ⩾10, 0, otherwise	3.74[c]

Sources: Jimenez and Lockheed 1989; Lockheed, Fonacier and Bianchi 1989; Lockheed, Fuller and Nyirongo 1989

a Statistically significant at 1 percent level b 5 percent level c 10 percent level d Not significantly different than zero e These estimates pertain only to girls. Estimates for boys are not significantly different than zero. Mother's education is defined as a dummy variable equal to 1 if the highest attainment is primary schooling and 0. For females in coeducational schools, the variable pertains to secondary schooling

255

in education in explaining cross-national variations in income per capita and social indicators. Starting off with scatter plots of levels of Gross National Product (GNP) per capita and social indicators in 1985 against female enrollment rates in primary education in 1975,

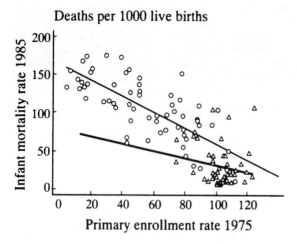

Deaths per 1000 live births

Infant mortality rate 1985

Primary enrollment rate 1975

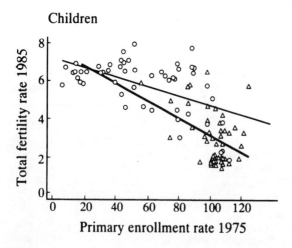

Children

Total fertility rate 1985

Primary enrollment rate 1975

Figure 2
Levels of development indicators by size of education gender gap
a These graphs plot 1985 values of indicators against 1975 data on female primary enrollment rates   b The countries represented by circles have a larger education gender gap—that is, the female enrollment rate is less than 75 percent of that for males—while those represented by triangles have a smaller gender gap—that is, the female enrollment rate is more than 75 percent of that for males   c The two lines are regression lines estimated from the scatter plots of the two groups of countries; the thicker line relates to countries with a smaller gender gap

they found the expected negative correlation between education and fertility and infant mortality, and the expected positive association between education and income and life expectancy (see Fig. 2). When countries are categorized by the size of the education gender gap as measured by the ratio of male to female enrollment rates, a much improved picture emerges. The levels of fertility and infant mortality associated with a particular level of female education are much lower, and GNP per capita and life expectancy much higher, in countries with greater equity between the sexes. It is also noteworthy that in the graph for total fertility, the slope for countries with a larger gender gap is significantly flatter than for countries with greater equity. This means that the widely recognized negative effect of education on fertility will be weaker when the education gender gap is larger.

These graphs strongly suggest that the large gender gap in education leads to significant welfare losses. Furthermore, multivariate analyses which consider the influence of other variables that determine income and social indicators for more than 100 developing countries support the conclusions from these simple correlations, and establish causality (Hill and King 1993).

The mechanisms by which gender inequality in education affects development are not well-understood, however. Sen (1984) illuminates the potential for conflict that men and women may have in distribution of family resources. It is possible that the gender gap in education affects the relative earnings potential of husband and wife and, thus, the division of labor between them. To benefit most from higher male wages, the husband and wife will specialize more in their respective family responsibilities, increasing the husband's hours of work in the market at the expense of home work and the wife's home activities at the expense of her market work. As a result, the wife and the rest of the family can benefit from the returns to her husband's education through income transfers from him, but they cannot benefit as easily from the non-monetary returns to his education, such as his skills and technical knowledge.

In certain sub-Saharan African countries, men and women also maintain separate budgets, and there are well-established conventions concerning which expenditures are to be met from each income. In West Africa, polygyny makes this practice necessary; women in polygamous marriages must find independent ways to support themselves and their children (Fapohunda 1988, Oppong 1983). Although men are expected to support their wives, this support varies widely among groups. This separation of budgets implies that women's expenditures—for their farms, their children, and themselves—can be severely limited by their own productivity and their access to credit and technology, which are influenced by their own education, not their husbands'.

The gender gap effect also reflects the wife's weaker

role in decision-making when the husband's education is much greater than the wife's. Little control by women over their reproductive outcomes and over the allocation of resources for childcare could mean larger families and poorer health status of children.

4. Explaining the Paradox of Female Education

If the benefits of educating women are so great, why does the gender gap persist? The explanation for this paradox lies in a complex mix of factors. Culture, institutions, and level of economic development jointly give rise to both barriers and incentives to education for women in countries around the world. Some cardinal factors that help explain the situation are given below.

4.1 Family and the Home

A sharp distinction between male and female socialization still persists in many countries. The socialization of girls typically emphasizes the predominant sex role where marriage and family, rather than employment in the labor market, are the ultimate goals of women. Greenhalgh (1988) argued that traditional intergenerational contracts between parents and children in Taiwan allowed parents to treat sons and daughters differently. While parents encouraged their sons to develop the knowledge and skills that would raise their future incomes, they increased their control over daughters. Parish and Willis (1993) argued that credit constraints facing households resulted in investment strategies that worked against older children, especially daughters. Girls' education rose during Taiwan's economic expansion, but parents took their older daughters out of school so that daughters could help support the schooling of their younger siblings.

Parents' education shapes gender differences in education, as discussed earlier in this entry, but what does parental education represent? The literature interprets its effect in different ways. First, parents' education may represent the value that parents attach to formal education. The expected relationship is that more educated parents value formal education for their daughters as much as for their sons. Cochrane et al. (1986) found that, given the level of family income, parental education had the greatest influence on educational aspirations for children in both rural and urban areas in Egypt. Second, it measures the degree to which parents may be open to influences outside tradition. Third, parents' education is a limited measure of family income or wealth when more direct measures are not available. When estimates of family income are available, as in Malaysia, income was found to have three times as great an influence on the probability of enrollment of girls aged 12 to 18 as on that of boys.

The greater effect of the mother's education on

daughters than on sons could be a result of the traditional sexual division of labor within families. Mothers tend to spend more time with their daughters, especially in the context of performing household work, while fathers spend more time with their sons. However, this result might also reflect differences in the preferences of mothers and fathers, and the stronger influence of the more educated mother on the allocation of family resources.

Another home factor that affects girls' education is the demand that their time be put to alternative uses. Parents may not be able to afford the opportunity costs of educating children, which vary by sex. With few exceptions, girls do more home and marketplace work than boys (Hill and King 1993). They cook, clean the house, fetch water, and help their mothers care for younger children, especially those who are ill. In Nepal and Java, for example, most young girls spend at least one-third more hours per day working at home and in the market than boys of the same age, and in some age groups as much as 85 percent more hours (Nag et al. 1980). In Taiwan, a study of the determinants of education indicates that having an older sister means that a child could delay work or marriage and remain in school (Parish and Willis 1993).

Besides lost work, parents may feel that girls are forgoing important training at home if they go to school. The relative importance of these forgone training opportunities will differ across countries depending, in particular, on the expected adult occupation. If women are expected to enter the informal labor market by continuing in a crafts tradition (or in agriculture), the skills for which are imparted by their mothers, then the cost of attending formal schooling must include not only the opportunity cost of current time, but also the lost alternative training.

In addition to the financial costs and opportunity costs of schooling, educating girls may exact nonpecuniary or "psychic" costs as well. In certain settings, sociocultural factors (such as norms proscribing the societal, economic, and familial roles of women) and religion strongly influence the behavior of parents by imposing a heavy cost on nonconformist behavior. In countries in which females are usually secluded, girls may only attend schools that do not admit boys or only those that employ female teachers. The importance of preserving a young girl's reputation in such cultures leads to high dropout rates of girls at the onset of puberty (Caldwell et al. 1985, Papanek 1985).

Parents may also consider education itself as a negative factor because the suitability of more highly educated women as good wives is held in doubt. With economic development and the corresponding expansion of work opportunities for women, however, tension grows between these traditional social norms and the family's desire to benefit from changing conditions. But how much, when, and which families or individuals will respond to these environmental shifts? Economic theory does not deal formally with the impact of sociocultural forces on individual behavior, and there is little empirical work on this, except insofar as parental education reflects family values.

4.2 Schools and Teachers

Although education is public and tuition is supposedly free in most countries around the world, school attendance still entails cost outlays from family resources. Contributions to the school, learning materials, uniforms, transportation, and boarding fees are some of the nontuition costs of sending children to school. For a variety of reasons, these out-of-pocket expenses may be different for boys and girls. For example, parents' greater reluctance to send daughters to school without proper attire raises the cost of school attendance for girls.

Evidence from many developing countries suggests that parents are reluctant to send their daughters to distant schools because of the fear that they will be placed in moral or physical danger, thus necessitating different boarding and lodging arrangements costs for girls. Even in the relatively more open societies of Malaysia and the Philippines, distance to school is a greater deterrent to girls' enrollment than to boys' (King and Lillard 1987). Moreover, school facilities themselves can be hostile to girls. In Bangladesh, parents have withdrawn girls (but not boys) from schools without latrines; in Pakistan, many parents worry about enrolling girls in schools without boundary walls which provide privacy for them (Khan 1991).

The school environment exerts its own influence on female education. Despite compulsory education legislation and open admissions policies, schools may be inaccessible to girls and women. There are barriers at the postprimary education level with gender-specific admissions policies in certain areas of study. In addition, the barriers to girls' education begin earlier—at the primary-school level where teachers and textbooks may project attitudes that discourage achievement by girls, or promote stereotypes of girls as less capable than boys at learning technical subjects or mathematics. Studies have found that single-sex schools may be more effective for girls' learning. In Thailand, these schools certainly make a difference; even after controlling for such factors as socioeconomic home background and school resources, girls achieved more in single-sex schools than in coeducational schools, while boys did better in the latter (Jimenez and Lockheed 1989).

4.3 Employment and Marriage

Finally, although the nonmarket benefits from education are manifold, returns to education in the labor market influence the degree of education which women acquire. Due partly to choice, the inflexibility of employers, or the unavailability of reliable childcare, women are removed from the workforce for substantial periods (or even permanently) by pregnancy, childbirth, and parenting duties, and are thus denied paid work. This labor supply pattern then feeds back into employers' wage-setting decisions, causing them to place a lower value on women workers than on men workers. Yet the withdrawal from the labor force by married women is due partly to the fact that education increases women's productivity in nonmarket activities, and that unless more highly paid jobs outside the home are available to those with secondary education, staying at home is often a superior option.

In East Asia and Latin America, where more women are entering the formal labor market, women workers are still concentrated in a few jobs which are generally characterized as requiring low skill, and offering low wages and low mobility. In Malaysia, Wang (1982) found that girls expected their salaries to be lower than those of boys and believed that the range of jobs open to them was more restricted. These expectations, in turn, affected educational aspirations.

Taken together, these various factors determine whether girls enter school, how long they remain in school, and how well they perform. Whereas supply variables such as the availability of schools or distance to schools have been found to be significant determinants of school participation, past studies have not adequately examined the differential impact of textbooks, curriculum content, or sex and attitude of teachers on male and female students. The knowledge base for these areas consists largely of anecdotal and fragmented evidence. Moreover, the focus of empirical work in the economic literature has been almost exclusively formal education, and very little is available on those factors which influence women's postschool or on-the-job training.

See also: Gender and Occupational Segregation; Education and Female Labor Force Participation in Industrializing Countries; Gender Differences in Earnings; School Choice: Market Mechanisms

References

Barrera A 1990 The role of maternal schooling and its interaction with public health programs in child health production. *J. Dev. Econ.* 32(1): 69–91

Becker G 1974 A theory of social interactions. *J. Pol. Econ.* 82(6): 1063–91

Becker G 1976 Altruism, egoism, and genetic fitness: Economics and sociobiology. *J. Econ. Lit.* 14(3): 817–26

Behrman J R, Deolalikar A B 1990 The intrahousehold demand for nutrients in rural south India: Individual estimates, fixed effects and permanent income. *J. Hum. Resources* 25(4): 665–96

Caldwell J C, Caldwell P, Reddy P H 1985 Educational transition in rural south India. *Popul. Dev. Rev.* 11(1): 29–51

Cochrane S, Mehra K, Osheba I T 1986 *The Educational*

Participation of Egyptian Children. EDT Discussion Paper No. 45, The World Bank, Washington, DC

Cochrane S, Sai F T 1991 *Excess Fertility*. Population and Human Resources Department, The World Bank, Washington, DC

Fapohunda E R 1988 The nonpooling household: A challenge to theory. In: Dwyer D, Bruce J (eds.) 1988 *A Home Divided*. Stanford University Press, Stanford, California

Folbre N 1986 Cleaning house. *J. Dev. Econ.* 22(1): 5–40

Glewwe P 1991 *Schooling, Skills, and the Returns to Government Investment in Education: An Exploration Using Data from Ghana*. LSMS Working Paper No. 76, The World Bank, Washington, DC

Greenhalgh S 1988 Intergenerational contracts: Familial roots of sexual stratification in Taiwan. In: Dwyer D, Bruce J (eds.) 1988 *A Home Divided*. Stanford University Press, Stanford, California

Hill M A, King E 1993 Women's education in the Third World: An overview. In: King E M, Hill M A (eds.) 1993 *Women's Education in Developing Countries (Barriers, Benefits and Policy)*. Johns Hopkins University Press, Baltimore, Maryland.)

Jamison D T, Lau L J 1982 *Farmer Education and Farm Efficiency*. Johns Hopkins University Press, Baltimore, Maryland

Jimenez E, Lockheed M E 1989 Enhancing girls' learning through single-sex education: Evidence and a political conundrum *Educ. Eval. Pol. Anal.* 11(2): 117–42

Khan S 1991 South Asia. In: King E M, Hill M A (eds.) 1991 *Women's Education in Developing Countries (Barriers, Benefits and Policy)*. Document PHREE/91/40, The World Bank, Washington, DC

King E M, Peterson J, Adioetomo S M, Domingo L, Syed S 1986 *Change in the Status of Women Across Generations in Asia*. Report No. R–3399–RF. The Rand Corporation, Santa Monica, California

King E M, Lillard L A 1987 Education policy and schooling attainment in Malaysia and the Philippines. *Econ. Educ. Rev.* 6(2): 167–81

King E M, Bellew R T 1989 *The Effects of Peru's Push to Improve Education*. Policy, Planning, and Research Working Paper Series No. 472, The World Bank, Washington, DC

Lockheed M E, Fonacier J, Bianchi L J 1989 *Effective Primary Level Science Teaching in the Philippines*. PPR Working Paper Series No. 208, The World Bank, Washington, DC

Lockheed M E, Fuller B, Nyirongo R 1989 Family effects on students' achievement in Thailand and Malawi. *Sociol. Educ.* 62(4): 239–56

Manser M, Brown M 1980 Marriage and household decision making: A bargaining analysis. *Int. Econ. Rev.* 21(1): 31–44

McElroy M B 1990 The empirical content of nash-bargained household behavior. *J. Hum. Resources* 25(4): 559–83

Nag M, White B, Peet R C 1980 An anthropological approach to the study of the economic value of children in Java and Nepal. In: Binswanger H, Evenson R, Florencio C, White B (eds.) 1980 *Rural Household Studies in Asia*. Singapore University Press, Singapore

Oppong C (ed.) 1983 *Female and Male in West Africa*. Allen and Unwin, London

Papanek H 1985 Class and gender in education—employment linkages. *Comp. Educ. Rev.* 29(3): 317–46

Parish W L, Willis R J 1993 Daughters, education, and family budgets. *J. Hum. Resources* 28(4): 863–98

Psacharopoulos G, Tzannatos Z 1991 *Women's Employment and Pay in Latin America*. Regional Studies Program Report No. 10, The World Bank, Washington, DC

Rosenzweig M R, Schultz T P 1982 Market opportunities, genetic endowments and the intrafamily resource distribution. *Am. Econ. Rev.* 72(4): 803–15

Schultz T P 1993 Investments in the schooling and health of women and men. *J. Hum. Resources* 28(4): 694–734

Sen A 1984 *Resources, Value and Development*. Blackwell, London

Wang B L C 1982 Sex and ethnic differences in educational attainment in Malaysia: The effect of reward structure. In: Kelly G, Elliot C (eds.) 1982 *Women's Education in the Third World: Comparative Perspectives*. State University of New York Press, Albany, New York

World Bank 1991 *World Development Report 1991*. Oxford University Press, New York

Further Reading

Arriagada A M 1989 *The Effect of Job Training on Peruvian Women's Employment and Wages*. PPR Working Paper Series No. 241, The World Bank, Washington, DC

Lillard L A, Tan H W 1986 *Private Sector Training. Who Gets It and What Are Its Effects?* Report R–3331–DOL/RC. The Rand Corporation, Santa Monica, California

Schultz T P 1993 Returns to women's education. In: King E M, Hill M A (eds.) 1993 *Women's Education in Developing Countries (Barriers, Benefits and Policy)*. Johns Hopkins University Press, Baltimore, Maryland.)

Thomas D 1991 *Gender Differences in Household Resource Allocations*. LSMS Working Paper No.79, The World Bank, Washington, DC

Immigrants' Economic Performance and Education

B. R. Chiswick

The economic performance of immigrants has been studied through analyses of earnings, employment, occupational status, linguistic skills, education, and other variables. These studies have been carried out for several countries and in different time periods. They suggest that immigrants experience a decline

259

in their occupational status at the time of immigration, compared to their occupation prior to migration. However, with increased duration of residence in the destination, their occupational status, earnings, and employment increase. This arises from the adjustment of pre-immigration skills and from additional post-immigration investments in human capital, in particular, language skills, schooling, on-the-job training, and labor market information.

1. Characteristics of Immigrants

The economic adjustment of immigrants is most easily understood through two models (Chiswick 1978a, 1979). One is the favorable self-selection of immigrants and the other is the international transferability of skills.

1.1 Self-selection

There is a tendency for migrants to higher income areas to be favorably self-selected in comparison with those who remain in the place of origin. In the historical literature, migrants have been variously described as more able, ambitious, and entrepreneurial, or, by those preferring pejorative terms, too crafty, aggressive, and avaricious.

A favorable self-selection of immigrants as a general proposition is not difficult to explain. Consider a simple model in which the ratio of earnings of those of high ability to those of lesser ability are approximately the same across countries. Then the more able receive a larger absolute increase in income from migration. The value of a unit of time devoted to the migration and readjustment in the destination is roughly proportionate to income, and hence ability. There are, however, many aspects of the move which involve costs that do not vary with ability or for which the more able have lower costs. The cost of purchased inputs (for example, an airline ticket) generally do not vary with ability. In addition, the more able may also be more efficient in migration, thereby requiring fewer resources. As a result of the higher ratio of benefits to costs from migration for the more able, they have a greater incentive to migrate.

Immigrants are likely to be particularly well-endowed with "allocative skills" (decision-making capability), in contrast to "worker skills" (task performance). Allocative skills are particularly valuable in a new environment in which many decisions need to be made regarding the labor market, training, and consumption behavior. This may also explain the greater propensity for immigrants to enter self-employment, an activity in which allocative skills are particularly important.

The intensity of the favorable self-selection of immigrants varies by reason for migrating. It is expected to be strongest for persons whose primary motive is economic betterment. It is expected to be less intense for those for whom factors other than anticipated relative success in the labor market are important influences on the migration decision, such as refugees, tied movers, and ideological migrants. Refugees are those whose migration decision is largely influenced by concerns for personal freedom or safety because of political, ideological, racial, ethnic, religious, or social class reasons. Tied movers are those whose migration decision is largely influenced by the desire to join or accompany a migrating family member. Ideological migrants are those whose migration decision is influenced by a political or nationalistic ideology, even when there is no threat to their personal freedom or safety.

1.2 International Transferability of Skills

Immigrants have skills acquired in the country of origin. Those migrating to a country in which the language, level of development, and structure of labor markets are similar to the country of origin have greater international transferability of skills. For example, immigrants to Canada from the United Kingdom can be expected to have more highly transferable skills than immigrants from Thailand. The extent of the transferability of skills for a cohort of immigrants will also vary by reason for migrating. More highly transferable skills facilitate the economic adjustment. Since economic migrants have earnings as the primary motive for migrating, they have generally planned for the move and made internationally transferable investments in skill. Only those who anticipate doing well in the destination would move. Refugees, on the other hand, generally do not anticipate the move and tend to have made more human capital investments specific to their country of origin. Most refugees would not have left the country of origin if not for the noneconomic factors. For example, physicians have internationally transferable skills and are to be found among economic migrants and refugees, while lawyers and judges have country-specific skills and are found in refugee populations, but seldom among economic migrants.

If skills were perfectly transferable internationally there would be no difference in the effects on earnings for years of schooling and labor market experience between immigrants and natives in the destination, and among the immigrants earnings would not depend on whether the schooling and labor market experience were acquired in the origin or destination. The weaker the international transferability of skills, however, the smaller is the effect of pre-immigration schooling and experience on labor market earnings, the lower the earnings on entering the labor market in destination, and the greater the favorable effect on earnings of labor market experience and other human capital investment acquired in the destination. Similar implications emerge for other measures of labor market outcomes, such as employment and occupational status.

2. Findings for the United States and Elsewhere

These models may be applied to immigrants in any country. The discussion focuses on the United States because most of the research has used United States data. Immigrants to the United States may be classified by the transferability of their skills, such as coming from either English-speaking developed countries (e.g., the United Kingdom, Republic of Ireland, Canada, and Australia) or other countries, and on the reason for migrating, such as being economic migrants or refugees and tied movers.

2.1 Earnings

Among economic migrants from English-speaking developed countries the effects on earnings in the United States of schooling and labor market experience are similar to those for native-born workers. In addition, there is no differential effect on United States earnings of labor market experience in the country of origin and experience in the United States. Among economic migrants from other countries, however, schooling has a smaller effect on earnings than it does for native-born workers, and this is also true of labor market experience received in the country of origin. Their earnings in the United States rise more steeply with United States labor market experience than do the earnings of native-born workers. For the refugee populations that have been studied (primarily Cuban and Chinese immigrants) the effects of schooling on United States earnings are very small, and there is no effect on United States earnings of labor market experience in the country of origin. There is, however, a very sharp rise in earnings with duration of residence in the United States.

The earnings of immigrant men tend to catch up with and then exceed those of native-born men, when all other factors are equal (Chiswick 1979, 1980a, 1986). Male economic migrants initially have lower earnings than native-born men. As a result of the steeper rise in earnings with United States experience, their earnings reach those of native-born (or native-parentage) men of the same race or ethnic origin after about 11 to 15 years of residence in the United States, after which the immigrants tend to have higher earnings. For example, in the 1980 Census data, white male immigrants in the United States reach earnings equality with native-born workers at about 15 years of residence, and those resident in the United States for 20 years have earnings 5 percent higher than native-born workers, a pattern nearly identical to the findings of the 1970 Census and other data (Chiswick 1986). The earnings of Black, Filipino, Japanese, and Mexican immigrants also catch up with the earnings of native-born (or native-parentage) workers of the same origin in about the 11- to 15-year interval, after which the immigrants have higher earnings. For the two immigrant populations with the largest proportion of refugees, the Cuban and Chinese, when all other things are equal, earnings also rise with duration of residence and approach those of native-born workers, yet the crossover occurs either later or not at all. The earnings of immigrants from developed countries exceed those from less developed countries, even when other factors are the same, presumably due in part to higher wage opportunities in the country of origin.

It might seem curious that the earnings of economic migrants would eventually exceed those of native-born workers. With the passage of time in the destination the disadvantages of the less-than-perfect international transferability of skills diminish, and any remaining disadvantage may be dominated by the effects of the more favorable self-selection of economic migrants. This interpretation is strengthened by the finding that in the United States the sons of immigrants earn 5 to 10 percent more than the sons of native-born parents of the same racial and ethnic origin. At least some of the favorable self-selection is passed on to the migrants' children.

Studies of immigrants to the United States at the turn of the century which use modern statistical analyses have also found that earnings and occupational status increase rapidly with duration. One study has shown that earnings parity with native-born workers was reached at about 11 to 13 years of residence, after which the immigrants had higher earnings (Blau 1979).

Most econometric analyses of immigrant adjustment have used cross-sectional data. This raises the question as to whether declines in unmeasured immigrant quality over time are responsible for the apparently universal improvement in earnings and other labor market characteristics with duration of residence, where all other factors are equal (Chiswick 1980a, Borjas 1985). Tests using longitudinal data, following synthetic cohorts over time in cross-sectional data, and other statistical procedures, suggest that this is not the case. There does not appear to be a systematic bias in the effect of duration of residence on labor market outcomes in cross-sectional data (Chiswick 1978b, 1980a, 1986).

2.2 Employment, Occupation, and Investments in Language Skills and Education

Analyses of employment (weeks worked in a year) and unemployment emphasize the "new labor market entrant" characteristics of recent immigrants (Chiswick 1982). Very recent immigrants work fewer weeks and have higher unemployment rates than native-born workers, all other things being equal. The differential narrows with duration of residence and essentially disappears after about five years of residence. The employment differential for new immigrants is larger for refugees than for economic migrants, and is larger during a recession than during a year of full employment.

These patterns reflect behavior that is also observed in the occupational status of immigrants (Chiswick 1978b). Using longitudinal data it has been found that there is a decline in the occupational status of immigrants when comparing the last occupation in the country of origin with the early occupation in the United States, but after entering the United States the immigrants experience more rapid upward occupational mobility. This U-shaped pattern is least intense for immigrants from English-speaking developed countries (high international transferability of skills) and is most intense for refugees (weak international transferability of skills).

Recent research has analyzed the determinants among immigrants of fluency in the dominant destination language (literacy and speaking skills), and the impact of dominant language fluency in the labor market, primarily on earnings (see Chiswick and Miller 1992). Destination language skills are found to be greater for those (a) in the destination a longer period of time, (b) with greater annual pre- and postmigration exposure to the dominant language, (c) who immigrated at a younger age, (d) who have a higher level of education, (e) who are more likely to remain in the destination, and (f) who are economic migrants rather than refugees. Other things being equal, dominant language skills are important determinants of economic success (earnings) in the destination. Language skills and earnings appear to have an endogenous relationship; those with greater language proficiency have higher earnings and those who can anticipate higher earnings if they were to become proficient in the dominant language do acquire greater proficiency in the dominant language.

Another dimension of the economic performance of immigrants is their investment in education. In part because of the depreciation of country-specific skills after migrating, immigrants have an incentive to make greater investments in the destination. The extent of these investments is apparently positively related to the level of premigration skills and expected duration of residence, and negatively related to age at arrival. In the United States, refugees undertake greater postmigration schooling investments than economic migrants, but the opposite is observed in Australia (Hashmi 1987, Chiswick and Miller 1991).

2.3 Other Countries

Studies of immigrants in Canada and Australia have found patterns remarkably similar to those for the United States. Studies for the United Kingdom reveal that most of the immigrants have highly transferable skills. As would be expected, however, immigrants in Israel demonstrate adjustment characteristics associated with non-economic migrants (refugees and ideological migrants).

See also: Internal Migration and Education

References

Blau F D 1979 Immigrant and labor earnings in early twentieth-century America. *Res. Popul. Econ.* 2: 21–41

Borjas G 1985 Assimilation, changes in cohort quality and the earnings of immigrants. *J. Labor Econ.* 3(4): 463–89

Chiswick B R 1978a The effects of Americanization on the earnings of foreign-born men. *J. Pol. Econ.* 86: 897–921

Chiswick B R 1978b A longitudinal analysis of the occupational mobility of immigrants. In: Dennis D (ed.) 1978 *Proc. 30 Annual Winter Meeting, Industrial Relations Research Association.* IRRA, Madison, Wisconsin

Chiswick B R 1979 The Economic progress of immigrants: Some apparently universal patterns. In: Fellner W (ed.) 1979 *Contemporary Economic Problems.* American Enterprise Institute for Public Policy Research, Washington, DC

Chiswick B R 1980a *An Analysis of the Economic Progress and Impact of Immigrants.* Report submitted to US Department of Labor, Employment, and Training Administration, NTIS No. PB80–200454. National Technical Information Service, Washington, DC

Chiswick B R 1982 *The Employment of Immigrants in the United States.* American Enterprise Institute, Washington, DC

Chiswick B R 1986 Is the new immigration less skilled than the old? *J. Labor Econ.* 4(2): 168–92

Chiswick B R, Miller P W 1991 *Post-Immigration Qualifications in Australia: Determinants and Consequences.* Bureau of Immigration Research, Canberra

Chiswick B R, Miller P W 1992 Language in the labor market: The immigrant experience in the United States and Canada. In: Chiswick B R (ed.) *Immigration, Language and Ethnicity: United States and Canada.* American Enterprise Institute, Washington, DC

Hashmi A 1987 Post-migration investment in education by Immigrants in the United States. Ph D dissertation, University of Illinois at Chicago, Chicago, Illinois

Further Reading

Chiswick B R 1980b The earnings of White and Coloured male immigrants in Britain. *Economica* 47: 81–87

Chiswick B R, Miller P W 1985 Immigrant generation and income in Australia. *Econ. Record* 61 (173): 540–33

Chiswick B R, Miller P W 1988 Earnings in Canada: The role of immigrant generation, French ethnicity and language. *Res. in Popul. Econ.* 6: 183–228

Douglas P H 1919 Is the new immigration more unskilled than the old? *J. Am. Stat. Assoc.* (June) 393–403

Grossman J B 1984 The occupational attainment of immigrant women in Sweden. *Scan. J. Econ.* 83(3): 337–51

Richard A H, Kalbach W E 1980 *Factors in the Adjustment of Immigrants and Their Descendants.* Statistics Canada Ottawa

Schwartz A 1976 Migration, age, and education. *J. Pol. Econ* 84: 701–19

Tandon B B 1978 Earnings differentials among native-born and foreign-born residents of Toronto. *Int. Migration Rev.* 12(3): 406–10

Kinship and Investment in Education

J. R. Behrman and P. Taubman

Analysis of kin data provides valuable insights into four questions about education: (a) To what extent is there intergenerational mobility in schooling? (b) What role does family background, and in particular genetic endowments and family-determined environment, play in determining educational attainment? (c) What determines the family's expenditures on each child? (d) How are estimates of education's impact on socioeconomic outcomes biased by not controlling for factors such as ability and motivation?

While several kin data sets permit exploration of the first question, few adult sibling data sets permit full investigation of the last three questions. Most analysis has been on samples that are not representative. In most studies education is represented by grades of schooling. Some potentially important statistical issues affect the estimates based on kin samples.

Intergenerational variability is less for schooling than for other observed measures of welfare, such as socioeconomic status (SES) and may be a brake on socioeconomic mobility. Sibling studies suggest that, for the United States, the variance in family background accounts for about three-fourths of schooling's intragenerational variance for White males born in the early twentieth century. Twin data indicate this family background contribution can be decomposed into genetic and family-determined environmental factors of about equal impact. Sibling studies indicate that the pattern of intrafamily expenditures on children's education reflects a mixture of expected returns and inequality aversion. Intrafamilial allocations are not consistent with pure investment models of education. Analyses of sibling data suggest that standard estimates of increased earnings due to education may be overstated—perhaps by a factor of two to three—because there was no controlling for partially unobserved abilities and motivations.

Kin data generally imply considerably less optimism than standard analyses about the extent to which education affects socioeconomic outcomes and leads to greater equality of opportunity.

1. Siblings, Twins, and Other Kin Data for Studies of Education

Education is the process through which individuals learn about their environment, how it functions, and how it can be altered. On-the-job training, reading, exposure to media of communication, verbal interchange, and many other experiences may make important contributions to education. Different individuals have different learning aptitudes because of differing genetic and nonschooling endowments. Individuals with identical grades of schooling may have highly varying education. Nevertheless, most studies define education in terms of grades of formal schooling completed.

Schooling is a better representation of education the more it is associated with the capacity for learning from other experiences. Schooling is of particular interest because it is amenable to policy.

In many surveys, respondents provide information on their parents' and their own schooling that can be used to study intergenerational mobility. Although some data sets are for special populations, others are representative of large populations and have sufficient observations to permit statistical testing of hypotheses. Contemporaneously collected (as opposed to recalled) data on more than two generations are relatively rare.

Many data sets do not have sufficient information to examine many dimensions of the last three questions in the introductory paragraph of this entry, which require information on adult socioeconomic outcomes. Brief descriptions of most of the major relevant data sets are given below (more details concerning the first five items and item (k) are in Taubman 1977, and details on items (b), (d), and (h)–(j) are in Jencks and Bartlett 1979).

(a) 156 pairs of brothers from Indianapolis with income measured in 1927 (Gorseline data, Chamberlain and Griliches 1975).

(b) 2,478 pairs of White male twins (about half identical) born in the United States in 1917–27, both veterans; health and some socioeconomic data from military records and repeated surveys from 1967 onwards (National Academy of Science–National Research Council [NAS–NRC]), Twin Registry (Behrman et al. 1977, 1980). Offspring data are available so it is possible to obtain correlations for other kin groups such as first cousins (Behrman and Taubman 1989).

(c) 292 pairs of brothers from the United States surveyed in 1966–71 and biannually (National Longitudinal Survey of Young Men, Chamberlain and Griliches 1975).

(d) 346 pairs of brothers in sixth grade between 1928 and 1950 in Kalamazoo, Michigan with socioeconomic data collected in 1973–74

(Olneck 1977).

(e) 2,000 brothers and sisters, one member a senior in secondary school in Wisconsin, United States, in 1957, with socioeconomic data from school records, parental income tax data, and surveys over the next two decades (Wisconsin Data, Sewell and Hauser 1977).

(f) About 500 pairs of sisters from Nicaragua in 1977–78 with socioeconomic data (Behrman and Wolfe 1984, 1989).

(g) About 80,000 people in some 270 "families" one member of which was institutionalized in 1900–18 because of mental retardation. A family contains all the descendants and spouses of each set of grandparents over the period 1800 to 1960. The data includes education, occupation, and IQ scores. (Reed and Reed 1965).

(h) 150 pairs of brothers in the United States age 35–64 in 1973 (National Opinion Research Center, Eagersfield 1979).

(i) 50 pairs of brothers in grades 11 and 12 in 1960 in the United States interviewed in 1971–72 (Jencks and Brown 1977).

(j) 151 individuals from 66 families in which one of the parents died in Cleveland, United States, in 1964–65 (Lindert 1977, Brittain 1976).

(k) 312 New Jersey 55–61-year old male employees of a utility company who gave information on their siblings' age, sex, education, and most recent occupation (Lindert 1977).

(l) About 5,000 siblings in the National Longitudinal survey of young men and women studied from the late 1960s through the early 1980s (Neumark 1988, Altonji and Dunn 1990).

(m) About 4,000 siblings, brothers and sisters, in the Panel Study of Income Dynamics (PSID) studied from 1968 through 1987 (Solon et al. 1987, Behrman and Taubman 1990).

(n) About 8,400 male and female twin pairs born in Minnesota between 1936 and 1955 with some 1,200 male pairs born between 1971 and 1981 (Lykken et al. 1990).

Thus sibling data sets with information on adult outcomes are few in number, come largely from the United States, and are often small and based on sample designs that may not be representative of larger populations. The sibling samples cannot be completely random since they do not include representatives of single-child households. Most of the relevant studies address the question of representativeness by comparing sample characteristics or regression coefficients with those from random samples. Such comparisons indicate that most of these data sets have more general validity. Within-sibling estimates

control for selectivity based on unobserved family characteristics.

2. Kin Data and Intergenerational Schooling Mobility

Intergeneration mobility refers to the relative position of a family in one generation versus their children's relative position. If the absolute value of the correlation between generations is close to one, there is almost no intergenerational mobility. If it is close to zero, there is considerable intergenerational mobility. Social mobility is usually regarded as a desirable characteristic.

Intergenerational correlations for schooling from a number of quite different samples—including (b), (d), (f), (h), (l), (m), and (n) in Sect. 1 and several others in Jencks and Bartlett 1979—are in the 0.3–0.5 range. The intergenerational correlations for SES are never larger, and are in the 0.2–0.4 range. Thus there is considerable intergenerational mobility for schooling. Fewer samples are available to make comparisons for income or earnings measured at the same point in the life cycle. Dwyer and Phelan (1976) estimate the intergenerational earnings correlation in sample (e) at about 0.33. Behrman and Taubman (1985) estimate this correlation R as no more than 0.2 using sample (b) augmented with children's data. However, these estimates are based on a single year's earning measure that can be atypical of a person's average income because of life cycle and business cycle factors. Adjusting for these in the PSID leads to an R of up to about 0.7 (Behrman and Taubman 1990).

3. Investment Model of Education and Role of Family

The economic analysis of education often focuses on its investment dimension (but see Sect. 7). There is an expected return to education, which depends on motivations and abilities that vary with genetic endowments and nonfamily environment. The downward sloping curve (DD) in Fig. 1 gives an individual's locus of such returns.

An individual with greater capabilities has a curve above the indicated one. The horizontal curve (SS) in Fig. 1 gives the marginal cost of investment in education. The maximizing investment is E_0, where the expected marginal return is equal to the marginal cost. This framework has been refined to explore more complex issues (Becker 1967, Rosen 1976), but Fig. 1 captures its essence.

Across families there may be differences in capabilities that imply systematic differences in average family marginal return curves and (given capital market imperfections) in marginal costs of educational investments.

Siblings may have different expected returns because of different capabilities or because of imperfections in labor markets (discrimination against women implies that a girl's expected returns may be less than those for her equally capable brother).

4. Variance Decomposition Estimates

The simplest form of variance decomposition analysis assumes that the optimal schooling (S) for a given individual reflects his or her genetic endowments (G), family-determined environment (N), and other random environmental determinants (U) in an additive relation:

$$S = G + N + U \qquad (1)$$

Taubman (1981) argues that variation in N may be an important component of inequality of opportunity, the elimination of which improves economic efficiency. Generally, it is not possible to determine how important each of the right-side components are in determining schooling, because these variables are unobserved.

Data on twins make possible one somewhat controversial approach to at least a partial decomposition of the variance of each of the right-side variables. First rewrite equation (1) with the environmental variables combined into one (N + U = V):

$$S = G + V \qquad (2)$$

Schooling is an observed phenotype that equals the sum of G and N, which are assumed to be uncorrelated. The total phenotypic variance is:

$$\sigma^2_S = \sigma^2_G + \sigma^2_V \qquad (3)$$

The alphabetical order of first names can be used to designate twin 1 and twin 2. By arranging all twin 1's by family number and doing the same for all twin 2's, the cross-twin covariance can be calculated by treating schooling for twin 1 and twin 2 as two separate variables. Then, by calculating the covariance separately for monozygotic (identical) and dizygotic (fraternal) twins, each of the two twin covariances can be expressed in terms of σ^2_G and σ^2_V and other unknown parameters. In the most general form, there are seven unknown parameters. The observed variance and covariances can be used to estimate no more than three unknowns; therefore a much simpler model must be employed (or more outcomes observed; see Sect. 5).

Heritability is defined as the proportion of the observed variance that comes from genotypic variation:

$$h^2 = \frac{\sigma^2_G}{\sigma^2_S} \qquad (4)$$

The calculation and interpretation of heritability estimates has generated considerable controversy

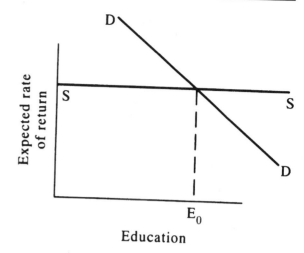

Figure 1

Determinants of education within investment model with horizontal marginal costs

(Goldberger 1977, 1979, Taubman 1978, 1981). In the simplest model, h^2 is estimated as twice the difference in the two twin correlations.

The assumption that the expected covariance in environments does not vary between types of twins is critical. There is some direct evidence that monozygotic twins are more alike in some respects than are dizygotic twins (for example, clothing). However, environmental differences may be in response to genetic differences and not just a desire to treat identical twins more alike. Scarr-Salapatck (1965) has examined cases in which parents have been mistaken regarding their twins' zygosity and has concluded that the parental choices are responsive to genetic factors whether or not parents correctly know the twin type.

While some researchers have been comfortable with this assumption, others have been extremely critical and have argued that heritability is overestimated since more similar environments for monozygotic twins are wrongly attributed as genetic effects. However, Taubman (1981) and Behrman et al. (1980) argue that it is legitimate to count that part of the environment that is a response to genetic differences as due to genetic differences.

Some researchers have interpreted high heritability estimates to mean that the phenotypic outcome could not be changed by variations in the environment. Such an inference is clearly wrong. Figure 2 provides an illustrative example.

The horizontal axis measures the environment (V), the vertical axis a phenotypic outcome such as schooling, and the curves A and B give the reaction of schooling to different environments for the only two genetic groups in the relevant population. Assuming that environment is identical for everyone, say at V_0, in this case a calculation of heritability indicates that all of the variance in schooling is due to genetic differences between group A and group B. However, that does not imply that environmental changes are ineffective, since these are measured by the slope of the curves A and B. Schooling inequality could almost be eliminated, for example, by changing everyone's environment to V_1, or the inequality could be reversed by changing only group B's environment to V_2. Heritability refers to a given distribution of other factors. It describes a particular situation, but does not indicate what phenotypic changes would occur if there were environmental changes.

5. Extended Latent Variable–Variance Decomposition Models

Heritability studies have been extended to a multi-equation context that allows better control for, and estimation of, the effects of unobserved or "latent" variables, such as family background, genetic endowments, and environment (Behrman et al. 1980, Chamberlain and Griliches 1975). This extension provides better estimates both of the determinants of schooling and of possible biases in the estimation of the impact of schooling.

If a latent variable is associated with enough observed variables, its variance may be estimated. For example, in Eqn. (3) above there are two unobserved variances that cannot be estimated since the only observable datum is the variance of schooling. But suppose that in addition to Eqn. (2) there were a series of other outcomes (Y_i) that depend on the same genetic endowments (G), schooling (s) and independently distributed environmental factors (V_i) in an additive manner:

$$Y_i = a_i s + b_i G + V_i \qquad (5)$$

For each additional relation three unknowns are added (i.e., a_i, b_i, and σ^2_v) However, observable data also increase; there are variances of the new variables, and their covariances with all other observed variables. With enough relations there are enough data points to estimate all of the unknown parameters. For example, with Eqn. (2) and 4 additional observed indicators determined as in Eqn. (5), there are 15 observed variances or covariances and 15 unobserved variances to be estimated (i.e., 4 a_i's, 4 b_i's, and 5 σ^2_v, σ_{SG}, and σ^2_G).

The latent variable methodology requires a relatively large number of observed variables to identify a fairly simple model (for example, genetic and environmental factors are uncorrelated, and environmental factors are independent across relations). However, sibling data increase substantially the observed covariances for a given number of Y_i because of the additional covariances among siblings. Related models have been developed by Chamberlain and Griliches (1975) for siblings and by Behrman et al. (1977) for twins. In the sibling models the researchers identify the latent variables as family factors (common to all siblings) and individual factors. In the twin models the researchers identify them as genetic endowments and family environmental factors.

The latent variable twins model is a more satisfactory framework for obtaining heritability estimates than the procedures reviewed in this section because it requires weaker assumptions. However, the controversial assumption regarding equal expected environmental correlations for the two types of twins still cannot be tested.

Behrman and Taubman (1989) adopt a model proposed by Fisher (1918) and use a larger group of kin groups to obtain heritability estimates. Fisher develops a three-parameter model of genotypic correlation of various kin groups under the assumption that (except for assortative mating) there is no correlation in the environments of kin. Behrman and Taubman partial out the effects of measured "environmental" variables such as father's occupation using a regression and then apply Fisher's method. They exploit the fact that first cousins whose fathers are identical twins are, from a genetic viewpoint, half sibs. They use both generations in the NAS–NRC sample to estimate an h^2 for years of schooling of about 0.8.

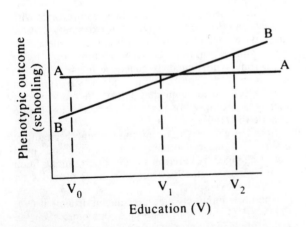

Figure 2
Reaction functions for genetic groups A and B with environment to determine schooling

6. The Family Role in the Intragenerational Variance of Schooling

While there are a large number of estimates of heritability of IQ based on the model in Sect. 4 (Jencks et al. 1972), estimates for schooling are much less common. The correlations for schooling for monozygotic and dizygotic twins are 0.78 and 0.53 in the NAS–NRC sample used by Behrman et al. (1980). About half of the intragenerational variance in schooling for white males is accounted for by variance in the genetic components (h^2 about 0.5).

With the latent variable extended-twin model (Sect. 5) and a distinction in the schooling relation between family-determined environment and other environment as in Eqn. (1), Behrman et al. (1980) decompose this same schooling variance into 32 percent from genetic variance, 45 percent from family-determined environmental variance, and 23 percent from other environmental variance.

7. Pure Investment versus Inequality Aversion

The investment model of education in Sect. 3 assumes pure maximization of expected returns from education without any consideration of allocation within the family.

Behrman et al. (1982) develop a model that permits the testing of whether a family's allocation of schooling among children reflects pure maximization of expected returns, pure inequality aversion, or some combination. The model posits that the distribution of schooling among children in a family is the outcome of the maximization of parental utility that depends upon each child's earnings capacity. The utility function is maximized subject to both a budget constraint and the earnings production function that depends on schooling, other parental investments, and genetic endowments. Figure 3 illustrates this model.

The axes refer to expected earnings of the ith

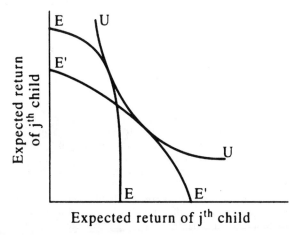

Figure 3
Parental preferences (UU) and two alternative expected returns frontiers (EE, E′E′) reflecting differential relative genetic endowments

and j^{th} children in a family. The curve UU is a parental indifference curve based on the distribution of expected returns between these children. The case drawn reflects a balance between pure investment and pure inequality aversion concerns. If the parents were concerned only with the child with the lowest expected earnings, this curve would be square-cornered along the 45 degree line from the origin. If the parents were indifferent about the distribution of expected earnings, this curve would be a straight line from a given expected earnings level for one child to an identical level for the other.

The curve EE is the expected earnings frontier between these two children, given the budget- and earnings-capacity production-function constraints and the relative genetic endowments of the two children. This curve is drawn to reflect the relatively better genetic endowment of the ith child. Curve E′E′ is for a different family in which the genetic endowment of the jth child is relatively better. The variance in such relative genetic endowments across families enables one to trace the curvature of the parental indifference curve, and to estimate the parental weight on inequality aversion versus pure investment maximization in their allocation of schooling among their children.

The extent of parental inequality aversion can be estimated with data on siblings' education and their expected earnings. Behrman et al. (1982) estimate this model using adult earnings as a proxy for expected earnings for the adult male United States dizygotic twins in item (b) in Sect. 1. The estimates are substantially and significantly different from the extremes of complete inequality aversion (Rawls 1971) and of pure returns maximization. Such estimates imply that parental allocation of resources to their children's schooling mitigates substantially the intrafamilial inequality of genetic endowments as compared with the pure investment model outcome.

Becker and Tomes (1976) have proposed a similar model in which parents' utility derived from each child depends on the sum of that child's expected earnings and returns from financial bequests. Since it is assumed that there are no diminishing returns to financial investments but diminishing returns to schooling investments, parents who plan to leave bequests should only spend for schooling on each child to a point where its return equals the return earned on financial investments. Parents should invest efficiently in each child's education and then compensate the less able with larger financial bequests.

Behrman et al. (1991) show that the Becker–Tomes conclusion only holds if parents have enough wealth to equalize children's income. Since they find that average annual absolute differences in siblings' earnings are in the US $6,000 to US $10,000 ranges, very large wealth differentials would be needed to generate offsetting annual returns from capital. They evaluate the available empirical evidence regarding patterns of bequest differentials, earnings differentials, and transfer differentials to discriminate between these models. They conclude that the evidence is less consistent with the Becker and Tomes (1976) model than with the Behrman et al. (1982) model.

8. Biases in Standard Estimates of the Impact of Schooling

There are many estimates of the impact of schooling on earnings, and other factors. However, such estimates may be biased because of the failure to control for unobserved variables (e.g., ability and motivation). Consider estimation of Eqn. 5. With ordinary estimation techniques, estimates of the schooling coefficient are biased upward if significant genetic and environmental variables, which are positively correlated with schooling, are omitted. In multivariate estimates of the impact of schooling, an attempt has been made to include available measures of ability and of family background. Generally, the inclusion of these variables has resulted in lower estimates of the effects of schooling. These findings suggest that there are important variables that are positively correlated with schooling (Jencks and Bartlett 1979).

Sibling data permit controlling for certain dimensions of family background that are usually unobserved and that may cause biases. For the special case of monozygotic twins, Eqn. (6) controls for genetic background and common environment (where ΔU_i is assumed to be noncommon environment):

$$\Delta Y_i = a_i\Delta S + \Delta U_i \qquad (6)$$

For fraternal twins and other siblings, the differenced version controls for common environment, but not for differences in genetic background:

$$\Delta Y_i = a_i\Delta S + b_i\Delta G + \Delta U_i \qquad (7)$$

The latent variable models of Sect. 5 provide a somewhat more satisfactory control for unobserved variables (they permit combining monozygotic twins with other siblings in the same estimate).

Measurement error also leads to biased estimates. Such "noise" in independent variables tends to bias their estimated coefficients toward zero (Griliches 1979). When sibling differences are the unit of observation, measurement error may be more prominent, and biases from this source may be increased. However, measurement error does not seem to account for most of the difference between the differenced siblings estimates and the nondifferenced estimates (Behrman et al. 1980, Jencks and Bartlett 1979). Moreover, if measurement error is correlated between the siblings (due to schooling quality, for

example), the bias is much smaller and may be in the other direction (Behrman 1984)

The estimated results from sibling data do not suggest large omitted variable bias if applied to samples (a) and (c) in Sect. 1 (Chamberlain and Griliches 1975). However, it is not possible to generalize from the samples since the former is regionally localized with overrepresentation of occupations in which nonpecuniary returns are relatively important (e.g., teaching), and the latter is of men at very early stages of their life cycle with expected, not actual, occupations used in the analysis.

Other sibling studies suggest that standard methods overestimate considerably the impact of education on later socioeconomic outcomes (Olneck 1977, Behrman et al. 1977, 1980, Behrman and Wolfe 1984, 1989, Wolfe and Behrman 1986, 1987). For sample (d), controlling for common background of brothers reduces the estimated schooling impact on early occupational status by 11 percent, on mature occupational status by 20 percent, and on earnings by 33 percent. For sample (b), controlling for common environment and common genetics reduces the estimated schooling impact on early occupation status by about 33 percent and on earnings by about 25 percent. In the same sample controlling for all genetic endowments and common environment reduces the estimated schooling effect on early occupational status by 50 percent, on mature occupational status by 12 percent, and on earnings by 70 percent. For sample (f), controlling for common genetics and common environment reduces the estimated schooling effect on income by about 40 percent and on fertility and child health by 100 percent.

Such evidence is not conclusive because of the special nature of existing sibling samples and possible measurement bias and contradictory results. However, it does suggest the possibility that standard estimates substantially overestimate the impact of education on important socioeconomic outcomes.

9. Conclusion

Samples of twins, siblings, and other kin have been used to study issues related to the determinants of schooling and subsequent socioeconomic outcomes. There is considerable but incomplete intergenerational schooling mobility. The family plays a major role in determining intragenerational inequality in schooling and in earnings. There is some evidence, not accepted by all researchers, that much of this inequality is attributable to differences in genetic endowments. Evidence also exists that parents care about inequality of earnings capacity among their offspring, and provide more schooling to the less able than would be the case if they were only concerned about the total earnings of their offspring.

Finally, these kin-related samples have been used to eliminate or reduce the bias in estimates of the impact of schooling. While the evidence is mixed, these studies suggest the possibility that studies of the schooling effects based on individuals may be strongly biased upward.

References

Altonji J, Dunn T 1990 Relationships among the family incomes and labor market outcomes of relatives. Northwestern University, Evanston, Illinois (mimeo)

Becker G S 1967 *Human Capital and the Personal Distribution of Income: An Analytical Approach* (Woytinski Lecture). Institute of Public Administration, Ann Arbor, Michigan

Becker G S, Tomes N 1976 Child endowments and the quantity and quality of children. *J. Pol. Econ.* 84(4 Pt.2): S143–62

Behrman J R 1984 Sibling deviation estimates, measurement error and biases in estimated returns to schooling. University of Pennsylvania, Philadelphia, Pennsylvania (mimeo)

Behrman J R, Hrubec Z, Taubman P, Wales T J 1980 *Socioeconomic Success: A Study of the Effects of Genetic Endowments, Family Environment, and Schooling.* North-Holland, Amsterdam

Behrman J R, Pollak R A, Taubman P 1982 Parental preferences and provision for progeny. *J. Pol. Econ.* 90 (1): 52–73

Behrman J R, Pollak R A, Taubman P 1991 Some causes and consequences of death. University of Pennsylvania, Philadelphia, Pennsylvania (mimeo)

Behrman J R, Taubman P 1985 Intergenerational earnings mobility in the US: Some estimates and a test of Becker's intergenerational endowments model. *Rev. Econ. Stat.* 67: 144–51

Behrman J R, Taubman P 1989 Is schooling "mostly in the genes"? Nature nurture decomposition using data on relatives. *J. Pol. Econ.* 97(6): 1425–46

Behrman J R, Taubman P 1990 The intergenerational correlation between children's adult earnings and their parents income: Results from the Michigan panel survey of income dynamics. *Review of Income and Wealth* 36(2): 115–27

Behrman J R, Taubman P, Wales T J 1977 Controlling for and measuring the effects of genetics and family environment in equations for schooling and labor market success. In: Taubman P (ed.) 1977

Behrman J R, Wolfe B L 1984 The socioeconomic impact of schooling in a developing country. *Rev. Econ. Stat.* 66(2): 296–303

Behrman J R, Wolfe B L 1989 Does more schooling make women better nourished and healthier? Adult sibling random and fixed effects estimates for Nicaragua. *J. Hum. Resources* 24(4): 644–63

Brittain J 1976 *The Inheritance of Economic Status.* Brookings Institution, Washington, DC

Chamberlain G, Griliches Z 1975 Unobservables with a variance-component structure: Ability, schooling and the economic success of brothers. *Int. Econ. Rev.* 16(2): 422–49

Dwyer J, Phelan T 1976 Education in America and the reproduction of social inequality: A method divergent model of indicator error. State University of New York, Stony Brook, New York (mimeo)

Eagersfield D 1979 The NORC brothers sample. In: Jencks C S, Bartlett S (eds.) 1979

Fisher R A 1918 The correlation between relatives on the supposition of Mendelian inheritance. *Transactions of the Royal Society Edinburgh* 52(2): 399–433

Goldberger A 1977 Twin methods: A skeptical view. In: Taubman P (ed.) 1977

Goldberger A 1979 Heritability. *Economica* 46(184): 327–47

Griliches Z 1979 Sibling models and data in economics: Beginnings of a survey. *J. Pol. Econ.* 87(5 Pt. 2): S37–64

Jencks C S, Bartlett S 1979 *Who Gets Ahead? The Determinants of Economic Success in America.* Basic Books, New York

Jencks C S, Brown M 1977 Genes and social stratification: A methodological exploration with illustrative data. In: Taubman P (ed.) 1977

Jencks C S et al. 1972 *Inequality: A Reassessment of the Effect of Family and Schooling in America.* Basic Books, New York

Lindert P 1977 Sibling position and achievement. *J. Hum Resources* 12(2): 198–219

Lykken D T, Bouchard T J Jr, McGue M, Tellegen A 1990 The Minnesota twin family registry: Some initial findings. *Acta Geneticae Medicae et Gemellologiae* 39(1): 35–70

Neumark D 1988 Employer's discriminatory behavior and the estimation of wage discrimination. *J. Hum. Resources* 23(2): 279–95

Olneck M 1977 On the use of sibling data to estimate the effects of family background, cognitive skills and schooling: Results from the Kalamazoo study. In: Taubman P (ed.) 1977

Rawls J 1971 *A Theory of Justice.* Belknap Press, Cambridge, Massachusetts

Reed E, Reed S 1965 *Mental Retardation: A Family Study.* Saunders, Philadelphia, Pennsylvania

Rosen S 1976 A theory of life earnings. *J. Pol. Econ.* 84(4 Pt. 2): 545–67

Scarr-Salapatck S 1965 Twin method: Defense of a critical assumption. University of Minnesota, Minneapolis, Minnesota (mimeo)

Sewell W, Hauser R 1977 On the effects of families and family structure on achievement. In: Taubman P (ed.) 1977

Solon G et al. 1987 The effect of family background on economic success: A longitudinal analysis of sibling correlations. NBER Working paper 2282, Cambridge, Massachusetts (mimeo)

Taubman P (ed.) 1977 *Kinometrics: Determinants of Socioeconomic Success Within and Between Families.* North-Holland, Amsterdam

Taumab P 1978 What we learn from estimating the genetic contribution to inequality in earnings: Reply. *Am. Econ. Rev.* 68(5): 970–76

Taubman P 1981 On heritability. *Economica* 48(192): 417–20

Wolfe B L, Behrman J R 1986 Child quantity and quality in a developing country: The importance of family background endogenous tastes and biological supply factors. *Economic Development and Cultural Change* 34: 703–20

Wolfe B L, Behrman J R 1987 Women's schooling and children's health: Are the effects robust with adult sibling control for the women's childhood backgrounds?

Journal of Health Economics 6(3): 239–54

Further Reading

Husén T 1974 *Talent, Equality and Meritocracy.* Nijhoffi, The Hague

Family Status and Economic Status

P. Taubman

The process by which people attain high economic status in modern industrial or postindustrial societies is a complex one. In preindustrial societies inheritance or ascription of occupations and status were the norm. Capitalism and industrialism required a more effective utilization of talent. Ideally, jobs are to be allocated according to the match between competence and tasks. Formal education is the key instrument of such matching. However, apparently family status is an important predictor of economic status, even in industrial societies that define themselves as capitalist and meritocratic. What goes on in families and the relationship of families to the labor market seem to translate into more schooling and greater success in the labor market even when schooling is accounted for.

This entry reviews the literature on the relationships between the family, education, and economic status. It focuses on developed countries, but much of the conceptual and empirical work also applies to developing countries. Although economic status can be defined either in terms of a person's income, earnings, wealth, or the quality or ranking of his or her occupation, the emphasis here is on family status, education, and occupational status. Comparisons of results are made using other concepts of status, such as earnings.

1. Occupational Status and Economic Status

1.1 Defining Occupational Status

Occupational status has been defined in a variety of ways. Duncan (1961) created an index from prestige rankings for 45 occupational titles. Using regression analysis he related these rankings to census measures of both the percentage of male workers in each occupation who were at least high school graduates and the percentage in each occupation with a certain minimum level of income. The regression results were then used to assign status values to nearly 500 occupations. This index is stable across time and in other countries. For the 40–50 year old age group, the correlation of the index with the natural logarithm of

current earnings is about 0.25 to 0.34 (Behrman et al. 1980 p.144). However, this observed correlation with earnings is lower than it might actually be. The scale of occupational status is forced into a range of 0–100 while earnings will often vary from hundreds of dollars to hundreds of thousands of dollars. Annual earnings also often have a great deal more statistical noise in them arising from the business cycle and bad or good luck in a particular year.

Occupational scales have also been created using measures of earnings and other criteria from census data in a selected year. Chamberlain and Griliches (1975), for example, used average earnings in the three-digit occupation "desired at age 30" for young men in the United States National Longitudinal Survey (NLS). (A three-digit code can specify a person's occupation and industrial sector, as well as their status as a "skilled" worker.) Alternatively, dummy (dichotomous) variables have been used, with the dummy set equal to 1 if the occupation meets a certain definition, namely "skilled" or falling between occupational code numbers N to (N + X). For example, Polachek (1981) explained women's selection into mutually exclusive occupations defined on the basis of wage level and attrition in wages when women are out of the labor force (for criticism of the Polachek model, see England 1982).

1.2 Adjusting Earnings for Occupational Characteristics

Attempts have also been made to "correct" earnings differences by adjusting them for occupational characteristics that reflect particularly dangerous or undesirable work, which therefore requires higher compensation. The theoretical basis for this "compensating differential" approach is presented in Thaler and Rosen (1975). They examine a labor market in which some jobs have a greater probability of resulting in an early death because of on-the-job accidents, murder, or ingestion of harmful substances (e.g., alcohol, asbestos, or coal dust).

They show that utility-maximizing individuals and profit-maximizing firms will adjust wages paid (to equally skilled workers) and expenditures on safety, health, and so on, until the supply and demand for each job are equalized. In this adjustment process riskier jobs pay a wage premium. The premium paid to induce the last needed worker—the worker who makes supply equal demand in any particular occupation and firm—to bear the extra risk can be estimated by comparing the wage rates of two persons alike in all other respects. However, if tastes differ, the least risk-averse individuals will be found in the most risky occupations and their premium will not be useful in determining how much more an *average* person would have to be paid to switch from the less to the more risky occupation under study.

The compensating variable scheme has been applied to characteristics other than likelihood of death. Examples include fluctuations in the wage or profit stream (see Taubman 1975, Weiss 1972, Hause 1974, Drazen and Matilla 1986, Garen 1988); job injuries (Viscusi 1978), job turnover (Topel 1984), and disamenities (Lucas 1977). Often, controlling for these compensation variations substantially changes the estimate of the extra earnings associated with schooling.

1.3 Occupational Status during the Life Cycle

Both earnings and occupational status vary greatly during the life cycle. Mincer (1974) provided a thorough analysis for earnings changes over lifetime. Occupational status also changes over the life cycle. For example, Behrman et al. (1980 p.146) indicated that in a sample of White male twins born between 1917 and 1927, their initial full-time civilian job status index (on a scale from 0 to 100) averaged about 35, whereas in the 1960s the index averaged about 50. This difference is statistically significant. Olneck (1977), in a sample of men age 35 to 59 who attended school in Kalamazoo, Michigan, reported initial occupation scores of 40 and current occupational status (at age 46) of 50. He also reported results from a national representative sample—"Occupational Change in a Generation II"—for the same age range of 34 and 44. The initial status occupation measured 34 and the later status 43.

2. Explaining Occupational Success

Studies have been undertaken to "explain" both the level of occupational success and occupational success *within* family achievement. The analysis generally uses educational attainment, family socioeconomic status, and ability as key variables. In the within-family studies only variables that differ by individuals can be examined. Yet it is possible to adjust individual data for differences from the mean for the within variable, and then study the effects of common variables for individuals. Some of these studies estimate reduced form and/or structural equations

using ordinary least squares (OLS) or some simultaneous equations method while others use path analysis (see Duncan 1966, Jencks et al. 1972). In some instances all these methods yield the same coefficients. In other cases, when the model is not statistically "just identified," the numerical estimates differ.

The studies generally focus on men. Women's occupational status and earnings are much more difficult to explain. A few studies have examined the determinants of female earnings, but the problem is complicated by the (changing) tendency of married women to drop out of the labor force. As Gronau (1974) and Heckman (1974) have shown, it is necessary to adjust for selectivity in estimating such earnings equations for women because those that stay in the labor force are a special group. Most studies of women have concentrated on earnings or wage rates and hours worked. Only a few have examined occupational status.

2.1 Occupational Success and Education

Education has been shown by many studies to exert a strong influence on the occupational attainment process. In a meritocratic society, education was assumed to be the dominant factor in social mobility. However, in the early 1960s the validity of this assumption was challenged by Anderson (1961), who argued that only a small part of a person's prospects of mobility can be explained by education. Boudon (1974) argued that a highly meritocratic society does not necessarily give those who have reached a high level of education more chance of promotion than those whose level is lower. Jencks et al. (1972) used a modification of the Duncan (1966) model to show that education is not as strong a factor in promoting social mobility as has been traditionally assumed. Using a similar model on Swedish (Malmö) longitudinal data, Fägerlind (1975) showed that the explanatory power of education and other variables of education and other variables varied according to the stage of the career being considered. Tuijnman (1989) took the same Malmö data and verified this finding, but also showed that youth education has a consistent and powerful effect on both occupational status and earnings throughout the life cycle.

2.2 Correcting for Other Variables

The relationship between occupational status and education may arise because of the underlying relationship of other variables. A major issue, therefore, in estimating the effects of education on occupational success is the bias arising from the omission of necessary controls from the equation. Controls can be either variables such as parental education or measures of family background as represented by family means or within sibling or twin pair representations. The findings in developed countries suggest that controlling for measured family background has little effect but controlling for measured ability or for genotype has a much greater effect on this relationship.

The usual measures of family background include parents' education, occupation, religion, the gender of the head of the family when the child was 14, birth order, number of siblings (which may be an endogenous variable), and residential location. When measures of the subject's own intelligence are included, most studies show that the coefficient on education decreases; yet overall, these controls generally do not have a large impact on the estimated effect of education on occupational status. However, occupational status is in part scored on the basis of average education, which may both bias the estimate of educational effects and minimize the intervening effect of other variables. Moreover, when earnings are the dependent variable, these controls reduce the effect of education by 10 percent to 25 percent, depending on what is measured and the stage of the life cycle when earnings are measured (Taubman 1989).

Several studies have tried to explain empirically occupational success using education and family background—broadly and narrowly defined—as controls. This section will consider the estimated relationships and any trends over the life cycle and time, and over generations. Many of the results are drawn from nonrandom samples, although results shown for occupational status and other dependent variables appear to be similar to those based on random samples.

The empirical results surveyed cover a wide span of years. For the United States the effect of education on occupational status is relatively time- and cohort-invariant, though there is a small negative association with age in a cohort. The major exception to this is the Chamberlain and Griliches (1975) study.

Research on occupational success was initiated in the 1960s with a study in the United States by Duncan (1961), and continued with Duncan et al. (1972). These studies mostly used the "Occupational Change in a Generation" (OCG) data, which was based on the March 1962 Current Population Survey. This was supplemented with some additional data. They obtained correlations from non-Black males in 10-year age cohorts beginning at age 25 and ending with age 64. The simple correlations between education and occupational status ranged from 0.56 to 0.65 and decreased slightly with age. The coefficient of education was about 0.5 to 0.6 when controlling for the number of siblings, father's education, and father's occupation. This coefficient decreased with age. The same sample was analyzed by Bowles and Nelson (1974). Duncan et al. also replicated their findings in other samples, such as the Detroit Area Study of 1966 (Duncan et al. 1972).

More sophisticated results using samples with more

interesting data began in the 1970s. Jencks et al. (1972) provided an excellent summary of then extant work on inequality in education, occupation, and income. They also extended much of the previous research and assembled results from previous studies using path analysis. They found that the correlation between father's and son's occupational status does not exceed 0.5. There was nearly as much status differential between fathers and sons or brothers as between randomly selected men. However, they also found that differences in education (not related to cognitive development) explained about 30 of the 60-point difference between the top and bottom fifth in occupational status. Each year of schooling added about 6 points to a status measure that had a standard deviation of 25 points. Jencks et al. (1972) also argued that some of the occupational success occurred because education is a credential rather than an enhancer of cognitive and other skills. They also presented some estimates of the impact of school quality on occupational quality. The best high school education could lead on to one more year of schooling and 5 points more in occupational status than the worst education.

Both earnings and occupational status have been correlated across the generations. Jencks et al. (1972) reported a correlation for status of about 0.5. Behrman et al. (1993) reported that the annual correlation was about one half that when earnings were averaged over time or when earnings were drawn from the same part of the life cycle for both generations.

Although estimates for parent–child correlation have focused on education, such estimates also exist for economic status. Most calculations for income or earnings are summarized in Behrman et al. (1980), Taubman (1989), or in Behrman et al. (1993). Using a year's measure of earnings taken from any point in which both generations were reporting, the correlation tended to be no higher than 0.25. However, if average earnings were used or if (in one sample) the earnings in both generations were taken from about age 40, the correlation coefficient (r) increased to more than 0.5.

Olneck (1977) presented results for both the Occupational Change in a Generation II (OCG-II), a United States random sample, and the Kalamazoo sample—data he collected. He showed that for the OCG-II sample of men aged 35 to 59, both initial occupation and current occupation displayed a positive simple correlation with test score (Kalamazoo only), father's education, and own education, whereas there were negative correlations with age and number of siblings. Moreover, the sibling correlation for initial occupation was about the same—near 0.4—for brothers born 3 or fewer years apart and more than 3 years apart. The simple sibling correlation for current occupational status was smaller for those born more than 3 years apart, but he did not control for the effect of age or experience in these calculations. Using number of siblings and father's education and occupation as independent variables, he found (in the Kalamazoo sample) a predicted sibling correlation for occupational status of 0.2 for initial occupation and 0.09 for current occupational status (with no control for age or experience). He also found sibling correlation for current and initial occupation of 0.4 and 0.3. This suggested that there were important sources of sibling occupational similarity not captured by his measured variables.

The coefficients of years of schooling in initial and current occupation (in Kalamazoo) were about 0.5 when no other variables were controlled for. The coefficient was essentially unchanged when the above measures of family background were included. When regressions were estimated for pairs of siblings, the size of the impact of education on current occupation was reduced from 4.2 to 3.5, when no controls were included.

The Wisconsin Longitudinal Study (WLS), initially consisting of Wisconsin high school seniors who were administered the Hemon-Nelson intelligence test in the late 1950s, has been another important source of data in such studies (see Hauser and Mossel 1985). In the WLS, parental income was taken from the 1957 to 1960 Wisconsin tax returns and earnings were obtained from social security files (with an adjustment for the date at which the Old Age and Survivor's Disability Insurance (OASDI) tax reached its ceiling).

The results using the WLS showed—in the mid-1960s—substantial earnings returns to education. Hauser and Mossel (1985) reported that completed education (as reported by the respondent in 1975) had a correlation with 1970 and 1975 occupation of 0.6 and 0.6. They found slightly lower correlations with parent education (as reported by the parent). The slope coefficient for education was in the 0.6 and 0.7 range and was about the same when the respondents were treated as individuals or when within-sibling pair data were used.

Tuijnman's work on the Swedish data (1989), following on from Fägerlind's earlier study (1975), showed that occupational status at various ages was significantly related to adult ability, youth education, home background (family status), and adult education. Youth education continued to be highly significant even when these other variables were accounted for. This was also the case for earnings, except that neither adult or early ability (test score) were significant explainers and that family background was only significant in the prime of working life (age 35–43).

2.3 Controlling for Family Environment and Genetic Endowments

The WLS data have also been used to estimate the earnings–education relationship within and between families. In the sample of about 500 pairs, they found no significant differences in these estimates.

It is possible to use data on relatives to control for family environment and genetic endowments.

Within-pair differences of identical twins control for genetic endowments and common environment. If the unmeasured specific endowment is uncorrelated with schooling, and if schooling is measured without error, the schooling coefficient estimate is unbiased. Taubman (1975) introduced the use of identical (MZ) and fraternal (DZ) twin data to economics. The difference between DZ twins and siblings is that the former are born much closer in time. For both groups, within-pair differences eliminate common environment and about half of the genetic endowment differences. In principle, the estimated coefficients need not be less biased than those based on individuals. The necessary conditions for a reduction in the bias are spelled out in Griliches (1979).

It is also possible to use other kin groups to construct controls for family environment and/or genetic endowments. For example, Scarr and Weinberg (1977) used data on adopted children. They showed that standard measures of family background have much smaller effects on children's occupational status than in data sets based on children living with their biological parents. Behrman and Taubman (1989) also showed how data on many different kin groups, including siblings and cousins, can be used to control for genotypic differences. However, they only applied their model to years of schooling.

Chamberlain and Griliches (1975) constructed a model using data for brothers, collected in 1927. They found that schooling had a coefficient of about 0.1 both in equations for individuals and in within-sibling pairs.

Behrman et al. (1980) used a large sample of White male twins (all veterans) born between 1921 and 1927 to formulate a latent variable decomposition model. The dependent variables were schooling, initial occupation, occupation in 1967, and the natural logarithm of earnings in 1973. When the twins were treated as individuals, the coefficient on schooling was 0.4 for initial occupation and 0.35 for 1967 occupation. When a long list of family background measures was included, the two coefficients fell to 0.37 and 0.33 (with the latter including the indirect effects from initial occupation).

The within-pair results were calculated separately for identical (MZ) and fraternal (DZ) twins. The effects of educational differences for initial occupation were 0.3 and 0.2 for DZ and MZ pairs respectively. For 1967 occupation, the total effect was 0.3 and 0.3 respectively. The system estimates were similar to those of the MZ within equation.

2.4 Conclusion

The statistical analyses indicate that education is strongly related to occupational status and earnings especially for men. However, much though not all of the relationship is attributable to the more educated differing in important characteristics from the less educated. Various techniques have been used to control for these characteristics including measures of intelligence, parental education, and studying outcomes within family groupings such as twins or brothers. Intergenerational correlations for education and economic status are positive and relatively large.

See also: Benefits of Education

References

Anderson C A 1961 A skeptical note on education and mobility. In: Halsey A H, Floud J, Anderson C A (eds.) 1961 *Education, Economy, and Society: A Reader in the Sociology of Education.* Free Press, New York

Behrman J R, Hrubec Z, Taubman P, Wales T J 1980 *Socioeconomics Success: A Study of the Effects of Genetic Endowments, Family Environment, and Schooling.* North-Holland, Amsterdam

Behrman J R, Pollak R A, Taubman P 1993 *From Parent to Child: Inequality and Immobility in the USA.* University of Chicago Press, Illinois

Behrman J R, Taubman P 1989 Is schooling mostly in the genes? Nature–nurture decomposition using data on relatives. *J. Pol. Econ.* 97(6): 1425–46

Boudon R 1974 *Education, Opportunity, and Social Inequality: Changing Prospects in Western Society.* Wiley, New York

Bowles S, Nelson V 1974 The inheritance of IQ and the intergenerational reproduction of economic inequality. *Rev. Econ. Stat.* 56: 39–51

Chamberlain G, Griliches Z 1975 Unobservables with a variance components structure: Ability, schooling and the economic success of brothers. *Int. Econ. Rev.* 16(2): 422–29

Duncan O D 1961 A socioeconomic index for all occupations. In: Reiss A J (ed.) 1961 *Occupations and Social Status.* Free Press, New York

Duncan O D 1966 Path analysis: Sociological examples. *Am. J. Sociol.* 72(1): 1–16

Duncan O, Featherman D, Duncan B 1972 *Socioeconomic Background and Achievement.* Seminar Press, New York

England P 1982 The failure of human capital theory to explain occupational sex segregation. *J. Hum. Resources* 17(3): 358–70

Fägerlind I 1975 *Formal Education and Adult Earnings: A Longitudinal Study on the Economic Benefits of Education.* Almqvist and Wiksell, Stockholm

Garen J 1988 Compensating wage differentials and the endogeneity of job riskiness. *Rev. Econ. Stat.* 70(1): 9–16

Griliches Z 1979 Sibling models and data in economics: Beginnings of a survey. *J. Pol. Econ.* 87(5 pt.2): 537–64

Gronau R 1974 Wage comparison—A selectivity bias. *J. Pol. Econ.* 82(6): 1119–43

Hause J 1974 The risk element in occupation and educational choices: Comment. *J. Pol. Econ.* 82(4): 803–7

Hauser R, Mossel P 1985 Fraternal resemblance in educational attainment and occupational status. *Am. J. Sociol.* 91(3): 650–73

Heckman J 1974 Shadow prices, market wages, and labor supply. *Econometrica* 42(4): 679–94

Jencks C S et al 1972 *Inequality: A Reassessment of the Effect of Family and Schooling in America.* Basic Books, New York

Lucas R E B 1977 Hedonic wage equations and psychic wages in the returns of schooling. *Am. Econ. Rev.* 67(4): 549–58

Mincer J 1974 *Schooling Experience and Earnings.* National Bureau of Economic Research, New York

Olneck M 1977 On the use of sibling data to estimate the effects of family background, cognitive skills, and schooling: Research from the Kalamazoo brothers study. In: Taubman P (ed.) 1977 *Kinometrics: Determinants of Socioeconomic Success Within and Between Families.* North-Holland, Amsterdam

Orazen P, Matilla J 1986 Occupational entry and uncertainty: Males leaving high school. *Rev. Econ. Stat.* 68(2): 265–73

Polachek S 1981 Occupational self-selection: A human capital approach to sex differences in occupational structure. *Rev. Econ. Stat.* 58(1): 60–69

Scarr S, Weinberg R 1977 The influence of "family background" on intellectual attainment: The unique contribution of adoptive studies to estimating environmental effects. Yale University, New Haven, Connecticut, Minnesota (mimeo)

Taubman P 1975 *Sources of Inequality in Earnings: Personal Skills, Random Events, Preferences towards Risk, and other Occupational Characteristics.* North-Holland, Amsterdam

Taubman P 1989 Role of parental income in educational attainment. *Am. Econ. Rev.* 79(2): 57–61

Thaler R, Rosen S 1975 The value of saving a life: Evidence from the labor market. In: Terleckyj N (ed.) 1975 *Household Production and Consumption.* National Bureau of Economic Research, Cambridge, Massachusetts

Topel R 1984 Equilibrium earnings, turnover and unemployment: New evidence. *J. Labor. Econ.* 2(4): 500–22

Tuijnman A 1989 *Recurrent Education, Earnings, and Well-being: A Fifty-Year Longitudinal Study of a Cohort of Swedish Men.* Almqvist and Wiksell, Stockholm

Viscusi W 1978 Wealth effects and earnings premiums for job hazards. *Rev. Econ. Stat.* 60(4): 408–16

Weiss Y 1972 The risk element in occupational and educational choices. *J. Pol. Econ.* 80(6): 1203–13

SECTION VI

The Production of Education

Introduction

M. Carnoy

Some of the most interesting departures from earlier economics of education approaches are in the way economists study the production of education.

Once sociologist James Coleman attempted to explain the variation in school achievement in the mid-1960s, economists jumped on the bandwagon and applied neoclassical theories of the firm to try to extend and improve on Coleman's results. The analysis has flourished to this day, and has been applied to educational systems in developed and developing countries, as Eric Hanushek shows in his lead entry in this section. Hanushek makes a good case that explaining the variation of school output with production function techniques does yield insights into the predicted effect on individual pupil performance of teacher characteristics (such as preservice preparation, in-service preparation, and experience) and physical educational inputs, such as books and laboratory equipment. Further, estimates of school production functions in resource-poor developing countries were successful in focusing attention on the particular effectiveness of nonteacher inputs and additional school time.

But despite these insights, standard production function analyses failed to yield consistent and meaningful explanations of the variation in pupil achievement in school or other measures of school quality, especially when these were measured in "value added" terms. This led many economists to criticize the approach. Further, as Henry Levin and Martin Carnoy suggest in their entries, production function analysis applied to schools as firms has been marked by severe theoretical problems. In using such functions, economists seem to feel no need to reveal any theory of learning underlying their function specification, nor to make clear what the decision-making unit is in school production. Is it the classroom, headed by a classroom teacher, the school, headed by a principal, the school district, the parents/family, or the pupil? Different units may have decision power over different aspects of the schooling process. Third, as economists changed their approaches to understanding firms' production processes in the private real goods

and services sector, the new approaches yielded insights into the way economists could explain school production. Specifically, organization and agency theories as applied to private firms put more emphasis on manager–employee relations, which appeared more relevant to the analysis of educational services delivery than traditional production function assumptions.

Furthermore, as David Monk shows in his contribution, alternative approaches to educational production that use microeconomic principles such as substitutability of inputs and the law of diminishing marginal productivity to derive insights into educational phenomena and decision-making within educational systems suggest that many of the policy conclusions that emerge from more traditional estimates would not hold were resource allocations in schools actually changed.

The limitations of production function estimates become obvious when these other approaches are used. Levin argues in his entry on educational improvement that effective school studies have shown that schools producing higher achievement for pupils of similar socio-economic backgrounds did so largely because the teachers had a clear vision of what they wanted to accomplish, had high standards for pupil achievement, developed a supportive atmosphere in the school, and applied effective teaching techniques to develop student learning. None of these variables have ever been included in typical input–output school production functions.

Further, as Carnoy points out in his two entries, the production of schooling is complicated by the fact that it is carried out in a political environment where academic achievement is only one of many outputs expected by the multilevel constituency which schools serve. Schooling is also produced in "series" between family and school, since the child is "educated" wholly in the family until entering preschool or kindergarten, and then in "parallel" between family and school as the family interacts with the school to help (or hinder) pupils in their acquiring cognitive and affective skills. Economists have long recognized this complex relationship, but at best only modeled the "series" part. So economists (and others) have never developed a clear understanding of how school inputs and processes relate to the family education environment or to other groups putting pressure on schools to produce employment and socialization outcomes desired by families and community. School personnel should have the most concrete understanding of their teaching techniques to family and the community environment, but it turns out that schools vary enormously in their ability to coordinate parental and community involvement with school achievement goals. Nor do central educational decision-making organizations, schools, or teachers do very well in fitting their teaching techniques to family and community environmental conditions in order to maximize pupil performance. Indeed, the opposite may very well be the case, where schools force teaching–learning models into environmental modes in ways that almost guarantee poor pupil performance. There is even some evidence that unless other "process" conditions prevail, both in the school and in the relationship between parents and teachers, raising the quality of teacher preparation alone does not produce higher achievement among low-income pupils.

In many countries of the world, however, important as process variables are, most schools have very poorly prepared school personnel, pupils and teachers meet a relatively short number of hours per day and days per year, and there are almost no school books and other materials available to students to follow the lessons and to work at home after school. Books are scarce, pupils sit on the dirt floor or at crowded, rudimentary desks, and rote learning predominates. Under such conditions, the main sources of improved school achievement would almost certainly come from more teacher training, more books, more relevant, child- and community-centered curriculum, and more time on task. Yet, even in those primitive circumstances, better managed schools, including greater teacher participation and commitment, seem to make a great difference in pupil performance.

In this section, these issues are covered "in the large" by the three introductory entries and then in detail by a series of entries that cover critical subissues of educational production, including the role of education in the home (Carnoy), time in learning (Millot), and classroom conditions (Monk). The largest of these

subissues is the supply of teacher skills and how teachers participate in the enterprise of schooling. Teachers are tenured and unionized in almost every country of the world. Since the traditional means of extracting effort from employees through threat of firing is effectively absent in the public school setting (although teacher control through school inspectors is widely used to insure teacher conformity to behavioral rules), training teachers to be effective, organizing them to exert effort voluntarily, and working with teacher organizations to produce higher quality education is a crucial task of the public educational enterprise. These issues are discussed in the entries by Murnane, Ebert and Stone, Brown, and Wagner.

The alternative to public school, of course, is to privatize education and have education production ruled by market mechanisms. Levin discusses this alternative and its consequences for educational production. A private market for teachers would tend to undermine union influence in schools, and could well lower teacher salaries, particularly in schools that serve lower-income populations (unless compensatory public finance mechanisms allocated higher educational vouchers to low-income families and public regulation prevented schools in high income areas from collecting additional tuition). However, whether putting schools into the marketplace would improve school outcomes is highly controversial. For example, private management may not be any more likely to organize teachers to produce more learning either for those students now served reasonably well by public schools or those disadvantaged students now not doing well in school and too high cost for privately-run schools to handle.

Alternatives within the current educational delivery framework exist as well: early preparation for schooling through high quality day care (Strober) and preschool education (Barnett), bringing the workplace more effectively into public secondary schools through improved school-to-work transition, such as school enterprises (Stern), and developing much greater consciousness regarding the underlying reasons for school dropouts (Kelly).

The debate between those who believe in developing such "public" alternatives and those who feel that the public system can never deliver schooling as effectively as the private market will certainly dominate the educational production debate for many years to come.

Education Production Functions

E. A. Hanushek

Although research into the determinants of students' achievement takes various approaches, one of the most appealing and useful is what economists call the "production function" approach. (In other disciplines it is known as the input-output or cost-quality approach.) In this, attention is focused primarily on the relationship between school outcomes and measurable inputs into the educational process. If the production function for schools were known, it would then be possible to predict what would happen if resources were added or subtracted, and to analyze what actions should be taken if the prices of various inputs were to change. The problem is that the production function for education is unknown and must be inferred from data on students and their schools.

1. The Coleman Report and its Influence

The origin of estimating input–output relations in schools is usually traced to the monumental United States study *Equality of Educational Opportunity* (commonly known as the Coleman Report—Coleman et al. 1966). Designed explicitly to study equity, this report was the United States Office of Education's response to a requirement of the Civil Rights Act of 1964, namely to investigate the extent of inequality (by race, religion, or national origin) in the nation's schools. The study's fundamental contribution was to direct attention to the distribution of student performance—the outputs under consideration in this entry. Instead of addressing questions of inequality simply by producing an inventory of differences among schools and teachers by race and region of the country, the Coleman Report sought to explain those differences; it delved into the relationship between inputs and outputs of schools.

The Coleman Report was widely interpreted as finding that schools have little importance in determining student achievement. Families and, to a lesser extent, peers were seen to be the primary determinants of variations in performance. The findings were clearly controversial (see critiques by Bowles and Levin 1968 and Hanushek and Kain 1972) and immediately led to an extensive research effort to compile additional evidence about the relationship between school resources and school performance. As described below, the common interpretation of the Coleman Report in fact results from a misinterpretation of the statistical findings.

The underlying model guiding the Coleman Report and most subsequent studies is straightforward. It postulates that the output of the educational process—that is, the achievement of individual students—is directly related to a series of inputs. Policymakers directly control some of these inputs; for instance, the characteristics of schools, teachers, and curricula. Other inputs—those of families and friends plus the innate endowments or learning capacities of the students—generally cannot be affected by public policy. Further, although achievement is usually measured at discrete points in time, the educational process is cumulative; past inputs affect students' current levels of achievement.

Starting with this model, statistical techniques, typically some form of regression analysis, are employed to identify the specific determinants of achievement and to make inferences about the relative importance of the various inputs into student performance. The accuracy of the analysis and the confidence the answers warrant depend crucially on a variety of issues regarding measurement and technical estimation. This summary sets aside these issues (see Hanushek 1979, 1981, 1986). Instead it highlights the overall findings and the major unanswered questions from this research.

Most studies of educational production relationships measure output by students' scores on standardized achievement tests, although significant numbers have used other quantitative measures, such as student attitudes, school attendance rates, and college continuation or dropout rates. The general interpretation is that they are all plausible indicators of future success in the labor market.

The reason for concentrating on achievement for students in school is straightforward. The policy question centers on how different teachers and school resources affect student performance. It would be generally impractical to have to wait a decade or two after observing educational inputs to measure any subsequent outcomes that will be related to those inputs. Data and analytical necessities dictate concentration on immediate measures of student performance such as test scores. Other research, however, indicates that these in-school measures are related to subsequent performance in the labor market and that they are thus reasonable proxies of economically pertinent skills.

Test measures have been included in standard models that explain earnings differences in the population. Studies of adult earnings in developed countries typically show significant direct effects of achievement. These come, however, in statistical models that also include years of schooling, and test achievement is an important determinant of continuation in schooling, implying an important additional indirect effect. The

277

evidence on returns to different measured skills has tended to be stronger in developing countries (see review in Harbison and Hanushek 1992). Second, studies have found direct links with productivity, particularly in agriculture (Welch 1970, Jamison and Lau 1982). In short, there is reasonably broad support for the notion that school quality as measured during schooling is directly related to productivity and earnings when students enter the labor force. Thus, although most attention is focused on the ability of schools to raise students' academic performance, there is reason to interpret this in the broader context of increasing economic performance of the students and of the overall economies.

Empirical specifications of production functions have varied widely in details, but they have also had much in common. Family inputs tend to be measured by sociodemographic characteristics of families, such as parental education, income, and family size. Peer inputs, when included, are typically aggregate summaries of the sociodemographic characteristics of other students in the school. School inputs include measures of the teachers' characteristics (education level, experience, sex, race, and so forth), of the schools' organization (class sizes, facilities, administrative expenditures, and so forth), and of district or community factors (e.g., average expenditure levels). Except for the original Coleman Report, most empirical work has relied on data, such as the normal administrative records of schools, that were constructed for other purposes.

2. Schools, Expenditures, and Achievement in the United States

The production function approach has been employed broadly to investigate the effect on school performance of the core factors that determine expenditure on education. Instructional expenditures make up about two-thirds of total school expenditures in the United States. Instructional expenditures are, in turn, determined mostly by teacher salaries and class sizes. Finally, in most United States school districts, teacher salaries are directly related to the years of teaching experience and the educational level of the teacher. Thus, the basic determinants of instructional expenditures in a district are teacher experience, teacher education, and class size. Most studies, regardless of what other school characteristics might be included, analyze the effect of these factors on outcomes. (These are also the factors most likely to be found in any given data set, especially if the data come from standard administrative records.)

Because the analyses have such common specifications, the effects of the expenditure parameters can easily be tabulated. An exhaustive search through 1988 publications uncovered 187 separate qualified studies found in 38 separate published articles or books. (Qualified studies satisfy certain minimal quality standards—being published in a book or journal, providing direct information about the effects of school resources on student performance, and providing information about the statistical significance of any findings.) These studies, while restricted to public schools, cover all regions of the United States, different grade levels, different measures of performance, and different analytical and statistical approaches. About one-third draw their data from a single school district, while the remaining two-thirds compare school performance across multiple districts. A majority of the studies (104) use individual students as the unit of analysis; the remainder rely upon aggregate school, district, or state level data. The studies are split about evenly between primary schooling (Grades 1–6) and secondary schooling (Grades 7–12). Over 70 percent of the studies measure school performance by some kind of standardized test. However, those that use nontest measures (such as dropout rates, college continuation, attitudes, or performance after school) are for obvious reasons concentrated in studies of secondary schooling. There is no indication that differences in sample and study design lead to differences in conclusions.

Table 1 summarizes the expenditure components of the 187 studies (Hanushek 1989). Since not all studies include each of the expenditure parameters, the first column in the table presents the total number of studies for which an input can be tabulated. For example, 152 studies provide information about the relationship between the teacher–pupil ratio and student performance. The available studies all provide regression estimates of the partial effect of given inputs, holding constant family background and other inputs. These estimated coefficients have been tabulated according to two pieces of information: the sign and the statistical significance (5 percent level) of the estimated relationship. Statistical significance is included to indicate confidence that any estimated relationship is real and not just an artifact of the sample of data employed.

According to both conventional wisdom and generally observed school policies, each tabulated factor should have a positive effect on student achievement. More education and more experience on the part of the teacher cost more and are presumed to improve individual student learning; smaller classes (more teachers per student) are also expected to be beneficial. More spending in general, higher teacher salaries, better facilities and better administration should also lead to better student performance. The quantitative magnitudes of estimated relationships are ignored here; only the direction of any effect is analyzed.

Of the 152 estimates of the effects of class size, only 27 are statistically significant. Of these, only 14 show a statistically significant positive relationship, whereas 13 display a negative relationship. An additional

Table 1
Summary of estimated expenditure parameter coefficients from 187 studies of educational production functions: United States

Input	Number of studies	Statistically significant			Statistically insignificant			Unknown sign
		Total	+	−	Total	+	−	
Teacher–pupil ratio	152	27	14	13	125	34	46	45
Teacher education	113	13	8	5	100	31	32	37
Teacher experience	140	50	40	10	90	44	31	15
Teacher salary	69	15	11	4	54	16	14	24
Expenditures/pupil	65	16	13	3	49	25	13	11
Administration	61	8	7	1	53	14	15	24
Facilities	74	12	7	5	62	17	14	31

Source: Hanushek 1989

25 estimates show that class size is not significant at the 5 percent level. Nor does ignoring statistical significance help to confirm the benefits of small classes. By a margin of 46 to 36 the insignificant coefficients are negative, the wrong sign according to conventional wisdom.

The entries for teacher education tell a similar story. The statistically significant results are split between positive and negative relationships, and in a vast majority of cases (100 out of 113) the estimated coefficients are statistically insignificant. Forgetting about statistical significance and looking just at estimated signs again does not make a case for the importance of added schooling for teachers.

Teacher experience is possibly different. A clear majority of estimated coefficients point in the expected direction, and about 29 percent of the estimated coefficients are both statistically significant and of the conventionally expected sign. These results, however, are hardly overwhelming; they only appear strong relative to the other school inputs. Moreover, they are subject to interpretative questions. Specifically, these positive correlations may result from senior teachers having the ability to locate themselves in schools and classrooms with good students. In other words, causation may run from achievement to experience and not the other way around.

Overall, the results are startlingly consistent. No compelling evidence emerges that teacher–pupil ratios, teacher education, or teacher experience have the expected positive effects on student achievement. It cannot be stated with confidence that hiring teachers with more education or having smaller classes will improve student performance. Teacher experience appears only marginally stronger in its relationship.

The remaining rows of Table 1 summarize information on other expenditure components, including administration, facilities, teacher salaries, and total expenditure per student. The quality of administration is measured in a wide variety of ways, ranging from

characteristics of the principal to expenditure per pupil on noninstructional items. Similarly, the quality of facilities is identified through both spending and many specific physical characteristics. The absence of a strong relationship between these two components and performance may result in part from variations in how these factors are measured. If only because of the preponderance of positive signs among the significant coefficients, administration appears marginally stronger in its relationship than facilities. Nevertheless, the available evidence on both again fails to support convincingly the conventional wisdom.

Finally, explicit measures of teacher salaries and expenditure per student are tabulated. These measures are less frequently available and are more difficult to interpret because they are included along with their underlying determinants. Nevertheless, it is not surprising that they do not suggest that they have a potentially important role in determining achievement. After all, the underlying components of this expenditure were themselves unrelated to achievement.

The research reveals no strong or systematic relationship between school expenditures and student performance. This is the case both when expenditure is decomposed into underlying determinants and when it is considered in the aggregate.

3. Other Inputs into Education–United States Studies

Since the publication of the Coleman Report, intense debate has surrounded the fundamental question of whether schools and teachers are important to the educational performance of students. That report has been commonly interpreted as finding that variations in school resources explain only a negligible portion of the variation in students' achievement.

A number of studies provide direct analyses of this

overall question of differential effectiveness of teachers and schools (Hanushek 1971, 1992; Murnane 1975; Armor et al. 1976; Murnane and Phillips 1981). They do this by estimating differences in the average performance of each teacher's (or school's) students after allowing for differences in family backgrounds and initial achievement scores. The findings are unequivocal: teachers and schools differ dramatically in their effectiveness. The formal statistical tests employed in these studies confirm that there are striking differences in average gain in student achievement across teachers. The faulty impressions left by the Coleman Report and by a number of subsequent studies about the importance of teachers have resulted primarily from a confusion between the measures of effectiveness and true effectiveness itself.

These production function analyses have also investigated a wide variety of other school and nonschool factors. Although it is difficult to be specific in any summary of other factors because the specifications are quite idiosyncratic, three generalizations are possible. First, family background is clearly very important in explaining differences in achievement. Second, while considerable attention has been given to the characteristics of peers or other students within schools, the findings are ambiguous. Finally, studies have examined many additional measures of the effects of schools, teachers, curricula, and, especially, instructional methods on achievement, but few consistent results have emerged.

4. Schooling in Developing Countries

Research on school achievement in developing countries is less extensive, less rigorous, and more difficult to interpret than that for the United States. Nevertheless, some conclusions can be drawn from school operations in developing countries from such research.

Dissimilar findings about the determinants of school performance in developing countries, as contrasted with developed countries, might be expected. The dramatic differences in the level of educational support provided by families and schools imply that the educational production process could be very different in developed and developing countries. In particular, while the effect of marginal resources on achievement may be hard to discern when average school expenditure in the United States is US$6,000 per year per pupil, they might be much larger and more noticeable when expenditure is one tenth or one hundredth that level.

At the same time, the standards of data collection and analysis are so variable that the results from this work tend to be uncertain. Much of the analysis of input–output relationships for developing countries is not published in standard academic journals, and thus it does not have that basic level of quality control. Even more important, the data for many of these studies do not come from regular collection schemes, are difficult to check for quality, and miss key elements of the educational process.

Different researchers have attempted to summarize key aspects of these studies, frequently providing qualitative discussions of the analyses, their results, and their interpretation. Here, however, an overall quantitative summary of the available analyses will be presented, which parallels that for the United States studies. The starting point is the comprehensive review of studies by Fuller (1985). This is supplemented by additional studies that have appeared since that review or were omitted from it. There are limitations, however. Because this discussion and analysis relies chiefly on secondary materials, the reporting of results has to be accepted. Consequently, the results cannot be presented in the same depth as those for the United States. Additionally, there is virtually no control over the selection of papers (i.e., according to explicit minimal quality standards) or over the interpretation of the statistical results.

Table 2
Summary of estimated expenditure parameter coefficients from 96 studies of educational production functions: developing countries

Input	Number of studies	Statistically significant +	Statistically significant −	Statistically insignificant
Teacher–pupil ratio	30	8	8	14
Teacher education	63	35	2	26
Teacher experience	46	16	2	28
Teacher salary	13	4	2	7
Expenditures/pupil	12	6	0	6
Facilities	34	22	3	9

Source: Harbison and Hanushek 1992

A total of 96 underlying studies form the basis for the analysis (about half the number utilized in the United States analysis). Table 2 divides the available studies into statistically significant (by sign) and statistically insignificant. (The insignificant findings, unfortunately, cannot be divided by direction of effect.) The table is laid out similarly to that for the United States studies. It begins with the characteristics directly related to instructional expenditure per student and then treats other attributes of schools.

The studies differ from the United States studies in terms of the overall significance of the estimated school effects. Simply put, compared with the results presented in Table 1, a higher proportion of the tabulated coefficients for the 96 studies in developing countries is statistically significant. (It must be emphasized, however, that the proportion of results that are "correct"—statistically significant by conventional standards and in the right direction—never reaches two-thirds; moreover, the general conclusion of no strong evidence of a systematic relationship between these factors and performance will not change.) The relative robustness in statistical findings could reflect analysis of settings where there is either greater variation in the tabulated educational inputs or greater sensitivity to these inputs by students. Alternatively, the differences could reflect attributes and, specifically, biases of the analyses themselves.

The evidence in Table 2 from developing countries provides no support for policies of reducing class sizes. Of the 30 studies investigating teacher–pupil ratios, only eight find statistically significant results supporting smaller classes; an equal number are significant but have the opposite sign; and almost half are statistically insignificant. These findings are particularly interesting because class sizes in the studies of developing countries are considerably more varied than those in the United States studies and thus pertain to a wider set of environments.

The analysis of the effect of teacher experience yields results that are roughly similar to those in the United States studies. Although 35 percent of the studies display significant positive benefits from more teaching experience (the analogous figure for United States studies is 29 percent), the majority of the estimated coefficients still are statistically insignificant. The primary difference between the two sets of tabulations arises from the relative support implied for the different school inputs. The United States studies are the most supportive of the conventional wisdom regarding the effects of teacher experience on performance. Similar support compared to other factors is not found in developing country studies.

The results for teacher education, on the other hand, diverge in relative terms from those seen for the United States. A majority of the studies (35 out of 63) support the conventional notion that providing more education for teachers is valuable. In the United States

studies, teacher education provided the least support of all the inputs for the conventional wisdom. Although still surrounded by considerable uncertainty (since 26 estimates are insignificant and 2 display significantly negative effects), these noticeably stronger results in developing countries clearly suggest a possible differentiation by stage of development and general level of resources available.

The teacher salary findings in developing countries contain no compelling support for the notion that better teachers are systematically paid more. Since the studies aggregate findings across very different countries, school organizations, and labor markets, however, it is difficult to take these results too far. For policy purposes, it would be desirable to seek information on what happens if the entire salary schedule is altered (as opposed to simply moving along a given schedule denominated, say, in experience, education, or other attributes of teachers). It is impossible to distinguish, however, between studies reflecting differences in schedules and those reflecting movements along a schedule.

Data for total expenditure per pupil are rarely available in analyses of education in developing countries. The 12 studies in which estimates can be found are evenly split between statistically significant and statistically insignificant. Given questions about the quality of the underlying data, not too much should be inferred from the findings for direct expenditure measures.

One of the clearest divergences between the two sets of findings is for facilities, again suggesting that differences in school environments are of some importance. The measures of facilities in developing countries (which incorporate a wide range of actual variables in specific studies) indicate more likely effects on student performance than found in United States studies. Some 22 of the 34 investigations demonstrate support for the provision of quality buildings and libraries.

In summary, the results of studies in developing countries do not make a compelling case for specific input policies. They do, however, indicate that direct school resources might be important in developing countries. Nevertheless, as in the United States research, the estimated models of educational performance undoubtedly fail to capture many of the truly important inputs to the educational process.

5. Other Factors—Developing Countries

As with the United States studies, a variety of other factors has been investigated in the course of the analyses of developing countries, including an assortment of curriculum issues, instructional methods, and teacher training programs. Many of these are difficult to assess (at least in a quantitative, comparative way) given the evidence from many countries and the probable importance of local institutions.

One intervention that has widespread endorsement, although as much for conceptual reasons as for solid empirical ones, is the provision of textbooks. The relationship of textbooks and writing materials to student performance is found with reasonable consistency to be important in developing countries, but there are relatively few studies of this (see Lockheed and Hanushek 1988, Lockheed and Verspoor 1989).

Investigations of technological or organizational differences have led to mixed results. Because of scattered settlement in many rural areas, several approaches to "distance education" have been investigated. In three extensive investigations (Nicaragua, Kenya, and Thailand), the use of interactive radio has proved effective (Lockheed and Hanushek 1988). However, this conclusion should not be generalized to all possible uses of new technology. In particular, there is little evidence at this time that the widespread introduction of computers is sensible (Lockheed and Verspoor 1989).

6. Conclusion—Implications for Policy

Somewhat surprisingly, perhaps, the available research from both developed and developing countries leads to many of the same conclusions. Two potential policy conclusions spring immediately from the overall results. First, since within the current institutional structure expenditures are not systematically related to performance, policies should not be dictated simply on the basis of expenditure. Second, since common surrogates for teacher and school quality—class size, teachers' education, and teachers' experience being among the most important—are not systematically related to performance, policies should not be dictated simply on the basis of such surrogates.

Moreover, these results strongly suggest that policies based solely on inputs—such as general reductions in class size or uniform increases in spending—are unlikely to be successful. This underscores the importance of moving toward policies based on performance; that is, output-based policies. Such policies would emphasize the importance of performance incentives (see, e.g., Chubb and Hanushek 1990).

See also: Economics of Educational Time and Learning; Political Economy of Educational Production; Joint Production of Education; Microeconomics of School Production; Cost-Benefits Analysis

References

Armor D et al. 1976 *Analysis of the School Preferred Reading Program in Selected Los Angeles Minority Schools.* R-2007-LAUSD, Rand Corporation, Santa Monica, California

Bowles S, Levin H M 1968 The determinants of scholastic achievement: An appraisal of some recent evidence. *J. Hum. Resources* 3(1): 3-24

Chubb J E, Hanushek E A 1990 Reforming educational reform. In: Aaron H J (ed.) 1990 *Setting National Priorities: Policy for the Nineties.* Brookings Institution, Washington, DC

Coleman J S et al. 1966 *Equality of Educational Opportunity* US Government Printing Office, Washington, DC

Fuller B 1985 *Raising School Quality in Developing Countries: What Investments Boost Learning?* Report No. EDT7, Education and Training Series, World Bank Washington, DC

Hanushek E A 1971 Teacher characteristics and gains in student achievement: Estimation using micro-data. *Am. Econ. Rev.* 61(2): 280-88

Hanushek E A 1979 Conceptual and empirical issues in the estimation of educational production functions. *J. Hum. Resources* 14(3): 351-88

Hanushek E A 1981 Throwing money at schools. *Journal of Policy Analysis and Management* 1(1): 19-41

Hanushek E A 1986 The economics of schooling: Production and efficiency in public schools. *J. Econ. Lit.* 24: 1141-77

Hanushek E A 1989 The impact of differential expenditures on school performance. *Educ. Res.* 18(4): 45–51

Hanushek E A 1992 The trade-off between child quantity and quality. *J. Pol. Econ.* 100(1): 84–117

Hanushek E A, Kain J F 1972 On the value of "equality of educational opportunity" as a guide to public policy. In: Mosteller F, Moynihan D P (eds.) 1972 *On Equality of Educational Opportunity.* Random House, New York

Harbison R W, Hanushek E A 1992 *Educational Performance of the Poor: Lessons from Rural Northeast Brazil.* Oxford University Press, New York

Jamison D, Lau L 1982 *Farmer Education and Farm Efficiency.* Johns Hopkins University Press, Baltimore Maryland

Lockheed M E, Verspoor A 1989 *Improving Primary Education in Developing Countries: A Review of Policy Options.* World Bank, Washington, DC

Lockheed M E, Hanushek E A 1988 Improving Educational efficiency in developing countries: What do we know? *Compare* 18(1): 21–38

Murnane R J 1975 *Impact of School Resources on the Learning of Inner City Children.* Ballinger, Cambridge, Massachusetts

Murnane R J, Philips B 1981 What do effective teachers of inner-city children have in common? *Social Science Research* 10(1): 83–100

Welch F 1970 Education in production. *J. Pol. Econ.* 78(1): 35–59

Raising Educational Productivity

H. M. Levin

This entry provides a survey of studies of educational production with emphasis on raising educational productivity. The educational sector draws upon a prodigious share of national, regional, and local resources. Industrialized countries typically allocate 6 percent or more of their national income to the provision of formal education. In countries such as the United States this figure amounted to over US$460 billion in 1992–93, almost 8 percent of gross domestic product, not including the foregone income of students. Schools require substantial facilities, large numbers of talented personnel, materials, equipment, and the considerable time of students that—at least for older students— could be devoted to productive work in the labor force. Also, education must compete for resources with other demands such as health, transportation, defense, the environment, and so on, typically under conditions of severe economic pressure.

A central question is one of educational productivity. Are these resources being used efficiently to produce education? Can one obtain greater educational results by using a different set of resources or using the present set in a different way? Even small gains in efficiency, on the order of 1–2 percent, can release prodigious resources which can reduce educational costs or be used to improve education. In the United States such gains would amount to billions of dollars. However, in order to begin to answer these questions, one must have information on the productivity of existing educational operations as well as insights on how to improve them. Thus, it is not surprising that economists and other social scientists have attempted to use their research tools to answer these questions. In what follows, a brief picture will be provided of these types of studies and their conclusions.

1. Educational Production Functions

The earliest attempts to understand educational production were based upon attempts to estimate educational production functions. These have their analogy with industry production functions which have a long history in economic research. Any particular firm in an industry produces an output which is a product or service. To produce this output, it uses inputs such as labor and capital which are transformed according to the existing technology into goods and services. To maximize profits, firms must use their resources efficiently and purchase inputs in the appropriate combinations relative to their costs and productivities in producing outputs. Using these concepts, economists

have engaged in studies to estimate the characteristics of production functions for different goods and services (Shephard 1970).

Schools also produce educational outputs in the form of student achievement and other valued results. To do this they use facilities, equipment, teachers, support personnel, supervisors, and administrators. Thus, there is an obvious analogy between attempts to estimate industry production functions and the possibility of estimating educational production functions. What are the relative productivities of different inputs relative to their costs in producing educational outcomes. The educational production function is a statistical relation between inputs and outputs. A general formulation is as follows (see Hanushek 1986):

$$A_t = f (F_t, T_t, OS_t) \qquad (1)$$

A_t represents the achievement of a student at period t; F_t represents the family inputs of students cumulative to t that affect achievement including such indicators as parental education, income, race, and language spoken in the home; T_t represents teacher inputs for a student, cumulative to t including teacher qualifications; and OS_t represents other school inputs including class size, materials, curriculum, and so on.

This function is estimated statistically using a multivariate regression model where multiple measures of each input are obtained. The most common measures of family input are race and socioeconomic status as reflected in parental income and education. The most common measures of teacher inputs include their licensing credentials, teaching experience, and education in terms of degrees completed. Other inputs typically include class size and facilities such as library books and laboratories. Although production functions do not normally include teachers' salaries or expenditures per student, sometimes these measures are substituted for the inputs that they purchase.

1.1 Research Results

The earliest forms of the educational production function are found in the Coleman Report, published in the mid-1960s (Coleman et al. 1966). This government study collected achievement data and school inputs for over 700,000 students in the United States and estimated statistical relationships that reflect the production function concept. The study found that family background characteristics seemed to predict student achievement more fully than teacher and other school characteristics. However, the statistical analysis was critiqued by others who argued that the techniques of the report could not adequately separate the impact of different inputs (Bowles and Levin 1968). Further studies using the data generated by this report found somewhat more evidence of school effects and particularly the apparent impact of teacher verbal skills as measured by a short vocabulary test taken by the teachers (Hanushek 1972).

Over time, many other educational production function studies were carried out using data from local school districts or states. These were summarized first by Bridge et al. (1979) for the United States and later by Hanushek (1986); a good summary is also found in Cohn and Geske (1990).Such studies have also been carried out for other societies, especially developing ones (Fuller and Clark 1994). The most influential summary was that of Hanushek (1986) which reviewed the educational production methodology and attempted to summarize the results for over 100 studies. Hanushek found that the pattern of effects of different inputs were inconsistent from study to study. He concluded that the typical input policies used by schools to improve student achievement (e.g., reducing class size, obtaining more experienced teachers or ones with higher educational qualifications, raising teachers' salaries, and raising per pupil expenditures) did not show a consistent relation to student achievement. This publication and subsequent summaries such as Hanushek (1989) gained wide publicity and created widespread skepticism among educational policymakers that education could be improved with greater spending.

However, a more recent reassessment using the statistical technique of meta-analysis was applied to the same studies used in the Hanushek analysis (Hedges et al. 1994). This reanalysis found that, contrary to Hanushek's findings, the traditional input strategies showed the pattern of expected relationships with student achievement with a particularly large impact for per-pupil expenditures. A 10 percent rise in per-pupil expenditures was associated—across studies—with about two-thirds of a standard deviation increase in achievement, a gain in achievement equal to about seven months of schooling at the elementary level. This is equivalent to raising achievement scores from the 50th percentile to almost the 76th percentile. Since Hedges and his colleagues used a more sophisticated analysis of the same body of studies used by Hanushek, it appears that standard inputs do make more of a difference in student achievement than Hanushek asserted. However, as will be seen in later studies, there is still room for increased efficiency in how schools use those inputs.

1.2 Cost-effectiveness

In general, the educational production literature has found that teacher experience, qualifications, and class size can be statistically related to achievement, although not always. Further, teacher education and teacher proficiency as measured by test scores on teacher examinations can also be important. However, such studies do not provide insights into which inputs represent more effective strategies for increasing achievement within a given budget constraint. In order to fulfill that goal, it is necessary to compare the costs and effectiveness of the different inputs or strategies.

An early study represented an attempt to use the results of production functions to compare the regression coefficients (marginal products or effects) of hiring more experienced teachers or teachers with higher verbal achievement relative to the costs of these strategies (Levin 1970). It found that hiring more verbally able teachers provided five to ten times as much increase in student achievement per unit cost as hiring more experienced teachers. A study for Tunisia found that hiring teachers with greater teaching experience was more cost-effective than hiring more teachers from France or increasing the proportion of boarding students (Carnoy et al. 1977). More recent cost-effectiveness studies have compared the impacts of reduced class size, computer-assisted instruction, peer tutoring, and a longer school day (Levin et al. 1987). Peer tutoring followed by computer-assisted instruction were found to be far more cost-effective in increasing student achievement in mathematics and reading at the elementary level than were reductions in class size and expansions in the length of the school day. However, there are still relatively few cost-effectiveness studies in education.

1.3 Frontier Production Functions

A further refinement of the educational production function has been the search for frontier production functions. The typical production function represents a statistical fit between inputs and output among a sample or population of schools. In this sense, the educational production relation that is estimated is an "average" among a sample of schools with different levels of productive efficiency rather than among efficient schools. But, if the educational production function is to reflect the maximum output that can be produced with each and every combination of inputs, it should be fitted only to those schools that are maximally efficient, that is, operating at the production frontier. Instead of using a statistical procedure to estimate the equation, the frontier function requires the use of mathematical programming or data envelopment analysis which fits only the extremes.

The earliest application of this technique to education found that the marginal products of the different input variables differed considerably when one compared those at the frontier with those for the average statistical production function (Levin 1974, Levin 1976). Later work using the frontier approach to measure the relative efficiency of schools has found high variability in efficiency among samples of schools (Bessent et al. 1982, Grosskopf et al. 1992). But, one must be cautious in drawing policy conclusions from this work because the results are highly susceptible to measurement errors and other vagaries (Silkman 1986).

1.4 Difficulties in Interpretation

In addition to these issues, there are difficulties in interpreting educational production functions for policy purposes. The normal industry production function assumes that with a given technology the presence of a given set of inputs can produce a given output. Such an assumption is predicated upon the close monitoring of labor productivity through supervision and the ability to recontract with workers (e.g., Alchian and Demsetz 1972, Williamson 1975). In contrast, it is difficult to monitor the work of teachers, since most of it takes place behind closed doors; outputs are largely psychological, produced over the long term, and measurement is highly problematic; and teacher contracts are long-term and difficult to modify on an individual basis. Furthermore, teachers are not inert inputs into production and can use their de facto property rights over school resources in ways that may not support the objectives of the school. Therefore, school policies that attempt to control teacher activity are important mediating devices in transforming teacher inputs into specific educational outcomes, but these are almost never considered in educational production functions (Levin 1980). In addition, educational production functions are probably subject to management bias in which more efficient managers use more of some inputs than others. Although it may appear that certain input combinations are more efficient statistically, they may simply be choices made by more efficient managers (Massell 1967). Using the same input combinations might not provide the same results with less efficient managers.

2. Effective Schools Methodology

Although the educational production function approach continues to be pursued, results since the 1960s have provided little consistency in findings. Family inputs are always important statistically in explaining student achievement, but there is wide variability from study to study in terms of which teacher and other school inputs are related to achievement. As was noted above, one explanation is that inputs in a complex production organization such as a school that produces psychological outputs through a largely psychological transformation process can never be converted routinely and that a variety of organizational characteristics determine their effectiveness (Levin 1980). Unfortunately, these characteristics vary considerably among schools and in ways that are not easily measured using the production function method. Thus, it is not surprising that alternative methods for understanding and improving educational production have been sought.

One of the most influential of these in both the United States and the United Kingdom has been the effective schools methodology. This approach grew out of a realization that schools with similar student populations were achieving very different results. The focus of the research was to compare the operations of effective schools with ineffective ones to understand the differences and employ that to improve school effectiveness. In general, this meant carrying out a statistical analysis of school achievement for schools with similar students to see which had achievement that was substantially higher or lower than the average achievement for the schools (Brookover and Lezotte 1979, Edmonds 1979, Rutter et al. 1979, Mortimore et al. 1979). High-achieving schools were compared with low-achieving schools to see how they differed. These differences were called "effective school correlates," and it was asserted that if ineffective schools could adopt these correlates they would become effective.

2.1 Effective Schools Research Results

In the United Kingdom, researchers studied a group of secondary schools and concluded that the following were correlates of effective schools: group management in the classroom, high expectations, positive teacher models, feedback on student performance, consistency of school values, and pupil acceptance of school norms (Rutter et al. 1979). A study of elementary schools by Mortimore et al. (1979) tended to overlap with these characteristics, but added a number of additional ones. Early studies in the United States by Edmonds (1979) focused on strong leadership of the principal, emphasis on mastery of basic skills, a clean and orderly school environment, high teacher expectations of student performance, and frequent assessments of student progress. In an influential article evaluating the earlier effective schools literature, Purkey and Smith (1983) identified a number of other organizational and process features. A study of effective schools case studies and research in developing countries found that such schools are characterized by a central philosophy and strategy; deep community involvement; responsibility for decisions or their consequences at the level of teachers, students, and parents rather than at centralized levels; a strategy of active learning in which students create and produce rather than memorize; a clear focus in terms of curriculum and goals; high teacher expectations; and adequate funding and other resources (Levin and Lockheed 1993).

2.2 Methodological Challenges

The effective school methodology has been heavily criticized on a number of counts. Typically, the test scores of students with similar socioeconomic backgrounds are compared among different schools. Schools with test scores that differ substantially from the expected values (e.g., one standard deviation above and below the mean) are identified. The high-achieving schools are compared with low-achieving schools to see how they differ. These differences are typically identified through surveys of school characteristics. Those characteristics that differentiate high-achieving from low-achieving schools are considered to be the correlates of effective schools. These correlates are then used to set up interventions that are designed to transform ineffective schools into effective ones.

Among the criticisms of the methodology are the following: The schools that are found to be effective are highly sensitive to which grade levels and subject areas are tested (e.g., Madaus et al. 1987, Reynolds 1982). Furthermore, the results differ from year to year, even for the same grade level. The correlates of effectiveness vary among studies, and there is little evidence that schools can be "taught" to be effective by receiving training in the correlates. Although about half of the schools in the United States had taken or were planning to take training in the effective schools correlates (US General Accounting Office 1989), a systematic search of sources on the subject was unsuccessful in finding evaluations documenting that ineffective schools had become effective as a result of the effective schools interventions (Felton 1990).

The result is that effective schools research has become less prominent, and the effective schools training has given way to a merger with total quality management (TQM) as a way of improving schools. TQM represents an attempt to apply the quality improvement techniques that statistical sampling expert Edward Deming made famous for improving performance in industry. The emphasis is on worker involvement in continuous improvement by providing a focus on client needs and on problem-solving on a regular basis to improve product quality. There is virtually no research that could be identified on the efficacy of this process to improving education, but there is a groundswell of involvement on the part of school personnel in attending workshops and reading materials on TQM.

3. Market and Public Choice Solutions

The lack of progress in using production function and effective school approaches to improve education in the 1970s and 1980s led to a new search for educational productivity solutions. A general departure was that of educational choice in order to get schools to compete for students and to tailor their offerings for particular student needs. This was less a research-based approach than a theoretical approach for improving public education. This perspective is premised on the view that if schools compete for students rather than requiring them to attend in their local neighborhoods and school districts, parents will seek the best education and schools for their students. The result will be that schools will become more client-oriented and will tailor their offerings to student needs and compete for students by trying to offer the best educational services consistent with their resources.

3.1 Choice Alternatives

The general movement towards educational choice has stimulated a large number of choice plans (Clune and Witte 1990). In some cases, magnet schools are designed to attract students with particular interests or learning needs. In other cases, parents are given the choice of any school within a district or a more restricted range of choices depending upon transportation provisions and the racial compositions of available schools. Yet in other cases, they are permitted to draw upon higher educational alternatives at the secondary level or to select a school district for their children beyond the borders of the one that they live in. The most ambitious approaches to choice are those that would create a market of educational alternatives in which private schools would be eligible for public subsidies.

Milton Friedman (1962) proposed such a plan in the early 1960s. Under his plan, students would be eligible for vouchers that could be used at any school that met minimal requirements in curriculum. Eligible schools would be able to redeem their vouchers with the state, and would have incentives to meet student needs by competing for their vouchers. Momentum for creating an educational market based upon vouchers was stimulated in the 1980s by research comparing the achievement in public and private schools.

3.2 Research Results

Coleman and Hoffer (1987) found that achievement for apparently comparable students (adjusting for race and social class) was higher in private high schools than in public ones. Their conclusions that private schools were more efficient than public schools were challenged with three arguments (Haertel et al. 1987, Witte 1992).

(a) It was asserted that children who go to private schools are more educationally oriented and come from more highly motivated families than children in public schools, even after adjusting for race and family income. The detractors were not convinced that private school advantages in achievement were due to school effects rather than selection effects.

(b) The above argument was strengthened by the very small difference in achievement between public and private schools, about 3–4 percentiles which could easily be accounted for by selection effects. Empirical studies suggest that such small differences in achievement are unlikely to have a strong impact on employment, earnings, or admission to a more selective university.

c) The interpretation was questioned by further analysis of the data. Bryk and Lee (1992) found that there were no obvious sectoral differences between public and private schools that could not be accounted for by differences in school practices in either sector. Thus, although differences in school operations in either sector had an apparent influence on student achievement, there was no difference between the two sectors beyond these practices. Thus, it was not surprising to find that more than 46 percent of public school students were performing above the average of private school students, even if private school achievement was slightly higher, on average, than that of public schools.

The argument has also been made that a large segment of private schools are less costly than public ones, even though the most elite segment of independent schools is considerably more expensive (Levin 1991a). But, the problem is that the comparisons are made between private school tuition and fees and public school expenditures rather than a careful accounting of total costs in the two sectors. Further, the output mix differs considerably with private schools less likely to provide expensive remedial, bilingual, and special educational services. Unfortunately, rigorous studies attempting to measure costs in a consistent manner and adjusting for different service mixes are nonexistent.

Research on the effects of educational choice approaches to schooling provide largely ambiguous results. Relatively few parents take advantage of such choices, unless they are required to send their child to a choice school. Moreover, the results have been ambiguous in terms of effects of choice on student achievement. However, a prominent publication by Chubb and Moe (1990) in combination with the earlier research on public–private differences did stimulate considerable political activity to create voucher arrangements for financing education in the United States. In several states, there were voter initiatives to get support for vouchers, but all were defeated soundly. However, the Wisconsin Legislature established such a plan for poor students in Milwaukee. After three years it appeared that students who took advantage of vouchers did not perform better academically than students in the Milwaukee Public School system and that only about half of the eligible places in private schools were actually used by students (Witte et al. 1993). On a more positive note, the parents and students expressed greater satisfaction with their schools than comparable respondents in the public school system.

4. Redesigning Public School Organization

Work in this area has begun to address the issue of educational productivity by pursuing a different strategy than earlier, the organizational transformation of

schools to make them more efficient, whether in the public or private sector. This work redesigns schools along the lines of productive firms, while taking account of the special nature of educational activities. It then proceeds to establish a process of change for schools that will incorporate the new design. The goal is to identify features of efficient production organizations outside of the educational arena and to make those features integral to the design and operations of schools.

4.1 Organizational Conditions for Efficiency

Economic analysis suggests that efficient firms must meet the following conditions (more detail is found in Levin 1994):

(a) a clear objective function with measurable outcomes;

(b) incentives that are linked to success on the objective function;

(c) efficient access to useful information for decisions;

(d) adaptability to meet changing conditions;

(e) use of the most productive technology consistent with cost constraints.

4.1.1 Objective Function. Every efficient firm must be clear about what it is attempting to achieve in the sense that there is a widespread understanding by all participants of what needs to be done as well as a collective focus on that objective. Moreover, this objective must be associated with measurable outcomes in order to appraise how well the firm is doing (Cyert 1988). Schools seem far removed from this standard as the objectives of the school often vary from teacher to teacher with some placing more emphasis on some subjects than others and some pushing for rote memorization while others stress thinking skills and problem-solving. There is also considerable evidence that many schools set different goals for different groups of students according to ethnicity, race, and socioeconomic origins, practices that are encrusted in tracking or streaming of students, each track associated with different expectations (Oakes 1985).

4.1.2 Organizational Incentives. The principal strategy for inducing employees to pursue the objectives of the firm is to link employee rewards to their performance in contributing to those objectives. In the case of schools, there is little evidence of incentives tied to student success. Salary increases are provided according to seniority and qualifications, not effectiveness. Incentives can be intrinsic (e.g., a sense of accomplishment) or extrinsic (e.g., financial rewards or recognition); they can be individual or collective. But, even if individual teachers receive some intrinsic satisfaction from the accomplishments of their students, the fact that there is little connection among teachers' efforts or objectives means that school outcomes are likely to be poorer than could be produced with a highly articulated effort towards a single objective function.

4.1.3 Useful Information. To succeed, firms need continuous and systematic information on their overall success to see if they are meeting objectives. They need rapid feedback on challenges, problems, bottlenecks, and impending obstacles as well as changes in market environments, production technologies, and prices that may affect them. Comparable information in schools is not readily available at the school level. Indeed, schools rarely have accurate information on alternatives or strategies and channels to obtain that information. Even the test score data on students are usually not available until the end of the school year or the beginning of the following one, limiting the ability to learn through trial and error as suggested by Murnane and Nelson (1984).

4.1.4 Adaptability. Firms that are in situations where their markets, products, technologies, costs, and prices are largely stable do not need to adapt to succeed and survive. They can continue to follow the same practices that have brought them success in the past. In contrast, firms facing rapid changes in these dimensions must be prepared to adapt to meet changing conditions. This becomes even more challenging when the technology of production is uncertain and requires considerable trial and error to get it right (Murnane and Nelson 1984). Many schools typically face unstable and unpredictable situations with changes in student populations as neighborhoods change; precipitous changes in budgets from year to year; rapid changes in electronic technologies and their capabilities; changing teacher supplies as relative salaries change (Murnane et al. 1991); and new demands, such as AIDS education. However, schools are typically faced with centrally adopted curricula, rules, regulations, and mandates which create obstacles to change and no internal decision mechanism which could adapt to change, even if greater involvement in decision-making were permitted. Schools need to have the ability to make decisions on resource allocation in order to adjust to disequilibria (Schultz 1975).

4.1.5 Efficient Technology of Production. Finally, efficient firms need to adopt the most productive technologies consistent with cost constraints. Unfortunately, schools tend to follow historical approaches despite attempts to change them through educational reforms (Cuban 1990). Although most schools still use approaches that require student to simply memorize material as it is presented considerable research finds that this is an inefficient teaching and learning technique (e.g., Peterson 1989 Gardner 1983, Gardner and Hatch 1990, Knapp et al. 1992). A more effective approach seems to be to provide active learning situations in which student can build on previous experiences and engage in new activities which allow them to construct their own understanding through research, hands-on projects and other applications. In many respects, this is the approach used for gifted and talented students, but it is becoming increasingly recognized that it works effectively for all students (Feldhusen 1992).

4.2 Redesigned Schools

According to the five dimensions of a firm that are generally considered to be required for an efficient productive organization, schools seem to be ill-equipped to produce educational services efficiently. The Accelerated Schools Project was designed to improve school productivity dramatically by altering these five dimensions. Starting with only two pilot schools in 1986–87, the Project comprised more than 800 elementary and middle schools in 39 states in the United States by 1995–96. The Project was designed to transform public schools with high concentrations of at-risk students, students who are unlikely to succeed educationally because of poverty, minority or immigrant status, broken families, and so on. These schools have relied primarily on remedial education and have been notoriously unsuccessful in bringing these students into the educational mainstream.

Schools are provided with a process to establish a unity of purpose among all staff, parents, and students around accelerated academic outcomes for all children. This unity was buttressed with a system of decision-making that provides input and incentives for all of the participants to become actively engaged in problem-solving methods that will lead to those outcomes. In addition, the entire school staff, with student and parent participation, is provided with training in problem-solving and group dynamics with a focus on assessment of results and the use of powerful learning strategies. Thus, schools develop an objective function, collective incentives to address that objective, shared information, and an ability to adjust to disequilibria. In addition, the accelerated agenda shifts the school to a more powerful technology of learning, that which is usually reserved only for the most gifted and talented students in traditional schools and which is built upon constructivist learning approaches (Brooks and Brooks 1993).

In order to induce these deep changes, schools are introduced to a philosophy and set of practices which require deep changes in the values and expectations of all participants, a substantial transformation of school culture (Hopfenberg et al. 1993). Such changes in school culture have been found to be particularly problematic in the past (Sarason 1982, 1990). However, (Finnan 1992, 1994) has documented such a cultural transition in Accelerated Schools. Moreover, evaluations of Accelerated Schools indicate impressive improvements in student achievement, attendance, and parent participation, and reductions in costly policies such as students retained in grade and special education placements (e.g., see McCarthy and Still 1993). Moreover, the costs of these reforms are rather minimal with a typical marginal cost of about US$30 a year per student in the first year of school transformation and less in ensuing years as most of the changes are accomplished through reallocation of existing resources.

It would seem that the transformation of school organizations, or what is broadly called, "school restructuring" (Fullan 1991, Murphy and Hallinger 1993), is a promising direction to explore to improve educational productivity, an approach that might also be extended to higher education (Levin 1991b). Such changes will require major policy alterations in the educational system, whether reforms are contained in the public sector or shifted to a market environment. That is, issues of educational choice through exit mechanisms or public school transformation through greater voice mechanisms (Hirschman 1970) will both require decentralization and a supportive infrastructure to provide information, technical assistance, and assessment of results.

5. Conclusion

Historically, the attempt to study and improve educational productivity has comprised two fundamentally different approaches. Early attempts were based upon research that might uncover the most productive inputs or effective school practices. Economists hoped to ascertain the most efficient combinations of inputs from a cost-effectiveness perspective through linking educational production function or effective school results to the costs of the inputs and school practices. These led to prescriptive policy recommendations with regard to the types of inputs that are most efficient, or school practices that are correlated with effectiveness. In both cases, the empirical research has been based upon correlational analysis which has tried to identify conditions for educational effectiveness. But, in order to apply the knowledge base, it is necessary to establish interventions under somewhat controlled conditions to see if the recommendations from such research actually improve educational productivity. This type of evidence is not readily available.

Inconsistent findings and the difficulties of using what was learned to change school practices from educational production function and effective schools research has shifted the emphasis to educational choice and school restructuring approaches. The concept behind the development of school choice strategies through educational vouchers and public choice policies is to change the environment within which schools operate to build greater incentives to meet client needs. In essence, it is assumed that if schools were to become more client-oriented because of their need to attract students for survival and profitability, they would discover the most efficient practices and appropriate output mixes to maintain clientele. In this case, those who wish to improve productivity should worry less about prescribing internal school policies than in creating the conditions that will induce schools to search continuously for ways to improve their operations.

According to this view, it is more important to establish efficient systems of educational choice with provisions for information and (if necessary) transportation than to address the internal operations of schools. Successful schools will have incentives to search for and identify those practices on a continuous basis in order to compete successfully for students. However, at this point neither public nor market choice in education has produced a consistent and substantial base of empirical support for improving educational productivity (see *Economics of Education Review* 1992).

The call for redesign or restructuring of school organizations within the public sector is an outgrowth of this early history. Much of the pressure for institutional change implicit in choice approaches also guides the redesign or restructuring movement. Although there have been substantial evaluation results from the one particular intervention that is presented in this article, that is, Accelerated Schools, it is too early to draw conclusions on the general effectiveness of the school redesign strategy. Market choice advocates would also question whether such redesign can even be implemented in public schools on a more universal basis or whether it is limited to ideosyncratic situations. Whether such organizational changes can and should be done within the public sector or through the creation of a publicly funded educational marketplace is a source of great debate (e.g., compare Levin 1991a, 1991c with West 1991a, 1991b). Of particular controversy is the degree to which public schools produce social benefits that exceed those of private schools and the value of those additional social benefits. Also under debate is whether private schools have intrinsic characteristics which enable them to be more productive than public schools. These issues are reflected in comparisons of public and private schools (James and Levin 1988 and Haertel 1987) as well as debates on the relative merits of government versus markets in education. For example, compare Brown (1992) and Frey (1992) on the one hand with Coleman (1987), Coons and Sugarman (1978), Chubb and Moe (1990), and Friedman (1962) on the other.

What is particularly important to note, in summary, is that educational production has peculiar characteristics which do not simply fit into the standard production function and cost minimization literature. Definitions and measurements of inputs and outputs, understanding of the technology of production, and the distributional implications of student composition for both educational production and outcomes are just three areas in which there is great controversy, but little, robust empirical evidence. Clearly, the same glaring gaps in knowledge underlie the debate over market approaches to educational production and school redesign. It is readily apparent that continuing research will be necessary to provide a better understanding for policy directions.

References

Alchian A, Demsetz H 1972 Production, information costs, and economic organization. *Am. Econ. Rev.* 62(5): 777–95

Bessent A M, Bessent E W, Kennington J, Reagan B 1982 An application of mathematical programming to assess productivity in the Houston Independent School District. *Management Science* 28: 1355–67

Bowles S, Levin H M 1968 The determinants of scholastic achievement: An appriaisal of some recent evidence. *J. Hum. Resources* 3: 3–24

Bridge G, Judd C, Moock P 1979 *The Determinants of Educational Outcomes: The Impact of Families, Peers, Teachers and Schools.* Ballinger, Cambridge, Massachusetts

Brookover W, Lezotte L 1979 *Changes in School Characteristics Coincident with Changes in Student Achievement.* College of Urban Development, Michigan State University, East Lansing, Michigan

Brooks J G, Brooks M G 1993 *The Case for Constructivist Classrooms.* Association for Supervision and Curriculum Development, Alexandria, Virginia

Brown B W 1992 Why governments run schools. *Econ. Educ. Rev.* 11(4): 287–300

Bryk, A S, Lee V E 1992 *Catholic Schools and the Common Good.* Harvard University Press, Cambridge, Massachusetts

Carnoy M, Sack R, Thias H 1977 *The Payoff to Better Schooling: A Case Study of Tunisian Secondary Schools.* World Bank, Washington, DC

Chubb J E, Moe T M 1990 *Politics, Markets, and America's Schools.* The Brookings Institution, Washington, DC

Clune W H, Witte J F (eds.) 1990 *Choice and Control in American Education,* Vols. 1 & 2. Falmer Press, New York

Cohn E, Geske T G 1990 Production and cost functions in education. In: Cohn E, Geske T G (eds.) 1990 *The Economics of Education,* 3rd edn. Pergamon Press, Oxford

Coleman J S 1987 Families and schools. *Educ. Researcher* 16(6): 32–38

Coleman J S et al. 1966 *Equality of Educational Opportunity.* Report prepared for the US Office of Education. US Government Printing Office, Washington, DC

Coleman J S, Hoffer T 1987 *Public and Private High Schools.* Basic Books, New York

Coons J E, Sugarman S 1978 *Education by Choice.* University of California Press, Berkeley, California

Cuban L 1990 Reforming again, again, and again. *Educ. Researcher* 19: 3–13

Cyert R 1988 *The Economic Theory of Organization and the Firm.* New York University Press, New York

Economics of Education Review 1992 11(4): entire issue

Edmonds R 1979 Effective schools for the urban poor. *Educ. Leadership* 37(1): 15–24

Feldhusen J F (1992) *Talent Identification and Development in Education.* Center for Creative Learning, Sarasota, Florida

Felton M K 1990 The effective schools movement: A review of its research and implementation (unpublished honors thesis). Stanford University, Stanford, California

Finnan C 1992 *Becoming an Accelerated Middle School: Initiating School Culture Change.* Report prepared for the accelerated Schools Project. School of Education, Stanford University, Stanford, California

Finnan C 1994 Studying an accelerated school. In: Spindler G, Spindler L (eds.) 1994 *Pathways to Cultural Awareness: Cultural Therapy with Teachers and Students.* Corwin Press, Thousand Oaks, California

Friedman M 1962 The role of government in education. In: Friedman M (ed.) 1962 *Capitalism and Freedom.* University of Chicago Press, Chicago, Illinois

Frey D E 1992 Can privatizing education really improve achievement? *Econ. Educ. Rev.* 11(4): 417–26

Fullan M 1991 *The New Meaning of Educational Change.* Teachers College Press, New York

Fuller B, Clarke P 1994 Raising school effects while ignoring culture? Local conditions and the influence of classroom tools, rules, and pedagogy. *Rev. Educ. Res.* 64(1): 119–58

Gardner H 1983 *Frames of Mind.* Basic Books, New York

Gardner H, Hatch T 1990 Multiple intelligences go to school: Educational implications of the theory of multiple intelligences. *Educ. Researcher* 19: 4–10

Grosskopf S, Hayes K, Taylor L, Weber W 1992 *Budget-constrained Frontier Measures of Fiscal Equality and Efficiency in Schooling.* Working paper no. 9206. Federal Reserve Bank, Dallas, Texas

Haertel E H 1987 Comparing public and private schools using longitudinal data from the HSB study. In: Haertal E H, James T, Levin H M (eds.) 1987 *Comparing Public and Private Schools.* Falmer Press, New York

Haertel E H, James T, Levin H M 1987 *Comparing Public and Private Schools: School Achievement,* Vol. 2. Falmer Press, New York

Hanushek, E 1972 *Education and Race.* Health, Lexington, Massachusetts

Hanushek E 1986 The economics of schooling: Production and efficiency in public schools. *J. Econ. Lit.* 24: 1141–71

Hanushek E 1989 The impact of differential expenditures on school performance. *Educ. Researcher* 18(4): 45–65

Hedges L V, Laine R D, Greenwald R 1994 Does money matter? A meta-analysis of studies of the effects of differential school inputs on student outcomes. *Educ. Researcher* 23: 5–14

Hirschman A O 1970 *Exit, Voice, and Loyalty.* Harvard University Press, Cambridge, Massachusetts

Hopfenberg W et al. 1993 *The Accelerated Schools Resource Guide.* Jossey-Bass, San Francisco, California

James T, Levin H M (eds.) 1988 *Comparing Public and Private Schools: Institutions and Organizations,* Vol. 1. Falmer Press, New York

Knapp M S, Shield P M, Turnbull B J 1922 *Academic Challenge for the Children of Poverty,* Vols. 1 & 2. US

Department of Education, Office of Policy and Planning, Washington, DC

Levin H M 1970 A cost-effectiveness analysis of teacher selection. *J. Hum. Resources* 5: 24–33

Levin H M 1974 Measuring efficiency in educational production. *Public Finance Quarterly* 2: 3–24

Levin H M 1976 Economic efficiency and educational production. In: Froomkin J, Jamison D, Radner R (eds.) *Education as an Industry*. Ballinger Press, Cambridge, Massachusetts

Levin H M 1980 Educational production theory and teacher inputs. In: Bidwell C, Windham D (eds.) 1980 *The Analysis of Educational Productivity: Issues in Macroanalysis*, Vol. 11. Ballinger Press, Cambridge, Massachusetts

Levin H M 1991a The economics of educational choice. *Econ. Educ. Rev.* 10: 137–58

Levin H M 1991b Raising productivity in higher education. *J. Higher Educ.* 62(3): 241–62

Levin H M 1991c Views on the economics of educational choice: A reply to West. *Econ. Educ. Rev.* 10: 171–76

Levin H M 1994 The necessary and sufficient conditions for achieving educational equity. In: Berne R (ed.) in press *The Road to Outcome Equity in Education*. Corwin Press, Thousand Oaks, California

Levin H M, Lockheed M (eds.) 1993 *Effective Schools in Developing Countries*. Falmer Press, Brighton

Levin H M, Glass, G V, Meister G R 1987 Cost-effectiveness of computer-assisted instruction. *Eval. Rev.* 11(1): 50–72

Madaus G, Kellaghan T, Rakow E A, King D J 1987 The sensitivity of measures of school effectiveness. *Harv. Educ. Rev.* 49(2): 207–30

Massell B F 1967 Elimination of management bias from production functions fitted to cross-section data: A model and an application to African agriculture. *Econometrica* 35(3–4): 495–508

McCarthy J, Still S 1993 Hollibrook accelerated elementary school. In: Murphy J, Hallinger P (eds.) 1993 *Restructuring Schools: Learning From Ongoing Efforts*. Corwin Press, Monterey Park, California

Mortimore P et al. 1979 *School Matters*. University of California Press, Berkeley, California

Murnane R J, Nelson R R 1984 Production and innovation when techniques are tacit. *Journal of Economic Behavior and Organization* 5: 353–73

Murnane R J et al. 1991 *Who Will Teach? Policies that Matter*. Harvard University Press, Cambridge, Massachusetts

Murphy J, Hallinger P, (eds.) 1993 *Restructuring Schools: Learning from Ongoing Efforts*. Corwin Press, Thousand Oaks, California

Oakes J 1985 *Keeping Track: How Schools Structure Inequality*. Yale University Press, New Haven, Connecticut

Peterson J M 1989 Remediation is no remedy. *Educ. Leadership* 46(6): 24–25

Purkey S C, Smith M S 1983 Effective Schools: A review. *Elem. Sch. J.* 83: 427–53

Reynolds D 1982 The search for effective schools. *School Organizations* 2(3): 215–37

Rutter M et al. 1979 *Fifteen Thousand Hours*. Harvard University Press, Cambridge, Massachusetts

Sarason S B 1982 *The Culture of the School and the Problem of Change*, 2nd edn. Allyn and Bacon, Boston, Massachusetts

Sarason S B 1990 *The Predictable Failure of Educational Reform: Can We Change Course Before it's Too Late?* Jossey-Bass, San Francisco, California

Schultz T W 1975 The value of the ability to deal with disequilibria. *J. Econ. Lit.* 13(3): 827–46

Shephard R W 1970 *Theory of Cost and Production Functions*. Princeton University Press, Princeton, New Jersey

Silkman R (ed.) 1986 *Measuring Efficiency*. Jossey-Bass, San Francisco, California

US General Accounting Office of the US Congress 1989 *Effective Schools Programs: Their Extent and Characteristics*. US Government Printing Office, Washington, DC

West E G 1991a Public schools and excess burdens. *Econ. Educ. Rev.* 10: 159–70

West E G 1991b Rejoinder. *Econ. Educ. Rev.* 10: 177–78

Williamson O 1975 *Markets and Hierarchies*. Free Press, New York

Witte J F 1992 Private school versus public school achievement: Are there findings that should affect the educational choice debate? *Econ. Educ. Rev.* 11(4): 371–94

Witte J F, Bailey A B, Thorn C A 1993 *Third-Year Report: Milwaukee Parental Choice Program*. Department of Political Science and the Robert La Follette Institute of Public Affairs, University of Wisconsin, Madison, Wisconsin

Political Economy of Educational Production

M. Carnoy

"Traditional" analyses of educational production are based on the premise that schools function like private firms, with either the classroom or the school as the producing unit and with the teacher, the principal, or the district/municipality superintendent, as the decision-maker who controls and shapes the teaching–learning process.

Literature in the 1980s and early 1990s argues that this premise is fundamentally flawed. First, it contends that production function analysis neglects the key variable of educational administrative organizations (whether the administrative organization is in the school itself, a politically-defined school administrative district, a municipality, or a regional or national ministry) and its impact on teacher effectiveness (Meyer et al. 1985). Second, schools and school administrative districts do *not* function like private firms. They are part of the public sector, subject to different conditions and organizational imperatives. Schools' "workers" (teachers) and "supervisors" (principals) are not like workers and supervisors in the private sector, in that teachers and principals do have some control over the learning (production) process (Levin 1980). Nor do teachers, principals, or superintendents act like entrepreneur/decision makers directing the allocation of resources and choosing production technology. School administrations are bureaucracies (see e.g., Meyer 1985, Corwin and Edelfelt 1978), that are part of a larger public bureaucracy subject to complex political pressures and operating much more according to political than to economic rules (Offe 1973). As non-profit, public firms, schools have value functions that weigh outputs and inputs according to institutional values as well as market prices (Hopkins and Massy 1981). These values are affected not only by a school administration's own preferences among objectives, but by each administrative district's and school's constituencies' "political power." In addition, schools are different from private firms in terms of planning production. The director of a firm knows the desired specifications of a firm's inputs to produce a desired output, and aims to attain those inputs. On the other hand, a school principal and classroom teachers have little control over one of the main inputs into schooling—pupils' competencies—and hence have to adjust constantly to changing inputs in the production process. The decision-making process is much more complex and discretionary for a principal or teacher than for a factory manager. How educational administrations function is therefore subject as much to political and educational criteria as to economic criteria.

1. School Production

The typical measure of educational outcome has been performance on standardized achievement tests (although some studies have used noncognitive measures, such as student attitudes or test scores that reflect other cognitive domains). The measures of inputs include those related to student characteristics (socioeconomic status, race, ethnic group, and gender) and those directly related to schools: class size, teacher experience and education, and school facilities (see Brown and Saks 1975, and Averch et al. 1974).

If school production equations truly represented the educational process, they should provide some indication of whether a school district administration is organized to maximize school outcomes. The definition of school "district" varies from country to country and includes political entities known as school districts, municipalities that govern all the schools within them (for example, Sweden, primary schools in Brazil and the People's Republic of China), or regional governments (secondary schools in many countries). However it is defined, the district would choose to invest in those inputs that resulted in the largest contribution to the achievement of pupils with different social class background.

Estimates of such equations have shown that pupil socioeconomic characteristics have an important impact on school achievement and specific teacher characteristics vary in their effect on school performance depending on pupils' social class and race (Averch et al. 1974, Hanushek 1986).

School production studies fail to provide the basis either for school resource allocation decisions or for judging administrative organization. This is in part due to a lack of an underlying theory of schooling— either a theory of how inputs relate to outputs or a theory of organizational behavior which forms the basis of understanding how schools are organized for learning and how resource decisions are made (Levin 1980).

Although school production models recognize that school performance is a joint product of the school and the family, a theoretical basis for specifying the joint production relationship is lacking. Joint production is assumed to take place in a series of stages, first in the family, then—when the pupil enters school—in the classroom or school. But learning is a complex process that includes "production" in the family, community, and the school, even after the child enters school (see *Joint Production of Education*).

Even assuming that the learning process could be specified, however, education production estimates have generally ignored the issue of specificity of school administration, assuming that school "firms" are administered either or both at the school level (in which school administrators choose and allocate teacher *capacity* and *time*) and at the classroom level, in which case individual teachers themselves are assumed to organize the teaching–learning process, including the allocation of capacity, effort, and time (Levin 1980). Levin argues that the approach to educational production must shift from an "autonomous classroom" assumption to one which centers on educational administration and its relation both to teachers (educational workers) and to exogenous factors influencing school production.

There is no evidence that schools or school districts have as a singular or even primary objective the increase of average student performance or average "value added" (the increase in pupil performance over the previous year), as a firm would to increase earnings (Cyert and March 1963). Rather, pupil achievement is usually seen in terms of achieved standards or a target, influenced heavily by social expectations inside and outside the school and district, and that target is one of several institutional objectives, including primarily teacher satisfaction, administrative "prestige" (control, power), and compliance with state performance criteria. These other objectives may have as much to do with bureaucratic accountability and control as with pupil performance (Meyer et al. 1985).

2. The School as a "Public Sector" Organization

If school districts do not operate as private firms maximizing profit (real value added in the form of increased student performance), what do they do and how do they do it? Public schools are part of the political system and are therefore political institutions. As public institutions, they do not seek to maximize profit or output in the "private" sense. The institution itself values outputs and inputs in ways that alter the school district's or school's decision as to how much of any given output to produce (Hopkins and Massy 1981). Even if parents in every district sent their children to school only to improve their academic achievement, the administration and teachers of each school or school district might place different amounts of emphasis or weight on pupil achievement compared to other outputs, such as discipline or childcare. This different emphasis reflects the diverse institutional values in schools.

There are two sides to the effect that institutional values have on the production of achievement. On the positive side, institutional values of public institutions in a democracy are responsive to direct public pressure and to more indirect changes in social values (public ideology). Public schools may, by putting emphasis on pupil achievement in their own objective functions, increase achievement gains beyond those demanded by parents alone. The schools' objective functions should also be subject to influence from broader political and professional educators' expectations about pupil performance. In this sense, the assumption has always been that the public sector would provide more and better education than individual families would be willing to pay for privately because of the "externalities" associated with that education (Blaug 1970).

On the negative side, public bureaucracies are well-equipped for allocative functions but poorly equipped for productive activities (Buchanan and Tullock 1965), Niskanen 1973, Offe 1973, Tullock 1979):

> the problem is that the application of predetermined rules through a hierarchical structure of neutral officials is simply insufficient to absorb the decision load that is implied by productive state activities ... the administration of productive state activities requires more than the routinized allocation of state resources like money and justice ... is beyond the scope and responsibility of a bureaucracy in the strict sense. (Offe 1973 p. 136)

This negative argument implies that school districts as institutions are much better suited to judge who is capable of meeting particular standards and who is not than to increase average performance (in Offe's terms, to present information and then to "allocate" pupils to different levels of performance). As public bureaucracies, they are not well-organized to "produce"—that is, to increase the output of—academic performance beyond the gains that pupils now achieve.

3. An Alternative Model of Schools and School Districts as Public Firms

A school or school district as an autonomous political decision-making unit, subject to parent (client) pressures, internal bureaucratic demands, and external social, political (value), and bureaucratic pressures can be viewed as a "mini-democratic-state." Understanding the school or school district's institutional demand function requires a political–economic theory of that "mini-state." The key elements of such a theory are the following: First, schools and school districts have the complex but rather clearly (and externally) defined mandate of socializing and training pupils both as future workers in the economy and as citizens of the nation (Carnoy and Levin 1985). Second, this demand is conveyed to school administrators directly from the community (consumers), as represented by the school board or parent representatives, and is measured by pupil performance. Third, demand is also conveyed through the state central administration. The level of school district funding from local, regional, and central government sources is, to some extent, based on the degree to which schools are viewed as fulfilling their mandate, but it is also based on the ability of the district (in some countries) to maintain financial solvency and (in all countries) to fulfill bureaucratic requirements associated with flows of funds from the region or central government to the school or district. Fourth, since the school or school district is a public enterprise with a semipermanent set of employees—tenured teachers—school administrations also rely on "demand" from their teacher corps, which also depends in part on their success in allowing or helping teachers achieve "acceptable" pupil performance. Fifth, school district administrations have a tendency to try to "control" their own destiny by centralizing functions in the district, regional, or central ministry office. This tendency is exacerbated by bureaucratic demands from outside the local school or district, usually connected with administrative styles and the social acceptability of large bureaucracies. Finally, school districts and schools are, to some extent, affected by larger national and state ideological characterizations of the schooling "problem." Although the ideological effect is interpreted through the lens of school politics and institutional values, external pressures can change local district values enough to force bureaucracies to change.

The school or school district as "mini-state" is different from a democratically elected government because school administrators are appointed professionals rather than elected officials. However, the fact that school boards and parent representatives are elected and school officials must be responsive to

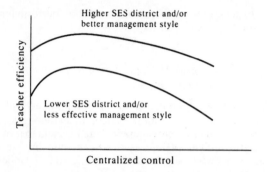

Figure 1
Teacher efficiency and administrative centralization

school boards does mean that a superintendent or a principal would have a difficult time remaining in a decision-making position without community legitimacy. At the same time, because district and school administrators are not elected and have an important professional constituency, their power is also a function of professional legitimacy, specifically related to their ability to deliver higher wages, better working conditions, and professional pride and participation to the district's teachers and staff.

Such "political" considerations condition the school or district's institutional value function. The function can be written as follows:

$$V = V(X_i)$$

X_i = school district objectives

(1)

For simplicity's sake, school or district objectives discussed here are reduced to three: pupil achievement (assuming that this results in community and parent satisfaction), teacher efficacy and satisfaction, and administrative control (power). The last of these is assumed to respond both to bureaucratic demands external to schools and school districts and to the desire of district administrators to exert control over school affairs.

Administrators are faced with trade-offs, and complementarities between these objectives. For example, Hannaway (1991) suggests that increased teacher participation in school and school district decision-making, including setting curriculum, new forms of teaching, and even school management, increases teacher efficacy and that efficacy is higher for all levels of participation in districts with higher pupil socioeconomic class. Similar results obtain for rural Colombia (see UNICEF 1991 for a description of the *Escuela Nueva* project). This means that giving teachers more control over educational decision-making (and the skills to make such decisions in an organized fashion) and giving up central administrative control would increase teacher self-efficacy. Teacher self-efficacy (or efficacy, for short) is defined as the sense

that a teacher has about his or her influence and control over professional environment.

Although correlated with teacher job satisfaction, efficacy is more a measure of influence than contentment, at least in a certain range of administrative control (see Fig. 1). It can also easily be argued that without some centralized district administration and strong leadership at the school level, teacher efficacy would decline (McLaughlin and Talbert 1991). Figure 1 suggests that the relation between teacher efficacy and centralized administrative control is an inverted "U", with the height of the curve influenced by the district's socioeconomic conditions and by the central administration's overall management effectiveness.

Although there are no hard data that show a positive relation between teacher efficacy and pupil achievement gains (value added), such a relationship is not far-fetched, at least in a certain range of efficacy change, with the caveat that those teachers with better tools and clearer objectives for increasing learning for a particular group of students will produce higher pupil performance at all levels of efficacy (see Fig. 2). (Achievement gain as defined here is the absolute gain in tested knowledge during the school year(s).) The main assumption behind the teacher efficacy–pupil achievement relation is that efficaciousness is associated with positive involvement with pupils, a belief in their capability, and a belief in the worthiness of the teacher's role in the learning process (Hannaway 1991). However, the small amount of empirical data available suggests that it is the interaction between increased efficacy and clarity of objectives and methods that produces achievement gains. Fig. 2 also suggests that the effect of increased efficacy should be greater in lower income schools and districts where the quality of teaching would logically have more of an impact on pupil achievement gains than in higher income districts.

If the curves in Figs. 1 and 2 are realistic characterizations of the relationships between teacher efficacy and centralized control and teacher efficacy and achievement gain, then school districts with pupils from lower income families—for example,

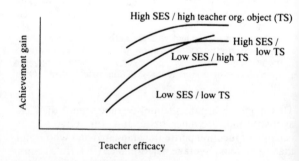

Figure 2
Teacher efficacy and student achievement

low-income urban schools in all countries or rural schools in developing countries—could have much more to gain from an effective decentralization and much more to lose from centralization, mainly because of the sharper effect that increased teacher efficacy interacting with clear school objectives at the school level has on gains in lower income than in higher income schools. The lower achievement orientation in lower income schools is the result both of the increased emphasis on administrative control over such schools (Chubb and Moe 1990, Figueroa, 1986) and the much greater effect of the lower teacher efficacy–disoriented objectives interacion on pupils' achievement. Schools with higher income pupils have less to lose or gain from greater or less centralization of administrative control. So even if such a school or school district is as centrally administered as one in a low-income neighborhood or region, its achievement trade-off is much lower (Fig. 3).

For low-income urban and rural schools, attaining higher pupil achievement requires choosing less centralized administrative control than a suburban district or in wealthier urban neighborhoods, since teacher efficacy and educational clarity for a given amount of administrative control tend to be lower than in surburban school districts because of the difficult social conditions in urban schools and the weaker preparation of the pupils before they get to school (Figueroa 1986). If low- and high-income districts chose the same amount of administrative control, achievement gain would be lower in the low-income district, but probably not that much lower (al compared to a2). In practice, however, the value function of low-income urban or rural schools places the administrative control objective far above teacher efficacy and higher achievement, dropping achievement gain to a3.

3.1 Institutional Demand

A school or school district's "effectiveness" is very much the result of the level of its institutional demand for achievement, which depends on the value that

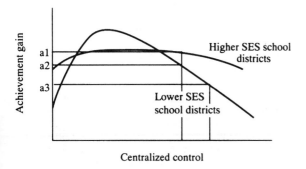

Figure 3
Administrative centralization and student achievement

schools and school districts have for pupil achievement compared to other goals. Institutional demand for achievement is the result of administrative choices based on a complex set of subjective norms negotiated politically between administrators, parents, and teachers. This negotiation has much greater consequences for low-income pupils, and, it turns out, usually ends up producing a greater centralized control in low-income districts and a lower institutional demand for achievement.

Institutional demand and total demand for schooling output, according to Hopkins and Massy (1981), can be expressed as:

$$EMIV_i = \frac{V_i}{\mu} \qquad (2)$$

$$Total\ Demand = MR + EMIV_i \qquad (3)$$

Why do low-income, urban schools and school districts end up with a greater emphasis on centralized control and less on school achievement gain, even though centralized control could produce more achievements gain? Alternatively, why is institutional demand for achievement gain higher in the higher income districts? At least part of the answer lies in the value functions of the school or school district administrations. Until the late 1980s administrators were able to argue that it is inherently necessary to develop complex bureaucracies to handle all the "special problems" of low-income children. Such schools and districts have a high fraction of their funding in the form of compensatory funding from central sources (either the central or regional government), and these require considerable accountability. Teachers and school administrators beset by pupil difficulties (which, in some countries, can include truancy, crime, drugs, and teacher–student or teacher–parent conflicts) tend to kick pupil problems "upstairs." Thus, it is easy for low-expectation administrators and teachers to believe that they are achieving maximum possible pupil achievement with large bureaucracies. Any failure to do better is blamed on factors outside the school district's control.

However, school administrators could not do this without teachers accepting low achievement on the part of their students and a low sense of efficacy on their own part. Neither can such administrative choices be explained without the complicity of low academic expectations for these pupils from society at large and the limited political ability of the parents in these districts to affect administration decisions. Often, in the name of "professional control," the centralization of school administration is used to convince low-income parents to reduce participation, in order to distance the school from the parents.

From any school or school district administration's point of view, the optimal administrative configuration is one that maximizes its legitimacy with its employees and the various community constituencies, especially pupils' parents and taxpayers (including businesses), as represented by the school board. It is usually when one or both of these groups stress pupil achievement (and, in the case of a diverse community, when all its elements put similar pressure on the school district) that pupil achievement standards in the *district as a whole* reach dominant importance in the district's value function.

There is also frequently a wide variation of parental pressure within districts. When this variation is "clustered" in certain schools (high pressure parents concentrated in one or more schools and low pressure parents in other schools), the district administration has the option of setting differential pupil achievement standards for different schools and focusing primarily on meeting the higher standards in the high pressure parent schools. School district goals are therefore themselves subject to variation, and setting goals and developing incentives to meet them become the most important variables in reforming administrative procedures. In this sense, critiques of education at the national level (for example, the National Commission on Excellence in Education 1983) are correct in focusing directly on raising educational standards as a principal precondition to raising pupil performance. However, the issue of linking raised academic goals to the means of achieving such standards for all pupils in a diverse ethnic and racial constituency are not directly addressed in such reports.

A school district administration itself may raise institutional demand for pupil achievement even in the absence of constituent pressures. It may choose to organize schooling (curriculum, teaching methods, the distribution of administrative responsibilities between schools and the district, and the administrative style within schools) in a way that tries to raise average pupil performance. This would probably increase the administration's community legitimacy and perhaps legitimacy with teachers. But if the district raises ex-

pectations more than it can actually raise performance, the administration's legitimacy may actually decline even though pupil performance rises. Therefore, the safer administrative route to follow is simultaneously to reduce community expectations and maintain average pupil performance, even if it is low. This is what most lower income districts (and indeed most districts) do.

School districts with low-income clientele usually tend to have about the same costs per student as those in high-income areas (see *Private and Public Costs of Schooling in Developing Nations*), but the costs per unit of achievement gain may be higher. The reasons for this are many, including the much longer time in school needed for students coming from low-income homes and the greater teacher dedication required to meet students' learning gaps. This is especially true in public schools, where all students, regardless of motivation or behavior or parent involvement, are taken into the school. Finding dedicated teachers to spend more time either means higher teacher salaries, or providing an exciting working environment, or both. This results in higher costs per unit of achievement gain.

Assuming a relatively uniform cost per unit of pupil achievement curve among school districts, the higher the parents' demand for higher achievement (MR versus MR' in Fig. 4) and the higher the institutional demand (EMIV versus EMIV'), the higher the pupil achievement in the district (MR+EMIV versus MR'+EMIV' in Fig. 4), where Hopkins and Massy (1981) define MR as the marginal revenue product of higher achievement, or private demand for achievement—both expressed in dollar terms. If school cost per unit of achievement is higher in low-income districts, even the same parent and institutional demand would not result in the same level of gains in low-income and high-income districts, but low-income districts could still be seen as "effective" if their institutional demand for achievement is high (Goodlad 1983). In addition, some higher income districts could be seen as "ineffective" if their institutional demand is low. Figure 4 suggests that not only may expressed community demand for pupil achievement be lower in low-income school districts, but that institutional demand is also low, and for reasons that usually make good political sense, though not good educational sense.

School district policy-making in this model can be viewed as the attempt to establish a dynamic equilibrium among constituent elements inside and outside the district. Unless there is a clear, uncompromising pressure on the district administration from somewhere (including inside the administration itself) to do something about pupil achievement, it is unlikely that the organization of achievement production in the district will change. Yet, if the community's (parents, taxpayers),

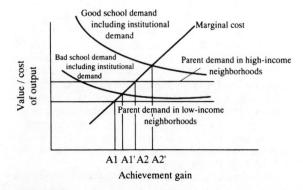

Figure 4
Parent and institutional demand for higher achievement

teachers', or administrative expectations of average pupil performance increase, trade-offs will have to take place, particularly if there are limited funds available to hire more personnel.

See also: Education Production Functions; Microeconomics of School Production; Economics of School Enterprise

References

Averch H et al. 1974 *How Effective is Schooling? A Critical Review and Synthesis of Research Findings.* Educational Technology Publications, Englewood Cliffs, New Jersey
Blaug M 1970 *An Introduction to the Economics of Economics.* Penguin, Harmondsworth
Brown B, Saks D 1975 The production and distribution of cognitive skills within schools. *Journal of Political Economy* 83(3): 571–93
Buchanan J, Tullock G 1965 *The Calculus of Consent: Logical Foundations of Constitutional Democracy.* University of Michigan Press, Ann Arbor, Michigan
Carnoy M, Levin H M 1985 *Schooling and Work in the Democratic State.* Stanford University Press, Stanford, California
Chubb J, Moe T 1990 *Politics, Markets, and America's Schools.* The Brookings Institution, Washington, DC
Corwin R G, Edelfelt R A 1978 *Perspectives on Organizations: Schools in the Larger Social Environment.* American Association of Colleges for Teacher Education, Washington, DC
Cyert R M, March J 1963 *A Behavioral Theory of the Firm.* Prentice-Hall Englewood Cliffs, New Jersey
Figueroa 1985 Methodological explorations on schooling and the reproduction of the social division of labor. Unpublished PhD dissertation, School of Education, Stanford University, Stanford, California
Goodlad J 1983 *A Place Called School: Prospects for the Future.* McGraw-Hill, New York
Hannaway J 1991 Restructuring: A tale of two districts. Stanford University, Stanford, California (mimeo)
Hanushek E A 1986 The economics of schooling: Production and efficiency in the public schools. *Journal of Economic Literature* 24 (3): 1141–77
Hopkins D, Massy W 1981 *Planning Models for Colleges and Universities.* Stanford University Press, Stanford, California
Levin H M 1980 Educational production theory and teacher inputs. In: Bidwell C, Windham D (eds.) 1980 *The Analysis of Educational Productivity. Vol. 2: Issues in Macro Analysis.* Ballinger, Cambridge, Massachusetts
McLaughlin M, Talbert J 1991 CRC report to the field sites. Stanford Center for Research on context, Stanford, California (mimeo)
Meyer J, Scott W R, Strang D, Creighton A 1985 Bureaucratization without centralization: Changes in the organizational system of American public education, 1940–1980. CERAS, Stanford University, Stanford, California (mimeo)
National Commission on Excellence in Education 1983. *A Nation at Risk: The Imperative for Educational Reform.* Department of Education, Washington, DC
Niskanen W 1973 *Bureaucracy—Servant or Master? Lessons from America.* Institute of Economic Affairs, London.
Offe C 1973 The theory of a capitalist state and the problem of policy formation. In: Linberg L, Alford R, Crouch C, Offe C (eds.) 1973 *Stresses and Contradictions in Modern Capitalism.* Health, Lexington, Massachusetts
Tullock G 1979 *Efficient Government Through Decentralization.* Bureau for Economic Policy Analysis, University of Pretoria, Pretoria
UNICEF 1991 *Education.* Thematic Kit No. 1, UNICEF, New York.

Further Reading

Bowles S, Gintis H 1987 *Democracy and Capitalism: Property Community, and the Contradictions of Modern Social Thought.* Basic Books, New York
Coleman J, Hoffer T, Kilgore S 1982 *High School Achievement: Public Catholic, and Private Schools Compared.* Basic Books, New York
Dornbusch S 1987 The relations of parenting style to adolescent school performance. *Child Development* 58(5): 1244–57
Hannaway J 1989 *Managers Managing: The Workings of an Administrative System.* Oxford University Press, New York
Levin H 1991 Building school capacity for effective teacher empowerment: Applications to elementary schools with at-risk students. Stanford School of Education, Stanford, California (mimeo)
Murnane R 1983 How clients' characteristics affect organization performance: Lessons from education. *Journal of Policy Analysis Management* 2 (3): 403–17
Useem E 1986 *Low Tech Education in a High Tech World: Corporations and Classrooms in the New Information Society.* Free Press, New York

Joint Production of Education

M. Carnoy

The production of education takes place both in schools and families. Key decisions about children's school attendance and the degree of their school effort, for example, are influenced both by family conditions and by schools. How well prepared the child is to do school work when he or she first enters school ("cultural capital") is also a function of the family's ability and willingness to provide education in the early years when the family is completely responsible for the child's intellectual formation (Bourdieu and Passeron 1977).

A child's performance in school, generally viewed as his or her school achievement, is therefore closely related to two very different "firms" concerned with the production of its production: families and schools. Furthermore, the school "firm" counts on the family "firm" to cooperate in the production of school achievement, by motivating and enforcing school attendance, completion of homework, a positive attitude toward learning, cooperation with teachers, and so forth. Through their policies, schools can also promote more effective family production of school achievement by teaching parents to be better "producers." The process of achievement attainment at two separate sites in this interactive manner is called "joint production."

Economists have dealt with the family's role in educational production in two ways: (a) In the analysis of school production, they have traditionally included the pupil's socioeconomic background (parent's education, occupation, income) as a variable in educational production functions (see Hanushek 1986; *Education Production Functions*). Yet, although socioeconomic background (SES) does provide a proxy of sorts for family inputs into school achievement, it does not capture the complex relation between family and school. (b) They have analyzed parents' investment in children at home through models of the allocation of parental time to improving the human capital of their children (Becker 1965). Becker's model argues that home time is both labor and leisure, and that part of the labor time is allocated to investing in children's learning. Gronau (1977, 1986) extends Becker's theory to develop a more easily testable model of home-time use. He assumes that an individual equalizes the marginal value of market production, home production, and leisure. His and Becker's models are useful in understanding the trade-offs between home work and market work, and the way that parents choose to invest in their children's human capital. However, as in the case of production functions, these parent time models do not capture the complexity of school–home production once children are in school.

In order to capture such school–home investment interactions, development of extensions of these two types of models began at the end of the 1980s.

1. Parental Demand for Children's Schooling

Glewwe and Jacoby (1991) pose the problem of the family's role in educational production in developing countries as a threefold set of choices: (a) whether to send the child to school at all, and if so, at what age; (b) how to partition the child's school attendance between full-time and part-time; and (c) how high a quality of school to choose for the child, where quality is a function of cost (distance to school, school fees).

The first two of these choices are analyzed as a capital investment problem that maximizes present and future consumption. Glewwe and Jacoby have developed a human capital model in which students can augment their stock of human capital by attending school at a certain intensity, best thought of as the fraction of days of school attended per year. The cost of augmenting this human capital consists of school fees that vary with the quality of school chosen plus income forgone (the opportunity cost of the time devoted to schooling). A child's school attendance pattern consists of three phases: (a) an initial phase in which the child is old enough to attend school but may not begin until a later time—the child can earn income during this phase or begin school immediately, (b) a second phase in which the child attends school, and (c) a third phase when the child quits school and works.

When there are no credit constraints, finding the school starting and ending points is relatively simple, because they depend only on school fees, the market rate of interest, the initial child wage, and the time horizon of the family. Assuming no diminishing returns to human capital investment, children will always attend school full-time because in that way the family has the longest period of time to collect a return on its investment (Glewwe and Jacoby 1991 pp. 6–7). If there are credit constraints, part-time school attendance has some advantage, since the family can accumulate some savings during nonattendance periods and smooth out the fall in income with these savings during attendance periods. Credit constraints also complicate the choice of the child's school starting time. If families have more than one child, the model becomes even more complex. The number and spacing of siblings are:

> crucial determinants of each child's human capital investment. The more children are bunched together in time, the more parents, desiring a smooth consumption profile, will attempt to space them out by adjusting their school attendance. Children in larger families will tend to receive a smaller share of the total resources devoted to human capital investment, but birth order and the age gap between adjacent children will matter as well. (Glewwe and Jacoby 1991 p. 9)

The third decision is choosing a school, which in many developing countries means choosing among schools at varying distances from home, with varying school fees, and with perceived differences in quality of instruction. According to Glewwe and Jacoby's model, families choose the school that maximizes the child's human capital subject to cost constraints and the child's innate ability. It is assumed that higher quality schools produce more human capital (greater achievement added).

The Glewwe–Jacoby model discusses parental choice of timing in sending their children to school and of school choice, but does not deal with the issue of joint production—the interaction of learning in the home and learning at school. In their model, parents play their role in educational production by making investment and consumption choices through the timing and type of schooling they choose for their children. This implicitly assumes that, as far as schooling choices are concerned, families regard their children primarily in terms of income–earning capacity (present versus future income).

However, the view of children as income providers declines when a family's socioeconomic level goes up. Instead, children become increasingly appreciated for the pleasure they bring to parents and other family members (Fawcett 1983). This should not be surprising. Low-income families have to be more concerned about economic survival in all aspects of their lives. In low-income, rural situations, there are far fewer earning opportunities available to parents, so children constitute one of the few ways for the family of investing in economic security. Higher income families earn more for their work and are much more likely to be aware of the restrictions and opportunity costs imposed by children. As income (and consumption) opportunities increase with more agricultural development, more education, and industrialization and urbanization, so parents view children less as sources of future income and more as sources of psychic satisfaction. In deciding family size, they weigh such satisfaction against their own possibilities of earning more income and consuming more.

In a six-country comparative study, Fawcett (1977) found that "... urban parents (especially the more educated) emphasize the psychological and emotional benefits that derive from interacting with children and observing and guiding their growth and development ... Rural parents, by contrast, emphasize the economic and practical benefits to be derived from children, including the long-term benefit of old-age security" (Fawcett 1983 p. 434). However, most children go to school near home for reasons other than cost (parents prefer to have their children nearby in order to enjoy them), and the relationship between what happens at school and in the home on a day-to-day basis is an important one.

These two factors point to the need for a model that is more oriented to parental preferences and possibilities concerning the use of their own time rather than to children's earning capacity constrained by the cost of schooling. This aspect of joint production will now be discussed.

2. Parental Demand for Educational Quality

Unquestionably all parents, regardless of social class, want the best education for their children. Logic and surveys suggest that this is so. However, the issue in the marketplace is not what people say but how they behave. Since education is largely a public good, the demand for it is at least partly determined by "voice" (Hirschman 1970)—parents' *revealed* willingness and ability to influence their children's education, either through direct efforts at home or by pressuring the system in favor of their children.

The greater voice of higher educated, education-wise families expresses itself in three important forms: (a) in the greater school-relevant experience that families provide to their children *before* they enter school, (b) in the greater school-relevant support they provide their children once in school, and (c) in the greater weight they bring to affecting decisions about their children by school authorities.

Nevertheless, since education is delivered unequally even as a public good (Carnoy and Levin 1985) and is provided privately (under public scrutiny), how much children get is also a function of income and price. Higher income parents have greater possibility, in Hirschman's terms, of "exit" into alternative (higher quality) educational situations, either by moving to higher priced neighborhoods or by buying higher priced private schooling.

It is possible to break this problem down into two parts: (a) how the family allocates its time among activities producing material consumption (C), leisure (L), and children's school-relevant achievement gain (Q); and (b) how the family allocates its consumption between material goods and increased achievement for its children. This choice among activities takes place before the child goes to school and while the child is in school (Becker 1965, Gronau 1977).

Achievement gain in such a model is defined as an *absolute* gain in achievement in each school year or group of school years. One way to measure such gain net of parents' contribution would be to estimate achievement in a given school year as a function of achievement in an earlier year and a function of a student's socioeconomic level (if the school were the unit of observation, the relevant variables would be average achievement and average socioeconomic level of students in the school). The measured achievement versus the "predicted" achievement of students of similar socioeconomic background could be interpreted as the gain resulting from school contribution.

The family earning unit maximizes the utility function:

$$U = F[C, \quad (L + Q)] \tag{1}$$

subject to the budget constraint

$$Pc*C = w*(T - L - Q)) \tag{2}$$

Where T = total time available for work, leisure, and achievement-producing activities; w = wages; and Pc = prices of consumption goods.

In this formulation, voice would only be a function of Q. It is also a function of parents' educational "wisdom", highly correlated with parents' education, but

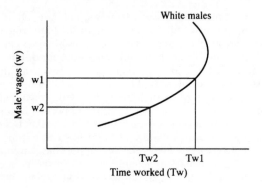

Figure 1
Supply of Labor (White males)

for the moment the assumption is made that it is only a question of time spent on achievement-enhancing activities.

The voice function is complex and highly nonlinear. Figure 1 shows that Tw bends backwards as a function of wages, and Fig. 2 shows that over the last 15 years, as women's wages have risen and men's fallen, women have increased the average hours they work. In addition, the women's curve has shifted to the right as families attempt to maintain real income and the percentage of single head of household females increases (see Fig. 2).

Under quite usual assumptions about the trade-off between leisure (L) and time spent with children on school-related activities (Q), the time available for educational functions in the parents' day is greater among low-wage earners than among middle-wage earners, at least comparing two-parent families and one-parent families as separate categories (see Fig. 3). However, once account is taken of the higher incidence of female-headed households among those of low income, and the possibility that low-income fathers may be less likely to substitute for traditional female roles (see Hill and Stafford 1974, 1980 on

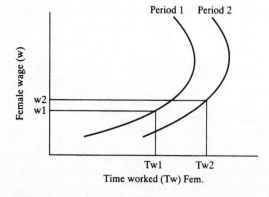

Figure 2
Supply of Labor (females)

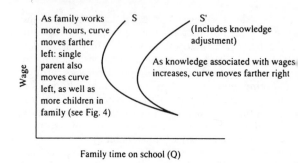

Figure 3
Supply of parent time for child's intellectual development

the greater shift from market to home work by less educated females), this shifts the low end of the Ts curve to the left (see Fig. 4). Finally, in both Figs 3 and 4, when parents' educational wisdom (K) is added into the curve, the upper end is shifted far to the right. A good example of the power of K is that college-educated female heads of households—even where the father has been absent from an early age—may have more voice (influence over their children's education) than lower educated, often higher income, two-parent families with more time to devote to schooling matters.

Once children are old enough to go to school, parents can also choose to spend their income on schooling of children or material goods. In this case, they maximize the utility derived from consuming material goods and the increased quality they get from purchasing better public schooling (higher taxes and home payments, or, under a choice program, more distant, higher quality schooling) or private schooling for their children. Following Gertler and Glewwe (1989):

$$U = g(C, Su, Sv), \qquad (3)$$

where Su = public schooling, and Sv = private schooling; subject to the budget constraint

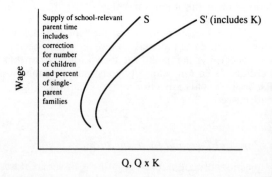

Figure 4
Adjusted supply of parent time for child's intellectual development

$$Pc*C + Pu*Su + Pv*Sv = Y, \qquad (4)$$

where Pu = the cost of public schooling, and Pv = the cost of private schooling.

Since parents are assumed to be buying additional quality of schooling, it is possible to express schooling as some function of a vector of school quality factors, Xu in public school, and Xv in private school. Thus:

$$Su = AuXu \qquad (5)$$

and

$$Sv = AvXv. \qquad (6)$$

Even assuming that all parents have the same utility function for schooling quality and other goods, higher income parents could purchase more schooling quality with their higher income and would have more "exit" potential because of the availability of more income to spend on schooling, even if they did not exercise exit.

When put together, the equations suggest that both voice and the income available for buying higher quality schooling—hence the demand for educational quality—is considerably higher among higher educated parents, and that two-parent families—with more income and/or more time—are more likely to have a higher demand for educational quality than single parents, all other factors being equal. Higher income parents also have the greatest possibility to substitute the purchase of higher quality schooling for spending time with their children, although it is likely that, on average, voice and spending on school quality is higher among higher income parents.

All this is hypothetical, but measurable. If the formulation of the voice curve is correct, the demand for educational quality is lower among low- and middle-educated, low-income parents on two counts: they are likely to have less expressed voice and certainly have less "exit" than higher education, higher income parents. They are also likely to invest less in their children before they enter elementary education. The difference in school-relevant investment for children coming from less and more educated households comes from three sources: (a) the greater V in higher educated households ($Q \times K$), (b) better nutrition in the crucial early childhood years, and (c) more school-relevant resources at home. The latter two are a function of income as well as parents' education and school wisdom. Therefore, children from higher educated, school-wise homes may come to school "easier to teach," increasing institutional demand for higher achievement gains through higher academic expectations by teachers and parents.

2.1 Some Empirical Estimates of the Effect of Adult Time on Children's Achievement

There have been attempts to measure the relationship between parent time inputs and children's achievement in the United States, but establishing the link is difficult and the effects vary widely from study to study (for a review, see Kelley 1992). Leibowitz (1974, 1977) finds that mother's education affects children's achievement by enhancing both the quantity and quality of time that mothers spend with their children. Benson (1982) finds that parent involvement has little direct effect on achievement except for middle socioeconomic class (SES) children: high SES children have high achievement independent of parent time, and low SES children show little improvement even with more parent time. Datcher-Loury (1988) finds a significant effect of childcare hours on childrens years of schooling completed for mothers with more than 12 years of schooling, but no impact at lower levels of mother's schooling.

3. School Quality and Family Production of Education

Children from higher educated, school-wise homes may come to school "easier to teach," increasing institutional demand for higher achievement gains through higher academic expectations by teachers and parents (see *Political Economy of Educational Production*) for an analysis of institutional demand). But at the same time, schools and school districts with high expectations for pupils' academic achievement irrespective of children's home educational environment can increase parents' ability to improve pupil's school performance (Levin 1991). Indeed, school administrators' and teachers' willingness to engage less school-wise, lower-voice parents in the schooling process may be a key to improving school quality.

This potential effort by schools and the resulting effect on pupil achievement can be modeled as follows:

$K = f$ (school administration, parents initial knowledge);

$K = bK$ (O)

Parents' $V = g(Q, K)$;

Achievement in school = $h(Xi,$ parents' $V)$;

where parents' voice (V) is expressed as a function of time spent on school-related activities at home (Q) and knowledge about schooling and school learning (K), and K is a function of some initial parental knowledge plus school administration efforts to add to that initial knowledge, as measured by b.

This accounts for the fact that some of the more recent efforts to raise school achievement among disadvantaged children, such as the *Escuela Nueva* in Colombia that targets rural children (UNICEF 1991) or the Accelerated Schools model in the United States (Levin 1991) that targets low-income, minority children, put a significant focus on involving the community in the schools. Parents in these efforts are motivated and instructed by teachers in helping the children at home. In turn, these types of parental involvement programs enable teachers to raise expectations concerning the amount of work children are supposed to do for school.

3.1 Empirical Estimates of School Quality and Joint Production

Estimates of the functions described are sparse, especially when it comes to parents' use of time by level of income and its relationship to voice. But both Glewwe and Jacoby (1991) and Gertler and Glewwe (1989) have estimated school choice functions for Ghana and Peru, respectively, and Glewwe and Jacoby (1991) have estimated the school timing and attainment function for Ghana.

In the Ghana case study, urban and rural children are mixed in one sample, which may cause problems since the variables affecting choices about schooling may be quite different between the two groups. There is some indication that this is so. Children outside Accra start schooling significantly later, so much so that living outside Accra has a larger negative impact on late starting than three standard deviations of innate ability have on lowering the school starting age (Glewwe and Jacoby Table 5). Higher male agricultural wage also raises starting age, as does lower parent income. But it is not clear from their results whether parental income has a significant effect on children in urban areas.

To some extent school quality (as measured by teachers' experience and the physical characteristics of the school) also affects starting age, as do enrollment fees. As would be expected, many of these same variables affect school attainment. Interestingly enough, when school variables, religion, and place of residence are taken into account, parents' education is relatively unimportant in affecting either starting age or school attainment.

In choosing secondary schools (middle schools in Ghana), both case studies found that "better educated parents derive higher utility from sending their children to faraway schools," and that, in Ghana, "more able children are also more likely to be sent away," as are those from higher income families. Higher quality schools are more attractive to parents than less attractive schools. Since in the Ghana case, these are all fee-charging schools, parents do appear to make choices based on economic and quality considerations.

This suggests that the choice models have some validity. But the results also suggest that powerful locational and cultural variables may be more influential than either school or income variables in determining school attendance and selection choices. It would be interesting to test whether choices differ in rural and urban areas and whether they vary among different ethnic groups, and to explain why. One good reason may be that the view of children varies considerably according to ethnicity, location,

and family education and income. This suggests that joint production between family and school depends critically on family values and the role the school plays in those values. This is hardly a spectacular revelation, but economists still do not take it very seriously.

See also: Education Production Functions; Political Economy of Educational Production

References

Becker G 1965 A theory of the allocation of time. *Economic Journal* 75 (September): 493–517
Benson C S 1982 Household production of human capital: Time uses of parents and children as inputs In: McMahon W W, Geske T G (eds.) 1982 *Financing Education: Overcoming Inefficiency and Inequity.* University of Illinois Press, Urbana, Illinois
Bourdieu P, Passeron C 1977 *Reproduction in Education, Society, and Culture.* Sage, Beverly Hills, California
Carnoy M, Levin H 1985 *Schooling and Work in the Democratic State.* Stanford University Press, Stanford, California
Datcher-Loury L 1988 Effects of mother's home time on children's schooling. *Rev. Econ. Stat.* 70(3): 367–73
Fawcett J T 1977 The value and cost of children: Converging theory and research. In: Ruzicka L T (ed.) 1977 *The Economic and Social Supports for High Fertility.* Australian National University, Department of Demography, Canberra
Fawcett J T 1983 Perceptions of the value of children. In: Bulatao R, Lee R (eds.) 1983 *Determinants of Fertility in Developing Countries.* Academic Press, New York
Gertler P, Glewwe P 1989 The willingness to pay for education in developing countries: Evidence from rural Peru. Living Standards Measurement Study, Working Paper No. 54, World Bank, Washington, DC
Glewwe P, Jacoby H 1991 Student achievement and schooling choice in low income countries: Evidence from Ghana. World Bank, Washington, DC (mimeo)
Gronau R 1977 Leisure, home production, and work—the theory of the allocation of time revisited. *J. Pol. Econ.* 85(6): 1099–1123
Gronau R 1986 Home production—a survey. In: Ashenfelter O C, Layard R (eds.) 1986 *Handbook of Labor Economics,* Vol. 1. North-Holland, Amsterdam
Hanushek A 1986 The economics of schooling: Production and efficiency in public schools. *J. Econ. Lit.* 24(3): 1141–77
Hill C R, Stafford F P 1974 Allocation of time to preschool children and educational opportunity. *J. Hum. Resources* 9(3): 323–41
Hill C R, Stafford F P 1980 Parental care of children: Time diary estimates of quantity, predictability, and variety. *J. Hum. Resources* 15(2): 219–39
Hirschman O 1970 *Exit, Voice, and Loyalty: Responses to Decline in Firms, Organizations, and States.* Harvard University Press, Cambridge, Massachusetts
Kelley C 1992 How does society invest in its children? Estimating the value of non-school adult time. Unpublished dissertation proposal, Stanford University, Stanford, California (mimeo)

Leibowitz A 1974 Home investments in children. In: Schultz T W (ed.) 1974 *Economics of the Family: Marriage, Children, and Human Capital.* University of Chicago Press, Chicago, Illinois

Leibowitz A 1977 Parental inputs and children's achievements. *J. Hum. Resources* 12(2): 242–51

Levin H 1991 Building school capacity for effective teacher empowerment: Applications to elementary schools with at-risk students. Consortium for Policy Research in Education, Rutgers University, New Brunswick, New Jersey

UNICEF 1991 *Education.* Thematic Kit, No. 1. UNICEF, New York

Microeconomics of School Production

D. H. Monk

Economists have a characteristically macro orientation toward school productivity issues. Certainly, the early attempts to estimate education production functions focused on macro policy issues and relied heavily on survey-based data aggregated to school and even district levels. For a period, during the late 1970s and early 1980s, it appeared that frustration with the inconsistent and largely insignificant results of these early production function studies (Hanushek 1986) would give rise to more micro-oriented production function studies in which analysts would measure actual inputs supplied to individual students. The work of Brown and Saks (1987), Hanushek (1971), Rossmiller (1986), and Thomas and Kemmerer (1983) pointed in this direction.

However, it has become increasingly clear that economically oriented research on school productivity has not moved in this direction (Monk 1992). Instead, several alternative responses have emerged. For example, analysts have retained highly aggregated data but have worked to achieve refinements in the attributes of schools and schooling that are being measured. Examples include the work of Card and Krueger (1990) and Ferguson (1991).

Analysts have also improved estimation techniques. Important advances have occurred in the statistical treatment of nested production processes, wherein relevant phenomena transpire simultaneously at several levels of aggregation (Bryk and Raudenbush 1988). Analysts have also begun to explore alternative research strategies. In particular, there have been a number of economically oriented evaluations of educational innovations which provide explicit treatment of costs in relation to benefits (Barnett 1985, Levin et al. 1984).

Finally, there have been efforts that are less focused on estimating the properties of education production functions and more focused on the microeconomics of the education production *process* itself (Akin and Stewart 1982, Arnott and Rowse 1987, Becker 1982, Brown 1988, Brown and Saks 1980, Correa and Gruver 1987, Farkas and Hotchkiss 1989, Hoenack 1988, Hoenack and Monk 1990, Lima 1981, McKenzie 1979, McKenzie and Staaf 1974, Monk 1984, 1991a,

Mulligan 1984, Murnane and Nelson 1984, Snellings 1987). An important rationale for this work has been an awareness that much of the disappointment associated with the earlier production-function estimation studies can be traced to the inapplicability of standard economic production models to the study of education. Analysts contributing to this line of research set for themselves the daunting task of adapting standard economic models of production to the peculiarities of educational processes. These economically oriented assessments of the educational process will be the subject of this entry.

The work is primarily conceptual, and for a variety of reasons is not well-known within educational policy circles. This is due in part to the recent origin of the work, partly because the analysis can become quite technical fairly quickly, and partly because the messages the work generates tend to point in unconventional directions that sometimes work to the disadvantage of influential stakeholders in the policy debate. It is, nevertheless, important and promising work. By focusing on conceptual issues, it has the potential to lay down highly informative groundwork for the next generation of production function studies. It also has important and more immediate implications for the direction of public policy.

1. Interdependence of Substitutable Inputs

An important part of this research involves the use of principles drawn from productivity theory to examine educational practice. Many of the earlier and ongoing efforts to estimate educational production functions make use of highly simplified production models which sacrifice sensitivity to relevant economic phenomena (e.g., the substitutability of inputs) for the sake of easy (or relatively easy) statistical estimation.

A common goal for production function analysts is to identify school resources that have high levels of marginal productivity. Once these resources are identified, the often implicit message is that policymakers simply need to increase the supply of more productive inputs and to reduce or at least hold constant the supply of the less productive inputs.

While such a policy implication may appear to be straightforward, the potential for inputs to be substituted coupled with the self-evident fact that school officials (teachers and administrators) are not the only agents who allocate educational resources make the actual policy implications much less clear, even in cases where there is no ambiguity surrounding which school input is the most productive. Becker (1982), Correa and Gruver (1987), and McKenzie (1979) have all explored the reasons for this.

These analysts stress the fact that students themselves make important resource allocation decisions regarding the production of educational outcomes. To the extent that students respond to the increased supply of a more productive school input by withdrawing the supply of inputs over which they have discretion (most notably their time and effort), the expected positive effect on outcomes will not materialize. The recognition that students have interests in life other than the production of school-related learning gains which compete for students' time and energy makes the envisioned withdrawal more than a remote possibility.

Moreover, the substitution can work in the opposite direction. In as much as teachers respond to increased work and effort on the part of students (or to better preparation embodied in students) by withdrawing their own time and effort in order to pursue alternative interests in research, other teaching, or leisure, the expected positive effects on student outcomes can be severely diminished.

2. Diminishing Marginal Returns of Inputs

A second microeconomic principle which has been applied to the study of educational productivity is the proposition that most production processes are characterized by inputs with variable rather than constant levels of marginal productivity. The idea here is that while a given resource may be productive at one level of supply, this need not continue to be the case if the level changes.

There has been some recognition of this principle by those whose goal it is to estimate relationships between educational resources and achievement gains of students. For example, among those who study the effects of class size on achievement, there has evolved a recognition that the effects of a change in class size will likely vary depending on its absolute level. In particular, Glass and Smith (1979) reached the conclusion that the strength of the negative relationship between class size and achievement diminishes as the absolute level of class size increases.

However, this is a principle that can also be applied in interesting ways by analysts who are more directly concerned with the economics of educational

processes. For example, questions may arise about the allocation of resources that are perceived to have great productivity. A good example of such a resource would be an individual teacher in a school who is widely agreed to be superior relative to his or her peers (Monk 1991, Snellings 1987).

One of Murnane's findings was that principals are able to differentiate among their teachers on the basis of their respective levels of productivity (Murnane 1975). If teachers vary widely in this way, their allocation raises a number of difficult issues. The allocation problem can be approached in at least two ways. First, it can be viewed as an equity problem, and the goal becomes one of distributing teachers so that the good, the bad, and the mediocre are equitably apportioned among students. In his interviews with principals, Monk (1987b) found evidence suggesting that this is how the issue is conceived by principals in a sample of United States elementary schools.

Alternatively, the issue can be viewed from an efficiency perspective, and the principle of diminishing marginal returns introduced. The variable productivity of teachers may be regarded as evidence of inefficiency in the distribution of students among teachers. An alternative distribution strategy could be devised which would involve assigning students so as to equalize the marginal productivities of the various teachers on-staff. Such an alternative distribution might involve assigning larger numbers of students to the more productive teachers. On the other hand, it might entail assigning a larger proportion of more difficult students to the more productive teachers. In so doing, the equity issue evaporates, since it would be equally acceptable to parents and others with an interest in the matter whether a child was assigned to a smaller class with a teacher initially judged to be less productive or whether it was assigned to a larger class with a teacher initially judged to be more productive. This indifference would obtain to the degree that the marginal productivities of the teachers were truly equalized.

Gains in efficiency would be realized insofar as the additional students in the initially more productive teachers' classes learn more than would otherwise be the case, and also insofar as the classmates they leave in the previously less productive teachers' classes gain from the reduction in class size.

Of course, the initially more productive teachers would probably object to increases in their class sizes, but whatever additional compensation becomes necessary to offset their displeasure could be financed via reductions in salaries paid to the less productive teachers with the smaller (or otherwise easier) classes. In the final outcome, it is possible for policies designed to equalize the marginal productivities of teachers to improve the efficiency of educational systems.

The analysis may be taken a step further. The prevailing practice of viewing the allocation of superior teachers as an equity rather than as an efficiency issue so that each teacher, regardless of competence ceives roughly the same number of students not selected on the basis of how difficult they are to teach, may result in placing an unnecessarily low ceiling on teachers' own incentive to seek improvement in their performance. As Becker, Correa and Gruver, and McKenzie have made clear, a teacher who makes gains in competence has to strike a balance between improving the performance of students (subject to the students' willingness to continue supplying their own time and energy) and gaining more time for leisure and other pursuits.

A reasonable strategy for a teacher to pursue in the face of the prevailing equity practice would be to improve the performance of his or her students (or some segment of them) only to the point where it becomes apparent that he or she is a cut above the average teacher in the school. Such a teacher would receive the benefits of being sought after by parents and others concerned about the welfare of students, and the balance of the gain could be devoted to freeing time and energy for other pursuits. Going beyond this point would seem to have much less appeal. Thus, it would appear that prevailing practice imposes a potentially quite limiting ceiling on teachers' ambitions to improve their performance as instructors.

. Microeconomics of Grouping

Economic models have also been applied to various aspects of grouping within educational settings (Arnott and Rowse 1987, Brown 1988, Monk 1984, 1991a). From an economic perspective it is important to balance whatever gains a student realizes from spending time in a small group setting with his or her instructor against whatever drawbacks are associated with the accompanying time spent making use of seatwork or other types of resources at greater distance from the instructor. The two uses of time are linked because teachers are responsible for collections of students, and time spent in small group settings with some students necessarily entails time spent by the remaining students in instructional settings that are less proximate to the instructor.

This need not imply that the learning resources supplied to students in these large group settings are necessarily less productive, but if they are not it becomes less than obvious why teachers spend any time at all in small group settings with their students. The grouping phenomena becomes interesting from an economic perspective to the degree that small group time is more productive than large group time, and to the degree that large group (seatwork) time is less productive than direct instruction provided to the whole class.

Most of the applications of economic models to grouping issues rely heavily on ad hoc assumptions about the differing levels of resource (especially teacher resource) productivities in different size contexts.

In contrast, Mulligan (1984) draws on queuing theory to justify differences in the productivity of teacher resources in different group size settings.

What makes the phenomena even more interesting from an economic perspective is the fact that the terms of trade between small group and large group (seatwork) time are generally not one-to-one. If a teacher forms three groups and spends an equal amount of time with each group, a minute of small group time for a given student translates into 2 minutes of large group (seatwork) time.

Thus, to the extent that time spent in small group settings is sufficiently more productive to offset the loss (relative to what would have been realized in the absence of the grouping strategy), the grouping strategy is desirable.

This test of the wisdom of grouping is far removed from the usual evaluation of whether students learn more in small group settings than in large. The microeconomic approach takes more explicit account of the trade-offs such as strategy entails. It also points out the sources of the losses, and generates implications for both future research and policy. In particular, although not immediately apparent in this approach, it highlights the importance of attending to the productivity of student time in the large groups that accompany grouping strategies.

4. Microeconomics of Cooperation

Correa and Gruver (1987) have applied aspects of game theory to the study of how teachers and students interact. These researchers pay explicit attention to the structural difficulties surrounding serious efforts to foster cooperation within educational systems. More specifically, they show that equilibrium with interaction (between students and teachers) but without cooperation will result in too little effort being allocated to academic achievement for optimal satisfaction. In other words, they demonstrate that the resultant equilibrium is such that it would be possible for both the student and the teacher to benefit more. They trace the difficulty to the fact that student achievement is commonly regarded simply as a public good, which they assume enters the utility functions of both teachers and students.

They also show that the realization of these improvements will require enforced cooperation where explicit attention is paid to counteracting the incentives which will exist for both teachers and students to break the agreement. This focus on the difficulties associated with achieving cooperation contrasts sharply with the more typical naive, ill-researched optimism which presents cooperation as a cure-all which will be relatively easy to accomplish.

Correa and Gruver were prescient in their recognition that students can make use of perverse threats in their bargaining with teachers. Picus (1991) reports anecdotal evidence suggesting that students in Californian high schools sought to extract concessions from their teachers in exchange for student cooperation on state-imposed examinations. These teachers in California had a more than casual interest in their students' cooperation, since monetary rewards were attached by the state to the students' performance. Hoenack (1988) also anticipated this result when he advocated including students in the rewards provided as part of incentive systems intended to improve educational productivity.

The role parents can play in fostering cooperation between teachers and students was passed over too quickly by Correa and Grover. Some of the most promising interventions by other authors place considerable emphasis on strengthening the parental role in schools (Comer 1988, Levin 1989). Moreover, Coleman (1988) extends the economist's notion of human capital to capture parental and other community influences on students' intellectual and social growth. He uses the term "social capital" to encompass these external influences and the role they can play within schools.

Correa and Gruver's analysis can also be extended to examine cooperation among students as part of their instruction. This topic attracted considerable attention during the 1980s, although the perspective is typically that of the psychologist rather than the economist (see Slavin 1989 for an example). This is an area where the economist's sensitivity and insights into the tradeoffs associated with cooperation might prove very helpful.

Other researchers employing microeconomic models have been attentive to the problems of fostering cooperation at more centralized levels of schooling systems. In particular, Galvin (1990) studied cooperation among local education agencies and was able to discern both costs and benefits accruing in the short, as well as in the longer, term. He makes it clear that meaningful cooperation is not easily accomplished and can require institutional support from more centralized levels of government.

5. *Microeconomics of Teacher Deployment and Development*

By differentiating among the numerous skills teachers bring to their craft, and by recognizing that teachers can vary enormously in the aptitudes they possess, it is possible to gain further insights into the microeconomics of educational processes.

For example, it is possible to conceive of a teacher-productivity profile wherein a given teacher's ability to teach in a variety of different subject areas is assessed. One teacher might be capable of teaching at a high level of competence in a relatively large range

of subjects (e.g., algebra, geometry, earth science, biology, and chemistry); another teacher might be more of a specialist, and hence competent to teach in a much narrower range. Various propositions can be advanced about the character of these profiles, including the reasonable assumption that, as a general rule, breadth in the range of subjects taught at a given level of competence will come at the expense of the degree of competence in the teaching of any given subject. Thus, the first teacher's profile might be depicted as a blunter, less elevated surface, while the second teacher's profile would have a narrower, steeper, and perhaps more spiked appearance.

Variation in productivity across subject areas takes on added significance when it is recognized that secondary school teachers tend not to specialize in the teaching of even broadly conceived subject areas (Monk 1987a). Microeconomic analysis draws attention to the complexity surrounding the assignment of teachers to their classes under these circumstances. It proposes that attention be paid to teachers' competence levels outside their major subject area specialization. Indeed, the analysis suggests the counterintuitive result that under certain conditions, the overall productivity of a school might be enhanced by having at least some teachers *not* teach in their area of greatest competence. Such a conclusion would obtain in situations where some faculty members' productivity profiles were blunter while others were quite spiked.

The characteristics of the productivity profiles themselves are outcomes of policies affecting the development of teaching talent. The current emphasis within the United States, and the traditional emphasis in most other countries, of strengthening the subject matter preparation of high school teachers by requiring undergraduate majors in subject areas (Holmes Group 1986) could further contribute to the spiked character of teachers' productivity profiles, with the attendant resource-allocation challenges examined above.

Economists are also growing in their sensitivity to the likely reality that there exists no unique solution to the question of what constitutes a "good" teacher, or what constitutes "good teaching" (Hanushek 1986, Lima 1981, Murnane and Nelson 1984). Lima conceived of good teaching as a stochastic learning process in which the individual begins with some model of what a good teacher does in the classroom and has this supplemented with accurate feedback about what has worked and what has not worked. According to Lima, the key to developing effective teachers is a diet of constructive feedback coupled with the opportunity to practice different styles.

The optimal allocation of teaching talent within schools is linked in complicated ways to supply as well as demand phenomena. On the supply side questions arise over why limits exist on the degree to which secondary school teachers specialize in the subjects they teach. On the demand side, there are questions about the determinants of student demand for one type of course rather than another. Farkas and Hotchkiss (1989) connect student demand for courses to perceptions about grading difficulty. They report evidence suggesting that teachers of more advanced courses impose more rigorous grading standards, and they observe that the expected negative effects of such practice on course-taking can be offset by the high demand academically oriented students can have for such courses

6. Conclusion

One of the primary lessons to be learned from the work in this area during the 1980s is that the microeconomic analysis of education productivity is not synonymous with attempts to estimate education production functions using highly disaggregated data intended to measure actual resource flows to individual students. Rather than move in this direction, economists and others applying economic models have pursued a more conceptually rooted approach and have used microeconomic principles such as the substitutability of inputs and the law of diminishing marginal productivity to derive insights into educational phenomena which occur deep within educational systems. Analysts have also developed economically oriented examinations of widespread educational practices such as grouped instruction, cooperation in the production of education, and the distribution of teachers and students among instructional settings.

The interest in establishing the properties of education production functions continues (see the relevant entries in this encyclopedia), and the micro approach to estimation, although assigned a low priority during the 1980s, remains a viable, if costly, strategy. It will be interesting to see if this line of research makes a reappearance during the 1990s and beyond. In the meantime, the microeconomic approach to the study of the educational process has established itself as an important and promising source of new insights into pressing educational policy issues.

See also: Economics of School Enterprise; Economics of Educational Time and Learning

References

Akin J S, Stewart J F 1982 The time allocation decision and achievement patterns of young children. *Econ. Educ. Rev.* 1(4): 307–30

Arnott R, Rowse J 1987 Peer group effects and educational attainment. *J. Pub. Econ.* 32: 287–305

Barnett S W 1985 Benefit–cost analysis of the Perry preschool program and its policy implications. *Educ. Eval. Policy Anal.* 7(4): 333–42

Becker W E 1982. The educational process and student achievement given uncertainty in measurement. *Am. Econ. Rev.* 72: 229–36

Brown B W 1988 The microeconomics of learning: Students, teachers, and classrooms. In: Monk D H, Underwood J (eds.) 1988 *Microlevel School Finance: Issues and Implications for Policy.* Harper and Row, New York

Brown B W, Saks D H 1980 Production technologies and resource allocations within classrooms and schools: Theory and measurement. In: Dreeben R, Thomas J A (eds.) 1980 *The Analysis of Educational Productivity Vol. 1: Issues in Microanalysis.* Ballinger, Cambridge, Massachusetts

Brown B W, Saks D H 1987 The microeconomics of the allocation of teachers' time and student learning. *Econ. Educ. Rev.* 6(4): 319–32

Bryk A S, Raudenbush S W 1988 Toward a more appropriate conceptualization of research on school effects: A three-level hierarchical linear model. *Am. J. Educ.* 97(1): 65–108

Card D, Krueger A 1990 Does school quality matter? Returns to education and the characteristics of public schools in the United States. National Bureau of Economic Research Working Paper No. 3358, Cambridge, Massachusetts

Coleman J S 1988 Social capital in the creation of human capital. *Am. J. Sociol.* 94: S95–S120

Comer J P 1988 Educating poor minority children. *Sci. Am.* 259(5): 42–48

Correa H, Gruver G W 1987 Teacher-student interaction: A game theoretic extension of the economics theory of education. *Mathematical Social Sciences* 13: 19–47

Farkas G, Hotchkiss L 1989 Incentives and disincentives for subject matter difficulty and student effort: Course grade determinants across the stratification system. *Econ. Educ. Rev.* 8(2): 121–32

Ferguson R F 1991 Paying for public education: New evidence on how and why money matters. *Harvard Journal on Legislation* 28(2): 465–98

Galvin P 1990 The structure of school district cooperatives: Factors that influence participation in cooperative ventures. Doctoral dissertation, Cornell University, Ithaca, New York

Glass G V, Smith M 1979 Meta-analysis of research on the relationship of class size and achievement. *Educ. Eval. Policy Anal.* 1(1): 2–16

Hanushek E A 1971 Teacher characteristics and gains in student achievement: Estimation using micro data. *Am. Econ. Rev. Papers and Proceedings* 61: 280–88

Hanushek E A 1986 The economics of schooling: Production and efficiency in the public schools. *J. Econ. Lit.* 24(3): 1141–78

Hoenack S A 1988 Incentives, outcome-based instruction, and school efficiency. In: Monk D H, Underwood J (eds.) 1988 *Microlevel School Finance: Issues and Implications for Policy.* Ballinger, Cambridge, Massachusetts

Hoenack S A, Monk D H 1990 Economic aspects of teacher evaluation. In: Millman J, Darling-Hammond L (eds.) 1990 *Handbook of Teacher Evaluation: Assessing Elementary and Secondary School Teachers*, 2nd edn. Sage Publications, Newbury Park, California

Holmes Group 1986 *Tomorrow's Teachers: A Report of the Holmes Group.* Holmes Group Inc., East Lansing, Michigan

Levin H M 1989 Financing the education of at-risk students. *Educ. Eval. Policy Anal.* 11(1): 47–60

Levin H M, Glass G V, Meister G R (1984) Cost-effectiveness of four educational interventions. Report 84-A11. Stanford University Institute for Research on Educational Finance and Governance, Stanford, California

Lima A K 1981 An economic model of teaching effectiveness. *Am. Econ. Rev.* 71(5): 1056–59

McKenzie R B 1979 *The Political Economy of the Educational Process*. Marinus Nijhoff, Boston, Massachusetts

McKenzie R B, Staaf R I 1974 *An Economic Theory of Learning*. University Publications, Blacksburg, Virginia

Monk D H 1984 Interdependencies among educational inputs and resource allocation in classrooms. *Econ. Educ. Rev.* 3(1): 65–73

Monk D H 1987a Secondary school size and curriculum comprehensiveness. *Econ. Educ. Rev.* 6(2): 137–50

Monk D H 1987b Assigning elementary pupils to their teachers. *Elem. Sch. J.* 88(2): 167–87

Monk D H 1991 Microeconomic aspects of schooling: An overview with implications for policy. In: Verstegen D A, Ward J G (eds.) 1991 *Spheres of Justice in Education*. Harper Collins, New York

Monk D H 1992 Education productivity research: An update and assessment of its role in education finance reform. *Educ. Eval. Policy Anal.* 14(4): 307–332

Mulligan J G 1984 A classroom production function. *Economic Inquiry* 22(2): 218–26

Murnane R J 1975 *The Impact of School Resources on the Learning of Inner City Children*. Ballinger, Cambridge, Massachusetts

Murnane R J, Nelson R R 1984 Production and innovation when techniques are tacit: The case of education. *Journal of Economic Behavior and Organization* 5: 353–73

Picus L O 1991 Using incentives to stimulate improved school performance: An assessment of alternative approaches. Paper presented at the annual meeting of the American Educational Research Association, Boston, Massachusetts

Rossmiller R A 1986 *Resource Utilization in Schools and Classrooms: Final Report*. Wisconsin Center for Education Research, School of Education, University of Wisconsin, Madison, Wisconsin

Slavin R E 1989 *Cooperative Learning: Student Teams*, 2nd ed. Prentice-Hall, Englewood Cliffs, New Jersey

Snellings E C 1987 Classrooms as commons. *Atlantic Economic Journal* 15(3): 76

Thomas J A, Kemmerer F 1983 *Money, Time, and Learning*. School of Education, State University of New York, Albany, New York

School Dropouts

D. M. Kelly

Economists have traditionally viewed school dropout and grade repetition as measures of inefficiency or wastage. Other analysts are more interested in which groups suffer the most as a result of inefficient schooling systems, and their work focuses on how schooling often operates to the greater disadvantage of groups on the margins of power in society. Before taking up this theme, this entry will discuss whether students drop out or get pushed out, how to measure school disengagement, the incidence of the problem, and some key variables that explain it.

1. Dropouts, Pushouts, and the Concept of Disengagement

Much of the research on students who fail to complete school can be divided into two imperfect schools of thought. The dominant school—which fits within the traditions of neoclassical economics, status attainment, and social psychology—conceives of early school leaving as dropping out. Researchers who use this framework favor correlation models in which students' behavior, performance in school, psychological states, and family background are independent variables (e.g., Ekstrom et al. 1986). This approach generally casts dropping out as an individual act, signifying individual, or perhaps family or cultural, failure.

The other school of thought conceives of noncompleters as pushouts. Such researchers see the variables emphasized by the status-attainment school as symptoms, not causes. They focus on unequal economic, political, and social structures and certain schooling practices like tracking and expulsion that serve to stigmatize, discourage, and exclude children. Researchers using this model have tended to document the inequities in the economic and political system and then postulate that pushouts are functional to the reproduction of the capitalist order (e.g., Bowles and Gintis 1976; for a review of Brazilian writers in this tradition, see Vershine and Pita de Melo 1988). Viewed through this lens, the way in which the schooling system achieves this and why the pushouts comply is relatively straightforward.

Both frameworks recognize that a certain failure rate is built into most schooling systems and that schools sort children hierarchically, but there is disagreement over the basis. The dropout school believes that, ideally, the sorting of students is based on merit. The curriculum basically works the same way for everyone and provides a fair means of selection nto different areas of the workforce. In contrast, the pushout school argues that schools exclude students on the basis of class, race, ethnicity, and other markers of power and status, and that they rationalize this as being done on the basis of ability. So-called merit-based standards, set by the most powerful in society, serve mainly to perpetuate inequality. Wealthy children, for example, often attend high-quality schools, and their parents can afford to provide outside help and tutoring.

The term "dropout" puts inordinate blame on the individual; the term "pushout" puts inordinate blame on the institution. Dropout implies that the student makes an independent, final decision, while pushout implies that the institution acts inexorably to purge unwilling victims. Some recent work on early school leaving has emphasized that it is a mutual process of rejection (e.g., Fine 1990), or what can be called "disengagement." The metaphor underlying engagement is that of two toothed wheels of a gear, student and school, meshed together so that the motion in one is passed on to the other.

The concept of disengagement connotes a long-running, interactive process which may be reversible. It therefore encourages researchers to connect events in students' lives over time and look for cumulative effects. It also acknowledges the spectrum of ways in which students are engaged: one who recognizes the need for a diploma can be very different from one who likes school. The terms dropout and pushout retain some usefulness in characterizing an exit from school—often the final outcome—as more student- or school-initiated. For others—and in North America and elsewhere this is a significant group—the decisive moment of dropout or pushout never occurs; these students attend infrequently, leaving and returning several times, and thus may be more aptly described as fade-outs (Kelly 1993).

2. Measuring School Disengagement

Disengagement can be difficult to document because it occurs over time and may not always be observable (e.g., passive resistance to learning) or may be open to different interpretations. The literature on dropouts and pushouts suggests signs and styles of disengagement primarily displayed within school settings. These indicators of disengagement can be grouped under four major domains: academics (including teacher–student relations), peer relations, extracurricular activities, and the schooling credential itself (e.g., certificate, diploma).

Indicators of disengagement from academics include: poor academic progress, classroom withdrawal (e.g., few instructional interactions), participation in nonacademic or remedial classes and programs, grade repetition, and suspension and expulsion.

Ethnographic research has shown that peer cultures mediate student outcomes like dropout and pushout. These outcomes are not simply a function of within-school factors, as economic models often imply. Indicators of disengagement related to peers include: fighting, inability to make friends, alienation from and opposition to peer groups accorded status by the school, and bonding with peers marginalized by institutional practices.

Indicators of disengagement from extracurricular activities include lack of participation in and dislike of school-sponsored clubs, teams, and events. An example of disengagement from the credential is the belief that a diploma is either not necessary to realize future plans or will not bring promised rewards.

While school administrators keep records of some of these indicators, only recently have researchers and educators begun to think of systematically linking patterns of disengagement to individual students in an effort to identify and re-engage those "at risk" of dropping out or being pushed out. Instead, most attempts to define and measure disengagement have focused on the final outcome of the process, with one exception: grade repetition.

Dropout statistics vary widely, depending in part on the definition of dropout, the source of the data, and the method of calculating the rate (Rumberger 1987). Students who transfer to another school, who obtain an alternative certificate of achievement, or who stop attending but eventually return to school, are sometimes counted as dropouts. On the other hand, students who leave school at a young age, who leave to get married or join the military, or who pass the legal compulsory school attendance age are sometimes not counted as dropouts or pushouts. Nor are students who attend regularly but do not learn to read and write.

True dropout rates are difficult to obtain because few countries collect data on who actually drops out and who gets promoted (UNESCO 1984). Two common, but crude, proxies derive from attrition and census data. Typically, attrition rates are constructed for a class cohort out of enrollment and graduation numbers. One of the difficulties of the approach lies in determining membership in the cohort. Transfers and repeaters may get counted twice, overstating the number of students initially enrolled. Thus, attrition rates tend to overestimate the true dropout rate. One can use census data to calculate what percentage of a given age cohort has not completed, say, primary or secondary school and is not enrolled in school. But because census data are usually self-reported or second-hand and undercount marginalized groups like low-income and ethnic minorities, this approach can underestimate the true dropout rate.

3. Worldwide Patterns of Dropout/Pushout and Repetition

In general, primary school dropout rates are low in countries with a high gross national product per capita. These countries, primarily the industrialized countries of Europe, North America, Japan, Australia, and New

Zealand, have also achieved universal primary school enrollment. Table 1 shows that 40 percent of students who enrolled in primary school in low-income countries such as Haiti and Mali dropped out or were pushed out before the terminal year of that cycle. Moreover, primary school completion rates declined over the 1980s in the poorest countries (Lockheed and Verspoor 1990).

Repetition rates show a similar pattern: they are highest in the poorest countries. Yet these aggregate data mask differences among countries due to educational structure and promotion practices. For example, low-income countries like Sudan and middle-income countries like the Republic of Korea, Zimbabwe, and Malaysia now practice automatic promotion. Although most industrialized countries follow automatic promotion either by law or in practice (UNESCO Office of Statistics 1984), many states in the United States have ended social promotion in response to concern over standards, making the country's annual repetition rate comparable to such low-income countries as Kenya (Shepard and Smith 1989 pp. 7–9).

In many countries of Africa and Asia, except the poorest, girls' repetition rates are lower than those of boys (UNESCO 1984). However, girls tend to drop out at higher rates and earlier, regardless of their repetition rate. Further, in many countries with limited access to primary school, girls are enrolled at lower rates, so dropout and repetition rates alone tend to understate gender inequities (Deble 1980 pp. 47–50). Several studies have shown that girls (or their parents) are more easily discouraged by repetition. In countries where access to further schooling is limited, parents more often encourage boys to repeat a grade in the hope that they will obtain better entrance exam scores (UNESCO 1979, Lewis et al. 1990, Anderson 1988).

4. Repetition: A Pushout Factor or Indicator of Academic Failure?

Many studies show that repetition and dropout/pushout are correlated. The relationship of repeating a grade to final disengagement is complex

and shaped by the context of particular schooling systems and countries. Researchers, particularly those using a dropout framework, have commonly assumed that repetition and dropout were both largely attributable to academic failure. In contrast, those using a pushout framework have argued that being retained a grade sends an institutional message of rejection that contributes directly to students' disengagement from school, above and beyond their actual ability or achievement level (Fine 1991). In one of the few studies to examine the causal relationship between repetition and dropout, Grissom and Shepard (1989) found that repetition increased the probability of eventually dropping out of school—across three city school districts in the United States—by 20 to 30 percent, after achievement, socioeconomic status and gender were controlled.

Repetition may also contribute to dropping out when it results in students being overage for their grade. As they approach the age of adulthood, which varies by culture, some students, especially girls and low-income youths, face increased domestic and work responsibilities and the prospects of early marriage and pregnancy that may pull them out of school. In some Third World countries, students may be overage for their grade due not to repetition but to late enrollment. For example, a study of 37 schools in Argentina found that eventual dropouts enrolled in school late and had irregular attendance compared with primary school completers, but they were not more likely to have repeated (Patty and Tobin 1973).

5. Key Variables Explaining Disengagement

Before discussing some key variables that help to explain disengagement, a few preliminary observations are in order. First, most school dropout research has been descriptive, either based on correlation models or surveys of dropouts and educators. The former cannot show that the factors associated with early school leaving actually cause the phenomenon. Survey

Table 1
Median primary school dropout and repetition rates 1985

Countries by GNP per capita	Dropout Rates (in %)		Repetition Rates (in %)		
	Total	No. Countries	Total	Female	No. Countries
Low	40.8	13	16.3	16.5	23
Lower middle	19.5	11	10.6	8.7	20
Upper middle	14.1	7	7.5	5.5	14
High (oil exporters)			5.7	5.2	3
High (market economies)			1.5	1.1	10

Source: UNESCO database 1989, cited in Lockheed and Verspoor 1990 pp. 205–16

data must also be interpreted with caution. Dropouts and pushouts, influenced by norms regarding socially acceptable behavior, may answer vaguely or lie. The responses of teachers and administrators also tend to reflect self-interest. As Davico (1990) found in her study of eight Brazilian schools, teachers identified the low socioeconomic conditions of students and families—seen to limit students' ability to learn—as the primary reason for dropout. This deflected attention from their own behavior and other in-school factors.

A second caveat has to do with differences among regions and countries. Much of the Third World data focuses more broadly on access and participation issues and thus has examined such factors as the number of, and distance to, schools (Stromquist 1989), whereas in highly industrialized countries like the United States, researchers have placed more emphasis on student behavior and achievement in relation to disengagement (Rumberger 1987). Nevertheless, a number of the factors that determine initial access to schooling also affect survival once enrolled, and these factors have been shown to interact with each other in roughly similar ways across countries.

Among these factors are markers of power and status such as social class, ethnicity and race, gender, and community type (urban or rural). Usually these have been treated as demographic variables, but with demands for democratization increasing, recent research has included more systematic analysis of how various disadvantaged groups have fared through the schooling system as well as in the labor and marriage markets. These outcomes have been seen to shape perceptions of the worth of further schooling.

5.1 Socioeconomic Status

Children living in poverty are less likely to complete school (for reviews, see Anderson 1988, Lockheed and Verspoor 1990, Rumberger 1987). Socioeconomic status, correlated with dropout/pushout, is often measured by parental education, father's occupation, family income, and household items available. Rumberger (1983), in a United States study, found that differences in dropout rates among ethnic groups could be explained mostly by differences in family background. The most uniform predictor among the various ethnic/gender groups was the presence in the home of reading materials.

Surveys of early school leavers underscore the importance of socioeconomic reasons (e.g., Verhine and Pita de Melo 1988). Some families cannot afford to pay for school fees, books and supplies, transportation, and uniforms. Others cannot afford the opportunity costs, that is, the earned income and domestic labor that parents forego when their children are enrolled in school. Still other children report shame at their relative poverty, reflected in their clothes or lack of lunch. In Brazil, where the dropout rate exceeds 80 percent at the primary level, low-income families make up the majority in the public school system. Davico (1990) identified a number of school-related factors that seemed to influence the disengagement process, including inadequately prepared teachers and low expectations for student success.

5.2 Race and Ethnicity

Race and ethnicity also influence who persists in school. Research has shown that groups that have been disadvantaged historically tend to leave school early. In a qualitative study in Canada, most First Nations (aboriginal) people who left school without graduating said racism, including discriminatory practices and attitudes on the part of teachers and peers, had affected their decision to leave (Canada 1990 p. 11). Ethnic and other minority groups may be faced with curricular content that does not reflect their living conditions or presents as truth a certain history and a set of personal experiences that for them is alien. Teaching in a language other than that used by students outside of school may contribute to their disengagement, although this is complicated by socioeconomic status and other factors. For example, Morocco introduces French, a nonindigenous language, in third grade, and a Ministry of Education study there found that knowledge of French was the single largest determinant of success at the end of primary school (Lockheed and Verspoor 1990 p. 106).

Discrimination in the job market and ethnic quotas in educational selection can promote disengagement. In Malaysia, the Malays saw university attendance and better job prospects as more possible and thus continued their schooling. In contrast, the Chinese, who came from higher socioeconomic backgrounds and had better examination scores, tended to discontinue their schooling more often because they perceived fewer payoffs (Wang 1982).

5.3 Gender

The sex-role division of labor within the family and society influences the persistence in school by gender. In some regions boys drop out more often and earlier to herd grazing animals and do other tasks (Stromquist 1989 p. 150). But more often, girls—particularly those in low-income and rural families—seem to be needed at home to care for younger siblings and do housework and agricultural tasks (Anderson 1988, Stromquist 1989, Lewis et al. 1990).

Recognizing that parents in Bangladesh have greater elasticity of demand for girls' schooling, a pilot project offered low-income girls scholarships to encourage them to remain in school. In the project area, the secondary school dropout rate for girls dropped from 15 percent before the program started to 3.5 percent in 1987. Interviews with parents of children both in and out of school confirmed that lack of financial resources was the single most important reason that girls do not attend secondary school (Thein et al. 1990).

Research in the United States and elsewhere has clearly demonstrated the link between early marriage and childbearing and dropping out, the magnitude of which is much stronger for low socioeconomic status youths (Rumberger 1983, Anderson 1988 p. 11). Surveys in developing countries reveal that a number of reasons for girls leaving school are related to the onset of puberty. Girls and parents cite sexual attention from, or involvement with, boys and male teachers, concerns about girls' safety due to distance from school, as well as cultural and religious values concerning early marriage and pregnancy (for a review, see Stromquist 1989 p. 153–58). It is common for schools around the world to exclude girls who become pregnant or get married. In Malawi, for example, institutional policy and practice support the permanent expulsion of pregnant and married girls from formal schooling (Lewis et al. 1990 p. 13).

Do girls leave school due to early pregnancy and marriage, or do these options emerge as a means of escape from an institution—the school—that has failed to offer them a sense of purpose and competence? Scholars and policymakers have often assumed that the school has little influence on girls taking on adult roles early. Yet recent research indicates that pregnancy and marriage may be partly symptoms of, and attempts to deal with, disaffection with school. In the United States a substantial minority of female dropouts or pushouts become pregnant after they leave school. Likewise, several studies done in developing countries have challenged the widely held view that the main reason females drop out of school is due to pregnancy; this may only be the proximate cause or a post hoc explanation (Anderson 1988 p. 11, Lewis et al. 1990 p. 19).

5.4 Community Type

Rural residents, especially in developing countries and particularly in Latin America, drop out at higher rates than their urban counterparts (Anderson 1988, Stromquist 1989, Lockheed and Verspoor 1990). Lack of schools and a complement of grades, large distances between school and home, lack of flexible scheduling of classes and the school year to meet the local (typically agrarian) population's needs are some of the reasons cited by rural residents who have disengaged. Even in industrialized countries like Canada and Australia, rural dropouts say transportation difficulties and a lack of options within school contributed to their disengagement (Canada 1990). In the United States and presumably other highly industrialized countries, dropouts and pushouts more often live in urban areas (Ekstrom et al. 1986), where schools are typically overcrowded, underfunded, and bureaucratically run. For example, Fine (1990) undertook an ethnographic study of a public high school in New York where over

two-thirds of the student body dropped out or were pushed out.

6. Conclusion

Resources are limited, and demands for equality of access to schools and treatment are high. Given restricted numbers of places at higher levels of schooling, informal and formal practices have emerged as a means of rationing access and survival. These practices can convey messages of rejection to students, who, in turn, may decide to resist or leave an institution that does not engage them. Among the most easily discouraged are disproportionate numbers of those with limited access to power and resources in the wider society.

References

Anderson M B 1988 *Improving Access to Schooling in the Third World: An Overview.* Project BRIDGES Research Report No. 1. Harvard University, Cambridge, Massachusetts
Bowles S, Gintis H 1976 *Schooling in Capitalist America: Educational Reform and the Contradictions of Economic Life.* Basic Books, New York
Canada 1990 *Qualitative Research on School Leavers.* Employment and Immigration Canada and Statistics Canada, Queen's Printer, Ottawa
Davico M I 1990 The repeat and drop-out problem: A study in Brazil on the role of the teacher. *Prospects* 20(1): 107–13
Deble I 1980 *The School Education of Girls: An International Comparative Study on School Wastage Among Girls and Boys at the First and Second Levels of Education.* UNESCO, Paris
Ekstrom R B, Goertz M E, Pollack J M, Rock D A 1986 Who drops out of high school and why? Findings from a national study. *Teach. Coll. Rec.* 87(3): 356–73
Fine M 1990 *Framing Dropouts: Notes on the Politics of an Urban High School.* State University of New York Press, Albany, New York
Grissom J B, Shepard L A 1989 Repeating and dropping out of school. In: Shepard L A, Smith M L (eds.) 1989 *Flunking Grades: Research and Policies on Retention.* Falmer Press, Lewes
Kelly D M 1993 *Last Chance High: How Girls and Boys Drop In and Out of Alternative Schools.* Yale University Press, New Haven, Connecticut
Lewis S G, Horn R, Kainja C, Nyirenda S, Spratt J 1990 *Constraints to Girls' Persistence in Primary School and Women's Employment Opportunities in the Education Service.* Report No. PN-ABH-289. United States Agency for International Development, Washington, DC
Lockheed M E, Verspoor A M 1990 *Improving Primary Education in Developing Countries: A Review of Policy Options.* World Bank, Washington, DC
Patty M, Tobin A 1973 *La Desercion Escolar en la Primeria de Rio Negro, Argentina.* Centro de Investigaciones Educativas, Buenos Aires
Rumberger R W 1983 Dropping out of high school: The influence of race, sex, and family background. *Am. Educ. Res. J.* 20(2): 199–220

Rumberger R W 1987 High school dropouts: A review of issues and evidence. *Rev. Educ. Res.* 57(2): 101–22

Shepard L A, Smith M L 1989 Introduction and overview. In: Shepard L A, Smith M L (eds.) 1989 *Flunking Grades: Research and Policies on Retention.* Falmer Press, Lewes

Stromquist N P 1989 Determinants of educational participation and achievement of women in the Third World: A review of the evidence and a theoretical critique. *Rev. Educ. Res.* 59(2): 143–83

Thein T M, Kabir M, Islam M 1990 *Evaluation of the Female Education Scholarship Program.* Report No. PD-ABB-512. United States Agency for International Development, Washington, DC

UNESCO 1979 *Etude du problème de déperdition d'effectifs*

scolaires parmi les jeunes syriens et syriennes inscrit dans les cycles de l'enseignement préuniversitaire. UNESCO, Paris

UNESCO Office of Statistics 1984 Wastage in Primary Education from 1970 to 1980. *Prospects* 14(3): 347–68

Verhine R E, Pita de Melo A M 1988 Causes of school failure: The case of the State of Bahia in Brazil. *Prospects* 18(4): 557–68

Wang B L C 1982 Sex and ethnic differences in educational investment in Malaysia: The effects of reward structures. In: Kelly G P, Elliott C M (eds.) 1982 *Women's Education in the Third World: Comparative Perspectives.* State University of New York Press, Albany, New York

Economics of Preschool Education

W. S. Barnett

From an economic perspective, preschool education is similar to the education of older children. It provides a safe, healthy, and enjoyable environment that contributes to the happiness of a child and makes it possible for the child's parents to engage in other activities. In addition, it provides experiences that contribute to the child's learning and development. As with education generally, there are both public and private benefits from preschool education, but government involvement in the education of preschoolers has tended to develop in the late twentieth century and to be smaller than private provision.

1. Public Interests in Preschool Education

Government involvement in preschool education has usually been motivated by public interest in providing an adequate level of welfare for young children, facilitating the labor force participation of women, and increasing the level of investment in human capital. These interests derive from the different products of preschool education and tend to lead to the development of different program emphases and orientations toward different constituencies.

The public interest in child welfare provides a stimulus for the development of programs for children whose home environments are judged to be undesirable, often because of problems associated with poverty. Such programs are a means of providing for a child's safety, health, nutrition, and happiness out of a desire to improve the child's life situation. These programs may be provided primarily for children who come to the attention of a public health or social service agency on account of poverty or because of family problems that have resulted in abuse and neglect.

The interest in women's labor force participation has led to the development of programs that meet the needs of mothers who work outside the home. The emphasis is on caretaking during the hours of "regular" employment. Public interest in such programs may arise from a desire to increase the size of the labor force, to improve women's access to jobs and income (which tends to be hindered by their greater responsibilities for childcare), or to increase birthrates which may have suffered due to high costs of caring for young children (whether purchased or provided by parents).

The interest in human capital investment generates support for programs that seek to advance early learning and development. Such programs tend to emphasize the provision of special learning experiences for the child and have tended to focus on children at risk of delayed or limited development or who may be expected to have problems at school. This has led to special programs for children with disabilities, for children from families in poverty, and for children who score low on tests of "readiness" or developmental assessments. Interest in more general provision may stem from beliefs that many children are unprepared for the social or academic demands of school, beliefs that children with few or no siblings need peer experiences for social development, a desire to accelerate the learning of young children, and fears that the private childcare arrangements of even well-off working parents underinvest in learning and development.

Programs arising from interest in child welfare and maternal employment have tended to provide full-day services and be called "childcare." Programs arising from an interest in human capital investment have tended to be part-day and be called "preschool education." Despite these tendencies, most programs provide some of both outputs—care and education—as joint products. (Education programs for the child at home or in short individual sessions at clinics are exceptions.) However, the output mix can be varied, with some programs producing large numbers of convenient hours of low-quality education and others producing high-quality education for only a few hours which are inconvenient for working parents. These patterns are not the only ones possible, but they tend to result from the specialization of public services according to agency mission and constituency as well as from the high cost of producing substantial amounts of both types of outputs. Recent usage of the term "early childhood care and education" to refer to all types of programs for young children reflects a recognition of the joint nature of production.

Government interest in the provision of preschool education has generated a set of public policy questions that can be addressed by economic analysis. These are as follows.

(a)   How much does preschool education cost?

(b)   What are the benefits of preschool education?

(c)   Which approaches are most cost-effective?

The answers to these questions have important implications for preschool education policy. This entry will summarize the knowledge regarding answers to each of these questions. However, it should be emphasized that there are no simple answers. The answers depend on three factors: the characteristics of the children involved and their families; the characteristics of the programs; and the characteristics of the social context.

2. Costs of Preschool Education

The issues with respect to the costs of preschool education are fundamentally the same as those for the education of older children. The direct costs of preschool education tend to be higher (per hour) than for primary school education because higher staff–children ratios are desirable, making it more labor intensive. As a result, preschool education can be much more expensive than primary education in countries with high labor costs. For example, in Sweden the cost per child of quality full-day programs is twice that of early primary education (Gustafsson and Stafford 1992). In countries with inexpensive labor (or even surplus labor) the cost of preschool education may be nearly the same or lower than for primary education, especially if formal educational qualifications are lower for preschool teachers.

The indirect costs of preschool education are the value of the activities the child forgoes to participate in the preschool program. In most cases, this does not involve the loss of earnings or contributions to household production through helping other family members. Thus, indirect costs may be best viewed as a comparison of the relative benefits (or disadvantages) of a particular preschool education program compared with the experiences the child would have had in the absence of the program.

The cost of preschool education is to a great extent determined by policy choices. In most countries, the total public cost is limited by government budget allocations which are insufficient to provide quality full-day programs for every child, though several European countries approach universal coverage of children from the age of three. Several strategies are used to allocate available resources. Public provision may be limited to children and families with specific needs. Programs with an educational focus tend to limit hours; preschool teachers may serve two sessions of children daily and serve each child less than five days per week. Because different trade-offs are chosen in different places, teacher–child ratios and qualifications vary substantially between countries with roughly comparable income levels (Tietze and Ufermann 1989).

The characteristics of children affect costs, usually as a result of differences in the intensity of services thought desirable. The younger the children, the higher the staff–children ratio considered appropriate. Where children suffer from disabilities, developmental delays, and other problems that pose risks to learning and development, a program's resource needs are thought to be more intensive, requiring more staff that are better trained. A broader range of activities may be required which will demand specialists or specialized staff training.

The effects of program characteristics on costs have been more frequently studied, although even here the number of sound studies remains small. There is little empirical basis for international comparisons or generalizations about costs. Estimation of cost functions for preschool education programs of various types could make valuable contributions to the understanding of resource allocation decisions and the determinants of program costs. Cost studies confirm that staff–children ratios and staff qualifications are key determinants of costs. Other obvious influences on costs are hours of operation, the amount of space per child, and the quality of facilities. Interestingly, the limited evidence available does not indicate that private programs tend to be more cost-efficient than public programs in provision of preschool education.

For some kinds of programs, particularly programs aiming to improve the development of children with disabilities or developmental delays, it can be argued that the production technology is not yet well-defined or understood. Thus, not only are classroom approaches of various types used, but nonclassroom approaches such as home visits, one-to-one therapy in a clinic, and training of parents as teachers of their own children are common. Nonclassroom approaches may be used in conjunction with classroom programs or on their own. One appeal of nonclassroom programs is that they tend to have lower costs per child, especially for government. Escobar and Barnett (in press) suggest that nonclassroom programs have lower costs primarily because they provide fewer hours of service. Even adjusting for the intensity of adult–child interaction, they tend to provide less service per child than classroom programs. Programs that train parents as teachers keep down costs to the government by shifting much of the cost burden to parents who provide the labor by giving up other activities. Unfortunately, by imposing substantial time costs on parents, programs can discourage participation, which may explain the high dropout rates experienced by many programs which rely heavily on parents.

3. Benefits of Preschool Education

As the subject is treated in a separate entry (see *Economics of Childcare*), only a brief summary is provided regarding benefits for maternal labor force participation and earnings. From several studies in industrialized countries, it appears that maternal labor force participation can be quite responsive to public provision and subsidization of childcare (Gustafsson and Stafford 1992). In some circumstances the monetary value of mothers' employment-related benefits might exceed the costs of high-quality, full-day programs for preschoolers. However, the evidence is limited and results vary. One small experiment failed to find employment benefits from a preschool education and care program for low-income families.

Most research on the benefits of preschool education has focused on benefits to the child. Obviously, it is possible for preschool programs to provide safe, healthy, and pleasant environments. In addition, hundreds of studies have evaluated the effects of preschool programs on children's learning and development. Most of these studies were conducted with children known or anticipated to have problems with development. Overwhelmingly, preschool programs have produced substantial improvements in current developmental status in a wide variety of domains for children who are at risk because of biological conditions and/or home environment (Barnett 1992).

Research on children not at special risk has tended to focus on potential negative consequences from out-of-home care. The evidence suggests that low-quality programs can be detrimental to the current learning and development of average children (Lamb and Sternberg 1990). At the same time, high-quality programs may provide at least short-term social and cognitive benefits compared with home environments and lower-quality programs (Clarke-Stewart 1991).

The evidence is less uniform regarding the long-term persistence of benefits from preschool education. Some have concluded that benefits are transitory (Clarke-Stewart 1991). However, a more accurate conclusion would appear to be that high-quality programs produce some permanent benefits, but these vary with the characteristics of the children and social environment (Barnett 1992).

3.1 Long-term Benefits to At-risk Children

The most important evidence of the long-term benefits of preschool education comes from about 30 studies that have examined the effects of preschool programs on children beyond age 8. A somewhat larger number of studies has examined the effects of preschool education one or two years beyond the preschool level. It is frequently found that the benefits fade over time and disappear after several years. This finding is nearly universal for intelligence as measured by IQ tests. Preschool education has not demonstrated success in permanently raising IQ scores.

There is more support for the view that preschool education can produce permanent effects on other aspects of children's lives, in particular academic achievement and school success as measured by test scores, grade retention, special education placement, and graduation. A review of studies that examined long-term effects on these variables in the United States (Barnett 1992) concluded that the evidence strongly supports the view that preschool can produce long-term educational benefits for children who are at-risk due to poverty. The failure of some studies to find persistent effects on academic achievement and progress can be attributed to weaknesses of research design and analysis that tend to underestimate program effects. Studies using the Linear Structural Relations Analysis (LISREL) approach to statistical estimation to address some of these problems have provided further evidence of the benefits of preschool education and support for the view that methodological limitations in earlier studies are an important source of null findings (e.g., Tietze 1987).

The most comprehensive evidence of the benefits of preschool education comes from a small experiment ($n = 123$) in the United States with children from low-income families (Berrueta-Clement et al. 1984). The experimental group attended an extremely high-quality preschool program for two and a half hours per day (the Perry Preschool Program). Most attended for two school years beginning at age 3, a few for one year beginning at age 4. The control group did not attend.

Extensive follow-up of both groups until age 19 revealed a pattern of effects that began with increased IQ scores. The experimental group's IQ advantage began to decline after school entry and ceased to be statistically significant by second grade (age 7). However, the experimental group scored higher on achievement tests and teachers' ratings in the early primary grades and higher achievement continued through adolescence. Substantial effects were found with regard to special education placement, high school graduation, postsecondary education, employment and earnings, use of public welfare, delinquency and crime, and teenage pregnancy.

The benefit–cost analysis of the Perry Preschool Program provides a complete cost estimate and extensive, but less complete, benefit estimates. For example, there are no estimates of the value of improvements in the preschoolers' quality of life, the intrinsic value of increased school success and satisfaction, or reduced teenage pregnancy. Benefits were estimated for: childcare provided, public school cost savings, reduced crime costs, increased earnings, and reduced public welfare costs. Mothers' labor force participation did not appear to increase (the short attendance each day may have been as much a hindrance as a help), and the value of child care is a negligible contribution to benefits in this case.

The conclusion of the benefit–cost analysis was that the present value of benefits minus costs (i.e., after discounting) of preschool education was positive. This indicates that preschool education for poor children can be a sound economic investment for society as a whole based on the benefits to children alone. This conclusion was found to hold under a wide range of assumptions about the discount rate and possible errors in the estimation of benefits.

The benefit–cost analysis also produced an important conclusion about the distribution of costs and benefits between study participants and the general public. It is in the taxpayers' interest to provide preschool education to children from low-income families at little or no cost to the children's families. Not only would the inability of low-income families to pay preclude attendance, but even if they could afford preschool education, it would not be in their economic interest. The largest gain to participants—increased earnings—was largely offset by reductions in welfare payments. On the other hand, the taxpayers profit even if they bear the entire cost because the present value of decreased government program costs and increased tax revenues exceeds costs.

Generalization from this economic analysis to other children and contexts presents difficulties, but a logical basis for extrapolating potential benefits can be constructed. The initial effects of preschool education appear to be on achievement and school success. Thus, the first question to be asked in any extrapolation is: for these children, what is the potential to improve their academic achievement and school success? The second question is: what are the potential economic benefits from those improvements?

It appears that wherever poor children perform poorly in school and a significant percentage repeat grades, require special education programs, and complete fewer years of school, there is the potential for substantial economic benefits from reduced educational costs and increased earnings. Additional economic benefits could be obtained to the extent that educational success leads to other benefits only a few of which were measured in the Perry study (see *Consumption Benefits of Education; External Benefits of Education; Benefits of Education*).

Several interesting propositions have been advanced regarding the potential benefits from investment in preschool education in less developed countries. First, less developed countries appear to overallocate resources to higher levels of education and underallocate to lower levels, especially preschool education, as empirical evidence suggests that the contribution of primary and secondary schooling to earnings is an increasing function of the level of preschool ability (Pinera and Selowsky 1981). Second, preschool ability would appear to increase earnings by increasing the productivity of a given number of years of schooling and by increasing the number of years of schooling obtained (Selowsky 1981). Third, there appear to be important interactions among nutrition, health, and education for preschoolers such that comprehensive programs addressing all three of these would be more productive than programs addressing only one (McKay and McKay, 1983).

3.2 Long-term Benefits to More Advantaged Children

A few studies have examined the long-term benefits of preschool education for children who are not at risk on account of biology or environment. These indicate that preschool education can contribute to improved academic ability and social behavior in the early primary grades (Clarke-Stewart 1991, Zaslow 1991, Osborn and Milbank 1987). A large national study in Great Britain suggests that effects on academic test scores may be somewhat smaller than for disadvantaged children (Osborn and Milbank 1987). Although these studies have not investigated later benefits, the most likely would be increased earnings due to gains in the quality and quantity of education. Large public sector cost savings would not be expected, as advantaged children have relatively low rates of grade retention, special education needs, crime and delinquency, unemployment, and welfare dependency. Of course, such benefits would not be expected to end abruptly at some arbitrarily defined poverty line, but to decline gradually as income level rises.

4. Cost-effectiveness of Alternative Approaches

Research on the relative economic efficiency of alternative approaches to the provision of preschool programs could produce much useful information. For the most part, generalizations based on existing studies are not useful because of methodological limitations (Barnett and Escobar 1987). Some evidence indicates that the benefits of preschool education increase with the number of years provided, the educational intensity of the program, and the quality of the program as measured by direct observation of the process or inputs to the program (primarily teacher–child ratio and teacher quality). These variables have important impacts on cost, however, and the trade-offs have not been assessed. The effects of these variables and childcare-related variables such as hours of service should be the subject of comparative economic analyses that examine costs and the benefits to both parents and children.

References

Barnett W S 1992 Benefits of compensatory preschool education. *J. Hum. Resources* 27(2): 279–312

Barnett W S, Escobar C M 1987 The economics of early educational intervention: A review. *Rev. Ed. Res.* 57: 387–414

Berrueta-Clement J R, Schweinhart L J, Barnett W S, Epstein A S, Weikart D P 1984 *Changed Lives: The Effects of the Perry Preschool Program on Youths through Age 19*. Monographs of the High/Scope Foundation, Ypsilanti, Michigan

Clarke-Stewart K A 1991 A home is not a school: The effects of child care on children's development. *J. Soc. Issues* 47(2): 105–124

Escobar C M, Barnett W S in press Costs of early childhood special education. In: Barnett W S, Walberg H in press *Cost Analysis for Educational Decisions: Methods and Examples*. JAI Press, Greenwich, Connecticut

Gustafsson S, Stafford F 1992 Child care subsidies and labor supply in Sweden. *J. Hum. Resources* 27(1): 204–30

Lamb M, Sternberg K 1990 Do we really know how day care affects children? *J. of Appl. Devel. Psychol.* 11: 351–79

McKay H, McKay A 1983 Primary school progress after preschool experience: Troublesome issues in the conduct of follow-up research and findings from the Cali, Columbia study. In: King K, Myers R (eds.) 1983 *Preventing School Failure: The Relationship Between Preschool and Primary Education*. International Development Research Center, Ottawa

Osborn A F, Milbank J E 1987 *The Effects of Early Education: A Report from the Child Health and Education Study of Children in Britain born 5–11 April 1970*: Oxford University Press, Oxford

Pinera S, Selowsky M 1981 The optimal ability–education mix and the misallocation of resources within education magnitude for developing countries. *J. Dev. Econ.* 8: 111–31

Selowsky M 1981 Nutrition, health, and education: The economic significance of complementarities at early age. *J. Dev. Econ.* 9: 331–46

Tietze W 1987 A structural model for the evaluation of preschool effects. *Early Child. Res. Q.* 2(2): 133–54

Tiezte W, Ufermann K 1989 An international perspective on schooling for 4-year olds. *Theory Pract.* 28(1): 69–77

Zaslow M J 1991 Variation in child care quality and its implications for children. *J. Soc. Issues* 47(2): 125–38

Further Reading

Barnett W S 1985 Benefit–cost analysis of the Perry Preschool Program and its policy implications. *Educ. Eval. Policy Anal.* 7(4): 333–42

Barnett W S 1985 *The Perry Preschool Program and its Longterm Effects: A Benefit–cost analysis*. High/Scope, Ypsilanti, Michigan

Selowsky M 1976 A note on preschool-age investment in human capital in developing countries. *Econ. Dev. and Cult. Change* 24(4): 707–20

Supply of Teachers

R. J. Murnane

A recurring policy concern in many countries is whether there will be enough skilled teachers to educate all children. This entry describes economic factors that affect the supply of teachers, and summarizes evidence on how these factors impact on the career decisions of potential teachers, current teachers, and former teachers. It is these decisions that determine the supply of teachers.

1. Factors Affecting Teacher Supply

Key determinants of the supply of teachers in a particular country are salaries and working conditions for teachers relative to those in other occupations, and the cost of preparing to become a teacher relative to the cost of preparing for other occupations.

1.1 Salaries and Working Conditions for Teachers

At the center of the economics perspective on the determinants of teacher supply are salaries in teaching relative to salaries in other occupations. Barro and Suter (1988) have documented that the ratios of teachers' salaries to those in other occupations vary widely across countries, suggesting that the attractiveness of teaching as an occupation of choice also varies across countries. Table 1 presents Barro's estimates for ten industrialized countries of the average elementary school teacher salary and the average secondary school teacher salary expressed as a percentage of per capita gross domestic product.

Two patterns are evident from the Table. First, the attractiveness of teaching salaries relative to a measure of per capita income level varies enormously across countries, ranging from relatively low levels in Sweden and the United States to quite high levels in South Korea. Second, while in some countries, such as the United States and Sweden, elementary and secondary school teachers are paid approximately the same salaries, in other countries, such as the

Table 1
Average salaries of elementary and secondary school teachers relative to per capita gross domestic product, selected countries and years

Country	Year	Ratio (elementary)	Ratio (secondary)
Sweden	1984	1.15	1.37
United States	1984	1.37	1.44
Netherlands	1982	1.54	2.33
United Kingdom	1984	1.62	1.69
Denmark	1982	1.67	2.40
West Germany	1982	1.72	1.96
Japan	1984	1.84	2.03
Canada	1984	1.90	2.14
New Zealand	1986	2.02	2.54
South Korea	1984	3.32	3.32

Source: Barro and Suter 1988 Table 3

Netherlands and Denmark, secondary school teachers earn considerably more than elementary school teachers. As the next section documents, there is evidence that the supply of teachers is sensitive to relative salary levels.

The limited evidence from developing countries suggests the importance of living and working conditions in determining teacher supply. Ankhara-Dove (1982) and Klitgaard et al. (1985) point out that difficult living and working conditions in rural areas make it difficult to attract teachers to these areas, even when there is a surplus of teachers in cities.

In principle, working conditions should also influence the supply of teachers in industrialized countries. It has proven difficult, however, to collect meaningful data on working conditions because, as Johnson (1990) has explained, teachers care about difficult-to-measure variables such as the availability of materials, and the quality of administrative support. As a result, there is almost no solid evidence on the impact of working conditions on teacher supply in industrialized countries.

1.2 Opportunities in Other Occupations

In evaluating whether salaries and working conditions in teaching are sufficient to attract an adequate supply of skilled teachers, the critical concept is how well they stack up against the best alternatives available to potential teachers. In most countries, teachers are paid according to a uniform scale in which salaries depend on amount of formal education and years of teaching experience, and *not* on the field of subject specialization. Since college graduates trained in certain fields, such as chemistry and physics, can earn more in business and industry than graduates trained in the liberal arts, any single salary scale for teachers will appear more competitive for liberal arts graduates than for chemistry and physics graduates. For this reason, some countries, including the United States, have greater difficulty in staffing the schools with an adequate supply of chemistry and physics teachers than they do in finding a sufficient number of history teachers (Murnane et al. 1991). This illustrates the importance of identifying subject fields in analyzing teacher supply. Because of differences in opportunities in other occupations, the teaching profession is much more attractive to college graduates with certain subject specialties than to graduates with other specialties.

In some countries, the teaching profession has been able to attract relatively large numbers of women and minority group members because they have been denied access to occupations with better pay. Social changes resulting in improved access to other professions for women and minorities reduces the ability of the education sector to attract women and minority groups at relatively low salaries. One illustration of this phenomenon is the change in the occupational choices of Black female college graduates. Among those graduating in the late 1960s and entering the full-time work force, seven in ten became teachers. By 1980, the comparable figure was one in four (Murnane et al. 1991). While the attraction of teaching also declined for other groups of college graduates during the 1970s, for no other group is the change so great. This illustrates the general point that the supply of teachers is influenced not only by salaries and working conditions in the teaching profession, but also by the quality of alternative career opportunities available to potential teachers. As a result, changes in opportunities in other fields are likely to have a significant impact on teacher supply.

1.3 Cost of Preparation

Many countries specify that potential teachers must satisfy certain conditions before obtaining a license permitting them to teach. Typically, these conditions include completion of a minimum number of years of formal education, and also frequently include completion of particular training programs, or achieving above a prespecified score on a test of subject matter knowledge or knowledge of pedagogy. The goal of these regulations is to assure that students are taught by competent teachers. However, they also restrict the number of people who choose to teach, by increasing the cost of entering the profession. The costs include not only tuition and fees for the formal education required for entry, but also forgone income during the training period. In addition, test score requirements reduce the supply of teachers by eliminating potential teachers who score below the cutoff score, and by deterring from teacher training potential teachers who fear that they may not pass the licensing test.

1.4 The Quality Dilemma

A major limitation in research on teacher supply is the difficulty in measuring quality. This is important because, in many countries, the primary adjustment mechanism when there is a shortage of "skilled" teachers is not that schools are closed; instead, the schools are staffed with teachers who lack the skills to teach effectively. A consequence of this adjustment mechanism is that research should focus on the supply of skilled teachers, recognizing that the need to staff schools with unskilled teachers may be almost as great a cost as denying schooling to children altogether. The difficulty in implementing this idea is that it has proven very difficult to identify variables that reliably distinguish skilled teachers from unskilled teachers. As Harbison and Hanushek (1992) explain, the number of years of formal education is not a strong predictor of teaching effectiveness, especially in industrialized countries where all teachers have completed at least 14 years of schooling. Teachers' scores on tests of cognitive skills are positively related to teaching effectiveness, as measured by students' test score gains. But even these variables explain only a small part of the variance in teachers effectiveness, as measured by the test score gains of students. Consequently, available research evidence suggests that the criteria many nations use to license teachers do not reliably distinguish competent teachers from incompetent ones.

This inability to study the supply of skilled teachers is a major limitation of existing research. In particular, in interpreting research on teacher supply, one should be aware that almost no studies shed light on the impact of salaries and working conditions on the quality of the teaching force.

2. The Career Pipeline

The supply of teachers is determined by the career decisions of potential, current, and former teachers. This section summarizes the evidence on the roles which salaries, working conditions, and training costs play in influencing these career decisions.

2.1 Whether to Become a Teacher

Dolton (1990) has shown that the occupational decisions of college graduates in the United Kingdom are extremely sensitive to salaries. The more favorably teacher salaries compare to salaries in other occupations, the more likely graduates are to choose teaching.

Manski (1987) used information on college students in the United States in the 1970s to explore the role of salaries and test scores in the decision to become a teacher. He found that teaching salaries have marked effects on the size of the pool of college graduates who enter teaching: the higher the salaries, the larger the pool. He also found that salary levels did not have a marked impact on the ability distribution of the set of college graduates who enter teaching. The inference Manski drew from his analysis is that a strategy for upgrading the quality of new entrants to teaching must include salary increases and entry requirements that screen out weaker applicants. The difficulty in implementing Manski's strategy is identifying a variable that reliably distinguishes weaker candidates from stronger ones.

Murnane et al. (1991) have shown that the representation of Black college graduates in the pool of newly licensed teachers is extremely sensitive to test score requirements. They report that in the first four years after the state of North Carolina reinstituted a test score requirement for obtaining a teaching license, the proportion of Black graduates in the pool of new licensees fell from 20 percent to 10 percent. Smith (1987) has shown that even small changes in the minimum passing scores on written licensing tests have a large impact on the number of minority group applicants who obtain teaching licenses.

2.2 How Long to Stay in Teaching

The length of time teachers remain in teaching has a marked influence on the adequacy of the supply of teachers. For example, if two million teachers are needed to staff a nation's schools, and 20 percent of the existing stock leaves the classroom each year, then 400,000 replacements are needed each year. If the attrition rate is 5 percent, only 100,000 replacements are needed.

As Grissmer and Kirby (1991) have explained, the average attrition rate for a stock of teachers is highly sensitive to the age and experience distribution. The reason is that the attrition rate is relatively high for novice teachers, especially young ones. The attrition rate is low for middle-aged, experienced teachers, and rises only as teachers approach retirement age. As a result, changes in the age and experience distribution of a stock of teachers affects the attrition rate even when there is no change in the attrition rate for teachers of a specific age with a specific amount of teaching experience.

Recent studies by Murnane et al. (1991) and Grissmer and Kirby (1991), based on data from the United States, have shown that the attrition rate of novice teachers is very sensitive to salaries and opportunities in other fields. Novice teachers who are relatively well-paid are less likely to leave teaching after only one or two years than are less well-paid novices. Novice chemistry and physics teachers, who tend to have well-paying alternative career options, are more likely to leave teaching than novice social studies and language arts teachers, who face less well-paying career alternatives. Novice teachers who score well on standardized tests, and who consequently are most likely to do well on the examinations required for entry to training programs for highly paid fields such as the legal profession, are more likely to leave teaching than are novices with lower test scores.

While the effects of salaries in teaching and in other occupations have strong effects on the decisions of novice teachers, they do not significantly affect the career decisions of teachers with more than seven or eight years of experience. As a result, the effect of salaries on the overall attrition rate is very sensitive to the proportion of novice teachers and very young teachers in the teaching stock: the larger the proportion of novices and young teachers, the larger the impact salary changes will have on the average attrition rate.

2.3 Where to Teach

A number of studies have shown that, as a result of geographical differences in salaries and working conditions, teacher surpluses and teacher shortages within a country can exist simultaneously. For example, Klitgaard (1985) reports the coexistence in Pakistan of an aggregate unemployment rate of more than 50 per cent for licensed teachers and a shortage of teachers in rural areas. Ankhara-Dove (1982) describes the conditions in rural areas of developing countries that make it difficult to attract skilled teachers and lead to extremely high teacher turnover rates.

Ferguson (1991) examined the role of salaries in attracting academically talented teachers in 900 local school districts in Texas, each of which sets its own salary scale. He documents that districts paying high salaries attract higher percentages of teachers who score well on standardized tests than do neighboring districts paying low salaries. Moreover, Ferguson shows that teachers' scores on this test predict student test scores. As a result, this study differs from almost all other studies of teacher supply in that it indicates that salaries affect teacher quality, as well as the number of college graduates who want to teach.

2.4 Whether to Return to Teaching

One of the surprising findings of recent studies on teacher supply in the United States is that the majority of newly hired teachers are not new college graduates making an initial career choice. Instead, they are older graduates either returning to teaching after a career interruption, or entering teaching after either raising children or working in another occupation (Kirby et al. 1991). This has led to significant interest in the concept of the "reserve pool," defined as individuals licensed to teach, but not currently teaching.

While the evidence on the reserve pool is restricted to the United States the lessons for teacher supply about the importance of demographic trends are generally applicable and significant. In the United States, the reserve pool is large for two related reasons. First, as a result of the baby boom of the 1950s and 1960s, the age cohorts currently in their late thirties and early forties are very large. Second, many college graduates in these age groups obtained teaching credentials in the late 1960s and early 1970s when jobs in teaching still seemed abundant, but were not able to find or retain teaching jobs in the late 1970s when the earlier baby boom was followed by a marked declined in the birthrate.

As the United States looks ahead to growing demand for teachers in the 1990s, a critical question is whether the reserve pool will continue to be the major source of supply that it was during the 1980s. It is unlikely that this will be the case because the large baby boom cohorts will be followed by smaller cohorts, reducing the size of the reserve pool, and also because the projected slow rate of labor force growth should create strong alternative career opportunities for college graduates, giving members of the reserve pool a variety of occupational choices.

3. Conclusion

The literature on teacher supply provides three basic lessons. The first is that incentives matter. Evidence from a variety of countries shows that the supply of teachers is sensitive to salaries and working conditions in teaching relative to those in other occupations. Second, demographics play a major role. Trends in birthrates and cohort sizes have long-term effects on the supply of teachers, both by influencing the number of potential teachers, and by influencing the likelihood that individuals who do prepare to teach will find teaching positions. Third, the important policy questions do not concern the generic issue of teacher supply, but rather the more detailed issues of: the supply of teachers of particular subjects, the quality of individuals entering and staying in the teaching profession, and the willingness of teachers to work in particular geographical areas.

Important questions concerning teacher supply about which little is known, and which are in critical need of study include: the effects that changes in licensing requirements have on the supply of teachers, factors influencing the timing of teachers' retirement decisions, the impact of working conditions on teacher supply, and the extent to which geographically specific pension plans inhibit teacher mobility.

See also: Economics of Teacher Unionization; Demand and Supply Elasticities for Educated Labor

References

Ankhara-Dove L 1982 The deployment and training of teachers for remote rural schools in less-developed countries. *Int. Rev. Educ.* 28(1): 3–27

Barro S M, Suter L 1988 *International Comparisons of Teachers' Salaries: An Exploratory Study*. National Center for Education Statistics, Washington, DC

Dolton P 1990 The economics of UK teacher supply: The graduate's decision. *Economic J.* 100(5): 91–104

Ferguson R F 1991 Paying for public education: New evidence on how and why money matters. *Harvard J. Legislation* 28(2): 465–98

Grissmer D W, Kirby S N 1991 *Patterns of Attrition Among Indiana Teachers, 1965–1987*. The Rand Corporation, Santa Monica, California

Harbison R W, Hanushek E A 1992 *Educational Performance of the Poor: Lessons from Rural Northeast Brazil*. Oxford University Press, New York

Johnson S M 1990 *Teachers at Work: Achieving Excellence in Our Schools*. Basic Books, New York

Kirby S N, Grissmer D W, Hudson L 1991 *New and Returning Teachers in Indiana: Sources of Supply*. The Rand Corporation, Santa Monica, California

Klitgaard R E 1985 The economics of teacher education in Pakistan. *Comp. Educ. Rev.* 29(1): 97–110

Manski C F 1987 Academic ability, earnings, and the decision to become a teacher: Evidence from the national longitudinal study of the high school class of 1972. In: Wise D A (ed.) 1987 *Public Sector Payrolls*. University of Chicago Press, Chicago, Illinois

Murnane R J, Singer J D, Willett J B, Kemple J J, Olsen R J 1991 *Who Will Teach: Policies That Matter*. Harvard University Press, Cambridge, Massachusetts

Smith G P 1987 *The Effects of Competency Testing on the Supply of Minority Teachers*. National Education Association and the Council of Chief State School Officers, Washington, DC

Further Reading

Bobbitt S A et al. 1991 Characteristics of stayers, movers, and leavers: Results from the teacher followup survey, 1988–89. National Center for Education Statistics, Washington, DC

Hafner A, Owings J 1991 Careers in teaching: Following members of the high school class of 1972 in and out of teaching. National Center for Education Statistics, Washington, DC

Kershaw J A, McKean R N 1962 *Teacher Shortages and Salary Schedules*. McGraw-Hill, New York

Murnane R J, Olsen R J 1989 Economics of the education industry: Will there be enough teachers? *American Economics Review Papers and Proceedings* 79(2): 242–46

Economics of Teacher Education

A. Wagner

Policies aimed at improving compulsory education in Organisation for Economic Co-operation and Development (OECD) member countries include proposals for reform in teacher education. The reforms have important economic dimensions, although the economic aspects have not always figured prominently in the research or policy debates (see, e.g., Neave 1987, Blackburn and Moisan 1987, OECD/CERI 1993). Nonetheless, costs and financing, and their relationship to effectiveness, are essential elements for informed choices among alternative options for teacher education. This entry presents an elaboration of these elements, drawing on the situation and experiences in OECD member countries with regard to the education of primary and secondary school teachers.

1. Demand for and Supply of Teacher Education

As with all forms of education, the demand for teacher education can be regarded principally as a derived demand. It is derived from the demand for teachers or, more appropriately, for teaching services. From this perspective, the stocks of knowledge and skills to be embodied in teachers are seen to depend both on the expectations placed on schools (what children are expected to learn) and on the ways in which teaching and learning are organized within schools. It is important to note that differences exist among and within countries on these matters (see, e.g., Hanushek 1981). Furthermore, school "inputs" (teacher effort, student effort, materials, equipment, and facilities) can be combined in different ways to achieve comparable schooling results. It follows that, for any given school level and subject specialization of teacher, there is no single profile for the specific mix of the stocks of knowledge and skills. The profiles demanded may differ from one school to another, and these demands may change over time.

One key aspect which influences the demand for teacher education is the cyclical pattern of growth in the size of the teaching force in most OECD countries. Particularly during the postwar period (and dating back to the nineteenth century in Germany), large increases in the number of teachers have been followed by years in which the increases were relatively low. The cycles result from particular demographic trends (in pupil numbers and in the age distribution of the teaching force), a volatile pattern of policy-driven changes in curricula and educational standards, and trends in opportunities and conditions in teaching as compared to other occupations (OECD 1990). Annual new entrant teacher requirements in the United Kingdom (England and Wales only), for example, were estimated at 14,800 for 1980–81 to 1984–85, 11,400 for 1985–86 to 1989–90 and 16,400 for 1990–91 to 1994–95 (with most of the differences expected at the secondary level). In the states which formerly constituted the Federal Republic of Germany, owing in part to declines in new teacher demand, the absolute volume of students enrolled in teacher-training programs fell by more than 50 percent from 1977 to 1988 (OECD 1992).

The supply of teacher education differs both among and within countries, with respect to structure (e.g., by level and timing over the teaching career), content, and methods. In the area of the OECD, the most common pattern has been to elaborate different initial teacher education requirements by level and type of teacher. While there are exceptions, aspiring primary school teachers receive their training in non university higher education and the study program devotes particular attention to pedagogy and child development. Candidates seeking posts as secondary teachers commonly follow a regular first degree course at university, with specialized study in education and practical training taken either as part of their coursework (Japan and the United States, for example) or mostly on completion of the first degree (as in Germany, France, and the Postgraduate Certificate of Education (PGCE) course in the United Kingdom). Within the area of the OECD, the trend has been to move toward an "all graduate" profession, by requiring all aspiring primary school teachers to complete university or university-level education. Greece, Spain, and France have implemented reforms which take just this step.

Differences also exist among and within countries in the nature and scale of organized inservice education and training (INSET) activities. Such activities extend from long, credit-bearing courses to short, formal off-site training for individual teachers, to on-site school development activities for the entire school staff. Relatively greater weight appears to be given in Belgium (Flemish community) to formal courses than to school-based activities, although there is a general trend in the area of the OECD toward INSET which is provided in short sessions, at the school site, and in relation to overall school development.

2. Costs of Teacher Education

A full economic accounting of the costs of teacher education includes direct program expenses (wages of training staff, use of equipment and facilities, and certain "overhead" costs), direct expenses incurred by the participants (books and materials, relevant transportation costs), the costs of the participants' time, and the implicit costs of the time devoted by the staff to the activity. The calculation of these costs is not easy for methodological and practical reasons (see, e.g., Drake 1973, Bolam 1982, Levin 1983, Ryan 1991). As a result, comprehensive, detailed comparative infor-

mation in the area of the OECD on program-level and system-wide costs of teacher education are not readily available.

2.1 Costs of Participants' and Staff Time

In estimating the costs of teacher education, the costs of participants' and trainers' time are the most difficult to gauge and the most frequently miscalculated.

In Germany, for example, teacher candidates in the second phase of initial teacher training receive stipends. As these candidates will teach during part of this phase of their training, some portion of the stipend should be considered as payment for service rather than as a cost of training. In contrast, for beginning teachers who take part in induction activities (as in Australia, Japan, and the United States among other countries), a portion of their salaries should be considered as a cost of training. With regard to INSET, provision is often made for full or partial replacement of teachers who participate in training during regular school hours. However, to the extent that the replacements are not full and complete substitutes (in the economic sense) for those in training, the budgeted costs may understate the actual costs as other teachers are required to make up the difference (if levels of student learning are to be maintained).

Available estimates suggest that the costs of participants' time are considerable, ranging in the United Kingdom (England and Wales) from 33 percent of annual costs of university-based initial teacher education to 56 percent of the annual costs of initial teacher education provided in colleges (Drake 1973). One implication of these estimates is that changes in resources used directly by teacher education programs (reflected, for example, in student – staff ratios or program "unit" costs as conventionally measured) will have a limited effect on the full economic costs of initial teacher education. The length of initial teacher education is perhaps the most important determinant of its costs.

In Germany and other OECD countries, the costs of staff time set aside in schools for supervision and mentoring of teacher candidates are not always calculated. These costs may be explicit, such as when the difference between the regular class load and the reduced class load is assigned to supervising teachers, as well as implicit, for instance, when other teachers assume heavier class loads to cover for the reduced loads of both the supervising teacher and the teacher candidate. Proposals in the United Kingdom (England and Wales) to increase the "school-based" component in initial teacher education to 80 percent have brought this question to the surface. While it is envisaged that schools which accept teacher candidates for such training will be compensated, the level of compensation has not been worked out. Apart from increased costs during an implementation period, there are indications that the recurrent costs of locating a larger share of initial teacher training in the schools are as considerable as, and may be greater than, the costs of traditional, formal initial teacher education courses (OECD/CERI 1993).

2.2 Forms of Teacher Education

Estimates from England and Wales also reveal large differences in costs according to the type of the initial teacher-training program: annual student costs in colleges were half of student costs at universities and 77 percent of student costs in advanced full-time further education (Drake 1973). The sources of differences are to be found in the running and capital costs of the different programs. It should be pointed out that such annual cost differences may be justified by differences in the results or effectiveness of the programs (i.e., differences in amounts and mixes of the stocks of knowledge and skills acquired by graduates, dropout rates and "jointly produced" results such as improved knowledge about teaching and learning which accompanies, and is accompanied by, the production of qualified teachers).

Cost considerations, as well as considerations of effectiveness, are raised by the introduction of "alternative routes" to teaching. Initial teacher education provided under alternative route schemes found in the United States and the United Kingdom (England and Wales) are relatively short in duration and combine actual teaching with part-time training. In the mid-1980s, the mean cost per participant for United States "alternative route" programs was about US$5,000; the median cost was about US$2,200 (Adelman 1986). Most participants had completed first degrees. The costs of participants' time are not included in these figures; the average salary in 1985–86 for beginning teachers was about US$17,500 (part of which, as noted above, should be considered as payment for service).

2.3 Scale and Variation in Participant Flows

The teacher education effort in most OECD member countries is large. One indication of the magnitude of the effort is simply the relative size of the teaching force. Other things being equal, even modest rates of replacement and new teacher demand imply significant recruitment from initial teacher training. Graduates with teaching credentials account for 12 percent of new graduates in the United States and 8 percent of new graduates in Germany, although not all of these graduates will become teachers (OECD 1992).

The scale of requirements for the inservice education and training of teachers is similarly large. Quite apart from the development and delivery costs of such training, the direct and indirect costs of teacher participation can be considerable. In Japan, the equivalent of an estimated 8 percent of the total work year is given over to various inservice activities. In the Nordic countries, it is estimated that 1.5 to 2.5 percent of the working year is given over to INSET. In Sweden, about 12 percent of the teaching force annually follow inservice education courses each year, and all teachers must take part in five days of school-based inservice training each year. In the Netherlands, the cost of inservice training in education amounts to an estimated 1 percent of the education wage bill, a share that is nonetheless smaller than the 4 to 6 percent share found in some Dutch industry training budgets. The volume of training to be delivered implies that alternative approaches need to be judged in terms of cost-feasibility as well as cost-effectiveness.

Given the magnitude of the overall teacher education effort, less costly alternatives are being sought. Such options include distance learning and the use of new information technologies. While these strategies can reduce the overall unit cost of training, it is not clear that this is always the case (Nielsen and Tatto 1991). Moreover, such approaches also may lead to an increase in the economic costs borne by some participants (see, e.g., Kemmerer and Wagner 1985, 1986; Kurland 1984).

Attention should be given to changes in the Netherlands, Finland, and Sweden, where steps have been taken to widen both the age-span and subject coverage of teacher education and teacher qualifications. The development reverses a trend toward greater specialization in teaching. The impact on the effectiveness of teaching and learning aside, such changes enable education authorities to minimize the extent of underutilization and overutilization of the available capacity of teacher education, with consequent moderation of effects on unit costs (per student, per graduate, or per new teacher placement). Indirectly, these changes respond to the limits of basing teacher education provision on detailed forecasts of teacher demand and supply, and to the rigidities present in most countries which prevent rapid adaptation of teacher employment and teacher education to conditions found at different levels and segments of the education system.

3. Sources and Methods of Financing

In most OECD member countries, the course of studies of a student pursuing initial education for entry into teaching is financed in ways similar to studies in other postsecondary education fields. Direct study costs are subsidized, to a greater or lesser extent, through grants made directly to the institutions providing the education or through grants to students who then must pay fees. There are different approaches to financing participants' time. Similar to other postsecondary students, those following courses in initial teacher education have at least part of the costs of their time subsidized by below-cost provision of housing and meals (e.g., in France), stipends (e.g., second phase of teacher education in Germany, and also France) and/or subsidies implicit in student loans. Earnings forgone in excess of these subsidies are borne by students or their families.

The trend in most OECD member countries is to reduce subsidies, and so increase the share of costs—instruction and forgone earnings—borne by students and their families. However, authorities in some countries offer additional support or subsidies for students in initial teacher education. In the United States, such students may qualify for special grants, scholarships, or loans which offer forgiveness of principal and interest if the student, upon graduation, enters and remains in teaching for a minimum number of years. In France, special grants are offered in regions and subject areas experiencing shortages.

With respect to the inservice education and training of teachers, the variation in provision among and within OECD member countries is accompanied by wide differences in the ways in which the costs are financed. Dedicated budgets for inservice education cover principally the salaries of the trainers (whether they are employed full-time for this purpose or they are employed in other jobs and take on specific, short-term assignments for nominal fees). The salary costs of teachers participating in training during working hours are sometimes absorbed within the teacher salary budget at the appropriate level (but, as noted above, replacements may only partly substitute for teachers undergoing training during regular working hours and thus require other teachers to share the training costs through their own additional effort). Teachers participating in INSET outside of regular class hours bear the implicit costs of the time spent in training and, as in the United Kingdom (England and Wales) among other countries, sometimes the fees as well.

Since INSET is usually provided as an expectation or requirement for the continued employment or career progression of the teacher, the share of costs borne by the employers (education authorities) is usually not treated as personal income of the participating teacher for the purposes of income taxation. This tax treatment implies another "partner" in the costs of INSET, namely the finance authorities which forgo tax payments on the value of inservice training provided by education authorities to teachers.

Notwithstanding how the costs of teacher education are shared among the various stakeholders, the methods of financing are being changed in a number of OECD countries in the early 1990s. The most recent trend is to provide clearer signals and incentives to providers of inservice education via criteria included in categorical funding mechanisms, as in Norway and the United Kingdom (England and Wales), and to introduce competition by allowing authorities at the appropriate levels in the countries concerned (schools, municipalities, regions) to purchase inservice training from a provider offering the best training at the lowest cost (as in Sweden, Denmark, and the United Kingdom). These financing methods are believed to promote efficiency in the sense that provision has been

"steered" toward priority areas, new knowledge or techniques have been diffused widely in the schools, and budgeted costs per participant appear to have been reduced in various ways.

4. Internal Efficiency

Much of the extant research in teacher education in OECD member countries focuses on the effectiveness of different approaches, although the results of this work are seldom presented in ways which permit comparisons among approaches or the assessment of internal and external efficiency (the latter requires cost data). In these studies, the outputs —the knowledge and skills to be learned by prospective or practicing teachers—are defined by teacher education faculty or teacher trainers and shaped to a greater or lesser extent by criteria set down by relevant education authorities.

One key issue in this area is the balance to be struck between on-site, "practical" training and education provided in formal courses in professional education subjects such as sociology of education or child psychology. The debates have centered on questions of changes in observed teaching practice (e.g., to what extent does broad knowledge of educational theory enable and encourage teachers to employ specific teaching techniques? To what extent does greater attention to practical training at the expense of the study of educational theory foreclose the development in the teacher of an ability to "work through" solutions to the unique educational situations confronted by individual students?). On these matters, the research base is limited and diverse, but suggestive (see, e.g., Smith and O'Day 1988, Gran 1989). The main conclusions with regard to teacher education are that there needs to be a balance between theoretical subjects and practical training (neither extreme appears to be appropriate), and that teachers acquire skills best when the training is grounded in the reality of schools and classrooms.

The implications of the present and likely future profile of the teaching force for the internal efficiency of teacher education, including the balance between its theoretical and practical elements, has been studied less. Under quite reasonable assumptions, it may well be that new entrants into teaching will be more diverse in abilities, interests, background, and motivation. In these circumstances, the balance to be struck between formal courses in education subjects as opposed to practical training might differ according to the characteristics of prospective teachers and the ways teachers with different characteristics will be employed within individual schools.

A second key issue concerning internal efficiency is the balance between initial teacher preparation and inservice education and training. The question here is whether the knowledge and skills required by teachers might be best acquired over a longer period of time, rather than through the "front-loaded" approach characteristic of teacher education in most OECD member countries in the early 1990s. Differences exist among countries, with Japan placing relatively less weight on preservice and more weight on inservice than is the case in Sweden. One view is that appropriate, substantial, and in-depth initial teacher education may equip teachers with the stocks of knowledge and skills which enable more efficient inservice education and training, that is, fewer instances of formal inservice training, of shorter duration, which are more effectively assimilated by the participating teacher (see, e.g., Eraut 1989). However, a shift in the timing of teacher education toward inservice could provide a more effective and less costly response to evolving career paths and profiles in the teaching force, including a growth in part-time teaching, intermittent periods inside and outside of the profession, mid-career recruitment in some countries, and cyclical patterns of new teacher demand.

One important consequence of a shift toward inservice teacher education and training is that it may be possible to use the system's present capacity for initial teacher training more effectively. This capacity could be applied to inservice education and so reduce the costs arising from the tendency of programs aimed at initial teacher preparation to operate above or below capacity.

5. External Efficiency

Teacher education can also be evaluated with respect to outcomes, particularly the effects on pupils attributable to the stocks of knowledge and skills acquired by teachers via teacher education. In the United States, experiments have shown that training teachers to behave in effective ways did lead to changes in classroom practice which were associated with relatively greater increases in student achievement than alternative approaches (in which teachers continued to use their conventional ways of teaching). However, the effects apparently vary by school level, student characteristics, subject matter, and the type of achievement being measured. Moreover, such a specific approach to training seems to lead to diminishing returns; that is, the gains decrease as certain teacher behaviors are more intensively and comprehensively used. More generally, teacher education in the United States (and other OECD member countries) is criticized because it has failed to develop in prospective or practicing teachers the knowledge and skills required for effective teaching in actual classrooms (Smith and O'Day 1988). In other words, programs may be internally efficient, in that teachers acquire the skills and knowledge imparted by the programs, but these programs nevertheless fail to meet external efficiency criteria, inasmuch as knowledge and skills are either inappropriate for

the settings or pupils, or are inappropriately used (Cohen 1990).

Evidence exists with regard to another dimension of the outcomes of teacher education, namely the employment experiences of those who are qualified to teach. Compared to other fields of study, initial teacher education develops skills and abilities which are more directly linked to a specific employment sector and job (e.g., in France, the number of openings in teacher training courses are set according to estimates of new teacher demand). As a result, teacher education graduates are more likely to be found in teaching, either initially or at mid-career, than graduates of other fields are to be found in occupations closely related to their training (OECD 1992). Evidence on the effect of inservice training on the subsequent careers of teachers is limited. Apart from systems in which additional formal training is a prerequisite for advancement (and so provides clear benefits to the individual teacher), wider effects commonly have neither been gauged nor weighed against costs. A study in the United Kingdom suggested that successful participation in long, award-bearing courses provides a signal to authorities about the enhanced skills and abilities of the participant (Howard and Bradley 1992).

However, owing both to the particular structure of the labor markets for graduates with qualifications and to the requirements for entry into teaching, differences in the employment experiences of newly qualified graduates can be seen among countries. In Japan, for example, about 2 out of 10 recipients of teaching certificates in the mid-1980s were placed into teaching posts; the ratio for Finland is estimated to be about 8 out of 10. Those who do not enter teaching appear to be able to find employment in other sectors, and in posts which draw upon the knowledge and skills acquired in teacher education. In Germany, for example, a mid-1980s study revealed that unemployed teacher education graduates who subsequently were employed outside of teaching often found jobs related to their training. About two-thirds (64 percent) of these graduates considered their jobs to be satisfactory; 34 percent regarded their jobs as a provisional expedient (OECD 1992).

Moreover, teacher education may enable students to acquire field-specific knowledge which is of value outside of formal paid work. In this case, such training might prepare parents to contribute more effectively to the intellectual and social development of their own children as a complement to the teaching and learning which takes place in schools and classrooms. Indeed, the profiles of teachers and their careers (female, married, part-time, intermittent employment) imply that the perceived value of the use of the acquired skills and abilities in the home or family may be one of the motivations for following a course in teacher education.

Finally, initial teacher education programs are seen by some to serve purposes other than enabling prospective teachers to acquire the skills and abilities necessary for teaching per se. One of these purposes is to convey a status commensurate with the perceived requirements of the job of teaching. In this view, completion of teacher education at the university level will lead to a more appropriate level of remuneration (as provided in public sector pay schedules which are differentiated by educational qualifications) as well as to confer on teaching a status that makes teaching more attractive. The effects on recruitment of differences in the educational level required for entry into teaching have not been fully explored. Raising entry qualifications is a costly way to improve recruitment and retention, although strengthening the content and rigor of teacher education by raising it to university level has been advocated on the grounds of improved effectiveness of teaching. An interesting issue is the extent to which individuals differ in their valuations of the status conferred by different levels of qualifications. Different forms and requirements of teacher education might discriminate better among pools of prospective teachers than salaries or other monetary incentives.

Another purpose set out for initial teacher education programs is to provide for the orderly development of the knowledge base on teaching and learning. While the effects and costs of this aspect of existing teacher education programs are difficult to gauge, some general issues regarding the efficiency of different structures can be developed.

6. Conclusion

While teacher education assumes a vital role in the development and improvement of schooling in OECD member countries, careful analyses of the costs, financing and efficiency of provision are limited in number and breadth. This entry has drawn on developments in the area of the OECD in teacher education and training in an attempt to set out more clearly their economic dimensions. Four conclusions have emerged as crucial to an evaluation of teacher education from such a perspective. First, a full accounting of economic costs includes the costs of participants', trainers', and other staff time. These costs are the most difficult to gauge and most frequently miscalculated. Second, the scale of provision introduces an important issue of cost feasibility. Some effective and efficient approaches may be impossible to implement system-wide. Third, the efficiency of provision must be gauged against the organization of schooling and labor market structures in individual countries. Finally, the effectiveness and efficiency of alternative forms of teacher education are related to the characteristics and abilities of participants; the particular way in which the teaching force evolves will determine the choice of approach to teacher education.

See also: Benefits of Improving the Quality of Education

References

Adelman N E 1986 *An Exploratory Study of Teacher Alternate Certification and Retraining Programs.* Policy Studies Associates, Washington, DC
Blackburn V, Moisan C 1987 *The In-Service Training of Teachers in the Twelve Member States of the European Community.* Presses InterUniversitaires Européennes, Maastricht
Bolam R 1982 *In-Service Education and Training of Teachers: A Condition of Educational Change.* OECD/CERI, Paris
Cohen D K 1990 A revolution in one classroom: The case of Mrs. Oublier. *Educ. Eval. Policy Anal.* 12(3): 327–45
Drake K 1973 The economics of teacher education. In: Lomax D E (ed.) 1973 *The Education of Teachers in Britain.* Wiley, London
Eraut M 1989 Review of research on in-service education: A UK perspective. In: Wilson J (ed.) 1989 *The Effectiveness of In-Service Education and Training of Teachers and School Leaders.* Swets and Zeitlinger, Amsterdam
Gran B 1989 *Research on Swedish Teacher Training.* School of Education, University of Lund, Malmö
Hanushek E 1981 Throwing money at schools. *Journal of Policy Analysis and Management* 1: 19–41
Howard J, Bradley H 1992 *Patterns of Employment and Development of Teachers after INSET Courses.* Cambridge Institute of Education, Cambridge
Kemmerer F, Wagner A 1985 The economics of educational reform. *Econ. Educ. Rev.* 4(2): 111–21
Kemmerer F, Wagner A 1986 *Limits on the Use of Educational Technology in Developing Countries: A Reappraisal of the Costs.* IREDU, University of Dijon, Dijon
Kurland N D 1984 *The Role of Technology in the Education, Training and Retraining of Adult Workers.* Kurland & Associates, Delmar, New York
Levin H M 1983 *Cost-Effectiveness: A Primer.* Sage, Newbury Park, California
Neave G 1987 Challenges met: Trends in teacher education 1975–85. In: Council of Europe Standing Conference of European Ministers of Education 1987 *New Challenges for Teachers and their Education.* Council of Europe, Strasbourg
Nielsen H D, Tatto M T 1991 *The Cost-Effectiveness of Distance Education for Teacher Training, Bridges Research Report Series,* No. 9. USAID, Washington, DC
OECD 1990 *Teacher Demand and Supply: The Labour Market for Teachers.* (Restricted), OECD, Paris
OECD 1992 *From Higher Education to Employment,* Vol. I–III (country reports). OECD, Paris
OECD/CERI in press *The Training of Teachers.* OECD/CERI, Paris
Ryan P 1991 How much do employers spend on training? An assessment of the 'Training in Britain' estimates. *Human Resource Manag. J.* 1: 55–76
Smith M S, O'Day J 1988 *Teaching Policy and Research on Teaching.* Stanford University Press, Stanford, California

Economics of Teacher Unionization

R. W. Eberts and J. A. Stone

1. Introduction

Teacher unionization, defined as the formal organization of teachers for the purpose of bargaining collectively with their employer, is a relatively recent phenomenon. However, organizations representing the interests of teachers both in schools and in the political arena have been well-established in most industrialized countries for a longer period of time. Freedom of association for teachers is enunciated, for example, in the "Recommendation Concerning the Status of Teachers" adopted at an intergovernmental conference convened by UNESCO in 1966 (Pepin 1990). Again, formal collective bargaining is typically a more recent phenomenon. In the United States, for example, organizations representing public-school teachers experienced phenomenal growth in the 1970s, despite a general decline in enrollment during the same period. The two major teacher unions in the United States, the American Federation of Teachers (AFT) and the National Education Association (NEA), increased their ranks from 770,000 in 1960 to over 2 million by 1990, representing about 86 percent of the public-school teachers in the United States. Evidence provided by Saltzman (1985) suggests that the rapid growth of teacher unionization in the United States during this period was both a result and a cause of the public-sector bargaining laws enacted during that period.

Teacher unions are even more prevalent in other industrialized countries. For example, 95 percent of Australia's 180,000 teachers are formally represented and virtually all government-employed teachers in France are members of a national union. Although almost all teachers are covered by some form of collective bargaining contract in many industrialized countries, the nature and geographical scope of the bargaining process differs substantially. The United States, in particular, has very fragmented bargaining compared to other industrial countries, reflecting the autonomy of its more than 15,000 school districts. Even though many local bargaining units are members of state and national umbrella organizations, each local bargaining unit negotiates directly with the district and bargaining outcomes differ across these districts. France provides an example of the other extreme in which a national teacher association bargains with a centralized national educational system and yields a uniform contract for all teachers (Duclaud-Williams, 1985). Australia represents an intermediate case. Teacher unions have formed around the state- and territory-wide educational systems. Within each Australian territory or state (except Victoria) unions

have emerged as dominant bargaining and policy-making organizations (Blackmore and Spaull, 1987).

Teacher unions affect the educational system in various ways, each one with a magnitude that depends upon its bargaining strength. For example, labor unions affect the salaries and working conditions of their members and provide a process to redress grievances. Unions also influence the availability of funds to education and the policies determined at local, state, and national levels. Results in these areas, in turn, have ramifications for the outcomes of schools—the educational achievement of students. Most of the literature on teacher unions has focused on the bargaining process and bargaining outcomes as they relate to salaries, fringe benefits, and hiring practices. However, the general public's concern lies principally with the ultimate effects of unions on the cost and quality of education.

This entry reviews the theory and empirical results of the effects of teacher unionization, with particular emphasis on student outcomes. It offers an evaluation of the effects of collective bargaining on student achievement within a framework based on educational production functions, which link the resources available to education to the various results of education. The evaluation proceeds in four stages. First, the entry surveys a list of primary determinants of student outcomes (typically measured by gains in standardized test scores) emphasized in the literature. Second, it examines the effects of collective bargaining on these various determinants. Third, it reviews studies that directly estimate the effects of collective bargaining within an educational production function framework. Finally, it summarizes evidence on the effects of teacher unionization on the cost of instruction.

2. Determinants of Educational Outcomes

The framework for looking at the possible effects of teacher unions is embedded in the literature on the determinants of educational outcomes, as described by what are referred to as "educational production functions," which are also sometimes called "input–output functions." These functions relate differences in student achievement gains to differences in school resources and other relevant factors.

Within this framework, the linkage may be traced between collective bargaining and student achievement. For instance, if collective bargaining increases class size, and students do not perform as well in larger classes, then slower student progress can be traced to teacher unions, and the same with other factors.

Making the connection requires two significant relationships: the link between educational "inputs" and educational outcomes, and the link between collective bargaining and educational inputs.

The educational process is sufficiently complex that concentrating only upon class size or teachers, or aspects of the interaction between teacher and student, is not sufficient to assess the overall effect of collective bargaining. However, space does not permit a discussion of the details of educational production functions; the theory and empirical findings in this area are included in several entries in this *Encyclopedia* (see *Education Production Functions; Joint Production of Education; Political Economy of Educational Production*). In addition, the literature abounds with empirical studies of this sort. Hanushek (1986) reports that between 1966 and 1986 some 147 separate factors affecting educational outcomes were reported in the literature. Despite the widespread interest in educational production functions, only a handful of researchers have included union representation as a factor in formal educational production analysis.

It is, however, sufficient to posit a simple model of the educational process that identifies five basic groups of determinants of student outcomes and then to summarize briefly their relative importance as described in the literature. The groups are: (a) student and student-background characteristics, (b) teacher characteristics, (c) time spent by teachers and students performing various tasks, (d) modes of instruction, and (e) administrator characteristics.

At the risk of misrepresenting the richness of the results reported in the educational production function literature, it is nevertheless useful to summarize the findings and isolate the most important classes of determinants. A study by Eberts and Stone (1984) utilizes a nationwide sample of 14,000 fourth-graders in 328 elementary schools that was collected under the Department of Education's Sustaining Effects Study (SES). Student achievement is measured by the gains on standardized mathematics pre- and post-test.

Findings by Eberts and Stone are generally consistent with other studies and point to a number of teacher- and principal-related factors that are important determinants of the educational process. The factors that contribute most positively to achievement gains are the time teachers spend in instruction and preparation, the teacher–student ratio, the total experience of teachers, and the time principals spend assessing and evaluating math programs. The positive effects related to the teacher–student ratio and teacher experience are not found by all studies, as noted by Hanushek (1986). The evidence found by Eberts and Stone may be stronger because of their ability to link individual student achievement to explicit measures of the resources devoted to that student (e.g., instructional time, teacher attributes, and class size). Most studies attempt to link average student achievement to school

or district averages to obtain broad determinants of student achievement.

3. Effects of Unionization on Determinants of Student Outcomes

The literature on the effects of unionization deals primarily with the effects on various immediate or intermediate determinants of student outcomes, rather than directly upon educational outcomes for students. These studies may be divided into those that address issues of resource allocation (e.g., salaries, class sizes, instructional modes, and the like), those that address attitudes among teachers and administrators important to their effectiveness, and those that address broader issues related to local and national policies.

3.1 Resource Allocation

The majority of studies of the effects of unionization on determinants of student outcomes deal directly or indirectly with issues of resource allocation. For example, several studies of teacher markets in the United States show that teacher unions increase the wages of their members (or those in the bargaining unit) relative to nonmembers. However, in the early 1970s, when teacher organizing efforts were relatively new, the effect was only marginal (see Kasper 1970, Perry 1979). Baugh and Stone (1982) show that the union-wage premium increased dramatically during the 1970s, from a 7 percent premium in 1974 to a 14 percent premium in 1977. The 14 percent union wage differential is comparable to the average union wage premium in the private sector. Baugh and Stone attribute the higher union wage premium to the growth in legislation favorable to teacher collective bargaining and the maturation of relatively new teacher unions during the 1970s.

Teacher unionization also affects staffing ratios through shifts in resources caused by higher salaries and through explicit contractual constraints, such as restrictions on class size and mandated preparation time. Using data from the Sustaining Effects Study of 6,000 elementary teachers Eberts (1984) shows that districts in which collective bargaining is practiced have more teachers and administrators per student but employ fewer clerical staff and aides per student. Estimates reveal that union districts have 10 percent more teachers per student and 5 percent more administrators per student. These increases are partly offset by a 7 percent reduction in clerical staff.

In addition, collective bargaining affects the composition and attributes of the instructional staff. Higher union salaries attract and retain teachers, and the negotiated salary structure rewards teachers for obtaining additional years of education. Eberts (1984) shows that elementary teachers covered by a collective bargaining contract have one to two years of additional teaching experience. Milkman (1989) finds similar results for a national sample of high-school teachers.

By establishing rules and procedures that govern

a teacher's time, collective bargaining can affect the amount of time in which teachers engage in productive, instruction-related activities. For example, contracts commonly contain provisions that explicity specify the amount of time for class preparation, guarantee a duty-free lunch, and discourage participation in after-school meetings. Using the SES database, Eberts (1984) finds that teachers covered by collective bargaining agreements spend less time in instruction, more time in preparation and performing administrative and clerical duties. Based on a 180-day school year, collective bargaining reduces instruction by an equivalent of 5 schooldays a year and increases class preparation time by an equivalent 6.5 schooldays.

3.2 Attitudes of Teachers and Administrators

Attitudes among teachers and administrators can also be important, if intangible, factors in student achievement. The impact of collective bargaining on such attitudes is complex and subtle. Collective bargaining provides teachers with both the opportunity to voice their opinions on a wide range of district and school issues and with some degree of power to make their opinions count. Indeed, it is the union function as a voice for its members that specialists in industrial relations typically highlight as the most fundamental contribution of collective bargaining (see Hirschman 1970, Freeman and Medoff 1984).

Studies confirm that teachers derive great psychological value from pedagogical and professional activities (Lortie 1977). Relationships between teacher and student, relationships between teacher and administrator, organization of the classroom, selection of curriculum and materials, nonteaching responsibilities, and the perceptions and pressures of parents and community are all important.

According to Eberts and Stone (1984), union and nonunion teachers perceive the importance of these various issues differently. For instance, union and nonunion teachers differ in their views about the ingredients that make schools a satisfying place in which to work. Teachers covered by collective bargaining appear less concerned with the personnel policies of the district than their nonunion colleagues. It is possible that this decline in interest is due to a greater reliance on the part of union members on the union to take care of personnel matters, as well as to more structured personnel practices in union districts. Union teachers, on the other hand, appear more sensitive to class size than nonunion teachers. Unionized teachers also appear to be less satisfied in general with their workplace than their nonunionized counterparts, although the lower level of satisfaction may be an explanation rather than a consequence of collective bargaining.

3.3 Local and National Policy

Collective bargaining can also affect the educational process by influencing the formulation of state and local educational policy. For example, in the United States the two major teacher unions—the American Federation of Teachers and the National Education Association—have launched national lobbying and media campaigns that stress the importance of quality education to the national economy and individual well-being. Teacher unions in the United States have also become involved in the movement toward more choice in education, typically taking a stance opposing this initiative. In Australia, teacher unions have influenced, and often initiated, progressive educational policies on curriculum innovation, school organization, noncompetitiveness assessment, and participation of students, teachers, and parents in local and regional administrative bodies (Blackmore and Spaull 1987). Consequently, by influencing national policy and resource allocation decisions, teacher unions can affect the educational process. Indeed, in many countries the primary focus of national teacher unions is on issues of educational finance and policy at the national level.

4. Effect of Unionization on Student Outcomes

It is not possible to assess the overall effect of teacher unionization on student achievement from simply looking at the effects of components of the educational production process. Collective bargaining works in many opposing directions. For example, it appears to reduce student achievement on the one hand by reducing time spent in instruction, but increases it on the other by increasing the time teachers spend in preparation and the teacher–student ratio.

Several studies have analyzed the net effect of collective bargaining on student achievement for a variety of student groups. Most studies find that students in union districts perform better on average than students in nonunion districts. The basic approach in most studies has been to enter a measure of union representation into a standard educational production function. Eberts and Stone (1984, 1987) estimate a variant of this approach, by estimating separate equations for *individual* fourth-grade students in union and nonunion school districts. The student outcome measure records the difference in the pre- and post-test scores of each of 14,000 fourth-grade students on a standardized mathematics test. The educational production functions account for differences in student, teacher, administrator, and district characteristics, as well as the home environment. By controlling for these factors, the predominant factor explaining remaining differences in student test-score gains between students in union and nonunion districts should be teacher unionization.

Test-score gains of students in union districts are on average 8 percent higher than those of students in nonunion districts. Half of the net effect is attributable to union-induced differences in resources and other educational factors between the two types of districts; half is due to union–nonunion differences in the effectiveness of these resources.

The effects of collective bargaining found by Eberts and Stone appear to vary for students of different achievement levels: union districts do better with average students. However, union districts do less well with students either well above or well below average; nonunion schools are more productive with these students, by about the same margin. These differences appear to arise from two major factors. First, union districts rely to a greater degree than nonunion districts on standard classroom instructional techniques, which work best for the majority of "average" students. However, the exposure for significantly below or above average students to specialized programs and instructional techniques is significantly greater in nonunion districts. This standardization of instructional techniques is similar to union behavior in many private sector industries. A second major source of union advantage is the greater effectiveness of instructional leadership activities by school principals in union districts. In organized districts, for example, instructional leadership by school principals may be much more effective both because specific principal actions are conditioned by teacher opinion and because the effectiveness of particular actions is enhanced by improved communication and coordination.

Milkman (1989) follows the same approach as Eberts and Stone in examining the effects of collective bargaining on the achievement gains of high school students. However, Milkman emphasizes the effect of collective bargaining on achievement of social minority group students. In schools and districts where minority group students are in the numerical minority, teacher unionization is associated with decreases in achievement by these students. However, in schools and districts where minority group students are in the numerical majority, unionization is associated with increases in their achievement. Milkman interprets this set of findings as further confirmation of the hypothesis that the standardization of curriculum and instructional techniques associated with collective bargaining explains the gains by average students in unionized districts, as well as the losses by the atypical students in the same districts.

A related study by Grimes and Register (1991) finds that Black high school students attending union districts perform better on SAT tests than Black students in nonunion districts. Their results show that a Black student in a union district scores 13.11 percent higher than a comparable Black student in a nonunion district. Register and Grimes do not distinguish whether the effects differ according to whether minority group students are in the numerical minority or majority. The use of SAT scores is also problematic because students taking SAT tests for college admission are typically above average achievers. Register and Grimes attribute their results to the fact that union work rules reduce the possibility of discriminatory practices by school staff.

Kleiner and Petree (1988), using aggregate state-level data for the period 1972–82, find that students in union districts score higher on SAT and ACT scores than students in nonunion districts. However, Kurth (1987) reports the opposite result: a negative relationship between union strength and SAT scores across states and time. This finding by Kurth has been criticized for the absence of controls for trend or regional factors, which are used in the study by Kleiner and Petree.

5. *Effect of Unionization on Costs of Instruction*

The higher average productivity of teacher unions is not without cost. The smaller classes and higher salaries enjoyed by union teachers require additional resources, or a significant shift away from other resources. The question is whether or not the additional gains in student achievement exceed the costs of obtaining these gains.

Evidence on the influence of teacher unionization on district expenditures is mixed, but most find, not surprisingly, that collective bargaining increases expenditures. Gallagher (1979) estimates that union districts have an operating budget approximately 9 percent larger than that of nonunion districts. In contrast, Hall and Carroll (1975) conclude that higher salaries negotiated in union districts are completely offset by larger class sizes, resulting in no significant difference in total operating expenditures between the two district types. Chambers (1977) also finds that collective bargaining reallocates resources within the district without significant increase in total operating expenditures.

However, none of these studies deals directly with the issue of overall union–nonunion cost differentials with the quality of education held constant. To do this, Eberts and Stone (1986) estimate an expenditure equation that specifies district operating expenditures per pupil as a function of variables that reflect the quality of education, community preferences and fiscal capacity, the size of the district, and urban and geographical characteristics. The results indicate that organized districts spend on average 12 percent more per pupil than nonorganized districts, even with achievement measures and student and community characteristics held constant.

The cost effects of teacher unions can be classified into three categories: compensation effects, factor-use effects, and productivity effects. The first two appear to increase the cost of education per unit of output, while the last effect appears to reduce the unit cost of providing education services. The factor-use effect relates to contract constraints placed on school administrators that may prevent them from allocating resources in the most efficient manner. As reported earlier, class-size restrictions, reduction-in-force limitations, and other contract provisions significantly affect the use of resources in unionized districts.

The three effects can be placed in perspective by using the estimates reported by Eberts and Stone. Of the three union effects considered, the productivity and factor-use effects appear roughly to offset one another. That is, the cost advantage associated with the higher productivity of unionized districts is of roughly the same magnitude as the cost disadvantage associated with higher teacher–student ratios in unionized districts. Because the productivity and factor-use effects tend to cancel each other out in this way, the union-induced teacher compensation premium dominates the estimated cost differential. This conclusion is further supported by the fact that multiplying the midrange estimate of the union salary premium (about 17 percent) by the typical ratio of teacher personnel costs to total costs (about 0.7) yields an estimate of the union cost differential (12 percent) consistent with the midrange of the direct estimates presented by Eberts and Stone. Thus, the union cost differential appears primarily to represent a transfer from taxpayers to teachers, with little detrimental change in average student achievement.

On a more speculative note, over a much longer period of time the higher compensation in unionized districts could enable such districts to attract and retain more productive teachers, partially offsetting the union cost differential.

6. Conclusion

Teacher unionization is a crucial force in the operation, effectiveness, and cost of public schools. Evidence to date, primarily from the United States, suggests that unionized teachers receive higher salaries, teach smaller classes, spend less time in instructing students, and have more time for classroom preparation. The net effect of teacher unions on these important factors in the educational process is to make unionized districts slightly more effective than nonunionized districts in educating the average student. This gain appears to be related to a greater standardization of instruction in unionized districts. Atypical students appear to do worse on average in unionized districts as a result of the greater standardization of instructional modes and techniques. For example, unionization is associated with decreased achievement for social minority group students who attend schools where they make up a minority of the students, but with increased achievement for minority group students who attend schools where they make up a majority of the students. Despite the overall productivity advantage for unionized schools, other costs associated with unionization, particularly in the form of higher teacher salaries and benefits, more than offset the productivity advantage of unionized schools, so that the cost of a given quality and quantity of instruction is higher in unionized schools, where all other factors are the same. In many countries, but to a lesser extent in the United States, national teacher unions focus on national issues of educational finance and policy, and place less emphasis on local bargaining.

See also: Education Production Functions; Economics of Educational Time and Learning; Microeconomics of School Production

References

Baugh W H, Stone A 1982 Teachers, unions, and wages in the 1970s: Unionism now pays. *Industrial and Labor Relations Review* 35(3): 368–76
Blackmore J, Spaull A 1987 Australian teacher unionism: New directions. In: Boyd W L, Smart D (eds.) 1987 *Educational Policy in Australia and America: Comparative Perspectives*. Falmer Press, New York
J G Chambers 1977 The impact of collective bargaining for teachers on resource allocation in public school districts. *Journal of Urban Economics* 4(3): 324–39
Duclaud-Williams R 1985 Teacher unions and educational policy in France. In: Lawn M (ed.) 1985 *The Politics of Teacher Unionism: International Perspectives* Croom Helm, London
Eberts R W 1984 Union effects on teacher productivity. *Industrial and Labor Relations Review* 37(3): 346–58
Eberts R W, Stone J A 1984 *Unions and Public Schools: The Effect of Collective Bargaining on American Education.* Lexington Books, Lexington, Massachusetts
Eberts R W, Stone J A 1986 Teacher unions and the cost of public education. *Economic Inquiry* 24 (October): 631–43
Eberts R W, Stone J A 1987 The effect of teacher unions and the productivity of public schools.
Freeman R B, Medoff J L 1984 *What Do Unions Do?* Basic Books, New York
Gallagher D G 1979 Teacher negotiations, school district expenditures, and taxation levels. *Educ. Admin. Q.* 15(1): 67–82
Grimes P W, Register C A 1991 Teacher unions and black students' scores on college entrance exams. *Ind. Rel.* 30(3): 492–500
Hall W C, and Carroll N 1975 The effect of teachers' organizations on salaries and class size. *Ind. Lab. Rel. Rev.* 26(2): 834–41
Hanushek E A 1986 The economics of schooling: Production and efficiency in the public schools *J. Econ. Lit.* 24(3): 1141–77
Hirschman A O 1970 *Exit, Voice, and Loyalty: Responses to decline in Firms, Organizations, and States.* Harvard University Press, Cambridge, Massachusetts
Kasper H 1970 The effect of collective bargaining on public teachers' salaries. *Industrial and Labor Relations Review* 24(1): 52–72
Kleiner M M, Petree D L 1988 Unionism and licensing of public school teachers: Impact on wages and educational output. In: Freeman R B, Ichniowski C (eds.) 1988 *When Public Sector Workers Unionize.* The University of Chicago Press, Chicago, Illinois

Kurth M 1987 Teachers' unions and excellence in education: An analysis of the decline in SAT scores. *J. Lab. Res.* Vol. 8, Fall, pp. 351–67

Lortie D C 1977 *Schoolteacher: A Sociological Study.* University of Chicago Press, Chicago, Illinois

Milkman M I 1989 Teacher unions and high school productivity, unpublished PhD dissertation, University of Oregon, Eugen, Oregon

Pepin L 1990 The defense of teachers' trade union rights. *Int. Lab. Rev.* 129(1): 59–71

Perry C 1979 Teacher bargaining: The experience in nine-systems. *Industrial and Labor Relations Review* 33(1): 3–17

Saltzman G M 1985 Bargaining laws as a cause and consequence of the growth of teacher unionism. *Industrial and Labor Relations Review* 38(3): 335–51

Teacher Involvement and Educational Restructuring

C. Brown

1. Introduction

In the 1970s and 1980s, productivity growth slowed in the United States while the productivity of its OECD trading partners continued to climb. During that time, school children in the United States lost ground in certain test scores to school children in other industrialized countries. (Inkeles 1977, Rohman 1987, Walberg 1983, Commission on Skills of the American Workforce 1990.) These two trends inspired educators and managers in the United States to search for ways to improve the educational process and the work process in order to improve educational performance and firm performance.

One idea that was reconsidered by both educators and managers is that of employee involvement (EI) in the decision-making process. This form of decentralization is not new, its application in the past was largely confined to managerial employees, however. Extending employee involvement in decision-making to nonmanagerial employees has become popularized as part of the highly touted Japanese management system (Hashimoto 1990, Koike and Saso 1988, OECD 1990). Brown et al. (1992) argue that EI must be analyzed as part of the broader employment system and that its success depends on including training and security programs.

This entry addresses the following question: In what ways has decentralization been used in the private sector to improve the efficiency of decision-making and increase the quality of labor input by drawing on employees' knowledge, and what can the public schools learn from these experiences?

2. Conceptual Framework

The central issue of decentralization is whether managers should make decisions after collecting information from employees, or whether employees should make those decisions themselves. The economist's conceptual framework identifies and compares the alternative decision-making processes with the attendant costs and returns.

Here, employee involvement is seen as a form of decentralized decision-making undertaken by employees in nonmanagerial ranks. The employee involvement process can be viewed as a subset of the larger organizational control process. The broader issue of decentralizing decision-making among various levels of management will not be addressed in this entry, however. In general, the literature has been concerned with the application of decentralization to managerial employees only. Extending the process to nonmanagerial employees affects the analysis in important ways, including legal and other institutional constraints.

Most economic models of organizational decision-making emphasize the costs associated with collecting, transmitting, and assimilating information and the costs associated with coordinating various divisions (monitoring and transactions costs), the costs associated with divergence in goals of the organizations and the employees involved in decision-making (agency costs), as well as the difficulties involved with measuring outcomes resulting from the decisions made (moral hazard) (Anandalingam et al. 1987, Arrow 1964, De Groot 1988, Lazear 1991, Williamson 1985). Sociological theories of bureaucracy make an important contribution by delineating the unintended consequences associated with different control techniques (March and Simon 1958). This is the result whenever the control mechanism affects the institutions (i.e., rules and customs) that structure behavior within the organization.

Decentralization, then, includes these identifiable (although perhaps not measurable) costs and benefits as well as the possible unknown risks of unintended consequences. Theoretically, an incentive structure exists for optimal decentralized decision-making or for revealed knowledge required for centralized decision-making. However, the costs associated with monitoring or gathering information usually make such an incentive scheme impractical. In addition, the agency costs associated with the discrepancy between the objectives of the organization and the employees are often unknown because of the problem of unintended consequences.

In order for an organization to know which decisions should be delegated to nonmanagerial employees, the organization needs to know three things:

a) The objective or production function. It is assumed that the goals or outcomes can be measured (the monitoring system) and that the system of control (usually either a system of performance-based compensation or a system of rules regulating procedures or outcomes) is well-defined. It is further assumed that the impact of the decentralized decisions on the objective as well as the impact of the new system on behavior within the system (including unintended consequences) is known.

b) The information system. It is assumed that the value of the employees' knowledge, and the transaction costs associated with acquiring, disseminating, and processing this information, is known. Specifically, it is important to know what type of information is needed for what types of decisions.

c) The decision-making structure. The primary factor in the decision-making structure is the presence or absence of a union. In a unionized organization, a cooperative union–management relationship at the centralized level is a necessary, but not sufficient, step in implementing decentralized decision-making, which includes union–management cooperation at the site or shopfloor level. Whether the union–management relationship is adversarial or cooperative affects the decisions made as well as the costs of decision-making. In the absence of a union, the decentralization process lacks an important mechanism for employee input, for voicing discontent, and ensuring trust in employer's commitments. The managers of a nonunion work force must find alternative ways to gather information, process grievances, and negotiate commitments.

Neither of the first two items is common currency in the real world, and all three items involve a complex relationship of important underlying structural variables. Since the overall impact of decentralizing decision-making depends in crucial ways on the objective function, the information system, and the decision-making structure, this triad is used to analyze decentralization in private organizations and to compare private organizations to public schools.

Decentralization in decision-making is a complex economic and managerial process and there are no simple rules for what decisions should be decentralized under what conditions. However, enough experience has been gathered to enable some crude generalizations to be made about the process and prospects of decentralization of decision-making.

3. Company Practices

Since employees have always been involved to some extent in decision-making, the concern in this entry is with the innovations in employment systems that *increase* employee input in decision-making. In general, three specific types of employee involvement can be categorized: (a) traditional, which includes the types of decisions traditionally made by employees in unionized firms; (b) innovative, which includes the types of decisions made by employees in companies that increase employee involvement on the shop floor; and (c) advanced, which includes employee involvement in strategic decision-making and personnel activities.

Operationally, certain characteristics are discernible in these three types of decision-making categories:

(a) The *traditional* involves: solving routine (recurring) problems; being involved in scheduling vacations, shifts, work assignments, and transfers (usually by seniority); resolving conflict among co-workers; processing grievances against management for contract violations; training co-workers.

(b) The *innovative* involves: solving nonroutine problems; suggesting improvements in the work or production process; suggesting improvements in the service or product; being involved in the design and assignment of work; monitoring one's own work.

(c) The *advanced* involves: evaluating the performance of co-workers; selecting leaders or supervisors; working without supervision; being involved in strategic planning of output, investment, and budgeting.

Each category builds on the previous category, so that a company introducing innovative EI will be adding the activities listed under (b) to those under (a).

Workers and their unions sometimes participate in nonproductive types of "decision-making," such as absenteeism, nuisance grievances against an unpopular supervisor, and rigid enforcement of detailed job classifications. This behavior is matched by similar types of adversarial behavior by supervisors, such as rigid enforcement of break procedures and policies regulating shopfloor behavior. In practice, decentralization of policy making often means changing the type of employee involvement at the shopfloor level so that workers and supervisors work cooperatively to reach production and quality goals. These innovative EI activities require a basis of trust and a sense of shared interests between employees and employers.

In manufacturing, the expansion from traditional EI to innovative EI for production workers often begins in an atmosphere in which feedback is viewed by foremen as obstructionism, and where working informally outside narrow job descriptions is viewed by union shop stewards as rate-busting. Although there are exceptions to these stereotypical descriptions, in general workers do not believe that their input is wanted (and believe they may be punished), the union believes that strict work rules are required to constrain arbitrary (and undesirable) management actions, and managers believe that they have to protect their decision-making prerogatives in order to ensure control over production.

The implementation of innovative EI requires the company and the union to build an industrial relations structure that increases the trust between management and worker on the shop floor and between union and company at the bargaining table, and that enlarges the area of shared interests between these parties. Traditionally, the union has short-run power over production standards, job assignment, and layoff procedures, but it has no long-run power over the size of labor force, the location of plants, automation, or any other strategic decisions. The company has little short-run control over who does what job, although it controls the size of the labor force through short-run layoffs. The company controls its long-run investments, and its ultimate power rests with its ability to determine plant locations and the size of its domestic work force.

In order to implement innovative EI, the company needs to share more of its long-run power with the union and workers in exchange for greater short-run power over production standards, use of the work force, and involvement of workers in making quality and productivity improvements. Even though the workers' long-run economic interests may lie with the financial success of their company, the traditional industrial relations structure prevents their trading in short-run benefits associated with exercising shop-floor power for long-run benefits associated with a guaranteed share in the company's success. With an excess of short-run power for the union and an excess of long-run power for the company, the area of shared interests is small indeed.

The innovations desired by companies involve the union accepting fewer job classifications while adopting a flexible approach to job assignment (i.e., giving up control over job assignment) and encouraging worker input into daily decision-making (balancing workloads, solving problems, suggesting improvements). In return for the advantages to them of these innovations, companies usually provide a commitment to employment security. The issue that arises with a policy of job security is the company's need to ensure that workers remain motivated when they have secure jobs. However, motivation, which is a form of agency cost, is a problem under the alternative employment system, which does not have employment security but has seniority-based layoffs and transfers.

Since job titles do not usually change as workers become more involved in making suggestions and solving problems, they are not usually paid for these skills except through an awards program and the commitment to job security. Long-run job security usually provides the motivation as well as the reward for employee involvement. Although the goals of the company, union, and workers do not change, the structure of power within which they function does, and their area of shared interest is enlarged. Conflict is not eradicated, since employees and the company still have areas of divergent interests. However, with a greater exchange of information and the shared goal of short-run improvements to ensure long-run success (without tit-for-tat bargaining), outcomes can be negotiated that formerly might not even have been considered and that benefit both sides to a greater extent than was the case under adversarial bargaining. Successful implementation of cooperative union–management relations lowers transaction and agency costs.

4. Policy Implications of Observed Decentralization in Manufacturing

Do companies implementing innovative EI tend to fulfill the three criteria presented in the conceptual framework? Three private companies were studied in order to answer this question (see Table 1). Two implemented EI—one company was unionized (MU) whereas the second was not (MN). A third company did not implement EI but attempted union–management cooperation in a centralized fashion (SU). Comparison can also be made with the Japanese managed system (JS) and with schools (SH) (Brown 1992).

In general, the observations made of these companies suggest that they can monitor output and quality at a low marginal cost since this information is automatically collected by the information technology that controls the production process. However, the system of control is less well-defined. Pay for performance is not found in nonmanagerial jobs, except in one nonunion company. Instead, companies rely on systems of rules whose workings are often not fully understood. Because of the large number of intervening variables, such as changes in orders, personnel, and product design, the relationship between the impact of decentralized decisions on measured outcomes is difficult to isolate. Even with pay for performance, pay is tied more to potential than actual performance, so that the impact of decisions on outcomes is not clearly established. In addition, management often seems unable to predict the consequences of the system on variables such as morale and attitudes toward supervisors.

Decentralizing decision-making clearly increases the input of employees' knowledge. The transaction

Table 1
Types of employee involvement in decision-making

	MU	MN	SU	JS	SH
Traditional					
Solving routine problems	×	×	×	×	×
Scheduling and transfers	×	—	×	—	×
Resolving conflict among co-workers	×	—	×	×	×
Processing grievances	×	—	×	×	×
Training co-workers	×	×	×	×	×
Innovative	×	×	×	×	×
Solving nonroutine problems					
Improving work design	×	×	—	×	×
Suggesting product improvements	×	×	—	×	×
Design and assignment of work	×	—	—	×	×
Monitoring own work	×	×	—	×	×
Advanced	—	—	—	—	×
Evaluating co-workers' performance					
Selecting leaders/supervisors	×	—	—	—	—
Working without supervision	—	—	—	—	—
Strategic planning	—	—	—	—	×

costs associated with the collection and processing of workers' knowledge appear to be less than the gains from innovative EI. In general, the transaction costs are minimal when part of the information process is embedded in the production process (e.g., team activities, and job rotation). However, some of the information process is formal (e.g., team meetings), and so has a direct cost.

Agency costs increase with decentralization, and so monitoring and control costs also exist; these have a direct component (e.g., awards for suggestions) and an indirect component (e.g., supervision). In a unionized setting, the difference between the net increase in information or transaction costs and the net increase in agency costs depends to a large extent on the union—management (U–M) relationship at the local level, which is itself influenced by the relationship at the central level. A cooperative U–M relationship at the plant level will greatly reduce the agency costs. At the central level, U–M cooperation seems to be a necessary but insufficient condition for U–M cooperation at the local level in the long run. Innovative EI cannot be implemented until a cooperative union—management structure has been implemented at both the central and local levels.

Cooperation is often the product of adversity. This is hardly surprising, since changing the structure of decision-making under the condition of imperfect information implies taking risks. Both the union and management appear adverse to risk; often the two sides will experiment with innovations only when faced

with a structure that is no longer economically viable. The fact that these changes are made during a period of economic crisis does not necessarily mean that they benefit management and harm the union or workers.

A cooperative relationship is often tried by the union and management independently of the goal of increasing employee involvement at the shop-floor. Cooperation is tried if the parties believe that cooperation would lower the net transaction cost of bargaining without changing the size and division of the pie. Such a windfall gain, including a possible increase in the size of pie, can be split between the parties through negotiation so that both sides gain (thus its designation as "win-win"; see Fisher and Brown 1989).

5. Lessons for Public Schools

What are the similarities and differences in decentralization of decision-making in public schools compared with the observed case studies from the private sector? First the objective function, the information system, and the structure of decision-making should be considered. Then the possible types of decentralized decision-making that would involve teachers in innovative or advanced EI in the public schools must be taken into account.

The economic, political, and social structure within which the public schools operate differs from the structure governing the private sector in important ways that affect the process of decentralizing decision-making. Since market exchange does not provide a connection between demand for the product and the cost of production in public education, output and unit costs cannot be used to evaluate the impact of changing inputs, including the employment system. As scholars of education are acutely aware, educational reforms are hard to evaluate on a large scale because the objective of "educated people" is hard to define and measure. Proxy measures, such as dropout rates, college-bound rates, absentee rates, or standardized test scores, are less than satisfactory because the relationship between these proxies and the broader goal is not known. However, if these factors were defined as subgoals of the educational process, then they could be used to measure changes in inputs. Until some measures of output can be designated, rational evaluation remains impossible.

Once a way to measure output(s) is agreed upon, then the effect of decentralized decisions on output should be known. Here the schools differ from the private sector in that the relationship between inputs and outputs is even less well-established. The production process in education is vastly more complicated than it is in the private sector because of the large number of intervening social, political, and economic variables that are outside the control of the schools. Although researchers might assume the existence of a stable production function in manufacturing in order to predict the impact of changes in inputs on output, such an assumption cannot be made with any confidence in education, since variations in the intervening variables will cause the assumed function to be in flux. The researcher is left with the unsatisfactory prospect of evaluating the impact of EI by evaluating the decision-making process (e.g., the number of meetings or number of suggestions made) or the decisions themselves (e.g., the actual suggestions made). The former type of evaluation can provide an excuse for wasteful meetings or useless suggestions. The latter type of evaluation can easily degenerate into a simple comparison between teachers' decisions and the decisions that would have been made centrally by the principal or the superintendent, and such a comparison negates any potential gain from EI.

The involvement and treatment of production workers in the Japanese employment system has been characterized as the "white collarization of blue collar workers" (Koike and Saso 1988). In contrast, the centralization of decision-making has resulted in the "blue collarization of white collar work" in many occupations and industries, including education. Normally, professional workers would be expected to be involved in decision-making with responsibility for their decisions and to have performance standards and a pay system that rewards experience and skill. The movement to increase EI in decision-making is partially a response to the earlier centralization of decision-making throughout the economy, and as such it allows experimentation with forms of organization that may be more

efficient. However, increasing the decision-making of teachers is only one aspect of their employment system, which should be an integrated system including standards, accountability for decisions, and payment dependent on skills and experience. Caution is needed in applying to teachers any generalizations from the private sector for nonprofessional workers, since it differs in important ways from the process of education. As teachers are professionals who provide a public good within a politicized process, the agency costs and the monitoring problems are more complicated than they are in the private sector. Although the potential of advanced EI is greater for these professionals than for production workers, the difficulties of managing EI are much greater because of the problems of defining and measuring the objective goal in education. The agency costs are magnified by the provision of employment security in an employment system that does not relate workers' performance to the organization's long-term performance.

Security functions differently in the schools compared to private industry. Exchanging employment security for innovative EI in the private sector increases the employees' stake in the company since the promise of security and the ability to raise wages depends on the company's long-run performance. When security is provided, Japanese companies have motivated workers with a performance-related component for pay and promotion. Since a school's costs and revenues are not affected by performance in the short or long run, security commitments do not increase the teachers' stake in the school. Budgets are formed in an unreliable political process and changing economic environment. Teachers find that budgets can be lowered unexpectedly resulting in a decline in the quantity and quality of education and in the quality of their working conditions. Demand is formed primarily by demographics.

In this situation, where job security is granted and budgets are unrelated to long-term performance, the question is how to provide motivation. Without inextricably linking the performance of schools to it, teachers' performance should be partially related to their pay, including pay for skills and experience, job assignments, and tasks undertaken.

What types of additional EI might be used in the schools that would lower transaction costs to a greater extent than they would raise monitoring or agency costs? Innovative EI at the site level requires a budget to pay for meeting times, training for communication and problem-solving skills, and costs associated with the implementation of improvements. Over time, these costs should be offset by output (quality and quantity) improvements and unit cost reductions, or the innovative EI is not performing efficiently. However, as mentioned above, it may be impossible to measure these costs and improvements accurately, so the costs and returns to EI programs may not be quantified.

Teachers know a vast amount about their students

and their classroom dynamics. This type of information cannot be economically transmitted and used in a centralized fashion. However, teachers may or may not know as much about subject matter as the centralized authorities. For this reason, decision-making has tended to be divided, with teachers making decisions concerning individual students and classroom dynamics and districts making decisions on curriculum. This approach precludes the possibility of using teachers' knowledge about the subject matter and introduces the problem of monitoring teachers to ensure the subject matter is well-taught. Decentralization that increases teachers' control over the curriculum addresses the first problem, but it worsens the second. Less ambitious types of EI, such as development of training programs for staff development days, use teachers' knowledge in an efficient way without incurring monitoring costs. Perhaps for this reason, EI experiments have successfully focused on topics such as teacher development.

Teachers already engage in traditional EI activities. (see Table 1, column SH). By the nature of their jobs, they also already engage in nonroutine problem-solving, and they monitor the quality of their work because external monitoring is too difficult. Many districts in California have implemented innovative and advanced EI activities at site level. Beside transforming the U–M relationship into a cooperative one at the district level, districts have experimented with programs to decentralize decision-making so that principals have more decision-making power and can accordingly involve their teachers in the decision-making process. The types of decisions usually made are those that would be categorized as suggesting improvements or design and assignment of work. Although there are discussions about how to monitor the quality of work, peer review has been limited to new teachers.

As Smith and O'Day (1991) argue, effective site-level restructuring (that is, innovative EI) must have a well-defined structure within which to function. (Benson and others prefer to emphasize that college-bound and noncollege-bound students should be taught different materials in a different manner. Students planning to enter the labor market after high school would be better prepared by high schools that integrate academic and vocational learning, use cooperative learning and teacher collaboration, and create a school connection with a company .) This is equivalent to having a well-designed production system in the private sector. Smith and O'Day believe that the state must provide the structure with an instructional guidance system, including a curriculum framework, student achievement goals, teacher professional development, and student assessment.

In the budget crisis of the early 1990s, some school districts in California used EI in the budget-cutting process. Several districts reported that EI activities resulted in finding creative solutions to help minimize the impact of the cuts. The use of EI appears to have increased teachers' willingness to take on larger burdens as budgets are cut. Although the use of teachers' knowledge to find creative solutions is valuable, the use of EI to impose additional burdens must be carefully evaluated in a labor market where some policymakers would like to increase the flow of highly qualified candidates. These increased burdens may not be sustainable in the short run for the impacted teachers or in the long run for the labor market for teachers. In either case, the public, who pay for education, may be misled about the true impact of budget cuts on the quantity and quality of education being provided.

In summary, the impact of decentralization of decision-making on the performance of an organization may be viewed with cautious optimism. An executive of Xerox, a company that has successfully implemented innovative EI, summarized the contribution of decentralization as being "the systematic integrated changes it can support, perhaps enable, and stimulate." However, decentralization as a sole strategy in education should not be expected to have any direct impact on learning, although it may have a direct impact on the working conditions of teachers.

Perhaps the most important lesson learned from the private sector is that EI is a complement to, and not a substitute for, well-designed products and a well-functioning production system. EI cannot solve deep-rooted problems of inoperative communication systems, poorly designed products, or defective or broken equipment. Neither can EI solve the problems caused by poor macroeconomic performance. Decentralization of decision-making appears to work effectively when it is part of an already well-functioning organization, in which case innovative EI allows marginal improvements to the overall system. Over time, the accumulation of many small decisions amount to a potentially large payoff to innovative EI.

A growing economy is important in order to support high performance workplaces and schools. Without sufficient demand, companies are not able to honor employment security commitments and workers are not motivated to make improvements in productivity. Without the promise of jobs that use their education, students are not motivated to learn. Literacy, which includes mathematical, linguistic, and analytical skills, prepares students to be trained on the job in order to become productive workers who can increase their skills over their lifetime. However, a growth in demand is required for employers to hire and train new entrants and to provide them with opportunities to improve their skills and be promoted. Improvement in the education provided by high schools will not by itself solve the weak labor market and low returns to schooling faced by high-school graduates (Cutler and Katz 1991).

Over time innovative EI can have a powerful impact in a well-functioning school, including cooperative industrial relations at the district and site level, adequate and well-maintained physical facilities, adequate books and supplies, well-trained teachers, and healthy and eager students with grade-level skills. Innovative EI cannot be expected to overcome serious shortcomings. However, once the schools are at a functional baseline innovative EI can be a powerful tool for making continual improvements and maintaining high performance.

See also: Economics of School Enterprise

References

Anandalingam G, Chatterjee K, Gangolly J S 1987 Information, incentives, and decentralized decision-making in a Bayesian framework. *J. Op. Res. Soc.* 38(6): 499–508

Arrow K J 1964 Control in Large Organizations. *Management Science* 10(3): 397–408

Benson C S 1991 Current state of occupational and technical training: The need for integration and high quality programs. Working paper, National Center for Research in Vocational Education, University of California, Berkeley, California

Brown C 1992 Employee involvement in industrial decision-making: Lessons for public schools. In: Hanaway J, Carnoy M (eds.) 1992 *Decentralization and School Improvements: Can we Fulfill the Promise?* Jossey-Bass, San Francisco, California

Brown C, Reich M, Stern D 1992 Becoming a high-performance organization: The role of security, employee involvement, and training. Working paper, Institute of Industrial Relations, University of California, Berkeley, California

Commission on the Skills of the American Workforce 1990 *America's Choice: High Skills or Low Wages*. National Center on Education and the Economy, Rochester, New York

Cutler D M, Katz L F 1991 Macroeconomic performance and the disadvantage. *Brookings Papers on Economic Activity*, No.2

De Groot H 1988 Decentralization decisions in bureaucracies as a principal–agent problem. *J. Pub. Econ.* 36: 323–37

Fisher R, Brown S 1989 *Getting Together*. Business, London

Hashimoto M 1990 *The Japanese Labor Market*. Upjohn, Washington, DC

Inkeles A 1977 The international evaluation of educational achievement: A review of international studies in evaluation, *Proc. National Academy of Education* 11

Koike K, Saso M 1988 *Understanding Industrial Relations in Japan*. Macmillan, Basingstoke

Lazear E 1991 Labor economics and the psychology of organizations, *J. Econ. Perspectives* 5(2): 89–110

March J G, Simon H A 1958 *Organizations*. Wiley, New York

Organisation for Economic Co-operation and Development (OECD), 1990 *Labor Flexibility and Work Organization: Japan*. OECD, Paris

Rothman R 1987 Foreigners outpace american students in science. *Education Week* February 28, p.1

Smith M S, O'Day J 1991 Systemic school reform. In: Fuhram S H, Malen B 1991 *The Politics of Curriculum and Testing: The 1990 Yearbook of the Politics of Education Association*. Falmer Press, London

Walberg H J 1983 Science literacy and economic productivity in international perspective. *Daedalus*, 111

Williamson O 1985 *Economic Institutions of Capitalism: Firms, Markets, Relational Contracting*. Free Press, New York

Further Reading

Clarke F H, Barrough M N 1983 Optimal employment contracts in a principal–agent relationship. *J. Econ. Behav. Org.* 4: 69–90

Economics of School Enterprise

D. Stern

Possibly every country in the world contains some examples of school enterprise, defined here as school-sponsored activity that engages groups of students in producing goods or services for sale or use to people other than the students involved. In capitalist industrialized nations students build houses, run restaurants, operate child-care centers, repair automobiles, cultivate crops and livestock, manage retail shops, and carry out small manufacturing projects, among other things. Socialist societies have combined work with schooling from the primary grades through to the polytechnics. Many developing countries involve students in agriculture, construction, or crafts. However, school enterprise generally plays only a marginal role in the curriculum or in the financing of schools, despite the potentially significant educational and economic benefits of making productive work a bigger part of students' activity. This entry reviews the potential benefits, lists some examples, and describes constraints on the growth of school enterprise.

1. Rationale

The most self-evident, and in some contexts the most important, potential benefit of school enterprise is that it recovers some or all of the cost of schooling through the sale or use of goods or services produced by students. In addition, engaging students in work that is immediately productive can contribute to the development of students' knowledge and skill. Moreover, combining education with production can yield tangible and intangible benefits for the local community and society at large.

1.1 Cost Recovery

According to von Borstel's (1991a) historical review of the concept of productive education, one of its earliest proponents was the English political philosopher John Locke. In his 1696 *Plan for Working-Schools for Poor Children*, Locke envisioned an institution that would train and care for indigent children, supported by the work of the children themselves. Self-sufficiency through sale of goods produced by the schools was a salient feature of the plan. Von Borstel finds a similar idea later in the English socialist Robert Owen's 1818 *Report to the Committee of the Association for the Relief of the Poor*. Owen put the idea of productive education into practice in the community he founded at New Lanark. A more recent application of the same concept was the Supported Work Demonstration in the United States during the 1970s, which created enterprises for the purposes of training welfare recipients, former drug addicts, unemployed youth, and former prison inmates (Manpower Demonstration Research Corporation 1980).

Von Borstel (1991b) credits the Soviet educator Anton Semenovitch Makarenko with the first actual demonstration of cost-recovery through school enterprise. At the Gorky Colony during the 1920s and 1930s, students operated a number of successful enterprises, starting with the cultivation of grain, vegetables and fruit, and animal husbandry, and eventually including the manufacture of clothing, furniture, and cameras. These were able to generate profits, with students working four hours a day and devoting the rest of their time to studies.

Cost-recovery tends to be a more important objective for school enterprise in situations where resource scarcity is more pressing. Accordingly, revenues from school enterprises in developing countries often cover a large proportion of school costs. Von Borstel's (1982) survey of 27 productive education projects in developing countries found that nine of them generated enough revenue to pay all the costs of the school, another five supported between 60 and 90 percent of school costs, and six more recovered between 25 and 45 percent. This implies that the enterprises produced enough not only to cover the cost of production itself but also, in many instances, to cover the cost of education. Similarly, in the rural southeastern United States, several colleges have traditionally used school enterprises to help support themselves (Mullinax et al. 1991). One of these, Berea College, has had students working in more than 60 different departments, including a bakery, wood shop, farm, dairy, restaurant, and hotel, in addition to the college's power plant, and its maintenance and housekeeping, library, and administrative offices (Peck 1989).

In more affluent settings, the potential for profitable school enterprise also exists. For instance, there are schools in the United States that operate profitable hotels, hair styling salons, and food catering services. However, enterprises in relatively well-to-do schools usually do not try to maximize output, revenues, or profits, in part because such an emphasis would require students to do too much repetitive work, and would therefore detract from their educational development.

1.2 Enhancing Education

On the other hand, productive activity, if properly organized, can contribute to schools' educational effectiveness. The educational benefit of combining education with actual production has been suggested by recent research on the value of "situated learning" (Resnick 1987a, 1987b; Brown et al. 1989; Raizen 1989; Sticht 1979, 1987; Lave and Wenger 1991). This research has produced new evidence that learning through the work process itself is an effective method for acquiring work-related knowledge. In contrast, what is learned in classrooms, while useful in classrooms, does not always transfer to actual work situations. A number of empirical studies have demonstrated the lack of correlation between school-taught knowledge on the one hand, and problem solving in the context of actual production on the other. These studies corroborate the value of learning by doing. In economic terms, they imply that productive activity can be a substitute for classroom instruction. Lave and Wenger go so far as to define learning as "legitimate peripheral participation in communities of practice" (1991 p. 31). School enterprises are natural settings for learning in this sense.

According to von Borstel (1991a), the eighteenth-century French philosopher Jean-Jacques Rousseau was the first to assert the pedagogical benefits of productive education. Rousseau's ideas were applied and refined by the Swiss-German educator Johann Heinrich Pestalozzi, who opened a school in 1774 where education was organized around productive labor. Among other nineteenth-century proponents of the pedagogical value of work were the French utopian socialist Charles Fourier and the German schoolmaster Georg Kerschensteiner. The American philosopher John Dewey brought this idea into the twentieth century, consistently arguing that students learn best when productive experience is an integral part of their education.

Contemporary education at the secondary level and beyond commonly includes work as an adjunct to classroom instruction in programs that are explicitly occupational. For instance, apprenticeship programs combine training on the job with classroom instruction, and education for professions including medicine and architecture usually requires a period of internship. In the United States, vocational programs in high schools and two-year colleges often feature cooperative education, which provides part-time jobs related to students' coursework (US Department of Education 1991, US Congress, General Accounting Office 1991). In cooperative education, a written training plan details what each student is expected to learn on the job, and the student's performance is jointly monitored by the classroom teacher and the job supervisor.

Apprenticeship, cooperative education, and professional internship all appear to use work experience to complement classroom instruction, not to substitute for it. Students are evidently presumed to learn more from the combination of classroom instruction and work experience than they would from either one alone. The work experience gives students an opportunity to apply, extend, and better understand what they have been taught in the classroom. It also confronts them with real problems that can motivate them to seek the knowledge their courses are offering.

School enterprise may offer more of these educational benefits than work experience in jobs outside the school. The supply of outside job placements depends on the business cycle and the prosperity of local employers. Thus, for instance, work opportunities on a school farm, restaurant, or automobile repair shop may be more predictable than in similar enterprises outside the school. School enterprises can provide instructive employment even if they do not make money.

Teachers also have more control over the content of students' activities in a school enterprise than in outside jobs. There is less danger in a school enterprise that students will be confined to simple, repetitive tasks with little educational value, or that they will be asked to sacrifice quality for speed. Since they are not required to make a profit, school enterprises can afford to let students work slowly and carefully, try out a number of different jobs, and take more collective responsibility for managing the operation (Stern 1984).

Use of productive activity as a context for education may be especially effective in preparing students for work that requires continual learning and problem–solving. These cognitive demands are a traditional feature of many professional and managerial jobs, and some researchers have concluded that computerization also results in greater demand for thinking on the part of clerical and production workers (Hirschhorn 1984, Zuboff 1988, Koike and Inoki 1990, Adler 1992). Learning by doing in a school enterprise may be highly appropriate preparation for the "doing by learning" which characterizes some contemporary workplaces (Stern and Benson 1991). Some advanced forms of school enterprise—for example, the teaching hospital attached to a medical school—embody elements of the "learning enterprise" which may grow more predominant as basic and applied research, product development, and continual process improvement become more important parts of work for more people.

1.3 External Benefits

In addition to benefits for students themselves, school enterprise can also create positive externalities. One externality for the local community, region, or nation is adding to the export base. Schools can organize students to produce for export, as in Cuba's *Escuelas en el Campo*, directly earning foreign exchange and contributing to the country's economic growth. Schools can also serve as seedbeds for new export enterprises, either turning them over to local businesses or enabling students themselves to form independent ventures. Jonathan Sher (1977) proposed the concept of school-based community development corporations that would perform this function in rural communities. Subsequently, Sher helped Paul DeLargy to create an organization called REAL (Rural Entrepreneurship through Action Learning), which has enabled rural schools in several parts of the United States to spawn new businesses that add to the local export base.

Information is another external benefit that may be produced by school enterprise. For example, Mullenax (1982) has described a school in rural Colombia called the FUNDAEC Rural University, which offered a six-year program to train "engineers for rural development." As part of the program, the school developed and demonstrated more productive methods for agriculture in the region. Students helped local farmers implement the new techniques. The school thus took on the function of an agricultural extension service, dispensing free information. Similarly, in the urban United States, schools have engaged students in giving information to local communities about issues including health and nutrition, energy conservation, and disaster preparedness.

School enterprises provide tangible external benefits whenever they provide goods or services to people for less than they are willing to pay. Student-run restaurants, child-care centers, automobile repair services, and other enterprises that cater to the general public usually charge a price that is less than the going market rate. If the price reduction is still greater than that warranted by the lower value of the product or service itself—for example, less convenient location or schedule, slower service, or less varied menu compared to commercial providers—then the customers are receiving an extra benefit.

A less tangible external benefit is the inculcation of pro-social values in students. In particular, combining education with production has been advocated as a method to teach appreciation for all labor, and to prevent elitist attitudes from developing among students who are privileged to receive more than the average amount of schooling. This has been an explicit objective for school enterprise in socialist countries, but it has also been emphasized by non-socialists including Kerschensteiner and Dewey (von Borstal 1991a, 1991b). On the other hand, school enterprise has been used to teach about capitalist business, as in the Junior Achievement program in the United States and the mini-enterprise initiative in the United Kingdom during the 1980s (Jamieson et al. 1989).

In economic terms, a positive externality would occur if students, after being educated through school enterprise, decided to use their talents in occupations or locations where they provided a greater amount of unremunerated service to other people. The rural engineers trained at FUNDAEC in Colombia are an example: if they stay in the countryside and spend much of their time giving free or inexpensive technical assistance to farmers, rather than going to the city and taking jobs where their productivity is no greater but their salary is, then there is a positive externality.

1.4 Summary of Normative Theory

In a market economy it would be considered justifiable for school enterprises to undertake activities that are socially beneficial but would not be feasible for profit-seeking enterprises. This includes two main categories. In one category are activities from which the benefit to people other than the students involved exceeds the true cost of production including students' time, but which cannot be profitably undertaken by a private enterprise because the benefit is a pure public good or the activity yields significant positive externalities. The use of a pure public good by one person does not diminish its availability for use by other people. Restoration of a historic landmark is an example. Although many people might appreciate the benefit of having the restoration done even if they never visit the site, their potential willingness to pay could not be captured in the form of user fees. The conventional means of financing such projects is either through donations to a nonprofit organization, or through taxation to support a public agency doing the work. A public school is, in fact, a public agency, and the expenditure of resources necessary for a school enterprise to produce the public good is justified if the benefit to citizens exceeds the project's cost. The same can be said of activities such as energy conservation and environmental enhancement, which may not be pure public goods but do yield positive spillover benefits to people other than the actual customers or clients. For example, installing more energy-efficient lighting not only reduces electricity bills for the property owner but also reduces environmental damage caused by production of electricity.

In the second category are labor-intensive services from which the benefit to customers or clients does not exceed the cost of production, but which are of sufficient educational value to participating students that the sum of the educational benefit and the benefit to consumers does exceed production cost. Examples might be caring for small children, restoring wrecked houses or cars, or providing low-volume retail or food services. A profit-seeking enterprise would not be able to break even on such activities, but the school enterprise would be justified in undertaking them because of the educational benefit to the students involved.

The logic of these calculations becomes clearer if one uses some explicit symbols. Let B stand for the benefit from a proposed activity to people other than the students involved. Let S denote the benefit to participating students and C the true cost of production including students' time. B, C, and S are all measured per unit of product or service. Suppose M is the price that could be charged in a competitive market. If M > C, the activity could be performed by a profit-seeking business, and need not be conducted by a school enterprise. In a market economy an activity would generally be considered appropriate for a school enterprise if and only if

$$S + B > C > M$$

In the first category of justifiable activities are public goods or activities with positive spillover benefits, where B > C, but where C > M because an ordinary business enterprise relying on user fees could not capture all of the benefits. In the second category are labor-intensive services where B < C, but S + B > C > M.

In practice it is not usually possible to measure these quantities with any precision. However, these principles provide general guidance in analyzing existing or potential school enterprises.

2. Examples

Some instances of school enterprise have already been mentioned. In order to provide further concrete examples, several cases are listed here in slightly more detail. Table 1 gives some of the information from von Borstel (1982) on the 10 largest productive education programs in developing countries, among the 27 he studied. Shown in the table are the numbers of students and sites involved in each program, the highest school grade level at which instruction is offered, the percentage of school costs recovered from enterprise revenues, and the ratio of scheduled class time to work time for students.

In the United States, most school enterprises are connected with vocational education. A good example is the construction enterprise operated by the public schools in Montgomery County, Maryland (US Department of Education 1991). This program builds one or two houses each year. The Montgomery County Students Construction Trades Foundation was formed as a nonprofit corporation in 1976. The board of directors has included local real estate developers, construction contractors, realtors, attorneys, and architects. In its first year the Foundation secured a US$100,000 bank loan to buy land and materials. The loan was repaid from the sale of the first house, which sold for US$106,000 in 1977. Since then, the Foundation has been able to finance subsequent purchases of land and materials from preceding years' profits.

Table 1
Ten large productive education programs in developing countries

Country: Name of program	Students	Sites	Highest grade	Cost % recovered	Class/ work time
Sri Lanka: Prevocational studies	1,000,000	5,500	9	5	3.37
Philippines: Barrio High Schools	310,000	2,000	12	5	1.80
Cuba: *Escuelas en el Campo*	150,000	300	12	100	1.33
Panama: *Escuelas de Produccion*	48,000	110	9	100	0.55
Tunisia: *Initiation au Travail Manuel*	28,600	892	8	25	1.00
Upper Volta[a]: Rural Education Centers	27,000	737	3	25	1.00
Kenya: Craft Training Centers	10,500	214	8	28	1.33
Papua New Guinea: Vocational Centers	4,400	63	7	100	0.27
Botswana: Brigades	1,100	12	9	100	0.52
Cameroon: Zones of Community and Cultural Activity	950	19	6	12	1.33

a Subsequently named Burkina Faso

The Foundation sold houses on the open market for six years. Then for four years it built one or two houses a year under a county program that provided free land, restricted the selling price of the houses built, and limited eligible purchasers to households with incomes below a certain level. In 1988 the Foundation returned to operating on the open market, building a large suburban house that was expected to sell for about US$250,000. In addition to building a total of 16 houses by the end of 1988, the Foundation has also engaged students in construction projects for the school system, including a solar demonstration house and a covered bridge at an outdoor education center.

The students most intensively involved in the construction project are those enrolled in carpentry, masonry, plumbing, heating and air conditioning, or electricity courses. At the construction site, students work under the supervision of their classroom teachers as well as a site coordinator and the resource teacher for the Construction Trades Project. Some work is contracted out to professionals. Students are not expected to engage in work for which they receive no instruction, such as pouring concrete, plastering, or operating earth-moving equipment. In addition, if work is behind schedule, subcontractors are hired for such tasks as taping drywalls and painting. The aim is to finish the house or houses started each year, so that students have the satisfaction of seeing the finished product, even if some of the work has to be contracted out. If possible, two houses are built each year instead of one, so that there will always be plenty of work for students.

Although most school enterprises in the United States are part of vocational education, some grow out of the academic curriculum. One well-known example is Foxfire, a literary enterprise that started in an English class and has published a series of magazines and books (Wigginton 1985). Another example is an enterprise at Mt Edgecumbe High School in Sitka,

Alaska, where students produce smoked salmon for export to Asia (Knapp 1989). The purpose of the enterprise is not just to teach students how to slice, smoke, and package fish, but more importantly to engage them in thinking about product development, analyzing the cultures and languages of the Pacific Rim and confronting the challenge of continuous quality improvement.

3. Obstacles

Since the idea of school enterprise is well-known, and the potential benefits seem great, it is evident that there must be constraints which prevent more students from becoming involved. One such constraint is the lack of instructional resources. Designing an enterprise that will be productive and at the same time provide significant learning opportunities for students is not a trivial task. Von Borstel (1982) observed that even in established school enterprises the curriculum often fails to meet the promise of using work as a context for students to analyze technical and social problems. Good instructional materials for this purpose are scarce. Also, few teachers have the know-how to organize productive enterprises without additional training.

However, the problem is larger than that. Sinclair (1977) reported that, even when the idea of combining education with production has been supported by central governments in developing countries, it has often been resisted. Parents want schools to make their children upwardly mobile; they oppose programs that involve students in low-status manual work. Teachers and school administrators likewise may consider such activities demeaning to their own position as educated individuals. The resistance seems most intense when school enterprise is explicitly linked to school programs that limit students' opportunity for upward mobility, such as the Rural Education Centers in the former state of Upper Volta (now Burkina Faso).

Competition with private firms and labor unions is another constraint. Schools have to be careful that their productive activities do not threaten local businesses. Unions also oppose any encroachment of student labor into unionized sectors. As long as one function of schools is to keep children out of the labor market—a role given to schools following industrialization and urbanization—school enterprise is likely to remain a limited option.

On the other hand, policy initiatives in the 1980s and 1990s in numerous countries attempted to create more opportunities for students to experience learning through work. These initiatives were primarily oriented towards placing students in work settings outside the school, but there was a recognition that outside employers might not be able to provide a sufficient number of high-quality placements. In some countries, including Denmark and the United States, laws have encouraged the use of school enterprise for work-based learning. In this context, the role of school enterprise may expand.

See also: Joint Production of Education; Political Economy of Educational Production; Microeconomics of School Production; Education Production Functions

References

Adler P (ed.) 1992 *Technology and the Future of Work.* Oxford University Press, New York

Brown J S, Collins A, Duguid P 1989 Situated cognition and the culture of learning. *Educ. Researcher* 18(1): 32–42

Hirschhorn L 1984 *Beyond Mechanization: Work and Technology in a Postindustrial Age.* MIT Press, Cambridge, Massachusetts

Jameison I, Miller A, Watts A G 1989 *Mirrors of Work.* Falmer Press, Philadelphia, Pennsylvania

Knapp M R 1989 Alaska's young entrepreneurs. *Vocational Educational Journal* 64(8): 40–41

Koike K, Inoki T (eds.) 1990 *Skill Formation in Japan and Southeast Asia.* University of Tokyo Press, Tokyo

Lave J, Wenger E 1991 *Situated Learning, Legitimate Peripheral Participation.* Cambridge University Press, Cambridge

Manpower Demonstration Research Corporation 1980 *Summary and Findings of the National Supported Work Demonstration.* Ballinger, Cambridge, Massachusetts

Mullenax P B 1982 *Education for Rural Development FUNDAEC. A Case Study.* Doctoral thesis, Department of Educational Administration and Supervision, Bowling Green State University, Bowling Green, Ohio

Mullinax M F, Stephenson J B, Denman W, Davis J, Canon A 1991 Labour, learning, and service in five American colleges. *Education with Production* 7(2): 83–104

Peck E 1989 Labour for education. *Education with Production* 6(2): 5–28

Raizen S A 1989 *Reforming Education for Work. A Cognitive Science Perspective.* National Center for Research in Vocational Education, University of California, Berkeley, California

Resnick L B 1987a The 1987 Presidential address Learning in school and out. *Educ. Researcher* 16(9): 13–20

Resnick L B 1987b *Education and Learning to Think.* National Academy Press, Washington, DC

Sher J P (ed.) 1977 *Education in Rural America. A Reassessment of Conventional Wisdom.* Westview Press, Boulder, Colorado

Sinclair M E 1977 Introducing work-experience programmes in Third World schools. *Prospects* 7(3): 362–78

Stern D 1984 School-based enterprise and the quality of work experience. A study of high school students. *Youth & Society* 15(4): 401–27

Stern D, Benson C S 1991 Firms' propensity to train. In: Stern D, Ritzen J M M (eds.) 1991 *Market Failure in Training? New Economic Analysis and Evidence on Training of Adult Employees.* Springer-Verlag, Heidelberg and New York

Sticht T G 1979 Developing literacy and learning strategies in organizational settings. In: O'Neil H F Jr., Spielberger C D (eds.) 1979 *Cognitive and Affective Learning Strategies.* Academic Press, New York

Sticht T G 1987 *Functional Context Education. Workshop Resource Notebook.* The Applied Behavioral & Cognitive Sciences, Inc., San Diego, California

US Congress, General Accounting Office 1991 *Transition from School to Work. Linking Education and Worksite Training.* GAO/HRD-91-105. General Accounting Office, Washington, DC

US Department of Education, Office of Vocational and Adult Education 1991 *Combining School and Work. Options in High Schools and Two-Year Colleges.* Department of Education, Washington, DC

von Borstel F 1982 *Productive Education. A Comparative Study of the Present Day Experience in Developing Nations.* Doctoral thesis, Department of Educational Theory, University of Toronto, Toronto

von Borstel F 1991a Development of the concept of productive education, Pt. I. *Education with Production* 7(2): 19–51

von Borstel F 1991b Development of the concept of productive education, Pt. II. *Education with Production* 8(1): 5–36

Wigginton E 1985 *Sometimes a Shining Moment. The Foxfire Experience.* Doubleday, New York

Zuboff S 1988 *In the Age of the Smart Machine: The Future of Work and Paver.* Basic Books, New York

Further Reading

Collins C, Gillespie R 1987 *Contemporary Issues in International Education. Booklet No. 4: School and Work.* Department of Education, School of External Studies and Continuing Education, University of Queensland, St. Lucia

Morsy Z 1979 *Learning and Working.* UNESCO, Paris

Stern D, Stone J, Hopkins C, McMillan M, Crain R 1994 *School-based Enterprise: Productive Learning in American High Schools.* Jossey-Bass, San Francisco, California

van Rensburg P 1974 *Report from Swaneng Hill: Education and Employment in an African Country.* Almqvist and Wiksell, Stockholm

Economics of Childcare

M. H. Strober

As a result of the remarkable increase in women's labor force participation and women's participation in education and training in all Western industrialized countries, mothers no longer routinely care for their young children on a full-time basis. Arrangements for the care of infants and young children during the working or school hours of their parent(s) have now become matters of public policy. Economic issues include the supply and demand for childcare; its cost, quality, and external benefits; and alternative systems of finance, governance, and regulation.

Except for the United States, industrialized countries have developed extensive policies for dealing with the care of young children, including paid periods of maternal and parental leave (Kahn and Kamerman 1987). Bergman (1993) provided a full discussion of the French system. Kamerman (1991) provided a summary of policies and programs in an international context. The United States situation is of particular policy interest because numerous decisions have been debated at the national, state, and local levels.

1. Overview of the United States Childcare Market

The diversity of care options for preschool children is extraordinary. Children whose parent(s) are in school or in the labor force can be cared for informally or formally. Within the formal sector there is great variation in the auspices and ownership of care options. Moreover, within any given week, many parents often use combinations of types of care.

Informal care includes both paid and unpaid care: the child can accompany one or both parents to school or work; the parents can split their work and school time so that one of them is always available to care for the child in the child's own home (often referred to as "splitting shifts"); a relative (including an older sibling) can care for the child in the child's home or in the relative's home, either paid or unpaid; and a nonrelative (housekeeper, nanny, or au pair) can care for the child for pay in the child's own home, and either live in that home or not. Children also sometimes care for themselves; these are the so-called "latch-key children."

Formal care always involves payment and includes care in a family daycare home or in a childcare center. Family daycare services are offered in the home of the child care-provider; in general 2 to 12 children of mixed ages are cared for in such homes (Hayes et al. 1990). According to the 1990 National Child Care Survey (National Association for the Education

of Young Children (NAEYC 1991) there are an average of six children in regulated family day homes, and an average of three in nonregulated homes. Often, the provider cares for her or his own child as well as for other children.

A childcare center generally cares for a substantial number of children, who are grouped by age or developmental stage. The average number of children cared for ranges from 50 in Head Start programs to 91 in for-profit chains (NAEYC 1991). Centers may be public, private nonprofit, or private for-profit. Some centers are operated by employers, primarily for the children of their employees, and some are operated by school districts.

In the United States in 1988, almost two-thirds of children under the age of 5 whose mothers worked full-time were cared for in group care; about one-third (32.6 percent) in childcare centers, nursery schools, kindergartens, extended daycare or day camp; and about one-third (31.2 percent) in family daycare homes (Blau and Ferber 1992). The percentage of care provided by these two types of institutions increased greatly after the Second World War. For example, in 1958 less than 20 percent of children under 5 with full-time employed mothers were cared for in these two types of institutions (Hayes et al. 1990). The NAEYC (1991) study estimated that at the beginning of 1990 there were about 80,000 childcare centers serving about 4 million children, and about 118,000 regulated family daycare homes serving about 700,000 children. Estimates of unregulated family daycare homes ranged widely from 550,000 to 1.1 million (Hayes et al. 1990). The number of children served by unregulated family daycare homes was estimated to be about 5 million (Kahn and Kamerman 1987).

2. The Market for Formal Care

2.1 Supply

It is difficult to obtain precise estimates of the supply of childcare workers in the United States. Because many childcare workers, especially those who provide unregulated services in their own homes, do not report employment and income, it is likely that the Current Population Surveys underestimate the number of childcare workers (Blau 1992). The National Child Care Staffing Study, (Whitebrook et al. 1989) found that 97 percent of teachers and assistant teachers were female.

Relative to the female labor force as a whole, childcare workers are well-educated (NAEYC 1985). In the civilian labor force as a whole, less than half of all women have attended college, but Whitebrook et al. (1989) found that in their sample of childcare centers, more than half of assistant teachers and almost three-fourths of teachers had some college education. The NAEYC (1991) study found that among teachers in centers almost half (47 percent) had a four-year college degree, about 13 percent had a two-year college degree, about 12 percent had a Child Development Associate credential, and 15 percent had some college experience (NAEYC 1991).

Family daycare providers were found to be less well-educated than childcare center teachers and assistant teachers. Among United States parents who used family daycare facilities, less than half of those responding to a survey reported that their provider had childcare training (the survey had an 88 percent response rate). When providers were asked about their own training, only about two-thirds of regulated providers and one-third of unregulated providers said they had any training in child care (NAEYC 1991).

Relative to their education level, childcare workers were found to be poorly paid. The average hourly wage of teachers in childcare centers in the United States in 1990 was US$7.49; for providers in regulated family daycare homes, US$4.04; and for providers in unregulated homes, US$1.25 (NAEYC 1991). Moreover, the earnings structure was exceedingly flat: there was little wage variation by job level or by education. For example, the National Childcare Staffing study found that among those with some college education, aides were paid on average US$4.45 per hour, while teacher/directors were paid only about one dollar more (US$5.66) per hour. Among teachers, those with 12 years of schooling or less were paid US$4.74 per hour while those with a postcollege degree were paid only about three dollars per hour more (US$7.49) (Whitebrook et al. 1989).

A study of the determinants of earnings for childcare workers, using data from the Current Population Survey, found the surprising result that geographic location, race, and age were unrelated to earnings (Blau 1992). The result for geographic location was unexpected given the variation in fees by geographic area. The relationship between earnings and race needs further investigation.

The childcare market appears to be highly segregated by race. For example, the National Day Care Home Study found that 80 percent of children in family daycare centers were of the same race and ethnicity as their caregiver (Fosburg 1981). Given this segregation, it may be that there is an absence of the usual wage discrimination faced by minority workers, since, with all other factors held constant, female Black providers who cared for Black children appeared to be paid the same as female White providers who cared for White children.

Reasoning from a human capital framework, the absence of a significant relationship between earnings and age suggests that there may be little on-the-job learning in childcare. Alternatively, it may be that in the case of childcare workers, age is not a good proxy for experience: older workers in the field may not be any more experienced than younger workers.

The absence of a strong relationship between education and earnings for childcare workers was even more surprising. Among private household workers (including both nannies and family daycare providers) and among those who defined themselves as teachers (including teachers in childcare centers, nursery school teachers and kindergarten teachers), there was no significant relationship between education and earnings; however, for staff members in childcare centers who did not designate themselves as teachers (assistant teachers, aides, etc.) the wage rate was significantly related to education. Blau (1992) suggested that while teachers used their higher education to enter the more highly paid sector of the childcare market, once they did so their wage rate was not related to their education level.

Not only have wages been low among childcare workers, but benefits have also been minimal. In the National Childcare Staffing sample, even among full-time staff, only about 40 percent had employment-related health insurance and only about 20 percent had retirement benefits. Moreover, those earning the lowest wages had the poorest benefits packages (Whitebrook et al. 1989).

Partly as a consequence of low wages and poor benefits, turnover among childcare workers has been very high, a worrisome finding since continuity of care is an important element of childcare quality and children's well-being (Hayes et al. 1990). Moreover, high turnover increases the level of stress in the work environment and negatively affects the job performance and quality of care provided by remaining staff (Whitebrook et al. 1989, Strober et al. 1989). While the average turnover rate for all occupations is about 20 percent (Hayes et al. 1990), the estimates of turnover rates for childcare workers in centers ranged between 25 percent (NAEYC 1991) and 41 percent (Whitebrook et al. 1989).

The elasticity of the supply of childcare workers has been estimated by looking at the pattern of real earnings over time. Blau (1992) concluded that because real earnings remained constant over the period 1976–86, despite increases in government subsidies and regulation, the supply of childcare workers has been relatively elastic. Walker (1992), looking specifically at the elasticity of supply of family daycare providers, found that unlicensed providers had less attachment to the labor market than their licensed counterparts; they had less training, less experience, cared for fewer children per establishment, and were less involved in marketing their services.

The matter of supply elasticity deserves further research. If the elasticity of supply is indeed high, government attempts to improve quality of services by mandating higher educational requirements and requiring licensure could result in fewer childcare slots, and especially family daycare slots, as providers respond to these regulations and requirements by leaving the field altogether. The absence of a payoff to education among childcare workers also suggests that increased educational requirements may drive providers out of the market.

2.2 Demand for Childcare

Two key issues on the demand side of the market are the responsiveness of parental demand to changes in price and the effect of the availability and price of childcare on mothers' decisions to seek employment.

The price elasticity of the demand for childcare and the effect of price of childcare on mothers' employment decisions vary with the age of the child, in part because childcare costs are higher for younger children (Leibowitz et al. 1992), and with the marital status of the mother—single mothers are more responsive to changes in price than are married mothers (Michalopoulos et al. 1992).

Price has an important (negative) effect on parents' choice of type of care (Hofferth and Wissoker 1992). It also has a large and significant negative effect on mothers' labor supply, although researchers disagree on its size (Ribar 1992, Connelly 1991, Michalopoulos et al. 1992).

About one-fourth of mothers aged 21–29 who were not in the United States labor force in 1988 cited childcare problems as the major reason for their non-participation. Among poor women, the percentage was about one-third (Cattan 1991). Connelly's estimates suggest that universal no-cost childcare in the United States would cause an increase of about 10 percentage points in women's labor force participation (Connelly 1991 p. 110).

In Sweden, research on the price elasticity of demand for childcare suggests that if the price of care were to fall (as a result of an increased subsidy), the effect on labor force participation would be small. Most of the effect would consist of mothers moving from private to public care (Gustafsson and Stafford 1992).

The income elasticity of demand for childcare is complex. An increase in family income that comes from wife's own earnings has a positive effect on labor force participation, but does not significantly increase childcare expenditures. On the other hand, increases in family income derived from husband's earnings or nonwage sources decreases wives' labor force participation but increases expenditures on center care (but not on care by a nanny or relatives) (Hofferth and Wissoker 1992).

2.3 Cost of Childcare

Childcare is labor-intensive, with personnel costs accounting for between 50 and 80 percent of childcare centers' budgets (Willer 1987). Kagan and Glennon

(1982) found that nonprofit centers spent about 73 percent of their budgets on wages, while profit centers spent about 63 percent. Since young children require a great deal of individual attention, especially if they are in childcare all day, quality care requires relatively low child–staff ratios. As a result, even though childcare providers receive low pay, childcare is expensive.

The cost of care ranges widely, by region of a country, age of child, and auspices of ownership. In 1990, average center fees in the United States ranged from US $1.29 per hour in the South to US $2.18 per hour in the Northeast. Average fees for regulated family daycare ranged from US $1.32 per hour in the South to US $2.02 per hour in the Northeast. Average fees in unregulated family daycare homes ranged from US $0.89 per hour in the South to US $1.83 per hour in the Midwest and Northeast (NAEYC 1991).

Among employed mothers with a child under 5, childcare costs represent about 10 percent of family income, about what the average family allocates to food expenditures (Hayes et al. 1990). For lower-income families, the fraction is even higher: in 1990, for those in families with an income less than US $15,000 per year, childcare costs were almost one-fourth (23 %) of income. For those in families with income between US $15,000 and US $25,000, childcare costs were 12 percent of family income (NAEYC 1991).

Infant care is even more expensive: The National Childcare Staffing Study in the United States found that in 1988 in 227 centers in the five metropolitan areas surveyed, full-time infant care fees ranged from US $62.00 to US $150 per week (Whitebrook et al. 1989).

2.4 Quality of Care

Child development experts agree that the primary ingredients of quality care are caregivers who interact with children frequently and responsively (Hayes et al. 1990). Certain structural arrangements promote such interactions: small group size, low child–adult ratios, child-related training for the caregiver, caregiver stability and continuity, hygienic physical care and food preparation, safe and attractive physical space, and a program that promotes children's emotional, social, and cognitive growth (Hayes et al. 1990). The effects on quality of parental involvement, caregiver autonomy, overall size of the facility, and multicultural curricula are still being studied (Hayes et al. 1990).

Many children in United States family daycare homes and childcare centers do not receive quality care because they are in programs that have high child–adult ratios and/or caregivers without training in group care of children. Although almost all states regulate child–staff ratios in centers, the stringency of their requirements varies greatly, from 6:1 for 3-year olds to 25:1 for 5-year olds. For children cared for in centers, the child–staff ratio for those under one year old is on average about 4:1; for those aged one to three, about 6–8:1; and for those aged three to five, about 10:1. For children up to 5 years old cared for in family daycare homes (both regulated and unregulated), the child–staff ratio is about 4:1 (NAEYC 1991).

Only 14 states in the United States require that family daycare providers have training in group care of children. Only 28 states specify educational requirements for teachers in centers, and only eight states have such requirements for teacher assistants (aides) (Hayes et al. 1990). Even where states have stringent requirements, because the turnover rate among childcare workers has been so high, and because centers have had difficulty finding adequately educated workers, teachers and teacher aides who do not have requisite training have often been hired on an "emergency" basis (Strober et al. 1989).

The evidence on the relationship between the cost of care and its quality is mixed (Hayes et al. 1990, Hofferth and Wissoker 1992, Kisker and Maynard 1991). In some instances high-quality care is relatively low cost; low-paid teachers in effect subsidize the high-quality care. However, over time, these teachers tend to leave, contributing to discontinuity of teacher–child relationships.

Price appears to have a stronger effect on parental choice than does quality. However, Hofferth and Wissoker (1992) found that, given price, parents were more likely to choose a higher-quality center (as measured by child–staff ratio.) Others found that parents trade off quality attributes from a child-development point of view for attributes such as convenience of location or hours of operation (Blau 1991).

Some argue that parents are often poorly informed about what constitutes good quality care from a child-development point of view (Blau 1991) and cannot (or do not) seek information about quality (Hayes et al. 1990). Others (Hofferth and Wissoker 1992) have suggested that even when parents choose family daycare, they may be better informed about quality than researchers think.

3. Policy Issues

The major policy issue in childcare concerns government intervention: should governments intervene in childcare markets, and if so, how?

In 1988 in the United States about $16 billion were spent on childcare by parents, other private sources, and government. The federal government spent about US $7 billion, slightly more than half of that through the dependent care tax credit. The states spent approximately US $500 million (Hayes et al. 1990). For purposes of comparison, it is useful to note that if all children under 6 years old were in full-time paid care, all children 6–14 years old were in paid care during non school hours, and all care measured up to quality standards that promoted emotional, social, and cognitive development (likely to cost about US $4,000 per year per preschooler and US $2000 per year per school-age child) the total cost of care would be US $126 billion (Hayes et al. 1990).

There are two economic justifications for increased government subsidization of childcare: increased efficiency and increased equity. The increased efficiency argument is that there is currently underinvestment in childcare, that parents spend too little on quality childcare, and that the negative effects of this underinvestment accrue not only to children and parents but also to society as a whole. This argument suggests that childcare has external benefits and that the populace as a whole has an interest (or should have an interest) in ensuring that young children whose parent(s) work receive high-quality childcare (Strober 1975).

External benefits of childcare include: enhanced social, emotional, and cognitive learning for young children which would reduce public social and educational expenditures for remediation later in childhood and in adulthood; improved ability for women to plan their education and employment with the expectation that market work can realistically be a permanent feature of their adult lives, even if they choose to have children; and increased productivity for employers as they experience decreases in employee turnover and absenteeism (Strober 1975).

With respect to equity, since children who come from families where there is economic and psychological stress are more often enrolled in low-quality childcare than are other children (Hayes et al. 1990), subsidy of childcare for these children has been seen as righting an existing inequality.

Because childcare produces private as well as social benefits, an economic case can be made for cost sharing between the private and public sectors. Moreover, since employers are one of the beneficiaries of a high-quality, reliable childcare system, it is sensible to require that they pay part of the costs, either through the provision of direct services or through taxation.

Government subsidization of childcare may take one of four forms: subsidies to parents for childcare; subsidies to parents for parental leave to care for their own children; subsidies to providers, including tuition benefits for their own training and assistance with liability insurance; and subsidies for the infrastructure of the childcare system, including the improvement of provider training facilities and information networks for parents and providers.

The costs and benefits of each of these alternatives need to be studied. Each will have different effects on quality of care and different external benefits. For example, existing evidence does not suggest that subsidization of childcare on the demand side would lead parents to purchase higher-quality care. In addition, each alternative needs to be considered in conjunction with possible more stringent state regulation of staff–child ratios, group and facility size, and caregiver training. Decisions also need to be made about the levels of government that should collect taxes and provide subsidies (Yeager and Strober 1992).

Questions concerning organization and productivity of resources also need attention. For example, care in Swedish childcare centers was found to be twice the cost of such care in the other Nordic countries, in part because Swedish centers operated for longer hours, even though few children attended during early morning and evening hours (Jansson and Strömquist 1988). The Swedish authors questioned the productivity implications of these organizational arrangements.

There are other important questions. Could costs be reduced without compromising quality if childcare centers were combined with family daycare homes in integrated systems (Strober 1975)? Should states and localities be encouraged to place childcare systems under the aegis of existing school boards? What should be the role of employer-sponsored care in the larger childcare system? How can sick children best be cared for? Finally, what should be the role of parents in the governance of childcare systems?

References

Bergmann B B 1993 The French welfare system: An excellent system we could adapt and afford. In: Wilson W J (ed.) 1993 *Sociology and the Public Agenda*. Sage, Los Angeles, California

Blau D M 1991 Introduction. In: Blau D M (ed.) 1991 *The Economics of Child Care*. Russell Sage Foundation, New York

Blau D M 1992 The child care labor market. *J. Hum. Resources* 27(1): 9–39

Blau F D, Ferber M A 1992 *The Economics of Women, Men and Work*. Prentice-Hall, Englewood Cliffs, New Jersey

Cattan P 1991 Child care problems: An obstacle to work. *Month. Lab. Rev.* 114(10): 3–9

Connelly R 1991 The importance of child care costs to women's decisionmaking. In: Blau D M (ed.) 1991 *The Economics of Child Care*. Russell Sage Foundation, New York

Fosburg S 1981 *Family Day Care in the United States: Summary of Findings*. DHHS Pub. No. 80–30382. US Department of Health and Human Services, Washington, DC

Gustafsson S, Stafford F 1992 Child care subsidies and labor supply in Sweden. *J. Hum. Resources* 27(1): 204–30

Hayes C D, Palmer J L, Zaslow M J (eds.) 1990 *Who Cares for America's Children?: Child Care Policy for the 1990s*. National Academy Press, Washington, DC

Hofferth S L, Wissoker D A 1992 Price, quality and income in child care choice. *J. Hum. Resources* 27(1): 70–112

Jansson T, Strömquist S 1988 *Child Care in the Nordic Countries: Costs, Quality, Management*. The Swedish Agency for Administrative Development, Stockholm

Kagan S, Glennon T 1982 Considering proprietary child care. In: Zigler E, Gordon E (eds.) 1982 *Day Care: Scientific and Social Policy Issues*. Auburn House, Boston, Massachusetts

Kahn A J, Kamerman S B 1987 *Child Care: Facing the Hard Choices*. Greenwood Press, New Haven, Connecticut

Kamerman S B 1991 Child care policies and programs: An international overview. *J. Soc. Issues* 47(2): 179–96

Kisker E, Maynard R 1991 Quality, cost, and parental cost of child care. In: Blau D M (ed.) 1991 *The Economics of Child Care*. Russell Sage Foundation, New York

Leibowitz A, Klerman J A, Waite L J 1992 Employment of new mothers and child care choice: Differences by children's age. *J. Hum. Resources* 27(1): 112–33

Michalopoulos C, Robins P K, Garfinkel I 1992 A structural model of labor supply and child care demand. *J. Hum. Resources* 27(1): 166–203

National Association for the Education of Young Children (NAEYC) 1985 *In Whose Hands?: A Demographic Fact Sheet on Child Care Providers*. National Association for the Education of Young Children, Washington, DC

National Association for the Education of Young Children (NAEYC); Administration on Children, Youth and Families of the US Department of Health and Human Services; Office of Policy Planning of the US Department of Education 1991 *The Demand and Supply of Child Care in 1990: Joint Findings from The National Child Care Survey, 1990 and A Profile of Child Care Settings*. National Association for the Education of Young Children, Washington, DC

Ribar D C 1992 Child care and the labor supply of married women: Reduced form evidence. *J. Hum. Resources* 27(1): 134–65

Strober M H 1975 Formal extrafamily child care: Some economic observations. In: Lloyd C B (ed.) 1975 *Sex, Discrimination, and the Division of Labor*. Columbia University Press, New York

Strober M H, Gerlach-Downie S, Yeager K E 1989 Child care centers as workplaces. Paper presented to Annual Meeting of the American Educational Research Association, Boston, Massachusetts

Walker J R 1992 New evidence on the supply of child care: A statistical portrait of family providers and an analysis of their fees. *J. Hum. Resources* 27(1) 40–69

Whitebrook M, Howes C, Phillips D 1989 *Who Cares?: Child Care Teachers and the Quality of Care in America*. Child Care Employee Project, Oakland, California

Willer B 1987 *The Growing Crisis in Child Care: Quality, Compensation and Affordability in Early Childhood Programs*. National Association for the Education of Young Children, Washington, DC

Yeager K E, Strober M H 1992 Financing child care through local taxes: One city's bold attempt. *Journal of Family Issues*

Further Reading

Hartmann H, Pearce D 1989 *High Skill and Low Pay: The Economics of Child Care Work*. Institute for Women's Policy Research, Washington, DC

Spalter-Roth R, Hartmann H 1988 *Unnecessary Losses: Costs to Americans of the Lack of Family and Medical Leave: Executive Summary*. Institute for Women's Policy Research, Washington, DC

School Choice: Market Mechanisms

H. M. Levin

There has been an increasing trend during the 1990s toward creating greater choice in education. In most public educational systems, students are assigned to schools according to their neighborhoods or other criteria. Critics have argued that such assignment tends to make schools inefficient in two respects. The first is that schools do not have to be successful to survive because they have a monopoly clientele that has no other options. In this respect, they have no incentives to improve, a fact that would change if schools had to compete for students. Second, it is argued that different types of families seek different types of schooling opportunities, a diversity that cannot be provided for in a single approach. By choosing among a plethora of schools, families could select schools that best serve the unique values of families and the needs of their children.

1. Choice Approaches

In response to these arguments, two types of choice strategies have arisen, public and market choice approaches. Public choice approaches represent an attempt to provide options to parents and students by giving them opportunities to choose among different schools or school districts within the public sector (Clune and Witte 1990 Nathan 1989). The rationale for public choice is to obtain greater schooling efficiency through matching students to schools that reflect family preferences as well as to increase competition among schools for students. Typical public choice approaches include choices among programs or "minischools" within school sites, choices among schools within a school district, and choice among school districts. In the United Kingdom parents have been given a right to express a school preference which the local educational authority is required to take into account for school placement (Walford 1992).

Market choices refer to approaches in which schools compete in the marketplace for students and are rewarded according to the numbers of students they attract or the numbers of students who succeed. Market choices can be financed from family resources and other private sources of finance or by public financing mechanisms that promote market approaches. For example, the World Bank has relied increasingly on "privatization" of funding for schools to increase family choice, in part as a practical response to the lack of public resources for expansion. James (1987) has provided a cogent explanation for the division of public and private schools within nations and has concluded that barriers to public expansion are an extremely important determinant of private school growth.

Most market choice schemes in education are based upon establishing funding mechanisms that will use public support to enable market choice. The two most common of these approaches are tuition tax credits or educational vouchers. Tuition tax credits represent a reduction in tax payments for some portion of tuition or other costs paid for children in private schools (James and Levin 1983).

The more important thrust toward market choice has been embodied in the formulation of schemes involving educational vouchers. Educational vouchers are certificates that can be used to pay tuition at schools eligible to redeem such certificates from the state. Eligible schools would have to meet some minimal standards to participate. Families would be given vouchers for each student, and schools would compete for students and their vouchers.

Educational vouchers have a long history. For example, West (1967) has documented a plan proposed by the British–American political philosopher Thomas Paine some two centuries ago. A related scheme was the "payment by results" approach used in English and Welsh elementary schools from 1862 until 1897 (Rapple 1992). Schools and teachers were paid according to the numbers of students who were able to pass examinations administered by school inspectors, who worked for the state.

Even the "modern" voucher scheme goes back almost 40 years to Milton Friedman's original essay of 1955 on the role of government in education (Friedman 1955). That essay became more widely circulated when Friedman published a revised version of it in his important work *Capitalism and Freedom* (Friedman 1962). Although this work rapidly attained the status of a classic in graduate-level courses in public finance, it did not attract many adherents at the policy level. However, it was a source of important debate in the United Kingdom by the mid-1960s (Beales et al. 1967).

By 1966 the voucher plan was touched as a potential solution to the problems of education in the inner cities of the United States. Jencks (1966), Sizer and Whitten (1968), and Levin (1968) all suggested experimentation with vouchers in the inner city to find ways of improving education for poor and minority students. By 1969 the United States Office of Educational Opportunity (OEO) took up the challenge by asking the noted sociologist Christopher Jencks to design a voucher experiment in which the claims of voucher advocates could be tested. Jencks proposed a "pro-poor" approach, in which larger or compensatory vouchers would be provided to poor children and a certain portion of admissions would be made by lottery in oversubscribed schools to give "disadvantaged" students a fair choice (Center for Study of Public Policy 1970). What was proposed was a highly regulated voucher plan that would protect the interests of the poor in terms of the size of the voucher, eligibility criteria for schools, and a substantial information system.

The OEO was unable to obtain the state legislation or local cooperation that would enable private schools to participate, so it settled on a public choice approach in San Jose, California, to test the voucher concept. Some 13 neighborhood schools generated 51 alternatives for families within the school district. While many saw positive gains from such a system, it was clearly restricted to public choice rather than market choice (Weiler 1974).

In the late 1970s an active campaign was established in California to hold a referendum to pass a state constitutional amendment that would establish family choice or vouchers under a plan based upon the work of Coons and Sugarman (1978). That campaign failed, but in 1990 the voucher issue arose with great fanfare with the publication of a book, *Politics, Markets, and America's Schools* by Chubb and Moe (1990). They argued that democratic control of schools was the obstacle, rather than the solution, to the creation of better schools. According to these authors, democracy leads to complex demands on schools and large bureaucracies to carry out those demands. As a result, existing public schools had become unwieldy, inefficient, and unresponsive organizational dinosaurs. Only by providing greater autonomy and a distinct break from both democratic demands and their inevitable bureaucracies could schools become more productive. Although some of these arguments for greater autonomy and decentralization were also at the root of the public choice and restructuring movement (Murphy 1992), Chubb and Moe argued that, in principle, public schools and public choice could not work and market solutions were the only alternative.

Chubb and Moe's book was characterized by a substantial amount of statistical analysis. Both the interpretation of the statistical evidence and its ties to educational vouchers or "scholarships," as the authors termed them, were questioned by experts (e.g., Witte 1992). Coleman and Hoffer (1987) also found that students in private high schools reached achievement levels higher than those in public schools, even after adjusting statistically for differences in student race and social class. Yet this evidence has been questioned because of the very small size of the differences and the difficulty of adjusting for self-selection of students in the two sectors (Levin 1991, Witte 1992).

2. The Voucher Debate

The voucher debate revolves around two sets of issues. The first considers schooling from the individual perspective and whether a voucher plan would improve individual educational outcomes through greater choice and competition. The second considers schooling from the social perspective and whether a voucher plan would improve outcomes from the perspective of social outcomes of educational investment. In general, those who advocate vouchers view schooling primarily from the individual perspective in terms of consumer choice. In contrast, those who oppose vouchers tend to place more weight on the social goals of schooling.

2.1 The Inherent Conflict

The inherent conflict arises because schooling lies at the intersection of two sets of concerns in democratic and market-oriented societies. From the perspective of families, schooling represents the prime institution for social mobility and reinforcement of family values for their children. Accordingly, from a family or individual perspective, it is rational to provide the family with the ability to choose the "best" schooling experience for a child. This will, however, necessarily lead to different schools for different children, based upon philosophical, religious, and political differences among families, particularly in heterogeneous societies with large differences among families along these dimensions.

From the perspective of society, schooling is directed at creating a common set of educational experiences to assure a common language, civic values, and preparation for participation in the dominant social, economic, and political institutions. In a democracy, there must be an understanding and acceptance of established forums for self-expression, political mechanisms for participation and representation in the democratic process, and institutions for adjudicating conflict. Citizens must engage in rational discourse and tolerate dissent. They must accept the tenets of the economic system and use a common language for commerce and discourse—even if subgroups in society also use other languages for their affairs.

The result is that the social goals of schooling require a set of common features in which students from different backgrounds are exposed to a common set of values and social practices which all will be expected to accept. To the degree that parents choose schools that represent their own political beliefs, philosophies, religions, and social class, this common experience will be undermined by one that may satisfy narrow family goals without meeting the social goals of schooling. It is this tension between private and social goals that is at the heart of the voucher debate.

2.2 The Main Arguments

Advocates refer to the primacy of choice in the marketplace and ask if anything less should be expected for schools in a free society. They also believe that competition for students will improve the academic outcomes of schooling by creating incentives for schools to meet he needs of their clientele. Opponents refer to the fact that as families seek schools that emphasize values similar to their own, and as schools enroll students from similar families, schooling will become stratified into many different types with little concern for common social interests. This will lead to the balkanization of society, without a common basis for democratic participation.

Each side marshals its own evidence. Advocates of vouchers refer to empirical evidence of greater academic achievement by students in private schools (Coleman and Hoffer 1987, Chubb and Moe 1990). Opponents argue that measured effects are small or nonexistent and can be accounted for by selection effects that are not accounted for by crude statistical controls (Witte 1992). Further, they argue that if private school children are at the 53rd percentile relative to public school students at the 50th percentile, some 47 percent of private school students are performing below the average of those in public schools (Levin 1991).

Advocates of vouchers assert that the poor who are captives in the worst schools will benefit the most from choice. Opponents point out that the poor are least likely to take advantage of existing public schooling choices and they lack the resources to obtain the information and transportation that will provide meaningful choices (Levin 1991). Finally, opponents point to the need for public schools to provide elements of a common experience for reproducing democratic institutions, practices, and participation. What is clear is that families of different religions or political persuasions would be able to select those environments for their own children and avoid the influences of other religions, political perspectives, and philosophies. Advocates of market approaches either denigrate the benefits of a common public experience (West 1965), assume that such benefits are produced as readily in private schools, or assume that they must be subordinate to consumer choice (Chubb and Moe 1990, Coons and Sugarman 1978, Friedman 1962).

3. Understanding Voucher Plans

A crucial tenet for understanding vouchers is that there is no single voucher system, but a large number of different approaches using the voucher mechanism. The various voucher proposals differ substantially from each other in ways that have different implications for choice and educational outcomes. Voucher plans differ on three dimensions: (a) finance; (b) regulation; and (c) information (Levin 1980). Since almost all of the concrete proposals have their origins in the United States, the examples that follow will be based primarily on the debate in the United States.

3.1 Finance

The finance component of a voucher plan refers to such factors as the size of the educational voucher,

what it can be used for, whether a school can charge more than the voucher or obtain additional funding through gifts, whether costs of transportation are covered, and the basic sources of funding. The treatment of each of these aspects has different impacts on choice in general, but specifically among groups with different private capabilities to use their resources for schooling.

For example, Friedman (1962) proposed providing a uniform voucher to parents for each child, with parents themselves providing "add-ons" to the voucher to purchase more expensive education for their children. Obviously, wealthier families and those with fewer children would benefit the most from this arrangement. In contrast, the voucher proposal that was the basis for the proposed voucher experiment would have provided the largest vouchers to children in poorer families to help compensate for the lack of educational resources in their homes. Other approaches have advocated setting the level of the voucher according to grade level, curriculum, bilingualism, special needs and handicaps, variations in local cost, or other social priorities, as in a prospective state constitutional initiative proposed by Coons and Sugarman for the State of California in 1979 and summarized in Levin (1980).

Differences in provision for the costs of transportation are also important determinants of the impact of a voucher plan. In the absence of transportation allowances, the poor are limited to schools in their immediate neighborhoods relative to those with more substantial family resources. Transportation costs can be very high, diluting the amount of educational expenditure that can be assigned to the costs of instruction. Accordingly, a plan with substantial transportation provision can provide greater equality in choices among families with different family incomes; but the cost of greater equality in choice will be a smaller portion of education expenditure, for instruction.

3.2 Regulation

Although the voucher approach represents a shift from government production of educational services to the private marketplace, that market would consist of schools that had to meet particular regulations in order to be eligible to receive vouchers. Differences in regulatory requirements would create differences in the range of choices. Among the major areas of regulation are those of curriculum content, personnel, and admissions standards.

Regulation of schools under a voucher system is designed to make certain that the social benefits of schooling are captured under the market approach. Any given definition of social benefits, such as those associated with a common educational experience, will generate a set of regulations for all schools to ensure that those benefits are generated. Obviously, the greater the degree of regulation, the smaller the diversity of voucher-eligible schools in the educational marketplace.

The present system of public education provides a highly detailed and articulated set of curriculum requirements with respect to the areas in which instructions must be provided and students must have instructional experiences. In addition, there are many areas in which teaching is proscribed, most notably religious instruction. Different voucher plans vary with respect to curriculum requirements. Friedman (1962) is vague on this dimension, but it is apparent from his short discussion that such requirements would be minimal, with emphasis on instruction in basic skills and a common set of civic values. The OEO voucher plan (Center for the Study of Public Policy 1970) is more detailed, but leaves the specifics to the state implementing the voucher experiment. The California Initiative tended to limit curriculum requirements to those that were required of private schools in the state, a fairly minimal standard.

Both the Friedman (1962) and Coons and Sugarman (1978) versions would permit a large diversity of schools with respect to underlying values and content in curriculum. The state would not intervene or attempt to regulate instruction, except to insure that no laws were being violated. Since the constitutional protection of free expression is the implicit standard, public support for schools could extend to fairly extreme political, religious, philosophical, and ideological sponsorship and content as long as the Supreme Court interpreted an educational voucher plan as aiding children and families rather than institutions. Separation of church and state would preclude direct public support for religious instruction.

Personnel requirements for voucher plans vary from no requirements—permitting each school to set its own standards—to the use of existing standards for the licensing of public school teachers and administrators. The regulation of admission practices shows similar diversity. Friedman advocates complete autonomy for schools in setting admissions policies. In contrast, the OEO plan establishes relatively detailed requirements including nondiscriminatory practices, possible quotas for racial composition, and a lottery approach to choosing some portion of the student body for schools that have more applications than places.

3.3 Information

The competitive efficiency of market systems of choice depends crucially upon knowledge of alternatives. In fact, the perfectly competitive market assumes the existence of perfect knowledge of all pertinent information for making efficient decisions on the part of both potential consumers and producers. Unfortunately, the educational marketplace presents an unusual challenge.

Two particular difficulties emerge in the area of educational information, whether provided in the context of the educational marketplace or that of public choice. First, education represents a rather complex service. It cannot easily be summarized in ways that will reflect accurately the nature of the educational experience a particular child might face. Second, available methods of providing appropriate information on a large number of educational alternatives to a wide variety of audiences in a constantly changing situation—as new schools open and others fail—is likely to be costly and problematic. This challenge is particularly severe for the least advantaged families, such as those in which parents are poorly educated, do not speak English, and who tend to move frequently because of marginality in housing markets.

With respect to the first of these dimensions, it is probably possible to provide accurate information on such prominent dimensions as religious, political, or ideological sponsorship or orientation of a school as well as emphases on particular curricula such as the arts, sciences, sports, and so on. However, qualitative aspects of education are much more difficult to characterize. It cannot easily be ascertained how well educational institutions carry out their mission and how appropriate a particular environment is for a particular student. Unfortunately, it is difficult for students to sample different schools before making a choice. There is also the problem of advertising and promotional distortions that are found in most industries.

The second problem is the cost of establishing and maintaining an up-to-date system of information in a form that will be understandable and accessible to potential producers and consumers. This challenge is especially important for addressing the information needs of disadvantaged populations. Such persons are characterized by low educational attainments, higher probabilities of speaking a language other than English, and a higher incidence of mobility because of a lack of housing and job stability. In essence the system of information will have to be constructed according to the needs of local populations and the specific options in each of hundreds of local educational markets in each state. Bilingual services need to be available in many settings, and counselors will need to be available to interpret the information. Such a decentralized approach to information, with its many services and needs for data collection, is likely to have a high cost. Alternatively, as with an adequate transportation system, the cost of a suitable information system may discourage its provision because of the substantial resources that it siphons off from the level of the voucher and instructional resources.

4. Summary

The movement toward market choice in education, and especially vouchers, is fueled by concerns about public school quality and efficiency, an insufficiency of resources for public school expansion, and the ideology of greater consumer choice and less government involvement in the economy. These are trends that have

haracterized the last part of the twentieth century and
vill probably continue to be evident in the early part
f the twenty-first century.

Opposition is largely fueled by those who see such
narket mechanisms as undermining the ability of
chools to prepare all young people to participate in
democratic society. Opponents do not believe that
narket choice along philosophical, political, religious,
cademic, and socioeconomic lines can serve to main-
ain the historic contribution of education in providing
he common set of values and knowledge required
or democratic functioning. In the educational arena,
his struggle between opposing contentions is likely
o be played out for the foreseeable future, in both
ndustrialized and industrializing countries.

ee also: Political Economy of Educational Pro-
uction; Private and Public Costs of Schooling in
Developing Nations; Educational Financing; School
finance; International Aspects of Financing Educa-
ion; Public-Private Division of Responsibility for
education

References

Seales A C F, Blaug M, Veale D, West E G 1967 *Education:
A Framework for Choice*. Institute of Economic Affairs,
London
Center for the Study of Public Policy 1970 *Education Vouch-
ers: A Report on Financing Elementary Education by
Grants to Parents*. Center for the Study of Public Policy,
Cambridge, Massachusetts
Chubb J E, Moe T M 1990 *Politics, Markets, and America's
Schools*. The Brookings Institution, Washington, DC
Clune W H, Witte J F (eds.) 1990 *Choice and Control in
American Education. Vol. 2: The Practice of Choice, De-
centralization and School Restructuring*. Falmer Press,
London
Coleman J S, Hoffer T 1987 *Public and Private High
Schools: The Impact of Communities*. Basic Books,
New York
Coons J E, Sugarman S D 1978 *Education By Choice: The
Case for Family Control*. University of California Press,
Berkeley, California
Friedman M 1955 The role of government in education. In:
Solo R A (ed.) 1955 *Economics and the Public Interest*.
Rutgers University Press, New Brunswick, New Jersey
Friedman M 1962 The role of government in education. In:
Friedman M 1962 *Capitalism and Freedom*. University
of Chicago Press, Chicago, Illinois
James E 1987 The public/private division of responsibility
for education: An international comparison. *Econ. Educ.
Rev.* 6(1): 1–14
James T, Levin H M 1983 *Public Dollars for Private
Schools: The Case of Tuition Tax Credits*. Temple
University Press, Philadelphia, Pennylvania
Jencks C 1966 Is the public school obsolete? *Public Interest*
2: 18–27
Levin H M 1968 The failure of the public schools and the free
market remedy. *Urban Rev.* 2: 32–37
Levin H M 1980 Educational vouchers and social policy.
In: Haskins R, Gallagher J J (eds.) 1980 *Care and Edu-
cation of Young Children in America*. Ablex, Norwood,
New Jersey
Levin H M 1991 The economics of educational choice. *Econ.
Educ. Rev.* 10(2): 137–58
Murphy J 1992 *Restructuring Schools: Capturing and As-
sessing the Phenomena*. Teachers College Press, New
York
Nathan J 1989 *Public Schools by Choice: Expanding Oppor-
tunities for Parents, Students, and Teachers*. Institute for
Teaching and Learning, St Paul, Minnesota
Rapple B A 1992 A Victorian experiment in economic
efficiency in education. *Econ. Educ. Rev.* 11(4)
Sizer T, Whitten P 1968 A proposal for a poor children's bill
of rights. *Psychol. Today* 2(3): 59–63
Walford G 1992 Educational choice and equity in Great
Britain. *Educ. Policy* 6(2): 123–38
Weiler D 1974 *A Public School Voucher Demonstration: The
First Year at Alum Rock*. The Rand Corporation; Santa
Monica, California
West E G 1965 *Education and the State: A Study in Political
Economy*. Institute of Economic Affairs, London
West E G 1967 Tom Paine's voucher scheme for public
education. *Southern Economic Journal* 33(3): 378–82
Witte J F 1992 Public subsidies for private schools: What we
know and how to proceed. *Educ. Policy* 6(2): 206–27

Economics of Educational Time and Learning

B. Millot

nvestment in education scarcely compares with any
other investment from the point of view of duration or
hat of maturity of pay-off. This specificity has many
mportant consequences, at the level of individual stra-
egies and choices, and in terms of educational policy.
t also has financial implications because, whatever
he societal system, time is not a free commodity.
For this reason, one might expect economists to
have explored this intriguing characteristic of education. This is not the case, however—educators, child
psychologists, and sociologists have gone further in
exploring this dimension in the field of education. Yet
the conventional economic paradigm can help explain
the interplay between time, education, and social differentiation. This entry underscores the potentialities
of the economic perspective to interpret the temporal

dimension of education. The first section investigates the question within a nonmonetary, purely academic context, with a time horizon limited to that of the education process itself, and with the emphasis on administrative decisions. The second section treats the issues within a longer time frame, and includes financial and social considerations, while shifting the perspective to students as decision makers.

1. Time as an Ingredient of the Schooling Process

1.1 Time as a Proxy for Exposure

Although it is a plain fact that education is a lengthy process, there is no real consensus on how long it takes to educate a child, even if only primary education is considered. In part, this is due to the lack of a totally standardized concept of the product "primary education" itself, and therefore of what is necessary to produce it. In the case of secondary education, the picture becomes even more unclear, let alone that of postsecondary studies. Indeed, time is a proxy, and is not in and of itself what children need to be educated. In education, time stands for exposure, in the same way as it stands for experience in the employment realm. However, school attendance is not synonymous with learning, and high enrollment rates can mask poor instruction.

This is well recognized by education specialists who insist that time is only one of the ingredients of a sound instructional process, in which other factors such as personal effort and teachers' ability play a key role. Likewise, economists consider time as an input to be combined with other inputs in the production of instruction. Most of the research conducted by educationalists has been influenced by the mastery learning model developed by Bloom (1976). According to this model, mastery in any given subject can be achieved, provided enough time is allowed and that the teacher aims at reducing the time differential required between the fastest and the slowest students. Educationalists have developed various types of statistical model (particularly path analysis) to weigh the respective roles of various factors, including time, on school performance. Sociologists have done the same to document not only school achievements but also occupational status. Similarly, economists have included school time both in education production functions and in earning functions (Hanushek 1979).

In the United States, faced with the declining quality of education, researchers from various fields have accorded a new value to the time element, claiming that an increase in the length of the school year would place the quality of United States schooling on a par with that of other nations. However, as was rightly emphasized by Levin (1984) and Levin and Tsang (1987), the relationship is not as straightforward as it

seems, and much methodological caution is needed if one is to draw conclusions on the optimum duration of exposure and on the optimum mix of time and other factors to achieve better performance, and hence to recommend reforms.

1.2 Administrative Time

There are several divisions of schooling time which can be manipulated by educational authorities: (a) the "hour" of class, an hour being the minimal unit of administrative time that students spend in the same classroom, with the same teacher, working on one subject; (b) the school day; (c) the school week; (d) the school year; and (e) the official minimum number of years required to complete a cycle, for example primary education.

Each of these administrative schedules is subject to considerable variation within and among countries, even at the level of primary education. The "hour" itself corresponds to portions of time ranging from 30 to 60 minutes. The school day typically represents 5 to 8 hours. Where the double shift system applied to teachers is used, the school day is reduced to 4 "clock" hours. In turn, the school week can vary from 4.5 to 6 days. The school year can be as short as 180 school days (in the United States) or as long as 243 days (Japan). In fact, data gathered from over 60 countries indicate that mean official instructional time amounts to 849 hours per year of primary schooling in less developed countries, and 917 in more developed countries (Benavot 1991). Finally, primary school education requires between 5 to 8 years until graduation. Aggregated, these figures demonstrate an extensive range of practices: the total minimum number of hours necessary to graduate from primary school (the cumulation of minimum instructional time at all levels) in the fast scenario would be 2,250 hours, while the slow scenario (the cumulation of all maximum instructional times) would require 15,450 hours. This 1:7 ratio is only illustrative, and educational authorities throughout the world play on the various scales (i.e., hour, day, week, year, or cycle) to organize scenarios which fall somewhere between the two extremes.

Time differentials reach a 1:9 ratio if no repetition is assumed in the fast scenario, and if three repetitions are allowed in the slow scenario (which then totalizes 19,200 hours). Although usually seen through the negative filter of its cost (Haddad 1979), repetition can also be viewed as a strategy to compensate for short official contact time, for instance to make up for a double shift system, as observed in Burundi (Eisemon et al. in press).

As educators are well aware, beside the total number of official hours, what counts is the distribution of these hours within the day, the week and the year and their combination with interruptions. On the higher rings of the educational ladder, at the level of secondary and tertiary education, the picture becomes more complex, especially if alternative periods of study and work are taken into account.

1.3 Real Instructional Time

The official time is only partially devoted to instruction, and substantial differences exist between this administrative time and real instructional, or academic learning time. Preparation, interruptions, and discipline-oriented activities consume a share of this official time, thus reducing what is left for genuine teaching and learning. The discussion so far has considered only teachers' teaching time, which has been assimilated to students' learning time. But at least three additional factors need to be examined.

First, while teachers teach, students do not necessarily learn. They may miss classes, either because of sickness, or as often happens in rural areas of less developed countries, because their parents periodically keep them home for seasonal work in the field. Even when they attend class, many reasons can prevent students from even listening, let alone benefiting from the lesson. Undernourished, fatigued children are frequently found in poor countries where endemic diarrhea or malaria contribute to reduce actual learning time. Likewise, children with emotional problems and children from low socioeconomic background do not profit as much from the time they spend in the classroom.

Second, a classroom is comprised of more than one student, and teachers make implicit choices on how to allocate their time across the classroom population. Depending on teachers' preferences, their time is either asymmetrically allocated to a small subset of students, most likely the brightest, or evenly distributed over the total population they are supposed to serve (Brown and Saks 1987).

Third, both students' nonlearning time and teachers' nonteaching time have a bearing on school achievements. A portion of that time is spent on the school premises, for evaluation, or compensatory additional contact hours for example. Therefore, time spent by school supervisors and school principals on such activities should also be incorporated in education production functions, as well as time devoted to tutorial activities. Mention should also be made of the time spent by students on out-of-school activities which have an impact on their educational achievement such as homework, and even television time (the negative effect of which is now documented across countries, see Lapointe et al. 1989). Finally, the time parents devote personally to the education of their children is an obvious input in the education process; it is also one of the least equally distributed.

Thus, time as an input in the education process is a stake for distinct decision-making units whose interest might not necessarily converge, and may even be conflicting. These units include students and their parents, teachers and their unions, public education authorities (with several layers in federal systems), private education authorities when they play a significant role, school principals and supervisors, not to mention employers. The interests of all these constituencies contribute to define the total duration of the school day, week, and year, and to shape the pattern of these time divisions. The power of these respective actors over the temporal dimension of education varies with the level of education. Generally speaking, students' own preferences carry more weight as one gets higher on the education ladder.

1.4 Time and Achievement

The various difficulties inherent in the concept and the measure of time as an educational input do not really demonstrate how efficient it is to manipulate this input in order to achieve better performance. Undoubtedly, methodological obstacles to singling out the impact of time on achievement are enormous, and it is fair to say that there is no conclusive statistical study on the subject. Studies in the United States suggest that substantial increases in instructional time are associated with rather small improvements in educational achievement. Other studies suggest that the pay-off of increasing instructional time depends on the subject matter, for instance that it improves the teaching of foreign languages (Levin, 1984).

Empirical research on the effect of time on school achievement has also shown the importance of differentiating between the quantity and the quality of time. Even if all conditions were met to make teaching time identical to learning time, and if the slow scenario were in effect, it does not follow that this time would be efficiently used for learning purposes by the student. In other words, the amount of effort put in any unit of learning/teaching time can vary considerably. The same holds true for the productivity of time, which is related to the intensity of the effort engaged for instructional purposes. Indeed, students' attributes such as innate talent or aptitude also influence the amount of time needed to perform a given academic task. There are indications, at least at the postelementary level, that students adjust the degree of their effort according to the perception they have of the relationship between these efforts and their academic successes, based on past experiences (Perrot 1987). They also modulate their efforts on the basis of the value they attribute to the diploma they are pursuing.

1.5 Considerations in Increasing Instructional Time

Other things remaining equal, bureaucratic decisions to increase the supply of teaching time do not guarantee a proportional increase of the final academic output since both students and teachers might resist this decision, either by deliberately reducing their effort, or because of sheer fatigue. It may also be that an excessive increase of mandatory class attendance time provokes dropouts, for financial or other reasons. The threshold for these counterproductive effects clearly fluctuates with countries, level of education, and socioeconomic status of students.

In order to be productive, instructional time requires the availability of other resources, including in the first place, teachers' skills. Lack of complementary resources may transform teachers into mere child-minders. Some kind of infrastructure, school books and instructional material are other necessary ingredients which give to teaching/learning time its value, and they constitute incentives for both students and teachers to make the best use of their time. Consequently, any reform which aims at increasing instructional time as a means to raise academic achievement ought at the same time to ensure that these other inputs are available in sufficient quantities.

2. Time as a Device of Differentiation

2.1 Time is Money

To obtain a more realistic picture, the financial dimension of time has to be introduced. It has two aspects, depending on whether teachers and other resources on the one hand, or students on the other, are concerned.

Any increase in the duration of instruction is likely to translate into additional total costs, starting with a larger wage bill. This is why education authorities usually seek first to intensify the use of instructional time before trying to increase its supply. Two types of strategies are available. The first is to squeeze more effective contact hours into the school day or more effective days into the school year, if possible without increasing teachers' annual remuneration. Another possibility is to provide more complementary inputs in the instructional process, in order to boost incentives for both students and teachers and to make each hour more productive.

From the student's standpoint, what is sacrificed while being enrolled in school is the price of time. It is the opportunity cost which is embedded in any use of time, and indeed in the education process, which represents a particularly high opportunity cost. Forgone earnings are theoretically nil at the level of universal and compulsory education. However, they become positive even at that level in situations where a seasonal labor force is in great demand, and where parents are reluctant to give up their children's free labor. Forgone earnings become more and more substantial as higher levels of education are reached. In postprimary education, especially in public systems where student contribution to the direct costs of education is low, forgone earnings constitute the bulk of private costs. In this respect they are the main elements against which the benefits of education are weighed, and along with the latter, determine the private rate of return to education. However, once again there are serious methodological problems linked with estimating forgone earnings, and thus rates of return, which reduce the predictive power of the latter indicator, already flawed by the difficulty of assessing the benefits attributable to any given level of education (Carnoy and Marenbach 1975).

One of the main issues associated with the estimate has to do with the selection of the correct control group from which to derive the forgone earnings. It is difficult to pretend that those who have not continued to the education level under consideration have, all else being equal, the same characteristics and attitudes towards the labor market, and that their earnings potential is only a function of the number of years of training they receive. Yet this assumption is needed to carry out the estimate, and it is indeed similar to the general assumption found in human capital theory about the relationship between education and earnings. Second, if the graduates whose forgone earnings are estimated were actually entering the labor market, an oversupply would occur, and earnings would fall. There is no real solution to this problem, which arises from applying a method which is only valid at the margin. It is possible, though, to adjust estimates so as to take into account the unemployment factor, and deflate forgone earnings by the proportion of those unemployed in the control group.

2.2 Credential Inflation

The most dramatic effect on social costs linked to the time factor is undoubtedly repetition. Because of repetition, unit costs become misleading indicators for planning purposes, and should always be twinned with actual per graduate costs, which in turn should be compared with theoretical per graduate costs, that is, what it would cost to turn out one graduate without repetition.

If one excepts elementary school, where decisions on attendance are made entirely by parents, students' strategies at the university level and even at the secondary level are largely based on the observation of the private cost of time, and can be understood within the rate-of-return approach. In the case of public higher education institutions in countries where labor market expectations are on the low side and where consequently, actual forgone earnings, as adjusted for unemployment, are also low, it is rational from the students' standpoint, and especially if direct private costs are slight, to stay as long as possible at university, regardless of what they learn. One efficient way to manage this is to repeat grades. A second method is to transfer to another institution when there are restrictions on repetition within a given institution; yet another is to continue as far as possible up the academic scale. The first strategy is likely to be less demanding in terms of effort, while the third remains an investment in terms of knowledge. At any rate, all three strategies (they can be combined) are an attempt by students to position themselves in the job search queue, while strengthening their credentials at low individual cost. It is rational to do so because, despite the disadvantage of joining the queue, returns to higher education remain higher than those associated with secondary education.

The above illustrates the divorce between the social cost of repetition and other longer duration forms of formal education on the one hand, and the benefits which can be drawn from it from a private perspective on the other. More generally, it exemplifies how social demand for free education tends to entertain its own upward motion, without a rationale either on academic, equity, or skill requirement grounds (Millot 1982). Certainly, the trend toward lengthening the duration of formal education is not seen as totally negative by political authorities in spite of its budgetary consequences, because it provides a *de facto* instrument for postponing the effects of unemployment, at least in the short run. These private and social costs and benefits must be weighed in both the short and long run. In doing so, it is important to remember that, like monetary inflation, credential inflation does not equally harm all individuals; instead, it is a highly socially biased mechanism. While the value of diplomas (or even of an additional year of schooling) is eroding, those who strive the hardest to graduate often come from a lower socioeconomic background, with less information on the market, and competing with obsolete instruments.

2.3 Competition Through Differentiation

The analysis above can be brought a step further, and incorporated into a more general dynamic: that of competition through differentiation. Although there is no sound way to test this assumption empirically, it is reasonable to state that in many instances, if private investment in education were made solely for the sake of qualifying to fill all available jobs, much less would be invested in education. The difference between the hypothetical level of investment in education granted solely on the basis of skill needs, and the much higher actual general level of education, is the result of competing via differentiation. As the level of education of the general population rises, and in particular as universal primary education is realized, individuals strive to acquire attributes which will single them out for good jobs and high pay. One straightforward strategy to achieve this is to spend more years in the school system, which then becomes a screening or filtering apparatus, in addition to being a supplier of knowledge. However, what is rational for one person is also rational for other individuals competing for the best jobs, and the result is the irresistible trend of most open educational systems towards longer studies. In this process, which reflects the normal struggle to obtain a scarcity rent which is forever moving away, the gap between demand and supply for high level graduates progressively widens. Most competitors delude themselves, however, since the pay-off tied to a given level of education, taken as a basis for investment keeps depreciating as education expands. This may be likened to standing in an elevator, amid a group of people, and aiming to reach a point above oneself which is not fixed, but also moving upwards. When the elevator rises, one feels that one is going to reach the target. Yet everybody else has simply moved upwards as well and relative positions have not changed:

this is the illusion created by the mass extension of education. Because of the general expansion of the education system and because of the general rise of the level of education, returns to education must be seen in a dynamic framework which takes intergenerational effects into account (Knight and Sabot 1990).

Within this dynamic, time (or the number of years of schooling) is admittedly a gross yardstick, and it begins to lose its signaling power when it becomes clear that it does not differentiate any more, or when employers start realizing that the number of school years, far from signaling a potentially talented job candidate, may rather indicate that a candidate is ill-suited for work. A shift then occurs, away from time signaling to qualitative differentiation, in particular through tracking, selection, and institutionalization. More sophisticated strategies use horizontal, qualitative vehicles, in order to achieve a more accurate degree of differentiation, for the satisfaction of both employers and graduates. Moreover, the social price of alternative strategies is often lower, although they typically claim a higher private contribution in terms of direct costs. This shift is by no means exclusive, as vertical, quantitative differentiation does not disappear. The coexistence of open, long university tracks and selective, often shorter "grandes écoles" in France are a perfect example of this dualistic differentiation process. So is the North American system, where highly selective universities share the market with higher education institutions which are barely above college level. In socially hierarchized societies (France, Japan), the existence of this double-track system reflects unequal positions vis à vis the screening process which is operating. On the one hand, students of higher social status avoid as far as possible the elevator trap, choose horizontal and qualitative forms of differentiation that their own peer group (including public and private executives/employers) helps to define, and so try to enter selective schools. On the other hand, families from lower social groups are directly hit by credential inflation, and frequently fall into the elevator trap, which they perceive as the only vehicle for upward mobility. They send their children into long, general, and free studies, failing to realize that screening devices change as the elevator ascends.

In many poor countries, the vertical, quantitative, and lengthy pattern is more commonly observed, with consequences both in budgetary terms, because of the high public costs implied, and in social terms, because of frustrated expectations. In both poor and developed countries, a perverse trend is frequently observed, namely towards attributing higher rewards to occupations linked to general qualifications and studies than to technical occupations linked to vocational education. This reward scheme thus provides a strong incentive to embark on the former kind of studies, which feed the inflationary process. However, even in countries where higher education enrollment is still limited, but where the diploma disease has already spread, forms of horizontal differentiation are often encountered, either through selective national institutions, or through studies abroad, rather than in local universities.

3. Conclusion

Reforms which aim at increasing time to boost school achievements should be weighed cautiously against efforts to increase time productivity and reforms to buttress other educational inputs. While the effect of bureaucratic manipulations of instructional time on achievements might remain marginal or uncertain, time often plays a major role in strategies to differentiate labor supply. As education expands and demand for skilled labor is rationed, with employers seeking clear signals to select the best candidates, longer studies become less and less profitable as a differentiating device. Adjustment lags on both the supply and demand sides, and intergenerational effects, distort expectations linked to given educational levels. As a result of both administrative efforts to lengthen teaching time and social pressure for longer studies, the total duration of the education investment tends to increase beyond desirable levels.

See also: Education Production Functions; Political Economy of Educational Production; Economics of School Enterprise

References

Benavot A 1991 *Curricular Content, Educational Expansion, and Economic Growth*. The World Bank, Population and Human Resources Department. Working Paper No. 734, World Bank, Washington, DC

Bloom B 1976 *Human Characteristics and School Learning*. McGraw-Hill, New York

Brown B W, Saks D H 1987 The Microeconomics of the allocation of teachers' time and student learning. *Econ. Educ. Rev.* 6(4): 319–32

Carnoy M, Marenbach D 1975 The return to schooling in the United States, 1939–69. *J. Hum. Resources* 10 (3): 313–31

Eisemon T O, Schwille J, Prouty R, Ukobizoba F, Kana D, Manirabona G in press *Empirical Results and Conventional Wisdom: Primary School Effectiveness in Burundi*. Falcum Press, Stanford, California

Haddad W D 1979 *Educational and Economic Effects of Promotion and Repetition Practices*. World Bank Staff Working Paper No. 319, World Bank, Washington, DC

Hanushek E A 1979 Conceptual and empirical issues in the estimation of educational production functions. *J. Hum. Resources* 14 (3): 351–88

Knight J, Sabot R 1990 *Education, Productivity and Inequality: The East African Natural Experiment*. World Bank Oxford University Press, New York

Lapointe A E, Mead N A, Phillips G W 1989 *A World of Differences. An International Assessment of Mathematics and Science*. Educational Testing Service, Report No. 19-CAEP-011, Princeton, New Jersey

Levin H M 1984 About time for educational reform. *Educ. Eval. Policy Anal.* 6(2): 151–63

Levin H M, Tsang M C 1987 The economics of student time. *Econ. Educ. Rev.* 6(4): 357–64

Millot B 1982 Educational potlatch as a mode of social regulation in France. In: Archer M (ed.) 1982 *The Sociology of Educational Expansion*. Sage, Beverly Hills, California

Perrot J 1987 *L'influence de l'utilisation du temps sur la réussite des étudiants en France*. LABREV, UCAM, Cahier 8714L, Montreal

Evaluating Educational and Training Investment

Introduction

M. Carnoy

Not much has changed since the 1980s or even the 1960s in the way that economists evaluate educational investments. The two forms of evaluation, "external" and "internal," referring to evaluating educational investment in terms of the payoff to individuals in the form of higher productivity, hence higher wages (external) and evaluating the payoff to alternative investments in improving educational outcomes or "quality" (internal).

The entries in this section review the methodologies that comprise these two types of evaluation. For those readers who have followed the evolution of such evaluations, there should be few surprises, but many excellent reviews of the fundamentals. Henry Levin provides a detailed review of cost-benefit analysis, Martin Carnoy, of rate of return analysis, and Keith Hinchliffe, of manpower analysis. The last of these is now probably the least favored by economists, but still the most favored by ministries of labor and education. It is well to ask why. Manpower analysis, most effectively of any "evaluative" technique, conveys a government's political agenda to its constituencies. For example, in South Africa today, the government wants to deliver a message to the Black majority that it will develop cadres of Black South Africans to staff higher and middle management positions, teachers, and skilled technicians, and that these jobs will no longer be reserved for Whites. What better way to do this than through a manpower plan? Similarly, in countries competing in high tech or the space race, scientific manpower is a crucial political symbol of the country's ability to compete. Economists would do well to take account of such evaluation politics even though manpower analysis is an inaccurate predictor of an economy's educational investment pattern.

The rate of return to educational investment as a measure of education's value has never been taken very seriously except in certain international lending agencies. A major reason for this, Carnoy argues, is that the enormous amount of information available from accurately estimated rate of return studies has not been used creatively to understand how "usual"

national patterns of educational investment over time produce changing patterns of payoffs to various levels of schooling. Further, rates of return are rarely used for educational planning, mainly because educational investment is carried out in accordance with political goals rather than investment efficiency criteria. Nevertheless, such estimates do yield much *post hoc* insight into individual educational investment behavior, government subsidies to different groups of individuals, the relationship between public sector macroeconomic policy and public education policy, and, to some extent, information on the changing demand and supply of skills. Gaining such understandings makes the estimates useful, if they are done accurately.

John Bishop's entry on overeducation deals with this last issue of the changing demand and supply of skills in more detail. In it he assesses the meaning of "too much" or "too little" investment in education in terms of whether the wage premiums paid to workers with certain levels of education and those who complete certain fields of study are historically high or low and rising or falling. He shows how difficult it is to pin down whether there is indeed an oversupply or undersupply of education in the nation's labor force.

The "internal" evaluation of educational investment is carried out primarily using cost-effectiveness analysis, either from production function estimates discussed in Section VI of this volume, or a "partial" analysis that directly compares the costs and effectiveness of alternative strategies for producing improved achievement outcomes. Levin's second entry discusses this methodology. Levin also discusses the major problems of cost-effectiveness analysis and how they can be overcome.

Both in cost-benefit and cost-effectiveness analysis, most of the emphasis in past years has been on measuring material benefits to education or the outcomes of alternative strategies for school improvement. All too frequently, Mun Tsang argues in the first of his entries, cost measurements are taken rather lightly. For example, economists now tend to estimate rates of return using "Mincer" regression coefficients for level of schooling dummies in equations that relate the logarithm of individual earnings to individual schooling and experience. This is a convenient way to estimate private rates assuming that the only private cost is income foregone. Yet, in most countries, individuals and their families bear a surprisingly high fraction of the total cost of schooling in the form of direct private contributions and other private costs over and above income foregone. This is true even at the primary school level. Excluding such direct private costs at lower levels of schooling, where income foregone is low, seriously overestimates the private rate of return at those levels compared to university, for example.

Errors in cost estimates are generally much more frequent and larger than errors in benefits simply because we know much less about family expenses on schooling and about the incomes of the young than incomes during prime labor force years. Cost errors have a much larger impact on benefit-cost estimates than errors in measuring returns, especially returns farther out in the benefit stream. Similarly, in cost-effectiveness, there has traditionally been much greater inaccuracy in measuring costs than achievement gains. Analysts often seriously underestimate the costs of alternative improvement strategies they favor.

In the second of his entries, Tsang makes a similar point, but this time as it applies to cost-effectiveness analysis—specifically, in the public–private school comparisons. Tsang argues that in most of these comparisons, costs are incorrectly estimated, seriously influencing the comparisons and biasing the results and policy conclusions. The more favored treatment (in this case, private schooling) is often given a cost break that results in a higher effectiveness–cost ratio than the less favored treatment. The major reason this can happen in otherwise seemingly sophisticated analyses is because of economists' less-than-careful approach to costs.

Steven Klees takes a somewhat different position on cost-effectiveness analysis in his entry on evaluating educational technology. Klees contends that the entire analysis is clouded by an "efficiency" perspective that is untenable in a world of conflicting interests. Technologies, he claims, have been applied in schools in ways that advance the interests of some but hurt the interest of others. Specifically, educational technologies have been used to substitute for effective training of teachers and to decrease the control that teachers have over classrooms. The fact that certain technologies have been cost-effective in the short-run in raising some pupils' achievement scores begs the question of whether, in the long-run, better-trained teachers employing teacher-centered innovations would do considerably better than the technology. If the two strategies are substitutes, then cost-effectiveness analysis must compare longer-range educational *strategies*, not substitutable inputs in a given production process.

Cost–Benefit Analysis

H. M. Levin

Cost–benefit analysis represents an important tool for analyzing the desirability of social investments. It has been applied widely to educational investments at the national and sub-national levels, particularly in evaluating the ability of such investments to raise productivity and earnings. Cost–benefit analysis compares the costs and outcomes of alternatives when the outcomes can be assessed in monetary terms (Mishan 1976).

Cost–benefit analysis enables a direct comparison of the costs and benefits of an alternative or a comparison of their magnitudes with those of other types of social investments in education or in other sectors. Not only is it possible to ascertain which educational investment has the largest benefits relative to costs; it is also possible to compare these results with investments in health, transportation, physical capital such as plant and equipment, and other sectors. In this way governmental units can use cost–benefit analysis to compare the desirability of alternative educational investments, as well as in determining the balance between investing in education and other sectors. In contrast, cost-effectiveness can only evaluate alternatives with the same goals and measures of effectiveness, such as improvements in student achievement (see *Cost-effectiveness Analysis*).

Cost–benefit analysis was developed in the 1930s by the United States Corps of Army Engineers. The US Congress was overwhelmed with requests for massive regional investments in water-resource projects (e.g., hydroelectric dams, deep-water harbors, major canals) which the various regional interests viewed as powerful stimuli for reducing unemployment at a time of national economic depression. A bewildered Congress asked the Corps of Army Engineers to recommend only projects whose benefits were at least equal to costs (Eckstein 1958). By the 1960s, cost–benefit analysis was used widely by economists to assist in the search for efficiency in government spending. At the same time it began to be used to scrutinize educational investments.

1. Measuring Costs and Benefits

In contrast to cost-effectiveness analysis, cost–benefit analysis requires that both costs and benefits be expressed in monetary terms. In this respect, the costs are measured in the same way for both types of analyses using the ingredients or resource-recovery approach (Levin 1983). However, benefits must be measurable in terms of their monetary value rather than in terms of educational effectiveness as reflected in cost-effectiveness analysis.

1.1 Assessing Benefits

Since cost–benefit analysis requires that benefits be measured in monetary units, it is only possible to apply it to subjects where that is feasible. This means that cost–benefit analysis lends itself especially well to those alternatives or interventions in which the outcomes are market-oriented. For example, educational and training programs that are designed to improve employment and earnings or reduce poverty can be evaluated with a cost–benefit approach when the benefits are the additional earnings associated with the interventions (Ribich 1969).

Many educational projects and investments are dedicated to raising labor force productivity and income. These include commitments to vocational education, workforce training, dropout prevention and even much of the effort at general education which is dedicated to improving the labor force (Becker 1964, Psacharopoulos and Woodhall 1985). Thus, educational programs that have labor market outcomes are the most appropriate ones for using cost–benefit analysis. The most typical method of measuring the benefits of such interventions is to compare the earnings of similar persons with different amounts of education. Under assumptions of the competitive marketplace, long-run differences in earnings associated with education are equivalent to the higher productivity of such persons.

It is difficult to estimate such benefits through experimental studies in a democratic society. An experiment would require that persons be assigned randomly to different levels of education—and perhaps their lives would have to be controlled in other ways—to assure comparability in examining the role of education. More typically the studies observe cross-sections of workers or follow them longitudinally in attempting to measure the connection between specific levels and types of educational investments and earnings. However, it is reasonable to expect that persons with more education also have other resources that can account for higher earnings. For example, persons with more education are generally of a higher social origin, leading to better connections in labor markets. They may also have higher ability and discipline, two factors which are associated with greater educational attainments and which should also reap dividends in labor markets. Accordingly, the measurement of benefits in cost–benefit analysis must attempt to control statistically for noneducational differences that may affect earnings and that are associated with education.

Thus, the benefits of a specific vocational education program relative to an alternative can be measured according to the earnings associated with participation in that program rather than the alternative. The benefits of expanding schooling can be assessed according to the additional earnings of those who benefit from that expansion. Of course, these represent the gross benefits to the investment. Net benefits can only be determined after subtracting the cost.

There are a number of other concerns in the measurement of benefits. The first is that the additional earnings that represent the benefits of more education or training are not received immediately. They are distributed over the working lives of the educated labor force following education and training. Yet economists and psychologists have long recognized that benefits that are received over time have a lesser value than those received at present. In order to make the value of benefits indifferent to the time pattern over which they were conferred, it is important to obtain a standard measure of their value. Accordingly, the stream of benefits from an investment that is generated over time is converted to a single measure of "present value" by penalizing or discounting future benefits by an interest rate to make them comparable with benefits received at present. This is a fairly straightforward conversion which provides a present value of benefits that can be compared directly with a present value of costs (Mishan 1976 pp. 199–224).

A second concern is that the benefits of educational investments extend beyond increases in productivity and earnings to improvements in health, consumption, labor market information, and reductions in criminal justice and public assistance burdens. Haveman and Wolfe (1984) have estimated that the total value of benefits from educational investments is probably double that of the additional earnings alone. Therefore it is likely that the education-induced increase in earnings will understate the true value of benefits from educational investments.

A final concern is that the aggregate benefits and costs that comprise a cost–benefit estimate reveal nothing about the distribution of who pays the costs and receives the benefits. The question of who receives the benefits and who pays the costs may be an important issue. For example, if social investments tend to redistribute income, most democracies prefer investments that are redistributive from wealthier to poorer populations. There is some evidence that educational subsidies in higher education represent a net transfer of resources from lower-income groups to upper-income ones (Fields 1980, Leslie and Brinkman 1988. pp. 107–21). Lower-income groups participate less in higher education than upper-income groups, but they must still pay taxes to support such a system. In this case, the investment may have high benefits relative to costs, but may redistribute income from the poor to the rich. Accordingly, the distributive consequences of investments must be analyzed as well as the ratio of costs to benefits (Psacharopoulos and Woodhall 1985 pp. 244–86).

1.2 Measuring Costs

The costs of an intervention are defined as the value of the resources that are given up by society to effect the intervention. These resources are referred to as the ingredients of the intervention, and it is the social value of those ingredients that constitute its overall cost. At a later stage one can assess the distribution of these costs between the decision-making agency and other entities. Accordingly, the method sets out systematically to identify and ascertain the value of the ingredients that are required for each alternative that is under consideration. From an economic perspective the costs of an action are determined by the value of the resources that are entailed in their best alternative use. This is known as "opportunity cost," in the sense that it is the value of the forgone opportunities that must be considered when one refers to the cost of an endeavor. The ingredients method represents a straightforward way of estimating cost within this framework.

The ingredients approach to cost estimation entails three distinct phases: (a) identification of ingredients; (b) determination of the value or cost of the ingredients and the overall costs of an intervention; and (c) an analysis of the costs in an appropriate decision-oriented framework. These three phases are discussed more fully elsewhere (see *Cost-effectiveness Analysis*), but they hold some particular implications for cost–benefit analysis.

1.3 Identification of Ingredients

The identification of ingredients refers to the delineation of all of the resources that are required for the particular intervention that forms the basis for the cost–benefit analysis. For example, in the case of a study of expansion of technical education, the personnel, facilities, materials, and other ingredients required for the activity need to be identified.

Educational interventions use not only these resources, but also the time of students who might otherwise be able to use their time productively in the workplace or through self-employment. Even the time of primary school youngsters in developing societies is likely to have some value in terms of household or farm tasks. If a student is required to spend four additional academic years in the educational system, those years could have been used for other productive activities that, when forgone, have a cost to both the individual and society. Accordingly, an important element of specifying ingredients for cost–benefit analysis is that of student time.

1.4 Determination of Costs

Once the ingredients have been identified and stipulated, it is necessary to ascertain their costs (Levin 1983 Chap. 4). In doing this, all ingredients are assumed to have a cost, including donated or volunteer resources. That is, they have a cost to someone, even if the sponsoring agency did not pay for them in a particular situation. At a later stage the costs will be distributed among the constituencies who paid them, but at this stage the aim is to ascertain the total costs of the intervention.

Ingredients can be divided into those that are purchased in reasonably competitive markets, and those that are obtained through other types of transactions. In general, the value of an ingredient for costing purposes is its market value. In the case of personnel, market value may be ascertained by determining what the costs would be for hiring a particular type of person. Such costs must include not only salary, but also fringe benefits and other employment costs that are paid by the employer. Many of the other inputs can also be costed by using their market prices. There are a number of techniques for determining the values of resources that cannot be readily priced in the marketplace (see *Cost-effectiveness Analysis*).

Of particular concern is the value of student time. The usual measure of the value of student time is the earnings forgone by the student by enrolling in school or a training program rather than being employed in the workplace. This should approximate to the value of productive activity that was lost because the student was in school. Typically the cost of student time is estimated from the earnings of persons of similar gender, race, and socioeconomic status who are in the workforce rather than in schools or training programs. Of course, such estimates must be adjusted for the probability of unemployment.

1.5 Combining Benefits and Costs

Costs and benefits can be combined in several ways in order to do a cost–benefit analysis. The most common forms of cost–benefit comparison are rate of return, cost–benefit (or benefit–cost) ratios, and net present values. One form of cost–benefit analysis is that of estimating internal rates of return on investment, that rate of interest that equates the present values of benefits and costs (Psacharopoulos and Woodhall 1985 pp. 31–41) In general, no investment should be undertaken that does not have a rate of return that is at least equal to that of other alternatives (see *Rates of Return to Education*).

A more typical cost–benefit analysis takes the form of a comparison of cost–benefit ratios among alternative endeavors. The necessary condition for considering an educational investment is that its benefits exceed costs where both benefits and costs represent present values, that is, benefit and cost streams that are properly discounted. The sufficient condition is that the benefit–cost ratio is greater than that of all alternative investments, both educational and noneducational.

The third form of cost–benefit analysis is the calculation of net present values of investments. Net present value is simply the difference between the present benefits and present costs, using the same discount rate to ascertain present values of each. The necessary condition for considering an investment is that its net present value be positive. The sufficient condition is that the net present value of an alternative exceed the net present value of all other alternative investments whose costs are of the same magnitude.

2. Examples of Cost–Benefit Studies

Cost–benefit studies have been carried out in many areas of education. These include the prevention of dropouts, preschool education for disadvantaged children, vocational education, and college loan programs among others.

2.1 Dropout Prevention

A study of dropout prevention found large net present benefits (Stern et al. 1989). This evaluation was based upon the success in reducing dropouts among 11 academies created in public high schools in California. These academies were special programs or schools within the larger high school setting that provided vocational training for careers in which students stood a good chance of placement, as well as academic training. Students were given special attention from their teachers and representatives of local employers. When students were matched with a similar group of students in the regular school programs, it was estimated that the academies had saved 29 persons who would have been expected to drop out.

The marginal costs of the academy program beyond the costs of the regular school program for all 327 students were compared to net present benefits in terms of the additional earnings of the 29 persons who were "saved" from dropping out. The overall net present benefits of the program were found to exceed overall costs by considerable amounts, the specifics depending upon which assumptions were used regarding benefits.

In contrast to studies of a single dropout program, Levin undertook a national study on the economic consequences of high school dropout (Levin 1972).

This study calculated the additional lifetime earnings and tax revenues that would have been generated if the entire cohort of 25- to 34-years old males in 1970 had graduated from high school. It was assumed that, even if existing dropouts had graduated, they would not have done as well as those who had actually graduated from high school. Thus, additional earnings of dropouts who would be induced to graduate were assumed to be only 75 percent of those of conventional high school graduates. However, it was also assumed that a portion of the induced graduates would continue into higher education with additional earnings from that source as well.

The total loss of lifetime earnings for this group as a result of failure to complete at least high school was estimated at about US $237 billion. The additional cost for achieving this result was comprised of two parts: first, there was the cost of the additional years of schooling undertaken by members of the group; second, there was the cost of the additional expenditures to prevent dropping out. It was assumed that it would have been necessary to increase annual schooling expenditures on those at risk of dropping out by 50 percent a year for all of their elementary and secondary schooling to keep them in school until completion of high school. On this basis it was estimated that the total costs of achieving at least high school graduation for all members of the cohort was about US $40 billion, producing a benefit of six dollars for each dollar of cost. The additional lifetime earnings would have generated about US $71 billion in government revenue or about US $1.75 in tax revenues for each US $1.00 in cost. The study also estimated that inadequate education was contributing about US $6 billion a year to the costs of welfare and crime in 1970.

2.2 Preschool Educational Investment

Barnett (1985) undertook a cost–benefit analysis of the Perry Preschool Project in Ypsilanti, Michigan. The Perry Preschool approach is one that has been studied since its inception in the 1960s, and it has been used as a model for hundreds of preschools for disadvantaged students across the United States, including the national Head Start Program. Students who had been enrolled in the preschool project were followed until age 19. It was found that relative to a matched control group, enrollees in the project experienced better school achievement, educational placement, educational attainment, and employment. Monetary values for the benefits were calculated on the basis of the apparent effect of these advantages on the value of childcare during the programs; reduced school expenditures for remediation, special services, and grade repetition; reduced costs of crime, delinquency, and welfare; and higher earnings and employment.

It was found that the benefits exceeded the costs by a large margin under a wide range of assumptions. The one-year program showed benefits of seven dollars for every dollar of costs, a benefit–cost ratio of about 7:1, and the two-year program showed a benefit-cost ratio of about 3.6:1 (Barrueta-Clement et al. 1984 p. 60). About 80 percent of the net benefits were received by taxpayers in the form of higher tax contributions and lower expenditures on education, crime, and welfare and by potential crime victims in the form of lower costs for property losses and injuries.

2.3 Higher Educational Loans

A study of benefits and costs for financial aid to stimulate participation in higher education for low-income students has also indicated high benefits relative to costs for government investment (St. John and Masten 1990). This study compared tax revenues generated by the additional income produced by the higher levels of college participation among low-income students with the costs of financial aid that induced these higher enrollments. The net present value of additional tax revenues was four times as great as the cost of the aid program for students in the high school class of 1980. In other words, from the perspective of the federal treasury, such programs had a benefit–cost ratio of 4:1.

2.4 Developing Countries

Cost–benefit analysis has been carried out in education for developing countries by several international agencies including The World Bank (Psacharopoulos and Woodhall 1985). But, usually the analysis is done in the form of a rate-of-return analysis rather than a cost–benefit ratio or net present value. That is, the benefits of the investment are expressed in terms of the equivalent of an annual return on investment rather than in the form of a cost–benefit ratio or a net present value. However, the basic data that are used to estimate internal rates-of-return can be used to calculate net present values or cost–benefit ratios.

See also: Consumption Benefits of Education; Education and Economic Growth; Benefits of Education; Cost Analysis in Education; Returns to Vocational Education in Developing Nations

References

Barnett W S 1985 Benefit-cost analysis of the Perry Preschool Program and its Policy implications. *Educational Evaluation and Policy Analysis* 7(4): 333–42

Becker G S 1964 *Human Capital.* Columbia University Press, New York

Berrueta-Clement J R, Schweinhart L J, Barnett W S, Epstein A S, Weikart D P 1984 *Changed Lives: The Effects of the Perry Preschool Program on Youths Through Age 19.* High/Scope Press, Ypsilanti, Michigan

Eckstein O 1958 *Water-Resource Development: The Economics of Project Evaluation.* Harvard University Press, Cambridge, Massachusetts

Fields G S 1980 Education and income distribution in developing countries: A review of the literature. In: King T (ed.) 1980 *Education and Income.* Staff Working Paper No. 402, The World Bank, Washington DC

Haveman R, Wolfe R 1984 Schooling and economic well-being: The role of nonmarket effects. *J. Hum. Resources* 19(3): 377–407

Leslie L L, Brinkman P T 1988 *The Economic Value of Higher Education.* Macmillan, New York

Levin H M 1972 *The Costs to the Nation of Inadequate Education.* Report of the Select Senate Committee on Equal Educational Opportunity, 92nd US Congress. Government Printing Office, Washington DC

Levin H M 1983 *Cost-Effectiveness: A Primer.* Sage, Beverly Hills, California

Mishan E J 1976 *Cost-Benefit Analysis: An Informal Introduction.* Praeger, New York

Psacharopoulos G, Woodhall M 1985 *Education for Development: An Analysis of Investment Choices.* Oxford University Press, New York

Ribich T I 1969 *Education and Poverty.* Brookings Institution, Washington, DC

St John E P, Masten C L 1990 Return on the federal investment in student financial aid: An assessment for the high school class of 1972. *J. Stud. Financial Aid* 20(3): 4–23

Stern D, Dayton C, Paik I W, Weisberg A 1989 Benefits and costs of dropout prevention in a high school program combining academic and vocational education: Third-year results from replications of the California Peninsula Academies. *Educ. Evaluation and Policy Analysis* 11(4): 405–16

Rates of Return to Education

M. Carnoy

1. Introduction

The rate of return to investment in education is a measure of the future net economic payoff to an individual or to society of increasing the amount of education taken. As a measure of profitability, the rate is equivalent to the interest paid on savings or the rate of return to investing in a machine, real estate, or any other form of capital requiring a stream of investment over time and an income return over time.

The rate of return is found by setting the discounted value of costs and benefits over time equal to zero and solving for the implicit discount rate, r,

$$0 = \sum \frac{C_i}{(1 + r)^i} + \sum \frac{B_i}{(1 + r)^i} \tag{1}$$

where what the individual spends for education or other costs incurred (*C*) in this equation are negative and the additional income or other benefits the individual gains from the education (*B*) are positive.

From the individual's standpoint (the private rate of return), the benefits of the additional education are the additional income the individual earns because of it, the nonpecuniary consumption benefits educational investment provides over a person's life, such as greater enjoyment of cultural activities or higher social status, and the direct consumption derived from taking the education. However, in measuring private rates of return, economists have limited themselves to the earnings benefits of education. They have assumed that such a measure underestimates the real rate, since consumption benefits are considered positive (see *Consumption Benefits of Education*). Yet, in practice, the direct consumption effect of attending school could be highly negative for those children who are not particularly successful or are members of a lower status minority. A negative unmeasured consumption effect implies that earnings differences would overestimate the true rate of return.

Private costs of education include the income forgone by students while they attend school or other educational activities, the additional expenditures associated with taking education, such as uniforms, books, transportation, and fees, and possibly a negative consumption effect of sitting in classes.

Since costs occur early in the temporal stream of costs and benefits, they necessarily have a much greater weight both in the educational investment decision process and in the estimated rate of return. However, private costs are much more difficult to measure than private benefits (e.g., how great is the amount of income forgone by teenagers in developing countries?), and direct private costs are usually significantly underestimated. Families in many countries bear a large proportion of the total cost of even public primary school (see *Private and Public Costs of Schooling in Developing Nations*).

From society's point of view (social rate of return) the benefits of additional education are the additional productivity of those who have taken more schooling and engaged in other educational activities, the collective consumption value of the education, and the "externalities" of education (see *External Benefits of Education*) accruing to society in nonmaterial forms, such as more civilized collective behavior, a more productive environment, and a wiser choice of political leadership. The social costs of additional education equal the private costs plus any costs borne collectively through taxes or voluntary donations used for public spending on education.

Although the social benefits of education are usually estimated by using the same average earnings streams as in the private rate estimates but corrected for income taxes, such approximations of social benefits are problematic. Earnings differences do not necessarily equal productivity differences, especially when a

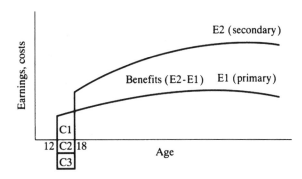

Figure 1
Earnings streams by level of education

significant percentage of those with certain levels of education, such as university, work in the public sector or in oligopolized sectors of private industry and services. From a private individual's standpoint, it makes little difference what the additional earnings represent, since private investment decisions are based on expected returns. If employers pay higher salaries to those with more schooling, the benefits as seen by individuals are the additional wages, whatever the reason for paying them. Yet for society, the reason behind higher incomes makes a difference in assessing whether to invest in more education or not.

One way in which economists have approached the productivity/earnings quandary is to correct estimated earnings streams for factors other than education and experience (Thias and Carnoy 1972, Blaug 1972). For the private individual, it makes sense to look at the educational benefits and costs for his or her gender, race, or ethnic group, assuming that these differences are structural and persistent (see *Race Earnings Differentials; Gender Differences in Earnings*). However, earnings corrected for race and gender differences may result in "misleading" estimates of social rates, since such corrections may reflect political power relations rather than productivity differences.

2. Estimating Rates of Return

There are two principal methods used in estimating rates of return to education, known respectively as "traditional" and "Mincer." The traditional method uses calculated annual costs and earnings by education level (see Fig. 1). Earnings forgone are estimated as the income the individual could have earned while attending school (C1 in Fig. 1). Direct costs borne by the family (C2) are added to earnings forgone for the private rate of return estimate. Public costs (C3) are added to earnings forgone and direct private costs to estimate annual social costs (C1+C2+C3) for the social rate of return estimate. Costs are estimated over the length of the schooling period. If the average primary school student takes 8 years to

Table 1
Cost–benefit stream for typical private rate of return estimate comparing secondary school completion (12 years of schooling) to primary school completion (6 years of schooling)

Year	Age	Income 1[a]	Income 2	Benefit[b]	Direct cost	Total
1	13	345	0	−259	−100	−359
2	14	350	0	−262	−100	−362
3	15	370	0	−278	−100	−378
4	16	400	0	−300	−150	−450
5	17	450	0	−338	−150	−488
6	18	500	0	−375	−150	−525
7	19	600	900	300		300
.						
.						
.						
27	39	800	1300	500		500
.						
.						
.						
47	59	750	1600	850		850

a Hypothetical incomes provided by author   b Income forgone calculated as 0.75 of Income 1

finish 6 years of primary school because of repetition, for example, costs should be calculated over 8 years, not 6. This also means, however, that more advantaged pupils may have lower costs of schooling than less advantaged students. Annual private and social benefits are calculated from the difference in average earnings of those who have different levels of education (E2 minus E1 in Fig. 1). The year-by-year costs and benefits are inserted into Eqn. (1) above to estimate the discount rate that equalizes costs to benefits.

Usually, such annual benefits and costs are estimated directly from average earnings calculated at various ages for men and women in the labor force and the estimated direct private and public costs of schooling. Yet they have also been estimated from log earnings regressions for different education groups (Carnoy 1965, Hanoch 1967, Thias and Carnoy 1972). This has allowed for "corrections" of the education coefficients for each age group for other factors, such as social class background, region, and time worked (Eckaus 1973). The "corrected" earnings streams yield rate of return estimates "corrected" for these other factors (Thias and Carnoy 1972).

In either case, the average income difference (negative in the case of income forgone and positive in the case of income benefits) between two proximate schooling levels is estimated for each year from the initial year of schooling at the level being evaluated—for example, the first year of upper secondary, if upper secondary completion is being compared with lower secondary completion. Direct costs are added to income forgone during the school years to obtain the private rate, and other costs are added to private costs to obtain the social rate. Income differences are estimated net of taxes for the private rate, but not for the social rate.

Table 1 shows a typical cost and benefit stream calculation. The rate of return is estimated by putting such costs and benefits into Eqn. (1).

The Mincer method uses regression analysis to fit a Mincerian human capital earnings function to individual data on earnings (Y), years of schooling (S), and years of labor market experience (E)—equal to age minus years of schooling minus age of starting school—in a semilogarithmic form (Mincer 1974). The average private rate of return to schooling is estimated as the estimated (b) regression coefficient of schooling from the log income regression equation:

$$LnY = a + bS + cE + dE^2 \qquad (2)$$

The reasoning of this procedure is that partial differentiation of LnY with respect to S gives the definition of a "short-cut" method-calculated rate of return:

$$b = \frac{\partial LnY}{\partial S} \qquad (3)$$

or in discrete form for expository purposes

$$b = \frac{LnY_s - LnY_o}{\Delta S} \qquad (4)$$

where Y_s and Y_o refer to the earnings of those with s and o years of schooling, respectively.

Marginal rates of return to particular levels of schooling can be estimated from Mincerian regressions by substituting a string of dummy variables for each level of schooling. In this case, the coefficient of the dummy

Table 2
Rates of return by country type, level of education, gender, and university subject studied (in percent)

		Social			Private	
	Primary	Secondary	Higher	Primary	Secondary	Higher
Region						
Africa	28	17	13	45	26	32
Asia	27	15	13	31	15	18
Latin America	26	18	16	32	23	23
Country type						
Intermediate	13	10	8	17	13	13
Advanced	—	11	9	—	12	12
Gender						
Male				19	16	15
Female				17	21	14
Subject						
Economics			13			
Law			12			
Social sciences			11			
Medicine			12			
Engineering			12			
Sciences, mathematics, physics			8			
Agriculture			8			

Source: Psacharopoulos 1985 Tables 1, 5, and 7

variable will yield the total return to that level minus the excluded dummy. For example, if the excluded level is "no schooling," the coefficient of the "high school completed" dummy represents the total return to all the years of schooling up to completion of high school. To estimate an annualized rate of return, the coefficient must be divided by the number of years of schooling (in this case, primary plus lower secondary plus higher secondary).

In both methods, the earnings by experience and education are generally estimated using cross-sectional rather than longitudinal cohort data. In other words, earnings are estimated for different age groups of income earners with different amounts of education in the labor force in a given calendar year. On the one hand, this is a fair representation of what private individuals consider when deciding to invest in additional education or not—they use what older individuals earn at that point in time as a single best estimate of what they might earn in the future. On the other hand, it is a misleading indicator for both private and public investment, since cross-sectional earnings represent the payoff to past schooling, past economic growth rates, and past income distribution policies (see *Education and Earnings*). They may or may not be accurate estimates of future earnings, or hence of future payoffs to education.

In light of these limitations, researchers have attempted to find more dynamic measures of rates of return. Longitudinal rates have been estimated for the United States using cohort earnings across census years. These estimates suggest that longitudinal rates are affected by the economic growth rate (Carnoy and Marenbach 1975). Another way of getting around the cross-sectional problem is to estimate a series of rates of return based on cross-sectional earnings in the same country over time. Using a time series of rates provides a historical picture of changing payoffs to different levels of schooling. Although such time series do not predict short-term fluctuations in rates based on short-term fluctuations in the relative earnings of more and less educated groups, they do suggest secular trends in payoffs to different levels of schooling. On the basis of these trends, insights can be gained into the effect on the relative value of different kinds of educational investment as the economy and educational system expand.

3. Empirical Results

3.1 Cross-sectional Rates

Rates of return to education have been estimated for a large number of countries, by level of schooling, by gender, and—for some countries—over time. Table 2 shows the latest summary of rates (Psacharopoulos 1985). They should be interpreted with some care, since they are averages of estimates using different kinds of data, different assumptions about costs, and referring to different populations.

These estimates show that the rates to primary education are higher than the rates to secondary and higher education, that the rates are higher in developing countries than in advanced industrial countries, that the rate of return to women's education may be higher than to men's even though women are paid less in absolute terms than men, and that the rates to studying social sciences in universities are as high or higher than the rates to medicine and engineering.

3.2 Rates of Return over Time

The more interesting estimates of rates are those made in the same country over time (see Psacharopoulos 1989). They reveal not only the differing payoffs to different levels of schooling, but also provide insight into how school expansion affects payoffs under varying economic conditions.

Although time-series within-country rate of return estimates using comparable data over time are available for only a few countries, the results there indicate that rates fall with expanded schooling, and that they fall first at lower levels of schooling as the educational system expands.

In the United States, for example, the annualized social rate of return to secondary education for males fell from 18 percent to 11 percent between 1939 and 1969 during a period of major expansion in secondary enrollment and graduation (Carnoy and Marenbach 1975). The social rate to college completion remained constant at about 11 percent over the same period (Carnoy and Marenbach 1975) but then fell sharply in the early 1970s and rose again in the 1980s (Murphy and Welch 1989). This suggests that rates of return to lower levels of schooling fall relative to higher level rates when the school system expands. Except for the fall in college rates in the early 1970s with the Vietnam War bulge in college attendance and graduation, rates to college have remained stable, but the absolute number of male college graduates has grown slowly since 1975.

Rates of return measured over time in other countries have shown a similar tendency. Estimates in Bogota, Colombia (Mohan 1986) show that in a period of relatively rapid growth during the 1970s (1973–78), the estimated private rate to each level of education fell, and that even at the beginning of the period, the rate of return to primary education was lower than to secondary and higher education, and remained so throughout the decade (Mohan 1986 Table 8-3). Private rates to secondary education fell significantly and more rapidly than those to higher education in these 5 years, so that the secondary rates end up lower than higher rates by 1978. Chung's research in Hong Kong (1990) shows payoffs to primary and secondary education falling below the rate of return to investment in university and dropping more rapidly than the rate of return to university in the late 1970s and early 1980s, a period of rapid industrialization and educational expansion. Two separate studies in Kenya (Thias and Carnoy 1972, Knight and Sabot 1990) suggest that private and social rates of return to primary school fell rapidly in the 1960s and rates to secondary education then fell in the 1970s, in the face

Table 3
Republic of Korea: Mincer (private) rates of return, by level of schooling, gender, and year, all employed and manufacturing workers 1974–88 (in percent)[a]

	All workers							
	MS/PS[b]		HS/MS		JC/HS		COL/HS	
Year	M	F	M	F	M	F	M	F
1976(N)[c]	2.4	1.6	9.1	11.9	13.6	19.2	16.8	19.6
1981(N)	1.7	1.2	6.5	9.1	13.0	26.6	15.4	19.4
1986(N)	2.8	3.4	4.6	5.6	8.3	17.3	14.4	19.3
1988(N)	1.9	2.7	3.9	5.2	6.5	14.0	12.2	15.0

	Manufacturing sector							
	MS/PS		HS/MS		JC/HS		COL/HS	
Year	M	F	M	F	M	F	M	F
1974(R)[d]	8.0	7.5	14.8	14.8	12.5	20.2	16.5	15.1
1976(N)	3.2	1.6	8.7	9.3	14.7	15.8	17.5	16.7
1979(R)	6.1	3.1	11.7	12.4	15.0	17.4	17.8	18.8
1981(N)	2.9	1.0	6.0	6.5	12.8	19.3	16.1	18.7
1986(R)	4.2	2.2	10.0	9.0	12.2	15.4	17.8	20.3
1986(N)	3.4	2.3	4.6	4.0	9.0	8.5	13.4	20.0
1988(N)	2.7	1.8	4.4	4.4	6.3	6.2	11.0	11.8

Sources: Ryoo 1988, Nam in press. Human capital regression estimates from Occupational Wage Survey, 1974, 1976, 1979, 1981, 1986, 1988 a The rates are annualized coefficients of education in human capital regression equations. Ryoo used educational dummy variables, experience and experienced squared in his equation; Nam used education dummies, experience dummies, tenure in the firm (years) and tenure squared. The difference in the definition of the human capital equation accounts for at least part of the difference in Mincer rates for the one year (1986) in which both Ryoo and Nam estimate rates. The annual rates were obtained by dividing the coefficients of education dummies by the number of years of schooling associated with that level of education b MS/PS: middle school (3 yrs)/primary school; HS/MS: high school (3 yrs)/middle school; JC/HS: junior college (2 yrs)/high school; COL/HS: college (4 yrs)/high school c (N) = estimates by Nam d (R)=estimates by Ryoo

of bottom-up rapid expansion of education over the two decades.

However, the most convincing evidence for sequential declines (primary, then secondary, then university) in rates of return as the economy grows and the educational system expands comes from South Korea. A number of rate-of-return estimates are available for the past 20 years (see Psacharopoulos 1985, 1989), but they are generally not appropriate for intertemporal comparisons because of inconsistent treatment of the data and different methods used. Nevertheless, recent studies of Korean rates do specifically make intertemporal comparisons using the same data source for all years (Ryoo et al. in press). Table 3 presents the Mincer private rates of return estimates for Korea, by level of schooling, gender, and year. They show that in Ryoo's and Nam's estimates both for all Koreans employed and for those employed in manufacturing, the Mincer rates of return to investment in middle school were already low in 1974, but declined further in the 14 years of rapid economic growth from 1974 to 1988. This was true for both males and females. Rates to investment in higher secondary school in 1974 were much more equal to rates to investment in four-year college. However, secondary rates dropped sharply in the mid- and late 1970s for both males and females so that by the 1980s, they were much lower than college rates. The Mincer rates to investing in junior college appear to have risen in the 1970s (or at least stayed constant) and fell in the 1980s. Junior college private rates by the late 1980s were not much higher for males than the low rates to investing in high school, but remained much higher for females, especially outside manufacturing. The private rates to college completion remained fairly constant or may have even increased until the late 1980s, when they, too, began to fall. College rates were already as high or higher in 1974 than rates to investment in other levels.

3.3 Implications of Patterns of Rates of Return over Time

The rate of return estimates for comparable groups taken as a series of cross sections over time in various countries (United States, Colombia, Hong Kong, Kenya, and Korea) suggests that where there is rapid industrialization and simultaneous rapid expansion of schooling toward the universal completion of primary, junior and senior high school (lower and upper secondary school), rates of return to various levels of schooling decline over time, and tend to decline first at the primary level, then at the secondary level, and finally at the university level. There is evidence that in almost all these countries this process has left the rates to university higher than those to secondary, and those to secondary higher than those to primary.

The pattern of rate changes revealed by these time comparisons has several implications: (a) earlier conclusions regarding relatively high rates to primary education and low rates to higher education may be relevant only to economies and educational systems at the early stages of development; (b) rates of return estimated over time using comparable groups are valuable for understanding changes in the economic and social role that education plays at various points in historical time; and (c) during periods of rapid industrialization and expansion of the educational system, the main restriction on students taking further education may not be self-selection as suggested by the pattern of declining rates from primary to higher education in earlier cross-sectional comparisons. Rather, it may reflect imposed selection, either through highly imperfect capital markets, or restrictions on the number of places available in secondary school in some countries or four-year colleges in more advanced countries. Hence, where rates rise with education level (as in Korea, Hong Kong, and Colombia), schooling may well act as a screening mechanism.

See also: Education and Economic Growth; Education and Productivity; Benefits of Education; Education, Occupation, and Earnings; Education and Earnings; Cost–Benefit Analysis; Consumption Benefits of Education

References

Blaug M 1972 The correlation between education and earnings. What does it signify? *High. Educ.* 1(1): 53–76

Carnoy M 1965 The cost and return to schooling in Mexico: A case study. Doctoral dissertation, University of Chicago, Chicago, Illinois

Carnoy M, Marenbach D 1975 The return to schooling in the United States, 1939–1969. *J. Hum. Resources* 10(3): 312–31

Chung Y-P 1990 Changes of rates of return to education over time: The case study of Hong Kong. Paper presented at the Comparative and International Education Society, Atlanta, Georgia (mimeo)

Eckaus R 1973 *Estimating the Rates of Return to Education: A Disaggregated Approach.* A technical report sponsored by the Carnegie Commission on Higher Education, Carnegie Commission on Higher Education, Berkeley, California

Hanoch G 1967 An economic analysis of earnings and schooling. *J. Hum. Resources* 2(3): 310–30

Knight J B, Sabot R 1990 *Education, Productivity, and Inequality: The East African Natural Experiment.* Published for the World Bank by Oxford University Press, Oxford

Mincer J 1974 *Schooling, Experience, and Earnings.* National Bureau of Economic Research, New York

Mohan R 1986 *Work, Wages, and Welfare in a Developing Metropolis: Consequences of Growth in Bogotá, Colombia.* Oxford University Press for the World Bank, New York

Murphy K, Welch F 1989 Wage premiums for college graduates: Recent growth and possible explanations. *Educ. Researcher* 18(4): 17–26

Nam Y-S in press Educational expansion and changes in the structure of earnings inequality by gender among young workers: The case of South Korea. Doctoral dissertation, Stanford University, Stanford, California

Psacharopoulos G 1985 Returns to education: A further international update and implications. *J. Hum. Resources* 20(4): 583–604

Psacharopoulos G 1989 Time trends of the returns to education: Cross-national evidence. *Econ. Educ. Rev.* 8(3): 225–39

Ryoo J-K 1988 Changes in the rate of return to education over time: The case of Korea. Doctoral dissertation, Stanford University, Stanford, California

Ryoo J-K, Nam Y-S, Carnoy M 1993 Changing rates of return to education over time: A Korean case study. *Econ. Educ. Rev.* (March)

Thias H, Carnoy M (1972) *Cost-benefit Analysis in Education: A Case Study of Kenya.* Johns Hopkins University Press, Baltimore, Maryland

Manpower Analysis

K. Hinchliffe

From the early 1940s, but most particularly since the late 1950s, estimates have been made of future manpower requirements for the purposes of educational planning, across highly divergent societies in terms of their economic structure and political ideology. This entry focuses mainly on mixed economy, less developed countries which, following political independence, largely embraced the concept of managed economic development, including comprehensive development planning. In this context, the development of manpower forecasting has been closely associated with the view that the degree and structure of postbasic educational expansion ought, to a significant extent, to be explicitly geared to the prospective demand for labor across the economy. This view, it is argued, requires direct state intervention in the provision of educational services and the methodology of manpower forecasting is best equipped to provide the necessary guidance. Both the need for manpower forecasting and the assumptions and methodology underlying its practice have been subject to considerable criticism since the 1960s, particularly from neoclassical economists. As a consequence some advocates and practitioners of manpower forecasting have qualified their approaches; others have carried on regardless. In some respects, the manpower forecasting debate of the 1960s and 1970s can be seen as a forerunner of the more generalized critique of development planning which emerged during the early 1980s.

1. Introduction

The central rationale behind national manpower forecasting is that shortages and surpluses of differently qualified groups of labor will constantly arise in the absence of planning, with a detrimental result to individuals and to society as a whole. Manpower forecasts, it is argued, can provide useful estimates of future demands for different types of labor and action can then be taken in time to ensure appropriate supplies. The removal of potential imbalances leads to increased national economic production and a higher level of average earnings. For the less developed countries (LDCs) that aim to make fundamental structural changes in their economies, forecasting the shifts in demand for different skills is held to be particularly necessary.

The government of the former Soviet Union was the first to make manpower forecasts which were then fed into educational decision-making. Following the Second World War and throughout the 1950s, governments and researchers in other countries gradually began producing forecasts. In Eastern Europe

these tended to have a comprehensive focus, while in the developed market economies forecasts tended to be limited to a small number of highly qualified occupations. One of the greatest upsurges in manpower forecasting in Europe occurred between 1962 and 1965 when six countries (Italy, Spain, Portugal, Yugoslavia, Greece, and Turkey) were the subject of a major Organisation for Economic Co-operation and Development (OECD) initiative to study the educational requirements for economic growth up to 1975 following a common methodology.

Among the LDCs, India was from early on a leading exponent of manpower forecasting in line with the overall comprehensive planning approach adopted. However, it was the decolonization measures taken in Africa at the end of the 1950s and in the early 1960s that provided the major stimulus to the growing concern with the economic dimension of education in general, and the manpower forecasting approach in particular. Many governments inherited only rudimentary educational structures, particularly at the postprimary level, and the numbers of qualified workers were small. As a result educational expansion was invariably given a high priority, and in most countries the search for an appropriate methodology on which to base this expansion led to some form of manpower forecasting. By 1970, 20 African governments had produced estimates of manpower requirements and there was a similarly widespread adoption of the approach throughout Southeast Asia and the countries of South America. The overall dominance of the manpower forecasting approach to educational planning in the early and mid-1960s was demonstrated by UNESCO. Of the 91 countries surveyed, 73 had education plans and 60 of these were based on forecasts of future manpower requirements. Blaug (1970) justly commented that "the concept of forecasting manpower requirements is today the leading method throughout the world for integrating educational and economic planning." This dominance has not been allowed to proceed uncontested.

2. The Theoretical Base of Manpower Forecasting

The purpose of making manpower forecasts is to ensure that supplies of manpower are available when new requirements arise. As a result, manpower shortages and surpluses can be avoided and output increased. An immediate question is why manpower demand and supply cannot simply be left to market mechanisms to be brought into equilibrium. Neoclassical economics suggests that any shortage of a particular type of manpower is only temporary. The immediate impact is an increase in wages. When this occurs, demand will fall as employers substitute other types of labor or other factors of production and a new short-run equilibrium will be reached. Simultaneously, the higher wage rate will increase supply. The process of adjustment will continue until the particular labor market is once again in long-term equilibrium. Two sets of assumptions are central to this line of argument. The first is that in disequilibrium the labor market produces the appropriate signals, for instance an increase in wages, to which both employers and the labor force react in the ways predicted—for instance, by substituting factors and increasing supply respectively. The second assumption is that it is possible for different factors of production to be easily substituted for each other without any substantial reduction in output. Advocates of manpower forecasting argue that both sets of assumptions are false.

To understand the objections to the market-clearing analysis, it is necessary to place the forecasting approach in its wider conceptual context. Essentially, manpower forecasting is grounded in a structuralist interpretation of the world (Colclough 1990). In contradiction of the neoclassical view of perfect markets and unconstrained, infinite flexibility in the economic system, structuralists argue that a series of inflexibilities and rigidities provide significant barriers to the efficient workings of the markets. These barriers are stable and systematic, and seriously influence market outcomes. Some of the barriers, such as lack of perfect knowledge, imperfect substitutabilities, and immobility of factors, may be termed "market imperfections." In addition, historical factors and institutional structures are also capable of constraining the various economic markets in their pursuit of efficient resource use. Generally, the structuralist interpretation of the world leads to a view that governments need to intervene in markets, and not merely for the provision of public goods.

Returning to the labor market, and to manpower forecasting, structuralists argue that a large number of rigidities are present which prevent wages being raised immediately in times of excess demand and that, when they do eventually increase, labor force reactions are not those postulated by neoclassicists. For instance, the facilities for increasing supply may simply not exist, and the mobility of labor between geographical areas and jobs may be low for a variety of cultural reasons. In addition, labor market information on wages, employment vacancies, and labor availability is often restricted. Most importantly, the training periods required for specialized manpower are of such a length that even if individuals do respond to higher wages by commencing a period of training, by the time they are trained either demand has fallen or so many others have responded in a similar way that an excess supply occurs.

The inadequacy of market forces to bring about equilibrium in the labor market may be used to justify state intervention in the provision of education, but is insufficient alone to justify long-term manpower forecasting as the basis for educational planning. Important here is the assumption that each level of national income and rate of economic growth requires specific types and levels of skills and that these, in turn, have quite precise implications for the educational system. Behind these assumptions are the concepts of fixed occupation–output coefficients and a direct connection between each occupation and a specific level of education. Even with perfect information in the labor market and no rigidities in its operation, potential output may be reduced by limited possibilities of substitution in the production process. Not surprisingly, the issue of substitution came to dominate the theoretical controversies relating to manpower forecasting. As Ahamad and Blaug (1973) point out, substitution is not solely a question of the effectiveness of different types of manpower; it is also one of their relative cost. The appropriate measure of substitution is, therefore, the partial elasticity of substitution as measured by the percentage change in the relative quantities of two types of manpower employed resulting from a 1 percent change in their relative earnings. If this is infinite, shortages of manpower will not constitute bottlenecks to increased output; if it is zero, output will fall substantially. However, efforts to measure elasticities of substitution, either directly by estimating derivatives of production functions, or through the use of international cross-sectional data, while suggesting that elasticities are positive, have as yet proved inconclusive. Proponents of the forecasting approach continue to maintain that substitution possibilities between various types of labor in particular, and between labor and capital in general, are low.

In summary, two main reasons are given for making manpower forecasts: (a) the imperfections and inadequacies in the labor market for coping with shortages and surpluses, and (b) the limited possibilities of substitution. Together, these are said to result in a reduced level of national output if shortages of manpower occur. Therefore, it is argued that attempts should be made to forecast future manpower requirements to enable appropriate supplies to be created. These forecasts can, in turn, provide the base for planning educational expansion.

3. Types of Manpower Forecasting

Although a common rationale underlies all attempts to forecast manpower requirements, several different approaches have been taken, largely on account of the varying degrees of data availabile. The approaches described below are employers' survey, international comparisons, labor–output ratios, and the Mediterranean Regional Project method. Full critical discussion of these approaches, and others, is to be found in Blaug (1970), Ahamad and Blaug (1973) and Psacharopoulos and Woodhall (1985).

3.1 Employers' Survey

One of the simplest methods of assessing manpower requirements is to ask employers directly to forecast their own labor requirements for the future. In the absence of data on past trends in the labor market, governments of LDCs have regularly used this approach. It has also been used in the United States, the United Kingdom, Canada, Sweden, and France, particularly with reference to technical and scientific manpower. In general, forecasts resulting from this approach tend to be short-term and more geared to overall employment policy than to manpower forecasting as a guide for educational planning.

The employer survey approach to manpower forecasting has a number of specific conceptual and operational difficulties. The usual approach taken is simply to ask employers to forecast their manpower requirements on, or up to, a particular date. Since employers are unlikely to make common assumptions about the future growth and structure of output, inconsistencies are very likely. Another problem concerns the weighting to give to individual employer's responses. While some may take much time and care in arriving at their estimates, and may even consider the impact of new technology, trends in relative salaries, and so on, others may simply guess. A simple aggregation will not reflect the variety in quality of forecast.

3.2 International Comparisons

A second approach to forecasting manpower requirements, and one which again largely owes its existence to a lack of domestic labor market information, particularly in the LDCs, is the use of international comparisons. These may either take the form of time-series data from a single country with experience that is regarded as particularly relevant, or of cross-sectional data from a range of countries. In the early years of manpower forecasting, what came to be known as the "Harbison rules of thumb" were particularly influential. These rules, which were said to be based on a number of countries' experiences, state that the growth of degree-equivalent and secondary-school manpower needs to be respectively two and three times the growth rate of national income. This approach to manpower forecasting and educational planning was followed particularly closely in Nigeria between 1960 and 1964 and formed the basis of the Ashby Report, one of the most widely publicized early educational planning exercises (Hinchliffe 1973). It was also applied in several East African and Southeast Asian countries. Later use of international comparisons resulted in the calculation of regression equations, relating levels of manpower stocks to variables such as levels of economic output or labor productivity.

The central problem of this whole approach to educational planning is that the jump from demonstrating existing relationships between, say, university graduates and the level of per capita income, to presuming that such relationships are necessary is not plausible. Stocks of manpower employed in individual countries at a single point in time are likely to be a result of both demand and supply. There is no way in which these stocks can be described as optimal. Using positions on the regression lines constructed from other countries' experiences as ones for which an individual country should aim assumes that each of these countries has a manpower structure perfectly suited to its level of national income. There is very little reason to believe that this will be the case.

3.3 Labor–Output Ratios

Labor–output ratios have mainly been used for forecasting requirements in single occupations requiring advanced qualifications: engineers, doctors, scientists, and teachers. The approach is basically simple and is founded on extrapolations of manpower per unit of output and the level of output. At its most sophisticated, this requires time-series data on output per worker cross-classified by sector, occupation, and educational qualification. More simply, linear regression equations relating an occupation, for instance, engineering, to national income have been utilized.

A variant of the labor–output approach is the use of density ratios. Here the ratio of a particular occupation to the total sectoral labor force is calculated. The size of this labor force is then forecast for future dates (on the basis of output and productivity forecasts) and divided by the ratio to give the occupational requirements. Calculations of output are central to all these approaches. In some cases, attempts are made to calculate value added, while in others, such as those of doctors and teachers, physical norms such as total population or school-age population are used. In the latter case, judgments concerning desirable doctor–patient and teacher–pupil ratios have to be made. If this is done on the basis of existing ratios, some conception of "best practice" (highest existing ratios), or extrapolation of past trends, any present disequilibria will simply be continued. Several discussions of single-occupation forecasting exercises that have used some type of labor–output ratio approach are included in Ahamad and Blaug (1973) and Youdi and Hinchliffe (1985).

3.4 The Mediterranean Regional Project

Forecasting requirements for occupations on an individual and independent basis could result in the aggregate requirements being greater than the anticipated size of the labor force. It is partly for this reason, and also because the whole occupational structure is relevant for purposes of educational planning, that attempts have been made to produce forecasting models that result in estimates of manpower requirements across the whole labor force simultaneously. An early and widely known model was that developed by Parnes for the OECD's Mediterranean Regional Project

(MRP). This approach follows six major steps. First, an estimate of total output in the economy and its composition between sectors at the target date is estimated. Second, so as to transform output targets to labor requirements by sector, estimates of future labor productivity are required. Third, each projected sectoral labor force needs to be disaggregated into occupational groups. At this point, numbers of workers in each occupation in each sector have been forecast. These are then aggregated across sectors. Finally, for the purposes of estimating requirements, the occupational requirements are converted into required educational stocks and again aggregated across occupations. From these requirements of educational stocks it is then necessary to subtract those workers in the current labor force who can be expected still to be working at the target date and the expected flows of graduates from the existing educational and training system. The result is the manpower gap and hence the base for changes to the system.

Although there are problems associated with most of these steps, the major criticisms of the MRP method have concentrated on those that involve forecasting occupational profiles and the required educational level of each occupation. In practice, shifts in occupational structures within sectors have been estimated by a variety of methods including international comparisons, extrapolation of past trends, and assumptions concerning "best practice" in leading firms and agencies. This diversity of approach simply reflects the fact that there is no agreement on the most successful way of estimating future occupational structures.

3.5 Summary

While each of the approaches to forecasting manpower requirements summarized above is distinctive, all, in their most basic forms, share the following positions: that it is possible to forecast levels of labor productivity with reasonable accuracy; that past, present, and future structures of employment are determined predominantly by demand or technically determined requirements and hardly at all by available supply; that only one occupational structure is likely to be consistent with each level and structure of output and/or labor productivity; that for a large number of occupations a specific optimal educational profile exists for each occupation; and that shortages in specific occupational categories requiring specific educational qualifications will result in significant falls in economic output.

As a result of adopting these positions, the approach has often been regarded as a technological rather than an economic one. However, it is possible to place the approach within a standard economic framework, although this requires a number of stringent assumptions. In its most extreme formulation these are that: (a) the demand for, and supply of, individual categories of labor are inelastic; and (b) the elasticity of substitution between different labor categories is zero. Critical in each of these is the supposition that wages have little or no effect on the demand for and supply of labor. Advocates of forecasting are, in practice, unlikely to take such extreme positions, but would rather argue that there is a tendency toward them. Similarly, critics of manpower forecasting do not generally assume infinite elasticities across the whole range of occupations and skills but, again, maintain there is a tendency in that direction. As suggested in Sect. 1, while tests of these assumptions derived from estimates of production functions in individual industries or from cross-sectional international data remain defective the debate will continue on the basis of only very partial evidence.

A further way in which the requirements approach departs from a standard economic framework is in the treatment of costs. Particular stocks of manpower are said to be required to reach specific social and economic targets. If the costs of meeting these requirements are judged to be too high the implication is that the targets are then revised down. However, the literature says little about the nature of this judgment and implies that in meeting social and economic targets the costs are always justified. In the event of resource constraints occurring at levels which could not allow all the required manpower to be produced, little direction is given in the approach regarding how to decide which categories to expand and which to curtail.

4. Evaluations of the Manpower Forecasting Approach

Three cross-national evaluations of manpower forecasting have been made since the early 1970s. The first, by Jolly and Colclough (1972), examined 33 manpower studies from 20 African countries made between 1960 and 1970. In these, projections of requirements were most often made by a simple expansion of the existing number of posts with no allowance made for changes in occupational or educational structures. Combining the effects of errors in projected economic growth rates with those for labor–output elasticities (on the basis of the 1970 OECD study), the conclusion was drawn that the requirements were considerably overestimated in a large majority of countries.

Recalculating manpower requirements on the basis of what were considered more reliable assumptions concerning the growth of output, elasticity of demand for manpower in relation to output growth, changes in real wages, and the elasticity of demand for manpower with respect to wage changes, Jolly and Colclough concluded that almost a quarter of the actual projections were within 10 percent of these, and almost all within 50 percent. Much of this apparent degree of reliability, however, appears to have resulted from compensating errors rather than from accuracy at each step of the calculation. Jolly and Colclough also discussed the extent to which manpower plans affected policy and whether the effects were positive or negative. One conclusion was that the plans had generally been used to influence opinion rather than as bases for action. Another was that the preoccupation with quantifiable aspects of labor policy often diverted attention from those aspects of training and informal education which could not be so easily treated in this way.

The second evaluation of manpower-requirements forecasting was made by Ahamad and Blaug (1973) in a review of 10 case studies covering the United States, the United Kingdom, France, Sweden, Thailand, India, and Nigeria. A general conclusion was that forecasts based on some form of the MRP approach demonstrated considerable errors in the forecasts of employment by occupation. These resulted not only from assumptions of fixed coefficients but also from errors in projecting total employment and labor productivity. For single occupation forecasts of teachers, doctors, and engineers forecasting errors were, again, often large. Not surprisingly, errors were generally greater in the longer term exercises. A central argument of the Ahamad and Blaug evaluation was that too much use had been made of the assumption that manpower inputs per unit of output are fixed parameters. The assumed nonexistence of substitutability, they contended, was unjustified. More generally, they argued that the case studies showed that forecasts of manpower imbalances are very sensitive to changes in each of the central assumptions of the manpower-requirements approach. When forecasts are short-term in nature, aimed at employment policy, the assumptions utilized are plausible and the resulting forecasts may be reasonably accurate. For purposes of educational planning, manpower-requirements forecasts need to be long-term. Increasingly over time, however, the central assumptions of low substitutability and malfunctioning of labor markets become less plausible. The final conclusion of the evaluation was that manpower structures cannot be accurately predicted 10 to 15 years ahead, and that forecasting has not so far proved useful for educational decision-making.

A more recent set of evaluations covered the experiences of 11 Western industrialized, East European, and less developed countries, mainly through the 1970s and early 1980s (Youdi and Hinchliffe 1985). Among the editors' conclusions were the following: the increased concentration of forecasts on single occupations; the diminished role of forecasting in countries where labor surpluses exist for all but a very few occupations; the continuing methodological problems associated with determining work norms and the degree of "specialist saturation" in East European countries; while forecasts of employment at a sectoral level have proved to be reasonably accurate, their conversion to educational and occupation requirements remains problematic, and there is a growing reluctance among practitioners to disaggregate the more global forecasts; job switching causes significant difficulties for assessing the need for newly trained workers; cost analyses continue to be virtually absent from manpower forecasting exercises; and that, despite the theoretical criticisms and negative evaluations of manpower forecasting, most less developed countries in the sample continue to follow the basic single forecast model. Half of the authors of the individual case studies were practicing manpower forecasters and half were academics. Despite the problems and acknowledged inaccuracies in many of the studies, none of the authors concluded that the activity should be totally rejected. The studies, however, did provide an additional impetus to a growing, though still only partially held view, that manpower forecasters needed to respond to their critics.

5. Reforms in Manpower Forecasting

The criticisms of manpower forecasting made essentially but not only by neoclassical economists, and the sets of relatively negative evaluations of the assumptions and outcomes led to some changes in focus from the early 1980s. Two trends can be distinguished in the early 1990s: first, a move away from an emphasis solely on techniques of planning to one which stresses the importance of planning as a process; and second, a shift from concentrating on a single approach and technique to a wider use of several modes of labor market analysis. Dougherty (1983) and Hollister (1983) were early exponents of this first trend, while Psacharopoulos (1991), as a forecasting critic, and Richter (1984), as a practitioner, have argued for the second trend. While the view that manpower forecasting needs to be an activity which responds to and informs policymakers in an orderly way is likely to strengthen, its replacement by a mixture of ad hoc studies and surveys coming under a general title of "labor market analysis" is less likely to do so. Labor market information systems have spread through the less developed countries since the early 1980s. However, proponents have so far made little headway in imparting the knowledge of how the information in these systems is to be used to inform education policymakers in investment choices. Perhaps more generally, the ultimate fate of manpower forecasting in the near future will depend on the form and outcome of the wider debate regarding neoclassical and structuralist views of the world.

References

Ahamad B, Blaug M (eds.) 1973 *The Practice of Manpower Forecasting: A Collection of Case Studies.* Elsevier, Amsterdam

Blaug M 1970 *An Introduction to the Economics of Education.* Penguin, Harmondsworth

Colclough C 1990 How can the manpower planning debate be resolved? In: Amjad R et al. 1990 *Quantitative Techniques in Employment Planning: Five Papers.* International Labour Organisation, ILO, Geneva

Dougherty C 1983 Manpower development planning from three points of view. In: Psacharopoulos G et al. 1983

Hinchliffe K 1973 Nigeria. In: Ahamad B, Blaug M (eds.) 1973

Hollister R 1983 A perspective on the role of manpower analysis and planning in developing countries. In: Psacharopoulos G et al. 1983

Jolly A, Colclough C 1972 African manpower plans: An evaluation. *Int. Lab. Rev.* 106(3): 207–64

Organisation for Economic Co-operation and Development (OECD) 1965 *The Mediterranean Regional Project.* OECD, Paris

Psacharopoulos G 1991 From manpower planning to labour market analysis. *Int. Lab. Rev.* 130: 459–70

Psacharopoulos G, Hinchliffe K, Dougherty C, Hollister R 1983 *Manpower Issues in Educational Investment: A Consideration of Planning Processes and Techniques.* World Bank Staff Working Paper No. 624. World Bank, Washington, DC

Psacharopoulos G, Woodhall M 1985 *Education for Development: An Analysis of Investment Choices.* Oxford University Press, New York

Richter L 1984 Manpower planning in developing countries: Changing approaches and emphases. *Int. Lab. Rev.* 123(6): 677–92

Youdi R, Hinchliffe K (eds.) 1985 *Forecasting Skilled Manpower Needs: The Experience of Eleven Countries.* UNESCO/IIEP, Paris

Overeducation

J. Bishop

"Overeducation" is a term which implies a judgment that a society (or an individual) has more education than is *required* or desirable. It is not a new idea, but can be found in *Ecclesiastes* (1:18): "He that increaseth knowledge, increaseth sorrow," and in the vernacular, "he knows more than is good for him." "Undereducation" implies the opposite judgment. This view is also not new; a Chinese proverb says "The schools of the country are its future in miniature." Whether a society is "undereducated," "overeducated," or neither of the above depends, of course, on the standard used to define required or desirable. Not surprisingly, analysts operating in the two main research traditions analyzing the economic role of education—manpower requirements and human capital—have different ways of defining overeducation and undereducation.

1. Manpower Requirements Perspective

In the manpower requirements paradigm, jobs and occupations have specific schooling requirements and the occupational skill demands of the economy are driven by forces external to the education sector such as consumer demand and technology. Training for skilled occupations takes many years so supplies of skilled workers cannot quickly adjust to current economic needs. Shifts in relative wage rates are not sufficient to equilibrate supply and demand for educated labor. An oversupply results in many workers having more schooling than is required by their job. This is presumed to cause job dissatisfaction, job turnover, lower productivity, and political discontent. An undersupply of skilled workers, "undereducation," creates bottlenecks which constrain economic growth. Two research programs unique to the manpower require-

ments paradigm employ this concept of overeducation:

(a) Estimates of the aggregate number of overeducated workers are made by counting mismatches between reported occupation and reported schooling.

(b) The impacts of overeducation on wages, productivity, job satisfaction, turnover, political alienation, and activism are studied.

1.1 Counting Aggregate Overeducation

Most studies define overeducation objectively as a mismatch between occupation and schooling in which the individual's reported schooling exceeds the amount that is presumed to be required by that job. This approach, however, suffers from two very serious measurement problems.

The reporting and coding of occupation and schooling is quite unreliable, so counts of mismatches significantly overstate their true frequency. United States Census Bureau studies have found that between 18.3 and 27.3 percent of individuals recorded as professionals, technicians, or managers in one interview, are recorded in a lower occupational category in a later interview. Furthermore, between 5.5 and 9 percent of respondents who are recorded as having 16 years of schooling or more in one interview are recorded as having fewer than 16 years of schooling in a later interview. These measurement problems mean that counts of mismatches between occupation and schooling derived from household survey data can produce truly incredible estimates. Tabulations of United States labor force surveys indicate, for example, that between 5.4 and 6.5 percent of the people who claim to be lawyers, physicians, and elementary/secondary school teachers also claim not to have completed 16 years of schooling (Bishop and Carter 1991). Given the laws regulating entry into these professions, these estimates of undereducation are clearly not credible. Neither are the corresponding estimates of overeducation. In United States labor force surveys conducted during the 1980s about 17 percent of those reporting 16+ years of schooling also said they worked in a retail sales, clerical, service, or manual job. Mismatches of this type occur frequently, but they are less common than the 17 percent figure suggests.

The second problem with interpreting mismatches as indicators of overeducation is that they might just as easily be the result of the poor quality of the education received by some college graduates. Seventeen percent of young American college graduates read at a level below the typical 11th grader (Bishop and Carter 1991). Isn't a college educated secretary with an 11th grade reading level undereducated rather than overeducated?

Countries outside North America also have quality control problems in higher education and difficulties measuring schooling and occupation, so educational leaders throughout the world need to be skeptical of national estimates of aggregate undereducation or overeducation based on counts of occupation–schooling mismatches.

1.2 Effects of Being Overeducated

A number of studies have been conducted of the effects of being overeducated on attitudes and wage rates. When you compare people in the same occupation, those with substantially above average schooling (those who are overeducated for the job) are paid more but not as much more as someone with the same level of schooling who has obtained a job that conventionally employs people with greater schooling. This is neither a new nor a surprising finding. Essentially the point is that, when people with the same amount of schooling are compared, those who are less successful in gaining access to high status occupations are paid less. This has been a common-place of the status attainment literature for two decades.

It has also been hypothesized that "overeducation" causes political alienation, job dissatisfaction and lower productivity. Burris (1983) examined many of these hypotheses and found that while modest levels of overeducation had no effects, the highly overeducated (the 3.6% of his American sample in which schooling exceeded the norm by at least 3 years) were less satisfied with their job and less likely to affirm an achievement ideology. There was, however, no tendency for highly overeducated workers to be more liberal, to vote Democratic or to be more politically alienated, and they were substantially more likely to identify themselves as middle class and to oppose welfare spending.

Tsang et al. (1991) report finding a tendency for highly overeducated males (but not females) to be more dissatisfied with their job and more likely to plan to leave it for another. They also tested for an effect of overeducation on drinking at work, energy level, and health, but found none. They appear to believe these results have great significance because they conclude "This study suggests that such action may be ineffective at best and counterproductive at worst" (p. 228). This statement is completely unjustified. Job satisfaction and plans to quit are not measures of worker productivity and are only weakly correlated with direct measures of productivity. There have been thousands of studies of specific jobs on the relationship between direct measures of productivity—supervisory ratings and work samples and years of schooling and key outcomes of schooling such as reading and mathematics achievement tests, together with meta analyses of this literature, have established that both of these correlations are positive. Indeed in most jobs, measures of the quality and output of schooling—reading, vocabulary and mathematical achievement test scores—are better predictors of job performance than interviews, references, ratings of training and experience, personality tests, and comprehensive background questionnaires (Hunter and Hunter 1984).

This literature further demonstrates that a core assumption of the manpower requirements framework—that specific jobs require particular minimum levels of basic reading and mathematical skills and that once those thresholds are reached, further improvements in basic skills yield sharply diminishing productivity benefits—is invalid. The hypothesis of diminishing returns to basic skills has been tested many times and about 95 percent of the time, it has been rejected. A recent test of this hypothesis in data on 31,000 workers found significant diminishing returns only for sales clerk jobs (Bishop 1993).

These results imply that the economic case for upgrading the basic skills of the general population does not rest solely on the pace at which high skill jobs replace low skill jobs or the extent to which "high performance" work systems replace conventional Tayloristic work systems. The fact that employment in high skill occupations grows much faster than employment in low skill occupations and high performance work sites are replacing Tayloristic work sites just strengthens the case for improving the quality of elementary and secondary education.

2. Human Capital Perspective

Most research on the economic role of education employs a human capital framework. Human capital theory tends to be more optimistic about the ability of the economy to put additional skill to good use if the price employers must pay for it declines. It focuses instead on what determines the supply of skilled labor. It starts with the premise that investments of the student's time, energy, and money in learning yield benefits over many years that are both pecuniary and onpecuniary. Expected benefits influence the decisions of some students about whether to attend, what to study, and how hard to study. When the demand for graduates in a particular field exceeds supply at current wage rates, relative wage rates rise stimulating employers to hire fewer workers trained in the field and attracting students into it and inducing them to accelerate their course of study. These student responses increase future supply and an equilibrium is established with a larger wage premium for the skill. Hence, if students are free to choose their field of study, there will be a tendency for the relative supplies of workers with different kinds of educational credentials to produce wage differentials which translate into rates of return comparable to those on alternative investments.

Rates of return will tend to be low if schools are free and easily accessible. If tuition is high, loans unavailable and admission requirements difficult to meet, high rates of return and substantial wage differentials will be necessary to attract enough students into university to supply future needs for college graduate workers. Deviations from this standard occur when large shifts in demand for or supply of graduates push the market into temporary disequilibrium, when barriers to entry (e.g., limits on the number of university places) or market failures prevent enrollment decisions from equalizing rates of return and when nonpecuniary benefits are particularly large or small.

Within the human capital paradigm terms like overeducation, oversupply, undereducation, and shortage have two quite different meanings. In the first usage these terms are descriptions of the general level of rates of return to schooling relative to historical patterns. The theme of Richard Freeman's 1976 book, *The Overeducated American*, was that rates of return to university education had fallen below previous levels. The human capital model predicts that periods of oversupply or undersupply will be temporary. There are two reasons for this. First, the circumstances that cause these disequilibria (the baby boom and the Vietnam War in the case of the 1970s oversupply of college graduates in the US) are themselves generally temporary. Second, very low (or high) rates of return set in motion a supply response (e.g., male college attendance rates in the US fell during the late 1970s) which, with a lag, tends to bring supply and demand back into balance.

Three research programs (which with modifications are shared by manpower requirements analysts) are implied by this concern for disequilibria in the balance between the supply and demand for skill:

(a) Assessments are made of the supply-demand balance for specific fields of study or occupations. (Manpower requirements analysts do this by counting the number of graduates in a field who are overeducated for their current job. Researchers operating in the human capital tradition focus on levels and rates of change of

wage premiums for skill and rates of return to training.)

(b) Historical trends in the supply-demand balance for skilled workers are analyzed.

(c) Planners forecast future skill needs and advise policymakers on how to adjust the supply of training slots to these forecasts.

Each of these research programs will be discussed in turn. Then the second usage of the terms "undereducation" and "overeducation" will be examined.

2.1 Supply-Demand Balance for Specific Fields of Study

Graduates from different university fields of study are not close substitutes for one another in the labor market. Consequently, there is not one labor market for college graduates, there are hundreds. At any given point in time some of these markets are likely to be oversupplied and others undersupplied.

The best indicators of whether a field is in oversupply or undersupply are the level and rate of change of the relative wages of people trained in that field. Unemployment rates and proportions of graduates from a program who take jobs that do not appear to require a college degree also provide useful information. Table 1 presents US and UK data on these indicators of the supply-demand balance by field of study. In both the United States and the United Kingdom, graduates in engineering, physical science, mathematics, business and economics fare the best. Unemployment was lower; proportions taking nonprofessional, nontechnical, and nonmanagerial (non-PTM) jobs were lower; and earnings premiums were higher than for other fields. These areas of study have two things in common: a substantial mathematics content and employment destinations primarily in the private sector.

Graduates in education and health fields have relatively low earnings but they apparently had little difficulty finding work in their field. Rates of unemployment and of taking non-PTM jobs were very low in these fields.

Graduates in humanities, social sciences other than economics, psychology, and biological sciences fared least well. Recent graduates experienced higher unemployment, higher rates of employment in non-PTM jobs, and lower monetary returns to a college degree. Humanities graduates, for example, were clearly in disequilibrium surplus during the 1970s. In 1976 starting pay was 10 percent below the wage of recent high school graduates. As a result, the share of American BAs awarded in English and foreign languages fell from 9 percent in 1971 to 3.7 percent in 1984. Since then, however, the share of BAs awarded in these two fields has risen and in 1990 it was 4.7 percent. This suggests that the nonpecuniary benefits of studying

Table 1
Wage premiums and underemployment of university graduates by field of study in the US and the UK

	United States						United Kingdom		
	1986/90 BA Recipients		BA Full-time starting salary premium over high school graduates working full-time with 1–5 yeas of experience			Earnings premium BAs over highschool graduates	Premium of university graduates' salaries 5 years after graduation over average earnings of all workers		
	Unemployment rate 1987/91	Full-time employment in non professional technical-management 1987/91	1991 Fem.	1987 M&F	1976 M&F	1984/87	1986	1976	1966
University Major	%	%	%	%	%	%	%	%	%
Engineering	4/3	6/7	165	130	89	180	49	41	102
Physical science and mathematics	4/5	12/10	124	95	8	120	48	30	91
Health	2/2	4/4	172	96	33	45	36	40	64
Business management and accounting	4/5	20/28	105	83	57	155	54	57	—
Law (7-yr degree in US)	—	—	—	—	—	(313)	62	27	124
Social science	8/5	28/31	76	76	3	72	26	25	—
economics						184	65	44	108
Biological science	7/4	26/16	79	42	0	81	28	23	74
Psychology	6/6	29/28	66	50	—	81	22	14	53
Humanities	8/6	32/33	61	40	−10	34	25	23	56
Education	3/2	13/11	63	37%	−3	24	6	13	37

Sources: Column 1–5 were calculated from National Center for Educational Statistics 1993 Tables 371, 372, and 375. Column 1 is the percent of those in the labor force who were unemployed. Column 2 is the share of graduates with fulltime jobs who were employed outside of professional, technical and managerial occupations and who report they did not need a college degree to get their job. Columns 3, 4, and 5 are the percentage by which the salary of bachelors degree recipients one year after graduation exceeded that of high school graduates with 1–5 years of work experience. Column 6 is derived from Kominski (1990). Table A and B. Columns 7–9 are from Table 1 of Dalton (1992)

English and foreign languages (and the 34–40% wage premium over high school graduates that prevailed since 1984) may be sufficient to induce 4 to 5 percent of American college students to major in the field even though a third of young humanities graduates are likely to be forced into non-PTM jobs, and earnings over their career are likely to be only one half of those of graduates in engineering, business, and economics.

What are the policy implications of these numbers? A manpower requirements economist would probably say there are still too many humanities majors. She would doubt that most students making this choice are aware that they have less than a one-third chance of getting a job "closely related" to their field of study. The number of jobs which use the writing and language skills developed by majors in these fields is limited, she would argue, so fewer graduates would mean fewer disappointed graduates and no change in the number finding related jobs.

From human capital economists would come a proposal to inform students of the job prospects of different fields of study. Many would also support scholarships for students in shortage fields such as engineering which aid competitiveness and technological progress. Most, however, would oppose placing caps on the number of humanities majors. They would be more inclined to think that students are aware of the economic consequences of majoring in English or a foreign language and are entering the field largely for nonpecuniary reasons. Poor as the job prospects may be for humanities BAs, high school graduates have it worse, they would argue. Recent high school graduates had 19 percent unemployment rates in 1987 and almost no chance of getting a job in a humanities field such as writing. To the point that the marginal humanities major will end up in a clerical job rather than a humanities job, they would respond that even if that is the true, job performance will improve somewhat as a result of the college experience.

2.2 Trends in the Supply-Demand Balance for Highly Educated Labor

The supply of college educated workers has been increasing rapidly all over the world. During the 1970s and 1980s the university graduate share of the population of working age grew at an annual rate of 3.34 percent in the United States, 3.55 percent in Japan, 2.75 percent in Germany, 5.6–5.8 percent in Sweden and Norway, 3.07 percent in Belgium, and 3.97 percent in Canada (OECD 1989).

Demand has also been growing rapidly. Occupations at the top of the skill continuum such as professionals, technicians, and managers (PT & M) jobs have been growing much more rapidly than manual (service, craft, operative, laborer, and farm occupations) jobs. In the United States the growth rate differential between PTM and manual jobs was 1.6 percent per year during the first half of the twentieth century, 1.9 percent per year between 1950 and 1970, 2.8 percent per year between 1970 and 1981, and 2.46 percent per year during the 1980s. The growth rate advantage of PTM jobs is even more striking in Europe and Japan. Japan's rate was 4.27 percent per year in the 1970s and 3.26 percent per year in the 1980s. Germany's rate was 3.67 percent per year in the 1970s and 2.53 percent per year in the 1980s (Bishop 1992).

Demand for highly educated workers also grows when employers decide that new hires should have greater amounts of previous training either because (a) the job has become more complex; (b) quality and job performance targets have increased; or (c) workers with school provided training have become less costly. Looking over a 70-year period, one can clearly see that most occupations—management, medicine, teaching, engineering, construction, social services, military, financial services, and manufacturing—have become more complicated. Only a few occupations—laborers, retail sales clerks, photographers, musicians, and truck drivers—have apparently not increased in complexity.

As sales, transactions, and output per worker grow, so do the costs of making mistakes and the benefits of higher quality. This has meant that it pays to strive for higher standards of performance and quality even when tasks remain unchanged. For many years there was controversy about the effect of technological progress on skill demands of specific occupations. Now, however, the predominant view is that complexity, responsibility, abstractness, and interdependence have risen in most occupations (Hirschorn 1986).

The third source of increased demand for educated workers is the transfer to schools of training tasks formerly the province of apprenticeships and employer training. The switch of training functions to schools is a natural part of the life cycle of a technology and its associated skills. As a technology matures and its use grows, the technology and its associated skills become standardized (i.e., general rather than firm specific), the demand for formal training grows, and schools enter the market as training providers. Once skills become standardized, schools have natural advantages as competitors in this market: (a) they offer students flexibility in scheduling and the choice of courses, (b) hourly costs of training are lower because teaching staff are specialized and economies result from spreading the cost of developing courses over many students,

(c) school certification of skills makes them more portable, and (d) schools and students have access to public subsidies not available when training takes place at a firm. When schools become major training providers, barriers to entry into the occupation and the industry fall, the supply of skilled workers grows, the costs of employing people with the skill fall, and expanded use of the technology is facilitated. Almost every medium and high level occupation (e.g., typists, computer programmers, lawyers, and plumbers) has been through this evolution (Flynn 1988).

In most countries and most historical periods, percentage growth rates of highly educated workers have been higher than the percentage growth rates of high level occupations. Some researchers have attempted to measure other sources of increased demand for highly educated workers and then, comparing their measure of increased demand to the growth of supply, have claimed to have evidence of secular increases in "overeducation" (Rumberger 1981). This exercise is futile, however. There is no way of measuring independently how employer hiring standards are influenced by technical progress and the entry of schools into new training markets. The only way to know what has happened to the supply–demand balance for highly educated workers is to infer it from changes in the rate of return to schooling, relative unemployment rates, and proportions of graduates reporting their job does not make use of the skills developed in college. The wage premium for university graduates declined in most European countries during the 1960s and 1970s but has tended to stabilize or rise during the 1980s. At the end of the 1980s the average of the male and female earnings premiums for 45- to 64-year old university graduates was 42 percent in Denmark, 52 percent in Sweden, 66 percent in the United Kingdom, 70–72 percent in Australia and Canada, and 81–82 percent in Finland, the Netherlands, and the United States (OECD 1992).

2.3 Forecasting the Supply–Demand Balance for Highly Educated Workers

It is extremely difficult to make accurate forecasts of the supply–demand balance for highly educated labor. Small errors in forecasting rates of change of either demand or supply translate into big errors in projections of the gap between supply and demand.

An accurate forecast requires not only accurate predictions of the growth rates of hundreds of occupations, it requires accurate predictions of changes in the hiring standards for these occupations. Innovations such as high performance micro-computers, fiber optic telecommunications, global sourcing of parts and high performance work systems are bound to influence skill demands in the year 2005. But who knows how big the effects will be?

It should come as no surprise, therefore, that published forecasts of the balance between supply and demand for highly educated workers based on the

379

manpower requirements paradigm have almost always been far off the mark. Seymour Harris's forecast of the United States labor market for college graduates was one of the first. He predicted in 1949 that:

> a large proportion of the potential college students within the next twenty years are doomed to disappointment after graduation, as the number of coveted openings will be substantially less than the numbers seeking them. (Harris 1949 p. 64)

As predicted the number of college educated workers grew dramatically, but the predicted oversupply failed to materialize because professional–technical share of the workforce grew dramatically as well, from 8.4 percent in 1950 to 13.7 percent in 1970. In fact, demand for college graduates must have grown faster than supply because the wage premium of college graduates with 1–10 years of work experience over high school graduates with similar levels of experience rose from 45 percent to 76 percent.

The US Bureau of Labor Statistics projections of the supply–demand balance for college graduates have been similarly flawed. In 1970 they predicted demand and supply would be in balance during the 1970s; a surplus ensued and college wage premiums fell. In 1980 they predicted a surplus for the 1980s; a shortage ensued and the wage premium for college graduates rose dramatically (Bishop and Carter 1991).

Richard Freeman, an economist whose work reflects the human capital perspective, has a much better forecasting record. He correctly predicted in 1976 that the college wage differential would continue to decline during the 1970s and then turn up during the 1980s (Freeman 1976).

3. Chronic Undereducation

In the second usage of terms like "undereducation" and "overeducation", a claim is being made that there is a *chronic* tendency for individuals to underinvest or overinvest in education relative to some social standard. Student decisions are motivated by the expectation of benefits that will accrue to themselves and their families, not by benefits that may accrue to others. Yet we all benefit when those we interact with have real expertise. Not only do such individuals pay more taxes and receive fewer government transfer benefits, they are more likely to make discoveries or innovations which benefit others, more likely to fix the car correctly the first time, and less likely to make mistakes which injure co-workers, customers, or the public. Economists call social benefits such as these "spillovers" or "externalities." Private decisions will lead to an insufficient quantity and quality of education and training and insufficient achievement by students, unless public agencies subsidize costs or add to the rewards. The optimal amount and character of public intervention in the education market depends on the size and character of these spillover benefits.

3.1 Years Spent in School Margin

By compelling attendance, subsidizing instructional costs, building schools in convenient locations, and providing financial aid, society induces students to choose more years of schooling than they would choose on their own. In the absence of such interventions, we would clearly live in a world of chronic underschooling. Is the current level of government support for schooling the correct level? That is much more difficult to say. Some of the spillover benefits of schooling—the tax and social insurance effects—are measurable, but most are not. Economists have tackled this issue by calculating a *lower bound* on the social rate of return to schooling. Lower bound social rates of return are calculated by comparing the impact of schooling on before tax earnings (substracting that component of the earnings differential actually due to ability and family background advantages) to the total costs (both instructional costs and student time costs) of schooling. Since the benefits of schooling accrue over many years, they must be discounted to the present before they can be compared to costs. The lower bound social rate of return to schooling is the interest rate which exactly equates discounted measurable social benefits and social costs. If this lower bound social rate of return is equal to or above the social rate of return on physical capital, a society might be said to be underschooled. If, on the other hand, the lower bound social rate of return is below the social rate of return on physical capital, we are left uncertain about whether the society is underschooled or overschooled. The answer depends on the importance of the unmeasured spillover benefits of schooling—the discoveries and innovations; greater political, racial, and religious tolerance; and so on.

3.2 Achievement Margin

Spending too few years in school is only one of the ways students may underinvest in education. How much is learnt and how expert a student becomes depends as much on individual study effort, as on the number of years spent in school. Society tries to encourage students to study harder by recruiting inspiring teachers, by conditioning access to higher levels of schooling and well-paid fields of study on performance in school, by awarding credentials only to those who achieve a minimum level of competency in their field, and by providing references for graduates who are entering the labor market. Expertise is notoriously difficult to measure, however, and the credentials that schools award do a poor job of signaling it (particularly the kinds of expertise that employers are seeking). Credentials are well rewarded by the labor market. Holding credentials constant, however, greater expertise is under-rewarded. The incentives facing students are thus to put sufficient effort into their studies to get the credential, but to do little more. This is the outcome in the United States where the

igh school diploma signals time spent in school and
tot educational achievement. Such an outcome can be
egitimately characterized as chronic undereducation.

When educational systems provide finely graded
certifications of academic accomplishment but ignore
accomplishments relevant to employment such as
computer literacy, teamwork, and occupational skills,
the likely result is chronic miseducation—students
studying subjects which schools think are important
but the labor market does not. Japan, the United
Kingdom and many developing countries suffer from
this kind of problem. The German dual-system and
the new French *baccalauréat* (with its technical Bacs)
should be less subject to these problems. However, it
is very difficult to keep instruction and credentialing
up to date and in line with a nation's economic and social needs, so miseducation and undereducation along
some important dimensions can never be banished
from an educational system.

The question "What should our youth learn?" inevitably sparks controversy. What is miseducation or
overeducation to one individual is "proper regard for
our cultural heritage" to another. Those who claim that
overeducation is chronic use a "Does your job require
that you know it?" standard to judge what should be
taught. Even if one were to accept their analysis of economic demand for learning and skills, this would be
a very limiting conception of the nature of education.
Surely better jobs are not the only reason for getting an
education. What about desires to appreciate literature
better or to make a discovery that will improve the
lives of others?

The analysis just completed implies that
overeducation can occur only when government gets
too aggressive in promoting and subsidizing it. In
the absence of such subsidies a society will be both
underschooled and undereducated. Surely it is possible
for governments to make mistakes. But how else is a
society to make collective value judgements regarding
the importance of spillovers such as discoveries, innovations and political, religious, and racial tolerance—
other than through democratic political institutions?
Those who want to prove that chronic overeducation
exists would be well advised, therefore, to focus their
efforts on a political theory showing why democratic
political systems should have a systematic tendency to
overinvest in education. The job requirements theory that
has been used in the past appears to be a dead end.

See also: Manpower Analysis; Education and Productivity; Demand and Supply Elasticities for Educated Labor; Education and Technological Change

References

Bishop J 1993 Improving job–worker matching in the US labor market: What is the role of the Employment Service? In: Bailey M, Winston C (eds.) *Brookings Papers on Economic Activity; Microeconomics.* The Brookings Institution, Washington, DC
Bishop J, Carter S 1991 The worsening shortage of college graduate workers. *Educational Evaluation and Policy Analysis* 13(3): 221–55
Burris V 1983 The social and political consequences of overeducation. *American Sociological Review* 48(4): 454–67
Dalton P 1992 The market for qualified manpower in the UK. *Oxford Review of Economic Policy* 8(2): 103–29
Harris S 1949 *The Market for College Graduates and Related Aspects of Education and Income*: Harvard University Press, Cambridge, Massachusetts
Hunter J, Hunter R F 1984 Validity and utility of alternative predictors of job performance *Psycho. Bull.* 96(1): 72–98
Kominski R 1990 *What's it Worth? Educational Background and Economic Status: Spring 1987.* US Bureau of the Census, Current Population Reports, P–70, No. 21
National Center for Educational Statistics 1993 *Digest of Education Statistics: 1993.* Department of Education, Washington, DC.
Organisation of Economic Co-operation and Development 1989 OECD *Employment Outlook July 1989.* OECD, Paris
Organisation of Economic Co-operation and Development 1992 *Education at a Glance: OECD Indicators.* OECD, Paris
Rumberger R 1981 The changing skill requirements of jobs in the US economy. *Industrial and Labor Relations Review* 34(4): 578–90
Tsang Mun, Rumberger R, Levin H 1991 The impact of surplus schooling on worker productivity. *Industrial Relations* 30(2): 209–28
Bishop J 1992 Schooling, learning and worker productivity. In: Asplund R (ed.) *Human Capital and Scandinavian Labor Markets.* Elinkeinoelaman Tutkimuslaitos Näringslivets Forskningsinstitut (ETLA), Helsinki
Flynn P 1988 *Facilitating Technological Change: The Human Resource Challenge.* Ballinger, Cambridge, Massachusetts
Freeman R 1976 *The Overeducated American.* Academic Press, New York
Hirschorn L 1986 *Beyond Mechanization* MIT Press, Cambridge, Massachusetts

Cost-effectiveness Analysis

H. M. Levin

Cost-effectiveness analysis refers to the consideration of decision alternatives in which both their costs and consequences are taken into account in a systematic way. It is a decision-oriented tool, in that it is designed to ascertain which means of attaining particular educational goals are most efficient. For example, there are many alternative approaches for pursuing such goals as raising reading or mathematics achievement. These include the adoption of new materials or curriculum, teacher training, educational television, computer-assisted instruction, smaller class sizes, and so on. The cost-effective solution to this challenge is to ascertain the costs and effects on reading or mathematics achievement of each alternative and to choose that alternative which has the greatest impact on raising achievement scores for any given resource outlay.

Cost-effectiveness analysis is closely related to cost–benefit analysis in that both represent economic evaluations of alternative resource use and measure costs in the same way (see *Cost–Benefit Analysis*). However, cost–benefit analysis is used to address only those types of alternatives where the outcomes can be measured in terms of their monetary values. For example, educational alternatives that are designed to raise productivity and income, such as vocational education, have outcomes that can be assessed in monetary terms and can be evaluated according to cost–benefit analysis. However, most educational alternatives are dedicated to improving achievement or some other educational outcome that cannot be easily converted into monetary terms. In these cases, one must limit the comparison of alternatives to those that have similar goals by comparing them through cost-effectiveness analysis.

The purpose of cost-effectiveness analysis in education is to ascertain which program or combination of programs can achieve particular objectives at the lowest cost. The underlying assumption is that different alternatives are associated with different costs and different educational results. By choosing those with the least cost for a given outcome, society can use its resources more effectively. Those resources that are saved through using more cost-effective approaches can be devoted to expanding programs or to other important educational and social endeavors.

Cost-effectiveness analysis was developed in the 1950s by the United States Department of Defense as a device for adjudicating among the demands of the various branches of the armed services for increasingly costly weapons systems with different levels of performance and overlapping missions (Hitch and McKean 1960). By the 1960s it had become widely used as a tool for analyzing the efficiency of alternative government programs outside of the military, although its applications to educational decisions have been much slower to develop. Indeed, in the early 1990s the use of the tool in considering educational resource allocation is restricted largely to the United States and has not emerged as a decision approach to resource allocation in other countries.

1. Measuring Cost-effectiveness

The basic technique has been to derive results for educational effectiveness of each alternative by using standard evaluation procedures or studies (Rossi and Freeman 1985) and to combine such information with cost data that are derived from the ingredient approach. The ingredients approach was developed to provide a systematic way for evaluators to estimate the costs of social interventions (Levin 1983). It has been applied not only to cost-effectiveness problems, but also to determining the costs of different educational programs for state and local planning (Hartman 1981).

1.1 Assessing Effectiveness

Before starting the cost analysis, it is necessary to know what the decision problem is, how to measure effectiveness, which alternatives are being considered and what their effects are. If a problem has risen on the policy agenda that requires a response, a careful understanding of the problem is crucial to addressing its solution (Levin 1983 pp. 34–35). Once the problem has been formulated, it will be necessary to consider how to assess the effectiveness of alternatives. For this purpose, clear dimensions and measures of effectiveness will be needed. Table 1 shows examples of effectiveness measures that respond to particular program objectives.

Given the problem and criteria for assessing the effectiveness of proposed solutions, it is necessary to formulate alternative programs or interventions. The search for such interventions should be as wide ranging and creative as possible. This procedure sets the stage for the evaluation of effectiveness of the alternatives, a process which is akin to the standard use of evaluation methods (e.g., Rossi and Freeman 1985). Estimates of effectiveness can be derived from previous evaluations or from tailored evaluations for the present purpose.

It is important to emphasize that the evaluation of effectiveness is separable from the evaluation of costs. Most standard evaluation designs for assessing the effectiveness of an intervention are also suitable for incorporation into cost-effectiveness studies. These can be found in the standard evaluation literature (see e.g., Cook and Campbell 1979, Rossi and Freeman 1985). The cost analysis is not typically found in the general evaluation literature and has been developed independently as a subspecialization (Levin 1983).

1.2 Cost Estimation

The costs of an intervention are defined as the value of the resources that are given up by society to effect the intervention. These are referred to as the ingredients of the intervention, and it is the social value of those ingredients that constitute its overall cost. At a later stage the distribution of these costs among the decision-making agency and other entities can be assessed. Accordingly, the method sets out systematically to identify and ascertain the value of the ingredients that are required for each alternative that is under consideration.

The ingredients approach to cost estimation entails three distinct phases: (a) identification of ingredients; (b) determination of the value or cost of the ingredients and the overall costs of an intervention; and (c) an analysis of the costs in an appropriate decision-oriented framework.

The first step is to ascertain which ingredients are required for an intervention (Levin 1983 Chap. 3). Most educational interventions are labor-intensive, so an initial concern is to account for the number and characteristics of personnel. It is important to stipulate whether personnel are part-time or full-time and the types of skills or qualifications that they need. Beyond this it is necessary to identify the facilities, equipment, materials, and other ingredients or resources which are required for the intervention.

Identification of ingredients requires a level of detail that is adequate to ensure that all resources are included and are described adequately to place cost values on them. For this reason, the search for ingredients must be systematic rather than casual.

The primary sources for such data are written reports, observations, and interviews. Written reports usually contain at least a brief history and description of the intervention. Other sources of information must be used to corroborate and supplement data on ingredients from evaluations and descriptive reports. If the intervention is present at a nearby site, it may be possible to visit and gather additional data on ingredients through observation. A third valuable source is that of interviews, where present or former personnel are asked to identify resources from among a

number of different classifications. The three principal types of information—reports, observations, and interviews—can be used to assure the accuracy of the data by comparing the findings from each source and reconciling differences, the process of triangulation.

Once the ingredients have been identified and stipulated, it is necessary to ascertain their costs (Levin 1983 Chap. 4). In doing this, all ingredients are assumed to have a cost, including donated or volunteer resources. That is, they have a cost to someone, even if the sponsoring agency did not pay for them in a particular situation. At a later stage the costs will be distributed among the constituencies who paid them, but at this stage the need is to ascertain the total costs of the intervention.

Ingredients can be divided into those that are purchased in reasonably competitive markets, and those that are obtained through other types of transactions. In general, the value of an ingredient for costing purposes is its market value. In the case of personnel, market value may be ascertained by determining what the costs would be for hiring a particular type of person. Such costs must include not only salary, but also fringe benefits and other employment costs that are paid by the employer. Many of the other inputs can also be costed by using their market prices. These include the costs of equipment, materials, utilities, and so on. Clearly the cost of leased facilities can also be ascertained in this way.

Although the market prices of some ingredients such as personnel can often be obtained from accounting data for educational enterprises, such data are not reliable sources for ascertaining overall program costs. The accounting systems that are used by schools were designed for ensuring consistent reporting to state agencies rather than for providing accurate and consistent cost data on educational interventions. For example, they omit completely or understate the cost of volunteers and other donated resources. Capital improvements are charged to such budgets and accounts during the year of their purchase, even when the improvements have a life of 20–30 years. Normal cost accounting practices would ascertain the annual costs of such improvements by spreading them over their useful lives through an appropriate method (Levin 1983 pp. 67–71). Thus, data from accounting and budgetary reports must be used selectively and appropriately and cannot be relied upon for all ingredients.

There exist a variety of techniques for ascertaining the value of ingredients that are not purchased in competitive markets. For example, the method for ascertaining the value of volunteers and other contributed ingredients is to determine the market value of such resources if they had to be purchased. The value of facilities can be determined by estimating their lease value. The annual value of facilities and equipment can be estimated through a relatively

Table 1

Examples of effectiveness measures

Program objective	Measure of effectiveness
Program completions	Number of students completing program
Reducing dropouts	Number of potential dropouts who graduate
Employment of graduates	Number of graduates placed in appropriate jobs
Student learning	Test scores in appropriate domains utilizing appropriate test instruments
Student satisfaction	Student assessment of program on appropriate instrument to measure satisfaction
Physical performance	Evaluation of student physical condition and physical skills
College placement	Number of students placed in colleges of particular types
Advance college placement	Number of courses and units received by students in advance placement, by subject

simple approach that takes account of depreciation and interest foregone by the remaining capital investment. Details for these techniques are found in Levin (1983 Chap. 4).

1.3 Combining into Cost-effectiveness

Once each of the ingredients is costed, these can be added to obtain a total cost for the intervention. The next stage entails the use of these costs in an analytic framework (Levin 1983 Chap. 5). The two most important concerns for cost summary and analysis are (a) the appropriate unit for expressing costs and (b) who pays the costs.

Clearly, the question of the appropriate unit for expressing costs depends upon how effectiveness is measured and the nature of the decision. Usually, educational effectiveness is measured in terms of achievement gains per student or some other per-student measure. In that case, it is necessary to convert total costs to a per-student cost figure for comparing cost-effectiveness of alternative interventions. Cost-effectiveness ratios are usually based upon the average effects and costs per student. However, it is possible to do an analysis on total project or program costs and effects. In other cases it may be the additional or marginal costs versus additional or marginal effectiveness that is the subject of scrutiny. For example, one may want to ascertain the number of additional students who will graduate from high school relative to the additional costs of alternative approaches for reducing dropouts.

A very different issue is who pays the costs. The overall cost-effectiveness ratio may be irrelevant to a decision-maker who pays only part of the costs for one intervention, but all of the costs for an alternative. For this reason, it is important to ascertain total costs of an intervention and to separate out those that are borne by the decision-maker in considering different alternatives. However, it should be remembered that since different decision-making units have different opportunities to obtain volunteers and contributed resources, it is inappropriate to assume any particular cost subsidy to the decision-maker. The basic estimate of costs that is used for all subsequent cost analyses is the overall cost of the intervention. Subsequent analyses can distribute the costs among those who will bear them to ascertain the implications of that distribution for decisions.

The most common measure of cost-effectiveness is the cost-effectiveness ratio, namely, the effectiveness of an alternative divided by its cost. When this is done for each alternative, it is possible to see which of the alternatives yields the best outcomes per unit of cost. For example, one might wish to examine different alternatives for raising student achievement by comparing the cost per additional achievement gains. In principle, the alternative with the lowest cost per achievement gain would be the

most desirable. However, it is important to know if differences in cost-effectiveness ratios are large or small. If the differences are small, it is probably wise to weigh more fully other criteria in making the decision such as the ease of implementation or previous experience of staff. If the differences in cost-effectiveness are large, it is important to place greater weight on the cost-effectiveness criteria while still considering other factors that were not considered in the analysis.

Finally, it is important to mention the issue of scale. In general, those alternatives with high fixed costs such as those with large investments in facilities and equipment will require a high enrollment or utilization to reach their best cost—effectiveness ratios. The reason for this is that fixed costs represented by a building or an educational television network of transmitters and receiving stations cannot be readily adjusted to demand and must be fully utilized to obtain the lowest level of cost per unit of output. In contrast, alternatives that are constituted largely of variable costs such as personnel will have costs that are less sensitive to the scale of output. Variable costs are derived from inputs or ingredients that can be readily increased or decreased. Thus, a comparison of cost-effectiveness of alternatives that differ in terms of their intensities of fixed versus variable costs may produce very different results depending upon the scale of enrollment or output. Accordingly, estimates should be made among the alternatives for the specific levels of output that are pertinent rather than assuming a general pattern from cost estimation at only one level of scale.

2. Educational Applications

Cost-effectiveness studies have been carried out on teacher training (Tatto et al. 1991), teacher selection (Levin 1970), educational television and radio (Jamison et al. 1978), choice of a mathematics curriculum (Quinn et al. 1984), computer-assisted instruction (Levin et al. 1987) and also increasing the school day, reducing class size, and cross-age tutoring (Levin et al. 1987). Lockheed and Hanushek (1988) have provided a good summary of cost-effectiveness studies of educational radio and of textbook provision for several countries. Their comparisons among studies and interventions should be viewed cautiously given that the studies were done independently for different years (with no standardization for changes in price levels or exchange rates) and are not necessarily based upon the same cost methodology.

2.1 Educational Television

The 1970s witnessed a great interest in educational television as a way of improving educational quality in developing countries, as well as expanding their educational systems (Mayo et al. 1975, Jamison et al. 1978). In many developing societies adequate numbers of trained teachers are unavailable—particularly in rural areas—or populations are so sparsely distributed that there are not adequate numbers of students in school attendance boundaries to justify minimum personnel requirements. Educational television has been viewed as an alternative for delivering instruction that might be less costly and that also might raise the quality of education. Studies were undertaken of educational television as a partial replacement for teachers in rural areas where examination test scores were used as a basis for effectiveness. Such studies found that the television was relatively cost-effective in comparison with traditional schools in that it produced comparable student achievement at lower cost (Mayo et al. 1975). However, these results depended heavily on certain assumptions which were highly controversial, illustrating the fact that cost-effectiveness comparisons must be reviewed carefully before using them for decision-making (Carnoy and Levin 1975).

2.2 Curriculum

Curriculum is an area that is very appropriate for cost-effectiveness analysis. In the quest for educational improvement, schools face numerous ways in which they can organize the pace, content, and method of instruction. Some are likely to be more effective than others, and there may also be substantial differences in resource requirements with respect to such ingredients as teacher time, materials, equipment, and so on. As with many other areas of education, the potential for using cost-effectiveness analysis has barely been tapped in the curriculum field.

An excellent cost-effectiveness study of fifth grade mathematics curriculum was carried out by Quinn et al. (1984). Their evaluation compared two approaches to teaching mathematics, a traditional curriculum and an alternative one. Using the ingredients method, the researchers found that the alternative mathematics program cost about 50 percent more than the traditional mathematics program, but the effectiveness of the alternative program was also higher. Depending upon how student achievement was measured, the alternative mathematics program was found to be from 60 percent to 300 percent more cost-effective—cost per point of achievement score—than the traditional program.

2.3 Teacher Training

A study of teacher training in Sri Lanka compared the cost-effectiveness of training in colleges of education and in teachers' colleges as well as through distance education (Tatto et al. 1991). Teacher performance and pupil achievement were used as measures of effectiveness. Teachers who had received distance education were almost as effective as those trained in colleges of education and teachers' college, but the costs of their training were a small fraction of the costs of institutional training. In a country that has a shortage of teachers, it appears that expansion of qualified teachers could be done more efficiently using distance education.

2.4 General Comparisons of Reform Alternatives

An attempt was made to compare a variety of educational reforms that had been suggested for improving schools in the United States. In the early 1980s, such reports suggested a general reform agenda that included a large variety of alternatives. Levin et al. (1987) investigated four of these for which there were adequate effectiveness data as well as a basis for estimating costs. These four alternatives included computer-assisted instruction (CAI), a longer school day, smaller class sizes, and peer tutoring. Each was associated with acceptable effectiveness studies that had assessed the effects of the reform on student achievement scores at the elementary level in both mathematics and reading.

More specifically, the CAI consisted of daily sessions of 10 minutes of drill and practice on a computer using an approach that has received wide adoption both in the United States and in other countries. The increase in the length of the school day comprised a total of one hour, divided equally between instruction in mathematics and reading. Changes in class size were evaluated for reductions from 35 to 30 students; 30 to 25 students; 25 to 20 students; and 35 to 20 students. Peer tutoring was evaluated for a program in which fifth and sixth grade students tutored second grade students for 15 minutes a day.

Costs were estimated by using the ingredients approach. They were summarized according to the cost per student for each subject. The least costly interventions were reductions in class size of five students and increasing the length of the school day. The most costly was peer tutoring because it requires adult coordinators. The costs of peer tutoring were about four times as great as reducing class size by five students or increasing instructional time by one half hour a day per subject and twice as great as the daily sessions of CAI.

In terms of effectiveness, peer tutoring showed the largest effects, nearly a year of achievement gain in mathematics and about one-half year in reading. The longer school day and reduction of class size by five students showed the smallest effects. CAI was associated with gains in the middle of the range of results.

Cost-effectiveness was determined by combining costs and effectiveness in terms of the estimated annual costs to obtain an additional month of student achievement per year of instruction. According to this study, an additional month of mathematics achievement would cost about US$200 a year with a longer school day, but only about US$22 a year with peer tutoring. In fact, a longer school day was less than half as cost-effective in raising mathematics achievement as was CAI or reducing class size, despite the prominence of calls for longer school days in the national reports on educational reform. The most cost-effective approach, peer tutoring, required only one-ninth of the resources to obtain the same effect on mathematics achievement as increasing the school day.

To obtain an additional month of reading achievement would cost about twice as much for increasing the school day as using peer tutoring, with CAI almost as efficient as the latter. Reducing class size appears to be particularly inefficient with respect to raising reading achievement. Although its effectiveness is very high, its cost is also high. These results provide useful information in comparing instructional strategies to raise achievement.

See also: Education Production Functions; Cost Analysis in Education; Cost-Benefit Analysis

References

Carnoy M, Levin H M 1975 Evaluation of educational media: Some issues *Instr. Sci.* 4(3/4): 385–406
Cook T D, Campbell D T 1979 *Quasi-Experimentation.* Houghton Mifflin, Boston, Massachusetts
Hartman W T 1981 Estimating the costs of educating handicapped children: A resource–cost model approach summary report. *Educ. Eval. Policy Anal.* 3(4): 33–48
Hitch C J, McKean R N 1960 *The Economics of Defense in the Nuclear Age.* Harvard University Press, Cambridge, Massachusetts
Jamison D, Klees S, Wells S 1978 *The Costs of Educational Media: Guiddiness for Planning and Evaluation.* Sage, Beverly Hills, California
Levin H M 1970 Cost-effectiveness analysis of teacher selection. *J. Hum. Resources* 5(1): 24–33
Levin H M 1983 *Cost-Effectiveness: A Primer.* Sage Beverly Hills, California
Levin H M, Glass G V, Meister G 1987 A Cost-effectiveness analysis of computer-assisted instruction. *Eval. Rev.* 11(1): 50–72
Lockheed M E, Hanushek E 1988 Improving educational efficiency in developing countries: What do we know? *Compare* 18(1): 21–38
Mayo J, McAnany E, Klees S 1975 The Mexican telesecundaria: A cost-effectiveness analysis. *Instr. Sci.* 4(3/4): 193–236
Quinn B, VanMondfrans A, Worthen B R 1984 Cost-effectiveness of two math programs as moderated by pupil SES. *Educ. Eval. Policy Anal.* 6(1): 39–52
Rossi P H, Freeman H E 1985 *Evaluation: A Systematic Approach*, 3rd edn. Sage, Beverly Hills, California
Tatto M T, Nielsen D, Cummings W, Kularatna N G, Dharmadasa K H 1991 *Comparing the Effects and Costs of Different Approaches for Educating Primary School Teachers: The Case of Sri Lanka.* Bridges Project, Harvard Institute for International Development, Cambridge, Massachusetts

Cost Analysis in Education

M. C. Tsang

Many important decisions in education are concerned with the costs of education. Cost analysis can reveal the cost implications of an educational policy, assess the financial feasibility of an educational reform, provide diagnosis of past and current resource utilization in education, project future educational cost requirements, and evaluate the relative efficiency of alternative educational policies or interventions. Cost studies can contribute significantly to decision-making, planning, and monitoring in education. The purpose of this entry is to introduce the different types of educational cost analysis and explain how they can contribute to improved policy-making in education. The discussion is grounded in a review of educational cost studies in both developed and developing countries in order to provide a brief summary of the current state of knowledge and gaps in educational cost analysis.

1. An Economic Classification of Cost Studies in Education

An economic framework is useful for analysis of costs and efficiency in education (Hanushek 1979). According to this framework, educational production is likened to economic production, whereby inputs to education (such as students, teachers, instructional materials, school facilities, equipment, etc.) are transformed through an educational process (encompassing, e.g., the curriculum, pedagogical methods, school organization, management and monitoring procedure) into educational outputs (schooling effects such as cognitive and noncognitive skills, and schooling benefits such as higher productivity and earnings). The costs of education refer to the economic value of the inputs used in education. The cost or economic value of an educational input is defined as its opportunity costs and is measured by the value of the input in its best alternative use. This definition of cost implies that the costs of education consist not only of public educational expenditures on personnel, school facilities, supplies, and equipment, but also parental and students' expenditures on education (direct private costs, such as tuition and other education-related fees, textbooks, uniform, transportation, etc.), students' forgone opportunities (indirect private costs, such as forgone earnings or other productive activities), as well as private contributions to education (contributions in cash or in kind, by individuals, parents, or private organizations).

Efficiency in education production is concerned with a comparison of the costs of education to the output of education. Educational production is said to be efficient when the maximum amount of educational output is produced for given educational costs; or alternatively, the least amount of educational cost is required to achieve a given level of educational output.

There is a large body of literature on educational cost studies in both developing countries and developed countries that demonstrates the applications of cost analysis to improved policy-making in education (Tsang 1988, Levin 1983, Cohn and Geske 1990). It is a diverse literature which includes studies that vary in the type of cost analysis, the purposes and applications in education, and in the scope of analysis. Nevertheless these studies can be conveniently classified into three categories based on the economic framework described above: costing and feasibility-testing studies, behavioral studies of educational costs, and input–output studies.

2. Educational Costing and Feasibility Testing Studies

Studies in the first category are concerned with educational inputs only. Their major tasks are to identify, classify, and measure the costs of various inputs to education. They are conducted for purposes of costing, and testing the financial feasibility of an educational activity.

Educational costing is one of the earliest and most common applications of cost analysis in education. There are numerous studies which illustrate the broad scope of cost estimation in traditional education (Coombs and Hallack 1972). They range from the costing of an educational intervention in the classroom, an education project, or an education program, to the costing of the reform in a subsector of education, or the five-year plan for the entire education system. They demonstrate that for a given educational activity, cost estimation can inform the policy-maker about: (a) the total cost and thus financial requirement of the activity, (b) the economic feasibility and thus the likelihood of successful implementation of the activity, (c) the short-term and long-term cost implications (such

as start-up costs and recurrent costs of the activity when fully operated), and (d) the distribution of the cost burden among various parties involved and thus equity/inequity in cost sharing. All such information is relevant to the decision about whether or not to undertake the educational activity.

The estimation of the costs of new educational technology is another important area of educational costing. A significant number of cost studies have been conducted on new educational media projects (Eicher et al. 1982). They indicate that such projects have high start-up costs, but the cost per student generally decreases with student enrollment. Depending on how the operation is conducted, the cost per broadcast hour can vary significantly among countries. A positive result of these cost studies is the standardization of the measurement and classification of the various costs of new educational media. Estimating the costs of new educational media is a necessary part of the comparison of its cost-effectiveness with that of traditional education.

The costing of quality basic education programs for marginalized or disadvantaged populations is also an important and timely application, given the recent and on-going world wide effort to provide basic education for all. The costs of these programs for marginalized populations are likely to be different from those for the average or nonmarginalized populations because of differences in input prices, program design, and other factors (Tsang 1994: 18–19).

A number of conceptual and methodological advances have been made in the understanding of educational costs. First, the cost of an education input is defined in terms of its opportunity costs and is thus not necessarily equal to public expenditure on the input. Consideration of public educational expenditures alone can significantly underestimate the real cost of an educational activity, usually due to omission of direct and indirect private costs of education, as well as private contributions. Second, care has to be exercised in estimating capital costs. In particular, the facilities and equipment purchased through a capital investment can last for many years; thus the annualized costs of such capital inputs have to depend on the expected life of service of the items, the rate of discount, and the opportunity cost of the undepreciated part of the items. Also, if future expenditures that are required as a result of capital investment (such as maintenance, repair, and staff) are ignored, the total cost of an educational activity will be underestimated. Third, it is useful to distinguish between educational costs in current dollars and educational costs in constant dollars; the latter reflect real resources to education and are obtained by adjusting the former with price indexes showing changes in the price level. If the rates of inflation are high, the cost figures in current dollars will differ substantially from those for in constant dollars. Teachers are often victimized by inflation as their salary increases fall behind the rates of inflation.

To assess the amount of real resources to education, educational costs in constant dollars should be estimated. Finally, since the prices of education inputs can vary significantly among regions, cost-of-education indexes reflecting such price disparities are needed in determining the costs of education for different regions (Chambers 1978). Failure to take account of these conceptual/methodological issues can lead to error in costing and in the choice of policies based on such costing information.

Despite these advances and the obvious relevance of cost analysis for informed decision-making in education, "technical" and "sociopolitical" barriers do exist that could limit the usefulness of cost analysis in education. On the technical side, a major barrier is the lack of relevant cost data. There are tremendous gaps between what data are required and what data are available for cost analysis, especially for studies in developing countries. For example, data are often available for public educational expenditures, but not for the other costs of education. Even public educational expenditures are sometimes available in terms of planned public expenditures, not actual public expenditures. Public educational expenditures by the central government are available, but not necessarily those by lower levels of education. Similarly, educational expenditures by the ministry of education are available, but not necessarily those by noneducation ministries or departments. Finally, expenditures on a number of items are sometimes lumped together; such aggregated data are not useful when information on individual items is needed.

Besides data-related difficulties, a failure in the evaluation of educational activities may result from a lack of awareness of the relevance of cost analysis on the part of decision-makers or a shortage of competent cost analysts.

On the sociopolitical side, policymakers may not have genuine interest in determining the financial requirements and feasibility of an educational plan. Educational plans may be drawn up by policy-makers for symbolic purposes, for legitimizing the power and actions of a regime, or for complying with the requirements for obtaining external financial assistance. Analysis of educational costs may yield findings inconsistent with the hidden agenda of such policymakers. It may also expose glaring inequalities or inequities in the distribution of educational resources by social class, gender, ethnicity, and region, which a regime would like to cover up. Obviously, technical barriers are easier to overcome than the sociopolitical ones.

3. Behavioral Studies of Educational Cost

Studies in the second category are concerned with the relationships among inputs and the utilization of inputs in the educational production process. They are conducted for purposes such as ascertaining behavioral patterns in educational costs, revealing the extent of underutilization of inputs in educational production process, and uncovering problematic cost patterns in education. They provide "diagnostic" signals to policymakers about existing or potential problems in education. Their scope of analysis also ranges widely, from "macro" investigations of national education systems to "micro" investigations of individual schools. These studies can be further subdivided into two groups: studies of educational expenditures and unit costs of education, and studies of resource utilization in education.

3.1 Studies of Educational Expenditures and Unit Costs

These studies are based largely on national data over time. The major tasks are focused on understanding the trend in educational expenditures, and uncovering the determinants of educational expenditure and unit costs.

Most cross-national studies on educational expenditures are concerned with public educational expenditures. There are three major findings on the trend of public educational expenditures in developing and developed countries over time (Eicher 1984 pp. 45–47). First, despite variation among countries and regions, the overall effort in favor of education in the 1960s and 1970s has been phenomenal. Total public educational expenditure increased by 250 percent in real terms. Public educational expenditure as a proportion of gross national product ("national-effort" cost indicator) increased by 75 percent in developing countries and by 50 percent in developed countries. Public educational expenditure as a proportion of total public expenditure ("fiscal-effort" cost indicator) increased by over 30 percent in both developing and developed countries. Second, there are discernible trends in the national-effort and fiscal-effort cost indicators. The average national-effort cost indicator increased from 2.9 percent to 4.2 percent during the 1960s; it continued to increase at a slower rate between 1970 and 1974. However, after 1974 the pattern between countries differed: the national-effort cost indicators began to stabilize for developed countries and Asian countries, but continued the upward trend for sub-Saharan African countries. As for the fiscal-effort cost indicators, the trend was rising for all countries between 1960 and 1974 (from about 11% to 15%). Developed countries began to reduce their fiscal effort in the 1970s. In contrast, developing countries stabilized their fiscal effort after the mid-1970s. Third, the effort in favor of educational expenditure is now leveling off for all countries except the sub-Saharan African region. The slowdown in national and fiscal efforts is widespread.

The changes in public educational expenditures are due to both supply factors (such as the growth rate of the national economy, the ranges of competing demands of other public services, etc.) and demand factors (such as demographic changes, the importance of education for national development, etc.) which are often outside the locus of control of educational policy-makers and school administrators. The slowdown in public educational expenditures can be attributed to three factors: slower rates of economic growth, a relative decrease in the demand for education, and a change in government attitude toward education (Eicher 1984 p. 55).

Lack of data makes cross-national comparison of private costs of education difficult. Available evidence indicates that the direct and indirect costs of schooling are significant compared to public costs (Wolff 1985, Tilak 1985, Tsang and Kidchanapanish 1992). The costs of private schools relative to those of government schools may be significantly underestimated if private costs are omitted (Tsang and Taoklam 1992).

Unit costs of education have been estimated for a wide range of situations, usually in terms of expenditure per student. Two major findings are obtained from unit cost studies: there are significant disparities in unit costs for different situations, and there are identifiable patterns in unit costs. For example, significant differences often exist in unit costs between rural areas and urban areas, between states or provinces in a country, and among countries. There are also significant differences in unit costs between different levels of education, between different types of curriculum or subjects, and between different types of schools (e.g., boarding schools vs. day schools; government schools vs. private schools).

On the other hand, per-student expenditure exhibits common patterns across education systems: (a) it rises with the level of education, (b) it is dominated by personnel costs with higher proportion for personnel costs at lower levels of education, (c) it is higher for boarding schools than for day schools at the secondary level, (d) it is generally higher for vocational/technical education than for academic/general education at the secondary level, (e) it is higher for engineering and science subjects than for arts and humanities at the tertiary level, and (f) it has a built-in tendency to rise over time (Psacharopoulos 1982, Tsang 1988, Coombs and Hallak 1988). These common patterns can be understood by examining the determinants of unit costs.

An important factor affecting unit cost is the technology of educational production. Education in countries across the world takes place predominately in the traditional school and university, with similar organization, curriculum, pedagogy, management, and monitoring procedure. The adoption of a common technology is the major reason for the similar patterns of unit costs. The labor-intensive technology of traditional education accounts for the dominance of teacher costs. Different provisions in terms of class size, staffing pattern, and facilities explain the cost differences among levels of education, types of curriculum, and types of schools. Furthermore, pay scales based on qualifications, years of service, and automatic promotion practice make personnel costs rise over time.

3.2 Studies of Resource Utilization in Education

The other group of studies assesses the rates of utilization of inputs in educational institutions, and the findings have direct implications for unit costs and educational efficiency. If there is considerable underutilization of resources, the number of students served can be increased without incurring additional cost; alternatively, cost can be reduced without affecting the number of students served. In either situation, unit cost is lowered and educational efficiency is raised.

Survey studies have been conducted to study the utilization rates of resources in educational institutions in a number of developing countries, based on measures such as the number of contact hours per week for a teacher, the student–teacher (or student–faculty) ratio, the building area per student, and the percentage use of laboratory time and equipment. Low rates of utilization are reported for both secondary schools and for universities, indicating real potential for cost savings and efficiency improvement.

Econometric studies have also been conducted to assess resource utilization by estimating education cost functions (ECFs) and determining the presence or absence of economies of scale in educational production. An ECF relates the minimum cost of education to the level of educational output, given input prices and the technology of production; it shows how the cost of education varies with educational output. Education cost functions can be estimated statistically, though there are a number of theoretical and methodological difficulties (Tsang 1988 p.208). The presence or absence of economies of scale can be determined from an estimated ECF. Educational production is said to exhibit economies (or diseconomies) of scale if each additional unit of output becomes cheaper (or more expensive) to produce.

Studies of ECFs in developed countries (Canada, the US, and the UK) show that there are economies of scale in primary and secondary education, and in higher education (Kumar 1983, Fox 1981, Verry and Davies 1976, Brinkman and Leslie 1987). There are very few studies of ECFs in developing countries. Available evidence indicates that higher education production demonstrates economies of scale (Psacharopoulos 1982), but no definite conclusion can be drawn for primary and secondary education in developing countries.

Studies of cost functions of new educational-media projects in developing countries indicate the presence of economies of scale (Jamison et al. 1978, Perraton 1982). They found that these projects have large start-up costs, so that large enrollments and a long period of operation are needed to lower their unit costs to levels comparable to that of the traditional school. In addition, "small" media (such as radio) are much less costly than "big" media (such as television).

3.3 Behavioral Cost Studies and Educational Policy-making

Studies in the second category illustrate how cost analysis can contribute to improved policy-making in a number of ways. First, examination of cost patterns and resource utilization can uncover opportunities for improving the efficiency of educational investment, for example, in terms of reallocation of resources between levels or types of education, improved utilization of existing personnel or facilities, or the adoption of alternative technologies of education.

Second, the studies find considerable disparities in educational expenditures and unit costs across diverse settings. This finding has several policy implications. Policymakers should be warned against designing an "average" policy to be applied to diverse settings. Schools in different settings may have different needs and thus require different treatment. The diversity of educational setting also implies the need to base policies on disaggregated data. Moreover, disparities in educational costs often reflect inequities in access to educational resources; reducing such inequities can be a desirable policy objective. Finally, differences among countries and regions warn against uncritical adoption of practices found useful elsewhere.

Third, indicators of education costs can be used in an anatomical examination of resource utilization in education. They include, for example, measures of national effort and fiscal effort, unit costs by level of education, type of education, curriculum, region, and time, as well as indicators related to the distribution of costs by sources and input categories. From a policy perspective, indicators are useful for a number of diagnostic purposes: they indicate the state of affairs in education, uncover areas of abnormalities, and provide the bases for gauging progress in educational interventions. They should be regularly constructed and examined.

4. Input–Output Studies in Education

In contrast to the previous two categories of cost studies which examine input costs and characteristics of educational costs only, studies in the third category consider both the costs and outputs of education. They are conducted for the purposes of choosing among alternative educational investment so that educational resources are allocated efficiently. These studies can be divided into two distinct groups: cost-benefit studies which compare the benefits of education (such as increased productivity and earnings) to the costs of education, and cost-effectiveness studies which compare the effects of education (such as student learning)

to the costs of education. A brief summary of the findings of these studies and their policy implications is presented here. More detailed discussion of the theory and methodology of these analyses is available elsewhere (Cohn and Geske 1990, Levin 1983).

4.1 Cost–Benefit Studies in Education

These studies use the rates-of-return approach to evaluation. The measurement of educational benefits is based on human capital theory. According to this theory, education enhances the skills (human capital) of individuals and thus raises their productivity; and in a competitive labor market, a more productive individual is paid a higher wage. Thus differences in education among individuals result in differences in earnings, other things being equal. Since human capital is durable, the productive benefits of education can be measured in terms of lifetime earning differentials. One can distinguish between private rates of return and social rates of return. Private rates of return compare the benefits of education to an individual to the costs of education to the individual; they inform investment decisions for an individual. Social rates of return compare the benefits of education to society to the costs of education to society; they inform public investment decisions to achieve "external" efficiency in education.

A large literature on cost-benefit studies in education exists for both developing countries and developed countries. The major findings are: (a) educational investment is very profitable, with rates generally above the benchmark rate for physical capital (10%); (b) primary education has the highest rates of return among all education levels; (c) private rates of return are higher than social rates of return, especially at the level of higher education; (d) at a given level, the rate of return to education in developing countries is higher than that in developed countries; (e) the rates of return to women's education are higher than those for men in developing countries; and (f) at the secondary level, academic education has a higher rate of return than that of vocational/technical education (Psacharopoulos 1985).

The implications for educational policies are obvious, if one accepts human capital theory and the rates-of-return approach. The findings suggest a top priority of investment in primary education, increasing private costs of university education, expanding access to schooling for females, and offering academic education at the secondary level.

The social rates-of-return approach to public investment is adopted by some cost analysts because it is grounded in economic theory, is analytically straightforward, and has clear policy implications. Yet it is not without its limitations, especially with regard to the measurement of educational benefits. Besides, there are alternative explanations of the relationship between education, productivity, and earnings (Tsang 1988 pp. 213–15). Policymakers should be informed

Table 1
Applications of cost analysis in education

Type of cost studies	Domains of	Applications	
	Educational policy analysis	Educational planning	Educational monitoring
Costing/feasibility studies			
Cost estimation	Costing	Costing	-
Economic feasibility	Evaluating feasibility	Evaluating feasibility	-
Behavioral studies of costs			
Expenditure/unit costs	-	Costing and cost projection	Diagnosis
Other cost indicators and indices	-	Cost projection	Diagnosis
Resource utilization surveys	Improving efficiency	-	Assessing resource utilization
Estimation of cost functions and economies of scale	Improving efficiency	-	-
Input–output studies			
Cost-benefit studies	Improving efficiency	-	-
Cost-effectiveness studies	Improving efficiency	-	-

about both the advantages and limitations of cost-benefit analysis.

4.2 Cost-effectiveness Studies in Education

Cost-effectiveness analysis in education is used to choose among alternative educational interventions so as to maximize educational effects given cost, thus improving "internal" efficiency in education.

A prominent application of cost-effectiveness analysis is in new educational media. Despite some methodological difficulties, several tentative conclusions can be drawn on the cost-effectiveness of new educational media (Eicher et al. 1982, Jamison and Orivel 1982): (a) students do learn from new educational media, but their use within the traditional school setting is not cost-effective; (b) small media have been found to be more cost-effective than big media; (c) distance teaching may be the only way to educate children in thinly populated areas; (d) distance teaching projects for school equivalency appear to be effective and cost-effective; (e) the effective use of new educational media requires technical staff for operation and maintenance; and (f) in any given situation, it is difficult to determine which particular medium is most suitable; in practice several media are used together in a project.

Compared to cost-benefit analysis, the applications of cost-effectiveness to traditional education are relatively few, especially in developing countries. Most studies on school improvement have focused on educational effectiveness (primarily measures of cognitive outcomes), without also considering educational costs. Among the few applications, a conspicuous

example is studies on textbooks which find that the provision of textbooks is a cost-effective strategy to improve student achievement (Heyneman et al. 1984). Another example includes the study of alternative approaches to computer-assisted instruction (Levin et al. 1987). The cost-effectiveness information on other traditional education inputs or processes is lacking, incomplete, or not yet generalizable.

In short, not much has been learned about alternative school interventions for improving the internal efficiency of traditional education. This state of affairs is indeed unsatisfactory given the pressing need to improve educational efficiency under conditions of tight fiscal constraints and unmet social demand for education. This situation may be improved by efforts to strengthen the research basis of cost-effectiveness analysis and the utilization of research findings in educational policy-making. In particular, educational evaluation should be based on the cost-effectiveness approach, efforts should be made to collect reliable cost data, and measures of school effectiveness should include not only cognitive effects, but noncognitive effects as well.

5. Summary and Recommendations

Table 1 summarizes the applications of cost analysis in education. It shows that there are eight common types of cost studies (within the three categories discussed) which can be used in at least three domains of educational analysis, for different purposes or type of applications in each domain. The scope of cost analysis can be very broad; it may range from the analysis of school activities and educational institutions to the analysis of a subsector of education and the system of education.

While cost analysis can contribute significantly to informed decisions in education, its use in the different domains of educational analysis remains inadequate to date. This state of affairs is especially unsatisfactory in light of the need to improve educational quality and provide basic education to all, the severe fiscal constraints facing many countries, and the importance of raising the efficiency of educational investment in the years to come. At least three tasks are necessary to alter this situation. One task is to strengthen the informational basis of cost analysis. As indicated previously, there often exist wide gaps between what cost data are available and what cost data are needed. The need to develop a database for cost analysis is both self-evident and urgent (Tsang 1988 pp. 223–24). Another task is to encourage research on educational costs. Studies of cost-effectiveness in traditional education are especially limited and should be encouraged. Studies of unit costs and other cost indicators and indexes should be conducted periodically to monitor and diagnose resource allocation and utilization in education. The third task is to heighten the awareness of educational decision-makers about the usefulness of cost analysis and to encourage them to incorporate the findings of cost studies in educational policymaking (Levin 1988).

See also: Education Production Functions; Cost–Benefit Analysis; Cost-effectiveness Analysis.

References

Brinkman P, Leslie L 1987 Economics of scale in higher education: Sixty years of research. *Rev. Higher Educ.* 10(1): 1–28

Chambers J 1978 Educational cost differentials and allocation of state aid for elementary secondary education. *J. Hum. Resources* 13(4): 459–81

Cohn E, Geske T 1990 *The Economics of Education*, 3rd edn. Pergamon, Oxford

Coombs P, Hallak J 1972 *Educational Cost-Analysis in Action: Case Studies for Planners*, Vols. 1–3. UNESCO/IIEP, Paris

Coombs P, Hallak J 1988 *Cost Analysis in Education: A Tool for Policy and Planning.* Johns Hopkins University Press, Baltimore, Maryland

Eicher J C 1984 *Educational Costing and Financing in Developing Countries: Focus on Sub-Saharan Africa.* World Bank Staff Working Paper No. 655, World Bank, Washington, DC

Eicher J C, Hawkridge D, McAnany E, Mariet F, Orivel F (eds.) 1982 *The Economics of New Educational Media, Vol. 3: Cost and Effectiveness. Overview and Synthesis.* UNESCO, Paris

Fox W 1981 Reviewing economies of size in education. *J. Educ. Finance* 6: 273–96

Hanushek E 1979 Conceptual and empirical issues in the estimation of educational production functions. *J. Hum. Resources* 14(3): 351–88

Heyneman S, Jamison D, Montenegro X 1984 Textbooks in the Philippines: Evaluation of the pedagogical impact of a nationwide investment. *Educ. Eval. Policy Anal.* 6(2): 139–150

Jamison D, Klees S, Wells S 1978 The costs of eductional media: Guidelines for planning and evaluation. Sage, Beverly Hills, California

Jamison D, Orivel F 1982 Cost-effectiveness of distance teaching for school equivalency. In: Perraton H (ed.) 1982

Kumar R 1983 Economies of scale in school operation: Evidence from Canada. *Appl. Econ.* 15: 323–40

Levin H 1983 *Cost-effectiveness: A Primer.* Sage, Beverly Hills, California

Levin H 1988 Cost effectiveness and educational policy. *Educ. Eval. Policy Anal.* 10(1): 51–69

Levin H, Glass G, Meister G 1987 Cost-effectiveness of computer-assisted instruction. *Eval. Rev.* 11(1): 50–72

Perraton H (ed.) 1982 *Alternative Routes to Formal Education.* Johns Hopkins University Press, Baltimore, Maryland

Psacharopoulous G 1982 The economics of higher education in developing countries. *Comp. Educ. Rev.* 26(2): 139–59

Psacharopoulos G 1985 Returns to education: A further international update and implications. *J. Hum. Resources* 20(4): 583–604

Tilak J 1985 Analysis of costs of education in India. Occasional Paper No. 10, National Institute of Educational Planning and Administration (India), New Delhi (ERIC Document Reproduction Service No. ED 261 946)

Tsang M 1988 Cost analysis for educational policymaking: A review of cost studies in education in developing countries. *Rev. Educ. Res.* 58(2): 181–230

Tsang M, Kidchanapanish S 1992 Private resources and the quality of primary education in Thailand. *Int. J. Educ. Res.* 17(2): 179–98

Tsang M, Taoklam W 1992 Comparing the costs of government and private primary education in Thailand. *Int. J. Educ. Dev.* 12(3): 177–90

Tsang M 1994 *Cost Analysis of Educational Inclusion of Marginalized Populations.* International Institute for Educational Planning, UNESCO, Paris

Verry D, Davies B 1976 *University Costs and Output.* Studies on Education 6, Elsevier, Amsterdam

Wolff L 1985 Controlling the Costs of Education in Eastern Africa: A Review of Data, Issues, and Policies. World Bank Staff Working Paper No. 702, World Bank, Washington, DC

Private and Public Costs of Schooling in Developing Nations

M. C. Tsang

The costs of schooling include not only public expenditures on teachers, supplies, school buildings, and equipment, but also the private resources devoted by parents and the community to schooling. Private resources are an important factor to consider because they are related to a number of important educational issues that concern educators, educational researchers, educational administrators and policy-makers alike: demand for and quality of education, inequality and inequity in education, as well as a comparison of the costs and relative efficiency of public and private schools. By drawing up empirical studies of primary and secondary schools in developing countries, this entry examines the relationship of private resources to these issues. The major tasks are to summarize what is known about such relationships and to indicate the knowledge gaps.

1. Private and Public Costs of Schooling

Educational costs at the school level can be divided into two groups: institutional costs, and private resources devoted to education. Institutional costs refer to costs incurred by the school on educational inputs and services. They are usually divided into two categories for accounting purposes: recurrent costs and capital costs. Recurrent costs are costs of educational inputs or services which are expended in a period of one year; they consist of personnel costs (salaries, employment benefits and supplementary benefits paid to teachers, school administrators, and other school staff) and nonpersonnel costs (costs of instructional materials, teaching aids, school supplies, minor repair and regular maintenance, utilities, and student welfare). Capital costs are costs of inputs which last for more than one year; they include the costs of buildings, equipment, and land. Public expenditures on such educational inputs and services constitute the bulk of the public costs of schooling.

Private resources for education can be classified into three categories: direct private costs of education, household contributions to school, and indirect private costs of education. Direct private costs of education (DPC) are expenditures by parents on their children's schooling, such as expenditures on school fees (tuition and other school fees), textbooks and supplementary study guides, writing supplies, uniform, school bag, transportation, and boarding (for boarding schools). Expenditures on school fees are part of the revenue for education to finance institutional costs. Nonfee expenditures are additional financial resources to

schooling not captured in institutional costs. Household contributions to school are contributions, in cash or in kind, from families to the school, or to school personnel (e.g., teachers). Contributions to school can be used in a variety of ways, for example to purchase library books or to construct a school building. Indirect private costs of education refer to the economic value of the forgone opportunities of schooling. The opportunities forgone can be a child's labor in family production, in looking after younger siblings, and/or in performing other household chores. These three categories constitute the private costs of schooling.

The institutional costs of public schools are supported by public expenditures on education, fee-related direct private costs (usually nontuition school fees), and household contributions to school. Usually, public educational expenditures constitute the largest share of such costs. The institutional costs of private schools are supported by school fees, and household contributions to school (and by public educational expenditures on government-subsidized private schools); with school fees supporting a major share of such costs. Public schools and private schools both depend on private resources.

Educational costs above the school level consist of the costs of running educational bureaucracies (administrative, supervisory, planning, and research-related) at the central, provincial, and local levels. Such costs are usually small compared to school-level costs, on a per-student basis.

2. Private Resources, Educational Quality, and Educational Demand

Available empirical evidence suggests that private resources constitute a very significant part of the total resources (sum of public and private resources) devoted to educational production, that they are the major sources of support for important inputs to education, and that they affect educational demand, especially for children from disadvantaged backgrounds.

2.1 Comparison with Public Educational Expenditure

Although there is large variation among countries, studies of Asian, Latin American, and African countries generally find that private resources are significant compared to public educational expenditures, at both the primary and secondary levels.

First, some Asian countries may be considered. In Thailand, total private resources (sum of three categories of private resources) amounted to 28 percent of institutional cost in government primary schools in

1987 (Tsang and Taoklam 1992). In Pakistan, direct private costs amounted to about 30 percent of the per-student public recurrent expenditure in 1979–80, at the primary level (Tsang et al. 1990). A World Bank study of education in two provinces in the People's Republic of China found that in 1988, direct private cost equaled about 70–75 percent of total public institutional expenditure at the primary level, and 50–70 percent of total public institutional expenditure for secondary general education (World Bank 1991 Vol. 2 pp. 70, 77). In 1979–80 in India, public educational expenditure (all levels of education) amounted to 3.9 percent of GNP, while private educational expenditure (mostly DPC) and indirect private cost were estimated to be 1.9 percent of GNP and 4.2 percent of GNP respectively (Tilak 1985).

Two studies of Latin American countries also provide supportive evidence. The ratio of private educational expenditure (mostly DPC) to the total public expenditure of the ministry of education was reported to be 1.11, 0.51, 0.32, 0.13, and 0.04 for Brazil, Colombia, Chile, Venezuela, and Argentina respectively (Schiefelbein 1986 p. 29). For rural primary schools in Colombia, household contributions to school amounted to an average of 30 percent of total education cost per pupil (Paulsen 1981).

For secondary schools in nine East African countries, direct private costs constituted about one-third of the total cost per pupil. But this ratio varies widely among the countries and among different types of schools; it ranged from 0 percent for day schools in Somalia in 1981–82 to 81 percent for assisted Harambee schools in Kenya in 1981–82. The ratio for boarding schools was found to be consistently larger than that for day schools (Wolff 1985 pp. 51–55).

In short, information on public educational expenditures alone substantially underestimates total resources to education. Given their magnitude and the fiscal constraints faced by many developing countries, private resources will continue to be an indispensable source of financing of education.

2.2 Relationship to Educational Quality

Studies in some developing countries show that direct private costs and household contributions to schools are the major sources of support for quality-related educational inputs.

In the People's Republic of China, parents are required to pay the school twice a year for the costs of textbooks and workbooks, and the school purchases such materials for students. In 1988, such costs amounted to 10–24 yuan (US $2.7–6.5) at the primary level, 30–43 yuan at the lower-secondary level, and 30–40 yuan at the upper-secondary (general education) level, the cost being lower in rural areas than in urban areas. Although the government does provide subsidies to some families from very disadvantaged backgrounds to cover the costs of textbooks and school fees, such

public expenditure is, relatively speaking, very small. Overall, parents contribute almost all of the costs of textbooks and workbooks (World Bank 1991 Vol. 1 pp. 67–68).

For primary education in 1987 in Thailand, parents with children in government schools spent an average of 125 baht (about 5 US dollars) per year on textbooks and workbooks while the corresponding figure for private-school parents was 353 baht per year (Tsang and Kidchanapanish 1992). The government provides textbooks to one-fourth of the students (mainly from poor backgrounds) in government primary schools. In the same year, parental expenditure accounted for about 80 percent of total expenditure on these inputs in 1987. In some other countries, the government still bears all or most of the costs of textbooks.

Household or community contributions may play an important role in school construction, especially in rural areas. For example, in the People's Republic of China, primary schools are built from resources (especially materials and labor) obtained from the village. The mayor of the village provides the leadership in collecting contributions from households in the village and in coordinating the construction of a school. With the decentralization of educational financing in the 1980s (known as "local responsibility and administration by levels"), households can more easily identify themselves with the schools in their community and are thus willing to build their own schools. Data from two provinces in 1988 indicate that 35–55 percent of all capital expenditure on primary and secondary education were used to perform major school repair or replacement, and household contributions were a major source for such expenditure (World Bank 1991 Vol. 1 Chap. 4). The important role of community contributions in school construction and maintenance is also found in the African countries of Nigeria, Kenya, Zambia, and Botswana (Bray and Lillis 1987 Chap. 9–12).

Teachers receive varying degrees of financial support from the community. In China, 45 percent of the primary school teachers are *minban* (nongovernment) teachers who rely heavily on living subsidies provided by the local community. Community subsidies amount to about 40 percent of total subsidy (community plus government) to these teachers (World Bank 1991 vol. 1 p. 87). In Thailand, teachers receive relatively little community contribution. Contributions to teachers amounted to 8–16 baht per year, which is a tiny fraction of the average annual salary of a government school teacher (57,600 baht).

The Thai study does show the importance of household contributions in kind: 39 percent of the total value of household contributions to primary education was derived from in-kind contributions, and the proportion was higher for rural/agricultural households; a strong relationship among the school, the Buddhist temple, and the community facilitates such contributions (Tsang and Kidchanapanish 1992).

For educational policymakers and administrators, how to encourage community contributions and to channel such resources to effective uses are important tasks for financing quality-related improvement in primary and secondary education.

2.3 Relationship to Educational Demand

The private costs of schooling can be an economic burden for households, especially for poor households. In public primary schools in Thailand, for example, direct private costs, household contributions, and indirect private costs averaged 5.8, 1.4, and 7.2 percent of household income respectively in 1987; but the corresponding figures for the households in the lowest 20 percent of the income distribution were 16.3, 4.3, and 25.9 percent (Tsang and Kidchanapanish 1992). In Malaysia, direct private costs of education (all levels) alone accounted for 18 percent of household income for the lowest income group, as compared to 6 percent for the top income group. The economic burden will be much higher for low-income households if indirect costs are included (Meerman, 1979). In 1988 in China, direct private costs (excluding boarding costs) alone amounted to 5.6, 11, 19 percent of the average household income at the primary, lower-secondary, and upper-secondary levels respectively for the "poor" counties (as defined by the central government, with a per capita income of less than 50 US dollars). Boarding costs for some schools would add another 15–20 percent of household income (computed from data in World Bank 1991 vol. 1 Chap. 4).

The burden of private costs can adversely affect the demand for education. For example, in Taijiang county (per capita income of about US $50) in Guizhan province, China, 673 of the 1,034 students who dropped out of primary school in 1988 reported economic difficulty to be the major reason for their departure. A recent experiment to reduce the costs of textbooks and school fees by 50 percent conducted in two primary schools in the same county showed marked improvement in attendance; in particular, female enrollment increased from 20 to 50 percent of the student population (World Bank 1991 vol. 1 p. 67). Similarly, in India, poor parents attributed their failure to send their children to school to high direct private costs (Psacharopoulos and Woodhall 1985 p. 113).

It has to be pointed out that there are other noneconomic factors affecting the private demand for education. In some developing countries, cultural traditions adversely affect the participation of girls in education. But the evidence presented here does document the heavy burden of private costs on poor households; reduction of the private-cost burden for such households will likely raise their demand for education.

3. Private Resources, Educational Inequality, and Educational Inequity

Besides the important role of private resources in supporting educational production, empirical studies also indicate that private financing of education can exacerbate existing inequality and inequity in education. A proper balance has to be maintained between public and private financing of education. Intergovernmental education grants can be designed to mitigate the negative effects of private resources on education.

3.1 Inequality in Educational Resources

Private resources to education vary significantly among households of different socioeconomic backgrounds and the pattern is different for different categories of private resources.

Consider first direct private costs. Studies in Thailand and Pakistan show that urban, higher income, more wealthy, more educated, and professional/managerial households spent much more than rural, lower income, less wealthy, less educated, and agricultural households respectively; and the differences between the top group and the bottom group are substantial (the ratio ranges from 2:1 to 16:1; see Tsang and Kidchanapanish 1992, Tsang, et al. 1990). A related finding is that private-school parents spend much more than government-school parents. This comes about not only because the former have to pay tuition costs, but also because they spend significantly more than the latter group on learning-related inputs (such as textbooks, workbooks, and writing supplies) and on transportation (Tan 1985, Tsang and Kidchanapanish 1991).

The findings regarding direct private costs on boys and girls are mixed. Analysis of 1981 data on secondary schools in Tanzania found that the direct private costs for girls were significantly higher than that for boys, for both government schools and private schools (Tan 1985). For primary education in Thailand, analysis of 1987 data found that in government schools, the costs for girls are higher than those for boys; but in private schools, the costs for boys are higher. In either case, the difference is statistically insignificant (Tsang and Kidchanapanish 1992). For public primary schools in Pakistan, girls had higher costs in urban areas but lower costs in rural areas (Tsang et al. 1990). More research is needed to clarify the findings.

The situation is different for indirect private costs. For primary education in Thailand, as expected, households from higher socioeconomic backgrounds demand less time from their children and had lower indirect private cost (Tsang and Kidchanapanish 1992).

As for household contributions, higher socioeconomic groups generally contribute more to school than lower socioeconomic groups (Bray and Lillis 1988, Tsang and Kidchanapanish 1992).

In short, children from lower socioeconomic back-

Table 1
Per-student costs of government and private primary schools in Thailand 1987 (baht/student/school year)

	ONPEC schools (1)	Government Bangkok schools (2)	Schools Municipal schools (3)	All govt. schools (4)	Private schools (5)	Cost ratio (5)/(4) (6)	Cost ratio (5)/(3) (7)
Recurrent cost per student	3,630	2,778	2,208	3,505	1,663	0.47	0.75
Capital cost per student	766	8,228	1,156	1,290	899	0.70	0.78
Institutional cost per student	4,396	11,006	3,364	4,795	2,562	0.53	0.76
Private resources per student	1,291	1,700	1,743	1,353	3,568	2.64	2.04
Total cost per student	5,540	12,533	5,028	6,003	4,667	0.78	0.93

Source: Tsang and Taoklam 1992

grounds are confronted with a number of educational inequalities: they have less direct private resources available to them when they are in school, and face stronger pressure to stay out of school. Private resources are thus a means for perpetuating social class-based inequality in education. Further research is needed to demonstrate the linkage between private resources and student achievement.

3.2 Inequity in Educational Financing

Not only do private resources contribute to educational inequality, they are also an inequitable means for financing education. The studies on Thailand, Malaysia, and the People's Republic of China discussed in Sect. 2.3 show that lower income households bear a much heavier economic burden than higher income households. The significant role of private resources in financing education and their negative inequity (and inequality) effects present a dilemma for educational policy-makers in developing countries. In some countries, stagnant economic growth, tight fiscal constraints, and unmet educational demand combine to create strong pressure to mobilize additional resources to education, whether they are private resources or public resources. Despite the negative effects of private resources, reality in these countries dictates that private resources will continue to play a significant role in educational financing. The problem at hand is not whether or not to encourage private resources to education. Obviously, both public and private resources to education should be encouraged. Rather, the challenge is to obtain additional resources and distribute these resources more equally and equitably. The existing scheme for raising public revenue may not be efficient or fair and there are alternative ways of allocating and distributing available resources. For example, while households are encouraged to contribute additional private resources to education, additional public revenue can be targeted at disadvantaged populations for equalization, through the use of intergovernmental educational grants (Tsang and

Levin 1983); the goal is to ensure that the minimum package of educational inputs and services needed for effective learning is available to such population groups (Windham 1991). Since private resources are strongly related to household income, poor households should receive more (and not less) government subsidies in education during periods of economic downturn.

4. Private Resources and Relative Efficiency of Government Schools and Private Schools

A key consideration in the debate about privatization of schooling is the relative efficiency of government schools and private schools. Proponents of private schools claim that private schools are more efficient than government schools. Yet most discussion of relative efficiency focuses on student achievement, with little analysis of costs. However, information on costs is needed to compare cost-effectiveness, to estimate resource requirements, and to assess the financial feasibility of the development of government schools and private schools. There are very few comparative studies of the costs of government schools and private schools. This is partly due to the fact that some cost data are not easily available or accessible, especially data on costs of private education and data on private resources to education. Even in published studies of comparative education costs, the cost data can be quite crude; for example, they are not disaggregated into costs for different types of government schools and private schools, and they concern institutional costs only; and some of the data used are school revenue data, not cost data (Jimenez et al. 1988).

A study of comparative education costs in Thailand (Tsang and Taoklam 1992) shows that, if private resources are not taken into account, the cost of private schools relative to government schools will be substantially underestimated and that the relative efficiency of private schools will correspondingly be overstated. Moreover, since there are different types of government schools and private schools that operate in different social contexts, cost comparison that treats government schools and private schools as two homogeneous systems will not lead to meaningful evaluation of the relative efficiency of the two types of schools; comparison should rather be made of schools which operate in similar social contexts.

In Thailand, most of the government primary schools are administered by the Office of the National Primary Education Commission (ONPEC) and most of these ONPEC schools are located in rural areas which are remote from urban areas. The rest of the government primary schools are administered by educational bureaucracies in the capital (Bangkok Metropolitan schools) and in other municipalities (municipal schools). Both Bangkok schools and municipal schools are primarily urban schools, and a great majority of the private schools are located in urban areas. Using a multistage cluster sampling of schools, the study selected 301 schools with a primary section only (248 ONPEC schools, 19 Bangkok schools, 14 municipal schools, and 20 private schools) and 2,075 parents. The per-student costs of different types of schools are shown in Table 1. Column (6) gives the cost ratio between private schools and governments by treating the two types of schools as homogeneous systems. If, like most cost studies, comparison is based on recurrent costs, the cost ratio is only 0.47, that is, private schools are less than half as costly as government schools. When capital costs are also included, the cost ratio based on total institutional cost increases to 0.53. But private-school parents devote much greater private resources to education than government-school parents (a cost ratio of 2.64). When private resources are also included in the analysis, the ratio of per-student total cost jumps to 0.78. Cost-effectiveness comparison of the two types of schools should be based on per-student total cost. The efficiency of private schools relative to government schools would be substantially overstated (by 66%) if per-student recurrent costs were used.

However, the two systems of schools are not homogeneous. The ONPEC schools cater to students from rural and agricultural backgrounds; the remoteness of these schools and the traditionally strong community–temple–school relationship (thus a small catchment area) means that these schools are much smaller in enrollment and have a lower student–teacher ratio than the urban government schools in Bangkok and in other municipalities. Bangkok schools are the most costly primarily because of the high cost of land. Municipal schools and private schools are much more similar in their social settings in terms of locality, backgrounds of students, school size, and student–teacher ratio. The

figures in column (6) essentially compare the costs of mostly urban private schools to the costs of mostly rural ONPEC schools. Such a comparison is not meaningful as these two types of schools operate in different social settings, cater to different students, and thus are not genuine alternatives from a policy viewpoint. Column (7) presents cost ratios between private schools and municipal schools. The per-student total costs of these two types of school which operate in similar social settings are actually quite similar.

In short, a proper accounting of all the resources utilized in educational production and a contextual comparison of the costs of private schools and government schools are necessary in properly assessing the relative efficiency of the two types of school. Further research on this topic in other countries, and at both the primary and secondary levels should be encouraged, in light of the dearth of such studies and the recurrent interest in privatization of schooling.

5. Conclusion

In summary, private resources to education constitute a significant share of the total resources devoted to schooling, are the major source of support for some quality-related educational inputs, and affect the demand for education. They also contribute to inequality of educational resources and inequitable educational financing with regard to different socioeconomic groups. If they are omitted in analysis of the relative efficiency of government and private schools, significant bias will result.

The empirical findings also have a number of policy implications. Both educational policy-makers and planners should take private resources into account in issues concerning financing, school quality, and educational demand, whenever appropriate. In particular, intergovernmental grants targeted at disadvantaged populations may be necessary to ensure a minimally accepted level of educational quality for such populations and to raise their demand for basic education, as well as to mitigate the negative inequality and inequity effects of private resources. How to direct private resources to effective uses is also a relevant concern for educational policy-makers and administrators. Furthermore, policy discussion regarding privatization is misleading without a proper cost comparison.

Since there are significant gaps in the literature, further research on private resources is needed. Future research areas might include: the utilization of private resources in educational production, the gender-related effects of private resources, the comparative studies of costs of government schools and private schools, and the economic and other aspects of the school–community relation, in different social/national contexts and for both primary and secondary education. The research effort should be paralleled by the development of a database on educational costs, including data on private resources.

See also: Educational Financing; Community Financing of Education; Cost Analysis in Education; Public-Private Division of Responsibility for Education

References

Bray M, Lillis K 1988 *Community Financing of Education: Issues and Policy Implications in Less Developed Countries*. Pergamon Press, Oxford

Jimenez E, Lockheed M, Wattanawaha N 1988 The relative efficiency of public and private schools: The case of Thailand. *World Bank Econ. Rev.* 2(2): 139–64

Meerman J 1979 *Public Expenditures in Malaysia: Who Benefits and Why*. Oxford University Press, New York

Paulsen A 1981 *The Unit Costs of Education*. OFISEL, Bogota

Psacharopoulos G, Woodhall M 1985 *Education for Development: An Analysis of Investment Choices*. Oxford University Press, New York

Schiefelbein E 1986 *Education Costs and Financing Policies in Latin America: A Review of Available Research*. World Bank, Education and Training Department, Washington, DC

Tan J-P 1985 The private direct cost of secondary schools in Tanzania. *Int. J. Educ. Dev.* 5(1): 1–10

Tilak J 1985 *Analysis of costs of education in India*. Occasional Paper No. 10, National Institute of Educational Planning and Administration (India), New Delhi. (ERIC Document Reproduction Service No. ED 261 946)

Tsang M, Levin H 1983 The impacts of intergovernmental grants on educational expenditures. *Rev. Educ. Res.* 53(3): 329–67

Tsang M, Zaki M, Ghafoor A 1990 *Household Educational Expenditures in Pakistan*. College of Education, Michigan State University, East Lansing, Michigan

Tsang M, Kidchanapanish S 1992 Private resources and the quality of primary education in Thailand. *Int. J. Educ. Res.* 17(2): 179–98

Tsang M, Taoklam W 1992 Comparing the costs of government and private primary education in Thailand. *Int. J. Educ. Dev.* 12(3): 177–90

Windham D 1991 The role of basic education in promoting development: Aggregate effects and marginalized population. In: Chapman D, Walberg H (eds.) 1991 *Strategies for Enhancing Educational Productivity*. JAI Press, Greenwich, Connecticut

Wolff L 1985 Controlling the costs of education in Eastern Africa: A review of data issues, and policies (Staff Working Paper No. 702). World Bank, Washington, DC

World Bank 1991 *China: Provincial Education Planning and Finance Sector Study*. Asian Department, World Bank, Washington, DC

Economics of Educational Technology

S. J. Klees

Economists generally use the term "technology" to refer to any way of combining inputs in a production process. In education, processes that make different uses of teachers, texbooks, radio, computers, or peer tutoring are all technologies. This entry focuses on the more capital-intensive hardware associated with the vernacular meaning of educational technology, examining the use of radio, television, the computer, and multimedia distance education systems.

1. Economists, Educators, and Technologies

Economic perspectives on educational technology are best understood as part of larger social, political, and academic debates. In the twentieth century, new technology has increasingly been viewed as the principal means for raising productivity and making economic progress. In education, this belief has translated into considerable enthusiasm for the transformative powers of each new technology: film in the 1920s, radio in the 1930s, television in the 1950s, and computers in the 1980s. Throughout this history, extravagant claims were often made, from Thomas Edison's assertion that, with film "books will soon be obsolete" (Cuban 1986 p.11), to more recent speculations on likely "computopias" (Masuda 1985). Less visionary but more common among educators has been an optimism that new technologies could be used to improve the quality of education, to extend access to educational opportunities, and to serve as catalysts to revitalize teaching and learning (Schramm 1977). Neoclassical economists complemented this optimism by pointing out how, as teacher salaries rise and the costs of alternative technologies fall, technology use becomes increasingly cost-effective.

The enthusiasm and optimism with which many educators and economists greeted new technologies has been dampened by experience and considerable criticism. Overall, Cuban (1986) argued that the same historical cycle has been repeated for each new educational technology: great enthusiasm, early research support, later research showing failure, and the eventual discarding of the technology. Technology failures, especially of high-profile educational television projects, seriously challenged early optimism (Emery 1985). Media advocates such as Schramm (1977) rethought the attention being given to "big media" such as TV, especially in developing countries, and argued for greater use of less expensive "little media," such as radio. Despite such reassessments, critical analysts, often using a political economy perspective, have argued that most new educational technologies have been applied in ways that increased inequalities, took power away from teachers, and had problematic economic and cultural consequences (Arnove 1976; Carnoy and Levin 1975, 1985; Klees and Wells 1983).

A new dominant wisdom has been emerging, however. It still argues that alternative educational technologies may have a high payoff, but it adopts a more modest approach to their application than in previous eras. It should not be presumed that all problems have technological solutions; rather, the educational problem should be the starting point for finding solutions (Anzalone 1987, Lockheed and Middleton 1991). Applications of educational technology should be specific and targeted, and not seen as general catalysts for reform (Lockheed and Middleton 1991, Nettleton 1991). The question should no longer be whether educational technologies can work; research and experience has shown some situations where they do, and others must be examined on a case-by-case basis. Particular attention needs to be paid to conditions for sustainable use (Oliveira 1988, Lockheed and Middleton 1991, Nettleton 1991).

The remainder of this entry focuses on how contrasting economic perspectives on educational technology support or challenge this new dominant wisdom of "qualified optimism" (Oliveira 1988). It is organized around the media—television, radio, multimedia distance education, and the computer—while recognizing that their impact is due not to the characteristics of the media themselves but to the specifics of the applications (Clark 1983). Each section is divided in two, beginning with an examination of the prevailing wisdom and how a neoclassical economics perspective and related research have supported it, followed by a discussion of how a political economy perspective and related research yield a much more critical view (recognizing, of course, that this dichotomy is a useful simplification).

2. Television

2.1 The Dominant View

Apart from the use of television as a component of open university systems, the new conventional wisdom is uniformly negative about the potential of television to contribute substantially to educational systems. In wealthier countries, such as the United States, educational television (ETV) never got off the ground. Few major applications were made, and those few were usually short-lived. For the most part, the televisions purchased for schools ended up in storerooms, largely neglected by teachers and students (Cuban 1986). For less industrialized countries (LICs), more substantial experimentation was undertaken, but in the main was not considered successful. Anzalone (1991 p. 55) summed up the dominant view: "The use of television in classrooms in developing countries has generally proved to be an expensive addition to educational budgets, but little evidence has been gathered to show that the expenditure brought results that were worthwhile."

The idea that master teachers, superior teaching, and an endless variety of audiovisual aids could be brought to every classroom overnight was a powerful argument for early ETV enthusiasts, especially in Third World countries. However, in practice, most large-scale uses of ETV did not involve very creative programming. In a project in Niger, one of the few where programming was acclaimed as creative, the project did not proceed far beyond the pilot stage, consequently had very high costs, about US$1200 per student, and had mixed evaluation results (Carnoy 1976, Anzalone 1987).

Mixed evaluation results, in terms of the relative gains in cognitive achievement for ETV versus non-ETV students, also characterized most of the large scale ETV projects studied in the 1960s and 1970s. Early evaluations were often positive. In American Samoa, the location of one of the first big ETV projects, early evaluations reported achievement gains, while later ones showed that ETV student achievement declined over time (Emery 1985, Cuban 1986, Anzalone 1987). In El Salvador, early evaluations reported mixed results but considered ETV a success, while later re-analyses suggested that the gains were novelty effects and that no clear advantage could be substantiated for ETV (Klees and Wells 1983, Cuban 1986, Anzalone 1987, Mayo 1990). Similar conclusions have been drawn for projects in Colombia and the Ivory Coast (Anzalone 1987).

There were also no cost advantages to ETV. In these large-scale projects, television was an add-on to the educational system, often one part of a larger reform package. The add-on cost of the ETV component varied considerably: US$4 per student in Colombia, US$13 in the Ivory Coast, US$26 in El Salvador, and US$166 in Samoa (Carnoy 1976; Anzalone 1987, 1991).

The only large project that actually reduced costs by substituting ETV for teacher quality (i.e., capital for labor) was *Telesecundaria* in Mexico. In order to reach an unserved population it used primary school teachers in secondary school classrooms, in which they were adjuncts to an intensive use of televised instruction. Achievement was evaluated as equal between the regular secondary school students and ETV system students. Initially there was a substantial cost advantage to the ETV system, leading to assessments of the system as cost-effective. However, this was eroded early on by a teachers' strike and subsequent contract agreements that put ETV teachers' salaries on a par with those of qualified secondary school teachers

(Carnoy and Levin 1975, Anzalone 1987, Mayo 1990, Nettleton 1991).

Almost all of these projects were started with large amounts of foreign aid, with the exception of Mexico's, which may account for its cost-saving structure. Mexico also seems to be the only project that has continued, actually expanding considerably during the 1970s and 1980s (Nettleton 1991). The reasons for the limited effectiveness of ETV are often seen as due to logistical, mechanical, and training problems, teacher resistance, a focus on hardware instead of software, and overall poor planning and implementation. While the assessment is not uniformly negative (Jamison and Orivel 1982), the new prevailing wisdom does not envisage television as a major educational tool for the future.

2.2 The Critical View

For ETV the dominant and critical perspectives have similar conclusions, although for largely different reasons. Issues of cost and achievement gain play a part in a critical assessment of ETV, with critics sometimes claiming monetary costs to be even higher, and the achievement picture worse, than other research had indicated (Carnoy 1976, Klees and Wells 1983). However, most of the negative conclusions reached by the critics stem from other dimensions of costs, effects, and benefits.

In educational and social terms, ETV systems continued to transmit what many regarded as inappropriate curricula. The structure of an ETV system is seen as leading almost inevitably to a lockstep curriculum imbued with a one-way, hierarchical view of the teaching–learning process (Arnove 1976, Emery 1985). Critics have emphasized how strongly teachers resisted many of these ETV experiments, with anything from strikes to refusal to turn on the television set. This point has also been made by mainstream researchers who generally attribute it to lack of teacher involvement in planning and to poor implementation strategies (Anzalone 1991). Critics from a political economy perspective usually interpret the resistance as more fundamental. In part, it is seen as arising from the very nature of ETV projects, which are premised on a lack of teacher competence and the belief that ETV can circumvent this. More broadly, critics have viewed teacher resistance as part of the general struggle between labor and capital: ETV systems are resisted because they disadvantage and deskill teachers (Arnove 1976, Carnoy 1976, Klees and Wells 1983).

The foreign aid-supported nature of many ETV projects is also seen as problematic. Aid came with conditions that turned foreign manufacturers and experts into the major beneficiaries; donor political agendas determined the nature of projects; once begun, donors had too much control over project decision-making (Klees and Wells 1983). Related challenges to national sovereignty came from the cultural effects of ETV systems: the influence of foreign cultures on

the curriculum and structure of these projects, the devaluing of nonmodern cultures, and the tendency to increase the market penetration of commercial television (Arnove 1976). In broad development terms, ETV projects have been seen as not helping to remedy educational or social inequalities and as running counter to necessary improvements in the capabilities and status of teachers in their roles in education and local development (Arnove 1976, Carnoy 1976).

3. Radio

3.1 The Dominant View

While radio has been used in a variety of educational ways since the 1920s, it has been around one particular application to primary schools in the mid-1970s that the new dominant wisdom has coalesced. The interactive radio instruction (IRI) approach used in the Nicaragua Radio Mathematics Project has come to be seen as a "major breakthrough" in educational technology use, with very low costs and large achievement gains (Anzalone 1987 p. 20). The success of IRI is attributed to its careful attention to instructional design and its "interactive," conversational style that elicits responses (often 100 in a half-hour lesson) from the classes listening (Anzalone 1987). Similar projects have been started in at least 14 countries, aimed chiefly at primary school mathematics and language. In the early 1990s these projects were reaching as many as 600,000 children in 10 countries (Anzalone 1991). Presented as three times more cost-effective than textbooks (Lockheed and Middleton 1991), it is no surprise that IRI strategies have become the epitome of the new wisdom: they have been seen as targeted interventions for specific contexts with a proven track record of high cost-effectiveness.

Evaluations of these projects have often shown substantially larger achievement gains than those found for other educational interventions. Reported effect sizes (gains in standard deviation units) range from 0.24 for reading in Kenya to 0.91 for mathematics in Bolivia, with most results toward the higher end (Anzalone 1991). Costs have generally been seen as modest, with estimates ranging from US$0.34 per student per year in Kenya to US$3.05 per student per year in Nicaragua (Anzalone 1987, 1991). For all but one of these IRI projects, radio has been an add-on cost to the existing educational system. The exception is Radio-assisted Community Basic Education (RADECO) in the Dominican Republic, which uses IRI in combination with monitors who have minimal education, to offer the equivalent of the first four grades of primary school to about 1,500 children in an unserved rural area. An evaluation reported that achievement levels were equal with conventional schools, but RADECO students learned the material in half the time at half the cost (Anzalone 1987).

There have been other significant uses of radio in

education, but many were never evaluated and those evaluated did not yield results as positive as those of IRI, often having unclear effects and/or high costs. Nonetheless, there have been many applications that could well have been cost-effective. Thailand has used radio since the 1950s to enrich formal schooling, at times reaching close to a million students (Anzalone 1987). In Colombia, radio has also been used for as long as an integral part of the nonformal education efforts of the ACPO (Popular Cultural Action) community development organization. Overall, the dominant consensus has been generally favorable to radio applications, but has principally championed IRI.

3.2 The Critical View

Few critical analyses of educational radio applications have been conducted (Byrram 1981, Arias-Godinez and Ginsburg 1984), partly because the small scale and low funding of educational radio has limited evaluation of any kind. IRI has been heavily evaluated only because evaluation has been integral to its testing and marketing campaign, and the evaluations therefore have primarily been undertaken in-house. Nonetheless, the picture that emerges of IRI from the few critical accounts and from the discussion of problems by system advocates bears little resemblance to the dominant view: costs may have been considerably underestimated, achievement gains overestimated, the whole IRI approach has not proven sustainable, and, more broadly, it has carried much of the same development strategy baggage for which ETV was criticized.

Several analysts have pointed out how IRI costs have been underestimated. Some estimates have omitted the costs of important components: start-up and development, program revision, delivery of printed materials, radio repair, transmission, or even initial radio purchase. Furthermore, most of the lower estimates of IRI costs have been based on hypothetical project expansion to an entire nation (Wagner and Kemmerer 1986, Mayo 1990). While some argue that IRI can actually substitute for printed materials, needing neither workbooks nor texts, many IRI projects have used printed materials along with radio lessons, reportedly doubling the cost of IRI (Nettleton 1991). The wide 1:8 variation observed in IRI project cost estimates reported earlier underscores how different assumptions may yield very different cost pictures of an IRI project.

There is also the possibility that the phenomenal achievement gains reported for IRI have been overstated. First, a portion of the gain may well have been caused by novelty effects: almost all the data are from the first few years of pilot project operations (Anzalone 1991). Second, since all the data are from pilot projects, it is unclear what will happen to those achievement gains in an expanded system, which is a less accessible and controllable environment (Wagner and Kemmerer 1986). Third, in most cases, achievement tests were constructed by IRI project implementors. While there is no reason to suspect overt

bias, the formulation and selection of questions could implicitly favor IRI. The implementors themselves recognized some related problems (Friend et al. 1988) and if the tests had been constructed by the respective ministries of education, the achievement advantage of IRI may have been considerably smaller.

Even if IRI has the cost-effectiveness that its proponents claim, it has not been sufficient to overcome IRI's biggest practical problem: getting a country to agree to expansion beyond the pilot. Since around 1975 the United States Agency for International Development (USAID) has invested more than US$50 million to test and market IRI globally. Yet of the 14 IRI projects initiated, only two have expanded nationwide, in Honduras and Lesotho, and the latter on the basis of voluntary use by teachers.

This problem with "sustainability" is openly acknowledged by IRI proponents and critics alike, and an array of explanations have been proffered. One problem, common to many innovations, has been the lack of specific attention paid to institutionalization during the pilot phase. The independent management and budgets that are such an advantage to pilot project operations often make it difficult later to find a permanent organizational home, as well as to function within government budgetary limits (Wagner and Kemmerer 1986, Mayo 1990).

There have also been several explanations for expansion and sustainability problems specific to an IRI system, mostly centered on how IRI may be much more difficult to operate in less accessible and controllable contexts. Technical problems will be magnified when operating on a large scale: radio repair, battery replacement, radio signal strength, delivery of printed materials, and so forth (Wagner and Kemmerer 1986). The centralized nature of an IRI system yields other problems for educational operations on a large scale. A fixed national broadcast schedule does not function easily with local variations in schedules and school calendar. Teacher and student absenteeism, more prevalent in remoter regions, can make large-scale IRI systems less effective or even unusable (Wagner and Kemmerer 1986; Anzalone 1987, 1991).

Even if the costs of IRI are judged reasonable, the financing of those costs on a large scale may be difficult or impossible. Recognizing this, some IRI pilot projects experimented with alternative financing mechanisms: e.g., getting teachers to buy the radios by offering them a price substantially below retail, or getting communities to buy batteries. However, these strategies met with mixed success in pilot projects and could be even more problematic nationwide (Wagner and Kemmerer 1986; Anzalone 1987, 1991).

There has not been the overt teacher resistance to IRI that characterized some ETV efforts, but it has been suggested that resistance comes from other stakeholders, such as "textbook writers and publishers, local curriculum specialists, teacher trainers, or expatriate educational advisors" (Anzalone 1987 p.

30). From a more explicitly political economy perspective there are some additional problems with IRI: the use of radio programming from other countries; IRI's centralized structure, which takes responsibility and control away from the classroom teacher and often makes it harder to meet the needs of disadvantaged groups (Anzalone 1987); and its regressive financing strategy when teachers and communities have to pay a substantial portion of the add-on costs.

4. Distance Education

4.1 The Dominant View

At least some, and perhaps all, of the projects discussed above could be classified as distance education systems. The essential meaning of distance education is that a substantial amount of teaching is done by someone at a distance from the learner. Usually the term is applied to out-of-school systems that are alternatives to conventional schooling (Nettleton 1991). Distance education systems originated in the 1800s and most today still rely almost exclusively on print media. When broadcast technologies are included, they are usually not used as significant teachers, but in a more minor role for "variety, enrichment and motivation," curriculum "pacing," and, increasingly, for advertising (Nettleton 1991 p. 111).

The new dominant wisdom believes that distance education is potentially a very cost-effective alternative to conventional schooling, especially to extend access to hard-to-reach populations. The rapid proliferation of open universities, enrolling almost four million students worldwide, is seen as efficient and equity-promoting because of the costs and problems associated with opening conventional universities to a diffuse population that, for the most part, must work full-time (Oliveira 1988, Lockheed and Middleton 1991). The Open University in the United Kingdom has been generally evaluated as having lower costs per student, per graduate, and per pass rate on standardized exams than traditional universities. Evaluations of open universities in LICs have provided less information. Costs per student have been generally one-third to two-thirds of the cost of conventional universities. However, dropout rates are usually high, sometimes amounting to 40–50 percent a year. This could make costs per graduate relatively high, but comparisons with conventional schooling are unavailable (Nettleton 1991).

Distance education at the primary and secondary level has not grown as much as have open universities. However, many substantial applications exist, such as the *Telesecundaria* and RADECO systems mentioned earlier. Evaluations at these levels have shown mixed results: costs per student have been usually lower than those for conventional schooling, but sometimes learning and graduation rates have also been lower (Jamison and Orivel 1982, Nettleton 1991).

Teacher training has been a major specialized application of distance education and has been considered very successful. Studies have often been cited of projects in Tanzania and Brazil, where costs were one-sixth and one-fourth of conventional teacher training costs respectively, and which were evaluated as being at least as effective. Yet the evidence is also somewhat mixed here, with studies showing other distance education teacher-training systems, in Kenya and South Africa, not to be cost-effective (Nettleton 1991).

Some of the mixed results can be attributed to economies of scale. Jamison and Orivel (1982) judge that for secondary, and perhaps postsecondary schooling, distance education systems require enrollments of at least 10,000 before their costs drop below the costs of conventional schooling. For more specialized applications, such as teacher training, some analysts have argued that distance education can be cost-effective with enrollments as low as 1,000 to 2,000 (Jamison and Orivel 1982).

Even with large enrollments, costs may vary substantially because of a wide array of contextual factors and policy choices. In particular, the relative costs of distance education diminish the more reliance there is on independent study instead of on local teachers, and the higher the opportunity costs students face in attending a conventional institution (Jamison and Orivel 1982). While for these and other reasons, the costs of distance education can vary greatly, the new conventional wisdom generally regards distance education as both cost-effective and a factor in reducing inequity in a variety of proven applications.

4.2 The Critical View

Many analysts have been skeptical of the claims made for distance education. For the most part, the cost-effectiveness claims have been based on costs alone. Little outcome data have been available on achievement or even graduation rates; what exists is problematic because noncomparable groups are usually compared. Distance education students generally must be more highly motivated than the average student in conventional schooling—this may be the explanation for any superior results. Tsang (1988 pp. 217–18) concludes that, given the "fragmentary" information available on outcomes, "firm conclusions are unwarranted" about the cost-effectiveness of distance education.

The other major claim made for distance education systems is their "clear, positive impact on educational equity—in terms of making quality education more widely available, and in terms of making access to any education at all possible for previously excluded groups" (Jamison and Orivel 1982 p. 267). It appears equitable to extend access to education, but what are these latecomers getting? In an early critique from a political economy perspective, Carnoy and Levin (1975 p. 390) pointed out that assessment by "a narrow measure of educational attainment" misses the important ways in which the socialization and teaching–learning processes in a traditional education setting offer many advantages to students over distance education substitutes such as the United Kingdom's Open University or Mexico's *Telesecundaria* (also see Mayo 1990). Even advocates have recognized that distance education is often perceived "as second choice, indeed second rate" (Oliveira 1988 p. 15).

The issue is not one of narrow cost-effectiveness. From a political economy perspective, the massive expansion of education since the 1950s in part reflects gains that have been made by the poor and the working classes, but expansion has also served to maintain the inequities of a global capitalist system. Over time, ever higher educational credentials are needed to get the same economic rewards. Disadvantaged populations are the last to be incorporated into the education system and generally get a lower economic return to schooling than did their predecessors. Moreover, as schooling has expanded over time, its nature has often changed so that the expectations of these latecomers are "cooled out," moving away from the desire for more schooling that brought success to their predecessors and toward more vocational goals (Carnoy and Levin 1985).

Distance education systems, from a political economy perspective, have thus usually been seen as giving a second-class, inferior education to those allowed into education last, namely, those who are hardest to reach and frequently the most disadvantaged. To add insult to injury, cost-recovery efforts have usually been higher in distance education systems, so disadvantaged students have ended up paying more for their education than those in conventional schools (Oliveira 1988, Nettleton 1991). Moreover, the independent study nature of distance education lets fewer students through the education pipeline. Those who do not get through are often "cooled out" from higher expectations, and society is absolved of blame for not having given them a fair chance. Indeed, more broadly, distance education systems have been seen to help maintain the stability of unfair societies by legitimating what is only a pretense of equal opportunity. More directly, especially for authoritarian regimes, stability can be enhanced because, with distance education, students do not congregate and are therefore less likely to be a political force.

5. Computers

5.1 The Dominant View

Given the relative newness of computers there is less of a consensus about computer uses in education than for other technologies, but overall expectations are positive. For wealthier countries, it has been argued that high technology in the workplace will increasingly be a source of productivity and international competitive advantage and that this requires that schools teach computer literacy and skills as basic competencies (Levin and Rumberger 1989). In addition, it is believed that computers can be effective, and increasingly cost-effective, in augmenting cognitive achievement, perhaps in developing creativity and higher-order thinking skills, and, certainly, in teaching some vocational and technical skills. For LICs, the conventional wisdom has argued that the relatively high costs of computers has severely restricted applications. Nonetheless, LICs too must move toward high technology in the workplace for reasons of economic competitiveness, and therefore they too must have enough computer applications in schools to move toward this future (Carnoy et al. 1987, Papagiannis et al. 1987, Anzalone 1991).

Evidence for the positive effect of microcomputer use on cognitive achievement comes principally from one application—computer-assisted instruction (CAI) drill and practice. There is no evidence that computer use in education has any advantage in teaching higher-order thinking skills (Carnoy et al. 1987, Papagiannis et al. 1987). Very little research is available on the cost-effectiveness of microcomputer applications, although Niemec et al. (1986) claimed that, compared to a number of educational interventions (a longer school day, reduced class size, and peer or adult tutoring) CAI was by far the most cost-effective.

In the United States research on CAI has also been used to argue that computers can contribute to a more equitable educational system: they can be effective in compensatory education strategies; are generally more effective for minorities; and may be perceived by disadvantaged populations as fairer than teachers. Moreover, United States survey data have been interpreted as showing an equitable distribution of in-school access to and use of computers not particularly biased according to gender, race, or social class (Clark 1983, Carnoy et al. 1987, Papagiannis et al. 1987).

Many analysts have pointed out that computer technologies will not be like film, radio, and television, which have not played major roles in education. To an ever greater degree, computers are a pervasive part of cultures and workplaces around the world, they are a leading symbol of modernity, they often have the support of teachers and parents, and they thus have a sizable political constituency (Cuban 1986, Papagiannis et al. 1987, Anzalone 1991). The new conventional wisdom has argued that while some of this optimism is exaggerated, computers will become more and more integrated into education in cost-effective and equitable ways. What is needed is more R&D, experimentation, and analysis to discover how computer technologies may best enhance education.

5.2 The Critical View

Critics have argued that the evidence does not support most of the past or current efforts to use computer technologies in education. Even for CAI, the research shows mixed and inconsistent results. At best, only modest effects have been observed, and these may result from biases in studies using inappropriate control groups, tests that are tailored to the intervention, and evaluator involvement in the intervention (Levin et al. 1986, Papagiannis et al. 1987). Clark (1983) argued that novelty effects and content differences may also account for such gains; any leftover is due to method, not medium. If the effort put into designing computer instruction was put into designing conventional instruction the gains might even be greater.

Even if CAI were effective, it has not been seen as cost-effective. Niemec et al.'s (1986) claim that CAI is cost-effective compared to other interventions is a critique of work by Levin, Glass, and Meister which argued the contrary; in particular that peer tutoring is about twice as cost-effective as CAI. Niemec et al. (1986) drew on meta-analysis results showing lower peer-tutoring effects and higher CAI effects, thus yielding the reverse finding: that CAI is twice as cost-effective as peer tutoring. In a pointed response entitled "The Political Arithmetic of Cost-Effectiveness Analysis," Levin et al. (1986) argued that the meta-analysis averages their critics use "exaggerate the effects of CAI" (p. 71). Such political arithmetic, they continue, is "invoked to bolster a political position in lieu of carefully subjecting that position to scientific scrutiny" (p. 72).

The critics argue that the application of computer technologies in education *has* contributed to greater inequalities along gender, race, and class lines. In the United States studies may show some improvements over time, but they have also indicated that disadvantaged groups still face substantial disadvantages in access to computers, in their uses of the computer, and in the competencies they acquire through computer use (Sutton 1991). These disadvantages come about through many mechanisms: poorer schools can afford fewer computers and teachers competent in their use, while richer individuals can afford computers in their homes; the bias toward computer applications in mathematics and science combines with the biases that keep women and minorities away from precisely these subjects, so disadvantaging them further; the content of computer magazines, textbooks, and software reinforces these same racial and gender biases; and schools segregated by race and wealth, tracking, and teacher prejudices combine to give lower status computer applications to disadvantaged groups (Apple 1986, Carnoy et al. 1987, Grubb 1987, Papagiannis et al. 1987). Sutton's (1991 p. 94) review of these issues in the United States concluded: "children who were minority, poor, female or low achieving were likely to be further behind after the introduction of computers into schools."

Although little information is available about computer use in education in LICs, it is clearly much more prevalent in private schools and learning centers and in higher grade levels, with the concomitant biases

that favor boys, the wealthy, dominant racial and ethnic groups, and the urban (UNESCO 1986, Anzalone 1987, Carnoy et al. 1987, Papagiannis et al. 1987). Papagiannis et al. (1987) pointed out the inequality double bind that LICs face: using computers in education will necessarily increase inequalities within a country, while restricting their use will necessarily increase inequalities between nations, as the technological gap between LICs and the industrialized world grows (also see Anzalone 1987).

Finally, the critics have pointed out that there is no reason to believe that computers in education can further the development of a hi-tech economy and there are reasons to worry that their use will have harmful educational and social consequences. The deskilling of jobs and the simplification of computers leave little need to develop computer skills at school (Levin and Rumberger 1989). The fact-oriented and programmed reasoning nature of computer uses in education exacerbates the neglect of the ambiguity, morality, creativity, critical understanding, and human interrelationships necessary to improving individual, social, and economic life. Moreover, in the aggregate, the money spent on computers has been generated by reductions in the numbers of teachers, their training and salaries, and from increased cutbacks in programs targeted to the disadvantaged (Apple 1986). Therefore, from a political economy perspective, for most microcomputer applications in education the broad costs have outweighed any narrow benefits.

6. Conclusion

The perspectives taken on the economics of educational technology depend on interpretations of theory, research, and experience. The dominant neoclassical economics perspective sees alternative educational technologies as means to improving efficiency, inside and outside the educational system, and, sometimes, to improving equity. The excessive optimism about past technologies has been rejected in favor of a new wisdom that argues that certain technologies have proven themselves, under certain conditions, to be efficient and equitable, particularly IRI and distance education, and perhaps some computer applications. Whether these interventions will remain advantageous, or whether others will become more attractive, will have to be determined by evaluation and monitoring activities, as with any educational or other governmental intervention.

From a political economy view of educational technology, the above framework is untenable. In a world of conflicting interests, technologies have been applied in schools (and workplaces) in ways that chiefly advance the interests of the more privileged. The disadvantaged receive fewer computers and less valued applications, second-class distance education systems, and problematic band-aids, such as IRI, to overcome the major obstacles that keep them from educational and social success. Between countries, education and social inequalities have been increasing; educational technology differences are a part of the gap.

A major problem with educational technology from a political economy perspective is that it has been governed by the same antilabor logic as technology choice in the workplace. Educational technology applications usually run counter to teacher interests: for example, hi-tech schools are planned with a lower teacher-to-student ratio in order to pay for the technology; distance education gives disadvantaged groups minimal teacher contact; and IRI gives minimal teacher training. Most educational technology systems have assumed that teachers are not competent to deliver the curriculum and therefore delivery needs to be "teacher-proofed" (Apple 1986). Nicaragua's IRI was designed explicitly to get around the poor training of the rural teacher (Wagner and Kemmerer 1986). In the United States in the 1950s and 1960s, the "needs" of the Cold War led to packaged curricula to get around the inadequacies of United States teachers. Microcomputer applications in the schools, although increasing the skills of some teachers, widened the gap among teachers and limited teacher control over an increasingly centralized curriculum (Apple 1986, Carnoy et al. 1987). Overall, educational technology use has been an alternative to investing in teachers, to training them, to paying them a good salary, and to giving them more professional control of their classrooms. Political economists, and others, would suggest that investment in teachers, not teacher substitution and deskilling, is essential to education and development success (Carnoy 1976, Carnoy et al. 1987, Papagiannis et al. 1987).

Political economists should not be seen as antitechnology. Technologies that are used as part of more participative education strategies, that enhance teacher skills and control, and that empower disadvantaged groups may be very worthwhile. To design and choose better technologies, political economists argue that better mechanisms for analysis and choice are needed. While there are no simple solutions, employing broader criteria and more participatory processes of investigation and choice can help progress toward more constructive and fairer analyses and uses of educational technology (Klees and Wells 1983, Arias-Godinez and Ginsburg 1984, Carnoy and Levin 1985, Apple 1986, Carnoy et al. 1987, Papagiannis et al. 1987).

References

Anzalone S 1987 Using instructional hardware for primary education in developing countries: A review of the literature. Project BRIDGES, Harvard University, Cambridge, Massachusetts

Anzalone S 1991 Educational technology and the improvement of general education in developing countries. In:

Lockheed M, Middleton J, Nettleton G (eds.) 1991 *Education Technolgy: Sustainable and Effective Use*. World Bank, Washington, DC

Apple M 1986 *Teachers and Texts: A Political Economy of Class and Gender Relations in Education*. Routledge and Kegan Paul, New York

Arias-Godinez B, Ginsburg M 1984 Nonformal education and social reproduction/transformation: Educational radio in Mexico. *Comp. Educ. Rev.* 28(1): 116–27

Arnove R (ed.) 1976 *Educational Television: A Policy Critique and Guide for Developing Countries*. Praeger, New York

Byram M 1981 Popular participation in the mass media: An appraisal of a participatory approach to educational radio. *Canadian and International Education* 10(2): 48–63

Carnoy M 1976 The economic costs and returns to educational television. In: Arnove R F (ed.) 1976

Carnoy M, Daley H, Loop L 1987 Education and computers: Vision and reality. Stanford University School of Education, Stanford, California (mimeo)

Carnoy M, Levin H 1975 Evaluation of educational media: Some issues. *Inst. Sci.* 4(3/4): 385–406

Carnoy M, Levin H 1985 *Schooling and Work in the Democratic State*. Stanford University Press, Stanford, California

Clark R E 1983 Reconsidering research on learning from media. *Rev. Educ. Res* 53(4): 445–60

Cuban L 1986 *Teachers and Machines: The Classroom Uses of Technology since 1920*. Teachers College Press, New York

Emery M 1985 Another exciting learning revolution? A rejoinder to Kupisiewicz and White. *Prospects* 15(4): 493–572

Friend J, Galda K, Searle B 1988 From Nicaragua to Thailand: Adopting interactive radio instruction. *Development Communications Report* (Special Issue): 8–9

Jamison D, Orivel F 1982 The cost-effectiveness of distance teaching for school equivalency. In: Perraton H (ed.) 1982 *Alternative Routes to Formal Education: Distance Teaching for School Equivalency*. Johns Hopkins University Press, Baltimore, Maryland

Klees S, Wells S 1983 Economic evaluation of education: A critical analysis in the context of applications to educational reforms in El Salvador. *Educ. Eval. Policy Anal.* 5(3): 327–45

Levin H, Glass G, Meister G 1986. The political arithmetic of cost-effectiveness analysis. *Phi Del. Kap.* 69–72.

Levin H, Rumberger R 1989 Education, work and employment in developed countries: Situation and future challenges. *Prospects* 19(2): 205–24

Lockheed M, Middleton J 1991 Education technology: Towards appropriate and sustainable use. In: Lockheed M, Middleton J, Nettleton G (eds.) 1991 *Education Technology: Sustainable and Effective Use*. World Bank, Washington, DC

Masuda Y 1985 Computopia. In: Forester T (ed.) 1985 *The Information Technology Revolution*. MIT Press, Cambridge, Massachusetts

Mayo J 1990 Unmet challenges: Educational broadcasting in the Third World. In: Chapman D W, Carrier C A 1990 *Improving Educational Quality: A Global Perspective*. Greenwood Press, New York

Nettleton G 1991 Uses and Costs of educational technology for distance education in developing countries.

In: Lockheed M, Middleton J, Nettleton G (eds.) 1991 *Education Technology: Sustainable and Effective Use.* World Bank, Washington, DC

Niemec R, Blackwell M, Walberg H 1986 CAI can be doubly effective. *Phi Del. Kap.* 67(10): 750–51

Oliveira J 1988 Can technology advance education? EDI Seminar Report Series, World Bank, Washington, DC

Pagiannis G, Douglas C, Williamson N, LeMon R 1987 *Information Technology and Education: Implications for Theory, Research and Practice.* International Development Research Centre, Ottawa

Schramm W 1977 *Big Media. Little Media: Tools and Technologies for Instruction.* Sage, Beverly Hills, California

Sutton R 1991 Equity and computers in the schools: A decade of research. *Rev. Educ. Res.* 61(4): 475–503

Tsang M 1988 Cost analysis for educational policymaking: A review of cost studies in education in developing countries. *Rev. Educ. Res.* 58(2): 81–230

UNESCO 1986 *Informatics and Education: A First Survey of the State-of-the-Art in 43 Countries.* UNESCO, Paris

Wagner A, Kemmerer F 1986 Limits of the use of educational technology in developing countries: A reappraisal of the costs. Paper presented at the conference on Economics of Education: Tackling the New Policy Issues, Dijon

Further Reading

Bock J, Papagiannis G (eds.) 1983, *Nonformal Education and National Development: A Critical Assessment of Policy, Research and Practice.* Praeger, New York

Campen J T *Benefit, Cost and Beyond: The Political Economy of Benefit–cost Analysis.* Harper & Row, New York

Clark R 1986 Evidence for confounding in computer-based instruction studies: Analyzing the meta-analyses. *Educ. Comm. & Tech. J.* 33 (4): 249–62

Easton P, Klees S 1990 Education and the economy: Considering alternative perspectives. *Prospects* 20(4): 413–28

Goulet D 1977 *The Uncertain Promise: Value Conflicts in Technology Transfer.* IDOC, New York

Grubb W 1987 Responding to the constancy of change New technologies and future demands on US education In: Burke G, Rumberger R (eds.) 1987 *The Future Impact of Technology on Work and Education.* Falmer New York

Jamison D, McAnany E 1978 *Radio for Education and Development.* Sage, Beverly Hills, California

Kozma R 1991 Learning with media. *Rev. Educ. Res.* 61(2) 179–212

Mayo J, Hornik R, McAnany E 1976 *Educational Reform with Television: The El Salvador Experience.* Stanford University Press, Stanford, California

Orivel F 1987 Educational technology. In: Psacharopoulos G (ed.) 1987 *Economics of Education: Research and Studies.* Pergamon Press, Oxford

Papagiannis G, Klees S, Bickel R 1982 Toward a political economy of educational innovation. *Rev. Educ. Res* 52(2): 245–90

Perraton H (ed.) 1986 *The Cost of Distance Education* International Extension College, Cambridge

Tilson T, Jamison D, Fryer M, Godoy-Kain P, Imhof M 1991 Sustainability in four interactive radio projects: Bolivia Honduras, Lesotho, Papua New Guinea. In: Lockheed M, Middleton J, Nettleton G (eds.) 1991 *Education Technology: Sustainable and Effective Use.* World Bank Washington, DC

United States Agency for International Development (USAID) 1990 *Interactive Radio Instruction: Confronting Crisis in Basic Education.* USAID, Washington, DC

Webster F, Robins K 1986 *Information Technology: A Luddite Analysis.* Ablex Publishing, Norwood, New Jersey

SECTION VIII

Financing Education

Introduction

M. Carnoy

Financing education, like financing any public good, has involved searching for amounts and sources of funds that "match" the public's view of how much should be spent and who should bear the costs of education. This welfare approach to educational finance has not changed fundamentally in the past generation. It is appropriate that Charles Benson, who did much of the seminal work in this field and whose untimely death in 1994 ended a long career in the economics of education, should have written the opening entry in this section. In it he outlines the three main criteria by which systems of education are traditionally judged: whether the level of provision of educational services is adequate, whether the distribution of educational resources is efficient, and whether the distribution of educational resources is equitable. All three are marked by a number of complexities. What is the definition of "adequacy"? When does the free market (the decisions of individual students and their families responding to prices of education that reflect the real cost of schooling) result in an "efficient" allocation of resources to education? What should be the proper role of centralized tax collection and financing in a society marked by geographic and social inequalities?

Henry Levin's entry expands on each of these criteria. He concludes that the greatest challenge to educational finance is presented by rising costs at a time of economic difficulties. He sees the greatest hope in attempting to maintain educational quality while reducing costs per unit of output or increasing quality while maintaining costs. The other challenge is to find new sources of funding in ways that do not increase inequality. Both these challenges are discussed in the entries that follow.

The changes in educational financing issues that occurred in the late 1980s and 1990s were the result of a major slowdown in world economic growth and the drastic declines in gross economic product per capita in a number of African and Latin American countries during the 1980s. Many of these countries had been heavy international borrowers in the 1970s, so the decline in their growth in the 1980s subjected them to considerable pressure from developed countries and international financial institutions to cut public spending, including privatizing public industries, and finding new sources of public revenues. Jean-Claude Eicher's entry on trends in international spending on education document these changes, and Fernando Reimers reviews the implications of the economic crisis for educational financing in developing countries. Both Eicher and Reimers conclude that the economic decline had a strong negative effect on educational spending per pupil. Reimers further argues that structural adjustment measures, whether self-imposed by the country itself or by external lending agencies, tended to reduce funding to basic education more than to university education and reduced spending on school supplies more than on teacher salaries—precisely the opposite of the policy recommended by the external lending agencies but inevitable given the politics of educational finance.

As Doug Windham shows, international agencies have played an increasing role in funding education in developing countries, and in shaping educational policy. Part of the rethinking of educational financing necessarily entailed searching for ways to expand education at lower cost to the general public but in ways that fulfilled the goal of using education to improve equity.

The most popular way to cut public spending yet maintain the availability of schooling to growing school-age populations has been to privatize schooling. A number of economists in the international agencies, as shown in Emmanuel Jimenez's entry, have argued that forced cuts in public spending could provide greater equity in educational finance by increasing the fraction of university costs borne by fees (private financing) and shifting public spending from tertiary level elite education to basic primary and secondary schooling—levels serving low- and middle-income school populations. The main outlines of this strategy are described in Maureen Woodhall's two entries on student loans and student fees.

Yet, despite pressure from international organizations, the opposite has generally occurred; with increased pressure to reduce public spending on education, primary and secondary schooling in Africa and Latin America has increasingly become privately funded, whereas university education has continued to maintain its share of public funding.

Estelle James suggests that the privatization of public education occurs in two principal forms. First, families bear an increasing share of the total cost of public schooling in the form of fees, contributions to the school, and the required expenditures on books, school supplies, and uniforms. Second, as public funding for education declines and conditions in public schools worsen, an increasing percentage of pupils attend privately-run schools, usually subsidized by the public sector. James's argument is that because of such arrangements, the private/public school dichotomy is a false one, privately-managed schools are generally supported partly or wholly by public assistance, and public schools are financed to an increasing extent by private fees and other spending.

As Jimenez points out, however, private financing of education, while more closely approaching user fees for user services at lower levels of schooling, does impact low-income families much more than higher-income families. The result is that enrollment rates may be affected in a highly inequitable fashion.

The other side of the financing coin, as described by Benson and Levin, is the issue of community control—centralized versus decentralized financing and centralized/decentralized school management. Allegedly, the more decentralized funding and management are (the purely private school), the more the school will serve directly the needs of the school clientele. The more centralized funding and control are, the less the likelihood that client needs will be served. The problem with the highly decentralized funding and control market model, however, is that it can result in a highly unequal provision of educational services. But a centralized model does not guarantee equity either. Jimenez deals with some of these trade-offs in his entry, but it is in Mark Bray's piece on community financing of education that the full implications of the trade-off between the centralization of financing and client control are discussed. Community financing represents a more collective manifestation of raising private funds (and donated time) locally for educating the children of the community. The advantage of such community financing is the possibility of community influence over the educational process—indeed Bray outlines a topology of financing/community control possibilities along a decentralized/centralized management/financing continuum. But its disadvantage is that poor communities clearly have less to donate than rich communities. It is this conundrum of control versus more equal resources that is at the heart of the decentralization debate.

Educational Financing

C. S. Benson

Education in almost all countries is provided in both the private and public sectors. Thus education is not purely a public good; the exclusion principle, barring students who fail to pay fees to a particular educational institution, can be readily applied (even though it rarely is in the lower grades). Education consumes a significant amount of resources in almost all countries, running between 6 and 10 percent of gross national product. A certain minimum level of educational provision is generally assumed to be necessary in order for a country to attain a reasonably high rate of economic growth. The distribution of educational opportunities to different groups of the population has consequences for social justice. As a result of the size of the set of educational activities in a country, and because educational provision affects economic growth and the distribution of income, systems of educational finance are likely to be complicated. This complexity is reinforced by the fact that education is carried forward in both public and private sectors and might best be described as a quasi-public good.

There are three main criteria by which systems of educational finance are traditionally judged: whether the level of provision of educational services is adequate, whether the distribution of educational resources is efficient, and whether the distribution of educational resources is equitable. These three criteria are interrelated.

1. Adequacy of Funding

During the 1960s and the first half of the 1970s, adequacy was defined in terms of the percentage of gross national product devoted to education (the figure of 8 percent was often deemed "adequate"), and in terms of the share of the central government's budget spent on education (20 percent was an appropriate figure). These kinds of measures are not thoroughly satisfactory because they sometimes ignore private education and educational revenues generated in provincial and local authorities. Their meaning was also ambiguous because they failed to address the question of the efficiency with which a given government ran its educational programs.

Since the late 1970s, following the lead taken by the World Bank, a new set of adequacy measures has come to be accepted. These measures are intended to get somewhat closer to outcomes of educational systems. One measure is the proportion of the relevant age group enrolled in primary school (in Ethiopia, a figure of 36 percent was reported in 1985; in the same year in Turkey, it was 116 percent). A second set of measures related to balance by gender, that is, whether educational opportunities are provided to women (in Morocco, 98 percent of the age cohort of males were enrolled in primary school but only 63 percent of females). A third criterion of adequacy is the proportion of the age cohort enrolled in secondary school (in the industrialized nations, this runs from 70 percent to over 90 percent; in the poorer nations, a figure of around 35 percent is typical). A fourth criterion is the adult literacy rate (the industrialized nations report no adult illiteracy to speak of, with the literacy rate typically at 99 percent; poorer nations have literacy rates of 50 percent or less, generally speaking).

To assure (a) near-universal enrollment in the elementary grades, (b) sufficient retention in the elementary grades to supply a sizable and sexually balanced group of students for the secondary grades, and (c) a quality of instruction for the whole population to sustain lifelong literacy, it is demanded that teachers and classrooms be generously available in both cities and rural areas. The objectives by which adequacy of education is defined also require at least a minimum level of commitment on the part of teachers. In turn, the requirements for real resources to meet standards of adequacy set the financial requirements. Required cost per capita will vary from country to country, depending on the degree of efficiency with which the educational system is operated.

For the industrialized nations, and for nonindustrialized countries characterized by a relatively equal distribution of income, the question of adequacy needs no further general discussion. However, when a large part of the youth population of a country is affected by malnutrition, or poor health, or where many parents find it necessary to exploit the labor of their very young children, then an "adequately financed" system of education, as defined by conventional standards, may fail to yield the objectives of educational adequacy mentioned above (near-universal primary enrollment, gender balance in secondary schools, high rates of adult literacy, etc.) It

may be necessary to expend public resources to protect the nutritional status, health, and so forth, of students and intending students in order that they be physically able to benefit from the instruction offered to them in an "adequately financed" educational system.

Like an international airline, a university system is an indispensable symbol of status the world over. It is generally expected that universities will be financed at some level beyond the requirements of the economy to provide a nation with liberal arts graduates and lawyers. When adequacy is viewed in terms of less glamorous sectors of higher education, such as polytechnical institutes, the situation is often different. Many countries fail to provide themselves with sufficient graduates in technical fields, a problem that could be ameliorated by adjusting program enrollments to workforce requirements projections.

2. Efficiency

Publicly financed institutions, whether at the school, technical institute, or university level, ordinarily claim a certain degree of autonomy in managing their affairs. In some instances, institutional views of educational policy may be contrary to the dictates of efficiency, as seen from a national perspective. There are two main criteria for judging efficiency in education: cost–benefit and cost-effectiveness. To raise standards of educational efficiency, it is necessary that central governments use the power of the purse string to shape local policy.

The cost–benefit ratio can be reduced (implying an improvement in efficiency) by reducing cost while holding output constant or by ensuring that graduates at any level have been prepared, or are being prepared, to maximize the present discounted value of their lifetime income streams.

In free market economies, it might at first seem that one could leave the problem of income maximization in the hands of the individual student. However, it is not always true that the market, even where it is competitively organized, gives sufficient heed to long-term needs for trained personnel. Hence, for example, the government might judge that the country was offering excessively high rewards to business managers and inadequate rewards to scientists and engineers, with the result that the country was in danger of losing whatever degree of technological superiority it had attained. The government might then offer grants to postsecondary institutions for improvement of their science and engineering facilities and offer additional fellowships in these fields, while cutting back on fellowships provided to students in management fields. Use by the government of financial incentives to produce a relative shift of real resources among specialties in postsecondary institutions may be unavailing, however, if the basic salary structure in the economy is unyielding (e.g., if employers continue to give preference in pay to managers over scientists and engineers). This illustrates the point that improvements in educational efficiency may require exercise of economic power beyond that which is held within the educational community itself.

Another type of cost–benefit problem may be more amenable to government policy: for example, if it is determined that rural youth are being provided a lower standard of educational provision than city youth, and that the educational deficiencies in the countryside prevent graduates of rural institutions from making their full contribution to the economy. The government could then use its financial powers to improve the physical facilities of rural schools, and offer salary supplements to well-trained teachers who might be induced to work in rural schools. A similar problem occurs when the education of females is neglected, with the result that a country can be deprived of the services of up to one-half of its human talent. The government, seeking to change such a condition, might give special grants to institutions that enroll women in nontraditional fields, and offer extra fellowships to female applicants. The government may, and has the power to, redirect resources toward these target groups. It may also need to follow up and put pressure on private employers to hire graduates of rural schools and to hire women to work in nontraditional roles.

It is necessary to consider cost-efficiency and how efforts to raise the cost-effectiveness of an educational system might be reflected in a government's financial policy. Cost-effectiveness refers to the yield of educational outputs relative to consumption of real resources by educational institutions. Lapses from an acceptable standard of efficiency generally take one or more of the following forms: (a) an excessive rate of student wastage; (b) an excessive rate of student repetition of classes; (c) a high rate of student failure in examinations (whether as actually recorded, or as perceived by potential employers); and (d) a progress of instruction which is too slow and drawn out.

Student wastage, repetition, and failure may have a number of different causes, and the causes may differ from one institution to another. To attack these problems by using financial incentives requires a government to have a good management information system and a certain freedom from political influence. In the lower grades, children in rural areas and in urban slums may drop out of school or study poorly on account of problems of health and diet. In postsecondary institutions, problems of student performance may reflect primarily that students were not well-prepared for academic studies in the feeder institutions they attended. In some countries these difficulties appear to be massive in scale, and the government then faces a choice of trying to do a little for all the students who are in academic difficulty, or to marshal substantial resources to help students in certain development zones or pilot projects, leaving the rest to wither on the vine.

3. Equity

The effects of a search for equity in the design of most systems of educational finance are so strong, and the approaches to finance of primary and secondary schools on the one hand, and to finance of postsecondary institutions on the other, are sufficiently different, that it is necessary to distinguish clearly between these two main sectors of education.

In the administration of primary and secondary schools, most central governments seek an arrangement which is neither wholly centralized nor wholly decentralized. Complete centralization implies an excessive amount of bureaucratic delay in making decisions, and it is also likely to entail an incapacity to take proper account of changes in local needs and desired practices. It may forestall experiment and progress based on experiment. Yet complete decentralization destroys the capacity of the central government to direct local authorities to meet long-range national needs for training personnel. It also prevents a progressive administration from imposing higher standards of public morality on backward local authorities. Finally, complete decentralization leaves the pattern of local financial provision to be determined by the pattern of local financial resources. Given that localities often show vast differences in fiscal capacity, the result is likely to be a situation where some children receive more than adequate care, while others are taught in shacks by untrained teachers, working in large groups and lacking instructional materials.

A mixed system of provision, one which is subject to decision rules about the presence of both central and local powers, calls for a financial arrangement within the category of "intergovernmental fiscal relations." The money flows from the larger governments to the smaller, regardless of the number of levels. (In England and Wales, there are two main levels— the center and the local authorities; in the United States, there are three main levels—federal, state, and local.) The general rule for the distribution of funds is as follows: the larger unit of government distributes funds to the smaller unit directly in accordance with the needs of students in the smaller unit and, inversely, with regard to the fiscal capacity of the smaller unit of government.

Needs of students are measured in the first instance by a census of the age cohort eligible to attend a particular level of education. This age cohort may then be adjusted in various ways, and the more sophisticated the adjustments, the higher the degree of equity likely to be attained. First, the age cohort may be reduced to recognize the number of students for whom parents choose private education. Second, the number may be fictionally increased, that is "weighted," to take account of the fact that some students are more expensive to educate than others. The more expensive categories may include children who are academically or economically disadvantaged, the handicapped, students who do not speak the language of the host country, students who seek those kinds of vocational training that require special equipment or specially trained teachers, and gifted students. Third, the age cohort may be further weighted to recognize the fact that market power is not uniform among local authorities. Local authorities that have a pleasant climate in which the students are exclusively middle-class may be able to attract a teacher of given competence at a lower salary than disadvantaged industrial suburbs.

Measurement of local financial capacity is ordinarily a simpler process. Having determined what the local tax base consists of, whether income, trade, or property, a total is taken for this local area and is then divided by the number of eligible students.

Using their estimates of local needs and resources, the central government is likely to employ one of three main fiscal devices to link together central and local support for education. The first of these is called a "foundation program plan." The foundation program is a money figure representing the government's estimate of the cost of educating a typical student in a typical local authority. It is a per-student figure. The value of the foundation program is multiplied by the weighted student enrollments in each local authority, in order to derive a set of estimates of local needs. The government then determines a "fair rate of local contribution" and in the case of each local authority applies this national fair rate of local contribution to the local tax base. The positive difference, if any, between the government's estimate of local needs and the government's estimate of appropriate local contribution represents the government's grant to a given local authority. The intention under this arrangement is to ensure that any local authority can provide an adequate educational program at a rate of local taxation no higher than is required of a wealthy authority.

A second main type of grant is known as "percentage equalizing." Under this arrangement, the government agrees to share in the costs of a locally determined education budget and, using a complicated formula, to share local budgets in such a way that any two local authorities that levy the same local school tax rate are provided with the same sum of money to spend per student. In effect, the state grant equalizes local fiscal capacity, while leaving the decision about the size of the budget to local discretion. Obviously, the percentage share of state money will be higher in a poor local authority than in a rich one.

The third main type of grant is the "weighted-population grant." This is the simplest arrangement of the three and the one that is the most flexible, that is, that requires least commitment of future resources on the part of the state. A given local authority's share of funds appropriated by the state for some stated purpose is equal to that local authority's proportionate share of total weighted population statewide, with the "weights" reflecting such factors as grade level of students or needs of certain types of students for extra resources. If the appropriation for a particular educational program is 10 million dollars, pounds, or pesos, and if local authority X represents 10 percent of the state's total weighted student population, then authority X is entitled to one million dollars, pounds, or pesos.

In the United States, efforts in some parts of the country to produce financial equalization have proceeded to the point that an unusual number of middle-class families have deserted the public schools for the private. This, in turn, has led to a demand that the state deal directly with parents, giving them "vouchers" for educational services that could be redeemed in either public or private institutions. So far, none of the various voucher proposals has found sufficient favor with the voters to be passed into law.

There are two main approaches to the problem of equity in finance of higher education. In Europe, and in most developing countries, the central government pays most of the costs of postsecondary education, including student maintenance, and the necessary funds are distributed directly to the institutions. The systems are hierarchical, with one or more major universities at the top, and various forms of technical institutes and institutions of further education at the bottom. The intending student finds a place in the structure in accordance with his or her measured academic abilities. Analysts at the World Bank and elsewhere have suggested that an increasing proportion of the costs of higher education in developing countries should be shifted from government to parents, citing both efficiency and equity arguments.

In the United States the main support of higher education is found in a system of grants and loans made directly to students. The size of individual grants is related (inversely) to parental income. The student is free to use the grant or loan in any approved institution to which he or she can gain admission. The United States approach is apparently more conducive than the European to privately administered expansion of higher education and "openness" of admissions. However, some observers express concern about academic standards in the lower tier of institutions in the United States.

Periodically, there is interest in shifting the cost of United States higher education from government and parents to students themselves, using the device of "income-contingent loans." Through those loans students would be able to borrow practically unlimited sums for their education and pay the money back over their working lifetime, relative to the extra income that is estimated to be attributable to their additional schooling. Under conservative fiscal policy and high rates of inflation of the costs of higher education, devices of this kind may well be adopted. In the meantime, a majority of students meet a share of their expenditures on higher education by working for wages on a part-time basis.

See also: Private and Public Costs of Schooling in Developing Nations

Bibliography

Balderston J, Wilson A, Freire M, Simonen M 1981 *Malnourished Children of the Rural Poor: The Web of Food, Health, Education, Fertility, and Agricultural Production.* Auburn House, Cambridge, Massachusetts
Benson C 1978 *The Economics of Public Education,* 3rd edn.
Houghton Mifflin, Boston, Massachusetts
Benson C 1991 Definitions of equity in school finance in Texas, New Jersey, and Kentucky *Harv. J. Legislation* 28 (2): 401–22
Cohn E, Geske T G 1990 *The Economics of Education,* 3rd edn. Pergamon Press, Oxford
McMahon W W 1988 Potential resource recovery in higher education in the developing countries and the parents' expected contribution. *Econ. Educ. Rev.* 7 (1): 135–52
Psacharopoulos G, Tan J-P, Jimenez E 1986 *Financing Education in Developing Countries: An Exploration of Policy Options.* World Bank, Washington, DC

School Finance

H. M. Levin

The term "school finance" refers to the process by which tax revenues and other resources are derived for establishing and operating elementary and secondary schools as well as the process by which those resources are allocated to schools in different geographical areas and to types and levels of education. The term, school finance, has generally been limited to the elementary and secondary levels, although it has also been applied to preprimary institutions.

The area of school finance draws heavily from other fields. Since laws must be passed and administered, it is closely related to the politics of education and educational law. Since various aspects of economics and finance are involved, it must draw upon principles from the economics of education and government finance (Monk 1990). And, since the overall plans for financing education must be translated into the operations of schools, it must necessarily relate to school administration.

1. Structural Features of School Finance

It is important to provide brief definitions of a number of terms that are commonly used in school finance. School revenues refer to the financial receipts of schools for supporting their operations. Such revenues can be derived from taxation, tuition charges, and student fees as well as from contributions and income from the provision of goods and services. School expenditures refer to the financial disbursements of schools for the purchase of the various resources or inputs of the schooling process such as administrators, teachers, materials, equipment, and facilities. Costs represent the value of all resources used in the schooling process, whether reflected in school budgets and expenditures or not. The costs of school resources

include the values of any inputs that are used, even if they are donated or not reflected accurately in expenditure accounts.

Capital expenditures are those incurred for providing school plant and facilities. Although capital investment requires a large initial expenditure, the plant and facilities have a lifetime that extends over many years. In contrast, operating or recurrent expenditures refer to financial outlays for school resources that are used each year for the operations of the schools, such as teacher salaries and disposable supplies. Budgetary provisions must be made for operating expenditures each year.

School finance begins with the major decisions about education, such as who will be educated in what ways. The financial aspects must necessarily be based on the translation of these decisions into resource requirements, which will be satisfied through tax revenues, family expenditures, and donated resources. Since these decisions will differ substantially from society to society, so too will school finance arrangements. Although the principles of school finance can be applied to many different societies, their actual application must reflect the unique economic, political, social, and cultural attributes of each setting. There is no universal tax or expenditure approach for schools that will be found appropriate for all situations.

One reason for the importance of school finance is the fact that a considerable part of the gross national product (GNP) of nations is devoted to education. Available sources of data such as those in the UNESCO *Statistical Yearbook* (e.g., UNESCO 1991) tend to combine expenditure at all levels, including those for higher education. In the 1980s, about 2–9 percent of GNP was devoted to public educational expenditures among nations. In general, those countries with higher proportions of their young enrolled in school and with higher per capita incomes spent a larger proportion of GNP on education. In a worldwide survey of this phenomenon, Eicher (1982) found that for every 1 percent increase in GNP, there was an increase of over 2 percent in public educational expenditure among countries from all major regions of the world in 1960–65. This declined to about a 1.3 percent increase in the 1965–76 period, but educational expenditures still maintained a faster rate of growth than did GNP.

There are at least two reasons why educational expenditures tend to increase at a faster rate than GNP. First, at relatively low levels of per capita income, most of what is produced must be used for consumption with little surplus available for investments in schooling or other areas. But at higher per capita incomes the available resources for both social and private investment rise. Second, as countries become more industrialized, there is a greater private and social demand for schooling. What is clear is that education makes a prodigious demand on the resources of almost all societies, and even these amounts do not reflect the sizeable private expenditures on schooling and related educational needs such as books, transportation, and uniforms (Schiefelbein 1987, Tsang and Kidchanapanish 1992).

2. Decisions in School Finance

The best way to understand the field of school finance is to consider it as a decision-oriented phenomenon in which educational decisions must be translated into ways of financing schools. Each society has its own educational priorities, system of government finance, political mechanisms for making decisions, and administrative structures for implementing them. School finance reflects these structures and processes.

2.1 How Much Schooling?

Every society must decide who will be educated and how much education will be provided? Depending upon the answers to these questions, particular populations will be eligible, or even compelled, to attend school. Further, given the availability of schools, noncompulsory schooling (e.g., upper-secondary and higher education) will rise over time as more and more persons complete the compulsory years. When these phenomena are combined with the size and growth of the eligible youth populations, financial provision must be made for adequate numbers of places in elementary and/or secondary schools. The financial implications arising from who will be educated represent the most fundamental building blocks of a system of school finance. Both the projection of capital costs and operating costs depend upon an understanding of who will be eligible to attend school and who will actually participate.

The ability to ascertain the number of students that

should be planned for at each level is essential to designing an adequate system of school finance. The most basic tool is that of demographic studies of the population which transform birth rates and the size of the youth population at each schooling level into anticipated enrollments for specific target dates in the future (Davis 1980b). To a large extent, this type of analysis must ascertain not only who is eligible to attend each schooling level, but what proportion will actually attend if schools are available. Social demands for schooling can be developed statistically to make these estimates (Davis 1980a).

In wealthier societies it may be suitable to let schooling expand as rapidly as the demands for it grow, particularly if there is evidence that the additional benefits of that schooling exceed the additional costs. However, most countries are subject to severe constraints in following this approach, given the dearth of resources, and even the richer industrial societies face serious problems of unemployment among their educated populations. Accordingly, some societies may choose to plan the expansion of schooling beyond the compulsory years according to some sense of social or economic need for the nation.

The personnel planning approach attempts to estimate the required number of workers with different levels of schooling according to the occupational needs for meeting specific objectives of economic output at some future target period. It has been criticized severely for the lack of realism of its assumptions and its projections (Blaug 1972). (See *Manpower Analysis*.)

The rate-of-return approach provides a method of assessing the expansion of schooling in terms of an investment where the future increase in economic output from an investment in education is compared with the cost of additional schooling (Becker 1964, Psacharopoulos 1973). In this way one can compare the returns for social investments in schooling with investments in other public goods such as health or capital investment in plant and equipment. Presumably, further investment in schooling should proceed only when its rate of return exceeds those for alternatives. This technique has been criticized because of its crucial assumption that increases in social productivity of workers can be assessed according to higher earnings that they receive when they have obtained more schooling (Berry 1980). Further, the lack of data availability on future earnings may also introduce distortions into the estimates (Eckaus 1973). These analytical tools are considered to be helpful, primarily, at a heuristic level, in planning for future enrollments, even if they cannot be applied mechanically to the issue (Blaug 1972).

2.2 How will People be Educated?

Once having established who will be educated and how much education will be provided, it is necessary to ask what types of education will be provided. There are at least three basic dimensions to this question. First, what type of education will be offered at each level? Of particular concern is the nature of the primary curriculum and the emphasis on vocational versus academic education at the secondary level as well as the specific requirements of each. Second, what quality of education will be offered? Clearly a system of large classes using minimal facilities with modest instructional material and poorly trained teachers will require fewer resources than one with greater qualitative depth. Third, what provisions will be made for children with special educational needs, such as the physically and mentally handicapped, intellectually gifted, immigrants, and those from impoverished backgrounds? It is widely recognized that such groups have particular educational requirements that may necessitate supplementary resources (Kakalik et al. 1981, Levin 1973).

The nature of the primary educational curriculum and the division of secondary students between academic and vocational training have major cost consequences, since each is associated with different resource needs (Hu and Stromsdorfer 1979). This is obviously true for differences in school quality, with the cost per student increasing as a function of teacher preparation, reduction in class size, and the facilities and instructional materials that are provided. Because of the predominance of teacher costs, the decision on class size alone can dominate cost patterns. Essentially, a reduction in class size by 50 percent will tend to increase the cost per student by almost 100 percent. Finally, the greater the attention to the special needs of particular students, the more resources will be required to meet educational commitments (Kakalik et al. 1981).

The quality issue must be assessed with respect to the benefits of any particular level of resource utilization in meeting the goals of schooling relative to the costs of those resources. One criterion that has been used on an international basis is that of the contribution of educational resources to cognitive achievement as reflected in test scores (Heyneman and Loxley 1982). The literature on this subject, that of educational production functions, seeks to determine how changes in different educational inputs such as class size and teacher quality create differences in student achievement (Hanushek 1986). However, it is important to note that the quality of education should not be judged on the basis of test scores alone.

One major concern is the impact of public school investment on the relation between public and private sectors. In many societies, the low investment in and resulting quality of the public schools relegates them as institutions for the poor who have no other alternatives. Middle- and upper-income families send their children to private schools which are more highly endowed with educational resources. Often there are substantial public investments in these private schools. The result is the existence of a dual system of

schools: a low-quality public one with large classes, modestly trained teachers, poor materials, and inferior facilities that is attended by children from low-income families, and a higher quality private system with smaller classes and better teachers and other amenities. The latter charges fees that are beyond the resources of poor families.

A related issue is what provision of educational resources will be made to those students with special needs such as the handicapped, intellectually gifted, immigrants, and the poor? This is a matter of social and political priorities which may require considerable economic resources to address fully.

2.3 Who Should Pay?

The resources that are required for elementary and secondary schools include those that are used directly to provide instruction and those that must be present in the schooling process. Included in the first category are teachers, buildings, materials, equipment, and so on. Within the second category are the time and efforts of students to undertake instruction and to study. In many societies the use of student time at the upper-primary level and secondary level represents a cost because children who are attending school must reduce their provision of productive labor for the support of families and society. Thus the student's time must be considered as a resource that is usually "paid" for by the family and society in terms of reduced income, and the total cost of schooling must include this element as well as the direct instructional costs.

Each society must decide which constituencies should pay the costs of the resources that are required for schooling. One principle that is used is that of benefits received. That is, the various constituencies should bear the costs of schooling according to the benefits they receive. For example, schooling is supposed to have considerable benefits for the entire society in the form of a more literate and productive nation with a common language and common set of values (Weisbrod 1964, Bowen 1977). Schooling also provides advantages for individual students and their families in the form of higher status, earnings, and access to opportunities. The problem of allocating costs between the larger society and the individual participants in the schools is that it is difficult to determine in a precise sense the social and private benefits for schooling.

2.4 What is the Appropriate Government Structure?

The appropriate government structure for the sponsorship of schools has important implications for school finance. Different societies rely on different principles of school organization. Some societies provide a highly centralized form of school organization and governance in order to maximize the uniformity of school operations and to benefit from presumed economies of scale. Others are organized largely according to region and locality within certain national laws or guidelines. One based upon regional and local sponsorships provides greater potential for responding to the specific needs of the school populations that are being served. The balance between central and regional or local governance of schools will determine the balance between uniformity and diversity. Such a decision on governance can have profound implications for school finance, since decision-making responsibilities at any governmental level often entail financing responsibilities as well.

To the degree that there is some reliance upon regional and local authorities in the finance of education, issues of school finance inequalities arise. Units of government may differ in the level of educational support for their students according to their relative priorities for education as well as their wealth and tax bases relative to the number of school-eligible children. Especially important in this regard are differences between urban and rural areas, where the latter are usually considerably poorer than the former.

In many cases central governments take responsibility for providing grants to states and local governments to provide a minimally acceptable quality of schooling for all eligible youth (Sherman 1980). The state or regional governments may also provide such equalizing grants to individual local schools. In some cases higher levels of government will also provide categorical grants to their decentralized school authorities to induce them to provide specific categories of educational services such as those for disadvantaged and handicapped children.

A final aspect of governmental structure is the choice between government and private sponsorship of schools. Friedman (1962) has argued that although the government should provide resources for schooling because of its important benefits for the society as a whole, the actual operation of schools should be under private auspices to create choice and competition among schools. This issue will be addressed below.

3. Obtaining and Allocating Resources

How will resources be obtained and allocated to different levels of schooling, different types of students, and different regions and locality? There are two criteria that can be used to analyze each of these issues: efficiency and equity. Efficiency refers to using available resources in a way that maximizes the welfare of a society (Levin 1976). Equity refers to distributing the benefits and costs of any endeavor in a way that is considered to be fair. It is clear that both concepts are socially determined in that what is assumed to be efficient and equitable in one society might be considered to be inefficient and inequitable in another. However, the two criteria are of great assistance for any particular society in evaluating

the most appropriate methods for both obtaining and allocating resources for the schools.

3.1 Obtaining Resources for Schooling

The first issue that arises with respect to obtaining resources for schooling is how the burden of support will be distributed between the government and families. Even when the government pays the direct cost of instruction, families must often pay for the costs of books, uniforms, athletic equipment, and the loss of forgone earnings of their older children who are enrolled in school rather than being employed.

In general, it is argued that primary and most secondary education provides social benefits of such an important nature that the entire society should support them (Friedman 1962, Weisbrod 1964). These benefits include a common set of values, knowledge, a standard language, skills for modern work enterprise, the development of latent scientific and cultural talents, and many more. Further, widespread participation in modern societies requires that all individuals be exposed to a set of common experiences that are requisite to obtaining access to available opportunities. This democratization of access to opportunities is considered to be an important social benefit in itself. Because of the perception that elementary and secondary schooling are necessary for the functioning of modern societies, most nations take the view that the direct costs of providing schooling should be subsidized through public funds.

A central question that arises is what type of tax system is most appropriate for the support of elementary and secondary schools from the perspectives of efficiency and equity. In general, there are two concepts of tax equity that might be considered: benefits received and ability to pay (Musgrave and Musgrave 1976). The benefits-received principle assumes that the tax burden ought to be levied according to the benefits received by different constituencies. Unfortunately, the very nature of most social benefits means that they are difficult or impossible to apportion to different constituencies.

The ability-to-pay principle assumes that those taxpayers with greater ability to support the tax system— usually those with greater income and wealth—ought to provide larger contributions to tax revenues than those with lesser resources. The actual application of this principle will depend upon the specific tax base and the particular assumptions regarding how to minimize social sacrifice for obtaining a given level of revenue (Musgrave and Musgrave 1976).

Efficiency in taxation refers to the effects of the tax system on the entire economy as well as the collection and compliance costs for raising any particular revenues. If one believes that the "natural" workings of a free economy produce the most efficient allocation of resources, then it is important that any system of taxation minimizes the distortions to that system (Musgrave and Musgrave 1976). Of course, monopoly concentration in many industries and the effects of trade unions and government raise serious questions about the existence of a free and competitive economy. Further, sometimes the tax system is used to provide "desirable" distortions such as taxation on tobacco products, liquor, and luxury goods, which is designed to reduce consumption of those products. However, the design of a tax system should always be scrutinized to minimize any distortions that are considered to be undesirable.

Efficiency in collection and compliance refers to minimizing the costs required to obtain a given level of revenue. In this respect, costs refer not only to the governmental resources that are required to collect the tax, but also the cost to the taxpayer of complying with the demands of the tax system. Different taxes are associated with different costs of collection and compliance.

Thus far the discussion has referred to the characteristics of systems of taxation in general terms rather than with regard to school finance. A system of public revenues for school finance has two other characteristics that are desirable: stability and growth. Stability refers to the yield of a tax system from year to year. An educational system will have predictable revenue needs, and it is important that the tax system provide those needs with high reliability. Some systems of taxation will be characterized by large fluctuations from year to year depending upon economic conditions. For example, a tax on the export of primary commodities will tend to be highly unstable as market conditions vary.

To the degree that school enrollments are expanding or improvement of school quality is desired, it is also necessary that tax revenues grow adequately to meet the rising resource requirements. Some tax bases have greater growth potential than others. Any tax approach should be assessed for whether the tax revenues that it will produce will keep pace with the rising demands upon it.

The most widely used taxes are corporate and personal income taxes, sales and consumption taxes, and property taxes. Each is associated with different equity and efficiency consequences, depending upon how it is applied. In general, equity in taxation is determined by ascertaining the incidence of a tax on households in different income classes (Musgrave and Musgrave 1976). For purposes of defining tax equity, a tax may be characterized as progressive, proportional, or regressive. A progressive tax represents an increasing proportion of household income as income rises; a proportional tax is a constant proportion of income at all income levels; and a regressive tax is one that carries a greater proportional burden on lower incomes than on upper ones.

Business taxes and some property and sales taxes are not levied directly on households, so it is not always possible to know in any precise sense how the tax is shifted to different income groups in higher prices or lower incomes. However, there is a vast literature which has provided broad conclusions on the equity consequences of different taxes (Musgrave and Musgrave 1976, Break 1974, Pechman and Okner 1974).

The personal income tax is highly flexible and can be progressive, proportional, or regressive depending upon the structure of tax rates, the definition of taxable income, and provisions for tax deductions, exemptions, and credits. Typically, the official tax rates reveal little about the actual incidence of the tax. For example, the United States has a highly progressive income tax on the basis of the official tax rates, but the large numbers of tax loopholes that are to the particular advantage of upper income taxpayers have meant that the actual incidence has been more nearly proportional (Pechman and Okner 1974).

It is difficult to know who ultimately pays business taxes since they can be shifted to the consumer in higher prices or to their workers in lower wages. One type of income tax that is commonly used is the payroll tax. This tax tends to be highly regressive, because it is a tax on the earnings from labor, while not taxing property income. Since property income is concentrated among the highest income groups, a payroll tax does not tax a major source of income for these groups while taxing the major or only income source for lower income households.

Sales taxes can be divided into specific excise taxes and broad-based or general sales taxes (Musgrave and Musgrave 1976). The former are usually levied on luxury goods or those for which a society wishes to discourage consumption such as cigarettes, liquor, and gasoline. General sales taxes or consumption taxes—as they are called—apply to a much larger set of goods and services. These include the turnover tax or value-added tax which is a tax applied to the increased value of goods at each stage of production. Such taxes are common throughout Europe and other industrialized countries. The incidence of the excise tax will obviously depend upon the incomes of families that consume the taxed goods. If the tax is on luxury goods, it will tend to be progressive. Sales or consumption taxes are generally considered to be regressive, because a low income household must allocate a higher proportion of its income to consumption than a richer one. However, the incidence can be made less regressive by excluding such necessities from the tax base as food, basic clothing, shelter, and medical care.

The property tax can be applied to both real property (land and its attachments) and personal property. A tax on real property is particularly attractive at the local level, since local taxes on sales and income may induce rapid shifts in location of household and purchases to avoid the tax. A tax on real property is less subject to such avoidance, especially over the short run. To the degree that the property tax is a tax on shelter it is believed to be regressive, since shelter constitutes a higher proportion of income when income is low. To the degree that the tax is on capital, it may be progressive, since capital ownership is concentrated heavily among high income households (Aaron 1975).

In general, the personal income tax is considered the most efficient with respect to its economic impact in that it does not distort prices of goods and services and market allocations, although very high marginal rates of taxation could reduce the incentive to work or invest. Each of the other taxes does alter the relative prices and returns to different goods and services or sources of income with some effect on the after-tax allocation of resources (Musgrave and Musgrave 1976).

Collection and compliance costs will differ from country to country. In most nations the collection and compliance costs are lowest for payroll and turnover taxes because the collection mechanism can be routinized among the firms providing employment and producing goods and services. Sales taxes and property taxes generally require a more elaborate administrative apparatus for the government. In countries where the income tax has had a long history of acceptance, as in the United States, it too will have relatively low costs of collection and compliance relative to its yield. However, in countries where such a tax is not well-accepted, there may be great difficulties in collection.

3.2 Allocating Resources for Schooling

In addition to the concern for how resources will be obtained for schooling, decisions must also be made on how to allocate resources to different levels and types of schooling, different types of students, and different regions. These decisions, too, can be analyzed according to the criteria of equity and efficiency where public expenditure is the principal measure of resource distribution. Equity in school expenditures refers to fairness in the distribution of subsidies to students with different educational needs and from different educational and geographical backgrounds. Efficiency in school expenditures refers to using them in the most effective way to meet particular goals, such as economic growth or citizen participation.

When defined in this way, equity and efficiency may be complementary to each other, or may be in conflict. As with the case of taxation, each society must determine what is meant by equity in schooling expenditures. For example, if all students are to be given an equal public subsidy for schooling, then it is only necessary to provide equal expenditures for each student, adjusted for differences in the cost of resources from region to region (Chambers 1978). However, equal expenditures will not provide an appropriate or adequate education for each child if some children need different and more costly resources than others. Children from poor backgrounds often lack the investments in health, nutrition, and intellectual stimulation that will enable them to succeed in school

(Levin 1973). Such students may need compensatory resources such as health services, meals, and remedial assistance in order to benefit from the schooling experience (Levin 1989). Of course, this is also a potential efficiency argument in that it is conceivable that much of the standard instruction is wasted on such youngsters without ensuring their basic well-being. A similar case can be made for children from immigrant backgrounds who must develop linguistic competence to be able to benefit fully from instruction.

However, not all cases will be characterized by such a compatible relation between equity and efficiency implications of school expenditure patterns. In some cases, equity will require greater investment in the schooling of a particular group of students without contributing in the most efficient way to other educational goals. In those instances, the issue of equity must be viewed as an end in itself, rather than a means to greater efficiency. For example, some physical and mental impairments among handicapped children may be so serious that no amount of schooling will prepare the young for productive work or to take care of their own needs. They will always require a high level of custodial care. Yet, providing access to special educational programs that will assist them in caring for many of their needs and developing social skills and relations may be considered to be a high priority, even though it will be a relatively expensive undertaking that cannot be defended on narrow efficiency grounds.

In the situation where equity and efficiency considerations are in conflict, a particularly important issue is that of cost. If the costs of the resources required to achieve equity detract only nominally from the achievement of other schooling goals, equity is easier to pursue than if the conflict between the use of resources is substantial. In this case one must examine the trade-offs in using resources for one goal rather than the other (Levin 1991b).

In addition to the equity decisions among different types of students, there is a particular issue that arises when schools are financed at several levels of government. Since regional and local governments will have different capacities to provide schooling based upon their income and wealth, the same tax effort will create rather different amounts of school revenues among governmental entities. In general, urban areas will have more taxable wealth income, so at the same tax effort they will be able to provide higher expenditures for the schooling of each student. Inequalities in expenditure that emanate from differences in the taxable resources of subunits of government do not have an educational rationale, even though they may reflect accurately the regional distribution of income and wealth. Accordingly, many societies make at least some attempt to equalize expenditures among regions and municipalities (Oates 1972).

One view about equalizing school finance capacity among decentralized units within a country has stressed the concept of fiscal neutrality. Under this approach, the amount of funding spent on each student should be neutral with respect to the fiscal capacity of the unit of government (Feldstein 1975). One method of ensuring a measure of fiscal neutrality is for the central government to assume all responsibility for funding the schools, but such a change also removes much of the source of autonomy and responsiveness of regional and local schools. An alternative method that preserves this autonomy is to permit the decentralized governments to determine their level of tax effort with respect to the tax rate that they choose for supporting the schools. The central government can guarantee that at any level of tax effort the same amount of funding will be available for each child, regardless of the income or wealth of the subunit of government (Coons et al. 1970). In essence, the central government provides a grant to the regional or local government which represents the difference between what is guaranteed at a particular tax rate and what is raised by the state or local government at that rate.

One of the major efficiency questions in allocating schooling expenditures is that of supporting different levels and types of schooling. For example, what should be the appropriate ratio between expenditures on elementary and secondary schooling? Given an expansion of secondary schooling, what proportion of the additional resources should be placed in vocational versus academic education? One method that has been used to address these issues is to look at each type and level of schooling as an alternative investment in which earnings and employability of graduates represent a major benefit and the costs of instruction and forgone earnings of students during the period of schooling represent the major costs (see *Rates of Return to Education*; also Psacharopoulos 1973, 1981). In principle, those levels and types of schooling with the highest rate of return on investment will represent the best candidates for expansion. However, such analyses do not account for equity issues or other benefits that are not reflected in employment and earnings.

A different type of concern is the effect of different forms of financing on the efficiency of resource use. The most provocative proposal in this regard is that of Friedman (1962) to provide a system of educational vouchers to finance elementary and secondary education. Under a voucher system, parents would be given certificates that could be used to pay a specified maximum level of tuition at any school approved by the state. Schools would be sponsored under both public and private auspices to compete for the vouchers. Presumably, the increased competition for students and greater choice would lead to a more responsive and efficient educational system as the marketplace replaces government decisions on schooling. The dearth of voucher experience means that this contention is largely untested. The voucher approach has been criticized as having the potential to destroy the social and democratic benefits of schooling by stratifying schools according to social class, race, political orientation, and religion. It has also been asserted that the administrative arrangements for centralized record-keeping and administration of a voucher plan that must account for every school-age child would be extremely costly, offsetting any gains in efficiency from competition. These arguments have been strongly debated (e.g., Levin 1991a, West 1991).

4. Summary and Future Issues

School finance is tied intimately to both educational and social commitments of a society as well as the resources for meeting those commitments. There is no overall model that provides the most appropriate approach to financing schools for all situations. Each society will need to consider its own educational and social priorities as well as its means for addressing them. However, there exist a number of analytic concepts and tools for evaluating different approaches to school finance from the perspectives of both equity and efficiency.

Perhaps the most important challenge to school finance is presented by the rising costs of schooling at a time when world economic crisis has limited severely the capabilities of most societies to meet concomitantly all of their aspirations. Schooling is a labor-intensive activity, and as the costs of labor rise, educational salaries must keep pace. If enrollments increase at the same time that expenditures per student are maintained, the overall cost of schooling must continue to rise. Even this phenomenon does not allow for raising quality at a time when it is believed that educational quality is too low.

There exist three ways to constrain such costs: restricting the growth in enrollments; reducing the quality of instruction; and finding ways to maintain or increase quality at lower cost per student. The first of these has severe political and ethical implications, but it may be unavoidable in the long run unless other alternatives emerge. The second seems to be an unwise choice at a time when most countries are concerned that existing quality is too low. The third represents the challenge of our times. Can new technologies such as computers and educational television as well as new organizational arrangements reduce or contain costs, while maintaining or even improving quality (Levin and Lockheed 1993)? The future agenda of school finance must necessarily be preoccupied with the search for answers to this question (Schiefelbein 1986, Wolff 1984).

In the meantime, much public policy in the 1990s and beyond seems to be directed toward encouraging greater responsibilities by local communities and families for the financing of education. The potential of greater community contributions—even among poorer communities—seems great in terms of contributed labor for facilities and other functions (Bray and Lillis 1987). However, dependence upon this source of financing would tend to exacerbate the differences in opportunities between rich and poor communities. Likewise, empirical studies have found that considerable funding of education from family resources already exists in some countries, and it leads to systematic differences in educational resources among children from different economic backgrounds (Tsang and Kidchanapanish 1992). Accordingly, the shift in emphasis by agencies such as the World Bank may have severe repercussions for equity.

See also: International Aspects of Financing Education

References

Aaron H J 1975 *Who Pays the Property Tax? A New View*. Brookings Institution, Washington, DC
Becker G S 1964 *Human Capital: A Theoretical and Empirical Analysis, with Special Reference to Education*. Columbia University Press, New York
Berry A 1980 Education, income productivity, and urban poverty: A background study for World Development Report. In: King T (ed.) 1980 *Education and Income*. World Bank, Washington, DC
Blaug M 1972 *An Introduction to the Economics of Education*. Penguin, Harmondsworth
Bowen H R 1977 *Investment in Learning: The Individual and Social Value of American Higher Education*. Jossey-Bass, San Francisco, California
Bray M, Lillis K 1987 *Community Financing of Education: Issues and Policy Implications in Less Developed Countries*. Pergamon Press, Oxford
Break G F 1974 The incidence and economic effects of taxation. In: Blinder A S, Solow R M, Break G F, Steiner P O, Netzer R (eds.) 1974 *The Economics of Public Finance: Essays*. Brookings Institution, Washington, DC
Chambers J G 1978 Educational cost differentials and the allocation of state aid for elementary/secondary education. *J. Hum. Resources* 13(4): 459–81
Coons J E, Clune W H, Sugarman S D 1970 *Private Wealth and Public Education*. Belknap, Cambridge, Massachusetts
Davis R G 1980a *Planning Education for Development. Vol 1: Issues and Problems in the Planning of Education in Developing Countries*. Center for Studies in Education and Development, Harvard University, Cambridge, Massachusetts
Davis R G 1980b *Planning Education for Development. Vol. 2: Models and Methods for Systematic Planning of Education*. Center for Studies in Education and Development, Harvard University, Cambridge, Massachusetts
Eckaus R S 1973 *Estimating the Returns to Education: A Disaggregated Approach*. McGraw-Hill, New York.
Eicher J C 1982 What resources for education? *Prospects* 12(1): 57–68
Feldstein M S 1975 Wealth, neutrality, and local choice in public education. *Am. Econ. Rev.* 65: 75–89
Friedman M 1962 *Capitalism and Freedom*. University of Chicago Press, Chicago, Illinois
Hanushek A E 1986 The economics of schooling: Production and efficiency in public schools. *J. Econ. Lit.* 24(3): 1141–77
Heyneman S P, Loxley W A 1982 Influences on academic achievement across high and low income countries: A re-analysis of IEA data. *Soc. Educ.* 55:(1) 13–21
Hu T-W, Stromsdorfer E W 1979 Cost–benefit analysis of vocational education. In: Abramson T Y, Tittle C K, Cohen L (eds.) 1979 *Handbook of Vocational Education Evaluation*. Sage, Beverly Hills, California
Kakalik J W, Furry W S, Thomas M A, Carney M F 1981 *The Cost of Special Education*. Rand Corporation, Santa Monica, California
Levin H M 1973 Equal educational opportunity and the distribution of educational expenditures. *Educ. Urb. Soc.* 5(2): 149–76
Levin H M 1976 Concepts of economic efficiency and educational production. In: Jamison D T, Froomkin J T, Radner R (eds.) 1976 *Education as an Industry: A Conference of the Universities National Bureau Committee for Economic Research*. Ballinger, Cambridge, Massachusetts
Levin H M 1989 Financing the education of at-risk students. *Educ. Eval. Policy Anal.* 11: 47–60
Levin H M 1991a The economics of educational choice. *Econ. Educ. Rev.* 10(2): 137–58
Levin H M 1991b The economics of justice in education. In: Verstegen D, Ward J G (eds.) 1991 *Spheres of Justice in American Schools*. Harper Business, New York
Levin H M, Lockheed M (eds.) 1993 *Effective Schools in Developing Countries*. Falmer Press, New York.
Monk D H (1990) *Educational Finance: An Economic Approach*, McGraw-Hill, New York
Musgrave R A, Musgrave P B 1976 *Public Finance in Theory and Practice*, 2nd edn. McGraw-Hill, New York
Oates W E 1972 *Fiscal Federalism*. Harcourt Brace Jovanovich, New York
Pechman J A, Okner B A 1974 *Who Bears the Tax Burden?* Brookings Institution, Washington, DC
Psacharopoulos G 1973 *Returns to Education: An International Comparison*. Jossey-Bass, San Francisco, California
Psacharopoulos G 1981 Returns to education: An updated international comparison. *Comp. Educ.* 17(3): 321–41
Schiefelbein E 1987 *Education Costs and Financing Policies in Latin America: A Review of Available Research*. World Bank, Washington, DC
Sherman J D 1980 Equity in school finance: A comparative case study of Sweden and Norway. *Comp. Educ. Rev.* 24(3): 389–99
Tsang M C, Kidchanapanish S (1992) Private resources and the quality of primary education in Thailand. *Int. J. Educ. Res.* 17: 179–98
UNESCO 1991 *Statistical Yearbook, 1990*. UNESCO, Paris
Weisbrod B A 1964 *External Benefits of Public Education: An Economic Analysis*. Department of Economics, Princeton University, Princeton, New Jersey
West E G 1991 Public schools and excess burdens. *Econ. Educ. Rev.* 10(2): 159–69
Wolff L 1984 *Controlling the Costs of Education in Eastern Africa: A Review of Data, Issues, and Policies*. World Bank, Washington, DC

Student Loans

M. Woodhall

Students in higher education in many developed and less developed countries receive financial aid in the form of loans, which must be repaid after the students graduate or complete their education. Student loans, together with scholarships, grants, bursaries, or fellowships represent one of the main ways in which governments or private institutions provide financial support for students, to enable them to pay tuition fees or living expenses. However loans, unlike other forms of student support, must ultimately be repaid. There are a wide variety of student loan schemes operating in different countries, and the conditions under which the loan schemes are administered differ substantially.

Student loans are the subject of great controversy in several countries, because there is disagreement about whether students should be subsidized by means of loans or grants and scholarships. There is disagreement about the effects of loans and disagreement about the best way of providing financial aid for students. Advocates and opponents of loans argue fiercely, often ignoring the actual experience of various countries with student loan schemes. However, there is a considerable body of experience, since student loans have been widely used as a means of supporting students in higher education since at least the early 1960s. This entry will therefore summarize the type of student loan schemes operating in various countries, consider the arguments for and against loans, and review the evidence on the effects of student loans as a means of financing higher education.

The arguments about student loans concern the effect of loans compared with other forms of financial aid on access to higher education, particularly for poor students from low-income families, the equity of different methods of financing students, the effects of loans on student motivation and performance, the feasibility and costs of administering loan programs, and administrative issues such as which institutions should provide the loan, how to organize repayment, what rate of interest should be charged, how to deal with students who default on repayment, and so on.

1. Different Types of Financial Aid for Students

Governments throughout the world provide financial support for students in higher education. The extent of subsidization of education and the way in which subsidies are provided differ substantially in different countries, but in every country, both developed and less developed, governments provide a large part of the financial resources for higher education, as well

as for primary and secondary education. Subsidies for higher education may be given to institutions, that is schools, colleges, or universities, or to students, to cover part or all of their living costs.

The majority of countries provide both kinds of subsidy, but there are considerable differences between countries in the balance between aid to institutions and aid to students. The following types of financial aid are provided, in various countries:

(a) Payments to institutions to cover direct costs of tuition, and therefore reduce or eliminate fees to students.

(b) Unconditional payment to all students in the form of a grant.

(c) Payments to selected students, in the form of a scholarship, grant, or bursary awarded on the basis of academic ability.

(d) Payments to selected students, in the form of means-tested grants or scholarships, awarded on grounds of financial need.

(e) Repayable loans provided to students from public funds at interest rates below the market rate, or at zero interest.

(f) Government guarantees for loans provided by banks or other private institutions, and interest subsidies to enable loans to be offered at less than market rates of interest.

(g) Payments to students for part-time work provided under special employment schemes for students.

(h) Provision of meals, accommodation, or travel at prices below market rates.

(i) Tax concessions to students or graduates.

(j) Tax concessions to students' parents.

Governments subsidize higher education for a number of different reasons. Since investment in education is judged to bring economic and social benefits, one objective of government aid to education is to ensure that there is sufficient investment in education, and another is to promote equality of opportunity by ensuring that financial barriers do not prevent students from enrolling in higher education.

Student loan programs also have a number of different objectives. In some countries the primary aim is to secure sufficient educated personnel to serve the needs of the economy, whereas in other countries the question of equality of opportunity is of crucial importance. Many countries provide a number of different types of financial aid for students. In particular, many countries provide a mixture of grants and loans, in some cases accompanied by tax concessions for students or their parents, or subsidized employment opportunities for students.

Student loans are an important form of financial aid for students in various European countries, throughout Scandinavia, in Canada, the United States, and in Japan, and they are widely used in Latin America. Some developing countries in Africa and Asia have student loan programs, but many developing countries make little use of loans, providing instead the bulk of financial aid for higher education by means of grants to institutions and grants, scholarships, or bursaries to students. Very few countries rely exclusively on student loans. Japan is one of the few countries which provides nearly all financial aid to students in the form of loans, although there has been a trend toward greater reliance on loans in several countries in the 1980s, and some countries, including the United Kingdom, have recently introduced loan programs in the early 1990s. However, there is still controversy in many countries about the desirability of introducing student loans. A few countries, for example, Japan and Sweden, provide loans for students in upper-secondary schools. However, in most cases, loans are mainly provided for students in higher education (postsecondary, technical, or vocational) rather than for those in primary or secondary education.

There have been several comparative studies of student support in Europe and the United States (Woodhall 1970, 1978, 1982, 1989, 1990; Johnstone 1986) and extensive analysis of student aid policy in individual countries, particularly the United States and the United Kingdom. From the late 1980s, the feasibility of student loans in developing countries has also attracted attention, and the International Institute for Educational Planning (IIEP) has organized a series of educational forums on student loans in the United States and Europe (Woodhall 1990), Asia (Woodhall 1991a), Africa (Woodhall 1991b), and Latin America (Woodhall 1993). The World Bank has also conducted research on student loans in developing countries, and a special issue of *Higher Education* is entirely devoted to student loans in developing countries. These studies are summarized below.

2. Student Loan Programs

In some countries, private institutions operate student loan programs, for example, some individual colleges or universities offer loans to their students, and some charitable funds have been established to provide loans for poor students. In the majority of cases, however, student loan schemes are operated by or for central or state governments. Many countries, including Canada, Denmark, Norway, Sweden, and Japan established government loan programs in the 1960s, while others, including Germany and the United Kingdom, have introduced loans more recently.

In the United States there are various student loan programs, operated by commercial banks, individual colleges, universities, or private agencies, but with government guarantees and interest subsidies. The first scheme was set up in 1958 and called the National Direct Student Loan Program (NDSLP), now known as "Perkins loans." This was followed by the Guaranteed Student Loan Program (GSLP) in 1965, now known as "Stafford loans", and the most recently established schemes, set up in 1981, are Parent Loans for Undergraduate Students (PLUS), and Supplementary Loans for Students (SLS). In the United Kingdom, student loans known as "top-up loans" were introduced in 1990, to supplement grants covering students' maintenance or living expenses.

In South America, the first student loans were offered in 1950 when the Colombian Institute for Advanced Training Abroad (*Instituto Colombiano de Crédito Educativo y Estudios Técnicos en el Exterior*, or ICETEX) was established. The term "educational credit" (*crédito educativo*) is used in Latin America to refer to student loans and any type of financial aid for students involving a repayment obligation. The scheme in Colombia was originally intended to help students finance higher education abroad, but in 1968 ICETEX began to provide loans to students for study in Colombia. The student loan scheme in Colombia was followed, during the 1960s and 1970s, by the establishment of student loan institutions in many Latin American countries, for example EDUCREDITO in Venezuela, and the *Instituto Nacional de Crédito Educativo* (INCE) in Argentina. The various student loan institutions in Latin America have formed the Pan American Association of Educational Credit Institutions (*Asociación Panamericana de Instituciones de Crédito Educativo*, or APICE).

3. The Main Features of Student Loan Programs

The majority of student loan programs provide long-term low-interest loans for students to enable them to finance tuition fees and/or living expenses. In Scandinavia and in other European countries loans are provided for maintenance costs only, since tuition is generally free, but in Japan and the United States loans are given to help students pay tuition fees. Most student loans have to be repaid within 10 or 20 years, but there are considerable differences in the terms of repayment, and in the rate of interest charged on student loans. Many governments subsidize student loans so that students do not usually have to pay interest while they are studying, and after graduating or completing their course the interest charged on the money borrowed is usually below market rates of interest. In the United States the different loan schemes charge different rates of interest. The most highly subsidized loans are Perkins loans, intended for students from low-income families; borrowers must pay 5 percent on Perkins loans, but 8–10 percent on Stafford loans, and between 12 and 14 percent on SLS and PLUS loans. In Canada the rate of interest varies with market rates and in Sweden and Japan interest is below commercial rates. In most cases, students undertake to repay their loans over a fixed period of time, at a fixed rate per year. Thus student loans resemble mortgages in most cases. However, in a few instances graduates may vary the rate at which they repay their loans and in several countries graduates can postpone repayment in the eventuality of illness or unemployment. The government provides guarantees in many countries, so that if a borrower dies or becomes seriously ill or handicapped, and so cannot repay the loan, the debt is written off, although in some cases borrowers must have personal guarantors.

In several countries there have been proposals to introduce income-contingent loans. This would mean that students would undertake to pay a fixed proportion of their income each year until their debt was repaid. Very few countries have so far introduced income-contingent loans, but Sweden introduced income-related repayment in 1989, which means that graduates are expected to pay 4 percent of their income until their loan is repaid. Australia has introduced a Higher Education Contribution Scheme (HECS) under which students must pay a charge which represents about 20 percent of average tuition costs; this may be deferred until after graduation and then paid, through the tax system, by means of 2 to 4 percent of gross taxable income. This scheme has been wrongly described by some commentators as a graduate tax, but in fact it resembles an income-contingent loan, collected through the tax system. The essential difference between student loans and a graduate tax is that the former involves repayment of a debt, and payment comes to an end when the debt is fully discharged, whereas a graduate tax involves a permanent obligation. In Australia a graduate's payments come to an end when the total liability is repaid.

Income-contingent loans have been advocated in the United Kingdom by Barr (1988, 1991) on the grounds that they are both more efficient and more equitable than mortgage-type loans. There have been several such proposals in the United States, but a short-lived experiment with income-contingent loans in the United States—the so-called "Yale Plan" in the 1970s—was not a success. Nevertheless, some United States economists, notably Reischauer (1989) have advocated income-related repayments, and the idea is again being examined in the United States.

In most countries, eligibility for student loans depends on the level of a student's family income, that is, they are means-tested. In many cases loans are specifically intended for needy students who would otherwise be unable to afford to pay fees or living expenses. However, in Sweden all students are entitled to receive loans, regardless of parental income, and in the United Kingdom the new "top-up loans" are also available to all students regardless of family income. In the United States the Middle Income Student Assistance Act (MISAA) of 1978 removed any income ceiling, so that all students became eligible for GSLP loans. The result was such an increase in demand for subsidized loans, and such a heavy burden on federal government funds, that in 1981 GSLP loans were again confined to students from lower income families.

This brief summary of existing student loan programs shows that there are wide variations in the type of loan available to students in different countries. The effects of student loans will, therefore, depend on the type of loan scheme adopted, and there is still considerable controversy among economists about the relative merits of different types of loan.

4. The Question of Loans versus Grants

One of the fiercest controversies in the field of educational finance is whether financial aid for students should be given in the form of loans or grants. Economists in the United States and the United Kingdom have disagreed, over many years, on the subject of the desirability of student loans, as well as the advantages or disadvantages of particular types of loan. Arguments center around the following factors: (a) the supply of finance for higher education, (b) the financial benefits of higher education, (c) the equity of alternative methods of financing education, (d) the effect of loans or grants on equality of opportunity, (e) the efficiency of higher education, and (f) practical and administrative questions about the operation of student loan programs.

Advocates of student loans argue that governments should subsidize higher education on grounds of national welfare, since education brings both economic and noneconomic benefits to the community, but that a system of loans will impose less of a burden on public funds than a system of grants or scholarships, and it will also be more equitable than grants, since those who will themselves benefit from higher education, in the form of higher lifetime earnings, will contribute to the costs of their education through repaying their loans. Opponents of loans, on the other hand, argue that student loans will be less effective than grants in encouraging low-income students to continue their education, since the fear of debt may discourage poor students or women. They also argue that student loans will increase the risk of wastage or dropout, since students will be concerned about the size of their debts, and furthermore that the costs of administering loan scheme and the problem of students who default on repayments will reduce the potential savings from introducing a loan scheme.

Much of the argument depends on what type or level of student aid is available in a country. So, for example, in the United Kingdom where the majority of university students receive a grant to cover maintenance expenses and have free tuition, the opponents of loans argue that loans will discourage working-class students, and that the threat of a "negative dowry" will discourage women from enrolling in higher education. In the United States on the other hand, where very little student aid was available until the mid-1970s, advocates of student loans argued that they would help to equalize educational opportunities by making it possible for even the poorest students to finance higher education by borrowing.

The question of equity is raised in many of the debates about loans versus grants. Advocates of loans argue that it is students from upper income families who are most likely to benefit from subsidies for higher education, and this involves a transfer of income from taxpayers with average or below average income to those who will enjoy above average income in the future as a result of their education. Thus, it is argued that loans are more equitable than grants because they ensure that those who directly benefit from higher education will ultimately pay when they repay their loans. A system of loans, it is argued, provides financial aid when it is needed, but does not involve a transfer of income from taxpayers to graduates. In the United Kingdom, for example, Prest (1966), Blaug (1970), Maynard (1975), and Woodhall (1982) all argued that a system of student loans is more equitable than a system of outright grants, as well as being more flexible and imposing less of a burden on public funds. In addition, Barr (1988, 1991) argues that income-contingent loans, collected through the national insurance or social security systems, are supported by both the "benefit principle" of taxation and ability to pay.

5. Student Loans in Developing Countries

The arguments about loans versus grants as a means of student support have recently been extended to developing countries. Severe financial constraints which limit public expenditure mean that governments in many developing countries have been forced to reduce public funding for higher education. Many economists have argued for increased cost-recovery in higher education, on the grounds that it is a profitable private investment, with private returns exceeding social returns, so that high levels of subsidy, including grants, involve a transfer of income from poor taxpayers to those who will in the future enjoy high earnings as a result of their higher education. Moreover, in many

developing countries students in higher education are likely to come from privileged backgrounds, so that increased cost-recovery together with a substitution of loans for grants have been advocated, both for their efficiency and their equity. (Psacharopoulos and Woodhall 1985, Psacharopoulos et al. 1986).

Experience of student loans in developing countries is more limited than in industrialized countries, but loan schemes now operate throughout Latin America and increasingly in Africa and Asia. However, many of these have encountered serious administrative problems, in particular high rates of default, so that critics contend that loans are not feasible in developing countries that lack an efficient banking system or other financial infrastructure. There is a growing body of literature dealing specifically with the problems of designing student loan programs for developing countries (Woodhall 1987, Albrecht and Ziderman 1991). This depends crucially on evaluations of existing loan programs, including experience in industrialized and developing countries. This research is summarized in the following section.

6. Evaluations of Student Loans

There have been a number of recent evaluations of student loans as a means of financing higher education. Some of these have been carried out in the context of debates about how to reform student aid policy in particular countries. For example, in Canada a Federal-Provincial Task Force on Student Assistance presented a report in 1980 which included an evaluation of the Canada Student Loan Program (CSLP). In the United States there have been many evaluations and assessments of loans as a means of student support (Hartman 1971, Rice 1977, Hansen 1989, Gladieux 1989). An early study concluded: "The student loan program is not an unmixed blessing, nor an entirely unmitigated evil ... In today's fiscal and educational policy circumstances loans are needed" (Rice 1977 p. 9).

More recently, Hansen concluded that "The existence of loans gives students wider access to financial assistance than would be possible if the aid were in the form of outright, non-repayable grants ... Fiscal realities demand that we continue to rely on loans as a major source of funding for students in postsecondary education" (Hansen 1989 p. 67).

The two main concerns identified by Hansen are the fear of excessive debt burdens and high default rates, particularly in proprietary schools. These problems are partly due to the very rapid growth in student loans in the United States. Between 1978 and 1981, as a result of the increase in eligibility of GSLP loans, the total volume of lending to students rose from US$2 billion to US$8 billion, and the cost of interest subsidies rose from US$600 million in 1978 to US$2.5

billion in 1981. By 1989, total lending under federal government programs had risen to over US$12 billion, and defaults cost the federal government over US2$1 billion per annum. However, Hansen concludes that this is mainly due to the rapid increase in borrowing, rather than a growing unwillingness to repay student loans. If debtors with very low incomes could be protected by means of income insurance, the default problem would be greatly reduced.

In addition to evaluations of individual countries, there has been a considerable growth throughout the 1980s and early 1990s of comparative studies which draw conclusions about the effects of different types of 1983 student loans on the basis of international experience (Rogers 1972, Johnstone 1986, Woodhall 1970, 1982, 1989, 1992, 1993, Barr 1991, Albrecht and Ziderman 1991).

Research shows that student loans are feasible in developed countries, but that certain problems remain, and many countries are still actively changing their systems of student support, and the terms of conditions of loans.

An early study of student loans in Scandinavia concluded:

> A perfect system of student aid has not yet been developed in any country. What is clear from this examination of Scandinavian experience is that to regard a system of student loans as either a panacea for educational and financial ills, or as an evil to be avoided at all costs, is equally mistaken. Some of the more exaggerated statements of both the opponents and advocates of student loans fall into perspective when viewed in the light of the working experience of other countries. (Woodhall 1970 pp. 1983–84)

This conclusion was based on the relatively early experience of several countries which had introduced student loans in the mid-1960s. At that time the rate of inflation was low in Europe and there was full employment, so that graduates experienced little difficulty in finding and keeping jobs, and the problem of default on loan repayments was not severe. A more recent evaluation of experience in Canada, Sweden, and the United States concluded:

(a) Student loan schemes can be devised to satisfy any objective of government policy, but trade-offs exist between the costs of a program and the number of students who can be assisted.

(b) The degree of subsidy involved in student loans is variable, and depends upon political decisions, but it is advisable to make both students and the public aware of the size of the subsidy, rather than have a system of "hidden grants."

(c) Default rates need not be high, provided that there are special provisions for those who are unable to pay their loans because of illness, unemployment, or low incomes.

(d) Student loans do not automatically deter working-class students or women from participating in higher education.

(e) There are no significant savings in the short run from introducing student loans, but in the long run a system of loans can produce significant saving of public funds, which can then be used to provide other forms of financial assistance—for example, for 16–19-year olds or for adults taking part-time courses.

(f) Evaluations of student loans have shown that they are popular among students and the general public, that problems have arisen in the last 10 years as a result of inflation and high interest rates, but that these can be controlled. High rates of default, particularly in the United States, have demonstrated the importance of providing some element of insurance, such as exists in Sweden for those who are unable to repay their loans as a result of low incomes. (Woodhall 1982 p. 7)

Johnstone (1986) showed that because most loan programs involve a substantial interest subsidy, the present value of loan repayments is actually considerably below the real value of the funds borrowed, so that there is a substantial "hidden grant" in the Swedish and German loan programs, and to a lesser extent in the United States. Albrecht and Ziderman (1991) have extended this analysis and calculated the implicit subsidy involved in 20 countries where student loans are offered at less than market interest rates. They conclude that in half the programs examined, the implicit subsidy or "hidden grant" is more than half the value of the loan, and in a few cases such as Kenya and Venezuela, the combined effects of interest subsidies, high rates of default, and administrative costs mean that it would actually be cheaper for the government to give grants to students. Thus the study concludes that loan programs have so far had only marginal impacts on educational finance, and that "loans have been operating only at the margins of cost recovery." Nevertheless, the authors emphasize:

> It should not be concluded from disappointing results of past experience that loan programs should be abandoned. On the contrary, we argue that reform and improvement in several key elements of program design are necessary conditions for well-functioning loan programs. (Albrecht and Ziderman 1991 p. 23)

In particular three major issues are identified: effective targeting (for example to concentrate resources on needy students); reducing subsidies while limiting debt burdens (by increasing interest rates, but linking repayments to income, as in Sweden since 1989) and finally minimizing evasion (by designing efficient recovery mechanisms, for example using the tax system as in Australia, or the social security system). Albrecht and Ziderman conclude:

Student loans and alternative forms of deferred payments present an important policy option to assist in cost recovery, without deterring access to qualified students. In order to achieve these twin goals, however, programs require careful planning, particularly to ensure recovery. (1991 p. 49)

Another important issue is the effect of student loans on equality of opportunity and equity. Advocates of loans believe that they will be more equitable than grants because they involve less transfer of income from poor taxpayers to potentially rich students. Critics, on the other hand, believe that loans will deter working-class students. Once again, the evidence from evaluations of student loan programs shows that loans are neither as effective nor as damaging as these views suggest. On the one hand, studies in the United States and Sweden show that low-income students are not discouraged from entering higher education by the fear of incurring debts. On the other hand, the fact that loan programs are so heavily subsidized in most countries means that there is still a substantial transfer of income. So, for example, Jallade's evaluation (1974) of student loans in Colombia concluded that the loan scheme "can hardly be considered as a tool to shift the burden of higher education away from taxpayers to students, but rather as a cheaper way to channel additional funds to private universities" (Jallade 1974 p. 35).

Thus, the general conclusion of these evaluations of student loans in both developed and developing countries is that student loans can be an effective way of providing financial assistance for students but the extent to which they contribute toward cost recovery, equality of opportunity, or toward redistributing the costs of higher education depends critically on the terms and conditions of the loans and the general educational and economic situation within which a student loan scheme operates.

See also: Cost–Benefit Analysis

References

Albrecht D, Ziderman A 1991 *Deferred Cost Recovery for Higher Education: Student Loan Programs in Developing Countries*. Discussion Paper No. 137, World Bank, Washington DC

Barr N 1988 *Student Loans: The Next Steps*. Aberdeen University Press, Aberdeen

Barr N 1991 Income-contingent student loans: An idea whose time has come. In: Shaw G K (ed.) 1991 *Economics, Culture and Education: Essays in Honour of Mark Blaug*. Edward Elgar, Aldershot

Blaug M 1970 *An Introduction to the Economics of Education*. Penguin, Harmondsworth

Gladieux L (ed.) 1989 *Radical Reform or Incremental Change? Student Loan Policies for the Federal Government*. College Entrance Examination Board, New York

Hansen J 1989 Cost-sharing in higher education: The United States experience. In: Woodhall M (ed.) 1989

Hartman R W 1971 *Credit for College: Public Policy for Student Loans*. McGraw-Hill, New York

Jallade J-P 1974 *Student Loans in Developing Countries: An Evaluation of the Colombian Performance*. Staff Working Paper No. 182, World Bank, Washington, DC

Johnstone D B 1986 *Sharing the Costs of Higher Education: Student Financial Assistance in the United Kingdom, the Federal Republic of Germany, France, Sweden and the United States*. College Entrance Examination Board, New York

Maynard A K 1975 *Experiment with Choice in Education: An Analysis of New Methods of Consumer Financing to Bring More Resources into Education by Vouchers and Loans*. Institute of Economic Affairs, London

Prest A R 1966 *Financing University Education: A Study of University Fees and Loans to Students in Great Britain*. Institute of Economic Affairs, London

Psacharopoulos G, Woodhall M, 1985 *Education for Development: An Analysis of Investment Choices*. Oxford University Press, New York

Psacharopoulos G, Tan J-P, Jimenez E 1986 *Financing Education in Developing Countries: An Exploration of Policy Options*. World Bank, Washington, DC

Reischauer R 1989 HELP: A student loan program for the twenty-first century. In: Gladieux L (ed.) 1989

Rice L (ed.) 1977 *Student Loans: Problems and Policy Alternatives*. College Entrance Examination Board, New York

Rogers D C 1972 *An Evaluation of Student Loan Programs*. US Agency for International Development, Washington, DC

Woodhall M 1970 *Student Loans: A Review of Experience in Scandinavia and Elsewhere*. Harrap, London

Woodhall M 1978 *Review of Student Support Schemes in Selected OECD Countries*. Organisation for Economic Co-operation and Development, Paris

Woodhall M 1982 *Student Loans: Lessons from Recent International Experience*. Policy Studies Institute, London

Woodhall M 1983 *Student Loans as a Means of Financing Higher Education: Lessons from International Experience*. World Bank Staff Working Paper No. 599, World Bank, Washington DC

Woodhall M 1987 *Lending for Learning: Designing a Student Loan Programme for Developing Countries*. Commonwealth Secretariat, London

Woodhall M 1989 (ed.) *Financial Support for Students: Grants, Loans or Graduate Tax?* Kogan Page, London

Woodhall M 1990 *Student Loans in Higher Education 1: Western Europe and USA*. International Institute for Educational Planning, Paris

Woodhall M 1991a *Student Loans in Higher Education 2: Asia*. International Institute for Educational Planning, Paris

Woodhall M 1991b *Student Loans in Higher Education 3: English-speaking Africa*. International Institute for Educational Planning, Paris

Woodhall M 1992 Student loans in developing countries: Feasibility, experience and prospects for reform. *Higher Education* 23 (4): 347–56 (special issue devoted to student loans)

Woodhall M 1993 *Student Loans in Higher Education 4: Latin America*. International Institute for Educational Planning, Paris.

Student Fees

M. Woodhall

Student fees are payments of money which are made to cover all or part of the costs of tuition in schools, colleges, universities, or other educational institutions. Fees may be paid by students themselves, or by their parents, families, or some other agency such as an employer or a central, state, or local government. In all cases the payment is made in return for tuition received by the student. However, not all educational establishments charge fees and the question of whether institutions should charge fees and what their level should be has been the subject of considerable debate in many countries.

One of the points at issue is the role of public and private institutions. In many countries public and private schools or colleges exist side by side, but the question of ownership does not necessarily determine the way in which the institutions are financed. In some countries publicly owned colleges or universities do charge fees, whereas in other cases a school or college is privately owned and administered—by a religious or charitable body, for instance—but nevertheless receives funds from central or local government and therefore does not charge fees. Elsewhere however, the debate about the level of fees is primarily concerned with the question of whether educational institutions should be under public or private ownership.

In other cases, where both public and private institutions exist, there is debate about whether publicly owned schools or colleges should charge fees. In many European countries, universities, colleges of higher education, and technical and vocational schools are owned and controlled by the government, and financed entirely out of public funds by means of institutional grants. In other countries, such as the United Kingdom, higher education institutions do charge fees, even when they are publicly owned and administered, but central or local government provide financial assistance to students to enable them to pay the fees, and in some cases the fees are paid entirely out of public funds. In the United States there has been some controversy about whether government funds should be given to public institutions to enable them to abolish or reduce fees, or whether governments should simply provide financial assistance for students to enable them to pay fees. In fact, the majority of public institutions in the United States do charge fees, but are subsidized by state governments.

The third area of disagreement concerns the question of fee differentials. Differential fees can be charged which reflect cost differences. For example, fees may be higher for graduate than for undergraduate courses, or different fees may be charged for different subjects: thus, fees for engineering may be higher than for economics on the grounds of cost differences. In some countries differential fees do not reflect cost differences but differences between students' place of residence. As a result, in many parts of the United States a student attending a public university will pay higher fees if he or she lives outside the state where the university is situated. The reason for this is that the university is partly financed by the state government, and it is argued that state government subsidies should be used primarily to benefit the residents of that state, since the funds are derived from taxing local residents. In the United Kingdom students whose normal place of residence is outside the United Kingdom or the European Community pay higher fees than "home students," and in Australia and Canada foreign students pay higher fees than home students. All these differential fee policies have aroused controversy.

The question of whether students pay fees, and how those fees should be determined, therefore raises a number of issues concerning the finance of education and its control. Also relevant is the question of how governments provide financial assistance for students. There has been considerable debate in some countries about whether student aid should be given in the form of grants or subsidized loans, and whether governments should provide students or their parents with vouchers which can be used to pay tuition fees.

1. Student Fees in Private Institutions

Although in some countries the majority of educational institutions are publicly owned and administered, there are many private institutions where student fees represent the predominant or, in some cases, the only source of finance. In many countries private schools and colleges play a significant role in the provision of higher education and postsecondary vocational education and training. Some of these institutions are run by charitable organizations, but others are profit-making establishments, charging fees which are intended to cover all costs and provide a profit for the owners.

There exist a number of studies of private higher education in Asia, particularly in Japan (James and Benjamin 1988) and the Philippines (James 1991) also in Latin America (Levy 1986) and several international comparisons of the role of private institutions (Geiger 1986; James 1987, 1989; James et al. 1988) Many of these studies provide information and data on fees in private institutions. Attempts to assess the significance of private vocational schools and colleges in the United States and the United Kingdom have reavealed a great variety in the size and quality of institutions, and a similar diversity in the level of fees charged.

Economists have suggested that private institutions are likely to be more efficient than publicly owned schools or colleges, because they are wholly dependent on student fees for their income, and will therefore be more responsive to the needs of students, or employers, as well as attempting to maximize efficiency. Comparisons between public and private schools in the United States (e.g., Coleman et al. 1982, Coleman and Hoffer 1987) have generated considerable controversy. Since the late 1980s, there have been several comparative studies of public and private schools in developing countries (Psacharopoulos 1987, Jimenez et al. 1988, 1991) which concluded that private schools "are relatively more cost-effective (that is, efficient) than public schools" (Jimenez et al. 1988 p. 162), although critics argue that differences in pupil achievement are the result of selection bias and other social factors rather than greater efficiency. This issue remains controversial and it is impossible to demonstrate any general relationship between the charging of fees in private schools and efficiency. More extended treatment of this topic will be found in the section on the public–private division of education.

2. Student Fees in Public Institutions

In many countries all education in publicly owned institutions is provided free, including both compulsory and higher education. In some cases both current and capital expenditure is financed by means of direct grants from central or local government and no fees are charged.

Throughout Scandanavia, for example, and in many European countries, schools, colleges, and universities which are publicly owned do not charge any tuition fees. However, there are a number of countries where colleges and universities do charge fees, despite the fact that they are public institutions.

In Canada, Spain, and Japan, for example, tuition fees provide between 15 and 20 percent of the income of public universities (Williams and Fulth 1990), and Australia introduced a new Higher Education Contribution Scheme (HECS) in 1989, under which students must pay a charge of about 20 percent of average university costs, either as an "up-front fee" or by means of a deffered payment, collected through the tax system. There has been extensive debate in Australia, as in other countries, about the effects of the introduction of tuition fees on equality of opportunity and access. Tuition fees were abolished in Australia in 1974, but the Wran Committee, which recommended the

introduction of HECS, quoted research which showed that "the abolition of fees had a marginal effect at best, on the accessibility of higher education for socially and economically disadvantaged groups. At worst, it provided a further benefit to the economically advantaged" (Wran Committee 1988 p. 5). The imposition of charges for tuition therefore represented, in the view of the Wran Committee, an improvement rather than a reduction in equity: "The advantaged who use and benefit directly from higher education ought to contribute more directly to the cost of the system" (p. xi).

In the United States there are wide differences between the states in the proportion of income derived from tuition fees in public universities and colleges, but on average tuition fees represent about 25 percent of average instructional costs and in many states this proportion increased in the 1970s and 1980s. The question of the role of student fees in public institutions of higher education is still very controversial in the United States. One commentator sums it up as follows:

> Two opposing doctrines have vied for acceptance: one holds that higher education is like elementary and secondary schooling, a public good whose benefits accrue to the entire nation and whose costs should therefore be written into the Social Contract and financed by the public sector through taxation; the other asserts that because higher education enhances the lives of those receiving it, they should pay for it themselves. The crazy-quilt pattern of financing higher education today reflects the inability to agree on either doctrine and the resultant compromises that have been made. Postsecondary schooling, it appears, is regarded as both a public good and a private investment and is paid for accordingly. (Finn 1978 p. 46)

In many countries the same two principles are debated among economists. On the one hand, it is argued that higher education provides benefits for the whole of society and so should be financed out of general taxation. On the other hand, since individuals gain both financial and noneconomic benefits from their education, it is argued that they should contribute to its cost by paying fees. Governments can still provide subsidies in the form of grants or loans to help students who could not afford to pay the fees without financial assistance. The argument is not about whether government subsidies should be provided for education, but whether it is better to subsidize institutions or individuals.

In the United Kingdom, for example, the Robbins Committee (1963) argued for an increase in tuition fees on the grounds that it was a source of strength that public finance should come from more than one channel, and that it was better to subsidize students than institutions. The arguments put forward for individual rather than institutional subsidies include the fact that institutions will be more efficient if they have to compete directly for students, and it is suggested that they will be more responsive to the

427

needs of students, or their future employers, if they are dependent on student fees for their income. It is also suggested that if institutions charge fees, and governments provide financial aid to students, this will encourage institutional autonomy and diversity.

The British government introduced a new policy in 1990, which involved substantial increases in tuition fees in higher education, even though the majority of British students still have their fees paid in full from public funds. The rationale for this change is that it will give universities and other higher education institutions a greater incentive to recruit additional students and thus reduce unit costs, that it will increase the responsiveness of institutions to student demand, and will diversify sources of institutional income and reduce dependence on a single central government grant (Department of Education and Science 1989).

Tuition fee policy in Canada has been reviewed by Stager (1989), who not only provides a historical summary of the development of tuition fees, particularly in the province of Ontario, but also a detailed analysis of alternative approaches to setting tuition fees, together with a summary of research on fees and student financial aid policy in Canada and other countries.

In some developing countries tuition fees are charged at primary, secondary, and higher levels, but many governments have tried to maintain a policy of free education, despite serious financial constraints. The provision of free education is usually justified on grounds of equity, but several economists have argued that tuition fees, combined with student aid, are in fact more equitable and more efficient than universal subsidies that often favor the children of rich parents at the expense of poor taxpayers. This view has been strongly emphasized by Psacharopoulos et al. (1986), and Bray (1988) provides a useful summary of economic, philosophical, and operational issues concerning tuition fees in developing countries.

3. Differences between Public and Private Institutions

In countries such as Japan and the United States, where both public and private institutions exist side by side, there are often very considerable differences between fees in public and private colleges or universities.

Many private institutions have expressed concern about the growing differential between public and private fees which is known as the "tuition gap" in the United States. A number of proposals have been made in the United States for increased federal or state government subsidies to private institutions to overcome this problem.

There has been some research on the likely effects of different proposals (Breneman and Finn 1978) but there is still major political disagreement about the desirability of providing public subsidies to reduce differentials between public and private institutions.

4. Fee Differentials between Students

Not only are there considerable differentials between public and private institutions in several countries, but there is an increasing trend in some countries to differentiate between students in the level of fees charged in the same institution. There are two possible ways of introducing such differentials. If tuition fees represent the main source of income for colleges or universities, then it can be argued that fees should reflect differences in the costs of courses. For example, where the costs of graduate courses of study exceed the costs of undergraduate courses, then institutions may charge fees which reflect these cost differences. The problem is that it is difficult to obtain accurate cost data for different levels of education or for different subjects, even though it is well-established that some courses—for example, science, engineering, and medicine—have higher costs than others such as arts or social studies. Another problem is that the average costs of higher education may be higher or lower than the marginal costs of educating one additional student or an incremental group of students. If tuition fees are supposed to reflect cost differences, then strictly speaking they should be based on marginal, rather than average costs. Yet very little information is available on the marginal costs of different courses of study.

In the United Kingdom the government introduced a policy of "full-cost fees" for overseas students in 1980. Tuition fees for home students and those from the European Community are still subsidized, but all other overseas students pay fees which are intended to cover the full costs of their courses. In 1990 these ranged from £4,560 (US$6,980) for arts and social studies, £6,050 (US$9,260) for science and engineering, to £11,150 (US$17,060) for medicine.

This policy of full-cost fees for overseas students has attracted great controversy in the United Kingdom and in other countries. There has been extensive research on the effects of the introduction of full-cost fees for overseas students in the United Kingdom (Williams 1981; Williams 1982; Overseas Students Trust 1987; Williams et al. 1986). Fee differentials for overseas students have also been introduced in Australia and Canada, and Throsby (1986) has analyzed the economic implications of fee differentials in Australia.

The question of whether there should or should not be a fee differential for overseas students is not one which can be answered by research. It is a political question which raises a number of difficult issues concerning equity and the proper role of educational subsidies. Many people would prefer to see the same fees charged to all students, regardless of origin. Others argue that it is right that public subsidies should be provided mainly for the country's taxpayers, or children of taxpayers, but that selective aid can be provided for particular groups of students on the basis of agreed criteria. In the United States the policy in many states of charging higher fees for students whose normal residence is not in the state where they are studying raises many similar issues.

The question of fee differentials therefore brings to light a number of issues concerning who benefits from education and who should bear the cost. Countries differ in the policies which determine how these costs are shared between individuals and the public purse, and between taxpayers and citizens from other states or countries.

5. Student Aid

Countries also differ in their policies on financial aid for students, to enable them to pay tuition fees and other charges. Since the mid-1980s there have been significant changes in the type and level of financial aid for students in many countries and several comparative studies have analyzed student aid policy in detail (Johnstone 1986, Woodhall 1989).

Even where no tuition fees are charged, as in many European countries, there is still a need for student aid in order to help students pay their living expenses. Where students must pay tuition fees, however, the question of what is the most efficient and equitable method of providing financial aid for students takes on an even greater importance (see *Student Loans*).

See also: Benefits of Education; Cost–Benefit Analysis; Cost Analysis in Education

References

Bray M 1988 School fees: Philosophical and operational issues. In Bray M, Lillis K (eds.) 1988 *Community Financing of Education: Issues and Policy Implications in Less Developed Countries*. Pergamon Press, Oxford

Breneman D W, Finn C E Jr (eds.) 1978 *Public Policy and Private Higher Education*. Brookings Institution, Washington, DC

Coleman J, Hoffer T, Kilgore S 1982 *High School Achievement: Public, Catholic and Private Schools Compared*. Basic Books, New York

Coleman J, Hoffer T 1987 *Public and Private High Schools: The Impact of Communities*. Basic Books, New York

Department of Education and Science (DES) 1989 *Shifting the Balance of Public Funding of Higher Education to Fees: A Consultation Paper*. DES, London

Finn C E Jr 1978 *Scholars, Dollars and Bureaucrats*. Brookings Institution, Washington, DC

Geiger R 1986 *Private Sectors in Higher Education: Structure, Function and Change in Eight Countries*. University of Michigan Press, Ann Albor, Michigan

James E 1987 The public/private division of responsibility for education: An international comparison. *Econ. Educ. Rev.* 6(1):1–14

James E 1989 *The Non-profit Sector in International Perspective: Studies in Comparative Culture and Policy*. Yale Studies on Non-profit Organizations, Oxford University Press, New York

James E 1991 Private higher education: The Philippines as a Prototype. *Higher Educ.* 21 (2): 189–206

James E, Benjamin G 1988 *Public Policy and Private Education in Japan*. Macmillan, Basingstoke

James T, Levin H, Haenel E (eds.) 1988 *Comparing Public and Private Schools*. Falmer Press, London

Jimenez E, Lockheed M, Wattanawaha N 1988 The relative efficiency of private and public schools: The case of Thailand. *World Bank Econ. Rev.* 2 (2): 139–64

Jimenez E, Lockheed M, Paqueo V 1991 The relative efficiency of private and public schools in developing countries. *World Bank Res. Obs.* 6 (2):205–18

Johnstone D B 1986 *Sharing the Costs of Higher Education: Student Financial Assistance in the United Kingdom, the Federal Republic of Germany, France, Sweden, and the United States*. College Entrance Examination Board, New York

Levy D 1986 *Higher Education and the State in Latin America: Private Challenges to Public Dominance*. University of Chicago Press, Chicago, Illinois

Overseas Students Trust (OST) 1987 *The Next Steps: Overseas Student Policy into the 1990s*. OST, London

Psacharopoulos G 1987 Public versus private schools in developing countries: Evidence from Colombia and Tanzania. *Int. J. Educ. Dev.* 7 (1): 59–67

Psacharopoulos G, Tan J-P, Jimenez E 1986 *Financing Education in Developing Countries: An Exploration of Policy Options*. World Bank, Washington, DC

Robbins Committee 1963 *Higher Education. Report of the Committee under the Chairmanship of Lord Robbins 1961–63*. HMSO, London

Stager D 1989 *Focus on Fees: Alternative Policies for University Tuition Fees*. Council of Ontario Universities, Toronto

Throsby C D 1986 Economic aspects of the foreign student question. *Econ. Rec.* 62 (179): 400–14

Williams G, Woodhall M, O'Brien U 1986 *Overseas Students and Their Place of Study*. Overseas Students Trust, London

Williams G, Fulth D 1990 *Financing Higher Education: Current Patterns*. OECD, Paris

Williams P (ed.) 1981 *The Overseas Student Question: Studies for a Policy*. Heinemann, London

Williams P 1982 *A Policy for Overseas Students: Analysis Options, Proposals*. Overseas Student Trust, London

Woodhall M (ed.) 1989 *Financial Support for Students: Grants, Loans or Graduate Tax?* Kogan Page, London

Wran Committee 1988 *Report of the Committee on Higher Education Funding*. Australian Government Publishing Service, Canberra

Community Financing of Education

M. Bray

Issues relating to community financing of schools have come increasingly to the fore in many countries. The chief reason is negative: governments find themselves financially hard-pressed, and admit that they cannot shoulder the total cost of education by themselves. Communities generate their own resources to bridge the gap, for they realize that the alternative to self-help is no help at all.

More positively, expanded community financing may encourage participants to value education more highly, and greater parental involvement can promote the effectiveness of school systems. However, in official policy statements these positive rationales generally receive less weight than the negative economic one, except as justifications when governments find themselves gaining unfavourable publicity.

In this entry the term "community" is defined broadly and includes geographic, religious, ethnic and racial groups. It also includes alumni and parents. The entry commences with comments on the scope and potential for community financing. It then turns to mechanisms for raising funds, issues of quality, social and geographic inequalities, and questions of guidance and control.

1. The Scope and Potential for Community Financing

Community support is heavily influenced by cultural and economic factors, and similar amounts of finance cannot be generated in all contexts. Nevertheless, a few examples can illustrate the scope and potential.

One of the best examples is the *harambee* movement in Kenya (Anderson 1973, 1975). *Harambee* is a Swahili word meaning "let's pull together," and the concept has been strongly promoted by the nation's politicians. In the mid-1980s, 50 percent of Kenya's secondary schools were unaided *harambee* institutions, and another 20 percent were aided *harambee* or private schools. Most primary schools also had a strong element of community funding, especially in the physical infrastructure. As well as providing cash, communities contributed land, labor and materials.

Zimbabwe is also well-known for its community support. Chung (1990 p. 192) states that between 1979 and 1989 the number of primary schools increased from 2,401 to 4,504, and the number of secondary schools from 177 to 1,502. Construction was heavily dependent on community financing. Communities also contributed significantly to running costs.

Other statistics from Trinidad and Tobago, the Dominican Republic, Panama, Honduras, and Cuba indicate that between 15 and 30 percent of both recurrent and capital costs may be financed by community inputs. In Nepal, 60 percent of the labor for school construction is said to be provided free of charge by communities; and in parts of China over 60 percent of primary school teachers are community-employed (Bray and Lillis 1988 p. 7).

The industrialized countries of Europe, North America, and Australasia also have important elements of community financing, particularly through Parent–Teacher Associations (PTAs) and comparable bodies. In most of these countries, communities only supplement government provision but nevertheless provide some important "extras." Parallel systems of profit-making private schools may also exist, though these cannot be classified as community efforts.

2. Mechanisms for Raising Resources

2.1 School Fees

In most self-help institutions, fees are the greatest source of income. Fees can of course be put to any use, but are particularly important for financing recurrent expenditure because it is often difficult to find other ways to do so. Fund-raising schemes for capital works have the advantage that they aim at visible outcomes. Moreover, donors like to think that their gifts will have a lasting impact rather than being dissipated on salaries or materials. Most schools therefore set the fees aside for recurrent needs, and utilize other mechanisms for generating capital resources.

2.2 Levies

It might be argued that the difference between a fee and a levy is merely semantic, particularly when levies are imposed every year and are destined for expenditure that would otherwise be covered from a general fee. Certainly there are cases in which communities have been prohibited from charging fees, and have therefore changed the name to levies but have used the money for the same purposes. Fees are sometimes conceptualized as payments for services, however, whereas levies are more commonly methods of raising funds for specific projects. In many systems, levies are particularly important for capital works.

2.3 Launching Ceremonies

When properly managed, launching ceremonies can generate considerable funds for capital works. Mbithi and Rasmusson (1977) describe practices in Eastern Kenya:

> In a typical self-help project, participants walk to the project site from the sublocation and surrounding areas. Those representing special groups such as clans are provided with transport by their groups .... The dignitaries such as the chief, headman, clan leaders, project committee members, visiting politicians and wealthy businessmen and citymen sit near the table of the Master of Ceremonies. The local clans normally prepare food and supply water, and young men act as marshals, dance partners and general handymen.
>
> As all expected participants arrive the tempo of work and dance increases as each group attempts to out-perform its neighbour .... All contributions are announced publicly and all sing songs of praise to the contributor. If contributions are meagre, the songs will exalt the wealth of the conspicuously rich and appeal to their love for their local area .... Donations which continue to pour in may be money, eggs, poultry, food, cement, a lorry full of sand or even the land on which the project stands. (Mbithi and Rasmusson 1977 pp. 27–28)

This account is culturally specific. However, some of the general principles, for example, of encouraging competition to donate, and of making the event highly visible, are applicable in many other cultures.

2.4 Community Taxation

Communities sometimes raise additional resources by imposing taxes on members. Igwe (1988 pp. 112–3) indicates that community members in Eastern Nigeria are taxed by Councils of Elders. The men generally pay higher rates than the women, and age groups are a valuable instrument for collection of the dues. Sons and daughters who are no longer resident in the village may also be taxed, with the sanction of ostracism in the event of nonpayment.

Religious communities may also impose taxes on themselves. In Indonesia, for example, part of the funds for the *pesantrens*, which teach both Islamic religious knowledge and secular subjects, comes from tithes (Bray and Lillis 1988 p. 41). Donation of the compulsory tax known as *zakat* is one of the pillars of Islam, and other religions also emphasize the importance of charity.

2.5 PTA Collections

Collections by Parent–Teacher Associations can be another major source of income in both industrialized and less developed countries. While not focusing specifically on financing, Beattie (1985) presents extensive information on parental participation in the education systems of France, Italy, Germany, and England and Wales. Examples from less developed countries are provided by Berthe (1985) who focuses on Mali, and Kaluba (1988) on Zambia.

2.6 Other Mechanisms

Other types and sources of community funds include contributions from alumni, grants from cooperatives, assistance from overseas churches, and donations from local business people.

3. Implications for Quality

When communities supplement the resources of government schools, one may assume that their efforts improve the quality of education. Many churches also have a reputation for strong discipline and high-quality teaching. However, major problems have arisen in some countries from the poor quality of independent self-help schools. Wellings (1983 p. 24) concluded that the quality of education in Kenya's *harambee* schools was "low, and quite often abysmally low" in both relative and absolute terms. These schools have suffered from poor resource bases, untrained teachers, and academically weak students. Wellings considers *harambee* schools more a blight than a blessing.

Mkandawire (1985) was not so forceful about the situation in Malawi, but reached a similar conclusion:

> Community financing of schools has indeed helped to expand the school system, but the variation in its financing has made it difficult to achieve acceptable standards ... It would appear that unless there is an expansion in central government financing of schools, we shall live with a situation where high academic standards are hard to achieve. (Mkandawire 1985 p. 3)

One should of course distinguish between the quality of the school intake and the quality of the teaching process, and recognize that many self-help schools are handicapped at the outset by their inability to attract the best students. However, Kenyan research shows that *harambee* schools have compounded the problems of poor intakes by giving their students poor teaching. Robinson's (1988) comments on the People's Republic of China imply that similar factors have operated there.

4. Social and Geographic Inequalities

In some countries, community financing of education has exacerbated social inequalities. To cite just one example, Galabawa (1985) indicates that Tanzanian nongovernment secondary school fees exceed 2,000 Tanzanian shillings (TShs) per pupil per annum.

> The ordinary peasant in Tanzania cannot afford this amount. But many of the schools are built with the help of money or labor of the very poor peasant ... A striking example is that of Omumwani Secondary School in Kagera which was opened by TAPA in 1968. The school fees are exorbitant and yet the Kagera Region Cooperative Union was paying TShs 600 per annum for every pupil. Here one

may question the justification for the common cooperative funds being used to educate children of the few members of the cooperative. (Galabawa 1985 p. 18)

Self-help operations can also exacerbate regional inequalities, for the rich areas are in a better position to fund operations than poor ones. It has been shown in Kenya, for example, that the *harambee* movement has widened the gap between the economically developed central highlands and poorer regions in the rest of the country. Similar findings appear in the literature from Tanzania and elsewhere.

5. Central Guidance and Control

The problems of quality and equity emphasize the need for central guidance and control. However, strong control raises the danger that local initiatives will be stifled, and governments have to seek an appropriate balance. The nature of this balance varies in different societies. In Eastern Nigeria, for example, the tradition of self-help is so great that it seems to flourish under almost all circumstances. Elsewhere, seeds might require more careful nurture.

Government control on community initiative may be direct, through regulations on registration of schools, class size and fees. Alternatively, influence may be indirect, through provision of grants, training programs for teachers, general advice through district education officers, and so on.

In most systems, regulations lay down a series of steps which communities must follow before a school can gain full approval. Community leaders must first secure approval in principle before proceeding with construction, and they must secure final approval before they are allowed to operate the school. The initial stage allows the government to check whether the location and nature of the school matches its own priorities, and the second stage allows it to see whether the facilities meet required standards.

Governments may also set regulations on accounting procedures. Misuse of money, or allegation of misuse, is one of the most common causes of strife in community-funded projects. Improved record-keeping could discourage the temptation to embezzle funds and could protect the innocent. Even when individuals have not stolen school money, they often find it difficult to demonstrate that fact when they have poor accounts, and allegations of theft can severely damage community spirit.

Indirect influences may be exerted through grants of various kinds. The grants encourage the communities to provide the facilities for which the money is intended, and allow the government to set requirements on the types and nature of facilities. Special grants may be made for disadvantaged communities in order to reduce social and regional inequalities, and help may be in the form of government-paid staff.

Governments may also hold workshops for boards of governors and PTA officials. Experience in Papua New Guinea has suggested that at least in some contexts these need not be costly (Bray 1988). Communities are often willing to provide accommodation and travel expenses for their own nominees, and the workshops can be valuable forums for headteachers, community leaders, and government officers to exchange views.

Offers of government takeover of community schools may also be an effective indirect influence. Most Kenyan communities are very keen for the government to take over their institutions and to relieve them of heavy financial burdens. The government sets clear criteria on which it decides whether or not to take over a school, among which are the nature of the facilities and the standard of academic achievement. This acts as a guideline and incentive for the communities.

However, many of these controls are limited. Bureaucracies are frequently overworked and inadequately staffed, and it is hard to devote optimum attention to these matters. Governments often find it difficult to encourage communities which are fragmented and do not have strong traditions of self-help. Occasionally, they also find it difficult to restrain eager communities, the activities of which may have a detrimental effect on social and regional inequalities.

Some governments operate through overcentralized administrations. Hanson (1986) indicates that, prior to a 1968 reform, the Venezuelan Ministry of Education was responsible for all major and minor decisions about schools, personnel, and instructional programs. The ministry, Hanson contends, became a huge bureaucratic job bank which often took 9–12 months even to reply to simple requests on such matters as building repairs or payment of teachers in newly opened institutions. It would be hard in such a structure either to encourage desirable community initiatives or to discourage undesirable ones.

6. Conclusion

Mechanisms for community financing are diverse and dependent on local conditions. Nevertheless, in many parts of the world community financing plays a crucial role in supporting education systems and sometimes in providing an alternative track to the mainstream. Too often, government figures are quoted as if they represent the only expenditure on education. In many settings a full picture of financing would have to include community and private expenditures.

Although governments and international agencies have become more interested in community financing, it is not a panacea. Authorities would be unwise to allow schools to be starved of government funds on the assumption that communities would necessarily bridge gaps. Furthermore independent self-help schools are sometimes of inferior quality, and can exacerbate social and regional imbalances. Only a heavily qualified recommendation could be made to other governments to try to emulate Kenya's strategy of *harambee*, even assuming that it can be emulated and that its roots are not exclusive to that country. Authorities also need to pay careful attention to guidance and controls, yet to be sufficiently flexible to avoid stifling initiatives.

See also: Private and Public Costs of Schooling in Developing Nations

References

Anderson J 1973 *Organization and Financing of Self-Help Education in Kenya.* International Institute for Educational Planning (IIEP), Paris

Anderson J 1975 The organisation of support and the management of self-help schools: A case study from Kenya. In: Brown G N, Hiskett M (eds.) 1975 *Conflict and Harmony in Education in Tropical Africa.* George Allen and Unwin, London

Beattie N 1985 *Professional Parents: Parent Participation in Four Western European Countries.* Falmer, London

Berthe A 1985 *Participation des Communautés Locales au Financement de l'Education au Mali.* Division of Educational Policies and Planning, UNESCO, Paris.

Bray M 1988 Community management and financing of schools in Papua New Guinea. In: Bray M, Lillis K (eds.) 1988

Bray M, Lillis K (eds.) 1988 *Community Financing of Education: Issues and Policy Implications in Less Developed Countries.* Pergamon, Oxford

Chung F 1990 Government and community partnership in the financing of education in Zimbabwe. *Int. J. Educ. Dev.* 10(2/3): 191–94

Galabawa J C J 1985 Community financing of schools in Tanzania. Paper presented at the Commonwealth Secretariat workshop on community financing of schools, Gaborone

Hanson M 1986 *Educational Reform and Administrative Development: The Cases of Colombia and Venezuela.* Hoover Institution Press, Stanford, California

Igwe S O 1988 Community financing of schools in Eastern Nigeria. In: Bray M, Lillis K (eds.) 1988

Kaluba L H 1988 Education and community self-help in Zambia. In: Bray M, Lillis K (eds.) 1988

Mbithi P M, Rasmusson R 1977 *Self-Reliance in Kenya: The Case of Harambee.* Scandinavian Institute for African Studies, Uppsala

Mkandawire D 1985 Academic standards in Malawi schools. Paper presented at the Commonwealth Secretariat workshop on community financing of schools, Gaborone, Botswana

Robinson J C 1988 State control and local financing of schools in China. In: Bray M, Lillis K (eds.) 1988

Wellings P A 1983 Unaided education in Kenya: Blessing or blight? *Res. Educ.* 29(1): 11–28

Further Reading

Bray M 1986 *New Resources for Education: Community Management and Financing of Schools in Less Developed Countries.* Commonwealth Secretariat, London

Kemmerer F 1992 Community support of schools. In: Chapman D W, Walberg H J (eds.) 1992 *International Perspectives on Educational Productivity.* JAI Press, Greenwich, Connecticut

Okoye M 1986 Community secondary schools: A case-study of a Nigerian innovation in self-help. *Int. J. Educ. Dev.* 6(4): 263–74

Ota C C 1986 Community financing of schools in Zimbabwe. *Prospects* 16(3): 355–68

Shaeffer S 1991 *School and Community Collaboration for Educational Change: Report of an IIEP Seminar.* International Institute for Educational Planning, Paris

Williams P 1986 Non-government resources for education with special reference to community financing. *Prospects* 16(2): 231–41

International Financing of Education

D. M. Windham

Since the 1960s the amount of money provided by international assistance agencies for the support of education in developing nations has increased dramatically. However, in the 1980s the provision of specific development assistance for schooling, and for educational development activities generally, has faced competition from emerging concerns with environmental, health, and population issues as well as the continuing pressure of demands from what have been called the "immediately productive" economic sectors (industry, transportation, and support of market infrastructure). In addition, as the decade of the 1980s progressed, the greater use of domestic funds in some countries for defense, internal security, and international debt servicing meant that an increased amount of foreign assistance to education may have replaced rather than complemented domestic human development efforts. The rapid changes which have occurred in the world's political and economic environment during the 1980s and 1990s provide a critical opportunity to reconsider the forms and level of support provided for international educational

Table 1
International aid for education (in billions US$)

Type of assistance	1986	1987	1988	1989	1990
Total ODA[a]	36.7	41.6	48.1	46.7	—
Total ODA[b]	41.2	41.6	44.8	43.6	—
Education ODA[a]	4.0	4.4	5.3	5.0	—
Education ODA[b]	4.5	4.4	4.9	4.7	—
Total multilateral finance[a]	31.2	36.1	38.1	42.4	—
Education multilateral finance[b]	1.6	2.8	1.6	2.2	—
Lending by IBRD/IDA[a] Total	16.3	17.7	19.2	21.4	20.7
Education	0.8	0.4	0.9	1.0	1.5

Sources: Organisation for Economic Co-operation and Development and The World Bank 1990
a current prices   b 1987 prices

finance and to assess the vital concerns about this form of assistance.

1. Forms and Levels of Support

It has been estimated that approximately US$2.5 billion is provided annually to developing countries for direct educational assistance; while this may appear impressive in aggregate, it amounts to less than US$4.00 per child for the estimated 700 million pupils in these countries (Orivel and Sergent 1990). Enormous variation exists between countries in the receipt of aid and, within the countries, in the purposes to which it is directed. A study covering the period from 1981 to 1986, concludes that aid receipts varied within sub-Saharan Africa by a factor of 200:1 and the ratio of foreign educational assistance per primary pupil versus that given to higher education students was almost 1:500 (Millot et al. 1987). The same study reports that only US$180 million per year was provided specifically for primary education; an amount that is in sharp contrast to the US$100 billion estimated to have been spent by the developing countries themselves on such educational programs.

In 1989, an estimated 10.7 percent of international bilateral aid was allocated to education and 5.1 percent of multilateral aid; the bilateral figure compares with 12.7 percent in 1980–81 while the multilateral figure has been stable since 1985–86, the period for which comparable data is available (World Bank 1990). Table 1 presents available data on the period from 1986 to 1990 for the provision of official development assistance (ODA) in total and to education by bilateral agencies and the same finances as provided by multilateral agencies. The working definition of ODA is any assistance related to economic development with a grant element greater than 25 percent. Since 1986 total ODA has increased in both real and purchasing power terms and education assistance has formed a relatively stable proportion of the whole. The

ODA figures in Table 1 are for the country members of the Organisation for Economic Co-operation and Development's Development Assistance Committee (DAC).

The figures for total multilateral finance reflect an increase in aid of over one-third at current prices with, again, a proportional increase in support for education. The lending for education activities by the International Bank for Reconstruction and Development (IBRD) and the International Development Association (IDA) has increased from US$0.8 billion to US$1.5 billion between 1986 and 1990; this represents an increase in the proportion of total IBRD/IDA finance going to education from 5.1 percent to 7.2 percent over the period.

The figures cited here must be interpreted in terms of the rapidly escalating populations of school-age children, especially in sub-Saharan Africa and the Indian subcontinent. However, it might also be noted that these data do not yet reflect the effects of the increased allocations to education pledged by the assistance agencies at the World Conference on Education for All held in Jomtien, Thailand in March 1990. Even so, a summary interpretation must be that international financing of education is not impressive in aggregate and meeting the burgeoning demand for educational support that will occur in developing countries during the period from 1991–2010. The impact of international finance for education will also be constrained by several critical concerns related to the provision and use of such foreign assistance.

2. Critical Concerns

Educational development takes place within a complex environment of political, economic, and cultural constraints as well as one of multisectoral competition for political attention and financial resources. Domestic support for education depends upon the relative prosperity of the economy and political priorities, including national defense and internal security, established by the government leadership. Similarly, international assistance for education depends on the economic and political conditions existing in the financing countries. Of all the critical concerns that might be identified within both the developed and developing countries, four will be emphasized here: international debt burdens; fungibility of assistance; conditionality of assistance; and changes in the world political environment. Each of these will be discussed in terms of how they might affect the provision, receipt, or use of international financial assistance for education.

2.1 International Debt Burden

For many developing countries, the impact of foreign debt and the requirements of structural adjustment programs have often had a dramatic impact on educational planning activities (Conference of Commonwealth Education Ministers 1991). Debt servicing removes a substantial amount of potential resources from the national budget; research is questioning whether education as a public activity suffers disproportionately from such budget reductions. In Latin America, for example, one study concluded that educational support declined both absolutely and in relative terms, and this led to concomitant reductions in indicators of school performance (Reimers 1991).

Debt burdens also affect education through their generalized negative impact upon economic development. Over time the effect of substantial debt servicing requirements is to constrain general economic development. This reduces the revenue base for all public services including education. However, the effect on the demand for educated labor, which is also negative, is often overlooked. A depressed market for educated labor reduces the immediate financial benefits of education and discourages educational participation, especially among the socially disadvantaged, who can least afford to engage in highly speculative investments in education and training.

International attention to the debt crisis has been slow in developing and has not led to a consensus of the most effective strategy. Debt swaps, loan forgiveness, and refinancing suggestions have been both modest in their extent and excessively narrow in their coverage. There has also been a failure to deal with the debt issue in the larger context of the equity of international trade and financial relationships. Unless a broad, comprehensive debt strategy is evolved, debt burdens may be expected to continue to constrain future domestic investments in, and benefits from, the education sector and to further constrain the impact of foreign assistance.

2.2 Fungibility of Aid

It has long been argued (see Singer 1965, Krueger

1986) that, because money is inherently fungible, international assistance cannot be effectively targeted to a particular sector or activity. If a government receives US$10 million in international assistance for education, the reaction may be to reduce domestic financial support by an amount proportional or even equal to this amount. The result is that assistance dedicated to a specific purpose—education—may be converted to general budget support because of the fungibility of financial aid.

Financing organizations may attempt to control for this by providing in-kind assistance or by requiring the receiving government to provide evidence of "maintenance of effort" in the domestic support of education. However, in-kind assistance can still release funds that would have been expended on the goods or services provided, and there are both conceptual and practical difficulties in the design and fair administration of maintenance-of-effort requirements.

The argument can be advanced that the best international support for educational activities may be general macroeconomic and infrastructural support for the economy (Krueger et al. 1989). As was noted above, general economic conditions determine both the fiscal capacity of a government to support education and the returns to educational investments that may be earned in the labor market. To the extent that fungibility promotes effective macroeconomic investments rather than waste or political misappropriation of funds, the "problem" of fungibility may be overstated.

The core issue here is the conflict between the provider's interest in helping a specific activity and the recipient's interest in using all available funds to meet domestic political priorities. The 1980s saw increased attempts by multilateral and bilateral agencies to use financial assistance for education as a means to promote domestic policy reform; the fungibility of assistance meant that this could be achieved only through increased "conditionality" of aid—the requirement for certain actions by the receivers of aid as a condition to its provision.

In recognition of these issues, donors such as the World Bank, the United Nations Development Programme, and the United States Agency for International Development have begun to support increased "program" over "project" aid. Program aid is normally provided on a sector-wide basis and allows much greater discretion for local decision-making about the use of funds. This new strategy represents a shift from the innovation and experimentation that has characterized project support to a greater concern with the sustainability of the central activities of the education system. By creating an emphasis on intrasystem incentives for effectiveness, and by increasing the opportunity for local rather than expatriate personnel to gain the experience of managing these activities, the supporters of the program alternatively hope to minimize the transitory effects common to many externally financed education projects. However, the program approach does not fully remove the possible conflict that may exist between the policy priorities of the financing agency and those of the receiving country.

2.3 Conditionality

Krueger (1986) points out that the literature on foreign assistance often asserts either that such activities can create dependency and divert domestic policy from its proper path or can be seen as allowing developing countries to continue counterproductive development policies by facilitating the avoidance of the consequences of their own bad decisions. It is within polar views such as these that the debate over the conditionality of education assistance takes place.

Conditions are placed on assistance for three primary reasons. First, there are technical justifications for certain requirements which attempt to assure that the aid is used for the intended purpose and that the policy environment for education is supportive of the financial assistance provided. Second, conditions are often imposed in order to gain political support for aid within the financing country (some such requirements—for example, to purchase equipment from the financing country—often reduce the real value of the assistance provided). Finally, there may be an ideological basis for conditionality in that certain individuals or agencies will attempt to use international assistance to promote specific economic or political agendas.

The World Bank has been a leader in examining the policy context for educational assistance (World Bank 1988, Hadded 1980, Lockheed and Verspoor 1990). In its 1988 review of sub-Saharan Africa, the World Bank notes appropriately that variations among individual countries are too great for any single set of comprehensive solutions to be universally applicable. However, it is also asserted that three dimensions of education policy—adjustment (diversifying finance while controlling costs), revitalization (enhancing quality), and selective expansion (broadened access)—will need to be tailored to the particular context of each country. These are the three dimensions which will form the center of the debate over conditionality of all financing agencies into the twenty-first century. The success and acceptability of the conditionality process will be determined not just by the nature of the conditions on financing, but by whether these conditions are mutually determined in a context of partnership, or are imposed because of differences in economic power.

2.4 Changes in the World Political Environment

A major determinant of the future availability of international financing assistance for education will be the world political environment. The nature and direction of changes in this environment have become increasingly difficult to forecast. The reduction in East–West tensions, the fragmentation of the former Soviet Union, the hopes for increased stability in the Middle East, Central America, and Southeast Asia are all factors that will influence both the capacity for foreign assistance and the willingness to provide it. However, the promises of a "peace dividend" that could be channeled into development assistance for education and other social support activities have been largely unrealized.

In fact, the developing nations of Africa, Asia, and Latin America appear to have lost rather than gained from political changes in the world since the late 1980s. First, the requests for financial assistance from Eastern Europe and the newly autonomous parts of what was the Soviet Union will compete with the long-standing needs of the developing countries that traditionally have benefited from such aid. The political influence of these new demands will be substantial; the countries of Eastern Europe and the former republics of the Soviet Union have strong ties of geographic proximity and economic and historical interaction with Western Europe. Equally strong ties exist with the United States because of the substantial number of American citizens descended from immigrants from these areas. Thus, considerable political pressure is growing to assign priority to these countries within a stable or shrinking pool of financial assistance. As the provider of significant new financial support for the traditional developing countries, Japan is the notable exception among the major financing countries (Hotta 1991).

Second, the reduction of international tensions may accelerate tendencies toward isolationist attitudes and insular policies. Both the United States and the European Community contain political elements that demand a greater attention to internal needs, even at the sacrifice of traditional external responsibilities. The 1992 levels of unpaid obligations to international organizations, the failure of the United States Congress to approve foreign aid legislation between 1985 and 1991, and the reduced levels of assistance being earmarked for the traditional recipient nations all suggest a change in the political priorities of the economically advantaged countries.

The effect of these trends can be offset only through improved efficiency in the use of both domestic and international educational assistance by the receiving nations. Such efficiency improvements will immediately increase the effect of existing levels of support and may even lead to relatively higher levels of future support by assuring financing sources that funds will be used properly. However, the conclusion cannot be avoided that the aggregate increase in international aid to education over the 1990s is unlikely to offset the collective impact of demographic growth, quality enhancement needs, and an increased competition for assistance.

3. New Structures and Means for International Educational Finance

Meeting the increased financial requirements for international educational assistance and dealing with the aforementioned critical concerns with education aid will require new structural relationships between and among financing and recipient nations. A key step will be to develop effective partnerships at the international, regional, and national level. Increasingly, nongovernmental organizations (NGOs) may be expected to play an important role (Williams 1990). These NGOs (representing such organizations as voluntary agencies, religious groups, trade unions, and professional associations) have the potential to promote higher levels of educational support through their international structures. At the national and subnational levels NGOs will play a key role in the design, implementation, and evaluation of educational projects and programs.

Another important form of partnership has been noted above: it is necessary for the financing organizations and the receiving countries to deal as more equal partners in the specification of international financing goals. If both parties can agree on the policy outcomes to be sought from educational investments, there is a greater chance for congruence on the necessary changes in the policy environment and on specific conditionalities to be attached to any assistance project or program.

Another form of partnership that can promote more effective use of international finance for education is regional educational structures. Especially in the least developed countries, there is no practical means to provide all the types and forms of education that modern sector development may require. Regional cooperation based on country institutions with specialized curricula is one method of overcoming the small-scale diseconomies faced by many countries in tertiary education and in certain forms of vocational/technical education. In the past, political barriers to such partnerships have constrained the development of multicountry educational institutions. The financial conditions of the twenty-first century will reward those countries which are able to forge joint educational strategies despite political barriers.

The issue of the level of international finance is not a question of the fiscal capacity of economically advantaged countries to provide more educational support to developing countries; rather, it is an issue of their political willingness to do so. The ability to overcome insular domestic priorities, competition for aid from the "new democracies," and the needs of the other social interests such as health and the environment require that investments in education be rationalized in a broader context. Education may be asserted to be both a right of the individual and a responsibility of government, but evidence must still be presented to show the value of specific educational expenditures to both the agency providing and the country receiving the assistance. Also, broad program approaches that plan activities in sector-wide or multisectoral contexts are more likely to receive support and use resources effectively. These changes, combined with reforms of educational policy and practice within countries and with more equitable economic arrangements among countries in terms of trade and finance, offer some basis for optimism about the future levels and effectiveness of international educational assistance.

See also: International Aspects of Financing Education; International Educational Expenditures

References

Conference of Commonwealth Education Ministers 1991 *Report of the Eleventh Conference of Commonwealth Education Ministers.* Commonwealth Secretariat, London

Hotta T 1991 Japanese educational assistance to developing countries. *Comp. Educ. Rev.* 35(3): 476–90

Krueger A O 1986 Aid in the development process. *The World Bank Research Observer* 1(1): 57–78

Krueger A O, Michalopoulos C, Ruttan V W (eds.) 1989 *Aid and Development.* Johns Hopkins University Press, Baltimore, Maryland

Lockheed M E, Verspoor A M 1990 *Improving Primary Education in Developing Countries: A Review of Policy Options.* World Bank, Washington, DC

Millot B, Orivel F, Rasera J-B 1987 *L'Aide exterieure à l'education en Afrique sub-Saharienne.* World Bank, Washingon, DC

Orivel F, Sergent F 1990 International support for education. UNESCO *Sources* 13(1): 7–9

Reimers F 1991 The impact of economic stabilization and adjustment on education in Latin America. *Comp. Educ. Rev.* 35(2): 319–53

Singer H W 1965 External aid: In plans or projects? *Economics Journal* 75(3): 539–45

Williams A 1990 A growing role for NGOs in development. *Finance and Development* 27(4): 31–33

World Bank 1988 *Education in sub-Saharan Africa: Policies for Adjustment, Revitalization, and Expansion.* World Bank, Washington, DC

World Bank 1990 *World Development Report 1990.* Oxford University Press, Oxford

World Conference on Education for All 1990 *Meeting Basic Learning Needs: A Vision for the 1990s.* World Conference on Education for All, New York

Further Reading

Bird G (ed.) 1989 *Third World Debt: The Search for a Solution.* Gower, Aldershot

Curry R L 1990 A review of contemporary US foreign aid policies. *Journal of Economic Issues.* 24(3): 813–23

Heller P S, Diamond J 1990 *International Comparisons of Government Expenditure Revisited: The Developing Countries, 1975–86.* International Monetary Fund, Washington, DC

Lipton M, Toye J 1990 *Does Aid Work in India? A Country Study of the Impact of Official Development Assistance.* Routledge, London

Psacharopoulos G, Steier F 1987 *Foreign Debt and Domestic Spending: An International Comparison.* World Bank, Washington, DC

Reimers F 1990 *Deuda Externa Y Financiamento de la Educacion: Su Impacto en Latinamerica.* UNESCO, Santiago

Hadded W D 1980 *Education in sub-Saharan Africa: Policies for Adjustment, Revitalization, and Expansion.* World Bank, Washington, DC

International Aspects of Financing Education

E. Jimenez

Most of education—particularly at the primary level—around the world is government-funded. It is estimated that, in 1984, 87 percent of all primary school and 79 percent of all secondary school enrollment was in public schools (UNESCO).

How are these schools financed? It is difficult to obtain a comprehensive picture of the sources of financing across all the world's countries. Usually, only data from direct central government spending on education are recorded systematically by international organizations, such as the UNESCO *Statistical Yearbooks* and the IMF's *Government Finance Statistics*. However, these data and case-study materials (e.g., Jimenez 1986, World Bank staff 1988, Tan and Mingat 1992, Winkler 1989) are sufficient to conclude that, with only a few notable exceptions (such as the United States), most countries in the world finance the large majority of public schools through allocations from the central government budget. Although there are state-run and locally run schools in federal systems, in many such systems (particularly in developing countries), the revenue-raising capacity of lower tiers to finance major expenditures such as education is limited and they, too, must perforce rely heavily on central government transfers (World Bank Staff 1988 Chap. 7).

This entry will discuss the principal ways in which education is financed internationally. Rather than limiting itself to describing practices prevalent in the early 1990s, the discussion will also highlight some developments in the literature. These focus on the need to consider alternative financing sources (such as fees, earmarked taxes, and community financing), in the face of constraints on the popular practice of relying on general taxes and deficit financing. Such a focus is important given the need for expanding education in developing countries and in improving its quality in almost all countries.

1. General Financing Sources

It is generally accepted that education is a shared responsibility between the family (or student) and the state. The latter's role is important for a number of reasons. First, when one individual's consumption of a good affects others (an externality), the individual must be induced to consider the social rather than the private costs and benefits of behavior. It is often argued that this is true for many aspects of education, at least at the primary level. Second, government intervention may be necessary because limited financial markets do not allow students to borrow sufficient amounts on the basis of enhanced future earnings to cover costs. Third, if human resource investment is a principal strategy in poverty alleviation then this must also be a government concern (World Bank Staff 1990).

These objectives provide an economic justification for the most common financing practice found in most countries—a reliance on general revenues to finance education. For these general sources (deficit financing and taxes), there is almost no link between the amount an individual pays and the benefits received. However, as discussed below, it is also important to consider the limits to each of these general sources as a way to increase financing for education.

1.1 Deficit Financing

Governments need not raise revenue if they can run a deficit. Such a deficit can be financed by printing money or by borrowing (either domestically or through foreign sources). Deficits can be prudently managed, depending upon the size and growth rate of the economy. The countries with the largest deficits are industrialized countries that have a strong and growing economic base. Even for developing countries, a sizable debt to GNP ratio will be manageable as long as the economy is growing. For example, countries such as India (US $41 bn), Malaysia, Pakistan (US $13 bn), and Thailand (US $18 bn) were able to run sizable deficits without inflation as they grew at rates of over 5 percent in the period (World Bank 1988). There are, however, limits to which deficits can be used to finance an expansion of a major expenditure item such as education. Deficit financing through money creation and borrowing, if not prudently managed,

Table 1
Tax composition by country income group 1985

	Low income	Type of country Middle income	Industrial
Domestic income taxes	25	32	35
Personnel	9	10	27
Company	15	17	7
Other	1	5	1
Other direct	4	17	34
Social security	1	11	31
Property tax	1	2	2
Other	2	4	1
Domestic Commodities tax	32	30	29
Sales VAT	17	13	17
Excise	13	12	10
Other	2	5	2
Trade taxes	38	19	2
Import	29	17	2
Export	8	1	0
Other	1	1	0

Source: World Bank 1988

can cause macroeconomic imbalances and ultimately reduce growth.

Printing money accrues resources to government because it is like a tax on money holders—this is called seniorage. The process in unstable: eventually, as price increases make the money worth less, the government must print even more to obtain the same revenue, possibly resulting in hyperinflation. This, in turn, has economic costs, since it raises transactions costs and uncertainty regarding returns to long-term productive investment. Borrowing is not a long-term panacea either. Heavy domestic borrowing will lead to high interest rates (through the crowding-out effect) and eventually to depressed private investment. An inordinate amount of external borrowing or drawing down foreign reserves might precipitate a debt crisis or capital flight as domestic savers anticipate devaluation or new taxes. The prevalent practice of running arrears jeopardizes new financing.

Some countries have been more successful at evading these problems than others (see Fischer and Easterly 1990). The bottom line is prudence; as of 1992 many countries cannot afford to do this, nor will they be able to in the near future (particularly those countries in Latin America that are already highly indebted or those which have poor growth prospects, such as many African countries).

1.2 General Taxes

Taxes are unrequited compulsory payments collected primarily by the central government. They are, by far,

the principal source of financing for the central government, constituting 80–90 percent of all revenue for most developing and industrial countries (World Bank Staff 1988 Chap.4). They differ from minor revenue sources, such as user charges which are payments in exchange for specific goods and services (note their voluntary nature), and other forms of revenue raising such as licenses, fines, and public property rental.

The main types of taxes are: direct taxes, such as taxes on personal income, payroll, or wealth; and indirect or commodity taxes, such as sales, turnover, and trade. One of the principal differences between developing and developed countries is in the composition of taxes (see Table 1). Industrial countries draw their main source of revenue from direct taxes. Developing countries rely heavily on commodity taxes, primarily excises or import taxes (trade taxes contribute negligible amounts to revenue in developed countries). They are relatively easier to collect than direct taxes, but, as discussed below, may impose higher economic costs.

One major concern in attempting to raise more revenue through taxes is the potentially adverse impact on efficiency or growth. Changing a tax base or rate changes incentives—economic activity shifts from heavily taxed activities to lightly taxed ones. Unless these shifts correct for market imperfections, they are likely to make resource allocation worse. This is called the "deadweight" or excess burden of the tax— a loss of welfare above and beyond the tax revenues collected. They are particularly inimical for indirect taxes that affect goods used in the production of other

Table 2
Taxation by income group in selected countries 1970s[a]

| Country | Percentage of income paid in taxes | | |
	Lowest income	Middle income	Highest income
Argentina	17.2	19.8	21.4
Brazil	5.2	14.3	14.8
Chile	18.5	16.2	26.7
Colombia	17.1	13.1	29.9
Kenya	11.5	8.8	12.7
Korea, Rep. of	16.4	15.7	21.6
Lebanon	8.4	20.2	20.3
Malaysia	17.7	16.5	42.1
Mexico	40.2	22.7	14.9
Pakistan	15.0	9.6	25.3
Peru	4.8	17.4	26.6
Philippines	23.0	16.9	33.5

Source: Various sources quoted in Jimenez 1987
a Figures include direct and indirect taxes

commodities since the tax would have a cascading effect on those other commodities. As regards the tax structutre in the United States, for example, some observers estimate that US $1 of additional revenue raised costs the economy US $0.15–US $0.50 (Ballard et al. 1985). No comparable figures have been systematically compiled for developing countries, but they are probably higher, given the heavier reliance on indirect taxes on trade and intermediate goods. These countries typically have a narrower tax base which leads to a higher economic cost—since the economic cost rises with the rate, and the narrower the base, the higher the tax rate has to be.

Another major concern is with the pursuit of equity. Many countries maintain a personal income tax structure that is nominally progressive. However, such a nominal structure may be completely at odds with actual tax incidence, particularly in countries where such direct taxes constitute only a small portion of revenue and are often difficult to collect administratively and politically. Actual tax incidence depends on the types of taxes being collected (direct or indirect), their rates, and, most important, assumptions regarding "shifting" behavior. Taxes change the price at which transactions take place, and the burden is borne by both seller and buyer (e.g., a tax on candy at the store would raise its price but the burden is shared by the storeowner with the consumer to the extent that demand falls as a result of the higher price). Thus, nominally progressive tax structures in most countries do not reflect actual incidence once all of these factors are taken into account. As Table 2 shows, this is true for many developing countries for which data are available.

A final concern of great importance is the need for simplicity. Administration of taxes is one of the most important problems in developing countries. Compliance and enforcement are both critical issues. Most important, countries often confront a trade-off: while broadly based taxes on income or consumption are the least costly to apply, they are also among the most difficult to implement and enforce. As a result, many countries rely on trade, production, and company income taxes—which are cheaper to administer but more inefficient in terms of economic costs.

These concerns have led to proposals to reform the tax system in order to get the most revenue while minimizing damage to economic efficiency, equity, and administrative cost (World Bank 1991). These include measures such as the following: shifting from taxation of production to the taxation of consumption (such as a value added tax), in order to avoid cascading effects of distortionary behavior; shifting from international trade taxes to taxes on domestic transactions in order to avoid tariffs that protect industry but penalize consumers and promote inefficient patterns of production; restructuring income taxes to broaden the base by including all sources of income and simplifying the structure; and strengthening tax administration.

Although many countries, including some poor ones, have made remarkable progress in implementing some of these reform measures, many others have yet to start. Moreover, even if the funds were raised, there are no assurances that they would be spent for education. At the same time, the education sector in many countries confronts burgeoning demand due to population pressures. There is also a sense that reliance on centrally generated funds does not give any incentives for providers of education to minimize costs; and that patterns of government spending reserve a large proportion of the subsidies for the well-off anyway.

Table 3
Percentage of government education subsidies received by income group (selected countries)

Country and sector	Year of survey	Income group Lower 40 percent	Middle 40 percent	Upper 20 percent
All education				
Argentina	1983	48	35	17
Chile	1983	48	34	17
Colombia	1974	40	39	21
Costa Rica	1983	42	38	20
Dominican Republic	1976–7	24	43	14
Uruguay	1983	52	34	14
Indonesia	1978	46	25	29
Malaysia	1974	41	41	18
Higher education				
Argentina	1983	17	45	38
Chile	1983	12	34	54
Colombia	1974	6	35	60
Costa Rica	1983	17	41	42
Dominican Republic	1976–7	2	22	76
Uruguay	1980	14	52	34
Indonesia	1978	7	10	83
Malaysia	1974	10	38	51

Source: Various sources quoted in Jimenez 1990

2. Alternative Financing Sources

For the reasons given above, analysts have recently taken a closer look at alternative funding mechanisms. They have given particular attention to user charges, earmarked taxation, and local/community-level financing. Although no practical analyst has concluded that these can (or should) play the primary role in educational financing, there has been some interesting debate about the extent to which they can contribute to the financing problem.

2.1 Private Financing Through User Charges

The recent debates on increased user charges have been spawned by the following problems: the fact that fiscal problems plague most governments and their ability to do much about it is limited, as outlined above; contrary to stated policy, social subsidies are not adequately directed towards the poor; and the limited resources devoted to education are badly used—too little goes to relatively cheap and cost-effective alternatives (World Bank 1986).

These problems have generated a series of proposals to replace the *de facto* policy of uniformly low (or zero) prices by policies that differentiate prices by type of service and by type of consumer (Jimenez 1990 discusses this in greater detail). The policies propose that:

(a) User fees ought to be selectively raised at higher levels so that subsidies are cut for services that have large private benefits and that are consumed mostly by people with high income; in the meantime, to the extent necessary, subsidies should be targeted more effectively on poor households.

(b) Expenditure reform ought to go along with financing reform, so that high-return educational investments such as primary education are given priority (Lockheed 1990, Lockheed et al. 1991).

(c) The extent of the price increase ought to be commensurate with the ability of countries to develop scholarship and loan schemes to protect the poor.

It is worth noting that the proposals generally argue that charges for primary education are for the most part excluded from the proposed price increase. In fact, increased subsidies are called for, in some cases. Most proponents of user charges are also very careful to argue that, while subsidies can be cut, this should be done only when consumption is not going to be severely affected and the poor can be adequately protected. Finally, this type of reform argues that educational subsidies are essential because education is a public good, for the reasons outlined above. However, these subsidies can be targeted better, since not all components of education benefit society more than the individual beneficiary.

One issue is whether user fees would worsen the

access of the poor to services. Most analysts agree that, under highly subsidized financing arrangements, the poor do not obtain access to high-cost education services; and do not obtain a share of government subsidies that is necessarily greater than that of any other group. For example, the poor tend not to consume higher education in many developing countries because of its high private cost (books and materials, opportunity cost) and rationing often hinders them (they cannot afford private tutors to help them pass entrance exams). And yet the ratio of unit subsidies of higher education to primary education (where the poor are abundantly represented) is about 25:1 for all developing countries; more than 50:1 for Africa. The result is that the distribution of government subsidies in overall education is not heavily skewed towards the poor (see Table 3). In fact, access to these subsidies is roughly proportional to the population. Thus, present policies distribute subsidies to rich and poor alike, with the rich getting access to high-cost services.

Raising fees at higher levels is therefore unlikely to affect poor people very much, and yet many governments still want to ensure that the poor are given incentives to attend. As a result, most proponents of user charges argue that the charges should be accompanied by targeted subsidies to ensure that the poor have access. Targeting through differential pricing is not enough. Other ways of directing subsidies towards consumers have to be found, such as means-tested scholarships. The viability of such schemes is only beginning to be tested.

Do user fees improve efficiency by increasing the availability and use of social services and by lowering unit cost? Without the benefit of actual experience (few countries have tried this type of comprehensive pricing reform), most of the literature has constructed its arguments from simulations of behavioral responses. These pieces of evidence are often dramatic. It has been estimated that, by merely eliminating living allowances to university students in several African countries, an 18 percent average expansion in yearly primary education budget can be financed (Psacharopoulos et al. 1986). The impact of individual behavior, however, is only beginning to be studied. The point of these initial studies is that there is willingness to pay for health and education. When given the choice, households seem to be willing to pay; not as much as full cost recovery but certainly enough to improve quality (Gertler and Glewwe 1989).

In sum, there is much merit and adequate empirical support for the proposals to increase prices in the social sectors. Yet there are some weak links, including the feasibility of measures to protect the poor, based on actual experience; information about cost structure of service provision; and systematic evaluations of actual attempts to raise prices (Jimenez 1990).

2.2 Earmarked Taxes for Education and Training

The issue of earmarking taxes for education and training has arisen because of the following questions: (a) how to ensure that, even if resources can be raised, they will be devoted to education; and (b) how to generate additional resources for education aside from general taxes. Again, this is discussed elsewhere in this *Encyclopedia* so only a brief summary of issues will be given here.

Earmarking is the practice of assigning revenues from specific taxes or groups of taxes to specific or broad areas of government activity in contrast to general funds that are pooled. Earmarking reduces discretion by reducing central command over resource allocation, and is thus unpopular with many fiscal experts. Recent reviews indicate that while the practice theoretically provides greater assurances of minimum levels of financing for worthwhile public services, in reality governments have been able to circumvent such levels through inflation and other means. Many analysts agree that earmarking is most effective when there is a close link between the incidence of the taxes paid and the incidence of the benefits for which the tax is earmarked. This is called the "benefit principle" (see McCleary 1991 for a more thorough review).

In principle, earmarked payroll taxes to finance training approximate benefit-related taxes. The burden of a payroll tax is shared by the employer and the employee, depending on labor-supply elasticities. Indeed, some claim that, because labor supply is empirically inelastic, most of the burden falls on the employee, who is likely to be the main beneficiary of training anyway. In practice, however, the capacity of countries to finance a national training system through payroll taxes varies and must be compared to alternatives in the private sector. The use of payroll taxes to finance formal education is less alluring because the link to the labor market from more general education is tenuous (Whalley and Ziderman 1989).

2.3 Community-based Financing

Can schools rely on local communities to finance more of their education, as is the case in the United States? The answer depends on the extent to which localities are autonomous and can raise their own revenues. The international practice is too varied to draw any general conclusions. However, in developing countries, significant improvements in local administration are necessary even if constitutions were to permit localities to contribute to funding education. This improvement is particularly important in the case of property taxes, which is the principal way local schools are financed in North America. These taxes are relatively efficient and equitable, but they are also difficult to implement (because of valuation and other issues), and are not used extensively in many developing countries.

3. Conclusion

Governments play a major role in financing education around the world. Although country circumstances vary, most countries (and particularly poor ones) are confronted with major challenges in the area of further educational expansion and improvement, and, given the constraints, must consider nontraditional (user charges, payroll taxes, community finance) as well as traditional (general central taxation) methods of mobilizing resources. Moreover, these efforts must be combined with a more efficient and equitable allocation of existing finances.

References

Ballard C L, Shoven B, Whalley J 1985 General equilibrium computations of the marginal welfare costs of taxes in the United States. *Am. Econ. Rev.* 75(1): 128–38
Fischer S, Easterly W 1990 The economics of the government budget constraint. *The World Bank Research Observer* 5(2): 127–42
Gertler P, Glewwe P 1989 *The Willingness to Pay for Education in Developing Countries: Evidence from Rural Peru.* Living Standards Measurement Study Working Paper No. 54. The World Bank, Washington, DC
International Monetary Fund (IMF) (various years) *Government Finance Statistics* IMF, Washington, DC
Jimenez E 1987 *Pricing Policy in the Social Sectors: Cost Recovery for Education and Health in Developing Countries.* Johns Hopkins University Press, Baltimore, Maryland
Jimenez E 1990 Social sector pricing policy revisited: a survey of some recent controversies. Proceedings of the World Bank Annual Conference on Development Economics 1989. Supplement to *World Bank Economic Review and World Bank Research Observer.* World Bank, Washington, DC
Lockheed M E 1990 *Primary Education: A World Bank Policy Paper.* The World Bank, Washington, DC
Lockheed M E et al. 1991 *Improving Primary Education in Developing Countries.* Oxford University Press, New York
McCleary W 1991 The earmarking of government revenue: A review of some World Bank experience. *World Bank Research Observer* 6(1): 81–104
Psacharopoulos G, Tan J P, Jimenez E 1986 *Financing Education in Developing Countries: An Exploration of Policy Options.* The World Bank, Washington, DC
Tan J P, Mingat A 1992 *Education in Asia: A Comparative Study of Cost and Financing.* Regional and Sectoral Studies Series, The World Bank, Washington, DC
UNESCO (various years) *Statistical Yearbook* UNESCO, Paris
Whalley J, Ziderman A 1989 *Payroll Taxes for Financing Training in Developing Countries.* World Bank Policy and Research Working Paper WPS No. 141, World Bank, Washington, DC
Winkler D 1989 Decentralization in education: an economic perspective. Policy, Planning and Research Working Paper 143. The World Bank
World Bank Staff 1988, 1990 *World Development Report.* The World Bank, Washington, DC
World Bank 1991 *Lessons of Tax Reform.* The World Bank, Washington, DC

International Educational Expenditures

J-C. Eicher

International comparisons of expenditures for education are made difficult by the lack of reliable and homogeneous data. Public expenditures are better documented than private expenditures. Compared to total national resources they show a sharply rising trend in public spending on education from the early 1960s to the mid-1970s; a trend that is now reversing itself. Comparisons by level of education show that some developing countries, especially in Africa, spend up to 100 times more for a university student than for a primary-school student. No such inequality is observed in other regions. Private expenditures are known only for a few countries and are generally incomplete, but the information available shows that the contribution of households is extremely unequal between countries.

1. Data Availability and Limitations

It is the aim of economists to measure and compare the sacrifices of scarce resources made by different individuals or constituencies. In other words, they attempt to observe costs; however, they can make direct observations only on financial flows or expenditures.

Although incomplete and sometimes misleading, data on expenditures are still of interest. They give information on trends and also allow for comparisons between different sources of finance and between different countries. Yet international comparisons are hampered by a lack of reliable information for many countries. Education is not provided though the market. Those who demand it do not, as a rule, pay a price for it equal to its cost. The main source of finance for education is generally the state. Firms are also involved, mostly in vocational and adult education. Voluntary support by foundations or private individuals may be important, especially in higher education, while foreign aid sometimes makes a substantial contribution to the education budget of developing countries. Information on the volume of resources coming from each one of these constituencies derives from different sources and is unevenly available.

Public expenditures on education may be observed in official budgetary documents, but it is not always the case that the figures represent the total amount of what has been effectively spent by all public bodies during a given year. The three main causes of discrepancy between the official figures and this total are as follows:

(a) Published data sometimes only concern the ministry (or ministries) of education. In all countries, other ministries do spend money on education, and even in highly centralized countries, local communities are also involved in the financing of education (in France, for instance, the Ministry of Education covers only 75 percent of total public expenditures on education).

(b) Transfers between bodies are sometimes not taken into account, which leads to double counting.

(c) The ministry of education budget sometimes includes expenditures not for education (e.g., social subsidies).

Household expenditures on education are not fully measured anywhere by the usual household surveys. Specific and costly surveys are required, which are organized at regular intervals only in very few countries, and which, even when they do exist, do not have the same coverage from one country to the next, thereby making international comparisons hazardous. The only source of comparative data is the Organisation for Economic Co-operation and Development (OECD), but this data is not continuous through time and concerns only around a dozen developed countries.

Expenditures by firms may concern many types of training activities; those which take place on-the-job are not usually identified in the financial accounts while, in contrast, some are compulsory by law and hence easy to evaluate. Here again, institutional arrangements differ between countries and make international comparisons problematic.

Private voluntary support is given to institutions. National consolidated accounts are not available, but, except in some countries' higher education (7.3 percent of total expenditures in the United States in 1986, according to the 1989 *Digest of Education Statistics*) this source of finance is insignificant compared with the others.

Foreign aid comes from many sources, public and private, multilateral and bilateral. No consolidated accounts were attempted before 1989.

For all the reasons cited above, comprehensive international comparisons are unavailable as things stand in 1992. On the other hand, data on public expenditures are available for many countries; some limited comparisons can be drawn concerning the contribution of households, and foreign aid can now be estimated for many developing countries.

2. Public Expenditures on Education

The only statistical source on educational expenditures giving normalized information for virtually all countries of the world over a fairly long timespan is the *Statistical Yearbook* published annually by UNESCO. It is based on the official replies by member states to a questionnaire sent by UNESCO, but the information is checked by the UNESCO Statistical Office and is, when necessary, complemented by other elements provided by the countries themselves.

The information on expenditures concerns public expenditures on education, that is, public expenditure on public education plus subsidies for private education. It does not include information on foreign aid received for education except, in footnotes, for some countries.

The first issue of the UNESCO *Statistical Yearbook* was published in 1963. It gave information on total expenditure both in 1950 (or, in the case of some countries, the early 1950s) and in 1960 for 125 countries and, for the mid-1950s and/or 1960, for 20 more. The 1991 issue has data on total public expenditures for 179 countries and territories and more detailed information for around 150 countries. This series of yearbooks is not always homogeneous but it is the only one which covers such a long timespan.

The World Bank also gives yearly information on expenditures on education. However, its series, published in the *World Development Report*, starts only with the 1983 report. The data are not homogeneous and relate only to the year 1972, and then the years from 1980 onwards. The data published by the Organisation for Economic Co-operation and Development (OECD) in its series on national accounts and in special publications on education concern only the 24 developed countries which are members of that organization.

2.1 Total Expenditures

The absolute level of expenditures cannot be compared meaningfully. It is determined largely by external factors. Prominent among these are the size of the country and its level of development. Not surprisingly, in 1987, the United States spent 69,400 times more on education than Bhutan. It is more interesting to compare the percentage of resources which various countries devote to education. It would be logical to

Table 1

Public expenditures on education as a percentage of Gross National Product by world region (averages are arithmetic and unweighted)

	1960	1965	1970	1974	1976	1980
Developed countries	3.47	4.30	4.86	5.24	5.45	5.55
Market economies	3.21	4.04	4.94	5.35	5.63	5.74
Europe (north)[a]	3.43	4.15	5.30	5.86	6.18	6.20
Europe (south)[b]	2.32	3.26	3.49	3.38	3.74	3.77
North America[c]	4.14	5.66	7.70	6.88	7.11	7.28
Anglo-Saxon countries[d]	3.69	4.70	5.92	6.44	6.40	6.33
Nonmarket economies	4.28	5.12	4.62	4.89	4.88	4.97
Developing countries	2.55	3.13	3.63	3.69	4.13	4.35
Africa (excluding Arab states)	2.50	3.11	3.56	3.86	4.35	4.70
Latin America	2.75	3.32	4.09	4.29	4.56	4.77
Asia (excluding Arab states)	2.46	3.00	3.32	2.93	3.49	3.54
Arab states	3.01	3.39	3.93	3.59	4.20	4.28

Source: Calculations based on UNESCO *Statistical Yearbook* data
a Austria, Belgium, Denmark, Finland, Germany (Fed. Rep.), Luxembourg, Ireland, Netherlands, Norway, Sweden, Switzerland, United Kingdom b France, Greece, Italy, Portugal, Spain c Canada, United States d Australia, Canada, Ireland, New Zealand, United Kingdom, United States

compare *total* expenditures on education with *total* resources, since estimates of private expenditures are generally not available, but are, in most instances, known to be small compared with public expenditures, it makes sense to look at the percentage of national product spent *publicly* on education. It is also interesting to compare the amount spent by the public sector on education with the total public budget.

These comparisons may be made between regions or between countries. Tables 1 and 2 summarize the evolution by regions between 1960 and 1980. Table 1 shows that the percentage of national resources spent on education increased considerably during these 20 years, but that the increase was much greater during the 1960s (40 percent and 42 percent respectively for

developed and developing countries) than during the 1970s (14 and 32 percent).

On the whole, developing countries spend a smaller portion of their resources on education than do developed countries, but the former have bridged part of the gap during the 20 years recorded in the tables. The overall increase was 71 percent for developing countries versus slightly less than 60 percent for the developed countries. Significant differences exist between regions. In the developed world, northern countries, and especially the Anglo-Saxon ones, spend much more than southern countries. Among developing regions, Latin America comes first in educational expenditure and Asia last. Africa has increased its effort faster than the other regions, though, by 88 percent

Table 2

Public expenditures on education as a percentage of public budgets by world region[a]

Region	1965	1970	1974	1976	1980
Western Europe	16.5	15.8	14.4	13.7	13.7
Other developed market economies	16.1	15.6	14.8	13.8	13.3
Africa	16.6	17.7	18.2	18.4	15.6
Asia (excluding Japan)	14.7	13.3	13.0	12.3	11.6
Latin America	18.7	21.2	17.7	17.8	16.0

Source: Calculation based on UNESCO *Statistical Yearbook* data
a In 1960 the number of countries for which this information was available was too small in most regions to make the averages meaningful

Table 3
Trends in educational effort by region (percentage of countries in each region)

Region	1960–65			1965–70			Period 1970–74			1974–80			1980–85			1985–88		
	+a	=b	–c	+	=	–	+	=	–	+	=	–	+	=	–	+	=	–
Developed countries	86.5	4.5	9	65	26	9	62	24	14	62	33.5	4.5	41.5	27.5	31	40	36	24
Developing countries	82	9.5	8.5	59.5	23.5	17	41.5	24.5	34	64.5	14	21.5	43.5	14	42.5	33	29	38
Africa	86	7	7	62	19	19	50	31	19	69.5	9	21.5	37.5	12.5	50	44	32	24
Latin America	94	0	6	62.5	31	6.5	44	22	34	66.5	15	18.5	37.5	16.5	46	32	16	52
Asia	66	22	12	53	22	25	28	19	53	55.5	19.5	25	66.5	13.5	20	6.5	53.5	40

Source: Calculations by the author and UNESCO *Statistical Yearbook* 1991
a The percentage of GNP spent publicly on education has increased by more than 0.2 points during the period   b The percentage has changed by 0.2 points or less   c The percentage
has decreased by more than 0.2 points

etween 1960 and 1980 compared with 73 percent for Latin America, 44 percent for Asia, and 42 percent for the Arab states. The economic crisis seems to have increased the priority given to education in all regions. The percentage spent on education was significantly higher in 1976, the first year when the full impact of the crisis was felt on public budgets, than in 1974, the last "normal" budgetary year, yet this is due mainly to the fact that the budget for education, mostly made up of expenditures for wages and salaries, is much more rigid in the short run than most other budgets.

This hypothesis is confirmed by Table 2. It shows that the portion of the overall public budget going to education tended to decrease in most regions during the 1970s. The earlier trend was also slightly downward in most regions, with the exception of Africa, where relative spending on education was increasing until 1976. The table also shows, though, that a substantial part of the budget is spent on education everywhere.

It would be interesting to extend these observations to the 1980s. For many developing and some developed countries, however, information has deteriorated so much that these averages have become less reliable. Fortunately, there is another way to observe trends: by classifying countries according to the direction in which their educational effort has gone over time. These trends are shown in Table 3.

During the early 1960s, the upward trend was almost universal in all regions. Only countries that had very specific problems reduced their effort. From 1965 to 1974 a majority still increased relative educational spending but there was a significant increase in the number of countries tending to spend less resources on education. Just after the onset of the economic crisis, many countries temporarily reversed the trend by stepping up their effort, but this did not last beyond the 1970s. In the early 1990s, it has become clear that the real tendency is downward. Closer scrutiny shows that actual expenditures have decreased much

Table 4

Comparison between enrollments and public expenditures by level of education in selected countries 1989

Country	Enrollment by level (%)			Expenditures by level (%)		
	Preprimary and primary	Secondary	Higher	Preprimary and primary	Secondary	Higher
Developed						
France	49.0	39.4	11.6	35.7	49.2	15.1
Germany (Fed. Rep.)	34.0	51.9	14.1	20.3	55.3	24.4
Japan	45.7	43.8	10.5	34.8	38.4	26.8
Portugal	61.7	29.5	8.6	48.6	34.7	16.7
United Kingdom	48.4	41.1	10.5	30.8	48.9	20.3
United States	55.7	33.1	21.2	36.3	23.7	40.0
Developing						
Burkina Faso	83.3	15.9	0.8	41.9	25.9	32.2
Congo	70.3	28.2	1.5	30.0	35.6	34.4
Malawi	97.2	2.4	0.4	55.4	23.5	21.1
Mali	81.9	16.7	1.4	51.6	25.1	23.3
Senegal	78.7	19.6	1.7	49.0	25.3	23.7
Sierra Leone	78.7	20.8	0.5	24.2	36.1	39.8
Togo[a]	81.5	17.4	1.1	35.3	37.3	27.4
Zimbabwe	76.2	21.9	1.9	59.4	32.3	8.3
Brazil	86.3	9.5	4.2	67.9	9.3	22.8
Colombia	62.2	31.3	6.5	42.0	36.0	22.0
Cuba	40.2	48.8	11.0	31.7	50.3	18.0
Mexico	68.0	26.8	5.2	35.7	40.7	23.6
India	63.5	33.6	2.9	47.6	33.0	19.4
Korea (Rep. of)	46.2	39.6	14.2	54.2	36.5	9.3
Pakistan	68.5	29.0	2.5	42.2	36.5	21.3
Thailand	68.7	21.4	9.9	62.4	24.8	12.8

Source: UNESCO *Statistical Yearbook* 1991
a 1987

more than the provisional figures shown in official budgets.

These average trends by region do not reveal the large differences between individual countries. For instance, in 1960 Surinam spent 7.3 percent of its national resources on education and Iraq 6.8 percent, while Niger and Pakistan spent only 1 percent; in 1988, Algeria spent 10.3 percent, but Zaire only 0.9 percent. Also in 1988, 27.0 percent of total government expenditure went to education in Algeria, but only 6.4 percent in Hungary and Iraq. Within the same regions, differences are also important. For instance, in 1988 in Western Europe, Denmark spent 7.8 percent of its Gross National Product (GNP) on education but Germany only 4.2 percent.

2.2 The Distribution of Expenditures

The UNESCO *Statistical Yearbooks* contain a table showing distribution between current expenditures and capital expenditures, a table distributing current expenditures according to purpose, and a table distributing current expenditures by level of education.

For many countries, capital expenditures are either not available or patently unreliable. The distribution of expenditures according to purpose is not homogeneous from country to country. On the other hand, distribution by level of education is more reliable and

Table 5
Public expenditure per student in higher education and in primary education (expenditure per student in primary education = 1) around 1989

Developed countries	
France	1.78
Germany (Fed. Rep.)	2.88
Japan	3.36
Portugal	2.46
United Kingdom	3.02
United States	3.36
Developing countries	
Burkina Faso	109.2
Congo	53.3
Malawi	92.5
Mali	26.4
Senegal	27.0
Sierra Leone	65.3
Togo	57.9
Zimbabwe	5.6
Brazil	6.9
Colombia	5.0
Cuba	2.1
Mexico	5.7
India	8.9
Korea (Rep. of)	0.59
Pakistan	13.7
Thailand	1.42

more interesting, in that it is an indication of the level of development of education and, when one compares it with the distribution of enrollment, it shows the priorities of each country.

Table 4 shows, for selected countries, that the distribution of expenditures by level differs very significantly among countries, even those at the same level of development. Among advanced countries, France spends relatively much less than the others on higher education and the United States relatively much more. In the developing world, Brazil and Thailand distribute more than 60 percent of their budgets to primary and preprimary education whereas Sierra Leone devotes less than 25 percent to that level. The difference is more striking if one compares the distribution of spending with the distribution of enrollment.

Table 5 shows that some countries in Africa spend around 100 times as much per university student as per primary-school student. Around the beginning of the 1980s, this ratio was between 60:1 and 100:1 in almost all sub-Saharan countries but, as the table shows, several of them such as Mali and Senegal have successfully attempted to reduce the ratio. On the other hand, Zimbabwe has always been an exception within Africa, with a ratio close to that observed in Latin America. The case of the Republic of Korea should also be noted. This results from a combination of a very high enrollment ratio in higher education and a predominantly private system of financing university studies.

The situation of sub-Saharan Africa is peculiar indeed. As Table 4 shows, some countries like Sierra Leone and Congo spend a larger part of the educational budget on the elite 1 percent of the school population than on the three-fourths in primary education. The ratio between expenditure per university student and expenditure per primary-school student is almost 10 times as high as in Asia, 15 times as high as in Latin America, and 24 times as high as in Europe. It is therefore to be hoped that all countries of that region will endeavor to correct this gross imbalance.

In developed countries, the ratio is on average around 3:1, with the exception of France.

3. Private Expenditures on Education

Private expenditures on education come from three sources: households, firms, and private donors.

3.1 Private Donors

Very little is known about this source. It is safe to say that it represents a very small portion of total expenditures except, in some countries, for higher education.

In the United States, according to the *Digest of Education Statistics* published by the United States Department of Education, private gifts, grants, and contracts represented 5.4 percent of the current fund revenue of institutions of higher education in the period 1985–86 (3.2 percent in public institutions versus

9.3 percent in private institutions). Endowment income amounted to 2.3 percent of current fund revenue during the same year (0.6 percent in public institutions versus 5.3 percent in private institutions).

3.2 Firms

Firms contribute to many types of education and training programs. Their contribution takes many forms, ranging from the compulsory levies for apprenticeship and/or for adult education which exist in several countries to costs incurred by on-the-job training activities.

No comprehensive survey is available for any country and no meaningful comparison may be made of the incomplete surveys existing in a handful of countries. However, two examples may be produced to give an idea of the importance of this source of finance for education. In France, where a survey of total expenditures was first made in 1974, it is estimated that firms contribute approximatively 5 percent of this total. In the United States, studies tend to show that firms spend more on higher education programs outside university than the total budget of universities.

3.3 Households

Households incur high costs for the education of their children. Forgone earnings, which cannot be measured accurately and objectively, are estimated as representing a large part of these costs.

Expenditures largely exceed tuition and fees paid to institutions of education. They include also all types of household expenditures (on food, clothing, transportation, and so forth) that are the result of the enrollment of one or more members of the family in a school. Total expenditure by households can be obtained only through special surveys, which are conducted only in a few countries and often not on a regular basis. Comparative data are published only by the OECD. As the coverage of the original surveys is highly variable

from country to country, no definitive conclusions may be drawn from them.

Table 6 gives information on the level of tuition and fees in higher education in some developed countries. Two groups of countries stand out: countries with high fees (Japan and the United States), and countries with low fees (Europe). There are significant differences among European nations, however, and the trend is toward an increase in fees of up to US$400–600 per year. In some countries, such as Japan, the cost supported by students and their families is extremely high. In 1982, it was estimated that tuition, fees, and living expenses represented 25 percent of the average family income for children in public institutions of higher education and 30 percent for those in private institutions. In upper-secondary education the cost was estimated respectively at 5 and 10 percent. These figures did not include the private tutoring costs which were incurred by most families and which amounted to 3 to 5 percent of family income per child.

In Europe, on the other hand, this cost is much lower. In France, for instance, it is estimated that households contribute less than 10 percent of total expenditures to education.

The contrast is also striking in developing countries. Almost exclusively public institutions levy no tuition fees in Africa. However, a high proportion of students are in private high-fee institutions in many Latin American countries.

4. Foreign Aid

The only detailed survey on foreign aid according to donor and to recipient is published by the OECD. Unfortunately it is incomplete (multilateral aid is not included), and it does not isolate aid to education. The first systematic survey to include all sources and all types of aid to education (e.g., loans of teachers and scholarships abroad) was commissioned by the World Bank in 1987. It originally concerned only sub-Saharan Africa but has since been extended to other regions. The latest evaluation yields the following information:

(a) Total amount of aid to education (average 1981–86): US $5.96 million, of which:

(i)	Aid registered by UNDP	1.73
(ii)	Non-governmental organizations (NGOs)	0.42
(iii)	Former USSR and other socialist countries	0.46
(iv)	Enrollment of Third World students in developed countries	1.15
(v)	Training linked with projects in other sectors	2.20

(b) Percentage distribution of aid to education by level:

(i)	Basic education	14.74
(ii)	Secondary education	24.53
(iii)	Higher education	31.63
(iv)	Teacher training	2.95

Table 6
Tuition and fees in higher education in selected developed countries (in US$)[a]

	Public	Private
Japan (1982)[b]	3,950	4,380
USA (1987)	1,414[cd]	6,658[d]
France (1988)	75	[e]
Germany (F.R.) (1988)	23–40[f]	—
Netherlands (1988)	660	660
Spain (1987)	285–405	—

a Amounts in local currency have been converted to US$ at the official rate of exchange   b Includes living expenses   c For instate students only   d Only 4-year institutions, undergraduate students   e Range from US$100 to US$5,000 but concerns few students   f No tuition, only social contributions

(v) Nondistributed or not identified   16.15

(c) Distribution by region and by level of development (as defined by the World Bank):

Region
(i) sub-Saharan Africa	48.7
(ii) North Africa	9.4
(iii) Central America	6.7
(iv) South America	4.4
(v) Middle East	5.7
(vi) South Asia	3.9
(vii) East Asia (including China)	19.5
(viii) Oceania	1.6
Total	100.0

Level of development
(i) Low-income countries	43.2
(ii) Middle-income countries	
Lower middle	50.2
Upper middle	6.0
(iii) Oil-exporting countries	0.1
(iv) Income undetermined	0.5
Total	100.0

Sub-Saharan Africa is the main recipient of foreign aid. This is not surprising as the majority of low-income countries are in that part of the world. More surprising is the fact that basic education receives barely 15 percent of the total and even less (7.2 percent) in Africa.

These evaluations still need to be improved but they give, for the first time, an overview of the global situation.

See also: Educational Financing

Bibliography

Caillods F (ed.) 1989 *The Prospects for Educational Planning.* IIEP, Paris, Chaps. 2 and 3
Eicher J-C 1990 The financial crisis and its consequences in European higher education. *Higher Educ. Policy* 3(4):26–29
Eicher J-C, Orivel F 1979 *The Allocation of Resources to Education Worldwide* UNESCO Office of Statistics, Paris
Organisation for Economic Co-operation and Development (OECD) 1990 *Education in OECD Countries 1987/88.* OECD, Paris
Organisation for Economic Co-operation and Development (OECD) in press *Education at a Glance.* OECD, Paris
Orivel F, Sergent F 1988 Foreign aid to education in sub-Saharan Africa: How useful is it? *Prospects* 18(4):459–69
UNESCO 1963–91 *Statistical Yearbook.* UNESCO, Paris
US Department of Education 1989 *Digest of Education Statistics.* US Government Printing Office, Washington, DC
US Department of Education 1991 *The Condition of Education,* 2 vols. US Government Printing Office, Washington, DC
US Department of Education 1987 *Japanese Education Today.* US Government Printing Office, Washington, DC

Public–Private Division of Responsibility for Education

E. James

Education yields both private benefits to the student and public benefits to society at large. As a result, it can be financed through the public or private sectors. Even when government funding predominates, management can be carried out through the public hierarchy or through private groups, as when schools founded and operated by nongovernmental organizations are subsidized. Thus a wide range is observed in the public–private division of funding, management, and enrollments.

What factors account for these differences across societies? How does the process of economic development affect the public–private division of responsibility for education? This entry investigates these closely related questions. The answers are important because private schools behave differently from public schools; a system that is largely private may provide a different educational service from one that is largely public, and the underlying *raison*

d'être for the private sector helps to explain these differences.

Before beginning the discussion it is necessary to define what is meant by "private." This is by no means clear-cut in situations where many "private" schools are heavily funded and regulated by the state. In most developing countries private schools depend mainly on private funding, but in many developed countries subsidies cover a large proportion of total expenses, and government control over hiring and firing of teachers and student admissions criteria accompanies these subsidies. "Source of funding" and "degree of decision-making authority" then yield different public–private categories, and many mixed rather than polar cases. In this entry "private" schools are defined as those that were privately founded and are privately managed; they usually have some private funding, although considerable funding and control may also come from the government. Section 1 presents a model used to analyze the role of the private sector in many countries and Section 2 presents supporting empirical evidence.

1. Determinants of Private Sector Size and Other Characteristics

The private share of total enrollments at the primary and secondary levels of education covers the entire spectrum, from 1 percent to 100 percent, and the variation is almost as wide at the level of higher education. Examination of these data reveals two outstanding observations: first, at the secondary level the relative size of the private sector is much larger in developing rather than in developed countries; and second, within a given level of education and stage of development there is a large, seemingly random variation.

How are these two observations to be explained? This section sets forth a conceptual framework for answering that question. (For details about the model used see James 1986a, 1987, 1993.) The first observation is attributed to limited public spending, which creates an "excess demand" from people who would prefer to use the public schools but are involuntarily excluded and pushed into the private sector. The second observation is attributed to differentiated demand stemming from cultural (i.e., religious, linguistic) heterogeneity or differentiated tastes about quality which lead people voluntarily to opt out of the public system to secure the kind of education they prefer. In both cases, the supply of nonprofit entrepreneurship by diverse religious organizations in their competition for a larger market share of "souls" is hypothesized to play an important role in determining private sector size and other characteristics.

1.1 Excess Demand

Suppose that, through some collective choice process, each country decides how much and what kind of public education to provide (see below for determinants of this choice). Each family then has three options for its children, namely that they attend a public school if available, attend a private school, or do not attend any school at all. The private sector can be thought of as a market response to situations where a public school place is not available for everyone or where some people are dissatisfied with the type of government schools provided, and where other people are willing to supply alternative schools, often for nonpecuniary reasons. Two very different patterns of private education have evolved around the world, depending on whether the motivation is excess demand or differentiated demand.

Excess demand for education often exists when the capacity of the public school system is less than full enrollment; that is, the option of attending a free or low-price public school is not available to everyone.

If the private benefits from education are high (e.g., because of labor market rewards), many people who are left out of the public schools will seek places in private schools as a "second best" solution.

The "excess demand" model most clearly applies to education in Western countries in the nineteenth century and to many developing countries at the end of the twentieth century. Examples are Kenya and Indonesia where, until recently, the majority of secondary school enrollments were private, and Brazil and the Philippines, where the majority of college enrollments are private. Among industrialized countries in the 1990s, Japan best fits the "excess demand" model; over three-fourths of higher education students attend private institutions, mainly because of limited space in the preferred public universities. (See Levy 1986a; Winkler 1990; James 1986a, 1986b, 1991b; James and Benjamin 1988.)

In these situations, a political coalition of groups with high tax rates and low benefits from education has limited the supply of government schools, especially at the secondary and higher levels. At the same time, because of the large private benefits of education, many families are anxious to send their children to school, even if they must pay themselves. Under these circumstances, the smaller the capacity of the public sector is, relative to the size of the age cohort, the larger will be the excess demand for the private sector.

A number of predictions follow about the characteristics of excess-demand-driven private sectors. Since the basic cause is postulated to be limited government spending, excess-demand-driven, privately managed schools are also likely to be privately funded. In order to attract low- and middle-income students, and because of competitive pressures, many of these schools will keep their fees low, that is, lower than the costs per student in public schools. This, in turn, means that their expenditures per student must be low. If the limited spaces in public schools are rationed by academic criteria, the private sector will cater to students with lower incoming qualifications than public schools and will therefore also have lower outgoing results. Since academic performance is highly correlated with socioeconomic status, the income bias in the private sector (due to price barriers) may be no greater than in the public sector (due to academic barriers). Excess-demand-driven private schools may be considered lower in quality than public schools, but they will still be utilized by students who cannot get into the latter.

At the higher education level some additional predictions may be made about the product mix that will be chosen by excess-demand-driven private universities. Since families are more likely to pay for products with private rather than social benefits, undergraduate schooling will be stressed over graduate training and research. For similar reasons, low-cost vocational fields will be emphasized, for instance, business management and law rather than laboratory science.

1.2 Differentiated Demand

Excess demand cannot be the motivation for private schools in advanced industrial societies which guarantee a place for everyone in their public schools. The alternative explanation—differentiated demand—views private schooling as a response to differentiated tastes about the kind of education to be consumed. This model hypothesizes that important taste differences about education stem from religious and linguistic differences that concern group identification. In such cases, the greater the cultural diversity of the population and the more uniform the public educational system, the larger will be the differentiated demand for private education. If cultural minorities have sufficient political power, they may obtain subsidies for their schools, which further increase private sector size (see below).

Private sectors driven by differentiated tastes exist both in developing and developed countries. For example, the "melting pot theory" and a general belief in assimilation of minorities led to the "common school" movement in the United States in the nineteenth and twentieth centuries, but the growth of Catholic private schools was a response by a group that did not want to be fully assimilated. In India, too, many private schools and colleges accommodate religious or linguistic minorities, such as Muslims, Parsees, and Sikhs. The same is true of the Chinese and Indian minorities in Malaysia. However, the best example of the "cultural heterogeneity" model is the Netherlands, where two-thirds of the population attend privately managed, publicly funded schools, a response to the pervasive religious cleavage which dominated that country at the turn of the nineteenth and twentieth centuries (see James 1984, 1989).

Since a public school alternative is available, consumers who choose differentiated private schools (in contrast to those who attend excess-demand-driven private schools) must feel these are "better" in some respect. For cultural minorities the relevant dimension may be related to socialization, ideology, or value-formation, rather than cognition. However, differential preferences about academic quality can also lead to development of private schools; a low quality public sector may stimulate the growth of a high quality private sector, meeting the demand of those willing and able to pay for academic quality. This might be the case, for example, if political pressures led public quantity to expand by taking in more students without a commensurate increase in educational spending. The phenomenon of private schools differentiated from public schools along academic quality lines has been observed at the secondary level in the Unite States, the United Kingdom, India, the Philippines, and Brazil, and at the university level in many Latin American countries. Since demand for academic quality is highly income-elastic, for any given public quality the academic quality-driven private sector is expected to be larger in areas with greater income inequality, especially those with more families in the upper tail of the income distribution.

1.3 Nonprofit Supply

While the size and nature of the private sector in a society is thus partially determined by the source of demand, supply forces also play a crucial role. If for-profit schools are permitted and supplies of educational inputs are elastic, it might be expected that the supply of private school places will simply respond to demand. Private schools are often established as nonprofit organizations, that is, as organizations that cannot distribute a monetary dividend. Indeed, nonprofit status is legally required for educational institutions in many countries.

Therefore, one cannot be sure that private schools will spring up wherever a pecuniary profit exists, since nonprofit capital and entrepreneurship may not be available. On the other hand, nonprofit schools may spring up in situations where for-profit schools could not break even, because of their lower cost functions due to donated capital, voluntary labor, and tax advantages. The availability of nonprofit entrepreneurs, therefore, may strongly influence the growth of the private education sector. It is necessary to enquire what the motives are of people who start nonprofit schools, and what the factors are that determine their availability.

An answer to these questions is suggested by the observation that most founders of private schools (and other nonprofits) are "ideological" organizations: political groups, socialist labor unions, and, first and foremost, religious groups. Examples are sectarian schools in the United States and United Kingdom, Catholic schools in France and Latin America, Calvanist schools in the Netherlands, ultra-orthodox Jewish schools in Israel, missionary activities in developing countries, services provided by Muslim *waqfs* (religious trusts) in the Middle East, and so forth. Usually these are proselytizing religions, which use schools as a mechanism for shaping values, socializing old members, and attracting new ones. Competing ideologies have often been forced to start their own schools, as a defensive strategy (e.g., the "independence schools" in Africa and the caste-dominated schools in India were started partly to keep their members out of the Western-dominated Christian schools). This model hypothesizes that these nonprofit founders concentrated on education because schools are one of the most important institutions of value formation and socialization. It follows that the private educational sector will be larger in countries with many strong, independent religious organizations competing for members and member loyalty, through their schools, historically or currently. Nonprofit theory further predicts that nonprofit schools will tend to be higher in quality than for-profit schools, but their relative standing vis-à-vis public schools is *a priori* ambiguous. (For a fuller discussion of the motivations and behavior of nonprofit organizations see James 1983, 1989; James and Rose-Ackerman 1986; Levy 1986b.)

1.4 Government Policies

Finally, government policies influence the demand for and supply of private schools. As mentioned above, excess demand and differentiated demand for private education depend critically on the size and nature of the public school system, as determined in part by public educational spending. A second type of policy concerns government regulation of private schools, which may increase their costs and decrease their availability. In extreme cases, private schools have been virtually prohibited; this was the case, for example, with respect to Catholic schools in the eighteenth century in the United Kingdom and the Netherlands, and private schools in Pakistan and Tanzania during the 1970s. A final important policy concerns the provision of public subsidies to private schools, which increases the total effective demand that they face. Most advanced industrial states heavily subsidize their private schools and this is probably one reason why private education has not disappeared as free public schools have become available.

2. Empirical Data

The various hypotheses set forth above—that the private educational sector will be large where public educational spending is small, where cultural heterogeneity and religious competition are great, and where the government subsidizes private schools—have been tested statistically at the primary and secondary educational levels and consistent results have been obtained.

2.1 Interstate Comparisons

For example, the demand and supply-side forces have explained differences in private sector size across states or provinces in the Netherlands, India, Japan, and the United States (James 1986a, 1987). In all these cases, a "religious competition" variable was included and proved to be highly significant. In the United States, the private sector is relatively large in states where per capita income is high, public expenditures per student are low, and the proportion of Catholics and Blacks are high, consistent with the differentiated demand and nonprofit entrepreneurship theories of private school formation. In the Netherlands, the proportion of Catholics and Calvinists in the provinces examined proved to be the most important variable. In Japan and India, the early presence of Christian missionaries was central. In Brazil, where the private secondary sector is quality-driven and many for-profit schools exist, interstate differences in income in-

equality are the most significant explanatory variable (James et al. 1995).

2.2 Cross-national Comparisons

These hypotheses were also tested across a sample of 50 countries, using OLS, logit, and 2SLS (James 1993). Once again, the most consistently important factor explaining the relative size of the private sector was cultural heterogeneity, particularly religious heterogeneity, which combines both demand and supply-side effects. Linguistic heterogeneity, too, had a positive although somewhat weaker effect. Income diversity, on the other hand, was insignificant (possibly because public school quality was not controlled). Taken as a group, the heterogeneity variables explained 25 percent of the variance in private enrollments.

These findings have important implications for the behaviour of private schools. For example, they suggest that private schools often segment the population along religious, linguistic, national, or ideological lines, because of the motivations of their nonprofit producers and differentiated consumers. Many countries, particularly those trying to build a sense of national unity out of disparate groups, may fear these divisions.

While basic cultural factors play a large role, public policies are also crucial. Thus, the presence of "large" subsidies to the private sector (i.e., subsidies that cover more than 70 percent of total expenses) increases the private enrollment share by 10 percentage points. In contrast, public educational expenditures have a strong negative effect on private enrollments, and, once this variable is taken into account, the difference between developed and developing countries in relative private sector size disappears (i.e., low public educational spending at the secondary level in developing countries "explains" the large excess demand there). This suggests that if developing countries increase their public spending some private schools will be crowded out, so total enrollments may not rise as fast as spending or as much as was anticipated.

This result holds whether public spending is treated as exogenous or as endogenous, simultaneously determined with private sector size. The key variables that explain public spending in the simultaneous model are per capita income, noneducational governmental spending, an index of political and civil rights, and proportion of the population aged 0–14. The first three have a positive effect; the latter has a positive effect on primary spending but not on secondary spending, evidence of the quantity–quality trade-off in family size decisions. Private sector size does not seem to influence public educational spending, although the converse is clearly true.

2.3 Evidence on Characteristics of Excess-Demand-Driven Private Sectors

The limited empirical evidence on characteristics of excess-demand-driven private sectors is descriptive and case-study rather than econometric in nature, but it is consistent with the predictions made above. For example, studies of nongovernmental secondary schools in Japan and Kenya (1960s and 1970s), and in Tanzania (1980s) indicate they are (or were) largely funded by private fees and spend much less per student than do public schools (see James 1986a, James and Benjamin 1988, Samoff 1991). Cost economies are achieved by offering large classes, using meager supplies and equipment, and paying teachers low salaries. (To a lesser extent, differentiated-demand-driven private sectors also exhibit these cost economies. See James 1991c, Jimenez, Lockheed and Wattanawaha 1988, Jimenez, Lockheed and Paqueo 1988, Jimenez et al. 1991.) Their ability to function with lower costs has been variously attributed to lower quality, greater efficiency, selection of more motivated students or reduced power of teachers to obtain rents. Often their students have lower entrance scores and, consequently, lower outgoing scores. Even after controlling statistically for examination scores, schools with a large share of funding from local government or private sources seem to incur lower cost per student, evidence of greater efficiency (see Jimenez and Paqueo 1993, James, King and Suryadi 1995). Religious nonprofit schools appear to be higher in cost and quality than for-profit schools. However, careful value-added measures of quality in excess-demand-driven private sectors have not been made (in contrast to the large controversial literature on relative value added in differentiated-demand-driven private sectors).

A similar picture concerning revenues, costs, and student ability holds for excess-demand-driven universities in Brazil, the Philippines, and Japan (see Levy 1986a, Winkler 1990, James 1991b, James and Benjamin 1987, 1988). As expected, these universities concentrate on undergraduate teaching of low-cost vocationally oriented fields such as law, management, and economics. (In contrast, public universities in these countries and elite private universities in other countries place greater emphasis on graduate education, research, and science, financed largely by public funds.) The socioeconomic distribution of their student body is income-biased, but not more so than in the more selective public universities.

2.4 Impact of Large Subsidies and Regulations

Another study investigates in greater detail the impact of large subsidies on the size and characteristics of the private sector in a sample of 35 countries (James 1991a). It turns out that this relationship is quite complex. First of all, the majority of countries in the overall sample provide little or no subsidy. However, disaggregation of the developing and developed countries changes the picture: most of the latter provide large subsidies (covering more than 70 percent of total expenses) to their private primary and secondary

schools, while most of the former provide only small subsidies. Empirically, it seems that private schools depend mainly on fee financing in the early stages of development, while government funding displaces private funding later on.

Second, at the secondary level many developing countries have "large" private sectors, even though they offer little or no subsidy. In contrast, all developed countries with large private sectors have large subsidies. Thus, subsidies appear to be a necessary condition for the growth of large private sectors in modern industrial states, while large fee-financed private sectors seem viable in developing countries. This is consistent with the hypothesis that excess demand is driving private education in many developing countries, while differentiated demand is the driving force in developed countries; people are more willing to pay fees for the former than the latter.

Finally, it should be noted that substantial regulations usually accompany large subsidies. These regulations are similar to those applied to public schools; typically they specify hiring and firing procedures, credentials and salaries of teachers, criteria for selecting students, price and expenditures per student, and participants in the school's decision-making structure. In particular, they raise salaries and other costs while lowering private price and contributions (see James 1984, 1991a, 1991c). This is the origin of the public–private hybrid mentioned at the beginning of this entry. Large private sectors in developed countries are heavily subsidized and heavily controlled and, in fact, these forces lead them to behave very much like the public sector.

References

James E 1983 How nonprofits grow: A model. *Journal of Policy Analysis and Management* 2(3): 350–65

James E 1984 Benefits and costs of privatized public services: Lessons from the Dutch educational system. *Comp. Educ. Rev.* 28(4): 605–24

James E 1986a The private nonprofit provision of education: A theoretical model and application to Japan. *J. Comp. Econ.* 10: 255–76

James E 1986b The private educational sector: A case study of Kenya. Report for the Agency for International Development (USAID), Washington, DC

James E 1987 The public/private division of responsibility for education: An international comparison. *Econ. Educ. Rev.* 6(1): 1–14

James E 1989 *The Nonprofit Sector in International Perspective: Studies in Comparative Culture and Policy.* Oxford University Press, New York

James E 1991a Public policies toward private education: An international comparison. *Int. J. Educ. Res.* 15(5): 359–76

James E 1991b Private higher education: The Philippines as a prototype. *High. Educ.* 21: 189–206

James E 1991c Private education and redistributive subsidies in Australia. In: Gormley W (ed.) 1991 *Privatization and*

Its Alternatives. University of Wisconsin Press, Madison, Wisconsin

James E 1993 Why do different countries choose a different public–private mix of education services? *J. Hum. Resources* 28(3): 571–92

James E, Rose-Ackerman S 1986 *The Nonprofit Enterprise in Market Economies*. Harwood Academic Publishers, New York

James E, Benjamin G 1987 Educational distribution and income redistribution through education in Japan. *J. Hum. Resources* 22(4): 469–89

James E, Benjamin G 1988 *Public Policy and Private Education in Japan*. Macmillan, Basingstoke

James E, Braga C P, Andre P 1995 Private education and public regulation in Brazil. In: Birdsall N, Sabot R (eds.) 1995 Education, Growth, and Inequality in Brazil. The World Bank, Washington, DC

James E, King E, Suryadi A 1995 Finance management and costs of public and private schools in Indonesia. Econ. Educ. Rev.

Jimenez E, Lockheed M, Paqueo V 1988 The relative efficiency of private and public schools in developing countries. *World Bank Res. Obs.* 6(2): 205–18

Jimenez E, Lockheed M, Wattanawaha N 1988 The relative efficiency of public and private schools: The case of Thailand. *World Bank Econ. R.* 2(2): 139–64

Jimenez E, Lockheed M, Luna E, Paqueo V 1991 School effects and costs for private and public schools in the Dominican Republic. *Int. J. Educ. Res.* 15(5): 393–410

Jimenez E, Paqueo V 1993 Do local contributions affect the efficiency of public primary schools? Paper presented at the International Symposium on Economics of Education, Manchester

Levy D 1986a *Higher Education and the State in Latin America*. University of Chicago Press, Chicago, Illinois

Levy D (ed.) 1986b *Private Education and Public Policy: Studies in Choice and Public Policy: Private Challenges to Public Dominance*. Oxford University Press, New York

Samoff J 1991 Local initiatives and national policies: The politics of private schooling in Tanzania. *Int. J. Educ. Res.* 15(5): 377–92

Winkler D 1990 Higher education in Latin America: Issues of efficiency and equity. World Bank Discussion Paper No. 77. The World Bank, Washington, DC

World Bank 1986 *Financing Education in Developing Countries: An Explanation of Policy Options*. The World Bank, Washington, DC

List of Contributors

Contributors are listed in alphabetical order together with their affiliations. Titles of articles which they have authored follow in alphabetical order, along with the respective page numbers. Where articles are co-authored, this has been indicated by an asterisk preceding the article title.

457

FERBER, M. A. (University of Illinois, Urbana, Illinois, USA)
Gender Differences in Earnings 242–48

FIELDS, G. S. (Cornell University, Ithaca, New York, USA)
Educational Expansion and Labor Markets 101–07

FREEMAN, R. B. (Harvard University, Cambridge, Massachusetts, USA)
Demand and Supply Elasticities for Educated Labor 63–69

GIBNEY, L. (Stanford University, Stanford, California, USA)
Education and Fertility 164–68

GINTIS, H. (University of Massachusetts, Amhurst, Massachusetts, USA)
*Agency and Efficiency Wage Theory 52–58

GLOVER, R. (University of Texas, Austin, Texas, USA)
*Economics of Apprenticeship 181–85

GROOT, W. (Leiden University, Leiden, The Netherlands)
*Screening Models and Education 34–39

GRUBEL, H. G. (Simon Fraser University, Burnaby, British Columbia, Canada)
Economics of the Brain Drain 80–86

HAMILTON, S. F. (Cornell University, Ithaca, New York, USA)
*Economics of Apprenticeship 181–85

HANUSHEK, E. A. (University of Rochester, Rochester, New York, USA)
Education Production Functions 277–82

HARRIS, D. J. (Stanford University, Stanford, California, USA)
Endogenous Learning and Economic Growth 199–205

HARTOG, J. (University of Amsterdam, Amsterdam, The Netherlands)
*Screening Models and Education 34–39

HICKS, N. L. (World Bank, Washington, DC, USA)
Education and Economic Growth 192–98

HINCHLIFFE, K. (University of East Anglia, Norwich, UK)
Education and the Labor Market 20–24; *Manpower Analysis* 370–75; *Public Sector Employment and Education* 87–90

JAMES, E. (World Bank, Washington, DC, USA)
Public–Private Division of Responsibility for Education 450–55

JIMENEZ, E. (World Bank, Washington, DC, USA)
International Aspects of Financing Education 438–43

KELLY, D. M. (University of British Columbia, Vancouver, British Columbia, Canada)
School Dropouts 308–13

KING, E. M. (World Bank, Washington, DC, USA)
Economics of Gender and Occupational Choices 252–59

KLEES, S. J. (Florida State University, Tallahassee, Florida, USA)
Economics of Educational Technology 398–406

LEVIN, H. M. (Stanford University, Stanford, California, USA)
Cost–Benefit Analysis 360–64; *Cost-effectiveness Analysis* 381–86; *Raising Educational Productivity* 283–91; *School Choice: Market Mechanisms* 349–53; *School Finance* 412–19; *Work and Education* 10–19

LLAMAS, I. (Universidad Autónoma Metropolitana, Mexico City, Mexico)
Education and Labor Markets in Developing Nations 90–95

McMAHON, W. W. (University of Illinois, Urbana, Illinois, USA)
Consumption Benefits of Education 168–72

MILLOT, B. (World Bank, Washington, DC, USA)
Economics of Educational Time and Learning 353–58

MIN, WEIFANG (Beijing University, Beijing, People's Republic of China)
Vocational Education and Productivity 140–45

MIRANDA, G. V. DE (Federal University of Minas Gerais, Belo Horizonte, Brazil)
Education and Female Labor Force Participation in Industrializing Countries 95–101

MONK, D. H. (Cornell University, Ithaca, New York, USA)
Microeconomics of School Production 303–08

MOOCK, P. R. (World Bank, Washington, DC, USA)
*Education and Agricultural Productivity 130–40

Name Index

The Name Index has been compiled so that the reader can proceed directly to the page where an author's work is cited, or to the reference itself in the bibliography. For each name, the page numbers for the bibliographic section are given first, followed by the page number(s) in parentheses where that reference is cited in text. Where a name is referred to only in text, and not in the bibliography, the page number appears only in parentheses.

The accuracy of the spelling of authors' names has been affected by the use of different initials by some authors, or a different spelling of their name in different papers or review articles (sometimes this may arise from a transliteration process), and by those journals which give only one initial to each author.

Subject Index

The Subject Index has been compiled as a guide to the reader who is interested in locating all the references to a particular subject area within the Encyclopedia. Entries may have up to three levels of heading. Where the page numbers appear in bold italic type, this indicates a substantive discussion of the topic. Every effort has been made to index as comprehensively as possible and to standardize the terms used in the index. However, given the diverse nature of the field and the varied use of terms throughout the international community, synonyms and foreign language terms have been included with appropriate cross-references, As a further aid to the reader, cross-references have also been given to terms of related interest.